COLLECTIVE BARGAINING IN PRIVATE EMPLOYMENT

Second Edition

Unit One
of

Labor Relations and Social Problems
A Course Book

COLLECTIVE BARGAINING IN PRIVATE EMPLOYMENT

Second Edition

Unit One

of

Labor Relations and Social Problems
A Course Book

Prepared by

James B. Atleson, Chairman, Unit One
State University of New York, Buffalo

Robert J. Rabin
Syracuse University

George Schatzki
University of Washington

Herbert L. Sherman, Jr.
University of Pittsburgh

Eileen Silverstein
University of Connecticut

for

The Labor Law Group

The Bureau of National Affairs, Inc., Washington, D.C.

Library of Congress Cataloging in Publication Data

Main entry under title:
Collective bargaining in private employment.
(Labor relations and social problems: a course book; unit 1)
Includes bibliographical references and index.
1. Trade-unions—Law and legislation—United States. 2. Collective labor
agreements—United States. I. Atleson, James B. II. Labor Law Group (U.S.)
III. Series: Labor relations and social problems; unit 1.
    KF3389.C645 1984   344.73'0189   84-1767
    ISBN 0-87179-424-1   347.304189

Printed in the United States of America
International Standard Book Number: 0-87179-424-1

LABOR LAW GROUP

Foreword

Starting in 1971, the Labor Law Group made a sharp break from the traditional format and content of law school teaching materials in the area of labor relations and social problems.

The Group had its genesis in a paper delivered at the 1946 meeting of the Association of American Law Schools by Willard Wirtz, then a professor of law at Northwestern University. Inspired by the vision of this address, a group of law teachers obtained a grant from the Carnegie Corporation of New York. With the cooperation of the University of Michigan Law School, the group held, at Ann Arbor in June of 1947, a two-week "Conference on the Training of Law Students in Labor Relations."

After the conference, the law teachers began the preparation of teaching materials. Eventually the materials were published in 1953 by Little, Brown and Co. under the title Labor Relations and the Law. All of the preparation of the preliminary drafts and the first published edition were under the general editorship of Professor Robert E. Mathews.

The law teachers soon thereafter established a common law trust, obtained recognition of tax-exempt status, and assumed the name "Labor Law Group." The original membership was 31. Over the years some teachers have dropped out and others have become members. Altogether almost 70 persons, including some practitioners and government officials, have been members of the Group. Three of the original members—Benjamin Aaron, Donald H. Wollett, and Edwin R. Teple—are still active. All royalties from Group publications have gone into a trust fund to finance the Group's planning and editorial activities. No member of the Group has ever received personal financial remuneration.

In 1958 Professor Mathews, to whom we continue to pay honor as the foremost of our founding fathers, resigned as head of the group, and he was succeeded by Professors Benjamin Aaron and Donald H. Wollett as co-chairmen and co-editors of the second edition of Labor Relations and the Law, which appeared in 1960. They in turn were succeeded by Professor Jerre Williams, who was general editor of the third edition in 1965 and Group chairman through 1967. The Group has also published Employment Relations and the Law (1957, Benjamin Aaron, Editor) and Readings in Labor Law (1955). Professor William P. Murphy served as chairman of the Group's Executive and Editorial Committees from 1967 to 1972. Professor Herbert L. Sherman, Jr. served as chairman from 1973 to 1978, and Professor James E. Jones, Jr. served as chairman from 1978 to 1982. Professor Robert N. Covington became the chairman in 1982.

The Group reexamined the teaching of labor law at a one-week conference held at Boulder, Colo., in 1969. The conference was attended by law teachers, academic authorities from other disciplines, and management and labor spokesmen. As a result of this meeting and others, the Group decided to publish a series of books on Labor Relations and Social Problems. Between 1971 and 1977 ten books, and subsequent editions of several of these books, were published by the Group.

In 1976 the Group decided to reorganize the materials for future books (starting in 1978), and to publish six books, including a substantial amount of nondoctrinal material, on the following subject matter: Collective Bargaining in Private Employment, Social Legislation, Discrimination in Employment, Collective Bargaining in Public Employment, Negotiation, and Arbitration and Conflict Resolution. Each of these books is designed so that it may be used by itself, but two or more of these books may be used in the same course or seminar.

The following characteristics distinguish this series of books from standard labor law casebooks:

1. The format of separate units (each dealing with a separable topic in the general field) in recognition of the fact that it is impossible to teach all of these subjects in one course.

2. For each subject a book which is shorter in length than a standard casebook, thus making it more practical to use in a typical course.

3. Frequent updating of units to keep abreast of a fast-changing field of law.

4. Inclusion of a separate unit on social legislation.

5. Coverage of matters not covered in standard casebooks, e.g., the art and techniques of negotiation and the myth of expertise.

6. Inclusion of material on professional responsibility and comparative law.

7. A blending of legal and nondoctrinal materials so that a greater appreciation of the "law" can be achieved.

8. Meeting of the need for legal materials for seminars and advanced courses.

9. Meeting of the need for legal materials in the labor-management area for use in undergraduate courses.

10. Greater flexibility for the law teacher in putting together a course or courses of the teacher's own liking.

It is our hope that these books will give students an idea of industrial relations law and practices, and also shed light on the variety of techniques which are available for the peaceful resolution of significant social disputes.

THE EDITORIAL POLICY COMMITTEE

Summary Table of Contents

Detailed Table of Contents

1. Introduction to Labor Law*

A. LABOR IN EARLY AMERICA**

In the eighteenth century stable labor organizations or trade unions were beginning to emerge from the industrialization of England. In colonial America, however, laborers generally procured the desired terms of employment without having to combine with others. Some concerted action did occur, but it was usually directed at specific goals and did not result in permanent organizations. Even servants bound by various types of employment contracts sometimes struck or deserted. Almost invariably such actions were ruthlessly put down by the authorities. Concerted action by slaves was viewed as an insurrection, even though the particular activity might be a form of labor protest.

Combinations by employers for the purposes of trade monopoly, price fixing, and control of the labor market were not regulated by law and were more common in colonial times than combinations of journeymen. "Collective action by journeymen workmen in colonial towns, as distinguished from combinations by licensed trades, guild groups or employers' trade associations, were comparatively rare. . . ." R. Morris, Government and Labor in Early America 195 (1946).

Even during this period, however, the law regulated the employment relationship. Throughout the colonial period free labor remained in short supply, a situation which settlers sought to remedy through particular legal or social relationships. First, several forms of bound labor were created for white Europeans, and a coercive labor system was adopted for black Africans. Thus, although only apprentices were bound by contract for a period of years under English law, apprenticeship in America was only one form of bound labor.

---

*The user of this book should be aware that some citations to statutes and to other cases have been edited from the opinions of many of the principal cases in this book without any symbol to designate the omission, and that footnotes to cases and articles which are included are numbered in accordance with the original. The user should also be aware that the primary research for this book was completed in mid 1983.

**This note is based largely upon the writings of Richard Morris in GOVERNMENT AND LABOR IN EARLY AMERICA; *The Emergence of American Labor*, THE U.S. DEPARTMENT OF LABOR BICENTENNIAL HISTORY OF THE AMERICAN WORKER (R. Morris ed. 1976); *Preface* to 3, 4 J. Commons and E. Gilmore, DOCUMENTARY HISTORY OF AMERICAN INDUSTRIAL SOCIETY (1958). See also D. Galenson, WHITE SERVITUDE IN COLONIAL AMERICA (1981); G. Nash, THE URBAN CRUCIBLE: SOCIAL CHANGE, POLITICAL CONSCIOUSNESS AND THE ORIGINS OF THE AMERICAN REVOLUTION (1979).

1

Apprentices agreed to serve their masters loyally and faithfully, a condition found in all formal and informal bound labor relationships. As this listing suggests, free workers were the least numerous and perhaps least important group of American workers throughout the colonial era.

Indentured servitude, another form of bound labor, included persons bound to labor for periods of years, determined either by a written agreement or by the custom of the colony. During the indenture period, freedom of movement and occupation were restricted, and the master possessed a property interest in the laborer which could usually be assigned or sold.

White immigrants, called redemptioners or "free willers," bound themselves as servants for varying periods in return for their passage to America. It has been estimated that redemptioners composed almost 80 percent of the total British continental immigration to America prior to the Revolution. Redemptioners were sometimes shipped to America through coercive practices, often packed in unsanitary ships. They suffered high mortality rates. Once ashore, families might be broken up, husbands and wives could be sold to different masters, and parents were frequently forced to sell their children.

The transportation of convicts, perhaps amounting to 50,000 persons, provided another source of bound labor in the colonies. The labor market was also supplied through apprentices, a system which was also designed to provide training in a trade.

Other legal devices were employed to increase labor supply as well as restrict workers' bargaining power. Prisoners unable to make restitution after being convicted of larceny, for instance, would normally be bound out to service by the courts. Absentee or runaway servants would often be punished by requiring them to serve as many as 10 days for every day of unauthorized leave. No distinction was made between runaway indentured servants and absentee freeworkers under contract. The debtor was also an important source of bound labor in American colonies, servitude being more economically useful than imprisonment. In addition, workers could be impressed for a variety of public works projects, including road and highway construction and repair. The wages for such work were set by local authorities. The colonies also experimented with wage and price regulation, placing a ceiling on wages and a floor on hours of employment. See R. Morris, Government and Labor in Early America 55–92 (1965).

For black Africans a very special bound labor evolved, based upon practices along the West African coast existing for nearly two centuries before the settlement of Virginia. As the English empire expanded to the new world, slave traders grasped the chance to make huge profits from this immoral business. When the first blacks came to Virginia in 1619, they were treated as bound servants and were freed when their terms expired. In the 1640s, however, blacks began to be sold as servants for life, a system of de facto slavery which preceded formal, legalized slavery. In the 1660s and 1670s statutes in Virginia and Maryland gave slavery its formal distinguishing features, an inheritable status of servitude for life. Soon restrictions on slave mobility, along with a harsh system of discipline, were written into the "Black Codes" of all the Southern colonies.

The fact that many early laborers were bound, unfree to leave or change their circumstances, may have affected the way Americans viewed the employment relationship even after such forms faded away. Some forms of bound labor began to disappear, not because they were necessarily inconsistent with democratic principles, but because employers found that in periods of excess labor and especially during depressions, it was advantageous to substitute the market for status-contractual relationships. Nevertheless, the American view of the employment relationship may intuitively have been affected by the substantial number of bound workers which previously existed.

The basic problem is that possible connections between bound labor and conceptions of the modern "free" worker have not been explored. Many forms of bound labor seem to have faded away after the American revolution, but this does not mean that assumptions had not already been formed as to the obligations and status of all laborers. Slavery in the north, after all, existed for some time after the revolution. Northern legislators were extremely conservative on this issue, and freedom only came slowly to northern slaves. The legislators of the northeastern states rejected what David Brion Davis refers to as the "most cautious proposals for gradual abolition." From 1784 to 1804, emancipation acts won grudging assent in Connecticut, Rhode Island, New York and New Jersey. New York's first emancipation act in 1799 left all existing slaves in "perpetual servitude," and New Jersey's statute of 1804 was "so conservative and slow in operation that the state still contained slaves, euphemistically called 'apprentices,' at the time of the Civil War." Thus, not only did slavery itself exist in northern states into the nineteenth century, but a clear connection was perceived between slavery and at least one form of bound labor, apprenticeship. See D.B. Davis, The Problem of Slavery in the Age of Revolution, 1770–1823, at 87–89 (1975).

Eventually, forms of bound labor and indentured servitude ended, and nineteenth century law emphasized the contractual rather than the social ties between master and servant. Workers were to be left to their own devices, to drive the best bargain they could but possessing no claims beyond those growing out of the employment contract. These changes may have speeded the rate of economic growth, but the system increased the risks of survival for workers. The risks of unemployment due to injury or economic downturns were shouldered by the employee or, eventually, partially shared by the community. See J. Atleson, Values and Assumptions in American Labor Law 11–16 (1983).

In the early nineteenth century, workers first turned to more permanent types of trade union organization. In this period critical decisions were no longer made by master artisans who owned the means of production, but were increasingly made by manufacturers "whose control derived exclusively from ownership of property, raw materials, and finished products." A. Dawley, Class and Community: The Industrial Revolution in Lynn 223 (1976). The owner's power was exercised through the creation of central shops and, later, factories. The factory system and concurrent technological advances permitted vastly increased productivity, and the accumulation of capital ultimately destroyed the old order based upon household production.

The rise of the factory, the transition from custom work to wholesale work, and the resulting concentration of workers in certain expanding industries served to bring about more distinct class stratifications. Widening markets, combined with intense competition, induced employers to hire journeymen, to lower wages, and to subdivide work tasks, thereby stressing speed and cheapness rather than skill. The extension of markets should not be viewed as a causal factor for the rise of manufacturing; owners did not simply respond to market conditions but, rather, the businessmen created the new markets. This period, then, was marked by the decline of the apprenticeship system, the lowering of wages for goods produced for marketing, and the reduction of standards of workmanship. Correspondingly, the period included the growth of a work force with a greater consciousness of common interests.

Rising fortunes increased the degree of felt separation, even among property owners, and artisans and journeymen became wage earners, clearly separating those who owned productive property and those who did not. The changing character of inequality was clearly perceived by workers, especially those who remembered a past rooted in household and skill relationships. The awareness of change is clearly demonstrated in the following extracts from the *Awl*, a Massachusetts labor newspaper:

> "The division of society into the producing and non-producing classes, and the fact of the unequal distribution of value between the two, introduces us at once to another distinction—that of capital and labor. . . . Labor now becomes a commodity, wealth capital, and the natural order of things is entirely reversed. Antagonism and opposition of interest is introduced in the community; capital and labor stand opposed." (Quoted in Dawley, *supra* 63–64.)

Employees turned to labor organizations as they abandoned hope of occupational mobility and acquired fears for job security. Although geographical and some occupational mobility did occur, the most usual form of advancement was movement within a class. It was rare for a worker, or an offspring, to enter the managerial ranks, and property accumulation would rarely involve substantial wealth. See, *e.g.*, A. Dawley, Class and Community: The Industrial Revolution in Lynn, Ch. 2 (1976).

It is common in American scholarship to discuss problems of status and occupational mobility, but it should be equally stressed that the majority of factory workers found themselves working under oppressive and unsafe conditions. Labor contracts, usually verbal in form, permitted entrepreneurs to maintain control over workers. Substantial fines could be imposed, for instance, for tardiness. Acceptance of employment was thought to mean acquiescence in often detailed work rules. Employees, for example, could be required to give two weeks notice prior to departure, a condition not deemed applicable to employers. A blacklist was commonly maintained, and an employee not receiving an "honorable discharge" would find it impossible to find work in the area. See, *e.g.*, W.

Sullivan, The Industrial Worker in Pennsylvania, 1800–1840, 34–57 (1955, reprint. 1972); C. Ware, The Early New England Cotton Manufacture: A Study in Industrial Beginnings 260-68 (1966).

"[T]he [main] difference between the labor story of the colonial and post-Revolutionary periods is that the acts of combination in the earlier period were temporary, spurred on by special and local problems of competition, low wages, or other unfavorable working conditions. The strikes that at times resulted are too scattered in area and time to suggest any consistent pattern." Morris, *Preface* to 3, 4 J. Commons and E. Gilmore, Documentary History of American Industrial Society i (1958) [hereinafter cited as Commons and Gilmore]. What is significant for the later development of the doctrine of criminal conspiracy is the attitude of colonial authorities to such strikes. Although public authorities sometimes intervened, strikes and strike activity were not normally considered illegal in the colonial period—the reason is probably that employers had recourse to other legal mechanisms, such as statutes authorizing compulsory labor, heavy penalties for absenteeism and desertion, and specific enforcement of labor contracts. See R. Morris, Government and Labor in Early America 221 (1946).

> "To seek an answer to the question why strikes were suddenly prosecuted by the machinery of the criminal law in the Jeffersonian and early national periods, we must consider the change which was swiftly occurring in American manufacturing. We must bear in mind that both employers and employees found competition far more acute than at any time previously. Trade union organization was taking on a permanent character, closed shop demands became frequent, and strikes seemed to lead a normal pattern of labor protest. After the close of the Revolution, and particularly after the new national government under the federal Constitution went into effect, the factory system expanded and custom or bespoke work in various fields, such as shoemaking, was being supplanted by wholesale order work for an outside market. To meet new and severe competition employers introduced green hands or cheap and less skilled labor, sought to keep open their labor supply and to keep down the cost of production, including wages, even if it meant cheapening their product. To meet this formidable threat the skilled craftsmen turned to the trade union. As the trade union movement spread employers in city after city looked to the courts to choke its growth. In the absence of state statutes making trade-union activity illegal precedents were found in the common law of England. Though these precedents were of dubious validity and of still more doubtful application to America, they were quickly seized by conservative groups who saw the threat to their status posed by the growing power of labor." (Morris, *Preface* to 3, 4 J. Commons and E. Gilmore, Documentary History of American Industrial Society iii–iv (1958).)

Thus, by the early nineteenth century, organizations of skilled workers began to emerge in northeastern cities, particularly among printers, carpenters, shoemakers, or cordwainers. Journeymen cordwainers and printers had lost faith in older hopes of becoming masters, and they increasingly realized that they were likely to remain journeymen. These organizations were often primarily benevolent organizations, although some of their aims went beyond "mutual aid societies." The societies supplemented benevolent programs with basic economic demands—a minimum wage, either a stated daily rate or a minimum wage for each task or piece of work completed—and they demanded the equivalent of a closed shop. Thus, they sought to compel employers to hire and retain society members only, and insisted that outsiders be made to join if they hoped to work. Since maintenance of union-set terms turned basically upon internal union discipline, the closed shop was a key demand. Early strikes, or "turn-outs," typically lasted several hours to several days and were often unorganized, yet peaceful. Many of these organizations were created in response to specific grievances, and they dissolved when the dispute was resolved or when efforts were unsuccessful. Wider aims were involved as well—strikes involved employees, many of them skilled artisans, who "worried that the transformation of the American social and economic structure threatened settled ways of work and life and particular visions of a just society." H. Gutman, Work, Culture and Society in Industrializing America 54 (1977).

The nation's second surge of unionism occurred at mid-century as journeymen once more combined. These unions concentrated on the closed shop, rules of apprenticeship, wages and methods of payment, and other benefits.

The unilateral adoption of "rules" indicating the price of labor was a common device for workers who were in passage from journeymen artisans to factory laborers. Unskilled workers, having no monopoly of special skills, tended to rely upon different tactics, e.g., "massive solidarity supplemented by intimidation of dissenters through social ostracism, threats, or riots. Their actions were more frequently community-based than workshop-based, all inhabitants of a residential neighborhood becoming involved in the strike action." D. Montgomery, Beyond Equality: Labor and the Radical Republicans 1862–1872, at 142–47 (1967).

The goals of these unions should not be seen as exclusively materialistic. The attempt to achieve shorter hours, as in the 10-hour movement, was inspired by a desire to secure an opportunity for leisure and self-improvement. The persistent concern over the lack of individual status and equality also led many workers into utopian, religious, and political movements.

No thumbnail sketch of labor in America could do justice to the richness of this history of turbulence and conflict. Numerous excellent histories exist, however, including histories of specific periods, areas, industries, and unions. The impact of law in the nineteenth century is difficult to document. It is clear that courts did not favor union organization or collective employee action, but numerous obstacles to organization existed which may well have been far more critical than legal barriers. The repeated depressions of the nineteenth century, the determined opposition of employers, and the effect of immigration resulting in a work force containing differences in culture, language, and religion may have been far more serious obstacles to union organization. Judicial doctrines, however, severely restricted the economic weapons early unions could employ to encourage organization or to pressure employers to cease particular practices. Employers, on the other hand, were free to use their economic power to hire or fire at will to discourage unionism.

The legal response, however, tells us something about the role of the legal system in regulating explosive economic combat. Labor law is one of the few law school courses which deals with collective economic action and focuses in large part upon the question whether these economic conflicts should be left to private resolution or regulated by the state.

The question whether terms and conditions of employment should be set by individual bargaining or collective negotiations, and whether the law should support one method or the other, is also involved in many of the early labor cases. Although collective bargaining is now supported by federal policy, most of the current issues of labor regulation can be found in early labor cases. These cases, for instance, involve the extent to which law should limit the scope and types of weapons available for economic combat. Attempts to secure a monopoly of the labor supply, to strengthen the union as an institution, especially against nonunion employees or rival unions, and the use of various economic weapons are all present in early cases. Indeed, many of our labor "problems" have not changed even though some of the legal answers have.

1. The Criminal Conspiracy Doctrine

Problem

Journeymen tailors, presenting themselves as a committee of workers, requested higher pay for the work they were then engaged in completing. To get the work done, the employer agreed to pay the price demanded. When the work was finished, the higher wages were paid, but committee members were then summarily discharged. A short time later, the remaining journeymen demanded that the discharged workmen be reemployed, threatening otherwise to cease work and quit immediately. The employer refused to reinstate the discharged employees, and the remaining journeymen left the store. The strikers engaged in picketing in an attempt to induce prospective employees not to accept jobs. When the employer attempted to send his work to other employers, the strikers threatened to strike any employer who performed the "struck work." Indeed, the tailors struck two firms which accepted the struck work.

How should the law respond to the demand that wages be raised, the discharge of the employees, the strike demanding their reinstatement, the picketing and the inducement of other employees not to "scab," and the pressure on the other employers not to perform struck work?

The Philadelphia shoemaker (or cordwainer) strike of 1805 led to what is often considered the first American labor case. The shoe trade had passed from the production of custom work by master cordwainers to quantity production for retail sales. Output was still centered around household production, and pressure was generally directed only to maintain or increase piecework rates. When Philadelphia manufacturers began to sell shoes and boots in the South in competition with English goods, journeymen had initially aided the effort by agreeing to a 25-cent reduction on the regular piecework rate for boots made for export. The strike was aimed both at increasing the regular piecework rate and eliminating the rebate for export products. The strikers held out for several weeks, but the arrest of the strike leaders for criminal conspiracy ended the effort in failure.

Nelles, The First American Labor Case*†

The practice of arguing law as well as fact to juries in criminal cases was still universal at the time of the cordwainers' trial. There was no controversy as to the facts. The question of law involved was novel in the United States. It would have been rash, therefore, for the court to undertake to prevent counsel from appealing to the jury on grounds of public policy as well as by citation of English authorities. And since the issues of public policy with respect to organized labor have not changed greatly in a century and a quarter, the most interesting of the arguments of counsel are those which touched them.

The major premise of the prosecution's case was that unlimited expansion of manufactures is beneficial to the community. It is therefore proper, said Hopkinson, "to support this manufacture. Will you permit men to destroy it who have no permanent stake in the city; men who can pack up their all in a knapsack, or carry them in their pockets to New York or Baltimore?" The journeymen's confederacy, said Ingersoll, will destroy the industry, to the ruin, not of the masters, who could stand the shock, but of the journeymen themselves.

Another of the prosecution's scarecrows may have seemed to the jury more perturbing: if the masters pay higher wages, "you must pay higher for the articles." From this was drawn the inference, perhaps plausible if the export trade had not yet become important to the masters, that the masters "have no interest to serve in the prosecution. . . . They, in truth, are protecting the community."

That the prosecution was subversive of American freedom was the main contention of the defense. Even if it were conceded (as of course it was not) that at English common law the cordwainers' society would be a criminal conspiracy, that common law was not American common law. In support of this, counsel argued, relying upon Tucker's Blackstone, that if a doctrine of labor conspiracy had been used in this country during the colonial period—which it had not—it could not survive as law in one of the United States, even under a constitution or statute which continued "the

*Nelles, *First American Labor Case*, 41 YALE L.J. 165, 166–70, 173–79, 182–83, 190 (1931). Copyright 1932 by the Yale Law Journal Co., Inc. Used by permission.
  †Footnotes omitted.

common law" in general terms. For it would be in derogation of the natural and unalienable rights of man, and inconsistent with democracy.

A safe and sensible position for a court in 1806 might have been this: The question is of American public policy and cannot be deemed controlled by English authorities. Society is divided with respect to it; there is no such approach to unanimity as might justify a court in feeling that it had a mandate from society to decide it, and no such indifference as to make a decision either way preferable to none at all. Such a question of policy is more appropriate for legislative than for judicial consideration; and so long as the legislature has not spoken, society may be presumed to will that the subject shall remain unregulated by law.

A different position, however, was taken by Recorder Levy. In his charge to the jury such sensitiveness as he showed to considerations which have been here adduced was not catholic.

A Brief Sketch of the Criminal Conspiracy Doctrine*

The journeymen shoemakers in Philadelphia were convicted, and fined $8 each when they "did combine, conspire and confederate, and unlawfully agree together . . . that they . . . would not . . . work . . . but at certain large prices and rates." Philadelphia Cordwainers' Case of 1806 (*Commonwealth* v. *Pullis,* Phila. Mayor's Court), 3 Commons and Gilmore, A Documentary History of American Industrial Society 59–248 (1910). The pattern which was developed here, involving the identification of the most common activity of employee groups as a "criminal conspiracy," was followed in eight of the ten similar cases which arose during the next 20 years in Pennsylvania, Maryland, New York, and Massachusetts. See Nelles, *Commonwealth* v. *Hunt,* 32 Colum. L. Rev. 1128, 1166 (1932).

In the charge which Moses Levy, one of the judges of the Mayor's Court in Philadelphia and its Recorder, made to the jury in the Cordwainers' Case he summed up "the law" as follows (3 Commons and Gilmore 228–33):

> "It is proper to consider, is such a combination consistent with the principles of our law, and injurious to the public welfare? The usual means by which the prices of work are regulated, are the demand for the article and the excellence of its fabric. Where the work is well done, and the demand is considerable, the prices will necessarily be high. Where the work is ill done, and the demand is inconsiderable, they will unquestionably be low. . . . To make an artificial regulation, is not to regard the excellence of the work or quality of the material, but to fix a positive and arbitrary price, governed by no standard, controlled by no impartial person, but dependent on the will of the few who are interested; this is the unnatural way of raising the price of goods or work. . . . It is an unnatural, artificial means of raising the price of work beyond its standard, and taking an undue advantage of the public. Is the rule of law bottomed upon such principles, as to permit or protect

*Some of this material has been adapted from an earlier publication of the Labor Law Group, LABOR RELATIONS AND THE LAW 18–23 (3d ed. 1965).

such conduct? Consider it on the footing of the general commerce of the city. Is there any man who can calculate (if this is tolerated) at what price he may safely contract to deliver articles, for which he may receive orders, if he is to be regulated by the journeymen in an arbitrary jump from one price to another? . . . Can he fix the price of his commodity for a future day? It is impossible that any man can carry on commerce in this way. There cannot be a large contract entered into, but what the contractor will make at his peril. He may be ruined by the difference of prices made by the journeymen in the intermediate time. . . . Consider these circumstances as they affect trade generally. Does this measure tend to make good workmen? No: it puts the botch incapable of doing justice to his work, on a level with the best tradesman. The master must give the same wages to each. Such a practice would take away all the excitement to excel in workmanship or industry. Consider the effect it would have upon the whole community. If the masters say they will not sell under certain prices, as the journeymen declare they will not work at certain wages, they, if persisted in, would put the whole body of the people into their power. Shoes and boots are articles of the first necessity. If they could stand out three or four weeks in winter, they might raise the price of boots to thirty, forty, or fifty dollars a pair, at least for some time, and until a competent supply could be got from other places. In every point of view, this measure is pregnant with public mischief and private injury . . . tends to demoralize the workmen . . . destroy the trade of the city, and leaves the pockets of the whole community to the discretion of the concerned. . . .

"It is in the volumes of the common law we are to seek for information in the far greater number, as well as the most important causes that come before our tribunals. . . . It says there may be cases in which what one man may do with [out] offence, many combined may not do with impunity. It distinguishes between the object so aimed at in different transactions. If the purpose to be obtained, be an object of individual interest, it may be fairly attempted by an individual. . . . Many are prohibited from combining for the attainment of it.

"What is the case now before us? . . . A combination of workmen to raise their wages may be considered in a two fold point of view: one is to benefit themselves . . . the other is to injure those who do not join their society. The rule of law condemns both. If the rule be clear, we are bound to conform to it even though we do not comprehend the principle upon which it is founded. We are not to reject it because we do not see the reason of it. It is enough, that it is the will of the majority. It is law because it is their will—if it is law, there may be good reasons for it though we cannot find them out. But the rule in this case is pregnant with sound sense and all the authorities are clear upon the subject. Hawkins, the greatest authority on the criminal law, has laid it down, that a combination to maintaining one another, carrying a particular object, whether true or false, is criminal. . . ."

Another factor in the evolution of the criminal conspiracy doctrine was suggested in *People* v. *Faulkner*, 4 Commons and Gilmore, Documentary

History of American Industrial Society 315 et seq. (1910), decided in the court of Oyer and Terminer of New York City in 1836. Tailors had struck first for wages and then (after they had received substantial increases) for a kind of seniority system. Highhanded tactics were used against employers of "dungs," tailors who took work when more senior tailors were without jobs. The trial was on an indictment for conspiring to injure trade and commerce (based on a New York statute) and was apparently not based on another indictment for "riot, and assault and battery." The tailors were convicted of conspiracy. In imposing fines totaling $1150, Judge Edwards addressed the tailors at length, in part as follows (4 Commons and Gilmore at 330–31):

> "Associations of this description are of recent origin in this country. Here, where the government is purely paternal, where the people are governed by laws of their own creating; where the legislature proceeds with a watchful regard to the welfare not only of the whole, but of every class of society; where the representatives ever lend a listening ear to the complaints of their constituents, it has not been found necessary or proper to subject any portion of the people to the control of self-created societies. Judging from what we have witnessed within the last year, we should be led to the conclusion that the trades of the country, which contribute immeasurably to its wealth, and upon which the prosperity of a most valuable portion of the community hinges, [are] rapidly passing from the control of the supreme power of the state into the hands of private societies. . . . Every American knows, or ought to know, that he has no better friend than the laws, and that he needs no artificial combination for his protection. . . . They [the "private societies" of the journeymen groups] are of foreign origin, and I am led to believe are mainly upheld by foreigners. . . .
>
> "Self-created societies are unknown to the constitution and laws, and will not be permitted to rear their crest and extend their baneful influence over any portion of the community."

Judge Edwards' observation that the union movement of his time was largely supported by "foreigners" was as questionable as his paternalistic view of American government in which the association was not to intervene and mediate between the individual and the state. Alexis de Toqueville was touring America about the time Judge Edwards lectured the tailors. Of the associational life of the nation, he wrote, in his Democracy in America 319 (Oxford ed. 1947):*

> "The political associations that exist in the United States are only a single feature in the midst of the immense assemblage of associations in that country. Americans of all ages, all conditions, and all dispositions, constantly form associations. They have not only commercial and manufacturing companies, in which all take part, but associations of a thousand other kinds—religious, moral, serious, futile, extensive or restricted, enormous or diminutive. . . . The English often perform great things singly; whereas the Americans form associations for the

*Reprinted with permission of the Oxford University Press.

smallest undertakings. It is evident that the former people consider associations as a powerful means of action, but the latter seem to regard it as the only means they have of acting.

"Thus the most democratic country on the face of the earth is that in which men have in our time carried to the highest perfection the art of pursuing in common the object of their common desires, and have applied this new science to the greatest number of purposes. Is this the result of accident? or is there in reality any necessary connection between the principle of association and that of equality? Aristocratic communities always contain, among a multitude of persons who by themselves are powerless, a small number of powerful and wealthy citizens, each of whom can achieve great undertakings single-handed. In aristocratic societies men do not need to combine in order to act, because they are strongly held together. . . . Among democratic nations, on the contrary, all the citizens are independent and feeble; they can do hardly anything by themselves, and none of them can oblige his fellow men to lend him their assistance. They all, therefore, fall into a state of incapacity, if they do not learn voluntarily to help each other."

The courts' application of the criminal conspiracy doctrine to early employee group activities eventually aroused a storm of public protest. The people felt that the courts had overreached their authority. The public concern was not limited to working groups; it included also those who voted Federalist, wanted high tariffs, and owned mills and factories which would be closed if labor feeling grew too strong. Labor was already recognized as a strong, if not cohesive, economic and political force.

These, some suggest, were among the considerations which prompted the Supreme Judicial Court of Massachusetts, in 1842, to set aside the conviction (for criminal conspiracy) of seven members of the Boston Journeymen Bootmakers' Society who had indicated that they would refuse to work in shops where nonmembers of the Society were employed at less than the scheduled rate (obtained by the Society in a recent strike) of $2 per pair of boots. *Commonwealth* v. *Hunt,* 4 Metc. 111 (1842). The court, while not rejecting the doctrine of criminal conspiracy as being inapplicable to organized employee activity, cut the heart from the old approach by insisting that it was the *purpose* of the concerted action rather than the fact of such concert itself which was important. Chief Justice Shaw wrote (p. 129): "The manifest intention of the association is, to induce all those engaged in the same occupation to become members of it. Such a purpose is not unlawful. It would give them a power which might be exerted for useful and honorable purposes, or for dangerous and pernicious ones. If the latter were the real and actual object, and susceptible of proof, it should have been specially charged. . . . In this state of things, we cannot perceive, that it is criminal for men to agree together to exercise their acknowledged rights, in such a manner as best to subserve their own interests."

In the same volume of the Massachusetts reports, Justice Shaw decided *Farwell* v. *Boston and Worcester Railroad Corp.,* 4 Metc. 49 (Mass. 1842), adopting the "fellow servant rule," which denied an employee recovery against his employer for injuries caused by the negligence of another employee. This rule and the hardships which it imposed on employees was replaced 70 years later by a series of Workmen's Compensation and Employer Liability Laws. In adopting the fellow servant rule, which had previously been developed in only one English case and accepted in a South Carolina decision, Justice Shaw wrote in terms which seem equally applicable to his decision in *Commonwealth* v. *Hunt* (p. 58):

> "In considering the rights and obligations arising out of particular relations, it is competent for courts of justice to regard considerations of policy and general convenience, and to draw from them such rules as will, in their practical application, best promote the safety and security of all parties concerned."

Comment on the Role of the Doctrine

The role of conspiracy prosecutions and their scope have probably often been overstated. A significant number of strikes occurred in the first half of the nineteenth century, apparently undeterred by the threat of criminal prosecution. The threat of prosecution may have been an ineffective threat, paralleling the modern attempts to bar strikes by public workers. Few recorded prosecutions resulted in anything other than minor fines. The Philadelphia strike leaders, for instance, were each fined $8. In the cases reported in 3, 4 Commons and Gilmore, no worker received a jail sentence. See also J. Landis and M. Manoff, Cases on Labor Law 32–33 n. 88 (2d ed. 1942). Would greater penalties have deterred strikes? Can the threat of criminal prosecution nevertheless be a deterrent even though the penalties are likely to be modest?

A corrective on the traditional history of the early period is provided by Professor Edwin E. Witte who noted that underlying legal theories had actually changed little up to the 1920s when he was writing.

Witte, Early American Labor Cases*†

Prior to the eighties there were but few reported decisions in cases which arose in connection with labor disputes in the United States. In consequence, all writers who discuss the beginnings of American labor law have devoted considerable attention to the early unreported cases in inferior courts which preceded *Commonwealth* v. *Hunt* in 1842.

These early unreported cases have usually been interpreted as reflecting "a spirit of medievalism with its antagonism to the working classes." It is commonly believed, as one writer puts it, that "in the early part of the nineteenth century, peaceable combinations of workingmen to better

*Witte, *Early American Labor Cases*. Reprinted by permission of the Yale Law Journal Co., Inc., and Fred B. Rothman & Co. from THE YALE LAW JOURNAL, Vol. 35, pp. 825–30, 832, 836–37.
†Footnotes omitted.

their conditions of employment were illegal both in England and the United States;" or, as expressed by another, that "combinations of workmen to raise their wages, shorten hours and compel the employment of their own members were held unlawful conspiracies by the courts at common law and even under some of the statutes one hundred years ago." *Commonwealth* v. *Hunt* is usually regarded as the case which overthrew these archaic doctrines and which marks the beginning of the modern law of labor combinations, in which "the legal battle ground has shifted from a fight over the right of labor unions to exist to a contest as to what means may lawfully be used by labor organizations in the economic struggle over the price of labor."

This interpretation of the early American labor cases will not stand the test of an examination of the original sources. It is supported only by a few expressions of hostility to the newly founded labor unions by judges and prosecutors, which have been mistaken for established legal doctrines. It was never the law in the United States that labor unions are illegal per se, or that all strikes are unlawful. The unreported cases of the early nineteenth century did not turn upon the legality of the unions per se, but on the methods which they employed to gain their ends. Nor were the views expressed in these early cases as to the methods which might lawfully be employed less liberal than those now [the 1920s] generally held by the courts.

In one respect, indeed, these early cases differed radically from present-day legal actions in connection with labor disputes. This was that all these early cases, with one exception, involved criminal indictments for conspiracy, not injunctions or damage suits, as do most present-day cases. This is a difference, however, only in the character of the actions, not in underlying legal theories. As to these, there is little to distinguish the unreported cases of the early nineteenth century from the law today.

Only one of the legal theories which played a role in the early cases has been entirely abandoned. This was the theory that it is illegal for workingmen to combine to raise wages. This doctrine had the support of numerous English precedents; but in this country it never attained the status of generally accepted law. In about one half of the early conspiracy cases, one of the counts in the indictment was to the effect that the defendants had combined to raise wages. In all of these cases, however, there were also charges of violence, picketing or closed shop rules and practices; and it was these charges which the prosecution emphasized rather than the combination to raise wages.

In the earliest case, that of the Philadelphia cordwainers in 1806, the prosecution, indeed, made the point that a combination to raise wages is illegal at common law; but it also argued that the defendants were not indicted "for regulating their own individual wages, but for undertaking by a combination to regulate the price of labor of others as well as their own." [*Philadelphia Cordwainers*, 3 Commons and Gilmore 68]. Recorder Levy, however, was more positive, and squarely instructed the jury that a combination to raise wages was illegal.

This case was followed by eighteen other prosecutions of working-men for conspiracy in the next three decades. In only one of them, however, did the court take the same view of the illegality of combinations to raise wages as did Recorder Levy. This was the New York case of *People* v. *Fisher* [14 Wend. 9, reprinted in 4 Commons and Gilmore 275] in 1835, in which Chief Justice Savage at some length developed the same thesis, although the case involved not merely a combination to raise wages, but the threat of a strike to procure the discharge of non-union workmen.

The defendants in all of the cases prior to *Commonwealth* v. *Hunt* used means to effect their ends which are generally regarded as unlawful even now. In nearly all of these cases the star witnesses for the prosecution were non-union workmen who had lost their jobs because the indicted union members refused to work with them. Some cases involved even more doubtful practices. In the Buffalo tailors' case in 1824 the defendants sent a list of "black legs" to unions throughout the country to prevent the hated non-unionists from getting work anywhere. The Baltimore weavers' case in 1829 arose because the defendants had taken an oath that none of them would work for a certain master for two years; and, as has been noted, the Hudson shoemakers in 1826 went on strike to compel a master to pay a heavy fine for employing a non-union workman. Yet in none of these cases nor in any other conspiracy cases prior to the Civil War was a single workman sentenced to jail, and only in the New York tailors' case were heavy fines imposed; while a considerable number of these cases resulted in acquittals.

In several of these early conspiracy cases the prosecution or the court, or both, stated that it was the methods which the defendants had used which rendered their combination illegal; but it was not until *Commonwealth* v. *Hunt* that the distinction vaguely hinted at in these early cases, between the legality of the combination per se and the methods which it employs was clearly expressed. This famous case, like many of the cases which preceded it, involved a strike to procure the discharge of a non-union workman. Today, such a strike is illegal in Massachusetts, but in this case in 1842 the Supreme Court of that state in a unanimous decision written by Chief Justice Shaw held the conduct of these strikers to have been entirely lawful.

This decision, however, did not, as some writers have stated, mark the end of the application of the conspiracy doctrine to labor combinations. Even today this doctrine is the most important of all legal theories which figure in labor cases. Far from repudiating this doctrine, *Commonwealth* v. *Hunt* expressed it in the form in which it usually has been expressed since, namely, that the legality of a combination depends upon the purposes sought to be accomplished and the means used to effect these ends.

CONSPIRACY CASES AFTER *COMMONWEALTH* V. *HUNT*

Except for its influence upon the form of the statement of the conspiracy doctrine, *Commonwealth* v. *Hunt* seems to have had comparatively little effect upon the development of the law of labor combinations in this country. In the next twenty years, indeed, only three conspiracy cases are known to have occurred in connection with labor disputes; but that there were not more such cases is readily explained by the almost complete absence of strikes during this period. With the general revival of trade unionism in the closing years of the Civil War, conspiracy cases once more became of frequent occurrence. From 1863 to 1880 there were at least seven conspiracy cases in Pennsylvania, five in New York, three in New Jersey and one each in Connecticut, Illinois and Missouri.

These prosecutions led the labor organizations of this period to demand "the repeal of the conspiracy laws," by which was meant the enactment of legislation to nullify the conspiracy doctrine of the common law. Such legislation was won in Pennsylvania, New York, New Jersey and Maryland, and in part, also in Illinois. It proved a great disappointment in operation, however, actually making practically no change in the law, and failing to end prosecutions for conspiracy premised upon participation in strikes.

. . .

Criminal prosecutions for conspiracy became infrequent after the "eighties" not because of any changes in the substantive law, but solely because injunctions became the usual form of action in legal controversies growing out of labor disputes.

. . .

Notes

1. Witte notes that although criminal conspiracy prosecutions faded from the legal scene, substantive legal rules remained unchanged through the 1920s.

". . . The decisions of the courts today upon what conduct in the furtherance of the objects of labor unions is lawful, are not one wit more liberal than the doctrines announced in the earliest cases; and the statutes enacted have been practically without effect. As regards substantive rights, the law of labor combinations in the United States has remained unchanged, except as to details, throughout its entire history.

"The fundamentally important changes which have occurred, related to remedies, not to substantive rights. For more than three quarters of a century after the first American labor case, practically the only remedy was a criminal prosecution for conspiracy. Then in the 'eighties' was developed the injunction, and within the last fifteen years the damage suit. From a practical point of view it is the stages in the development of these remedies which constitute the most important chapters in the history of American law of labor combinations."

2. How can the theoretical equality of individuals stressed by early judges be reconciled with the real life inequality of individual power? To what extent should disparity in bargaining or economic power affect the result when economic harm is caused?

3. In *Commonwealth* v. *Hunt*, Chief Justice Shaw refused to find illegality in a combination not to work for employers who employed nonmembers of the organization. He based this conclusion on the notion that such a

combination might have worthy objectives such as the promotion of safety, and no particular unworthy objective had been set forth in the indictment. The same reasoning was applied to the second charge, noting that no unsocial end was set forth in the attempt to discharge a co-worker. Yet, Shaw's "demolition of the indictment pursues a highly technical course, and he avoids carefully any characterization of the true activity of the strikers as sanctioned by law. Nowhere in his judgment is there any indication that the earlier common law authorities are being rejected; instead, even though they be accepted, technical construction of the indictment fails to disclose a case within the ambit—the pursuit by a combination of an unlawful end or of a lawful end by unlawful means." J. Landis and M. Manoff, Cases on Labor Law 35 (2d ed. 1942). Moreover, in *State* v. *Donaldson*, 32 N.J.L. 151, 90 A.M. Dec. 649 (1867), a case remarkably like *Commonwealth* v. *Hunt*, the court was able to narrowly distinguish that decision on the ground "that the aim of the combination was unlawful because 'the effort was to dictate to this employer whom he should discharge from his employ.' The doctrine of the *Donaldson* case found practically unanimous application in a series of cases that featured the growing labor unrest of the early seventies, an unrest that was to culminate in the Railway Strike of 1877." Landis and Manoff 36–37.

Justice Shaw's opinion in *Commonwealth* v. *Hunt* has generally been reported as a critically important decision in the history of American labor law as well as a reflection of a master judicial craftsman at work. See Nelles. *Commonwealth* v. *Hunt*, 32 Colum. L. Rev. 1128 (1932); L. Levy, The Law of the Commonwealth and Chief Justice Shaw 183–206 (1967). As Professor Witte has argued, however, this view overstates the harshness of earlier decisions as well as the legal significance of *Hunt*. Moreover, the *Donaldson* decision suggests that there was no great difficulty in refurbishing the doctrine in the turbulent labor struggles of the 1860s and 1870s.

How does one determine the effect of a decision such as *Commonwealth* v. *Hunt*? Could the absence of strikes in the 20 years after *Hunt*, used by Witte to explain the absence of conspiracy prosecutions, be due to "the probability that a good many employers, on the advice of counsel . . . , put up with labor unions which, had *Commonwealth* v. *Hunt* gone the other way, the law would have been invited to crush?" Nelles, *Commonwealth* v. *Hunt*, 32 Colum. L. Rev. 1128, 1163 (1932).

4. Although the early courts routinely condemned action by employees to alter the "natural" operation of the market system, the focus of concern, except for a few trials such as that of Philadelphia Cordwainers, was generally the effect of union power on nonunion members. A number of cases suggest that concerted action became criminal only if the union attempted to use economic pressure to force unwilling employees to comply with union rules. See, *e.g.*, *Baltimore Weavers Case* (Balt. City Ct. 1829), 4 Commons and Gilmore 269–72; *Commonwealth* v. *Grinder* (Phila. Rec. Ct. 1836), 4 Commons and Gilmore 335–41; *People* v. *Melvin*, 2 Wheeler Crim. Cas. 262 (N.Y. Ct. Gen. Sess. 1809), 3 Commons and Gilmore 251–385.

Assuming that nonmembers present a threat to union-determined wages and labor conditions, on what grounds can courts decide which set of conflicting interests to protect?

2. TORT, EQUITY, AND THE RISE OF THE UNLAWFUL MEANS-UNLAWFUL ENDS DOCTRINE

After the Civil War, the legality of collective economic action was occasionally determined in tort actions for money damages. The issue raised in these cases concerned the extent to which associations could restrain the operation of the "free market place" by regulating prices, supply of labor, and the terms of employment. The first cases involved a combination of employers. *Master·Stevedores' Ass'n* v. *Walsh*, 2 Daly 1 (N.Y.C.P. 1867), held that an incorporated association of master stevedores (who were the entrepreneurs of that business) could penalize any member of the association who charged less than the association's schedule of prices. The New York Court of Common Pleas declared that, "It is better for the law to leave such matters to the action of the parties interested—to leave master workmen or journeymen free to form what associations they please in relation to the rate of compensation, so long as they are voluntary." *Id.* 12. The labor cases in the Cordwainers tradition were distinguished as involving coercion of nonmembers of the group.

In *Walker* v. *Cronin*, 107 Mass. 555 (1871), however, a shoemakers' union program of permitting its members to work only in shops which provided acceptable terms and conditions of employment was held an actionable tort. In this and other cases of the period, the courts developed the principle that organized labor's pressures constituted a prima facie tort. The intentional infliction of harm upon employers or nonunion employees, usually present in these cases, was in itself wrong unless justifiable cause could be shown. If the purpose of the infliction of harm was the procuring of higher wages, for instance, most courts deemed the activity as having a justifiable cause, and therefore the strike was not tortious. Some courts felt the same way about action designed to enlarge union membership; others, notably those in Massachusetts, considered such strikes to be without justification and, therefore, a sufficient basis for recovery of damages.

Toward the end of the nineteenth century, however, another phase of judicial participation in the evolution of the employment relationship began. Labor activities which had first been considered as the subject of criminal proceedings, and then as torts, were identified, almost suddenly, as matters enjoinable in the equity courts.

It was only by accident that the courts in this country stumbled into a departure from what had always been the English rule against the issuance of injunctions in labor disputes. The American practice developed in the 1880s and 1890s when many railroads were in receivership, under the control of agents of the courts of equity. When railroad employees struck, the equity courts' traditional weapon was turned on them. The technique worked so well and so quickly that it was almost immediately applied to strikes at plants where the equity court had no interest until the strike broke.

Of this era of the law, Professor Gregory has written:*

"[P]erhaps the most alarming feature of the labor injunction . . . was the ease with which its use increasingly tempted judges to dispense with any well-founded independent theory of illegality. . . . They came to look at much of organized labor's economic coercive activity as enjoinable in itself, without bothering to find or to state in their opinions that it was also unlawful. This was an unfortunate tendency which fed on itself. It seemed to lead many courts to grant sweeping injunctions on the basis of personal or class dislike of organized labor's economic program instead of in accordance with settled standards of law. A process of this sort lent itself admirably to the use of the illegal purpose doctrine.

". . . [S]ince no generally recognized body of law existed, aside from that governing various specific types of conduct, by which to judge the legality of purposes and contexts, many courts asked to issue injunctions unfortunately slipped into the custom of using as standards their own notions of what they believed to be good or bad as a matter of policy. In this way too many judges began to think of labor union activity as something enjoinable in itself. . . . This unwholesome state of affairs, where labor unionists never knew just where they stood under the shadow of a brooding and undefined judicial power, involved an almost certain threat of suppression to most of organized labor's bargaining and organizational program, without benefit of any legislative declaration of policy or, indeed, of any rules of the game that might be called law." (Gregory 102–03.)

The procedures under which injunctions were issued often failed to afford unions a fair opportunity to establish a defense prior to the issuance of the writ. These procedures included the issuance of injunctions ex parte, based upon affidavits of a type which many deemed utterly untrustworthy. See Judge Amidon's opinion in *Great Northern Ry.* v. *Brosseau*, 286 Fed. 414 (D.N.D. 1923); F. Frankfurter and N. Greene, The Labor Injunction (1930) [hereinafter cited as Frankfurter and Greene].

The language commonly found in complaints added to the problem. Whereas violence was forbidden, "intimidation," "threats," or "coercion" could be similarly treated if one assumed that violence would be the inevitable result. A "threat," however, might merely warn that legally permissible pressure would be directed at uncooperative employers. Similarly "coercion" might have suggested permissible economic pressure. The "persuasive" aspects of a picket line might have sought to communicate and encourage the exercise of free judgment. "Unwittingly a court may be pronouncing judgment upon the implications of a label, instead of weighing the elements of an industrial conflict as it actually transpired." Frankfurter and Green 34–35 (footnote omitted).

---

*Selections are reprinted from LABOR AND THE LAW, by Charles O. Gregory, Second Revised Edition, with the permission of the publisher, W.W. Norton & Co., Inc. Copyright 1946, 1949, Second Edition Copyright © 1958 by W.W. Norton & Co., Inc.

Just as in criminal conspiracy, where unlawfulness was expanded beyond criminal conduct, labor activity in tort or equity actions did not have to fall within established prohibitions to be deemed unlawful. The boundaries were vague and included all conduct deemed socially objectionable by the courts. Justice Holmes saw clearly that judgments concerning privilege or justification to cause harm were matters of economic and social policy. In Holmes, *Privilege, Malice and Intent*, 8 Harv. L. Rev. 1, 3, 7, 9 (1894), he said:

"But whether, and how far, a privilege shall be allowed is a question of policy. Questions of policy are legislative questions, and judges are shy of reasoning from such grounds. Therefore, decisions for or against the privilege, which really can stand only upon such grounds, often are presented as hollow deductions from empty general propositions like *sic utere tuo ul alienum non laedas*, which teaches nothing but a benevolent yearning, or else are put as if they themselves embodied a postulate of the law and admitted of no further deduction, as when it is said that, although there is temporal damage, there is no wrong; whereas, the very thing to be found out is whether there is a wrong or not, and if not, why not.

. . .

"Perhaps one of the reasons why judges do not like to discuss questions of policy, or to put a decision in terms upon their views as lawmakers, is that the moment you leave the path of merely logical deduction you lose the illusion of certainty which makes legal reasoning seem like mathematics. But the certainty is only an illusion, nevertheless. Views of policy are taught by experience of the interests of life. Those interests are fields of battle. Whatever decisions are made must be against the wishes and opinion of one party, and the distinctions on which they go will be distinctions of degree. Even the economic postulate of the benefit of free competition, which I have mentioned above, is denied by an important school.

. . .

"I make these suggestions, not as criticisms of the decisions, but to call attention to the very serious legislative considerations which have to be weighed. The danger is that such considerations should have their weight in an inarticulate form as unconscious prejudice or half conscious inclination. To measure them justly needs not only the highest powers of a judge and a training which the practice of the law does not insure, but also a freedom from prepossessions which is very hard to attain. It seems to me desirable that the work should be done with express recognition of its nature."

Vegelahn v. Guntner

Supreme Judicial Court of Massachusetts, 1896
167 Mass. 92, 44 N.E. 1077

[The defendant union was enjoined *pendente lite* from picketing the plaintiff's factory after a preliminary hearing. The hearing on the merits was before Holmes, J, who reported the case for the consideration of the full court. The proposed final decree enjoined the union from interfering with plaintiff's business "by obstructing or physically interfering with any persons in entering or leaving the plaintiff's premises . . . , or by intimidating, by threats, express or implied, of violence or physical harm to body or property, any person or persons who now are or hereafter may be in the employment of the plaintiff, or desirous of entering the same, from entering or continuing in it. . . ." Holmes dissented, however, and refused to enjoin the union's use of "social pressure and persuasion" to prevent plaintiff from hiring workers, on the ground that such means were lawful even though economically harmful.]

ALLEN, J.

The principal question in this case is whether the defendants should be enjoined against maintaining the patrol. The report shows that, following upon a strike of the plaintiff's workmen, the defendants conspired to prevent him from getting workmen, and thereby to prevent him from carrying on his business, unless and until he should adopt a certain schedule of prices. The means adopted were persuasion and social pressure, threats of personal injury or unlawful harm conveyed to persons employed or seeking employment, and a patrol of two men in front of the plaintiff's factory, maintained from half past six in the morning till half past five in the afternoon, on one of the busiest streets of Boston. The number of men was greater at times, and at times showed some little disposition to stop the plaintiff's door. The patrol proper at times went further than simple advice, not obtruded beyond the point where the other person was willing to listen; and it was found that the patrol would probably be continued, if not enjoined. There was also some evidence of persuasion to break existing contracts.

The patrol was maintained as one of the means of carrying out the defendants' plan, and it was used in combination with social pressure, threats of personal injury or unlawful harm, and persuasion to break existing contracts. It was thus one means of intimidation indirectly to the plaintiff, and directly to persons actually employed, or seeking to be employed, by the plaintiff, and of rendering such employment unpleasant or intolerable to such persons. Such an act is an unlawful interference with the rights both of employer and of employed. An employer has a right to engage all persons who are willing to work for him, at such prices as may be mutually agreed upon; and persons employed or seeking employment have a corresponding right to enter into or remain in the employment of any person or corporation willing to employ them. These rights are secured by the Constitution itself. . . . No one can lawfully interfere by force or intimidation to prevent employers or persons employed or wishing to be employed from the exercise of these rights. In Massachusetts, as in some other States, it is even made a criminal offense for one by intimidation or force to prevent or seek to prevent a person from entering into or continuing in the employment of a person or corporation. Pub. Sts. c. 74, § 2. Intimidation is not limited to threats of violence or of physical injury to person or property. It has a broader signification, and there also may be a moral intimidation which is illegal. . . . The patrol was an unlawful interference both with the plaintiff and with the workmen, within the principle of many cases, and, when instituted for the purpose of interfering with his business, it became a private nuisance. See *Carew* v. *Rutherford*, 106 Mass. 1; *Walker* v. *Cronin*, 107 Mass. 555. . . .

The defendants contend that these acts were justifiable, because they were only seeking to secure better wages for themselves by compelling the plaintiff to accept their schedule of wages. This motive or purpose does not justify maintaining a patrol in front of the plaintiff's premises, as a means of carrying out their conspiracy. A combination among persons merely to regulate their own conduct is within allowable competition, and is lawful, although others may be indirectly affected thereby. But a combination to do injurious acts expressly directed to another, by way of intimidation or constraint, either of himself or of persons employed or seeking to be employed by him, is outside of allowable competition, and is unlawful. . . .

Nor does the fact that the defendants' acts might subject them to an indictment prevent a court of equity from issuing an injunction. It is true that ordinarily a court of equity will decline to issue an injunction to restrain the commission of a crime; but a continuing injury to property or business may be enjoined, although it may also be punishable as a nuisance or other crime. *Sherry* v. *Perkins*, 147 Mass. 212. *In re Debs*, 158 U.S. 564, 598, 599. . . .

A question is also presented whether the court should enjoin such interference with persons in the employment of the plaintiff who are not bound by contract to remain with him, or with persons who are not under any existing contract, but who are seeking or intending to enter into his employment. A conspiracy to interfere with the plaintiff's business by means of threats and intimidation, and by maintaining a patrol in front of his premises in order to prevent persons from entering his employment, or in order to prevent persons who are in his employment from continuing therein, is unlawful, even though such persons are not bound by contract to enter into or to continue in his employment; and the injunction should not be so limited as to relate only to persons who are bound by existing contracts. . . .

In the opinion of a majority of the court the injunction should be in the form originally issued. So ordered.

FIELD, C.J., dissenting [omitted].
HOLMES, J. [dissenting] . . .

In the first place, a word or two should be said as to the meaning of the report. I assume that my brethren construe it as I meant it to be construed, and that, if they were not prepared to do so, they would give an opportunity to the defendants to have it amended in accordance with what I state my meaning to be. There was no proof of any threat or danger of a patrol exceeding two men, and as of course an injunction is not granted except with reference to what there is reason to expect in its absence, the question on that point is whether a patrol of two men should be enjoined. Again, the defendants are enjoined by the final decree from intimidating by threats, express or implied, of physical harm to body or property, any person who may be desirous of entering into the employment of the plaintiff so far as to prevent him from entering the same. In order to test the correctness of the refusal to go further, it must be assumed that the defendants obey the express prohibition of the decree. If they do not, they fall within the injunction as it now stands, and are liable to summary punishment. The important difference between the preliminary and the final injunction is that the former goes further, and forbids the defendants to interfere with the plaintiff's business "by any scheme . . . organized for the purpose of . . . preventing any person or persons who now are or may hereafter be . . . desirous of entering the [plaintiff's employment] from entering it." I quote only a part, and the part which seems to me most objectionable. This includes refusal of social intercourse, and even organized persuasion or argument, although free from any threat of violence, either express or implied. And this is with reference to persons who have a legal right to contract or not to contract with the plaintiff, as they may see fit. Interference with existing contracts is forbidden by the final decree. I wish to insist a little that the only point of difference which involves a difference of principle between the final decree and the preliminary injunction which it is proposed to restore, is what I have mentioned, in order that it may be seen exactly what we are to discuss. It appears to me that the judgment of the majority turns in part on the assumption that the patrol necessarily carries with it a threat of bodily harm. That assumption I think unwarranted, for the reasons which I have given. Furthermore, it cannot be said, I think, that two men walking together up and down a sidewalk and speaking to those who enter a certain shop do necessarily and always thereby convey a threat of force. I do not think it possible to discriminate, and to say that two workmen, or even two representatives of an organization of workmen, do,—especially when they are, and are known to be, under the injunction of this court not to do so. . . . I may add, that I think the more intelligent workingmen believe as fully as I do that they no more can be permitted to usurp the State's prerogative of force than can their opponents in their controversies. But if I am wrong, then the decree as it stands reaches the patrol, since it applies to all threats of force. With this I pass to the real difference between the interlocutory and the final decree.

I agree, whatever may be the law in the case of a single defendant, *Rice* v. *Albee*, 164 Mass. 88, that when a plaintiff proves that several persons have combined and conspired to injure his business, and have done acts producing that effect, he shows temporal damage and a cause of action, unless the facts disclose, or the defendants prove, some ground of excuse or justification. And I take it to be settled, and rightly settled, that doing that damage by combined persuasion is actionable, as well as doing it by falsehood or by force. . . .

Nevertheless, in numberless instances the law warrants the intentional infliction of temporal damage because it regards it as justified. It is on the question of what shall amount to a justification, and more especially on the nature of the considerations which really determine or ought to determine the answer to that question, that judicial reasoning seems to me often to be inadequate. The true grounds of decision are considerations of policy and of social advantage, and it is vain to suppose that solutions can be attained merely by logic and the general propositions of law which nobody disputes. Propositions as to public policy rarely are unanimously accepted, and still more rarely, if ever, are capable of unanswerable proof. They require a special training to enable any one even to form an intelligent opinion about them. In the early stages of law, at least, they generally are acted on rather as inarticulate instincts than as definite ideas for which a rational defence is ready.

To illustrate what I have said in the last paragraph, it has been the law for centuries that a man may set up a business in a country town too small to support more than one, although he expects and intends thereby to ruin some one already there, and succeeds in his intent. In such a case he is not held to act "unlawfully and without justifiable cause," as was alleged in *Walker* v. *Cronin* and *Rice* v. *Albee*. The reason, of course, is that the doctrine generally has been accepted that free competition is worth more to society than it costs, and that on this ground the infliction of the damage is privileged. *Commonwealth* v. *Hunt*, 4 Met. 111, 134. Yet even this proposition nowadays is disputed by a considerable body of persons, including many whose intelligence is not to be denied, little as we may agree with them.

I have chosen this illustration partly with reference to what I have to say next. It shows without the need of further authority that the policy of allowing free competition justifies the intentional inflicting of temporal damage, including the damage of interference with a man's business, by some means, when the damage is done not for its own sake, but as an instrumentality in reaching the end of victory in the battle of trade. In such a case it cannot matter whether the plaintiff is the only rival of the defendant, and so is aimed at specifically, or is one of a class all of whom are hit. The only debatable ground is the nature of the means by which such damage may be inflicted. We all agree that it cannot be done by force or threats of force. We all agree, I presume, that it may be done by persuasion to leave a rival's shop and come to the defendant's. It may be done by the refusal or withdrawal of various pecuniary advantages which, apart from this consequence, are within the defendant's lawful control. It may be done by the withdrawal, or threat to withdraw, such advantages from third persons who have a right to deal or not to deal with the plaintiff, as a means of inducing them not to deal with him either as customers or servants. *Commonwealth* v. *Hunt*, 4 Met. 111, 132, 133. *Bowen* v. *Matheson*, 14 Allen, 499.

I pause here to remark that the word "threats" often is used as if, when it appeared that threats had been made, it appeared that unlawful conduct had begun. But it depends on what you threaten. As a general rule, even if subject to some exceptions, what you may do in a certain event you may threaten to do, that is, give warning of your intention to do in that event, and thus allow the other person the chance of avoiding the consequences. So as to "compulsion," it depends on how you "compel." *Commonwealth* v. *Hunt*, 4 Met. 111, 133. So as to "annoyance" or "intimidation." *Connor* v. *Kent, Curran* v. *Treleaven*, 17 Cox C.C. 354, 367, 368, 370. In *Sherry* v. *Perkins*, 147 Mass. 212, it was found as a fact that the display of banners which was enjoined was part of a scheme to prevent workmen from entering or remaining in the plaintiff's employment, "by threats and intimidation." The context showed that the words as there used meant threats of personal violence, and intimidation by causing fear of it.

I have seen the suggestion made that the conflict between employers and employed is not competition. But I venture to assume that none of my brethren would rely on that suggestion. If the policy on which our law is founded is too narrowly expressed in the term free competition, we may substitute free struggle for life. Certainly the policy is not limited to struggles between persons of the same class competing for the same end. It applies to all conflicts of temporal interests.

So far, I suppose, we are agreed. But there is a notion which latterly has been insisted on a good deal, that a combination of persons to what any one of them lawfully might do by himself will make the otherwise lawful conduct unlawful. It would be rash to say that some as yet unformulated truth may not be hidden under this proposition. But in the general form in which it has been presented and accepted by many courts, I think it plainly untrue, both on authority and on principle. *Commonwealth* v. *Hunt*, 4 Met. 111. *Randall* v. *Hazelton*, 12 Allen, 412, 414. There was combination of the most flagrant and dominant kind in *Bowen* v. *Matheson* and in the Mogul Steamship Company's case, and combination was essential to the success achieved. But it is not necessary to cite cases; it is plain from the slightest consideration of practical affairs, or the most superficial reading of industrial history, that free competition means combination, and that the organization of the world, now going on so fast, means an ever increasing might and scope of combination. It seems to me futile to set our faces against this tendency. Whether beneficial on the whole, as I think it, or detrimental, it is inevitable, unless the fundamental axioms of society, and even the fundamental conditions of life, are to be changed.

One of the eternal conflicts out of which life is made up is that between the effort of every man to get the most he can for his services, and that of society, disguised under the name of capital, to get his services for the least possible return. Combination on the one side is patent and powerful. Combination on the other is the necessary and desirable counterpart, if the battle is to be carried on in a fair and equal way. . . .

If it be true that workingmen may combine with a view, among other things, to getting as much as they can for their labor, just as capital may combine with a view to getting the greatest possible return, it must be true that when combined they have the same liberty that combined capital has to support their interests by argument, persuasion, and the bestowal or refusal of those advantages which they otherwise lawfully control. I can remember when many people thought that, apart from violence or breach of contract, strikes were wicked, as organized refusals to work. I suppose that intelligent economists and legislators have given up that notion today. I feel pretty confident that they equally will abandon the idea that an organized refusal by workmen of social intercourse with a man who shall enter their antagonist's employ is wrong, if it is dissociated from any threat of violence, and is made for the sole object of prevailing if possible in a contest with their employer about the rate of wages. The fact, that the immediate object of the act by which the benefit to themselves is to be gained is to injure their antagonist, does not necessarily make it unlawful, any more than when a great house lowers the price of certain goods for the purpose, and with the effect, of driving a smaller antagonist from the business. Indeed, the question seems to me to have been decided as long ago as 1842 by the good sense of Chief Justice Shaw, in *Commonwealth* v. *Hunt*, 4 Met. 111.

Questions

1. What interests of the plaintiff-employer were thought by the majority to be harmed by the defendants' concerted activity? Were they all worthy of legal protection, *e.g.*, did the employer have an enforceable legal right to bar persuasion of prospective employees or to have non-striking employees show up for work each day?

2. What was defendants' object? Was it improper? What functions are served by picketing that are not served by the strike? Would a strike alone have been permissible? If so, what does this suggest about the extent to which the law will protect employers from economic harm?

Presumably, a strike alone would not have exerted sufficient pressure on the employer, perhaps because it would not have been 100 percent effective or because replacements were available. The picket line, then, was perceived by the strikers as vital to carry out their clearly legal objective. An injunction removed a vital weapon from the union's arsenal, yet the court avoids discussing the impact of its decision on the balance of power. Is the court aware that it is deciding the extent to which public regulation or private dispute resolution should be the mode for resolving labor-management disputes?

3. What is the difference between the injunction proposed by Holmes and that granted by the majority? Is the court assuming that picketing, but not strikes alone, necessarily results in violence? If so, what is the court's source of knowledge on this issue? Was evidence taken in the proceeding indicating strife or the likelihood of violence in the particular case?

Many courts felt that picketing was indeed inherently coercive and that violence was a likely result. Thus, there was no need to decide in any particular case whether violence was likely to occur. The vehemence and certainty with which this assumption was pursued can be seen in the following colorful and often dramatic statements quoted in C. Summers and H. Wellington, Cases on Labor Law 150–51 (1968):*

> " 'A picket, in its very nature . . . tends and is designed by physical intimidation, to deter other men from seeking employment in places vacated by the strikers. It tends and is designed to drive business away from the boycotted place, not by the legitimate methods of persuasion, but by the illegitimate means of physical intimidation and fear. Crowds

naturally collect, disturbances of the peace are always imminent and of frequent occurrence. Many peaceful citizens, men and women, are always deterred by physical trepidation from entering places of business so under a boycott patrol. It is idle to split hairs upon so plain a proposition, and to say that the picket may consist of nothing more than a single individual peacefully endeavoring by persuasion to prevent customers from entering the boycotted place. The plain facts are always at variance with such refinements of reason.' [*Pierce* v. *Stablemen's Union*, 156 Cal. 70, 103 P. 324 (1909).]

"[Similarly], other courts have declared that ' "peaceful picketing" is a self-contradiction and aptly describes nothing that is known to man.' *Cooper Co.* v. *Los Angeles Building Trades Council*, 3 C.C.H. Lab. Cas. 60, 728 at 731 (Cal. Super. Ct. 1941); and 'There is and can be no such thing as peaceful picketing, any more than there can be chaste vulgarity, or peaceful mobbing or lawful lynching.' *Atchison, T. & S.F. Ry. Co.* v. *Gee*, 139 F. 582 at 584 (C.C. Iowa, 1905). 'A single sentinel, constantly parading in front of a place of employment for any extended length of time may be just as effective in striking terror to the souls of employees, bound there by their duty, as was the swinging pendulum in Poe's famous story "The Pit and the Pendulum" to the victim chained in its ultimate path. In fact, silence is sometimes more striking and impressive than the loud mouthings of the mob. It is the show of force back of the demonstration, or the inevitableness of the impending disaster, which tries men's souls and drives them to desperation.' *Gevas* v. *Greek Restaurant Workers' Club*, 99 N.J. Eq. 770, 783, 134 A. 309, 314 (1926)."

The New York Court of Appeals, however, saw the matter quite differently. In holding that the picketers did not engage in disorderly conduct, the court noted:

"It has been said at times that picketing in large numbers near a place of business where a strike is in progress is in itself a threat of violence, and invites counter-violence. Circumstances may in particular cases justify a finding to that effect. . . . In the absence of evidence, we may not infer that the conduct of the defendants was intended as a threat, or be so construed, or was an incentive to violence by others." *People* v. *Nixon*, 248 N.Y. 182, 186–87, 161 N.E. 463–65 (1928).

Some courts limited the number of permissible picketers, others noted that pickets too needed protection from company agents or nonstrikers. How can one explain these differences? Were workers in Massachusetts more violent than in New York?

Query whether the threat of violence was the basic concern? What does the court mean by, "coercion of the will"? Is the court concerned about mere persuasion, that is, feelings of guilt or fear of being socially shunned engendered in those who seek to cross a picket line?

4. Is Holmes' notion that organization of employees is required so that the competition of labor and capital will be "carried on in a fair and equal way" a statement of Holmes' personal values, the view of a substantial

portion of the community, or implicit in legal doctrine? Holmes discusses
the law's recognition of competition as a justification for the causing of
severe economic harm. Was it necessary to build the defendants' case so
that activity would be viewed as "competition"?

5. In cases involving combinations of employers to weaken or destroy
competitors, the common law courts found justification in the values of
competition. Thus, in *Bowen* v. *Matheson,* 96 Mass. (14 Allen) 499 (1867),
the Massachusetts Supreme Court declined to aid a shipping master from
a combination of his rivals, who combined to secure a monopoly of the
business of boarding seamen and hiring them out. In an action resembling secondary boycott activity by unions, the conspirators allegedly
agreed to refuse to deal with sea captains who hired seamen from nonmembers of the combination. Their economic power stemmed from their
control over the supply of labor. Ignoring the charge of conspiracy, the
court noted that the conduct did not constitute any existing tort or crime.
"If their effect is to destroy the business of shipping masters who are not
members of the association, it is such a result as in the competition of
business often follows from a course of proceeding that the law permits."
Id. at 503–04. Competition as a justification for harm had been well
recognized in English law. See C. Gregory, Labor and the Law 31–51 (2d
rev. ed. 1958).

Compare this approach to the one taken in the following case.

Plant v. Woods

Supreme Judicial Court of Massachusetts, 1900
176 Mass. 492, 57 N.E. 1011

HAMMOND, J.

This case arises out of a contest for supremacy between two labor
unions of the same craft, having substantially the same constitution and
by-laws. The chief difference between them is that the plaintiff union is
affiliated with a national organization having its headquarters in Lafayette in the State of Indiana, while the defendant union is affiliated with a
similar organization having its headquarters in Baltimore in the State of
Maryland. The plaintiff union was composed of workmen who in 1897
withdrew from the defendant union.

. . .

The contest became active early in the fall of 1898. In September of that
year, the members of the defendant union declared "all painters not
affiliated with the Baltimore headquarters to be non-union men," and
voted to "notify the bosses" of that declaration. The manifest object of the
defendants was to have all the members of the craft subjected to the rules
and discipline of their particular union, in order that they might have
better control over the whole business, and to that end they combined and
conspired to get the plaintiffs and each of them to join the defendant
association, peaceably if possible, but by threat and intimidation if necessary. Accordingly, on October 7, they voted that "if our demands are not

complied with, all men working in shops where Lafayette people are employed refuse to go to work." . . .

A duly authorized agent of the defendants would visit a shop where one or more of the plaintiffs were at work and inform the employer of the action of the defendant union with reference to the plaintiffs, and ask him to induce such of the plaintiffs as were in his employ to sign applications for reinstatement in the defendant union. As to the general nature of these interviews the master finds that the defendants have been courteous in manner, have made no threats of personal violence, have referred to the plaintiffs as non-union men, but have not otherwise represented them as men lacking good standing in their craft; that they have not asked that the Lafayette men be discharged, and in some cases have expressly stated that they did not wish to have them discharged, but only that they sign the blanks for reinstatement in the defendant union. The master, however, further finds, from all the circumstances under which those requests were made, that the defendants intended that employers of Lafayette men should fear trouble in their business if they continued to employ such men, and that employers to whom these requests were made were justified in believing that a failure on the part of their employees who were Lafayette men to sign such reinstatement blanks, and a failure on the part of the employers to discharge them for not doing so, would lead to trouble in the business of the employers in the nature of strikes or a boycott, . . . and as a means to this end they caused strikes to be instituted in the shops where strikes would seriously interfere with the business of the shops, and in all other shops they made such representations as would lead the proprietors thereof to expect trouble in their business.
. . .

It is well to see what is the meaning of this threat to strike, when taken in connection with the intimation that the employer may "expect trouble in his business." It means more than that the strikers will cease to work. That is only the preliminary skirmish. It means that those who have ceased to work will, by strong, persistent, and organized persuasion and social pressure of every description, do all they can to prevent the employer from procuring workmen to take their places. It means much more. It means that, if these peaceful measures fail, the employer may reasonably expect that unlawful physical injury may be done to his property; that attempts in all the ways practised by organized labor will be made to injure him in his business, even to his ruin, if possible; and that, by the use of vile and opprobrious epithets and other annoying conduct, and actual and threatened personal violence, attempts will be made to intimidate those who enter or desire to enter his employ; and that whether or not all this be done by the strikers or only by their sympathizers, or with the open sanction and approval of the former, he will have no help from them in his efforts to protect himself.

However mild the language or suave the manner in which the threat to strike is made under such circumstances as are disclosed in this case, the employer knows that he is in danger of passing through such an ordeal as that above described, and those who make the threat know that as well as he does. Even if the intent of the strikers, so far as respects their own conduct and influence, be to discountenance all actual or threatened injury to person or property or business, except that which is the direct necessary result of the interruption of the work, and even if their connection with the injurious and violent conduct of the turbulent among them or of their sympathizers be not such as to make them liable criminally or even answerable civilly in damages to those who suffer, still with full knowledge of what is to be expected they give the signal, and in so doing must be held to avail themselves of the degree of fear and dread which the knowledge of such consequences will cause in the mind of those—whether their employer or fellow workmen—against whom the strike is directed; and the measure of coercion and intimidation imposed upon those against whom the strike is threatened or directed is not fully realized until all those probable consequences are considered.

Such is the nature of the threat, and such the degree of coercion and intimidation involved in it.

If the defendants can lawfully perform the acts complained of in the city of Springfield, they can pursue the plaintiffs all over the State in the same manner, and compel them to abandon their trade or bow to the behests of their pursuers.

It is to be observed that this is not a case between the employer and employed, or, to use a hackneyed expression, between capital and labor, but between laborers all of the same craft, and each having the same right as any one of the others to pursue his calling. In this, as in every other case of equal rights, the right of each individual is to be exercised with due regard to the similar right of all others, and the right of one be said to end where that of another begins.

The right involved is the right to dispose of one's labor with full freedom. This is a legal right, and it is entitled to legal protection. . . .

The same rule is stated with care and discrimination by Wells, J. in *Walker* v. *Cronin,* 107 Mass. 555, 564: "Every one has a right to enjoy the fruits and advantages of his own enterprise, industry, skill and credit. He has no right to be protected against competition; but he has a right to be free from malicious and wanton interference, disturbance or annoyance. If disturbance, or loss, come as a result of competition, or the exercise of like rights by others, it is *damnum absque injuria,* unless some superior right by contract or otherwise is interfered with. But if it come from the merely wanton or malicious acts of others, without the justification of competition or the service of any interest or lawful purpose, it then stands upon a different footing."

In this case the acts complained of were calculated to cause damage to the plaintiffs, and did actually cause such damage; and they were intentionally done for that purpose. Unless, therefore, there was justifiable cause, the acts were malicious and unlawful. *Walker* v. *Cronin, ubi supra. Carew* v. *Rutherford,* 106 Mass. 1, and cases cited therein.

The defendants contend that they have done nothing unlawful, and, in support of that contention, they say that a person may work for whom he pleases; and, in the absence of any contract to the contrary, may cease to work when he pleases, and for any reason whatever, whether the same be good or bad; that he may give notice of his intention in advance, with or without stating the reason; that what one man may do several men acting in concert may do, and may agree beforehand that they will do, and may give notice of the agreement; and that all this may be lawfully done notwithstanding such concerted action may, by reason of the consequent interruption of the work, result in great loss to the employer and his other employees, and that such a result was intended. In a general sense, and without reference to exceptions arising out of conflicting public and private interests, all this may be true.

It is said also that, where one has the lawful right to do a thing, the motive by which he is actuated is immaterial. One form of this statement appears in the first head-note in *Allen* v. *Flood,* as reported in [1898] A.C. 1, as follows: "An act lawful in itself is not converted by a malicious or bad motive into an unlawful act so as to make the doer of the act liable to a civil action." If the meaning of this and similar expressions is that where a person has the lawful right to a thing irrespective of his motive, his motive is immaterial, the proposition is a mere truism. If, however, the meaning is that where a person, if actuated by one kind of a motive, has a lawful right to do a thing, the act is lawful when done under any conceivable motive, or that an act lawful under one set of circumstances is therefore lawful under every conceivable set of circumstances, the proposition does not commend itself to us either logically or legally accurate.

In so far as a right is lawful, it is lawful, and in many cases the right is so far absolute as to be lawful whatever may be the motive of the actor, as where one digs upon his own land for water, (*Greenleaf* v. *Francis,* 18 Pick. 117,) or makes a written lease of his land for the purpose terminating a tenancy at will, (*Groustra* v. *Bourges,* 141 Mass. 7,) but in many cases the lawfulness of an act which causes damage to another may depend upon whether the act is for justifiable cause; and this justification may be found sometimes in the circumstances under which it is done irrespective of motive, sometimes in the motive alone, and sometimes in the circumstance and motives combined.

. . .

Still standing for solution is the question. Under what circumstances, including the motive of the actor, is the act complained of lawful, and to what extent?

In cases somewhat akin to the one at bar this court has had occasion to consider the question how far acts, manifestly coercive and intimidating in their nature, which cause damage and injury to the business or property of another, and are done with intent to cause such injury and partly in reliance upon such coercion, are justifiable.

[The court discusses *Bowen* v. *Matheson,* holding that business competition justifies the infliction of economic harm.]

. . .

On the other hand, it was held in *Carew* v. *Rutherford,* 106 Mass. 1, that a conspiracy against a mechanic,—who is under the necessity of employing workmen in order to carry on his business,—to obtain a sum of money from him which he is under no legal obligation to pay, by inducing his workmen to leave him, or by deterring others from entering into his employ, or by threatening to do this so that he is induced to pay the money demanded, under a reasonable apprehension that he cannot carry on his business without yielding to the demands, is an illegal, if not a criminal, conspiracy; that the acts done under it are illegal, and that the money thus obtained may be recovered back. Chapman, C.J., speaking for the court, says that there is no doubt that, if the parties under such circumstances succeed in injuring the business of the mechanic, they are liable to pay all the damages done to him.

That case bears a close analogy to the one at bar. The acts there threatened were like those in this case, and the purpose was, in substance, to force the plaintiff to give his work to the defendants, and to extort from him a fine because he had given some of his work to other persons.

Without now indicating to what extent workmen may combine and in pursuance of an agreement may act by means of strikes and boycotts to get the hours of labor reduced or their wages increased, or to procure from their employers any other concession directly and immediately affecting their own interests, or to help themselves in competition with their fellow-workmen, we think this case must be governed by the principles laid down in *Carew* v. *Rutherford, ubi supra.* The purpose of these defendants was to force the plaintiffs to join the defendant association, and to that end they injured the plaintiffs in their business, and molested and disturbed them in their efforts to work at their trade. It is true they committed no acts of personal violence, or of physical injury to property, although they threatened to do something which might reasonably be expected to lead to such results. In their threat, however, there was plainly that which was coercive in its effect upon the will. It is not necessary that the liberty of the body should be restrained. Restraint of the mind, provided it would be such as would be likely to force a man against his will to grant the thing demanded, and actually has that effect, is sufficient in cases like this. . . .

. . .

The necessity that the plaintiffs should join this association is not so great, nor is its relation to the rights of the defendants, as compared with the right of the plaintiffs to be free from molestation, such as to bring the acts of the defendants under the shelter of the principles of trade competition. Such acts are without justification, and therefore are malicious and unlawful, and the conspiracy thus to force the plaintiffs was unlawful. Such conduct is intolerable, and inconsistent with the spirit of our laws.

HOLMES, C.J. [dissenting]

. . . If the decision in the present case simply had relied upon *Vegelahn* v. *Guntner,* 167 Mass. 92, I should have hesitated to say anything, although I might have stated that my personal opinion had not been weakened by the substantial agreement with my views to be found in the judgments of the majority of the House of Lords in *Allen* v. *Flood,* [1898] A.C. 1. But much to my satisfaction, if I may say so, the court has seen fit to adopt the mode of approaching the question which I believe to be the correct one, and to open an issue which otherwise I might have thought closed. The difference between my brethren and me now seems to be a difference of degree, and the line of reasoning followed makes it proper for me to explain where the difference lies.

. . . To come directly to the point, the issue is narrowed to the question whether, assuming that some purposes would be a justification, the purpose in this case of the threatened boycotts and strikes was such as to justify the threats. That purpose was not directly concerned with wages. It was one degree more remote. The immediate object and motive was to strengthen the defendants' society as a preliminary and means to enable it to make a better fight on questions of wages or other matters of clashing interests. I differ from my brethren in thinking that the threats were as lawful for this preliminary purpose as for the final one to which strengthening the union was a means. I think that unity of organization is necessary to make the contest of labor effectual, and that societies of laborers lawfully may employ in their preparation the means which they might use in the final contest.

Although this is not the place for extended economic discussion, and although the law may not always reach ultimate economic conceptions, I think it well to add that I cherish no illusions as to the meaning and effect of strikes. While I think the strike a lawful instrument in the universal struggle of life, I think it pure phantasy to suppose that there is a body of capital of which labor as a whole secures a larger share by that means. The annual product, subject to an infinitesimal deduction for the luxuries of the few, is directed to consumption by the multitude, and is consumed by the multitude, always. Organization and strikes may get a larger share for the members of an organization, but, if they do, they get it at the expense of the less organized and less powerful portion of the laboring mass. They do not create something out of nothing. It is only by divesting our minds of questions of ownership and other machinery of distribution, and by looking solely at the question of consumption,—asking ourselves what is the annual product, who consumes it, and what changes would or could we make,—that we keep in the world of realities. But, subject to the qualifications which I have expressed, I think it lawful for a body of workmen to try by combination to get more than they now are getting, although they do it at the expense of their fellows, and to that end to strengthen their union by the boycott and the strike.

Questions

1. *Plant* represents a determination that the defendant union pursued an unlawful objective, although the court's stress on the possibly terrible consequences of the union's threat suggests the difficulty of distinguishing between unlawful means and ends.

The closed shop, a term not then in usage, forecloses the employer from hiring employees in the open labor market. The importance of the device to unions is due in part to the form of bargaining which was once common. As noted earlier, unions often determined for themselves the wage or piece rates at which they would work and enforced these terms by internal union discipline. In addition, however, unions seek to protect standards by securing a monopoly over labor supply, a monopoly which is threatened by rival unionists as much as by nonunionists. Was the end sought by the defendant union any less relevant or "direct" to collective interests than an allowable strike for higher wages?

2. Holmes states that an employee organization only "benefits employees at the expense of the less organized and less powerful portion of the laboring mass." How can Holmes justify the defendants' actions given the limited benefits he sees in employee organization?

3. To hold that labor activity or any allegedly tortious conduct is subject to liability unless defendants' acts are justified is merely to state the issue. If the basic inquiry focuses on the existence of privilege, how is the court to decide the purposes and means by which economic harm can be caused? Are determinations to be made in each case or is there a need for broad statements setting out the permissible bounds of economic conflict? Do these cases suggest that courts can separate the elements of justification from their concern over the harm which defendants seek to justify?

In *Plant* v. *Woods,* the union's purpose was held not to be sufficiently "direct." Is this a statement of fact or of law? Obviously the workers' concerns were sufficient to motivate a strike, but the court purports to determine whether the goal is directly related to "employee interests." Why are the employees not the best judge of "directness?" If not, what principle is the court actually applying? Can it avoid relying on economic and social judgments? If so, whose judgments should prevail—the views of the community, the business community, or the judges?

These decisions are generally criticized for stressing the court's own economic and social views. Would other formulations of legal doctrine avoid such policy making? Are considerations of "social advantage" foreign to judicial decision-making? Is the criticism of these cases based on the court's choice of the wrong set of policies? If so, then the criticism is not so much based on a criticism of economic policy making but, rather, the making of poor policy choices. Could courts have avoided making these policy choices? See H. Wellington, Labor and the Legal Process 7–46 (1968).

4. Bricklayers informed contractors that they would refuse to work unless they could "point" bricks (a finishing process) as well as lay them. This work had always been performed by pointers, who were not bricklayers and who had repeatedly been denied an AFL charter. The pointers were more skilled, yet cheaper than bricklayers, but the contractors had no choice but to accede to the pressure. The court viewed the case as a contest involving a trade advantage (the defendants' use of their monopoly of bricklaying skills to secure other work tasks). The harm could then be justified as competition. How can the case be distinguished from *Plant*? What about the court's recognition in *Plant* of the "right" to dispose of one's labor with full freedom? See *Pickett* v. *Walsh,* 192 Mass. 572 (1906).

5. The rigid doctrine of competition adopted by Massachusetts courts denied that employees competed with their employers, even for different allocations of profits, but, rather, held that they were engaged in a joint effort. Query: how could the court uphold strikes for "direct" benefits, such as higher wages or shorter hours, given this view? Can this be explained other than in terms of pure political expedience?

In the pointers' case, *Pickett* v. *Walsh*, the court was faced with a situation resembling business competition since two groups of workers were competing for the same work. The attempt to exclude one group of workers created a zero-sum game. The result is that the court upheld a refusal to work in a jurisdictional or work-assignment dispute, considered by many to be the most wasteful of all labor disputes. Would the Baltimore painters in *Plant* v. *Woods* have been successful if, instead of attempting to secure the allegiance of the breakaway unionists, they had sought to exclude those workers from available work?

The attempt to extend labor organization throughout a product or labor market and the attempt to secure closed shop arrangements are both motivated by a desire to protect established labor conditions from competition by unorganized workers or rival unionists. To the extent that the prices of goods reflect differences in labor standards, pressure is placed upon the labor standards of organized employees as well as their employers. Similarly, the bricklayers' union is stronger as an organization, and individual bricklayers are more economically secure, to the extent they can extend the variety and scope of work tasks within their jurisdiction. Were the Massachusetts courts simply unaware of these economic realities?

These decisions should be contrasted with the quite different development in New York. In 1902 the New York Court of Appeals upheld a union's right to strike for a closed shop, stating that concerted action was justifiable so long as self-interest was present. So long as the employees' conduct was lawful, that is, did not constitute a crime or tort, courts were not to pass upon the legality of the objectives sought or their wisdom. *National Protective Ass'n* v. *Cumming*, 170 N.Y. 315 (1902). This view implicitly assumed that regulations beyond existing crimes or torts were a legislative rather than a judicial function.

Other courts applied the doctrine that intentional infliction of economic harm was actionable unless justified, but adopted a far broader view of justification based primarily upon self-interest. Are any of these views clearly preferable or more suitable for judicial decision-making? See C. Gregory, Labor and the Law, Ch. III (2d ed. 1958).

Problems

Consider how the law should respond to the situations presented in the following problems.

1. Shoemakers strike and picket their employer to protest the introduction of a machine which will substantially reduce work opportunities and weaken the skill content of the trade. Is there any reason to treat this strike differently from a strike for higher wages or a strike to acquire work as in *Pickett* v. *Walsh*? Although courts permitted efforts to gain new work or to replace workers with union members, strikes to bar unemployment due to the introduction of machines were often enjoined. For instance, the efforts of the Musicians Union to bar the use of canned music was

declared an unlawful objective since it "bears no reasonable relation to wages, hours of employment . . . or any other condition of employment." *Opera on Tour, Inc.* v. *Weber,* 285 N.Y. 348, 357, 34 N.E.2d 349, 353 (1941). See also *Hopkins* v. *Oxley Stave Co.,* 83 F. 912 (8th Cir. 1897). See cases cited at J. Landis and M. Manoff, Cases on Labor Law 430–31 (2d ed. 1942).

The social costs of technical change are borne by workers and their families, and judicial intervention bars worker attempts to avoid such costs. When jobs are affected immediately, workers rarely take the long view that technical change is advantageous and efforts to oppose such change are futile or harmful to economic progress. What is the justification for judicial intervention? Can these cases be distinguished from the decisions mentioned above because the use of capital is involved? Surely there is no lack of directness in the relationship of machinery, jobs, and working conditions.

The difference between a strike to displace nonunion workers or to acquire new work, on one hand, and a strike against the introduction of machines on the other, may involve a sense that there is a greater social value supporting the employer's position in these cases. "Another object of the conspiracy, which was no less harmful, was to deprive the public at large of the advantages to be derived from the use of an invention which was not only designed to diminish the cost of making certain necessary articles, but to lessen the labor of human hands." *Hopkins* v. *Oxley Stave Co.,* 83 F. at 917. This object was held enjoinable, although the coopers' conception of the value of machines which lessened their labor differed substantially from the courts.

Are the courts the appropriate public agencies to make these determinations? Will workers, assuming they are apprised of the law, avoid such strikes because of the threat of an injunction? Such avoidance seems unlikely, although empirical evidence is lacking.

2. Assume that a strike has little effect upon the employer's operations, and the union urges the public to boycott the company's product. The boycott is aimed at securing a diminution or stoppage of production, a situation the strike alone could not accomplish. Should the employer's request for an injunction be granted?

What if strikers picket retail outlets, operated by seemingly neutral employers? What if the targeted retail outlets are located within a shopping plaza? These "secondary" activities have long been a source of legal confusion as later material in this volume will demonstrate. These pressure devices are economically harmful to the employer, but this cannot alone justify judicial action since all legitimate union pressure causes economic harm. Can it be argued that consumers are neutrals, uninterested parties in the dispute, and, therefore, the picketing cannot be justified on the grounds of self-interest? Can appeals to consumers, however, be justified on constitutional grounds since an injunction prohibits the public from deciding whether to become a party to the dispute?

The New York Court of Appeals permitted picketing of non-union-made goods when the retailer was in "unity of interest with the manufacturer." *Goldfinger* v. *Feintuch,* 276 N.Y. 281, 287, 11 N.E.2d 910, 913

(1937). Can one distinguish between urging the boycott of specific goods rather than the withholding of all patronage from a neutral retailer? How could such a distinction be justified? See Smith, *Coercion of Third Parties in Labor Disputes—The Secondary Boycott,* 1 La. L. Rev. 277 (1939).

Comment on the Role of the Courts and on Social Dynamics

The responses of many courts can justifiably be seen as attempts to preserve the existing social and economic order from change from social and economic forces. Concurrent with these decisions, ironically, was the rapid concentration of economic power in a few hands, a development actually encouraged by law. An individual case involves only a small slice of the social reality, yet judges were no doubt concerned about protecting property interests and the freedom to contract. In a time of rapid change involving the clash of class interests, can the courts stem the tide? Doesn't such action place the court in the position of an active supporter of the interests of a particular class, a position which to the nonchosen side generates disrespect for law?

On the other hand, is there any way for the courts to avoid involvement? Courts exist to decide specific disputes. Even a decision to deny an injunction, because no recognized legal standard exists to decide the case, or because the issue involved should be left to legislative deliberation, in fact promotes the union's interests in that case. Such abstinence, however, could encourage legislative action. The courts could have treated unions similarly to combinations of employers, although admittedly such a *laissez faire* position would also have involved a choice of values. Such an approach was taken in some states. Thus, the New York Court of Appeals held in effect that economic disputes were not necessarily legal disputes and employer harm was an insufficient reason for judicial action. "The interests of capital and labor are at times inimical and the courts may not decide controversies between the parties so long as neither resorts to violence, deceit or misrepresentation to bring about desired results." *Stillwell Theatre* v. *Kaplan,* 259 N.Y. 405, 410, 182 N.E. 63, 65, *cert. denied,* 288 U.S. 606 (1932).

The swamps of early labor law doctrine represent more than the failure to create rational rules to regulate social conflict, and caution should be exercised in using twentieth century labels to characterize late nineteenth and early twentieth century attitudes. The following comments suggest some of the social dynamics of this turbulent period, affecting both the economic interests of employers as well as legal thought.

Rapidly changing technological and economic forces troubled employers as well as employees during the late nineteenth century. New machines and production processes obliterated old crafts but also destroyed the competitiveness of some businesses. The economic depressions of the late nineteenth century caused workers to lose jobs by the millions and also brought business failure to thousands of enterprises. Unable to control a highly competitive and unsure marketplace or to manage employees as they chose, industrialists, like their workers, sought greater economic security.

Some industrialists sought economic security by corporate merger and concentration which effectively reduced marketplace competition in several key industries. Employers also exerted rigid control over employees' wages, hours, and working conditions. As the workers attempted to preserve or expand their position, employers sought additional authority over their employees, and a series of bitter battles ensued.

By challenging the right of managers to organize their labor force freely, unions threatened to introduce the same kinds of uncertainties entrepreneurs were attempting to eliminate. Professor Kirkland characterizes the common employer response: "This interference was not only unsettling and irresponsible, it was ignorant of business in general as well as of the affairs of the firm which employed it. Contrariwise, those in charge believed that 'brains and capital must be classed together.' In a humanitarian spirit the capitalist must do the business thinking for his men." K. Kirkland, Industry Comes of Age 355 (1961).

Cochran and Miller, The Age of Enterprise*

Unionization far more than radicalism was the continual worry of American employers. They all shared an almost psychopathic fear of having to meet the representatives of labor on a footing of equal authority, and a similar fear of labor gaining a position strong enough to influence management. "I do not believe," said President Meisel of the Kidder Press Company, "that a manufacturer can afford to be dictated to by his labor as to what he shall do, and I shall never give in. I would rather go out of business." His was the old conception of the employer as the host inviting the worker to come and make use of his property, but only on the conditions that the owner of the property should dictate. In the manager-owned plants of a hundred or fewer employees, the backbone of nineteenth century business, this dictatorship furthered the aim of American society for progress, expansion, and elimination of the "unfit." Saving for future investment was the prime requisite for the achievement of this aim, and such saving was most easily arranged under a system of high profits and low wages.

The transition to twentieth century conditions of big organizations, minute labor specialization, greater mechanization, and unused savings broke down the old situation and the old rationale. The employing official in the big company was a career man trying to make a reputation for efficiency as measured by the balance sheet. With capital no longer "scarce," low wages advanced only the interest of this official, not those of society in general. New managerial devices and new slogans were needed if morale was to be maintained, but management refused to believe that recognition of the A.F. of L. was the proper solution.

*T. Cochran and W. Miller, THE AGE OF ENTERPRISE 238 (rev. ed. 1961). Copyright by The Macmillan Company. Used by permission.

Wiebe, The Search for Order 1877–1920*

America in the late nineteenth century was a society without a core. It lacked those national centers of authority and information which might have given order to such swift changes. American institutions were still oriented toward a community life where family and church, education and press, professions and government, all largely found their meaning by the way they fit one with another inside a town or a detached portion of a city. As men ranged farther and farther from their communities, they tried desperately to understand the larger world in terms of their small, familiar environment. They tried, in other words, to impose the known upon the unknown, to master an impersonal world through the customs of a personal society. They failed, usually without recognizing why; and that failure to comprehend a society they were helping to make contained the essence of the nation's story.

. . .

. . . Often the transition from shop to factory had occurred so quickly that the executive who boasted his office was open to any man on the payroll deluded himself into believing the old paternalism still obtained. Or he resisted understanding, because the fatherly care of employees was still widely regarded as his Christian duty. Thus discontent became perversity or the influence of "outsiders," usually a form of personal disloyalty as well. . . . Absentee owners ignorant of life around the mines readily gave subordinates a free hand to eliminate troublemakers. Acting behind the shield of the corporation, underlings then shot and beat, trampled the strikers' rights as citizens, and blacklisted them throughout the region. Western laborers who came to sneer at the democratic process, who looked upon justice as synonymous with injunctions, martial law, and the bull pen, were absolutely correct in believing they had no peaceful, orderly recourse. They worked in a basically inhuman system made more brutal by its insidious anarchy. As late as 1913, when bullets raked a strikers' camp outside Ludlow, Colorado, who could say that the local agents of the Colorado Coal and Iron Company were more than bloody tools? Yet the owner, John D. Rockefeller, Jr., a kindly man busy with his philanthropies, really knew little about it. Shocked by the affair, he felt approximately the same responsibility that he might have for any unfortunate act of nature. The situation did not differ significantly in the steel and textile mills, the lumber camps and slaughtering houses. Henry Clay Frick, who made his fortune in coke and steel, "should not be allowed in the same room with children," an acquaintance once remarked. "I have always had one rule," a veteran employer announced from his New York office. "If a workman sticks up his head, hit it."

Inhumanity in no way depended upon physical distance. Traditionally urban slums had lain outside of the boundaries that most respectable citizens recognized as the true city. As long as a cordon sanitaire had

*R. Wiebe, THE SEARCH FOR ORDER 1877–1920, at 12, 20, 38, 76–79, 81–83 (1967). Copyright by Robert H. Wiebe. Used by permission. Many perceived unions as only one threat to the existing social order. This extract suggests that labor organization was perceived as only one component of a general breakdown of social order.

sealed the world of hovels from theirs, they did not have to concern themselves about the very poor. Officials, reflecting this attitude, had made little effort to police these outcast districts, only to contain them. With the rise of the industrial city, however, slums deepened and spread at an alarming rate. Slum dwellers were no longer mere pariahs; they comprised essential labor that had woven itself throughout the city's fabric. Trouble in the tenements potentially touched everyone, and knowing nothing about the slum except that it frightened them, respectable citizens demanded aggressive protection. Now officials were expected to break up gatherings, crack the heads of demonstrators, and generally show the masses that "society," as it was called, stood armed against any menace. Utterly ineffectual as law enforcement, these desultory acts of violence brought cheers from anxious men of property in and around the city, a kind of exultation over the brutality toward their fellow citizens.

. . .

Anxiety, like the common cold, was a most egalitarian malady which in many respects ran the same course wherever it struck. Men in formal authority, equally disturbed by their sprawling, impersonal society, also reached out for that essential, elusive mastery. Like the protectors of the community, they also underwent a basic shift in outlook which converted incidents into series, giving their worries that same cumulative, self-fueling quality.

Yet the differences were just as significant. Because many of the men in power tried initially to ignore signs of upheaval, they tended to enter the crisis spiral more slowly. Once they did, they moved through it that much more swiftly and savagely. Moreover, their themes of distress, while also phrased in the language of individualism and unity, had a distinctive ring. In the baldest sense, they came to fear that in a democratic society the people might rule. Individualism, except as a mode of implicit contempt for the scattered sheep below, almost always referred to the rights of an elite to retain what they held and to acquire more; cohesion meant an imposed order, one that would necessitate a sharp-edged enforcement. Rather than anticipating the good that would eventually arise from crisis, they wanted to quash all disorder now, to forestall catastrophe by fitting society into a safe, sturdy mold. "Law" and "property," the fundamental terms in their rhetoric, connoted a whole complex of social, economic, and political privileges. Finally, they responded more ingeniously on the whole than the leaders of apocalyptic reform. In a narrow and often coarse manner, they constructed some instruments that would outlast the period of crisis and serve as a basis for their expansion in the years ahead.

Champions of the community seemed to materialize everywhere all at once, swinging broadly at their enemies from the very beginning. Among the men in power, by contrast, an acute anxiety appeared first in the major cities and concerned issues immediately at hand. An urban leadership, already uneasy over the strange population swelling about them, reacted to the "great uprising of labor" in the mid-eighties as if an army of swords had been unsheathed. With incredible exaggeration, they interpreted the Knights of Labor as disciplined mass sedition and the brief epidemic of local labor parties in 1886 and 1887 as a preface to political revolution. References to an American Reign of Terror and a domestic version of the Paris Commune were now heard everywhere, and the most discussed wonder of modern science was the dynamite bomb, symbol of mob terror.

While the alarm spread rapidly through the cities, it penetrated the countryside more gradually. Both in the West and the South local oligarchs generally belittled the first indications of discontent around them, even attempting in many cases to maintain friendly relations with the challengers. That lag had vanished by the end of the eighties, however, and by the early nineties specific worries both in the cities and in the countryside had grown into generalized fears. Now danger lurked everywhere. Farmers and wage earners, dissenting ministers and angry editors, immigrants and ideologists, peaceful petitioners, and armed strikers, all blurred into visions of a society unhinged. The wells of panic, once tapped, flowed continuously.

Appropriately, the first significant changes in policy came from an urban elite. As labor disturbances swept across the country during the mid-eighties, employer associations organized in response. Such leagues had long been common during crises. In the past, however, they had dissolved as soon as the immediate danger passed; now a number of them remained as standing weapons against their employees, and more arrived in each succeeding year. Most of these associations promised mutual assistance to any firm facing labor difficulties. Some also invested in strike insurance, a novel policy introduced just for these anxious times, and a few attempted the systematic suppression of all unions throughout their plants. Seldom well-coordinated, these groups still marked an important departure, particularly at a time when distrust and uncertainty were undermining almost every other form of joint action among corporations.

Spreading to include the whole of the slums, the new concern affected other urban leaders just as deeply. Who could tell when someone might grab the torch and march? An explosion in May 1886 next to Haymarket Square in Chicago raised precisely that specter. Workers, aliens, radicals, mobs, and dynamite all had coalesced in one incident. A local strike had stirred resentment; German anarchists had called a meeting of protest; then when the police tried to disperse it, a bomb had risen out of the shapeless crowd, killing one and mortally wounding a half-dozen more. Immediate punishment was imperative. In the absence of a culprit, the state sped eight available anarchists through the processes of justice, convicting seven to die. Sanctity of human life had certainly not been the issue; within a few hours after the event the police had indiscriminately killed at least as many as the bomb. Nor had inviolability of the law; substantial citizens demanded death, not due process. Behind this insistence upon reprisals lay the assumption that fundamentally the masses could understand only the bared fist, that without the authority of an indisputable force—always visible, always ready—chaos would reign.

. . .

. . . Disorganizing change during the late nineteenth century had encouraged exactly the kind of broad, outlined guidance the judiciary could provide, just as it had inhibited a more detailed, daily direction through either legislation or administration. Moreover, the other two branches had regularly invited the judiciary to assume greater responsibilities. The leading judges of the late nineteenth century saw themselves as major policymakers and framed their important decisions with that purpose in mind.

Samuel F. Miller and Joseph P. Bradley, the dominant members of the Supreme Court until the nineties, were experiencing the same uncertainties that beset equally able men throughout America. Along with several of their colleagues, they were deeply disturbed by the deterioration of a familiar society. They worried about the irresponsible power of great corporations, especially about the financial wizards behind so many of them. "Modern Shylocks and Railroad Smashers," Bradley disgustedly called them. Consequently in the seventies the Court had on several occasions reaffirmed the right of state and local governments to regulate industry as essential to the public welfare. But while they opposed monopolies and manipulators, they also wanted the avenues of national commerce open to legitimate business, and that in turn led them to protect interstate corporations from what they considered excessively obstructive local regulation. They too regarded property as society's keystone, and they too revered law and order.

The result of these mixed attitudes during the eighties was to discourage precise declarations and leave a great deal to the discretion of the lower courts, including those of the states. Rather than abdication, it represented the cautious response of policymakers feeling for solid ground, a search that was naturally affected by the anxious climate of the later eighties. In general, the judiciary expressed its rising apprehension by a greater sensitivity to the claims of private property, a gradual shift toward defense, and, above all, the preparation of exceptionally broad rules of surveillance. In the area of corporation controls, for example, it had long been assumed that at some extreme point state regulation could deprive a company of its property without due process of law, in violation of the Constitution. For years, however, that remained a theoretical consideration, and the Supreme Court continued to treat due process solely as a matter of legal procedure. Then around the mid-eighties, worries about social stability began to cast shadows on business regulation that had once been considered a proper exercise of the community's police power. A time of trouble invested property with much higher importance, and in 1890 the Court officially reserved the right to invalidate any state action that set injuriously low railroad rates. When it saw fit, in other words, the Court could determine what was a reasonable and what an unreasonable return on capital, a vast, new province for judicial review.

With even greater vigor, lower courts were following a parallel route in labor law, a subject the Supreme Court had as yet largely left alone.

Injunctions against strikers and demonstrators, for instance, had for some years been granted in cases of immediate danger to physical property. Out of the turmoil of the mid-eighties and the fantasies of an irresistible union power, the meaning of both danger and property expanded into huge misty concepts. By the later eighties Federal courts were issuing injunctions to protect intangible as well as tangible property from potential as well as actual danger, rulings that essentially commanded a group of workers to avoid any hint of a disturbance. Just as they could determine the degree of business regulation commensurate with a proper return on capital, so the judges, a case at a time, would demarcate "the allowable area of economic conflict" between employer and employee. Both realms left the judges peculiarly free from any prior restraints in deciding extremely complicated social problems.

As long as the Justices of the Supreme Court believed that they were merely strengthening an outer wall, they could afford such large, gray areas of discretion. But many substantial citizens, growing frightened more rapidly than a majority of the Court, found that leeway intolerable. Lacking controls from above, a judge on the Court of Appeals in West Virginia could uphold state regulation of the coal industry because "the public tranquility and the good and safety of society" demanded it. The same sweeping logic they were employing, in other words, could be used to exactly the opposite conclusion. Other courts might demonstrate great resourcefulness in preserving order, as one did in 1892 when it used an obsolete statute on treason to demoralize the workers at Homestead, Pennsylvania, but the men in power were furious that such crucial matters should depend upon jerry-built law. Seeking the security of rigid, inclusive rules, an increasing number of them, including many prominent lawyers, undertook to extract that kind of certainty from the Supreme Court. The rationale for judicial intervention was now well developed. As soon as five Justices shared the feeling that the outer wall had been breached and the inner one was cracking, they could act with dispatch all along the line.

These attempts to tighten social control were never coordinated into a general campaign. Almost all of the employer associations remained local leagues that rarely communicated with one another. The same usually held true for those who tried to discipline the legislature, stiffen the executive's will, and win strict rulings from the Supreme Court. The movements were also crude, with a penchant for the bludgeon rather than the rapier. Yet whatever their failings, they enjoyed incalculable advantages of power. To the degree that anyone could marshall society's resources, these men sitting in or around the seats of authority qualified. Together they comprised the citizens whose goodwill and enterprise seemed essential to a community's prosperity, most of the strategic office-holders in government, and the best legal talent. They constituted the explorers in a new national power. They were the ones whose positions in finance and distribution placed countless Americans in an attitude of dependence; whose corporations could maneuver simultaneously around several city councils or state legislatures, playing one against the others and confusing the lot; whose positions in the major parties most closely approximated national leadership.

Note

It must be noted here that the history of labor-management controversies and violent labor struggle may tell us little about labor history and the lives of working people. Only a minority of American workers have belonged to labor unions at any time in our history. Little has been written about experiences and perspectives of workers themselves, and concern with skilled craft workers has tended to obscure the impact of industrialization on less skilled workers. Some beginnings can be found in H. Gutman, Industrial Workers Struggle for Power, The Gilded Age: A Reappraisal (H. Wayne Morgan ed., rev. ed., 1970); H. Gutman, Work, Culture and Society in Industrializing America (1977); S. Thernstrom, Poverty and Progress, Social Mobility in a Nineteenth Century City (1964); A. Dawley, Class and Community: The Industrial Revolution in Lynn (1976); D. Montgomery, Workers' Control in America (1979); D. Walkowitz, Worker City, Company Town (1978). Two useful documentary collections or anthologies are J. Auerbach, American Labor: The Twentieth Century (1969); L. Litwack, The American Labor Movement (1962).

B. APPLICATION OF ANTITRUST AND ANTI-INJUNCTION LAWS TO LABOR RELATIONS*

1. ACCOMMODATION OF COMPETING STATUTORY POLICIES

One of the irreconcilable conflicts in law is that which exists between labor relations policy and antitrust policy. In the former, the premise is that unions (combinations of employees to set wages and working conditions) are sometimes a good thing, and that collective bargaining (combinations between unions and employers—often competing employers—to set wages and working conditions, or to maximize job opportunities by not automating or not subcontracting) is also a good thing. On the other hand, pursuant to antitrust policy, it is a bad thing to have competitors (be they employees or employers) combine to reduce competition because, the theory goes, the consumer will end up paying more and getting less due to the loss of competition.

Virtually no one argues that unions should be abolished because of antitrust policy, or that collective bargaining should be abandoned. At the

---

*See, generally, Boudin, *The Sherman Act and Labor Disputes*, 39 COLUM. L. REV. 1281, 40 COLUM. L. REV. 14 (1939); Cox, *Labor and the Antitrust Laws—A Preliminary Analysis*, 104 U. PA. L. REV. 252 (1955); Winter, *Collective Bargaining and Competitions: The Application of Antitrust Standards to Union Activity*, 73 YALE L.J. 14 (1963); and Meltzer, *Labor Unions, Collective Bargaining, and the Antitrust Laws*, 32 U. CHI. L. REV. 659 (1965).

other end of the spectrum, virtually no one argues that unions and their activities should be wholly exempt from the reach of the antitrust laws. While Congress has given direction to the courts as to what the scope, if any, of a labor exemption should be, that direction has proven inadequate to give the courts answers in most cases. Early court decisions had little to use for precedent other than the common law of unfair competition. Over the years, of course, as federal antitrust precedents became numerous, some principles have developed. However, the following account will make clear that the principles are not settled, they do not resolve all cases, and they may reflect (at least in any one person's judgment) invalid premises or unreasonable balancing of legitimate and competing interests and policies.

a. Federal Labor and Antitrust Law, 1890–1940

While this book is not a study of the antitrust laws, the issues posed by the problem cannot be resolved without some idea of the purposes of the Sherman Act. It is overly simplistic to characterize the Sherman Act as being aimed at reducing combinations of economic entities where those combinations result in reductions in competition, but such a characterization should suffice for our purposes.

The background to the passage of the Sherman Act makes clear that Congress meant to outlaw business cartels. While the history of the Act is not entirely clear, the better view appears to be that Congress did not contemplate that the Act would apply at all to labor unions. See E. Berman, Labor and the Sherman Act (1930). That being so, and given the prevailing limited meaning of the Commerce Clause of the Constitution during the 1890s and the early twentieth century, the courts did not outlaw unions as such during the formative years of the Sherman Act, although there seems to be little doubt that unions are anticompetitive institutions made up of natural competitors, employees. This did not prevent the courts from applying antitrust law to labor unions in some situations. While the prevailing doctrine was that local strikes did not involve interstate commerce (thus leaving such strikes to the sole regulation of the state and local governments), in situations where the unions' actions occurred in states other than the location of the dispute between the union and the employer, the courts were prepared to apply the antitrust laws. In Loewe v. Lawlor, 208 U.S. 274 (1908), known popularly as the "Danbury Hatters' " case, the Supreme Court approved the application of the Sherman Act to a union that allegedly attempted to apply economic pressure to a manufacturer with whom it was having a dispute by boycotting the manufacturer's retail customers who were located in other states to stop doing business with the manufacturer. Was this the kind of reduced competition contemplated by the Sherman Act? Citing cases that involved business trusts, the Court concluded that the complaint was sufficient because it charged that the union was a combination to restrain directly the plaintiff's trade, the trade was interstate, means were used to attain the restraint, and as a consequence the plaintiff's business was injured. The Court offered no other analysis.

Following *Loewe* there were many years of lobbying by the labor movement and, as a result, the antitrust laws, so far as they applied to unions, were amended in 1914 by the Clayton Act's Sections 6 and 20. It was thought that the amendments were the "Magna Carta" for organized labor. Section 6 did make clear that the mere existence of labor unions did not violate the Sherman Act. The unions also believed, as did most commentators, that Section 20 freed unions from the reach of the antitrust laws. It was not to be. In *Duplex Co.* v. *Deering*, 254 U.S. 443 (1921), the Supreme Court held that behavior very similar to that of the union in *Loewe* v. *Lawlor* still violated the antitrust laws. Despite the rather extensive efforts of the labor movement and its sympathizers in Congress to create labor immunity through Section 20, the Court was able to find loopholes. The essence of the Court's refusal to grant the unions broad immunity can be summed up by the Court's observations: "[I]t must be borne in mind that the section imposes an exceptional and extraordinary restriction upon the equity powers of the courts of the United States and upon the general operation of the anti-trust laws, a restriction in the nature of a special privilege or immunity to a particular class, with corresponding detriment to the general public; and it would violate rules of statutory construction having general application and far-reaching importance to enlarge that special privilege by resorting to a loose construction of the section, not to speak of ignoring or slighting the qualifying words that are found in it." *Id.* at 471–72. On a more technical level, the Court deprived unions of freedom from Clayton Act injunctions and from the antitrust laws, generally, by interpreting the meaning of "employees" in Section 20 to mean only those people working for the employer involved in the labor dispute. Moreover, the Court made use of the limiting words "lawfully" and "lawful" to apply its own understanding of preexisting law to deem such boycotts independently unlawful and, thus, not exempt pursuant to Section 20.

Is this a proper way for a court to interpret the will of the legislature? Would it have been better if the Court had said that when Congress wants to do something that appears to make no sense at all, the burden is on Congress to say it clearly, or the Court will resolve ambiguities in favor of what the Court believes to be the only reasonable course of action? What ambiguities in Section 20 permitted the Court to conclude that the union had violated the antitrust laws? Justice Brandeis dissented. It was his view that Section 20 reflected a decision by Congress to free unions from the burden of the antitrust laws. Given that objective, the ambiguities (if there were any) should be resolved consistently with Congress' known objective. Do you think Brandeis' approach to resolving the ambiguities in the Act is better? Even if you agreed with the majority that the purpose of Congress was absurd?

Following *Duplex*, the lower courts as well as the Supreme Court proceeded for nearly two decades to apply the antitrust laws to labor unions with even greater vigor than had been the case in the past. For the first time, the Supreme Court applied the antitrust laws to labor activities aimed at the so-called primary employer (the employer involved in the dispute), at least where there was some evidence supporting a finding that a purpose of the union's efforts to organize the primary employer's employees was to protect the wage scale of organized employees in other states. In addition, the Court's vision of what constituted interstate commerce greatly expanded, thus making it easier for the federal courts to apply the antitrust laws to labor union activities.

In 1940, the Court decided *Apex Hosiery Co.* v. *Leader*, 310 U.S. 469, 6 LRRM 647. The case involved a violent strike and plant takeover by the employees. Since the strike was aimed at the employer with whom the union and employees had their dispute, the Court almost surely could have determined that the union had no interstate "purpose" (despite the fact that the strike's effect was to prevent stockings from being delivered from Pennsylvania to other states). However, the Court eschewed this approach to the case, at least partially, and said the following:

"A combination of employees necessarily restrains competition among themselves in the sale of their services to the employer; yet such a combination was not considered an illegal restraint of trade at common law when the Sherman Act was adopted, either because it was not thought to be unreasonable or because it was not deemed a 'restraint of trade.' Since the enactment of the declaration in § 6 of the Clayton Act that the 'labor of a human being is not a commodity or article of commerce . . . nor shall such [labor] organizations, or the members thereof, be held or construed to be illegal combinations or conspiracies in the restraint of trade under the antitrust laws,' it would seem plain that restraints on the sale of the employee's services to the employer, however much they curtail the competition among employees, are not in themselves combinations or conspiracies in restraint of trade or commerce under the Sherman Act." 310 U.S. at 502–503.

The Court went on to observe that a collective bargaining agreement that had the effect of fixing prices for employees' services, even if that price fixing had an effect on the cost of the employer's product to the consumer, did not violate the antitrust laws. Finally, the Court concluded that combinations and conspiracies are not within the Sherman Act unless their restraints are intended to have, or in fact have, the effects of market control of a commodity, such as monopoly of supply, control of price, or discrimination between would-be purchasers. Are these distinctions helpful in determining when unions violate the antitrust laws?

b. Federal Injunctions and Labor Law, 1914–1941

The *Apex* attempt to reconcile the antitrust laws and the emerging labor laws and policies of the nation was short-lived, or at least it was put on the sidelines for a number of years. Before considering the Court's effort only one year later, we must consider the history of the use of labor injunctions, often pursuant to the antitrust laws, in federal courts, and how these uses and abuses led to the Norris-LaGuardia Act of 1932.

Given the result in the *Duplex* case which had undone the congressional purpose attached to Section 20 of the Clayton Act, the unions were faced with the irony of being worse off under the Clayton Act than they had been under the unamended Sherman Act, because Section 16 of the Clayton Act made it possible for a private party to seek an injunction under the antitrust laws; prior to that time, only the government could seek such an injunction, while private parties were limited to seeking treble damages from the alleged violators of the law. During the next few years, the use of injunctions by federal (as well as state) courts proved to be one of the most effective employer weapons in undermining union activities. An injunction of union activities may abort entirely a union's efforts to organize employees. The ease with which employers were able to obtain these injunctions played a major role in union-management relations in the 1920s. Combined with the expanding meaning given the Commerce Clause, the injunctions could be used even to interfere with primary acts of unions. In the unlikely event that a union had the resources to attack an injunction, it would not help—as a practical matter—because by the time a court could hear the case on the merits (or on appeal), the labor dispute invariably had ended. The rules for obtaining these injunctions would, today, offend anyone's sense of fairness. These orders could be obtained *ex parte*. They could be obtained although supported only by affidavits. The orders of the courts often were aimed not only at the union but also at all persons working in concert with it or to abet it (despite the fact these many unnamed persons were never brought before the court), and the scope of the injunctions was usually extremely broad and vague. The contempt hearings were sometimes also *ex parte*, conducted by the same judges who had already issued the original injunctions, and often were also decided on affidavits alone.

It is no exaggeration to state that federal injunctions in labor disputes (usually in the name of the antitrust laws) spread like wildfire. Proposals for reform were frequent. In 1932, Congress passed the Norris-LaGuardia Act which set out to end the federal courts' role in interfering in labor disputes. It is probably not unfair to state that it was generally believed in 1932 that Norris-LaGuardia did end use of the labor injunction, but that it had no effect on the previously described substantive developments which applied the antitrust laws to labor activities.

Also consistent with the changing societal and political values of the 1930s, no doubt triggered to a significant extent by the Great Depression, Congress passed in 1935 the National Labor Relations Act (known as the Wagner Act for the law's chief sponsor). While patterned in part on the Railway Labor Act of 1926, there were many differences. Beginning with Section C of this chapter, we shall spend a great deal of time studying the NLRA. At the moment we should only note that the NLRA was a major statement by Congress that labor unions and collective bargaining were legitimate and important parts of our society, and could not be interfered with by other branches of government without serious and at least equally important cause.

United States v. Hutcheson*

Supreme Court of the United States, 1941
312 U.S. 219, 7 LRRM 267

MR. JUSTICE FRANKFURTER delivered the opinion of the Court.

Whether the use of conventional, peaceful activities by a union in controversy with a rival union over certain jobs is a violation of the Sherman Law, as amended, is the question. It is sharply presented in this case because it arises in a criminal prosecution. Concededly an injunction either at the suit of the Government or of the employer could not issue.

Summarizing the long indictment, these are the facts. Anheuser-Busch, Inc., operating a large plant in St. Louis, contracted with Borsari Tank Corporation for the erection of an additional facility. The Gaylord Container Corporation, a lessee of adjacent property from Anheuser-Busch, made a similar contract for a new building with the Stocker Company. Anheuser-Busch obtained the materials for its brewing and other operations and sold its finished products largely through interstate shipments. The Gaylord Corporation was equally dependent on interstate commerce for marketing its goods, as were the construction companies for their building materials. Among the employees of Anheuser-Busch were members of the United Brotherhood of Carpenters and Joiners of America and of the International Association of Machinists. The conflicting claims of these two organizations, affiliated with the American Federation of Labor, in regard to the erection and dismantling of machinery had long been a source of controversy between them. Anheuser-Busch had had agreements with both organizations whereby the Machinists were given the disputed jobs and the Carpenters agreed to submit all disputes to arbitration. But in 1939 the president of the Carpenters, their general representative, and two officials of the Carpenters' local organization, the four men under indictment, stood on the claims of the Carpenters for the jobs. Rejection by the employer of the Carpenters' demand and the refusal of the latter to submit to arbitration were followed by a strike of the Carpenters, called by the defendants against Anheuser-Busch and the construction companies, a picketing of Anheuser-Busch and its tenant, and a request through circular letters and the official publication of the Carpenters that union members and their friends refrain from buying Anheuser-Busch beer.

These activities on behalf of the Carpenters formed the charge of the indictment as a criminal combination and conspiracy in violation of the Sherman Act. Demurrers denying that what was charged constituted a violation of the laws of the United States were sustained and the case came here under the Criminal Appeals Act.

. . .

Section 1 of the Sherman Law on which the indictment rested is as follows:

---

*See Stiffen, *Labor Activities in Restraint of Trade: The Hutcheson Case*, 36 ILL. L. REV. 1 (1941); Nathanson and Wirtz, *The Hutcheson Case: Another View*, 36 ILL. L. REV. 41 (1941); and Gregory, *The New Sherman—Clayton—Norris—LaGuardia Act*, 8 CHI. L. REV. 503 (1941).

[The Court quoted the statute.] The controversies engendered by its application to trade union activities and the efforts to secure legislative relief from its consequences are familiar history. The Clayton Act of 1914 was the result. "This statute was the fruit of unceasing agitation, which extended over more than twenty years and was designed to equalize before the law the position of workingmen and employer as industrial combatants." *Duplex Co.* v. *Deering.* Section 20 of that Act, which is set out in the margin in full, withdrew from the general interdict of the Sherman Law specifically enumerated practices of labor unions by prohibiting injunctions against them—since the use of the injunction had been the major source of dissatisfaction—and also relieved such practices of all illegal taint by the catch-all provision, "nor shall any of the acts specified in this paragraph be considered or held to be violations of any law of the United States." The Clayton Act gave rise to new litigation and to renewed controversy in and out of Congress regarding the status of trade unions. By the generality of its terms the Sherman Law had necessarily compelled the courts to work out its meaning from case to case. It was widely believed that into the Clayton Act courts read the very beliefs which that Act was designed to remove. Specifically the courts restricted the scope of § 20 to trade union activities directed against an employer by his own employees. *Duplex Co.* v. *Deering, supra.* Such a view it was urged, both by powerful judicial dissents and informed lay opinion, misconceived the area of economic conflict that had best be left to economic forces and the pressure of public opinion and not subjected to the judgment of courts. Agitation again led to legislation and in 1932 Congress wrote the Norris-LaGuardia Act.

The Norris-LaGuardia Act removed the fetters upon trade union activities, which according to judicial construction § 20 of the Clayton Act had left untouched, by still further narrowing the circumstances under which the federal courts could grant injunctions in labor disputes. More especially, the Act explicitly formulated the "public policy of the United States" in regard to the industrial conflict, and by its light established that the allowable area of union activity was not to be restricted, as it had been in the *Duplex* case, to an immediate employer-employee relation. Therefore, whether trade union conduct constitutes a violation of the Sherman Law is to be determined only by reading the Sherman Law and § 20 of the Clayton Act and the Norris-LaGuardia Act as a harmonizing text of outlawry of labor conduct.

Were, then, the acts charged against the defendants prohibited, or permitted, by these three interlacing statutes? If the facts laid in the indictment come within the conduct enumerated in § 20 of the Clayton Act they do not constitute a crime within the general terms of the Sherman Law because of the explicit command of that section that such conduct shall not be "considered or held to be violations of any law of the United States." So long as a union acts in its self-interest and does not combine with non-labor groups, the licit and the illicit under § 20 are not to be distinguished by any judgment regarding the wisdom or unwisdom, the rightness or wrongness, the selfishness or unselfishness of the end of which the particular union activities are the means. There is nothing remotely within the terms of § 20 that differentiates between trade union conduct directed against an employer because of a controversy arising in the relation between employer and employee, as such, and conduct similarly directed but ultimately due to an internecine struggle between two unions seeking the favor of the same employer. Such strife between competing unions has been an obdurate conflict in the evolution of so-called craft unionism and has undoubtedly been one of the potent forces in the modern development of industrial unions. These conflicts have intensified industrial tension but there is not the slightest warrant for saying that Congress has made § 20 inapplicable to trade union conduct resulting from them.

In so far as the Clayton Act is concerned, we must therefore dispose of this case as though we had before us precisely the same conduct on the part of the defendants in pressing claims against Anheuser-Busch for increased wages, or shorter hours, or other elements of what are called working conditions. The fact that what was done was done in a competition for jobs against the Machinists rather than against, let us say, a company union is a differentiation which Congress has not put into the federal legislation and which therefore we cannot write into it.

It is at once apparent that the acts with which the defendants are charged are the kind of acts protected by § 20 of the Clayton Act. The refusal of the Carpenters to work for Anheuser-Busch or on construction work being done for it and its adjoining tenant, and the peaceful attempt to get members of other unions similarly to refuse to work, are plainly within the free scope accorded to workers by § 20 for "terminating any relation of employment," or "ceasing to perform any work or labor," or "recommending, advising, or persuading others by peaceful means so to do." The picketing of Anheuser-Busch premises with signs to indicate that Anheuser-Busch was unfair to organized labor, a familiar practice in these situations, comes within the language "attending at any place where any such person or persons may lawfully be, for the purpose of peacefully obtaining or communicating information, or from peacefully persuading any person to work or to abstain from working." Finally, the recommendation to union members and their friends not to buy or use the product of Anheuser-Busch is explicitly covered by "ceasing to patronize . . . any party to such dispute, or from recommending, advising, or persuading others by peaceful and lawful means so to do."

Clearly, then, the facts here charged constitute lawful conduct under the Clayton Act unless the defendants cannot invoke that Act because outsiders to the immediate dispute also shared in the conduct. But we need not determine whether the conduct is legal within the restrictions which *Duplex Co.* v. *Deering* gave to the immunities of § 20 of the Clayton Act. Congress in the Norris-LaGuardia Act has expressed the public policy of the United States and defined its conception of a "labor dispute" in terms that no longer leave room for doubt. This was done, as we recently said, in order to "obviate the results of the judicial construction" thereofore given the Clayton Act. Such a dispute, § 13 (c) provides, "includes any controversy concerning terms or conditions of employment, or concerning the association or representation of persons in negotiating, fixing, maintaining, changing, or seeking to arrange terms or conditions of employment, regardless of whether or not the disputants stand in the proximate relation of employer and employee." And under § 13 (b) a person is "participating or interested in a labor dispute" if he "is engaged in the same industry, trade, craft, or occupation, in which such dispute occurs, or has a direct or indirect interest therein, or is a member, officer, or agent of any association composed in whole or in part of employers or employees engaged in such industry, trade, craft, or occupation."

To be sure, Congress expressed this national policy and determined the bounds of a labor dispute in an act explicitly dealing with the further withdrawal of injunctions in labor controversies. But to argue, as it was urged before us, that the *Duplex* case still governs for purposes of a criminal prosecution is to say that that which on the equity side of the court is allowable conduct may in a criminal proceeding become the road to prison. It would be strange indeed that although neither the Government nor Anheuser-Busch could have sought an injunction against the acts here challenged, the elaborate efforts to permit such conduct failed to prevent criminal liability punishable with imprisonment and heavy fines. That is not the way to read the will of Congress, particularly when expressed by a statute which, as we have already indicated, is practically and historically one of a series of enactments touching one of the most sensitive national problems. Such legislation must not be read in a spirit of mutilating narrowness. . . . The appropriate way to read legislation in a situation like the one before us, was indicated by Mr. Justice Holmes on circuit: "A statute may indicate or require as its justification a change in the policy of the law, although it expresses that change only in the specific cases most likely to occur in the mind. The Legislature has the power to decide what the policy of the law shall be, and if it has intimated its will, however indirectly, that will should be recognized and obeyed. The major premise of the conclusion expressed in a statute, the change of policy that induces the enactment, may not be set out in terms, but it is not an adequate discharge of duty for the courts to say: We see what you are driving at, but you have not said it, and therefore we shall go on as before." *Johnson* v. *United States* 163 F. 30, 32.

The relation of the Norris-LaGuardia Act to the Clayton Act is not that of a tightly drawn amendment to a technically phrased tax provision. The underlying aim of the Norris-LaGuardia Act was to restore the broad purpose which Congress thought it had formulated in the Clayton Act but which was frustrated, so Congress believed, by unduly restrictive judicial construction. . . . The Norris-LaGuardia Act reasserted the original purpose of the Clayton Act by infusing into it the immunized trade union activities as redefined by the later Act. In this light § 20 removes all such allowable conduct from the taint of being a "violation of any law of the United States," including the Sherman Law.

There is no profit in discussing those cases under the Clayton Act which were decided before the courts were furnished the light shed by the

Norris-LaGuardia Act on the nature of the industrial conflict. And since the facts in the indictment are made lawful by the Clayton Act in so far as "any law of the United States" is concerned, it would be idle to consider the Sherman Law apart from the Clayton Act as interpreted by Congress. It was precisely in order to minimize the difficulties to which the general language of the Sherman Law in its application to workers had given rise, that Congress cut through all the tangled verbalisms and enumerated concretely the types of activities which had become familiar incidents of union procedure.

Affirmed.

MR. JUSTICE MURPHY took no part in the disposition of this case.

MR. JUSTICE STONE, concurring.

As I think it clear that the indictment fails to charge an offense under the Sherman Act, as it has been interpreted and applied by this Court, I find no occasion to consider the impact of the Norris-LaGuardia Act on the definition of participants in a labor dispute in the Clayton Act, as construed by this Court in *Duplex Printing Press Co.* v. *Deering*, 254 U.S. 443—an application of the Norris-LaGuardia Act which is not free from doubt and which some of my brethren sharply challenge.

. . .

MR. JUSTICE ROBERTS, dissenting.

I am of opinion that the judgment should be reversed.

. . .

By a process of construction never, as I think, heretofore indulged by this court, it is now found that, because Congress forbade the issuing of injunctions to restrain certain conduct, it intended to repeal the provisions of the Sherman Act authorizing actions at law and criminal prosecutions for the commission of torts and crimes defined by the antitrust laws. The doctrine now announced seems to be that an indication of a change of policy in an Act as respects one specific item in a general field of the law, covered by an earlier Act, justifies this court in spelling out an implied repeal of the whole of the earlier statute as applied to conduct of the sort here involved. I venture to say that no court has ever undertaken so radically to legislate where Congress has refused so to do.

The construction of the act now adopted is the more clearly inadmissible when we remember that the scope of proposed amendments and repeals of the antitrust laws in respect of labor organizations has been the subject of constant controversy and consideration in Congress. In the light of this history, to attribute to Congress an intent to repeal legislation which has had a definite and well understood scope and effect for decades past, by resurrecting a rejected construction of the Clayton Act and extending a policy strictly limited by the Congress itself in the Norris-LaGuardia Act, seems to me a usurpation by the courts of the function of the Congress not only novel but fraught, as well, with the most serious dangers to our constitutional system of division of powers.

THE CHIEF JUSTICE joins in this opinion.

Questions

1. Was the Court's use of the Norris-LaGuardia Act sound?
2. Does the decision make sense as a matter of labor policy? Antitrust policy?
3. Did the Court leave the door ajar for antitrust law to be applied to labor unions? If so, in what sorts of cases?

c. Federal Labor and Antitrust Law, 1945–1964

Having recreated the "Magna Carta," the Supreme Court indicated only four years later that there were limits on the labor exemption from the antitrust laws. In *Allen Bradley* v. *Local Union No. 3, IBEW*, 325 U.S. 797, 16 LRRM 798 (1945), the Court found a union violation of the antitrust laws. In that case, the real facts of the case involved an effort by a local union to assure its members in New York City of full employment and high wages. The device for accomplishing these acceptable and traditional labor goals was to force the electrical contractors of the construction industry in the city to buy materials only from manufacturers in the city, these manufacturers also having been organized by the same local union that represented the electrical construction employees. The result was that the largest construction market in the country, New York City, used only materials made in that city, and the employees who manufactured and who installed the materials were all represented by the defendant union. Of course, this also meant that competing manufacturers from other locals (even those with organized employees belonging to sister locals of the defendant local) could not sell their products in New York. For reasons that only the most sophisticated of Supreme Court watchers would attempt to explain, the Court described the arrangement as if it were employer instigated and dominated, and proceeded to declare the combination a violation of the antitrust laws. The qualifying words of *Hutcheson* had come back to haunt the labor movement only four years after Justice Frankfurter had written them. The *Allen Bradley* Court said, in an eerie reminder of *Duplex:*

"It must be remembered that the exemptions granted the unions were special exceptions to a general legislative plan. The primary objective of all the Anti-trust legislation has been to preserve business competition and to proscribe business monopoly. It would be a surprising thing if Congress, in order to prevent a misapplication of that legislation to labor unions had bestowed upon such unions complete and unreviewable authority to aid business groups to frustrate its primary objective. For if business groups, by combining with labor unions, can fix prices and divide up markets, it was little more than a futile gesture for Congress to prohibit price fixing by business groups themselves. Seldom, if ever, has it been claimed before, that by permitting labor unions to carry on their own activities, Congress intended completely to abdicate its constitutional power to regulate interstate commerce and to empower interested business groups to shift our society from a competitive to a monopolistic economy. Finding no purpose of Congress to immunize labor unions who aid and abet manufacturers and traders in violating the Sherman Act, we hold that the district court correctly concluded that the respondents had violated the Act.

"Our holding means that the same labor union activities may or may not be in violation of the Sherman Act, dependent upon whether the union acts alone or in combination with business groups." 325 U.S. at 809–10.

Does *Allen Bradley* leave unions free to do anything? It would seem that so long as unions do not combine with nonlabor groups, there may be no antitrust threat. See Section 6 of the Clayton Act. If the union joins with a nonlabor group, however, has the union violated the antitrust laws whenever there is any anticompetitive effect? For example, does the union violate the Sherman Act by joining with an employer to set wages of all the employees of that employer? Surely, the anticompetitive effect of setting the wages may force the employer to pay higher wages and thereby pass the cost on to the consumer. If the Court was not outlawing such a practice, what is the dividing line? Perhaps, and the language of the Court does suggest this, the conspiracy of several employers (with the union) was the key to the Court's decision. Would this mean that all multi-employer associations are precluded from joint negotiations with a single union? Even if the only "price fixing" was the setting of uniform wages? If this is not a violation of the antitrust laws, what does explain the Court's decision? Could it be that the Court ignored Justice Frankfurter's warning in *Hutcheson* that courts should not worry about the wisdom or rightness of unions' efforts? Or is the fact that the union did combine with nonlabor groups (as all collective bargaining must do), an invitation for the Court to explore the wisdom or rightness of the union's behavior? If that is what the Court did in *Allen Bradley*, what is the key to the Court's conclusion that what the union did in this case violates the antitrust laws? What made the union's acts "unwise," "wrong," or impermissibly "selfish?"

One would have thought, with the *Allen Bradley* opinion, that the number of antitrust suits against unions would increase substantially and immediately. That did not happen. There were only occasional antitrust lawsuits against unions. In such lawsuits, the issue raised was more often whether the "employees" or "labor groups" were protected by the labor exemption to the antitrust laws than whether the activities were protected by the labor exemption. While one can only speculate, a major reason for this lull in antitrust litigation may have been the availability of remedies provided by the 1947 Taft-Hartley amendments to the Wagner Act. Included in these amendments were a number of prohibitions against union activities, including bans on so-called "secondary boycotts." In 1959, the Landrum-Griffin amendments also outlawed hot cargo clauses—provisions under which the employer agreed not to buy from nonunion employers or employers with whom a union had a dispute. In the mid-1960s, the mood changed.

d. The "Modern" Era

Mine Workers v. Pennington

Supreme Court of the United States, 1965
381 U.S. 657, 59 LRRM 2369

MR. JUSTICE WHITE announced the judgment of the Court and delivered an opinion, in which THE CHIEF JUSTICE and MR. JUSTICE BRENNAN joined.

. . .

[The claim alleged the following, among other things:]

Prior to the 1950 Wage Agreement between the operators and the union, severe controversy had existed in the industry, particularly over wages, the welfare fund and the union's efforts to control the working time of its members. Since 1950, however, relative peace has existed in the industry, all as the result of the 1950 Wage Agreement and its amendments and the additional understandings entered into between UMW and the large operators. Allegedly the parties considered over-production to be the critical problem of the coal industry. The agreed solution was to be the elimination of the smaller companies, the larger companies thereby controlling the market. More specifically, the union abandoned its efforts to control the working time of the miners, agreed not to oppose the rapid mechanization of the mines which would substantially reduce mine employment, agreed to help finance such mechanization and agreed to impose the terms of the 1950 agreement on all operators without regard to their ability to pay. The benefit to the union was to be increased wages as productivity increased with mechanization, these increases to be demanded of the smaller companies whether mechanized or not. Royalty payments into the welfare fund were to be increased also, and the union was to have effective control over the fund's use. The union and large companies agreed upon other steps to exclude the marketing, production, and sale of nonunion coal. Thus the companies agreed not to lease coal lands to nonunion operators, and in 1958 agreed not to sell or buy coal from such companies. The companies and the union jointly and successfully approached the Secretary of Labor to obtain establishment under the Walsh-Healey Act of a minimum wage for employees of contractors selling coal to the TVA, such minimum wage being much higher than in other industries and making it difficult for small companies to compete in the TVA term contract market. At a later time, at a meeting attended by both union and company representatives, the TVA was urged to curtail its spot market purchases, a substantial portion of which were exempt from the Walsh-Healey order. Thereafter four of the larger companies waged a destructive and collusive price-cutting campaign in the TVA spot market for coal, two of the companies, West Kentucky Coal Co. and its subsidiary Nashville Coal Co., being those in which the union had large investments and over which it was in position to exercise control.

The complaint survived motions to dismiss and after a five-week trial before a jury, a verdict was returned in favor of Phillips and against the trustees and the union, the damages against the union being fixed in the amount of $90,000, to be trebled under 15 U.S.C. § 15 (1958 ed.). The trial court set aside the verdict against the trustees but overruled the union's motion for judgment notwithstanding the verdict or in the alternative for a new trial. The Court of Appeals affirmed. . . .

I.

We first consider UMW's contention that the trial court erred in denying its motion for a directed verdict and for judgment notwithstanding the verdict, since a determination in UMW's favor on this issue would finally resolve the controversy. The question presented by this phase of the case is whether in the circumstances of this case the union is exempt from liability under the antitrust laws. We think the answer is clearly in the negative and that the union's motions were correctly denied.

The antitrust laws do not bar the existence and operation of labor unions as such. Moreover, § 20 of the Clayton Act and § 4 of the Norris-LaGuardia Act permit a union, acting alone, to engage in the conduct therein specified without violating the Sherman Act.

But neither § 20 nor § 4 expressly deals with arrangements or agreements between unions and employers. Neither section tells us whether any or all such arrangements or agreements are barred or permitted by the antitrust laws. . . .

If the UMW in this case, in order to protect its wage scale by maintaining employer income, had presented a set of prices at which the mine operators would be required to sell their coal, the union and the employers who happened to agree could not successfully defend this contract provision if it were challenged under the antitrust laws by the United States or by some party injured by the arrangement. In such a case, the restraint on the product market is direct and immediate, is of the type characteristically deemed unreasonable under the Sherman Act and the union gets from the promise nothing more concrete than a hope for better wages to come.

Likewise, if as is alleged in this case, the union became a party to a collusive bidding arrangement designed to drive Phillips and others from the TVA spot market, we think any claim to exemption from antitrust liability would be frivolous at best. For this reason alone the motions of the unions were properly denied.

A major part of Phillips' case, however, was that the union entered into a conspiracy with the large operators to impose the agreed-upon wage and royalty scales upon the smaller, nonunion operators, regardless of their ability to pay and regardless of whether or not the union represented the employees of these companies, all for the purpose of eliminating them from the industry, limiting production and pre-empting the market for the large, unionized operators. The UMW urges that since such an agreement concerned wage standards, it is exempt from the antitrust laws.

It is true that wages lie at the very heart of those subjects about which employers and unions must bargain and the law contemplates agreements on wages not only between individual employers and a union but agreements between the union and employers in a multi-employer bargaining unit. The union benefit from the wage scale agreed upon is direct and concrete and the effect on the product market, though clearly present, results from the elimination of competition based on wages among the employers in the bargaining unit, which is not the kind of restraint Congress intended the Sherman Act to proscribe. We think it beyond question that a union may conclude a wage agreement with the multi-employer bargaining unit without violating the antitrust laws and that it may as a matter of its own policy, and not by agreement with all or part of the employers of that unit, seek the same wages from other employers.

This is not to say that an agreement resulting from union-employer negotiations is automatically exempt from Sherman Act scrutiny simply because the negotiations involve a compulsory subject of bargaining, regardless of the subject or the form and content of the agreement. . . . [T]here are limits to what a union or an employer may offer or extract in the name of wages, and because they must bargain does not mean that the agreement reached may disregard other laws.

We have said that a union may make wage agreements with a multi-employer bargaining unit and may in pursuance of its own union interests seek to obtain the same terms from other employers. No case under the antitrust laws could be made out on evidence limited to such union behavior.[2] But we think a union forfeits its exemption from the antitrust laws when it is clearly shown that it has agreed with one set of employers to impose a certain wage scale on other bargaining units. One group of employers may not conspire to eliminate competitors from the industry and the union is liable with the employers if it becomes a party to the conspiracy. This is true even though the union's part in the scheme is an undertaking to secure the same wages, hours or other conditions of employment from the remaining employers in the industry.

We do not find anything in the national labor policy that conflicts with this conclusion. This Court has recognized that a legitimate aim of any national labor organization is to obtain uniformity of labor standards and that a consequence of such union activity may be to eliminate competition based on differences in such standards. *Apex Hosiery Co.* v. *Leader.* But there is nothing in the labor policy indicating that the union and the employers in one bargaining unit are free to bargain about the wages, hours and working conditions of other bargaining units or to attempt to settle these matters for the entire industry. On the contrary, the duty to bargain unit by unit leads to a quite different conclusion. . . .

---

[2]Unilaterally, and without agreement with any employer group to do so, a union may adopt a uniform wage policy and seek vigorously to implement it even though it may suspect that some employers cannot effectively compete if they are required to pay the wage scale demanded by the union. The union need not gear its wage demands to wages which the weakest units in the industry can afford to pay. Such union conduct is not alone sufficient evidence to maintain a union-employer conspiracy charge under the Sherman Act. There must be additional direct or indirect evidence of the conspiracy. There was, of course, other evidence in this case, but we indicate no opinion as to its sufficiency.

On the other hand, the policy of the antitrust laws is clearly set against employer-union agreements seeking to prescribe labor standards outside the bargaining unit. . . . For the salient characteristic of such agreements is that the union surrenders its freedom of action with respect to its bargaining policy. Prior to the agreement the union might seek uniform standards in its own self-interest but would be required to assess in each case the probable costs and gains of a strike or other collective action to that end and thus might conclude that the objective of uniform standards should temporarily give way. After the agreement the union's interest would be bound in each case to that of the favored employer group. It is just such restraints upon the freedom of economic units to act according to their own choice and discretion that run counter to antitrust policy.

Thus the relevant labor and antitrust policies compel us to conclude that the alleged agreement between UMW and the large operators to secure uniform labor standards throughout the industry, if proved, was not exempt from the antitrust laws.

II.

The UMW next contends that the trial court erroneously denied its motion for a new trial based on claimed errors in the admission of evidence.

. . .

[The Court sustained the union's contention, reversed and remanded for a new trial.]

MR. JUSTICE DOUGLAS, with whom MR. JUSTICE BLACK and MR. JUSTICE CLARK agree, concurring.

. . .

Congress can design an oligopoly for our society, if it chooses. But business alone cannot do so as long as the antitrust laws are enforced. Nor should business and labor working hand-in-hand be allowed to make that basic change in the design of our so-called free enterprise system. If the allegations in this case are to be believed, organized labor joined hands with organized business to drive marginal operators out of existence. According to those allegations the union used its control over West Kentucky Coal Co. and Nashville Coal Co. to dump coal at such low prices that respondents, who were small operators, had to abandon their business. According to those allegations there was a boycott by the union and the major companies against small companies who needed major companies' coal land on which to operate. According to those allegations, high wage and welfare terms of employment were imposed on the small, marginal companies by the union and the major companies with the knowledge and intent that the small ones would be driven out of business.

The only architect of our economic system is Congress. We are right in adhering to its philosophy of the free enterprise system as expressed in the antitrust laws . . . until the Congress delegates to big business and big labor the power to remold our economy in the manner charged here.

Meat Cutters v. Jewel Tea

Supreme Court of the United States, 1965
381 U.S. 676, 59 LRRM 2376

MR. JUSTICE WHITE announced the judgment of the Court and delivered an opinion, in which THE CHIEF JUSTICE and MR. JUSTICE BRENNAN join.

Like *United Mine Workers* v. *Pennington,* this case presents questions regarding the application of §§ 1 and 2 of the Sherman Antitrust Act, as amended, to activities of labor unions. In particular it concerns the lawfulness of the following restriction on the operating hours of food store meat departments contained in a collective bargaining agreement executed after joint multi-employer, multi-union negotiations:

"Market operating hours shall be 9:00 a.m. to 6:00 p.m. Monday through Saturday, inclusive. No customer shall be served who comes into the market before or after the hours set forth above."

[During negotiation of the contract, the employer group of 9,000 Chicago retailers of fresh meat proposed deletion of the quoted language.[1] The union refused. Eventually the employer group agreed to the language, although Jewel Tea, a large food store chain, signed only under the duress of a threatened strike. Jewel Tea then sued the union.]

After trial . . . the District Judge ruled the "record was devoid of any evidence to support a finding of conspiracy" between Associated and the unions to force the restrictive provision on Jewel. Testing the unions' action standing alone, the trial court found that even in self-service markets removal of the limitation on marketing hours either would inaugurate longer hours and night work for the butchers or would result in butchers' work being done by others unskilled in the trade. Thus, the court concluded, the unions had imposed the marketing-hours limitation to serve their own interests respecting conditions of employment, and such action was clearly within the labor exemption of the Sherman Act. . . . Alternatively, the District Court ruled that even if this was not the case, the arrangement did not amount to an unreasonable restraint of trade in violation of the Sherman Act.

The Court of Appeals reversed the dismissal of the complaint as to both the unions and Associated. . . .

Here, as in *United Mine Workers* v. *Pennington,* the claim is made that the agreement under attack is exempt from the antitrust laws. We agree, but not on the broad grounds urged by the union.

It is well at the outset to emphasize that this case comes to us stripped of any claim of a union-employer conspiracy against Jewel. The trial court

---

[1] The practice in the Chicago area is for the employers and the butchers to execute separate, but similar, collective bargaining agreements for self-service and service markets. A self-service market is "one in which fresh beef, veal, lamb, mutton or pork are available for sale on a prepackage self-service basis." Semi-self-service markets, those in which fresh meat is made available on a prepackaged basis but there is also a service counter offering custom cutting for those who prefer it, are governed by the self-service contract. Service markets are those in which no fresh meat is made available on a self-service basis.

found no evidence to sustain Jewel's conspiracy claim and this finding was not disturbed by the Court of Appeals. We therefore have a situation where the unions, having obtained a marketing-hours agreement from one group of employers, have successfully sought the same terms from a single employer, Jewel, not as a result of a bargain between the unions and some employers directed against other employers, but pursuant to what the unions deemed to be in their own labor union interests.

Jewel does not allege that it has been injured by the elimination of competition among the other employers within the unit with respect to marketing hours; Jewel complains only of the union's action in forcing it to accept the same restriction, the unions acting not at the behest of any employer group but in pursuit of their own policies. It might be argued that absent any union-employer conspiracy against Jewel and absent any agreement between Jewel and any other employer, the union-Jewel contract cannot be a violation of the Sherman Act. But the issue before us is not the broad substantive one of a violation of the antitrust laws—was there a conspiracy or combination which unreasonably restrained trade or an attempt to monopolize and was Jewel damaged in its business?—but whether the agreement is immune from attack by reason of the labor exemption from the antitrust laws. The fact that the parties to the agreement are but a single employer and the unions representing its employees does not compel immunity for the agreement. We must consider the subject matter of the agreement in the light of the national labor policy.

We pointed out in *Pennington* that exemption for union-employer agreements is very much a matter of accommodating the coverage of the Sherman Act to the policy of the labor laws. Employers and unions are required to bargain about wages, hours and working conditions, and this fact weighs heavily in favor of antitrust exemption for agreements on these subjects. But neither party need bargain about other matters and either party commits an unfair labor practice if it conditions its bargaining upon discussions of a nonmandatory subject. . . .

Thus the issue in this case is whether the marketing hours restriction, like wages, and unlike prices, is so intimately related to wages, hours and working conditions that the unions' successful attempt to obtain that provision through bona fide, arm's-length bargaining in pursuit of their own labor union policies, and not at the behest of or in combination with nonlabor groups, falls within the protection of the national labor policy and is therefore exempt from the Sherman Act.[5] We think that it is.

. . .

Contrary to the Court of Appeals, we think that the particular hours of the day and the particular days of the week during which employees shall be required to work are subjects well within the realm of "wages, hours, and other terms and conditions of employment" about which employers and unions must bargain. . . .

Disposing of the case, as it did, on the broad grounds we have indicated, the Court of Appeals did not deal separately with the marketing-hours

---

[5]The crucial determinant is not the form of the agreement—*e.g.*, prices or wages—but its relative impact on the product market and the interests of union members. . . .

provision, as distinguished from hours of work, in connection with either service or self-service markets. The dispute here pertains principally to self-service markets.

The unions argue that since night operations would be impossible without night employment of butchers, or an impairment of the butchers' jurisdiction, or a substantial effect on the butchers' workload, the marketing-hours restriction is either little different in effect from the valid working-hours provision that work shall stop at 6 p.m. or is necessary to protect other concerns of the union members. If the unions' factual premises are true, we think the unions could impose a restriction on night operations without violation of the Sherman Act; for then operating hours, like working hours, would constitute a subject of immediate and legitimate concern to union members.

Jewel alleges on the other hand that the night operation of self-service markets requires no butcher to be in attendance and does not infringe any other legitimate union concern. Customers serve themselves; and if owners want to forgo furnishing the services of a butcher to give advice or to make special cuts, this is not the unions' concern since their desire to avoid night work is fully satisfied and no other legitimate interest is being infringed. In short, the connection between working hours and operating hours in the case of the self-service market is said to be so attenuated as to bring the provision within the prohibition of the Sherman Act.

If it were true that self-service markets could actually operate without butchers, at least for a few hours after 6 p.m., that no encroachment on butchers' work would result and that the workload of butchers during normal working hours would not be substantially increased, Jewel's position would have considerable merit. For then the obvious restraint on the product market—the exclusion of self-service stores from the evening market for meat—would stand alone, unmitigated and unjustified by the vital interests of the union butchers which are relied upon in this case. In such event the limitation imposed by the unions might well be reduced to nothing but an effort by the unions to protect one group of employers from competition by another, which is conduct that is not exempt from the Sherman Act. Whether there would be a violation of §§ 1 and 2 would then depend on whether the elements of a conspiracy in restraint of trade or an attempt to monopolize had been proved.

Thus the dispute between Jewel and the unions essentially concerns a narrow factual question: Are night operations without butchers, and without infringement of butchers' interests, feasible? The District Court resolved this factual dispute in favor of the unions. . . . Our function is limited to reviewing the record to satisfy ourselves that the trial judge's findings are not clearly erroneous.

. . .

The unions' evidence with regard to the practicability of night operations without butchers was accurately summarized by the trial judge as follows:

> "[I]n most of plaintiff's stores outside Chicago, where night operations exist, meat cutters are on duty whenever a meat department is open after 6 p.m. . . . Even in self-service departments, ostensibly oper-

ated without employees on duty after 6 P.M., there was evidence that requisite customer services in connection with meat sales were performed by grocery clerks. In the same vein, defendants adduced evidence that in the sale of delicatessen items, which could be made after 6 P.M. from self-service cases under the contract, 'practically' always during the time the market was open the manager, or other employees, would be rearranging and restocking the cases. There was also evidence that even if it were practical to operate a self-service meat market after 6 P.M. without employees, the night operations would add to the workload in getting the meats prepared for night sales and in putting the counters in order the next day."

Jewel challenges the unions' evidence on each of these points—arguing, for example, that its preference to have butchers on duty at night, where possible under the union contract, is not probative of the feasibility of not having butchers on duty and that the evidence that grocery clerks performed customer services within the butchers' jurisdiction was based on a single instance resulting from "entrapment" by union agents. But Jewel's argument . . . falls far short of a showing that the trial judge's ultimate findings were clearly erroneous.

Reversed.

MR. JUSTICE GOLDBERG, with whom MR. JUSTICE HARLAN and MR. JUSTICE STEWART join, dissenting from the opinion but concurring in the reversal in [*Pennington*] and concurring in the judgment of the Court in [*Jewel Tea*].

Stripped of all the pejorative adjectives and reduced to their essential facts, both *Pennington* and *Jewel Tea* represent refusals by judges to give full effect to congressional action designed to prohibit judicial intervention via the antitrust route in legitimate collective bargaining. The history of these cases furnishes fresh evidence of the observation that in this area, necessarily involving a determination of "what public policy in regard to the industrial struggle demands," *Duplex Co.* v. *Deering*, (dissenting opinion of Mr. Justice Brandeis), "courts have neither the aptitude nor the criteria for reaching sound decisions." Cox, *Labor and the Antitrust Laws—A Preliminary Analysis,* 104 U. Pa. L. Rev. 252, 269–70 (1955). . . .

Pennington presents a case of a union negotiating with the employers in the industry for wages, fringe benefits, and working conditions. Despite allegations of conspiracy, which connotes clandestine activities, it is no secret that the United Mine Workers, acting to further what it considers to be the best interests of its members, espouses a philosophy of achieving uniform high wages, fringe benefits, and good working conditions. As the *quid pro quo* for this, the Union is willing to accept the burdens and consequences of automation. Further, it acts upon the view that the existence of marginal operators who cannot afford these high wages, fringe benefits, and good working conditions does not serve the best interests of the working miner but, on the contrary, depresses wage standards and perpetuates undesirable conditions. This has been the articulated policy of the Union since 1933. . . .

Jewel Tea presents another and different aspect of collective bargaining philosophy. The Chicago Local of the Amalgamated Meat Cutters bargains for its members with small, independent service butchers as well as large automated self-service chains. It seeks from both a uniform policy that no fresh meat be sold after 6 p.m. . . . While it is claimed by Jewel Tea, a large operator of automated self-service markets, that it can operate beyond the set hours without increasing the work of butchers or having others do butchers' work—a claim rejected by the trial court and the majority of this Court—it is conceded, on this record, that the small, independent service operators cannot do so. Therefore to the extent that the Union's uniform policy limiting hours of selling fresh meat has the effect of aiding one group of employers at the expense of another, here the union policy, unlike that in *Pennington,* aids the small employers at the expense of the large.

Although evidencing these converse economic effects, both *Pennington* and *Jewel Tea,* as the Court in *Pennington,* and my Brother WHITE'S opinion in *Jewel Tea* acknowledge, involve conventional collective bargaining on wages, hours, and working conditions—mandatory subjects of bargaining under the National Labor Relations Act. Yet the Mine Workers' activity in *Pennington* was held subject to an antitrust action by two lower courts. This decision was based upon a jury determination that the Union's economic philosophy is undesirable, and it resulted in an award against the Union of treble damages of $270,000 and $55,000 extra for respondent's attorneys' fees. In *Jewel Tea,* the Union has also been subjected to an antitrust suit in which a court of appeals, with its own notions as to what butchers are legitimately interested in, would subject the Union to a treble damage judgment in an as yet undetermined amount.

Regretfully these cases, both in the lower courts and in expressions in the various opinions filed today in this Court, as I shall demonstrate, constitute a throwback to past days when courts allowed antitrust actions against unions and employers engaged in conventional collective bargaining, because "a judge considered" the union or employer conduct in question to be "socially or economically" objectionable. *Duplex Co.* v. *Deering* (dissenting opinion of MR. JUSTICE BRANDEIS).

. . .

[I]t seems clear that the essential error at the core of the Court's reasoning [in *Pennington*] is that it ignores the express command of Congress that "[t]he labor of a human being is not a commodity or article of commerce," and therefore that the antitrust laws do not prohibit the "elimination of price competition based on differences in labor standards." *Apex Hosiery Co.* v. *Leader.* This is made clear by a simple question that the Court does not face. Where there is an "agreement" to seek uniform wages in an industry, in what item is competition restrained? The answer to this question can only be that competition is restrained in employee wage standards. That is, the union has agreed to restrain the free competitive market for labor by refusing to provide labor to other employers below the uniform rate. Under such an analysis, it would seem to follow that the existence of a union itself constitutes a restraint of trade, for the object of a union is to band together the individual workers in an effort, by common action, to obtain better wages and working conditions—*i.e.,* to obtain a higher price for their labor. The very purpose and effect of a labor union is to limit the power of an employer to use competition among workingmen to drive down wage rates and enforce substandard conditions of employment. If competition between workingmen to see who will work for the lowest wage is the ideal, all labor unions should be eliminated. . . .

My Brother WHITE recognizes [in *Jewel Tea*] that the issue of the hours of sale of meat concerns a mandatory subject of bargaining based on the trial court's findings that it directly affected the hours of work of the butchers in the self-service markets, and therefore, since there was a finding that the Union was not abetting an independent employer conspiracy, he joins in reversing the Court of Appeals. In doing so, however, he apparently draws lines among mandatory subjects of bargaining, presumably based on a judicial determination of their importance to the worker, and states that not all agreements resulting from collective bargaining based on mandatory subjects of bargaining are immune from the antitrust laws, even absent evidence of union abetment of an independent conspiracy of employers. Following this reasoning, my Brother WHITE indicates that he would sustain a judgment here, even absent evidence of union abetment of an independent conspiracy of employers, if the trial court had found "that self-service markets could actually operate without butchers, at least for a few hours after 6 p.m., that no encroachment on butchers' work would result and that the workload of butchers during normal working hours would not be substantially increased. . . ." Such a view seems to me to be unsupportable. It represents a narrow, confining view of what labor unions have a legitimate interest in preserving and thus bargaining about. Even if the self-service markets could operate after 6 p.m., without their butchers and without increasing the work of their butchers at other times, the result of such operation can reasonably be expected to be either that the small, independent service markets would have to remain open in order to compete, thus requiring their union butchers to work at night, or that the small, independent service markets would not be able to operate at night and thus would be put at a competitive disadvantage. Since it is clear that the large, automated self-service markets employ fewer butchers per volume of sales than service markets do, the Union certainly has a legitimate interest in keeping service markets competitive so as to preserve jobs. Job security of this kind has been recognized to be a legitimate subject of union interest. . . .

My view that Congress intended that collective bargaining activity on mandatory subjects of bargaining under the Labor Act not be subject to the antitrust laws does not mean that I believe that Congress intended that activity involving all nonmandatory subjects of bargaining be similarly exempt. The direct and overriding interest of unions in such subjects as wages, hours, and other working conditions, which Congress has recognized in making them subjects of mandatory bargaining, is clearly lacking where the subject of the agreement is price-fixing and market allocation. Moreover, such activities are at the core of the type of anticompetitive commercial restraint at which the antitrust laws are directed.

. . .

MR. JUSTICE DOUGLAS, with whom MR. JUSTICE BLACK and MR. JUSTICE CLARK concur, dissenting.

If we followed *Allen Bradley Co.* v. *Union,* we would hold with the Court of Appeals that this multi-employer agreement with the union not to sell meat between 6 p.m. and 9 a.m. was not immunized from the antitrust laws and that respondent's evidence made out a prima facie case that it was in fact a violation of the Sherman Act.

If, in the present case, the employers alone agreed not to sell meat from 6 p.m. to 9 a.m., they would be guilty of an anticompetitive practice, barred by the antitrust laws. Absent an agreement or conspiracy, a proprietor can keep his establishment open for such hours as he chooses. . . .

My Brother WHITE's conclusion that the concern of the union members over *marketing* hours is "immediate and direct" depends upon there being a necessary connection between marketing hours and working hours. That connection is found in the District Court's finding that "in stores where meat is sold at night it is impractical to operate without either butchers or other employees." 215 F. Supp. 839, 846. It is, however, undisputed that on some nights Jewel does so operate in some of its stores in Indiana, and even in Chicago it sometimes operates without butchers at night in the sale of fresh poultry and sausage, which are exempt from the union ban.

It is said that even if night self-service could be carried on without butchers, still the union interest in store hours would be immediate and direct because competitors would have to stay open too or be put at a disadvantage—and some of these competitors would be non-self-service stores that would have to employ union butchers at night. But *Allen Bradley* forecloses such an expansive view of the labor exemption to the antitrust laws.

Questions

1. Given the three three-justice opinions, what can one say of the state of antitrust law as it applies to labor unions? Can one assume that the White opinion is "the law" since it was the swing vote which controlled the result in both *Pennington* and *Jewel Tea?* See *Ramsey* v. *United Mine Workers of America,* 401 U.S. 302, 76 LRRM 2549 (1971).

2. What are the principles that emerge from the White opinions? Are they noticeably different from Justice Goldberg's approach? In what way? Would Justice Goldberg ever find a union in violation of the antitrust laws? If so, how significantly different are the approaches? Is it only a matter of degree? If it is a difference in kind, what is it? At the other end, would Justice Douglas send every collective bargaining contract to the jury to determine whether it violated the antitrust laws? If so, is that feasible? Or, does Justice Douglas limit his position to multi-employer bargaining? If not, are the responses found in the two other opinions persuasive?

3. Should multi-employer bargaining be deemed a violation of the antitrust laws? If not, should the law be amended to accomplish that

objective? Are you persuaded that if there were no multi-employer bargaining, there would be more competition among employers and this would redound to the benefit of the consumer? Might it not also produce more competition among unions, or local unions, which would be injurious to the consumer?

4. Consider the dilemma of employers and unions after *Pennington*. Are not the difficulties immense for the parties engaged in collective bargaining? Reconsider this while you are studying the duty to bargain under the NLRA.

5. Can an employer agree with a union which does not represent its employees to pay the employees union-scale wages?

Connell Construction Company, Inc. v. Plumbers and Steamfitters Local Union No. 100*

Supreme Court of the United States, 1975
421 U.S. 616, 89 LRRM 2401

MR. JUSTICE POWELL delivered the opinion of the Court.

The building trades union in this case supported its efforts to organize mechanical subcontractors by picketing certain general contractors, including Petitioner. The union's sole objective was to compel the general contractors to agree that in letting subcontracts for mechanical work they would deal only with firms that were parties to the union's current collective-bargaining agreement. The union disclaimed any interest in representing the general contractors' employees. In this case the picketing succeeded, and Petitioner seeks to annul the resulting agreement as an illegal restraint on competition under federal and state law. The union claims immunity from federal antitrust statutes and argues that federal labor regulation pre-empts state law.

Local 100 is the bargaining representative for workers in the plumbing and mechanical trades in Dallas. When this litigation began, it was party to a multiemployer bargaining agreement with the Mechanical Contractors Association of Dallas, a group of about 75 mechanical contractors. That contract contained a "most favored nation" clause, by which the union agreed that if it granted a more favorable contract to any other employer it would extend the same terms to all members of the Association.

Connell Construction Company is a general building contractor in Dallas. It obtains jobs by competitive bidding and subcontracts all plumbing and mechanical work. Connell has followed a policy of awarding these subcontracts on the basis of competitive bids, and it has done business with both union and non-union subcontractors. Connell's employees are represented by various building trade unions. Local 100 has never sought to represent them or to bargain with Connell on their behalf.

*See St. Antoine, Connell: *Antitrust Law at the Expense of Labor Law*, 62 VA. L. REV. 603 (1976).

In November 1970, Local 100 asked Connell to agree that it would subcontract mechanical work only to firms that had a current contract with the union.

. . .

When Connell refused to sign this agreement, Local 100 stationed a single picket at one of Connell's major construction sites. About 150 workers walked off the job, and construction halted. Connell filed suit in state court to enjoin the picketing as a violation of Texas antitrust laws. Local 100 removed the case to federal court. Connell then signed the subcontracting agreement under protest. It amended its complaint to claim that the agreement violated §§ 1 and 2 of the Sherman Act, and was therefore invalid. Connell sought a declaration to this effect and an injunction against any further efforts to force it to sign such an agreement.

By the time the case went to trial, Local 100 had submitted identical agreements to a number of other general contractors in Dallas. Five others had signed, and the union was waging a selective picketing campaign against those who resisted.

The District Court held that the subcontracting agreement was exempt from federal antitrust laws because it was authorized by the construction industry proviso to § 8(e) of the National Labor Relations Act. The court also held that federal labor legislation pre-empted the State's antitrust laws. The Court of Appeals for the Fifth Circuit affirmed, with one judge dissenting.

. . .

The basic sources of organized labor's exemption from federal antitrust laws are §§ 6 and 20 of the Clayton Act, and the Norris-LaGuardia Act. These statutes declare that labor unions are not combinations or conspiracies in restraint of trade, and exempt specific union activities, including secondary picketing and boycotts, from the operation of the antitrust laws. See *United States* v. *Hutcheson.* They do not exempt concerted action or agreements between unions and nonlabor parties. *UMW* v. *Pennington.* The Court has recognized, however, that a proper accommodation between the congressional policy favoring collective bargaining under the NLRA and the congressional policy favoring free competition in business markets requires that some union-employer agreements be accorded a limited nonstatutory exemption from antitrust sanctions. *Meat Cutters Local 189* v. *Jewel Tea Co.*

The nonstatutory exemption has its source in the strong labor policy favoring the association of employees to eliminate competition over wages and working conditions. Union success in organizing workers and standardizing wages ultimately will affect price competition among employers, but the goals of federal labor law never could be achieved if this effect on business competition were held a violation of the antitrust laws. The Court therefore has acknowledged that labor policy requires tolerance for the lessening of business competition based on differences in wages and working conditions. Labor policy clearly does not require, however, that a union have freedom to impose direct restraints on competition among those who employ its members. Thus, while the statutory exemption allows unions to accomplish some restraints by acting unilaterally, *e.g.*, *American Federation of Musicians* v. *Carroll*, 391 U.S. 99, 68 LRRM 2230 (1968), the nonstatutory exemption offers no similar protection when a union and a nonlabor party agree to restrain competition in a business market.

In this case Local 100 used direct restraints on the business market to support its organizing campaign. The agreements with Connell and other general contractors indiscriminately excluded nonunion subcontractors from a portion of the market, even if their competitive advantages were not derived from substandard wages and working conditions but rather from more efficient operating methods. Curtailment of competition based on efficiency is neither a goal of federal labor policy nor a necessary effect of the elimination of competition among workers. Moreover, competition based on efficiency is a positive value that the antitrust laws strive to protect.

The multiemployer bargaining agreement between Local 100 and the Association, though not challenged in this suit, is relevant in determining the effect that the agreement between Local 100 and Connell would have on the business market. The "most favored nation" clause in the multiemployer agreement promised to eliminate competition between members of the Association and any other subcontractors that Local 100 might organize. By giving members of the Association a contractual right to insist on terms as favorable as those given any competitor, it guaranteed that the union would make no agreement that would give an unaffiliated contractor a competitive advantage over members of the Association. Subcontractors in the Association thus stood to benefit from any extension of Local 100's organization, but the method Local 100 chose also had the effect of sheltering them from outside competition in that portion of the market covered by subcontracting agreements between general contractors and Local 100. In that portion of the market, the restriction on subcontracting would eliminate competition on all subjects covered by the multiemployer agreement, even on subjects unrelated to wages, hours and working conditions.

Success in exacting agreements from general contractors would also give Local 100 power to control access to the market for mechanical subcontracting work. The agreements with general contractors did not simply prohibit subcontracting to any nonunion firm; they prohibited subcontracting to any firm that did not have a contract with Local 100. The union thus had complete control over subcontract work offered by general contractors that had signed these agreements. Such control could result in significant adverse effects on the market and on consumers, effects unrelated to the union's legitimate goals of organizing workers and standardizing working conditions. For example, if the union thought the interests of its members would be served by having fewer subcontractors competing for the available work, it could refuse to sign collective-bargaining agreements with marginal firms. Cf. *UMW* v. *Pennington*. Or, since Local 100 has a well-defined geographical jurisdiction, it could exclude "travelling" subcontractors by refusing to deal with them. Local

100 thus might be able to create a geographical enclave for local contractors, similar to the closed market in *Allen Bradley*.

This record contains no evidence that the union's goal was anything other than organizing as many subcontractors as possible. This goal was legal, even though a successful organizing campaign ultimately would reduce the competition that unionized employers face from nonunion firms. But the methods the union chose are not immune from antitrust sanctions simply because the goal is legal. Here Local 100, by agreement with several contractors, made nonunion subcontractors ineligible to compete for a portion of the available work. This kind of direct restraint on the business market has substantial anticompetitive effects, both actual and potential, that would not follow naturally from the elimination of competition over wages and working conditions. It contravenes antitrust policies to a degree not justified by congressional labor policy, and therefore cannot claim a nonstatutory exemption from the antitrust laws.

There can be no argument in this case, whatever its force in other contexts, that a restraint of this magnitude might be entitled to an antitrust exemption if it were included in a lawful collective-bargaining agreement. In this case, Local 100 had no interest in representing Connell's employees. The federal policy favoring collective bargaining therefore can offer no shelter for the union's coercive action against Connell or its campaign to exclude nonunion firms from the subcontracting market.

. . .

Reversed in part, affirmed in part, and remanded.

MR. JUSTICE STEWART, with whom MR. JUSTICE DOUGLAS, MR. JUSTICE BRENNAN, and MR. JUSTICE MARSHALL join, dissenting.

. . .

The relevant legislative history unmistakably demonstrates that in regulating secondary activity and "hot cargo" agreements in 1947 and 1959, Congress selected with great care the sanctions to be imposed if proscribed union activity should occur. In so doing, Congress rejected efforts to give private parties injured by union activity such as that engaged in by Local 100 the right to seek relief under federal antitrust laws. Accordingly, I would affirm the judgment before us.

. . .

In sum, the legislative history of the 1947 and 1959 amendments and additions to national labor law clearly demonstrates that Congress did not intend to restore antitrust sanctions for secondary boycott activity such as that engaged in by Local 100 in this case, but rather intended to subject such activity only to regulation under the National Labor Relations Act and § 303 of the Labor Management Relations Act. The judicial imposition of "independent federal remedies" not intended by Congress, no less than the application of state law to union conduct that is either protected or prohibited by federal labor law, threatens "to upset the balance of power between labor and management expressed in our national labor policy." *Local 20, Teamsters* v. *Morton*, 377 U.S., at 260, 56 LRRM at 2228. Accordingly, the judgment before us should be affirmed.

[The dissenting opinion of JUSTICE DOUGLAS is omitted.]

Questions

1. Does the Court accurately state your understanding of any of the opinions in *Pennington* or *Jewel Tea*? What is the distinction between a statutory exemption and an exemption that is due to accommodation of antitrust and labor policies? Does Section 20 of the Clayton Act cover only action by labor unions when it is taken by the unions alone (that is, without cooperation of nonlabor groups)? If the language is ambiguous, how should the question be resolved? Is it not turning back the clock for the Court to invite itself into weighing the good and bad (the wise and unwise, the reasonable and unreasonable) of the particular arrangement, at least without some sort of benchmark? Moreover, does it make sense for the Court to suggest that the antitrust exemption precludes the courts from interfering with the union's efforts to obtain an agreement, but not with the agreement itself? Once the Court embarked on its journey to weigh the pros and cons of what the union had done, what went into the balance? Does the Court explain, other than to say, "Ugh"? What did the "most favored employer" clause have to do with the Court's analysis? Would the result have been different without that clause?

In a part of the opinion omitted, as well as in the dissent, there is considerable discussion of whether the remedies contained in the 1947 and 1959 amendments to the original NLRA preempted all other, or at least antitrust, remedies available to the employer in this case. After we have studied secondary boycotts and hot cargo clauses in Chapter 7, a reading of that part of the *Connell* case may prove rewarding.

2. Do the antitrust laws forbid all union efforts to get nonconsumer customers to refrain from doing business with a struck employer? If so, is this a good development so far as labor policy is concerned? Ask yourself these questions as you go through the rest of the course. On the other hand, what antitrust policy does the possible development serve? Did the union in *Connell* have any objective other than the traditional goals of union standards in employment? The answer seems to be clearly in the negative. Did the union, however, attempt to obtain this objective in a manner which was more costly to the consumer than a mere strike of union employees? The answer to this question may be in the affirmative, since the union did not represent the employees of the general contractor in *Connell* and the union's economic weapons resulted in a strike by more than the employees who were represented by the union. Should this make a difference for application of the antitrust laws? What if the pickets of the general contractor merely advertised the fact that the contractor refused to use only union subcontractors? Would that have made any difference?

2. APPLICATION OF STATE ANTITRUST LAWS

In *Connell,* the plaintiff had originally sued pursuant to state antitrust law in the state courts. Would an action under such state laws have been effective? The answer is clearly in the negative. The Court said in *Connell*:

"The Court has held repeatedly that federal law preempts state remedies that interfere with federal labor policy or with specific provisions of the NLRA. The use of state antitrust law to regulate union activities in aid of organization must also be preempted because it creates a substantial risk of conflict with policies central to federal labor law.

"In this area, the accommodation between federal labor and antitrust policy is delicate. Congress and this Court have carefully tailored the antitrust statutes to avoid conflict with the labor policy favoring lawful employee organization, not only by delineating exemptions from antitrust coverage but also by adjusting the scope of the antitrust remedies themselves. State antitrust laws generally have not been subjected to this process of accommodation. If they take account of labor goals at all, they may represent a totally different balance between labor and antitrust policies. Permitting state antitrust law to operate in this field could frustrate the basic federal policies favoring employee organization and allowing elimination of competition among wage earners, and interfere with the detailed system Congress has created for regulating organizational techniques.

"Because employee organization is central to federal labor policy and regulation of organizational procedures is comprehensive, federal law does not admit the use of state antitrust law to regulate union activity that is closely related to organizational goals. Of course, other agreements between union and nonlabor parties may yet be subject to state antitrust laws. The governing factor is the risk of conflict with the NLRA or with federal labor policy." 421 U.S. at 635–37.

The Court cited *Teamsters* v. *Oliver*, 358 U.S. 283, 43 LRRM 2374 (1959), for the proposition that collective agreements may violate state antitrust laws sometimes. In that case, the union and employer set some conditions for drivers in violation of state antitrust law, although the conditions set were "wages" within the meaning of the National Labor Relations Act. The Court concluded that the state could not outlaw such an arrangement, although the Court did say: "We have not here a case of a collective bargaining agreement in conflict with a local health or safety regulation; the conflict here is between the federally sanctioned agreement and state policy which seeks specifically to adjust relationships in the world of commerce." The substance of the agreement reached by the employer and union in *Oliver* was not mandated by the federal labor laws. The federal labor laws require the employer and union to bargain about wages, but the law does not require that the wages be reflected in the manner they were in that case. Why cannot the states outlaw certain agreements between the employer and the union? If the states can do this, what standards are they to use? Does the language of either *Oliver* or *Connell* aid one in finding a solution to the question? Is it enough that the state regulation addresses economic issues (as do the federal labor laws)? Is it helpful, as the *Connell* opinion suggests, that the states may propose different remedies for acts condemned by both state and federal law (that was, quite possibly, the case in *Connell*)? By both state and federal antitrust laws? If the activity is lawful under federal law, but not required, why cannot the states forbid the activity? (This is close to the situation in *Oliver*.) Throughout the remainder of the course, you will be consistently exposed to the possible conflicts and overlapping commands of state and federal law. The doctrine of federal preemption of state law is probably as highly developed in labor relations as any field of law. Yet, you will find that the doctrine as applied to labor relations is extremely complicated, confused, and still primitive.

3. PERSONS ENTITLED TO THE "LABOR EXEMPTION"

Problem

In Austin, Texas, most barbers belong to the Barbers Union. The union sets prices for haircuts, shampoos, and shaves.

Barber shops (as businesses) are owned by individual barbers. These barbers must pay rental for their shops and buy considerable equipment to open and continue a shop. In addition, they may advertise. If an owner-barber is successful enough, he will hire some other barbers to work in his shop. All the barbers in the shop will charge the union-set prices. The employee-barbers get 75 percent of the revenues they bring in.

Is this arrangement a violation of the antitrust laws?

In *Teamsters* v. *Oliver*, 358 U.S. 283, 43 LRRM 2374 (1959), the Supreme Court was faced with a case very similar to the facts posed in the hypothetical problem. In that case, however, the issues were (1) whether a minimum rental regulation set out in a collective bargaining agreement for the use of the trucks "owned" by the owner-operators was "wages" within the meaning of the National Labor Relations Act, and (2) whether state antitrust laws could regulate the form of wages in a collective bargaining contract which had an effect on interstate commerce. The Court concluded that the minimum rental regulation was "wages" since the fee was in lieu of wages which would be paid "employee-drivers" for doing the same work. The Court reasoned that if the union could not make the arrangements it had made, the whole wage structure for which the union had worked over many years might be threatened. As already noted, the Court also concluded that state antitrust laws were preempted by federal labor policy and laws. The Court did not decide, however, since the issue was not before the Court, whether a union can engage in collective bargaining on behalf of these independent contractors (although the Court's reasoning about wages and minimum rental fees was very suggestive).

On the other hand, the Supreme Court has held that a group of independent contractors who perform "blue collar" work cannot fix prices, even though it may be clear to some observers that these persons are being "exploited" by others with whom they deal. See *Columbia River Co.* v. *Hinton*, 315 U.S. 143, 9 LRRM 403 (1942), and *Meat Drivers* v. *United States*, 371 U.S. 94, 51 LRRM 2448 (1962).

In *Federation of Musicians* v. *Carroll*, 391 U.S. 99, 68 LRRM 2230 (1968), the Supreme Court permitted a form of price fixing in circumstances where the Court concluded that the union's activities were designed almost entirely to protect employees' wages. The facts, as described by the Court, were as follows:

"The petitioners are labor unions of professional musicians. The union practices questioned here are mainly those applied to 'club-date' engagements of union members. These are one-time engagements of orchestras to provide music, usually for only a few hours, at such social events as weddings, fashion shows, commencements, and the like.[3] The purchaser of the music, *e.g.*, the father of the bride, the chairman of the events, etc., makes arrangements with a musician, or with a musician's booking agent, for an orchestra of a conductor and a given number of instrumentalists, or 'sidemen,' at a specified time and place. The musician in such cases assumes the role of 'leader' of the orchestra, obtains the 'sidemen' and attends to the bookkeeping and other details of the engagement. Usually the 'leader' performs with the orchestra, sometimes only conducting but often also playing an instrument. When he does not personally appear, he designates a 'subleader' who conducts for him and often also plays an instrument.

"A musician performing 'club-dates' may perform in different capacities on the same day or during the same week, at times as leader and other times as subleader or sideman. The four respondents, however, are musicians who usually act as leaders and maintain offices and employ personnel to solicit engagements through advertising and personal contacts. When two or more engagements are accepted for the same time, each of the respondents will conduct, and, except respondent Peterson, sometimes play, at one and designate a subleader to perform the functions of leader at the other.

"The four respondents were members of the petitioner Federation and Local 802 when this suit was filed. Virtually all musicians in the United States and the great majority of the orchestra leaders are union members. There are no collective bargaining agreements in the club-date field.[6] Club-date engagements are rigidly regulated by unilaterally adopted union bylaws and regulations. Under these bylaws and regulations

"(1) Petitioners enforce a closed shop and exert various pressures upon orchestra leaders to become union members.

"(2) Orchestra leaders must engage a minimum number of sidemen for club-date engagements.

"(3) Orchestra leaders must charge purchasers of music minimum prices prescribed in a 'Price List Booklet.' The prices are the total of (a) the minimum wage scales for sidemen, (b) a 'leader's fee' which is

---

[3]" 'Musical engagements are generally classified as either "steady," those lasting for longer than one week, or "single," usually one day or one performance affairs but including all engagements lasting less than one week. The much sought after steady engagements are rare in comparison with the number of single engagements.

" ' The predominant form of single engagement is the "club date." . . . Single engagements also include the "non-club date" field, consisting of television appearances or recording engagements, etc. . . .' " 372 F.2d at 158.

[6]" 'The distinction between the kinds of single engagements is vital; the non-club date engagements are ordinarily governed by collective bargaining agreements. . . . The same is usually true of the steady engagement field. Local 802 has collective bargaining agreements with the major users or "purchasers" of live music within its area such as recording companies, hotels, television and film producers, opera companies and theatres.' " 372 F.2d at 158.

double the sideman's scale when four or more musicians compose the orchestra, and (c) an additional 8 percent to cover social security, unemployment insurance, and other expenses. When the leader does not personally appear at an engagement, but designates a subleader and four or more musicians perform, the leader must pay the subleader one and one-half times the wage scale out of his 'leader's fee.'

"(4) Orchestra leaders are required to use a form of contract, called the Form B contract, for all engagements. In the club-date field, however, Local 802 accepts assurances that the terms of club-date engagements comply with all union regulations and provide for payment of the minimum wage. Union business agents police compliance.

"(5) Additional regulations apply to traveling engagements. The leader of a traveling orchestra must charge 10 percent more than the minimum price of either the home local or of the local in whose territory the orchestra is playing, whichever is greater.

"(6) Orchestra leaders are prohibited from accepting engagements from or making any payments to caterers.

"(7) Orchestra leaders may accept engagements made by booking agents only if the booking agents have been licensed by the unions under standard forms of license agreements provided by the unions.

"The District Court assumed, and the Court of Appeals held, that orchestra leaders in the club-date field are employers and independent contractors."

The key to the Court's conclusion was:

"[T]he price of the product—here the price for an orchestra for a club-date—represents almost entirely the scale wages of the sidemen and the leader. Unlike most industries, except for the 8 percent charge, there are no other costs contributing to the price. Therefore, if leaders cut prices, inevitably wages must be cut."

Do these cases suggest a rationale that would exempt the price fixing of the Barbers Union in the hypothetical problem from the antitrust laws? Are you persuaded?

4. A Proposed Legislative Reform

From time to time over the years, proposals have been made to do away with multi-employer bargaining and to limit labor unions to representing employees of a single employer. The proponents stress three arguments in support of their position:

1. If groups of unions and employers bargain and resort to strikes and lockouts on a joint basis, unions have greater power to obtain higher wages while employers find it easier to grant wage demands and pass on the cost in the form of higher prices.

2. Industrywide bargaining tends to standardize wage costs and thus prevent differences in wages based on variations in efficiency and local conditions (*e.g.*, cost of living, labor supply, local tax laws).

3. Centralized bargaining tends to increase the severity of strikes and permits a few powerful people to close down entire industries and cause harm to consumers, national defense, and the economy in general.

Do these arguments justify the proposals? Do these arguments recognize all the relevant factors? For example, what is the relevance of unions striking to keep up with the accomplishments of other unions? Of employers engaging in conscious parallelism to avoid competition in wages? Of the most efficient employer setting the standard for all competitors' wages, those wages being higher than they are under present conditions? Of national unions having well-educated, well-disciplined leaders who avoid the hysteria of the immediate labor dispute? Of national unions employing economists to advise the unions of the long-range effects of various opportunities? Of the impact of foreign markets and foreign competition? Of tariffs and quotas?

C. NATIONAL LABOR RELATIONS ACT

1. HISTORY

a. The Railway Labor Act

In 1894, a strike of the Pullman Company shut down the railroad yards in Chicago. There was considerable violence attached to the labor dispute. After the strike ended, President Cleveland appointed a U.S. Strike Commission to make recommendations for improvements in national labor relations. The Commission concluded that the number and severity of strikes would be reduced if employers recognized and bargained with labor unions. In response to this report, Congress passed the Erdman Act in 1898, 30 Stat. 424, imposing criminal penalties for the firing or threatened discharge of railway employees because of their union membership. The Act also provided for means to conciliate disputes between railway unions and railroad companies through mediation and the encouragement of arbitration. On the grounds that the law violated the Fifth Amendment's Due Process Clause and was not authorized by the Interstate Commerce Clause [ironic, given the fact that in the same term, the Court applied the Sherman Act to a union, *Loewe* v. *Lawlor*, 208 U.S. 274 (1908)], the prohibition against anti-union discrimination was held unconstitutional by the Supreme Court in *Adair* v. *United States*, 208 U.S. 161 (1908). The views of the initial U.S. Strike Commission were confirmed, however, by reports of subsequent commissions in 1902 and 1915. During World War I, President Wilson's National War Labor Board gave strong protection to the right of employees to organize and penalized employers who interfered with that right. At the time it was believed that unionization and collective bargaining would help to prevent disruptive labor disputes which interfered with the war effort.

Though these policies ended with the war, their spirit was revived in the Railway Labor Act of 1926, 44 Stat. 577 (1926), 45 U.S.C. Sections 161–163 (1964). The Act prohibits employer interference with union organization by railway employees and provides procedures to aid in the settlement of employment disputes in the industry. Its constitutionality was upheld in *Texas and New Orleans Railroad Co.* v. *Brotherhood of Railway and S.S. Clerks,* 291 U.S. 548 (1930). The Act was amended in several important respects in 1934, and most of its provisions were extended to the airline industry in 1936, 49 Stat. 1189 (1936), 45 U.S.C. Sections 181 *et seq.* (1954). The employer's bargaining obligation under the amended act was defined in *Virginian Ry.* v. *System Federation No. 40,* 300 U.S. 515, 1 LRRM 743 (1937), to include a duty to meet, confer, and make reasonable attempts to reach agreement though there was no absolute requirement that a contract be achieved.

The Railway Labor Act procedures distinguish between two different kinds of disputes—"major" disputes over proposed new contract terms and "minor" disputes concerning the interpretation of existing terms or contract "grievances." If a carrier or union desires to introduce a new contract term, it is required to give at least 30 days' written notice to the other party. The carriers and unions are then to hold conferences on the proposed changes. If the conferences are unsuccessful, either party may call on the National Mediation Board to help resolve the dispute or the Mediation Board may enter on its own initiative in the case of a potential national emergency. If mediation does not succeed, the Board will attempt to induce the two sides to turn to arbitration to resolve the matter. If arbitration is refused and there is a risk of a substantial interruption of interstate commerce, the President can convene an emergency board to study the situation and make recommendations. During this entire period and for 30 days after the emergency board makes its report, lock-outs and strikes are not permitted and the parties are forbidden to change the existing terms without mutual agreement. However, in "major disputes" the parties are eventually free to resort to self-help by the use of economic pressures.

The "minor dispute" provisions for disagreements over interpretation of existing contracts are similar in the early stages. The parties are initially to meet and confer in an attempt to resolve the conflict. If they are unable to reach an adjustment, however, either party to a railroad dispute may refer it to the National Railroad Adjustment Board. The Board holds hearings, makes findings, and issues a written award which is enforceable in court. There is no national adjustment board in the airline industry though the Act permits its eventual establishment. Instead, there is a board with similar powers for each air carrier. The Act's system of compulsory arbitration for union disputes replaces the parties' normal powers to resolve the dispute by self-help. A strike which occurs while the matters in dispute are before the Adjustment Board will be enjoined despite the Norris-LaGuardia Act's limitation on labor injunctions. The Supreme Court has held that the latter act must be accommodated to the specific and exclusive techniques of the Railway Labor Act for conflict resolution. *Brotherhood of Railroad Trainmen* v. *Chicago River and Indiana Railroad Co.,* 353 U.S. 30, 39 LRRM 2578 (1957). Until the 1940s the RLA was hailed as highly successful. Since then its procedures for dealing with "major" disputes have been increasingly eroded by extrastatutory Presidential interventions in railroad disputes and by political pressures. Other aspects of the Act's administration have also been severely criticized. By the late 1960s the Railway Labor Act was thoroughly discredited and had few defenders.

b. The National Labor Relations Act of 1935—The Wagner Act

The National Industrial Recovery Act of 1933 contained the following provision in Section 7(a): ". . . (1) That employees shall have the right to organize and bargain collectively through representatives of their own choosing, and shall be free from the interference, restraint, or coercion of employers of labor, or their agents, in the designation of such representatives or in self-organization or in other concerted activities for the purpose of collective bargaining or other mutual aid or protection; (2) that no employee and no one seeking employment shall be required as a condition of employment to join any company union or to refrain from joining, organizing or assisting a labor organization of his own choosing. . . ."

This statutory recognition of the rights of employees was of historic importance. The statute, however, provided no means for their enforcement. Pursuant to the NIRA, in 1933, by Executive Order, President Roosevelt created a National Labor Board chaired by Senator Wagner of New York. In 1934, again by Executive Order, the NLB was replaced by a National Labor Relations Board. Both the NLB and the original NLRB received complaints, held elections, made investigations, and wrote decisions. But they had no enforcement powers. In 1935 the Supreme Court found the NIRA unconstitutional. *Schechter Poultry Corp.* v. *United States,* 295 U.S. 495 (1935). Although these early labor boards were short-lived and powerless, they helped to create a new atmosphere in which union membership expanded rapidly. Furthermore, the knowledge and experience obtained under the early boards proved to be enormously valuable, and were reflected directly in the National Labor Relations Act, the brainchild of Senator Wagner, which was enacted one month after the demise of the NIRA.

Section 7 of the NLRA was derived directly from Section 7(a) of the NIRA. But where Congress in 1933 and 1934 had stopped with a pronouncement of principle, it went on in 1935 to provide for the effectuation of that principle. To this day, the statutory pattern it established has remained, with one major change in 1947, the pattern of federal regulation of collective bargaining.

First, a three-person National Labor Relations Board (enlarged to five in 1947) was set up, with provision made for staff and field organization, to administer the new law.

Second, provision was made for the Board to conduct elections by which employees would select "representatives of their own choosing" for bargaining purposes. The exercise of this function came to be known as the handling of "representation" procedures and cases.

Third, the new Act identified five types of employer practices which were deemed inimical to the exercise of the rights specified in Section 7.

These were listed, in Section 8, as "unfair labor practices." Today, they constitute the subsections of Section 8(a).

Finally, Section 10 provided for judicial enforcement of National Labor Relations Board decisions.

c. The Labor Management Relations Act of 1947— The Taft-Hartley Act

Under the protective aegis of the NLRA, the labor movement, which in 1933 numbered between two and three million members, by 1947 had swelled to 15 million, roughly one third of the work force.

As a result of many factors, the Labor Management Relations Act (Taft-Hartley) was passed in 1947. While the employer unfair labor practices were retained, Section 8(c) purported to give employers a greater privilege to speak freely in labor controversies than had been permitted by the original statute. Through the creation of new unfair labor practices, the freedom of unions to exercise economic pressures on employers and employees was restricted for the first time.

Under the original NLRA, employees had the privilege of rejecting unionization and choosing to remain unorganized. This privilege was expressly spelled out by the amendments as a right and was protected against union restraint and coercion except when a certain type of union-shop agreement was in existence.

Under the original statute employers were privileged to enter into closed-shop, union-shop, maintenance-of-membership, and other types of union security contracts, even though such agreements required employees to be union members and encouraged membership in one union and discouraged membership in others. The amendments limited union security agreements; unions were prohibited from attempting to cause illegal employer discrimination; unions were obliged to bargain collectively; and, unions were prohibited from engaging in certain types of secondary "boycotts," from engaging in strikes to force an employer to recognize any union other than the one certified by the Board as the bargaining agent in his plant, and from striking to force an employer to assign jurisdiction over particular work tasks to one union rather than to another.

An effort was made to regulate the admission policies of unions by prohibiting, under certain circumstances, the imposition of excessive or discriminatory fees. Featherbedding practices were restricted to some extent by prohibiting unions from extorting payments from employers for work not performed.

Administratively, the NLRB's functions became almost entirely judicial. The Board was increased from three members to five, and its administrative and prosecuting functions were vested in a General Counsel who was to "exercise general supervision over all attorneys employed by the Board" as well as over the "officers and employees in the regional offices." The General Counsel, appointed by the President with the advice and consent of the Senate, had final authority in relation to the investigation of unfair labor practice charges and the prosecution of complaints before the Board.

The Taft-Hartley Act not only amended the Wagner Act, but also marked the extension of federal legislation into new areas of labor relations which had previously been regulated, if at all, by state law and tribunals. Congress decreed that collective bargaining contracts were to be enforceable in the federal courts, and unions were to be suable entities. Congress also restricted payments to union officials; provided for civil actions, in addition to unfair labor practice sanctions, against unions conducting secondary boycotts; and restricted political contributions and expenditures of unions. In Title II of the Act, the Federal Mediation and Conciliation service was strengthened, and Congress indicated its support for arbitration processes. So-called "national emergency disputes" were to be subject to an 80-day cooling-off period prior to any strike which would imperil the national health or safety. During that time, a panel was to evaluate the dispute and make findings of fact, but not recommendations, and the employees were to vote on the employer's last offer.

In addition, states were authorized to outlaw union shops. Under the aegis of this section, 20 states (tending to be those less industrialized) have adopted "right to work" laws.

d. The Labor Management Reporting and Disclosure Act of 1959— The Landrum-Griffin Act

In the late 1950s, largely as a result of dramatization by Senator McClellan of certain abuses by union officers of the power they had acquired, Congress was prodded into the regulation of still another area of labor relations, the internal affairs of labor organizations. Spurred by concern for undemocratic practices within unions, and after much political maneuvering, the Labor Management Reporting and Disclosure Act of 1959 was adopted. Most of it deals with internal union matters.

Also, amendments were made to the National Labor Relations Act. The principal changes were in connection with the union unfair labor practices provisions. Restrictions on secondary boycotts were broadened, "organizational picketing" was limited, and so-called "hot cargo" contracts were proscribed.

2. COVERAGE OF NATIONAL LABOR RELATIONS ACT

It is easy for one involved in a labor dispute to make the mistake of determining immediately the substantive rights and duties under the NLRA. Consideration should first be given, however, to such matters as whether the NLRB has jurisdiction over the case; if so, whether the Board will exercise its jurisdiction; and what employers and employees are covered by the Act.

a. NLRB Jurisdiction

The jurisdiction of the NLRB extends to unfair labor practices and questions of representation affecting interstate commerce. Section 10(a) of the NLRA states that the Board "is empowered . . . to prevent any person from engaging in any unfair labor practice (listed in Section 8) affecting commerce." The Board has taken the position that its jurisdiction is co-extensive with Congressional power to legislate under the Commerce Clause (see NLRB, 1st Ann. Rep. at 135 (1936)). That position was upheld by the Supreme Court in *NLRB* v. *Jones & Laughlin Steel Corp.*, 301 U.S. 1, 1 LRRM 703 (1937).

Despite the broad jurisdictional license given to the NLRB by the NLRA, the Board has historically refused to exercise its jurisdiction over cases where the effect on interstate commerce is relatively insignificant. Beginning in 1950, the Board published "jurisdictional yardsticks" which stated minimum monetary requirements. The business of an enterprise had to satisfy these requirements for the Board to take jurisdiction. The 1950 standards (26 LRRM 51) were revised in 1954 (34 LRRM 75) and again in 1958 (NLRB, 23rd Ann. Rep. 163–64). In 1959, Congress amended Section 14 of the NLRA to provide that although the Board may decline to assert jurisdiction over any class of employers where, in the opinion of the Board, the labor dispute has an insubstantial effect on interstate commerce, the Board may not decline to assert jurisdiction in any labor dispute "over which it would assert jurisdiction under the standards prevailing upon August 1, 1959." The standards prevailing on that date are set forth in NLRB, 23rd Ann. Rep. 163–64 (1958). Through a case-by-case process, the Board has extended its jurisdiction to a variety of enterprises over which it had previously declined to assert jurisdiction. To the extent the Board chooses not to exercise its jurisdiction, the states are free to do so (Section 14(c)).

b. Employers and Employees Under the National Labor Relations Act

While Sections 2(2) and 2(3) of the Act define "employer" and "employee" in broad scope, there are several major exclusions from the coverage of the Act. Section 2(2) excludes all governmental units (including Federal Reserve Banks and wholly owned government corporations other than the Postal Service); these governmental institutions employed approximately 16,222,000 persons in 1980. The Act also excludes from its coverage all railroads and airlines, since they are covered by the Railway Labor Act. Section 2(3) defines "employee" as one who is an employee of any employer, but excludes from its definition a large number of persons, the most significant of whom are: (1) agricultural laborers (of whom there were 3,700,000 in 1982), (2) domestic workers (of whom there were 1,041,000 in 1982), (3) independent contractors, (4) supervisors, and (5) persons employed by employers excluded from the definition of "employer" in Section 2(2). Not surprisingly, the meaning of "employee" and its exclusions has posed problems for the Board and the Courts. The following cases highlight some of these issues.

i. "Independent Contractor" or "Employee"?

NLRB v. Hearst Publications, Inc.

Supreme Court of the United States, 1944
322 U.S. 111, 14 LRRM 614

MR. JUSTICE RUTLEDGE delivered the opinion of the Court.

These cases arise from the refusal of respondents, publishers of four Los Angeles daily newspapers, to bargain collectively with a union representing newsboys who distribute their papers on the streets of that city. Respondents' contention that they were not required to bargain because the newsboys are not their "employees" within the meaning of that term in the National Labor Relations Act presents the important question which we granted certiorari to resolve.*

. . .

The findings of the Board disclose that the Los Angeles Times and the Los Angeles Examiner, published daily and Sunday, are morning papers. Each publishes several editions. . . .

The papers are distributed to the ultimate consumer through a variety of channels, including . . . newsboys who sell on the streets of the city and its suburbs. . . .

The newsboys work under varying terms and conditions. . . .

The units which the Board determined to be appropriate [for an election and for collective bargaining] are composed of those who sell full-time at established spots. Those vendors, misnamed boys, are generally mature men, dependent upon the proceeds of their sales for their sustenance, and frequently supporters of families. Working thus as news vendors on a regular basis, often for a number of years, they form a stable group with relatively little turnover. . . .

Overall circulation and distribution of the papers are under the general supervision of circulation managers. But for purposes of street distribution each paper has divided metropolitan Los Angeles into geographic districts. Each district is under the direct and close supervision of a district manager. His function in the mechanics of distribution is to supply the newsboys in his district with papers which he obtains from the publisher and to turn over to the publisher the receipts which he collects from their sales, either directly or with the assistance of "checkmen" or "main spot" boys. The latter, stationed at the important corners or "spots" in the district, are newsboys who, among other things, receive delivery of the papers, redistribute them to other newsboys stationed at less important corners, and collect receipts from their sales. For that service, which occupies a minor portion of their working day, the checkmen receive a small salary from the publisher. The bulk of their day, however, they spend in hawking papers at their "spots" like other full-time newsboys. A

*[Section 2(3) as it was in 1944 did not expressly exclude "independent contractor" from the definition of "employee."]

large part of the appropriate units selected by the Board for the News and the Herald are checkmen who, in that capacity, clearly are employees of those papers.

The newsboys' compensation consists in the difference between the prices at which they sell the papers and the prices they pay for them. The former are fixed by the publishers and the latter are fixed either by the publishers or, in the case of the News, by the district manager. In practice the newsboys receive their papers on credit. They pay for those sold either sometime during or after the close of their selling day, returning for credit all unsold papers. Lost or otherwise unreturned papers, however, must be paid for as though sold. Not only is the "profit" per paper thus effectively fixed by the publisher, but substantial control of the newsboys' total "take home" can be effected through the ability to designate their sales areas and the power to determine the number of papers allocated to each. While as a practical matter this power is not exercised fully, the newsboys' "right" to decide how many papers they will take is also not absolute. In practice, the Board found, they cannot determine the size of their established order without the cooperation of the district manager. And often the number of papers they must take is determined unilaterally by the district managers.

In addition to effectively fixing the compensation, respondents in a variety of ways prescribe, if not the minutiae of daily activities, at least the broad terms and conditions of work. This is accomplished largely through the supervisory efforts of the district managers, who serve as the nexus between the publishers and the newsboys. The district managers assign "spots" or corners to which the newsboys are expected to confine their selling activities. Transfers from one "spot" to another may be ordered by the district manager for reasons of discipline or efficiency or other cause. Transportation to the spots from the newspaper building is offered by each of respondents. Hours of work on the spots are determined not simply by the impersonal pressures of the market, but to a real extent by explicit instructions from the district managers. Adherence to the prescribed hours is observed closely by the district managers or other supervisory agents of the publishers. Sanctions, varying in severity from reprimand to dismissal, are visited on the tardy and the delinquent. By similar supervisory controls minimum standards of diligence and good conduct while at work are sought to be enforced. However wide may be the latitude for individual initiative beyond those standards, district managers' instructions in what the publishers apparently regard as helpful sales techniques are expected to be followed. Such varied items as the manner of displaying the paper, of emphasizing current features and headlines, and of placing advertising placards, or the advantages of soliciting customers at specific stores or in the traffic lanes are among the subjects of this instruction. Moreover, newsboys are furnished with sales equipment, such as racks, boxes and change aprons, and advertising placards by the publishers. In this pattern of employment the Board found that the newsboys are an integral part of the publishers distribution system and circulation organization. And the record discloses that the newsboys and checkmen feel they are employees of the papers; and respondents' supervisory employees, if not respondents themselves, regard them as such.

In addition to questioning the sufficiency of the evidence to sustain these findings, respondents point to a number of other attributes characterizing their relationship with the newsboys[17] and urge that on the entire record the latter cannot be considered their employees. They base this conclusion on the argument that by common-law standards the extent of their control and direction of the newsboys' working activities creates no more than an "independent contractor" relationship and that common-law standards determine the "employee" relationship under the Act. They further urge that the Board's selection of a collective bargaining unit is neither appropriate nor supported by substantial evidence.

I.

The principal question is whether the newsboys are "employees." Because Congress did not explicitly define the term, respondents say its meaning must be determined by reference to common-law standards. In their view "common-law standards" are those the courts have applied in distinguishing between "employees" and "independent contractors" when working out various problems unrelated to the Wagner Act's purposes and provisions.

The argument assumes that there is some simple, uniform and easily applicable test which the courts have used, in dealing with such problems, to determine whether persons doing work for others fall in one class or the other. Unfortunately this is not true. . . .

II.

Whether, given the intended national uniformity, the term "employee" includes such workers as these newsboys must be answered primarily from the history, terms and purposes of the legislation. The word "is not treated by Congress as a word of art having a definite meaning. . . ."
. . .

Congress, on the one hand, was not thinking solely of the immediate technical relation of employer and employee. It had in mind at least some other persons than those standing in the proximate legal relation of employee to the particular employer involved in the labor dispute. It cannot be taken, however, that the purpose was to include all other persons who may perform service for another or was to ignore entirely legal classifications made for other purposes.
. . .

---

[17]E.g., that there is either no evidence in the record to show, or the record explicitly negatives, that respondents carry the newsboys on their payrolls, pay "salaries" to them, keep records of their sales or locations, or register them as "employees" with the Social Security Board, or that the newsboys are covered by workmen's compensation insurance or the California Compensation Act. Furthermore, it is urged the record shows that the newsboys all sell newspapers, periodicals and other items not furnished to them by their respective publishers, assume the risk for papers lost, stolen or destroyed, purchase and sell their "spots," hire assistants and relief men and make arrangements among themselves for the sale of competing or leftover papers.

It will not do, for deciding this question as one of uniform national application, to import wholesale the traditional common-law conceptions or some distilled essence of their local variations as exclusively controlling limitations upon the scope of the statute's effectiveness. To do this would be merely to select some of the local, hairline variations for nation-wide application and thus to reject others for coverage under the Act. That result hardly would be consistent with the statute's broad terms and purposes.

Congress was not seeking to solve the nationally harassing problems with which the statute deals by solutions only partially effective. It rather sought to find a broad solution, one that would bring industrial peace by substituting, so far as its power could reach, the rights of workers to self-organization and collective bargaining for the industrial strife which prevails where these rights are not effectively established. Yet only partial solutions would be provided if large segments of workers about whose technical legal position such local differences exist should be wholly excluded from coverage by reason of such differences. . . .

Unless the common-law tests are to be imported and made exclusively controlling, without regard to the statute's purposes, it cannot be irrelevant that the particular workers in these cases are subject, as a matter of economic fact, to the evils the statute was designed to eradicate and that the remedies it affords are appropriate for preventing them or curing their harmful effects in the special situation. Interruption of commerce through strikes and unrest may stem as well from labor disputes between some who, for other purposes, are technically "independent contractors" and their employers as from disputes between persons who, for those purposes, are "employees" and their employers. Inequality of bargaining power in controversies over wages, hours, and working conditions may as well characterize the status of the one group as of the other. The former, when acting alone, may be as "helpless in dealing with an employer," as "dependent . . . on his daily wage" and as "unable to leave the employ and to resist arbitrary and unfair treatment" as the latter. For each, "union . . . [may be] essential to give . . . opportunity to deal on equality with their employer." And for each, collective bargaining may be appropriate and effective for the "friendly adjustment of industrial disputes arising out of differences as to wages, hours, or other working conditions." In short, when the particular situation of employment combines these characteristics, so that the economic facts of the relation make it more nearly one of employment than of independent business enterprise with respect to the ends sought to be accomplished by the legislation, those characteristics may outweigh technical legal classification for purposes unrelated to the statute's objectives and bring the relation within its protections.

. . .

It is not necessary in this case to make a completely definitive limitation around the term "employee." That task has been assigned primarily to the agency created by Congress to administer the Act. . . .

In making that body's determinations as to the facts in these matters conclusive, if supported by evidence, Congress entrusted to it primarily the decision whether the evidence establishes the material facts. Hence in reviewing the Board's ultimate conclusions, it is not the court's function to substitute its own inferences of fact for the Board's, when the latter have support in the record. Undoubtedly questions of statutory interpretation, especially when arising in the first instance in judicial proceedings, are for the courts to resolve, giving appropriate weight to the judgment of those whose special duty is to administer the questioned statute. But where the question is one of specific application of a broad statutory term in a proceeding in which the agency administering the statute must determine it initially, the reviewing court's function is limited. . . .

Stating that "the primary consideration in the determination of the applicability of the statutory definition is whether effectuation of the declared policy and purposes of the Act comprehend securing to the individual the rights guaranteed and protection afforded by the Act," the Board concluded that the newsboys are employees. The record sustains the Board's findings and there is ample basis in the law for its conclusion.

[The concurring opinion of JUSTICE REED and the dissenting opinion of JUSTICE ROBERTS have been omitted.]

Questions

1. Was the Supreme Court agreeing with the Board or was it deferring to the Board's expertise? If the latter, did the deference apply to the Board's fact-finding, the Board's statement of the appropriate principle of law, the Board's application of that principle to the case, or more than one of these?

2. In 1947, Congress amended Section 2(3) to exclude explicitly "independent contractor" from the definition of "employee." Without knowing more, do you think this exclusion would change the result in *Hearst* if it were to arise again? While the legislative history of the amendment makes clear that the purpose of the amendment was to reverse the result in *Hearst*, the basis for congressional disapproval of *Hearst* is less clear. Some of the history, as well as the language of the amendment, suggests disagreement with the Court's apparent rejection of the common-law test. Other parts of the legislative debate suggest considerable dissatisfaction with the apparent limits placed on judicial review. (Indeed, in Section 10, Congress made amendments to encourage greater judicial review of the Board.) Finally, there is even some history which suggests members of Congress were of the view that the Court either misidentified—or should not have applied—the general purposes of the Act to the narrow issue before the Court. In all likelihood, there were many members of Congress who held different views of *Hearst*. If one were to assume Congress meant for the Court to ignore the purposes of the Act in making decisions like *Hearst*, how could the Court make any sense whatever out of the amendment to Section 2(3)? On the other hand, if Congress did not exclude consideration of the general purposes of the Act, did the amend-

ment to Section 2(3) change in any significant way the meaning of that section?

3. In *NLRB* v. *United Insurance Co. of America*, 390 U.S. 254, 67 **LRRM** 2649 (1968), the Supreme Court had to wrestle with the meaning of the amended Section 2(3) and its impact on the reasoning in the *Hearst* case. The facts centered around an insurance company's debit agents who had voted to be represented by the Insurance Workers Union. The company refused to bargain on the grounds that the agents were "independent contractors" rather than "employees" within the meaning of Section 2(3). The Board ordered the company to bargain. The Court of Appeals reversed the Board, but the Supreme Court reinstated the Board's decision. In resolving the dispute, the Court stated:

". . . [Following *Hearst*,] Congress passed an amendment specifically excluding 'any individual having the status of an independent contractor' from the definition of 'employee' contained in § 2(3) of the Act. The obvious purpose of this amendment was to have the Board and the courts apply general agency principles in distinguishing between employees and independent contractors under the Act. And both petitioners and respondents agree that the proper standard here is the law of agency. Thus there is no doubt that we should apply the common-law agency test here in distinguishing an employee from an independent contractor. . . .

"There are innumerable situations which arise in the common law where it is difficult to say whether a particular individual is an employee or an independent contractor, and these cases present such a situation. On the one hand these debit agents perform their work primarily away from the company's offices and fix their own hours of work and work days; and clearly they are not as obviously employees as are production workers in a factory. On the other hand, however, they do not have the independence, nor are they allowed the initiative and decision-making authority, normally associated with an independent contractor. In such a situation as this there is no shorthand formula or magic phrase that can be applied to find the answer, but all of the incidents of the relationship must be assessed and weighed with no one factor being decisive. What is important is that the total factual context is assessed in light of the pertinent common-law agency principles. When this is done, the decisive factors in these cases become the following: the agents do not operate their own independent businesses, but perform functions that are an essential part of the company's normal operations; they need not have any prior training or experience, but are trained by company supervisory personnel; they do business in the company's name with considerable assistance and guidance from the company and its managerial personnel and ordinarily sell only the company's policies; the 'Agent's Commission Plan' that contains the terms and conditions under which they operate is promulgated and changed unilaterally by the company; the agents account to the company for the funds they collect under an elaborate and regular reporting procedure; the agents receive the benefits of the company's vacation plan and group insurance and pension fund; and the agents have a permanent working arrangement with the company under which they may continue as long as their performance is satisfactory. . . .

"The Board examined all of these facts and found that they showed the debit agents to be employees. This was not a purely factual finding by the Board, but involved the application of law to facts—what do the facts establish under the common law of agency: employee or independent contractor? It should also be pointed out that such a determination of pure agency law involved no special administrative expertise that a court does not possess. On the other hand, the Board's determination was a judgment made after a hearing with witnesses and oral argument had been held and on the basis of written briefs. Such a determination should not be set aside just because a court would, as an original matter, decide the case the other way."

Did the Court ignore the amendment to Section 2(3)?

ii. "Managerial" and "Confidential" Employees

The exclusion of "supervisors" was an immediate Congressional response to the Supreme Court's decision, *Packard Company* v. *NLRB*, 330 U.S. 485, 19 LRRM 2397 (1947), in which the Court, by a five-to-four vote, upheld the Board's decision that supervisors (persons who had the authority to hire and fire) were "employees" within the meaning of the Act. Congress, in amending the Act to exclude supervisors from its coverage, had two concerns: first, that employers might place spies within unions or in other ways coerce employees through the participation of supervisors in concerted activities; and, second, that the employers were entitled to full loyalty from employees who performed the functions of supervisors, as that term is defined in Section 2(11) of the Act. This second reason for excluding supervisors from the coverage of the Act served as the Court's primary justification for similarly excluding, through judicial interpretation, so-called "managerial" employees. Was the extension of concern over employee loyalty appropriate?

NLRB v. Bell Aerospace Company, Division of Textron, Inc.

Supreme Court of the United States, 1974
416 U.S. 267, 85 LRRM 2945

MR. JUSTICE POWELL delivered the opinion of the Court.

This case presents two questions: first, whether the National Labor Relations Board properly determined that all "managerial employees," except those whose participation in a labor organization would create a conflict of interest with their job responsibilities, are covered by the National Labor Relations Act; and second, whether the Board must proceed by rulemaking rather than by adjudication in determining whether certain buyers are "managerial employees." We answer both questions in the negative.

I

Respondent Bell Aerospace Co., Division of Textron, Inc. (company), operates a plant in Wheatfield, New York, where it is engaged in research and development in the design and fabrication of aerospace products. On July 30, 1970, Amalgamated Local No. 1286 of the United Automobile, Aerospace and Agricultural Implement Workers of America (union) petitioned the National Labor Relations Board (Board) for a representation election to determine whether the union would be certified as the bargaining representative of the 25 buyers in the purchasing and procurement department at the company's plant. The company opposed the petition on the ground that the buyers were "managerial employees" and thus were not covered by the Act.

The relevant facts adduced at the representation hearing are as follows. The purchasing and procurement department receives requisition orders from other departments at the plant and is responsible for purchasing all of the company's needs from outside suppliers. Some items are standardized and may be purchased "off the shelf" from various distributors and suppliers. Other items must be made to the company's specifications, and the requisition orders may be accompanied by detailed blueprints and other technical plans. Requisitions often designate a particular vendor, and in some instances the buyer must obtain approval before selecting a different one. Where no vendor is specified, the buyer is free to choose one.

Absent specific instructions to the contrary, buyers have full discretion, without any dollar limit, to select prospective vendors, draft invitations to bid, evaluate submitted bids, negotiate price and terms, and prepare purchase orders. Buyers execute all purchase orders up to $50,000. They may place or cancel orders of less than $5,000 on their own signature. On commitments in excess of $5,000, buyers must obtain the approval of a superior, with higher levels of approval required as the purchase cost increases. For the Minute Man missile project, which represents 70% of the company's sales, purchase decisions are made by a team of personnel from the engineering, quality assurance, finance, and manufacturing departments. The buyer serves as team chairman and signs the purchase order, but a representative from the pricing and negotiation department participates in working out the terms.

After the representation hearing, the Regional Director transferred the case to the Board. On May 20, 1971, the Board issued its decision holding that the company's buyers constituted an appropriate unit for purposes of collective bargaining and directing an election. . . .

On June 16, 1971, a representation election was conducted in which 15 of the buyers voted for the union and nine against. On August 12, the Board certified the union as the exclusive bargaining representative for the company's buyers. . . .

The company stood by its contention that the buyers, as "managerial employees," were not covered by the Act and refused to bargain with the union. An unfair labor practice complaint resulted in a Board finding that the company had violated §§ 8(a)(5) and (1) of the Act and an order compelling the company to bargain with the union. Subsequently, the company petitioned the United States Court of Appeals for the Second Circuit for review of the order and the Board cross-petitioned for enforcement.

The Court of Appeals denied enforcement. . . .

II

We begin with the question whether all "managerial employees," rather than just those in positions susceptible to conflicts of interest in labor relations, are excluded from the protections of the Act. The Board's early decisions, the legislative history of the Taft-Hartley Act of 1947, and subsequent Board and court decisions provide the necessary guidance for our inquiry.
. . .

A

The Wagner Act did not expressly mention the term "managerial employee." After the Act's passage, however, the Board developed the concept of "managerial employee" in a series of cases involving the appropriateness of bargaining units. The first cases established that "managerial employees" were not to be included in a unit with rank-and-file employees. . . .

Whether the Board regarded all "managerial employees" as entirely outside the protection of the Act, as well as inappropriate for inclusion in a rank-and-file bargaining unit, is less certain. To be sure, at no time did the Board certify even a separate unit of "managerial employees" or state that such was possible. The Board was cautious, however, in determining which employees were "managerial." . . .

. . . [I]n *Packard Motor Car Co.*, 61 NLRB 4, 64 NLRB 1212 (1945), . . . the Board held that foremen could constitute an appropriate unit for collective bargaining. The Board's position was upheld 5-4 by this court in *Packard Co.* v. *NLRB*, 330 U.S. 485 (1947). . . .

B

The *Packard* decision was a major factor in bringing about the Taft-Hartley Act of 1947.

The House bill provided for the exclusion of "supervisors," a category broadly defined to include any individual who had authority to hire, transfer, promote, discharge, reward, or discipline other employees or effectively to recommend such action. It also excluded (i) those who had authority to determine or effectively recommend the amount of wages earned by other employees; (ii) those employed in labor relations, personnel, and employment departments, as well as police and time-study personnel; and (iii) confidential employees. The Senate version of the bill also excluded supervisors, but defined that category more narrowly than the House version, distinguishing between "straw bosses, leadmen, set-up men, and other minor supervisory employees, on the one hand, and the supervisor vested with such genuine management prerogatives as the right to hire or fire, discipline, or make effective recommendations with respect to such action." S. Rep. No. 105, 80th Cong., 1st Sess., 4 (1947). It was the Senate's view that employees such as "straw bosses," who had only minor supervisory duties, should be included within the Act's protections.

Significantly, both the House Report and the Senate Report voiced concern over the Board's broad reading of the term "employee" to include those clearly within the managerial hierarchy. Focusing on . . . [the] dissent in *Packard*, the Senate Report specifically mentioned that even vice presidents might be unionized under the Board's decision. It also noted that unionization of supervisors had hurt productivity, increased the accident rate, upset the balance of power in collective bargaining, and tended to blur the line between management and labor. The House Report echoed the concern for reduction of industrial output and noted that unionization of supervisors had deprived employers of the loyal representations to which they were entitled. And in criticizing the Board's expansive reading of the Act's definition of the term "employees," the House Report noted that "[w]hen Congress passed the Labor Act, we were concerned, as we said in its preamble, with the welfare of 'workers' and 'wage earners,' not of the boss." H.R. Rep. No. 245, 80th Cong., 1st Sess., 13 (1947). . . .

The legislative history of the Taft-Hartley Act of 1947 may be summarized as follows. The House wanted to include certain persons within the definition of "supervisors," such as straw bosses, whom the Senate believed should be protected by the Act. As to these persons, the Senate's view prevailed. There were other persons, however, who both the House and the Senate believed were plainly outside the Act. The House wanted to make the exclusion of certain of these persons explicit. In the conference agreement, representatives from both the House and the Senate agreed that a specific provision was unnecessary since the Board had long regarded such persons as outside the Act. Among those mentioned as impliedly excluded were persons working in "labor relations, personnel and employment departments," and "confidential employees." But assuredly this did not exhaust the universe of such excluded persons. The legislative history strongly suggests that there also were other employees, much higher in the managerial structure, who were likewise regarded as so clearly outside the Act that no specific exclusionary provision was thought necessary. For example, in its discussion of confidential employees, the House Report noted that "[m]ost of the people who would qualify as 'confidential' employees are *executives and are excluded from the act in any event.*" H.R. Rep. No. 245, p. 23 (emphasis added). We think the inference is plain that "managerial employees" were paramount among this impliedly excluded group. . . .

C

Following the passage of the Taft-Hartley Act, the Board itself adhered to the view that "managerial employees" were outside the Act. . . . [The

Court cited a line of Board decisions which excluded buyers, or managerial employees, from bargaining units of other employees. Two cases said that such buyers could not even have their own separate unit because they were "representatives of managements," *American Locomotive Co.*, 92 NLRB 115, 27 LRRM 1064 (1950), or "allied with management." *Swift & Co.*, 115 NLRB 752, 37 LRRM 1391 (1956). The Board offered no other explanation for its decisions.] Until its decision in *North Arkansas* in 1970, the Board consistently followed this reading of the Act. It never certified any unit of "managerial employees," separate or otherwise, and repeatedly stated that it was Congress' intent that such employees not be accorded bargaining rights under the Act. And it was this reading which was permitted to stand when Congress again amended the Act in 1959.

The Board's exclusion of "managerial employees" defined as those who "formulate and effectuate management policies by expressing and making operative the decisions of their employer," has also been approved by courts without exception. . . .

D

In sum, the Board's early decisions, the purpose and legislative history of the Taft-Hartley Act of 1947, the Board's subsequent and consistent construction of the Act for more than two decades, and the decisions of the courts of appeals all point unmistakably to the conclusion that "managerial employees" are not covered by the Act.[18] We agree with the Court of Appeals below that the Board "is not now free" to read a new and more restrictive meaning into the Act.

In view of our conclusion, the case must be remanded to permit the Board to apply the proper legal standard in determining the status of these buyers. We express no opinion as to whether these buyers fall within the category of "managerial employees."

III

The Court of Appeals also held that, although the Board was not precluded from determining that buyers or some types of buyers were not "managerial employees," it could do so only by invoking its rulemaking procedures under § 6 of the Act. We disagree.

. . .

The judgment of the Court of Appeals is therefore affirmed in part and reversed in part, and the cause remanded to that court with directions to remand to the Board for further proceedings in conformity with this opinion.

It is so ordered.

---

[18]The contrary interpretation of the Act urged by the dissent would have far-reaching results. Although a shop foreman would be excluded from the Act, a wide range of executives would be included. A major company, for example, may have scores of executive officers who formulate and effectuate management policies, yet have no supervisory responsibility or identifiable conflict of interest in labor relations. If Congress intended the unionization of such executives, it most certainly would have made its design plain. . . .

MR. JUSTICE WHITE, with whom MR. JUSTICE BRENNAN, MR. JUSTICE STEWART, and MR. JUSTICE MARSHALL join, dissenting in part.

I concur in Part III of the Court's opinion insofar as it holds that the Board was not required to resort to rule-making in deciding this case, but I dissent from its holding in Part II that managerial employees as a class are not "employees" within the meaning of the National Labor Relations Act.

Questions

1. (a) Given the facts that the Board had never ruled on the managerial-employee issue prior to 1947, that no one in Congress talked about managerial employees in debating the 1947 amendments to the Act, and that the four-Justice dissent in *Packard* (which had allowed supervisors to be protected by the Act) only protested the idea of protecting supervisory employees who were involved in labor relations policy, can the majority derive any support from the 1947 amendments to the Act?

(b) Did the Board's holdings on "managerial employees" prior to 1970 and some dictum amount to a well-established doctrine? Was it relevant to the *Bell Aerospace* case that the doctrine, well established or not, had been overruled by the Board in 1970? Is the Court holding that the Board cannot overrule its earlier decisions, even ones which have offered no substantive reasoning for their conclusions? Can the Court find any support or comfort from the absence of any other cases dealing with the issue in *Bell Aerospace*?

(c) Given that there were only the two unreasoned decisions dealing with the issue and that no one in Congress talked about the issue when the 1959 amendments were being debated, can one rationally argue that Congress approved of the old Board decisions? That Congress even knew them? Can Congress make legislation without writing it? Without the President having an opportunity to veto it? Think of the consequences for the development of law if we are to assume that a legislature approves of (and makes a part of the statutory law) all judicial or administrative decisions which are not altered whenever the legislature turns to one part of the existing law.

2. If neither the words of the Act, the legislative history, nor the pronouncements of the Board and the courts give much solace to the majority, what was the basis for the Court's decision? The Court made at least three attempts to explain. First, in a footnote, the Court stated: "Extension of the Act to cover true 'managerial employees' would . . . eviscerate the traditional distinction between labor and management. If Congress intended a result so drastic, it is not unreasonable to expect that it would have said so expressly." Second, in another footnote, and quoting a lower court opinion, the Court stated: " 'Congress intended to exclude from the protection of the Act those who comprised a part of "management" or were allied with it on the theory that they were the one(s) from whom the workers needed protection.' " And, third, the Court, in still another footnote, quoted the House Committee's Report: " 'It seems wrong, and it is wrong, to subject people of this kind, who have demon-

strated their initiative, their ambition and their ability to get ahead, to the leveling processes of seniority, uniformity and standardization that the Supreme Court recognizes as being fundamental principles of unions.' " (The House Committee was referring to supervisors, not managerial employees.) Are any of these reasons persuasive? Do they reflect an antiunion bias? Are they reflective of the idea that labor-management relationships in this country must be class warfare between classes of employees, even those who desire to join unions?

3. What policies of the Act was the majority vindicating? Did the majority even mention the policies or purposes of the statute it was interpreting? If the purposes of the Act are not relevant, how does one give meaning to statutory language? Was the purpose being applied by the Court to be found only in the heads of the majority members of the Court? If so, were they correct in imposing it upon the statute? Were they justified in keeping it a secret?

4. Think of all the employees who may be excluded by this decision from the coverage of the Act. Why would Congress have wanted to exclude all of them?

5. On remand, the Board held that Bell Aerospace had to negotiate with the union because the employees involved were not "managerial employees," which the Board defined as follows:

"[T]hose who formulate, determine, and effectuate an Employer's policies. . . . Moreover, managerial status is not necessarily conferred upon employees because they possess some authority to determine, within established limits, prices and customer discounts. In fact, the determination of an employee's 'managerial' status depends upon the extent of his discretion, although even the authority to exercise considerable discretion does not render an employee managerial where his decision must conform to the employer's established policy.

"The Board long has defined managerial employees as those who formulate and effectuate management policies by expressing and making operative the decisions of their employer, and those who have discretion in the performance of their jobs independent of their employer's established policy . . . managerial status is not conferred upon rank-and-file workers, or upon those who perform routinely, but rather it is reserved for those in executive-type positions, those who are closely aligned with management as true representatives of management." *Bell Aerospace* and *UAW*, 219 NLRB 384, 385, 89 LRRM 1664, 1665 (1975).

Has the Board substantially obviated, or evaded, the impact of the Court's decision in *Bell Aerospace*? Do you find it difficult to answer that question because you are not sure what the Board's definition means?

6. Assume that the Bell Aerospace engineers have a strong commitment to their union. If they are not to be employees within the meaning of the Act, what can they do to protect their interests? Does your answer to that question suggest that the Supreme Court's opinion may not have very much impact on people?

7. University professors typically vote in departmental, school, or college groupings to determine such matters as who is employed to teach, who earns tenure, what courses are taught, academic and course schedules, and what standards are to be applied to the admission of students. Some faculty groups may determine budgetary matters. While most of these votes need to be ratified by administrators, virtually all of these faculty determinations are carried into practice. In a five-to-four vote, the Supreme Court, in overruling the Board, held that university professors—at least in the litigated case—were managerial and therefore excluded from the coverage of the Act. *NLRB* v. *Yeshiva University*, 444 U.S. 672, 103 LRRM 2526 (1980). Much of the Court's opinion reflected deep concern that "the 'business' of a university is education, and its vitality ultimately must depend on academic policies that largely are formulated and generally are implemented by faculty governance decisions. Faculty members enhance their own standing and fulfill their professional mission by ensuring that the university's objectives are met. . . . It is fruitless to ask whether an employee is expected to conform to one goal or another when the two are essentially the same. The problem of divided loyalty is particularly acute for a university . . . which depends on the professional judgment of its faculty to formulate and apply crucial policies constrained only by necessarily general institutional goals. . . . It is clear that . . . universities must rely on their faculties to participate in the making and implementation of their policies." The Court was concerned that divided loyalties would result in undermining the very purpose of the university. The dissent suggested that this tension exists for all employees. In a footnote, the majority assured that "professors may not be excluded merely because they determine the content of their own courses, evaluate their own students, and supervise their own research. There thus may be institutions of higher learning unlike Yeshiva where the faculty are entirely or predominantly nonmanagerial." The Court also suggested that possibly a "rational line could be drawn between tenured and untenured faculty members."

Public university professors, who have responsibilities wholly similar to those held by Yeshiva faculty, are often authorized by state law to engage in collective bargaining. Does this suggest that the Court majority may have overstated the nature of the dilemma posed by placing university academics within the meaning of "employee"? Is it possible that *Yeshiva*, like *Bell Aerospace*, is another reflection of the taste of five members of the Court that certain types of people are "too good" or "not appropriate" for industrial-type unions?

NLRB v. Hendricks County Rural Electric Membership Corp.

Supreme Court of the United States, 1981
454 U.S. 170, 108 LRRM 3105

JUSTICE BRENNAN delivered the opinion of the Court.

The question presented is whether an employee who, in the course of his employment, may have access to information considered confidential by his employer is impliedly excluded from the definition of "employee" in § 2(3) of the National Labor Relations Act and denied all protections under the Act.

I

We have before us two cases under the same docket number. We shall first state separately the factual and procedural background of each.

THE HENDRICKS CASE

Mary Weatherman was the personal secretary to the general manager and chief executive officer of respondent Hendricks County Rural Electric Membership Corporation (Hendricks), a rural electric membership cooperative. She had been employed by the cooperative for nine years. In May 1977 she signed a petition seeking reinstatement of a close friend and fellow employee, who had lost his arm in the course of employment with Hendricks, and had been dismissed. Several days later she was discharged.

Weatherman filed an unfair labor practice charge with the National Labor Relations Board (NLRB or Board), alleging that the discharge violated § 8(a)(1) of the National Labor Relations Act (NLRA or Act), 29 U.S.C. § 158(a)(1). Hendricks's defense, *inter alia*, was that Weatherman was denied the Act's protection because as a "confidential" secretary she was impliedly excluded from the Act's definition of "employee" in § 2(3). . . .

[The Board found a violation of the Act, and the Court of Appeals for the Seventh Circuit reversed.]

THE MALLEABLE CASE

This case grew out of efforts of the Office and Professional Employees International Union (Union) to represent, as collective bargaining agent, various employees of respondent Malleable Iron Range Company (Malleable). In December 1978 the Union sought certification as the collective bargaining representative for a unit of office clerical, technical, and professional personnel employed at the respondent's facility in Beaver Dam, Wisconsin. At the subsequent representation hearing, Malleable challenged the inclusion of 18 employees in the unit on the ground that they had access to confidential business information. The Regional Director of the NLRB rejected Malleable's objection, concluding that none of the challenged 18 employees was a confidential employee under the Board's "labor nexus" test [which was inconsistent with the view of the Court of Appeals for the Seventh Circuit.]

We granted the Board's petition for certiorari in both cases to resolve the conflict among the Courts of Appeals respecting the propriety of the Board's practice of excluding from collective bargaining units only those confidential employees with a "labor nexus," while rejecting any claim that all employees with access to confidential information are beyond the reach of § 2(3)'s definition of "employee." We hold that there is a reasonable basis in law for the Board's use of the "labor nexus" test. We therefore reverse the judgment of the Court of Appeals, with direction in the *Hendricks* case to enforce the Board's order, and with direction in the *Malleable* case for further proceedings consistent with this opinion.

II

Section 2(3) of the NLRA provides that the "term 'employee' shall include *any* employee . . ." (emphasis added), with certain stated exceptions such as "agricultural laborers," "supervisors" as defined in § 2(11), and "independent contractors." Under a literal reading of the phrase "any employee," then, the workers in question are "employees." But for over 40 years, the NLRB, while rejecting any claim that the definition of "employee" in § 2(3) excludes confidential employees, has excluded from the collective bargaining units determined under the Act those confidential employees satisfying the Board's labor-nexus test. Respondents argue that contrary to the Board's practice, all employees who may have access to confidential business information are impliedly excluded from the definition of employee in § 2(3).

. . . We proceed to review the Board's determinations from 1940 to 1946 whether confidential employees were "employees" within § 2(3) of the National Labor Relations Act (the Wagner Act), and then determine whether Congress, when it considered those determinations in enacting the Taft-Hartley Act of 1947, intended to alter the Board's practice.

A

In 1935 the Wagner Act became law. . . . Although the Act's express exclusions did not embrace confidential employees, the Board was soon faced with the argument that all individuals who had access to confidential information of their employers should be excluded, as a policy matter, from the definition of "employee." The Board rejected such an implied exclusion, finding it to have "no warrant under the Act." But in fulfilling its statutory obligation to determine appropriate bargaining units under § 9 of the Act, for which broad discretion has been vested in the Board, the Board adopted special treatment for the narrow group of employees with access to confidential, labor-relations information of the employer. The Board excluded these individuals from bargaining units composed of rank-and-file workers. The Board's rationale was that

> "management should not be required to handle labor relations matters through employees who are represented by the union with which the [c]ompany is required to deal and who in the normal performance of their duties may obtain advance information of the [c]ompany's position with regard to contract negotiations, the disposition of grievances, and other labor relations matters."

. . .

In 1946, in *Ford Motor Co.*, 66 NLRB 1317, 1322, the Board refined slightly the labor-nexus test because in its view the "definition [was] too inclusive and needlessly preclude[d] many employees from bargaining collectively together with other workers having common interests." Henceforth, the Board announced, it intended "to limit the term 'confidential' so as to embrace only those employees who assist and act in a confidential capacity to persons who exercise 'managerial' functions in the field of labor relations." This was the state of the law in 1947 when Congress amended the NLRA through the enactment of the Taft-Hartley Act.

B

Although the text of the Taft-Hartley Act also makes no explicit reference to confidential employees, when Congress addressed the scope of the NLRA's coverage, the status of confidential employees was discussed. But nothing in that legislative discussion supports any inference, let alone conclusion, that Congress intended to alter the Board's pre-1947 determinations that only confidential employees with a "labor nexus" should be excluded from bargaining units. Indeed, the contrary appears.

. . .

Indeed, the Taft-Hartley Act's express inclusion of "professional employees" under the Act's coverage negates any reading of the legislative history as excluding confidential employees generally from the definition of employee in § 2(3). The definition of professional employees was intended to cover "such persons as legal, engineering, scientific and medical personnel together with their junior professional assistants." H.R.Conf.Rep. No. 510, 80th Cong., 1st Sess., p. 36 (1947), U.S.Code Cong.Serv. 1947, p. 1141. But surely almost all such persons would likely be privy to confidential business information and thus would fall within the broad definition of confidential employee excluded under the House bill. It would therefore be extraordinary to read an implied exclusion for confidential employees into the statute that would swallow up and displace almost the entirety of the professional-employee inclusion.

Plainly, too, nothing in the legislative history of the Taft-Hartley Act provides any support for the argument that Congress disapproved the Board's prior practice of applying a labor-nexus test to identify confidential employees whom the Board excluded from bargaining units. To the contrary, the House Managers' statement accompanying the Conference Committee Report indicates that Congress intended to leave the Board's historic practice undisturbed.

III

The Court of Appeals, and the respondents here, rely on dictum in a footnote to *NLRB* v. *Bell Aerospace*, 416 U.S. 267 (1974), to suggest that the Eightieth Congress believed that all employees with access to confidential business information of their employers had been excluded from the Wagner Act by prior NLRB decisions and that Congress intended to freeze that interpretation of the Wagner Act into law. The *Bell Aerospace* dictum is:

"In 1946 in *Ford Motor Co.*, 66 NLRB 1317, 1322, the Board had narrowed its definition of 'confidential employees' to embrace only those who exercised ' "managerial" functions in the field of labor relations.' The discussion of 'confidential employees' in both the House and Conference Committee Reports, however, unmistakably refers to that term as defined in the House bill, which was not limited just to those in 'labor relations.' Thus, although Congress may have misconstrued recent Board practice, it clearly thought that the Act did not cover 'confidential employees' even under a broad definition of that term." *Id.*, at 284, n. 12.

Obviously this statement was unnecessary to the determination whether *managerial* employees are excluded from the Act, which was the question decided in *Bell Aerospace*. In any event, the statement that Congress "clearly thought that the Act did not cover 'confidential employees,' even under a broad definition of that term," is error. The error is clear in light of our analysis above of the legislative history of the Taft-Hartley Act pertinent to the question. Moreover, the footnote erroneously implies that *Ford Motor Co.*, 66 NLRB 1317 (1946), marked a major departure from the Board's prior practice. To the contrary, that Board decision introduced only a slight refinement of the labor-nexus test which the Board had applied in numerous decisions from 1941 to 1946. Certainly the Conference Committee, in approving the Board's "prevailing practice," was aware of the Board's line of decisions. Thus the only plausible interpretation of the Report is that, in describing the Board's prevailing practice of denying certain employees the full benefits of the Wagner Act, the Report referred only to employees involved in labor relations, personnel and employment functions, and confidential secretaries *to such persons.* For that, in essence, is where the Board law as of 1947 stood. It follows that the dictum in *Bell Aerospace*, and the Court of Appeals' reliance upon it, cannot be squared with Congressional intent, and should be "recede[d] from" now that the issue of the status of confidential employees is "squarely presented."

. . .

In sum, our review of the Board's decisions indicates that the Board has never followed a practice of depriving all employees who have access to confidential business information from the full panoply of rights afforded by the Act. Rather, for over 40 years, the Board, while declining to create any implied exclusion from the definition of "employee" for confidential employees, has applied a labor-nexus test in identifying those employees who should be excluded from bargaining units because of access to confidential business information. We cannot ignore this consistent, long-standing interpretation of the NLRA by the Board. See *Bell Aerospace, supra*, 416 U.S., at 275.

IV

The Court's ultimate task here is, of course, to determine whether the Board's "labor nexus" limitation on the class of confidential employees who, although within the definition of "employee" under § 2(3), may be denied inclusion in bargaining units has "a reasonable basis in law." Clearly the NLRB's longstanding practice of excluding from bargaining units only those confidential employees satisfying the Board's labor-nexus test, rooted firmly in the Board's understanding of the nature of the collective bargaining process, and Congress' acceptance of that practice, fairly demonstrates that the Board's treatment of confidential employees does indeed have "a reasonable basis in law." We therefore return finally to the disposition of the cases before us.

[In both *Hendricks* and *Malleable*, no party argued that the disputed employees acted in a confidential capacity with respect to labor relations. The Court, thus, upheld the Board.]

JUSTICE POWELL, with whom THE CHIEF JUSTICE, JUSTICE REHNQUIST, and JUSTICE O'CONNOR join, concurring in part and dissenting in part:

I concur in the Court's holding that employees in the possession of proprietary or nonpublic business information are not for that reason excluded from the NLRA as "confidential" employees. By explicitly providing for the inclusion of professional employees, the Act itself indicates that Congress did not intend such a sweeping definition of the confidential employee exclusion. But because the majority's decision "tends to obliterate the line between management and labor," a line which Congress insisted be observed by enacting the Taft-Hartley Act, I dissent from the conclusion that the confidential secretary in this case is not a confidential employee excluded from the Act.

I

In *NLRB* v. *Bell Aerospace Co.*, 416 U.S. 267 (1974), we held that all managerial employees were excluded from the Act regardless of whether they had a "labor nexus." In reversing the Board, the Court found that a basic purpose of the Taft-Hartley Act was to establish a sharp line between management and labor. When the Board breached this line by deeming supervisors to be "employees" within the Act, Congress responded by passing the Taft-Hartley Act with its explicit exclusion of supervisory employees. And when the Board in *Bell Aerospace* departed from its own recognition that "[i]t was the clear intent of Congress to exclude from the coverage of the Act *all individuals allied with management*," this Court responded by again requiring the Board to adhere to the dividing line between management and labor—a line fundamental to the industrial philosophy of the labor laws in this country.

Indeed, it was to assure that those employees allied with management were not included in the ranks of labor that the Board originally developed the "supervisory," "managerial," and "confidential" employees exclusions from the Wagner Act. The Board recognized that employees who by their duties, knowledge, or sympathy were aligned with management should not be treated as members of labor. In the adversary system which our labor laws envision, neither management nor labor should be forced to accept a potential fifth column into its ranks. Thus, both before and after the Taft-Hartley Act, the Board excluded from bargaining units of the rank and file employees who like "expediters" are "closely related to management," or who like assistant buyers have "interests . . . more closely identified with those of management." The Board has excluded employees "who formulate, determine, and effectuate an employer's policies," and employees who because of their familial relation to management "are on an intimate relationship with officers of the company."

The "confidential employee" exclusion and the labor nexus which the Board insists upon must be viewed as part of this larger effort to keep the line between management and labor distinct. Certainly employees with knowledge of sensitive labor relations information or "who assist and act in a confidential capacity to persons who formulate, determine, and effectuate management policies in the field of labor relations," fall on the management side of the line and should be excluded from the Act. But useful as it may be in identifying employees who are allied to management, the "labor nexus" test is but a means to this end. By its rigid insistence on the labor nexus in the case of confidential secretaries, the Board, and now this Court, have lost sight of the basic purpose of the labor nexus test itself and of the fundamental theory of our labor laws. Thus, it makes little sense to exclude "expediters," "assistant buyers," and "employment interviewers" as managerial but include within the rank and file confidential secretaries who are privy to the most sensitive details of management decisionmaking, who work closely with managers on a personal and daily basis, and who occupy a position of trust incompatible with labor management strife. To include employees so clearly allied to management within the ranks of labor does a disservice to management and labor alike.

II

The Court's decision not only is in conflict with the basic framework of the labor laws, it conflicts with explicit expressions of congressional intent on this subject. Congress only forbore from including an explicit provision in the Taft-Hartley Act excluding confidential secretaries because of its belief that the Board had been treating, and would continue to treat, such employees as allied to management. . . .

. . .

After today's decision, labor must accept into its ranks confidential secretaries who are properly allied to management. And these confidential employees, who are privy to the daily affairs of management, who have access to confidential information, and who are essential to management's operation may be subjected to conflicts of loyalty when the essence of their working relationship requires undivided loyalty. The basic philosophy of the labor relations laws, the expressed intent of Congress, and the joint desire of labor and management for undivided loyalty all counsel against such a result.

Questions

Has *Bell Aerospace* survived the reasoning of *Hendricks*? Can one make a case that "managerial" employees are more tied to management in matters of labor relations than are "confidential" employees?

2. The Recognition Process

A. AN OVERVIEW

1. THE SIGNIFICANCE OF RECOGNITION

The early labor cases discussed in Chapter 1 revealed a lack of systematic procedures for resolving disputes in the workplace. The approaches to problems were *ad hoc*, often entailing the use of economic force. The responses of the courts, acting without the guidance of formal mechanisms for dispute resolution, were unpredictable.

Our early labor legislation was concerned with providing alternatives to labor unrest through structures designed to encourage collective bargaining. These sentiments, reflected in the "Findings and Policies" of the National Labor Relations Act, may be viewed by some as pious declarations of hope, or as mere boiler plate inserted to shore up the enactment of a statute of then-doubtful constitutional validity. The fact is, however, that industrial peace has been fostered through the creation of long-term collective bargaining relationships and through the institution of contractual procedures for resolution of grievances. Our labor legislation provides a framework under which a collective bargaining relationship may be established, and sets forth ground rules for the bargaining process itself and the administration and enforcement of the agreement. In later chapters we shall study in detail the extent of governmental regulation of these processes. Our purpose in this chapter is to consider the nature and consequences of recognition and the various ways in which it may be attained.

In order to understand the significance of recognition, you should reflect upon the fact that the employer who is not bound to recognize a union is under few legal restraints in operating his business. He may hire and fire employees at will, determine rates of pay as he sees fit, make work assignments and award overtime on whatever basis he chooses, and decide upon the nature and level of fringe benefits, guided, perhaps, by the realities of the employment marketplace and the tenets of good labor relations. There are statutory floors which the employer must observe, such as minimum wage provisions and requirements for overtime pay. And decisions as to hiring, discipline, dismissal, and granting or withholding benefits may not be made on the basis of race or sex or other grounds prohibited by federal and state laws against discrimination. Collateral statutory regulations (for example, the Social Security system, the

Occupational Safety and Health Act, the Rehabilitation Act, and the Military Selective Service Act) have their impact on the employment relationship. Yet the employer retains the basic freedom to run his business.

In contrast, most organized workers in America rely upon a negotiated collective bargaining agreement as the source of their employment rights and the means for enforcing them, usually through grievance and arbitration procedures. The employer, too, looks to the contract for the limitations on his freedom to run the business. But before a collective bargaining agreement is reached, there are ground rules that require the employer and the union to deal with one another in order to attempt to come to an agreement. These obligations are spelled out broadly in Sections 8(a)(5) and 8(b)(3) of the Act, along with Section 8(d), which fleshes out the nature of the duty to bargain. We shall explore the bargaining obligation in depth in Chapter 4. You should understand for now that the bargaining duty imposed by the Act not only requires the parties to meet and negotiate in good faith in an effort to conclude an agreement but precludes the employer from changing existing terms and conditions of employment without first bargaining with the union. These constraints may also be imposed upon the parties while a collective bargaining agreement is in effect and during the hiatus between agreements.

There are other less important corollaries of recognition. Section 8(b)(7) of the Act restricts the freedom of the union to use picketing and related economic pressures to secure recognition. If another union is recognized or certified, or a valid election has been conducted within the past 12 months, the union is barred absolutely from recognitional picketing under Sections 8(b)(7)(A), 8(b)(7)(B), and 8(b)(4)(B). Even if none of these conditions exists, the union's picketing may be limited under Section 8(b)(7)(C), which allows a union to picket for "a reasonable period of time not to exceed thirty days" prior to the filing of an election petition. Certain provisions regarding publicity picketing also affect the union's right to use pressure at this point. Section 8(b)(7) tends to defy analysis, and we have chosen to postpone detailed consideration of it to Chapter 7, A. For now, however, you should realize that until the union achieves recognition it may be prevented from utilizing the full range of economic weapons in support of its ultimate bargaining goals.

2. EXCLUSIVITY

Recognition of a union confers upon it the powerful status of exclusivity. Our statutory scheme, reflected in Section 9(a) of the Act, contemplates a single spokesperson for all employee interests within the represented group. This means first that within the bargaining unit the employer may deal with only a single union. Exclusivity vis-à-vis other unions carries with it certain rules against challenge by rival unions for fixed periods of time. More important, the principle of exclusivity extinguishes much of the freedom of the individual to make her own bargain with the employer.

J. I. Case Co. v. NLRB

Supreme Court of the United States, 1944
321 U.S. 332, 14 LRRM 501

MR. JUSTICE JACKSON delivered the opinion of the Court. . . .

The petitioner, J. I. Case Company, at its Rock Island, Illinois, plant, from 1937 offered each employee an individual contract of employment. The contracts were uniform and for a term of one year. The Company agreed to furnish employment as steadily as conditions permitted, to pay a specified rate, which the Company might redetermine if the job changed, and to maintain certain hospital facilities. The employee agreed to accept the provisions, to serve faithfully and honestly for the term, to comply with factory rules, and that defective work should not be paid for. About 75 percent of the employees accepted and worked under these agreements.

According to the Board's stipulation and finding, the execution of the contracts was not a condition of employment, nor was the status of individual employees affected by reason of signing or failing to sign the contracts. It is not found or contended that the agreements were coerced, obtained by any unfair labor practice, or that they were not valid under the circumstances in which they were made.

While the individual contracts executed August 1, 1941 were in effect, a C.I.O. union petitioned the Board for certification as the exclusive bargaining representative of the production and maintenance employees. On December 17, 1941 a hearing was held, at which the Company urged the individual contracts as a bar to representation proceedings. The Board, however, directed an election, which was won by the union. The union was thereupon certified as the exclusive bargaining representative of the employees in question in respect to wages, hours, and other conditions of employment.

The union then asked the Company to bargain. It refused, declaring that it could not deal with the union in any manner affecting rights and obligations under the individual contracts while they remained in effect. It offered to negotiate on matters which did not affect rights under the individual contracts, and said that upon the expiration of the contracts it would bargain as to all matters. Twice the Company sent circulars to its employees asserting the validity of the individual contracts and stating the position that it took before the Board in reference to them.

The Board held that the Company had refused to bargain collectively, in violation of § 8 (5) of the National Labor Relations Act; and that the contracts had been utilized, by means of the circulars, to impede employees in the exercise of rights guaranteed by § 7 of the Act, with the result that the Company had engaged in unfair labor practices within the meaning of § 8 (1) of the Act. It ordered the Company to cease and desist from giving effect to the contracts, from extending them or entering into new ones, from refusing to bargain and from interfering with the employees; and it required the Company to give notice accordingly and to bargain upon request. . . .

Contract in labor law is a term the implications of which must be determined from the connection in which it appears. Collective bargaining between employer and the representatives of a unit, usually a union, results in an accord as to terms which will govern hiring and work and pay in that unit. The result is not, however, a contract of employment except in rare cases; no one has a job by reason of it and no obligation to any individual ordinarily comes into existence from it alone. The negotiations between union and management result in what often has been called a trade agreement, rather than in a contract of employment. Without pushing the analogy too far, the agreement may be likened to the tariffs established by a carrier, to standard provisions prescribed by supervising authorities for insurance policies, or to utility schedules of rates and rules for service, which do not of themselves establish any relationships but which do govern the terms of the shipper or insurer or customer relationship whenever and with whomever it may be established. Indeed, in some European countries, contrary to American practice, the terms of a collectively negotiated trade agreement are submitted to a government department and if approved become a governmental regulation ruling employment in the unit.

After the collective trade agreement is made, the individuals who shall benefit by it are identified by individual hirings. The employer, except as restricted by the collective agreement itself and except that he must engage in no unfair labor practice or discrimination, is free to select those he will employ or discharge. But the terms of the employment already have been traded out. There is little left to individual agreement except the act of hiring. This hiring may be by writing or by word of mouth or may be implied from conduct. In the sense of contracts of hiring, individual contracts between the employer and employee are not forbidden, but indeed are necessitated by the collective bargaining procedure.

But, however engaged, an employee becomes entitled by virtue of the Labor Relations Act somewhat as a third party beneficiary to all benefits of the collective trade agreement, even if on his own he would yield to less favorable terms. The individual hiring contract is subsidiary to the terms of the trade agreement and may not waive any of its benefits, any more than a shipper can contract away the benefit of filed tariffs, the insurer the benefit of standard provisions, or the utility customer the benefit of legally established rates. . . .

Individual contracts, no matter what the circumstances that justify their execution or what their terms, may not be availed of to defeat or delay the procedures prescribed by the National Labor Relations Act looking to collective bargaining, nor to exclude the contracting employee from a duly ascertained bargaining unit; nor may they be used to forestall bargaining or to limit or condition the terms of the collective agreement. "The Board asserts a public right vested in it as a public body, charged in the public interest with the duty of preventing unfair labor practices." *National Licorice Co.* v. *Labor Board*, 309 U.S. 350, 364. Wherever private contracts conflict with its functions, they obviously must yield or the Act would be reduced to a futility.

It is equally clear since the collective trade agreement is to serve the purpose contemplated by the Act, the individual contract cannot be effective as a waiver of any benefit to which the employee otherwise would be entitled under the trade agreement. The very purpose of providing by statute for the collective agreement is to supersede the terms of separate agreements of employees with terms which reflect the strength and bargaining power and serve the welfare of the group. Its benefits and advantages are open to every employee of the represented unit, whatever the type or terms of his pre-existing contract of employment.

But it is urged that some employees may lose by the collective agreement, that an individual workman may sometimes have, or be capable of getting, better terms than those obtainable by the group and that his freedom of contract must be respected on that account. We are not called upon to say that under no circumstances can an individual enforce an agreement more advantageous than a collective agreement, but we find the mere possibility that such agreements might be made no ground for holding generally that individual contracts may survive or surmount collective ones. The practice and philosophy of collective bargaining looks with suspicion on such individual advantages. Of course, where there is great variation in circumstances of employment or capacity of employees, it is possible for the collective bargain to prescribe only minimum rates or maximum hours or expressly to leave certain areas open to individual bargaining. But except as so provided, advantages to individuals may prove as disruptive of industrial peace as disadvantages. They are a fruitful way of interfering with organization and choice of representatives; increased compensation, if individually deserved, is often earned at the cost of breaking down some other standard thought to be for the welfare of the group, and always creates the suspicion of being paid at the long-range expense of the group as a whole. Such discriminations not infrequently amount to unfair labor practices. The workman is free, if he values his own bargaining position more than that of the group, to vote against representation; but the majority rules, and if it collectivizes the employment bargain, individual advantages or favors will generally in practice go in as a contribution to the collective result. We cannot except individual contracts generally from the operation of collective ones because some may be more individually advantageous. Individual contracts cannot subtract from collective ones, and whether under some circumstances they may add to them in matters covered by the collective bargain, we leave to be determined by appropriate forums under the laws of contracts applicable, and to the Labor Board if they constitute unfair labor practices. . . .

Hence we find that the contentions of the Company that the individual contracts precluded a choice of representatives and warranted refusal to bargain during their duration were properly overruled. It follows that representation to the employees by circular letter that they had such legal effect was improper and could properly be prohibited by the Board. . . .

The union and employer are not required to deal with one another through collective bargaining until the union has achieved legally recognized status as the collective bargaining agent. Indeed, the employer may violate the Act if it deals with the union before this critical benchmark is reached.

There are several ways in which the union may achieve recognition. We explore first probably the most typical method, in which the union petitions for the Board to conduct a representation election to determine the choice of the employees. If the union wins the election, it is certified as the collective bargaining representative and the various consequences of recognition attach. Other methods of achieving recognition will be discussed in Part D of this Chapter.

B. ANATOMY OF A REPRESENTATION CASE

1. ENDERBY ELECTION PROBLEM

a. Introduction to the Enderby Problems

This casebook raises and explores many of the issues in the course through in-depth problems. Many of these problems trace the development of the labor relations between an imaginary company, Enderby Industries, Inc., and the union ultimately chosen to represent its employees, the United Factory Workers of America. While the problems are cumulative, they are designed to be used separately, without the need to refer to previous problems. However, in order to work with the problems, a brief description of the company is needed.

Enderby Industries is a medium-sized manufacturer of rubber and plastic component parts, such as plastic trim for television sets and rubber insulating parts in automobiles and airplanes. The volume of its manufacturing in interstate commerce is sufficient to bring it within the NLRB's jurisdiction. Enderby employs some 320 production and maintenance employees in two plants located approximately 300 yards apart in an industrial park complex in a rural area. Other companies also have facilities in this industrial park. The two plants each make up a separate division, along product lines. The larger plant, which manufactures plastics, employs 200 production and maintenance workers, while the smaller rubber division employs 120 employees on its production lines. In addition, office clerical and related staffs are attached to each division. Enderby employs 12 laboratory technicians, housed in the rubber plant, who perform a variety of design and testing functions for both divisions. In general, however, there is little product mix between the two divisions; that is, a particular product does not usually pass through both plants.

The rubber division was originally a separate company, Maxwell Rubber Products, located in nearby Mill City. It was bought out by Enderby several years ago, and it moved next door to Enderby's existing facility at the industrial park. The rubber division work force is on the average somewhat older than that of the plastics division, in terms of both age and years of service. This reflects the fact that Maxwell Rubber Products was started many years before Enderby. Day-to-day operations of the rubber division continue to be directed by the former owners of Maxwell Rubber, Rita and Max Maxwell. Both now function as plant managers of the rubber plant. However, overall control of labor relations policies has increasingly been centralized and directed by the office of employee relations for Enderby Industries. This office is located in the plastics plant and directed by Matthew Crickboom, Enderby Industries' vice president for personnel.

b. Problem: The NLRB Election Hearing

Several weeks ago Herb Swoboda, an injection mold operator in the rubber division of Enderby Industries, contacted Ruth Blair, an organizer for the United Factory Workers of America. Swoboda told Blair that a number of employees in the rubber division were interested in forming a union and wanted some guidance. Blair arranged to meet with Swoboda a couple of weeks later at a local restaurant, the Jolly Frog.

Swoboda explained that the impetus for organizing came from the rubber division employees. These employees were concerned that Enderby was putting its resources into the larger plastics division. There was an increasing number of short-term layoffs in rubber, and the work force was not expanding. The rubber employees were worried about job security over the long run. They particularly wanted a seniority system that would give them bidding rights into the plastics division, with its much junior work force, in the event of job reductions in rubber. They were also worried about the fairness of their day-to-day supervision. The Maxwells, Rita and Max, maintained a close, family-type relationsip. But the personnel decisions now coming from Enderby under the direction of Vice President Crickboom seemed to the rubber workers arbitrary and impersonal. The rubber workers were also interested in a pension program, while the younger work force in plastics preferred more immediate benefits such as substantial wage increases.

It soon became clear to Blair that the pro-union sentiment was strongest in the smaller rubber division, particularly among the technicians, who felt they were substantially underpaid. Blair and Swoboda doubted that a majority of the plastics employees would choose representation.

Thus Blair concentrated her organizing efforts in the rubber division. With Swoboda's help, she chose three employees in the rubber plant to serve as "captains" of the organizing team. These captains were given authorization cards and were told to solicit signatures from a majority of the employees in the rubber plant.

The card looks like this:

SAMPLE AUTHORIZATION CARD

Date of signing _____

I, _____, now employed by
(print your name here)

_____ (name of company)
have voluntarily accepted membership in the United Factory Workers
Union (AFL-CIO) and designate said Union as my collective bargaining
agent in all matters pertaining to wages, hours and other conditions of
employment. I hereby further subscribe to the dues deduction provisions
printed on the reverse side of this card.

Signed _____

_____   _____
                                      (Signer's home address)

                                      _____
                                      (Phone No.)

Within a couple of weeks, the employee organizing team obtained signed authorization cards from about 60 percent of the rubber department employees. Blair then sent the following demand for recognition:

UNITED FACTORY WORKERS OF AMERICA, AFL-CIO, CLC
17 Union Square
New York, N.Y. 10003

Matthew Crickboom
Vice-President, Personnel
Enderby Industries, Inc.
Brown's Pond Industrial Park
Hokum, Georgia

Dear Mr. Crickboom:

This is to advise you that a majority of the employees of the rubber division of Enderby Industries, Inc., have authorized the United Factory Workers of America, AFL-CIO, to represent them for the purposes of collective bargaining.

We are prepared to prove our majority by submitting our authorization cards to a mutually agreeable third person provided that under no circumstances will the names of those employees who signed cards be revealed. We, therefore, request an appointment to meet with you at your earliest convenience in order to commence collective bargaining.

Please be further advised that no changes in wages, hours, or terms and conditions of employment may be made without negotiation with the United Factory Workers of America.

Very truly yours,

Ruth Blair

RB/mhc   Chief Organizer

Crickboom's response was not unexpected. He stated in a letter to Blair that "the appropriate way to resolve matters of this sort is through an election conducted under the auspices of the NLRB."

Blair then met with the union's Assistant General Counsel, David Diamond. Their discussion follows:

DIAMOND: Now as I understand your strategy, Ruth, you feel your strength lies in the rubber division, among other reasons because of the very strong pro-union feelings of the laboratory technicians, who are housed in rubber.

BLAIR: That's right. I'm sure we could win an election held in the rubber division alone, but I think we'd lose in the plastics division. Of course, if we picked off the rubber division first, the workers in plastics could probably follow suit if they got to vote later. If we had to go to an election in a unit made up of both plants, it would be awfully close.

DIAMOND: That is what I thought. On that assumption I drafted an "RC" petition seeking an election in the rubber division. [The petition appears below at pages 114–115.] Notice that in the exclusionary portion of the unit sought I made clear that we consider leadmen to be supervisors as defined in the Act, hence ineligible for inclusion in the unit. Is that what you wanted?

BLAIR: Exactly. The leadmen are employees who have been with the company for quite a while and have been rewarded for their loyalty to Enderby. We'd have to write off most of their votes as promanagement. Do you think we'll be able to exclude them?

DIAMOND: The test of supervisory status is contained in the NLRA in Section 2(11). All we have to do under that section, since it is set out in the disjunctive, is to show that any one of the criteria is met. I don't think we'll have too much trouble on that score. And the Board has a presumption in favor of single-plant units. So I think we can get an election in the rubber division alone. But let me suggest something else. Maybe we can get the company to agree to our unit request on the fundamental question of the rubber division unit if we can trade off some other issues, say, the question of leadmen. Along these lines, why don't we create a couple of other issues that we really don't have a chance of winning on. Perhaps we could try to include some office clerical people or student part-timers. In return for our dropping those demands, the company might agree to our single-plant request without going to a hearing.

BLAIR: David, I don't think the company is going to give in on the single-plant issue no matter what concessions you make on any other issue. Not only do they want to avoid a single-plant election, but they would be foolish to agree to a unit rather than fight it out through an election hearing. The hearing process takes a long time, and delay usually works against the union. The delay gives the company time to work on employees and it wears the workers down.

DIAMOND: I guess I have an ethical problem too. I can't go and create a phony issue just so I'll have something to trade off later on.

BLAIR: Ethics? David, I'm surprised at you! I think the company is going to invent issues too, so it can manipulate the hearing process and control the timing of the election. I appreciate your feelings, but I don't want to lose this battle because of your ethics.

Blair and Diamond finally decide to send the petition as drafted. When it is received by Crickboom, he consults his attorney, Eskrow McCormick. Here is their reaction:

CRICKBOOM: I tell you, we'll lose an election in the rubber division alone. Can't we get an election in a unit consisting of both plants?

McCORMICK: In one sense the cards are stacked against us. The issue before the Board isn't whether the unit sought by the union is *the* most appropriate unit, but whether it is *an* appropriate unit. So the union has some leeway to impose a unit on us. Also, the Board has a presumption in favor of single-plant units over multiple-plant units.

CRICKBOOM: That sounds bad for us. Are we licked?

McCORMICK: Not really. We start with the fact that the two plants are right next to each other, unlike many of the reported single-plant cases, where they were miles apart. And we may be able to show employee and product interchange between the two plants, and common supervision and setting of policy, all of which weigh against separate units. Also, many of the factors which determine a unit question are solely within our own knowledge. For example, whether a leadman has the power to hire or fire an employee, a factor which would make him a supervisor, is a question that only you can answer. If you say that he has no such power, and that in fact hiring and firing is done by you, then the man isn't a supervisor. Similarly, if you say that you set policies for both plants rather than their being set by the individual plant managers, then it is very hard for the union to show otherwise.

CRICKBOOM: You're suggesting that I lie?

McCORMICK: I'm suggesting no such thing. I'm saying that we have no duty in this hearing to provide a mirror for the hearing officer, thus revealing our setup in a coldly objective way. Rather, as advocates, we utilize your testimony as a prism, highlighting those factors which we find favorable. If we believe that the leadmen are in fact not supervisors, then it is permissible for you to say that the leadmen have no power to hire and fire.

CRICKBOOM: If that statement is true.

McCORMICK: Yes, if it is true. But I suggest to you that some of these questions have no clear answer. I suspect that nobody has ever clearly said that leadmen have no power to hire and fire. But now when you say it, it will be a fact.

CRICKBOOM: Don't I have to say, if I'm to be truthful, that until now there has been no such determination?

McCORMICK: That is the difference between a mirror and a prism.

This problem may be used by your instructor as a simulated hearing before the NLRB. (Additional factual information may be developed if this format is used.) The only two issues in the hearing will concern the placement of the leadmen and the appropriateness of the single-plant unit in the rubber division. Students will interview key witnesses in advance of the hearing. Your instructor may prefer, however, to deal with the issues raised by this problem through more conventional classroom discussion.

However the problem is treated, the materials in the next few subsections will help you deal with both the substantive issues of unit placement and the tactical and ethical considerations raised by the dialogues.

c. The "Law" of Unit Determination

As the above dialogues reveal, unit placement questions come in several shapes and sizes. They may involve the status of individual employees (is the leadman a supervisor or employee?), the shared interests of two similar groups of employees in separate physical locations (the rubber plant and the plastics plant), or the specialized skills of a particular group of employees (the technicians).

The parties may, if they choose, work out these unit placement questions by mutual agreement. This is known as a "consent-election agreement," and is described in Section 101.19 of the Board's Statements of Procedure. Two types of consent-election arrangements are contemplated under the Board's administrative regulations, one culminating in a regional director's certification of representative, the other in a Board certification. Both allow the parties the same freedom in drawing up an acceptable unit for voting; the difference is that challenges to the eligibility of any given voter or objections to the overall conduct of the election are handled in the former case by the regional director, whose determination is binding upon the parties, while under the latter arrangement disputed matters following the election are resolved by the Board. These consent-election procedures, however, may deprive minority interests of proper unit placement. The only recourse, in such event, is for the dissatisfied group to force the matter into a formal hearing, in which the minority group may intervene if it has a proper showing of interest and seeks a different unit configuration.

If the parties are unable to work out a consent agreement, the unit question must go to a formal hearing, which is described in Section 101.20 (c) of the Board's Statement of Procedures as follows:

"(c) The hearing, usually open to the public, is held before a hearing officer who normally is an attorney or field examiner attached to the

FORM NLRB-502
(11-64)

UNITED STATES OF AMERICA
NATIONAL LABOR RELATIONS BOARD

FORM EXEMPT UNDER
44 U.S.C. 3512

PETITION

DO NOT WRITE IN THIS SPACE

CASE NO.

DATE FILED

INSTRUCTIONS.—Submit an original and four (4) copies of this Petition to the NLRB Regional Office in the Region in which the employer concerned is located.
If more space is required for any one item, attach additional sheets, numbering item accordingly.

The Petitioner alleges that the following circumstances exist and requests that the National Labor Relations Board proceed under its proper authority pursuant to Section 9 of the National Labor Relations Act.

1. Purpose of this Petition (If box RC, RM, or RD is checked and a charge under Section 8(b) (7) of the Act has been filed involving the Employer named herein, the statement following the description of the type of petition shall not be deemed made.)

(Check one)

[X] RC—CERTIFICATION OF REPRESENTATIVE —A substantial number of employees wish to be represented for purposes of collective bargaining by Petitioner and Petitioner desires to be certified as representative of the employees.

[ ] RM—REPRESENTATION (EMPLOYER PETITION)—One or more individuals or labor organizations have presented a claim to Petitioner to be recognized as the representative of employees of Petitioner.

[ ] RD—DECERTIFICATION—A substantial number of employees assert that the certified or currently recognized bargaining representative is no longer their representative.

[ ] UD—WITHDRAWAL OF UNION SHOP AUTHORITY—Thirty percent (30%) or more of employees in a bargaining unit covered by an agreement between their employer and a labor organization desire that such authority be rescinded.

[ ] UC—UNIT CLARIFICATION—A labor organization is currently recognized by employer, but petitioner seeks clarification of placement of certain employees: (Check one) [ ] In unit not previously certified
[ ] In unit previously certified in Case No. _____

[ ] AC—AMENDMENT OF CERTIFICATION—Petitioner seeks amendment of certification issued in Case No. _____

Attach statement describing the specific amendment sought.

2. NAME OF EMPLOYER	EMPLOYER REPRESENTATIVE TO CONTACT	PHONE NO.
Enderby Industries, Inc.	M. Crickboom	426-7000

3. ADDRESS(ES) OF ESTABLISHMENT(S) INVOLVED (Street and number, city, State, and ZIP Code)

Brown's Pond Industrial Park, U.S. Highway 81

4a. TYPE OF ESTABLISHMENT (Factory, mine, wholesaler, etc.)	4b. IDENTIFY PRINCIPAL PRODUCT OR SERVICE
Factory	Rubber and Plastic Products

5. Unit Involved (In UC petition, describe PRESENT bargaining unit and attach description of proposed clarification.)

Included   All production and maintenance employees, including technicians, in the employer's Rubber Division.

6a. NUMBER OF EMPLOYEES IN UNIT.
PRESENT 120
PROPOSED (BY UC/AC)

(If you have checked box RC in 1 above, check and complete EITHER item 7a or 7b, whichever is applicable) | RM, UC, and AC

7a. ☒ Request for recognition as Bargaining Representative was made on **February 18, 1984** and Employer
(Month, day, year)
declined recognition on or about **March 1, 1984.** (If no reply received, so state)
(Month, day, year)

7b. ☐ Petitioner is currently recognized as Bargaining Representative and desires certification under the act.

8. Recognized or Certified Bargaining Agent (If there is none, so state)

NAME	AFFILIATION
ADDRESS	DATE OF RECOGNITION OR CERTIFICATION

9. DATE OF EXPIRATION OF CURRENT CONTRACT, IF ANY (Show month, day, and year)
None

10. IF YOU HAVE CHECKED BOX UD IN 1 ABOVE, SHOW HERE THE DATE OF EXECUTION OF AGREEMENT GRANTING UNION SHOP (Month, day, and year)

11a. IS THERE NOW A STRIKE OR PICKETING AT THE EMPLOYER'S ESTABLISHMENT(S) INVOLVED?   YES .... NO **X**

11b. IF SO, APPROXIMATELY HOW MANY EMPLOYEES ARE PARTICIPATING?

11c. THE EMPLOYER HAS BEEN PICKETED BY OR ON BEHALF OF .... A LABOR

ORGANIZATION, OF .... SINCE ....
(Insert name)   (Month, day, year)
(Insert address)

12. ORGANIZATIONS OR INDIVIDUALS OTHER THAN PETITIONER (AND OTHER THAN THOSE NAMED IN ITEMS 8 AND 11c), WHICH HAVE CLAIMED RECOGNITION AS REPRESENTATIVES AND OTHER ORGANIZATIONS AND INDIVIDUALS KNOWN TO HAVE A REPRESENTATIVE INTEREST IN ANY EMPLOYEES IN THE UNIT DESCRIBED IN ITEM 5 ABOVE.   (IF NONE, SO STATE.)

NAME	AFFILIATION	ADDRESS	DATE OF CLAIM (Required only if Petition is filed by Employer)

I declare that I have read the above petition and that the statements therein are true to the best of my knowledge and belief.

United Factory Workers of America
(Petitioner and affiliation, if any)

By **/s/ Ruth Blair**   **Regional Organizer**
(Signature of representative or person filing petition)   (Title, if any)

Address **17 Union Square, New York, New York**   **(212) 498-8600**
(Street and number, city, State, and ZIP Code)   (Telephone number)

WILLFULLY FALSE STATEMENT ON THIS PETITION CAN BE PUNISHED BY FINE AND IMPRISONMENT (U.S. CODE, TITLE 18, SECTION 1001)

GPO 883-928

regional office but may be another qualified official. The hearing, which is nonadversary in character, is part of the investigation in which the primary interest of the Board's agents is to insure that the record contains as full a statement of the pertinent facts as may be necessary for determination of the case. The parties are afforded full opportunity to present their respective positions and to produce the significant facts in support of their contentions. In most cases a substantial number of the relevant facts are undisputed and stipulated. The parties are permitted to argue orally on the record before the hearing officer."

This then leaves the question of unit determination to the regional director, with limited review by the Board.

The statutory law on unit determination questions is for the most part maddeningly open-ended. The Board's basic mandate, in Section 9(b), is to "decide in each case whether, in order to assure employees the fullest freedom in exercising the rights guaranteed by this Act, the unit appropriate for the purposes of collective bargaining shall be the employer unit, craft unit, plant unit, or subdivision thereof." More detailed rules deal with specific categories of employees. For example, as mentioned in the dialogue in the Enderby Problem, the definition of a supervisor in Section 2(11) is more precise, perhaps because that section also determines the extent of the Act's coverage. Similarly, there are specific rules for placing professional employees and guards. See Sections 9(b)(1) and 9(b)(3) and the definition of professional employees in Section 2(12). Some direction for treatment of craft units is contained in Section 9(b)(2).

Most unit determination questions, however, must be dealt with under the broad guidelines of Section 9(b), and particularly the reported Board decisions on unit placement. This is a tricky proposition for the practitioner, for the mundane sorts of unit questions involved in the Enderby Problem are not extensively reported in the published decisions of the NLRB. This is because most unit determinations are made by the individual regional directors and are seldom reviewed by the full Board. Section 3(b) of the Act authorizes the Board to delegate to its regional directors the authority to deal with unit determination and election matters under Section 9. This amendment, in 1959, was designed to speed up the election machinery. Consult NLRB Rules and Regulations Section 102.67 to see the limited grounds for review by the Board of unit determinations of the regional director. The practitioner should consider obtaining relevant unpublished decisions from the region in which he or she is handling a representation case.

We see no point in burdening you with the dreary detail of unit placement rules for the huge variety of unit situations that may arise. Instead, we want you to get a feel for handling the two narrow issues presented in the Enderby Problem, for they are typical of problems you will face in practice and they raise larger questions worth discussing in class.

Assume that the only two issues in question are whether the leadmen are supervisors (hence excluded from the unit) and whether a unit consisting of just the rubber division is appropriate. Extensive research would most likely turn up decisions on each issue that go either way. As you study the following materials, consider how you would prepare your case in the Enderby representation hearing.

i. Supervisors

As indicated in the dialogue and text above, various indicia of supervisory status are set forth in the statutory definition in Section 2(11). Satisfaction of any of these tests will make the employee in question a supervisor. The inquiry is extremely factual, and the outcome of the case may turn on the skill of counsel in marshaling the relevant evidence. We do not wish to fetter your imagination in developing lines of investigation; presenting some mundane examples of supervisor cases would do just that. Consider instead the broader points made by a sensible Down East judge, Senior Circuit Judge Aldrich, who had to decide whether to affirm (he did) a Board conclusion that head pharmacists in a retail drug chain are not supervisors. *Stop and Shop* v. *NLRB*, 548 F.2d 17, 94 LRRM 2417 (1st Cir. 1977). He reasoned that, before looking mechanically at the facts, one should know

> "the reason for excluding supervisory employees from the bargaining process. It is not because they have personal interests at variance with other employees. Many employees have interests at variance with, or even antagonistic to, one another. The reason for excluding supervisors is that they must be representatives of the interests of their employer vis-à-vis other employees. An employee who can discharge other employees, or direct them in matters involving judgment, has a duty to put his employer's interest over the interests of subordinates.
>
> "The mere fact that an employee may give some instructions to others, or that he may command their respect, does not indicate that he must identify with the interests of the employer rather than the employees. The test must be the significance of his judgments and directions. It is precisely for this reason that the question of the effectiveness of the alleged supervisor's authority must normally be a question of fact. To put the issue in homely terms, do the other employees feel, assuming the alleged supervisor is one who reasonably respects his duties, 'Here comes that so-and-so, get to work,' or is he, basically, one of the gang who merely gives routine instructions?"

ii. Single-Plant Versus Multiple-Plant Units

The following cases contain guidelines for resolving the question as to whether the appropriate bargaining unit is a single plant or multiple plants.

Black & Decker Mfg. Co.

National Labor Relations Board, 1964
147 NLRB 825, 56 LRRM 1302

The Employer is presently engaged in the manufacture of power tools at its facilities located at Towson and Hampstead, Maryland. The

Employer contends that the petition requesting a unit of hourly rate production and maintenance employees at its Towson plant fails to set forth an identifiable unit appropriate for the purposes of collective bargaining under the Act. The Employer further contends that its Towson and Hampstead plants are so functionally integrated as to make both plants the only appropriate bargaining unit. Petitioner maintains that the Towson plant constitutes an appropriate bargaining unit.

The Employer's plants at Towson and Hampstead are located 24 miles apart. The Towson plant was built first and as the Company's volume expanded the Hampstead plant was built in 1951. In 1953 and 1956, operations which were formerly located at Towson were transferred to Hampstead. . . .

The Towson plant has approximately 775 maintenance and production employees and its principal production process is the bar stock machining operation. Towson produces a number of component parts for the basic motorized parts made by the Company and these are shipped to the Hampstead plant which assembles, packages, stores, and ships the finished products. . . .

Operations of the two plants are integrated with respect to executive, managerial, and engineering activities. Purchasing and sales are done centrally for both plants and there is one central payroll and one seniority list. For both plants there is one director of industrial relations, one safety and health manager, one wage administrator, one cafeteria manager, and one vice president for manufacturing. These officers are located at either one plant or the other and they handle the problems arising from either plant. In addition, the Company's two plants have numerous single service departments, e.g., one credit department, one advertising department, etc., which provides services for both plants. Both plants work the same hours, have the same lunch period, and are closed for the same periods of time during vacation periods. Employees at both plants receive substantially the same wages, hours, vacations, bonuses, and are covered by the same life insurance, accident and sickness insurance, and pension programs.

While the Employer has one personnel department, hiring of employees is done independently at each of the two plants. Immediate and intermediate supervision is largely autonomous in the respective departments of the two plants and decisions as to promotions, merit increases, and discipline, including discharges, are normally made by the foremen and assistant foremen subject to occasional overruling by the vice president of manufacturing.

With respect to the transfer and interchange of employees between the plants, the most relevant evidence in the record indicates that there were approximately 136 interplant transfers in the period from September 1962 to September 1963. Of that total, however, 83 were transfers of 30 days or less. A company station wagon makes three regular trips a day transporting hourly paid personnel between the plants. Salaried personnel are required to use their own cars for travel between the plants and maintenance people have two vehicles reserved for their transportation needs between the two plants.

The issue of whether a single or a multiplant unit is appropriate for bargaining is often difficult to resolve. In this case, operations appear integrated with respect to executive, managerial, and engineering activities. However, a plant manager or superintendent is responsible for the day-to-day operations of the Towson plant. Immediate and intermediate supervision is largely autonomous within the departments of each plant and questions as to promotions, merit raises, and discipline are handled primarily by foremen and assistant foremen. Although there is only one personnel department, interviewing and hiring is done separately at the respective plants.

We are aware that a substantial degree of product integration exists here and that the interchange of employees between the plants is more than minimal. However, product integration is becoming a less significant factor in determining an appropriate unit because modern manufacturing techniques combined with the increased speed and ease of transport make it possible for plants located in different States to have a high degree of product integration and still maintain a separate identity for bargaining purposes. The limited interchange of employees here does not preclude finding a single-plant unit appropriate inasmuch as there were only 83 transfers for 30 days or less over a 1-year period, and a relatively small number of other employees traveled between the two plants on a regular recurring basis.

As the Board has previously noted, a single-plant unit is presumptively appropriate absent a bargaining history in a more comprehensive unit or a functional integration so severe as to negate the identity of a single-plant unit. Moreover, it has been our declared policy to consider only whether the requested unit is an appropriate one even though it may not be the optimum or most appropriate unit for collective bargaining. We are convinced that such a policy is compatible with the objectives of the Act which seeks to encourage rather than impede the collective-bargaining process.

Upon consideration of the entire record, including particularly the relatively wide geographical separation of the plants, the substantial degree of autonomy reflected by the control exercised by departmental managers and foremen in day-to-day operations, the absence of any bargaining history, and the fact that no labor organization is seeking a larger unit, we are satisfied that the requested Towson plant constitutes an appropriate unit.

Petrie Stores

National Labor Relations Board, 1983
266 NLRB No. 13, 112 LRRM 1233

The Employer, a New York corporation, operates a chain of retail stores selling women's clothing and accessories throughout the United States, including 34 stores in New Jersey. . . . Most stores are located within shopping malls and in some cases the Employer has several stores trading within the same shopping mall. The greatest distance between any two New Jersey stores is approximately 125 miles. At each store, the employee complement consists of sales employees, porters, and cashiers, and varies from one to 14, for an approximate total of 200 such employees.

The Petitioner seeks elections in 10 separate units, one for each store located at Paramus, Wayne (two stores), Rockaway, Woodbridge (two stores), Eatontown, Toms River, and Lawrenceville (two stores), New Jersey. Of the 10 petitions for stores, all are located in a shopping mall with at least one other Petrie store not the subject of a petition. The Employer contends that the single store units are inappropriate. The Employer further argues that the smallest appropriate unit would be all of the Employer's stores located within the same and adjacent shopping malls which experience considerable employee interchange among them and whose employees together share a community of interest. There is no bargaining history among any of the employees in the New Jersey stores, except for the Newark store which has a collective-bargaining history dating back to 1965. . . .

The Employer's management hierarchy is located in the Employer's main office in Secaucus, New Jersey, and is dominated by founder, chairman of the board, and chief operating officer, Milton Petrie. As chief operating officer, Petrie takes personal interest and involvement in inventory control, daily salaries, staffing, and energy concerns, among other things. Reporting directly to Petrie are Hilda Kirshbaum-Gerstein, president, in charge of merchandising, and Robert Mandel, senior vice president, in charge of all areas other than merchandising. Management structure below Mandel in New Jersey consists of seven supervisors; six are responsible for a group of stores numbering three to 10 with at least one store in a neighboring State; the Newark store has its own supervisor. Each store manager is in daily telephone contact with his supervisor, who reports to Mandel. At least once every two weeks, a supervisor will personally visit each store under his or her control. When the store manager is not present in the store, an assistant manager assumes control with all managerial duties and authorities.

Most administrative and personnel functions are centralized at the main office. The financial records are kept at the main office, along with employee payroll. Daily cash receipts from each store are transferred to a central account at the main office. Inventory tickets are removed from each garment at the store level and are brought to the main office for inventory control. The same forms are used throughout. All the stores look the same and the signs are similar. All stores open and close at the same time, subject only to individual shopping mall restrictions. The stores carry the same categories of merchandise and frequently call each other for items. Merchandise is transferred daily between stores and is sold for the same price throughout the New Jersey stores.

Wage rates for each job classification, graduated annual wage increases, and a 30-day raise after initial hire with the Employer are centrally determined. There is companywide seniority. All employees receive the same benefits, *i.e.*, hospitalization, life insurance, and pension plan. . . . For the most part, at all the stores, the same jobs requiring the same skills can be found. Each store has a copy of the company manual which sets forth the basic operating procedures to be followed. The manual specifies, among other things, the procedures to be followed in assisting customers, handling cash, accepting credit cards or checks, granting refunds or exchanges, employee policy as to dress code, eating, drinking, or smoking on the job, and handling inquiries. The temporary transfer of sales personnel, cashiers, and porters occurs at a rate of three to four per week, particularly between adjacent stores. Within these classifications, 10 to 15 percent of the employee complement has been transferred permanently.

Each of the six supervisors has considerable authority, both in the operation of personnel matters and the store. A supervisor is responsible for hiring and determines who will work and when. If a supervisor authorizes a manager to hire an employee, the supervisor will also interview the individual after hire. A supervisor can terminate an employee for any reason; a manager can only make a recommendation that an employee be terminated, except for instances involving theft or assault in which the manager may discipline the offending employee. A supervisor may alter or override a manager's decision or recommendation regarding reprimands and merit salary increases. In each store, a supervisor has responsibility for displays, placement, and rearrangement of racks, and, during inventory, a supervisor must be present unless another home office representative is present.

In personnel matters, a manager's autonomy is severely circumscribed by the authority retained by the supervisor and centrally determined policies. Store managers are not even involved in scheduling of the store employees, cannot grant vacations, leaves of absences, or promotions. A manager can only hire an employee with prior authority. In addition, a manager is instructed to inform a supervisor of any employee grievance and then the supervisor usually handles the matter. A store manager has little authority to purchase merchandise, cannot open a company bank account, and cannot mark down merchandise or transfer merchandise without prior authority. From uncontradicted testimony, it is clear that a store manager's role is to insure that the procedures and policies contained in the Employer's manual are followed.

Not only does the lack of individual store manager's autonomy compel a finding that single-store units are inappropriate, so does the high degree of centralization of administration and control. There is centralized control over merchandising, purchasing, warehousing, distribution, and price tagging. All payroll functions and administration and inventory records are found at the main office. The main office establishes and the supervisors implement uniform labor relations policies. The employees have companywide seniority with identical work procedures and policies calling for identical job skills from store to store within each unit classification.

The single plant, or in the instant case retail store, is presumptively appropriate unless it is established that the single store has been effectively merged into a more comprehensive unit so as to have lost its individual identity. *Frisch's Big Boy Ill-Mar. Inc.*, 147 NLRB 551, 56 LRRM

1246 (1964). *Haag Drug Company, Inc.*, 169 NLRB 877, 67 LRRM 1289
(1968). "The Board has never held or suggested that to rebut the presumption a party must proffer 'overwhelming evidence . . . illustrating
the complete submersion of the interests of employees at the single store,'
nor is it necessary to show that 'the separate interests' of the employees
sought have been 'obliterated.' " *Big Y Foods, Inc.*, 238 NLRB 860, 861, fn.
4, 99 LRRM 1366 (1978).

The Regional Director found the requested single-store units appropriate based on the degree of autonomy possessed by the store managers,
the lack of compelling evidence of substantial employee interchange
between the stores, the geographic separation between many of the stores
in the proposed statewide unit, the absence of any history of collective
bargaining on an overall basis and the presence of a history of collective
bargaining on a single-store basis, and the fact that no labor organization
was seeking to represent a broader unit.

. . .

Of the 10 petitions for stores, all are located in a shopping mall with at
least one other Petrie store not the subject of a petition. The closeness of
these stores is reflected in the substantial interchange of employees on a
temporary basis, three to four employees per week, in addition to the
permanent transfers consisting of 10 to 15 percent of the employee
complement. . . .

In both *Super X [Super X Drugs of Illinois, Inc.*, 233 NLRB 114, 96 LRRM
1642 (1977)] and this case, the store manager's limited authority is established in that the district manager or supervisor, the next level of management, have the final decisionmaking authority in hiring by the store
managers and disciplinary actions, employee grievances must be discussed with their superior, and approval must be received from the
district manager or supervisor to grant store employees leaves of absences, promotions, and pay raises. Also in *Super X*, the store manager
participated in the scheduling of work hours for employees; whereas, in
the instant case, the supervisor has sole discretion in scheduling.

In *Petrie Stores Corp.*, 212 NLRB 130, 86 LRRM 1509 (1974), the
petitioner sought to represent the employees of the employer in a unit of
one store out of three stores in the Atlanta, Georgia, area. The Board
found appropriate for collective bargaining a unit consisting of all three
stores due to the common supervision, wage rates, benefits, and other
conditions of employment, extensive employee interchange, common job
skills, function, centralized administration and operation, and lack of
any substantial individual store autonomy. The facts in the instant case
establish that the New Jersey stores experience an equal degree of centralization and that a store manager's authority is similarly tightly circumscribed.

Upon these facts, we find, in disagreement with the Regional Director,
that the requested single-store units are inappropriate. Accordingly, we
find it unnecessary to pass on whether the Regional Director erred in his
finding that the classifications of assistant manager, manager trainee,
relief manager, department managers, and junior assistant managers are

not supervisory as defined in Section 2(11) of the Act, and, as the Petitioner has made no alternative unit request, we shall dismiss the petitions.

d. The "Reality" of Unit Determination

What is the relevance of the criteria relied upon by the Board in the decisions you have just read? For example, why does it make any difference in *Petrie Stores* that the ultimate responsibility for hiring rests with one of the six supervisors, rather than the store manager? Assuming that the supervisor rather than the store manager has the dominant voice in hiring decisions (a fact not made clear in the opinion), would this affect the employees' determination to vote for or against the union in the election? Would it have anything to do with the union's ability to negotiate and administer a contract or to represent the employees fairly? If not, why is it a factor in the decision?

The Board often explains its use of the factors listed in these decisions as assisting it to determine whether the unit sought encompasses employees with a "community of interest." Yet even this facile term obscures the question of just what it is the Board is looking for. For example, in *Black & Decker*, should it matter whether the employees in the two plants work the same hours and have the same lunch period? Does this mean the Board is concerned whether there is sufficient employee interchange for effective discussion of the issues within the voting constituency? Should the Board try to avoid approving a unit in which communication among employees would be difficult after certification? But isn't it really up to the union to determine what sort of constituency it wishes to serve? Or would that lead to submergence of individual interests or an inability to represent groups separated by physical distance or different working conditions? If the Board's goal is to preserve minority interests, why would it ever tolerate a situation in the Enderby Problem in which the larger plastics division with its younger work force is allowed to swallow up the older, smaller rubber division, where job security is a prime concern? Yet we do not find in the Board decisions any articulated concern to protect such disparate interests among employees.

Now consider Section 9(c)(5) of the Act, which prohibits the Board from determining that a bargaining unit is appropriate solely on the basis of extent of organization. If the Board in fact goes with the unit petitioned for in *Petrie Stores*, on the theory that it is *an* appropriate unit, is not the Board in effect ignoring the mandate of 9(c)(5)? But do you think Congress intended the Board to reject a union petition just because it is congruent with extent of organization? Perhaps the goal of Section 9(c)(5) is somewhat unrealistic. Think about that in the context of the following excerpt from the Board's decision in *Sav-On Drugs, Inc.*, 138 NLRB 1032, 1033, 51 LRRM 1152 (1962), in which the Board reversed a previous policy of favoring multi-location units in certain specialized industries, such as retail stores. Is the Board's position consistent with Section 9(c)(5)?

"The Regional Director in his decision agreed with the Employer's primary position, in reliance on the policy statement made in prior

Board decisions that 'in cases involving retail chainstore operations, absent unusual circumstances, the appropriate unit for collective bargaining should embrace employees of all stores located within an employer's administrative division or geographic area.'

"In its request for review of the Regional Director's unit determination Petitioner urged, inter alia, that there are compelling reasons for the Board to reconsider the above-stated policy. Reviewing our experience under that policy we believe that too frequently it has operated to impede the exercise by employees in retail chain operations of their rights to self-organization guaranteed in Section 7 of the Act. In our opinion that policy has overemphasized the administrative grouping of merchandising outlets at the expense of factors such as geographic separation of the several outlets and the local managerial autonomy of the separate outlets; and it has ignored completely as a factor the extent to which the claiming labor organization had sought to organize the employees of the retail chain. We have decided to modify this policy and to apply to retail chain operations the same unit policy which we apply to multiplant enterprises in general. Therefore, whether a proposed unit which is confined to one of two or more retail establishments making up an employer's retail chain is appropriate will be determined in the light of all the circumstances of the case."

Look at *Petrie Stores* again. Why is it significant that wage rates and benefits have been centrally determined? Should the employees at separate locations have the opportunity to negotiate different terms and conditions for their facility? What consequences would this have for employees at other stores in the chain? Why wasn't the Board concerned about this when it certified a single plant unit in *Black & Decker*?

While, as the Board states in *Black & Decker*, product integration has become less significant, why does it have any significance at all? Is the Board concerned that a strike at Black & Decker's Towson plant might interrupt operations in the Hampstead plant if a product had to go through both facilities? Would this tend to enmesh the "neutral" employees of the Hampstead plant in a labor dispute at Towson? Would a strike put undue economic pressure on the employer, or is this not an appropriate inquiry for the Board? We shall discuss the problem of economic activity which spills over to a neutral employer in Chapter 7, B.

Since the assumptions behind the Board's unit determination criteria are not easy to articulate, there is a want of certainty and predictability in these matters. Since the Board will approve *an* appropriate unit, and not limit the parties to the optimal, ideal unit, there is a good chance that the unit petitioned for by the union will prevail. On the other hand, because the Board's criteria are somewhat flexible, cases seem to turn on the ability of each party to marshal facts in support of its position. And, as the dialogues in the Enderby Problem reveal, the employer may have a substantial advantage in this respect, both because of greater access to the facts and an ability to shape ambiguous practices and policies to fit its needs. The leadman issue in the Enderby Problem illustrates this possibility.

The reality of the unit determination process is that the union probably does not care very much about what is an appropriate unit. Its initial concern is to obtain an election in a unit in which it can win. For example, the union in *Petrie Stores* undoubtedly petitioned for an election in only 10 of the 34 stores because it had majority support in only those stores. The facts strongly suggest that the union did not think it could win an election if the other store in each of the 10 malls concerned were included in the unit. Imagine how much more difficult it would be for the union to organize all 34 stores in the Petrie chain. Considering the likely turnover in this industry, the union would probably have to concentrate all its resources on simultaneously organizing all the stores. Doesn't this suggest the employer sought the larger unit because it didn't think the union would win?

Note that the union did not seek an alternative unit in *Petrie Stores*. And the employer did not insist that the only appropriate unit was one encompassing all 34 stores. What exactly was the employer's position? What unit configurations between the extremes of a single store unit and a unit of all 34 stores do you think the Board might have approved?

e. Effects of Unit Determination on Economic Power in Bargaining

In making their unit contentions the parties may have to look beyond the immediate problem of winning the election. For example, while in the Enderby Problem the union may have a better shot at winning an election in the rubber division alone, bargaining effectiveness may require it to represent the employees of both plants, for the threat of a strike in the rubber division alone may be ineffectual.

Consider the fact that the Enderby work force includes both unskilled laborers and skilled laboratory technicians. If the unskilled laborers were to strike, the employer might be able to operate the plant with replacements. But if the bargaining unit also included technicians, who joined the strike, the inability to obtain trained replacements in the market would make the strike quite effective, particularly if the technical work were essential to completion of the production tasks. On the other hand, if the unit consisted of technicians alone, their decision to strike could have a disproportionately heavy economic impact upon the employer by shutting down its entire operation. It may be argued that since the other employees would be put out of work by a strike of technicians, they should be placed in the same bargaining unit so they may have some say in the determination of whether to strike.

Suppose that the employer's work force were divided into a number of small, discrete units. A settlement by the employer with one group might put pressure on unions in other units to achieve at least parity if not a better settlement. A group of employees might be reluctant to settle early for fear that employees in the other units would achieve a more favorable settlement. And the various employee groups might turn to the strongest constituent unit to "whipsaw" the employer into better settlements all around. On the other hand, smaller groups of employees in separate, discrete units may wield less economic power than a unit covering most of the employees in the plant. These economic considerations, stemming from unit determinations, may have a profound effect upon the agreements finally negotiated. Are these factors properly taken into account in the case materials you just read?

f. Effects of Unit Determination on the Union's Ability to Represent Employees Fairly

The right of exclusive representation, which you studied in connection with *J.I. Case* at page 105 above, carries with it a far-reaching obligation: the duty of the union to represent fairly all employees in the bargaining unit. The duty of fair representation is a judicial construct, flowing from the grant of exclusivity in Section 9(a). It was first expounded in *Steele* v. *Louisville & Nashville R.R.*, 323 U.S. 192, 15 LRRM 708 (1944), a case arising under the Railway Labor Act, involving the exclusion of black employees from a recognized union. In deriving a duty of fair representation from Railway Labor Act language that is similar to the grant of exclusivity under the NLRA, the Court wrote:

> "The fair interpretation of the statutory language is that the organization chosen to represent a craft is to represent all its members, the majority as well as the minority, and it is to act for and not against those whom it represents. It is a principle of general application that the exercise of a granted power to act in behalf of others involves the assumption towards them of a duty to exercise the power in their interest and behalf. . . ."

The *Steele* principle, which was used to strike down a distinction in representation based on race, was subsequently imported into the NLRA. The major case expounding the doctrine under the NLRA is *Vaca* v. *Sipes*, 386 U.S. 171, 64 LRRM 2369 (1967). Under *Vaca* the duty of fair representation forbids a union to act arbitrarily, discriminatorily, or in bad faith with regard to individual interests. The doctrine is not confined to distinctions based on race, as in *Steele*, but, as in *Vaca*, extends to such questions as whether the union must pursue an individual's grievance to arbitration.

We shall explore the duty of fair representation in depth in Chapter 4, and you will have to wait until then to decide whether the doctrine as presently defined gives adequate protection to the individual employee. But think about the question of fair representation in the context of the unit determination questions we have just considered. For example, take the work force in the rubber division of Enderby Industries. Can a union adequately represent the interests of the 12 technicians if they are submerged in a larger unit of some 120 employees? What if, as the opening problem suggests, the impetus of the organizing effort is the fear of rubber division employees over job security. Can those interests be adequately protected by a union in a unit consisting of both the rubber division and the much larger plastics division? If the union's decisions as to bargaining agendas—for example, whether to sacrifice present wages for future job security—are determined by membership vote, can the union adequately represent the interests of the rubber workers?

If problems of fair representation are raised by such unit placement, are they outweighed by other considerations such as administrative convenience to the employer or disparity of bargaining power if the technicians of the rubber division constitute a separate unit? As you review the unit determination materials, consider whether the Board has taken adequate account of the question of fair representation. Compare the position of the dissenting Board members in *St. Francis Hospital,* page 140 *infra.*

The inherent problems when one group of interests is outweighed by another are well illustrated by the case of *Emporium Capwell Co.* v. *Western Addition Community Organization,* 420 U.S. 50, 88 LRRM 2660 (1975), discussed in detail in Chapter 4. For purposes of our present discussion it is enough to know that the Supreme Court held in *Emporium Capwell* that certain activities, such as picketing, undertaken by individual black employees in protest against the company's allegedly racist employment policies were not protected under Section 7 of the Act. Rather, these activities should have been channelled through the grievance process and handled by the union. Although no one would suggest that the black employees should have been placed in a separate unit in *Emporium Capwell,* consider the Court's underlying assumptions about unit determinations as one of its justifications for its conclusion:

"Section 7 affirmatively guarantees employees the most basic rights of industrial self-determination, 'the right to self-organization, to form, join, or assist labor organizations, to bargain collectively through representatives of their own choosing, and to engage in other concerted activities for the purpose of collective bargaining or other mutual aid or protection,' as well as the right to refrain from these activities. These are, for the most part, collective rights, rights to act in concert with one's fellow employees; they are protected not for their own sake but as an instrument of the national labor policy of minimizing industrial strife 'by encouraging the practice and procedure of collective bargaining.'

"Central to the policy of fostering collective bargaining, where the employees elect that course, is the principle of majority rule. If the majority of a unit chooses union representation, the NLRA permits it to bargain with its employer to make union membership a condition of employment, thereby imposing its choice upon the minority. In establishing a regime of majority rule, Congress sought to secure to all members of the unit the benefits of their collective strength and bargaining power, in full awareness that the superior strength of some individuals or groups might be subordinated to the interest of the majority. *Vaca* v. *Sipes,* 386 U.S. 171, 182 (1967); *J. I. Case Co.* v. *NLRB,* 321 U.S. 332, 338–339 (1944); H.R. Rep. No. 972, 74th Cong., 1st Sess., 18 (1935). As a result, '[t]he complete satisfaction of all who are represented is hardly to be expected.' *Ford Motor Co.* v. *Huffman,* 345 U.S. 330, 338 (1953).

"In vesting the representatives of the majority with this broad power Congress did not, of course, authorize a tyranny of the majority over minority interests. First, it confined the exercise of these powers to the context of a 'unit appropriate for the purposes of collective bargaining,' *i.e.,* a group of employees with a sufficient commonality of circumstances to ensure against the submergence of a minority with distinctively different interests in the terms and conditions of their employment.

"Second, it undertook in the 1959 Landrum-Griffin amendments, 73 Stat. 519, to assure that minority voices are heard as they are in the functioning of a democratic institution. Third, we have held, by the very nature of the exclusive bargaining representative's status as representative of *all* unit employees, Congress implicitly imposed upon it a duty fairly and in good faith to represent the interests of minorities within the unit. *Vaca* v. *Sipes, supra; Wallace Corp.* v. *NLRB,* 323 U.S. 248 (1944); cf. *Steele* v. *Louisville & N.R. Co.,* 323 U.S. 192 (1944). And the Board has taken the position that a union's refusal to process grievances against racial discrimination, in violation of that duty, is an unfair labor practice. Indeed, the Board has ordered a union implicated by a collective-bargaining agreement in discrimination with an employer to propose specific contractual provisions to prohibit racial discrimination."

The foregoing materials suggest, as a respected authority has observed, that the bargaining unit plays several distinct roles in labor relations: it serves as an election district to determine the selection of a representative, as a governing unit, particularly in light of the doctrine of exclusivity, and as an economic entity in terms of applying pressure in bargaining. C. Summers, H. Wellington, and A. Hyde, Labor Law Cases and Materials 604–5 (2d ed. 1982). Does the law of unit determination adequately reflect this spectrum of considerations?

2. USING PROCEDURES TO AFFECT THE OUTCOME OF THE ELECTION

The union's success in the organizing drive may depend on how quickly its efforts culminate in an election. Momentum is important in an organizing campaign. If it takes too long to hold an election employees may lose interest in the union or become frustrated with the slowness of the Board's processes and discouraged about the union's ability to achieve results. The procedural hurdles involved in moving to an election afford numerous opportunities for both union and employer counsel to manipulate the timing of the election.

a. The Manipulation of Unit Determination Issues

Suppose it were clear in the Enderby Problem that the two divisions constituted separate appropriate units. The union would want an election to be held in the rubber division first because, as indicated in the dialogue, a victory there might influence a subsequent election in the plastics division. May the employer raise unimportant or even bogus issues with respect to the rubber division petition so that a complicated hearing must be held? May the employer at the same time petition for an immediate election in the plastics division? Obviously its purpose would be to have the election in the plastics division held first. May the union raise bogus issues to force a delay of the election in plastics? What are the ethical constraints upon the lawyers for either side?

Some of the potential for delay would have been eliminated by the proposed Labor Law Reform Act of 1977, which provided for the holding of an election within 22 days after the filing of a petition, if the Board has already promulgated a rule dealing with the unit matter in issue, and within 45 days if such a rule has not been promulgated, except that in cases which the Board determines present "issues of exceptional novelty or complexity" up to 75 days may be taken.

b. Showing of Interest

The Board will not set the election machinery in motion unless the union makes an advance showing of support in the unit sought. The Board requires a "showing of interest" that at least 30 percent of the electorate favors unionization; short of that the Board considers it a waste of administrative resources to proceed to an election. The most common means of showing support is through authorization cards. But if the hearing to determine an appropriate unit results in a direction of election in a unit larger than petitioned for, the union must make a showing of interest in the expanded unit. Thus by diluting the requested unit the employer may defeat the representation claim simply by foreclosing an adequate showing of interest. (If a second union seeks to intervene in the representation hearing to provide input on the unit question, it needs only a 10-percent showing for this purpose, while to merely appear on the ballot as an alternative choice requires but a single authorization card.)

The determination of whether there is an adequate showing of interest is held to be an administrative matter not subject to challenge in the representation hearing. How may the employer effectively press a claim that the signatures on certain authorization cards are forged? Suppose the employer challenges certain cards on the ground that they are tainted through unlawful assistance in violation of Section 8(a)(2)? How may the union effectively meet this claim? Should these important questions be determined as an administrative matter?

c. Pending Unfair Labor Practice Charges

Since unfair labor practices which are not remedied may destroy the "laboratory conditions" thought to be the prerequisite of a fair election, the Board has the power to withhold directing an election pending resolution of such charges. This means that the union can affect the timing of the election by postponing it through a "blocking" charge.

Presumably the filing of spurious charges to achieve such a result will be curbed by the union lawyer's professional responsibility and by the Board's ability to promptly investigate and dismiss such charges. The rule has merit in that it does not force a union to proceed to an election that it is likely to lose on account of the employer's unfair labor practices; by filing a charge the union may obtain resolution of the unfair labor practices claim prior to the holding of an election. The Board has discretion to determine whether to hold up the election. In certain circumstances, for example, where the suspension of the election would deprive the employees of a self-determination election for an unreasonably long period, the Board may allow the election to proceed in the face of charges. But the union may prefer to take its chances on the election, knowing that if it loses, the pending charge would, if sustained, serve to set the election aside and perhaps even support a bargaining order. The union may in such a case proceed simultaneously with its charge and with the election by filing a "Request to Proceed." These are routinely honored by the Board, and the election is held in spite of the pending charges. Here too there is potential for abuse, however. The union may view the filing of a charge, even if nonmeritorious, and the triggering of an NLRB onsite investigation of the charge, complete with "government agents," as a potent organizing tool which symbolizes to the workers the union's power to protect their rights. What safeguards are there against such abuse?

d. Professional Responsibility Question

It is debatable whether the practice of labor relations affords more opportunity than most other litigation, civil or criminal, to manipulate rules of procedure to achieve substantive ends. In any event, the student should consider the many ethical problems raised in these materials, such as the "selection" of testimony to achieve favorable results and the use of procedural devices to delay or perhaps accelerate an election.

The Code of Professional Responsibility prepared by the American Bar Association sets out in Canon 7 the limitations of the duty to represent a client zealously. While some of the ethical considerations and disciplinary rules which implement Canon 7 suffer from the same open-endedness as the unit determination rules themselves, the following disciplinary rule should assist you in understanding your professional responsibility in the situations under discussion:

"DR 7–102 Representing a Client Within the Bounds of the Law.
"(A) In his representation of a client, a lawyer shall not:
"(1) File a suit, assert a position, conduct a defense, delay a trial, or take other action on behalf of his client when he knows or when it is obvious that such action would serve merely to harass or maliciously injure another.
"(2) Knowingly advance a claim or defense that is unwarranted under existing law, except that he may advance such claim or defense if it can be supported by good faith argument for an extension, modification, or reversal of existing law.

"(3) Conceal or knowingly fail to disclose that which he is required by law to reveal.

"(4) Knowingly use perjured testimony or false evidence.

"(5) Knowingly make a false statement of law or fact.

"(6) Participate in the creation or preservation of evidence when he knows or it is obvious that the evidence is false.

"(7) Counsel or assist his client in conduct that the lawyer knows to be illegal or fraudulent.

"(8) Knowingly engage in other illegal conduct or conduct contrary to a Disciplinary Rule."

The ABA's Commission on Evaluation of Professional Standards released its new recommended Model Rules of Professional Conduct in May, 1981. The Rules had not been put into effect when we went to press.

One of the proposed new rules which would shed light on the ethical questions raised follows:

"Rule 3.1. Meritorious Claims and Contentions. A lawyer shall not bring or defend a proceeding, or assert or controvert an issue therein, unless there is a reasonable basis for doing so, which includes a good faith argument for an extension, modification or reversal of existing law. . . ."

The Commission's comments state that the new rule is an advantage over its prior counterpart, DR7–102, set out earlier, in that it prohibits the lawyer from misusing defenses which not only "harass or maliciously injure another" but which have no "reasonable basis."

Another new rule which builds upon the prior DR7–102 provides:

"Rule 3.2. Expediting Litigation. A lawyer shall make reasonable effort consistent with the legitimate interests of the clients to expedite litigation."

The comment to the rule goes on to state "delay should not be indulged merely . . . for the purpose of frustrating an opposing party's attempt to obtain rightful redress or repose."

But ask yourself whether the drafters of the new rules had in mind procedures like the NLRB representation hearing, and whether its rules make sense in that context.

3. AFTERMATH OF CERTIFICATION

a. Post-Election Procedures

i. Before the Board

After the election is held, the Board will move promptly, within days, to certify the result. If the union is certified, the obligation to bargain commences. But the election is not always immediately dispositive. Either party may move to set aside the election on the ground that conduct occurred which interfered with a fair election. The substantive grounds for such a challenge are discussed in Chapter 3. Procedurally, the objecting party must quickly file, within five days of the election, a self-contained document detailing the grounds for objection. These objections are then resolved promptly, with or without a hearing, generally at the regional director's level, but occasionally by the full Board. See Board Regulations Sections 102.67(c) and 102.69(c). The aim, again, is a speedy resolution of all claims. The Board will also utilize this procedure to resolve challenges to individual ballots actually cast, for example, claims that a particular voter was in fact a supervisor or that a group of voters were replacements for unfair labor practice strikers, hence ineligible to vote.

If objections are sustained, the Board will order a rerun election in the near future. The challenging party, particularly if it is the union, may wish to claim that the same activity which invalidates the election also constitutes an unfair labor practice. In such a case the election challenges may be consolidated with the unfair labor practice claims and handled in accordance with the procedures of Section 10 of the Act.

It is worthwhile, at this point, to discuss briefly the voting rights of strikers. Section 9(c)(3) of the Act was amended in 1959 to provide that economic strikers are eligible to vote in any election held within 12 months of the commencement of the strike. Their replacements, if permanent employees, are also entitled to vote. But if the strike goes beyond 12 months, those strikers who have been permanently replaced lose their voting rights. However, when a strike is precipitated or prolonged by an employer's unfair labor practice, it is characterized as an unfair labor practice strike. In such a case the strikers are entitled to vote for an indefinite period, while their replacements may not vote at all. The distinction between an economic strike and an unfair labor practice strike is a difficult one, pursued in greater detail in Chapter 4.

These issues become particularly acute if a decertification petition is filed after a strike. The strikers are likely to continue to support the union, while the employees who replaced them, essentially in defiance of the union, are likely to vote to remove the union. Hence the voting status of the strikers is critical.

Procedurally, the voting eligibility of strikers is determined by post-election challenge to ballots, in the manner described above with respect to other objections to the election. To identify those ballots, of course, the voter must be challenged and her ballot segregated at the time of the election.

ii. Judicial Review of Unit Determinations

The Act does not contemplate direct judicial appeal from a unit determination of the Board. The aggrieved party has in the first instance only a one-step appeal, in limited circumstances, from a decision of the regional director to the full Board. See Section 3(b) of the Act and Board Regulations Section 102.67(c). A Board certification is not deemed to be a "final order" under Section 10(b), hence direct judicial review is precluded. This rule has the salutary effect of preventing time-consuming delays in judicially testing Board unit determinations.

The one major exception to this rule is articulated in *Leedom* v. *Kyne*, 358 U.S. 184, 43 LRRM 2222 (1958). In that case the Court held that if a Board determination in a representation proceeding violates "a specific prohibition of the Act," it may be vacated by a federal district court under Section 24 of the Judicial Code. The Board had included 122 professional engineers and nine nonprofessional employees in the same bargaining unit in violation of the specific prohibition of Section 9(b)(1). *McCulloch* v. *Sociedad Nacional de Marineros de Honduras*, 372 U.S. 10, 52 LRRM 2425 (1963), elaborates on *Leedom* v. *Kyne*. In *Sociedad* the Court said (at 16–17):

> "We are not of course precluded from reexamining the jurisdiction of the District Court in Sociedad's action, merely because no challenge was made by the parties. . . . [W]e hold that the action falls within the limited exception fashioned in *Leedom* v. *Kyne*. . . . In that case judicial intervention was permitted since the Board's order was 'in excess of its delegated powers and contrary to a specific prohibition in the Act.' While here the Board has violated no specific prohibition in the Act, the overriding consideration is that the Board's assertion of power to determine the representation of foreign seamen aboard vessels under foreign flags has aroused vigorous protests from foreign governments and created international problems for our Government. . . . [T]he presence of public questions particularly high in the scale of our national interest because of their international complexion is a uniquely compelling justification for prompt judicial resolution of the controversy over the Board's power. No question of remotely comparable urgency was involved in *Kyne*, which was a purely domestic adversary situation. The exception recognized today is therefore not to be taken as an enlargement of the exception in *Kyne*."

For an unsuccessful attempt to extend the rule of *Leedom* v. *Kyne*, see *Boire* v. *Greyhound Corp.*, 376 U.S. 473, 55 LRRM 2694 (1964), which turned on a claim that the Board had erroneously treated an independent contractor as an employer under the Act, and hence exceeded its jurisdiction. The Court's answer was that the contention involved essentially a factual issue, not subject to review in this fashion.

This is not the end of the road for the employer. By refusing to bargain with the certified union on the ground that the Board directed an election in an inappropriate unit or otherwise exceeded its authority, the employer will undoubtedly draw an 8(a)(5) charge. If the charge is sustained by the Board and enforcement sought in the courts, the employer may now raise the claim of an improper unit determination; however, the contention is likely to receive short shrift by the court, which will generally defer to the Board's expertise in making unit determinations.

This of course gives the employer a way to postpone bargaining on technical grounds of a deficiency in the Board's unit finding. Once again ethical restraints will dictate how far the lawyer may go in resisting a demand for bargaining where the claim of an erroneous unit determination, if not totally spurious, is likely to go nowhere in court. You will have occasion to consider a closely related question of the appropriate remedy for this kind of delay in bargaining in connection with the discussion of remedies for refusal to bargain in Chapter 4. Meanwhile you might ponder whether the union has any parallel avenue for raising a judicial challenge to a unit determination by the Board.

b. Duration and Effect of Certification

Brooks v. NLRB

Supreme Court of the United States, 1954
348 U.S. 96, 35 LRRM 2158

MR. JUSTICE FRANKFURTER delivered the opinion of the Court.

The National Labor Relations Board conducted a representation election in petitioner's Chrysler-Plymouth agency on April 12, 1951. District Lodge No. 727, International Association of Machinists, won by a vote of eight to five, and the Labor Board certified it as the exclusive bargaining representative on April 20. A week after the election and the day before the certification, petitioner received a handwritten letter signed by 9 of the 13 employees in the bargaining unit stating: "We, the undersigned majority of the employees . . . are not in favor of being represented by Union Local 727 as a bargaining agent."

Relying on this letter . . . , petitioner refused to bargain with the union. . . .

The issue before us is the duty of an employer toward a duly certified bargaining agent if, shortly after the election which resulted in the certification, the union has lost, without the employer's fault, a majority of the employees from its membership.

. . .

[Prior to the 1947 Taft-Hartley Amendments] the Board uniformly found an unfair labor practice where, during the "certification year," an employer refused to bargain on the ground that the certified union no longer possessed a majority. While the courts in the main enforced the Board's decision, they did not commit themselves to one year as the determinate content of reasonableness. . . .

Certain aspects of the Labor Board's representation procedures came under scrutiny in the Congress that enacted the Taft-Hartley Act in 1947. Congress was mindful that, once employees had chosen a union, they could not vote to revoke its authority and refrain from union activities, while if they voted against having a union in the first place, the union could begin at once to agitate for a new election. The National Labor Relations Act was amended to provide that (a) employees could petition the Board for a decertification election, at which they would have an opportunity to choose no longer to be represented by a union, (b) an employer, if in doubt as to the majority claimed by a union without formal election or beset by the conflicting claims of rival unions, could likewise petition the Board for an election, (c) after a valid certification or decertification election had been conducted, the Board could not hold a second election in the same bargaining unit until a year had elapsed, (d) Board certification could only be granted as the result of an election, though an employer would presumably still be under a duty to bargain with an uncertified union that had a clear majority.

The Board continued to apply its "one year certification" rule after the Taft-Hartley Act came into force, except that even "unusual circumstances" no longer left the Board free to order an election where one had taken place within the preceding 12 months. Conflicting views became manifest in the Courts of Appeals when the Board sought to enforce orders based on refusal to bargain in violation of its rule. Some Circuits sanctioned the Board's position. The Court of Appeals for the Sixth Circuit denied enforcement. The Court of Appeals for the Third Circuit held that a "reasonable" period depends on the facts of the particular case.

The issue is open here. No case touching the problem has directly presented it. In *Franks Bros. Co.* v. *National Labor Relations Board*, 321 U.S. 702, we held that where a union's majority was dissipated after an employer's unfair labor practice in refusing to bargain, the Board could appropriately find that such conduct had undermined the prestige of the union and require the employer to bargain with it for a reasonable period despite the loss of majority. And in *National Labor Relations Board* v. *Mexia Textile Mills, Inc.*, 339 U.S. 563, we held that a claim of an intervening loss of majority was no defense to a proceeding for enforcement of an order to cease and desist from certain unfair labor practices.

Petitioner contends that whenever an employer is presented with evidence that his employees have deserted their certified union, he may forthwith refuse to bargain. In effect, he seeks to vindicate the rights of his employees to select their bargaining representative. If the employees are dissatisfied with their chosen union, they may submit their own grievance to the Board. If an employer has doubts about his duty to continue bargaining, it is his responsibility to petition the Board for relief, while continuing to bargain in good faith at least until the Board has given some indication that his claim has merit. Although the Board may, if the facts warrant, revoke a certification or agree not to pursue a charge of an unfair labor practice, these are matters for the Board: they do not justify employer self-help or judicial intervention. The underlying purpose of this statute is industrial peace. To allow employers to rely on employees' rights in refusing to bargain with the formally designated union is not conducive to that end, it is inimical to it. Congress has devised a formal mode for selection and rejection of bargaining agents and has fixed the spacing of elections, with a view of furthering industrial stability and with due regard to administrative prudence.

We find wanting the arguments against these controlling considerations. In placing a nonconsenting minority under the bargaining responsibility of an agency selected by a majority of the workers, Congress has discarded common-law doctrines of agency. It is contended that since a bargaining agency may be ascertained by methods less formal than a supervised election, informal repudiation should also be sanctioned where decertification by another election is precluded. This is to make situations that are different appear the same. Finally, it is not within the power of this Court to require the Board, as is suggested, to relieve a small employer, like the one involved in this case, of the duty that may be exacted from an enterprise with many employees.

To be sure, what we have said has special pertinence only to the period during which a second election is impossible. But the Board's view that the one-year period should run from the date of certification rather than the date of election seems within the allowable area of the Board's discretion in carrying out congressional policy. See *Phelps Dodge Corp.* v. *Labor Board*, 313 U.S. 177, 192–197, *Labor Board* v. *Seven-Up Bottling Co.*, 344 U.S. 344. Otherwise, encouragement would be given to management or a rival union to delay certification by spurious objections to the conduct of an election and thereby diminish the duration of the duty to bargain. Furthermore, the Board has ruled that one year after certification the employer can ask for an election or, if he has fair doubts about the union's continuing majority, he may refuse to bargain further with it. This, too, is a matter appropriately determined by the Board's administrative authority.

We conclude that the judgment of the Court of Appeals enforcing the Board's order must be affirmed.

If the incumbent union negotiates an agreement during the insulated period noted in *Brooks*, or, for that matter, at any time without successful challenge to its representation status, freedom from challenge by a rival union is further extended under the "contract bar" doctrine. This rule, which has undergone some changes over the years, precludes the holding of an election if a collective bargaining agreement of a fixed and "reasonable" duration is in effect. At present the outside limit of a contract bar is three years; a longer contract is not invalid, but it does not serve as a bar to an election after three years. Exceptions abound to the contract bar rule; for example, if the incumbent union ceases to function—that is, is "defunct" under Board jargon—the bar to an election drops. We leave further exceptions to your research as a practitioner, if needed.

You should understand that filing a petition in the face of an existing contract is not like "shooting fish in a barrel." The "open season" under a contract bar is exceedingly short: the petition must be filed in the period between the 60th and the 90th day prior to the expiration of the contract or the end of the third year of a longer agreement. If no petition is filed during that period, a contract negotiated by the incumbent within the 60-day "insulated period" prior to expiration of the agreement will serve as a new bar for up to another three years. Again we have refrained from giving you all the details of this rule. You should realize, however, that the uninitiated or unsophisticated rival union or disgruntled employee is likely to miss the open period during which a challenge may be made. Moreover, the individual seeking to file a decertification proceeding may not lawfully be assisted by the employer. But if the "open" period were longer, inordinate pressure might be placed on the bargaining process, and the goal of industrial stability through bargaining would be threatened.

Under a recent change in Board law, even a petition filed during the appropriate open period does not necessarily affect the bargaining relationship between the employer and the incumbent union. In *RCA Del Caribe, Inc.*, 262 NLRB 963, 110 LRRM 1369 (1982), the Board held that "the mere filing of a representation petition by an outside, challenging union will no longer require or permit an employer to withdraw from bargaining or executing a contract with an incumbent union," 262 NLRB at 965, 110 LRRM at 1371. Under the prior *Midwest Piping* rule the mere filing of a petition during the open period required the employer to cease bargaining with the union. While under the new rule the employer and union may reach an agreement even in the face of a rival challenge, the agreement is nullified if the rival union prevails in an election challenge.

This issue is discussed further in Chapter 3 at page 269, in connection with employer assistance to unions under Section 8(a)(2).

While we do not explore them in detail in this book, you should at least be aware of the device of the unit clarification claim (a UC petition), which may be utilized to clarify or modify a unit description, particularly in light of changed circumstances, and the deauthorization election (a UD petition), a procedure to withdraw a previously negotiated contractual provision requiring employees to join the union as a condition of employment. You should also observe that the rules which protect the inchoate bargaining relationship from the challenges described above are somewhat parallel to the restrictions found in Section 8(b)(7) of the Act against one union mounting economic pressure upon the employer while another is recognized or certified. These problems are discussed in Chapter 7, A.

C. SPECIAL REPRESENTATION ISSUES

1. Professional, Technical, and Craft Interests

The union's petition in the Enderby Problem seeks to include the technicians in the overall unit of production and maintenance employees. But do these employees have specialized skills, training, and interests which make their inclusion in the overall unit inappropriate, or, at the very least, render a separate unit of technicians, if sought, appropriate?

The Act provides in Section 9(b) for special unit placement of professionals. However, the work of a laboratory technician may not involve the requisite criteria for professional status as defined in Section 2(12) of the Act. The Board has defined a technician as one "whose work is of a technical nature involving the use of specialized training usually acquired in colleges or technical schools or through special courses." *Litton Industries*, 125 NLRB 722, 45 LRRM 1166 (1959). Usually such work does not entail the independent discretion and judgment which are part of the statutory definition of a professional. A separate body of law has developed regarding placement of technicians, particularly under *Sheffield Corp.*, 134 NLRB 1101, 49 LRRM 1265 (1961). In that case the Board rejected an earlier policy of automatically excluding technicians from production and maintenance units upon request of the technicians or employer, and instead dealt with placement on a case-by-case basis, using a variety of criteria, such as desires of the parties, history of bargaining, similarity of skills and job functions, common supervision, interchange with other employees, similarity of working conditions, type of industry, organization and physical setup of plant, and whether any union seeks to represent the technicians separately. Craft employees are somewhat akin to technicians in that they too have special skills, training, and interests, though their work does not entail the status of professionals.

Craft placement issues usually do not arise in the context of initial unit determinations, but in attempted withdrawals by craft employees from existing, more comprehensive units. The attempt to carve out a craft unit from a larger unit is known as craft severance.

In its earliest decisions the Board denied craft severance except where the craft could show it maintained its separate identity within the larger unit, *American Can Co.*, 13 NLRB 1252, 4 LRRM 392 (1939). Congress responded to *American Can* by enacting Section 9(b)(2) of the Act in 1947. It provides

"The Board shall not . . . decide that any craft unit is inappropriate on . . . the ground that a different unit has been established by a prior Board determination, unless a majority of the employees in the proposed craft unit vote against separate representation."

The Board's initial response to Section 9(b)(2), in *National Tube Co.*, 76 NLRB 1199, 21 LRRM 1292 (1948), was to continue to give great weight to the craft's prior inclusion in the larger unit, particularly in industries with heavy functional integration, where a labor dispute could disrupt the entire operation. But several years later, in *American Potash & Chemical Corp.*, 107 NLRB 1418, 33 LRRM 1380 (1954), the Board took a more lenient view of craft severance, although it continued to follow *National Tube* in the four heavy industries—basic steel, wet milling, lumber, and aluminum—in which it was most frequently applied.

Then, seven years later, in *Mallinckrodt Chemical Works*, 162 NLRB 387, 64 LRRM 1011 (1966), the Board again revised its test for craft severance. It said:

"The *American Potash* tests do serve to identify and define those employee groups which normally have the necessary cohesiveness and special interests to distinguish them from the generality of production and maintenance employees, and place in the scales of judgment the interests of the craft employees. However, they do not consider the interests of the other employees and thus do not permit a weighing of the craft group against the competing interests favoring continuance of the established relationship. Thus, by confining consideration solely to the interests favoring severance, the *American Potash* tests preclude the Board from discharging its statutory responsibility to make its unit determinations on the basis of all relevant factors, including those factors which weigh against severance. In short, application of these mechanistic tests leads always to the conclusion that the interests of craft employees always prevail. It does this, moreover, without affording a voice in the decision to the other employees, whose unity of association is broken and whose collective strength is weakened by the success of the craft or departmental group in pressing its own special interests."

The Board concluded that

"[T]he *American Potash* tests do not effectuate the policies of the Act. We shall, therefore, no longer allow our inquiry to be limited by them. Rather we shall, as the Board did prior to *American Potash*, broaden our inquiry to permit evaluation of all considerations relevant to an informed decision in this area. The following areas of inquiry are illustrative of those we deem relevant:

"1. Whether or not the proposed unit consists of a distinct and homogeneous group of skilled journeymen craftsmen performing the functions of their craft on a nonrepetitive basis, or of employees constituting a functionally distinct department, working in trades or occupations for which a tradition of separate representation exists.

"2. The history of collective bargaining of the employees sought at the plant involved, and at other plants of the employer, with emphasis on whether the existing patterns of bargaining are productive of stability in labor relations, and whether such stability will be unduly disrupted by the destruction of the existing patterns of representation.

"3. The extent to which the employees in the proposed unit have established and maintained their separate identity during the period of inclusion in a broader unit, and the extent of their participation or lack of participation in the establishment and maintenance of the existing pattern of representation and the prior opportunities, if any, afforded them to obtain separate representation.

"4. The history and pattern of collective bargaining in the industry involved.

"5. The degree of integration of the employer's production processes, including the extent to which the continued normal operation of the production processes is dependent upon the performance of the assigned functions of the employees in the proposed unit.

"6. The qualifications of the union seeking to 'carve out' a separate unit, including that union's experience in representing employees like those involved in the severance action."

The Board emphasized the "illustrative" character of the listed areas of inquiry:

"In view of the nature of the issue posed by a petition for severance, the foregoing should not be taken as a hard and fast definition of an inclusive or exclusive listing of the various considerations involved in making unit determinations in this area. No doubt other factors worthy of consideration will appear in the course of litigation. We emphasize the foregoing to demonstrate our intention to free ourselves from the restrictive effect of rigid and inflexible rules in making our unit determinations. Our determinations will be made only after a weighing of all relevant factors on a case-by-case basis, and we will apply the same principles and standards to all industries." 162 NLRB at 396–98, 64 LRRM 1015–17.

Do the shifts in Board doctrine described in this section reflect principled policy choices or just changes in the political makeup of the Board? Do the *Mallinckrodt* rules provide you with much guidance in determining how to prepare a craft severance case?

2. HEALTH CARE UNITS

The National Labor Relations Act was amended in 1974 to bring nonprofit hospitals under its coverage, and to make special provisions for all health care institutions, particularly with respect to strikes, see NLRA Section 2(14) and Section 8(g). While the amendment was silent as to unit placement in hospital cases, both the Senate and House reports accompanying the amendment stated that "due consideration should be given by the Board to preventing proliferation of bargaining units in the health care industry." The reports cited with approval certain earlier Board decisions (involving proprietary hospitals) that had denied petitions for smaller units. A proposed amendment to Section 9(b), which failed of passage, would have limited health care bargaining units to four, encompassing professional, technical, clerical, and service and maintenance units, respectively.

We tell you about these provisions not so that you may develop expertise in this rather specialized area, but to provide you with insight into yet another approach to unit determination issues.

St. Francis Hospital, 265 NLRB No. 12, 112 LRRM 1153 (1982), represents the Board's current response to criticism by reviewing courts that it has ignored the 1974 Amendments and given too much weight in hospital cases to traditional community of interest criteria (the relevant cases are cited in Chairman Van De Water's dissenting opinion in *St. Francis Hospital*). In *St. Francis Hospital* the Board granted a petition for separate representation of 39 maintenance employees out of the hospital's total work force of about 1300. The employer had sought a service and maintenance unit, one of the four categories recognized by the proposed 1974 amendments, of some 438 employees. Portions of the Board's decision follow:

"These cases demonstrate that the Board has responded to the Congressional concern for special attention to the number of bargaining units at a health care institution. It has refined and limited the traditional unit principles applicable in other employment settings. In cases arising outside the health care industry, the Board applies only a community-of-interest test, in which we examine the petitioned-for unit for shared job characteristics and common workplace concerns to determine whether that group of employees comprises an appropriate unit for bargaining. However, in the health care industry, to guard against the possibility that each of the many subspecialties at a modern health care facility might seek a separate bargaining unit, we have added a preliminary step to our unit determination process. We have identified certain groups of employees commonly found in a health care institution: physicians, registered nurses, other professional employees, technical employees, business office clerical employees, service and maintenance employees, and skilled maintenance employees. Often these groups of employees constitute the entire employee complement, and, almost invariably, all employees will fall into one of these enumerated categories. Based on our experience in examining the employee complement at health care facilities, we have determined that these seven named classifications represent the groupings of employees that *may* constitute appropriate units for bargaining. Only after determining that the unit sought fits one of these classifications do we then apply our traditional unit principles to determine whether the specific employees involved do, in fact, display the requisite community of interest to warrant separate representation. Under this two-tiered approach, if a petitioner seeks to represent a unit comprised of one of these seven potentially appropriate units, we will analyze the proposed unit to determine whether it displays the requisite separate identity for individual representation. If, however, a petitioner seeks to represent a unit of employees smaller than one of these seven identified groups, for example, a unit consisting only of physical therapists or telephone operators, we will dismiss that petition before reaching the second stage of analysis, unless we are presented with extraordinary and compelling facts justifying allowance of a smaller unit. By restricting the number of potentially appropriate units in this way—despite the fact that many more units could be appropriate under our traditional community-of-interest analysis alone—we have met our statutory responsibility to ensure against unwarranted fragmentation of bargaining units in the health care industry." 112 LRRM at 1157–58.

Applying this test, the majority concluded that the maintenance unit was appropriate, largely on the basis of the specialized skills and training of these employees, most of whom performed traditional craft duties.

Chairman Van De Water and member Hunter dissented in separate opinions. Chairman Van De Water emphasized that the procedures set forth in Section 8(g) of the Act are designed to minimize strikes in hospitals, and that Congress' statements about proliferation of units were part of the same concern:

"The legislators desired . . . to limit the *incidence* of strikes and work stoppages by instructing the Board to minimize the number of bargaining units in this industry. Congress understood that the risk of disruptive work stoppages in a health care facility would be increased the larger the number of bargaining units, primarily because of the heightened possibility of jurisdictional disputes among competing unions and the traditional reluctance of many employees to cross picket lines erected even by unions other than their own." 112 LRRM at 1163.

Both dissenters would follow a "disparity of interest" test as suggested by several circuit court decisions. Member Hunter would "find that the requested unit is appropriate only where the record establishes that, because of a disparity of interest that prohibits fair and adequate representation, the requested employees are entitled to separate representation." 112 LLRM at 1174. Member Hunter would have approved of a health and maintenance unit under this test. The Chairman concluded that "in a health care institution, separate units composed of all professional employees and all nonprofessional employees are appropriate for purposes of collective bargaining." However, "a more limited unit of either professional or nonprofessional employees may be appropriate, but only where it is clearly established that the employees in the proposed unit have a notable disparity of interests from employees in the larger unit which would prohibit or inhibit fair representation for them if they were denied separate representation." 112 LRRM at 1167.

The student should be wary of viewing *St. Francis Hospital* as definitive, given both the courts' hostility to the Board's unit approach thus far in hospital cases and the significant changes in the membership of the Board since this decision.

Consider the relevance of the union's duty of fair representation as outlined by both dissenters. Is this a factor in any of the other unit determination materials you read? Should it be?

3. MULTIEMPLOYER UNITS

It is not uncommon for collective bargaining to take place within a multiple-employer unit, consisting of several employers in a single industry who bargain with a union which represents employees at all locations. The multiemployer unit is generally set up along geographic lines, but seldom on a nationwide basis, and its incidence varies from industry to industry. See Report of General Subcommittee on Labor, House Committee on Education and Labor, Multiemployer Association Bargaining, Committee Print, 88th Cong., 2d Session (1964).

Sometimes the multiemployer approach may be a matter of convenience, where individual bargaining between the union and the numerous small employers in the industry would be unnecessarily costly and time consuming. Multiemployer bargaining also enables the participants to pool negotiating resources, such as legal assistance and data for negotiations. Such bargaining may, however, favor uniformity of terms and conditions at the expense of resolution of particular problems in individual shops.

Multiemployer bargaining may be the result of a determination to alter the balance of economic power. For example, a bargaining stance taken by all publishers of newspapers in a given geographical area, through a multiemployer unit, prevents the union from making a single newspaper the target of its demands. The single newspaper might be vulnerable to economic pressure, as a strike against it would shift advertising and circulation revenues to its competitors. The single employer might then be forced to capitulate to an agreement which the other employers are "whipsawed" into accepting. Compare the situation in the automobile industry, where multiemployer bargaining is not practiced. In each contract year the UAW predictably seeks out a "target" employer and then attempts to impose that settlement as the pattern for the other major manufacturers. A possible response to this tactic is the "supportive" lockout, discussed in Chapter 4. Some have argued that multiemployer bargaining actually enhances the union's bargaining position, for the employer is free to grant concessions without fear that its economic position will be undercut by a competitor who obtains a more favorable contract.

Because multiemployer bargaining may have profound economic consequences, it is not surprising that the creation of such a relationship has been held to be a purely consensual matter. To begin with, the Act does not clearly authorize the establishment of multiemployer bargaining units; the Board's mandate in Section 9(b) to determine whether the appropriate unit is the "employer unit, craft unit, plant unit, or subdivision thereof" would appear by negative implication to preclude the larger multiemployer unit. However, the broad definitions of "employer" and "person" in Sections 2(2) and 2(1) of the Act counter this restrictive interpretation. In any event, the Board has concluded that a unit larger than the employerwide unit may be approved only if all parties consent to its formation. This consent may be express, as in a consent agreement to an initial representation election, or implied from a course of collective bargaining on a multiemployer basis.

Withdrawal from a multiemployer unit is not so consensual, as the following case illustrates:

Bonanno Linen Service v. NLRB

Supreme Court of the United States, 1982
454 U.S. 404, 109 LRRM 2257

JUSTICE WHITE delivered the opinion of the Court.

The issue here is whether a bargaining impasse justifies an employer's unilateral withdrawal from a multiemployer bargaining unit. The National Labor Relations Board (Board) concluded that an employer attempting such a withdrawal commits an unfair labor practice in violation of §§ 8(a)(5) and 8(a)(1) . . . by refusing to execute the collective bargaining agreement later executed by the union and the multiemployer association. The Court of Appeals for the First Circuit enforced the Board's order. 630 F.2d 25, 105 LRRM 2477 (1980). Both the Board and the Court of appeals recognized that several other Courts of Appeals had previously rejected the Board's position on this issue. We granted certiorari, 450 U.S. 979, to resolve the conflict among the circuits on this important question of federal labor law. We affirm the judgment of the Court of Appeals.

I

The factual findings of the Administrative Law Judge were affirmed by the Board and are undisputed. Petitioner, Charles D. Bonanno Linen Service, Inc. (Bonanno), is a Massachusetts corporation engaged in laundering, renting, and distributing linens and uniforms. Teamsters Local No. 25 (Union) represents its drivers and helpers as well as those of other linen supply companies in the area. For several years, Bonanno has been a member of the New England Linen Supply Association (Association), a group of 10 employers formed to negotiate with the Union as a multi-employer unit and a signatory of the contracts negotiated between the Union and the Association. On February 19, 1975, Bonanno authorized the Association's negotiating committee to represent it in the anticipated negotiations for a new contract. Bonanno's president became a member of the committee.

The Union and the Association held 10 bargaining sessions during March and April. On April 30, the negotiators agreed upon a proposed contract, but four days later the Union members rejected it. By May 15, according to the stipulations of the parties, the Union and the Association had reached an impasse over the method of compensation: the Union demanded that the drivers be paid on commission, while the Association insisted on continuing payment at an hourly rate.

Several subsequent meetings failed to break the impasse. On June 23, the Union initiated a selective strike against Bonanno. In response, most of [the] Association members locked out their drivers. Despite sporadic meetings, the stalemate continued throughout the summer. During this period two of the employers met secretly with the Union, presumably in an effort to reach a separate settlement. These meetings, however, never reached the level of negotiations.

Bonanno hired permanent replacements for all of its striking drivers. On November 21, it notified the Association by letter that it was "withdrawing from the association with respect to negotiations at this time because of an ongoing impasse with Teamsters Local 25." Petr. App., at 58. Bonanno mailed a copy of its revocation letter to the Union and read the letter over the phone to a Union representative.

Soon after Bonanno's putative withdrawal, the Association ended the lockout. It told the Union that it wished to continue multiemployer negotiations. Several negotiating sessions took place between December and April, without Bonanno participating. In the middle of April, the Union abandoned its demand for payment on commission and accepted the Association's offer of a revised hourly wage rate. With this development, the parties quickly agreed on a new contract, dated April 23, 1976, and given retroactive effect to April 18, 1975.

Meanwhile, on April 9, 1976, the Union had filed the present action, alleging that Bonanno's purported withdrawal from the bargaining unit constituted an unfair labor practice. In a letter dated April 29, the Union informed Bonanno that because the Union had never consented to the withdrawal, it considered Bonanno to be bound by the settlement just reached. In a reply letter, Bonanno denied that it was bound by the contract.

An Administrative Law Judge concluded, after a hearing, that no unusual circumstances excused Bonanno's withdrawal from the multi-employer bargaining unit. The Board affirmed, ordering Bonanno to sign and implement the contract retroactively. In a supplemental decision, the Board explained the basis of its decision that Bonanno's attempt to withdraw from the multiemployer was untimely and ineffective. The Court of Appeals enforced the Board's order.

II

The standard for judicial review of the Board's decision in this case was established by *Labor Board* v. *Truck Drivers Union*, 353 U.S. 87, 39 LRRM 2603 (1957) (*Buffalo Linen*). There, the Union struck a single employer during negotiations with a multiemployer bargaining association. The other employers responded with a lockout. Negotiations continued, and an agreement was reached. The Union, claiming that the lockout violated its rights under §§ 7 and 8 of the Act, then filed charges with the Board. The Board rejected the claim, but the Court of Appeals held that the lockout was an unfair practice.

The Court in turn reversed. That the Act did not expressly authorize or deal with multiemployer units or with lockouts in that context was recognized. Nonetheless, multiemployer bargaining had "long antedated the Wagner Act" and had become more common as employers, in the course of complying with their duty to bargain under the Act, "sought through group bargaining to match increased union strength." 353 U.S., at 94–95. Furthermore, at the time of the debates on the Taft-Hartley amendments, Congress had rejected a proposal to limit or outlaw multiemployer bargaining. The debates and their results offered "cogent evidence that in many industries multiemployer bargaining was a vital factor in the effectuation of the national policy of promoting labor peace through strengthened collective bargaining." 353 U.S., at 95.[3] Congress' refusal to intervene indicated that it intended to leave to the Board's specialized judgment the resolution of conflicts between union and employer rights that were bound to arise in multiemployer bargaining. In such situations, the Court said,

---

[3] As the Court of Appeals explained in this case, "Multiemployer bargaining offers advantages to both management and labor. It enables smaller employers to bargain 'on an equal basis with a large union' and avoid 'the competitive disadvantages resulting from non-uniform contractual terms.' At the same time, it facilitates the development of industry-wide, worker benefit programs that employers otherwise might be unable to provide. More generally, multiemployer bargaining encourages both sides to adopt a flexible attitude during negotiations; as the Board explains, employers can make concessions 'without fear that other employers will refuse to make similar concessions to achieve a competitive advantage,' and a union can act similarly 'without fear that the employees will be dissatisfied at not receiving the same benefits which the union might win from other employers.' Brief, at 10. Finally, by permitting the union and employers to concentrate their bargaining resources on the negotiation of a single contract, multiemployer bargaining enhances the efficiency and effectiveness of the collective bargaining process and thereby reduces industrial strife." 630 F.2d, at 28.

"The ultimate problem is the balancing of the conflicting legitimate interests. The function of striking that balance to effectuate national labor policy is often a difficult and delicate responsibility, which the Congress committed primarily to the National Labor Relations Board, subject to limited judicial review." 353 U.S., at 96.

Thus, the Court of Appeals' rejection of the Board's justification of the lockout as an acceptable effort to maintain the integrity of the multiemployer unit and its refusal to accept the lockout as a legitimate response to the whipsaw strike had too narrowly confined the exercise of the Board's discretion. 353 U.S., at 97.

Multiemployer bargaining has continued to be the preferred bargaining mechanism in many industries,[4] and as *Buffalo Linen* predicted, it has raised a variety of problems requiring resolution. One critical question concerns the rights of the union and the employers to terminate the multiemployer bargaining arrangement. Until 1958, the Board permitted both employers and the Union to abandon the unit even in the midst of bargaining. But in *Retail Associates, Inc.*, 120 NLRB 388, 41 LRRM 1502 (1958), the Board announced guidelines for withdrawal from multiemployer units. These rules, which reflect an increasing emphasis on the stability of multiemployer units, permit any party to withdraw prior to the date set for negotiation of a new contract or the date on which negotiations actually begin, provided that adequate notice is given. Once negotiations for a new contract have commenced, however, withdrawal is permitted only if there is "mutual consent" or "unusual circumstances" exist. *Id.*, at 395.

The Board's approach in *Retail Associates* has been accepted in the courts, as have its decisions that unusual circumstances will be found where an employer is subject to extreme financial pressures or where a bargaining unit has become substantially fragmented. But as yet there is no consensus as to whether an impasse in bargaining in a multiemployer unit is an unusual circumstance justifying unilateral withdrawal by the Union or by an employer. After equivocating for a time, the Board squarely held that an impasse is not such an unusual circumstance. *Hi-Way Billboards, Inc.*, 206 NLRB 22, 84 LRRM 1161 (1973). . . .

III

We agree with the Board and with the Court of Appeals. The Board has recognized the voluntary nature of multiemployer bargaining. It neither forces employers into multiemployer units nor erects barriers to withdrawal prior to bargaining. At the same time, it has sought to further the utility of multiemployer bargaining as an instrument of labor peace by limiting the circumstances under which any party may unilaterally withdraw during negotiations. Thus, it has reiterated the view expressed in

[4]A recent survey of major collective bargaining agreements (those covering 1,000 or more employees) found that of 1,536 major agreements, 648 (42%) were multiemployer agreements and that 3,238,400 employees were covered by these agreements. U.S. Bureau of Labor Statistics, Dept. of Labor, Bull. No. 2065, Characteristics of Major Collective Bargaining Agreements—January 1, 1978, at 12, table 1.8 (1980).

Hi-Way Billboards that an impasse is not sufficiently destructive of group bargaining to justify unilateral withdrawal. As a recurring feature in the bargaining process, impasse is only a temporary deadlock or hiatus in negotiations "which in almost all cases is eventually broken either through a change of mind or the application of economic force." *Charles D. Bonanno Linen Service,* 243 NLRB 1093, 1093–1094, 102 LRRM 1001 (1979). Furthermore, an impasse may be "brought about intentionally by one or both parties as a device to further, rather than destroy, the bargaining process." *Id.,* at 1094. Hence, "there is little warrant for regarding an impasse as a rupture of the bargaining relation which leaves the parties free to go their own ways." *Ibid.* As the Board sees it, permitting withdrawal at impasse would as a practical matter undermine the utility of multiemployer bargaining.[8]

Of course, the ground rules for multiemployer bargaining have not come into being overnight. They have evolved and are still evolving, as the Board, employing its expertise in the light of experience, has sought to balance the "conflicting legitimate interests" in pursuit of the "national policy of promoting labor peace through strengthened collective bargaining." *Buffalo Linen, supra,* at 96, 97. The Board might have struck a different balance from the one it has, and it may be that some or all of us would prefer that it had done so. But assessing the significance of impasse and the dynamics of collective bargaining is precisely the kind of judgment that *Buffalo Linen* ruled should be left to the Board. We cannot say that the Board's current resolution of the issue is arbitrary or contrary to law.

If the Board's refusal to accept an impasse, standing alone, as an unusual circumstance warranting withdrawal were the only issue in this case, we would affirm without more. But several Courts of Appeals have rejected *Hi-Way Billboards* on the grounds that impasse may precipitate a strike against one or all members of the unit and that upon impasse the Board permits the union to execute interim agreements with individual employers. These Courts of Appeals consider the possibility of such events as sufficient grounds for any employer in the unit to withdraw.

. . .

The Board's reasons for adhering to its *Hi-Way Billboards* position are telling. They are surely adequate to survive judicial review. First, it is said that strikes and interim agreements often occur in the course of negotiations prior to impasse and that neither tactic is necessarily associated with impasse. Second, it is "vital" to understand that the Board distinguishes "between interim agreements which contemplate adherence to a final unitwide contract and are thus not antithetical to group bargaining and individual agreements which are clearly inconsistent with, and destructive of, group bargaining." 243 NLRB at 1096. In *Sangamo Construction Co.,* 188 NLRB 159, 77 LRRM 1039 (1971), and *Plumbers and Steamfitters*

---

[8]The Board explains that if withdrawal were permitted at impasse, the parties would bargain under the threat of withdrawal by any party who was not completely satisfied with the results of the negotiations. That is, parties could precipitate an impasse in order to escape any agreement less favorable than the one expected. In addition, it is precisely at and during impasse, when bargaining is temporarily replaced by economic warfare, that the need for a stable, predictable bargaining unit becomes acute in order that the parties can weigh the costs and possible benefits of their conduct. Brief for Respondent 24–25.

Union No. 323 (P.H.C. Mechanical Contractors), 191 NLRB 592, 77 LRRM 1769 (1971), the agreements arrived at with the struck employers were only temporary: both the union and the employer executing the interim agreement were bound by any settlement resulting from multiemployer bargaining. "[I]n both these cases, since the early signers maintained a vested interest in the outcome of final union-association negotiations, the multiemployer unit was neither fragmented nor significantly weakened," 243 NLRB at 1096, and unilateral withdrawal was not justified.

On the other hand, where the union, not content with interim agreements that expire with the execution of a unit-wide contract, executes separate agreements that will survive unit negotiations, the union has so "effectively fragmented and destroyed the integrity of the bargaining unit," *id.,* as to create an "unusual circumstance" under *Retail Associates* rules. Cf. *Typographic Service Co.,* 238 NLRB 1565, 99 LRRM 1649 (1978). Furthermore, the Board has held that the execution of separate agreements that would permit either the union or the employer to escape the binding effect of an agreement resulting from group bargaining is a refusal to bargain and an unfair labor practice on the part of both the union and any employer executing such an agreement. *Teamsters Union Local No. 378 (Olympia Automobile Dealers Ass'n),* 243 NLRB 1086, 102 LRRM 1007 (1979). The remaining members of the unit thus can insist that parties remain subject to unit negotiations in accordance with their original understanding.

The Board therefore emphatically rejects the proposition that the negotiation of truly interim, temporary agreements, as distinguished from separate, final contracts, are "inconsistent with the concept of multiemployer bargaining units." *Charles D. Bonanno Linen Service,* 243 NLRB 1093, 1096, 102 LRRM 1001 (1979). Although interim agreements establish terms and conditions of employment for one or more employer members of the unit pending the outcome of renewed group bargaining, all employers, including those executing interim agreements, have an "equivalent stake" in the final outcome because "the resulting group agreement would then apply to all employers, including each signer of an interim agreement." *Ibid.* Such interim arrangements "preclude a finding that the early signers had withdrawn from the unit." *Ibid.* Although the Board concedes that interim agreements exert economic pressure on struck employers, this fact should no more warrant withdrawal than the refusal of one employer to join with others in a lockout. In any event, the Board's view is that interim agreements, on balance, tend to deter rather than promote unit fragmentation since they preserve a continuing mutual interest by all employer members in a final association-wide contract.

The Board also rests on this Court's admonition that the Board should balance "conflicting legitimate interests" rather than economic weapons and bargaining strength. Its conclusion is that the interest in unit stability, recognized as a major consideration by both *Buffalo Linen* and *NLRB* v. *Brown,* 380 U.S. 278, 58 LRRM 2663 (1965), adequately justifies enforcement of the obligation to bargain despite the execution of a temporary agreement.

Of course, no interim or separate agreements were executed in this case. But neither did the impasse initiate any right to execute an agreement inconsistent with the duty to abide by the results of group bargaining. Some Courts of Appeals, taking a different view of the interests involved, question the legitimacy of enforcing the duty to bargain where impasse has occurred and interim agreements have been or may be executed. We think the Board has confined itself within the zone of discretion entrusted to it by Congress. The balance it has struck is not inconsistent with the terms or purposes of the Act, and its decision should therefore be enforced.

CHIEF JUSTICE BURGER and JUSTICE REHNQUIST dissented.

Note on Unit Changes and Other Methods of Recognition

Bonanno Linen presents an example of a unit configuration determined by voluntary agreement of the parties. Once that unit is established, however, it may not be changed except in the limited circumstances described in the opinion. The factors which go into unit determinations generally, whether by voluntary agreement or through a Board certification, are not fixed for all time. For example, suppose Enderby built a large warehousing facility, adjacent to its factories, to handle warehousing for Enderby as well as other companies. Would newly hired warehouse employees come within the union's certification? This depends whether the change is so substantial that it impairs the validity of the original unit determination. These cases are usually discussed under the rubric of "accretions" to existing units, a matter which we leave to your own research should the need arise. See, for example, *Weatherite Co.*, 261 NLRB 667, 110 LRRM 1108 (1982); *NLRB v. St. Regis Paper Co.*, 674 F.2d 104, 109 LRRM 3327 (1st Cir. 1982). Changes in the employer's status, for example through corporate merger, are discussed in Chapter 5 in connection with the successorship doctrine.

D. ALTERNATIVE METHODS OF ACHIEVING RECOGNITION

1. VOLUNTARY RECOGNITION

You saw in the Enderby problem that the union began its organizing campaign by sending the employer a letter demanding recognition (a facsimile of the letter was set out at page 110). Perhaps you are wondering whether this isn't an idle act, as the employer is likely to ignore the request or simply reply with a resounding "no." In fact, as you will learn in the next subsection, the employer generally may refuse to recognize the union without giving any reasons at all. But even if the employer declines recognition, the demand may prove useful, for it is a means of imputing to the employer knowledge of the union's organizing activity. Establishing such knowledge may be essential if the union later files charges of unlawful employer conduct in response to the union activity. We will discuss this in greater detail in Chapter 3.

There may, however, be situations in which it is to the employer's advantage to grant voluntary recognition to the union. If the employer believes that the union in fact has majority support and that recognition is inevitable, it may make sense to recognize the union directly and begin negotiations. This avoids a costly election campaign, which in the long run may be detrimental to labor relations. Or the employer may believe that if this union fails to secure recognition, the employees will turn to a more militant union. If the employer thinks unionization of his employees is inevitable, he may welcome representation by a particular union which happens to represent employees at his other plants and with which he enjoys a relatively harmonious and constructive bargaining relationship. Finally, the employer may be under economic pressure to recognize the union.

But voluntary recognition poses threats to the principle of employee self-determination. Suppose the employer knows his employees prefer Union A, a more militant organization. Does the employer's recognition of Union B interfere with his employees' rights under Section 7 of the Act? Are there ethical constraints upon a lawyer's advising his client to recognize one union in the face of a potential claim of another? If Union A demands recognition, may the employer hold a conference with the union to see what kind of bargain could be struck if recognition were granted? May it condition recognition on reaching a favorable agreement? Should the employees be told about such a conference? Does the union which agrees to this arrangement violate any duty to the employees? What ethical problems are posed for the union or management lawyer who advises or participates in such a procedure?

We treat the matter of voluntary recognition further in Chapter 3 because we think it may be better understood in the context of the employer's overall response to a union-organizing campaign and the devices he may use to undermine the union's majority status. However, it is worthwhile for you to understand at this point a few fundamental limitations on the use of voluntary recognition.

First, the union seeking voluntary recognition must in fact have majority support; it would be prudent for the union in such a case to utilize a neutral third party to verify its card count, as suggested in the model demand letter. If the employer begins to negotiate with the union before it attains majority status, Section 8(a)(2) of the Act is violated. It makes no difference that the union eventually manages to secure majority support; it is presumed that such support was encouraged by the premature, unlawful recognition. The leading case on this point is *ILGWU* v. *NLRB*, 366 U.S. 731, 48 LRRM 2251 (1961), known in the trade as *Bernhard-Altmann*. We shall return to it in Chapter 3.

Second, the employer in an initial organizing situation may not recognize one union once another files a valid election petition with the Board, *Bruckner Nursing Home*, 262 NLRB No. 115, 110 LRRM 1374 (1982). But it may continue to negotiate with an incumbent union with which it has an established bargaining relationship even in the face of such a petition,

RCA Del Caribe, Inc., 262 NLRB No. 116, 110 LRRM 1369 (1982). This matter is discussed further in Chapter 3 at page 269.

Finally, the union demanding recognition must not have its genesis in employer support. The concept of a "company dominated" union arose at a time when some employers created "sweetheart" unions designed to thwart the organizing efforts of unions wholly independent of the employer. The line between unlawful assistance, barred under Section 8(a)(2), and cooperation with an existing employee group is a difficult one to draw and is postponed until Chapter 3. Bear in mind that an unlawfully assisted union may be barred from recognition even through the channels of an NLRB election and certification.

2. RECOGNITION THROUGH A BARGAINING ORDER

NLRB v. Gissel Packing Co., Inc.

Supreme Court of the United States, 1969
395 U.S. 575, 71 LRRM 2481

[*Gissel* involves four cases consolidated on appeal—three from the Fourth Circuit and one from the First Circuit. All four raise the same basic questions as to the authority of the Board to mandate recognition through a bargaining order. The First Circuit case involves additional issues as to the scope of protection accorded by Section 8(c) of the Act to statements made by the employer during the organizing campaign. In our presentation of *Gissel* in this chapter we omit discussion of the free speech issue, and shall return to this aspect of the case in Chapter 3.]

MR. CHIEF JUSTICE WARREN delivered the opinion of the Court.

These cases involve the extent of an employer's duty under the National Labor Relations Act to recognize a union that bases its claim to representative status solely on the possession of union authorization cards, and the steps an employer may take, particularly with regard to the scope and content of statements he may make, in legitimately resisting such card-based recognition. The specific questions facing us here are whether the duty to bargain can arise without a Board election under the Act; whether union authorization cards, if obtained from a majority of employees without misrepresentation or coercion, are reliable enough generally to provide a valid, alternate route to majority status; whether a bargaining order is an appropriate and authorized remedy where an employer rejects a card majority while at the same time committing unfair labor practices that tend to undermine the union's majority and make a fair election an unlikely possibility; and whether certain specific statements made by an employer to his employees constituted such an election-voiding unfair labor practice and thus fell outside the protection of the First Amendment and § 8(c) of the Act. For reasons given below, we answer each of these questions in the affirmative.

I. . . . In each of the cases from the Fourth Circuit, the course of action followed by the Union and the employer and the Board's response were similar. In each case, the Union waged an organizational campaign, obtained authorization cards from a majority of employees in the appropriate bargaining unit, and then, on the basis of the cards, demanded recognition by the employer. All three employers refused to bargain on the ground that authorization cards were inherently unreliable indicators of employee desires; and they either embarked on, or continued, vigorous antiunion campaigns that gave rise to numerous unfair labor practice charges. In *Gissel,* where the employer's campaign began almost at the outset of the Union's organizational drive, the Union (petitioner in No. 691), did not seek an election, but instead filed three unfair labor practice charges against the employer, for refusing to bargain in violation of §8(a)(5), for coercion and intimidation of employees in violation of § 8(a)(1), and for discharge of Union adherents in violation of § 8(a)(3). In *Heck's* an election sought by the Union was never held because of nearly identical unfair labor practice charges later filed by the Union as a result of the employer's antiunion campaign, initiated after the Union's recognition demand. And in *General Steel,* an election petitioned for by the Union and won by the employer was set aside by the Board because of the unfair labor practices committed by the employer in the pre-election period.

In each case, the Board's primary response was an order to bargain directed at the employers, despite the absence of an election in *Gissel* and *Heck's* and the employer's victory in *General Steel.* More specifically, the Board found in each case (1) that the Union had obtained valid authorization cards[4] from a majority of the employees in the bargaining unit and was thus entitled to represent the employees for collective bargaining purposes; and (2) that the employer's refusal to bargain with the Union in violation of § 8(a)(5) was motivated, not by a "good faith" doubt of the Union's majority status, but by a desire to gain time to dissipate that status. The Board based its conclusion as to the lack of good faith doubt on the fact that the employers had committed substantial unfair labor practices during their antiunion campaign efforts to resist recognition. Thus, the Board found that all three employers had engaged in restraint and coercion of employees in violation of § 8(a)(1)—in *Gissel,* for coercively interrogating employees about Union activities, threatening them with discharge, and promising them benefits; in *Heck's,* for coercively interrogating employees, threatening reprisals, creating the appearance of surveillance, and offering benefits for opposing the Union; and in *General Steel,* for coercive interrogation and threats of reprisals, including discharge. In addition, the Board found that the employers in *Gissel* and *Heck's* had wrongfully discharged employees for engaging in Union activities in violation of § 8(a)(3). And, because the employers had rejected

[4]The cards used in all four campaigns in Nos. 573 and 691 and in the one drive in No. 585 unambiguously authorized the Union to represent the signing employee for collective bargaining purposes; there was no reference to elections. Typical of the cards was the one used in the Charleston campaign in *Heck's,* and it stated in relevant part:

"Desiring to become a member of the above Union of the International Brotherhood of Teamsters, Chauffeurs, Warehousemen and Helpers of America, I hereby make application for admission to membership. I hereby authorize you, your agents or representatives to act for me as collective bargaining agent on all matters pertaining to rates of pay, hours, or any other conditions of employment."

the card-based bargaining demand in bad faith, the Board found that all three had refused to recognize the Unions in violation of § 8(a)(5).

Only in *General Steel* was there any objection by an employer to the validity of the cards and the manner in which they had been solicited, and the doubt raised by the evidence was resolved in the following manner. The customary approach of the Board in dealing with allegations of misrepresentation by the Union and misunderstanding by the employees of the purpose for which the cards were being solicited has been set out in *Cumberland Shoe Corp.*, 144 NLRB 1268 (1963) and reaffirmed in *Levi Strauss & Co.*, 172 NLRB No. 57, 68 LRRM 1338 (1968). Under the *Cumberland Shoe* doctrine, if the card itself is unambiguous (*i.e.,* states on its face that the signer authorizes the Union to represent the employee for collective bargaining purposes and not to seek an election), it will be counted unless it is proved that the employee was told that the card was to be used *solely* for the purpose of obtaining an election. In *General Steel*, the trial examiner considered the allegations of misrepresentation at length and, applying the Board's customary analysis, rejected the claims with findings that were adopted by the Board and are reprinted in the margin.[5]

Consequently, the Board ordered the companies to cease and desist from their unfair labor practices, to offer reinstatement and back pay to the employees who had been discriminatorily discharged, to bargain with the Unions on request, and to post the appropriate notices.

On appeal, the Court of Appeals for the Fourth Circuit, in *per curiam* opinions in each of the three cases (398 F.2d 336, 337, 339), sustained the Board's findings as to the §§ 8(a)(1) and (3) violations, but rejected the Board's findings that the employers' refusal to bargain violated § 8(a)(5) and declined to enforce those portions of the Board's orders directing the respondent companies to bargain in good faith. The court based its § 8(a)(5) rulings on [certain] 1967 decisions raising the same fundamental issues. The court in those cases held that the 1947 Taft-Hartley amendments to the Act, which permitted the Board to resolve representation disputes by certification under § 9(c) only by secret ballot election, withdrew from the Board the authority to order an employer to bargain under § 8(a)(5) on the basis of cards, in the absence of NLRB certification, unless the employer knows independently of the cards that there is in fact no representation dispute. The court held that the cards themselves were so inherently unreliable that their use gave an employer virtually an automatic, good faith claim that such a dispute existed, for which a secret

---

[5]"Accordingly, I reject Respondent's contention 'that if a man is told that his card will be secret, or will be shown only to the Labor Board for the purpose of obtaining election, that this is the absolute equivalent of telling him that it will be used "only" for purposes of obtaining an election.'

. . . .

"With respect to the 97 employees named in the attached Appendix B Respondent in its brief contends, in substance, that their cards should be rejected because each of these employees was told *one or more* of the following: (1) that the card would be used to get an election (2) that he had the right to vote either way, even though he signed the card (3) that the card would be kept secret and not shown to anybody except to the Board in order to get an election. For reasons heretofore explicated, I conclude that these statements, singly or jointly, do not foreclose use of the cards for the purpose designated on their face."

election was necessary. Thus, these rulings established that a company could not be ordered to bargain unless (1) there was no question about a Union's majority status (either because the employer agreed the cards were valid or had conducted his own poll so indicating), or (2) the employers' §§ 8(a)(1) and (3) unfair labor practices committed during the representation campaign were so extensive and pervasive that a bargaining order was the only available Board remedy irrespective of a card majority.

II. In urging us to reverse the Fourth Circuit and to affirm the First Circuit, the National Labor Relations Board contends that we should approve its interpretation and administration of the duties and obligations imposed by the Act in authorization card cases. The Board argues (1) that unions have never been limited under § 9(c) of either the Wagner Act or the 1947 amendments to certified elections as the sole route to attaining representative status. Unions may, the Board contends, impose a duty to bargain on the employer under § 8(a)(5) by reliance on other evidence of majority employee support, such as authorization cards. Contrary to the Fourth Circuit's holding, the Board asserts, the 1947 amendments did not eliminate the alternative routes to majority status. The Board contends (2) that the cards themselves, when solicited in accordance with Board standards which adequately insure against union misrepresentation, are sufficiently reliable indicators of employee desires to support a bargaining order against an employer who refuses to recognize a card majority in violation of § 8(a)(5). The Board argues (3) that a bargaining order is the appropriate remedy for the § 8(a)(5) violation, where the employer commits other unfair labor practices that tend to undermine union support and render a fair election improbable.

Relying on these three assertions, the Board asks us to approve its current practice, which is briefly as follows. When confronted by a recognition demand based on possession of cards allegedly signed by a majority of his employees, an employer need not grant recognition immediately, but may, unless he has knowledge independently of the cards that the union has a majority, decline the union's request and insist on an election, either by requesting the union to file an election petition or by filing such a petition himself under § 9(c)(1)(B). If, however, the employer commits independent and substantial unfair labor practices disruptive of election conditions, the Board may withhold the election or set it aside, and issue instead a bargaining order as a remedy for the various violations. A bargaining order will not issue, of course, if the union obtained the cards through misrepresentation or coercion or if the employer's unfair labor practices are unrelated generally to the representation campaign. Conversely, the employers in these cases urge us to adopt the views of the Fourth Circuit. . . .

[The Court traced the Board's development of the bargaining order doctrine. The Board's initial position, in *Joy Silk* (85 NLRB 1263 (1949)), allowed the employer to reject a bargaining demand if he had a "good faith doubt" as to the union's majority; failure to come forward with a compelling reason for refusing to recognize the union could be evidence of bad faith. In *Aaron Brothers*, 158 NLRB 1077, 62 LRRM 1160 (1966), the Board made clear that the burden was on the General Counsel to show bad faith and that the employer need not give reasons for rejecting a bargaining demand. But even under *Aaron Brothers*, independent evidence of the union's majority might show that the employer's refusal was in bad faith.]

Although the Board's brief before this Court generally followed the approach as set out in *Aaron Brothers, supra*, the Board announced at oral argument that it had virtually abandoned the *Joy Silk* doctrine altogether. Under the Board's current practice, an employer's good faith doubt is largely irrelevant, and the key to the issuance of a bargaining order is the commission of serious unfair labor practices that interfere with the election processes and tend to preclude the holding of a fair election. Thus, an employer can insist that a union go to an election, regardless of his subjective motivation, so long as he is not guilty of misconduct; he need give no affirmative reasons for rejecting a recognition request, and he can demand an election with a simple "no comment" to the union. The Board pointed out, however, (1) that an employer could not refuse to bargain if he *knew*, through a personal poll for instance, that a majority of his employees supported the union, and (2) that an employer could not refuse recognition initially because of questions as to the appropriateness of the unit and then later claim, as an afterthought, that he doubted the union's strength.

[The Court then addressed a further contention, pressed by the petitioning union in one of the Fourth Circuit cases but not by the Board, that the employer confronted with a bargaining demand may not simply reject it, but must himself file a petition for an election. Since the Court was able to resolve the case on the basis of the employer's interference with a fair election, it did not reach the union's contention. It thus reserved judgment on the appropriateness of a bargaining order where there is no interference with a fair election.]

III. A. The first issue facing us is whether a union can establish a bargaining obligation by means other than a Board election and whether the validity of alternate routes to majority status, such as cards, was affected by the 1947 Taft-Hartley amendments. The most commonly traveled route for a union to obtain recognition as the exclusive bargaining representative of an unorganized group of employees is through the Board's election and certification procedures under § 9(c) of the Act; it is also, from the Board's point of view, the preferred route. A union is not limited to a Board election, however, for, in addition to § 9, the present Act provides in § 8(a)(5), as did the Wagner Act in § 8(5), that "[i]t shall be an unfair labor practice for an employer . . . to refuse to bargain collectively with the representatives of his employees, subject to the provisions of section 9(a)." Since § 9(a), in both the Wagner Act and the present Act, refers to the representative as the one "designated or selected" by a majority of the employees without specifying precisely how that representative is to be chosen, it was early recognized that an employer had a duty to bargain whenever the union representative presented "convincing evidence of majority support." Almost from the inception of the Act, then, it was recognized that a union did not have to be certified as the winner of a Board election to invoke a bargaining obligation; it could establish majority status by other means under the unfair labor practice provision of § 8(a)(5)—by showing convincing support, for instance, by a union-called strike or strike vote, or, as here, by possession of cards signed by a majority of the employees authorizing the union to represent them for collective bargaining purposes.

We have consistently accepted this interpretation of the Wagner Act and the present Act, particularly as to the use of authorization cards. . . . We see no reason to reject this approach to bargaining obligations now, and we find unpersuasive the Fourth Circuit's view that the 1947 Taft-Hartley amendments, enacted some nine years before our decision in *United Mine Workers, supra,* require us to disregard that case. Indeed, the 1947 amendments weaken rather than strengthen the position taken by the employers here and the Fourth Circuit below. An early version of the bill in the House would have amended § 8(5) of the Wagner Act to permit the Board to find a refusal-to-bargain violation only where an employer had failed to bargain with a union "currently recognized by the employer or certified as such [through an election] under section 9." Section 8(a)(5) of H.R. 3020, 80th Cong., 1st Sess. (1947). The proposed change, which would have eliminated the use of cards, was rejected in Conference (H.R. Conf. Rep. No. 510, 80th Cong., 1st Sess., 41 (1947)), however, and we cannot make a similar change in the Act simply because, as the employers assert, Congress did not expressly approve the use of cards in rejecting the House amendment. Nor can we accept the Fourth Circuit's conclusion that the change was wrought when Congress amended § 9(c) to make election the sole basis for *certification* by eliminating the phrase "any other suitable method to ascertain such representatives," under which the Board had occasionally used cards as a certification basis. A certified union has the benefit of numerous special privileges which are not accorded unions recognized voluntarily or under a bargaining order[14] and which, Congress could determine, should not be dispensed unless a union has survived the crucible of a secret ballot election.

The employers rely finally on the addition to § 9(c) of subparagraph (B), which allows an employer to petition for an election whenever "one or more individuals or labor organizations have presented to him a claim to be recognized as the representative defined in section 9(a)." That provision was not added, as the employers assert, to give them an absolute right to an election at any time; rather, it was intended, as the legislative history indicates, to allow them, after being asked to bargain, to test out their doubts as to a union's majority in a secret election which they would then presumably not cause to be set aside by illegal antiunion activity. We agree with the Board's assertion here that there is no suggestion that Congress intended § 9(c)(1)(B) to relieve any employer of his § 8(a)(5) bargaining

---

[14] *E.g.,* protection against the filing of new election petitions by rival unions or employees seeking decertification for 12 months (§ 9(c)(3)), protection for a reasonable period, usually one year, against any disruption of the bargaining relationship because of claims that the union no longer represents a majority (see *Brooks* v. *NLRB,* 348 U.S. 96 (1954)), protection against recognitional picketing by rival unions (§ 8(b)(4)(C)), and freedom from the restrictions placed in work assignments disputes by § 8(b)(4)(D), and on recognitional and organizational picketing by § 8(b)(7).

obligation where, without good faith, he engaged in unfair labor practices disruptive of the Board's election machinery. And we agree that the policies reflected in § 9(c)(1)(B) fully support the Board's present administration of the Act, for an employer can insist on a secret ballot election, unless, in the words of the Board, he engages "in contemporaneous unfair labor practices likely to destroy the union's majority and seriously impede the election." Brief for Petitioner, the Board, in No. 573, p. 36.

In short, we hold that the 1947 amendments did not restrict an employer's duty to bargain under § 8(a)(5) solely to those unions whose representative status is certified after a Board election.

B. We next consider the question whether authorization cards are such inherently unreliable indicators of employee desires that, whatever the validity of other alternate routes to representative status, the cards themselves may never be used to determine a union's majority and to support an order to bargain. In this context, the employers urge us to take the step the 1947 amendments and their legislative history indicate Congress did not take, namely, to rule out completely the use of cards in the bargaining arena. Even if we do not unhesitatingly accept the Fourth Circuit's view in the matter, the employers argue, at the very least we should overrule the *Cumberland Shoe* doctrine and establish stricter controls over the solicitation of the cards by union representatives.[18]

The objections to the use of cards voiced by the employers and the Fourth Circuit boil down to two contentions: (1) that, as contrasted with the election procedure, the cards cannot accurately reflect an employee's wishes, either because an employer has not had a chance to present his views and thus a chance to insure that the employee choice was an informed one, or because the choice was the result of group pressures and not individual decision made in the privacy of a voting booth; and (2) that quite apart from the election comparison, the cards are too often obtained through misrepresentation and coercion which compound the cards' inherent inferiority to the election process. Neither contention is persuasive, and each proves too much. The Board itself has recognized, and continues to do so here, that secret elections are generally the most satisfactory—indeed the preferred—method of ascertaining whether a union has majority support. The acknowledged superiority of the election process, however, does not mean that cards are thereby rendered totally invalid, for where an employer engages in conduct disruptive of the election process, cards may be the most effective—perhaps the only— way of assuring employee choice. As for misrepresentation, in any specific case of alleged irregularity in the solicitation of the cards, the proper course is to apply the Board's customary standards (to be discussed more fully below) and rule that there was no majority if the standards were not satisfied. It does not follow that because there are some instances of irregularity, the cards can never be used; otherwise, an employer could

[18]In dealing with the reliability of cards, we should re-emphasize what issues we are not confronting. . . . [A] union's right to rely on cards as a freely interchangeable substitute for elections where there has been no election interference is not put in issue here; we need only decide whether the cards are reliable enough to support a bargaining order where a fair election probably could not have been held, or where an election that was held was in fact set aside.

put off his bargaining obligation indefinitely through continuing interference with elections.

That the cards, though admittedly inferior to the election process, can adequately reflect employee sentiment when that process has been impeded, needs no extended discussion, for the employers' contentions cannot withstand close examination. The employers argue that their employees cannot make an informed choice because the card drive will be over before the employer has had a chance to present his side of the unionization issues. Normally, however, the union will inform the employer of its organization drive early in order to subject the employer to the unfair labor practice provisions of the Act; the union must be able to show the employer's awareness of the drive in order to prove that his contemporaneous conduct constituted unfair labor practices on which a bargaining order can be based if the drive is ultimately successful. Thus, in all of the cases here but the Charleston campaign in *Heck's* the employer, whether informed by the union or not, was aware of the union's organizing drive almost at the outset and began its antiunion campaign at that time; and even in the *Heck's* Charleston case, where the recognition demand came about a week after the solicitation began, the employer was able to deliver a speech before the union obtained a majority. Further, the employers argue that without a secret ballot an employee may, in a card drive, succumb to group pressures or sign simply to get the union "off his back" and then be unable to change his mind as he would be free to do once inside a voting booth. But the same pressures are likely to be equally present in an election, for election cases arise most often with small bargaining units where virtually every voter's sentiments can be carefully and individually canvassed. And no voter, of course, can change his mind after casting a ballot in an election even though he may think better of his choice shortly thereafter.

The employers' second complaint, that the cards are too often obtained through misrepresentation and coercion, must be rejected also in view of the Board's present rules for controlling card solicitation, which we view as adequate to the task where the cards involved state their purpose clearly and unambiguously on their face. We would be closing our eyes to obvious difficulties, of course, if we did not recognize that there have been abuses, primarily arising out of misrepresentations by union organizers as to whether the effect of signing a card was to designate the union to represent the employee for collective bargaining purposes or merely to authorize it to seek an election to determine that issue. And we would be equally blind if we did not recognize that various courts of appeals and commentators have differed significantly as to the effectiveness of the Board's *Cumberland Shoe* doctrine to cure such abuses. . . .

We need make no decision as to the conflicting approaches used with regard to dual-purpose cards, for in each of the five organization campaigns in the four cases before us the cards used were single-purpose cards, stating clearly and unambiguously on their face that the signer designated the union as his representative. And even the view forcefully voiced by the Fourth Circuit below that unambiguous cards as well present too many opportunities for misrepresentation comes before us somewhat weakened in view of the fact that there were no allegations of irregularities in four of those five campaigns (*Gissel,* the two *Heck's* campaigns, and *Sinclair*). Only in *General Steel* did the employer challenge the cards on the basis of misrepresentations. There, the trial examiner, after hearing testimony from over 100 employees and applying the traditional Board approach (see n. 5, *supra*), concluded that "all of these employees not only intended, but were fully aware, that they were thereby designating the Union as their representative." Thus, the sole question before us, raised in only one of the four cases here, is whether the *Cumberland Shoe* doctrine is an adequate rule under the Act for assuring employee free choice.

In resolving the conflict among the circuits in favor of approving the Board's *Cumberland* rule, we think it sufficient to point out that employees should be bound by the clear language of what they sign unless that language is deliberately and clearly canceled by a union adherent with words calculated to direct the signer to disregard and forget the language above his signature. There is nothing inconsistent in handing an employee a card that says the signer authorizes the union to represent him and then telling him that the card will probably be used first to get an election. Elections have been, after all, and will continue to be, held in the vast majority of cases; the union will still have to have the signatures of 30 percent of the employees when an employer rejects a bargaining demand and insists that the union seek an election. We cannot agree with the employers here that employees as a rule are too unsophisticated to be bound by what they sign unless expressly told that their act of signing represents something else. . . .

We agree, however, with the Board's own warnings in *Levi Strauss & Co.,* 172 NLRB No. 57, 68 LRRM 1338, 1341, and n. 7 (1968), that in hearing testimony concerning a card challenge, trial examiners should not neglect their obligation to ensure employee free choice by a too easy mechanical application of the *Cumberland* rule.[27] We also accept the observation that employees are more likely than not, many months after a card drive and in response to questions by company counsel, to give testimony damaging to the union, particularly where company officials have previously threatened reprisals for union activity in violation of § 8(a)(1). We therefore reject any rule that requires a probe of an employee's subjective motivations as involving an endless and unreliable inquiry. We nevertheless feel that the trial examiner's findings in *General Steel* (see n. 5, *supra*) represent the limits of the *Cumberland* rule's application. We emphasize that the Board should be careful to guard against an approach any more rigid than that in *General Steel*. And we reiterate that

[27]In explaining and reaffirming the *Cumberland Shoe* doctrine in the context of unambiguous cards, the Board stated:

"Thus the fact that employees are told in the course of solicitation that an election is contemplated, or that a purpose of the card is to make an election possible, provides in our view *insufficent* basis in itself for vitiating unambiguously worded authorization cards on the theory of misrepresentation. A different situation is presented, of course, where union organizers solicit cards on the explicit or indirectly expressed representation that they will use such cards *only* for an election and subsequently seek to use them for a different purpose. . . ."

nothing we say here indicates our approval of the *Cumberland Shoe* rule when applied to ambiguous, dual-purpose cards. . . .

C. Remaining before us is the propriety of a bargaining order as a remedy for a § 8(a)(5) refusal to bargain where an employer has committed independent unfair labor practices which have made the holding of a fair election unlikely or which have in fact undermined a union's majority and caused an election to be set aside. We have long held that the Board is not limited to a cease-and-desist order in such cases, but has the authority to issue a bargaining order without first requiring the union to show that it has been able to maintain its majority status. And we have held that the Board has the same authority even where it is clear that the union, which once had possession of cards from a majority of the employees, represents only a minority when the bargaining order is entered. We see no reason now to withdraw this authority from the Board. If the Board could enter only a cease-and-desist order and direct an election or a rerun, it would in effect be rewarding the employer and allowing him "to profit from [his] own wrongful refusal to bargain," while at the same time severely curtailing the employees' right freely to determine whether they desire a representative. The employer could continue to delay or disrupt the election processes and put off indefinitely his obligation to bargain;[30] and any election held under these circumstances would not be likely to demonstrate the employees' true undistorted desires.[31]

The employers argue that the Board has ample remedies, over and above the cease-and-desist order, to control employer misconduct. The Board can, they assert, direct the companies to mail notices to employees, to read notices to employees during plant time and to give the union access to employees during working time at the plant, or it can seek a court injunctive order under § 10(j) as a last resort. In view of the Board's power, they conclude, the bargaining order is an unnecessarily harsh remedy that needlessly prejudices employees' § 7 rights solely for the purpose of punishing or restraining an employer. Such an argument

---

[30]The Board indicates here that its records show that in the period between January and June 1968, the median time between the filing of an unfair labor practice charge and a Board decision in a contested case was 388 days. But the employer can do more than just put off his bargaining obligation by seeking to slow down the Board's administrative processes. He can also affect the outcome of a rerun election by delaying tactics, for figures show that the longer the time between a tainted election and a rerun, the less are the union's chances of reversing the outcome of the first election. See n. 31, *infra*.

[31]A study of 20,153 elections held between 1960 and 1962 shows that in the 267 cases where rerun elections were held over 30% were won by the party who caused the election to be set aside. See Pollitt, *NLRB Re-Run Elections: A Study*, 41 N.C.L. REV. 209, 212 (1963). The study shows further that certain unfair labor practices are more effective to destroy election conditions for a longer period of time than others. For instance, in cases involving threats to close or transfer plant operations, the union won the rerun only 29% of the time, while threats to eliminate benefits or refuse to deal with the union if elected seemed less irremediable with the union winning the rerun 75% of the time. *Id.*, at 215–216. Finally, time appears to be a factor. The figures suggest that if a rerun is held too soon after the election before the effects of the unfair labor practices have worn off, or too long after the election when interest in the union may have waned, the chances for a changed result occurring are not as good as they are if the rerun is held sometime in between those periods. Thus, the study showed that if the rerun is held within 30 days of the election or over nine months after, the chances that a different result will occur are only one in five; when the rerun is held within 30–60 days after the election, the chances for a changed result are two in five. *Id.*, at 221.

ignores that a bargaining order is designed as much to remedy past election damage as it is to deter future misconduct. If an employer has succeeded in undermining a union's strength and destroying the laboratory conditions necessary for a fair election, he may see no need to violate a cease-and-desist order by further unlawful activity. The damage will have been done, and perhaps the only fair way to effectuate employee rights is to re-establish the conditions as they existed before the employer's unlawful campaign. There is, after all, nothing permanent in a bargaining order, and if, after the effects of the employer's acts have worn off, the employees clearly desire to disavow the union, they can do so by filing a representation petition. . . .

Before considering whether the bargaining orders were appropriately entered in these cases, we should summarize the factors that go into such a determination. Despite our reversal of the Fourth Circuit below in Nos. 573 and 691 on all major issues, the actual area of disagreement between our position here and that of the Fourth Circuit is not large as a practical matter. While refusing to validate the general use of a bargaining order in reliance on cards, the Fourth Circuit nevertheless left open the possibility of imposing a bargaining order, without need of inquiry into majority status on the basis of cards or otherwise, in "exceptional" cases marked by "outrageous" and "pervasive" unfair labor practices. Such an order would be an appropriate remedy for those practices, the court noted, if they are of "such a nature that their coercive effects cannot be eliminated by the application of traditional remedies, with the result that a fair and reliable election cannot be had."

The only effect of our holding here is to approve the Board's use of the bargaining order in less extraordinary cases marked by less pervasive practices which nontheless still have the tendency to undermine majority strength and impede the election processes. The Board's authority to issue such an order on a lesser showing of employer misconduct is appropriate, we should reemphasize, where there is also a showing that at one point the union had a majority; in such a case, of course, effectuating ascertainable employee free choice becomes as important a goal as deterring employer misbehavior. In fashioning a remedy in the exercise of its discretion, then, the Board can properly take into consideration the extensiveness of an employer's unfair practices in terms of their past effect on election conditions and the likelihood of their recurrence in the future. If the Board finds that the possibility of erasing the effects of past practices and of ensuring a fair election (or a fair rerun) by the use of traditional remedies, though present, is slight and that employee sentiment once expressed through cards would, on balance, be better protected by a bargaining order, then such an order should issue.

We emphasize that under the Board's remedial power there is still a third category of minor or less extensive unfair labor practices, which, because of their minimal impact on the election machinery, will not sustain a bargaining order. There is, the Board says, no *per se* rule that the commission of any unfair practice will automatically result in a § 8(a)(5) violation and the issuance of an order to bargain. . . .

Notes

1. *Extent of election interference necessary to support a bargaining order.* With the Court's general sanction of the bargaining order remedy, the critical question for the practitioner is the magnitude of employer misconduct that will support such relief. As indicated in Part III, C, of the opinion, *Gissel* does not endorse the use of a bargaining order where the employer's misconduct is likely to have only a "slight" impact on a new election. At the other extreme, in cases involving "outrageous" and "pervasive" unfair labor practices, the bargaining order may issue even without a showing of majority support through authorization cards. It is not easy to draw the line between each of these categories and the one in between, involving "less pervasive practices which nonetheless still have the tendency to undermine majority strength and impede the election process."

In Chapter 3 we shall explore in depth various examples of employer misconduct that may violate the Act and interfere with a fair election. As you consider them, you will have an opportunity to decide whether, separately or cumulatively, they would warrant a *Gissel* bargaining order.

2. *Linden Lumber. Gissel* left unanswered whether an employer who engages in no misconduct which would intefere with a fair election may nevertheless be subject to a bargaining order where the union presents him with compelling evidence of its majority status. In cases prior to *Gissel,* under the *Joy Silk* and *Aaron Brothers* approach, the Board had held that a bargaining order would be appropriate in some such circumstances, for example, where an employer reneged on an agreement to abide by a card check. See *Snow & Sons,* 134 NLRB 709, 49 LRRM 1228 (1961), *enf'd,* 308 F.2d 687, 51 LRRM 2199 (9th Cir. 1962), and *Harding Glass Industries,* 216 NLRB 331, 88 LRRM 1506 (1975).

In a five-to-four decision, the Court in *Linden Lumber Division, Sumner & Co.* v. *NLRB,* 419 U.S. 301, 87 LRRM 3236 (1974), held that, even if there is evidence that the union has majority support, the employer need not recognize the union absent an election and certification. Nor does the obligation fall upon the employer in such a situation to initiate the election process in order to preserve its position. Part of the Court's reasoning follows:

"[This] is not to say that authorization cards are wholly unreliable as an indication of employee support of the union. An employer concededly may have valid objections to recognizing a union on that basis. His objection to cards may, of course, mask his opposition to unions. On the other hand he may have rational, good-faith grounds for distrusting authorization cards in a given situation. He may be convinced that the fact that a majority of the employees strike and picket does not necessarily establish that they desire the particular union as their representative. Fear may indeed prevent some from crossing a picket line; or sympathy for strikers, not the desire to have the particular union in the saddle, may influence others. These factors make difficult an examination of the employer's motive to ascertain whether it was in good faith.

To enter that domain is to reject the approval by *Gissel* of the retreat which the Board took from its 'good faith' inquiries.

"The union which is faced with an unwilling employer has two alternative remedies under the Board's decision in the instant case. It can file for an election; or it can press unfair labor practices against the employer under *Gissel*. The latter alternative promises to consume much time. In *Linden* the time between filing the charge and the Board's ruling was about 4½ years; in *Wilder*, about 6½ years. The Board's experience indicates that the median time in a contested case is 388 days. *Gissel*, 395 U.S., at 611, n. 30. On the other hand the median time between the filing of the petition for an election and the decision of the regional director is about 45 days. In terms of getting on with the problems of inaugurating regimes of industrial peace, the policy of encouraging secret elections under the Act is favored. The question remains—should the burden be on the union to ask for an election or should it be the responsibility of the employer?"

The majority, however, did not reach the question of what to do if the employer breaches an agreement to permit majority status to be determined by a card check. What should be the answer?

The dissenting justices in *Linden Lumber* would have held that an employer, presented with "convincing evidence of majority support," violates Section 8(a)(5) by refusing to recognize the union, even if he engages in no other misconduct, unless he petitions for an election or consents to an expedited election.

3. Getman, Goldberg, and Herman, Union Representation Elections: Law and Reality 132–35 (1976):*

"CARD-SIGNING AS AN INDICATION OF EMPLOYEE CHOICE

"The data demonstrate that card-signing is an accurate indicator of employee choice at the time the card is signed. Forty-six percent of the voters (489/1067) signed union authorization cards. Of those, 82 percent reported that they wanted union representation at the time they signed the card, 14 percent said they were uncertain, and 4 percent said they did not want union representation.

"The data also support the assumption that employees who are asked, but do not sign cards, are generally opposed to union representation or uncertain. Thirty-eight percent (216/568) of the non-signers were asked to sign cards. Of these, 73 percent reported that they had not signed because they did not want union representation at the time or were undecided, 9 percent cited a desire for privacy, and 18 percent gave other reasons.

"Card-signing is a reasonably accurate predictor of vote ($r = .51$). Seventy-two percent (351/489) of the card-signers voted for union representation; 79 percent (448/568) of the non-signers voted against union representation. The tendency of non-signers to vote against

*Excerpted from UNION REPRESENTATIONS ELECTIONS: LAW AND REALITY, by Julius G. Getman, Stephen B. Goldberg, and Jeanne B. Herman, © 1976 by Russell Sage Foundation, New York.

union representation was similar whether or not they had been asked to sign. . . .

"EMPLOYER KNOWLEDGE OF CARD-SIGNING

"The employers also argued in *Gissel* that authorization cards should not be treated as evidence of union support, because they are frequently signed before the employer has had a chance to present his side of the unionization issue. The employers asserted that such cards do not accurately reflect employee choice, since they are based on incomplete information. The unstated assumption underlying this assertion is that many card-signers, after hearing the employer's arguments, will vote against union representation.

"The Court responded

" 'Normally, however, the union will inform the employer of its organization drive early in order to subject the employer to the unfair labor practice provisions of the Act; the union must be able to show the employer's awareness of the drive in order to prove that his contemporaneous conduct constituted unfair labor practices on which a bargaining order can be based if the drive is ultimately successful.'

"In eighteen elections we were able to determine the proportion of authorization cards signed before the employer knew about the card-signing drive. In ten of these elections, all cards were signed before the employer was aware of the card-signing drive; in four, 50-75 percent were signed before the employer found out; and in four others nearly all cards were signed after employer knowledge.

"It appears then, that in most elections the employer does not know about the card-signing drive in time to respond before a majority of the cards have been signed. It does not follow, however, that cards do not represent reasonably firm union sentiments. As noted previously, 72 percent of all card-signers voted for union representation, even though few of them had heard the employer's side of the unionization issue at the time they signed a card. Furthermore, . . . campaign familiarity was generally low. Those card-signers who did switch to the company were no more familiar with the company campaign than those who voted union.

"In sum, the voting decision, made after hearing the employer's arguments, is not substantially more informed than the card-signing decision. Nor, for most employees, are the two choices different. For those few employees for whom the card-sign choice and the election choice are different, that difference is not associated with greater familiarity with the company campaign. Accordingly, the fact that most employees sign cards before having heard the employer's arguments ought not prevent the issuance of a bargaining order based on cards."

Dialogue

Assume that an election was held in a unit consisting of the rubber plant at Enderby and that the union lost by a narrow margin. It was able to set the election aside on the basis of employer misconduct during the election campaign. It now seeks a bargaining order against Enderby under *Gissel.* It filed a charge, the Board investigated and issued a Complaint.

It is now the evening before the NLRB hearing before an Administrative Law Judge. Baldwin, the attorney representing the NLRB's General Counsel, has primary responsibility for presenting the case. But since the union is entitled to participate as a matter of right, Diamond, the union's attorney, approaches Baldwin to discuss their strategy. Here is their discussion:

DIAMOND: My union went about its card solicitation in a very systematic way. We had three "captains" in the rubber plant who handed out cards to all the employees. In each case the captain witnessed the employee signing the card. I suggest you call each of these captains to the witness stand, have each one look at all the cards, and then testify that he or she personally saw them signed. The authorization cards are very simple and very clear on their face. They make plain that the employee designates the union as his or her representative for bargaining. The cards don't say anything about an election [the card is the same as the one set out on page 110 of your text—Ed.].

BALDWIN: I'd rather have each card signer take the stand and explain exactly how he or she got the card and the circumstances in which it was signed.

DIAMOND: Look, that really isn't necessary. The procedure I'm suggesting is exactly the procedure okayed by the Court in *Gissel* [see part III-B of *Gissel* at pages 157 to 160 of the text]. Your way will take forever, and it raises some problems.

BALDWIN: What kind of problems?

DIAMOND: You know very well that if the individual card signers take the stand they can be exposed to some tough cross-examination. I'm very worried that Enderby's lawyer will ask them if they read the card.

BALDWIN: Well, didn't they? You said it's a pretty simple card.

DIAMOND: I doubt it. Do you read everything you sign? These are everyday people. Somebody, a friend, asks them to sign a union card, they sign it. They don't bother to read it. Either they're busy at the machines or don't want to take time out of their break. But they know what they're doing. It takes courage to sign a union card.

BALDWIN: Well, what did the captain say to them?

DIAMOND: I've spoken to the captains, and most of them said something like, "look, will you sign this card? It's for a union election." And then most of them signed.

BALDWIN: You mean the captains lied about the cards?

DIAMOND: Of course not! You know as well as I do that these cards serve a couple of purposes. We use them first of all to make a showing of interest. You need to have cards from 30 percent of the people to get an election. As a matter of policy we won't go to an election unless we have cards from more than 50 percent of the people. So the cards really are "for an election" in the first place. But if we lose that election, then we fall back on the plain language of the card, which is to designate the union as bargaining representative.

BALDWIN: But if the employee is told that the card is for an election, and if she doesn't read the card at all, how in the world can you claim that the employee knowingly designated the union as her bargaining representative? As far as I'm concerned, all that employee did was to ask for the chance to make her own decision in a secret ballot election.

DIAMOND: That isn't the law. As long as we didn't misrepresent the card, that is, tell the employee something entirely different from what's on the card, the card is valid. If our captain said something like, "never mind what the card says," or, "don't worry, it's *only* for an election," then the card is no good. But *Gissel* makes clear that in our situation the cards are perfectly valid. The Court said very clearly that "employees should be bound by the clear language of what they sign unless that language is deliberately and clearly cancelled by a union adherent with words calculated to direct the signer to disregard and forget the language above his signature." Our union adherents surely didn't go that far! And the Court made clear in *Gissel* that we don't want to get into "an endless and unreliable inquiry" about an employee's "subjective motivations" in signing a card.

BALDWIN: Yes, but where the employee never *read* the card, that's a different story. I have a text of *Gissel* with me, because I thought some problems might come up at the hearing, and it says, let me see, that administrative law judges "should not neglect their obligation to ensure employee free choice by too easy mechanical application of the rules." And isn't there a Third Circuit case which refused a bargaining order where the employees didn't read the cards?

DIAMOND: Yes, there was a short-lived decision in *NLRB* v. *Keystone Pretzel Bakery* [674 F.2d 197, 109 LRRM 3277 (1982)], but it was overruled by the full bench of the circuit [696 F.2d 257, 112 LRRM 2349 (1983)]. The earlier decision was unsound, in my view. Imagine an employee, two years after an election which the union lost, with many of the former union adherents now gone, asked by his boss' lawyer whether he read the card. Up until now his union sentiments were supposed to be secret. Now he's worried that his boss will do something to him because he supported the union. So, to appease the boss he says, "well, I never read that card. I thought it was for an election, that's all." The Supreme Court understood that reality in *Gissel*, and that's one reason for their rule.

BALDWIN: I just don't know. The way the Supreme Court is going, they just might accept the earlier Third Circuit view. Then we'd have to remand this case. Maybe we should have each employee testify, so we have a complete record whichever way the law goes. Tell you what. Let me call my Regional Attorney in the morning and she'll tell me what to do.

Questions

1. If you were the Regional Attorney, how would you advise Baldwin to proceed?

2. Are there any ethical problems faced by Baldwin, Diamond, and the Regional Attorney in dealing with this problem?

Note on Recognition Without Authorization Cards

In *United Dairy Farmers Cooperative Ass'n* v. *NLRB*, 633 F.2d 1054, 105 LRRM 3034 (3d Cir. 1980), the court of appeals held that the Board has the authority, in appropriate cases, to issue a bargaining order in favor of a union that has neither won a representation election nor secured authorization cards from a majority of the bargaining unit employees.

Among the violations of the Act found by the Board were the discharge of a strong union supporter, the distribution of cash bonuses to employees, interrogation, threatening of employees with discharge if the union won the election, and unlawful conversion of the drivers' status from employees to "independent contractors." Six drivers who refused to accept this change were discharged. Then Chairman Fanning and Member Jenkins concluded that a bargaining order should issue; Members Murphy and Truesdale agreed that the Board has authority to enter a bargaining order without a card majority but found no support for this remedy on the facts. Member Penello stated the Board has no authority to issue a bargaining order in the absence of a showing of majority support through a representation election or card majority. The Board's decision is reported at 242 NLRB 1026, 101 LRRM 1278 (1979).

The court of appeals' holding emphasizes that the Board's authority to issue a bargaining order where there is no card showing of majority support depends on the nature of the employer's unfair labor practices; the court remanded the case to the Board to determine whether the employer's conduct was "outrageous" and the unfair labor practices "pervasive." The rationale for authorizing a bargaining order in such circumstances is deterrence of the employer; if the majority of employees do not in fact support representation, so be it. The court acknowledges the superiority of the election process in selecting a majority representative of employees, but it says that the rationale for utilizing the election process "evaporates" when the employer has committed serious unfair practices which destroy the laboratory conditions for any election in the immediate future. Such conditions cannot be attained, the court observes, regardless of the "reparative action" which the Board may attempt, and other means must be pursued.

On remand, the Board issued a bargaining order, 257 NLRB No. 129, 107 LRRM 1577 (1981). In view of the continuing change in membership of the Board, the ongoing vitality of this view is uncertain. As of May, 1982, a 3–2 majority of the Board subscribed to the position that a bargaining order could issue, despite no majority showing, in cases of outrageous and pervasive employer unfair practices, *Conair Corp.*, 261 NLRB No. 178, 110 LRRM 161 (1982). But the Board's composition has changed since that decision.

The Court of Appeals for the District of Columbia has expressed doubt that the Board's authority includes issuance of a bargaining order where a union cannot demonstrate a card majority, *Teamsters Local 115* v. *NLRB*, 640 F.2d 392, 106 LRRM 2462 (D.C. Cir. 1981), although it did not expressly decide the issue.

3. Regulation of the Organizational Campaign

A. ACCOMMODATION OF ORGANIZING AND PROPERTY INTERESTS

1. RIGHTS OF EMPLOYEES

Problem

In the early stages of the organizing drive at Enderby Company some of the key union activists among the Enderby employees shouldered the burden of convincing their co-workers to support the United Factory Workers. Their activities included distributing authorization cards (like those set out in Chapter 2), various leaflets and other literature describing the union and its programs, and just general talk in the work areas, rest rooms, and cafeteria.

Shortly after this activity began, the following notice appeared on the bulletin board:

ATTENTION ALL EMPLOYEES

THERE WILL BE NO SOLICITATION OF ANY KIND ON THE PLANT PREMISES BY ANY EMPLOYEE DURING WORKING HOURS.

THERE WILL BE NO DISTRIBUTION OF ANY LITERATURE, NOTICES, CARDS, OR PAPER OF ANY KIND IN AND ABOUT THE WORK AREAS OF ANY EMPLOYEE AT ANY TIME. NONEMPLOYEES SHALL NOT COME UPON OR BE UPON THE PLANT PREMISES FOR THE PURPOSE OF MAKING SOLICITATIONS OR DISTRIBUTING LITERATURE, NOTICES, CARDS, OR PAPER OF ANY KIND.

EXCEPTIONS WILL BE ALLOWED TO THE ABOVE RULES IF APPROVED IN WRITING BY THE PLANT SUPERINTENDENT.

H.W. MAXWELL
Plant Manager

The explanation for the posting of this rule came out many months later in testimony at an NLRB proceeding after the Union lost the election and sought to have the results set aside.

Q. (To Plant Manager Maxwell) Now, I ask you, if you heard anything about any union organization activity in the month of February?

A. Yes, sir, I think it was the second week, I believe, in February. One of the employees called me at my home after she got home from work and told me there was some union activity going on.

Q. And what, if anything unusual, did you observe immediately after that, Mr. Maxwell?

A. Well, yes, sir. After that of course I naturally looked for a little more, to see what was going on because I figured something might be—problems in the plant, you know, if union activity was going on. So there was a bunch of people going to the rest room more often than usual, and they were at the machine a little more often and talked a little more often; and later I began to notice the quality of the work wasn't quite as good as it previously was. It dropped down.

Q. Now did you, after that time, cause to be posted on the bulletin board a rule with reference to solicitation?

A. Yes, sir.

Questions

Does the rule bar employees from handing out union authorization cards on the plant floor? During working hours? In the rest rooms? At the picnic area? (See location of picnic area on the map at page 177.) Are these limitations lawful under the Act? Is the validity of the rule affected by Maxwell's explanation?

Republic Aviation Corp. v. NLRB

Supreme Court of the United States, 1945
324 U.S. 793, 16 LRRM 620

Mr. Justice Reed delivered the opinion of the Court.

In the *Republic Aviation Corporation* case, the employer, a large and rapidly growing military aircraft manufacturer, adopted, well before any union activity at the plant, a general rule against soliciting which read as follows:

"Soliciting of any type cannot be permitted in the factory or offices."

The Republic plant was located in a built-up section of Suffolk County, New York. An employee persisted after being warned of the rule in soliciting union membership in the plant by passing out application cards to employees on his own time during lunch periods. The employee was discharged for infraction of the rule and, as the National Labor Relations Board found, without discrimination on the part of the employer toward union activity.

. . .

The Board determined that the promulgation and enforcement of the "no solicitation" rule violated § 8(1) of the National Labor Relations Act as it interfered with, restrained and coerced employees in their rights under § 7 and discriminated against the discharged employee under § 8(3). . . . As a consequence of its conclusions as to the solicitation . . . , the Board entered the usual cease and desist order and directed the reinstatement of the discharged employees with back pay and also the rescission of "the rule against solicitation in so far as it prohibits union activity and solicitation on company property during the employees' own time." The Circuit Court of Appeals for the Second Circuit affirmed, and we granted certiorari, because of conflict with the decisions of other circuits.

In the case of *Le Tourneau Company of Georgia*, two employees were suspended two days each for distributing union literature or circulars on the employees' own time on company owned and policed parking lots, adjacent to the company's fenced-in plant, in violation of a long standing and strictly enforced rule, adopted prior to union organization activity about the premises, which read as follows:

> "In the future no Merchants, Concern, Company, or Individual or Individuals will be permitted to distribute, post, or otherwise circulate handbills or posters, or any literature of any description, on Company property without first securing permission from the Personnel Department."

The rule was adopted to control littering and petty pilfering from parked autos by distributors. The Board determined that there was no union bias or discrimination by the company in enforcing the rule.

The company's plant for the manufacture of earth-moving machinery and other products for the war is in the country on a six thousand acre tract. The plant is bisected by one public road and built along another. There is one hundred feet of company-owned land for parking or other use between the highways and the employee entrances to the fenced enclosures where the work is done, so that contact on public ways or on non-company property with employees at or about the establishment is limited to those employees, less than 800 out of 2100, who are likely to walk across the public highway near the plant on their way to work, or to those employees who will stop their private automobiles, buses or other conveyances on the public roads for communications. The employees' dwellings are widely scattered.

The Board found that the application of the rule to the distribution of union literature by the employees on company property which resulted in the lay-offs was an unfair labor practice under § 8(1) and 8(3). Cease and desist, and rule rescission orders, with directions to pay the employees for their lost time, followed. The Circuit Court of Appeals for the Fifth Circuit reversed the Board, and we granted certiorari because of conflict with the *Republic* case. 323 U.S. 698.

These cases bring here for review the action of the National Labor Relations Board in working out an adjustment between the undisputed right of self-organization assured to employees under the Wagner Act and the equally undisputed right of employers to maintain discipline in their establishments. Like so many others, these rights are not unlimited in the sense that they can be exercised without regard to any duty which the existence of rights in others may place upon employer or employee. Opportunity to organize and proper discipline are both essential elements in a balanced society.

The Wagner Act did not undertake the impossible task of specifying in precise and unmistakable language each incident which would constitute an unfair labor practice. On the contrary, that Act left to the Board the work of applying the Act's general prohibitory language in the light of the infinite combinations of events which might be charged as violative of its terms. Thus a "rigid scheme of remedies" is avoided and administrative flexibility within appropriate statutory limitations obtained to accomplish the dominant purpose of the legislation. *Phelps Dodge Corp.* v. *Labor Board*, 313 U.S. 177, 194. So far as we are here concerned, that purpose is the right of employees to organize for mutual aid without employer interference. This is the principle of labor relations which the Board is to foster.

The gravamen of the objection of both *Republic* and *Le Tourneau* to the Board's orders is that they rest on a policy formulated without due administrative procedure. To be more specific it is that the Board cannot substitute its knowledge of industrial relations for substantive evidence. The contention is that there must be evidence before the Board to show that the rules and orders of the employers interfered with and discouraged union organization in the circumstances and situation of each company. Neither in the *Republic* nor the *Le Tourneau* cases can it properly be said that there was evidence or a finding that the plant's physical location made solicitation away from company property ineffective to reach prospective union members. Neither of these is like a mining or lumber camp where the employees pass their rest as well as their work time on the employer's premises, so that union organization must proceed upon the employer's premises or be seriously handicapped.

. . .

In the *Republic Aviation Corporation* case the evidence showed that the petitioner was in early 1943 a non-urban manufacturing establishment for military production which employed thousands. It was growing rapidly. Trains and automobiles gathered daily many employees for the plant from an area on Long Island, certainly larger than walking distance. The rule against solicitation was introduced in evidence and the circumstances of its violation by the dismissed employee after warning was detailed.

. . .

No evidence was offered that any unusual conditions existed in labor relations, the plant location or otherwise to support any contention that conditions at this plant differed from those occurring normally at any other large establishment.

The *Le Tourneau Company of Georgia* case also is barren of special circumstances. The evidence which was introduced tends to prove the simple facts heretofore set out as to the circumstances surrounding the discharge of the two employees for distributing union circulars.

These were the facts upon which the Board reached its conclusions as to unfair labor practices. The Intermediate Report in the *Republic Aviation* case, 51 NLRB at 1195, set out the reason why the rule against solicitation was considered inimical to the right of organization.[6] This was approved by the Board. *Id.*, 1186. . . . In the *Le Tourneau Company* case the discussion of the reasons underlying the findings was much more extended. We insert in the note below a quotation which shows the character of the Board's opinion.[8] Furthermore, in both opinions of the Board full citation of authorities was given, including *Matter of Peyton Packing Co.*, 49 NLRB 828, 50 NLRB 355, hereinafter referred to.

The Board has fairly, we think, explicated in these cases the theory which moved it to its conclusions in these cases. The excerpts from its opinions just quoted show this. The reasons why it has decided as it has are sufficiently set forth. We cannot agree, as Republic urges, that in these present cases reviewing courts are left to "sheer acceptance" of the Board's conclusions or that its formulation of policy is "cryptic."

Not only has the Board in these cases sufficiently expressed the theory upon which it concludes that rules against solicitation or prohibitions against the wearing of insignia must fall as interferences with union organization, but, in so far as rules against solicitation are concerned, it had theretofore succinctly expressed the requirements of proof which it considered appropriate to outweigh or overcome the presumption as to rules against solicitation. In the *Peyton Packing Co.* case, 49 NLRB 828, at 843, hereinbefore referred to, the presumption adopted by the Board is set forth.[10]

. . .

JUSTICE ROBERTS dissented.

[6]51 NLRB 1195:
"Thus, under the conditions obtaining in January 1943, the respondent's employees, working long hours in a plant engaged entirely in war production and expanding with extreme rapidity, were entirely deprived of their normal right to 'full freedom of association' in the plant on their own time, the very time and place uniquely appropriate and almost solely available to them therefor. The respondent's rule is therefore in clear derogation of the rights of its employees guaranteed by the Act."

[8]54 NLRB at 1259–60: "As the Circuit Court of Appeals for the Second Circuit has held, 'It is not every interference with property rights that is within the Fifth Amendment. . . . Inconvenience, or even some dislocation of property rights, may be necessary in order to safeguard the right to collective bargaining.' The Board has frequently applied this principle in decisions involving varying sets of circumstances, where it has held that the employer's right to control his property does not permit him to deny access to his property to persons whose presence is necessary there to enable the employees effectively to exercise their right to self-organization and collective bargaining, and in those decisions which have reached the courts, the Board's position has been sustained. Similarly, the Board has held that, while it was 'within the province of an employer to promulgate and enforce a rule prohibiting union solicitation during working hours,' it was 'not within the province of an employer to promulgate and enforce a rule prohibiting union solicitation by an employee outside of working hours, although on company property,' the latter restriction being deemed an unreasonable impediment to the exercise of the right to self-organization."

[10]49 NLRB at 843–44: "The Act, of course, does not prevent an employer from making and enforcing reasonable rules covering the conduct of employees on company time. Working time is for work. It is therefore within the province of an employer to promulgate and enforce a rule prohibiting union solicitation during working hours. Such a rule must be presumed to be valid in the absence of evidence that it was adopted for a discriminatory

Notes on Organizing Activities by Employees on Company Property

1. In footnote 10 of the *Republic Aviation* case, the Court quotes with approval the Board's holding that "a rule prohibiting union solicitation during working hours" is presumptively valid. For many years the Board upheld no-solicitation rules when the bar was couched in the terms "working hours" or "working time," but in *T.R.W., Inc.*, 257 NLRB 442, 107 LRRM 1481 (1981), the Board changed its position and insisted upon greater specificity in the wording of a no-solicitation rule:

> "[T]he majority in *Essex International* held that rules which prohibit solicitation and distribution during "working times" are presumptively valid, but that rules prohibiting solicitation and distribution during 'working hours' are presumptively invalid. The latter presumption, however, could be overcome in any particular case by a presentation of extrinsic evidence that such 'working hours' rules were communicated or applied in such a way as to convey an intent clearly to *permit* solicitation during breaktime or other periods when employees are not actually at work. These conclusions concerning the distinctions between 'working time' and 'working hours' were predicated entirely upon what the *Essex International* majority saw as the 'clear distinction' to be drawn between the terms; that is, 'working hours' connoted the period of time from the beginning to the end of a workshift, including breaktime and mealtime, while 'working time,' on the other hand, connoted only the period of time that is spent in the performance of actual job duties, thereby excluding breaktime and mealtime from its scope.
>
> "We, however, see no inherent meaningful distinction between the terms 'working hours' and 'working time' when used in no-solicitation rules. Both terms are, without more, ambiguous, and the risk of such ambiguity must be borne by the promulgator of the rule. Either term is reasonably susceptible to an interpretation by employees that they are prohibited from engaging in protected activity during periods of the workday when they are properly not engaged in performing their work tasks (*e.g.*, meal and break periods). As such, either term tends unlawfully to interfere with and restrict employees in the exercise of their Section 7 organizational rights.
>
> "Inasmuch as employees may rightfully engage in organizational activities during breaktime and mealtime, rules which restrain, or which, because of their ambiguity, tend to restrain employees from engaging in such activity constitute unlawful restrictions against and

---

purpose. It is no less true that time outside working hours, whether before or after work, or during luncheon or rest periods, is an employee's time to use as he wishes without unreasonable restraint, although the employee is on company property. It is therefore not within the province of an employer to promulgate and enforce a rule prohibiting union solicitation by an employee outside of working hours, although on company property. Such a rule must be presumed to be an unreasonable impediment to self-organization and therefore discriminatory in the absence of evidence that special circumstances make the rule necessary in order to maintain production or discipline."

interference with the exercise by employees of the self-organizational rights guaranteed them by Section 7 of the Act."

Should a reviewing court insist upon some empirical data validating the Board's conclusion that employees no longer understand the distinction between working hours and working time? What sort of data would you suggest? On the other hand, does the Board's current position disserve any legitimate employer interest?

T.R.W. was a unanimous decision of a three-member panel of the Board. Compare *Intermedics, Inc.*, 262 NLRB No. 178, 110 LRRM 1441 (1982), in which two Board members expressed their disagreement with *T.R.W.* and urged a return to *Essex International*.

2. The Board takes a different view with respect to the treatment of literature distributed on company premises. The distinction is explained in *Stoddard-Quirk Manufacturing Co.*, 138 NLRB 615, 51 LRRM 1110 (1962):

"Solicitation and distribution of literature are *different* organizational techniques and their implementation poses *different* problems both for the employer and for the employees. Heretofore, the difference in result has been explained largely in terms of the employer's interests. Thus, it has been noted that solicitation, being oral in nature, impinges upon the employer's interests only to the extent that it occurs on working time, whereas distribution of literature, because it carries the potential of littering the employer's premises, raises a hazard to production whether it occurs on working time or nonworking time.

"The validity of this consideration cannot be gainsaid. But because it presents only one side of the employer-employee equation, it does not wholly resolve the problem. Thus, if employer interests alone were controlling, oral solicitation on plant premises could be denied altogether for no one would deny that the strong feelings frequently engendered by union solicitation inevitably carry over to some extent from nonworking time to working time. And, on the other hand, the employer's unquestioned right to make reasonable regulations governing the manner and volume of literature distribution in working areas of the plant if such distribution were allowed could be invoked to minimize any hazard to production raised thereby and, *pro tanto*, would abate the need for complete exclusion. . . .

"It does not follow, though, that an identical adjustment is appropriate where distribution of literature is involved. The distinguishing characteristic of literature as contrasted with oral solicitation—and a distinction too often overlooked—is that its message is of a permanent nature and that it is designed to be retained by the recipient for reading or re-reading at his convenience. Hence, the purpose is satisfied so long as it is received.

"This purpose, however, can, absent special circumstances, be as readily and as effectively achieved at company parking lots, at plant entrances or exits, or in other nonworking areas, as it can be at the machines or work stations where the employer's interest in cleanliness, order, and discipline is undeniably greater than it is in nonworking areas. . . . We believe organizational rights in that regard require only that employees have access to nonworking areas of the plant premises."

Into which camp would you place the distribution of union authorization cards?

3. The presumptions stated in the cases, while theoretically rebuttable, are not easily overcome. Employers have justified restrictions on solicitation even during nonworking hours and on distribution even in nonwork areas on the basis of special business needs. These exceptions usually arise in situations in which the employees are in frequent contact with the public or in situations where the areas which would be used for distribution are open to the public. The Board's rules for department stores are especially restrictive of employee communication, see *May Department Stores*, 59 NLRB 976, 15 LRRM 173 (1944), *enf'd.*, 154 F.2d 533, 17 LRRM 985 (8th Cir.), *cert. denied*, 329 U.S. 725, 18 LRRM 2469 (1946).

How would a union overcome the presumptive validity of a rule which prohibited solicitation during working hours? Suppose, for example, that an on-duty trucker is disciplined by the employer, under the rule in this problem, for attempting to solicit her partner in the rig to join the union?

How would you deal with an otherwise valid rule that is selectively enforced? For example, under the posted rule in this problem, suppose the employer routinely allows solicitation during working hours for certain charitable purposes?

Do the presumptions have such administrative utility that exceptions should rarely be allowed?

4. Union solicitation in hospitals is thought to present special problems because of its potential adverse impact on patient care. The Board has attempted to accommodate the various interests by holding that bans on solicitation are presumptively invalid in all areas of the hospital except "immediate patient care areas." The Court has upheld the application of this presumption to such areas as the cafeteria, gift shop, and lobbies not on patient care floors, *Beth Israel Hospital* v. *NLRB*, 437 U.S. 483, 98 LRRM 2727 (1978); *NLRB* v. *Baptist Hospital, Inc.*, 442 U.S. 773, 101 LRRM 2556 (1979). But a closer question is presented with respect to corridors and sitting rooms near patient care areas. In *Baptist Hospital, supra,* the Court held that the Board's presumption against the validity of a no-solicitation rule in such areas was overcome by the hospital's evidence that solicitation would affect patient care and disturb patients. The Court admonished the Board that "the experience to date raises serious doubts as to whether the Board's interpretation of its present presumption adequately takes into account the medical practices and methods of treatment incident to the delivery of patient care services in a modern hospital." 442 U.S. at 789, 101 LRRM at 2562.

5. Suppose the union succeeds in the Enderby Problem in invalidating the no-solicitation rule in an NLRB proceeding following the union's loss in the election. What is the appropriate remedy? What good does it do the union?

2. Rights of Outsiders

Problem

Blair, the union organizer, and Swoboda, the Enderby employee who has been one of the leaders of the organizing drive, have decided that the in-plant organizing techniques have run their course. Some employees are afraid to be seen taking union literature or conversing with known union adherents. Some have asked questions that are beyond the ken of the Enderby workers. What is needed now is an opportunity for union organizers, such as Blair, to talk with employees away from the workplace. Blair and Swoboda discuss the possibilities:

SWOBODA: What about visiting the employees in their homes?

BLAIR: I don't see how I could do that, Herb. This is a big, sprawling metropolitan area. What are there, a million people in the Greater Mill City area? With all the ground I'd have to cover, and people going bowling, or moonlighting, I'd be lucky to see three people a night.

SWOBODA: Can't the union put on more staff to help us win this thing?

BLAIR: Well, I suppose I could reassign a couple of my organizers. But our staff is stretched awfully thin. And I don't see how we could justify the costs. Putting on four or five organizers for a couple of months each, why it would take a lot of years of union dues to make that all back. What about calling some general meetings at our union hall?

SWOBODA: I just don't think you'd get much of a turnout. Some people are willing to talk about the union and support it as long as it isn't too much of a bother. When the company calls a meeting on working time and pays for it, then they'll go. But people want to go home after work and they don't want to travel a big distance for something they're not so sure about anyway. What about mailing literature to their homes?

BLAIR: The Board has made this easier for us under its *Excelsior* rule. We have to be given a list of employees' names and addresses. But I have never been convinced that written materials are effective. You need the personal touch. Even giving out a leaflet may be effective if you can shake the worker's hand, say a few words, and maybe answer questions.

SWOBODA: In that case I think you could do the most good in the parking lots and maybe on the access roads to the plant. If you look at the map of Brown's Pond Industrial Park (p. 177) you'll see that all workers for all the plants—our two plants and the other four that are now open—come in through the access road at entrance #1. There is enough of a slowdown for the guard house so that you could pass out literature there. Of course you can't tell at that point who belongs to Enderby and who doesn't, except that some of the starting times are different. The parking lots would be ideal because they are all Enderby cars near the two factories.

BLAIR: What concerns me is that this is all private property. I'm not sure we'll be able to stand there. What about standing on public property at entrances #2 and #3?

SWOBODA: The trouble is these are used only as exits in the evening and cars move out of there real quick. I doubt that we could stop enough

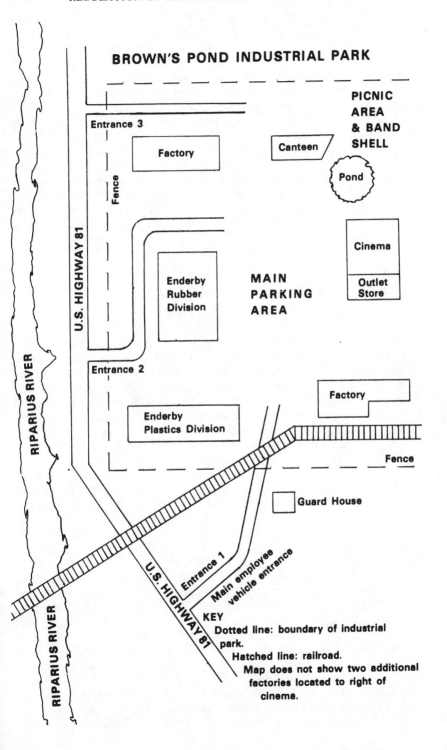

BROWN'S POND INDUSTRIAL PARK

KEY
Dotted line: boundary of industrial park.
Hatched line: railroad.
Map does not show two additional factories located to right of cinema.

cars, and even if we did, there'd be traffic hazards and people would resent us for holding them up. But what I don't understand is why you should think of this as private property. This industrial park is pretty much of a public place. It has six factories going, a seconds store which sells factory outlet goods to the public, and a movie house open to the public. The idea was not to let all this good parking space go to waste at night when the factories aren't working.

BLAIR: I think I'll take this up with our lawyers. Maybe there's a way we can lawfully get on this property to distribute literature. I'd especially like to be able to station myself in the parking lot so I can catch the Enderby workers when they park. And I wonder if there's some way the Enderby employees who support us can legally remain in the parking lots after their shifts are over to hand out literature. I think I also should check whether we can lawfully picket in the parking lot; this will be very important if we get bargaining rights and need to use economic pressure to get a contract.

NLRB v. Babcock & Wilcox Co.

Supreme Court of the United States, 1956
351 U.S. 105, 38 LRRM 2001

MR. JUSTICE REED delivered the opinion of the Court.

In each of these cases the employer refused to permit distribution of union literature by nonemployee union organizers on company-owned parking lots. The National Labor Relations Board, in separate and unrelated proceedings, found in each case that it was unreasonably difficult for the union organizer to reach the employees off company property and held that, in refusing the union's access to parking lots, the employers had unreasonably impeded their employees' rights to self-organization in violation of §8(a)(1) of the National Labor Relations Act.

The plant involved in No. 250, *National Labor Relations Board v. Babcock & Wilcox Co.,* is a company engaged in the manufacture of tubular products such as boilers and accessories, located on a 100-acre tract about one mile from a community of 21,000 people. Approximately 40 percent of the 500 employees live in that town and the remainder live within a 30-mile radius. More than 90 percent of them drive to work in private automobiles and park on a company lot that adjoins the fenced in plant area. The parking lot is reached only by a driveway 100 yards long which is entirely on company property excepting for a public right-of-way that extends 31 feet from the metal of the highway to the plant's property. Thus, the only public place in the immediate vicinity of the plant area at which leaflets can be effectively distributed to employees is that place where this driveway crosses the public right-of-way. Because of the traffic conditions at that place the Board found it practically impossible for union organizers to distribute leaflets safely to employees in motors as they enter or leave the lot. The Board noted that the company's policy on such distribution had not discriminated against labor organizations and that other means of communication, such as the mail and telephones, as well as the homes of the workers, were open to the union. The employer justified its refusal to allow distribution of literature on company property on the ground that it had maintained a consistent policy of refusing access to all kinds of pamphleteering and that such distribution of leaflets would litter its property.

The Board found that the parking lot and the walkway from it to the gatehouse, where employees punched in for work, were the only "safe and practicable" places for distribution of union literature. The Board viewed the place of work as so much more effective a place for communication of information that it held the employer guilty of an unfair labor practice for refusing limited access to company property to union organizers. It therefore ordered the employer to rescind its no-distribution order for the parking lot and walkway, subject to reasonable and nondiscriminating regulations "in the interest of plant efficiency and discipline, but not as to deny access to union representatives for the purpose of effecting such distribution." 109 NLRB at 486. . . .

. . . These holdings were placed on the Labor Board's determination in *LeTourneau Company of Georgia*, 54 NLRB 1253. In the *LeTourneau* case the Board balanced the conflicting interests of employees to receive information on self-organization on the company's property from fellow employees during nonworking time with the employer's right to control the use of his property and found the former more essential in the circumstances of that case. Recognizing that the employer could restrict employees' union activities when necessary to maintain plant discipline or production, the Board said: "Upon all the above considerations, we are convinced, and find, that the respondent, in applying its 'no-distributing' rule to the distribution of union literature by its employees on its parking lots has placed an unreasonable impediment on the freedom of communication essential to the exercise of its employees' right to self-organization," *LeTourneau Company of Georgia*, 54 NLRB at page 1262, 13 LRRM 227. This Court affirmed the Board. *Republic Aviation Corp.* v. *National Labor Relations Board*, 324 U.S. 793, 801 *et seq.*, 16 LRRM 620. The same rule had been earlier and more fully stated in *Peyton Packing Co.*, 49 NLRB 828, 843–844, 12 LRRM 183.

The Board has applied its reasoning in the *LeTourneau* case without distinction to situations where the distribution was made, as here, by nonemployees. The fact that our *LeTourneau* case ruled only as to employees has been noted by the Courts of Appeal in [various cases].

In these present cases the Board has set out the facts that support its conclusions as to the necessity for allowing nonemployee union organizers to distribute union literature on the company's property. In essence they are that nonemployee union representatives, if barred, would have to use personal contacts on streets or at home, telephones, letters or advertised meetings to get in touch with the employees. The force of this position in respect to employees isolated from normal contacts has been recognized by this Court and by others. We recognize, too, that the Board has the responsibility of " 'applying the Act's general prohibitory language in the light of the infinite combinations of events which might be charged as violative of its terms.' " *National Labor Relations Board* v. *Stowe*

Spinning Co., 336 U.S. 226, 231, 23 LRRM 2371, 2373–74. We are slow to overturn an administrative decision.

It is our judgment, however, that an employer may validly post his property against nonemployee distribution of union literature if reasonable efforts by the union through other available channels of communication will enable it to reach the employees with its message and if the employer's notice or order does not discriminate against the union by allowing other distribution. In these circumstances the employer may not be compelled to allow distribution even under such reasonable regulations as the orders in these cases permit.

This is not a problem of always open or always closed doors for union organization on company property. Organization rights are granted to workers by the same authority, the National Government, that preserves property rights. Accommodation between the two must be obtained with as little destruction of one as is consistent with the maintenance of the other. The employer may not affirmatively interfere with organization; the union may not always insist that the employer aid organization. But when the inaccessibility of employees makes ineffective the reasonable attempts by nonemployees to communicate with them through the usual channels, the right to exclude from property has been required to yield to the extent needed to permit communication of information on the right to organize.

The determination of the proper adjustments rests with the Board. Its rulings, when reached on findings of fact supported by substantial evidence on the record as a whole, should be sustained by the courts unless its conclusions rest on erroneous legal foundations. Here the Board failed to make a distinction between rules of law applicable to employees and those applicable to nonemployees.

The distinction is one of substance. No restriction may be placed on the employees' right to discuss self-organization among themselves, unless the employer can demonstrate that a restriction is necessary to maintain production or discipline. *Republic Aviation Corp.* v. *National Labor Relations Board*, 324 U.S. 793, 803, 16 LRRM 620. But no such obligation is owed nonemployee organizers. Their access to company property is governed by a different consideration. The right of self-organization depends in some measure on the ability of employees to learn the advantages of self-organization from others. Consequently, if the location of a plant and the living quarters of the employees place the employees beyond the reach of reasonable union efforts to communicate with them, the employer must allow the union to approach his employees on his property. No such conditions are shown in these records.

The plants are close to small well-settled communities where a large percentage of the employees live. The usual methods of imparting information are available. The various instruments of publicity are at hand. Though the quarters of the employees are scattered they are in reasonable reach. The Act requires only that the employer refrain from interference, discrimination, restraint or coercion in the employees' exercise of their own rights. It does not require that the employer permit the use of its facilities for organization when other means are readily available.

Note on Constitutional Rights of Access

For a period of about eight years, unions enjoyed a viable constitutional right of access to shopping centers and industrial parks. The doctrine was expanded most forcefully in *Amalgamated Food Employees Union* v. *Logan Valley Plaza*, 391 U.S. 308, 68 LRRM 2209 (1968), when the Court, building upon the decision almost 30 years earlier in *Marsh* v. *Alabama*, 326 U.S. 501 (1946), held that peaceful picketing within a large shopping center was protected by the First Amendment because the shopping center was the "functional equivalent" of a business district in a municipality. While the union in *Logan Valley* could have developed a theory of access under Section 7 of the Act, it based its case solely on the constitution. It may well be that the availability of a constitutional right of access discouraged development of a theory of access under the NLRA during that period.

However, *Logan Valley* was subsequently eroded by *Lloyd Corp.* v. *Tanner*, 407 U.S. 551 (1972), a case that did not involve union activity, and was finally put to rest in *Hudgens* v. *NLRB*, 424 U.S. 507, 91 LRRM 2489 (1976). The *Hudgens* court quoted portions of its earlier *Lloyd* opinion as the rationale for its refusal to continue to recognize a constitutional right of access, 424 U.S. at 520, 91 LRRM at 2494:

> "The argument reaches too far. The Constitution by no means requires such an attenuated doctrine of dedication of private property to public use. The closest decision in theory, *Marsh* v. *Alabama, supra*, involved the assumption by a private enterprise of all of the attributes of a state-created municipality and the exercise by that enterprise of semi-official municipal functions as a delegate of the State. In effect, the owner of the company town was performing the full spectrum of municipal powers and stood in the shoes of the State. In the instant case there is no comparable assumption or exercise of municipal functions or power." 407 U.S., at 568–569 (footnote omitted).
>
> . . .
>
> "We hold that there has been no such dedication of Lloyd's privately owned and operated shopping center to public use as to entitle respondents to exercise therein the asserted First Amendment rights. . . ." 407 U.S., at 570.

Although access is dead as a federal constitutional theory, union activity may well be protected on private property under state constitutional provisions. In *Pruneyard Shopping Center* v. *Robins*, 447 U.S. 74 (1980), a unanimous U.S. Supreme Court affirmed a decision of the California Supreme Court holding that the California state constitution protected "speech and petitioning, reasonably exercised, in [privately-owned] shopping centers."

The Supreme Court concluded that the state court's reading of the California constitution did not constitute a deprivation of petitioner's fifth, fourteenth, or first amendment rights.

The opinion by Justice Rehnquist reaffirmed the *Lloyd* statement that when tested against the United States Constitution a store does not lose its private character by being part of a shopping center. However, the states, pursuant to their police powers, may adopt different, if reasonable, restrictions on private property. The California court's ruling was predicated on the extensive public use of the center (25,000 persons daily) and the orderly activity of a small number of solicitors.

Dicta suggested a different result if the property belonged to an individual homeowner or "proprietor of a modest retail establishment," or if those soliciting did not follow "reasonable regulations adopted [by the store] to assure that these activities do not interfere with normal business operations."

Scott Hudgens *and Section 7*

As indicated in the previous note, the Court in *Hudgens* v. *NLRB*, 424 U.S. 507, 91 LRRM 2489 (1976), held that there is no constitutionally protected right of access to a privately owned shopping center. The litigation in *Hudgens* had taken a tortuous course until that point, with the parties shifting back and forth between Section 7 and constitutional theories in an attempt to anticipate the prevailing Supreme Court view. In denying the union's constitutional claim in *Hudgens*, the Court held that the case should be determined under Section 7 of the Act, and remanded for that purpose. In order to put the remanded case in its proper perspective, however, we first set out the portion of the Supreme Court's decision in *Hudgens* v. *NLRB* dealing with access under the NLRA.

. . .

"III

"From what has been said it follows that the rights and liabilities of the parties in this case are dependent exclusively upon the National Labor Relations Act. Under the Act the task of the Board, subject to review by the courts, is to resolve conflicts between § 7 rights and private property rights, 'and to seek a proper accommodation between the two.' *Central Hardware Co.* v. *NLRB*, 407 U.S. 539, 543, 80 LRRM 2769, 2770. What is 'a proper accommodation' in any situation may largely depend upon the content and the context of the § 7 rights being asserted. The task of the Board and the reviewing courts under the Act, therefore, stands in conspicuous contrast to the duty of a court in applying the standards of the First Amendment, which requires 'above all else' that expression must not be restricted by government 'because of its message, its ideas, its subject matter, or its content.'

"In the *Central Hardware* case, and earlier in the case of *NLRB* v. *Babcock & Wilcox Co.*, 351 U.S. 105, 38 LRRM 2001, the Court considered the nature of the Board's task in this area under the Act. Accommodation between employees' § 7 rights and employers' property rights, the Court said in *Babcock & Wilcox*, 'must be obtained with as little destruction of one as is consistent with the maintenance of the other.' 351 U.S., at 112, 38 LRRM, at 2004.

"Both *Central Hardware* and *Babcock & Wilcox* involved organizational activity carried on by nonemployees on the employers' property. The context of the § 7 activity in the present case was different in several respects which may or may not be relevant in striking the proper balance. First, it involved lawful economic strike activity rather than organizational activity. Second, the § 7 activity here was carried on by Butler's employees (albeit not employees of its shopping center store), not by outsiders. See *NLRB* v. *Babcock & Wilcox Co.*, 351 U.S., at 111–113. Third, the property interests impinged upon in this case were not those of the employer against whom the § 7 activity was directed, but of another.

"The *Babcock & Wilcox* opinion established the basic objective under the Act: accommodation of § 7 rights and private property rights 'with as little destruction of one as is consistent with the maintenance of the other.' The locus of that accommodation, however, may fall at differing points along the spectrum depending on the nature and strength of the respective § 7 rights and private property rights asserted in any given context. In each generic situation, the primary responsibility for making this accommodation must rest with the Board in the first instance. . . .

"For the reasons stated in this opinion, the judgment is vacated and the case is remanded to the Court of Appeals with directions to remand to the National Labor Relations Board, so that the case may be there considered under the statutory criteria of the National Labor Relations Act alone.

"*It is so ordered.*

"Vacated and remanded."

Scott Hudgens and Local 315, Retail, Wholesale and Department Store Union

National Labor Relations Board, 1977
230 NLRB 414, 95 LRRM 1351

SECOND SUPPLEMENTAL DECISION AND ORDER

. . . The court of appeals remanded the case to the Board on April 21, 1976.

On May 11, 1976, the Board invited the parties to file further statements of position. Subsequently, statements of position were filed by the General Counsel, by Respondent, and by the Charging Party, hereinafter called the Union.

Pursuant to the Court's remand, the Board has reconsidered its Supplemental Decision and Order, the statements of position, and the entire record in this case, and hereby reaffirms, for the reasons set forth below, its conclusion that Respondent violated Section 8(a)(1) of the Act.

The Supreme Court majority in *Hudgens* held that persons entering a private shopping center do not have a first amendment right to engage in

activity which would be accorded first amendment protection in public places. Therefore, if there is such a "right," it must have a source other than the Constitution. Accordingly, in remanding the case to the Board, the Court made it clear that any "rights and liabilities of the parties . . . are dependent exclusively upon the National Labor Relations Act."
. . .

The Court noted three factors distinguishing the instant case from *Central Hardware* and *Babcock & Wilcox* that "may or may not be relevant" in striking the *Babcock & Wilcox* balance:

"First, [the instant case] involved lawful economic strike activity rather than organizational activity. . . . Second, the § 7 activity here was carried on by Butler's employees (albeit not employees of its shopping center store), not by outsiders. . . . Third, the property interests impinged upon in this case were not those of the employer against whom the § 7 activity was directed, but of another. [Footnote omitted.]"

In sum, the issue in this case is whether, without reference to first amendment considerations, the threat by Hudgens' agent in the circumstances here to cause the arrest of Butler's warehouse employees engaged in picketing Butler's retail outlet in Hudgen's shopping center, herein also called the Center or the Mall, violated Section 8(a)(1) of the Act.

As was noted by the Court, both *Babcock & Wilcox* and *Central Hardware* involved organizational activity carried on by nonemployees on the employer's property, while the instant case involves lawful economic picketing conducted by Butler's warehouse employees on property owned by Hudgens, the lessor of the property on which Butler's retail store is located. In this case, the Court's distinction between organizational and economic strike activity is to some degree intertwined with its employee-nonemployee distinction, in that in *Babcock & Wilcox* and *Central Hardware* the organizational activity in question was by nonemployee union organizers, whereas the economic picketing here was carried on by employees of the struck employer. We conclude that the three factual differences, *i.e.*, the nature of the activity, the persons engaging therein, and the title to the property, do not preclude our finding that Hudgens violated Section 8(a)(1).[19]

Concerning the first distinction noted by the Court, that the instant case involves economic strike activity rather than organizational activity, it is fully recognized by Board and Court precedent, as well as by the parties to this proceeding, that both types of activity are protected by Section 7. Accordingly, economic activity deserves at least equal deference, and the fact that the picketing here was in support of an economic strike does not warrant denying it the same measure of protection afforded to organizational picketing.

[19]Member Murphy points out that, irrespective of fn. 30, the concurring opinion herein asserts, in effect, that the differences noted by the Supreme Court are of minimal importance in reaching the result. She disagrees with this approach. To the contrary, inasmuch as the Supreme Court pointed out the existence of these distinctions, it is essential that the Board consider and discuss their importance to the conclusion reached. Like her concurring colleague, she finds that they do not require a different result, but she has joined in attempting to explicate fully the reason for so finding.

With respect to the Court's second distinguishing factor, that the picketers were employees of the company whose store they were picketing rather than nonemployees, as were the union organizers in *Babcock & Wilcox*, it is basic that Section 7 of the Act was intended to protect the rights of employees rather than those of nonemployees. With this principle in mind, the employee status of the pickets here entitled them to at least as much protection as would be afforded to nonemployee organizers such as those in *Babcock & Wilcox*.

However, the fact that economic rather than organizational picketing is involved in this case may require a different application of the accommodation principle because of the different purposes sought to be served. It is clear that the Section 7 rights involved in *Babcock & Wilcox*, as in *Central Hardware*, are those of the employees rather than those of the nonemployees seeking to organize them. That is to say, if the employees are beyond the reach of reasonable union efforts to communicate with them, it is the employees' right to receive information on the right to organize that is abrogated when an employer denies nonemployee union organizers access to the employer's property. Similarly, where, as here, economic strike picketing is involved, the Section 7 rights at issue are those of employees, *i.e.*, the pickets' right to communicate their message both to persons who would do business with the struck employer and to those employees of the struck employer who have not joined the strike.

One difference between organizational campaigns as opposed to economic strike situations is that in the former the Section 7 rights being protected are those of the intended audience (the employees sought to be organized), and in the latter the Section 7 rights are those of the persons attempting to communicate with *their* intended audience, the public as well as the employees. A further distinction between organizational and economic strike activity becomes apparent when the focus shifts to the characteristics of the audience at which the Section 7 activity in question is directed. In an organizational campaign, the group of employees whose support the union seeks is specific and often is accessible by means of communication other than direct entry of the union organizers onto the employer's property, such as meeting employees on the street, home visits, letters, and telephone calls.

Here, the pickets' intended audience comprised two distinct groups: (1) those members of the buying public who might, when seeing Butler's window display inside the Mall, think of doing business with that one employer, and (2) the employees at the Butler store. Although the nonstriking employees at the Butler store were obviously a clearly defined group, the potential customers (the more important component of the intended audience) became established as such only when individual shoppers decide to enter the store. •

Hudgens contends that *Babcock & Wilcox* should be read to require that, if television, radio, and newspaper advertising is available, the picketers' Section 7 rights must yield to property rights regardless of the expense involved and regardless of the fact that such forms of communication, in order to reach the intended audience, necessarily must also reach the general populace. As to these contentions, the Administrative Law Judge found, and we agree, that the mass media, appropriately used by the North DeKalb Center and its merchants to attract customers from the Metropolitan Atlanta area, are not "reasonable" means of communication for employee pickets seeking to publicize their labor dispute with a single store in the Mall. Furthermore, Hudgens' suggested approach would undercut Board and Court precedent recognizing and protecting such picketing as the most effective way of reaching those who would enter a struck employer's premises, including situations in which the entrance to the employer's property is on land owned by another.

Hudgens further argues that the Union had other means of access to the public using the Mall in that it could have picketed on the private sidewalk around the Center building or on the public streets and sidewalks near the Center's parking lot. As to the first of these proposed locations, we find, in agreement with the Administrative Law Judge, that the only question the Board is called upon to decide was whether the employees had the right to picket immediately in front of the Butler store in the general walking area used by the invited public inside the Mall. Although the individual who was Hudgens' manager at material times in this proceeding testified that he told the pickets they could picket on the parking lot, the Administrative Law Judge discredited this testimony and noted that even in its brief Hudgens maintained that it had the right to eject pickets from the parking lot as well. As to Hudgens' suggestion that the pickets could have used public streets and sidewalks, the Administrative Law Judge pointed out that Butler is only 1 of 60 stores fronting on the same common inside walkways, that the closest public area—i.e., not privately owned—is 500 feet away from the store, and that a message announced orally or by picket sign at such a distance from the focal point would be too greatly diluted to be meaningful. Further, we find merit in the General Counsel's contentions that safety considerations, the likelihood of enmeshing neutral employers, and the fact that many people become members of the pickets' intended audience on impulse all weigh against requiring the pickets to remove to public property, or even to the sidewalks surrounding the Mall.

As for the third consideration noted by the *Hudgens* Court, that "the property rights impinged upon . . . were not those of the employer against whom the § 7 activity was directed, but of another," we find that, under the circumstances here, Hudgens' property right to exclude certain types of activity on his Mall must yield to the Section 7 right of lawful primary economic picketing directed against an employer doing business on that Mall. The walkways on the common areas of the Mall near the Butler store, although privately owned, are, during business hours, essentially open to the public and, as the General Counsel argues, are the equivalent of sidewalks for the people who come to the Center. Thus, the invitation to the public,[24] as recognized by Hudgens in the "Shopping Center Lease" form and publicized in various advertising and promotional campaigns, is simply "Come to the North DeKalb Center." Specific

[24]The invitation is to the public in the sense that all members of the public are considered potential customers.

intent to buy is not a prerequisite to invitee status; the fact that many people buy on impulse is explicitly recognized in the design and layout of the Center's commercial environment. As members of the public, the men who carried the signs were apparently within the scope of the invitation and welcome as long as they did not picket.[25]

Further, we find no merit to Hudgens' assertion that he is a completely neutral bystander in this situation. Although Hudgens is neutral in the sense that he is not the primary employer and is, therefore, not a party to the labor dispute, he is nonetheless financially interested in the success of each of the businesses in his Center inasmuch as he receives a percentage of their gross sales as part of his rental arrangement. He provides security and other services on a purportedly neutral basis to assure customer comfort and well-being in order that sales potential be maximized. Although in some ways the security services provided by Hudgens are analogous to those provided by police in the public shopping areas of any town, there are distinctions; *e.g.*, Hudgens' security force can, and as the record shows does, preclude certain types of behavior on the Mall that police could not prohibit on a public street. As the Court made clear, there is no first amendment right to enter such shopping centers to engage in activities that would be accorded first amendment protection in a public street or park.

To the extent that Hudgens' security force protects the Center and its businesses from such activities as, in Hudgens' view, might discomfit, discourage, or intimidate shoppers, Hudgens is protecting his own interests. To the extent that the businesses on the Mall have delegated to Hudgens responsibility for the maintenance of an environment that maximizes the shoppers' peace of mind, and therefore sales, those doing business at the Center are protecting their own interests through Hudgens. By the terms of the lease, part of the rent they pay Hudgens is for such protection.

Furthermore, although Hudgens owns the Mall, as long as the shopkeepers pay their rent, they have certain rights in the leased property. One of these is the right to have the walkways of the Mall accessible to persons who wish to shop there. Without that right, the leaseholds would, obviously, be worthless. In maintaining the comfort, cleanliness, and security of the Mall, Hudgens is, in a real sense, acting for the shopkeepers who lease their store locations from him. To this degree, he is their agent and, in light of his direct interest in seeing the shopkeepers' profits maximized, his interests in performing the above activities are mutual with those of the shopkeepers.

Picketing in support of an economic strike is intended to have, and certainly may have, economic effects on the struck business. This is true whether the picketing occurs on public or private property. Such activity is a corollary of the strike itself and is the means by which the striking employees communicate their message to those who would do business with the employer as well as to other employees of the employer. Here,

---

[25]Harold Glenn, one of the pickets, testified that they were told: "You can stay but those signs have got to go."

the activity of the pickets in front of the Butler store clearly could affect Hudgens' interests adversely: to the degree Butler's gross sales are diminished, Hudgens' rental percentage figure will likewise be reduced. Furthermore, as a result of our finding that in the circumstances here such picketing is permissible, businesses may find that mall locations are less desirable since such locations will be no more insulated from such Section 7 activity than are locations fronting a public sidewalk. To the extent that this makes mall locations less attractive to businesses seeking retail store sites, Hudgens' interests are further jeopardized.

However, in finding that the *Babcock & Wilcox* criteria are satisfied and that, in these circumstances, Hudgens' property rights must yield to the pickets' Section 7 rights, we are simply subjecting the businesses on the Mall to the same risk of Section 7 activity as similar businesses fronting on public sidewalks now endure. In leasing the shops to the merchants, Hudgens necessarily submitted his own property rights to whatever activity, lawful and protected by the Act, might be conducted against the merchants had they owned, instead of leased, the premises. The effect of our decision obviously is limited to such Section 7 activity and in no way requires Hudgens to open the Mall to any and all who may wish to demonstrate or solicit there. As the *Hudgens* Court made clear, no first amendment considerations are involved.

It is clear, then, that by our holding here we do no more than assure that employees of employers doing business in such malls will be afforded the full protection of the Act. In our view, the national labor policy requires that such employees be afforded that protection. A contrary holding would enable employers to insulate themselves from Section 7 activities by simply moving their operations to leased locations on private malls, and would thereby render Section 7 meaningless as to their employees.

On the basis of all the foregoing, we reaffirm our previous conclusion that the Respondent, by threatening to cause the arrest of Butler's warehouse employees engaged in picketing Butler's retail outlet in Respondent's shopping center violated Section 8(a)(1) of the Act. Accordingly, we shall reaffirm our original Order in this proceeding.

. . .

CHAIRMAN FANNING, concurring:

. . .

. . .That *Babcock* involved organizational activity and in this case peaceful, primary, and protected picketing is, in my judgment, irrelevant, and, notably, no litigant to the controversy contends otherwise. The Congress has repeatedly concluded "that a strike when legitimately employed is an economic weapon which in great measure implements and supports the principles of the collective bargaining system." As we stated in *Peddie*, it is a right "embodied in Section 7 and . . . given emphasis in Section 13." And, if the matter need be further underscored, it is a right specifically designed to foster the quality of bargaining power that is the entire statute's goal. The right to picket is so intertwined with the right to strike that the two amount to statutory equivalents.

That *Babcock* involved activity undertaken by nonemployees and this case that of employees is, on the other hand, relevant but only to the extent that it more persuasively points to the result reached. If, as in *Babcock*, the rights of the passive audience addressed were considered paramount, certainly, here, the rights of those actively asserting the statutory right should be accorded even greater deference.

Finally, that the property right in *Babcock* was vested in the employer against whom the protected activity was directed and, in this case, in a third party, matters, from the standpoint of those asserting the statutory right, little (*United Steelworkers* [*Carrier Corp.*] v. *NLRB*, 376 U.S. 492, 499), and from the standpoint of the property right holder who chooses to become a lessor not much, if any, more.

The balance to be struck in this case, therefore, no more favors this Respondent than the *Babcock* one. As our decisions in *Hudgens II* and *Peddie*, the case upon which we relied in *Hudgens II*, make, I believe, clear, a variety of considerations point toward finding a violation. The self-imposed limitations on exclusive use that Hudgens created, the significant diminishment of the employee right involved that the available alternatives for the picketing constitute, and the possibility that the available alternatives would enmesh a number of other employers surely more "neutral" to the dispute than Hudgens require striking the balance on the employees' side. I concur, therefore, in my colleagues' disposition.

3. THE PREEMPTION DOCTRINE

Problem: Two Lawyers and a Judge

Blair, the union organizer in the Enderby campaign, has asked the union's Associate General Counsel David Diamond to research the question whether, based upon the facts brought out in the earlier dialogues, union organizers are entitled to stand on company property to give out literature. Diamond concludes that the union has a strong case under Section 7 of the Act. It is arguable, if not clear, he says, that all other effective means of communication are foreclosed. Thus, Diamond advises the union that it may distribute literature on the property of the industrial park, but cautions against harassing people or disrupting traffic. The day after this activity begins, four state troopers arrive and advise the union people that they are trespassing and should take their activities elsewhere. The captain of the leafletting group telephones the union lawyer.

1. What kind of practical advice should you give at this point? Should you advise the handbillers to leave peacefully? If so, how will you initiate legal proceedings to test whether they have the right to be on private property? Should you suggest that they allow themselves to be arrested? If so, do you know how to find a bail bondsman and how to get to the jail? At this point do you want to reconsider whether the original advice as to the legality of this activity is sound?

2. What should the company do if the handbillers will not leave? Is it seemly to have them all arrested? Can the company initiate a legal proceeding against them at this point? How do you do this? Who are the parties? How do you serve process on them? Your course book does not

answer these questions. But when the time comes, you will need the answers promptly.

3. Assume that the industrial park and Enderby have brought a proceeding in state court against the union, seeking to enjoin it from further activity on private property. Proper service, whatever that entails, has been made. As is customary in matters of this sort, the judge has scheduled a hearing in his chambers the next day to consider whether to grant a preliminary injunction. We now join the proceedings in chambers. The company has first established that the activity has occurred on the private property of Brown's Pond Industrial Park, and that unless enjoined irreparable financial injury will result.

COMPANY LAWYER: Your Honor, the *Hudgens* case makes clear, if there ever was any doubt on this score, that a shopping center is not the functional equivalent of a company town, municipality, or other subdivision of government. The same should be true of an industrial park. Since neither public property nor state action is involved, the First Amendment is inapplicable to protect this activity, and it is a simple case of trespass.

UNION LAWYER: Judge, we realize the U.S. Constitution won't help us after *Hudgens*, though we hope that the Court will come around some day and restore *Logan Valley* as good law. And I'm not prepared in this short space of time to claim a state constitutional right of access of the sort upheld in *Pruneyard*.

But our activity is protected under Section 7 of the National Labor Relations Act. Both *Babcock & Wilcox* and *Hudgens* on remand hold that the union may engage in Section 7 activity on private property when other channels of communication aren't adequate.

JUDGE: Do you intend to establish that you can't reach the employees through telephone, the mails, meetings, and the like? I'm not sure I know enough about labor relations to decide these questions. Do I have authority to interpret Section 7 of the Act?

UNION LAWYER: That's the point, Judge. This question, of the adequacy of other channels of communication is one that the National Labor Relations Board must decide. They have the expertise in this area. In the landmark *Garmon* decision, 359 U.S. 236, 43 LRRM 2838 (1959), the Court said:

> "When an activity is arguably subject to § 7 or § 8 of the Act, the States as well as the federal courts must defer to the exclusive competence of the National Labor Relations Board if the danger of state interference with national policy is to be averted."

Therefore, Judge, we move to dismiss this case on the grounds that the matter is preempted under the NLRA and that this court has no jurisdiction.

JUDGE: What? I have no jurisdiction? To hear a simple trespass case? What?

COMPANY LAWYER: Your honor, whatever the force of the preemption doctrine, it has no application to a case like this. As you know, Your Honor, there is no way for the Company to bring a proceeding before the Board to challenge the Union's activity under the Act. That is why the

Supreme Court held in *Sears v. Carpenters Union*, 436 U.S. 180, 98 LRRM 2282 (1978), that the preemption doctrine does not apply to a trespass case, where the Company can't get the case before the NLRB. The state court retains jurisdiction, and we respectfully submit that you should enjoin this trespassory activity.

JUDGE: Hasn't the union filed a charge?

UNION LAWYER: We haven't, Judge, but the reason is that until yesterday there was nothing for us to file a charge about. Until the Company attempted to enjoin our activity, we had no claim of interference with Section 7 rights. Now I can't be two places at once, and as soon as we're done with this hearing, I intend to file a charge with the NLRB.

JUDGE: Well, if the union does file a charge, what does *Sears* say about my jurisdiction?

COMPANY LAWYER: Your Honor, while in *Sears* the union didn't file a charge, that's not the whole basis for the opinion. It also turns on the Court's view that trespass cases are part of the traditional concern of the states and that the likelihood of the union prevailing on a Section 7 claim is very slight.

UNION LAWYER: Judge, that's utter nonsense. First of all, the test under *Garmon*, which I already read to you, isn't whether we have a clear winning case under the NLRA, but whether it is *arguable* that we would prevail. And I think our right of access under the Act is arguable, if not clear. Second, Justice Blackmun's concurring opinion in *Sears* makes it clear that once we file a charge, the case should be handled exclusively by the Board. Otherwise, you know, we'll be sitting six months for a Board decision, and meanwhile this Company will break the back of our organizing campaign. And with your help, Judge, I should add, if you grant this injunction.

COMPANY LAWYER: My friend has hit on precisely the problem, but the answer is other than he suggests. Unless this court enjoins the union, it will tie us up for at least six months while the Board piddles with a hopeless claim. Justice Blackmun's position is way off base; indeed, Justice Powell concurred in *Sears* only on the understanding that the majority result would be no different even if the union filed a charge.

JUDGE: Well, just how strong a case does the union have under Section 7?

UNION LAWYER: Again, we say this isn't relevant. But we think we have a very strong case. The Board in *Hudgens* and other access cases is moving towards a much stronger access right under the Act. You see, while *Logan Valley* was in force, the Board didn't have to develop a statutory theory, and now with the *Hudgens* view of the constitutional situation, the Board is building a theory of Section 7 access. Recent cases like *Giant Food Markets, Inc.*, 241 NLRB 727, 100 LRRM 1598 (1979) and *Seattle First National Bank*, 243 NLRB 898, 100 LRRM 1624 (1979) upheld a right of access. And those were cases of picketing for economic purposes. Their reasoning applies even more forcefully to the present case, which involves core organizing rights under the Act.

COMPANY LAWYER: We disagree. Where the Board has found access it is in precisely those cases, as my friend points out, where the union must take its message to customers and suppliers coming to the store. There's no other way to reach them. But here the union is trying to communicate with employees of the factory. It has their names and addresses. There's no need to reach them on private property. If this was a case involving a remote logging camp, like *Husky Oil* v. *NLRB*, 669 F.2d 643, 109 LRRM 2548 (10th Cir. 1982), then the union might have something, for, as the *Husky* court put it, other methods of communication would be futile. But this case is just like *Hutzler Bros.* v. *NLRB*, 630 F.2d 1012, 105 LRRM 2473 (4th Cir. 1981), in which the court reversed the Board's finding of a violation because the Board had failed to consider the intensity of the union's organizing efforts. Said the court, "a union with a highly professional organizational department should at least make a serious attempt to organize a company before it can complain about the lack of access to the employer's property." We think the union's activity in this case is as "lackadaisical" as was the union's in *Hutzler*. And the other cases just mentioned by the union have been either reversed or questioned by appellate courts, so the Board's view isn't as solid as the union would have you think.

JUDGE: This is a difficult case. Judgment reserved until next Tuesday.

COMPANY LAWYER and UNION LAWYER: What do we do until then?

JUDGE (aside to her clerk): I haven't the foggiest idea. Get on this immediately. Read *Sears* in light of their contentions, and tell me how to decide this case.

Sears, Roebuck & Co. v. Carpenters Union

Supreme Court of the United States, 1978
436 U.S. 180, 98 LRRM 2282

MR. JUSTICE STEVENS delivered the opinion of the Court.

The question in this case is whether the National Labor Relations Act, as amended, deprives a state court of the power to entertain an action by an employer to enforce state trespass laws against picketing which is arguably—but not definitely—prohibited or protected by federal law.

I

On October 24, 1973, two business representatives of respondent Union visited the department store operated by petitioner (Sears) in Chula Vista, Cal., and determined that certain carpentry work was being performed by men who had not been dispatched from the Union hiring hall. Later that day, the Union agents met with the store manager and requested that Sears either arrange to have the work performed by a contractor who employed dispatched carpenters or agree in writing to abide by the terms of the Union's master labor agreement with respect to the dispatch and use of carpenters. The Sears manager stated that he would consider the request, but he never accepted or rejected it.

Two days later the Union established picket lines on Sears' property. The store is located in the center of a large rectangular lot. The building is surrounded by walkways and a large parking area. A concrete wall at one end separates the lot from residential property; the other three sides adjoin public sidewalks which are adjacent to the public streets. The pickets patrolled either on the privately owned walkways next to the building or in the parking area a few feet away. They carried signs indicating that they were sanctioned by the "Carpenters Trade Union." The picketing was peaceful and orderly.

Sears' security manager demanded that the Union remove the pickets from Sears' property. The Union refused, stating that the pickets would not leave unless forced to do so by legal action. On October 29, Sears filed a verified complaint in the Superior Court of California seeking an injunction against the continuing trespass; the court entered a temporary restraining order enjoining the Union from picketing on Sears' property. The Union promptly removed the pickets to the public sidewalks. On November 21, 1973, after hearing argument on the question whether the Union's picketing on Sears' property was protected by state or federal law, the court entered a preliminary injunction. The California Court of Appeal affirmed. While acknowledging the pre-emption guidelines set forth in *San Diego Building Trades Council* v. *Garmon*, the court held that the Union's continuing trespass fell within the longstanding exception for conduct which touched interests so deeply rooted in local feeling and responsibility that pre-emption could not be inferred in the absence of clear evidence of congressional intent.

The Supreme Court of California reversed. It concluded that the picketing was arguably protected by § 7 of the Act, because it was intended to secure work for Union members and to publicize Sears' undercutting of the prevailing area standards for the employment of carpenters. The court reasoned that the trespassory character of the picketing did not disqualify it from arguable protection, but was merely a factor which the National Labor Relations Board would consider in determining whether or not it was in fact protected. The court also considered it "arguable" that the Union had engaged in recognitional picketing subject to § 8(b)(7)(C) of the Act, which could not continue for more than 30 days without petitioning for a representation election. Because the picketing was both arguably protected by § 7 and arguably prohibited by § 8, the court held that state jurisdiction was pre-empted under the *Garmon* guidelines.

Since the Wagner Act was passed in 1935, this Court has not decided whether, or under what circumstances, a state court has power to enforce local trespass laws against a union's peaceful picketing. The obvious importance of this problem led us to grant certiorari in this case.

II

We start from the premise that the Union's picketing on Sears' property after the request to leave was a continuing trespass in violation of state law. We note, however, that the scope of the controversy in the state court was limited. Sears asserted no claim that the picketing itself violated any state or federal law. It sought simply to remove the pickets from its property to the public walkways, and the injunction issued by the state court was strictly confined to the relief sought. Thus, as a matter of state law, the location of the picketing was illegal but the picketing itself was unobjectionable.

As a matter of federal law, the legality of the picketing was unclear. Two separate theories would support an argument by Sears that the picketing was prohibited by § 8 of the NLRA, and a third theory would support an argument by the Union that the picketing was protected by § 7. Under each of these theories the Union's purpose would be of critical importance.

If an object of the picketing was to force Sears into assigning the carpentry work away from its employees to Union members dispatched from the hiring hall, the picketing may have been prohibited by § 8(b)(4)(D). Alternatively, if an object of the picketing was to coerce Sears into signing a prehire or members-only type agreement with the Union, the picketing was at least arguably subject to the prohibition on recognitional picketing contained in § 8(b)(7)(C). Hence, if Sears had filed an unfair labor practice charge against the Union, the Board's concern would have been limited to the question whether the Union's picketing had an objective proscribed by the Act; the location of the picketing would have been irrelevant.

On the other hand, the Union contends that the sole objective of its action was to secure compliance by Sears with area standards, and therefore the picketing was protected by § 7. Thus, if the Union had filed an unfair labor practice charge under § 8(a)(1) when Sears made a demand that the pickets leave its property, it is at least arguable that the Board would have found Sears guilty of an unfair labor practice.

Our second premise, therefore, is that the picketing was both arguably prohibited and arguably protected by federal law. The case is not, however, one in which "it is clear or may fairly be assumed" that the subject matter which the state court sought to regulate—that is, the location of the picketing—is either prohibited or protected by the Federal Act.

[Part III of the Court's opinion, reviewing the *Garmon* doctrine, is omitted.]

IV

. . . The leading case holding that when an employer grievance against a union may be presented to the National Labor Relations Board it is not subject to litigation in a state tribunal is *Garner* v. *Teamsters*, 346 U.S. 485. *Garner* involved peaceful organizational picketing which arguably violated § 8(b)(2) of the federal Act. A Pennsylvania equity court held that the picketing violated the Pennsylvania Labor Relations Act and therefore should be enjoined. The State Supreme Court reversed because the union conduct fell within the jurisdiction of the National Labor Relations Board to prevent unfair labor practices.

This Court affirmed because Congress had "taken in hand this particular type of controversy . . . [i]n language almost identical to parts of the Pennsylvania statute." Accordingly, the State, through its courts, was without power to "adjudge the same controversy and extend its own form of relief." This conclusion did not depend on any surmise as to "how the

National Labor Relations Board might have decided this controversy had petitioners presented it to that body." The precise conduct in controversy was arguably prohibited by federal law and therefore state jurisdiction was pre-empted. The reason for pre-emption was clearly articulated:

> "Congress evidently considered that centralized administration of specially designed procedures was necessary to obtain uniform application of its substantive rules and to avoid these diversities and conflicts likely to result from a variety of local procedures and attitudes toward labor controversies. Indeed, Pennsylvania passed a statute the same year as its labor relations Act reciting abuses of the injunction in labor litigations attributable more to procedure and usage than to substantive rules. A multiplicity of tribunals and a diversity of procedures are quite as apt to produce incompatible or conflicting adjudications as are different rules of substantive law. The same reasoning which prohibits federal courts from intervening in such cases, except by way of review or on application of the federal Board, precludes state courts from doing so.
> "The conflict lies in remedies. . . . [W]hen two separate remedies are brought to bear on the same activity, a conflict is imminent."

This reasoning has its greatest force when applied to state laws regulating the relations between employees, their union, and their employer. It may also apply to certain laws of general applicability which are occasionally invoked in connection with a labor dispute. Thus, a State's antitrust law may not be invoked to enjoin collective activity which is also arguably prohibited by the federal Act. In each case, the pertinent inquiry is whether the two potentially conflicting statutes were "brought to bear on precisely the same conduct."

On the other hand, the Court has allowed a State to enforce certain laws of general applicability even though aspects of the challenged conduct were arguably prohibited by § 8 of the NLRA. Thus, for example, the Court has upheld state-court jurisdiction over conduct that touches "interests so deeply rooted in local feeling and responsibility that, in the absence of compelling congressional direction, we could not infer that Congress had deprived the States of the power to act." *San Diego Building Trades Council* v. *Garmon*, 359 U.S., at 244. See *Construction Workers* v. *Laburnum Constr. Corp.*, 347 U.S. 656 (threats of violence); *Youngdahl* v. *Rainfair, Inc.*, 355 U.S. 131 (violence); *Automobile Workers* v. *Russell*, 356 U.S. 634 (violence); *Linn* v. *Plant Guard Workers*, 383 U.S. 53 (libel); *Farmer* v. *Carpenters*, 430 U.S. 290 (intentional infliction of mental distress).

In *Farmer*, the Court held that a union member, who alleged that his union had engaged in a campaign of personal abuse and harassment against him, could maintain an action for damages against the union and its officers for the intentional infliction of emotional distress. One aspect of the alleged campaign was discrimination by the union in hiring hall referrals. Although such discrimination was arguably prohibited by §§ 8(b)(1)(A) and 8(b)(2) of the NLRA and therefore an unfair labor practice charge could have been filed with the Board, the Court permitted the state action to proceed.

The Court identified those factors which warranted a departure from the general pre-emption guidelines in the "local interest" cases. Two are relevant to the arguably *prohibited* branch of the *Garmon* doctrine. First, there existed a significant state interest in protecting the citizen from the challenged conduct. Second, although the challenged conduct occurred in the course of a labor dispute and an unfair labor practice charge could have been filed, the exercise of state jurisdiction over the tort claim entailed little risk of interference with the regulatory jurisdiction of the Labor Board. Although the arguable federal violation and the state tort arose in the same factual setting, the respective controversies presented to the state and federal forums would not have been the same.

The critical inquiry, therefore, is not whether the State is enforcing a law relating specifically to labor relations or one of general application but whether the controversy presented to the state court is identical (as in *Garner*) or different from (as in *Farmer*) that which could have been, but was not, presented to the Labor Board. For it is only in the former situation that a state court's exercise of jurisdiction necessarily involves a risk of interference with the unfair labor practice jurisdiction of the Board which the arguably prohibited branch of the *Garmon* doctrine was designed to avoid.

In the present case, the controversy which Sears might have presented to the Labor Board is not the same as the controversy presented to the state court. If Sears had filed a charge, the federal issue would have been whether the picketing had a recognitional or work-reassignment objective; decision of that issue would have entailed relatively complex factual and legal determinations completely unrelated to the simple question whether a trespass had occurred.[28] Conversely, in the state action, Sears only challenged the location of the picketing; whether the picketing had an objective proscribed by federal law was irrelevant to the state claim. Accordingly, permitting the state court to adjudicate Sears' trespass claim would create no realistic risk of interference with the Labor Board's primary jurisdiction to enforce the statutory prohibition against unfair labor practices.

The reasons why pre-emption of state jurisdiction is normally appropriate when union activity is arguably prohibited by federal law plainly do not apply to this situation; they therefore are insufficient to preclude a State from exercising jurisdiction limited to the trespassory aspects of that activity.

V

The question whether the arguably protected character of the Union's trespassory picketing provides a sufficient jurisdiction for pre-emption of

---

[28]Moreover, decision of that issue would not necessarily have determined whether the picketing could continue. For the Board could conclude that the *picketing* was not prohibited by either § 8(b)(4)(D) or § 8(b)(7)(C) without reaching the question whether it was protected by § 7. If the Board had concluded that the picketing was not prohibited, Sears would still have been confronted with picketing which violated state law and was arguably protected by federal law. Thus, the filing of an unfair labor practice charge could initiate complex litigation which would not necessarily lead to a resolution of the problem which led to this litigation.

the state court's jurisdiction over Sears' trespass claim involves somewhat different considerations.

Apart from notions of "primary jurisdiction,"[29] there would be no objection to state courts' and the NLRB's exercising concurrent jurisdiction over conduct prohibited by the federal Act. But there is a constitutional objection to state-court interference with conduct actually protected by the Act. Considerations of federal supremacy, therefore, are implicated to a greater extent when labor-related activity is protected than when it is prohibited. Nevertheless, several considerations persuade us that the mere fact that the Union's trespass was *arguably* protected is insufficient to deprive the state court of jurisdiction in this case.

The first is the relative unimportance in this context of the "primary jurisdiction" rationale articulated in *Garmon*. In theory, of course, that rationale supports pre-emption regardless of which section of the NLRA is critical to resolving a controversy which may be subject to the regulatory jurisdiction of the NLRB. Indeed, at first blush, the primary-jurisdiction rationale provides stronger support for pre-emption in this case when the analysis is focused upon the arguably protected, rather than the arguably prohibited, character of the Union's conduct. For to the extent that the Union's picketing was arguably protected, there existed a potential overlap between the controversy presented to the state court and that which the Union might have brought before the NLRB. Prior to granting any relief from the Union's continuing trespass, the state court was obligated to decide that the trespass was not actually protected by federal law, a determination which might entail an accommodation of Sears' property rights and the Union's § 7 rights. In an unfair labor practice proceeding initiated by the Union, the Board might have been required to make the same accommodation.

Although it was theoretically possible for the accommodation issue to be decided either by the state court or by the Labor Board, there was in fact no risk of overlapping jurisdiction in this case. The primary-jurisdiction rationale justifies pre-emption only in situations in which an aggrieved party has a reasonable opportunity either to invoke the Board's jurisdiction himself or else to induce his adversary to do so. In this case, Sears could not directly obtain a Board ruling on the question whether the Union's trespass was federally protected. Such a Board determination could have been obtained only if the Union had filed an unfair labor practice charge alleging that Sears had interfered with the Union's § 7 right to engage in peaceful picketing on Sears' property. By demanding that the Union remove its pickets from the store's property, Sears in fact pursued a course of action which gave the Union the opportunity to file such a charge. But the Union's response to Sears' demand foreclosed the possibility of having the accommodation of § 7 and property rights made by the Labor Board; instead of filing a charge with the Board, the Union

[29]In this opinion, the term "primary jurisdiction" is used to refer to the various considerations articulated in *Garmon* and its progeny that militate in favor of pre-empting state-court jurisdiction over activity which is subject to the unfair labor practice jurisdiction of the federal Board.

advised Sears that the pickets would only depart under compulsion of legal process.

In the face of the Union's intransigence, Sears had only three options: permit the pickets to remain on its property; forcefully evict the pickets; or seek the protection of the State's trespass laws. Since the Union's conduct violated state law, Sears legitimately rejected the first option. Since the second option involved a risk of violence, Sears surely had the right—perhaps even the duty—to reject it. Only by proceeding in state court, therefore, could Sears obtain an orderly resolution of the question whether the Union had a federal right to remain on its property.

The primary-jurisdiction rationale unquestionably requires that when the same controversy may be presented to the state court or the NLRB, it must be presented to the Board. But that rationale does not extend to cases in which an employer has no acceptable method of invoking, or inducing the Union to invoke, the jurisdiction of the Board.[33] We are therefore persuaded that the primary-jurisdiction rationale does not provide a *sufficient* justification for pre-empting state jurisdiction over arguably protected conduct when the party who could have presented the protection issue to the Board has not done so and the other party to the dispute has no acceptable means of doing so.

This conclusion does not, however, necessarily foreclose the possibility that pre-emption may be appropriate. The danger of state interference with federally protected conduct is the principal concern of the second branch of the *Garmon* doctrine. To allow the exercise of state jurisdiction in certain contexts might create a significant risk of misinterpretation of federal law and the consequent prohibition of protected conduct. In those circumstances, it might be reasonable to infer that Congress preferred the costs inherent in a jurisdictional hiatus to the frustration of national labor policy which might accompany the exercise of state jurisdiction. Thus, the acceptability of "arguable protection" as a justification for pre-emption in a given class of cases is, at least in part, a function of the strength of the argument that § 7 does in fact protect the disputed conduct.

The Court has held that state jurisdiction to enforce its laws prohibiting violence, defamation, the intentional infliction of emotional distress, or obstruction of access to property is not pre-empted by the NLRA. But none of those violations of state law involves protected conduct. In contrast, some violations of state trespass laws may be actually protected by § 7 of the federal Act.

In *NLRB* v. *Babcock & Wilcox Co.*, 351 U.S. 105, for example, the Court recognized that in certain circumstances nonemployee union organizers

---

[33]Even if Sears had elected the self-help option, it could not have been assured that the Union would have invoked the jurisdiction of the Board. The Union may well have decided that the likelihood of success was remote and outweighed by the cost of the effort and the probability that Sears in turn would have charged the Union with violating § 8(b)(4)(D) or § 8(b)(7)(C) of the Act. Moreover, if Sears had elected this option, and the pickets were evicted with more force than reasonably necessary, it might have exposed itself to tort liability under state law. We are unwilling to presume that Congress intended to require employers to pursue such a risky course in order to ensure that issues involving the scope of § 7 rights be decided only by the Labor Board.

may have a limited right of access to an employer's premises for the purpose of engaging in organization solicitation. And the Court has indicated that *Babcock* extends to § 7 rights other than organizational activity, though the "locus" of the "accommodation of § 7 rights and private property rights . . . may fall at different points along the spectrum depending on the nature and strength of the respective § 7 rights and private property rights asserted in any given context." *Hudgens* v. *NLRB*, 424 U.S. 507, 522.

For purpose of analysis we must assume that the Union could have proved that its picketing was, at least in the absence of a trespass, protected by § 7. The remaining question is whether under *Babcock* the trespassory nature of the picketing caused it to forfeit its protected status. Since it cannot be said with certainty that, if the Union had filed an unfair labor practice charge against Sears, the Board would have fixed the locus of the accommodation at the unprotected end of the spectrum, it is indeed "arguable" that the Union's peaceful picketing, though trespassory, was protected. Nevertheless, permitting state courts to evaluate the merits of an argument that certain trespassory activity is protected does not create an unacceptable risk of interference with conduct which the Board, and a court reviewing the Board's decision, would find protected. For while there are unquestionably examples of trespassory union activity in which the question whether it is protected is fairly debatable, experience under the Act teaches that such situations are rare and that a trespass is far more likely to be unprotected than protected.

Experience with trespassory organizational solicitation by nonemployees is instructive in this regard. While *Babcock* indicates that an employer may not always bar nonemployee union organizers from his property, his right to do so remains the general rule. To gain access, the union has the burden of showing that no other reasonable means of communicating its organizational message to the employees exists or that the employer's access rules discriminate against union solicitation. That the burden imposed on the union is a heavy one is evidenced by the fact that the balance struck by the Board and the courts under the *Babcock* accommodation principle has rarely been in favor of trespassory organizational activity.

Even on the assumption that picketing to enforce area standards is entitled to the same deference in the *Babcock* accommodation analysis as organizational solicitation,[42] it would be unprotected in most instances. While there does exist some risk that state courts will on occasion enjoin a trespass that the Board would have protected, the significance of this risk is minimized by the fact that in the cases in which the argument in favor of protection is the strongest, the union is likely to invoke the Board's jurisdiction and thereby avoid the state forum. Whatever risk of an

---

[42]This assumption, however, is subject to serious question. Indeed, several factors make the argument for protection of trespassory area-standards picketing as a category of conduct less compelling than that for trespassory organizational solicitation. First, the right to organize is at the very core of the purpose for which the NLRA was enacted. Area-standards picketing, in contrast, has only recently been recognized as a § 7 right. *Hod Carriers Local 41 (Calumet Contractors Ass'n)*, 133 NLRB 512 (1961). Second, *Babcock* makes clear that the interests being protected by according limited-access rights to nonemployee union organiz-

erroneous state-court adjudication does exist is outweighed by the anomalous consequence of a rule which would deny the employer access to any forum in which to litigate either the trespass issue or the protection issue in those cases in which the disputed conduct is least likely to be protected by § 7.

If there is a strong argument that the trespass is protected in a particular case, a union can be expected to respond to an employer demand to depart by filing an unfair labor practice charge; the protection question would then be decided by the agency experienced in accommodating the § 7 rights of unions and the property rights of employers in the context of a labor dispute. But if the argument for protection is so weak that it has virtually no chance of prevailing, a trespassing union would be well advised to avoid the jurisdiction of the Board and to argue that the protected character of its conduct deprives the state court of jurisdiction.

As long as the union has a fair opportunity to present the protection issue to the Labor Board, it retains meaningful protection against the risk of error in a state tribunal. In this case the Union failed to invoke the jurisdiction of the Labor Board,[43] and Sears had no right to invoke that jurisdiction and could not even precipitate its exercise without resort to self-help. Because the assertion of state jurisdiction in a case of this kind does not create a significant risk of prohibition of protected conduct, we are unwilling to presume that Congress intended the arguably protected character of the Union's conduct to deprive the California courts of jurisdiction to entertain Sears' trespass action.

The judgment of the Supreme Court of California is therefore reversed, and the case is remanded to that court for further proceedings not inconsistent with this opinion.

MR. JUSTICE BLACKMUN, concurring.

I join the Court's opinion, but add three observations:

1. The problem of a no-man's land in regard to trespassory picketing has been a troubling one in the past because employers have been unable to secure a Labor Board adjudication whether the picketing was "actually protected" under § 7 of the National Labor Relations Act except by resorting to self-help to expel the pickets and thereby inducing the union to file an unfair labor practice charge. The unacceptable possibility of precipitating violence in such a situation called into serious question the practicability there of the *Garmon* pre-emption test, see *Longshoremen* v.

---

ers are not those of the organizers but of the employees located on the employer's property. The Court indicated that "no . . . obligation is owed nonemployee organizers"; any right they may have to solicit on an employer's property is a derivative of the right of that employer's employees to exercise their organization rights effectively. Area-standards picketing, on the other hand, has no such vital link to the employees located on the employer's property. While such picketing may have a beneficial effect on the compensation of those employees, the rationale for protecting area-standards picketing is that a union has a legitimate interest in protecting the wage standards of its members who are employed by competitors of the picketed employer.

[43]Not only could the Union have filed an unfair labor practice charge pursuant to § 8(a)(1) of the Act at the time Sears demanded that the pickets leave its property, but the Board's jurisdiction could have been invoked and the protection of its remedial powers obtained even after the litigation in the state court had commenced or the state injunction issued.

Ariadne Shipping Co., 397 U.S. 195, 202 (1970) (WHITE, J., concurring), despite the virtues of the *Garmon* test in ensuring uniform application of the standards of the NLRA.

In this case, however, the NLRB as *amicus curiae* has taken a position that narrows the no-man's land in regard to trespassory picketing, namely, that an employer's mere act of informing nonemployee pickets that they are not permitted on his property "would constitute a sufficient interference with rights arguably protected by Section 7 to warrant the General Counsel, had a charge been filed by the Union, in issuing a Section 8(a)(1) complaint" against the employer. Brief for NLRB as *Amicus Curiae* 18. Hence, if the union, once asked to leave the property, files a § 8(a)(1) charge, there is a practicable means of getting the issue of trespassory picketing before the Board in a timely fashion without danger of violence.

In this case, as the Court notes, the Union failed to file an unfair labor practice charge after being asked to leave. In such a situation pre-emption cannot sensibly obtain because the "risk of an erroneous state-court adjudication . . . is outweighed by the anomalous consequence of a rule which would deny the employer access to any forum in which to litigate either the trespass issue or the protection issue." *Ante*, at 206–207. It should be made clear, however, that the logical corollary of the Court's reasoning is that if the union *does* file a charge upon being asked by the employer to leave the employer's property and continues to process the charge expeditiously, state-court jurisdiction is pre-empted until such time as the General Counsel declines to issue a complaint or the Board, applying the standards of *NLRB* v. *Babcock & Wilcox Co.*, 351 U.S. 105 (1956), rules against the union and holds the picketing to be unprotected. Similarly, if a union timely files a § 8(a)(1) charge, a state court would be bound to stay any pending injunctive or damages suit brought by the employer until the Board has concluded, or the General Counsel by refusal to issue a complaint has indicated, that the picketing is not protected by § 7. As the Court also notes, *ante*, at 202, the primary-jurisdiction rationale articulated in *Garmon* "unquestionably requires that when the same controversy may be presented to the state court or the NLRB, it must be presented to the Board." Once the no-man's land has been bridged, as it is once a union files a charge, the importance of deferring to the Labor Board's case-by-case accommodation of employers' property rights and employees' § 7 rights mandates pre-emption of state-court jurisdiction.*

---

*MR. JUSTICE POWELL's concern, *post*, at 213, that there is an unacceptable delay in waiting for the General Counsel to act is answered in main part by this Court's previous holdings that any obstructive picketing or threatening conduct may be directly regulated by the State. See *Electrical Workers* v. *Wisconsin Employment Relations Bd.*, 315 U.S. 740 (1942); *Youngdahl* v. *Rainfair, Inc.*, 355 U.S. 131 (1957); cf. *Automobile Workers* v. *Russell*, 356 U.S. 634 (1958). There was no hint of such a problem in this case. As the California Supreme Court notes: "It is not disputed that at all times . . . the pickets conducted themselves in a peaceful and orderly fashion. The record discloses no acts of violence, threats of violence, or obstruction of traffic." 17 Cal.3d 893, 896, 553 P.2d 603, 606 (1976). There is no claim made that the pickets annoyed members of the public who wished to patronize the store of petitioner Sears; such conduct would be enjoinable, *Youngdahl, supra*, if it had occurred. And, of course, under current NLRB law, pickets would have no right to carry on their

2. The opinion correctly observes, *ante*, at 205, that in implementing this Court's decision in *Babcock* the NLRB only occasionally has found trespassory picketing to be protected under § 7. That observation is important, as is noted, *ante*, at 203, in that even the existence of a no-man's land may not justify departure from *Garmon's* pre-emption standard if the exercise of state-court jurisdiction portends frequent interference with actually protected conduct. But in its conclusion that trespassory picketing has been found in "experience under the Act" to be only "rare[ly]" protected and "far more likely to be unprotected than protected," *ante*, at 205, I take the opinion merely to be observing what the Board's past experience has been, not as glossing how the Board must treat the *Babcock* test in the future, either in regard to organizational picketing or other sorts of protected picketing. The *Babcock* test provides that "when the inaccessibility of employees makes ineffective the reasonable attempts by nonemployees to communicate with them through the usual channels, the right to exclude from property [is] required to yield to the extent needed to permit communication of information on the right to organize." 351 U.S., at 112. A variant of that test has been applied by the Board when communication with consumers is at stake. See *Scott Hudgens*, 230 NLRB 414 (1977). The problem of applying the test in the first instance is delegated to the Board, as part of its "responsibility to adapt the Act to changing patterns of industrial life." *NLRB* v. *Weingarten, Inc.*, 420 U.S. 251, 266 (1975); *Hudgens* v. *NLRB*, 424 U.S. 507, 523 (1976). When, for a number of years, the First Amendment holding of *Food Employees* v. *Logan Valley Plaza*, 391 U.S. 308 (1968), overruled in *Hudgens* v. *NLRB*, diverted the Board from any need to consider trespassory picketing under the statutory test of *Babcock*, it would be unwise to hold the Board confined to its earliest experience in administering the test.

3. The acceptability of permitting state-court jurisdiction over "arguably protected" activities where there is a jurisdictional no-man's land depends, as the Court notes, on whether the exercise of state-court jurisdiction is likely to interfere frequently with actually protected conduct. The likelihood of such interference will depend in large part on whether the state courts take care to provide an adversary hearing *before* issuing any restraint against union picketing activities. In this case, Sears filed a verified complaint seeking an injunction against the picketing on October 29, 1973. The Superior Court of California entered a temporary

---

activity within a store. *Marshall Field & Co.* v. *NLRB*, 200 F.2d 375 (CA 7 1953). With respect, I do not see what "danger of violence" remains in such a situation, any more than for a business that fronts upon a public sidewalk.

The possibility of delay to which my Brother POWELL adverts is a double-edged sword. The question really is upon whom the burden of delay should be placed. If it takes the General Counsel "weeks" to decide whether to issue a § 8(a)(1) complaint, by the same token there would be no relief available against an erroneous state-court injunction interfering with protected picketing for an equal length of time. Section 10(j) permits the Board to seek injunctive relief only after the issuance of a complaint. The Board arguably might seek dissolution of a state-court order under *NLRB* v. *Nash-Finch Co.*, 404 U.S. 138 (1971), but that remedy, too, would encompass some delay. It is worth noting that here by November 12, 1973, the picketing, confined to the public sidewalks by the California Superior Court's temporary restraining order, was abandoned as ineffective. Delay in remedy is desired by neither party in a labor dispute.

restraining order that day. So far as the record reveals, the Union was not accorded a hearing until November 16, on the order to show cause why a preliminary injunction should not be entered. The issue of a prompt hearing was apparently not raised before the Superior Court and was not raised on appeal, and hence does not enter into our judgment here approving the exercise of state-court jurisdiction. But it may be remiss not to observe that in labor-management relations, where *ex parte* proceedings historically were abused, see F. Frankfurter & N. Greene, The Labor Injunction 60, 64–66 (1930), it is critical that the state courts provide a prompt adversary hearing, preferably before any restraint issues and in all events within a few days thereafter, on the merits of the § 7 protection question. Labor disputes are frequently short lived, and a temporary restraining order issued upon *ex parte* application may, if in error, render the eventual finding of § 7 protection a hollow vindication.

Mr. Justice Powell, concurring.

Although I join the Court's opinion, Mr. Justice Blackmun's concurrence prompts me to add a word as to the "no-man's land" discussion with respect to trespassory picketing. Mr. Justice Blackmun, relying on the *amicus* brief of the National Labor Relations Board, observes that "there is a practicable means of getting the issue of trespassory picketing before the Board in a timely fashion without danger of violence," *ante*, at 209, if the union—having been requested to leave the property—files a § 8(a)(1) charge.

With all respect, this optimistic view overlooks the realities of the situation. Trespass upon private property by pickets, to a greater degree than isolated trespass, is usually organized, sustained, and sometimes obstructive—without initial violence—of the target business and annoying to members of the public who wish to patronize that business. The "danger of violence" is inherent in many—though certainly not all—situations of sustained trespassory picketing. One cannot predict whether or when it may occur, or its degree. It is because of these factors that, absent the availability of an equivalent remedy under the National Labor Relations Act, a state court should have the authority to protect the public and private interests by granting preliminary relief.

In the context of trespassory picketing not otherwise violative of the Act, the Board has no comparable authority. If a § 8(a)(1) charge is filed, nothing is likely to happen "in a timely fashion." The Board cannot issue, or obtain from the federal courts, a restraining order directed at the picketing. And it may take weeks for the General Counsel to decide whether to issue a complaint. Meanwhile, the "no-man's land" prevents all recourse to the courts, and is an open invitation to self-help. I am unwilling to believe that Congress intended, by its silence in the Act, to create a situation where there is no forum to which the parties may turn for orderly interim relief in the face of a potentially explosive situation.*

*It is true that under this Court's decisions, state courts are not precluded from providing relief against actual or threatened violence. But in light of the "danger of violence" inherent in many instances of sustained trespassory picketing, relief often may come too late to prevent interference with the operation of the target business. Cf. *People* v. *Bush*, 39 N.Y.2d 529, 349 N.E.2d 832 (1976). Moreover, as Mr. Justice Clark noted for the Court in *Linn* v.

I do not minimize the possibility that the Board may find that trespassory activity under certain circumstances is necessary to facilitate the exercise of § 7 rights by employees of the target employer. See *NLRB* v. *Babcock & Wilcox Co.*, 351 U.S. 105 (1956); *Central Hardware Co.* v. *NLRB*, 407 U.S. 539 (1972). The Union's conduct in this case, however, involved a publicity campaign maintained by nonemployees and directed at the general public. Such "area standards" trespassory picketing is certainly not at the core of the Act's protective ambit. In any event, it is open to the Board upon the issuance of a complaint to seek temporary relief under § 10(j) of the Act, 29 U.S.C. § 160(j), against the employer's interference with § 7 rights. Cf. *Capital Service, Inc.* v. *NLRB*, 347 U.S. 501 (1954). Moreover, it is not an unreasonable assumption that state courts will be mindful of the determination of an expert federal agency that there is probable cause to believe that conduct restrained by state process is protected under the Act. But I find no warrant in the Act to compel the employer to endure the creation, especially by nonemployees of a temporary easement on his property pending the outcome of the General Counsel's action on a charge.

In sum, I do not agree with MR. JUSTICE BLACKMUN that "the logical corollary of the Court's reasoning" in its opinion today is that state-court jurisdiction is pre-empted forthwith upon the filing of a charge by the union. I would not join the Court's opinion if I thought it fairly could be read to that effect.

MR. JUSTICE BRENNAN, with whom MR. JUSTICE STEWART and MR. JUSTICE MARSHALL joined, dissented.

Notes on Access

1. *Surmises on the ebb and flow of state power to regulate labor relations.* Interesting parallels may be found in the development of three lines of cases which first limited and then restored the power of the states to regulate labor relations.

The easiest to trace involves the reversal of the *Logan Valley* decision in *Scott Hudgens*, discussed on page 181. With private shopping centers and industrial parks no longer considered the "functional equivalent" of municipalities, the states are no longer barred by the constitution from regulating the location of picketing on private property.

A second line of cases involves regulation not of the location but of the nature of the picketing, particularly with respect to its objectives. The seminal case is *Thornhill* v. *Alabama*, 310 U.S. 88, 6 LRRM 697 (1940), in which the Supreme Court struck down a statute barring all picketing,

---

Plant Guard Workers, 383 U.S. 53, 64 n. 6 (1966), "[t]he fact that the Board has no authority to grant effective relief aggravates the State's concern since the refusal to redress an otherwise actionable wrong creates disrespect for the law and encourages the victim to take matters into his own hands." The "imminent threat of violence [that] exists whenever an employer is required to resort to self-help in order to vindicate his property rights," has prompted at least one state court to retain jurisdiction to enjoin trespassory picketing even after the filing of an unfair labor practice charge with the Board. *May Department Stores Co.* v. *Teamsters*, 64 Ill.2d 153, 162–163, 355 N.E.2d 7, 10–11 (1976).

declaring that "the dissemination of information concerning the facts of a labor dispute must be regarded as within that area of free discussion guaranteed by the Constitution," 310 U.S. at 102, 6 LRRM at 703. But subsequent cases qualified this constitutional right when the state could show a compelling basis to regulate the picketing. The retreat from the broad principles of *Thornhill* culminated in *Teamsters* v. *Vogt*, 354 U.S. 284, 40 LRRM 2208 (1957), in which the Court permitted the state to enjoin picketing for the purpose of compelling employees to join the union. Justice Frankfurter's opinion in *Vogt* traces the cases after *Thornhill* and characterizes them as establishing "a broad field in which a State, in enforcing some public policy, whether of its criminal or its civil law, and whether announced by its legislature or its courts, could constitutionally enjoin peaceful picketing aimed at preventing effectuation of that policy." Justice Frankfurter viewed these cases as granting "wide discretion to a State in the formulation of domestic policy, and not involving a curtailment of free speech in its obvious and accepted scope."

The dissenting justices in *Vogt*, in an opinion by Justice Douglas, charged that the Court had come "full circle" since *Thornhill*.

The *Thornhill* to *Vogt* line is of largely historical interest, as the interests asserted by the states in those cases were regulated, after 1959, under the NLRA, particularly under Section 8(b)(7), discussed in Chapter 7. If a state today were to attempt to regulate organizational picketing, the matter would likely be held preempted under the doctrines discussed in *Sears*.

But *Sears* in turn may be thought to represent a turnaround in the preemption doctrine. While we have omitted the dissenting opinion in *Sears*, the dissenters viewed the majority opinion as making a sharp break with the past. The qualified statement of preemption where no charge has been filed, coupled with the Court's statements about the strong local interests in regulating trespassory activity, may be viewed as a retreat from the Court's broad preemption principle set forth in *Garmon*. If so, *Sears* represents a further relaxation of doctrines which limit the state's power to regulate labor relations. Compare *Belknap, Inc.* v. *Hale*, 463 U.S. ___, 113 LRRM 3057 (1983). During an economic strike the employer promised permanent employment to employees hired as replacements for strikers. But when the strike was finally settled, the employer agreed with the union to reinstate some of the strikers, which resulted in the layoff of some of the strike replacements. In a divided opinion the Court held that a state cause of action by the strike replacements against the employer for breach of contract and misrepresentation was not preempted. The Court's opinion rests in part upon its concern for the state interest in protecting the rights of the strike replacements.

2. *Alternative means of communication.* In both *Babcock & Wilcox* and *Hudgens* the right of access under Section 7 turns in large part upon the availability of other channels of communication. The dialogue in the problem suggests some alternative means for the union to reach the employees. What additional opportunities for communication are provided by law? The answer is, precious few.

If the union thinks that it can achieve effective communications through the mails, then the Board's names-and-addresses rule is of some value. In a case with the prosaic name of *Excelsior Underwear, Inc.*, 156 NLRB 1236, 61 LRRM 1217 (1966), the Board set aside an election on the basis of the employer's refusal to provide the union with the names and addresses of employees eligible to vote. The Board set forth a requirement that in all elections the employer must provide the regional director of the Board with such a list within seven days of the direction of an election or the approval of a consent election agreement. The names and addresses are then made available to all parties. Consider the rationale for the rule, 156 NLRB at 1240–41:

> "As a practical matter, an employer, through his possession of employee names and home addresses as well as his ability to communicate with employees on plant premises, is assured of the continuing opportunity to inform the entire electorate of his views with respect to union representation. On the other hand, without a list of employee names and addresses, a labor organization, whose organizers normally have no right of access to plant premises, has no method by which it can be certain of reaching all the employees with its arguments in favor of representation, and, as a result, employees are often completely unaware of that point of view. This is not, of course, to deny the existence of various means by which a party *might* be able to communicate with a substantial portion of the electorate even without possessing their names and addresses. It is rather to say what seems to us obvious—that the access of *all* employees to such communications can be insured only if all parties have the names and addresses of all the voters. In other words, by providing all parties with employees' names and addresses, we maximize the likelihood that all the voters will be exposed to the arguments for, as well as against, union representation.
>
> "Nor are employee names and addresses readily available from sources other than the employer. . . ."

The Board has flirted with an "equal time" doctrine that would give the union the right under limited circumstances to address employees on company time and premises. Before you can evaluate this approach you must first become acquainted with the "captive audience" doctrine. A common technique used by employers in an organizing campaign is to call the employees together and address them on company time. While it is lawful under the Act to make such a "captive audience" speech, under the *Peerless Plywood* rule, 107 NLRB 427, 33 LRRM 1151 (1953), neither the union nor the employer may utilize this device within 24 hours prior to the election. This is designed to prevent a mass psychology from attaching to a last-minute speech and giving it undue weight; violation of the 24-hour rule will result in setting the election aside. But even where the employer's captive-audience speech is outside the 24-hour mark, unions have urged that it creates an imbalance in channels of communication. In *Bonwit-Teller*, 96 NLRB 608, 28 LRRM 1547 (1951), *remanded*, 197 F.2d 640, 30 LRRM 2305 (2d Cir. 1952), *cert. denied*, 345 U.S. 905, 31 LRRM 2444 (1953), the Board announced a short-lived rule that required an employer who delivered an otherwise proper captive-audience speech to allow the union equal time to respond. The Board reasoned that the employer's use of company time to campaign against the union rendered its no-solicitation rule discriminatory when applied to the union. But within two years, in *Livingston Shirt Corp.*, 107 NLRB 400, 33 LRRM 1156 (1953), the Board severely limited the *Bonwit-Teller* rule. The prevailing rule is that the employer is required to accede to a request to reply only if the employer makes a captive-audience speech while at the same time maintaining an unlawfully broad no-solicitation or no-distribution rule. (Special rules, which we will not discuss here, govern the application of this doctrine to department stores; see *May Department Stores*, 136 NLRB 797, 49 LRRM 1862 (1962).)

The Supreme Court has, in effect, upheld the Board's current accommodation in *NLRB* v. *Steelworkers* (*Nutone*), 357 U.S. 357, 42 LRRM 2324 (1958). In an opinion by Justice Frankfurter the Court held that the union is not "entitled to use a medium of communication simply because the employer is using it." However, there is a suggestion in the opinion that, if in view of the lack of alternative channels of communication the no-solicitation rule "truly diminished the ability of the labor organizations involved to carry their message to the employees," the captive-audience speech coupled with the no-solicitation rule might violate the Act. For a perceptive criticism of the Board's changing position on the equal-time doctrine, see Friendly, The Federal Administrative Agencies 36–41 (1962).

Access has also been granted to unions as a remedy for other violations of the Act, but the decisions on this point are in disarray. One line of cases holds that *Babcock* indeed controls and access must be predicated on the unavailability of alternative means. Another approach is to reject the applicability of *Babcock* altogether, on the theory that *Babcock* involved only the question of whether denial of access itself constitutes an unfair labor practice, rather than whether access is an appropriate remedial tool for other violations of the Act. The argument in favor of direct access as a remedial tool is summarized in *Steelworkers* v. *NLRB*, 646 F.2d 616, 106 LRRM 2573, 2589, 2590 (D.C. Cir. 1981) (a decision which also reviews the caselaw):

"We agree that there is a critical difference between access as an organizational tool and access as a remedial measure. Absent unfair labor practices, private property rights entitle an employer to restrict the ability of union organizers to enter company property and solicit for the union. As long as important employee rights may be exercised through other means, equally important private property rights need not be sacrificed. When an employer directly interferes with those employee rights, however, different considerations come into play. The Act contains a broad command that the Board take such affirmative action as is necessary to safeguard employee rights and thus effectuate the policies of the Act. As illustrated above, certain employer conduct may be of such a nature that some form of union access is needed to dissipate an atmosphere of fear and helplessness that has been created and to assure employees that fundamental rights exist and will be protected. In such a case, an employer cannot avoid the direct consequences of its own actions by invoking the talisman of private property rights. As employee rights have been violated, so too may private property rights be compromised. Private property rights are easily safeguarded, as decreed by *Babcock* and its progeny, by simple adherence to the structures of the Act. . . .

"The hallmark principle in each of these applications of access as a remedial measure is the necessity to offset coercive effects caused by an employer's unlawful campaign. As those effects spread and become entrenched, so too may an access remedy. In this way, grants of access are designed fully to effectuate the policies of the Act; access is ordered to remedy the effects of unlawful behavior and not to punish or deter an employer. It is clear that the principles of *Babcock* have no direct application in this setting.

"At the same time, we recognize that the presence of *Babcock* cannot be totally ignored. Access may be awarded as a remedial measure if necessary to offset the direct consequences or effects of an employer's unlawful conduct. Having produced such effects, an employer cannot hide behind the protection of *Babcock* or private property rights. If those effects are not present, however, the above analysis fails. Absent the necessity to counter these harmful consequences, access cannot be justified as a remedial measure and instead may directly affront the principles announced in *Babcock*. As a result, before access may be imposed, it is critical that a clear showing be made that access is needed to reassure employees of the existence and vitality of protected legal rights.

"In granting access as a remedial measure, therefore, a burden lies upon the Board to substantiate its conclusion that access is necessary to offset the consequences of unlawful employer conduct. In articulating the standard that the Board must meet, we are sensitive to the difficulty the Board faces in establishing that the exercise of employee rights has been chilled. Coercive effects are difficult to prove, yet at the same time the most important to dissipate. Certainly in this setting even more so than in other areas, the Board possesses an unmatched expertise in distilling and identifying the effects of unlawful employer conduct. We believe that the Board may rely on that expertise, and on the cumulative experience of past cases, to presume that certain employer conduct will inevitably produce certain effects on employees.

"Given the amount at stake in this setting, however, a conclusory statement by the Board that access is needed to neutralize effects is not sufficient to justify a grant of access. Assumptions must be supported by evidence in the record."

Other decisions ignore *Babcock*, regardless of whether remedial access is ordered (aggravated circumstances) or denied (lesser remedies are adequate and access to the losing union might suggest Board preference as against a rival union). If access is deemed necessary because the effects of the employer's prior unfair labor practices cannot be offset by tradi-

tional remedies, such as ordering another election under the rules generally applicable to first campaigns, a further question may arise: is the
union's direct access limited to the site at which the original election and
employer unfair labor practices occurred? The argument in favor of
broad access is that employees at other locations may learn of employer
unfair labor practices elsewhere and experience a "chilling effect" on
Section 7 rights to organize. Although rare, some courts have granted
companywide access to offset the effects of extensive, repeated, and well-
publicized unlawful employer conduct.

This line of cases is of no help to the union in establishing a right of
access when the employer is not otherwise in violation of the Act.

Throughout this entire discussion there is little factual data as to
whether access or lack of it actually affects the way employees vote.
Consider the following study:

Getman, Goldberg, and Herman, Union Representation Elections: Law and Reality*

THE IMPORTANCE OF MEETINGS

As shown by Tables 4–12 and 4–13, individual differences in familiarity related to campaign exposure are largely accounted for by attendance at meetings. Employees who attended company meetings were
significantly more familiar with the company campaign than those who
did not ($r = .33$); employees who attended union meetings were significantly more familiar with the union campaign than those who did not
($r = .43$).

A far larger proportion of employees attend company meetings (83
percent) than attend union meetings (36 percent). Furthermore, those
who attend union meetings tend to be union supporters ($r = .40$). This is
not true of company meetings ($r = -.03$). Regardless of intent, attendance at meetings is significantly related to familiarity. The company,
then, has a particular advantage in communicating with the undecided
and those not already committed to it.

In sum, when the employer can hold campaign meetings on working
time and premises and the union cannot, the union is at a substantial
disadvantage in achieving meaningful communication with employees,
even when all other means of campaigning are taken into account. This
disadvantage explains why company voters are less familiar than union
voters with the union campaign; it also explains why union voters are as
familiar with the company campaign as company voters.

In *NLRB* v. *United Steelworkers of America (Nutone, Inc.)*, the Supreme
Court asked whether an employer's use of company time and premises
for anti-union campaigning, combined with a refusal to allow the union to

*Excerpted from UNION REPRESENTATION ELECTIONS: LAW AND REALITY, by Julius G.
Getman, Stephen B. Goldberg, and Jeanne B. Herman, pp. 95–96, 156–59. © 1976 by
Russell Sage Foundation, New York.

Table 4–12

Correlations between Exposure to and Familiarity
with the Company Campaign, Intent, and Vote

Company Familiarity	Letters	Meetings	Personal Contact	Intent	Vote
1. 1.00					
2. .22	1.00				
3. .33	.21	1.00			
4. .19	.07	.01	1.00		
5. −.03	.09	.03	.14	1.00	
6. −.04	.09	.04	.15	.73	1.00

NOTE: $r = .08$; $p \leq .01$; $N = 955$.

Table 4–13

Correlations between Exposure to and Familiarity with the
Union Campaign, Intent, and Vote

Union Familiarity	Letters	Meetings	Personal Contact	Intent	Vote
1. 1.00					
2. .20	1.00				
3. .43	−.08	1.00			
4. .25	.11	−.02	1.00		
5. .35	−.10	.40	−.08	1.00	
6. .44	−.09	.46	−.08	.73	1.00

NOTE: $r = .09$; $p \leq .01$; $N = 888$.

engage in similar campaigning, created an "imbalance in opportunities
for organizational communication." The Board has held that except in
unusual circumstances, such as when the employees involved work on a
ship or are otherwise isolated, such conduct on the part of the employer
does not create an imbalance. The data suggest that the Board's answer
has been incorrect: when an employer uses company time and premises
for antiunion campaigning and the union must campaign off company
premises, the union is at a substantial disadvantage in communicating
with the voters.

EQUAL OPPORTUNITIES FOR ORGANIZATIONAL COMMUNICATION

In *NLRB* v. *United Steelworkers of America* (*Nutone, Inc.*), the Supreme
Court held that an employer did not necessarily violate the Act by campaigning against the union on working time or premises while preventing

similar campaigning on behalf of the union. The Court stated, however, that if the combined effect of the employer's campaigning and his refusal to allow similar union campaigning was to create an imbalance in opportunities for organizational communication, the Board could find the employer's conduct unlawful. The data show that such an imbalance normally exists. The employer who uses working time or premises to campaign against the union and denies those facilities to the union effectively communicates with a substantially greater proportion of the employees than does the union.

The employer's advantage is primarily due to the powerful correlation between campaign familiarity and attendance at meetings. Employees who attended meetings conducted by either party were significantly more familiar with that party's campaign than employees who did not attend meetings. The employer tends to be far more successful in attracting employees to meetings on working time and premises than does the union in attracting them to meetings outside working hours and away from company premises. Eighty-three percent of the sample attended company meetings, while only 36 percent attended union meetings. Furthermore, those employees who attended union meetings tended to be union supporters. The company, then, has a great advantage in communicating with the undecided and those not already committed to it. This advantage is particularly important since attendance at union meetings is significantly related to switching to the union. If the union could communicate with more of those not already committed to it, it might do significantly better in the election.

In order for each party to have an equal opportunity to present its views, an employer who holds campaign meetings on working time and premises should be required to allow the union (or unions) to hold such meetings on working time and premises. A similar requirement should be imposed on an employer who permits supervisors to campaign against the union on company premises, whether in individual or small group meetings with employees. Campaign familiarity is also significantly related to personal contacts. If employers could campaign individually or in small groups on company premises, without the necessity of offering the union an opportunity to campaign under similar circumstances, they would be tempted to switch to such campaigning. In view of the employer's ability to contact all employees on company premises, if the union were restricted to off-premises contacts, it would be at the same disadvantage as under existing law. Accordingly, if supervisors are allowed to engage in individual campaigning on company premises, union organizers must also be allowed to do so.

This recommendation does not rest solely on the evidence that campaign familiarity is related to switching to the union. It is fundamental to the democratic process that each party should have a roughly equal opportunity to communicate with the electorate, regardless of the effectiveness of that communication. This principle supports the employers' preference for determining employee choice by secret ballot election rather than authorization cards; it also supports the union's request for an opportunity to respond, on company time and premises, to employer campaigning on company time and premises.

―――――――

Agricultural Employees. Agricultural employees are not covered by the Act. See Section 2(3). Unless and until proposed federal legislation goes into effect, agricultural workers must rely on state laws for protection. California enacted a comprehensive Agricultural Labor Relations Act in 1975, and the Agricultural Labor Relations Board thereafter promulgated an access rule set out below.

"5. Accordingly, the Board will consider the rights of employees . . . to include the right of access by union organizers to the premises of an agricultural employer for the purpose of organizing, subject to the following limitations:

"a. Organizers may enter the property of an employer for a total period of 60 minutes before the start of work and 60 minutes after the completion of work to meet and talk with employees in areas in which employees congregate before and after working.

"b. In addition, organizers may enter the employer's property for a total period of one hour during the working day for the purpose of meeting and talking with employees during their lunch period, at such location or locations as the employees eat their lunch. If there is an established lunch break, the one-hour period shall include such lunch break. If there is no established lunch break, the one-hour period may be at any time during the working day.

"c. Access shall be limited to two organizers for each work crew on the property, provided that if there are more than 30 workers in a crew, there may be one additional organizer for every 15 additional workers.

"d. Upon request, organizers shall identify themselves by name and labor organizaton to the employer or his agent. Organizers shall also wear a badge or other designation of affiliation.

"e. The right of access shall not include conduct disruptive of the employer's property or agricultural operations, including injury to crops or machinery. Speech by itself shall not be considered disruptive conduct. Disruptive conduct by particular organizers shall not be grounds for expelling organizers not engaged in such conduct, nor for preventing future access.

"f. Pending further regulation by the Board, this regulation shall not apply after the results of an election have been certified."

The California Supreme Court upheld the validity of this rule in *Agricultural Labor Board* v. *Superior Court*, 91 LRRM 2657 (1976). Is this an accommodation that could sensibly be applied under the NLRA?

B. PROTECTION OF EMPLOYEE CHOICE

As described in *NLRB* v. *Gissel Packing Co., supra* p. 151, the representation election is intended to provide an opportunity for workers to assess for themselves the value of unionization. Laudable and simple as this goal may appear, the means for securing a reliable vote are not self-evident. One possibility is an election campaign in which union and company representatives are free to say and do whatever they feel will generate employee support. The approach traditionally taken by the Board has been quite different.

"In evaluating the interference resulting from specific conduct, the Board does not attempt to assess its actual effect on employees, but rather concerns itself with whether it is reasonable to conclude that the conduct tended to prevent the free formation and expression of the employees' choice." 33 NLRB Ann. Rep. 60 (1968).

"The Board has said that in election proceedings it seeks 'to provide a laboratory in which an experiment may be conducted, under conditions as nearly ideal as possible, to determine the uninhibited desires of the employees.' [General Shoe Corp., 77 NLRB 124, 127 (1948).] Where for any reason the standard falls too low the Board will set aside the election and direct a new one. . . ." Sewell Mfg. Co., 138 NLRB 66, 69–70, 50 LRRM 1532 (1962).

"We have thus opted for safeguards more rigorous than those applied in the arena of democratic procedures which lie at the very heart of our form of government." Modine Mfg. Co., 203 NLRB 527, 530, 83 LRRM 1133 (1973).

Considerable skepticism has been expressed about the Board's approach and its ability to judge the effects of campaign tactics on voting behavior.

"Although the Board aspires to 'laboratory conditions' in elections, we recognize that clinical asepsis is an unattainable goal in the real world of union organizational efforts. . . . Some degree of puffing and propagandizing must be permitted, else the laboratory would be found infected in every case." NLRB v. Sumter Plywood, 535 F.2d 917, 920 (5th Cir. 1976), cert. denied, 429 U.S. 1092, 14 FEP 702 (1977).

"The Board's rules concerning the circumstances under which it will find a tendency to coerce employee choice are . . . not grounded on factual data, but in guesses and assumptions. However, nothing in the collective activities or experience of the Board insures the accuracy of these assumptions."*

Even if the Board is able to determine which campaign techniques are conducive to reasoned choice, the value of the resulting regulation depends, in part, on the consequences of violating the rules. In the context of representation elections, the timing and extent of the Board's remedial authority are as essential to understanding the election process as are the standards by which the Board regulates the parties' tactics.

*Excerpted from UNION REPRESENTATION ELECTIONS: LAW AND REALITY, by Julius G. Getman, Stephen B. Goldberg, and Jeanne B. Herman, p. 5. © 1976 by Russell Sage Foundation, New York.

Although we reserve extended examination of remedial issues for the final section of this chapter, two observations may be helpful in evaluating the substantive legal rules.

"[D]elay is regarded as an employer weapon; the longer the period between initiation of an organization attempt and an election, the more discouraged employees become."*

"The main thrust of a union in organizing a nonunion shop is to win recognition and bargaining, not to win a victory in charges before the NLRB. Sometimes, however, successful charges can stop unlawful conduct that, unchecked, would virtually kill any chance of success in the drive. Moreover, the legal consequences of certain unfair employer conduct can, in some instances, provide useful vehicles for successful unionization."**

In addition, the techniques used in organizing campaigns have changed since passage of the Wagner Act and articulation of the major rules on campaigning. As expressed in the report of the House Subcommittee on Labor-Management Relations, extensive hearings uncovered "disturbing evidence" that the tactics of management consultants tend to "circumvent and nullify" existing worker protections. *Pressures in Today's Workplace: Oversight Hearings Before the House Subcommittee on Labor-Management Relations*, 96th Cong., 1st Sess. (1979). The problems which appear in this section illustrate the approach of attorneys and consultants who have recast campaign strategies in light of NLRA regulation. Before reading the materials immediately following each problem, evaluate the legality of each tactic. What does management hope to gain from the tactic? Is that goal consistent with the purpose of the election campaign? What statutory provision(s) applies to the conduct in question? As an attorney representing management, would you have any qualms about recommending the tactic under discussion? Reconsider your answers to these questions after you have examined the decisions and commentary following each problem.

1. CAMPAIGN PROPAGANDA

Problem

CONSULTANT: It's clear you have a communications problem here. There wouldn't be a union drive if the employees hadn't lost faith in management. Our job will be twofold: To stop the union cold and to make sure you develop employment policies that guarantee the union won't reappear.

MAXWELL: Sounds too good to be true. How do we go about it?

CONSULTANT: We identify the problems. Usually, employees are bothered by job security, arbitrary work rules or supervisors, and money.

*Payne, *The Consultants Who Coach the Violators*, AFL-CIO AMERICAN FEDERATIONIST 27 (Sept. 1977), quoting a management consultant.
**Stephen I. Schlossberg and Judith A. Scott, ORGANIZING AND THE LAW (1983) 68.

From what you've said, job security is a top priority here. We'll focus on that and on the consequences of having a union.

First, mail this letter to the homes of all your employees. Be sure to address it to the employee *and* the spouse:

"We can only survive if we work together to remain competitive and productive. We believe outside intervention can only hurt our ability to do this as well as threaten job security. Can any of us afford to risk steady, secure employment for the half-made promises which, if instituted, would most certainly add us to the list of others who have gone out of business and whose employees are now looking for work?

"If you think a union can do anything to protect your job, talk to employees at Ace, Brown, Dart, or other unionized plants nearby, that have gone out of business or laid people off.

"As long as we are able to control our prices and remain competitive in the market, we feel cutbacks can be kept to a minimum. Should we be forced to raise our rates beyond what the market will bear, our work load will continue to fall. We will not now nor will we ever dismiss a person because of political, religious, or moral beliefs."

Next, call a meeting of all the employees. Distribute this letter:

"This is a copy of a letter from our attorneys. It contains information we think you should know:

'You should make your employees aware of two facts. First, if your union calls a strike over contract negotiations—for example, to secure higher wages or an automatic dues checkoff—any employer is entitled to replace the strikers. The United States Supreme Court has ruled that strikers may be replaced permanently, so there's a real risk of job loss.

'Second, if the union gets a majority of the votes cast in this election, it will be extremely difficult, if not impossible, to ever get the union out of their plant. If the union loses, it will always be willing to come back and try again another year. *However, if it wins, it is virtually impossible to ever get the union out.* I have had personal experience in a case where almost every employee in the bargaining unit signed a request for an election to decertify the Union. However, because of a technical mistake they made in the proceedings, the NLRB would not even let them have the election.' "

Two days before the election, assemble the employees and give this speech:

"In less than 48 hours you will exercise your legal right to vote in this representation campaign. Throughout the campaign Enderby has tried to present our positions fairly and as the law allows. We believe you will not be swayed by the union's pie-in-the-sky promises. You know who signs your paychecks; a union won't change that.

"I want to emphasize finally that Enderby will honor any obligations under the law. If you vote against the Company, Enderby will bargain in good faith. This means, of course, that every wage rate, every benefit is open to negotiation. We start with a blank piece of paper. And in negotiations Enderby will act just like it's always been: tough but fair, since your best interests and the company's survival are tied together."

NLRB v. Gissel Packing Co.

Supreme Court of the United States, 1969
395 U.S. 575, 71 LRRM 2481

[Excerpts from this decision, which raise the question of the Board's authority to issue bargaining orders, appear at p. 151, *supra*.] . . .

MR. CHIEF JUSTICE WARREN delivered the opinion of the Court.

[The Sinclair Company was shut down for three months in 1952 as a result of a strike over contract negotiations with the American Wire Weavers Protective Association.]

The Company subsequently reopened without a union contract, and its employees remained unrepresented through 1964, when the Company was acquired by an Ohio corporation, with the Company's former president continuing as head of the Holyoke, Massachusetts, division. In July 1965, the International Brotherhood of Teamsters, Local Union No. 404, began an organizing campaign among petitioner's Holyoke employees and by the end of the summer had obtained authorization cards from 11 of the Company's 14 journeymen wire weavers choosing the Union as their bargaining agent. On September 20, the Union notified petitioner that it represented a majority of its wire weavers, requested that the Company bargain with it, and offered to submit the signed cards to a neutral third party for authentication. After petitioner's president declined the Union's request a week later, claiming, *inter alia*, that he had a good faith doubt of majority status because of the cards' inherent unreliability, the Union petitioned, on November 8, for an election that was ultimately set for December 9.

[The employer's anti-union efforts consisted solely of the communications described by the Court.]

When petitioner's president first learned of the Union's drive in July, he talked with all of his employees in an effort to dissuade them from joining a union. He particularly emphasized the results of the long 1952 strike, which he claimed "almost put our company out of business," and expressed worry that the employees were forgetting the "lessons of the past." He emphasized, secondly, that the Company was still on "thin ice" financially, that the Union's "only weapon is to strike," and that a strike "could lead to the closing of the plant," since the parent company had ample manufacturing facilities elsewhere. He noted, thirdly, that because of their age and the limited usefulness of their skills outside their craft, the employees might not be able to find re-employment if they lost their jobs as a result of a strike. Finally, he warned those who did not believe that the plant could go out of business to "look around Holyoke and see a lot of them out of business." The president sent letters to the same effect to the employees in early November, emphasizing that the parent company had no reason to stay in Massachusetts if profits went down.

During the two or three weeks immediately prior to the election on December 9, the president sent the employees a pamphlet captioned: "Do you want another 13-week strike?" stating, *inter alia*, that: "We have no doubt that the Teamsters Union can again close the Wire Weaving Department and the entire plant by a strike. We have no hopes that the Teamsters Union Bosses will not call a strike. . . . The Teamsters Union is a strike happy outfit." Similar communications followed in late November, including one stressing the Teamsters' "hoodlum control." Two days before the election, the Company sent out another pamphlet that was entitled: "Let's Look at the Record," and that purported to be an obituary of companies in the Holyoke-Springfield, Massachusetts, area that had allegedly gone out of business because of union demands, eliminating some 3,500 jobs; the first page carried a large cartoon showing the preparation of a grave for the Sinclair Company and other headstones containing the names of other plants allegedly victimized by the unions. Finally, on the day before the election, the president made another personal appeal to his employees to reject the Union. He repeated that the Company's financial condition was precarious; that a possible strike would jeopardize the continued operation of the plant; and that age and lack of education would make re-employment difficult. The Union lost the election 7 to 6, and then filed both objections to the election and unfair labor practice charges which were consolidated for hearing before the trial examiner.

[The Board set the election aside, entered a cease-and-desist order, and ordered the company to bargain on request; the Court of Appeals for the First Circuit enforced the Board's order. Noting the difficulties that arise when "an employer's anti-union efforts consist of speech alone," the Court continued:]

. . . [A]n employer's free speech right to communicate his views to his employees is firmly established and cannot be infringed by a union or the Board. Thus, § 8(c) merely implements the First Amendment by requiring that the expression of "any views, argument, or opinion" shall not be "evidence of an unfair labor practice," so long as such expression contains "no threat of reprisal or force or promise of benefit" in violation of § 8(a)(1). Section 8(a)(1), in turn, prohibits interference, restraint or coercion of employees in the exercise of their right to self-organization.

Any assessment of the precise scope of employer expression, of course, must be made in the context of its labor relations setting. Thus, an employer's rights cannot outweigh the equal rights of the employees to associate freely, as those rights are embodied in § 7 and protected by § 8(a)(1) and the proviso to § 8(c). And any balancing of those rights must take into account the economic dependence of the employees on their employers, and the necessary tendency of the former, because of that relationship, to pick up intended implications of the latter that might be more readily dismissed by a more disinterested ear. Stating these obvious principles is but another way of recognizing that what is basically at stake is the establishment of a nonpermanent, limited relationship between the employer, his economically dependent employee and his union agent, not the election of legislators or the enactment of legislation whereby that relationship is ultimately defined and where the independent voter may be freer to listen more objectively and employers as a class freer to talk. Cf. *New York Times Co.* v. *Sullivan,* 376 U.S. 254 (1964).

. . . Thus, an employer is free to communicate to his employees any of his general views about unionism or any of his specific views about a particular union, so long as the communications do not contain a "threat of reprisal or force or promise of benefit." He may even make a prediction as to the precise effects he believes unionization will have on his company. In such a case, however, the prediction must be carefully phrased on the basis of objective fact to convey an employer's belief as to demonstrably probable consequences beyond his control or to convey a management decision already arrived at to close the plant in case of unionization. See *Textile Workers* v. *Darlington Mfg. Co.,* 380 U.S. 263, 274, n. 20, 58 LRRM 2657 (1965). If there is any implication that an employer may or may not take action solely on his own initiative for reasons unrelated to economic necessities and known only to him, the statement is no longer a reasonable prediction based on available facts but a threat of retaliation based on misrepresentation and coercion, and as such without the protection of the First Amendment. We therefore agree with the court below that "[c]onveyance of the employer's belief, even though sincere, that unionization will or may result in the closing of the plant is not a statement of fact unless, which is most improbable, the eventuality of closing is capable of proof." 397 F.2d 157, 160, 68 LRRM 2720. As stated elsewhere, an employer is free only to tell "what he reasonably believes will be the likely economic consequences of unionization that are outside his control," and not "threats of economic reprisal to be taken solely on his own volition." *NLRB* v. *River Togs, Inc.,* 382 F.2d 198, 202, 65 LRRM 2987 (C.A. 2d Cir. 1967).

Equally valid was the finding by the court and the Board that petitioner's statements and communications were not cast as a prediction of "demonstrable 'economic consequences,' " 397 F.2d, at 160, but rather as a threat of retaliatory action. The Board found that petitioner's speeches, pamphlets, leaflets, and letters conveyed the following message: that the company was in a precarious financial conditon; that the "strike-happy" union would in all likelihood have to obtain its potentially unreasonable demands by striking, the probable result of which would be a plant shutdown, as the past history of labor relations in the area indicated; and that the employees in such a case would have great difficulty finding employment elsewhere. In carrying out its duty to focus on the question: "[W]hat did the speaker intend and the listener understand?" (A. Cox, Law and the National Labor Policy 44 (1960)), the Board could reasonably conclude that the intended and understood import of that message was not to predict that unionization would inevitably cause the plant to close but to threaten to throw employees out of work regardless of the economic realities. In this connection, we need go no further than to point out (1) that petitioner had no support for its basic assumption that the union, which had not yet even presented any demands, would have to strike to be heard, and that it admitted at the hearing that it had no basis for attributing other plant closings in the area to unionism; and (2) that the Board has often found that employees, who are particularly sensitive to rumors of plant closings, take such hints as coercive threats rather than honest forecasts.

Petitioner argues that the line between so-called permitted predictions and proscribed threats is too vague to stand up under traditional First Amendment analysis and that the Board's discretion to curtail free speech rights is correspondingly too uncontrolled. It is true that a reviewing court must recognize the Board's competence in the first instance to judge the impact of utterances made in the context of the employer-employee relationship, see *NLRB* v. *Virginia Electric & Power Co.*, 314 U.S. 469, 479, 9 LRRM 405 (1941). But an employer, who has control over that relationship and therefore knows it best, cannot be heard to complain that he is without an adequate guide for his behavior. He can easily make his views known without engaging in " 'brinkmanship' " when it becomes all too easy to "overstep and tumble [over] the brink," *Wausau Steel Corp.* v. *NLRB*, 377 F.2d 369, 372, 65 LRRM 2001 (7th Cir. 1967). At the least he can avoid coercive speech simply by avoiding conscious overstatements he has reason to believe will mislead his employees. . . .

[The Court affirmed the judgment of the Court of Appeals, enforcing the Board's order which required Sinclair to bargain on demand.]

Compare the analysis of Section 8(c) in Gissel with that in *NLRB* v. *Golub Corp.*, an earlier case in which the employer's anti-union efforts consisted solely of communications.

NLRB v. Golub Corp.

United States Court of Appeals, Second Circuit, 1967
388 F.2d 921, 66 LRRM 2769

FRIENDLY, Circuit Judge.
. . .

Under the Wagner Act, 49 Stat. 449 (1935), which contained § 8(a)(1) but nothing like § 8(c), the Board condemned almost any anti-union expression by an employer. It was sustained against First Amendment attack by some courts including this one, on the basis that employer arguments have "an ambivalent character." Since "what to an outsider will be no more than the vigorous presentation of a conviction, to an employee may be the manifestation of a determination which it is not safe to thwart," we held that "the Board must decide how far the second aspect obliterates the first," with the substantial evidence rule available to support its decision. *NLRB* v. *Federbush Co.*, 121 F.2d 954, 957, 8 LRRM 531 (2d Cir. 1941). The Supreme Court evidently thought otherwise. *NLRB* v. *Virginia Electric & Power Co.*, 314 U.S. 469, 9 LRRM 405 (1941), dealt with employer notices pointing out that in the fifteen years since an organization strike had failed, confidence and understanding had reigned without the existence of a labor organization in any department. It went on to state that the company would freely entertain employee grievances and that it believed the mutual interest of all could "best be promoted through confidence and cooperation." The Board found the communications a violation of § 8(1). The Court interpreted the words of the Wagner Act to avoid constitutional doubts arising from the First Amendment. It held that speech, which by its own terms was not coercive, did not violate the Act unless part of a course of conduct that was coercive.[12] As the Board appeared to have found that the employer's words had violated the Act in and of themselves, the Court remanded to the Board so that it could determine whether the totality of the employer's conduct, of which his communications were a part, coerced its employees in violation of the statute. The Board later held that it did. See *Virginia Electric & Power Co.* v. *NLRB*, 319 U.S. 533, 12 LRRM 739 (1943).

This decision and the Board's rather halting response to it, see, *e.g., A.J. Shawalter Co.*, 64 NLRB 573 (1945); *Clark Bros.*, 70 NLRB 802 (1946), *enforced on a limited basis* in 163 F.2d 373, 20 LRRM 2436 (2d Cir. 1947), constituted the background for § 8(c) of the Taft-Hartley Act, 61 Stat. 142 (1947). The Hartley bill as passed by the House provided that "Expressing any views, argument, or opinion, or the dissemination thereof, whether in written, printed, graphic or visual form, if it does not by its own terms threaten force or economic reprisal," shall not constitute or be evidence of an unfair labor practice. H.R. 3020, 80th Cong. 1st Sess., § 8(d)(1) (1947). The reference in the bill as passed by the Senate was less clear, reading:

"The Board shall not base any finding of unfair labor practice upon any statement of views or arguments, either written or oral, if such statement contains under all the circumstances no threat, express or implied, of reprisal or force, or offer, express or implied, of benefit; Provided, That no language or provision of this section is intended to nor shall it be construed or administered so as to abridge or interfere with the right of either employers or employees to freedom of speech as guaranteed by the first amendment to the Constitution of the United States." H.R. 3020, as passed Senate, § 8(c).

The Conference Committee eliminated both the "by its own terms" of the House bill and the "under all the circumstances" and the unnecessary proviso of the Senate bill. While the Act thus went less far than the House bill, the detailed analysis of the compromise which Senator Taft submitted makes clear that, at the very least, the final form limits the extent to which context can be used to impart sinister meanings to innocuous words:

"The House conferees were of the opinion that the phrase 'under all the circumstances' in the Senate amendment was ambiguous and might be susceptible of being construed as approving certain Board decisions

---

[12]The Court, in a dictum in *Thomas* v. *Collins*, 323 U.S. 516, 537, 15 LRRM 777 (1945), interpreted *Virginia Electric* as deciding that an employer's attempts to persuade employees to join or not to join a union are "within the First Amendment's guaranty" and can be restricted only when "other things are added which bring about coercion, or give it that character."

which have attempted to circumscribe the right of free speech where there were also findings of unfair labor practices. Since this was certainly contrary to the intent of the Senate, . . . the Senate conferees acceded to the wish of the House group that the intent of this section be clarified." 93 Cong. Rec. 6601 (1947).

. . .

. . . Only if respondent's words contained a "threat of reprisal" did they go beyond the bounds of § 8(c). But, as the dictionaries tell us, a "threat of reprisal" means a "threat of retaliation" and this in turn means not a prediction that adverse consequences will develop but a threat that they will be deliberately inflicted in return for an injury—"to return evil for evil." . . .

The error of the Board in finding violations of the Act in the two passages from the letter of February 2 and the second set of remarks in the speech of February 16 predicting loss of work, harder work, or even a close-down as a result of unionization is apparent. Nothing in these communications could reasonably be interpreted as a threat to make the employees' lot harder in retaliation for their voting for the union. . . . The only fair reading is that the employer would take these steps solely from economic necessity and with regret. *NLRB* v. *S & H Grossinger's, Inc.*, 372 F.2d 26, 64 LRRM 2295 (2d Cir. 1967), is very much in point. There the Board had found a violation of § 8(a)(1) in employer statements that unionization would result in "less steady work" and that, although the employees always had had the security of their jobs, "under union conditions, we never know." 156 NLRB 233, 241, 61 LRRM 1025 (1965). This court, speaking through Judge Hays, refused enforcement saying, in language equally applicable here, that "the statements did not suggest that the Grossinger management would seek to bring about any of the unfortunate conditions which they feared might occur." Still more recently, in *NLRB* v. *River Togs, Inc.*, 382 F.2d 198, 202, 65 LRRM 2987 (2d Cir. 1967), we noted that "Although the Board apparently thinks workers should be shielded from such disconcerting information, an employer is free to tell his employees what he reasonably believes will be the likely economic consequences of unionization that are outside his control, as distinguished from threats of economic reprisal to be taken solely on his own volition." While, as the last quoted extract suggests, what is in form a prediction could so far outrun any possible basis for it that the Board might be justified in concluding a threat was intended, . . . this is a principle that must be kept within narrow limits not here approached. Congress did not intend the Board to act as a censor of the reasonableness of statements by either party to a labor controversy even if it constitutionally could. . . .

HAYS, J., dissenting:

The majority opinion demonstrates once more the inescapable truth that United States Circuit Judges safely ensconced in their chambers do not feel threatened by what employers tell their employees. An employer can dress up his threats in the language of prediction ("You will lose your

job" rather than "I will fire you") and fool judges. He doesn't fool his employees; they know perfectly clearly what he means. . . ."
[The remainder of the dissenting opinion is omitted.]

Notes

1. If an employer fires a union supporter, the Board generally wants to know whether the employer's action was motivated by anti-union animus or by work-related considerations. Would an employer's privileged but anti-union communications during the election campaign aid the Board in making this determination? If so, why does Section 8(c) appear to prohibit the Board from utilizing these statements as evidence? If the concern is with chilling employer speech, would a more appropriate provision permit introduction of anti-union communications, but prohibit the Board from relying solely on the communications for a finding of animus? Compare the discussion of the role of Section 8(c) in the note on the aftermath of *Darlington*, *infra* at page 313.

2. As the Court recognizes in *Gissel*, the line between predictions and threats is hazy. Presumably threats of adverse economic consequences from unionization will chill employee support and skew election results, but objectively based predictions will aid employees in choosing whether to be represented. Consider the letters and speech at the beginning of this section. As an employee, would you feel that the employer had threatened reprisals if the union wins the election or that the employer was predicting the consequences of unionization? As a union leader, how would you respond to the statements? Could your response neutralize any perceived threat sufficiently to insure a fair election? As a policy matter, should the election be set aside even though an employer's threats, which initially disturbed the election atmosphere, were answered? Does your answer depend on the nature of the threat, *e.g.*, a threat to close as compared with a threat not to bargain with the union?

Election Interference

In *General Shoe Corp.*, 77 NLRB 124, 21 LRRM 1337 (1948), the Board determined that communication and conduct which do not constitute unfair labor practices may nevertheless interfere with employee choice. The Board assumed that it has the authority to review objections to the election process pursuant to the mandate of Section 9(c)(1)(A) and that well-founded objections require a new election.

When the challenged conduct does not involve the content of campaign propaganda, the Board may formulate a general rule based on inferences from objective events—such as the captive audience doctrine, under which an election is set aside if management required employees to attend a campaign speech held during working hours and within 24 hours of the election. See *Peerless Plywood Co.*, 107 NLRB 427, 33 LRRM 1151 (1953). When, however, the losing party objects to the campaign propaganda itself, the Board becomes involved in microscopic examination of the words (or pictures) as well as evaluation of the purported impact. For example, are materials highlighting race-related issues at the workplace the focus of, or one factor, in a campaign? Is the message an appeal for solidarity and pride among workers, or an inflammatory invitation to racial prejudice? See *Sewell Mfg. Co.*, 138 NLRB 66, 50 LRRM 1532 (1962); cf. *NLRB* v. *Sumter Plywood Corp.*, 535 F.2d 917, 92 LRRM 3508 (5th Cir. 1976), *cert. denied*, 429 U.S. 1092, 94 LRRM 2643 (1977).

The most difficult area for the Board has been the impact of campaign rhetoric which may not constitute an unfair labor practice but clearly trades on a party's economic position. In *Dal-Tex Corp.*, 137 NLRB 1782, 50 LRRM 1489, 1492 (1962), the Board held:

> "Conduct violative of Section 8(a)(1) is, *a fortiori*, conduct which interferes with the exercise of free and untrammeled choice in an election. This is so because the test of conduct which may interfere with the 'laboratory conditions' for an election is considerably more restrictive than the test of conduct which amounts to interference, restraint, or coercion which violates Section 8(a)(1). . . . [W]e shall look to the economic realities of the employer-employee relationship and shall set aside an election where we find that the employer's conduct has resulted in substantial interference with the election. . . . Congress specifically limited Section 8(c) to the adversary proceedings involved in unfair labor practice cases and it has no application to representation cases. . . . The strictures of the First Amendment, to be sure, must be considered in all cases."

Notes

1. Does the *General Shoe* doctrine accomplish its intended purposes? As an employer are you confident that, as the Supreme Court suggested in *Gissel*, you "are free to communicate to [your] employees any of [your] general views about unionism or any of [your] specific views about a particular union, as long as the communications do not contain threats of reprisal or promises of benefits . . ."? If not, what inducement is there for you to "make [your] views known without engaging in 'brinkmanship,' when it becomes all too easy to 'overstep and tumble [over] the brink' "? Is the threat of a bargaining order, as compared with the risk of an overturned election, sufficient to induce an employer to avoid "brinkmanship?"

2. Is the distinction between the remedies for unfair labor practices, including the possibility of a bargaining order, and the administrative overturning of an election sufficient to explain why regulation of noncoercive communication does not offend the First Amendment? Before answering a (qualified) yes, consider the following procedural point: Board orders in unfair labor practice proceedings are final orders under Section 10(f) of the Act and, therefore, reviewable by an appropriate court of appeals. Board determinations of election interference occur in connection with the representation procedures under Section 9. Such determinations, including orders directing a new election or certifying a

union, are deemed to be interlocutory and not appealable. See *NLRB* v. *Electrical Workers (IBEW), Local 876 (Consumers Power Co.)*, 308 U.S. 413, 5 LRRM 676 (1940). To secure judicial review of orders in Section 9 proceedings, the objecting party must engage in an unfair labor practice. For example, assume a union loses an election and the Board sustains the union's contention that noncoercive statements by company officials require that the election be set aside. If the union wins the rerun election and is certified, the company is obligated to bargain with the union. A refusal is an unfair labor practice, a "technical" Section 8(a)(5) violation, since the refusal is based on the same contentions raised in the Section 9 proceedings. After the Board issues an order in the unfair labor practice case, the employer may seek appellate review of the underlying issue. See *Boire* v. *Greyhound Corp.*, 376 U.S. 473, 55 LRRM 2694 (1964).

Industrial Disposal Svc.

National Labor Relations Board, 1983
266 NLRB No. 22, 112 LRRM 1257

[The union won the representation election by a vote of 6 to 5. In support of one of its objections, the employer proffered evidence "indicating that an agent of the Petitioner threatened employees that if anyone helped the Employer in a strike, they would 'be made an example of,' and added that during Petitioner's last strike, the Petitioner had a talk with an individual who 'worked both sides of the fence,' and the individual was 'still in the hospital.' "

[The Acting Regional Director overruled the objection, relying on a 1978 Board decision which held that statements by agents of a union directed at future contingent events are inadequate, as a matter of law, to set aside an election. In directing that the objections be set for hearing, the Board overruled its 1978 decision and adopted the approach taken in *Provincial House, Inc.*, 209 NLRB 215–16, 85 LRRM 1326, 1327 (1974), "that threats of picket line violence in the future [create the] impression that the Union could, and would, resort to whatever means—lawful or unlawful—[which] might be required effectively to exercise its power over employees."]

. . . [W]e believe it unrealistic to conclude that a union agent's threats of bodily harm, damage to personal property, or the like, cannot, as a matter of law, impact on an election merely because the threat in question is couched in terms of possible future conduct. Such an approach does not take into account the tendency of such threats to have a substantial and destructive effect on free and open campaign discussion, as well as freedom of choice at the polling place itself. A campaign environment in which a union threatens that violent repercussions will ensue, should employees choose to oppose it in the future, is one in which there is substantial likelihood that employees will be inhibited from expressing their actual views, and is surely one which jeopardizes the integrity of the election process. It can hardly be gainsaid that an employee faced with union threats of personal injury will think twice before pinning on a "vote no" button or passing out antiunion literature. A union can, by stilling the voices of just a few employees who oppose it, successfully paint a false picture of its support among the electorate and thereby influence the votes of those employees who find themselves undecided. Such threats may well have an additional indirect effect on other workers who might have been swayed against the union, had the voices of all employees been heard. Moreover, in any given case, depending on the number, nature, and severity of the threats involved, some employees who are either uncertain, or otherwise opposed to the union, will likely be inclined to opt for the safety of capitulation and decide to cast their lot with the union—the secrecy of the ballot box notwithstanding. . . .

. . . [W]e find that the allegations in Objection 1 pertaining to union threats of violent reprisals for refusing to cooperate with the Petitioner during a strike, if found to be true, constitute grounds for setting aside the election.

In this connection we note that the unit of approximately 11 employees was small and, though not controlling, that the election was decided by a single vote. Allegedly, the conduct occurred on the Employer's property within an hour of the election. Responsibility, according to the Employer, did not lie with an overzealous employee, but with an official of the Union itself. The union official, as noted previously, allegedly threatened that anyone who helped the Employer in a strike would be "made an example of." Rather than leave it to chance whether employees would take his remarks seriously, the evidence adduced by the Employer indicates that the official punctuated his threat with historical fact, *i.e.*, an individual who refused to toe the line during the Union's last strike was "still in the hospital." Inherent in statements such as these is the simple, unambiguous message that opposing the Union could be a very dangerous course for employees to pursue. If made, these statements would have destroyed the conditions for a free and fair election. . . .

JENKINS, Member, dissenting:

. . .

I refuse to join in the majority's blind leap of faith. I cannot equate rhetoric directed toward a union's ability to prevent strike-breaking, in the event of an election victory and a subsequent strike, with threats aimed at securing an election victory in the first place. The bridge between the two is nothing more than the majority's will that it should be so. . . .

It is a disservice and inaccurate to assert that employees tilt at windmills and shy at shadows. Employees are fully as capable of distinguishing between a present threat to personal safety and blustering campaign talk aimed at bolstering a union's image of its ability to bring effective pressure to bear against an employer in the event of a union victory and a possible subsequent strike. Principles of criminal law recognize this ability to distinguish such remote and conditional blusters from present threats, and hold them to constitute no provocation of or defense to unlawful conduct which they allegedly induce. As we noted in *Hickory Springs*, [239

NLRB 641, 99 LRRM 1715 (1974)], an employee made genuinely afraid by a union's claim to violent propensities during strikes would avoid the risk by voting against the union in the anonymity of the Board's secret-ballot election. To hold that elections may be set aside on this tenuous, conjectural basis lacks logical support.

Questions

Does the *General Shoe* doctrine, as applied in *Industrial Disposal*, serve its purpose? If, as the Board majority finds, the union's agents made threatening statements, which had the tendency to effect worker choice, has the union also violated Section 8(b)(1)(A)? In a situation like *Industrial Disposal*, would you recommend that an employer file a Section 8(b)(1)(A) charge? Before answering a (qualified) yes, consider these procedural questions:

If the employer's evidence supports its objections, the election in *Industrial Disposal* will be set aside and another election ordered. Is the Union able to secure appellate review of the Board's new rule prior to the rerun election?

Assume the Union loses the second election but that the employer does not engage in any unfair labor practices in the course of that election. Is the Union able to secure judicial review of the *Industrial Disposal* doctrine at this point? At any point?

If in order to secure judicial review of the Board's ruling, the union must point to a final order rather than an administrative ruling, is the Union's only option to resort to economic pressure? See Section 8(b)(7) of the Act. After reading that provision, would you advise the Union in *Industrial Disposal* to picket the Company to secure recognition?

Midland National Life Ins. Co.

National Labor Relations Board, 1982
263 NLRB No. 24, 110 LRRM 1489

[In an election on April 28, 1978, the vote was 127 to 75 against the union.

[A second election was ordered after the NLRB found that the employer had committed certain unfair labor practices, including threats of benefits and jobs losses; the Board's order was enforced.

[The second election, held on October 16, 1980, resulted in a tie vote of 107 to 107; there were 20 challenged ballots and one void ballot. The union filed objections. The objections to the challenged ballots were sustained. The administrative law judge recommended a third election.]

The facts are not complex. On the afternoon of October 15, 1980, the day before the election, the Employer distributed campaign literature to its employees with their paychecks. One of the distributions was a six-page document which included photographs and text depicting three local employers and their involvements with the Petitioner. The document also contained a reproduction of a portion of the Petitioner's 1979 financial report (hereinafter LMRDA report) submitted to the Department of Labor pursuant to the provisions of the Labor Management Reporting and Disclosure Act of 1959. The Petitioner learned of the document the next morning, 3½ hours before the polls were to open.

The first subject of the document, Meilman Food, Inc., was portrayed in "recent" pictures as a deserted facility, and was described in accompanying text as follows: "They too employed between 200 and 300 employees. This Local 304A struck this plant—violence ensued. *Now all of the workers are gone!* What did the Local 304A do for them? Where is the 304A union job security?" (Emphasis in original.) Jack Smith, the Petitioner's business representative, testified that Local 304A, the Petitioner, had been the representative of Meilman's employees, but that neither the Petitioner nor Meilman's employees had been on strike when the plant closed. He added that the employees had been working for at least 1½ years following the strike and prior to the closure of the facility.

The second and third employers pictured and discussed in the document were Luther Manor Nursing Home and Blue Cross/Blue Shield. The text accompanying the pictures of Luther Manor explained that:

> "[a]lmost a year ago this same union that tells you they will 'make job security' (we believe you are the only ones who can do that) and will get you more pay, told the employees of LUTHER MANOR (again, here in Sioux Falls) . . . the union would get them a contract with job security and more money. Unfortunately Local 304A did not tell the Luther Manor employees what year or century they were talking about. Today the employees have no contract. Most of the union leaders left to work elsewhere. Their job security is the same (depends upon the individual as it always has). There has been no change or increase in wages or hours. The union has sent in three different sets of negotiators. Again, promises and performance are two different things. All wages, fringes, working conditions are remaining the same while negotiations continue."

The text accompanying the pictures of Blue Cross stated that "this same Local union won an election at Blue Cross/Blue Shield after promising less restrictive policies, better pay and more job security. Since the election a good percentage of its former employees are no longer working there. Ask them! The employees have been offered a wage increase—*next year* of 5%. . . ." (Emphasis in original.)

Smith testified that the Petitioner took over negotiations at Luther Manor and at Blue Cross on or about July 1, 1980, after the Petitioner had merged with Retail Clerks, Local 1665, and that Retail Clerks, Local 1665, not the Petitioner, had conducted the prior negotiations and won the election at Blue Cross.

Assessing the statements concerning these local employers, the Hearing Officer concluded that, in its description of Meilman Food, the Employer intended to instill in the minds of its employees the false impression that the Petitioner had conducted a strike at Meilman, that violence had ensued, and that, as a direct result of the strike, all of the employees at Meilman were terminated. Evaluating the statements about Luther Manor and Blue Cross, the Hearing Officer found that the Employer had misrepresented the labor organization involved, and had implied that the Petitioner was an ineffectual and inefficient bargaining representative who would cause employees to suffer.

The Employer's distribution also included a portion of the Petitioner's 1979 LMRDA report which listed information concerning the Petitioner's assets, liabilities, and cash receipts and disbursements for the reporting period. Three entries on the reproduced page were underlined: total receipts, reported at $508,946; disbursements "On Behalf of Individual Members," reported at zero; and total disbursements, reported at $492,701. Other entries on the reproduced page showed disbursements of $93,185 to officers, and $22,662 to employees. The accompanying text stated that $141,000 of the Petitioner's funds went to "union officers and officials and those who worked for them," and that "NOTHING—according to the report they filed with the U.S. Government was spent 'on behalf of the individual members.' [sic]"

The Hearing Officer found that the report actually showed that the Petitioner disbursed only $115,847 to its officers and employees, a difference of $25,000, and that the Employer's statement attributed 19 percent more in income to the officials and employees than was actually received. He further found that, while the report showed that no sums had been spent "on behalf of the individual members," the instructions for the LMRDA report require that entry to reflect disbursements for "other than normal operating purposes," and that the Employer failed to include this fact in its distribution.

In accordance with his findings outlined above, the Hearing Officer concluded that the document distributed by the Employer contained numerous misrepresentations of fact of a substantial nature designed to portray the Petitioner as an organization staffed by highly paid officials and employees who were ineffectual as bargaining representatives, and that as a consequence employees would suffer with respect to job security and compensation. The Hearing Officer also determined that the document was distributed on the afternoon before the election, that the Petitioner did not become aware of it until approximately 10 a.m. election day, 2½ hours before the preelection conference and 3½ hours before the polls were to open, and that, owing to the nature of the misrepresentations, the Petitioner did not have sufficient time to respond effectively. Applying the standard found in *General Knit of California, Inc.*, and *Hollywood Ceramics Company, Inc.*, the Hearing Officer accordingly recommended that the objection be sustained and that a third election be directed.

We have decided to reject the Hearing Officer's recommendations and to certify the results of the election. . . .

. . .

. . . Overruling prior cases which indicated that intent to mislead was an element of the standard [*Hollywood Ceramics Co., Inc.*, 140 NLRB 221, 51 LRRM 1600 (1962)], the Board stated that "an election should be set aside only where there has been a misrepresentation or other similar campaign trickery, which involves a substantial departure from the truth, at a time which prevents the other party or parties from making an effective reply, so that the misrepresentation, whether deliberate or not, may reasonably be expected to have a significant impact on the election." *Id.* at 224.

In 1977, after 15 years of experience under this rule, a majority of the Board decided in *Shopping Kart Food Market, Inc.*, 228 NLRB 1311, 94 LRRM 1705 (1977), to overrule *Hollywood Ceramics.* . . . Thus, the board stated that it would "no longer probe into the truth or falsity of the parties' campaign statements," but would instead recognize and rely on employees "as mature individuals who are capable of recognizing campaign propaganda for what it is and discounting it." *Id.* at 1311, 1313. Consistent with this view, the majority also held that the Board would intervene "in instances where a party has engaged in such deceptive campaign practices as improperly involving the Board and its processes, or the use of forged documents which render the voters unable to recognize the propaganda for what it is." *Id.* at 1313.

A scant 20 months later, the Board reversed itself, overruled *Shopping Kart*, and reinstated the *Hollywood Ceramics* standard. *General Knit of California, Inc.*, 239 NLRB 619, 99 LRRM 1687 (1978). Finding that the rule propounded in *Shopping Kart* was "inconsistent with [the Board's] responsibility to insure fair elections," the Board stated that "there are certain circumstances where a particular misrepresentation . . . may materially affect an election," and that such an election should be set aside "in order to maintain the integrity of Board elections and thereby protect employee free choice." *Id.* at 620.

Many lessons and conclusions can be drawn from this summary of the Board's past practice regarding the role of misrepresentations in Board elections and, no doubt, many will be. However, one lesson which cannot be mistaken is that reasonable, informed individuals can differ, and indeed have differed, in their assessment of the effect of misrepresentations on voters and in their views of the Board's proper role in policing such misrepresentations. No one can or does dispute the ultimate purpose of this controversy, that is the necessity of Board procedures which insure the fair and free choice of a bargaining representative. The sole question facing us is how that "fair and free choice" is best assured.

. . .

For numerous reasons, we find that the rule we announce today constitutes just such a "justifiable and reasonable adjustment" of our democratic electoral processes. By returning to the sound principles espoused in *Shopping Kart*, not only do we alleviate the many difficulties attending the *Hollywood Ceramics* rule, but we also insure the certainty and finality of election results, and minimize unwarranted and dilatory claims attacking those results.

. . .

In sharp contrast to the *Hollywood Ceramics* standard, *Shopping Kart* "draws a clear line between what is and what is not objectionable." Thus, "elections will be set aside 'not on the basis of the *substance* of the representation, but the deceptive *manner* in which it was made.' . . . As long as the campaign material is what it purports to be, *i.e.*, mere propaganda of a particular party, the Board would leave the task of evaluating its contents solely to the employees." Where, due to forgery, no voter could recognize the propaganda "for what it is," Board intervention is warranted. Further, unlike *Hollywood Ceramics*, the rule in *Shopping Kart* lends itself to definite results which are both predictable and speedy. The incentive for protracted litigation is greatly reduced, as is the possibilty of disagreement between the Board and the courts. Because objections alleging false or inaccurate statements can be summarily rejected at the first stage of Board proceedings, the opportunity for delay is almost nonexistent.[18] Finally, the rule in *Shopping Kart* "furthers the goal of consistent and equitable adjudications" by applying uniformly to the objections of both unions and employers.

In addition to finding the *Hollywood Ceramics* rule to be unwieldy and counterproductive, we also consider it to have an unrealistic view of the ability of voters to assess misleading campaign progaganda. . . .

We appreciate that today's decision is likely to cause concern, just as did *General Knit's* quick retreat from *Shopping Kart* in 1978. Accordingly, we do not take this step lightly. . . .

In reaching this decision, we note that "[a]dministrative flexibility is . . . one of the principal reasons for the establishment of the regulatory agencies [because it] permits valuable experimentation and allows administrative policies to reflect changing policy views." As is obvious from today's decision, the policy views of the Board have changed. We cannot permit earlier decisions to endure forever if, in our view, their effects are deleterious and hinder the goals of the Act. The nature of administrative decisionmaking relies heavily upon the benefits of the cumulative experience of the decisionmakers. Such experience, in the words of the Supreme Court, "begets understanding and insight by which judgments . . . are validated or qualified or invalidated. The constant process of trial and error, on a wider and fuller scale than a single adversary litigation permits, differentiates perhaps more than anything else the administrative from the judicial process." *NLRB* v. *J. Weingarten, Inc.*, 420 U.S. 251, 265–266, 88 LRRM 2689 (1975).

Cumulative experience need not produce the same understanding and insight. Reasonable minds can and indeed have differed over the most appropriate resolution of this issue. That no one can dispute. However, we again express our emphatic belief that on balance the rule in *Shopping Kart* best accommodates and serves the interests of all.

---

[18]The figures cited by our dissenting colleagues purporting to compare the "number of elections in which allegations of misleading statements were ruled upon" before and after *Shopping Kart* hardly establish that the policy change we enunciate today will not have the desired effects. That parties continued to file misrepresentation objections in 1978 simply demonstrated their acknowledgment of the reality that *Shopping Kart* could be overturned by a shift of one Board Member. In fact, that is what occurred when former Member Truesdale replaced former Member Walther on the Board. In any event, had our dissenting colleagues been more amenable to giving *Shopping Kart* a reasonable chance to take life, perhaps their point might have some merit.

In sum, we rule today that we will no longer probe into the truth or falsity of the parties' campaign statements, and that we will not set elections aside on the basis of misleading campaign statements.[24] We will, however, intervene in cases where a party has used forged documents which render the voters unable to recognize propaganda for what it is.[25] Thus, we will set an election aside not because of the substance of the representation, but because of the deceptive manner in which it was made, a manner which renders employees unable to evaluate the forgery for what it is. As was the case in *Shopping Kart*, we will continue to protect against other campaign conduct, such as threats, promises, or the like, which interferes with employee free choice.

Accordingly, inasmuch as the Petitioner's objection alleges nothing more than misrepresentations, it is hereby overruled.[26] Because the tally of ballots shows that the Petitioner failed to receive a majority of the valid ballots cast, we shall certify the results.

FANNING and JENKINS, Members, dissenting:

For the second time in five years, a bare majority of the Board has abandoned the flexible and balanced *Hollywood Ceramics* standard for determining when election campaign misrepresentations have over-stepped the bounds of tolerability and substituted an ultra-permissive standard that places a premium on the well-timed use of deception, trick-ery, and fraud.[27] In reestablishing the *Shopping Kart* rule, the present majority adds nothing to the debate that has accompanied the seesawing

[24]In accordance with our usual practice, we shall apply our new policy not only "to the case in which the issue arises," but also "to all pending cases in whatever stage." *Deluxe Metal Furniture Company*, 121 NLRB 995, 1006–07, 42 LRRM 1470 (1958). See, generally, former Member Penello's dissenting opinion in *Blackman-Uhler Chemical Division—Synalloy Corporation*, 239 NLRB 637, 638, 99 LRRM 1702 (1978), applying the balancing test set forth by the Supreme Court in *Securities & Exchange Commission* v. *Chenery Corporation*, 332 U.S. 194, 203 (1947). As former Member Penello pointed out, applying the *Shopping Kart* standard retroactively imposes no substantial hardship on the objecting party. On the other hand, failure to do so would be contrary to the "statutory design." *Chenery, supra*. For, as discussed above, we believe that, on balance, the *Hollywood Ceramics* rule operates more to frustrate than to further the fundamental statutory purpose of assuring employee free choice.

[25]. . . Of course, as stated in *Shopping Kart*, we will also set elections aside when an official Board document has been altered in such a way as to indicate an endorsement by the Board of a party to the election. *Allied Electric Products, Inc.*, 109 NLRB 1270, 34 LRRM 1538 (1954).

[26]With respect to the LMRDA report, our dissenting colleagues' attempted analogy to the rule set forth in *Formco, Inc.*, 233 NLRB 61, 96 LRRM 1392 (1977), misses the mark by a wide margin. *Formco* clearly is inapposite, since here there is no Board document involved. In any event, there is no basis for describing—as the dissenters do—the Employer's presentation of the Form LM–2 excerpt as "an elaborately conceived fraud." The portion of the form distributed by the Employer appeared exactly as submitted by the Petitioner. We cate-gorically reject the dissenters' suggestion that any misrepresentation of any document constitutes a fraud. Their novel position in this regard finds no support in the law, and they make no attempt to muster such support.

[In *Affiliated Midwest Hospital, Inc.*, d/b/a *Riveredge Hospital*, 264 NLRB No. 146, 111 LRRM 1425 (1982), the Board overruled the *Formco* doctrine and held that mischaracterization of Board actions including misrepresentation of a Board decision, would be treated in the same manner as factual misrepresentations. Physical alteration of Board documents remains a basis for setting an election aside if "the document has been altered in such a way as to indicate an endorsement by the Board of a party to the election."—Ed.]

[27]Arguably, it is the present majority that for the first time establishes such a permissive standard. For then-Chairman Murphy, concurring in *Shopping Kart, supra*, 228 NLRB at 1314, 94 LRRM 1705, agreed with the "basic principles" set forth in *Hollywood Ceramics*, but worried that its "ruling has been expanded and misapplied as to have extended far from the original intent of the Board." Then-Chairman Murphy did not abandon analysis of the

of Board doctrine in this area. Instead, the majority reiterates the familiar theme of the "unrealistic view of the ability of voters to assess misleading campaign propaganda" (which it attributes to *Hollywood Ceramics*) and the promise of elimination of delays caused by the processing of misrepresentation objections. . . .

"The basic policy underlying this rule, as well as the other rules in this election field, is to assure the employees full and complete freedom of choice in selecting a bargaining representative. . . . It is obvious that where employees cast their ballots upon the basis of a material misrepresentation, such vote cannot reflect their uninhibited desires, and they have not exercised the kind of choice envisaged by the Act. . . .

"The Board has limited its intervention . . . because an election by secret ballot, conducted under Government auspices, should not be lightly set aside, and because we realize that additional elections upset the plant routine and prevent stable labor-management relations. We are also aware that absolute precision of statement and complete honesty are not always attainable in an election campaign, nor are they expected by the employees. Election campaigns are often hotly contested and feelings frequently run high. At such times a party may, in its zeal, overstate its own virtues and the vices of the other without essentially impairing 'laboratory conditions.' Accordingly, in reaching its decision in cases where objections to elections have been filed alleging that one party misrepresented certain facts, the Board must balance the right of the employees to an untrammeled choice, and the right of the parties to wage a free and vigorous campaign with all the normal legitimate tools of electioneering."

What the majority does now is to give up, in the interest of possibly reducing litigation, a speculative thing at best, any attempt to balance the rights of the employees and the campaigners.[30] However, their goal, which, as the Board noted in *General Knit*, must never take precedence over preservation of the integrity of the electoral process, seems to have eluded the Board's prior attempt under *Shopping Kart*. For, according to an internal audit conducted for the General Counsel, the number of elections in which allegations of misleading statements were ruled on increased from 327 in 1976, the year before *Shopping Kart* was decided, to

---

substance of the misrepresentation, as the present majority does. Rather, she sought to preserve some flexibility by taking the position that an election should be set aside "where a party makes an egregious mistake of fact." *Id.* at 1314. Moreover, she rejected the suggestion by her colleagues of the *Shopping Kart* majority that her concept of "egregious mistake of fact" was a very narrow one. *Id.* at 1314, fn. 24, and 1315, fn. 3. And, dissenting in *General Knit of California, supra,* then-Member Murphy, applying her "egregious mistake of fact" standard, characterized the issue presented in that case as "whether an accurate statement which is slightly ambiguous" could be the basis for setting aside the election. 239 NLRB at 633, 99 LRRM 1687. Thus, her departure from *Hollywood Ceramics* would appear to have been more rhetorically than empirically radical.

[30]We find incomprehensible the majority's additional suggestion that the *Shopping Kart* rule (presumably as compared with the *Hollywood Ceramics* rule) " 'furthers the goal of consistent and equitable adjudications' by applying uniformly to the objections of both unions and employers." To our knowledge, no rule ever contemplated by the Board has treated misrepresentations by unions and employers differently.

357 in 1978, the first full year after *Shopping Kart* was in effect, this despite a decrease (from 8,899 to 8,464) in the total number of elections conducted in those respective years.[31]

In return for the illusory benefits of speed and a speculative lightening of its workload, the majority today errs in relinquishing the Board's obligation to put some limits on fraud and deceit as campaign tools. It is apparent that the system contemplated by Section 9 of the Act for representation elections has survived reasonably well during the decades in which the Board has taken a role in insuring the integrity of its elections. Indeed, the majority does not suggest deregulating the election process other than with respect to misrepresentations. In this connection, we are especially puzzled by the distinction the majority draws between forgery, which it will regulate, and other kinds of fraud, which it will not. The majority states that forgeries "render the voters unable to recognize the propaganda for what it is." Yet it is precisely the Board's traditional perception that there are some misrepresentations which employees can recognize "for what they are" and others which, in the Board's considered judgment, they cannot, that has made the *Hollywood Ceramics* doctrine so effective. In place of this approach, under which judgments take into account the facts of each case, the majority creates an irrebuttable presumption that employees can recognize all misrepresentations, however opaque and deceptive, except forgeries. Employees' free choice in elections, the only reason we run elections, must necessarily be inhibited, distorted, and frustrated by this new rule. To the majority, this is less important than the freedom to engage in lies, trickery, and fraud. Under the new rule, important election issues will be ignored in favor of irresponsible charges and deceit. Under *Hollywood Ceramics,* the Board did not attempt to sanitize elections completely but only to keep the campaign propaganda within reasonable bounds. Those bounds have now disappeared. Why?

Albeit today's American employees may be better educated, in the formal sense, than those of previous generations, and may be in certain respects more sophisticated, we do not honor them by abandoning them utterly to the mercies of unscrupulous campaigners, including the expert cadre of professional opinion molders who devise campaigns for many of our representation elections. In political campaigns, which are conducted over a much longer period of time and are subject to extensive media scrutiny, the voters have ready access to independent sources of information concerning the issues. In representation campaigns, they do not. Thus, it has been observed that: "Promises are often written on the wind, but statements of fact are the stuff upon which men and women make serious value judgments . . . [and] rank and file employees must largely depend upon the company and union to provide the data. . . ."[32] As we

---

[31]The number of misrepresentation cases was even higher in 1977, the year in which *Shopping Kart* was decided. However, the total number of elections held in 1977 was substantially higher than in either 1976 or 1978.

[32]*J. I. Case Co.* v. *NLRB,* 555 F.2d 202, 205, 95 LRRM 2480 (8th Cir. 1977). As the cited case illustrates, the courts, although they have not hesitated to disagree with the Board's application of the *Hollywood Ceramics* standard to particular facts, have accepted its principles readily.

said in our dissent in *Shopping Kart*, the very high level of participation in Board elections as compared with political elections speaks well for the Board's role in insuring a measure of responsibility in campaigning. On the other hand, absent some external restraint, the campaigners will have little incentive to refrain from any last-minute deceptions that might work to their short-term advantage.
. . .

The majority through this decision is giving our election processes, possibly the most important part of installing a viable collective-bargaining relationship, over to the possible excesses of the participants and eliminating the Board from its statutory oversight responsibilities. Why? Accordingly, we must dissent.

Notes

1. In changing the misrepresentation doctrine for the third time in five years, the Board emphasizes that "reasonable, informed individuals can differ . . . in their assessment of the effect of misrepresentations . . . and in their views of the Board's proper role in policing such misrepresentations." Is it clear to you what factors led to the current Board's assessment? Consider:

a. Support for overruling the *Hollywood Ceramics* doctrine came from two academic studies, one of which concluded that the imprecise standards (*e.g.*, materiality, substantiality) invited routine objections and delayed certification of election results.* The other study found that the representation campaign had little impact on workers' votes. These authors concluded that in the 31 elections examined, the votes of 81 percent of the employees could be predicted on the basis of precampaign intent and attitudes; further, only 5 percent of voters admitted changing their minds on the basis of the campaign.**

Although discussion of these studies figures prominently in *Shopping Kart* and *General Knit*, the opinions in *Midland National Life* do not rely on them. Is this because the appearance of fairness is a major consideration in representation elections and empirical analysis tells us little about the value attached to the appearance of fairness? Is it because decision-makers are more comfortable evaluating policy than methodology?

b. "In fiscal 1976, the Board conducted 8,899 elections. In 84 elections *Hollywood Ceramics* type objections were filed against the employer. In only 18 cases was merit found and a new election directed. While it is difficult to get accurate statistics, we know very few such reruns result in victory for the objecting party. In any event, the average time for such rerun elections is many months, frankly only a few months less than a year, when the union could have gotten a new election anyway.

*Williams, Janus, and Huhn, NLRB REGULATION OF ELECTION CONDUCT (1974).
**Getman, Goldberg, and Herman, UNION REPRESENTATION ELECTIONS: LAW AND REALITY (1976).

"But let us count those 18 cases as on the merit side of the ledger. On the other side we find 223 *Hollywood Ceramics* objections filed against unions—almost 1 out of every 4 objections filed by employers, with only 8 rerun objections order(sic). Why so many employer objections based on *Hollywood Ceramics* issues when there is so little success?

"During 1976 employers appealed 9 bargaining order cases to Circuit Court decision opposing a Board Certification based on a *Hollywood Ceramics* issue. In 4 of those cases the courts reversed the Board and refused to order bargaining. In the 5 that were enforced, in 1 case the bargaining order came down 4 years after the election, in 2 cases, one and three-quarter years after the election, and in the last 2 cases, at least one and one-half years after. My guess is in all 5 of those victories the union won the legal battle but lost the war. I think we all realize that if effectuation of a certification can be delayed a year more for all practical purposes, the union's following is dissipated and its strength at the bargaining table nil. That is why employers filed *Hollywood Ceramics* type objections in many of the 223 cases.

"Of 127 summary judgment cases before the Board in 1976, 37 were 8(a)(5)'s arising out of Employer *Hollywood Ceramics* objections. Few of those would go on to enforcement proceedings before the Courts because it would not be necessary. The delay had already accomplished the objective, the union's following dissipated and its strength at the bargaining table destroyed by the time the Board's 8(a)(5) bargaining order comes down. Hence on the debit side opposite the Union's 18 rerun elections in *Hollywood Ceramics* cases we have 8 where the employer won, 9 which went to Court enforcement, and 37 through summary judgment at the Board. Fifty-four cases which the union concerned lost because of tactical manipulation of *Hollywood Ceramics*. . . . " 95 LRRM 205, 207–208 (1977) (remarks by then-Board member Walther).

c. The proponents of the *Shopping Kart-Midland Nat'l Ins.* approach are the Board members generally considered to be pro-management. Why would management prefer this approach?

d. Each change in the misrepresentation doctrine has occurred following a change in Board membership.

2. The information in the attorney's letter which introduces this section is accurate but incomplete. If an employer told organizing employees, "Strike and I'll replace you!", the Board would probably find an illegal threat of reprisal, even though the employer is entitled to replace strikers, see *NLRB* v. *Mackay* 304 U.S. 333, 2 LRRM 610 (1938). Is the information less threatening because it is conveyed to the employees in the guise of legal advice? If not threatening, is the letter nonetheless misleading because it is incomplete and therefore a misrepresentation of law which distorts the employees' ability to decide how to vote? Compare *Robbins & Myers*, 241 NLRB 102, 100 LRRM 1523 (1979) with *Eagle Comptronics*, 263 NLRB No. 70, 111 LRRM 1005 (1982), and *Beatrice Foods Co.*, 265 NLRB No. 193, 112 LRRM 1124 (1982).

Linn v. Plant Guard Workers of America

Supreme Court of the United States, 1966
383 U.S. 53, 61 LRRM 2345

MR. JUSTICE CLARK delivered the opinion of the Court.
. . .

I.

Petitioner Linn, an assistant general manager of Pinkerton's National Detective Agency, Inc., filed this suit against the respondent union, two of its officers and a Pinkerton employee, Leo J. Doyle. The complaint alleged that, during a campaign to organize Pinkerton's employees in Detroit, the respondents had circulated among the employees leaflets which stated *inter alia:*

> " (7) Now we find out that Pinkerton's has had a large volume of work in Saginaw they have had it for years.
>
> "United Plant Guard Workers now has evidence
>
> "A. That Pinkerton has 10 jobs in Saginaw, Michigan.
>
> "B. Employing 52 men.
>
> "C. Some of these jobs are 10 yrs. old!
>
> "(8) Make you feel kind sick & foolish.
>
> "(9) The men in Saginaw were deprived of their *right to vote* in three NLRB elections. Their names were not summitted [sic]. These guards were voted into the Union in 1959! These Pinkerton guards were *robbed* of pay increases. The Pinkerton manegers [sic] were *lying* to us—all the time the contract was in effect. No doubt the Saginaw men will file criminal charges. Somebody may go to Jail!"

The complaint further alleged that Linn was one of the managers referred to in the leaflet, and that the statements in the leaflet were "wholly false, defamatory and untrue" as respondents well knew. It did not allege any actual or special damage but prayed for the recovery of $1,000,000 on the ground that the accusations were libelous *per se.* Federal jurisdiction was based on diversity of citizenship.

All respondents, save Doyle, moved to dismiss, asserting that the subject matter was within the exclusive jurisdiction of the Board. The record indicates that prior to the institution of this action Pinkerton had filed unfair labor practice charges with the Regional Director of the Board, alleging that the distribution of the leaflets, as well as other written material, had restrained and coerced Pinkerton's employees in the exercise of their § 7 rights, in violation of § 8(b)(1)(A) of the Act. The Regional Director refused to issue a complaint. Finding that the leaflets were circulated by Doyle, who was "not an officer or member of the charged union, nor was there any evidence that he was acting as an agent of such union," he concluded that the union was not responsible for the distribution of the leaflets and the charge was, therefore, "wholly without basis." This ruling was sustained by the General Counsel of the Board some two months after this suit was filed.

In an unpublished opinion the District Judge dismissed the complaint holding, as we have already noted, that even if the union were responsible for distributing the material the case was controlled by *Garmon, supra.* The Court of Appeals affirmed, limiting its holding "to a suit for libelous statements growing out of and relevant to a union's campaign to organize the employees of an employer subject to the National Labor Relations Act." At 72.

II.

The question before us has been a recurring one in both state and federal tribunals, involving the extent to which the National Labor Relations Act, as amended, supersedes state law with respect to libels published during labor disputes. Its resolution entails accommodation of the federal interest in uniform regulation of labor relations with the traditional concern and responsibility of the State to protect its citizens against defamatory attacks. The problem is aggravated by the fact that the law in many States presumes damages from the publication of certain statements characterized as actionable *per se.* Labor disputes are ordinarily heated affairs; the language that is commonplace there might well be deemed actionable *per se* in some state jurisdictions. Indeed, representation campaigns are frequently characterizd by bitter and extreme charges, countercharges, unfounded rumors, vituperations, personal accusations, misrepresentations and distortions. Both labor and management often speak bluntly and recklessly, embellishing their respective positions with imprecatory language. *Cafeteria Union* v. *Angelos,* 320 U.S. 293, 295 (1943). It is therefore necessary to determine whether libel actions in such circumstances might interfere with the national labor policy.

Our task is rendered more difficult by the failure of the Congress to furnish precise guidance in either the language of the Act or its legislative history. As Mr. Justice Jackson said for a unanimous Court in *Garner* v. *Teamsters Union,* 346 U.S. 485, 488 (1953): "The . . . Act . . . leaves much to the states, though Congress has refrained from telling us how much. We must spell out from conflicting indications of congressional will the area in which state action is still permissible."

The Court has dealt with specific pre-emption problems arising under the National Labor Relations Act on many occasions, going back as far as *Allen-Bradley Local* v. *Wisconsin Employment Relations Board,* 315 U.S. 740 (1942). However, in framing the pre-emption question before us we need look primarily to *San Diego Building Trades Council* v. *Garmon,* 359 U.S. 236 (1959). There in most meticulous language this Court spelled out the "extent to which the variegated laws of the several States are displaced by a single, uniform, national rule. . . ." At 241. The Court emphasized that it was for the Board and the Congress to define the "precise and closely limited demarcations that can be adequately fashioned only by legislation and administration," while "[o]ur task is confined to dealing with classes of situations." At 242. In this respect, the Court concluded that the States need not yield jurisdiction "where the activity regulated was a merely peripheral concern of the Labor Management Relations Act . . . [o]r where the regulated conduct touched interests so deeply rooted in local feeling and responsibility that, in the absence of compelling congressional direction, we could not infer that Congress had deprived the States of the power to act." At 243–244. In short, as we said in *Plumbers' Union* v. *Borden*, 373 U.S. 690, 693–694 (1963):

> "[I]n the absence of an overriding state interest such as that involved in the maintenance of domestic peace, state courts must defer to the exclusive competence of the National Labor Relations Board in cases in which the activity that is the subject matter of the litigation is arguably subject to the protections of § 7 or the prohibitions of § 8 of the National Labor Relations Act. This relinquishment of state jurisdiction . . . is essential 'if the danger of state interference with national policy is to be averted,' . . . and is as necessary in a suit for damages as in a suit seeking equitable relief. Thus the first inquiry, in any case in which a claim of federal preemption is raised, must be whether the conduct called into question may reasonably be asserted to be subject to Labor Board cognizance."

We note that the Board has given frequent consideration to the type of statements circulated during labor controversies, and that it has allowed wide latitude to the competing parties. It is clear that the Board does not "police or censor propaganda used in the elections it conducts, but rather leaves to the good sense of the voters the appraisal of such matters, and to opposing parties the task of correcting inaccurate and untruthful statements," *Stewart-Warner Corp.*, 102 NLRB 1153, 1158 (1953). It will set aside an election only where a material fact has been misrepresented in the representation campaign; opportunity for reply has been lacking; and the misrepresentation has had an impact on the free choice of the employees participating in the election. *Hollywood Ceramics Co.*, 140 NLRB 221, 223–224 (1962); *F.H. Snow Canning Co.*, 119 NLRB 714, 717–718 (1957). Likewise, in a number of cases, the Board has concluded that epithets such as "scab," "unfair," and "liar" are commonplace in these struggles and not so indefensible as to remove them from the protection of § 7, even though the statements are erroneous and defame one of the parties to the dispute. Yet the Board indicated that its decisions would have been different had the statements been uttered with actual malice, "a deliberate intention to falsify" or "a malevolent desire to injure." *E.g.*, *Bettcher Mfg. Corp.*, 76 NLRB 526 (1948); *Atlantic Towing Co.*, 75 NLRB 1169, 1170–1173 (1948). In sum, although the Board tolerates intemperate, abusive and inaccurate statements made by the union during attempts to organize employees, it does not interpret the Act as giving either party license to injure the other intentionally by circulating defamatory or insulting material known to be false.

In the light of these considerations it appears that the exercise of state jurisdiction here would be a "merely peripheral concern of the Labor Management Relations Act," provided it is limited to redressing libel issued with knowledge of its falsity, or with reckless disregard of whether it was true or false. Moreover, we believe that "an overriding state interest" in protecting its residents from malicious libels should be recognized in these circumstances. This conclusion is buttressed by our holding in *United Construction Workers* v. *Laburnum Construction Corp.*, 347 U.S. 656 (1954), where Mr. Justice Burton writing for the Court held:

> "To the extent . . . that Congress has not prescribed procedure for dealing with the consequences of tortious conduct already committed, there is no ground for concluding that existing criminal penalties or liabilities for tortious conduct have been eliminated. The care we took in the *Garner* case to demonstrate the existing conflict between state and federal administrative remedies in that case was, itself, a recognition that if no conflict had existed, the state procedure would have survived." At 665.

In *United Automobile Workers* v. *Russell*, 356 U.S. 634 (1958), we again upheld state jurisdiction to entertain a compensatory and punitive damage action by an employee for malicious interference with his lawful occupation. In each of these cases the "type of conduct" involved, *i.e.*, "intimidation and threats of violence," affected such compelling state interests as to permit the exercise of state jurisdiction. *Garmon, supra,* at 248. We similarly conclude that a State's concern with redressing malicious libel is "so deeply rooted in local feeling and responsibility" that it fits within the exception specifically carved out by *Garmon*.

We acknowledge that the enactment of § 8(c) manifests a congressional intent to encourage free debate on issues dividing labor and management.[5] And, as we stated in another context, cases involving speech are to be considered "against the background of a profound . . . commitment to the principle that debate . . . should be uninhibited, robust, and wide-open, and that it may well include vehement, caustic, and sometimes unpleasantly sharp attacks." *New York Times Co.* v. *Sullivan*, 376 U.S. 254, 270 (1964). Such considerations likewise weigh heavily here; the most repulsive speech enjoys immunity provided it falls short of a deliberate or reckless untruth. But it must be emphasized that malicious libel enjoys no constitutional protection in any context. After all, the labor movement has grown up and must assume ordinary responsibilities. The malicious utterance of defamatory statements in any form cannot be condoned, and unions should adopt procedures calculated to prevent such abuses.

III.

Nor should the fact that defamation arises during a labor dispute give the Board exclusive jurisdiction to remedy its consequences. The malicious publication of libelous statements does not in and of itself constitute

---

[5]The wording of the statute indicates, however, that § 8(c) was not designed to serve this interest by immunizing all statements made in the course of a labor controversy. Rather § 8(c) provides that the "expressing of any views, argument, or opinion . . . shall not constitute or be evidence of an unfair labor practice . . . if such expression contains no threat of reprisal or force or promise of benefit." 61 Stat. 142 (1947), 29 U. S. C. § 158 (c) (1964 ed.). It is more likely that Congress adopted this section for a narrower purpose, *i.e.*, to prevent the Board from attributing anti-union motive to an employer on the basis of his past statements. See H. R. Rep. No. 510, 80th Cong., 1st Sess., 45 (1947).

an unfair labor practice. While the Board might find that an employer or union violated § 8 by deliberately making false statements, or that the issuance of malicious statements during an organizing campaign had such a profound effect on the election as to require that it be set aside, it looks only to the coercive or misleading nature of the statements rather than their defamatory quality. The injury that the statement might cause to an individual's reputation—whether he be an employer or union official—has no relevance to the Board's function. Cf. *Amalgamated Utility Workers* v. *Consolidated Edison Co.,* 309 U.S. 261 (1940). The Board can award no damages, impose no penalty, or give any other relief to the defamed individual.

On the contrary, state remedies have been designed to compensate the victim and enable him to vindicate his reputation. The Board's lack of concern with the "personal" injury caused by malicious libel, together with its inability to provide redress to the maligned party, vitiates the ordinary arguments for pre-emption.[6] As stressed by THE CHIEF JUSTICE in his dissenting opinion in *Russell, supra:*

"The unprovoked infliction of personal injuries during a period of labor unrest is neither to be expected nor to be justified, but economic loss inevitably attends work stoppages. Furthermore, damages for personal injuries may be assessed without regard to the merits of the labor controversy. . . ." At 649.

Judicial condemnation of the alleged attack on Linn's character would reflect no judgment upon the objectives of the union. It would not interfere with the Board's jurisdiction over the merits of the labor controversy.

But it has been insisted that not only would the threat of state libel suits dampen the ardor of labor debate and truncate the free discussion envisioned by the Act, but that such suits might be used as weapons of economic coercion. Moreover, in view of the propensity of juries to award excessive damages for defamation, the availability of libel actions may pose a threat to the stability of labor unions and smaller employers. In order that the recognition of legitimate state interests does not interfere with effective administration of national labor policy the possibility of such consequences must be minimized. We therefore limit the availability of state remedies for libel to those instances in which the complainant can show that the defamatory statements were circulated with malice and caused him damage.

The standards enunciated in *New York Times Co.* v. *Sullivan,* 376 U.S. 254 (1964), are adopted by analogy, rather than under constitutional compulsion. We apply the malice test to effectuate the statutory design with respect to pre-emption. Construing the Act to permit recovery of

---

[6]The fact that the Board has no authority to grant effective relief aggravates the State's concern since the refusal to redress an otherwise actionable wrong creates disrespect for the law and encourages the victim to take matters into his own hands. The function of libel suits in preventing violence has long been recognized. *Developments in the Law—Defamation,* 69 HARV. L. REV. 875, 933 (1956). But as to criminal libel suits see *Garrison* v. *Louisiana,* 379 U.S. 64 (1964).

damages in a state cause of action only for defamatory statements published with knowledge of their falsity or with reckless disregard of whether they were true or false guards against abuse of libel actions and unwarranted intrusion upon free discussion envisioned by the Act.

As we have pointed out, certain language characteristic of labor disputes may be held actionable *per se* in some state courts. These categories of libel have developed without specific reference to labor controversies. However, even in those jurisdictions, the amount of damages which may be recovered depends upon evidence as to the severity of the resulting harm. This is a salutary principle. We therefore hold that a complainant may not recover except upon proof of such harm, which may include general injury to reputation, consequent mental suffering, alienation of associates, specific items of pecuniary loss, or whatever form of harm would be recognized by state tort law.[7] The fact that courts are generally not in close contact with the pressures of labor disputes makes it especially necessary that this rule be followed. If the amount of damages awarded is excessive, it is the duty of the trial judge to require a remittitur or a new trial. Likewise, the defamed party must establish that he has suffered some sort of compensable harm as a prerequisite to the recovery of additional punitive damages.[8]

Since the complaint here does not make the specific allegations that we find necessary in such actions, leave should be given Linn on remand to amend his complaint, if he so desires, to meet these requirements. In the event of a new trial he, of course, bears the burden of proof of such allegations.

IV.

Finally, it has been argued that permitting state action here would impinge upon national labor policy because the availability of a judicial remedy for malicious libel would cause employers and unions to spurn appropriate administrative sanctions for contemporaneous violations of the Act. We disagree. When the Board and state law frown upon the publication of malicious libel, albeit for different reasons, it may be expected that the injured party will request both administrative and judicial relief. The Board would not be ignored since its sanctions alone can adjust the equilibrium disturbed by an unfair labor practice. If a malicious libel contributed to union victory in a closely fought election, few employers would be satisfied with simply damages for "personal" injury caused by the defamation. An unsuccessful union would also seek to set the election results aside as the fruits of an employer's malicious libel. And a union may be expected to request similar relief for defamatory statements which contribute to the victory of a competing union. Nor

---

[7]The Government, as *amicus curiae*, has urged us to go further. It would limit liability to "grave" defamations—those which accuse the defamed person of having engaged in criminal, homosexual, treasonable, or other infamous conduct. We cannot agree. This would impose artificial characterizations that would encroach too heavily upon state jurisdiction.

[8]It should be noted that punitive damages were awarded in *Laburnum* and *Russell*. In both instances there was proof of compensatory injury resulting from the defendants' violence.

would the courts and the Board act at cross purposes since, as we have seen, their policies would not be inconsistent.

As was said in *Garrison v. Louisiana,* 379 U.S. 64, 75: "[T]he use of the known lie as a tool is at once at odds with the premises of democratic government and with the orderly manner in which economic, social, or political change is to be effected." We believe that under the rules laid down here it can be appropriately redressed without curtailment of state libel remedies beyond the actual needs of national labor policy. However, if experience shows that a greater curtailment, even a total one, should be necessary to prevent impairment of that policy, the Court will be free to reconsider today's holding. We deal here not with a constitutional issue but solely with the degree to which state remedies have been pre-empted by the Act.

BLACK, J., dissenting.

The Court holds that an individual participant on the employer's side of a labor dispute can sue the union for libel on account of charges made by the union in the heat of the dispute. By the same token I assume that under the Court's holding, individual labor union members now have the right to sue their employers when they say naughty things during labor disputes. This new Court-made law tosses a monkey wrench into the collective bargaining machinery Congress set up to try to settle labor disputes, and at the same time exalts the law of libel to an even higher level of importance in the regulation of day-to-day life in this country.

. . . The object of the National Labor Relations Act was to bring about agreements by collective bargaining, not to add fuel to the fire by encouraging libel suits with their inevitable irritations and dispute-prolonging tendencies. Yet it is difficult to conceive of an element more certain to create irritations guaranteed to prevent fruitful collective bargaining discussions than the threat or presence of a large monetary judgment gained in a libel suit generating anger and a desire for vengeance on the part of one or the other of the bargaining parties. I think, therefore, that libel suits are not only "arguably" but inevitably in conflict with the basic purpose of the Act to settle disputes peaceably—not to aggravate them, but to end them. For this reason I would affirm the judgment of the two lower courts.

. . . It is rather strange for this Court to import its novel ideas on libel suits into the area of labor controversies where the effect is bound to abridge the freedom of the parties to discuss their disputes and to settle them through peaceful negotiations. It is strange because one of the hopes of those responsible for modern collective bargaining was that peaceful settlements among the parties working by themselves under the aegis of federal law would be substituted for the old-time labor feuds too frequently accompanied by bitter strife and wasteful, dangerous conflicts verging on private war. Because libel suits in my judgment are inconsistent with both the Constitution of the United States and the policies of the Act, I dissent from the holding of the Court reversing the judgment below.

FORTAS, J., with whom WARREN, C.J. and DOUGLAS, J. join, dissenting.
. . .

In my judgment, the structure provided by Congress for the handling of labor-management controversies precludes any court from entertaining a libel suit between parties to a labor dispute or their agents wnere the allegedly defamatory statement is confined to matters which are part of the fabric of the dispute. The present controversy is just such a case.

Petitioner Linn is an officer of the employer sought to be organized by respondent union. The allegedly defamatory statements, set out in the opinion of the Court, relate to management conduct during the course of the dispute. The leaflets in question allegedly accuse management of lying both to the NLRB and to employees in order to deprive some employees of their right to vote in NLRB elections and to certain pay increases.

As an illustration of the kind of hyperbole characteristic of labor-management strife, this "libel" is hardly incendiary. To the experienced eye, it is pale and anemic when compared with the rich and colorful charges freely exchanged in the heat of many labor disputes.[1]

In response to such a pallid "libel," the Court today holds that petitioner, perceiving himself the target of a purportedly false and defamatory statement, may sue the union and several of its officers for damages—so long as he pleads that the statement is defamatory, was made with malice, and caused some injury to him. Should he succeed in clearing the hurdles thus set in his path, he may recover not only compensation for his "injuries," but punitive or exemplary damages as well. These requirements that petitioner plead and prove both malice and special damages—arising from what I regard as the Court's well-founded concern that libel suits might otherwise "pose a threat to the stability of labor unions and smaller employers"—may be cold comfort to the potential defendant in a libel suit. "Malice," which the Court defines as a deliberate intention to falsify or a malevolent desire to injure, is, after all, a largely subjective standard, responsive to the ingenuity of trial counsel and the predilections of judge and jury. And "injury" resulting from words is not limited to tangible trauma. These requirements afford dubious defense on a battlefield from which the qualified umpire—the NLRB—has been removed. In a libel suit, the outcome is determined by standards alien to the subject matter of labor relations, by considerations which do not take into account the complex and subtle values that are at stake, and by a jury unfamiliar with the quality of rhetoric customary in labor disputes. The outcome, in fact, is more apt to reflect immediate community attitudes toward unionization than appreciation for the underlying, long-term perplexities of the interplay of management and labor in a democratic society.

Until today, the decisions of this Court have consistently held that the federal structure for resolving labor disputes may not be breached or

---

[1]Compare, for example, the considerably more imaginative use of vituperation reflected in the allegedly defamatory statement in *United Steelworkers of America* v. *R. H. Bouligny, Inc.*, 382 U.S. 145. A description of the statement is found in Brief for Respondent, p. 2 (No. 19, O.T. 1965). [The passage referred to reads: "White . . . in his complaint stated a cause of action for libel, alleging that the Union published in the . . . Union newspaper, a defamatory and scandalous cartoon caricature picturing him in the bowl of a commode."—Ed.]

encumbered by state remedies where the tortious conduct allegedly involved is either protected or prohibited by federal labor legislation, or even "arguably subject to" federal law[2]—and despite the inability of the NLRB to redress the pecuniary harm suffered by the victim.

In *Garner* v. *Teamsters Union*, 346 U.S. 485, the Court held that state courts may not enjoin peaceful picketing where plaintiff's grievance is within the jurisdiction of the NLRB. In *Guss* v. *Utah Labor Board*, 353 U.S. 1, the Court held that even where the NLRB declines to exercise its conceded jurisdiction over a labor dispute "affecting commerce," a parallel remedy before a state board is nonetheless pre-empted. And in *San Diego Building Trades Council* v. *Garmon*, 359 U.S. 236, the Court concluded that state courts may not award damages for peaceful picketing, although the conduct involved was only "arguably subject" to the federal statute and despite the NLRB's decision not to exercise jurisdiction.[3] Today marks the first departure from what has become a well-established rule that only where the public's compelling interest in preventing violence or the threat of violence is involved can the exclusiveness of the federal structure for resolving labor disputes be breached. As was said in *Garmon*, 359 U.S., at 247: "Even the States' salutary effort to redress private wrongs or grant compensation for past harm cannot be exerted to regulate activities that are potentially subject to the exclusive federal regulatory scheme." The majority's opinion fails to make clear why the participant's interest in protecting his reputation from the sting of words uttered as part of a labor dispute is a compelling concern which this Court must allow the States to protect, while his interest in preserving his economic well-being from illegal picketing is not.

By narrowly restricting the permissible exceptions to the general rule of pre-emption and by excluding generally the right to compensation for purely private wrongs, the Court has contributed to the Nation's success in domesticating the potentially explosive warfare between labor and management. The decision announced today threatens the degree of equilibrium which has been achieved. I think that the Court's decision both underestimates the damage libel suits may inflict on the equilibrium, and overestimates the effectiveness of the restraint which will result from superimposed requirements of malice and special damages. . . .[4]

The foregoing considerations do not apply to the extent that the use of verbal weapons during labor disputes is not confined to any issue in the dispute, or involves a person who is neither party to nor agent of a party to the dispute. In such instances, perhaps the courts ought to be free to

---

[2]Suits to enforce collective bargaining agreements have been held to arise under 29 U.S.C. § 185(a) (1964 ed.) and hence are not within the reach of the pre-emption doctrine. See *Smith* v. *Evening News Ass'n*, 371 U.S. 195; Sovern, *Section 301 and the Primary Jurisdiction of the NLRB*, 76 HARV. L. REV. 529 (1963).

[3]Subsequent to *Garmon* and *Guss*, Congress has explicitly removed the obstacles to state-court treatment of labor disputes as to which the NLRB has declined to exercise jurisdiction on the ground of insufficient effect on interstate commerce. 29 U.S.C. § 164(c)(2) (1964 ed.).

[4]Although libelous statements cannot serve as the predicate for an unfair labor practice charge, like any other misleading statement they may in certain circumstances induce the NLRB to set aside the results of an election. See Bok, *The Regulation of Campaign Tactics in Representation Elections Under the National Labor Relations Act*, 78 HARV. L. REV. 38, 82–84 (1964).

redress whatever private wrong has been suffered. But this is not such a case. The fact that the Court today rules that, after appropriate amendment of the complaint, a libel action may be maintained on the basis of the circumscribed accusation contained in the leaflet in question demonstrates how very substantial is the breach opened in the wall which has heretofore insulated labor disputes from the vagaries of lawsuits.[5] I would affirm the decision below.

Notes

1. Compare the definition of a scab, popularly attributed to Jack London:

> "After God had finished the rattlesnake, the toad, and the vampire, He had some awful substance left with which He made a *scab*.
>
> "A scab is a two-legged animal with a corkscrew soul, a water brain, a combination backbone of jelly and glue. Where others have hearts, he carries a tumor of rotten principles.
>
> "When a scab comes down the street, men turn their backs and Angels weep in Heaven, and the Devil shuts the gates of hell to keep him out.
>
> "No man (or woman) has a right to scab so long as there is a pool of water to drown his carcass in, or a rope long enough to hang his body with. Judas was a gentleman compared with a scab. For betraying his Master, he had character enough to hang himself. A scab has not.
>
> "Esau sold his birthright for a mess of pottage. Judas sold his Savior for thirty pieces of silver. Benedict Arnold sold his country for a promise of a commission in the British Army. The scab sells his birthright, country, his wife, his children and his fellowmen for an unfulfilled promise from his employer.
>
> "Esau was a traitor to himself; Judas was a traitor to his God; Benedict Arnold was a traitor to his country; a SCAB is a traitor to his God, his country, his family and his class."

Would you advise a union to distribute a list containing the names of strikebreakers under this definition? See *Old Dominion Branch, Letter Carriers* v. *Austin*, 418 U.S. 264, 86 LRRM 2740 (1974).

2. In *Linn* the Court resolves the tension between an open campaign and protecting reputation in favor of the latter. If the letter in Linn had stated that the company, rather than the manager, lied and stole from the employees, would the same considerations determine the Court's decision? Was the charge against the manager unrelated to the campaign? Should this make a difference, as the Government implicitly suggested in footnote 7?

---

[5] Resort to libel suits as an auxiliary weapon in resolving labor disputes presents much more than an abstract threat. For evidence of a growing tendency to invoke these suits see the list of such cases recently pending in the Fourth Circuit alone in Brief for Petitioner, p. 15, *United Steelworkers of America* v. *R. H. Bouligny, Inc., supra;* and those discussed at pp. 18–39 of the Appendix to the brief filed by respondents in Nos. 89 and 94, O. T. 1965, and in the present case as *amici curiae.*

3. Will the availability of a defamation suit have a chilling effect on speech? Assume that during the Enderby organizing campaign Swoboda addresses co-workers at a union rally and states:

"We all know just how unfair things are here. Just last week Supervisor Small robbed me of two days' pay by claiming that 'company policy' required her to change my time card to show two days of voluntary absences. Everyone knows that it's always been up to us to decide whether days off are vacation days or absences."

A union newsletter, distributed during the campaign, reports on the rally and includes the employee's remarks, along with the question: "How many others have the Supervisors robbed?" A few days before the election, Supervisor Small files a defamation action against the union local and Swoboda, seeking $100,000 in damages, including $50,000 in punitive damages. She alleges damage to her reputation and anxiety about "having publicly been called a crook."

What course of action do you recommend to the union? to Swoboda?

a. Would it be effective for the union to explain to the employees that the suit will be dismissed and that there is no chance that the local union treasury will be depleted by $100,000?

b. If the union loses the election, can the union challenge the results on the ground that the supervisor's suit was frivolous? Can the Board treat filing of the suit during the election as an unfair labor practice? Can the Board decide that management's talking about the suit during the campaign constitutes an unfair labor practice? That it constitutes sufficient grounds for setting the election aside?

c. If the suit is dismissed for not stating a cause of action, what remedies are available to the union? to Swoboda? Cf. *IBEW, Local 1805* v. *Mayo,* 281 Md. 475, 97 LRRM 2053 (1977).

4. Would the purposes of the Act and protection of individuals be served if the Board developed a rule invalidating elections on proof of malicious statements which cause specific injury? If the Board developed such a rule, would civil actions be preempted?

5. In *Bill Johnson's Restaurants, Inc.* v. *NLRB,* 461 U.S. ___, 51 USLW 4636, 113 LRRM 2647 (1983), the Supreme Court reviewed and overturned a Board doctrine which provided that employers violate the NLRA when they institute state court actions against employees in order to retaliate against their exercise of protected rights. The Court held that retaliatory intent alone was not sufficient.

The relevant facts were set out in the Court's opinion:

"The present controversy arises out of a labor dispute at 'Bill Johnson's Big Apple East,' one of four restaurants owned and operated by the petitioner in Phoenix, Arizona. It began on August 8, 1978, when petitioner fired Myrland Helton, one of the most senior waitresses at the restaurant. Believing that her termination was the result of her efforts to organize a union, she filed unfair labor practice charges against the restaurant with the Board.

"On September 20, after an investigation, the Board's General Counsel issued a complaint. On the same day, Helton, joined by three co-waitresses and a few others, picketed the restaurant. The picketers carried signs asking customers to boycott the restaurant because its management was unfair to the waitresses. Petitioner's manager confronted the picketers and threatened to 'get even' with them 'if it's the last thing I do.' Petitioner's president telephoned the husband of one of the picketing waitresses and impliedly threatened that the couple would 'get hurt' and lose their new home if the wife continued to participate in the protest. The picketing continued on September 21 and 22. In addition, the picketers distributed a leaflet that accused management of making '[u]nwarranted sexual advances' and maintaining a 'filthy restroom for women employees.' The leaflet also stated that a complaint against the restaurant had been filed by the Board and that Helton had been fired after suggesting that a union be organized.

"On the morning of September 25, petitioner and three of its co-owners filed a verified complaint against Helton and the other demonstrators in an Arizona state court. Plaintiffs alleged that the defendants had engaged in mass picketing, harassed customers, blocked public ingress to and egress from the restaurant, and created a threat to public safety. The complaint also contained a libel count, alleging that the leaflet contained false and outrageous statements published by the defendants with the malicious intent to injure the plaintiffs. The complaint sought a temporary restraining order and preliminary and permanent injunctive relief, as well as compensatory damages, $500,000 in punitive damages, and appropriate further legal and equitable relief. After a hearing, the state court declined to enjoin the distribution of leaflets but otherwise issued the requested restraining order. Expedited depositions were also permitted. The defendants retained counsel and, after a hearing on the plaintiffs' motion for a preliminary injunction on November 16, the court dissolved the temporary restraining order and denied preliminary injunctive relief.

"Meanwhile, on the day after the state-court suit was filed, Helton filed a second charge with the Board alleging that petitioner had committed a number of new unfair labor practices in connection with the dispute between the waitresses and the restaurant. Among these was a charge that petitioner had filed the civil suit in retaliation for the defendants' protected, concerted activities, and because they had filed charges under the Act. The General Counsel issued a complaint based on these new charges on October 23. As relevant here, the complaint alleged that petitioner, by filing and prosecuting the state suit, was attempting to retaliate against Helton and the others, in violation of §§ 8(a)(1) and (4) of the National Labor Relations [Act]. . . ."

Although the state court action might not be preempted, a retaliatory action could obviously interfere with the exercise of Section 7 rights or violate Section 8(a)(4) by discriminating against employees for invoking the procedures of the Board.

The Supreme Court recognized that a state court action could act as a "powerful instrument of coercion or retaliation."

". . . As the Board has observed, by suing an employee who files charges with the Board or engages in other protected activities, an employer can place its employees on notice that anyone who engages in such conduct is subjecting himself to the possibility of a burdensome lawsuit. Regardless of how unmeritorious the employer's suit is, the employee will most likely have to retain counsel and incur substantial legal expenses to defend against it. Furthermore, as the Court of Appeals in the present case noted, the chilling effect of a state lawsuit upon an employee's willingness to engage in protected activity is multiplied where the complaint seeks damages in addition to injunctive relief. Where, as here, such a suit is filed against hourly-wage waitresses or other individuals who lack the backing of a union, the need to allow the Board to intervene and provide a remedy is at its greatest."

Nevertheless, the Court noted that the "right of access to the courts is an aspect of the First Amendment right to petition the Government for redress of grievances." Moreover, the Court believed that the Board's doctrine was inconsistent with decisions such as *Linn* v. *Plant Guards*. The Court concluded that the "filing and prosecution of a well-founded lawsuit may not be enjoined as an unfair labor practice, even if it would not have been commenced but for the plaintiff's desire to retaliate against the defendant for exercising rights protected by the Act." Thus, the Court held that an employer commits an enjoinable unfair labor practice only when it prosecutes a lawsuit that is *both* retaliatory and baseless. The Court summarized its holding as follows:

"[W]e hold that the Board may not halt the prosecution of a state-court lawsuit, regardless of the plaintiff's motive, unless the suit lacks a reasonable basis in fact or law. Retaliatory motive and lack of reasonable basis are both essential prerequisites to the issuance of a cease-and-desist order against a state suit. The Board's reasonable basis inquiry must be structured in a manner that will preserve the state plantiff's right to have a state court jury or judge resolve genuine material factual or state-law legal disputes pertaining to the lawsuit. Therefore, if the Board is called upon to determine whether a suit is unlawful prior to the time that the state court renders final judgment, and if the state plantiff can show that such genuine material factual or legal issues exist, the Board must await the results of the state-court adjudication with respect to the merits of the state suit. If the state proceedings result in a judgment adverse to the plaintiff, the Board may then consider the matter further and, if it is found that the lawsuit was filed with retaliatory intent, the Board may find a violation and order appropriate relief. In short, then, although it is an unfair labor practice to prosecute an unmeritorious lawsuit for a retaliatory purpose, the offense is not enjoinable unless the suit lacks a reasonable basis."

Consider how the First Amendment or *Linn* leads to the outcome in *Bill Johnson's Restaurants*. For purposes of the First Amendment, is there a distinction between a retaliatory and baseless filing of a state court and a filing which is only retaliatory? Do the policies which led to the exception to the preemption doctrine in *Linn* support the result reached? Finally, consider the practical effects of the Court's decision.

6. If at this point you are uncertain about precisely what communications are shielded by Section 8(c), are sufficient to set an election aside, or are wholly acceptable to the Board, how do you advise a client on the legality of proposed campaign rhetoric? What ethical considerations further complicate this question?

2. Surveillance and Interrogation

Problem

Consultant: Now that we've set the campaign theme, we have to get the message out and find out how it's selling. Your supervisors are the best source. The employees trust them. What we do is explain the election laws to the supervisors, feed them lots of facts and figures, and send them out to do two things: talk and listen.

They say the things we want employees to hear day after day. In casual conversation they talk about strikes, possibilities of violence, union dues, pass out some of these newsclips we have about the corrupt union leadership. Most natural thing in the world for them to ask about the union's efforts, why employee X wants an outsider around, that kind of thing. They can also let us know what information we need to get out to the people, and they can count noses. On election day we should know the results before the NLRB does.

Maxwell: Will the supervisors do all that?

Consultant: Leave it to me. We'll get the supervisors together, explain that they're essential to our winning, and insure their cooperation by letting them know that if they're not good team players, out they go.

Maxwell: Isn't that against the law?

Consultant: Nope. Congress recognized that management needs the loyalty of supervisors in all kinds of situations. That's one of the reasons supervisors are excluded from the definition of employees in the statute.

NLRB v. Lorben Corporation

United States Court of Appeals, Second Circuit, 1965
345 F.2d 346, 59 LRRM 2184

[After an organizing campaign had started, the employer prepared a paper, with the question: "Do you wish Local 1922 of the Electrical Workers to represent you?" Under this were two columns—"yes" and "no." The plant superintendent handed these sheets to each employee telling each there was no obligation to sign. Each employee signed in the "no" column.]

MARSHALL, Circuit Judge.

. . .There is no evidence of any employee hostility to the union and the Trial Examiner found an absence of any "other unfair labor practices." However, the Examiner found that the respondent had violated the Act. While the Examiner mentioned the failure of respondent to advise the employees of the purpose of the interrogation and to assure them that no reprisals would follow, he based his decision primarily on his finding that the respondent had no legitimate purpose for the interrogation. The Board based its decision on the first two reasons and refused to rely on the third. We deny enforcement of the Board's order.

Employer interrogation of employees as to their desire to be represented by a particular union is not coercive or intimidating on its face. It is extremely difficult to determine how often and under what circumstances threats will be inferred by the employees . . . .

The problem of delineating what is coercion by interrogation has resisted any set rules or specific limitations. The Board's original determination that interrogation by the employer was unlawful per se, *Standard-Coosa-Thatcher Co.*, 85 NLRB 1358, 24 LRRM 1575 (1949), was disapproved by the courts and the Board retreated to the position that interrogation would only be unlawful where it was found to be coercive in the light of all surrounding circumstances. As the Board stated in *Blue Flash Express, Inc.*, 109 NLRB 591, 594, 34 LRRM 1384, 1386 (1954): "We agree with and adopt the test laid down by the Court of Appeals for the Second Circuit in the *Syracuse Color Press* case [209 F.2d 596, 33 LRRM 2334, *cert. denied,* 347 U.S. 966, 34 LRRM 2143 (1954)] which we construe to be that the answer to whether particular interrogation interferes with, restrains, and coerces employees must be found in the record as a whole." In *Bourne* v. *NLRB,* 332 F.2d 47, 48, 56 LRRM 2241 (2 Cir. 1964), this Circuit reaffirmed this comprehensive approach and we attempted to suggest some of the many factors that must be considered anew in each case to determine whether a particular interrogation is coercive:

"(1) The background, *i.e.,* is there a history of employer hostility and discrimination?

"(2) The nature of the information sought, *e.g.,* did the interrogator appear to be seeking information on which to base taking action against individual employees?

"(3) The identity of the questioner, *i.e.,* how high was he in the company hierarchy?

"(4) Place and method of interrogation, *e.g.,* was employee called from work to the boss's office? Was there an atmosphere of 'unnatural formality'?

"(5) Truthfulness of the reply."

Recently, the Board has withdrawn from this more comprehensive approach and has sought to establish the rule that employer interrogation is coercive in the absence of a showing that (1) there is a valid purpose for obtaining the information; (2) this purpose is communicated to the employees; and (3) the employees are assured that no reprisals will be taken, cf. *Johnnie's Poultry Co.,* 146 NLRB 770, 55 LRRM 1403

(April 17, 1964);[2] Bok, *supra,* at 107. In the instant case, the Board applied this rule. It acknowledged that respondent had a valid purpose in conducting the poll, namely, to determine whether the union repre-' sented a majority of its employees for the purpose of deciding whether recognition should be extended. Yet the Board found that respondent had committed an unfair labor practice simply because of "the manner in which the poll was conducted, particularly the fact that Respondent did not explain the purpose of the poll to all of the employees, and did not offer or provide any assurances to the employees that their rights under the Act would not be infringed."

To enforce the Board's order which rests on this narrow ground alone, would be to depart from the line of decisions of this Circuit cited above, once approved by the Board, and we are not so inclined. While it is true that questioning can very well have a coercive effect where the purpose is not explained and there are no assurances against retaliation, we hold that the absence of these two factors, without more and in the face of the undisputed facts in the record of this case, fails to show coercion within the meaning of section 8(a)(1).

FRIENDLY, C.J., dissenting.

The Board supported its conclusion that Lorben "violated 8(a) (1) of the Act in polling the employees" by saying that it relied "principally on the manner in which the poll was conducted, particularly the fact that Respondent did not explain the purpose of the poll to all of the employees, and did not offer or provide any assurances to the employees that their rights under the Act would not be infringed."

I fail to understand on what basis, in a case like this, we may properly reject the conditions to permissible interrogation which the Board has developed and here enforced. The Board's adoption, in *Blue Flash Express, Inc.,* 109 NLRB 591, 594, 34 LRRM 1384 (1954), of language used by this court in granting enforcement in *NLRB* v. *Syracuse Color Press, Inc.,* 209 F.2d 596, 599, 33 LRRM 2334 (2 Cir.), *cert. denied,* 347 U.S. 966, 34 LRRM 2143 (1954), did not prevent it from later concluding, in the light of experience, that proper administration demanded working rules for reconciling the employer's desire to know what was afoot and the employees' need to be free from harassment, which would provide a test more definite, and more readily applicable, than "whether, under all the circumstances, the interrogation reasonably tends to restrain or interfere with the employees in the exercise of rights guaranteed by the Act," 109 NLRB at 593. See *NLRB* v. *A.P.W. Prods., Inc.,* 316 F.2d 899, 905–906, 53 LRRM 2055 (2 Cir. 1963); Dickinson, Administrative Justice and the Supremacy of Law in the United States 143, 205 (1927). An agency

[2]However, in *Johnnie's Poultry Co.* there were findings that the employer had threatened to close the plant, showed evidence of "union animus" and demonstrated an absence of good faith, as well as an unlawful refusal to bargain in violation of section 8 (a) (5) of the Act. Similarly in *Frank Sullivan & Co.,* 133 NLRB 726, 48 LRRM 1704 (1961), there was a finding that the employer had "indicated an antipathy toward the Union"; and in *Orkin Exterminating Co.,* 136 NLRB 399, 49 LRRM 1781 (1962) it was recognized that the questioning occurred "in a context of threats to close the plant if the Union organized it" and after "pressure [had been] put on employees to withdraw their union cards."

receiving over 14,000 unfair labor practice charges a year, see 28 NLRB Ann.Rep. 161 (1963), ought not be denied the right to establish standards, appropriate to the statutory purpose, that are readily understandable by employers, regional directors and trial examiners, and be forced to determine every instance of alleged unlawful interrogation by an inquiry covering an employer's entire union history and his behavior during the particular crisis and to render decisions having little or no precedential value since "the number of distinct fact situations is almost infinite.". . . . The Board's powers to rule that certain types of conduct constitute unfair labor practices without further proof of motivation or effect has been sustained in cases too numerous for anything more than illustrative citation. *Republic Aviation Corp.* v. *NLRB,* 324 U.S. 793, 16 LRRM 620 (1945) (prohibition of union solicitation on company premises outside of working hours). . . .

Notes

1. In *Struksnes Construction Co.,* 165 NLRB 1062, 65 LRRM 1385 (1967), the Board again attempted to establish standards "that are readily understandable by employer, regional directors and trial examiners":

> "Absent unusual circumstances, the polling of employees by an employer will be violative of Section 8(a)(1) of the Act unless the following safeguards are observed: (1) the purpose of the poll is to determine the truth of a union's claim of majority, (2) this purpose is communicated to the employees, (3) assurances against reprisal are given, (4) the employees are polled by a secret ballot, and (5) the employer has not engaged in unfair labor practices or otherwise created a coercive atmosphere.
>
> "The purpose of the polling in these circumstances is clearly relevant to an issue raised by a union's claim for recognition and is therefore lawful. The requirement that the lawful purpose be communicated to the employees, along with assurance against reprisal, is designed to allay any fear of discrimination which might otherwise arise from the polling, and any tendency to interfere with employees' Section 7 rights. Secrecy of the ballot will give further assurance that reprisals cannot be taken against employees because the views of each individual will not be known. And the absence of employer unfair labor practices or other conduct creating a coercive atmosphere will serve as a further warranty to the employees that the poll does not have some unlawful object, contrary to the lawful purpose stated by the employer. In accord with presumptive rules applied by the Board with court approval in other situations, this rule is designed to effectuate the purposes of the Act by maintaining a reasonable balance between the protection of employee rights and legitimate interests of employers.
>
> "On the other hand, a poll taken while a petition for a Board election is pending does not, in our view, serve any legitimate interest of the employer that would not be better served by the forthcoming Board

election. In accord with long-established Board policy, therefore, such polls will continue to be found violative of Section 8(a)(1) of the Act."

2. In the problem on page 249, the consultant suggests that supervisors use informal contacts with workers to stress the hazards of unionization and to find out which employees support the union. What factors suggest that such supervisor contacts are coercive interrogations *or* casual conversations?

Compare *Graham Architectural Products*, 259 NLRB No. 153, 109 LRRM 1100 (1982), *enf'd in part*, 697 F.2d 534, 112 LRRM 2470 (3d Cir. 1983), in which the union lost the election 93 to 68. The administrative law judge, the Board, and the Court of Appeals reached startlingly different conclusions about the questioning of three employees. In each of the following excerpts, the Court of Appeals' analysis appears immediately after the Board's discussion:

a. *Stambaugh*

NLRB: "About three days before the July 16, 1979, election, Stambaugh was called to the desk of her supervisor, Greg Nash, and asked whether she was 'for the Union.' When she replied that she did not have to tell him, he said, 'No, you don't.' She went on, however, and stated that she planned to vote for the Union. The Administrative Law Judge, relying on *J.K. Electronics, Inc.*, d/b/a *Wesco Electrical Company*, [232 NLRB 479, 96 LRRM 1560 (1977)] found no violation in this conduct. We find that the facts here are significantly different from those in *Wesco*. In that case, a supervisor first asked an employee whether she had been to any union meetings, and then took the question back, saying that he could not ask her that question. The Board found no violation, finding that the supervisor immediately took the question back and that it was clear that he did not wish the employee to respond. Here, in contrast, Nash did not withdraw his question but simply conceded, when challenged, that Stambaugh was correct in saying she did not have to answer. By that time, he had already confronted Stambaugh and, if she did not answer, her silence could be construed as support for the Union. Accordingly, we find that, by Nash's conduct, Respondent violated Section 8(a)(1) of the Act."

Court of Appeals: ". . . The question itself contained no veiled threat or implication that the Company contemplated reprisals against union supporters.[4] And we fail to see how the circumstances here made Nash's inquiry coercive. Although Nash did call Stambaugh to his desk,

___

"[4]In *Hedstrom Co.* v. *NLRB*, 629 F.2d 305, 314–15, 105 LRRM 2183 (3d Cir. 1980) (*en banc*.), *cert. denied*, 450 U.S. 996, 106 LRRM 2817 (1981), this court viewed the supervisor's lack of assurances against reprisals and the lack of any valid reason for the inquiry as two factors indicative of coercion. Although these factors are also present here, they are outweighed by any other circumstances indicating that the statement did not tend to restrain the employee. The inquiries in *Hedstrom* were made in an environment of serious unfair labor practices by the company. There was no such background behind the inquiry of Stambaugh . . ."

this has little significance here because Nash's desk was located in an open area near Stambaugh's work station, not in a formal office. As Nash apparently was a low-level supervisor, it would not have been unusual for him to have in-plant conversations with the employees. We also note that the question led to a 90-minute conversation during which nothing improper was said. Moreover, it is important to bear in mind that there was no history of Company hostility to the Union. See *Lutheran Hospital of Milwaukee, Inc.* v. *NLRB*, 564 F.2d 208, 210–11, 96 LRRM 2515 (7th Cir. 1977), *vacated and remanded on other grounds*, 438 U.S. 902, 98 LRRM 2848 (1978). This inquiry was not part of a full scale 'antiunion campaign orchestrated by the highest levels of . . . management,' as was the case in *Ethyl Corp.*, 231 NLRB 431, 433, 97 LRRM 1465 (1977). Most important, by agreeing with Stambaugh that she did not have to answer the question, Nash effectively withdrew the question and removed any pressure on Stambaugh to respond.[5]"

b. *Shaeffer*

NLRB: "A few days before the election, Sonia Shaeffer was asked by her former supervisor, McArthur, what she thought the Union 'could get for her.' She replied that she expected better pay and benefits. The Administrative Law Judge found that this conversation did not constitute interrogation within the meaning of Section 8(a)(1) of the Act because Shaeffer was openly active on behalf of the Union and the question came up in the context of a personal conversation about McArthur's baby and included a general discussion of union benefits and wages around the country. The Board has held, however, that the coercive impact of such questions is not diminished by the employee's open union support or by the absence of attendant threats. *PPG Industries, Inc., Lexington Plant, Fiber Glass Division*, 251 NLRB 1146, 105 LRRM 1434 (1980), and that such an interrogation is not made lawful by being conducted in a 'friendly' manner, *Quemetco, Inc., a subsidiary of RSR Corporation*, 223 NLRB 470, 91 LRRM 1580 (1976). The fact that McArthur was no longer Shaeffer's supervisor does not require a different result, since he remained one of Respondent's supervisors and hence its agent."

Court of Appeals: ". . . McArthur's question is not inherently threatening or intimidating, and was asked in the course of a casual conversation that Shaeffer herself initiated. McArthur was not Shaeffer's supervisor and did not even work on the same shift with her. Moreover, because Shaeffer was openly active on behalf of the Union, there is no reason to think that McArthur was trying to discover her personal views. As the ALJ observed, the circumstances of the conversation do not suggest any element of coercion or possibility of reprisal."

"[5] . . . In the instant case, the Board distinguished *Wesco* [232 NLRB 479, 96 LRRM 1560 (1977)] on the ground that Nash 'did not withdraw his question but simply conceded, when challenged, that Stambaugh was correct in saying she did not have to answer.' We fail to appreciate the significance to this distinction. The important point is that Nash clearly communicated to Stambaugh that she need not respond to the inquiry."

c. *Jones*

NLRB: "On July 18, employee Rosa Jones was approached at her desk by Supervisor Danfelt, who asked her how she felt about the Union. She told Danfelt that she did not want to talk about it, and he replied that nothing would happen if she did. Jones testified that, when she replied that she thought the Union was 'all right,' Danfelt's complexion changed and he left the area. He returned shortly thereafter and asked her if she thought a union could get her more money. When she answered that she did not know, Danfelt asserted that it was by no means certain that it could. The Administrative Law Judge concluded that Danfelt's assurance that nothing would happen to Jones as a result of her answering his question rendered his conduct lawful. We do not agree. Contrary to the Administrative Law Judge, an inquiry into an employee's views toward a union, even in the context of assurances against reprisals, reasonably tends to interfere with the free exercise of an employee's Section 7 rights. We therefore conclude that Respondent additionally violated Section 8(a)(1) of the Act when Danfelt questioned Jones."

Court of Appeals: ". . . Even assuming that the casual inquiry into Jones' feelings about the Union can be described as 'interrogation,' the circumstances surrounding the questioning simply do not spell coercive activity. The discussion took place at Jones' work station. Again, Danfelt was not a high official in the Company. He conveyed no direct or implied threat or warning to Jones, nor was the question asked in the context of unlawful threats to other employees. Danfelt's assurances that nothing would happen to Jones if she revealed her feelings about the Union removed whatever minimal coercive influence the question might have had. Although Jones testified that she later learned that Danfelt made similar inquiries to other employees, we agree with the ALJ that the necessary element of coercion is lacking.

"In deciding whether questioning in individual cases amounts to the type of coercive interrogation that section 8(a)(1) proscribes, one must remember two general points. Because production supervisors and employees often work closely together, one can expect that during the course of the workday they will discuss a range of subjects of mutual interest, including ongoing unionization efforts. To hold that any instance of casual questioning concerning union sympathies violates the Act ignores the realities of the workplace. Moreover, as the United States Supreme Court recognized in *NLRB* v. *Gissel Packing Co.*, 395 U.S. 575, 71 LRRM 2481 (1969), the First Amendment permits employers to communicate with their employees concerning an ongoing union organizing campaign 'so long as the communications do not contain a threat of reprisal or force or promise of benefit.' *Id.* at 618. This right is recognized in section 8(c) of the Act. If section 8(a)(1) of the Act deprived the employers of any right to ask non-coercive questions of their employees during such a campaign, the Act would directly collide with the Constitution. What the Act proscribes is only those instances of true 'interrogation' which tend to interfere with the employees' right to organize. The Board has gone much further here."

The Board and the Court of Appeals agreed that two instances of questioning violated Section 8(a)(1). This is the court's description of the incident:

> "Employee Reisinger testified before the ALJ that on July 9 shortly after lunch supervisor Michael Lehr called him to Lehr's office. Reisinger met Lehr at the timeclock as he was on his way to Lehr's office. Lehr asked Reisinger several questions concerning Reisinger's activities during the preceding lunch hour, and Reisinger replied truthfully that he had been to the union hall. Lehr responded, 'Yes, I know you were at the union hall.' Lehr demanded to see the union literature Reisinger had obtained, but Reisinger refused to show Lehr the materials. The conversation continued for 15 to 20 minutes and covered a variety of subjects. Reisinger testified that he and Lehr were personal friends and often played basketball together at lunchtime.
>
> "Several aspects of this incident lead us to agree with the Board's finding that supervisor Lehr's questioning of employee Reisinger was unlawful. The inquiries were not part of an ordinary casual conversation; rather, Lehr specifically requested Reisinger to come to his office. Lehr indicated that he had prior knowledge of Reisinger's lunchtime visit to the union hall, implying that Reisinger's activities were under the Company's surveillance. Lehr demanded to see the materials Reisinger had picked up. Together, the circumstances created a risk from which Reisinger could reasonably conclude that if he engaged in further pro-union activities the Company might retaliate. Although Lehr's and Reisinger's friendship and the occurrence of the conversation in an open plant area tend to negate a coercive influence, considering all the evidence, including the peremptory demand for the union materials, the Board had a reasonable basis to find the interrogation coercive."

Are the factors which establish coercive interrogation clear to you? Is the basis for the Court of Appeals' disagreement with the Board clear to you?

3. What is the legal liability of the consultant who advises Enderby? In *St. Francis Hospital,* 263 NLRB No. 109, 111 LRRM 1153, 1157–58 (1982), the Hospital successfully countered the union's organizing drive, with the help of Modern Management, Inc., known as 2M, a management consulting firm. The Board found extensive unfair labor practices and ordered the hospital to bargain with the union. The consulting firm itself was not held legally responsible for the unfair labor practices. Portions of the administrative law judge's decision, affirmed by the Board, follow.

> "The supervisors violated Section 8(a)(1) of the Act by their interrogations and promises. Their feedback established condonation of this conduct by Respondent 2M and by Respondent St. Francis to whom Respondent 2M reported. Respondent St. Francis must bear the

entire responsibility for the 'anti-union' or 'union busting' campaign allegedly controlled and conducted by Respondent 2M. Respondent 2M was engaged by Respondent St. Francis as a consultant for advice and instructions to defeat the union organizing campaign. It chose to accept the advice and act upon it when it instructed its supervisory personnel to heed the advice and carry out the instructions of the representatives of Respondent 2M. By giving such instructions to its supervisory employees, Respondent St. Francis was, in effect, acting on the advice and pursuant to the instructions of its consultant, Respondent 2M.

"I am convinced that from a public policy viewpoint there is no basis for imposing liability upon Respondent 2M, inasmuch as the role of 2M in this case was that of a labor relations advisor to the hospital. There is no evidence that it advised its client to violate the Act. To hold Respondent 2M liable in these circumstances would constitute a serious intrusion into an employer's right to seek legal advice. In that regard, public policy has encouraged not discouraged obtaining professional assistance. If the General Counsel's theory is adopted, the effect would be to discourage a party from seeking such advice, whether it be from a law firm, labor relations consultant or any other professional source. The result would very well be the commission of more, rather than fewer, unfair labor practices by uninformed parties.

"The Board has held that an independent Respondent can be held liable for acts committed with respect to employees other than his own only if that Respondent possessed 'sufficient control over the Section 7 rights alleged to have been restrained or coerced.' *Fabric Services*, 190 NLRB 541, 77 LRRM 1236 (1971). . . .

"The evidence in the instant case demonstrates that Respondent 2M did not directly through its representatives, commit the unfair labor practices nor did it possess the requisite 'control' over the hospital or its employees, to effectuate the alleged unfair labor practices committed by the employees of the hospital. In addition, there is no evidence that Respondent 2M had instructed the supervisors to engage in unlawful interrogation although there is much evidence that it instructed the supervisors to engage in daily conversations with the staff nurses which resulted in unlawful interrogation committed by the hospital employees. Certainly, Respondent 2M knew what was going on as did Respondent St. Francis.

"I find that Respondent St. Francis had control of the anti-union campaign in the hospital and that it was acting on the advice and instructions of a consultant, Respondent 2M. Even if arguendo Respondent 2M's representatives advised the Respondent St. Francis' supervisors to commit unfair labor practices, whether such advice is per se an unfair labor practice and, as such, subjects a labor consultant to the Act's remedial process is a question which has not been resolved by the Board. Moreover, there is evidence that the Respondent 2M personnel did try educating the supervisors on how to obey the law. They were requested to 'report back' the nurses' 'general reactions' to the hospital campaign literature. There is no evidence that the supervisors were instructed to ask the nurses how they intended to vote (most of them wore buttons signifying their sympathies for or against). Likewise, there is no evidence that they were told to mention employee names when reporting the general reactions.

"In *National Lime and Stone Company*, 62 NLRB 282, 16 LRRM 188, the employer, whose employees were attempting organization, retained the services of Labor Relations Institute, a partnership engaged in the distribution of a semi-monthly publication entitled, 'Practical Problems in Labor Relations.' It maintained a field staff which performed various services such as wage and salary stabilization, negotiation of contracts with unions, installation of merit rating systems and personnel 'setups', foreman training, job evaluation and analysis, labor surveys, and the like. National employed the Institute for the purpose of making a survey of working conditions at its plant and to investigate the causes of dissatisfaction on the part of its employees. The Institute was solely a management representative organization. The Board in that case stated, 62 NLRB 298, fn. 26: 'There is no contention, as such, that National is not responsible for the conduct of the Institute or that the Institute is not an employer within the meaning of the Act. However, as indicated above, National employed the services of the Institute shortly after the Union had filed a petition for investigation and certification of representatives; General Manager Love authorized the Institute's representatives, Bladek and Hardy, to go among the employees and speak to them; Love introduced Bladek and Hardy to assembled groups of employees in National's plant, thereby sponsoring talks of the Institute's representatives to the employees on such occasions; and, Hardy signed the stipulation for consent election, mentioned above, as "agent" for National.' The Board concluded that under all the circumstances, the Institute acted in the interest of National and was therefore an employer within the meaning of Section 2(2) of the Act, and that National was also responsible for the acts and statements of the Institute. After finding that both were responsible for the unfair labor practices committed, it ordered both to cease and desist therefrom and to post notices for the employees of National.

"That case is distinguishable from the instant case in that the Institute's representatives dealt with the rank-and-file employees of National and committed the unfair labor practices against those employees directly and not through National's own supervisor employees. In addition, unlike the instant case, the Institute was alleged to be an agent of National and was so found."

3. INDUCEMENTS FOR SUPPORT

Problem

CONSULTANT: Now it's time to emphasize the positive. I read in the local paper that you've just received a defense contract worth millions. In next week's pay envelope, how about increasing everyone's wage rates by five percent?

MAXWELL: But production on that contract won't start for six months! I've never raised wages before production begins, because I don't get paid 'til then.

CONSULTANT: Never? Didn't you raise wages a couple of years ago without a new order? And aren't you worried. . .

MAXWELL: That was because of inflation.

CONSULTANT: about losing workers to your competitors?

MAXWELL: But . . .

CONSULTANT: If I read about the military contract, so have your employees. The union organizers will be screaming about profits and what they'll get in contract negotiations. And two years is a long time between raises. By giving the raise now we take over the issue. But you have to decide whether it's worth paying the money now.

The other thing we have to do is to figure out where to hold your election eve party. I have the invitation here. We'll get it out three days before the election.

"To all employees:
Enderby Company hopes you will join your colleagues for drinks, good food, and music tomorrow night.
As with any Enderby social occasion, attendance is voluntary. (If you are in doubt about coming, talk to someone who attended our annual Christmas party; tomorrow night's bash should be every bit as good.) We hope to see each of you.

E.V. Maxwell"

NLRB v. Exchange Parts Co.

Supreme Court of the United States, 1964
375 U.S. 405, 55 LRRM 2098

MR. JUSTICE HARLAN delivered the opinion of the Court.

This case presents a question concerning the limitations which § 8(a)(1) of the National Labor Relations Act, 49 Stat. 452 (1935), as amended, 29 U.S.C. § 158(a)(l), places on the right of an employer to confer economic benefits on his employees shortly before a representation election. The precise issue is whether that section prohibits the conferral of such benefits, without more, where the employer's purpose is to affect the outcome of the election.

. . .

The respondent, Exchange Parts Company, is engaged in the business of rebuilding automobile parts in Fort Worth, Texas. Prior to November 1959 its employees were not represented by a union. On November 9, 1959, the International Brotherhood of Boilermakers, Iron Shipbuilders, Blacksmiths, Forgers and Helpers, AFL-CIO, advised Exchange Parts that the union was conducting an organizational campaign at the plant and that a majority of the employees had designated the union as their bargaining representative. On November 16 the union petitioned the Labor

Board for a representation election. The Board conducted a hearing on December 29, and on February 19, 1960, issued an order directing that an election be held. The election was held on March 18, 1960.

At two meetings on November 4 and 5, 1959, C.V. McDonald, the Vice-President and General Manager of Exchange Parts, announced to the employees that their "floating holiday" in 1959 would fall on December 26 and that there would be an additional "floating holiday" in 1960. On February 25, six days after the Board issued its election order, Exchange Parts held a dinner for employees at which Vice-President McDonald told the employees that they could decide whether the extra day of vacation in 1960 would be a "floating holiday" or would be taken on their birthdays. The employees voted for the latter. McDonald also referred to the forth-coming representation election as one in which, in the words of the trial examiner, the employees would "determine whether . . . [they] wished to hand over their right to speak and act for themselves." He stated that the union had distorted some of the facts and pointed out the benefits obtained by the employees without a union. He urged all the employees to vote in the election.

On March 4 Exchange Parts sent its employees a letter which spoke of "the *Empty Promises* of the Union" and "the *fact* that *it is the Company that puts things in your envelope* . . . ." After mentioning a number of benefits, the letter said: "The Union can't put any of those things in your envelope—*only the Company can do that.*"[2] Further on, the letter stated: ". . .[I]t didn't take a Union to get any of those things and . . . it won't take a Union to get additional improvements in the future." Accompanying the letter was a detailed statement of the benefits granted by the company since 1949 and an estimate of the monetary value of such benefits to the employees. Included in the statement of benefits for 1960 were the birthday holiday, a new system for computing overtime during holiday weeks which had the effect of increasing wages for those weeks, and a new vacation schedule which enabled employees to extend their vacations by sandwiching them between two weekends. Although Exchange Parts asserts that the policy behind the latter two benefits was established earlier, it is clear that the letter of March 4 was the first general announce-ment of the changes to the employees. In the ensuing election the union lost.

The Board, affirming the findings of the trial examiner, found that the announcement of the birthday holiday and the grant and announcement of overtime and vacation benefits were arranged by Exchange Parts with the intention of inducing the employees to vote against the union. It found that this conduct violated § 8(a)(1) of the National Labor Relations Act and issued an appropriate order. On the Board's petition for enforce-ment of the order, the Court of Appeals rejected the finding that the announcement of the birthday holiday was timed to influence the out-come of the election. It accepted the Board's findings with respect to the overtime and vacation benefits, and the propriety of those findings is not in controversy here. However, noting that "the benefits were put into

---

[2]The italics appear in the original letter.

effect unconditionally on a permanent basis, and no one has suggested that there was any implication the benefits would be withdrawn if the workers voted for the union," 304 F.2d 368, 375, the court denied enforcement of the Board's order. It believed that it was not an unfair labor practice under § 8(a)(1) for an employer to grant benefits to its employees in these circumstances.

Section 8(a)(1) makes it an unfair labor practice for an employer "to interfere with, restrain, or coerce employees in the exercise of the rights guaranteed in section 7." Section 7 provides:

> "Employees shall have the right to self-organization, to form, join, or assist labor organizations, to bargain collectively through representatives of their own choosing, and to engage in other concerted activities for the purpose of collective bargaining or other mutual aid or protection, and shall also have the right to refrain from any or all of such activities except to the extent that such right may be affected by an agreement requiring membership in a labor organization as a condition of employment as authorized in section 8(a)(3)." 49 Stat. 452 (1935), as amended, 29 U.S.C. § 157.

We think the Court of Appeals was mistaken in concluding that the conferral of employee benefits while a representation election is pending, for the purpose of inducing employees to vote against the union, does not "interfere with" the protected right to organize.

The broad purpose of § 8(a)(1) is to establish "the right of employees to organize for mutual aid without employer interference." *Republic Aviation Corp.* v. *Labor Board,* 324 U.S. 793, 798. We have no doubt that it prohibits not only intrusive threats and promises but also conduct immediately favorable to employees which is undertaken with the express purpose of impinging upon their freedom of choice for or against unionization and is reasonably calculated to have that effect. In *Medo Photo Supply Co.* v. *Labor Board,* 321 U.S. 678, 686, this Court said: "The action of employees with respect to the choice of their bargaining agents may be induced by favors bestowed by the employer as well as by his threats or domination." Although in that case there was already a designated bargaining agent and the offer of "favors" was in response to a suggestion of the employees that they would leave the union if favors were bestowed, the principles which dictated the result there are fully applicable here. The danger inherent in well-timed increases in benefits is the suggestion of a fist inside the velvet glove. Employees are not likely to miss the inference that the source of benefits now conferred is also the source from which future benefits must flow and which may dry up if it is not obliged.[3] The danger may be diminished if, as in this case, the benefits are conferred perma-

---

[3] The inference was made almost explicit in Exchange Parts' letter to its employees of March 4, already quoted, which said: "The Union can't put any of those. . . [benefits] in your envelope—*only the Company can do that.*" (Original italics.) We place no reliance, however, on these or other words of the respondent dissociated from its conduct. Section 8(c) of the Act, 61 Stat. 142 (1947), 29 U.S.C. § 158(c), provides that the expression or dissemination of "any views, argument, or opinion" "shall not constitute or be evidence of an unfair labor practice under any of the provisions of this Act, if such expression contains no threat of reprisal or force or promise of benefit."

nently and unconditionally. But the absence of conditions or threats pertaining to the particular benefits conferred would be of controlling significance only if it could be presumed that no question of additional benefits or renegotiation of existing benefits would arise in the future; and, of course, no such presumption is tenable.

Other Courts of Appeals have found a violation of § 8(a)(1) in the kind of conduct involved here. See, *e.g., Labor Board* v. *Pyne Molding Corp., supra; Indiana Metal Products Corp.* v. *Labor Board, supra.* It is true, as the court below pointed out, that in most cases of this kind the increase in benefits could be regarded as "one part of an overall program of interference and restraint by the employer," 304 F.2d, at 372, and that in this case the questioned conduct stood in isolation. Other unlawful conduct may often be an indication of the motive behind a grant of benefits while an election is pending, and to that extent it is relevant to the legality of the grant; but when as here the motive is otherwise established, an employer is not free to violate § 8(a)(1) by conferring benefits simply because it refrains from other, more obvious violations. We cannot agree with the Court of Appeals that enforcement of the Board's order will have the "ironic" result of "discouraging benefits for labor." 304 F.2d, at 376. The beneficence of an employer is likely to be ephemeral if prompted by a threat of unionization which is subsequently removed. Insulating the right of collective organization from calculated good will of this sort deprives employees of little that has lasting value.

Notes

1. The Board's order in *Exchange Parts* reads, in pertinent part:

"Cease and desist from interfering with, restraining, or coercing its employees in the exercise of rights guaranteed in § 7 of the Act by granting them economic benefits or by changing the terms and conditions of their employment; provided, however, that nothing in this recommended order shall be construed as requiring Respondent to vary or abandon any economic benefit or any term or condition of employment which it has heretofore established." 131 NLRB 807 (1961).

2. In *NLRB* v. *Savair Mfg. Co.,* 414 U.S. 270, 84 LRRM 2929 (1973), a union that was seeking representation rights offered to waive the initiation fee for employees who signed authorization cards prior to the representation election. (Under the union bylaws the fee could be no higher than $10.00, but the employees who testified at the Board hearing either did not know of this limitation or had no knowledge regarding the amount of the fee.) The union won the election by a vote of 22 to 20. The company refused to bargain and the union filed unfair labor practice charges. Without deciding whether Section 8(b)(1)(A) applies to such union promises, the Supreme Court held that the offer to waive the initiation fee tended to interfere with the right of employee free choice

inherent in Section 9(c)(1)(A). Justice Douglas' opinion for the majority included the following observations:

"When the dissent says that '[t]he special inducement is to sign the card, not to vote for the union' and that treating the two choices as one is untenable, it overlooks cases like *NLRB* v. *Gissel Packing Co.*, 395 U.S. 575. There we held that the gathering of authorization cards from a majority of the employees in the bargaining unit may entitle the union to represent the employees for collective-bargaining purposes, even though there has been and will be no election, *id.*, at 582–583, and that rejection of that authorization by the employer is an unfair labor practice. Where the solicitation of cards is represented as being solely for the purpose of obtaining an election, a contrary result is indicated. *Id.*, at 584, 606. Thus the solicitation of authorization cards may serve one of two ends. Of course, when an election is contemplated, an employee does not become a member of the union merely by signing a card. But prior to the election if the union receives overwhelming support, the pro-union group may decide to treat the union authorization cards as authorizing it to conduct collective bargaining without an election. The latent potential of that alternative use of authorization cards cautions us to treat the solicitation of authorization cards in exchange for consideration of fringe benefits granted by the union as a separate step protected by the same kind of moral standard that governs elections themselves.

"The Board in its supervision of union elections may not sanction procedures that cast their weight for the choice of a union and against a nonunion shop or for a nonunion shop and against a union.

"In the *Exchange Parts* case we said that, although the benefits granted by the employer were permanent and unconditional, employees were 'not likely to miss the inference that the source of benefits now conferred is also the source from which future benefits must flow and which may dry up if it is not obliged.' 375 U.S., at 409. If we respect, as we must, the statutory right of employees to resist efforts to unionize a plant, we cannot assume that unions exercising powers are wholly benign towards their antagonists whether they be nonunion protagonists or the employer. The failure to sign a recognition slip may well seem ominous to nonunionists who fear that if they do not sign they will face a wrathful union regime, should the union win. That influence may well have had a decisive impact in this case where a change of one vote would have changed the result."

In a dissent joined by Justices Brennan and Blackman, Justice White articulated the differences between *Exchange Parts* and *Savair:*

"First, the employer actually gave his employees substantial increased benefits, whereas here the benefit is only contingent and small; the union glove is not very velvet. Secondly, in the union context, the fist is missing. When the employer increased benefits, the threat was made 'that the source of benefits now conferred is also the source from which future benefits must flow and which may dry up if it is not obliged.' *Ibid.* The Union, on the other hand, since it was not the representative of the employees, and would not be if it were unsuccessful in the election, could not make the same threat by offering a benefit which it would take away if it *lost* the election. A union can only make its own victory more desirable in the minds of the employees.[4"]

International Ladies Garment Workers Union v. NLRB (Bernhard-Altmann Texas Corp.)

Supreme Court of the United States, 1961
366 U.S. 731, 48 LRRM 2251

Mr. Justice Clark delivered the opinion of the Court.

We are asked to decide in this case whether it was an unfair labor practice for both an employer and a union to enter into an agreement under which the employer recognized the union as exclusive bargaining representative of certain of his employees, although in fact only a minority of those employees had authorized the union to represent their interests. The Board found that by extending such recognition, even though done in the good-faith belief that the union had the consent of a majority of employees in the appropriate bargaining unit, the employer interfered with the organizational rights of his employees in violation of § 8(a)(1) of the National Labor Relations Act and that such recognition also constituted unlawful support to a labor organization in violation of § 8(a)(2). In addition, the Board found that the union violated § 8(b)(1)(A) by its acceptance of exclusive bargaining authority at a time when in fact it did not have the support of a majority of the employees, and this in spite of its bona fide belief that it did. Accordingly, the Board ordered the unfair labor practices discontinued and directed the holding of a representation election. The Court of Appeals, by a divided vote, granted enforcement, 280 F.2d 616. We granted certiorari. 364 U.S. 811. We agree with the Board and the Court of Appeals that such extension and acceptance of recognition constitute unfair labor practices, and that the remedy provided was appropriate.

In October 1956 the petitioner union initiated an organizational campaign at Bernhard-Altmann Texas Corporation's knitwear manufacturing plant at San Antonio, Texas. No other labor organization was similarly engaged at that time. During the course of that campaign, on July 29, 1957, certain of the company's Topping Department employees went on

---

"[4]The Court cannot ignore the fact, as well, that § 1 of the National Labor Relations Act declared the congressional policy of 'encouraging the practice and procedure of collective bargaining' 29 U.S.C. § 151. The existence of unions is an inescapable corollary of this preference. To the extent that this Court prohibits the union from promising a fairer deal for unionized employees by describing the benefits to be obtained by unionization, this policy is seriously eroded. This preference is only one of opportunity and the free choice of the employee must be protected, but restrictions on the communications of the union as to potential benefits may unduly prevent the intelligent exercise of such choice. The employer may garner loyalty through his actions and record of past performance for his own employees; the union can only sell employees the future."

strike in protest against a wage reduction. That dispute was in no way related to the union campaign, however, and the organizational efforts were continued during the strike. Some of the striking employees had signed authorization cards solicited by the union during its drive, and, while the strike was in progress, the union entered upon a course of negotiations with the employer. As a result of those negotiations, held in New York City where the home offices of both were located, on August 30, 1957, the employer and union signed a "memorandum of understanding." In that memorandum the company recognized the union as exclusive bargaining representative of "all production and shipping employees." The union representative asserted that the union's comparison of the employee authorization cards in its possession with the number of eligible employee representatives of the company furnished it indicated that the union had in fact secured such cards from a majority of employees in the unit. Neither employer nor union made any effort at that time to check the cards in the union's possession against the employee roll, or otherwise, to ascertain with any degree of certainty that the union's assertion, later found by the Board to be erroneous,[4] was founded on fact rather than upon good-faith assumption. The agreement, containing no union security provisions, called for the ending of the strike and for certain improved wages and conditions of employment. It also provided that a "formal agreement containing these terms" would "be promptly drafted . . . and signed by both parties within the next two weeks."

Thereafter, on October 10, 1957, a formal collective bargaining agreement, embodying the terms of the August 30 memorandum, was signed by the parties. The bargaining unit description set out in the formal contract, although more specific, conformed to that contained in the prior memorandum. It is not disputed that as of execution of the formal contract the union in fact represented a clear majority of employees in the appropriate unit. In upholding the complaints filed against the employer and union by the General Counsel, the Board decided that the employer's good-faith belief that the union in fact represented a majority of employees in the unit on the critical date of the memorandum of understanding was not a defense, "particularly where, as here, the Company made no effort to check the authorization cards against its payroll records." 122 NLRB 1289, 1292. Noting that the union was "actively seeking recognition at the time such recognition was granted," and that "the Union was [not] the passive recipient of an unsolicited gift bestowed by the Company," the Board found that the union's execution of the August 30 agreement was a "direct deprivation" of the nonconsenting majority employees' organizational and bargaining rights. At pp. 1292, 1293, note 9. Accordingly, the Board ordered the employer to withhold all recognition from the union and to cease giving effect to agreements entered into

---

[4]The Board found that as of August 30 the union in fact had authority to represent either 70 employees out of a relevant total of 280, or 158 out of 368, depending upon the criteria used in determining employee eligibility. "Accordingly, the Union could not, under any circumstances, have represented a majority of the employees involved on August 30, 1957." 122 NLRB 1289, 1291–1292.

with the union;[7] the union was ordered to cease acting as bargaining representative of any of the employees until such time as a Board-conducted election demonstrated its majority status, and to refrain from seeking to enforce the agreements previously entered.

. . .

At the outset, we reject as without relevance to our decision the fact that, as of the execution date of the formal agreement on October 10, petitioner represented a majority of the employees. As the Court of Appeals indicated, the recognition of the minority union on August 30, 1957, was "a *fait accompli* depriving the majority of the employees of their guaranteed right to choose their own representative." 280 F.2d, at 621. It is, therefore, of no consequence that petitioner may have acquired by October 10 the necessary majority if, during the interim, it was acting unlawfully. Indeed, such acquisition of majority status itself might indicate that the recognition secured by the August 30 agreement afforded petitioner a deceptive cloak of authority with which to persuasively elicit additional employee support.

Nor does this case directly involve a strike. The strike which occurred was in protest against a wage reduction and had nothing to do with petitioner's quest for recognition. Likewise, no question of picketing is presented. Lastly, the violation which the Board found was the grant by the employer of exclusive representation status to a minority union, as distinguished from an employer's bargaining with a minority union for its members only. Therefore, the exclusive representation provision is the vice in the agreement, and discussion of "collective bargaining," as distinguished from "exclusive recognition," is pointless. Moreover, the insistence that we hold the agreement valid and enforceable as to those employees who consented to it must be rejected. On the facts shown, the agreement must fail in its entirety. It was obtained under the erroneous claim of majority representation. Perhaps the employer would not have entered into it if he had known the facts. Quite apart from other conceivable situations, the unlawful genesis of this agreement precludes its partial validity.

In their selection of a bargaining representative, § 9(a) of the Wagner Act guarantees employees freedom of choice and majority rule. *J.I. Case Co.* v. *Labor Board,* 321 U.S. 332, 339. In short, as we said in *Brooks* v. *Labor Board,* 348 U.S. 96, 103, the Act placed "a nonconsenting minority under the bargaining responsibility of an agency selected by a majority of the workers." Here, however, the reverse has been shown to be the case. Bernhard-Altmann granted exclusive bargaining status to an agency selected by a minority of its employees, thereby impressing that agent upon the nonconsenting majority. There could be no clearer abridgement of § 7 of the Act, assuring employees the right "to bargain collectively through representatives of their own choosing" or "to refrain from" such activity. It follows, without need of further demonstration, that the

---

[7]However, the terms and conditions of employment fixed by the agreement were not required to be varied or abandoned. We take it that the Board's order restraining the union and employer from dealing will, in any event, terminate after the election is held.

employer activity found present here violated § 8(a)(1) of the Act which prohibits employer interference with, and restraint of, employee exercise of § 7 rights. Section 8(a)(2) of the Act makes it an unfair labor practice for an employer to "contribute. . . support" to a labor organization. The law has long been settled that a grant of exclusive recognition to a minority union constitutes unlawful support in violation of that section, because the union so favored is given "a marked advantage over any other in securing the adherence of employees," *Labor Board* v. *Pennsylvania Greyhound Lines*, 303 U.S. 261, 267. In the Taft-Hartley Law, Congress added § 8(b)(1)(A) to the Wagner Act, prohibiting, as the Court of Appeals held, "unions from invading the rights of employees under § 7 in a fashion comparable to the activities of employers prohibited under § 8(a)(l)." 280 F.2d, at 620. It was the intent of Congress to impose upon unions the same restrictions which the Wagner Act imposed upon employers with respect to violations of employee rights.

The petitioner, while taking no issue with the fact of its minority status on the critical date, maintains that both Bernhard-Altmann's and its own good-faith beliefs in petitioner's majority status are a complete defense. To countenance such an excuse would place in permissibly careless employer and union hands the power to completely frustrate employee realization of the premise of the Act—that its prohibitions will go far to assure freedom of choice and majority rule in employee selection of representatives. We find nothing in the statutory language prescribing *scienter* as an element of the unfair labor practices here involved. The act made unlawful by § 8(a)(2) is employer support of a minority union. Here that support is an accomplished fact. More need not be shown, for, even if mistakenly, the employees' rights have been invaded. It follows that prohibited conduct cannot be excused by a showing of good faith.

This conclusion, while giving the employee only the protection assured him by the Act, places no particular hardship on the employer or the union. It merely requires that recognition be withheld until the Board-conducted election results in majority selection of a representative. The Board's order here, as we might infer from the employer's failure to resist its enforcement, would apparently result in similarly slight hardship upon it. We do not share petitioner's apprehension that holding such conduct unlawful will somehow induce a breakdown, or seriously impede the progress of collective bargaining. If an employer takes reasonable steps to verify union claims, themselves advanced only after careful estimate—precisely what Bernhard-Altmann and petitioner failed to do here—he can readily ascertain their validity and obviate a Board election. We fail to see any onerous burden involved in requiring responsible negotiators to be careful, by cross-checking, for example, well-analyzed employer records with union listings or authorization cards. Individual and collective employee rights may not be trampled upon merely because it is inconvenient to avoid doing so. Moreover, no penalty is attached to the violation. Assuming that an employer in good faith accepts or rejects a union claim of majority status, the validity of his decision may be tested in an unfair labor practice proceeding. If he is found to have erred in extending or withholding recognition, he is subject only to a remedial order requiring him to conform his conduct to the norms set out in the Act, as was the case here. No further penalty results. We believe the Board's remedial order is the proper one in such cases. *Labor Board* v. *District 50, UMW,* 355 U.S. 453.

Affirmed.

MR. JUSTICE DOUGLAS, with whom MR. JUSTICE BLACK concurs, dissenting in part.

I agree that, under the statutory scheme, a minority union does not have the standing to bargain for all employees. That principle of representative government extends only to the majority. But where there is no majority union, I see no reason why the minority union should be disabled from bargaining for the minority of the members who have joined it. Yet the order of the Board, now approved, enjoins petitioner union from acting as the exclusive bargaining representative "of any of the employees," and it enjoins the employer from recognizing the union as the representative of "any of its employees."

. . .

I think the Court is correct insofar as it sets aside the exclusive recognition clause in the contract. I think it is incorrect in setting aside the entire contract. *First,* that agreement secured valuable benefits for the union's members regarding wages and hours, work standards and distribution, discharge and discipline, holidays, vacations, health and welfare fund, and other matters. Since there was no duly selected representative for all the employees authorized in accordance with the Act, it certainly was the right of the employee union members to designate the union or any other appropriate person to make this contract they desired. To hold the contract void as to the union's voluntary members seems to me to go beyond the competency of the Board under the Act and to be unsupported by any principle of contract law. Certainly there is no principle of justice or fairness with which I am familiar that requires these employees to be stripped of the benefits they acquired by the good-faith bargaining of their designated agent. Such a deprivation gives no protection to the majority who were not members of the union and arbitrarily takes from the union members their contract rights.

Second, the result of today's decision is to enjoin the employer from dealing with the union as the representative of its own members in any manner, whether in relation to grievances or otherwise, until it is certified as a majority union. A case for complete disestablishment of the union cannot be sustained under our decisions. While the power of the Board is broad, it is "not limitless." *Labor Board* v. *Mine Workers,* 355 U.S. 453, 458. Thus a distinction has been taken between remedies in situations where a union has been dominated by the employer and where unions have been assisted but not dominated. *Id.,* 458–459.

The present case is unique. The findings are that both the employer and the union were in "good faith" in believing that the union represented a majority of the workers. Good-faith violations of the Act are nonetheless violations; and the present violation warrants disestablishment of the union as a majority representative. But this good-faith mistake hardly warrants full and complete disestablishment, heretofore reserved for flagrant violations of the Act. Its application here smacks more of a penalty than of a remedial measure.

I think this union is entitled to speak for its members until another union is certified as occupying the bargaining field. That is its common-law right in no way diluted or impaired by the Act.

Notes

1. Is the situation in Bernhard-Altmann the type of problem that Congress intended Section 8(a)(2) to cover? That provision reflects a rich history, which is nicely summarized in a statement by Senator Wagner when he introduced the bill that would become the NLRA:

"Nothing in the bill prevents employers from maintaining free and direct relations with the workers or from participating in group insurance, mutual welfare, pension systems, and other such activities. The only prohibition is against the sham or dummy union which is dominated by the employer, which is supported by the employer, which cannot change its rules or regulations without his consent, and which cannot live except by the grace of the employer's whims. To say that that kind of union must be preserved in order to give employees freedom of selection is a contradiction in terms. . . ."

Of equal significance, company unions were inconsistent with one goal of the labor movement, nationwide organization of industrial workers. Even if the representatives of a company union were not intimidated by their employers and were able to finance strikes, these unions were unlikely vehicles for bringing unionization into previously unorganized shops in the same industry. The argument most frequently made by proponents of company unions, that they promoted harmonious workplace relations, lost some of its force in the face of studies demonstrating that company unions were formed only after Congress mandated collective bargaining and employers were presented with claims for representation by independent, outside unions.

2. When two labor organizations seek to represent the same employees, is an election the only legitimate means for insuring that the question concerning representation is decided on the basis of majority will? From 1945 to 1982 the Board required strict neutrality from employers faced with claims from competing unions, see *Midwest Piping and Supply Co., Inc.*, 63 NLRB 1060, 17 LRRM 40 (1945). The courts of appeals frequently refused to enforce Board orders, on the ground that "the question concerning representation was resolved whenever an employer recognized a bona fide majority claimant and had not actually aided, in the traditional Section 8(a)(2) sense of that word, the recognized labor organization."

In *Bruckner Nursing Home*, 262 NLRB No. 115, 110 LRRM 1374 (1982), the employer recognized Local 144 on the basis of independently validated authorization cards and signed a collective bargaining agreement two months later. At the time of the card count, Local 144 had cards from

80 to 90 percent of the 125 employees, and the rival union possessed two authorization cards; no election petition had been filed. The Board held:

". . . [W]e will no longer find 8(a)(2) violations in rival union, initial organizing situations when an employer recognizes a labor organization which represents an uncoerced, unassisted majority, before a valid petition for an election has been filed with the Board.[13] However, once notified of a valid petition, an employer must refrain from recognizing any of the rival unions. Of course, we will continue to process timely filed petitions and to conduct elections in the most expeditious manner possible, following our normal procedures with respect to intervention and placement of parties on the ballot.

"Making the filing of a valid petition the operative event for the imposition of strict employer neutrality in rival union, initial organizing situations will establish a clearly defined rule of conduct and encourage both employee free choice and industrial stability. Where one of several rival labor organizations cannot command the support of even 30 percent of the unit, it will no longer be permitted to forestall an employer's recognition of another labor organization which represents an uncoerced majority of employees and thereby frustrate the establishment of a collective-bargaining relationship.[14] Likewise, an employer will no longer have to guess whether a real question concerning representation has been raised but will be able to recognize a labor organization unless it has received notice of a properly filed petition.

"On the other hand, where a labor organization has filed a petition, both the Act and our administrative experience dictate the need for resolution of the representation issue through a Board election rather than through employer recognition. When a union has demonstrated substantial support by filing a valid petition, an active contest exists for

---

"[13]Although an employer will no longer automatically violate Section 8(a)(2) by recognizing one of several rival unions before an election petition has been filed, we emphasize that an employer will still be found liable under Section 8(a)(2) for recognizing a labor organization which does not actually have majority employee support. *International Ladies' Garment Workers' Union, AFL–CIO* [Bernhard-Altmann Texas Corporation] v. *NLRB*, 366 U.S. 731, 68 LRRM 2251 (1961). This longstanding principle applies in either a single or rival union organizational context and is unaffected by the revised *Midwest Piping* doctrine announced in this case. For instance, if an occasion arises where an employer is faced with recognition demands by two unions, both of which claim to possess valid authorization card majority support, the employer must beware the risk of violating Section 8(a)(2) by recognizing either union even though no petition has been filed. In such a situation, there is a possibility that the claimed majority support of the recognized union could in fact be nonexistent. Consequently, the safe course would be simply to refuse recognition, as clearly authorized under *Linden Lumber Division, Summer & Co.* v. *NLRB*, 419 U.S. 301, 87 LRRM 3236 (1974). Either of the unions or the employer could then file a representation petition."

"[14]The filing of a valid petition by at least one of the competing unions indicates that it has substantial support in the petitioned-for unit. Based on broad experience in conducting elections, we have defined "substantial" in a representational context to mean that a union has at least 30-percent support in the unit sought. The 30-percent figure was arrived at pragmatically by the Board as a measure of whether or not there is sufficient union support to justify the effort and expense of a Board-conducted election. Experience showed that, when no labor organization had at least 30-percent support, the chances of achieving majority support for union representation were too remote to justify an election. We likewise regard the failure of a rival union to muster at least a 30-percent showing of interest to be a reliable indication that an election held solely at that union's request would be unnecessary."

the employees' allegiance. This contest takes on special significance where rival unions are involved since there an employer's grant of recognition may unduly influence or effectively end a contest between labor organizations. As long ago as 1938, the Supreme Court noted that, in enacting Section 8(a)(2) and (1) of the Act, Congress had been influenced by 'data showing that once an employer has conferred recognition on a particular organization it has a marked advantage over any other in securing the adherence of employees, and hence in preventing the recognition of any other.' Without questioning the reliability of authorization cards or unduly exalting election procedure, we believe the proper balance will be struck by prohibiting an employer from recognizing any of the competing unions for the limited period during which a representation petition is in process even though one or more of the unions may present a valid card majority.

"In addition to avoiding potential undue influence by an employer, our new approach provides a satisfactory answer to problems created by execution of dual authorization cards. It is our experience that employees confronted by solicitations from rival unions will frequently sign authorization cards for more than one union. Dual cards reflect the competing organizational campaigns. They may indicate shifting employee sentiments or employee desire to be represented by either of two rival unions. In this situation, authorization cards are less reliable as indications of employee preference. When a petition supported by a 30-percent showing of interest has been filed by one union, the reliability of a rival's expression of a card majority is sufficiently doubtful to require resolution of the competing claims through the Board's election process."

In a companion case, *RCA Del Caribe, Inc.*, 262 NLRB No. 116, 110 LRRM 1369, 1371 (1982), the Board reversed another long-standing policy and held that

"an employer will not violate Section 8(a)(2) by postpetition negotiation or execution of a contract with an incumbent, but an employer will violate Section 8(a)(5) by withdrawing from bargaining based solely on the fact that a petition has been filed by an outside union.

"This new approach affords maximum protection to the complementary statutory policies of furthering stability in industrial relations and of insuring employee free choice. It should be clear that our new rule does not have the effect of insulating incumbent unions from a legitimate outside challenge. As before, a timely filed petition will put an incumbent to the test of demonstrating that it still is the majority choice for exclusive bargaining representative. Unlike before, however, even though a valid petition has been filed, an incumbent will retain its earned right to demonstrate its effectiveness as a representative at the bargaining table. An outside union and its employee supporters will now be required to take their incumbent opponent as they find it—as the previously elected majority representative. Consequently, in the ensuing election, employees will no longer be presented with a distorted choice between an incumbent artificially deprived of the attributes of its office and a rival union artificially placed on an equal footing with the incumbent."

3. In order to establish a violation of Section 8(a)(2), the Board must find that the employer has unlawfully dealt with a labor organization within the meaning of Section 2(5). In *NLRB* v. *Cabot Carbon Co.*, 360 U.S. 203, 44 LRRM 2204 (1959), "Employee Committees" were established and supported by the company to discuss problems and raise grievances with management. An AFL-CIO union filed a Section 8(a)(2) charge alleging unlawful domination and support by the employer. While the court of appeals agreed with the Board that these committees had been dominated and supported by the employer, it held that they were not labor organizations as defined in Section 2(5). The Supreme Court reversed, holding that the phrase "dealing with" in Section 2(5) encompasses a range of conduct far broader than "bargaining with," and that while these committees did not actually negotiate with the employer, the company's recognition of their less formal dealings constituted a violation of Section 8(a)(2). The Court noted that Congress specifically rejected a House proposal for an amendment in 1947 which would have sanctioned employer formation of and dealings with employee committees. The Court's opinion concluded:

> "Respondents argue that to hold these employee committees to be labor organizations would prevent employers and employees from discussing matters of mutual interest concerning the employment relationship, and would thus abridge freedom of speech in violation of the First Amendment of the Constitution. But the Board's order does not impose any such bar; it merely precludes the employers from dominating, interfering with or supporting such employee committees which Congress has defined to be labor organizations."

The facts show that the employer drew up and published a set of bylaws for these committees; helped the committees to conduct their elections; and paid "all of the necessary expenses of the committees." Apart from the assistance, it met with the committees and occasionally acted favorably on their requests.

After *Cabot Carbon* the Board and the courts gave a liberal interpretation to the "dealing with" a labor organization language, noting that the Supreme Court had stated that "dealing with" employers meant more than collective bargaining. However, in *Sparks Nugget*, 230 NLRB 275, 95 LRRM 1298 (1977), Members Penello and Murphy, with Member Fanning in dissent, signaled a departure from the approach seemingly mandated by *Cabot Carbon*. Although finding that the employer instigated, assisted, and dominated an employee council, the majority found that the council was not a labor organization which dealt with management. The council was created by management to handle employee grievances; worker members of the council were elected by employees in each department; and council members sat with management (in a 1-to-2 ratio) in coming to a binding decision about a grievance.

4. Is a program giving employees some responsibility for traditional management functions in the ambit of Sections 8(a)(2) and (1)? Does your answer depend on the nature and degree of employee control? on the employer's motivation? on the timing of the decision?

MAXWELL: What happens after we win the election? Are we free to change things?

CONSULTANT: Depends whether the union files objections. We'll talk about timing later on. But it wouldn't hurt to start thinking about how you will structure work relations for the future. The union may be back and it's a good idea to develop a system that minimizes tensions. We suggest a policy of granting uniform benefits regardless of whether a plant or department is unionized. This should be combined with frequent, scheduled reviews of wages, benefits, working conditions, and adjustments where warranted.

Second, you should think about a job enrichment program. We've had a good deal of success with production teams. Each team has responsibility for one aspect of plant operations and has responsibility for making recommendations or decisions about some combination of work issues, for example: job assignments, interviewing job applicants and hiring, establishing and changing work rules, evaluating individual job performance and progression within the compensation system, resolving manufacturing problems that occur within or between the team's areas of responsibility, and selecting team operators to serve on plantwide committees or task forces. Team leaders can be elected or chosen by management.

MAXWELL: I've heard about those. Won't that be worse than a union, won't I have every employee telling me how to run things?

CONSULTANT: Not if we tie redesign to continued supervisor's training and personnel policies which screen out applicants who look like troublemakers. Also there's some evidence, although it's not convincing, that productivity increases—at least in the short run.

Would you advise Maxwell to adopt the team approach? At what point will the employees cease to be covered by Section 2(3) of the Act?*

4. DISCRIMINATION AGAINST UNION ACTIVITIES

"[M]anagement is for management. Neither Board nor Court can second-guess it or give it gentle guidance by over-the-shoulder supervision. Management can discharge for good cause, or bad cause, or no cause at all. It has, as the master of its own business affairs, complete freedom with but one specific, definite qualification: it may not discharge when the real motivating purpose is to do that which Section 8(a)(3) forbids." *NLRB* v. *McGahey*, 233 F.2d 406, 413, 38 LRRM 2142 (5th Cir. 1956).

*See Note, *Does Implementation of Employee Production Teams Violate Section 8(a)(2)?*, 49 IND. L.J. 516, 518–19 (1974).

Problem

CONSULTANT: The best way to defeat this union thing is to get rid of the most effective in-plant union supporters. Keep your eyes and ears open; go by the book. If someone's violating the rules, document it. But don't fire anyone without first talking to me.

SUPERVISOR SMALL: I have two candidates. Sam's always been a bit of a goldbrick; lots of absences, loafing on the job, practical jokes, that kind of thing. He's a rabid supporter, but I don't know how seriously the employees take him.

CONSULTANT: How long's always?

SUPERVISOR SMALL: Last ten years.

CONSULTANT: Any warnings before now?

SUPERVISOR SMALL: No.

CONSULTANT: And your other candidate?

SUPERVISOR SMALL: She's a good worker; but lately her kids have been pretty sick and she's been making unauthorized phone calls from my office, taking off a little early, trading lunch hours with co-workers without permission—minor things and they don't interfere with production the way Sam's antics sometimes do.

CONSULTANT: Influential with her co-workers?

SUPERVISOR SMALL: She sure is. This union thing would have never gotten anywhere in my department without her and I bet if she were gone, all the support would fold.

CONSULTANT: Warn her: once more and she's out.

MAXWELL: Is that legal? Production's not being interfered with . . .

CONSULTANT: As I told you before, the law in this area is unclear. But you shouldn't have to put up with a bad worker just because she's a union supporter. As long as there are legitimate grounds for the discharge you should be okay.

MAXWELL: What if the Board says the firing's no good?

CONSULTANT: The most you're facing is a reinstatement order and back pay. Not much of a price to pay if Small's right and the campaign fizzles.

Fairview Hospital

National Labor Relations Board, 1969

174 NLRB 924, 70 LRRM 1491

HERBERT SILBERMAN, Trial Examiner: These consolidated proceedings were heard at Chicago, Illinois, on July 31 and August 1 and 2, 1968. All parties were represented at the hearing by counsel. Following the close of the hearing briefs were submitted on behalf of the General Counsel and the Employer which have been carefully considered.

THE PLEADINGS

The complaint in Case 13–CA–8303, dated June 11, 1968, and amended on August 1, 1968, alleging that Fairview Hospital, herein referred to as the Employer or the Hospital, has engaged in and is engaging in unfair labor practices within the meaning of Sections 8(a)(1) and (3) and 2(6) and (7) of the National Labor Relations Act, as amended, is based upon a charge filed on February 29, 1968, by Hospital Employees Labor Program, Local 743, International Brotherhood of Teamsters, Chauffeurs, Warehousemen and Helpers of America, and Local 73, Building Service Employees International Union, AFL–CIO, jointly, herein called the Union. In substance, the complaint, as amended, alleges that the Employer discharged Melvin Gates, Louis Rodriquez, Lawrence Brown, and Clifford Williams on February 21, 25, and 26 and June 28, 1968, respectively, and constructively discharged Frank Rogers on February 21, 1968, because they had engaged in union or other concerted activities and, that by reason of said discharges and other conduct set forth in the complaint, the Employer has interfered with, restrained, and coerced employees in the exercise of the rights guaranteed to them by Section 7 of the Act. In its answer Respondent generally denies the allegations of the complaint. . . .

The tally of ballots shows that of approximately 42 eligible voters, 16 votes were cast for the Union, 17 votes were cast against the Union, and 5 ballots were challenged. [The ballots were impounded, pursuant to Board procedure.] The challenged ballots are sufficient in number to affect the results of the election.

On February 29, 1968, the Union filed timely objections to conduct affecting the results of the election.

The Regional Director caused an investigation of the challenges and the objections to be made and on June 19, 1968, issued his report thereon. The report shows that 4 of the 5 challenged ballots were cast by persons who are alleged in the complaint in Case 13–CA–8303 to have been unlawfully discharged and that the objections are substantially similar to some of the allegations set forth in the same complaint. . . . [The fifth ballot was impounded because of a question about the eligibility of a licensed practical nurse for inclusion in the bargaining unit.]

Upon the entire record in the cases, and from my observation of the witnesses and their demeanor, I make the following:

FINDINGS OF FACT

I. THE BUSINESS OF THE EMPLOYER

The Employer, an Illinois corporation, maintains a licensed proprietary psychiatric hospital in Chicago, Illinois. During the calendar year 1967, which is representative of Respondent's business activities, in the course and conduct of its hospital operations, the Employer received gross revenues in excess of $1 million. During this same period, the Employer received directly at its location in Chicago, Illinois, drugs and supplies from places in States of the United States other than the State of Illinois valued in excess of $3,000. The Employer admits, and I find, that it is engaged in commerce within the meaning of Section 2(6) and (7) of the Act.

II. THE LABOR ORGANIZATION INVOLVED

The Union is a labor organization within the meaning of Section 2(5) of the Act.

III. THE UNFAIR LABOR PRACTICES

A. INTERFERENCE, RESTRAINT, AND COERCION

In late fall of 1967 the Employer learned of the Union's drive to organize its employees. The Hospital's first response was to issue a directive, in November or December 1967, prohibiting its employees from discussing union matters during working hours.[1] Subsequently, on January 5, 1968, a representation petition was filed by the Union. The Employer and the Union on February 14, entered into a Stipulation for Certification Upon Consent Election pursuant to which an election was held on February 26, 1968. During the week preceding the election, and on the day of the election, the Employer is accused of having engaged in conduct which infringed on employee's statutory rights.

The first incident complained of occurred on February 21, 1968. In the afternoon of that day C. Geraldine Freund, executive director of the Hospital, held one of several meetings with employees. Present at this meeting, in addition to Mrs. Freund, were Anita Auerbach, assistant executive director, three nursing aides, and two orderlies, Lawrence Brown and Louis Rodriquez. Using some of the literature which had been distributed by the Union, Mrs. Freund compared the employees' wages and employment benefits with those the Union was promising to obtain for them. Such comparisons, if made with reasonable fairness, is a permissible preelection campaign tactic and is not statutorily offensive. However, Mrs. Freund used the occasion to voice numerous threats of loss of benefits should the Union become the employees' bargaining representative. Thus, Mrs. Freund said that if the Union got in the employees would no longer receive free meals, the Employer would discontinue giving loans to employees, the Employer would stop giving semiannual bonuses, and the employees who were being paid in excess of $2 per hour would suffer a wage reduction to the $2 figure. Mrs. Freund also discussed the employees' hospitalization insurance program. She told the employees that the Company was looking into improvements in its insurance program and that if the Union got in the employees probably would have to pay half the premiums for their hospitalization insurance (at the time of the meeting the Hospital's insurance program was noncontributory).[2]

---

[1] . . . As the complaint does not allege that the directive was unlawful and as General Counsel does not make any such contention in his brief, for the purposes of this case, I shall assume that the Hospital's rule prohibiting employees from discussing union subjects was limited to working areas during working hours and was lawfully promulgated.

[2] Brown, Rodriquez, and Mrs. Freund testified concerning the transactions at the February 21 meeting. I have credited the versions of Brown and Rodriquez. . . .

I do not credit Mrs. Freund's version of what she said at this meeting. Mrs. Freund impressed me as being an unreliable witness. Her memory of the events in issue appeared to be poor. In addition, she became excited as she testified which prevented her from giving a straightforward account of the transactions in question. When cross-examined by General

Despite the fact that during the meeting Mrs. Freund also told the employees, "If you want to join the Union, you're welcome to it," I find that by reason of the above-described conduct on the part of Mrs. Freund the Employer has violated Section 8(a)(1) of the Act.[3]

At the end of the February 21 meeting Mrs. Freund entered into a conversation with Brown and Rodriquez. She said to them that it was up to the employees if they wanted the Union or not, but they would be better off if they negotiated with her instead of doing so through the Union. She attempted to find out from them whether they favored the Union or not. Later in the same day Rodriquez met with Mrs. Freund alone. Mrs. Freund attempted to show Rodriquez that he had previously been given a $25 increase. The conversation then turned to the subject of the Union. Mrs. Freund, mentioning that Rodriquez was popular among the employees and spoke with everyone in the Hospital, asked him why the employees wanted the Union. She also asked whether there would be a lot of votes for the Union. Rodriquez answered in the affirmative. She inquired about the kitchen help and Rodriquez said that most of the kitchen help were going to vote against the Union. She then asked about the night shift and Rodriquez responded that the night shift was undecided. Mrs. Freund stated that "we got the Union out before . . . we'll get the Union out this time, too."

The questioning of Rodriquez and Brown regarding their attitudes toward the Union and her later questioning of Rodriquez concerning the attitudes of other employees occurring shortly after the meeting at which Mrs. Freund sought to dissuade the employees from supporting the Union and at which she had threatened the employees with various reprisals should the Union win the election, had a natural tendency to create the impression that she was considering reprisals against union supporters. In the circumstances, therefore, such conduct constituted unlawful interrogation in violation of Section 8(a)(1) of the Act.

About 2 hours after the February 21 employees' meeting concluded Mrs. Freund called Lawrence Brown to her office. She told him that she had heard that he was an agent for the Union and that he had been talking about the Union on the floor. She warned him that if she received any further reports about him "as far as union was concerned" he would be fired. The next day Mrs. Freund called Brown to the bookkeeping department where, in reviewing his wage records with him, she said to him that if the Union gets in his wage rate would be reduced from $2.20 an hour to $2 an hour. These threats made to Brown by Mrs. Freund

---

Counsel she assumed a combatatively [sic] defensive attitude, she tended to avoid giving direct and responsive answers to the questions asked and when finally compelled to answer his questions she did so generally in an argumentative manner. Even when questioned by the Employer's counsel her answers were more discursive than responsive. I am of the opinion that Mrs. Freund has been so affected by her involvement in the Union's organizational campaign and in the instant proceedings that her perspective has been distorted to such a degree as to have impaired her ability to recount the facts as they happened.

[3] According to Brown and Rodriquez, Mrs. Freund also said that she was looking into the purchase of new insurance for the employees and that it would be better if the employees negotiated with her rather than through the Union. Contrary to General Counsel, I do not find these remarks constitute unlawful promises of benefits.

constituted interference, restraint, and coercion of employees in violation of Section 8(a)(1) of the Act.

Clifford Williams, who was then employed by the Hospital as an elevator operator, testified that he attended a meeting of employees conducted by Mrs. Freund during which she said that she would like to know who was in favor of the Union and who was against the Union. During the same meeting she advised the employees that if the Union comes in the employees would lose their fringe benefits and "it is going to cost us to join the union." Williams further testified that on another occasion Mrs. Freund asked several employees including himself to name the people who had gone to the Holiday Inn where the Union had held a meeting. She remarked to Williams that she knew who had gone to the union meeting. These efforts on the part of Mrs. Freund to ferret information concerning which employees favored and supported the Union and which didn't and her threat that employees would lose fringe benefits if the Union should win the election constituted further violations of Section 8(a)(1) of the Act. . . .

B. THE DISCHARGE OF LOUIS RODRIQUEZ

Rodriquez, who was hired as an orderly on March 10, 1967, was discharged by Mrs. Freund on February 25, 1968, the day before the election. According to Rodriquez, on the date of his discharge, while he was working in the dining room he began a conversation with one of the kitchen employees (Mattie Freison) about the pending election. He inquired how long she had been working for the Hospital to which she replied for 8 months. He asked if she was going to vote. She did not answer, but just laughed. He then asked her whether she had been brainwashed. She still did not answer. Shortly thereafter Mrs. Freund sent for him. She asked what he had said to Mattie Freison. He repeated his conversation with Freison. Mrs. Freund responded that she was told that he had asked Freison whether or not she was going to vote for the Union and that he also had said to Freison that Mrs. Freund had been brainwashing her. Rodriquez denied that he had made those statements. Mrs. Freund then told him not to talk to anyone on the floor and to leave the floor.

Rodriquez went to the lobby of the building and there he had another encounter with Mrs. Freund. According to Rodriquez, "she started raving and talking very loud . . . and said I was for the union; and she called me a double agent. She said . . . I didn't think you were for the union, the way you talk and the way you act. . . . You're a double agent. . . . You're for the union, you're for the union . . . you're fired." During the same discussion Mrs. Freund also said, "[W]hy don't you go over [to the Presbyterian Hospital] and work for the union over there? I am paying you a salary over here. The union is not paying you. [I]f you wanted the union so bad, you should be working someplace else."

Mrs. Freund testified that over a period of several months the Employer had received complaints about Rodriquez' behavior, specifically, that he had been stealing drugs from the Hospital and had been engaging in serious improprieties with nurses in the Hospital. However, the immediate reason for his discharge was the incident involving Mattie Freison. According to Mrs. Freund, in the afternoon of February 25, Rodriquez came to speak with her and told her that he had been checking with some people in the Presbyterian—St. Luke's Hospital which was being unionized and that he heard that they were starting at very low salaries and were not happy and he is happy working here in a nonunion place. About 4:30 p.m., an hour later, Mattie Freison informed Mrs. Freund that Rodriquez had stopped her while she was on her way to the dining room with food and had asked her how she was going to vote and whether she favored the Union. Freison also complained that Rodriquez "sort of heckled me" and said, "You're being brainwashed by Mrs. Freund." Mrs. Freund went to the floor where Rodriquez was working and told him to report to her office. Her only conversation with him on the floor was to ask the rhetorical question, "Haven't you been told by Mrs. Auerbach and by me if you have to discuss anything on the floor to take it out of the hospital?" Before she met with Rodriquez in her office she called Dr. Freund and discussed Rodriquez with him. Dr. Freund, according to Mrs. Freund, advised, "knowing what we already know about him, knowing that he is provoking many situations, we don't think he is a good risk to be around patients." Dr. Freund instructed her to discharge Rodriquez, which she did.[7]

General Counsel does not contend that the Hospital's no-solicitation rule was invalid and presumably would not contend that had Rodriquez been discharged for a violation of the rule, the discharge would have been unlawful. However, it is General Counsel's argument that Mrs. Freund discharged Rodriquez because she learned that he was promoting the Union's cause rather than because of his violation of the Hospital's rule. The issue thus turns on whether the truth lies with Rodriquez' version or Mrs. Freund's version of what transpired on February 25, 1968. According to Mrs. Freund, on the Sunday in question Rodriquez interrupted her about 3 p.m. to tell her that he was happy "working here in a nonunion place." About an hour later Mrs. Freund learned from Mattie Freison that Rodriquez was promoting the Union's cause. Then, motivated by her concern for her patients because, according to her testimony, "mealtime for psychiatric patients [is] a very important part of the day . . . and psychiatric patients are very sensitive to disturbances on the floor," Mrs. Freund accosted Rodriquez on the floor where he was working and

---

[7]Mrs. Freund described Rodriquez' discharge twice. The version set forth above is a summary of her testimony given in response to questions asked her by Employer's counsel while presenting the Employer's defense. However, Mrs. Freund was questioned by General Counsel as an adverse witness and as his first witness. In response to his questions she gave a somewhat different version of Rodriquez' discharge. According to this version, Mattie Freison came to her office and told her that Rodriquez had stopped Freison while Freison was delivering food, asked Freison many questions about the union, and why Freison isn't joining the Union or signing up. Mrs. Freund approached Rodriquez and asked him whether Freison's story was true. Mrs. Freund was unable to remember Rodriquez' reply but did remember that Rodriquez admitted he had talked to Freison "about it." Mrs. Freund discharged him then or shortly thereafter. She informed Rodriquez that "he had repeatedly been told not to discuss union activities while he was taking care of patients, and he had been cautioned long before, and if they are doing it, this would be cause for dismissal." In this version Mrs. Freund does not refer to any conversation with Dr. Freund.

reproved him for speaking to Freison and for being away from the dining room. She told him to report to the office where, after talking to Dr. Freund, she discharged Rodriquez. She denied that she told Rodriquez that he was discharged because he was for the Union. This story does not ring true. Rodriquez, according to Mrs. Freund, was suspected of having engaged in serious derelictions over a period of several months. Nevertheless, no disciplinary action was taken against him. After receiving information that Rodriquez may have stolen drugs from the Hospital, Mrs. Freund testified that "I did not approach him. We sort of like to give an employee a chance . . . we like to be sure that he is guilty of what we are going to accuse [him]." Then when she later learned about Rodriquez' alleged improprieties with nurses the only action taken against him, according to Mrs. Freund, was that "we were observing him sort of without letting anyone know we knew about these things." Thus, with respect to the serious accusations made against Rodriquez, Mrs. Freund was willing to act slowly, cautiously, and only with certainty so that if Rodriquez was innocent he would not be unfairly penalized. However, in contrast, on a Sunday afternoon when the Hospital was operating "on skeleton staff" Rodriquez was peremptorily discharged for his alleged brief conversation with Mattie Freison about the latter's voting intentions the next day.

I credit Rodriquez' version of the events leading to his discharge on February 25. I find that he is a more reliable witness than Mrs. Freund. Furthermore, while Mrs. Freund's testimony is marked by incongruities and inconsistencies, Rodriquez' description of Mrs. Freund's behavior when she discharged him comports with the highly emotional and agitated manner Mrs. Freund displayed at the hearing. I find that Rodriquez was discharged on February 25, 1968, because Mrs. Freund had learned that he was supporting the Union in the pending election. Accordingly, I further find that the Employer thereby has violated Section 8(a)(3) and (1) of the Act.

C. THE DISCHARGE OF LAWRENCE BROWN

Lawrence Brown, who was hired as an orderly in July 1967, was discharged when he reported for work on Monday, February 26, 1968, the day of the election. The Employer's explanation is that Brown was not a satisfactory employee and that he was discharged because of his unexcused absence from work on the preceding day. General Counsel contends, however, that Brown was discharged not for the reason given by the Employer but because of Mrs. Freund's suspicions concerning his union sympathies and activities. Although Brown was not active in promoting the Union's organizational cause, he testified that he discussed the Union with other employees in the hospital premises particularly in the locker room and the dining room. Of more significance is the fact that on February 21 Brown was called to Mrs. Freund's office where he was accused by her of being "an agent for the union, double agent . . . [of] talking about the union on the floor" and was warned that he would be fired if she received any further reports about him "as far as union was concerned."

Brown was not discharged by Mrs. Freund but by Mrs. Auerbach, the assistant executive director of the Hospital. Mrs. Auerbach testified that Brown worked on the 3 to 11 p.m. shift and was chronically absent from work. According to Mrs. Auerbach, he would call to advise that he was going to be late and then would not appear at all so that on such occasions his department had to operate short of help. She spoke to him about the matter and following their conversation tried to schedule Brown's days off to accommodate his convenience. Nevertheless, Brown continued to remain away from work, particularly on Sundays. Mrs. Auerbach again spoke to him about his absenteeism. This time Brown informed her that he had another job and sometimes he was too tired to go to work. Mrs. Auerbach advised him that such excuse was unacceptable. About the same time she began to hear reports that Brown was using more physical restraint than necessary on patients. Mrs. Auerbach spoke to him about this matter and also about his tendency to be short tempered with the patients. Brown promised to be more careful. The week before he was discharged he again was absent on a scheduled work day. Mrs. Auerbach warned him that the next time he was absent he would be discharged. On Sunday, February 25, Brown again failed to report for work. According to Mrs. Auerbach, she received a report from the afternoon supervisor, Mrs. Frank, that Brown had telephoned to say that he had overslept and that he would get to work late. The next morning when Mrs. Auerbach arrived at the hospital she found a note from Mrs. Frank saying that Brown had not called back and had not reported for work. Accordingly, Mrs. Auerbach pulled his timecard thereby discharging him.[9]

I credit Mrs. Auerbach. As a witness at the hearing she gave her testimony, in response to questions directed to her on cross-examination as well as on direct examination, without equivocation, without embellishment, and with conviction. Her manner on the witness stand was sincere and straightforward. I am of the opinion that Mrs. Auerbach was a truthful and reliable witness. Furthermore, her testimony is uncontradicted. Accordingly, despite the suspicions generated by the transactions at the meeting on February 21 between Brown and Mrs. Freund, I

[9]Brown testified that on Sunday, February 25, he called and spoke with Mrs. Freund. He told Mrs. Freund that he had told Mrs. Frank, the afternoon supervisor, and "she said try to make it in, because they were short of help." He further testified that "the situation came up where the person that was driving me had car trouble, and was too late, and I didn't go in. But I had told Mrs. Frank that I wouldn't make it, and should I come in tomorrow, and she said, 'yes.'" On cross-examination Brown testified, "I had overslept and the person that was driving me had car trouble and I told Mrs. Frank that I'd try to get in, and she told me to try." General Counsel contends that the above-quoted testimony should be interpreted to mean that after Brown discovered that he would not be able to get to the hospital he telephoned Mrs. Frank a second time, informed her of his predicament and inquired whether he should report for work the next day to which she replied in the affirmative. While I find that Brown's testimony is less than clear I do not accept General Counsel's resolution of the ambiguities. If Brown had had a second telephone conversation with Mrs. Frank on the Sunday in question and had told her he would not be in at all that could have been brought out more clearly. Certainly, his review of the event on cross-examination does not even hint at the fact that he made more than one telephone call to Mrs. Frank or that he told her he would not be in at all.

find that General Counsel has failed to prove by a preponderance of the evidence that Brown was discharged for a reason prohibited by the Act.

D. THE DISCHARGES OF MELVIN GATES AND FRANK ROGERS

Frank Rogers and Melvin Gates were both hired by the Employer on February 3, 1968. Rogers was assigned to operate the elevator and Gates was assigned to work in the kitchen. Their employment terminated on February 21. They testified that several days earlier as they were walking through the lobby of the hospital from the locker room Gates asked Rogers whether he was going to vote for the Union and Rogers answered in the affirmative. They further testified that Mrs. Auerbach then was standing at the door to her office about 5 feet from them. General Counsel argues in his brief that there can be no question that Mrs. Auerbach heard this conversation because she was a witness at the hearing and did not deny having heard it. As further evidence that the Employer knew of their union sympathies General Counsel refers to the testimony of Gates and Rogers to the effect that as they were entering the hospital on February 21 to obtain their final paychecks following their terminations they overheard a supervisor, Mrs. Chapman, say to Mrs. Auerbach, "Melvin and Frank are for the union."

According to the Employer both Gates and Rogers were unsatisfactory employees. Gates was discharged following an insubordinate refusal to work overtime and Rogers quit his employment after he had been warned that if his performance did not improve he also would be discharged.

Josephine E. Oyler, dietary manager of the Hospital, who was Gates' immediate supervisor, testified about Gates' derelictions. One constant problem arose from the fact that Rogers repeatedly came into the kitchen and then he and Gates would begin "fooling around." She warned Rogers several times to stay out of the kitchen and to stop annoying Gates but Rogers, nevertheless, continued to come back. She criticized Gates on several occasions for leaving the kitchen without permission in order to smoke. She also testified to difficulties she had because of Gates' absence on one occasion and refusal to work overtime on another.

Mrs. Auerbach testified that she received several complaints about Gates from Mrs. Oyler. Following an occasion when Gates had promised to work overtime but nevertheless left the hospital without permission, she spoke with him about the occurrence and informed him that absenteeism was unforgivable. She agreed to give him another chance after he promised to do better. She spoke with him again at a later time after she had received a further complaint from Mrs. Oyler that Gates was "goofing off and fooling around with Frank Rogers and was not in the kitchen." On this occasion Gates again promised to do better. Lastly, on February 21, Mrs. Oyler reported that she had asked Gates to work overtime and he at first said he would, but later said he would not. Mrs. Auerbach sent for Gates and asked him whether he would stay, but he refused. She then asked if he would come to work the next day, which was his scheduled day off. He also refused to do this. After Gates left her office she discussed his work with Mrs. Oyler and decided to discharge him.[10] She called his home and left a message for him to telephone. When he called back Mrs. Auerbach told him that the Employer did not need his services any longer and that he was discharged.

During her final conversation with Gates the latter asked her if Rogers was also fired, she said, "No."[11]

Frank Rogers testified that Gates came to his home and told him he was discharged. He thereupon telephoned Mrs. Auerbach and asked her whether he was fired. She replied, "Not yet." Then according to Rogers, "I asked her how come I was going to be fired, and then she said that my work is not good. Then I asked her who told her that, and she told me my supervisor, Mrs. Chapman had told her, which I knew was not true. . . . Then I told her I'd be in to pick up my check."

According to Mrs. Auerbach, whom I credit, Rogers telephoned her shortly after her conversation with Gates. He mentioned that he understood that Gates was fired and inquired whether he too was fired. She answered, "No." But, she told him, "you are still on your three months' probation. I would expect now that Melvin is gone you can settle down and work well." He responded, "Well, I quit."

I credit the Employer's versions of the circumstances which led to the terminations of Gates and Rogers. I find that both employees were generally unsatisfactory, that Gates was discharged for his insubordinate refusal to work overtime and that Rogers voluntarily quit his employment.

E. THE DISCHARGE OF CLIFFORD WILLIAMS

Clifford Williams began working for the Hospital in 1964. About June 27, 1968, while he was on his vacation, he was notified by Mr. Kanter, the building superintendent, by telephone that he was discharged. No reason was given to Williams for his discharge. Williams testified that he was an elevator operator at the Hospital and during the period of the organizational campaign the topic of the Union was discussed widely among the employees. According to Williams, "it caused people to dislike people.

---

[10]Gates testified to a somewhat more dramatic version of the event, leading to his discharge. According to Gates, the previous day Mrs. Oyler had asked him to work overtime and he had responded that he was tired and could not work. She reported the incident to Mrs. Auerbach who spoke with him and asked him whether he wanted to work overtime, but when he told her he was tired Mrs. Auerbach said, "Okay." Then he continued his testimony, as follows:

"So the next day when I came back, she [Mrs. Oyler] asked me the same thing, would I work, and there wasn't anybody off and I said, 'No, I am not going to work.'

"And she told me the same thing and I said, 'I'll work.'

"She said, 'If you feel—If I tell you to work, you'll work.'

"I said, 'If you say it like that, I won't work. If you are going to tell me I have to work, I won't work.'

"Just like that."

[11]Gates testified that Mrs. Auerbach telephoned his home and left a message with his mother that the Employer would not need his services any more. When he returned, he telephoned Mrs. Auerbach and inquired why he was discharged. She gave him no reason. He then asked whether he could go to the hospital and pick up his check. She said yes, and she added, "If your friend, Frank, doesn't do any better, we are going to fire him, too." To the extent that they conflict, I credit Mrs. Auerbach's version of the event rather than Gates'.

And some of them wasn't speaking to one another. It was a terrible mess around there." Williams testified that there was a meeting of the employees in the maintenance department and that Mrs. Freund barred him from attending the meeting. According to Williams, she accused him of being an instigator of the Union. And told him that she should have fired him 2 years ago.

According to Williams' further testimony Mrs. Freund asked him, among others, who had attended a union meeting at the Holiday Inn and she remarked to him that she knew all the people who had gone to the meeting. He further testified that on the day of the election he was relieved from his duties as operator of the elevator by Mrs. Freund who said to him, "I don't want you on the elevator, because you are in favor of the Union."

Mrs. Freund testified that Williams' work performance had been bad for at least 6 to 8 months prior to his discharge. One of his offenses was to take food from the patients' food trays which was a violation of Board of Health rules. He was repeatedly warned to stop this practice and also to stop bringing sandwiches into the elevator. But he could not stop eating. Another practice he engaged in of which the Employer disapproved was to leave the elevator and listen to ball games in the emergency room so that he did not respond to elevator calls. He was warned many times about this fault. Still another offense of which he was guilty was to discuss medical problems with the families of patients. This tended to cause difficulties. In addition, he carried patients from floor to floor without first obtaining the clearance of the nurses in charge. According to Mrs. Freund, while Williams was on vacation in June 1968, Mr. Kanter, the building superintendent, advised her that he had hired a vacation replacement for Williams and found the replacement very capable and he wanted the new man to be Williams' permanent replacement. Mrs. Freund approved the change.

Williams did not deny that while he was employed by the Hospital he had engaged in the offenses described by Mrs. Freund. He was discharged 4 months after the election (objections to the election were pending at the time of his discharge). There is only minimal causal connection between the Employer's incriminatory conduct involving Williams which took place prior to February 21 and Williams' discharge. On the other hand, the Employer's reasons for Williams' discharge are plausible. Although the record gives rise to suspicions that Williams may have been discharged because of his suspected union activities, particularly as Kanter was not called as a witness to corroborate Mrs. Freund's testimony, nevertheless, I find that General Counsel has failed to prove by a preponderance of the evidence that Williams was discharged for his union sympathies or activities. . . .

VI. THE REMEDY

Having found that the Employer has engaged in unfair labor practices, I shall recommend that it cease and desist therefrom and that it take certain affirmative action designed to effectuate the policies of the Act.

Having found that the Employer unlawfully discharged Louis Rodriquez on February 25, 1968, I shall recommend that the Employer offer him immediate and full reinstatement to his former or to a substantially equivalent position, without prejudice to his seniority or other rights and privileges, and make him whole for any loss of earnings he may have suffered by reason of the discrimination against him by payment to him of a sum of money equal to that which he normally would have earned from the aforesaid date of his discharge to the date of the Employer's offer of reinstatement less his net earnings during such period. The backpay provided herein shall be computed on the basis of calendar quarters, in accordance with the method prescribed in *F.W. Woolworth Company*, 90 NLRB 289. Interest at the rate of 6 percent per annum shall be added to such net backpay* and shall be computed in the manner set forth in *Isis Plumbing & Heating Co.*, 138 NLRB 716. . . .

. . .

RECOMMENDED ORDER* *

Upon the basis of the foregoing findings of fact and conclusions of law and the entire record in the case, and pursuant to Section 10(c) of the Act, I hereby recommend that Fairview Hospital, its officers, agents, successors, and assigns, shall:

1. Cease and desist from:

(a) Discouraging membership in Hospital Employees Labor Program, Local 743, International Brotherhood of Teamsters, Chauffeurs, Warehousemen and Helpers of America, and Local 73, Building Service Employees International Union, AFL–CIO, Jointly, or any other labor organization, by discharging or by otherwise discriminating in regard to the hire, tenure of employment, or other term or condition of employment of any of its employees.

(b) Threatening its employees with loss of employment benefits if they should select or designate the above-named Union, or any other labor organization, as their collective-bargaining representative.

(c) Expressly or impliedly threatening its employees with a reduction in wages if they should select or designate the above-named Union, or any other labor organization, as their collective-bargaining representative.

(d) Interrogating employees about their union sympathies or attitudes or about the union sympathies or attitudes of other employees.

(e) Threatening its employees with discharge or other reprisals if they should support the above-named Union, or any other labor organization, as their collective-bargaining representative.

(f) In any like or related manner, interfering with, restraining, or coercing employees in the exercise of their right to self-organization, to form labor organizations, to join or assist the above-named Union, or any other labor organization, to bargain collectively through representatives of their own choosing and to engage in other concerted activities for the

---

*The Board uses the IRS' adjusted prime interest rate.—Ed.
**The entire order in this case is reproduced.—Ed.

purpose of collective bargaining or other mutual aid or protection or to refrain from any and all such activities.

2. Take the following affirmative action, which is deemed necessary to effectuate the policies of the Act.

(a) Offer to Louis Rodriquez immediate and full reinstatement to his former or to a substantially equivalent position, without prejudice to his seniority and other rights and privileges, and make him whole for any loss of earnings he may have suffered by reason of the unlawful discrimination against him in the manner set forth in the section of this Decision entitled "The Remedy."

(b) Preserve and, upon request, make available to the Board or its agents, for examination and copying, all payroll records, social security payment records, time cards, personnel records and reports, and all records relevant to a determination to the amount of backpay due to Louis Rodriquez.

(c) Notify Louis Rodriquez if presently serving in the Armed Forces of the United States of his right to full reinstatement upon application in accordance with the Selective Service Act and the Universal Military Training and Service Act, as amended, after discharge from the Armed Forces.

(d) Post at its hospital in Chicago, Illinois, copies of the attached notice marked "Appendix."[21] Copies of said notice, on forms provided by the Regional Director for Region 13, after being duly signed by its authorized representative, shall be posted by the Employer immediately upon receipt thereof, and be maintained by it for 60 consecutive days thereafter, in conspicuous places, including all places where notices to employees are customarily posted. Reasonable steps shall be taken by the Employer to insure that said notices are not altered, defaced, or covered by any other material.

(e) Notify the Regional Director for Region 13, in writing, within 20 days from the receipt of this Decision, what steps the Employer has taken to comply herewith.[22]

It is further recommended that the complaint in Case 13–CA–8303 be dismissed insofar as it alleges that Fairview Hospital has engaged in any unfair labor practices other than the conduct hereinabove specifically found to have constituted violations of Section 8(a)(1) or (3) of the Act.

It is also recommended that with respect to Case 13–RC–11360 the challenges to the ballots of Frank Rogers, Lawrence Brown, and Melvin Gates be sustained and that the challenges to the ballots of Louis Rodriquez and Wilma Mullins be overruled and that their ballots be opened and counted.

[21]In the event that this Recommended Order is adopted by the Board, the words "a Decision and Order" shall be substituted for the words "the Recommended Order of a Trial Examiner" in the notice. In the further event that the Board's Order is enforced by a decree of a United States Court of Appeals, the words "a Decree of the United States Court of Appeals Enforcing an Order" shall be substituted for the words "a Decision and Order."

[22]In the event that this Recommended Order is adopted by the Board, this provision shall be modified to read: "Notify said Regional Director, in writing, within 10 days from the date of this Order, what steps Respondent has taken to comply herewith."

It is further recommended that in the event that the revised tally of ballots in Case 13–RC–11360 shows that the Union has received a majority of the valid ballots cast a Certification of Representative shall issue. However, in the event that the revised tally of ballots shows that the Union has not received a majority of the valid ballots cast, the election conducted on February 26, 1968, shall be set aside and a second election shall be directed in accordance with the rules, regulations and practices of the Board.

APPENDIX

NOTICE TO ALL EMPLOYEES

Pursuant to the Recommended Order of a Trial Examiner of the National Labor Relations Board and in order to effectuate the policies of the National Labor Relations Act, as amended, we hereby notify our employees that:

We will not discourage membership in Hospital Employees Labor Program, Local 743, International Brotherhood of Teamsters, Chauffeurs, Warehousemen and Helpers of America and Local 73, Building Service Employees International Union, AFL–CIO, Jointly, or any other labor organization, by discharging or otherwise discriminating against any of our employees in regard to their hire, tenure or their employment, or any term or condition of their employment.

We will not threaten any of our employees with discharge or with other reprisals if they should join, assist, or support the above-named Union, or any other labor organization.

We will not threaten any of our employees with a reduction in their wages or with loss of other employment benefits or with discharge if they should select or designate the above-named Union, or any other labor organization, as their collective-bargaining representative.

We will not question any of our employees about their union sympathies or attitudes or about the union sympathies or attitudes of other employees.

We will not in any like or related manner interfere with, restrain, or coerce our employees in the exercise of their right to self-organization, to form labor organizations, to join or assist the above-named Union, or any other labor organization, to bargain collectively through representatives of their own choosing, to engage in concerted activities for the purpose of collective bargaining or other mutual aid or protection, or to refrain from any and all such activities.

We will offer Louis Rodriquez reinstatement to his former or to a substantially equivalent position, without prejudice to his seniority and other rights and privileges, and we will make him whole for any loss of earnings he may have suffered by reason of our unlawful discrimination against him.

We will notify Louis Rodriquez if presently serving in the Armed Forces of the United States of his right to full reinstatement upon application in accordance with the Selective Service Act and the Universal Military Training and Service Act, as amended, after discharge from the Armed Forces.

FAIRVIEW HOSPITAL
(Employer)

Dated   By

(Representative)   (Title)

This notice must remain posted for 60 consecutive days from the date of posting and must not be altered, defaced, or covered by any other material.

If employees have any question concerning this notice or compliance with its provisions, they may communicate directly with the Board's Regional Office (address and phone number omitted).

Notes

1. The Board summarily affirmed the trial examiner's decision, and issued the following order on March 20, 1969:

"Pursuant to Section 10(c) of the National Labor Relations Act, as amended, the National Labor Relations Board hereby adopts as its Order the Recommended Order of the Trial Examiner, as modified below, and hereby orders that Respondent, Fairview Hospital, Chicago, Illinois, its officers, agents, successors, and assigns, shall take the action set forth in the Trial Examiner's Recommended Order, as herein modified:

"1. Delete from paragraph 1(f) of the Trial Examiner's Recommended Order that part thereof which reads 'In any like or related manner' and substitute therefor 'In any other manner. . . .'

"2. Delete from the third to last paragraph of the Notice to All Employees the words 'in any like or related manner' and substitute therefor 'in any other manner. . . .'

"It is hereby further ordered that the complaint be, and it hereby is, dismissed insofar as it alleges violations not found herein."

2. The Court of Appeals for the Seventh Circuit enforced the Board's order on December 3, 1970. The hospital and Ms. Freund refused to comply with the Board's order, as enforced by the court of appeals, and did not attempt to have the order set aside. On April 9, 1971, Ms. Freund and the hospital were found in contempt of court and were fined $500 for each day they failed to purge themselves of the contempt. The hospital and Ms. Freund petitioned the court of appeals for an order staying the contempt order for 30 days and for remission and suspension of the fines, so that a petition for certiorari could be filed.

NLRB v. Fairview Hospital

United States Court of Appeals, Seventh Circuit, 1971
443 F.2d 1217, 77 LRRM 2137

PELL, Circuit Judge.

The hospital and its directress admit noncompliance but state that the discharged employee "had been breaking into the medicine room and stealing drugs and that he had sexual relations with hospital personnel on hospital premises." It is further claimed that Fairview Hospital is a psychiatric hospital, that many of the younger patients have drug-associated problems and that the retention of the employee constitutes a hazard to the operation of the hospital and is inimical to the welfare, mental health and treatment of the patients. It is further claimed that he was discharged at the earliest opportunity.

This court would not lightly impose upon a psychiatric hospital the necessity of hiring an employee who would be a threat to the proper treatment of mental patients. Because of this and because of the stubborn insistence of the hospital and its directress that there will be no rehiring, we have again reviewed the entire record in this cause. . . .

. . .

In the hearing before the trial examiner, Freund was called as an adverse witness by the General Counsel. When asked why the employee in question was fired, she did state on two counts that she would care "to discuss here now." The following then appears in testimony:

"Q. (By Mr. Maslanka) Why was [the employee] fired?
"A. That is because he was doing it.
"Q. Doing what?
"A. He was discussing the union during working hours.

. . .

"Q. What did you say to him?
"A. I just told him he had repeatedly been told not to discuss union activities while he was taking care of patients, and he had been cautioned long before, and if they are doing it, this would be cause for dismissal."

It was not until Freund testified on behalf of the hospital, nearly 300 pages of transcript later, that she first adverted to the charges of misconduct against the employee. At that time she said that they had been getting complaints "about some charges, about drugs." She further said that he had broken into a medicine room and had taken drugs: "I didn't see him do it, but it was told to me." This alleged occurrence, according to Freund's own testimony, was several months before he was discharged.

She then referred to his alleged relationship with the nurses when he was off duty late in the evening. This again was a charge which came to her and when asked when it had occurred, she replied: "Two, three months before. It was going on for several months." . . .

The trial examiner laid substantial significance on the fact that although serious accusations had been made against the employee, Freund was willing to act slowly, cautiously and only with a certainty so that if the employee were innocent he would not be unfairly penalized. In contrast, on a Sunday afternoon when the hospital was operating on a skeleton staff, the employee was peremptorily discharged for an alleged brief conversation with another employee about the latter's voting intentions the next day. The trial examiner found credibility in the employee's version of the events leading to the discharge and a lack of credibility on the part of the directress.

In the opinion-order of this court, the credibility determination was a reasonable one "under the circumstances of this case, which indicated other evidence of a background of anti-union activity on the part of" Geraldine Freund. . . .

At the juncture at which we now find ourselves, we find incredible the presently expressed concern of the executive directress over the re-employment of the discharged orderly, when with knowledge of the claimed derelictions on his part she permitted him to remain an employee for several months and until what she interpreted to be a display of union activity on his part.

In view of the clear support for the findings of the trial examiner, which were affirmed by the order of the Board and by the order of this court, that the immediate reason for the discharge of the employee was attributable to his union activities, the present position taken by the hospital and its executive directress would not prevail even though the claimed derelictions had been discovered shortly prior to the alleged discharge.

As this Court has long recognized, the existence of valid grounds for punitive action is no defense unless such action was predicated solely on these grounds and not by a desire to discourage protected activity. . . .

Here the continuance of employment after the discovery of the claimed malfeasance was of such duration as to provide inescapable indicia of afterthought.

Even if there were grounds, which we cannot now conceive, for not complying with the judgment directing the reinstatement, respondent's proper recourse would have been, as the court said in *Mastro, supra,* 261 F.2d at 148,

"in timely fashion to petition this court for a modification of its clear mandate, *McComb* v. *Jacksonville Paper Co.,* 1949, 336 U.S. 187, 191, 8 WH Cases 500; *National Labor Relations Board* v. *Republican Publishing Co.,* 1 Cir., 1950, 180 F.2d 437, 440, 25 LRRM 2559. The orderly administration of justice requires that respondents scrupulously avoid a unilateral determination that [the court's] orders need no longer be complied with."

Moreover, such grounds would have to be "based upon *subsequent events or subsequently discovered evidence* which would tend to show that reinstatement would no longer further the purpose of the Act." *NLRB* v. *Mastro*

Plastics Corp., supra, 261 F.2d at 149, and cases cited therein. (Emphasis added.) Respondents have not petitioned for modification. Nor did they seek review "by a petition for a rehearing, by a petition for a writ of certiorari, or conceivably by a petition for a writ of prohibition." *NLRB* v. *Local 282, IBT*, 428 F.2d 994, 999, 74 LRRM 2289 (2d Cir. 1970). They merely raise the same defense before this court for a second time.

Finally, the hospital and its directress claim that there should be no contempt holding because she is acting in good faith "solely to protect the best interests of the patients in the hospital.". . . As the Supreme Court stated in *Jacksonville Paper Co.*, 336 U.S. at 191:

> "Civil as distinguished from criminal contempt is a sanction to enforce compliance with an order of the court or to compensate for losses or damages sustained by reason of non-compliance. Since the purpose is remedial, it matters not with what intent the defendant did the prohibited act. The decree was not fashioned so as to grant or withhold its benefits dependent on the state of mind of respondents. It laid on them a duty to obey specified provisions of the statute. An act does not cease to be a violation of a law and of a decree merely because it may have been done innocently. The force and vitality of judicial decrees derive from more robust sanctions. And the grant or withholding of a remedial relief is not wholly discretionary with the judge. . . . The private or public rights that the decree sought to protect are an important measure of the remedy."

The hospital and its executive directress have been aware for more than six months that an order of the National Labor Relations Board entered in March of 1969 was to be enforced, which included reinstatement of the employee in question. Further delay would indeed make a mockery of lawful procedures established for the protection of labor. Expectation of and necessity for obedience to the law is not to be confined to marchers on the mall or confrontations on the campus. Respect for and observance of the law must pervade all strata of society.

The motion of Fairview Hospital, Inc. and Geraldine Freund for an order staying the effect of the contempt order issued by this court and requesting that this court remit and suspend fines and penalties which may have accrued heretofore is denied.

Notes

1. *NLRB* v. *Fairview* suggests the difficulty of deciding whether an employer's disciplining of employees is due to work-related considerations or to the employees' union activity. For example, in *Fairview* the trial examiner found that only Rodriquez was discharged for union activity. One could argue, however, that the dismissals of Gates, Brown, and Rogers were intended to eliminate pro-union votes for the coming election, and that the dismissal of Williams was in retaliation for pro-union sympathies and in anticipation of Williams' support for future organizational campaigns.

There was legally sufficient evidence on the record to find that the employer knew that Gates, Brown, Rogers, and Williams each supported the union. There was also substantial evidence on the record that until the election Fairview had tolerated Brown's unsatisfactory work record in the same way that it had tolerated Rodriquez's. The only objective difference in the two cases was that Brown had been warned that an additional absence would result in dismissal, whereas Rodriquez had not received a warning. In your view, should this have made a difference in the trial examiner's evaluation of the two cases? Should the trial examiner have considered more seriously the fact that Brown received the warning during the organizational campaign, that Brown's discharge occurred on the morning of the election, or that Brown was the fourth supporter fired?

Are you convinced that Rodriquez was fired because of his union activities and Brown because of his poor work record? If Auerbach had discharged Rodriquez and testified about the events described in the case "without embellishment and with conviction . . . [in a] sincere . . . straightforward [manner]," would the hearing officer have upheld the discharge?

Like Brown, Williams was warned that his work was unsatisfactory, but Williams was discharged after the election. If the discharge involved considerations of Williams' union support, should it make a difference that an election had already been held? Is it relevant that Williams had been an employee of the hospital for four years prior to the discharge? It appears that Williams was discharged, in part, because the hospital was able to hire someone that the supervisor preferred. Is this discharge for cause? Do the labor laws provide any protection for a discharge that is not for cause and is not shown to be motivated by anti-union bias?

Gates and Rogers present a more difficult case since they were probationary employees at the time of their discharges. Should this factor make a difference in the context of the anti-union campaign being conducted by Fairview? If Gates had been more active in the organizing campaign, would the trial examiner have scrutinized more closely the account of his discharge?

2. Did the court of appeals and the Board use the same standard in applying Section 8(a)(3)? If not, may Gates, Brown, Rogers, and Williams appeal the Board's conclusions on the ground that the Board applied the wrong standard? See Section 10(f).

3. Why is the analysis of discharges confined to Section 8(a)(3), even though the terms of Section 8(a)(1) seem to be applicable?

4. Should different standards of proof be used for ordering reinstatement and back pay? The Supreme Court rejected this approach in *NLRB v. Walton Mfg. Co.*, 369 U.S. 404, 49 LRRM 2962 (1962). Why is a discriminatee *required* to mitigate damages by finding substantially equivalent work or accepting alternative work when long-term efforts to find substantially equivalent work are not successful? Is it likely that Rodriquez was voluntarily unemployed during the more than three years between his discharge and compliance with the reinstatement order?

Wright Line, Inc.

National Labor Relations Board, 1980
251 NLRB 1083, 105 LRRM 1169

Respondent excepted, *inter alia*, to the Administrative Law Judge's conclusion that it violated Section 8(a)(3) and (1) of the Act when, on December 30, 1977, it discharged Bernard Lamoureux. We agree with the result reached by the Administrative Law Judge, but only for the reasons that follow.

In resolving cases involving alleged violations of Section 8(a)(3) and, in certain instances, Section 8(a)(1), it must be determined, *inter alia*, whether an employee's employment conditions were adversely affected by his or her engaging in union or other protected activities and, if so, whether the employer's action was motivated by such employee activities. As discussed *infra*, various "tests" have been employed by the Board and the courts to aid in making such determinations. These tests all examine the concept of "causality," that is, the relationship between the employees' protected activities and actions on the part of their employer which detrimentally affect their employment.

The Administrative Law Judge's Decision in the instant case reveals some uncertainty regarding the appropriate mode of analysis for examining causality in cases alleging unlawful discrimination. Indeed, similar doubts as to the applicable test appear to have become widespread at various levels of the decisional process primarily as a result of conflict in this area among the courts of appeals and between certain courts of appeals and the Board.

After careful consideration we find it both helpful and appropriate to set forth formally a test of causation for cases alleging violations of Section 8(a)(3) of the Act. We shall examine causality in such cases through an analysis akin to that used by the Supreme Court in *Mt. Healthy City School District Board of Education* v. *Doyle*, 429 U.S. 274 (1977).

It is our belief that application of the *Mt. Healthy* test[3] will maintain a substantive consistency with existing Board precedent and accommodate the concerns expressed by critics of the Board's past treatment of cases alleging unlawful discrimination. We further find the *Mt. Healthy* test to be in harmony with the Act's legislative history as well as pertinent Supreme Court decisions. Finally, in this regard, enunciation of the *Mt. Healthy* test will alleviate the confusion which now exists at various levels of the decisional process and do so in a manner that, we conclude, accords proper weight to the legitimate conflicting interest in this area, thereby advancing the fundamental objectives of the Act.

I. The Distinction Between Pretext and Dual Motive: It is helpful, initially, to distinguish between what are termed "pretext" cases and "dual motive"

---

[3]For ease of reference, we shall refer to this test of causality as the *Mt. Healthy* test. We note, however, that *Mt. Healthy* itself does not constitute a construction of the National Labor Relations Act and, accordingly, our Decision here is not compelled by *Mt. Healthy*. We do not view *Mt. Healthy* as at odds with our previous construction of the Act.

cases because it is in the dual motive situation where the legitimate interests of the parties most plainly conflict. Consequently it is in such situations that the existing controversy and confusion in this area are highlighted.[4]

In modern day labor relations, an employer will rarely, if ever, baldly assert that it has disciplined an employee because it detests unions or will not tolerate employees engaging in union or other protected activities. Instead, it will generally advance what it asserts to be a legitimate business reason for its action. Examination of the evidence may reveal, however, that the asserted justification is a sham in that the purported rule of circumstance advanced by the employer did not exist, or was not, in fact, relied upon. When this occurs, the reason advanced by the employer may be termed pretextual. Since no legitimate business justification for the discipline exists, there is, by strict definition, no dual motive.

The pure dual motive case presents a different situation. In such cases, the discipline decision involves two factors. The first is a legitimate business reason. The second reason, however, is not a legitimate business reason but is instead the employer's reaction to its employees' engaging in union or other protected activities. This latter motive, of course, runs afoul of Section 8(a)(3) of the Act. This existence of both a "good" and a "bad" reason for the employer's action requires further inquiry into the role played by each motive and has spawned substantial controversy in 8(a)(3) litigation.[5]

II. The "In Part" Test: For a number of years now, when determining whether the Act has been violated in a dual motivation case, the Board has applied what is termed the "in part" causation test. In its present form the "in part" test provides that if a discharge is motivated, "in part," by the protected activities of the employee the discharge violates the Act even if a legitimate business reason was also relied on. . . .

Since its inception, the "in part" test has been perceived by some to be, at least conceptually, at odds with the oftrepeated idea that:

> "Management can discharge for good cause, or bad cause, or no cause at all. It has, as the master of its own business affairs, complete freedom with but one specific, definite qualification: it may not discharge when the real motivating purpose is to do that which Section 8(a)(3) forbids."

[4]As is demonstrated herein, under the *Mt. Healthy* test, there is no real need to distinguish between pretext, and dual motive cases. The distinction is nonetheless useful in setting forth the controversy surrounding dual motive cases.

[5]Unfortunately, the distinction between a pretext case and a dual motive case is sometimes difficult to discern. This is especially true since the appropriate designation seldom can be made until after the presentation of all relevant evidence. The conceptual problems to which this sometimes blurred distinction gives rise can be eliminated if one views the employer's asserted justification as an affirmative defense. Thus, in a pretext situation, the employer's affirmative defense of business justification is wholly without merit. If, however, the affirmative defense has at least some merit a "dual motive" may exist and the issue becomes one of the sufficiency of proof necessary for the employer's affirmative defense to be sustained. Treating the employer's plea of a legitimate business reason for discipline as an affirmative defense is consistent with the Board's method of deciding such cases. See *Bedford Cut Stone Co., Inc.*, 235 NLRB 629, 98 LRRM 1003 (1978).

A conflict between this concept and the "in part" rationale is seen because in a dual motivation case, the employer does have a legitimate reason for its action. Yet, an improper reason for discharge is also present. Thus, the employer's recognized right to enforce rules of its own choosing is viewed as being in practical conflict with the employees' right to be free from adverse effects brought about by their participation in protected activities. Critics of the "in part" test have asserted that rather than seeking to resolve this conflict and accommodate the legitimate competing interests, the analysis goes only half way, in that once hostility to protected rights is found, the inquiry ends and the employer's plea of legitimate justification is ignored.

III. The Advent of the "Dominant Motive" Test and the Laws of the Circuits: In recent years, various courts of appeals have become increasingly critical of the "in part" analysis. The earliest, most outspoken critic of the "in part" test has been the First Circuit, which in *NLRB* v. *Billen Shoe Co., Inc.,* 297 F.2d 801, 68 LRRM 2699 (1st Cir. 1968), examined the Board's application of the "in part" analysis and found it lacking. Fundamental to its rejection of the "in part" test is the court's view that the test ignores the legitimate business motive of the employer and places the union activist in an almost impregnable position once union animus has been established.

. . .

. . . [T]he conflict over which test to apply in dual motive cases has now spread throughout the circuit courts to the extent that a review of the tests currently applied by the Board, our Administrative Law Judges, and the various courts of appeals reveals a picture of confusion and inconsistency.

. . .

We note that our citation of the foregoing cases is intended neither to explain nor vindicate the position expressed by any particular circuit court. Rather, it is intended to demonstrate that in an area fundamental to the Act, namely, Section 8(a)(3), disagreement and controversy are rampant among the various decisionmaking bodies.

IV. The Mt. Healthy Test: As the preceding two sections have demonstrated, the issue of what causation test is to be used to determine whether the Act has been violated in dual motivation cases is now in a position where some view the "in part" test as standing at one extreme, while the other extreme is represented by the "dominant motive" test first advanced by the First Circuit. Despite this perceived polarization, room for accommodation and clarification does exist in the test of causality set forth in the recent Supreme Court decision of *Mt. Healthy City School District Board of Education* v. *Doyle,* 429 U.S. 274.

The *Mt. Healthy* case arose when Doyle, an untenured teacher, brought suit against the Mt. Healthy School Board, alleging that it had wrongfully refused to renew his contract. The school board presented Doyle with written reasons for their refusal. The two reasons cited were: (1) Doyle's use of obscene language and gestures in the school cafeteria, and (2) Doyle's conveyance of a change in the school's policies to a local radio station. In his suit, Doyle alleged that the refusal to renew his contract violated his rights under the first and fourteenth amendments. He sought reinstatement and backpay.

The district court found that of the two reasons cited by the school board, one involved unprotected conduct while the second was clearly protected by the first and fourteenth amendments. The district court reasoned that since protected activity had played a substantial part in the school board's decision, its refusal to renew the contract was improper and Doyle was, therefore, entitled to reinstatement and backpay. The court of appeals affirmed, per curiam.

The Supreme Court reversed. In a unanimous opinion, the Court rejected the lower court's application of such a limited "in part" test and ruled that the school board must be given an opportunity to establish that its decision not to renew would have been the same if the protected activity had not occurred. The Court reasoned as follows:

"A rule of causation which focuses solely on whether protected conduct played a part, 'substantial' or otherwise, in a decision not to rehire, could place an employee in a better position as a result of the exercise of constitutionally protected conduct than he would have occupied had he done nothing. The difficulty with the rule enunciated by the District Court is that it would require reinstatement in cases where a dramatic and perhaps abrasive incident is inevitably on the minds of those responsible for the decision to rehire and does indeed play a part in that decision—even if the same decision would have been reached had the incident not occurred. The constitutional principle at stake is sufficiently vindicated if such an employee is placed in no worse a position than if he had not engaged in the conduct. A borderline or marginal candidate should not have the employment question resolved against him because of constitutionally protected conduct. But that same candidate ought not to be able, by engaging in such conduct, to prevent his employer from assessing his performance record and reaching a decision not to rehire on the basis of that record, simply because the protected conduct makes the employer more certain of the correctness of its decisions."

From this rationale, the Court fashioned the following test to be applied on remand:

"Initially, in this case, the burden was properly placed upon respondent [employee] to show that his conduct was constitutionally protected, and that this conduct was a 'substantial factor'—or, to put it in other words, that it was a 'motivating factor' in the [School] Board's decision not to rehire him. Respondent having carried that burden, however, the District Court should have gone on to determine whether the Board had shown by a preponderance of the evidence that it would have reached the same decision as to respondent's reemployment even in the absence of the protected conduct."

Thus, the Court established a two-part test to be applied in a dual motivation context. Initially, the employee must establish that the protected conduct was a "substantial" or "motivating" factor. Once this is accomplished, the burden shifts to the employer to demonstrate that it would have reached the same decision absent the protected conduct.

This test in *Mt. Healthy* is further explicatd by the Court in *Village of Arlington Heights* v. *Metropolitan Housing Development Corp.*, 429 U.S. 252 (1977), a case decided the same day as *Mt. Healthy*. A brief discussion of *Arlington Heights* is helpful in examining the parameters of the *Mt. Healthy* test.

Arlington Heights involved an effort by a real estate developer to obtain a zoning change enabling it to construct a housing development. During the zoning hearing, it became apparent that the new development would be racially integrated. The Village ultimately denied the rezoning and, in response, a group brought suit seeking injunctive and declaratory relief alleging that the decision was racially motivated. The Supreme Court ruled that plaintiffs had "failed to carry their burden of proving that discriminatory purpose was a motivating factor in the Village's decision."

In reaching its decision, the Court invoked the *Mt. Healthy* test. Thus, the Court, citing *Mt. Healthy*, stated that:

> "Proof that the decision by the Village was motivated in part by a racially discriminatory purpose would not necessarily have required invalidation of the challenged decision. Such proof would, however, have shifted to the Village the burden of establishing that the same decision would have resulted even had the impermissible purpose not been considered."

The *Arlington Heights* decision is instructive in one other respect as well. For in its decision, the Court recognized that efforts to determine what is the "dominant" or "primary" motive in a mixed motivation situation are usually unavailing. In this regard, the Court stated that a plaintiff is not required

> "to prove that the challenged action rested solely on racially discriminatory purposes. Rarely can it be said that a legislature or administrative body operating under a broad mandate made a decision motivated solely by a single concern, or even that a particular purpose was the 'dominant' or 'primary' one."

Assuming for the moment that the *Mt. Healthy* test is applicable to dual motive discharges under Section 8(a)(3), it is evident that *Mt. Healthy* represents a rejection of an "in part" test which stops with the establishment of a prima facie case or at consideration of an improper motive. Indeed, rejection of such an "in part" test is implicit in the Supreme Court's reversal of the district court's application of such an analysis.

The "dominant motive" test fares no better under *Mt. Healthy*. While a surface similarity between *Mt. Healthy* and the "dominant motive" test exists in that both reject a limited "in part" analysis and both require proof of how the employer would have acted in the absence of the protected activity, the similarity ends there. For the *Mt. Healthy* test and the "dominant motive" test place the burden for this proof on different parties.

As has been noted, under the "dominant motive" test it is the General Counsel who, in addition to establishing a prima facie showing of unlawful motive, is further required to rebut the employer's asserted defense by demonstrating that the discharge would not have taken place in the absence of the employees' protected activities. However, it is made abundantly clear in Mt. Healthy (and was specifically reiterated in Arlington Heights) that after an employee or, here, the General Counsel makes out a prima facie case of employer reliance upon protected activity, the burden shifts to the employer to demonstrate that the decision would have been the same in the absence of protected activity. This distinction is a crucial one since the decision as to who bears this burden can be determinative.

The "dominant motive" test is further undermined by the Arlington Heights decision. As noted above, the Court in Arlington Heights eschewed the "dominant motive" analysis by specifically stating that it is practically impossible to examine a dual motivation decision and arrive at a conclusion as to what was the "dominant" or "primary" purpose or motive. Finally, the shifting burden analysis set forth in Mt. Healthy and Arlington Heights represents a recognition of the practical reality that the employer is the party with the best access to proof of its motivation.

V. Application of the Mt. Healthy Test to Section 8(a)(3): In the final analysis, the applicability of the Mt. Healthy test to the NLRA depends upon its compatibility with established labor law principles and the extent to which the test reaches an accommodation between conflicting legitimate interests. . . .

. . .

Initially, support for the Mt. Healthy test of shifting burdens is found in the 1947 amendment of Section 10(c). That amendment provided that:

> "No order of the Board shall require the reinstatement of any individual as employee who has been suspended or discharged, or the payment to him of any backpay, if such individual was suspended or discharged for cause."

While the amendment itself does not address the "in part" or "dominant motive" analysis or the allocation of burdens, the legislative history does. In explaining the amendment Senator Taft stated:

> "The original House provision was that no order of the Board could require the reinstatement of any individual or employee who had been suspended or discharged, unless the weight of the evidence showed that such individual was not suspended or discharged for cause. In other words, it was turned around so as to put the entire burden on the employee to show he was not discharged for cause. Under provision of the conference report, the employer has to make the proof. That is the present rule and the present practice of the Board." [93 Cong. Rec. 6678, 2 Leg. Hist. 1595 (1947).]

The principle that "the employer has to make the proof" is also found in the Supreme Court's decision in NLRB v. Great Dane Trailers, Inc., 388 U.S. 26, 65 LRRM 2465 (1967). In that case the Court was concerned with the burden of proof in 8(a)(3) cases. It first noted that certain employer actions are inherently destructive of employee rights and, therefore, no proof of antiunion motive is required. Of course, the discharge of an employee, in and of itself, is not normally an inherently destructive act which would obviate the requirement of showing an improper motive. In this context, the Court in *Great Dane* stated that:

> "[I]f the adverse effect of the discriminatory conduct on employee rights is 'comparatively slight,' an antiunion motivation must be proved to sustain the charge *if* the employer has come forward with evidence of legitimate and substantial business justifications for the conduct. Thus . . . once it has been proved that the employer engaged in discriminatory conduct which could have adversely affected employee rights to *some* extent, the burden is upon the employer to establish that he was motivated by legitimate objectives since proof of motivation is most accessible to him."

Thus, both Congress and the Supreme Court have implicitly sanctioned the shift of burden called for in *Mt. Healthy* in the context of Section 8(a)(3).[11]

Indeed, as is indicated by the above quotation of legislative history and the citation of *Great Dane*, the shifting burden process in *Mt. Healthy* is consistent with the process envisioned by Congress and the Supreme Court to resolve discrimination cases, although the process has not been articulated formally in the manner set forth in *Mt. Healthy*. Similarly, it is the process used by the Board. Thus, the Board's decisional process traditionally has involved, first, an inquiry as to whether protected activities played a role in the employer's decision. If so, the inquiry then focuses on whether any "legitimate business reason" asserted by the employer is sufficiently proven to be the cause of the discipline to negate the General Counsel's showing of prohibited motivation.[12] Thus, while the Board's process has not been couched in the language of *Mt. Healthy*, the two methods of analysis are essentially the same.

Perhaps most important for our purposes, however, is the fact that the *Mt. Healthy* procedure accommodates the legitimate competing interests inherent in dual motivation cases, while at the same time serving to effectuate the policies and objectives of Section 8(a)(3) of the Act. . . .

. . .

Under the *Mt. Healthy* test, the aggrieved employee is afforded protection since he or she is only required initially to show that protected activities played a role in the employer's decision. Also, the employer is provided with a formal framework within which to establish its asserted legitimate justification. In this context, it is the employer which has "to

[11]It should be noted that this shifting of burden does not undermine the established concept that the General Counsel must establish an unfair labor practice by a preponderance of the evidence. The shifting burden merely requires the employer to make out what is actually an affirmative defense to overcome the prima facie case of wrongful motive. Such a requirement does not shift the ultimate burden.

[12]The absence of any legitimate basis for an action, of course, may form part of the proof of the General Counsel's case.

make the proof." Under this analysis, should the employer be able to demonstrate that the discipline or other action would have occurred absent protected activities, the employee cannot justly complain if the employer's action is upheld. Similarly, if the employer cannot make the necessary showing, it should not be heard to object to the employee's being made whole because its action will have been found to have been motivated by an unlawful consideration in a manner consistent with congressional intent, Supreme Court precedent, and established Board processes.

Finally, we find it to be of substantial importance that our explication of this test of causation will serve to alleviate the intolerable confusion in the 8(a)(3) area. In this regard, we believe that this test will provide litigants and the decisionmaking bodies with a uniform test to be applied in these 8(a)(3) cases.[13]

Thus, for the reasons set forth above, we shall henceforth employ the following causation test in all cases alleging violation of Section 8(a)(3) or violations of Section 8(a)(l) turning on employer motivation. First, we shall require that the General Counsel make a prima facie showing sufficient to support the inference that protected conduct was a "motivating factor" in the employer's decision. Once this is established, the burden will shift to the employer to demonstrate that the same action would have taken place even in the absence of the protected conduct.[14]

Finally, inherent in the adoption of the foregoing analysis is our recognition of the advantage of clearing the air by abandoning the "in part" language in expressing our conclusion as to whether the Act was violated. Yet, our abandonment of this familiar phraseology should not be viewed as a repudiation of the well-established principles and concepts which we have applied in the past. For, as noted at the outset of this Decision, our task in resolving cases alleging violations which turn on motivation is to determine whether a causal relationship existed between employees engaging in union or other protected activities and actions on the part of their employer which detrimentally affect such employees' employment. Indeed, it bears repeating that the "in part" test, the "dominant motive" test, and the *Mt. Healthy* test all share a fundamental common denominator in that the objective of each is to determine the relationship, if any, between employer action and protected employee conduct. Until now, in making this determination we frequently have employed the term "in part." But in so doing it only was a term used in pursuit of our goal which is to analyze thoroughly and completely the justification presented by the employer. It is, however, our considered view that adoption of the *Mt.*

---

[13]Still an additional benefit which will result from our use of the *Mt. Healthy* test is that the perceived significance in distinguishing between pretext and dual motive cases will be obviated.

[14]In this regard we note that in those instances where, after all the evidence has been submitted, the employer has been unable to carry its burden, we will not seek to quantitatively analyze the effect of the unlawful cause once it has been found. It is enough that the employees' protected activities are causally related to the employer action which is the basis of the complaint. Whether that "cause" was the straw that broke the camel's back or a bullet between the eyes, if it was enough to determine events, it is enough to come within the proscription of the Act.

Healthy test, with its more precise and formalized framework for making this analysis, will serve to provide the necessary clarification of our decisional processes while continuing to advance the fundamental purposes and objectives of the Act.

VI. Application of the Mt. Healthy Test to the Facts of the Instant Case: In the instant case, the General Counsel alleges that Respondent discharged Bernard Lamoureux in violation of Section 8(a)(3) and (1) of the Act. Respondent denies this allegation, asserting that Lamoureux was discharged for violating a plant rule against "knowingly altering, or falsifying production time reports, payroll records, time cards." The Administrative Law Judge found that Respondent's discharge of Lamoureux violated Section 8(a)(3) and (1) of the Act. For the reasons set forth below, we agree.

. . .

. . . [W]e conclude that the General Counsel made a prima facie showing that Lamoureux's union activity was a motivating factor in Respondent's decision to discharge him. Our conclusion is based on Respondent's union animus, as reflected in the hostility directed toward Lamoureux resulting from his active role in the union campaign, as well as the timing of the discharge, which occurred shortly after completion of the latest union election. Also of significance is Respondent's sudden and unexplained departure from its usual practice of declining to discharge employees for their first violation of this nature. Such action here is especially suspect in light of Lamoureux's admirable work record and the fact that his timesheet discrepancies neither inured to his benefit nor served to affect detrimentally Respondent's production control system.

We further find that Respondent has failed to demonstrate that it would have taken the same action against Lamoureux in the absence of his engaging in union activities. In this regard we note that the record discrepancies were only discovered by Forte following the plant supervisor's directive to "check" on Lamoureux, despite the fact that Respondent had no reason to believe that Lamoureux was untrustworthy. Under the circumstances, such actions suggest a predetermined plan to discover a reason to discharge Lamoureux and thus rid the facility of a union activist. Further undermining Respondent's defense is the evidence which demonstrates disparate treatment. As noted previously, the only instances where discharge was imposed by Respondent as a result of "record discrepancies" were where the employee in question sought to embezzle funds or collect fraudulent sales commissions. Lamoureux's infraction clearly did not rise to such a level. Indeed, the record demonstrates that such record discrepancies were commonplace and generally resulted in no discipline whatsoever. In those instances where discipline was imposed, Respondent issued warnings or other forms of discipline short of discharge.

Accordingly, for the reasons noted above, we find that Respondent's discharge of Bernard Lamoureux violated Section 8(a)(3) and (1) of the Act.

JENKINS, MEMBER, concurring:

I am willing to apply the shifting burden-of-proof standard my colleagues adopt for determining whether a discharge was caused by an unlawful purpose where the discharge may have had more than one cause, not all of them unlawful. This standard may suffice for most cases. However, there may remain a residue, perhaps small, of cases of mixed motive or cause, where the purposes are so interlocked that it is not possible to point to one of them as "the" cause. All of them, both lawful and unlawful, may have combined to push the employer to the decision he would not have reached if even one were absent. In such cases, it is plainly not the latest event, the most recent purpose, which is the cause of the discharge; rather, it is all of them together, from earliest to latest, which cause the discharge.

Where the evidence does not permit the isolation of a single event or motive as the cause of the discharge, then plainly the unlawful motive must be deemed to be part of the cause of the discharge, and the discharge is unlawful. . . .

Notes

1. Any legal rule should be viewed in light of its alternatives. For many years the Board held that a violation would be found even if the employer acted from both a legitimate as well as an illegitimate motive. The *Wright Line* standard conceptually begins from the assumption that unlawful discrimination exists when action is based in whole or in part on anti-union animus. Under the new standard, however, an employer who acted in part for unlawful reasons can nevertheless avoid an unfair labor practice charge by establishing that the discharge would have occurred even if the forbidden motive had been absent. The Supreme Court recently upheld the Board's placing of this burden upon the employer. *NLRB* v. *Transportation Management Corp.*, 462 U.S. ____, 113 LRRM 2857 (1983). As the Court noted:

"The employer is the wrongdoer; he has acted out of a motive that is declared illegitimate by the statute. It is fair that he bear the risk that the influence of legal and illegal motives cannot be separated, because he knowingly created the risk and because the risk was created not by innocent activity but by his own wrongdoing."

Apart from procedural issues, consider the functional difference between *Wright Line* and a rule holding that the presence of *any* anti-union animus constitutes an unfair labor practice. What difference does *Wright Line* make? As an initial proposition, why does Section 8(a)(3) require a showing of motive in the first place? Is it conceivable to consider Section 8(a)(3) violated whenever the *effect* instead of the intent of a discharge or other adverse action is to "discourage or encourage membership in any labor organization?"

2. The Board and courts treat Section 8(a)(1) as limited by the analytic framework imposed on Section 8(a)(3). Is this a matter of statutory construction or policy? What do you make of the following extracts from the Legislative History of the National Labor Relations Act of 1935?

"Section 8(1): This is a blanket unfair labor practice, to protect the rights cited in section 7. . . . Such a general unfair practice is necessary, since the courts may emasculate or construe very narrowly some one of the following specific unfair practices. Furthermore, employers will doubtless find methods of interference, etc., which are not specifically recited in the other unfair practices, but are just as effective in impeding self-organization and collective bargaining. Thus, subdivisions (2), (3), and (4) and [sic] are not exclusive, and, furthermore do not limit the general scope of subdivisions (1)." (Analysis prepared for Senate Committee on Education and Labor.)

"Long experience has proved . . . that courts and administrative agencies have difficulties in enforcing these general declarations of right in the absence of greater statutory particularity. Therefore, without in any way placing limitations upon the broadest reasonable interpretation of its omnibus guaranty of freedom, the bill refers in greater detail to a few of the practices which have proved the most fertile sources for evading or obstructing the purpose of the law." (Statement by Senator Wagner.)

Compare the decision in *NLRB* v. *Burnup & Sims*, 379 U.S. 21, 57 LRRM 2385 (1964), in which an employer fired two employees who reportedly threatened to use dynamite, if necessary, to achieve recognition of a union. The Board found that although the threat had never been made, the employer acted in good faith, and concluded that Sections 8(a)(3) and (1) were violated. The Supreme Court upheld the Board's order, requiring back pay and reinstatement, on the basis of the Section 8(a)(1) violation and did not discuss the application of Section 8(a)(3):

"Section 7 grants employees, inter alia, 'the right to self-organization, to form, join, or assist labor organizations.' Defeat of those rights by employer action does not necessarily depend on the existence of anti-union bias. . . . In sum, Section 8(a)(1) is violated if it is shown that the discharged employee was at the time engaged in protected activity, that the employer knew it was such, that the basis of the discharge was an alleged act of misconduct in the course of that activity, and that the employee was not, in fact, guilty of that misconduct.

"That rule seems to be in conformity with the policy behind Section 8(a)(1). Otherwise the protected activity would lose some of its immunity, since the example of employees who are discharged on false charges would or might have a deterrent effect on other employees. Union activity often engenders strong emotions and gives rise to active rumors. A protected activity acquires a precarious status, if innocent employees can be discharged while engaging in it, even though the employer acts in good faith. It is the tendency of those discharges to weaken or destroy the Section 8(a)(1) right that is controlling. . . . Had the alleged dynamiting threats been wholly disassociated from Section 7 activities quite different considerations might apply."

3. The traditional understanding of the employment relationship was that, absent a statutory restriction on employer discretion, companies were free to hire and fire at will. That understanding is being eroded by recent state court decisions recognizing tort and contract actions for wrongful discharge.* The basis for application of common law tort doctrines is explained in this excerpt from *Sheets* v. *Teddy's Frosted Foods,* 179 Conn. 471, 427 A.2d 385 (1980), in which the plaintiff alleged retaliatory dismissal for insisting that the company comply with a state statute regulating the labeling of foods:

"It would be difficult to maintain that the right to discharge an employee hired at will is so fundamentally different from other contract rights that its exercise is never subject to judicial scrutiny regardless of how outrageous, how violative of public policy, the employer's conduct may be. Cf. General Statutes § 31–126 (unfair employment practices). The defendant does not seriously contest the propriety of cases in other jurisdictions that have found wrongful and actionable a discharge in retaliation for the exercise of an employee's right to: (1) refuse to commit perjury; *Petermann* v. *International Brotherhood of Teamsters,* 174 Cal. App.2d 184, 189, 344 P.2d 25 (1959); (2) file a workmen's compensation claim; *Frampton* v. *Central Indiana Gas Co.,* 260 Ind. 249, 252, 297 N.E.2d 425 (1973); *Sventko* v. *Kroger Co.,* 69 Mich. App. 644, 648–49, 245 N.W.2d 151 (1976); *Brown* v. *Transcon Lines,* 284 Or. 597, 603, 588 P.2d 1087 (1978); (3) engage in union activity; *Glenn* v. *Clearman's Golden Cock Inn, Inc.,* 192 Cal. App.2d 793, 798, 13 Cal. Rptr. 769 (1961); (4) perform jury duty; *Nees* v. *Hocks,* 272 Or. 210, 216–19, 536 P.2d 512 (1975); *Reuther* v. *Fowler & Williams, Inc.,* 255 Pa. Super. 28, 386 A.2d 119, 120 (1978). While it may be true that these cases are supported by mandates of public policy derived directly from the applicable state statutes and constitutions, it is equally true that they serve at a minimum to establish the principle that public policy imposes some limits on unbridled discretion to terminate the employment of someone hired at will. See Blades, *Employment at Will vs. Individual Freedom: On Limiting the Abusive Exercise of Employer Power,* 67 Colum. L. Rev. 1404 (1967); Blumberg, *Corporate Responsibility and the Employee's Duty of Loyalty and Obedience: A Preliminary Inquiry,* 24 Okla. L. Rev. 279, 307–318 (1971). . . .

"The issue then becomes the familiar common-law problem of deciding where and how to draw the line between claims that genuinely involve the mandates of public policy and are actionable, and ordinary disputes between employee and employer that are not. We are mindful that courts should not lightly intervene to impair the exercise of managerial discretion or to foment unwarranted litigation. We are, however,

---

*This issue is explored in *Legislation Protecting the Individual Employee* which is Unit 2 of this Casebook series.

equally mindful that the myriad of employees without the bargaining power to command employment contracts for a definite term are entitled to a modicum of judicial protection when their conduct as good citizens is punished by their employers. . . ."

The "modicum of judicial protection" afforded employees in *Sheets* and other wrongful discharge cases does not require the employer to present a proper reason for dismissal. The employer is responsible in damages only if the former employee proves a demonstrably improper reason for dismissal.

The claim that termination of an employee constitutes a breach of contract rests on "whether the actions or omissions complained of constitute a violation of duties imposed by law, or of duties arising by virtue of the alleged expressed agreements between the parties." *Malone* v. *University of Kansas Medical Center*, 220 Kan. 371, 374, 552 P.2d 885, 888 (1976). For example, in *Weiner* v. *McGraw Hill, Inc.*, 57 N.Y.2d 458 (NYLJ, 12/1/82), the Court of Appeals (the State's highest court) recognized a cause of action for breach of contract based on a company's alleged failure to comply with the just cause dismissal provision in its personnel handbook. Does the availability of a contract action constitute a significant restraint on the exercise of managerial discretion since companies may be required to retain marginally productive employees? Or is the interference with business decisions illusory since the basis for the claim is the company's voluntary undertaking to its employees? What advice can you give to a company which desires to recruit talented personnel with assurances of continued employment, but also wants to retain the right to fire employees at will? Can a general disclaimer in a personnel handbook, reserving the company's right to amend or withdraw personnel policies, override a just cause dismissal provision?

Ought the law impose on companies the obligation to discharge employees only if good cause exists? Would such a provision limit a company's right to terminate employees because of a change in business operations? Because the company is able to hire other workers for less?

4. On June 22, 1982, the International Labor Organization adopted the "Termination of Employment Convention, 1982," which provides in Article 4 that: "The employment of a worker shall not be terminated unless there is a valid reason for such termination connected with the capacity or conduct of the worker or based on the operational requirements of the undertaking, establishment or service." However, Article 10 of the Convention provides, as a remedy, that: "If the bodies referred to in Article 8 of this Convention [a court, labor tribunal, arbitration committee or arbitrator] find that termination is unjustified and *if they are not empowered or do not find it practicable, in accordance with national law and practice, to* declare the termination invalid and/or *order* or propose *reinstatement of the worker, they shall be empowered to order payment of adequate compensation* or such other relief as may be deemed appropriate." (Emphasis added.)

Since this Convention makes the remedy of reinstatement for an unjust discharge dependent on national law and practice, it is interesting to compare the national law and practice of the U.S. on this legal issue with the national laws and practices of other industrialized countries. As shown by the following findings in a study of this issue, the national law and practice of the U.S. already provides more legal protection on this issue to unjustly discharged workers than the national laws and practices of the Common Market countries:

> "[T]he question [of] whether the U.S. should adopt a statute to protect unorganized employees against unfair dismissal has arisen in recent years. Some American authors have contended that such a statute should be adopted, and to some extent these proponents rely on the law of Western Europe to support their contention. However, the law as applied in actual practice in most Common Market countries does not provide a good model for the U.S. if reinstatement of unfairly dismissed non-union employees is an objective. Sherman, *Reinstatement as a Remedy for Unfair Dismissal in Common Market Countries*, 29 Am. J. Comp. L. 467 (1981). Under current law and practice the U.S. provides a remedy of reinstatement for unjustly discharged employees far more widely than is provided in most of Western Europe. *Id.* at footnote 161. [I]n actual practice no Common Market country requires employers to reinstate most of the employees who are found by a government body (court, tribunal or board) to have been unfairly dismissed. On the contrary, in every Common Market country (with the possible exception of Italy) only a small percentage of such employees, if any, are reinstated pursuant to government rulings. Thus in this sense the overwhelming majority of employees do not have job security. All Common Market countries provide by law for payment of monetary compensation to unfairly dismissed employees, at least in some circumstances. The amount of compensation varies considerably. In most Common Market countries an employer's liability in damages is so limited in practice that it does not provide much pressure to forego a contemplated dismissal. *Id.* at 507. Although the law as applied in most Common Market countries reflects the view that it is undesirable for a statute to require an employer to reinstate an unwanted employee . . . , it does not follow that a statute providing such a remedy would be socially undesirable for America. . . . American concepts of justice may call for the expansion of protection for unorganized employees. . . . *Id.* at footnote 163."

Textile Workers Union of America v. Darlington Manufacturing Co.

Supreme Court of the United States, 1965
380 U.S. 263, 58 LRRM 2657

MR. JUSTICE HARLAN delivered the opinion of the Court.

We here review judgments of the Court of Appeals setting aside and refusing to enforce an order of the National Labor Relations Board which found respondent Darlington guilty of an unfair labor practice by reason of having permanently closed its plant following petitioner union's election as the bargaining representative of Darlington's employees.

Darlington Manufacturing Company was a South Carolina corporation operating one textile mill. A majority of Darlington's stock was held by Deering Milliken, a New York "selling house" marketing textiles produced by others.[1] Deering Milliken in turn was controlled by Roger Milliken, president of Darlington, and by other members of the Milliken family.[2] The National Labor Relations Board found that the Milliken family, through Deering Milliken, operated 17 textile manufacturers, including Darlington, whose products, manufactured in 27 different mills, were marketed through Deering Milliken.

In March 1956 petitioner Textile Workers Union initiated an organizational campaign at Darlington which the company resisted vigorously in various ways, including threats to close the mill if the union won a representation election.[3] On September 6, 1956, the union won an election by a narrow margin. When Roger Milliken was advised of the union victory, he decided to call a meeting of the Darlington board of directors to consider closing the mill. Mr. Milliken testified before the Labor Board:

> "I felt that as a result of the campaign that had been conducted and the promises and statements made in these letters that had been distributed [favoring unionization], that if before we had had some hope, possible hope of achieving competitive [costs] . . . by taking advantage of new machinery that was being put in, that this hope had diminished as a result of the election because a majority of the employees had voted in favor of the union. . . ." (R. 457.)

The board of directors met on September 12 and voted to liquidate the corporation, action which was approved by the stockholders on October 17. The plant ceased operations entirely in November, and all plant machinery and equipment were sold piecemeal at auction in December.

The union filed charges with the Labor Board claiming that Darlington had violated §§ 8(a)(1) and (3) of the National Labor Relations Act by closing its plant, and § 8(a)(5) by refusing to bargain with the union after the election.[5] The Board, by a divided vote, found that Darlington had

[1]Deering Milliken & Co. owned 41 percent of the Darlington stock. Cotwool Manufacturing Corp., another textile manufacturer, owned 18 percent of the stock. In 1960 Deering Milliken & Co. was merged into Cotwool, the survivor being named Deering Milliken, Inc.

[2]The Milliken family owned only 6 percent of the Darlington stock, but held a majority stock interest in both Deering Milliken & Co. and Cotwool, see n. 1, *supra*.

[3]The Board found that Darlington had interrogated employees and threatened to close the mill if the union won the election. After the decision to liquidate was made (see *infra*), Darlington employees were told that the decision to close was caused by the election, and they were encouraged to sign a petition disavowing the union. These practices were held to violate § 8(a)(1) of the National Labor Relations Act . . . and that part of the Board decision is not challenged here.

[5]The union asked for a bargaining conference on September 12, 1956 (the day that the board of directors voted to liquidate), but was told to await certification by the Board. The union was certified on October 24, and did meet with Darlington officials in November, but no actual bargaining took place. The Board found this to be a violation of § 8(a)(5). Such a finding was in part based on the determination that the plant closing was an unfair labor practice, and no argument is made that § 8(a)(5) requires an employer to bargain concerning a purely business decision to terminate his enterprise. Cf. *Fibreboard Paper Products Corp.* v. *Labor Board,* 379 U.S. 203.

been closed because of the antiunion animus of Roger Milliken, and held that to be a violation of § 8(a)(3).[6] The Board also found Darlington to be part of a single integrated employer group controlled by the Milliken family through Deering Milliken; therefore Deering Milliken could be held liable for the unfair labor practices of Darlington. Alternatively, since Darlington was a part of the Deering Milliken enterprise, Deering Milliken had violated the Act by closing part of its business for a discriminatory purpose. The Board ordered back pay for all Darlington employees until they obtained substantially equivalent work or were put on preferential hiring lists at the other Deering Milliken mills. Respondent Deering Milliken was ordered to bargain with the union in regard to details of compliance with the Board order.

On review, the Court of Appeals, sitting *en banc*, set aside the order and denied enforcement by a divided vote. The Court of Appeals held that even accepting *arguendo* the Board's determination that Deering Milliken had the status of a single employer, a company has the absolute right to close out a part or all of its business regardless of antiunion motives. The court therefore did not review the Board's finding that Deering Milliken was a single integrated employer. We granted certiorari, 377 U.S. 903, to consider the important questions involved. We hold that so far as the Labor Relations Act is concerned, an employer has the absolute right to terminate his entire business for any reason he pleases, but disagree with the Court of Appeals that such right includes the ability to close part of a business no matter what the reason. We conclude that the cause must be remanded to the Board for further proceedings.

Preliminarily it should be observed that both petitioners argue that the Darlington closing violated § 8(a)(1) as well as § 8(a)(3) of the Act. We think, however, that the Board was correct in treating the closing only under § 8(a)(3).[8] Section 8(a)(1) provides that it is an unfair labor practice for an employer "to interfere with, restrain, or coerce employees in the exercise of clear" § 7 rights. Naturally, certain business decisions will, to some degree, interfere with concerted activities by employees. But it is only when the interference with § 7 rights outweighs the business justification for the employer's action that § 8(a)(1) is violated. See, *e.g*, *Labor Board* v. *Steelworkers,* 357 U.S. 357; *Republic Aviation Corp.* v. *Labor Board,* 324 U.S. 793. A violation of § 8(a)(1) alone therefore presupposes an act which is unlawful even absent a discriminatory motive. Whatever may be the limits of § 8(a)(1), some employer decisions are so peculiarly matters of management prerogative that they would never constitute violations of § 8(a)(1), whether or not they involved sound business judgment, unless they also violated § 8(a)(3). Thus it is not questioned in this case that an employer has the right to terminate his business, whatever the impact of such action on concerted activities, if the decision to close is motivated by

---

[6]Since the closing was held to be illegal, the Board found that the gradual discharges of all employees during November and December constituted § 8(a)(1) violations. The propriety of this determination depends entirely on whether the decision to close the plant violated § 8(a)(3).

[8]The Board did find that Darlington's discharges of employees following the decision to close violated § 8(a)(1). See n. 6, *supra*.

other than discriminatory reasons.[10] But such action, if discriminatorily motivated, is encompassed within the literal language of § 8(a)(3). We therefore deal with the Darlington closing under that section.

I.

We consider first the argument, advanced by the petitioner union but not by the Board, and rejected by the Court of Appeals, that an employer may not go completely out of business without running afoul of the Labor Relations Act if such action is prompted by a desire to avoid unionization.[11] Given the Board's findings on the issue of motive, acceptance of this contention would carry the day for the Board's conclusion that the closing of this plant was an unfair labor practice, even on the assumption that Darlington is to be regarded as an independent unrelated employer. A proposition that a single businessman cannot choose to go out of business if he wants to would represent such a startling innovation that it should not be entertained without the clearest manifestation of legislative intent or unequivocal judicial precedent so construing the Labor Relations Act. We find neither.

So far as legislative manifestation is concerned, it is sufficient to say that there is not the slightest indication in the history of the Wagner Act or of the Taft-Hartley Act that Congress envisaged any such result under either statute.

As for judicial precedent, the Board recognized that "[t]here is no decided case directly dispositive of Darlington's claim that it had an absolute right to close its mill, irrespective of motive." 139 NLRB, at 250. The only language by this Court in any way adverting to this problem is found in *Southport Petroleum Co.* v. *Labor Board*, 315 U.S. 100, 106, where it was stated:

> "Whether there was a *bona fide* discontinuance and a true change of ownership—which would terminate the duty of reinstatement created by the Board's order—or merely a disguised continuance of the old employer, does not clearly appear. . . ."

The courts of appeals have generally assumed that a complete cessation of business will remove an employer from future coverage by the Act. Thus the Court of Appeals said in these cases: The Act "does not compel a person to become or remain an employee. It does not compel one to become or remain an employer. Either may withdraw from that status with immunity, so long as the obligations of any employment contract

---

[10]It is also clear that the ambiguous act of closing a plant following the election of a union is not, absent an inquiry into the employer's motive, inherently discriminatory. We are thus not confronted with a situation where the employer "must be held to intend the very consequences which foreseeably and inescapably flow from his actions . . ." (*Labor Board* v. *Erie Resistor Corp.*, 373 U.S. 221, 228), in which the Board could find a violation of § 8(a)(3) without an examination into motive. See *Radio Officers* v. *Labor Board*, 347 U.S. 17, 42–43; *Teamster's Local* v. *Labor Board*, 365 U.S. 667, 674–676.

[11]The Board predicates its argument on the finding that Deering Milliken was an integrated enterprise, and does not consider it necessary to argue that an employer may not go completely out of business for antiunion reasons. Brief for National Labor Relations Board, p. 3, n. 2.

have been met." 325 F.2d, at 685. The Eighth Circuit, in *Labor Board* v. *New Madrid Mfg. Co.*, 215 F.2d 908, 914, was equally explicit:

"But none of this can be taken to mean that an employer does not have the absolute right, at all times, to permanently close and go out of business . . . for whatever reason he may choose, whether union animosity or anything else, and without his being thereby left subject to a remedial liability under the Labor Management Relations Act for such unfair labor practices as he may have committed in the enterprise, except up to the time that such actual and permanent closing . . . has occurred."

The AFL-CIO suggests in its *amicus* brief that Darlington's action was similar to a discriminatory lockout, which is prohibited " 'because designed to frustrate organizational efforts, to destroy or undermine bargaining representation, or to evade the duty to bargain.' " One of the purposes of the Labor Relations Act is to prohibit the discriminatory use of economic weapons in an effort to obtain future benefits. The discriminatory lockout designed to destroy a union, like a "runaway shop," is a lever which has been used to discourage collective employee activities in the future. But a complete liquidation of a business yields no such future benefit for the employer, if the termination is bona fide.[14] It may be motivated more by spite against the union than by business reasons, but it is not the type of discrimination which is prohibited by the Act. The personal satisfaction that such an employer may derive from standing on his beliefs and the mere possibility that other employers will follow his example are surely too remote to be considered dangers at which the labor statutes were aimed.[15] Although employees may be prohibited from engaging in a strike under certain conditions, no one would consider it a violation of the Act for the same employees to quit their employment *en masse*, even if motivated by a desire to ruin the employer. The very permanence of such action would negate any future economic benefit to the employees. The employer's right to go out of business is no different.

We are not presented here with the case of a "runaway shop,"[16] whereby Darlington would transfer its work to another plant or open a new plant in another locality to replace its closed plant.[17] Nor are we concerned with a shutdown where the employees, by renouncing the union, could cause the plant to reopen. Such cases would involve discriminatory employer action for the purpose of obtaining some benefit from

---

[14]The Darlington property and equipment could not be sold as a unit, and were eventually auctioned off piecemeal. We therefore are not confronted with a sale of a going concern, which might present different considerations under §§ 8(a)(3) and (5). Cf. *John Wiley & Sons, Inc.* v. *Livingston,* 376 U.S. 543: *Labor Board* v. *Deena Artware, Inc.,* 361 U.S. 398.

[15] Cf. NLRA § 8(c), 29 U.S.C. § 158(c) (1958 ed.). Different considerations would arise were it made to appear that the closing employer was acting pursuant to some arrangement or understanding with other employers to discourage employee organizational activities in their businesses.

[16]*E.g., Labor Board* v. *Preston Feed Corp.,* 309 F.2d 346; *Labor Board* v. *Wallick,* 198 F.2d 477. An analogous problem is presented where a department is closed for antiunion reasons but the work is continued by independent contractors. (Citations omitted.)

[17]After the decision to close the plant, Darlington accepted no new orders, and merely continued operations for a time to fill pending orders. 139 NLRB, at 244.

the employees in the future.[19] We hold here only that when an employer closes his entire business, even if the liquidation is motivated by vindictiveness toward the union, such action is not an unfair labor practice.[20]

II.

While we thus agree with the Court of Appeals that viewing Darlington as an independent employer the liquidation of its business was not an unfair labor practice, we cannot accept the lower court's view that the same conclusion necessarily follows if Darlington is regarded as an integral part of the Deering Milliken enterprise.

The closing of an entire business, even though discriminatory, ends the employer-employee relationship; the force of such a closing is entirely spent as to that business when termination of the enterprise takes place. On the other hand, a discriminatory partial closing may have repercussions on what remains of the business, affording employer leverage for discouraging the free exercise of § 7 rights among remaining employees of much the same kind as that found to exist in the "runaway shop" and "temporary closing" cases. See *supra*, pp. 272–273. Moreover, a possible remedy open to the Board in such a case, like the remedies available in the "runaway shop" and "temporary closing" cases, is to order reinstatement of the discharged employees in the other parts of the business. No such remedy is available when an entire business has been terminated. By analogy to those cases involving a continuing enterprise we are con-

[19]All of the cases to which we have been cited involved closings found to have been motivated, at least in part, by the expectation of achieving future benefits. . . . The two cases which are urged as indistinguishable from *Darlington* are *Labor Board* v. *Savoy Laundry*, 327 F.2d 370, and *Labor Board* v. *Missouri Transit Co.*, 250 F.2d 261. In *Savoy Laundry* the employer operated one laundry plant where he processed both retail laundry pickups and wholesale laundering. Once the laundry was marked, all of it was processed together. After some of the employees organized, the employer discontinued most of the wholesale service, and thereafter discharged some of his employees. There was no separate wholesale department, and the discriminatory motive was obviously to discourage unionization in the entire plant. *Missouri Transit* presents a similar situation. A bus company operated an interstate line and an intrastate shuttle service connecting a military base with the interstate terminal. When the union attempted to organize all of the drivers, the shuttle service was sold and the shuttle drivers were discharged. Although the two services were treated as separate departments, it is clear from the facts of the case that the union was attempting to organize all of the drivers, and the discriminatory motive of the employer was to discourage unionization in the interstate services as well as the shuttle service.

[20]Nothing we have said in this opinion would justify an employer's interfering with employee organizational activities by threatening to close his plant, as distinguished from announcing a decision to close already reached by the board of directors or other management authority empowered to make such a decision. We recognize that this safeguard does not wholly remove the possibility that our holding may result in some deterrent effect on organizational activities independent of that arising from the closing itself. An employer may be encouraged to make a definitive decision to close on the theory that its mere announcement before a representation election will discourage the employees from voting for the union, and thus his decision may not have to be implemented. Such a possibility is not likely to occur, however, except in a marginal business; a solidly successful employer is not apt to hazard the possibility that the employees will call his bluff by voting to organize. We see no practical way of eliminating this possible consequence of our holding short of allowing the Board to order an employer who chooses so to gamble with his employees not to carry out his announced intention to close. We do not consider the matter of sufficient significance in the overall labor-management relations picture to require or justify a decision different from the one we have made.

strained to hold, in disagreement with the Court of Appeals, that a partial closing is an unfair labor practice under § 8(a)(3) if motivated by a purpose to chill unionism in any of the remaining plants of the single employer and if the employer may reasonably have foreseen that such closing would likely have that effect.

While we have spoken in terms of a "partial closing" in the context of the Board's finding that Darlington was part of a larger single enterprise controlled by the Milliken family, we do not mean to suggest that an organizational integration of plants or corporations is a necessary prerequisite to the establishment of such a violation of § 8(a)(3). If the persons exercising control over a plant that is being closed for antiunion reasons (1) have an interest in another business, whether or not affiliated with or engaged in the same line of commercial activity as the closed plant, of sufficient substantiality to give promise of their reaping a benefit from the discouragement of unionization in that business; (2) act to close their plant with the purpose of producing such a result; and (3) occupy a relationship to the other business which makes it realistically foreseeable that its employees will fear that such business will also be closed down if they persist in organizational activities, we think that an unfair labor practice has been made out.

Although the Board's single employer finding necessarily embraced findings as to Roger Milliken and the Milliken family which, if sustained by the Court of Appeals, would satisfy the elements of "interest" and "relationship" with respect to other parts of the Deering Milliken enterprise, that and the other Board findings fall short of establishing the factors of "purpose" and "effect" which are vital requisites of the general principles that govern a case of this kind.

Thus, the Board's findings as to the purpose and foreseeable effect of the Darlington closing pertained *only* to its impact on the Darlington employees. No findings were made as to the purpose and effect of the closing with respect to the employees in the other plants comprising the Deering Milliken group. It does not suffice to establish the unfair labor practice charged here to argue that the Darlington closing necessarily had an adverse impact upon unionization in such other plants. We have heretofore observed that employer action which has a foreseeable consequence of discouraging concerted activities generally does not amount to a violation of § 8(a)(3) in the absence of a showing of motivation which is aimed at achieving the prohibited effect. See *Teamsters Local* v. *Labor Board*, 365 U.S. 667, and the concurring opinion therein, at 677. In an area which trenches so closely upon otherwise legitimate employer prerogatives, we consider the absence of Board findings on this score a fatal defect in its decision. The Court of Appeals for its part did not deal with the question of purpose and effect at all, since it concluded that an employer's right to close down his entire business because of distaste for unionism, also embraced a partial closing so motivated.

Apart from this, the Board's holding should not be accepted or rejected without court review of its single employer finding, judged, however, in accordance with the general principles set forth above. Review of that finding, which the lower court found unnecessary on its view of the cause, now becomes necessary in light of our holding in this part of our opinion, and is a task that devolves upon the Court of Appeals in the first instance. *Universal Camera Corp.* v. *Labor Board,* 340 U.S. 474.

In these circumstances, we think the proper disposition of this cause is to require that it be remanded to the Board so as to afford the Board the opportunity to make further findings on the issue of purpose and effect. See, *e.g., Labor Board* v. *Virginia Elec. & Power Co.,* 314 U.S. 469, 479–480. This is particularly appropriate here since the cases involve issues of first impression. If such findings are made, the cases will then be in a posture for further review by the Court of Appeals on all issues. Accordingly, without intimating any view as to how any of these matters should eventuate, we vacate the judgments of the Court of Appeals and remand the cases to that court with instructions to remand them to the Board for further proceedings consistent with this opinion.

MR. JUSTICE STEWART took no part in the decision of these cases.

MR. JUSTICE GOLDBERG took no part in the consideration or decision of these cases.

Notes

1. The Aftermath of *Darlington:* On remand the NLRB concluded that the record supported findings that Deering Milliken was a single employer, which satisfied the interest and relationship test; that the result of the election was a substantial cause of Darlington's closing; that the employer was motivated by a purpose to chill unionism at other Deering Milliken locations; and that the foreseeable effect of the Darlington closing would be fear of closings at other mills if those employees engaged in organizing. *Darlington Manufacturing Co.,* 165 NLRB 1074, 65 LRRM 1391 (1967). A majority of the Court of Appeals for the Fourth Circuit upheld the Board, 397 F.2d 760, 68 LRRM 2356 (4th Cir. 1968), *cert. denied,* 393 U.S. 1023 (1969).

Evidence which supported the position that the closing violated Section 8(a)(3) included:

1) Precampaign speeches to South Carolina government and business leaders, in which Roger Milliken indicated his intense concerns with the need to preserve "cooperation between management and labor. . . at all costs," and with unionism, which he regarded as a threat to the southern industrial community.

2) The dispatch with which Milliken closed the plant and auctioned off the machinery.

3) Evidence that news of the Darlington closing spread rapidly to other Deering Milliken plants and was discussed, frequently in terms of "Mr. Milliken would not operate a plant under a union."

4) Milliken's distribution of copies of published comments on the Darlington situation to all Deering mill officials, urging the officials to undertake a "public relations" program to make the community leaders understand the consequences of unionization. One reprint was an article from a trade magazine entitled, *Darlington Situation Becomes Object Lesson to*

All Concerned. Another reprint was an editorial from *America's Textile Reporter,* stating in part that for three generations of Milliken operations, management would not operate a profitless plant and would not "share the prerogatives of management with labor management leaders." The articles then detailed two instances of liquidation of Deering Milliken mills following unionization, and concluded: "We ourselves are small shareholders in Darlington. From experience and acquaintanceship, we knew the minute the union election vote was announced that we would receive a call for a special meeting to vote for a liquidation." [The Board commented that "the only way the community leaders could make use of this information would be by impressing upon employees the risk of unionism."]

These communications were admissible since Section 8(c) does not restrict admission of "instructions, directions or other statements which might be deemed admissible under ordinary rules of evidence." Senator Taft, 2 NLRA Legislative History 1947, pp. 1541, 1624 (1948). The Court of Appeals for the Fourth Circuit concluded that the speeches "clarify the scope and breadth of anti-union considerations which led to the Darlington closings, and we think that Section 8(c) was not intended to interdict evidence offered for this purpose." (This is a sensible reading of Section 8(c), particularly in light of Section 10(b) which requires the NLRB to follow federal court rules when they are "practical.") In addition, use of the speeches and memoranda was not banned by the six months limitation in Section 10(c); the communication was not an unfair labor practice in itself, and evidence arising before the six months period could be used to clarify and shed light on the events which occurred in the limitations period.

Darlington's evidence focused on the economic reasons for the closing. In 1956, a month before the closing, the mill treasurer reported an estimated loss of $40,000 for the current year; and the records showed an anticipated loss of $240,000 for the coming year. In rebuttal the General Counsel established that during the first nine months of 1956 the mill had a $400,000 capital improvements program; in September 1956 construction changes occurred to accommodate newly purchased looms; and Milliken did not call a special meeting of the board of directors to close the company or halt the capital improvements program when he learned of the prospective $40,000 loss.

Darlington argued that in determining whether the foreseeable effect of a closing is to chill unionism elsewhere, there must be evidence of ongoing organizing campaigns in the remaining part of an employer's business and of an actual chilling effect on remaining employees. The Board and Court of Appeals held that the traditional Section 8(a)(3) test applies.

Thus, in a *Darlington*-type case the Board must show that the employer's subjective motive is to chill unionism in other plants. The Board need not show, however, that the closing actually had a chilling effect on employees in the remaining plants; it is sufficient to show that a chilling effect would be a natural or foreseeable effect of a closing. Is this consistent with the Supreme Court decision in *Darlington*?

The Court of Appeals also enforced the Board's remedy: to offer to rehire the Darlington employees at other mills; to pay their transportation expenses, or if work was available, to put them on a preferential hiring list; to make whole all employees for any loss of pay until they obtained substantially equivalent employment, or, if jobs were not available, to place them on Deering Milliken's preferential hiring list.

In 1980 the employees, or (in one third of the cases) their heirs, voted 472 to 8 to accept a settlement of 5 million dollars in back pay. The individual awards ranged from $50 to $36,000. After 26 years, reinstatement was not an issue. For a discussion of the Board's role in remedying unfair labor practices, see Eames, *The History of the Litigation of Darlington as an Exercise in Administrative Procedure*, 5 Toledo L. Rev. 595 (1974).

2. In *Darlington,* Justice Harlan states that the Board was correct in analyzing the closing as a potential violation of Section 8(a)(3) rather than Section 8(a)(1). Do you agree? Justice Harlan also states that the legality of discharging the employees depends on the legality of the closing. Why should that be?

3. After *Darlington* how many employers are likely to announce and publicize the closing of one plant or department as a result of hostility to unions? Does the answer depend on whether the remedy to the terminated employee costs more than the savings (arguably) gained from maintaining a union-free work place elsewhere? How costly was the *Darlington* remedy if Deering Milliken realized the "benefit" of terminating the Darlington employees and operating its remaining 26 mills without a union?

4. (a) Are you persuaded by Justice Harlan's explanation of why a single employer can never violate Section 8(a)(3) by closing completely and permanently for avowedly anti-union reasons? Would a public purpose be served by finding such closings to violate Section 8(a)(3)? by making the displaced employees whole for lost wages until they secured substantially equivalent employment?

(b) Why would an employer who is closing permanently and totally, without any chance for future benefit from the decision, bother to announce its anti-union motivation? Does your answer depend on whether a union is actively organizing the employees at the facility being closed? Compare *Darlington,* n. 20; Section 8(c); and *Gissel,* page 216 *supra.*

(c) If the Court had held that Section 8(a)(3) is violated whenever a company closes permanently for avowedly anti-union reasons, how many employers would be unable to develop a paper record to support the decision to close on economic grounds?

5. In addition to ceasing operations, an employer may respond to unionization by transferring work to another location. Although this response involves considerations similiar to those found in *Darlington,* the Board and the courts have not applied the *Darlington* test of chilling effects elsewhere. Instead, transfers of work are unlawful if motivated by a desire to retaliate for union activity. But the concept of chilling effects elsewhere becomes relevant when dealing with the question of remedies. For example, in *Local 57, ILGWU* v. *NLRB* (Garwin Corp.), 374 F.2d 295,

64 LRRM 2159 (D.C. Cir.), *cert. denied,* 387 U.S. 942, 65 LRRM 2441 (1967), a New York clothing manufacturer moved its plant to Florida following unionization. The court of appeals agreed with the NLRB that there was sufficient evidence to find that the relocation was illegal because it was designed to show employees that unionization was foolish. However, the court set aside the order to bargain in Florida, noting that "the Board did not predicate its remedy on any finding that the unfair labor practices in New York precluded a fair and untainted vote by the Florida workers," and that "there is nothing in the record suggesting that the Florida workers were aware of what had occurred in New York." Does the court's approach make a mockery of the unfair labor practice finding?

In *NLRB* v. *Rapid Bindery, Inc.,* 293 F.2d 170, 48 LRRM 2658 (2d Cir. 1961), an employer moved its operations to new office space without bargaining with the newly certified union. During the election campaign the employer had predicted that operations would be moved. The Board found a violation of Section 8(a)(3), but the court of appeals reversed. It said:

> "All of the evidence points to motivation for sound business reasons. Though there may have been animosity between Union and Rapid, animosity furnishes no basis for the inference that this was the preponderant motive for the move when convincing evidence was received demonstrating business necessity. The decided cases do not condemn an employer who considers his relationship with his plant's union as only one part of the broad economic picture he must survey when he is faced with determining the desirability of making changes in his operations."

What of an employer who surveys "the broad economic picture" and finds that another company is able to provide the same service for less? Is a partial closing and termination of unionized employees solely because of "high labor costs" that which Section 8(a)(3) forbids?

NLRB v. Adkins Transfer Co.

United States Court of Appeals, Sixth Circuit, 1955
226 F.2d 324, 36 LRRM 2709

McAllister, Circuit Judge.

. . .

Respondent is a small truck line operator, carrying on its business between Chicago and Nashville, with the latter as the extreme southern point served. Its Nashville terminal utilized approximately eight trucks per day in transporting shipments to other cities, and four pick-up trucks for local work in Nashville. There is no evidence of any anti-union attitude on the part of the respondent, but, on the contrary, it has been on good terms with the local Teamsters Union, which is the charging party in the case. In fact, all of its road drivers are members of the Teamsters Union, and all of its local pick-up men and dock men are also members of the union. In addition, all extra employees engaged by respondent are procured by calling the local Teamsters union hall, whereupon the union sends such extra employees to respondent's place of business. This practice is followed in spite of the fact that there is in effect in the State of Tennessee the type of statute known as an open shop statute.

In November, 1953, respondent employed a mechanic and a helper whose duties were exclusively the maintenance and servicing of respondent's trucks. These are the employees involved in this case. In the same month that their employment commenced, the two employees joined the local Teamsters Union. Thereafter, the union demanded that respondent bargain with it for the purpose of entering into two contracts—one, a mechanic's contract for one of the employees, and the other, a service contract, for the other employee. At that time, one of the employees was paid at the rate of $1.25 per hour, and the other, 75 cents per hour. The union representative met with respondent's president and showed him copies of the union's uniform contracts covering mechanics and service men which were currently in effect between the union and other Nashville motor carriers. The various job classifications and the applicable wage rates specified in the contracts were discussed. As the union representative pointed out, under the contracts which he proposed that respondent adopt, one of the employees would receive $1.75 an hour, an increase of 50 cents over his current rate, and the other would receive between $1.25 and $1.40 per hour, an increase of between 50 and 65 cents over his current rate. There was no discussion as to whether a compromise could be reached on wage scales.

The first meeting between the union representative and respondent's president took place November 16. A second meeting occurred November 20. On the next day, the foreman came into the shop where the two employees were working, and stated that he had bad news for them—that the president was going to close the shop because he was not going to pay the union scale. At the direction of respondent's president, the foreman thereafter discharged the two employees. Respondent's president testified with regard to this incident, without contradiction or challenge, that it was "purely and simply a question of costs." Respondent's mechanical work since the discharge of the employees has been done on a job-by-job basis by local truck and automobile dealers, and the servicing has been done partly by its own operating employees and partly by independent business concerns. Respondent's president testified that he found this method of having the mechanical work done had resulted in even lower labor costs than those entailed by its former method of operation, under which respondent had paid $2.00 an hour for the combined services of the two employees. Respondent never replaced the two men, and its president testified on the hearing that it did not intend to.

. . . [T]he trial examiner . . . set forth in his findings that respondent's president testified, credibly, that, based upon his experience in dealing with the union, he believed that if respondent had continued its maintenance department at Nashville without raising the wages of the two employees to meet the union scale, a strike would have ensued which would have effectively closed down respondent's entire business operations. The examiner stated that the accuracy of such opinion was substantiated by the statement of the union respresentative who testified, on the hearing, that he knew of no instance when the union permitted a contracting employer to pay union members different wage rates than were provided in the union's uniform industry agreement for the particular employee classification. He found that respondent's president, rather than capitulating to the union demands and increasing the wages of the two employees, which he considered economically disadvantageous to respondent, had discontinued the maintenance department and discharged the two maintenance employees. He further found that respondent's president testified that the fact that the two employees joined the union did not motivate their discharge. The trial examiner concluded his findings with the following statement:

"This is not a case where an employer who is generally hostile towards unions and opposes employee organization seeks to defeat his employees' efforts to engage in collective bargaining by discontinuing a department in which a majority of the employees have selected a collective bargaining representative. . . . In this regard, it is significant that the complaint does not charge that the Respondent has refused to bargain in good faith with the Union. Here, the Respondent had only two practical choices, either to pay its maintenance employees the wage rates demanded by the Union, or discontinue its maintenance department. No area for bargaining with the Union existed."

The examiner then went on to point out that the union representative had testified that, if respondent had kept the maintenance department open but had declined to sign the union contract, the union procedure would have been to call a strike, and that a strike in which the Teamsters Union controlled the over-the-road men and the dock men—as in this case—usually resulted in a 100 percent shutdown of the company. The examiner, therefore, found that respondent had committed no unfair labor practice by choosing to discontinue its maintenance department and to discharge the two maintenance employees, especially in the absence of evidence of other unfair labor practices or animus toward the union; and that, accordingly, respondent did not discharge the employees to encourage or discourage membership in the labor organization, in violation of Section 8(a)(1) and (3) of the Act. He concluded by recommending that the complaint be dismissed.

The Board, however, rejected the recommendations of the trial examiner and his conclusions as to the alleged unfair labor practices. It held that the discharges established a prima facie case that the dismissal was violative of Section 8(a)(3) and (1) of the Act for the reason that the employees would not have been so summarily dismissed if they had not joined the union, and had not sought, through the union, to exercise the rights incident to union membership. The Board further said that respondent had not sustained its burden of dispelling the inferences fairly to be drawn, and that its claim that the dismissals represented an attempt to resolve a difficult economic position was supported "by nothing more than its subjective anticipation of what the Union might do, rather than upon what the Union actually did do in its representation of these employees." It, therefore, held that the dismissal was violative of the Act. . . .

. . .

We are of the view that the trial examiner was right and the Board was wrong in its decision and order. Only such discrimination as encourages or discourages membership in a labor organization is proscribed by the Act. *Radio Officers* v. *National Labor Relations Board,* 347 U.S. 17, 33 LRRM 2417. In order to establish an 8(a)(3) violation, there must be evidence that the employer's act encouraged or discouraged union membership. The section requires that the discrimination in regard to tenure of employment have both the purpose and effect of discouraging union membership, and to make out a case, it must appear that the employer has, by discrimination, encouraged or discouraged membership in a labor organization. There was no such discrimination in the instant case. A company may suspend its operations or change its business methods so long as its change in operations is not motivated by the illegal intention to avoid its obligations under the Act. *National Labor Relations Board* v. *Houston Chronicle Pub. Co.,* 211 F.2d 848, 33 LRRM 2847 (C.A. 5). An employer may discharge or refuse to reemploy one of his employees for any reason, just or unjust, except discrimination because of union activities and relationships, and the controlling and ultimate fact which determines an issue of the kind here presented is, what was the true reason back of the discharge. . . .

. . .

It is true that what might be termed the secondary reason for the discharge of the two employees was because they were members of the union, but the fact that they were members of the union was only incidental, and was not the real reason behind their discharge. The real reason was because the union wage scales were too high for respondent to operate profitably the department in question; and, since the employees were members of the union, respondent would be obliged to pay those rates, or close the department, or suffer a strike. It is plain that there was no interference or restraint or coercion of the employees in their rights to self-organization or collective bargaining, and there was no discrimination to encourage or discourage membership in a labor organization. Consequently, there was no violation of Section 8(a)(3) and (1) of the Act.

Respondent had no feeling against the labor union. All of his employees were already members of the union, and his relations with them and the union were friendly and cooperative. The only consideration that actuated respondent in dismissing the employees was, not that they were members of the union, but that the union wage scales were too high for this particular employment and that such services could be more cheaply performed by outside business concerns. All of these facts are indubitable from the evidence before us. It is our view that the trial examiner's finding and recommended disposition are both factually and legally correct, and that the Board's findings of fact to the contrary are not supported by substantial evidence on the record as a whole.

Note

What is the distinction between a decision based on labor costs associated with unionization and one based on anti-union animus? between a decision based on a legitimate business judgment apart from labor costs and one based on anti-union animus? Whatever your view of the decision in *Transportation Management, supra* at page 302, it is appropriate, is it not, to require companies to carry the burden of persuasion in cases like *Rapid Bindery, supra* at page 316, and *Adkins Transfer?*

5. REMEDIES

Problem

Enderby won the election by a vote of 154 to 150. The day after the election the Union filed objections and Sections 8(a)(3), (1), and (5) unfair labor practice charges. Enderby's counsel offered Enderby the following options:

1. Settle now to limit your monetary liability. Try to get the discharged employees to settle for back pay in lieu of reinstatement. Agree to a new election to be held immediately. Ninety percent of Board cases are settled within a median of 40 days without any formal litigation before the Board. The Regional Offices will try hard to mediate a settlement. They've a huge case load, too few staff members, and procedures under the Act subordinate private interests to achievement of a bargaining relationship if possible. There is also pressure to settle because the General Counsel estimates that each percentage point in the settlement rate represents about $1,000,000 saved annually from the Board's budget.

2. If you do not settle and the Regional Director issues a complaint on the unfair labor practices, there is a good chance the Administrative Law Judge and Board will uphold the charges; the General Counsel's success rate is about 80 percent. The time between issuing the complaint, a hearing, and an ALJ decision is about six months, eight months total since the election. If you file exceptions to the ALJ's recommendation, the case goes to the Board for a decision, which should have a decision in about four months. Using the totality of circumstances and laboratory conditions approach, I'd say some objections will be upheld; so at a minimum you'll be facing another election. Companies we continue to counsel win these elections about 95 percent of the time.

3. If the Board orders you to bargain, on the basis of findings of unfair labor practices, you can do so. But Board orders are not self-enforcing and you or the General Counsel may seek review from a court of appeals. It takes about 150 days for the agency's appellate division to file a brief in the court and about one year for the appeals court to issue a decision. Although the General Counsel is sustained in 80 percent of all cases, from reading the decisions it seems to me the rate's far lower when the Board seeks enforcement of bargaining orders. And if you lose the appeal, there's the possibility of a petition for certiorari—unlikely to be granted,

but given the conflicts in the circuits over what conduct justifies a bargaining order, filing a petition isn't frivolous.

4. One final point. Delay works to a company's advantage, most of the time. And unions know it. They might picket to force you to recognize and bargain now while there's still a good deal of employee enthusiasm. You should be able to stop them by filing a Section 8(b)(7) charge and asking the Regional Director to seek a 10(1) injunction.

In deciding which course to follow, what additional information does Enderby need?

NLRB v. Jamaica Towing, Inc.

United States Court of Appeals, Second Circuit, 1980
632 F.2d 208, 105 LRRM 2959

Mansfield, Circuit Judge.

For a second time the National Labor Relations Board (the Board) seeks enforcement of an order entered by it on July 18, 1978, after it found that respondent, Jamaica Towing, Inc. (Jamaica), violated §§ 8(a)(1) and 8(a)(5) of the National Labor Relations Act (the Act), 29 U.S.C. §§ 158 (a)(1) and (a)(5), immediately prior to a union representation election held on February 24, 1976, in which Local 917 of the International Brotherhood of Teamsters (the Union) was defeated. . . .
. . .
On December 8, 1977, the ALJ found that [Anthony] Giorgianni [Jamaica's president] had violated § 8(a)(1) of the Act by attempting to find out which employees had signed for the Union and by his individual meetings with each of three employees in which he expressed opposition to the Union and stated he would "use muscle" against it. The balance of Giorgianni's conduct was not found sufficiently egregious to constitute threats or promises of discharge, leading the ALJ to conclude that "the unlawful interrogations and threats. . . neither require nor justify the imposition of a bargaining order under the standards set forth by the Supreme Court in *NLRB* v. *Gissel Packing Co., Inc.*, 395 U.S. 575, 71 LRRM 2481 (1969). Two instances of interrogation, and three non-specific threats to resort to 'muscle,' do not, in any judgment, eliminate the possibility of a fair rerun election. . . ." Accordingly he recommended that Jamaica be ordered (1) to cease and desist from engaging in the activities found to be unfair labor practices, or from interfering with the employees' exercise of their rights under § 7 of the Act, and (2) to post a notice in conspicuous places to the effect that it would not engage in such activities and that employees were free to become and remain members of the Union.

Upon exceptions filed by the General Counsel the Board, on July 19, 1978 (more than 2 years and 5 months after the conduct complained of), agreed with the ALJ's findings of unfair practices but rejected his inference as to the relative insignificance of Giorgianni's meeting with employees at which he pointed out the disadvantages of unionization and stated that, although he could make no promises, he would consider the demands and benefits voiced by them. The Board held that this conduct amounted to direct dealing with the employees and repudiation of Jamaica's bargaining obligation, in violation of §§ 8(a)(1) and 8(a)(5) of the Act. It also concluded that Jamaica had "engaged in pernicious conduct which, by its nature, has long-lasting if not permanent effects on the employees' freedom of choice in selection or rejecting a bargaining representative" and that a bargaining order was required and justified.

On July 29, 1979, following the Board's initial petition for enforcement, we remanded with directions to consider the effect of the turnover of Jamaica's work force and to explain, in terms of standards or guidelines of general application consistent with its denial of bargaining orders in other similar cases, why such an order was required in this case rather than the preferred remedy of a Board-supervised second election held after entry of a cease-and-desist order of the type recommended by the ALJ. That order would require Jamaica to post notices that employees were free to remain or become members of Local 917. See 602 F.2d 1100, 101 LRRM 3011. Upon remand the Board, in a short "Supplemental Decision and Order," filed on January 17, 1980, for the most part regurgitated its prior decision, adding only that the impact of the employer's misconduct was pronounced and long-lasting because of the nature of the misconduct and the small size of the work force. No effort was made to ascertain the nature and extent of employee turnover during the period prior to or after its original decision. The Board simply concluded, without any evidentiary basis, that the prejudicial impact of the misconduct had not been dissipated, and that to hold otherwise would reward the employer, putting a premium on its continued litigation. It reaffirmed its July 18, 1978, order, enforcement of which is sought in this petition.

DISCUSSION

Where an employer's misconduct taints a prior union election by adversely affecting the employees' freedom of choice, the traditional remedy, frequently characterized as the "preferred" or "superior" remedy, . . . has been to (1) vacate the election, (2) enjoin the employer from engaging in such misbehavior, (3) require him to post "contrition" notices to his employees, disavowing any future interference, and (4) direct him to give union representatives reasonable access to the employees. This is then followed by a new Board-supervised election. The issuance by the Board of a bargaining order in lieu of a cease-and-desist order is only proper if, after an objective review of all of the relevant surrounding circumstances, including the nature of the employer's misbehavior and any later events bearing on its impact on the employees, it may reasonably be concluded that the employees will be unable to exercise a free choice in a Board-supervised rerun election.

In *NRLB* v. *Gissel Packing Co.*, 395 U.S. 575, 71 LRRM 2481 (1969), the Court held that under some circumstances the Board might find it necessary, because of the lasting adverse impact of the employer's misconduct upon the employees' freedom of choice, to require the employer to bargain directly with the union which had lost the election rather than simply to order a new election. The Court stated that in "exceptional" cases where the employer's unfair labor practices have been "outrageous" or "pervasive" a bargaining order would be justified because the coercive effects of the misbehavior would not be eliminated by the traditional remedy, 395 U.S. at 613–14. At the opposite end of the spectrum, "minor or less extensive unfair practices. . . will not sustain a bargaining order," 395 U.S. at 617. The Court noted that in between these two extremes there would be a group of "less extraordinary cases marked by less pervasive practices" where the Board would be called upon to "take into consideration the extensiveness of an employer's unfair practices in terms of their past effect on election conditions and the likelihood of their recurrence in the future." If the Board found "that the possibility of erasing the effects of past practices and of ensuring a fair election (or a fair rerun) by the use of traditional remedies, though present, is slight and that employee sentiment once expressed through cards would, on balance, be better protected by a bargaining order, then such an order should issue (see n. 32, *supra*)," 395 U.S. at 614–15. The Court left to the Board the task of fashioning a set of guidelines, 395 U.S. at 612 n. 32, by which the impact of the unfair practices upon employee free choice might objectively be ascertained.

Certain violations have been regularly regarded by the Board and the courts as highly coercive. These are the so-called "hallmark" violations and their presence will support the issuance of a bargaining order unless some significant mitigating circumstance exists. They include such employer misbehavior as the closing of a plant or threats of plant closure or loss of employment, the grant of benefits to employees, or the reassignment, demotion or discharge of union adherents in violation of § 8(a)(3) of the Act. In such cases the seriousness of the conduct, coupled with the fact that often it represents complete action as distinguished from mere statements, interrogations or promises, justifies a finding without extensive explication that it is likely to have a lasting inhibitive effect on a substantial percentage of the work force. The actual use of a "stick" in the form a plant closure, or the resort to physical force or discharge, pose no problem of assessing credibility or unlikelihood of implementation. They are complete acts which may reasonably be calculated to have a coercive effect on employees and to remain in their memories for a long period. The prospect of unionization is not a sure safeguard against such tactics.

". . .the reassignment, demotion, or discharge of union adherents will carry a message which cannot be lost on employees in the voting group. While there is some slight chance that a single 8(a)(3) violation will not be perceived as employer retribution, repeated violation will rarely if ever be misinterpreted. The impact on employees might be erased if our standard make-whole remedy could be swiftly obtained.

But unfortunately, in the usual litigated case, restoration to employment comes months or years later, if at all, and thus the coercive effect of the discrimination is unlikely ever to be undone. The Board, therefore, since *Gissel*, has regularly issued a bargaining order where a union majority was dissipated by such tactics. . . . *General Stencils, Inc.*, 195 NLRB 1109, 1112, 79 LRRM 1608 (1972, *upon remand*) (Chairman Miller, dissenting).

Similarly, the employer, by "remedying the very grievances which gave rise to the union interest, . . . destroy[s] for the moment at least the employees' need for greater strength. . . [so that] the employees cannot be said to have been free to fairly appraise the value of unionization." *Texaco, Inc. v. NLRB, supra,* 436 F.2d at 525. See, in accord, *NLRB v. Eagle Material Handling, Inc.,* 558 F.2d 160, 167, 95 LRRM 2934 (3d Cir. 1977). As for a threat of plant closure, it may not be completed action but it "is the one serious threat of economic disadvantage which is wholly beyond the influence of the union or the control of the employees." *General Stencils, supra.* 195 NLRB at 1113 (Chairman Miller dissenting). However, even with respect to these "hallmark" violations, a bargaining order may be denied for lack of proof of pervasiveness, such as where the discharge of an employee was unknown to most of the other employees or the discharged employee was not known to be a union adherent. See *Munro Enterprises, Inc.,* 210 NLRB 403, 86 LRRM 1620 (1974); *General Stencils, Inc., supra,* 195 NLRB 1112 (Chairman Miller dissenting).

   In contrast to the hallmark unfair labor practices just catalogued, which justify a bargaining order, there is an array of less serious violations which must either be numerous or be coupled with some other factor intensifying their effect before they will fall within *Gissel's* second category and support an order to bargain. These include such employer misconduct as interrogating employees regarding their union sympathies, holding out a "carrot" of promised benefits, expressing anti-union resolve, threatening that unionization will result in decreased benefits, or suggesting that physical force might be used to exclude the union. In such cases the Board may not presume an adverse effect, lasting or otherwise, upon the employees' free choice. The Board must undertake the task of investigating the circumstances thoroughly to determine the seriousness, extent, and longevity of any inhibitive impact. The reason for this requirement lies partly in the fact that talk is apt to be taken less seriously by employees than action. Promises of benefits may be viewed as mere ploys, never to be fulfilled without union bargaining pressures. Suggestions that unionization will lead to lesser benefits may be discounted by the employees' belief that effective collective bargaining will prevent them from ever being put into effect. Implementation of threats to increase work shifts or to adhere more strictly to work rules may not be in the employer's own economic self-interest. Moreover, failure to show that such promises or threats were widely disseminated among the work force may weaken any inference of coercive effect.

   In our view the Board must also, in considering the advisability of a bargaining order in response to these lesser violations, consider subsequent events bearing upon employee choice, including changes in the management as well as in the work force and the passage of time. . . .Although mere passage of time does not preclude a bargaining order, *NLRB* v. *Katz,* 369 U.S. 736, 738 n. 16, 50 LRRM 2177 (1962); *NLRB* v. *Gissel Packing Co., supra,* 395 U.S. at 610–11, and we must guard against rewarding an employer for his own misconduct or delaying tactics, there are cases where later relevant events are not of the employer's making and may, if ignored, result in unnecessarily thwarting the genuine desires of the current work force. If a new election would reliably reflect genuine, uncoerced employee sentiment, it does not reward the employer to hold one. Instead, it "effectuates employee rights," as *Gissel* requires, 395 U.S. at 612. An employer is "rewarded" by a new election only when the original authorization cards are a more reliable indicator of employee desires than a new election. In resolving this issue it is illogical not to consider all relevant factors, including employee turnover and lapse of time. As Judge Friendly pointed out in *NLRB* v. *General Stencils Inc., supra,* 472 F.2d at 176 n.5:

> "Where the focus is thus on ascertaining employee choice and examining the conditions likely to surround a future election, changes in personnel and the passage of time are relevant considerations in the Board's analysis. When the question whether the employer's conduct prevented a fair election is marginal in any view, as demonstrated by a dissent from one of its own members, it would seem that the Board should more carefully weight the deterrent effect of a bargaining order on an employer found to have violated § 8(a)(1) against the possibility of inflicting what may be a totally unwanted, and even largely unknown, union on a new work force. See *NLRB* v. *Staub Cleaners, Inc.,* 418 F.2d 1086, 1090, 72 LRRM 2755 (2 Cir. 1969) (Lumbard, Chief Judge, dissenting)."

Employee turnover and lapse of time may therefore become major factors in close cases such as the present one. Although new employees, who would be disenfranchised by bargaining, may gain some protection from their right to file a decertification petition after the Union bargains for a reasonable time with the employer, see *Gissel, supra,* 395 U.S. at 613; *Ex-Cell-O Corp.,* v. *NLRB,* 449 F.2d 1058, 1063, 77 LRRM 2547 (D.C. Cir. 1971); *NLRB* v. *Drives, Inc,* 440 F.2d 354, 367, 76 LRRM 2296 (7th Cir.), *cert. denied,* 404 U.S. 912, 78 LRRM 2585 (1971), such a burden should not be imposed upon them in a close case. The nature of the subsequent events and their importance in the particular case should be the yardstick. For instance, a heavy turnover within weeks after the employer's misconduct or a change in management to one which gives genuine and sincere assurances to the work force of noninterference by the employer would weigh heavily in favor of a new election rather than a bargaining order in a case where the misbehavior of the prior management had been marginal.

It is also significant that a refusal to give weight to subsequent events runs counter to the Board's own consideration of such events in determining, as directed by the Supreme Court in *Gissel,* 395 U.S. at 614, whether there is a likelihood that the employer would in the future repeat his unfair labor practices. The Board, for instance, has expressly taken into account an employer's later conduct revealing a "willingness to cooperate in bringing about a fair rerun election" (Brief of NLRB Gen. Counsel, 19). See *Peerless of America, Inc., supra,* 484 F.2d at 1121; *Restaurant Associates Industries,* 194 NLRB 1066, 79 LRRM 1145 (1972). In addition, the Board has refused to issue a bargaining order where the impact of the employer's misconduct "has, in part at least, likely been dissipated by [a] very considerable lapse of time," *May Department Stores Co.,* 211 NLRB 150, 152, 86 LRRM 1423 (1974).[5]

As we noted on the prior appeal in this case, 602 F.2d at 1104–05, review of the Board's rulings with respect to issuance of a bargaining order in the second *Gissel* category of cases is further complicated by the Board's ambivalence in the matter and the apparent inconsistencies in its case law on the subject. In some marginal cases the Board has granted bargaining orders, see *e.g., General Stencils, Inc.,* 195 NLRB 1109, 79 LRRM 1608 (1972); *Peerless of America, Inc., supra; Jamaica Towing Inc.,* 247 NLRB 1073, 103 LRRM 1294 (1980), and in other cases involving the same type or even more egregious misconduct it has denied such orders, see *Schrementi Brothers, Inc.,* 179 NLRB 853, 72 LRRM 1481 (1969); *Gold Circle Department Stores, Inc.,* 207 NLRB 1005, 85 LRRM 1033 (1973); *May Department Stores Co., supra; Stoutco, Inc.,* 180 NLRB 178, 73 LRRM 1107 (1969), all without rhyme, reason or differentiating factors other than the Board's conclusory statements. This has led us, in the interest of avoiding arbitrariness and insuring that like cases will receive like treatment, to direct the Board to articulate more precisely the standards employed and the facts found in those cases which in its opinion justify a bargaining order instead of a cease-and-desist order. *Jamaica Towing, Inc., supra,* 602 F.2d at 1105; *General Stencils, Inc.,* 438 F.2d 894, 904–05, 76 LRRM 2288 (2d Cir. 1971). Other circuits share our concern. See *Peerless of America, Inc., supra,* 484 F.2d at 1118–19 (7th Cir.); *NLRB v. Armcor Industries, Inc.,* 535 F.2d 239, 244–45, 92 LRRM 2374 (3d Cir. 1976); *NLRB v. Kaiser Agricultural Chemicals,* 473 F.2d 374, 383, 82 LRRM 2455 (5th Cir. 1973).

Applying these principles to the present case, we are satisfied that the bargaining portion of the Board's order is not justified. It is true that the employer's unfair labor practices here, which consisted of interrogation of employees, expressions of opposition to the Union, statements that unionization might result in loss of benefits through less overtime and stricter enforcement of work rules, implied promises that some of the employees' demands would be met, and statements that the employer might "use muscle" to oppose the Union, can hardly be dismissed out of hand or minimized. They were uttered by the chief executive in charge,

---

[5]The full statement of the Board in *May Department Stores Co.,* reads as follows:

"[W]hatever 'lingering effect' the Respondent's unfair labor practices may have had has, in part at least, likely been dissipated by the very considerable lapse of time here which time lapse also casts some doubt on the card signatures as evidence of majority status. We note, in this connection, that the record is at best unclear as to what portion of the cards are stale, a factor which further militates against finding a bargaining order to be an appropriate remedy in the circumstances of this case." 211 NLRB at 152.

Mr. Giorgianni, who had the capacity to carry them out, rather than by a lower-level supervisor, who might lack such authority. They were also uttered to members of a small work force of only 8 drivers where the likelihood of dissemination was greater than among a larger number of employees. All of these factors militate in favor of the Board's order.

On the other hand, the misbehavior definitely falls within the category of non-hallmark violations. The employer's conduct was limited entirely to Giorgianni's oral statements, none of which was ever put into effect. There was no plant closure or threat of closure, no actual grant of benefits, no discharge of employees or even threats of discharge in reprisal for union adherence (on the contrary, Mr. Giorgianni assured the employees that their jobs were secure), and no use of force. There was no evidence that any of the drivers, who were undoubtedly used to blunt talk, feared the loss of their jobs. On the contrary, four members attempted to bargain directly with Mr. Giorgianni by stating that they might dispense with unionization if he would meet certain demands. Recognizing that he was on a tightrope, Giorgianni gave an ambivalent response. Although the size of the work force is a relevant factor, the Board has not hesitated to find bargaining orders unwarranted in cases involving small employee groups. See *Restaurant Associates Industries*, 194 NLRB 1066, 79 LRRM 1145 (1972); *New Alaska Development Corp.*, 194 NLRB 830, 79 LRRM 1065 (1972); *Blade-Tribune Publishing Co.*, 180 NLRB 432, 73 LRRM 1041 (1969). Counterbalancing the smallness in size of the unit is the greater likelihood that any substantial employee turnover may radically change the desires of the majority of the current work force with respect to unionization.

The Board has not directed us to any case where it has issued a bargaining order under similar circumstances. The cases relied upon by it all involve more egregious misconduct. As we indicated in our first opinion, we are especially concerned over the effect of employee turnover, which was wholly unrelated to the employer's unfair labor practices. The three union adherents who left the company's employ represented 37½ percent of the unit. Assuming that the driver who did not originally sign a union authorization card remained in Jamaica's employ, only 50 percent of the original group who signed cards would remain. There is no evidence as to whether new drivers were hired to replace the three who had departed or, if so, whether they favored the Union. We are left to speculate regarding subsequent events bearing directly on the issue of the appropriate remedy. Since the departure of the three drivers occurred in September, 1976, which was only seven months after the election and more than nine months prior to the Board's issuance of a bargaining order (the ALJ having recommended against such an order in December, 1977), we do not believe that these events should be disregarded on the ground that to give them weight would somehow "reward" the employer for its misconduct or, in the Board's words, "put a premium upon continued litigation by the employer." In view of the immediacy with which the turnover occurred and its lack of any connection with the employer's behavior, the proper course for the Board on remand was to elicit evidence regarding the changed composition of the work force and determine whether the bargaining order might impair the rights of so large a percentage of the employee unit that it would now do more harm than good. This the Board has failed to do.

At this late date, almost five years after the events at issue, no useful purpose would be served by a second remand. In our view the Board, despite a full opportunity to remedy basic deficiencies in the record, has failed to do so.

Accordingly the order is enforced except for the bargaining requirement which is denied.

NLRB v. K & K Gourmet Meats, Inc.

United States Court of Appeals, Third Circuit, 1981

640 F.2d 460, 106 LRRM 2448

ROSENN, Circuit Judge.

The ALJ termed the violations he found in this case "minimal." The Board disagreed, calling those acts "serious" and concluding that their occurrence "precludes the holding of a fair election." The Board appears to have grounded its decision that a bargaining order was necessary primarily on its finding that there had been promises of benefits in exchange for the union's defeat, findings which we have upheld. . . . Here, the Board. . . found that K & K's actions were "designed to impress upon the employees the fact that they did not need a union to obtain satisfaction of their demands." The employer's conduct, the Board found, was such as "to undermine the Union's majority status" and "a bargaining order [was] necessary and appropriate to protect the majority sentiment expressed through authorization cards." With these talismanic words, *Gissel II* was invoked and, in the Board's mind, satisfied.

The selection of an exclusive collective bargaining agent is not a game of chance but a matter of the highest importance to employees and employers alike. Legislation and experience indicate that an employee's statutory right to select an exclusive bargaining agent should be determined by democratic process in a free and open election. The Board's responsibility for holding such elections was not meant to be supplanted by the authority found to exist in *Gissel.* Only in exceptional circumstances, where it is obvious that the extensive machinery and power of the NLRB is inadequate to ensure a free election, should employees be denied their right to cast a secret ballot for or against an exclusive bargaining agent.[4]

---

[4]The dissent submits that against the concern for employers and employees subject to bargaining orders must be weighed "the strong federal policy in favor of the formation of collective bargaining relationships." (Dissenting op., typescript, p. 28.) On the contrary, we believe that the federal policy with respect to the formation of collective bargaining relationships is neutral. We view the thrust of federal policy as the protection "of the right of employees to organize and bargain collectively" when they are so inclined. See 29 U.S.C. § 151 (1976). See also 29 U.S.C. § 157 (1976). Therefore, Congress in its declaration of national policy encouraging collective bargaining has also stated its policy in "protecting the

In this case, the Board indulges in the grossest kind of speculation to invoke *Gissel II*. The Supreme Court plainly stated that, before a *Gissel II* order should issue, the Board must make a determination that "the possibility of erasing the effects of past practices and of ensuring a fair election (or a fair rerun) by the use of traditional remedies, though present, is slight and that employee sentiment once expressed through cards would, on balance, be better protected by a bargaining order." 395 U.S. at 614–15. This is a determination of actual fact on the evidence received in each case. No room is left for automatic formulae under which, for example, one threat, two coerced interrogations and a promise of a wage increase will result in an order while another combination will not. The bargaining order is an extraordinary remedy and, because it operates to disenfranchise the workers in the choice of their representative, it is appropriate only when the harmful effects of that disenfranchisement are outweighed by the positive advancement of the policies underlying federal labor law. We agree with the ALJ and do not believe the Board has struck the appropriate balance in this case.

The record demonstrates that K & K's employees were not much impressed by Arthur Katz' speech on October 30. At a meeting that night, they collectively decided that his representations were not to be believed. They struck. Such are not the actions of cowering and coerced workers. Since the only unfair labor practices which we find to have occurred were promises by Weiler and Katz that certain benefits would be granted in exchange for the Union's defeat, and the employees did not believe those promises, we fail to perceive why the effects of those practices cannot be "erased. . . by the use of traditional remedies." Indeed, it appears to us that the effects of the unfair labor practices were easily and speedily erased by the evening of October 30, without any remedial action by the Board. We conclude that there was no basis in fact for the Board's determination that the extreme remedy of a bargaining order was necessary under these circumstances.

The Board's application for enforcement of its order requiring (a) K & K to cease and desist from promising employees benefits to discourage them from engaging in activities on behalf of the Union or any other labor organization; (b) that the Company refrain from in any like or related manner interfering with or restraining employees in the exercise of the rights guaranteed them by section 7 of the Act; and (c) that the Company post appropriate notices, will be enforced. In all other respects, enforcement of the order will be denied.

Each side to bear its own costs.

---

exercise of workers of full freedom of association, self-organization, and designation of representatives of their own choosing." 29 U.S.C. § 151. Freedom of association and free selection of a bargaining agent, however, may be substantially diminished by dependence on authorization cards.

. . .The Court in *Gissel* recognized that cards are "admittedly inferior to the election process," although they may perhaps be the only way of assuring employee choice when the employer engages in conduct disruptive of the election process, 395 U.S. at 602–03. As we note in the text, there is nothing in the record here to indicate that the Board could not conduct a fair election at the K & K plant.

GIBBONS, Circuit Judge, dissenting.

It is no secret that at least a significant minority of the members of this court believe that the Supreme Court in *NLRB* v. *Gissel Packing Co.,* 395 U.S. 575, 71 LRRM 2481 (1969), erred in interpreting the National Labor Relations Act to permit the National Labor Relations Board to enter a bargaining order as a remedy for unfair labor practices committed in the course of an organizing campaign. Nor is it any secret that those judges who are uncomfortable with the *Gissel* construction of the statute have been signalling the Board vigorously that bargaining orders are unwelcome in this circuit. . . . At the same time the Board is receiving from a different group of judges on this court a quite different signal. . . . Those different signals are that we acknowledge the primacy of the Supreme Court in interpreting the Act, at least until Congress speaks, that we acknowledge the primacy of the Board's role as a fact finder, and that if the Board decides to enter a *Gissel* order we will be satisfied with a statement of reasons reasonably identifying for us the basis, among several permissible bases, for choosing that remedy.

Until this case the guerilla warfare against *Gissel* orders has been carried out by insisting that the Board's opinion writing is so opaque that we cannot understand it, and remanding. See *NLRB* v. *Permanent Label Corp.,* No. 80–1617, slip op. at 28, 106 LRRM 2211 (Seitz, C.J., dissenting). With the present majority a new weapon is resorted to. The majority simply substitutes its fact finding for that of the Board. Perhaps the new tactic reflects a conclusion that finally the Board has devised a formula for stating its reasons satisfactorily. I hope so. The Board's statement follows:

"Respondent's unfair labor practices are serious in nature, and began on the day the Union demanded recognition. Its entire course of conduct, which included a promise of a wage increase, promises of better benefits, and solicitation of and a promise to remedy grievances, was designed to impress upon the employees the fact that they did not need a union to obtain satisfaction of their demands.[5]

"Under the principles set forth in *NLRB* v. *Gissel Packing Company, Inc.,* 395 U.S. 575, 71 LRRM 2481 (1969), a bargaining order is appropriate where a union's majority is established by cards and the nature and extent of the employer's unfair labor practices render unlikely a free choice by the employees in our election. As previously set forth, Respondent's unfair labor practices were clearly designed to undermine the Union's majority status. Here, the promises of a wage increase, increased benefits, and new approaches to resolve employee grievances, coupled with the threat that the organizational campaign would be futile, result in giving the employees much if not all of what they were seeking through union representation."

"[5]*Teledyne Dental Products Corp.,* 210 NLRB 435, 86 LRRM 1134 (1974)."

. . .

A comparison of the well written majority opinion with that of the Board discloses that the majority, looking at the same record evidence, has chosen to draw inferences from that evidence different from those the Board drew. Our scope of review under the National Labor Relations Act does not permit such action. See 29 U.S.C. § 160(e) (1976); *Universal Camera Corp.* v. *NLRB*, 340 U.S. 474, 27 LRRM 2373 (1951); *Tri-State Truck Service, Inc.* v. *NLRB*, 616 F.2d 65, 72, 103 LRRM 2640 (3d Cir. 1980) (Gibbons, J., dissenting).

Conscientious Board members reading our opinions from *Armcor Industries* in 1976 to *Permanent Label* in 1981 must be puzzled about what they should attempt to do in a *Gissel* bargaining order case to satisfy us. The answer to their puzzlement, I fear, is that for the judges uncomfortable with the *Gissel* interpretation of the statute nothing the Board does will be likely to appear satisfactory. I do not mean to suggest that discomfort over *Gissel* orders is an unreasonable judicial posture. We are all well aware that in recent years labor unions have been winning far fewer contested elections than heretofore. A *Gissel* order insulates a union from the hazards of an election, and arguably tilts the scale too far in the union's favor. But the Supreme Court interpreted the Act in the *Gissel* cases to give the Board that authority, and Congress has not chosen to react. If I were a congressman requested to vote on overruling *Gissel*, I am not sure how I would vote. The opponents of *Gissel* orders point out that they tend to undermine secret balloting in the choice of bargaining representatives. On the other hand, the keystone in the arch of federal labor policy is collective bargaining, which cannot take place until a bargaining representative has been recognized. A card majority is a legitimate means for such recognition. . . . If on the basis of a card majority a collective bargaining agreement resulted, we would not be overly concerned about the undermining of secret balloting in the choice of bargaining representatives. Thus one has to take at somewhat less than face value the oft-repeated concern that *Gissel* orders are inimical to the interests of employees. The real concern is for employers, but against that concern must be weighed the strong federal policy in favor of the formation of collective bargaining relationships. See 29 U.S.C. § 151 (1976). From that perspective *Gissel* orders do not look quite so threatening. In any event, it is not the role of an intermediate appellate court to substitute its balancing of the competing policies for that of the legislature, in the guise of requiring statements of reasons or of substituting its factual inferences for those made by the Board.

I would enforce the Board's order.

Notes

1. *Compare United Dairy Farmers Cooperative Ass'n* v. *NLRB*, 633 F.2d 1054, 105 LRRM 3034 (3d Cir. 1980), in which the union lost a representation election by a vote of 14 to 12. The court of appeals held that the Board has the authority to issue a bargaining order in the absence of a card majority. The employer's unfair labor practices included discriminatory discharges and threats to close, made before and after the election; following the vote, the company engaged in unlawful interrogations and attempted to change the status of some employees to independent contractors.

2. Is the distaste for bargaining orders revealed in *Jamaica Towing* and *K & K Gourmet* a product of:

(a) doubt about the reliability of authorization cards;
(b) doubt about the impact of the company's conduct on the employees;
(c) doubt about the expertise of the NLRB; or
(d) doubt about the desirability of collective bargaining and labor unions?

If (a), would the judges' views change after rereading *Gissel* (pp. 151 and 216 *supra*)? after learning that the Getman, Goldberg, and Herman study of 31 contested elections found authorization cards to be such reliable indicators of union support that elections are not really needed? (See Union Representation Elections: Law and Reality, pp. 125–53.)

If (b), would the judges' views change on being reminded that in one of the consolidated cases in *Gissel* (Sinclair Company), the Supreme Court upheld the use of a bargaining order where the only unlawful campaign conduct was the company's coercive communications?

If (c), would the judges' views change after considering that Congress has not acted to limit the Board's remedial power?

If (d), is there any evidence that could change the judges' views?

3. Compare the opinions in *Jamaica Towing* and *K & K Gourmet* with the following observations about remedies under the Act:

a. Orders to cease-and-desist from illegal conduct do no more than require adherence to existing legal obligations; posting of notices alerts employees to the company's prior conduct through artful language in which the company need not admit committing unfair labor practices. The deterrent value of these traditional remedies is questionable at best.

b. Back pay, as a remedy in Section 8(a)(3) cases, seems ineffective in preventing discriminatory discharges and in compensating discriminatees. Restitution may be costly, as in the *Darlington* settlement, but the expense may be more apparent than real. The back-pay award is reduced by an employee's interim earnings and by the amount the employee could have earned if she had engaged in a diligent job search. *Phelps Dodge Corp.* v. *NLRB* 313 U.S. 177, 8 LRRM 439 (1941). The employer's liability is tax deductible. A less easily quantified setoff is the savings attributed to defeat of the union. One economist has estimated that a firm with 10,000 employees saves $1 million dollars a year by avoiding a union. That figure is based on an extra direct labor cost of $0.05 per hour.* Finally, offers by employers to give discriminatees more than back pay in exchange for waiver of reinstatement rights suggest the limited deterrent value of monetary awards. As a means for restitution, back pay is equally unsuccessful. Employees are not compensated for expenses incurred because of discharge, such as interest on loans or loss of property for failure to meet installment payments. Those discriminatees who cannot be located, as many as 25 percent of the discharged workers, are never compensated.

---

*Testimony of Prof. B.R. Skelton, Hearings Before the Subcommittee on Labor-Management Relations of the Committee on Education and Labor, House of Representatives, 95th Cong., 1st Session. 219–20 (1977).

c. Reinstatement is considered a significant deterrent to unlawful conduct, since it returns union supporters to the workplace and provides a constant reminder to other employees that retaliation against union activity is unlawful. Although the NLRB Annual Report for 1980 reported that 89 percent of discriminatees accepted reinstatement, two studies raise questions about the effectiveness of the reinstatement remedy. Leslie Aspin examined a sample of 71 cases handled by the NLRB Boston office from 1962 to 1964.* Of 194 discriminatees, 64 (or 34 percent) refused reinstatement, in large part because of fear of company retaliation. In a study of all reinstatement cases arising in the Ft. Worth office, between 1971 and 1972, Warren H. Chaney found that 129 of 217 discriminatees (or 59 percent) declined reinstatement, with 114 persons citing fear of company backlash as a reason.** Fear of retaliation is sufficient in itself to cast doubt on the efficacy of the reinstatement remedy, but the employment histories of reinstated workers suggest that perception and reality are not far apart. In the Aspin group, 40 of the 85 reinstated employees left the companies, because of (unverifiable) bad treatment. Chaney's figures are even more dramatic. After eight years, only three reinstated workers remained in their jobs, with 65.3 percent of those who left citing "additional unfair company treatment" as a reason for their departures. (The companies identified "unfair company treatment" as the reason that 1.4 percent of the reinstated employees departed, while claiming that 62.5 percent of the reinstated discriminatees "left for unknown reasons.") Finally, the studies agree that the timing of reinstatement offers is critical. Aspin found that no one declined reinstatement when the case was settled within one month; Chaney's study showed acceptances by 93 percent of those offered reinstatement within two weeks, but of those offered reinstatement after six months, only five percent accepted.

Financial pressures on dischargees also undermine the deterrent value of the reinstatement remedy. If another job is not immediately available, many workers simply cannot afford to refuse a company's offer of back pay without reinstatement. (Unemployment insurance is unavailable in most states if a worker did not leave for "good cause"; claimants frequently find that state agents accept the company's reason for the discharge.) In the Aspin study only 10 of the discriminatees asserted the immediate need for back pay as their reason for accepting compensation without reinstatement. *But one of every three persons who refused reinstatement had not yet found another job.* It is more than reasonable to infer that pressing financial considerations compelled a substantial percentage of these working people to accept back pay in lieu of reinstatement.

d. Requiring a company to bargain with a union may lead to a collective bargaining agreement, but there is good reason to believe otherwise. The statute requires negotiations, not agreement; and it is a simple matter to meet the statutory obligation without ever signing a contract. One study estimates a 20 percent chance that employees who

---

*IRRA Proceedings (1970).
**The Reinstatement Remedy Revisited. 32 LAB. L.J. 357 (1981).

vote in a union will not secure a collective bargaining agreement. It is even less likely that employees whose desire for a union has dissipated because of illegal company conduct will be able to induce that company to sign a bargaining agreement. If the bargaining order is enforced four years after an election defeat, the union's ability to solidify support in the bargaining unit and to negotiate effectively is questionable.

e. Section 10(j) of the statute authorizes the Board to seek injunctive relief from the federal district courts after a complaint has been issued but before a decision by an administrative law judge or the Board itself. The General Counsel must present evidence that reasonable cause exists to believe that the Act has been or is being violated. In unfair labor practice cases involving election conduct, Section 10(j) injunctions could do much to deter illegal campaigning and to restore the status quo, by demonstrating the alacrity with which the NLRB acts to contain and neutralize the effects of allegedly illegal conduct. The Board has not chosen to exploit the potential of Section 10(j); in 1980–81 it authorized the General Counsel to seek only 71 10(j) injunctions.

f. Since 1957 the number of unfair labor practice charges has increased ninefold to 44,000. In 1980 the Board secured reinstatement for 1.3 employees in each representation election; in 1957 the figure was one employee for every six elections.

g. Even extraordinary remedies do not deter persistent violators. For example, from 1966 to 1980, the J.P. Stevens Company blatantly resisted union representation of any employees in its textile plants.* Company violations continued despite back-pay remedies in excess of $1 million dollars, numerous contempt citations by federal appeals courts, bargaining orders, requirements that union organizers have in-plant access to Stevens employees,** and awards to the NLRB of litigation costs. Fruitful bargaining did not occur until the Amalgamated Clothing and Textile Workers Union (ACTWU) adopted unusual pressure tactics. In addition to a consumer boycott (whose impact was questionable because Stevens' products are marketed under diverse labels), ACTWU identified companies with financial ties to the union and to Stevens. By threatening these companies with withdrawal of union pension funds or expensive proxy fights in usually uncontested elections for membership on the boards of directors, the union secured corporate cooperation in persuading Stevens to recognize and bargain with ACTWU. The 1980 contract between Stevens and ACTWU is significant not only because it presumably ends the 17-year-long labor dispute, but because it brings a company that had publicly vowed never to sign a collective bargaining agreement into compliance with national labor policy.

h. Whatever the direct financial benefit reaped by companies which resist unionization, there is an indirect gain: the expenditure of union resources. Ought one party be entitled to recover the costs associated with

---

*See e.g. NLRB v. J.P. Stevens & Co., 563 F.2d 8, 96 LRRM 2150 (2d Cir. 1977), cert. denied, 434 U.S. 1064, 97 LRRM 2747 (1978); and J.P. Stevens & Co. v. NLRB, 612 F.2d 881, 103 LRRM 2221 (4th Cir. 1980), cert. denied, 446 U.S. 956, 105 LRRM 2809 (1980).

**The access remedy has been applied to other repeat offenders, see United Steelworkers v. NLRB (Florida Steel Corp.), 646 F.2d 616, 106 LRRM 2573 (D.C. Cir. 1981), discussed supra at p. 207.

a rerun election? In considering your answer, would it make a difference if the reason for the second election was a change in Board law, if the contested conduct was not clearly an unfair labor practice, or if the violator was a repeat offender? Does the Act give the Board authority to order a reimbursement remedy?

In a somewhat different context, a union was awarded $10,000 as reimbursement for organizing expenses. A contractual pledge between the union and one of the company's facilities required the company to maintain a neutral position in any attempts to organize other facilities, provided that the company retained the right "to speak out in any manner appropriate when undue provocation" by the union occurred. During an organizing campaign, the union charged the company with violating the neutrality pledge. The arbitrator's discussion illustrates the difficulty of assessing damages.

"Wix's action undermined the UAW organizing effort and thus helped to force the UAW to withdraw its election petition temporarily. The UAW's momentum was halted and some part of its effort and expense were rendered useless. It will likely incur added expense when it returns to Gastonia to continue the campaign. Hence, the UAW has suffered money damages as a consequence of Wix's contract violation. But it is also true that the UAW organizing efforts have not been totally—or even largely—dissipated. No doubt substantial numbers of Wix employees maintain their interest in union representation because of the earlier UAW organizing effort. That interest is likely to rebound to the UAW's benefit when an election is finally held. The value to the UAW of its organizing campaign has not been lost. Moreover, no one can be certain what the outcome of the election would have been had Wix honored the neutrality pledge. Perhaps the UAW would have been defeated. The fact is that unions have not been successful in organizing Wix employees in the past.

"Nevertheless, it must be remembered that Wix is the wrongdoer here. Its contract violation has caused the UAW to lose the benefit of some of its organizing effort and will require the UAW to expend additional effort as well. There is money damage. While it is impossible to measure the degree of damage, I believe a proper money award of $10,000 to the UAW is justified." *Dana Corp.*, 76 LA 125 (1981).

4. The example of companies like J.P. Stevens and the increased use of management consultants whose tactics are inconsistent with the spirit if not the letter of the law have generated legislative proposals directed at strengthening the NLRB's remedial authority. The defeated Labor Law Reform Act of 1978 included provisions for a make-whole remedy, authorizing the Board to order any company that unlawfully refused to bargain on a first contract to compensate employees for lost wages and fringe benefits; double back pay for discriminatorily discharged employees; and debarment from federal contracts if a company willfully and repeatedly violated NLRB orders. Would the availability of such remedies deter companies like J.P. Stevens from engaging in illegal campaign-

ing? Or would these punitive measures alienate less intransigent companies and undermine the formation of bargaining relationships?

Another, but no less controversial, suggestion is to hold the representation election a few days after the filing of a petition. The goal of this approach is to secure an employee vote on unionization which is untainted by delay and unlawful campaigning. Questions about the appropriateness of a bargaining unit or the eligibility of particular employees would be resolved after the election itself. This procedure is used successfully in California, where a state statute gives farm workers organizing and bargaining rights, and in Canada. See California Labor Code section 1140 *et seq.*; and Weiler, *Promises to Keep: Securing Workers' Rights to Self-Organization Under the NLRA*, 96 HARV. L. REV. 1769 (1983). Is this proposal consistent with the goals of the NLRA? Or is it too powerful a response to the problem, given that the Board settles all but 4–5 percent of unfair labor practice charges? Or is it an appropriate cure, since each month of delay between filing a petition and holding an election means a 2.5 percent drop in union victories, and the more significant a company's preelection resistance, the less likely that a union election victory will be followed by the signing of a collective bargaining agreement?

How likely is it that companies which oppose dealing with a union will bargain instead of requesting hearings on voter eligibility and unit determination questions? Does the proposal to reduce delays by eliminating campaigns merely alter when delays occur?

4. Economic Warfare and Collective Bargaining

A. THE NATURE OF CONCERTED ACTIVITY*

Section 7 of the NLRA states that employees shall have the "right" to engage in "concerted activities for the purpose of . . . mutual aid or protection," and Section 8(a)(1) prohibits an employer from interfering with, restraining, or coercing employees in the exercise of that Section 7 right. Several questions arise immediately: What is a "concerted" activity? When is it for "mutual aid or protection"? Another question, already raised in earlier material in this book, is: What sorts of interference, restraint, or coercion will be permitted by Section 8(a)(1)? Are *all* concerted activities that fit the Section 7 description entitled to the protection of Section 8(a)(1)?

The NLRB and the courts, although the latter not quite so enthusiastically or consistently, have given "concerted activities" a fairly broad meaning. It is a concerted activity to refuse to be investigated by the employer without the presence of a union agent; it is concerted activity to complain about wages or other working conditions although the individual worker has not consulted with fellow employees (the courts have not been at all sure this is concerted activity); and it is concerted activity for an employee to complain about an alleged breach of a term of a collective bargaining contract.

The Board and the courts have also given very broad meaning to "mutual aid or protection," even extending that phrase to include activities which were aimed at helping workers of another employer, and even when those other workers were not "employees" within the meaning of the NLRA.

Eastex, Inc. v. NLRB

Supreme Court of the United States, 1978
437 U.S. 556, 98 LRRM 2717

MR. JUSTICE POWELL delivered the opinion of the Court.

Employees of petitioner sought to distribute a union newsletter in nonworking areas of petitioner's property during nonworking time urg-

*See Getman. *The Protection of Economic Pressure by Section 7 of the National Labor Relations Act,* 115 U. PA. L. REV. 1195 (1967); Schatzki, *Some Observations on a Misnomer—"Protected" Concerted Activities,* 47 TEX. L. REV. 378 (1969).

ing employees to support the union and discussing a proposal to incorporate the state "right-to-work" statute into the state constitution and a presidential veto of an increase in the federal minimum wage. The newsletter also called on employees to take action to protect their interests as employees with respect to these two issues. The question presented is whether petitioner's refusal to allow the distribution violated § 8(a)(1). . . .

I

Petitioner is a company that manufactures paper products in Silsbee, Tex. Since 1954, petitioner's production employees have been represented by Local 801 of the United Paperworkers International Union. It appears that many, although not all, of petitioner's approximately 800 production employees are members of Local 801. Since Texas is a "right-to-work" State by statute, Local 801 is barred from obtaining an agreement with petitioner requiring all production employees to become union members.

In March 1974, officers of Local 801, seeking to strengthen employee support for the union and perhaps recruit new members in anticipation of upcoming contract negotiations with petitioner, decided to distribute a union newsletter to petitioner's production employees. The newsletter was divided into four sections. The first and fourth sections urged employees to support and participate in the union and, more generally, extolled the benefits of union solidarity. The second section encouraged employees to write their legislators to oppose incorporation of the state "right-to-work" statute into a revised state constitution then under consideration, warning that incorporation would "weake[n] Unions and improv[e] the edge business has at the bargaining table." The third section noted that the President recently had vetoed a bill to increase the federal minimum wage from $1.60 to $2.00 per hour, compared this action to the increase of prices and profits in the oil industry under administration policies, and admonished, "As working men and women we must defeat our enemies and elect our friends. If you haven't registered to vote, please do so today."

. . .
On April 22, 1974, Boyd Young, president of Local 801, . . . asked [the Company] whether employees could distribute the newsletter in any nonworking areas of petitioner's property other than clock alley.[6] [The Company refused.]

---

[6]Young testified that he had asked "permission for employees of the Company to be allowed to distribute this on non-working hours, on non-production areas, and specifically outside the clock alley; and if that area posed a problem, we would be willing to move to any area convenient to the Company, out on the end of the walk or guardhouse or parking lot, that we would only hand it out to employees leaving the plant, and where it wouldn't cause a litter problem in the plant." The administrative law judge credited Young's testimony that the request was only for employees to distribute the newsletter.

At a hearing on [a] charge [of violation of § 8(a)(1), a Company official] testified that he had no objection to the first and fourth sections of the newsletter. He had denied permission to distribute the newsletter because he "didn't see any way in which [the second and third sections were] related to our association with the Union." [The Board held that the Company violated Section 8(a)(1) of the Act. The court of appeals enforced the Board's order.]

II

Two distinct questions are presented. The first is whether, apart from the location of the activity, distribution of the newsletter is the kind of concerted activity that is protected from employer interference by §§ 7 and 8(a)(1) of the National Labor Relations Act. If it is, then the second question is whether the fact that the activity takes place on petitioner's property gives rise to a countervailing interest that outweighs the exercise of § 7 rights in that location. . . .

A

Section 7 provides that "[e]mployees shall have the right . . . to engage in . . . concerted activities for the purpose of collective bargaining or other mutual aid or protection. . . ." Petitioner contends that the activity here is not within the "mutual aid or protection" language because it does not relate to a "specific dispute" between employees and their own employer "over an issue which the employer has the right or power to affect." In support of its position, petitioner asserts that the term "employees" in § 7 refers only to employees of a particular employer, so that only activity by employees on behalf of themselves or other employees of the same employer is protected. Petitioner also argues that the term "collective bargaining" in § 7 "indicates a direct bargaining relationship whereas 'other mutual aid or protection' must refer to activities of a similar nature. . . ." Thus, in petitioner's view, under § 7 "the employee is only protected for activity within the scope of the employment relationship." Petitioner rejects the idea that § 7 might protect any activity that could be characterized as "political," and suggests that the discharge of an employee who engages in any such activity would not violate the Act.

We believe that petitioner misconceives the reach of the "mutual aid or protection" clause. The "employees" who may engage in concerted activities for "mutual aid or protection" are defined by § 2(3) of the Act, 29 U.S.C. § 152(3), to "include any employee, and shall not be limited to the employees of a particular employer, unless the Act explicitly states otherwise. . . ." This definition was intended to protect employees when they engage in otherwise proper concerted activities in support of employees of employers other than their own. In recognition of this intent, the Board and the courts long have held that the "mutual aid or protection" clause encompasses such activity.[13] Petitioner's argument on this point ignores the language of the Act and its settled construction.

We also find no warrant for petitioner's view that employees lose their protection under the "mutual aid or protection" clause when they seek to improve terms and conditions of employment or otherwise improve their lot as employees through channels outside the immediate employee-employer relationship. The 74th Congress knew well enough that labor's cause often is advanced on fronts other than collective bargaining and grievance settlement within the immediate employment context. It recognized this fact by choosing, as the language of § 7 makes clear, to protect concerted activities for the somewhat broader purpose of "mutual aid or protection" as well as for the narrower purposes of "self-organization" and "collective bargaining." Thus, it has been held that the "mutual aid or protection" clause protects employees from retaliation by their employers when they seek to improve working conditions through resort to administrative and judicial forums, and that employees' appeals to legislators to protect their interests as employees are within the scope of this clause. To hold that activity of this nature is entirely unprotected—irrespective of location or the means employed—would leave employees open to retaliation for much legitimate activity that could improve their lot as employees. As this could "frustrate the policy of the Act to protect the right of workers to act together to better their working conditions," *NLRB* v. *Washington Aluminum Co.*, 370 U.S. 9, 50 LRRM 2235 (1962), we do not think that Congress could have intended the protection of § 7 to be as narrow as petitioner insists.[17]

It is true, of course, that some concerted activity bears a less immediate relationship to employees' interests as employees than other such activity.

---

[13]*E.g., Fort Wayne Corrugated Paper Co.* v. *NLRB*, 111 F.2d 869, 874 (CA 7 1940), *enforcing* 11 NLRB 1, 5–6 (1939) (right to assist in organizing another employer's employees); *NLRB* v. *J. G. Boswell Co.*, 136 F.2d 585, 595 (CA 9 1943), *enforcing* 35 NLRB 968 (1941) (right to express sympathy for striking employees of another employer); *Redwing Carriers, Inc.*, 137 NLRB 1545, 1546–1547 (1962), *enforced sub nom. Teamsters Union Local 79* v. *NLRB*, 117 U.S. App.D.C. 84, 325 F.2d 1011 (1963), *cert. denied*, 377 U.S. 905 (1964) (right to honor picket line of another employer's employees); *NLRB* v. *Alamo Express Co.*, 430 F.2d 1032, 1036 (CA 5 1970), *cert. denied*, 400 U.S. 1021 (1971), *enforcing* 170 NLRB 315 (1968) (accord); *Washington State Service Employees State Council No. 18*, 188 NLRB 957, 959 (1971) (right to demonstrate in support of another employer's employees); *Yellow Cab, Inc.*, 210 NLRB 568, 569 (1974) (right to distribute literature in support of another employer's employees). We express no opinion, however, as to the correctness of the particular balance struck between employees' exercise of § 7 rights and employers' legitimate interests in any of the above-cited cases.

[17]Petitioner relies upon several cases said to construe § 7 more narrowly than do we. . . . [The Court distinguished most of the cases relied upon by the employer.]

This leaves only *G&W Electric Specialty Co.* v. *NLRB*, 360 F.2d 873 (CA 7 1966), which refused to enforce a Board order because the concerted activity there—circulation of a petition concerning management of an employee-run credit union—"involved no request for any action upon the part of the Company and did not concern a matter over which the Company had any control." *Id.*, at 876. *G&W Electric* cites no authority for its narrowing of § 7, and it ignores a substantial weight of authority to the contrary, including the Seventh Circuit's own prior holding in *Fort Wayne Corrugated Paper Co.* v. *NLRB*, 111 F.2d 869, 874 (1940). See n. 13, *supra*. We therefore do not view any of these cases as persuasive authority for petitioner's position.

We may assume that at some point the relationship becomes so attenuated that an activity cannot fairly be deemed to come within the "mutual aid or protection" clause. It is neither necessary nor appropriate, however, for us to attempt to delineate precisely the boundaries of the "mutual aid or protection" clause. That task is for the Board to perform in the first instance as it considers the wide variety of cases that come before it. To decide this case, it is enough to determine whether the Board erred in holding that distribution of the second and third sections of the newsletter is for the purpose of "mutual aid or protection."

The Board determined that distribution of the second section, urging employees to write their legislators to oppose incorporation of the state "right-to-work" statute into a revised state constitution, was protected because union security is "central to the union concept of strength through solidarity" and "a mandatory subject of bargaining in other than right-to-work states." The newsletter warned that incorporation could affect employees adversely "by weakening Unions and improving the edge business has at the bargaining table." The fact that Texas already has a "right-to-work" statute does not render employees' interest in this matter any less strong, for, as the Court of Appeals noted, it is "one thing to face a legislative scheme which is open to legislative modification or repeal" and "quite another thing to face the prospect that such a scheme will be frozen in a concrete constitutional mandate." We cannot say that the Board erred in holding that this section of the newsletter bears such a relation to employees' interests as to come within the guarantee of the "mutual aid or protection" clause.

The Board held that distribution of the third section, criticizing a presidential veto of an increase in the federal minimum wage and urging employees to register to vote to "defeat our enemies and elect our friends," was protected despite the fact that petitioner's employees were paid more than the vetoed minimum wage. It reasoned that the "minimum wage inevitably influences wage levels derived from collective bargaining, even those far above the minimum," and that "concern by [petitioner's] employees for the plight of other employees might gain support for them at some future time when they might have a dispute with their employer." We think that the Board acted within the range of its discretion in so holding. Few topics are of such immediate concern to employees as the level of their wages. The Board was entitled to note the widely recognized impact that a rise in the minimum wage may have on the level of negotiated wages generally, a phenomenon that would not have been lost on petitioner's employees. The union's call, in the circumstances of this case, for these employees to back persons who support an increase in the minimum wage, and to oppose those who oppose it, fairly is characterized as concerted activity for the "mutual aid or protection" of petitioner's employees and of employees generally.

In sum, we hold that distribution of both the second and the third sections of the newsletter is protected under the "mutual aid or protection" clause of § 7.

B

The question that remains is whether the Board erred in holding that petitioner's employees may distribute the newsletter in nonworking areas of petitioner's property during nonworking time. . . .
. . .
Petitioner contends that the Board must distinguish among distributions of protected matter by employees on an employer's property on the basis of the content of each distribution. Echoing its earlier argument, petitioner urges that the *Republic Aviation* rule should not be applied if a distribution "does not involve a request for any action on the part of the employer, or does not concern a matter over which the employer has any degree of control. . . ." In petitioner's view, distribution of any other matter protected by § 7 would be an "unnecessary intrusio[n] on the employer's property rights," in the absence of a showing by employees that no alternative channels of communication with fellow employees are available.

We hold that the Board was not required to adopt this view in the case at hand. In the first place, petitioner's reliance on its property right is largely misplaced. Here, as in *Republic Aviation,* petitioner's employees are "already rightfully on the employer's property," so that in the context of this case it is the "employer's management interests rather than [its] property interests" that primarily are implicated. As already noted, petitioner made no attempt to show that its management interests would be prejudiced in any way by the exercise of § 7 rights proposed by its employees here. Even if the mere distribution by employees of material protected by § 7 can be said to intrude on petitioner's property rights in any meaningful sense, the degree of intrusion does not vary with the content of the material. Petitioner's only cognizable property right in this respect is in preventing employees from bringing literature onto its property and distributing it there—not in choosing which distributions protected by § 7 it wishes to suppress.

On the other side of the balance, it may be argued that the employees' interest in distributing literature that deals with matters affecting them as employees, but not with self-organization or collective bargaining, is so removed from the central concerns of the Act as to justify application of a different rule than in *Republic Aviation.* Although such an argument may have force in some circumstances, the Board to date generally has chosen not to engage in such refinement of its rules regarding the distribution of literature by employees during nonworking time in nonworking areas of their employers' property. We are not prepared to say in this case that the Board erred in the view it took.

It is apparent that the complexity of the Board's rules and the difficulty of the Board's task might be compounded greatly if it were required to distinguish not only between literature that is within and without the protection of § 7, but also among subcategories of literature within that protection. In addition, whatever the strength of the employees' § 7 interest in distributing particular literature, the Board is entitled to view the intrusion by employees on the property rights of their employer as quite limited in this context as long as the employer's management interests are adequately protected. The Board also properly may take into account the fact that the plant is a particularly appropriate place for the distribution of § 7 material, because it "is the one place where [employees] clearly share common interests and where they traditionally seek to persuade fellow workers in matters affecting their union organizational life and other matters related to their status as employees." *Gale Products*, 142 NLRB 1246, 1249 (1963).

We need not go so far in this case, however, as to hold that the *Republic Aviation* rule properly is applied to every in-plant distribution of literature that falls within the protective ambit of § 7. This is a new area for the Board and the courts which has not yet received mature consideration. It may be that the "nature of the problem, as revealed by unfolding variant situations," requires "an evolutionary process for its rational response, not a quick, definitive formula as a comprehensive answer." *Local 761, Electrical Workers* v. *NLRB*, 366 U.S. 667, 674, 48 LRRM 2210 (1961). For this reason, we confine our holding to the facts of this case.

Petitioner concedes that its employees were entitled to distribute a substantial portion of this newsletter on its property. In addition, as we have held above, the sections to which petitioner objected concern activity which petitioner, in the absence of a countervailing interest of its own, is not entitled to suppress. Yet petitioner made no attempt to show that its management interests would be prejudiced in any manner by distribution of these sections, and in our view any incremental intrusion on petitioner's property rights from their distribution together with the other sections would be minimal. Moreover, it is undisputed that the Union undertook the distribution in order to boost its support and improve its bargaining position in upcoming contract negotiations with petitioner. Thus, viewed in context, the distribution was closely tied to vital concerns of the Act. In these circumstances, we hold that the Board did not err in applying the *Republic Aviation* rule to the facts of this case. The judgment of the Court of Appeals therefore is

Affirmed.

Mr. Justice Rehnquist, with whom The Chief Justice joins, dissenting:

It is not necessary to determine the scope of the "mutual aid or protection" language of § 7 of the National Labor Relations Act to conclude that Congress never intended to require the opening of private property to the sort of political advocacy involved in this case. Petitioner's right as a property owner to prescribe the conditions under which strangers may enter its property is fully recognized under Texas law. . . .

The Court today cites no case in which it has ever held that anyone, whether an employee or a nonemployee, has a protected right to engage in anything other than organizational activity on an employer's property. The simple question before us is whether Congress has authorized the Board to displace an employer's right to prevent the distribution on his property of political material concerning matters over which he has no control. In eschewing any analysis of this question, in deference to the supposed expertise of the Board, the Court permits a " 'yielding' of property rights" which is certainly not "temporary"; and I cannot conclude that the deprivation of such a right of property can be dismissed as "minimal." It may be that Congress has power under the Commerce Clause to require an employer to open his property to such political advocacy, but, if Congress intended to do so, "such a legislative intention should be found in some definite and unmistakable expression." [*NLRB v. Fansteel Metallurgical Corp.*] 306 U.S. 240, 255. Finding no such expression in the Act, I would not permit the Board to balance away petitioner's right to exclude political literature from its property.

I would reverse the judgment of the Court of Appeals.

Questions

1. Implicit in the union's victory in *Eastex* is the notion, once again, that the courts (and the Board) retain the authority to evaluate what is "important" or "appropriate" for labor unions to do in our society. Is there any reason to believe that those governmental agencies understand better or have better insights into the labor movement than comparable institutions did nearly one hundred years ago?

2. Is the dissent's concern for the employer's property more than concern for symbolic values? Or is the dissent's concern more a matter of the employer's First Amendment interest in not giving support to political views with which its does not agree?

3. Would the result in *Eastex* have been the same if the newsletter supported specifically named candidates for public office?

4. Would the result in *Eastex* have been the same if the issue had been raised in the context of employees' protesting the employer's support for the right-to-work amendment to the state constitution?

NLRB v. Local Union No. 1229, International Brotherhood of Electrical Workers

Supreme Court of the United States, 1953
346 U.S. 464, 33 LRRM 2183

[The employer, a relatively new local television station named the Jefferson Standard Broadcasting Company, and the union, representing the company's 22 technicians, entered into collective bargaining. Primarily because of a failure to agree as to the jurisdiction an arbitrator would have in discharge cases, the parties did not enter into a contract. The union picketed. The employees did not strike.]

Mr. Justice Burton delivered the opinion of the Court.

. . . But on August 24, 1949, a new procedure made its appearance. Without warning, several . . . technicians launched a vitriolic attack on the quality of the company's television broadcasts. Five thousand handbills were printed over the designation "wbt technicians." These were distributed on the picket line, on the public square two or three blocks from the company's premises, in barber shops, restaurants and buses. Some were mailed to local businessmen. The handbills made no reference to the union, to a labor controversy or to collective bargaining. They read:

"IS CHARLOTTE A SECOND-CLASS CITY?

"You might think so from the kind of Television programs being presented by the Jefferson Standard Broadcasting Co. over WBTV. Have you seen one of their television programs lately? Did you know that all the programs presented over WBTV are on film and may be from one day to five years old. There are no local programs presented by WBTV. You cannot receive the local baseball games, football games or other local events because WBTV does not have the proper equipment to make these pickups. Cities like New York, Boston, Philadelphia, Washington receive such programs nightly. Why doesn't the Jefferson Standard Broadcasting Company purchase the needed equipment to bring you the same type of programs enjoyed by other leading American cities? Could it be that they consider Charlotte a second-class community and only entitled to the pictures now being presented to them?

"WBT TECHNICIANS"

This attack continued until September 3, 1949, when the company discharged ten of its technicians, whom it charged with sponsoring or distributing these handbills. The company's letter discharging them tells its side of the story.[4]

[4]"Dear Mr. . . . ,
"When you and some of our other technicians commenced early in July to picket against this Company, we felt that your action was very ill-considered. We were paying you a salary of . . . per week, to say nothing of other benefits which you receive as an employee of our Company, such as time-and-a-half pay for all work beyond eight hours in any one day, three weeks vacation each year with full pay, unlimited sick leave with full pay, liberal life insurance and hospitalization, for you and your family, and retirement and pension benefits unexcelled anywhere. Yet when we were unable to agree upon the terms of a contract with your Union, you began to denounce us publicly as 'unfair.'
"And ever since early July while you have been walking up and down the street with placards and literature attacking us, you have continued to hold your job and receive your pay and all the other benefits referred to above.
"Even when you began to put out propaganda which contained many untruths about our Company and great deal of personal abuse and slander, we still continued to treat you exactly as before. For it has been our understanding that under our labor laws, you have a very great latitude in trying to make the public believe that your employer is unfair to you.
"Now, however, you have turned from trying to persuade the public that we are unfair to you and are trying to persuade the public that we give inferior service to them. While we are struggling to expand into and develop a new field, and incidentally losing large sums of money in the process, you are busy trying to turn customers and the public against us in every possible way, even handing out leaflets on the public streets advertising that our operations are 'second-class,' and endeavoring in various ways to hamper and totally destroy our business. Certainly we are not required by law or common sense to keep you in our employment and pay you a substantial salary while you thus do your best to tear down and bankrupt our business.
"You are hereby discharged from our employment. Although there is nothing requiring

September 4, the union's picketing resumed its original tenor and, September 13, the union filed with the Board a charge that the company, by discharging the above-mentioned ten technicians, had engaged in an unfair labor practice. . . . The Board found that one of the discharged men had neither sponsored nor distributed the "Second-Class City" handbill and ordered his reinstatement with back pay. It then found that the other nine had sponsored or distributed the handbill and held that the company, by discharging them for such conduct, had not engaged in an unfair labor practice. The Board, accordingly, did not order their reinstatement. One member dissented. Under § 10(f) of the Taft-Hartley Act, the union petitioned the Court of Appeals for the District of Columbia Circuit for a review of the Board's order and for such a modification of it as would reinstate all ten of the discharged technicians with back pay. That court remanded the cause to the Board for further consideration and for a finding as to the "unlawfulness" of the conduct of the employees which had led to their discharge. 202 F.2d 186.[7]

The company's letter shows that it interpreted the handbill as a demonstration of such detrimental disloyalty as to provide "cause" for its refusal to continue in its employ the perpetrators of the attack. We agree.

Section 10(c) of the Taft-Hartley Act expressly provides that "No order of the Board shall require the reinstatement of any individual as an employee who has been suspended or discharged, or the payment to him of any back pay, if such individual was suspended or discharged for cause." There is no more elemental cause for discharge of an employee than disloyalty to his employer. It is equally elemental that the Taft-Hartley Act seeks to strengthen, rather than to weaken, that cooperation, continuity of service and cordial contractual relation between employer and employee that is born of loyalty to their common enterprise.

. . .

In the instant case the Board found that the company's discharge of the nine offenders resulted from their sponsoring and distributing the "Second-Class City" handbills of August 24–September 3, issued in their name as the "WBT TECHNICIANS." Assuming that there had been no pending labor controversy, the conduct of the "WBT TECHNICIANS" from August 24 through September 3 unquestionably would have provided

---

us to do so, and the circumstances certainly do not call for us doing so, we are enclosing a check payable to your order for two weeks' advance or severance pay.

"Very truly yours,
"Jefferson Standard Broadcasting Company
"By: CHARLES H. CRUTCHFIELD
"*Vice President*

"Enclosure"

[7]The Court of Appeals said:

"Protection under § 7 of the Act . . . is withdrawn only from those concerted activities which contravene either (a) specific provisions or basic policies of the Act or of related federal statutes, or (b) specific rules of other federal or local law that is not incompatible with the Board's governing statute. . . .

. . .

"We think the Board failed to make the finding essential to its conclusion that the concerted activity was unprotected. Sound practice in judicial review of administrative orders precludes this court from determining 'unlawfulness' without a prior consideration and finding by the Board."

adequate cause for their disciplinary discharge within the meaning of § 10(c). Their attack related itself to no labor practice of the company. It made no reference to wages, hours or working conditions. The policies attacked were those of finance and public relations for which management, not technicians, must be responsible. The attack asked for no public sympathy or support. It was a continuing attack, initiated while off duty, upon the very interests which the attackers were being paid to conserve. and develop. Nothing could be further from the purpose of the Act then to require an employer to finance such activities. Nothing would contribute less to the Act's declared purpose of promoting industrial peace and stability.[12]

The fortuity of the coexistence of a labor dispute affords these technicians no substantial defense. While they were also union men and leaders in the labor controversy, they took pains to separate those categories. In contrast to their claims on the picket line as to the labor controversy, their handbill of August 24 omitted all reference to it. The handbill diverted attention from the labor controversy. It attacked public policies of the company which had no discernible relation to that controversy. The only connection between the handbill and the labor controversy was an ultimate and undisclosed purpose or motive on the part of some of the sponsors that, by the hoped-for financial pressure, the attack might extract from the company some future concession. A disclosure of that motive might have lost more public support for the employees than it would have gained, for it would have given the handbill more the character of coercion than of collective bargaining. Referring to the attack, the Board said "In our judgment, these tactics, in the circumstances of this case, were hardly less 'indefensible' than acts of physical sabotage." In any event, the findings of the Board effectively separate the attack from the labor controversy and treat it solely as one made by the company's technical experts upon the quality of the company's product. As such, it was as adequate a cause for the discharge of its sponsors as if the labor controversy had not been pending. The technicians, themselves, so handled their attack as thus to bring their discharge under § 10(c).

The Board stated "We . . . do not decide whether the disparagement of product involved here would have justified the employer in discharging the employees responsible for it, had it been uttered in the context of a conventional appeal for support of the union in the labor dispute." This underscored the Board's factual conclusion that the attack of August 24 was not part of an appeal for support in the pending dispute. It was a concerted separate attack purporting to be made in the interest of the public rather than in that of the employees.

Mr. Justice Frankfurter, whom Mr. Justice Black and Mr. Justice Douglas join, dissenting.

. . .

---

[12]". . . An employee can not work and strike at the same time. He can not continue in his employment and openly or secretly refuse to do his work. He can not collect wages for his employment, and, at the same time, engage in activities to injure or destroy his employer's business." *Hoover Co.* v. *Labor Board*, 191 F.2d 380, 389, and see *Labor Board* v. *Montgomery Ward & Co.*, 157 F.2d 486, 496; *United Biscuit Co.* v. *Labor Board*, 128 F.2d 771.

[T]he Court, relying on § 10(c) which permits discharges "for cause,' points to the "disloyalty" of the employees and finds sufficient "cause" regardless of whether the handbill was a "concerted activity" within § 7. Section 10(c) does not speak of discharge "for disloyalty." If Congress had so written that section, it would have overturned much of the law that had been developed by the Board and the courts in the twelve years preceding the Taft-Hartley Act. The legislative history makes clear that Congress had no such purpose but was rather expressing approval of the construction of "concerted activities" adopted by the Board and the courts. Many of the legally recognized tactics and weapons of labor would readily be condemned for "disloyalty" were they employed between man and man in friendly personal relations. In this connection it is significant that the ground now taken by the Court, insofar as it is derived from the provision of § 10(c) relating to discharge "for cause," was not invoked by the Board in justification of its order.

To suggest that all actions which in the absence of a labor controversy might be "cause"—or, to use the words commonly found in labor agreements, "just cause"—for discharge should be unprotected, even when such actions were undertaken as "concerted activities, for the purpose of collective bargaining," is to misconstrue legislation designed to put labor on a fair footing with management. Furthermore, it would disregard the rough and tumble of strikes, in the course of which loose and even reckless language is properly discounted.

"Concerted activities" by employees and dismissal "for cause" by employers are not dissociated legal criteria under the Act. They are like the two halves of a pair of shears. Of course, as the Conference Report on the Taft-Hartley Act said, men on strike may be guilty of conduct "in connection with a concerted activity" which properly constitutes "cause" for dismissal and bars reinstatement. But § 10(c) does not obviate the necessity for a determination whether the distribution of the handbill here was a legitimate tool in a labor dispute or was so "improper," as the Conference Report put it, as to be denied the protection of § 7 and to constitute a discharge "for cause." It is for the Board, in the first instance, to make these evaluations, and a court of appeals does not travel beyond its proper bounds in asking the Board for greater explicitness in light of the correct legal standards for judgment.

The Board and the courts of appeals will hardly find guidance for future cases from this Court's reversal of the Court of Appeals, beyond that which the specific facts of this case may afford. More than that, to float such imprecise notions as "discipline" and "loyalty" in the context of labor controversies, as the basis of the right to discharge, is to open the door wide to individual judgment by Board members and judges. One may anticipate that the Court's opinion will needlessly stimulate litigation.

Section 7 of course only protects "concerted activities" in the course of promoting legitimate interests of labor. But to treat the offensive handbills here as though they were circulated by the technicians as interloping outsiders to the sustained dispute between them and their employer is a very unreal way of looking at the circumstances of a labor controversy. Certainly there is nothing in the language of the Act or in the legislative history to indicate that only conventional placards and handbills, headed by a trite phrase such as "UNFAIR TO LABOR," are protected. In any event, on a remand the Board could properly be asked to leave no doubt whether the technicians, in distributing their handbills, were, so far as the public could tell, on a frolic of their own or whether this tactic, however unorthodox, was no more unlawful than other union behavior previously found to be entitled to protection.

It follows that the Court of Appeals should not be reversed.

Notes

1. In what way were the employees in *Local 1229, IBEW,* more disloyal than employees who strike and use picket signs decrying their employer as unfair? Is the court suggesting that disloyalty in attacking the product cannot be considered protected activity? See *Patterson-Sargent Co.,* 115 NLRB 1627, 38 LRRM 1134 (1956), for an extension of *Local 1229's* reasoning to union-employee attacks on the quality of the employer's products because they were made by nonunion strikebreakers. Is the extension defensible?

What do you think the Court would have done if the employer had discharged the nonstriking employees for picketing during their "off" hours? Does the Court supply a basis upon which you can rationally answer the question?

2. As the Court indicates, unlawful concerted action, or action which is inconsistent with the policies of the Act, is traditionally deemed unprotected. For example, employees who engage in a violent sit-down strike in protest of their employer's unfair labor practices are not protected by the Act. *NLRB v. Fansteel Metallurgical Corp.,* 306 U.S. 240, 4 LRRM 515 (1939). On the other hand, a peaceful sit-down strike which ended at the request of the police is protected, *Pepsi-Cola Bottling v. NLRB,* 449 F.2d 824, 78 LRRM 2481 (5th Cir. 1971), although the act violated state law. Employees who violate the federal mutiny laws by striking are not protected. *Southern S.S. Co. v. NLRB,* 316 U.S. 31, 10 LRRM 544 (1942). Employees who engage in unfair labor practices are not protected. See *NLRB v. National Packing,* 377 F.2d 800, 65 LRRM 2507 (10th Cir. 1967). Employees who engage in activities to force the employer to violate the NLRA or another law are also unprotected. *Hoover Co. v. NLRB,* 191 F.2d 380, 28 LRRM 2353 (6th Cir. 1951); *American News Co.,* 55 NLRB 1302, 14 LRRM 64 (1944).

Before taking away the protection of the Act from certain concerted activities, is it relevant to ask whether the employees knew, or should have known, that what they were doing was unlawful, inconsistent with the policies of the Act, "disloyal," or "indefensible" to the extent there was "good cause" for discharge? Neither the Board nor the courts ask that question.

3. In *NLRB v. Washington Aluminum Co.,* 370 U.S. 9, 50 LRRM 2235 (1962), the Supreme Court affirmed the Board's determination that unrepresented and unorganized employees were protected by the Act

when they engaged in an unannounced strike to protest cold working conditions, despite the fact the group did not inform the employer of the purpose of the protest. The Court explained:

"We cannot agree that employees necessarily lose their right to engage in concerted activities under § 7 merely because they do not present a specific demand upon their employer to remedy a condition they find objectionable. The language of § 7 is broad enough to protect concerted activities whether they take place before, after, or at the same time such a demand is made. To compel the Board to interpret and apply that language in the restricted fashion suggested by the respondent here would only tend to frustrate the policy of the Act to protect the right of workers to act together to better their working conditions. Indeed, as indicated by this very case, such an interpretation of § 7 might place burdens upon employees so great that it would effectively nullify the right to engage in concerted activities which that section protects. The seven employees here were part of a small group of employees who were wholly unorganized. They had no bargaining representative and, in fact, no representative of any kind to present their grievances to their employer. Under these circumstances, they had to speak for themselves as best they could. . . . Having no bargaining representative and no established procedure by which they could take full advantage of their unanimity of opinion in negotiations with the company, the men took the most direct course to let the company know that they wanted a warmer place in which to work. So, after talking among themselves, they walked out together in the hope that this action might spotlight their complaint and bring about some improvement in that they considered to be the 'miserable' conditions of their employment. This we think was enough to justify the Board's holding that they were not required to make any more specific demand than they did to be entitled to the protection of § 7.

". . . The findings of the Board, which are supported by substantial evidence and which were not disturbed below, show a running dispute between the machine shop employees and the company over the heating of the shop on cold days—a dispute which culminated in the decision of the employees to act concertedly in an effort to force the company to improve that condition of their employment. The fact that the company was already making every effort to repair the furnace and bring heat into the shop that morning does not change the nature of the controversy that caused the walkout. At the very most, that fact might tend to indicate that the conduct of the men in leaving was unnecessary and unwise, and it has long been settled that the reasonableness of workers' decisions to engage in concerted activity is irrelevant to the determination of whether a labor dispute exists or not.[12] Moreover, the

---

[12]"The wisdom or unwisdom of the men, their justification or lack of it, in attributing to respondent an unreasonable or arbitrary attitude in connection with the negotiations, cannot determine whether, when they struck, they did so as a consequence of or in connection with a current labor dispute. *Labor Board* v. *Mackay Radio & Telegraph Co.*, 304 U.S. 333, 344."

evidence here shows that the conduct of these workers was far from unjustified under the circumstances. The company's own foreman expressed the opinion that the shop was so cold that the men should go home. This statement by the foreman but emphasizes the obvious— that is, that the conditions of coldness about which complaint had been made before had been so aggravated on the day of the walkout that the concerted action of the men in leaving their jobs seemed like a perfectly natural and reasonable thing to do. . . .

"It is of course true that § 7 does not protect all concerted activities, but that aspect of the section is not involved in this case. The activities engaged in here do not fall within the normal categories of unprotected concerted activities such as those that are unlawful, violent or in breach of contract. Nor can they be brought under this Court's more recent pronouncement which denied the protection of § 7 to activities characterized as "indefensible" because they were there found to show a disloyalty to the workers' employer which this Court deemed unnecessary to carry on the workers' legitimate concerted activities. The activities of these seven employees cannot be classified as "indefensible" by any recognized standard of conduct. Indeed, concerted activities by employees for the purpose of trying to protect themselves from working conditions as uncomfortable as the testimony and Board findings showed them to be in this case are unquestionably activities to correct conditions which modern labor-management legislation treats as too bad to have to be tolerated in a humane and civilized society like ours."

4. Is the line between "protected" and "unprotected" concerted activities reminiscent of the distinctions drawn in the common-law cases? Given the history you have read, can it be accurately said, for example, that *Washington Aluminum*, rather than *Local 1229*, more accurately reflects what Congress wanted to accomplish with Sections 7 and 8(a)(1)? Is it helpful in analysis to observe that a presumptively expert agency (rather than a court) is drawing the line between "protected" and "unprotected"?

Comment on Union Waiver of Section 7 Rights

In addition to the grounds already set out for denying concerted activities the protection of the NLRA, there is another of importance. In Chapter 5, you will be exposed to law dealing with the nature of the collective bargaining contract and its effect on the parties. It is necessary, however, to anticipate that chapter. Sometimes a union can "waive," through collective bargaining, some of the employees' Section 7 rights. Most important, the Board and the courts have consistently held that the collective bargaining contract can properly outlaw strikes; any employee who breaches the contract's no-strike clause is normally engaging in unprotected activity. See *NLRB* v. *Sands Mfg. Co.,* 306 U.S. 332, 4 LRRM 530 (1939); *Rockaway News Supply Co.,* 95 NLRB 336, 31 LRRM 2432 (1951), *enf. denied,* 197 F.2d 111, 30 LRRM 2119 (1952), *aff'd,* 345 U.S. 71

(1953). You will learn in the next chapter that a promise not to strike can be inferred from the promise to arbitrate the underlying dispute. You will also learn that the Supreme Court's love for arbitration (and its concomitant distaste for strikes during the term of the collective bargaining contract) is as close to an absolute as any in labor law.

When can employees strike during the term of a collective bargaining contract and still have the protection of the Act? Apparently, if the employer engages in serious unfair labor practices which, perhaps, threaten the status of the union representative, a general no-strike clause does not work as a waiver of the right to strike. *Mastro Plastics Corp.* v. *NLRB*, 350 U.S. 270, 37 LRRM 2587 (1956).

In *NLRB* v. *Magnavox Co.*, 415 U.S. 322, 85 LRRM 2475 (1974), a case not involving the right to strike, the Supreme Court upheld the Board's determination that it was unlawful for an employer to forbid employees' distribution of union literature during nonworking time and in nonworking areas. This would not be noteworthy but for the fact that the union that represented the employees apparently had authorized the employer to have such a rule. Why cannot the union waive the Section 7 right involved in *Magnavox?* How is it distinguishable from the waiver of the right to strike? The Court said:

"[A] different rule should obtain where the rights of the employees to exercise their choice of a bargaining representative is involved— whether to have no bargaining representative, or to retain the present one, or to obtain a new one. When the right to such a choice is at issue, it is difficult to assume that the incumbent union has no self-interest of its own to serve by perpetuating itself as the bargaining representative."

If this reasoning is sound, why shouldn't the union be able to waive the right of employees to distribute literature for that union? Moreover, does it follow that when the union is not representing some of the interests of some of the employees, the union cannot waive the rights of these employees? If so, would it be enough that the employees reasonably or in good faith believed they were not being represented?

In *Alexander* v. *Gardner-Denver Co.*, 415 U.S. 36, 7 FEP 81 (1974), an employee had charged his employer with discharging him for being black and, therefore, with violating Title VII of the Civil Rights Act of 1964. The employee had already litigated that issue in arbitration, pursuant to a collective bargaining contract, and the employer had been upheld in discharging the plaintiff-employee. The Court held that the arbitrator's determination was not a bar to a Title VII action. In the course of getting to that result, the Court reasoned:

"It is true, of course, that a union may waive certain statutory rights related to collective activity, such as the right to strike. These rights are conferred on employees collectively to foster the processes of bargaining and properly may be exercised or relinquished by the union as collective-bargaining agent to obtain economic benefits for unit members. Title VII, on the other hand, stands on plainly different ground;

it concerns not majoritarian processes, but an individual's right to equal employment opportunities."

Is this reasoning persuasive? Can a majoritarian union waive the rights of a minority of employees to strike? to protest to their employer? to have vacation breaks? to be free of arbitrary or unlawful employment practices? for any purpose?

Emporium Capwell Co. v. Western Addition Community Organization*

Supreme Court of the United States, 1975
420 U.S. 50, 88 LRRM 2660

Opinion of the Court by MR. JUSTICE MARSHALL, announced by MR. CHIEF JUSTICE BURGER.

This litigation presents the question whether, in light of the national policy against racial discrimination in employment, the National Labor Relations Act protects concerted activity by a group of minority employees to bargain with their employer over issues of employment discrimination. The National Labor Relations Board held that the employees could not circumvent their elected representative to engage in such bargaining. The Court of Appeals for the District of Columbia Circuit reversed and remanded, holding that in certain circumstances the activity would be protected. . . . We now reverse.

I

The Emporium Capwell Co. (Company) operates a department store in San Francisco. At all times relevant to this litigation it was a party to the collective-bargaining agreement negotiated by the San Francisco Retailer's Council, of which it was a member, and the Department Store Employees Union (Union) which represented all stock and marking area employees of the Company. The agreement, in which the Union was recognized as the sole collective-bargaining agency for all covered employees, prohibited employment discrimination by reason of race, color, creed, national origin, age, or sex, as well as union activity. It had a no-strike or lockout clause, and it established grievance and arbitration machinery for processing any claimed violation of the contract, including a violation of the antidiscrimination clause.

On April 3, 1968, a group of Company employees covered by the agreement met with the secretary-treasurer of the Union, Walter Johnson, to present a list of grievances including a claim that the Company was discriminating on the basis of race in making assignments and promotions. The Union official agreed to take certain of the grievances and to

*See Cantor, *Dissident Worker Action, After the* Emporium, 29 RUTGERS L. REV. 35 (1975); Meltzer, *The National Labor Relations Act and Racial Discrimination: The More Remedies the Better?* 42 CHI. L. REV. 1 (1974).

investigate the charge of racial discrimination. He appointed an investigating committee and prepared a report on the employees' grievances, which he submitted to the Retailer's Council and which the Council in turn referred to the Company. The report described "the possibility of racial discrimination" as perhaps the most important issue raised by the employees and termed the situation at the Company as potentially explosive if corrective action were not taken. It offered as an example of the problem the Company's failure to promote a Negro stock employee regarded by other employees as an outstanding candidate but a victim of racial discrimination.

Shortly after receiving the report, the Company's labor relations director met with Union representatives and agreed to "look into the matter" of discrimination and see what needed to be done. Apparently unsatisfied with these representations, the Union held a meeting in September attended by Union officials, Company employees, and representatives of the California Fair Employment Practices Committee (FEPC) and the local antipoverty agency. The secretary-treasurer of the Union announced that the Union had concluded that the Company was discriminating, and that it would process every such grievance through to arbitration if necessary. Testimony about the Company's practices was taken and transcribed by a court reporter, and the next day the Union notified the Company of its formal charge and demanded that the joint union-management Adjustment Board be convened "to hear the entire case."

At the September meeting some of the Company's employees had expressed their view that the contract procedures were inadequate to handle a systemic grievance of this sort; they suggested that the Union instead begin picketing the store in protest. Johnson explained that the collective agreement bound the Union to its processes and expressed his view that successful grievants would be helping not only themselves but all others who might be the victims of invidious discrimination as well. The FEPC and antipoverty agency representatives offered the same advice. Nonetheless, when the Adjustment Board meeting convened on October 16, James Joseph Hollins, Tom Hawkins, and two other employees whose testimony the Union had intended to elicit refused to participate in the grievance procedure. Instead, Hollins read a statement objecting to reliance on correction of individual inequities as an approach to the problem of discrimination at the store and demanding that the president of the Company meet with the four protestants to work out a broader agreement for dealing with the issue as they saw it. The four employees then walked out of the hearing.

Hollins attempted to discuss the question of racial discrimination with the Company president shortly after the incidents of October 16. The president refused to be drawn into such a discussion but suggested to Hollins that he see the personnel director about the matter. Hollins, who had spoken to the personnel director before, made no effort to do so again. Rather, he and Hawkins and several other dissident employees held a press conference on October 22, at which they denounced the store's employment policy as racist, reiterated their desire to deal directly with "the top management" of the Company over minority employment conditions, and announced their intention to picket and institute a boycott of the store. On Saturday, November 2, Hollins, Hawkins, and at least two other employees picketed the store throughout the day and distributed at the entrance handbills urging consumers not to patronize the store.[2] Johnson encountered the picketing employees, again urged them to rely on the grievance process, and warned that they might be fired for their activities. The pickets, however, were not dissuaded, and they continued to press their demand to deal directly with the Company president.

On November 7, Hollins and Hawkins were given written warnings that a repetition of the picketing or public statements about the Company could lead to their discharge.[4] When the conduct was repeated the following Saturday, the two employees were fired.

Western Addition Community Organization (hereinafter respondent), a local civil rights association of which Hollins and Hawkins were members, filed a charge against the Company with the National Labor Relations Board. The Board's General Counsel subsequently issued a complaint alleging that in discharging the two the Company had violated § 8(a)(1) of the National Labor Relations Act. After a hearing, the NLRB Trial Examiner found that the discharged employees had believed in good faith that the Company was discriminating against minority employees, and that they had resorted to concerted activity on the basis of that belief. He concluded, however, that their activity was not protected by § 7 of the Act and that their discharges did not, therefore, violate § 8(a)(1).

[2]The full text of the handbill read:

"* *BEWARE * * * * BEWARE * * * * BEWARE * *
"EMPORIUM SHOPPERS
" 'Boycott Is On' 'Boycott Is On' 'Boycott is On'
"For years at The Emporium black, brown, yellow and red people have worked at the lowest jobs, at the lowest levels. Time and time again we have seen intelligent, hard working brothers and sisters denied promotions and respect.
"The Emporium is a 20th Century colonial plantation. The brothers and sisters are being treated the same way as our brothers are being treated in the slave mines of Africa.
"Whenever the racist pig at The Emporium injures or harms a black sister or brother, they injure and insult all black people. THE EMPORIUM MUST PAY FOR THESE INSULTS. Therefore, we encourage all of our people to take their money out of this racist store, until black people have full employment and are promoted justly through out The Emporium.
"We welcome the support of our brothers and sisters from the churches, unions, sororities, fraternities, social clubs, Afro-American Institute, Black Panther Party, W. A. C. O. and the Poor Peoples Institute."
[4]The warning given to Hollins read:
"On October 22, 1968, you issued a public statement at a press conference to which all newspapers, radio, and TV stations were invited. The contents of this statement were substantially the same as those set forth in the sheet attached. This statement was broadcast on Channel 2 on October 22, 1968 and Station KDIA.
"On November 2nd you distributed copies of the attached statement to Negro customers and prospective customers, and to other persons passing by in front of The Emporium.
"These statements are untrue and are intended to and will, if continued, injure the reputation of The Emporium.
"There are ample legal remedies to correct any discrimination you may claim to exist. Therefore, we view your activities as a deliberate and unjustified attempt to injure your employer.
"This is to inform you that you may be discharged if you repeat any of the above acts or make any similar public statement."
That given to Hawkins was the same except that the first paragraph was not included.

The Board, after oral argument, adopted the findings and conclusions of its Trial Examiner and dismissed the complaint. Among the findings adopted by the Board was that the discharged employees' course of conduct

"was no mere presentation of a grievance but nothing short of a demand that the [Company] bargain with the picketing employees for the entire group of minority employees."[5]

The Board concluded that protection of such an attempt to bargain would undermine the statutory system of bargaining through an exclusive, elected representative, impede elected unions' efforts at bettering the working conditions of minority employees, "and place on the Employer an unreasonable burden of attempting to placate self-designated representatives of minority groups while abiding by the terms of a valid bargaining agreement and attempting in good faith to meet whatever demands the bargaining representative put forth under that agreement."

On respondent's petition for review the Court of Appeals reversed and remanded. . . .

II

Before turning to the central questions of labor policy raised by these cases, it is important to have firmly in mind the character of the underlying conduct to which we apply them. As stated, the Trial Examiner and the Board found that the employees were discharged for attempting to bargain with the Company over the terms and conditions of employment as they affected racial minorities. Although the Court of Appeals expressly declined to set aside this finding, respondent has devoted considerable effort to attacking it in this Court, on the theory that the employees were attempting only to present a grievance to their employer within the meaning of the first proviso to § 9(a).[12] We see no occasion to disturb the finding of the Board. The issue, then, is whether such

---

[5]192 NLRB, at 185. The evidence marshaled in support of this finding consisted of Hollins' meeting with the Company president in which he said that he wanted to discuss the problem perceived by minority employees; his statement that the pickets would not desist until the president treated with them; Hawkins' testimony that their purpose in picketing was to "talk to the top management to get better conditions"; and his statement that they wanted to achieve their purpose through "group talk and through the president if we could talk to him," as opposed to use of the grievance-arbitration machinery.

[12] . . .
Respondent clearly misapprehends the nature of the "right" conferred by this section. The intendment of the proviso is to permit employees to present grievances and to authorize the employer to entertain them without opening itself to liability for dealing directly with employees in derogation of the duty to bargain only with the exclusive bargaining representative, a violation of § 8(a)(5). The Act nowhere protects this "right" by making it an unfair labor practice for an employer to refuse to entertain such a presentation, nor can it be read to authorize resort to economic coercion. This matter is fully explicated in Black-Clawson Co. v. Machinists, 313 F.2d, 179 (CA2 1962). If the employees' activity in the present litigation is to be deemed protected, therefore, it must be so by reason of the reading given to the main part of § 9(a), in light of Title VII and the national policy against employment discrimination, and not by burdening the proviso to that section with a load it was not meant to carry.

attempts to engage in separate bargaining are protected by § 7 of the Act or proscribed by § 9(a).

A

Section 7 affirmatively guarantees employees the most basic rights of industrial self-determination. . . . These are, for the most part, collective rights, rights to act in concert with one's fellow employees; they are protected not for their own sake but as an instrument of the national labor policy of minimizing industrial strife "by encouraging the practice and procedure of collective bargaining."

Central to the policy of fostering collective bargaining, where the employees elect that course, is the principle of majority rule. If the majority of a unit chooses union representation, the NLRA permits it to bargain with its employer to make union membership a condition of employment, thereby imposing its choice upon the minority. In establishing a regime of majority rule, Congress sought to secure to all members of the unit the benefits of their collective strength and bargaining power, in full awareness that the superior strength of some individuals or groups might be subordinated to the interest of the majority. As a result, "[t]he complete satisfaction of all who are represented is hardly to be expected." . . .

In vesting the representatives of the majority with this broad power Congress did not, of course, authorize a tyranny of the majority over minority interests. First, it confined the exercise of these powers to the context of a "unit appropriate for the purposes of collective bargaining," *i.e.*, a group of employees with a sufficient commonality of circumstances to ensure against the submergence of a minority with distinctively different interests in the terms and conditions of their employment. Second, it undertook in the 1959 Landrum-Griffin amendments, to assure that minority voices are heard as they are in the functioning of a democratic institution. Third, we have held, by the very nature of the exclusive bargaining representative's status as representative of *all* unit employees, Congress implicitly imposed upon it a duty fairly and in good faith to represent the interests of minorities within the unit. And the Board has taken the position that a union's refusal to process grievances against racial discrimination, in violation of that duty, is an unfair labor practice. Indeed, the Board has ordered a union implicated by a collective-bargaining agreement in discrimination with an employer to propose specific contractual provisions to prohibit racial discrimination.

B

Against this background of long and consistent adherence to the principle of exclusive representation tempered by safeguards for the protection of minority interests, respondent urges this Court to fashion a limited exception to that principle: employees who seek to bargain separately with their employer as to the elimination of racially discriminatory employment practices peculiarly affecting them, should be free from the constraints of the exclusivity principle of § 9(a). Essentially because established procedures under Title VII or, as in this case, a grievance machinery, are too time consuming, the national labor policy against discrimination requires this exception, respondent argues, and its adoption would not unduly compromise the legitimate interests of either unions or employers.

Plainly, national labor policy embodies the principles of nondiscrimination as a matter of highest priority, and it is a commonplace that we must construe the NLRA in light of the broad national labor policy of which it is a part. These general principles do not aid respondent, however, as it is far from clear that separate bargaining is necessary to help eliminate discrimination. Indeed, as the facts of this litigation demonstrate, the proposed remedy might have just the opposite effect. The collective-bargaining agreement involved here prohibited without qualification all manner of invidious discrimination and made any claimed violation a grievable issue. The grievance procedure is directed precisely at determining whether discrimination has occurred. That orderly determination, if affirmative, could lead to an arbitral award enforceable in court. Nor is there any reason to believe that the processing of grievances is inherently limited to the correction of individual cases of discrimination. Quite apart from the essentially contractual question of whether the Union could grieve against a "pattern or practice" it deems inconsistent with the nondiscrimination clause of the contract, one would hardly expect an employer to continue in effect an employment practice that routinely results in adverse arbitral decisions.

The decision by a handful of employees to bypass the grievance procedure in favor of attempting to bargain with their employer, by contrast, may or may not be predicated upon the actual existence of discrimination. An employer confronted with bargaining demands from each of several minority groups would not necessarily, or even probably, be able to agree to remedial steps satisfactory to all at once. Competing claims on the employer's ability to accommodate each group's demands, *e.g.*, for reassignments and promotions to a limited number of positions, could only set one group against the other even if it is not the employer's intention to divide and overcome them. Having divided themselves, the minority employees will not be in position to advance their cause unless it be by recourse seriatim to economic coercion, which can only have the effect of further dividing them along racial or other lines. Nor is the situation materially different where, as apparently happened here, self-designated representatives purport to speak for all groups that might consider themselves to be victims of discrimination. Even if in actual bargaining the various groups did not perceive their interests as divergent and further subdivide themselves, the employer would be bound to bargain with them in a field largely pre-empted by the current collective-bargaining agreement with the elected bargaining representative. In this instance we do not know precisely what form the demands advanced by Hollins, Hawkins, et al. would take, but the nature of the grievance that motivated them indicates that the demands would have included the transfer of some minority employees to sales areas in which higher commissions were paid. Yet the collective-bargaining agreement provided that no employee would be transferred from a higher-paying to a lower-paying classification except by consent or in the course of a layoff or reduction in force. The potential for conflict between the minority and other employees in this situation is manifest. With each group able to enforce its conflicting demands—the incumbent employees by resort to contractual processes and the minority employees by economic coercion—the probability of strife and deadlock, is high; the likelihood of making headway against discriminatory practices would be minimal.

. . .

. . . The elimination of discrimination and its vestiges is an appropriate subject of bargaining, and an employer may have no objection to incorporating into a collective agreement the substance of his obligation not to discriminate in personnel decisions; the Company here has done as much, making any claimed dereliction a matter subject to the grievance-arbitration machinery as well as to the processes of Title VII. But that does not mean that an employer may not have strong and legitimate objections to bargaining on several fronts over the implementation of the right to be free of discrimination for some of the reasons set forth above. Similarly, while a union cannot lawfully bargain for the establishment or continuation of discriminatory practices, see *Steele* v. *Louisville & N. R. Co.*, 323 U.S. 192 (1944); 42 U.S.C. § 2000e-2(c)(3), it has a legitimate interest in presenting a united front on this as on other issues and in not seeing its strength dissipated and its stature denigrated by subgroups within the unit separately pursuing what they see as separate interests. When union and employer are not responsive to their legal obligations, the bargain they have struck must yield *pro tanto* to the law, whether by means of conciliation through the offices of the EEOC, or by means of federal-court enforcement at the instance of either that agency or the party claiming to be aggrieved.

. . .

Reversed.

MR. JUSTICE DOUGLAS, dissenting.

The Court's opinion makes these Union members—and others similarly situated—prisoners of the Union. The law, I think, was designed to prevent that tragic consequence. Hence, I dissent.

. . .

Questions

1. What was it the employees did that deprived them of the protection of the Act?

2. Are you persuaded the Court was bound to accept the Board's "finding" that the employees were not presenting a "grievance"? Having decided there was no "grievance," why did the Court address the proviso to Section 9(a)? See footnote 12. Does the Court's analysis of Section 9(a)'s proviso make sense, either as a matter of statutory construction or of

industrial relations practice? This question will be considered further in Chapter 5.

3. More fundamentally, why should employees be unprotected by the labor laws when they engage in what is clearly concerted activity for their own mutual benefit? Is the parade of horrors posed by the Court necessarily the outcome of protecting these employees? Note that the employer never objected to the employees' acts on the grounds the Court used to strip the employees of protection.

4. Whenever some members of an organized group of employees engage in concerted activities (related to their employment) without the consent (and, perhaps, approval) of their bargaining representative, they are said to be engaging in "wildcat" activities. Does *Emporium Capwell* mean that all wildcat activities, including especially wildcat strikes, are unprotected by the Act? Should it matter whether the union agrees with the wildcatters' objective? Conversely, should it matter if the union is ignoring the wildcatters' concern? Is it possible that wildcat activities may result in greater efficiency due to the outlet they provide employees for the frustrations they feel about their work, employer, and union?*

5. If there had been no union at Emporium Capwell, would the employees have been protected by the Act? If not, what was the real reason for their loss of statutory protection? If so, what should these employees do when they believe strongly, and over a long period of time, that the union will not adequately seek to correct the perceived employer wrong? If the employees believed reasonably and in good faith that the union was not representing their interests, should they be protected in their actions? Would the result of *Emporium Capwell* have been different if it had been proven that the employer engaged in race discrimination? If it had been proven that the union's efforts were not reasonable?

Comment on Section 502 of the LMRA**

Section 502 of the Act provides that "the quitting of labor by an employee . . . in good faith because of abnormally dangerous conditions of work [shall not] be deemed a strike under this Act." Given the Court's decision in *Washington Aluminum,* page 349, *supra,* Section 502 adds nothing to the rights of unorganized employees who believe, whether rightly or wrongly, that they should cease work because of what they perceive to be abnormally dangerous working conditions. For Section 502 to have any independent meaning, it must apply to cases where collective bargaining contracts are in effect, and where such contracts have provisions (explicit or implicit) that would otherwise outlaw strikes. The obvious purpose of Section 502 is to preclude any law from interfering with workers' efforts to avoid hazardous working conditions.

*See Atleson, *Work Group Behavior and Wildcat Strikes: The Causes and Functions of Industrial Disobedience,* 34 Ohio St. L. Rev. 751 (1973).

**See Atleson, *Threats to Health and Safety: Employee Self-Help Under the NLRA,* 59 Minn. L. Rev. 647 (1975).

In *Gateway Coal Co.* v. *United Mine Workers*, 415 U.S. 368, 85 LRRM 2049 (1974), three supervisory employees were falsifying records which were to reflect the performance of several safety devices used in the mines where the workers were employed. Despite their criminal behavior, these men were retained by their employer in their positions. Afraid that these supervisors might continue to falsify the records and thereby cause serious injury or loss of life, the workers refused to work in the mines. The Supreme Court held that by refusing to work these employees had breached the collective bargaining contract's implicit no-strike promise (there was only an explicit promise to arbitrate). It follows that the strikers could have been discharged for their behavior. The Court reasoned that there had to be objective evidence to support the employees' good faith fear that the working conditions were abnormally dangerous, and the presence of the dishonest supervisors was not the sort of dangerous conditions to which Section 502 referred. What were the employees supposed to do to avoid the serious injury they feared? Given the Court's assessment that there was no objective evidence to support the employees' good faith fear, what evidence would it take to prove the existence of abnormally dangerous conditions?

The Occupational Safety and Health Act (OSHA) was passed by Congress to make working conditions safer throughout the country. Pursuant to that Act, which did not explicitly authorize employees to refuse to do dangerous work, the Secretary of Labor issued the following interpretive regulation: among the rights that the OSH Act protects is the right of an employee to choose not to perform assigned tasks because of a reasonable apprehension of death or serious injury coupled with a reasonable belief that no less drastic alternative is available. In *Whirlpool Corp.* v. *Marshall*, 445 U.S. 1, 8 OSHC 1001 (1980), the Supreme Court affirmed the Secretary's authority to promulgate such a regulation. Is the distinction between *Gateway Coal* and *Whirlpool* merely a matter of form over substance?

B. ECONOMIC WEAPONS IN COLLECTIVE BARGAINING*

1. "BENIGN" BARGAINING

In the usual situation, once the employer has recognized the union as the collective bargaining representative of all its employees, or a group of its employees, representatives of the union and of the employer meet to negotiate a contract. The representatives of the employees may be one or more employees who work in the plant. Or they may be paid officials of the local union or of the international union. The representatives of the employer might be a personnel manager or the owner or some other official. Which of these individuals, or some other, is present at the bargaining depends to quite an extent on the size of the operation, the

*See Christensen and Swanoe, *Motive and Intent in the Commission of Unfair Labor Practices: The Supreme Court and the Fictive Formality.* 77 YALE L.J. 1269 (1968); Getman, *Section 8(a)(3) of the NLRA and the Effort to Insulate Free Employee Choice,* 32 CHI. L. REV. 735 (1965).

existing relationship between the union and the employer, and the relationships of particular individuals. An attorney may also be present for either or both sides. It is often disputed whether the presence of an attorney at the collective bargaining table is a desirable practice. Why should that be? Do you think lawyers can serve a useful function at the collective bargaining table? Might your answer depend upon the relationships of the parties? Upon the capacity of the attorneys to recognize what role they should be playing?

Usually, the bargaining process begins with the union's presentation of demands to the employer. These demands may involve wages, health and pension plans, hours, job security, grievance and arbitration procedures, working conditions, union status, union involvement in certain business affairs that affect the employees' interest, or a combination of many of these matters. The demands are made in writing.

What do you think the union takes into account in making its demands? Surely the union looks to environmental factors which delimit the employees' needs and desires. For example, the union undoubtedly considers the increases in the cost of living. But the union also looks to what comparable employees have in other industries in the same geographical area, or to what the union or employees in that industry have obtained in other areas. The particular requests or desires of the employees are relevant. Problems that have arisen at the employer's place of business and which involve the employees would be targets for negotiations. Do you think the union takes into account what the employer is likely to grant? And what price, if any, it is apt to exact for certain concessions? Do you think the union takes the possibility of a strike into account when it makes its initial demands? Or is that consideration postponed until the tenor of the negotiations themselves are determined? Is the union likely to know with some certainty what that tenor will be? If you think the union does, or ought to, take into account the possibility of a strike when it draws up its demands, how does it assess the likelihood of a strike? Of success? Do the answers to these questions turn to some extent on the issues that produce the strike? On the skills of the employees who will strike? On the status of the unemployment market? On the nature of the industry involved? On the potential cooperation of other unions? How much "puffing" on its demands do you think the union does, or ought to, engage in?

After receiving the union's requests, the employer will study them with some care. Some of the proposals may meet with approval. Others may also be acceptable, but perhaps the employer's view is to exact a price for making those concessions. Other proposals may be considered undesirable by the employer, but it might recognize that it would have to grant them to the union because the employer wants something else from the union and a "trade" would be possible. Or the employer might recognize that the union could force the concession in any event. Finally, there might be proposals which the employer finds truly unacceptable and to which it would agree only under the direst pressure.

Of course, if the employer is sophisticated, it will temper any reaction with an assessment of the union's and the employees' intensity of desire for each of the proposals. How can such an assessment be made? For example, should it be able to ask the employees? The employer also will have to assess what will happen if it balks on any or several of these bargaining issues. For example, can the union and the employees force the employer to make concessions? If so, will it be cheaper and less damaging to morale to make the concessions without a fight? Conversely, if the union cannot force the concessions, should the employer make them anyway in order to preserve harmony? Or is there some way to rid itself of the union, or at least greatly weaken its position, by putting up a stiff battle at the bargaining table? Is this the result the employer desires, or does it have more to gain by having a fairly healthy union to represent employees? What considerations should it take into account to resolve that question?

Many, if not most, of the union's proposals are economic in nature and will result in additional expense for the operation of the business. Should the employer take into account the ability to "pass on" the new expense to the public? What period of time should the employer take into account? This year? The future of the economy a decade hence? Are the questions related only to the consumers' willingness to pay the higher price? What about government intervention? Is this last consideration more relevant in some businesses than others?

After reaching at least tentative answers to these questions, the employer will start composing its own position on the many matters raised by the union's demands and on anything else it considers necessary for discussion. In the first discussions with the union, the employer may not yet have made any counterproposals, although in the course of discussions its position will be fairly clear about some of the union's proposals. Usually, at some point, the employer will also submit written counterproposals to the union.

A series of meetings may follow. How many, and for how long, will depend on the nature of the disagreements between the parties and the willingness of each to hold firm. Eventually, after considerable explaining, bartering, and compromising, and as a result of persuasion (at least in those situations where the employer and the union have a longstanding relationship with each other or at least some considerable familiarity with the collective bargaining process), as well as the ominous threat of some sort of coercion (what sort do you believe would be lawful?), agreement is reached. The parties reduce it to writing and sign it.

This is a brief description of the nonmalignant, nondisruptive, collective bargaining process. Most collective bargaining in this nation reflects, more or less, that description. Although the remaining materials do not deal directly with this most typical bargaining, many—if not all—of the elements described in the typical situation are present also in the cases where something "goes wrong" and overt coercion by the parties or by the legal system becomes necessary.

Of course, the nonmalignant bargaining does not exist in a vacuum. Much of its impetus comes from what the law allows or what the law requires. Much also turns on what the parties insist upon or what they must submit to. Finally, the mores of the industry, community, or the immediate plant may play a role. Thus, the bargaining process as described above does not tell us what must be bargained about, the manner of bargaining, or what can be done to effectuate one's bargaining position.

In any collective bargaining negotiations that are not productive of agreement, the parties must resort to some force if agreement is to be reached subsequently. Assuming that the parties have acted lawfully, or that they do not desire recourse through the NLRB, or that they are unwilling to await the outcome of whatever proceedings are available before the Board and the courts, what can each of the parties do to further the prospects of agreement?

What are the effects of a strike on the employees? The union? The employer? Can the employees insist on full pay while they are on strike? Although that solution does not seem impossible, neither the Board nor the courts have ever seriously considered it. Thus, during a strike, the employees would be forced to survive without their paychecks. What effect is this likely to have on the length of the strike? On the willingness of some employees to strike in the first place? What alternatives do you think are available to mitigate the pinch of the strike on the employees? Another job? Union strike funds? Unemployment benefits? In addition to considering the effect of a long strike on their pocketbooks, the employees undoubtedly take much more into account. For example, must they not ask themselves: How strongly do we feel about the unresolved issues at the bargaining table? Is the strike likely to be successful? How can the union and employees assess the likelihood of success?

What countermeasures, if any, has the employer to forestall the success of the strike? Can the employer's weapons have a greater or more direct effect on the employee than that necessary merely to remove the strike's sting to the employer?

2. Bargaining, Strikes, and Employer Responses

Enderby Company Problem

The Case of the Subcontracted Struck Work

Recently, the United Factory Workers of America was certified by the NLRB as the collective bargaining agent of the employees of Enderby Company. In the past, the company had delivered products to customers, and for this purpose it had employed 15 drivers and driver helpers.

The union submitted a proposed collective bargaining contract to the employer. Subsequently, the company responded with counterproposals. Ten or 11 meetings were held within two months. The parties were unable to reach agreement. A majority of the employees went on strike.

On the first day of the strike, the company sent a letter to all its employees announcing that the company was going to seek people to do the work of the strikers, that these replacements would have permanent status as employees of the company, that this meant the strikers would lose their jobs once they were replaced, and that the delivery work of the company had already been subcontracted and there were no longer any truck driver or helper jobs. In light of these actions, the company urged the strikers to return to work as soon as possible.

For several weeks prior to the strike and while negotiations with the union were progressing, the company also had been dealing with Fukumoto, who engaged in the delivery business. Three days before the strike the company and Fukumoto had reached the agreement that, if there were a strike, all the delivery needs of the company would be subcontracted to Fukumoto. A formal contract with Fukumoto was signed on the day of the strike's inception. Its term was indefinite and was terminable on 30 days' notice. The work was to be performed by Fukumoto employees, but Enderby trucks were to be used.*

You have been approached by the union officials, who ask you the following questions. What will your answers be?

First, was the company's threat to replace the strikers permanently at odds with the statute? Asked another way, can the employer lawfully replace the strikers permanently?

Second, what about the subcontracting? Can the employer lawfully terminate its employees in such a fashion? Is this different from mere permanent replacement?

Third, assuming the employer may be permitted to subcontract, did it violate the law by failing to negotiate with the union about such a drastic change in the collective bargaining unit before doing so?

Fourth, what responses are available to the union to bolster its chances of success in light of the employer's moves to reduce the impact of the strike on its business? Are your answers to this question related to your answers to the first three?

a. May Enderby Permanently Replace the Strikers?

NLRB v. Mackay Radio & Telegraph

Supreme Court of the United States, 1938
304 U.S. 333, 2 LRRM 6105

[After a strike, many employees sought to return to work. Since the employer had hired a number of replacements, he did not choose to reemploy all of the strikers. Rather, he discriminated between active union leaders and other strikers, refusing to hire back the leaders. The Board held that such discrimination violated the Act. The Court affirmed the Board's decision.]

MR. JUSTICE ROBERTS delivered the opinion of the Court. . . .

Fourth. It is contended that the Board lacked jurisdiction because respondent was at no time guilty of any unfair labor practice. Section 8 of

*The facts are taken from *Hawaii Meat Co.*, 139 NLRB 966, 51 LRRM 430 (1962), *enf. denied*, 321 F.2d 397, 53 LRRM 2872 (9th Cir. 1963).

the Act denominates as such practice action by an employer to interfere with, restrain, or coerce employees in the exercise of their rights to organize, to form, join or assist labor organizations, and to engage in concerted activities for the purpose of collective bargaining or other mutual aid or protection, or "by discrimination in regard to . . . tenure of employment or any term or condition of employment to encourage or discourage memberships in any labor organization: . . ." There is no evidence and no finding that the respondent was guilty of any unfair labor practice in connection with the negotiations in New York. On the contrary, it affirmatively appears that the respondent was negotiating with the authorized representatives of the union. Nor was it an unfair labor practice to replace the striking employees with others in an effort to carry on the business. Although § 13 provides, "Nothing in this Act shall be construed so as to interfere with or impede or diminish in any way the right to strike," it does not follow that an employer, guilty of no act denounced by the statute, has lost the right to protect and continue his business by supplying places left vacant by strikers. And he is not bound to discharge those hired to fill the places of strikers, upon the election of the latter to resume their employment, in order to create places for them. The assurance by respondent to those who accepted employment during the strike that if they so desired their places might be permanent was not an unfair labor practice nor was it such to reinstate only so many of the strikers as there were vacant places to be filled. But the claim put forward is that the unfair labor practice indulged by the respondent was discrimination in reinstating striking employees by keeping out certain of them for the sole reason that they had been active in the union. As we have said, the strikers retained, under the Act, the status of employees. Any such discrimination in putting them back to work is, therefore, prohibited by § 8.

Questions

1. Is the *Mackay* proposition—that permanent replacements of economic strikers is lawful—supported by the more obvious meaning of the language of Sections 7 and 13? With that of Sections 8(a)(1) and 8(a)(3)? If at first the ability to employ permanent employees cannot be reconciled with the more obvious meaning of the statute, one must look elsewhere for reasons to support the result dictated by the Supreme Court.

2. If you guessed that the purpose of the *Mackay* argument is to balance the economic power of the parties, are you curious why this was not articulated by the Court? You may be surprised to learn that neither the Board nor the Court has given that reason, or any other reason, for *Mackay*. What underlies the conclusion, speculative though it may be, that *Mackay* is desirable in order to balance the economic strength of the parties?

3. Are any of the assumptions apparently underlying *Mackay* clearly valid? Is it clear that all (most? many?) employers *need* the *Mackay* doctrine to keep their businesses from being destroyed? Or to keep them in

operation during a strike? Is it clear that the employer *should* be protected in this fashion from being closed down during the strike? Or from being destroyed?

4. Permanent replacements are not available to the employer when the employees are striking to protest unfair labor practices. In such a case, as a matter of remedy for the unlawful actions, the strikers are entitled to their jobs after the cessation of the work stoppage. If the employer's unfair labor practices are sufficiently egregious, the strikers may be entitled to reinstatement despite the fact that some of their own behavior constituted unprotected acts. See *NLRB* v. *Thayer Co.,* page 444, *infra.* Does it make sense to protect unfair labor practice strikers more than economic strikers? After all, unfair labor practices can be remedied through the Board and courts.

Since employees engaged in "economic" strikes (ones not protesting unfair labor practices of the employer) can be replaced but unfair labor practice strikers cannot, issues arise because of the difficulty of ascertaining the strike's purpose. Assume the employer sincerely believes it has not committed an unfair labor practice. (This is entirely plausible. For example, as you will soon discover, it is often difficult to categorize in advance, with any conviction, an employer's conduct as violative of Section 8(a)(5)'s mandate to bargain in "good faith.") If the employer assesses the situation incorrectly and refuses to reemploy the strikers because it has employed permanent replacements, think of the back-pay repercussions. On the other side of the coin, the union may have advised the employees that their conduct was protected from loss of employment. The employees may well lose their jobs because of the union's erroneous guess. If so, can the employees successfully sue the union? If not, think of the burden on the employees. If such a lawsuit is possible, what becomes of the union's treasury?

5. Does not *Mackay* help the employer who probably needs help the least, and offer little or no solace to the employer who is at the mercy of a powerful union?

NLRB v. Erie Resistor Corp.

Supreme Court of the United States, 1963
373 U.S. 221, 53 LRRM 2121

[During the period of negotiations, the company had 450 employees who had been previously laid off due to economic exigencies. When the parties were unable to reach a new contract, 478 employees who had been working during the negotiations went on strike. In an effort to hire permanent replacements, the employer promised the replacements that they would have 20 years of seniority for purposes of layoffs and recalls (but not for other employee benefits). Strikers who returned to work before the end of the strike were also given the superseniority. The NLRB held that the employer had violated the Act. The Court of Appeals reversed.]

MR. JUSTICE WHITE delivered the opinion of the Court. . . .

Though the intent necessary for an unfair labor practice may be shown in different ways, proving it in one manner may have far different weight and far different consequences than proving it in another. When specific evidence of a subjective intent to discriminate or to encourage or discourage union membership is shown, and found, many otherwise innocent or ambiguous actions which are normally incident to the conduct of a business may, without more, be converted into unfair labor practices. . . .

The outcome may well be the same when intent is founded upon the inherently discriminatory or destructive nature of the conduct itself. The employer in such cases must be held to intend the very consequences which foreseeably and inescapably flow from his actions and if he fails to explain away, to justify or to characterize his actions as something different than they appear on their face, an unfair labor practice charge is made out. But, as often happens, the employer may counter by claiming that his actions were taken in the pursuit of legitimate business ends and that his dominant purpose was not to discriminate or to invade union rights but to accomplish business objectives acceptable under the Act. Nevertheless, his conduct *does* speak for itself—it *is* discriminatory and it *does* discourage union membership and whatever the claimed overriding justification may be, it carries with it unavoidable consequences which the employer not only foresaw but which he must have intended. As is not uncommon in human experience, such situations present a complex of motives and preferring one motive to another is in reality the far more delicate task, reflected in part in decisions of this Court, of weighing the interests of employees in concerted activity against the interest of the employer in operating his business in a particular manner and of balancing in the light of the Act and its policy the intended consequences upon employee rights against the business ends to be served by the employer's conduct. This essentially is the teaching of the Court's prior cases dealing with this problem and, in our view, the Board did not depart from it.

The Board made a detailed assessment of super-seniority and, to its experienced eye, such a plan had the following characteristics:

(1) Super-seniority affects the tenure of all strikers whereas permanent replacement, proper under *Mackay*, affects only those who are, in actuality, replaced. It is one thing to say that a striker is subject to loss of his job at the strike's end but quite another to hold that in addition to the threat of replacement, all strikers will at best return to their jobs with seniority inferior to that of the replacements and of those who left the strike.

(2) A super-seniority award necessarily operates to the detriment of those who participated in the strike as compared to nonstrikers.

(3) Super-seniority made available to striking bargaining unit employees as well as to new employees is in effect offering individual benefits to the strikers to induce them to abandon the strike.

(4) Extending the benefits of super-seniority to striking bargaining unit employees as well as to new replacements deals a crippling blow to the strike effort. At one stroke, those with low seniority have the opportunity to obtain the job security which ordinarily only long years of service can bring, while conversely, the accumulated seniority of older employees is

seriously diluted. This combination of threat and promise could be expected to undermine the strikers' mutual interest and place the entire strike effort in jeopardy. The history of this strike and its virtual collapse following the announcement of the plan emphasize the grave repercussions of super-seniority.

(5) Super-seniority renders future bargaining difficult, if not impossible, for the collective bargaining representative. Unlike the replacement granted in *Mackay* which ceases to be an issue once the strike is over, the plan here creates a cleavage in the plant continuing long after the strike is ended. Employees are henceforth divided into two camps: those who stayed with the union and those who returned before the end of the strike and thereby gained extra seniority. This branch is re-emphasized with each subsequent layoff and stands as an ever-present reminder of the dangers connected with striking and with union activities in general.

In the light of this analysis, super-seniority by its very terms operates to discriminate between strikers and nonstrikers, both during and after a strike, and its destructive impact upon the strike and union activity cannot be doubted. The origin of the plan, as respondent insists, may have been to keep production going and it may have been necessary to offer super-seniority to attract replacements and induce union members to leave the strike. But if this is true, accomplishment of respondent's business purpose inexorably was contingent upon attracting sufficient replacements and strikers by offering preferential inducements to those who worked as opposed to those who struck. . . .

The Court of Appeals and respondent rely upon *Mackay* as precluding the result reached by the Board but we are not persuaded. Under the decision in that case an employer may operate his plant during a strike and at its conclusion need not discharge those who worked during the strike in order to make way for returning strikers. It may be, as the Court of Appeals said, "such a replacement policy is obviously discriminatory and may tend to discourage union membership." But *Mackay* did not deal with super-seniority, with its effects upon all strikers, whether replaced or not, or with its powerful impact upon a strike itself. Because the employer's interest must be deemed to outweigh the damage to concerted activities caused by permanently replacing strikers does not mean it also outweighs the far greater encroachment resulting from super-seniority in addition to permanent replacement.

We have no intention of questioning the continuing vitality of the *Mackay* rule, but we are not prepared to extend it to the situation we have here. To do so would require us to set aside the Board's considered judgment that the Act and its underlying policy require, in the present context, giving more weight to the harm wrought by super-seniority than to the interest of the employer in operating its plant during the strike by utilizing this particular means of attracting replacements. We find nothing in the Act or its legislative history to indicate that super-seniority is necessarily an acceptable method of resisting the economic impact of a strike, nor do we find anything inconsistent with the result which the Board reached. On the contrary, these sources are wholly consistent with, and lend full support to, the conclusion of the Board.

. . .

Questions

1. Which, if either, do you think has a greater adverse impact on the "right" to strike—the threatened and actual termination of strikers (*Mackay*) or superseniority for strikebreakers (*Erie Resistor*)? Is this an example of all-or-nothing weapons being the only lawful weapons allowed to the parties? What is the *Mackay* "privilege" worth to an employer in the position of Erie Resistor? Wasn't the lower court quite logical in extending *Mackay* to these circumstances?

2. What is the seniority status of Mackay's permanent replacements after the strike? Where does this status find its basis? In a collective agreement signed subsequently? In individual arrangements made with the employer? (*Erie Resistor* rejects this alternative.) Or in the statute itself? If the latter, under what provision of the Act?

NLRB v. Great Dane Trailers, Inc.

Supreme Court of the United States, 1967
388 U.S. 26, 65 LRRM 2465

MR. CHIEF JUSTICE WARREN delivered the opinion of the Court.

The issue here is whether, in the absence of proof of an antiunion motivation, an employer may be held to have violated §§ 8(a)(3) and (1) of the National Labor Relations Act when it refused to pay striking employees vacation benefits accrued under a terminated collective bargaining agreement while it announced an intention to pay such benefits to striker replacements, returning strikers, and nonstrikers who had been at work on a certain date during the strike.

The respondent company and the union entered into a collective bargaining agreement which was effective by its terms until March 31, 1963. The agreement contained a commitment by the company to pay vacation benefits to employees who met certain enumerated qualifications. In essence, the company agreed to pay specified vacation benefits to employees who, during the preceding year, had worked at least 1,525 hours. It was also provided that, in the case of a "lay-off, termination or quitting," employees who had served more than 60 days during the year would be entitled to pro rata shares of their vacation benefits. Benefits were to be paid on the Friday nearest July 1 of each year.

The agreement was temporarily extended beyond its termination date, but on April 30, 1963, the union gave the required 15 days' notice of intention to strike over issues which remained unsettled at the bargaining table. Accordingly, on May 16, 1963, approximately 350 of the company's 400 employees commenced a strike which lasted until December 26, 1963. The company continued to operate during the strike, using nonstrikers, persons hired as replacements for strikers, and some original strikers who had later abandoned the strike and returned to work. On July 12, 1963, a number of the strikers demanded their accrued vacation pay from the company. The company rejected this demand, basing its response on the assertion that all contractual obligations had been terminated by the strike and, therefore, none of the company's employees had a right to vacation pay. Shortly thereafter, however, the company announced that it would grant vacation pay—in the amounts and subject to the conditions set out in the expired agreement—to all employees who had reported for work on July 1, 1963. The company denied that these payments were founded on the agreement and stated that they merely reflected a new "policy" which had been unilaterally adopted.

The refusal to pay vacation benefits to strikers, coupled with the payments to nonstrikers, formed the bases of an unfair labor practice complaint filed with the Board while the strike was still in progress. . . .

[The Board found a violation of the Act.]

A petition for enforcement of the order was filed in the Court of Appeals for the Fifth Circuit. . . . Reviewing the substantive aspects of the Board's decision next, the Court of Appeals held that, although discrimination between striking and nonstriking employees had been proved, the Board's conclusion that the company had committed an unfair labor practice was not well-founded inasmuch as there had been no affirmative showing of an unlawful motivation to discourage union membership or to interfere with the exercise of protected rights. Despite the fact that the company itself had not introduced evidence of a legitimate business purpose underlying its discriminatory action, the Court of Appeals speculated that it might have been motivated by a desire "(1) to reduce expenses; (2) to encourage longer tenure among present employees; or (3) to discourage early leaves immediately before vacation periods." Believing that the possibility of the existence of such motives was sufficient to overcome the inference of an improper motive which flowed from the conduct itself, the court denied enforcement of the order. . . .

The unfair labor practice charged here is grounded primarily in § 8(a)(3) which requires specifically that the Board find a discrimination and a resulting discouragement of union membership. There is little question but that the result of the company's refusal to pay vacation benefits to strikers was discrimination in its simplest form. Some employees who met the conditions specified in the expired collective bargaining agreement were paid accrued vacation benefits in the amounts set forth in that agreement, while other employees who also met the conditions but who had engaged in protected concerted activity were denied such benefits. Similarly, there can be no doubt but that the discrimination was capable of discouraging membership in a labor organization within the meaning of the statute. Discouraging membership in a labor organization "includes discouraging participation in concerted activities . . . such as a legitimate strike." *Labor Board* v. *Erie Resistor Corp.* The act of paying accrued benefits to one group of employees while announcing the extinction of the same benefits for another group of employees who are distinguishable only by their participation in protected concerted activity surely may have a discouraging effect on either present or future concerted activity.

But inquiry under § 8(a)(3) does not usually stop at this point. The statutory language "discrimination . . . to . . . discourage" means that the finding of a violation normally turns on whether the discriminatory conduct was motivated by an antiunion purpose. *American Ship Building Co.* v. *Labor Board*, 380 U.S. 300 (1965). It was upon the motivation element that the Court of Appeals based its decision not to grant enforcement, and it is to that element which we now turn. . . .

First, if it can reasonably be concluded that the employer's discriminatory conduct was "inherently destructive" of important employee rights, no proof of an antiunion motivation is needed and the Board can find an unfair labor practice even if the employer introduces evidence that the conduct was motivated by business considerations. Second, if the adverse effect of the discriminatory conduct on employee rights is "comparatively slight," an antiunion motivation must be proved to sustain the charge *if* the employer has come forward with evidence of legitimate and substantial business justifications for the conduct. Thus, in either situation, once it has been proved that the employer engaged in discriminatory conduct which could have adversely affected employee rights to *some* extent, the burden is upon the employer to establish that he was motivated by legitimate objectives since proof of motivation is most accessible to him.

Applying the principles to this case then, it is not necessary for us to decide the degree to which the challenged conduct might have affected employee rights. As the Court of Appeals correctly noted, the company came forward with no evidence of legitimate motives for its discriminatory conduct. The company simply did not meet the burden of proof, and the Court of Appeals misconstrued the function of judicial review when it proceeded nonetheless to speculate upon which *might have* motivated the company. Since discriminatory conduct carrying a potential for adverse effect upon employee rights was proved and no evidence of a proper motivation appeared in the record, the Board's conclusions were supported by substantial evidence, *Universal Camera Corp.* v. *Labor Board*, 340 U.S. 474 (1951), and should have been sustained.

The judgment of the Court of Appeals is reversed and the case is remanded with directions to enforce the Board's order.

It is so ordered.

MR. JUSTICE HARLAN, whom MR. JUSTICE STEWART joins, dissenting. . . .

The Court begins by stating that vacation benefits had "accrued" under the contract, and implies that striking employees had a contractual right to such benefits which was arbitrarily disregarded by Great Dane in order to punish those employees for engaging in protected activity. Were these the properly established facts of the case, I would have little difficulty in concurring in the result reached by the majority. Employer action which undercuts rights protected by § 7 of the National Labor Relations Act, as amended, and has no inferable, legitimate business purpose has been held a violation of §§ 8(a)(3) and (1). *Republic Aviation Corp.* v. *Labor Board.* But the contract dispute is not so frivolous as to be determined without examination, and the issue framed by the Court is not properly before us. Moreover, contrary to the Court's assertion, neither the Board nor the lower court limited itself to considering this issue, and both recognized a limitation on the Board's contract interpretation powers in light of § 301(a) of the Labor Management Relations Act, 1947.

. . .

In these circumstances, I think the only issue properly before the Court is whether the employer's unilaterally declared vacation policy, considered on its own bottom, constitutes a violation of § 8(a)(3) absent a showing of improper motivation by evidence independent of the policy itself.

The Court attempts to resolve this issue as well as the contractual one. In the Court's view an employer must "come forward with evidence of legitimate and substantial business justifications" whenever any of his actions are challenged in a § 8(a)(3) proceeding. . . .

Under today's formulation, the Board is required to find independent evidence of the employer's antiunion motive only when the employer has overcome the presumption of unlawful motive which the Court raises. This alteration of the burden in § 8(a)(3) cases may either be a rule of convenience important to the resolution of this case alone or may, more unfortunately, portend an important shift in the manner of deciding employer unfair labor practice cases under § 8(a)(3). In either event, I believe it is unwise.

The "legitimate and substantial business justifications" test may be interpreted as requiring only that the employer come forward with a nonfrivolous business purpose in order to make operative the usual requirement of proof of antiunion motive. If this is the result of today's decision, then the Court has merely penalized Great Dane for not anticipating this requirement when arguing before the Board. . . .

On the other hand, the use of the word "substantial" in the burden of proof formulation may give the Board a power which it formerly had only in § 8(a)(3) cases like *Erie Resistor*. The Board may seize upon that term to evaluate the merits of the employer's business purposes and weigh them against the harm that befalls the union's interests as a result of the employer's action. If this is the Court's meaning, it may well impinge upon the accepted principle that "the right to bargain collectively does not entail any 'right' to insist on one's position free from economic disadvantage." *American Ship Building Co.* v. *Labor Board.* Employers have always been free to take reasonable measures which discourage a strike by pressuring the economic interests of employees, including the extreme measure of hiring permanent replacements, without having the Board inquire into the "substantiality" of their business justifications. *Labor Board* v. *Mackay Radio & Telegraph Co.* If the Court means to change this rule, though I assume it does not, it surely should not do so without argument of the point by the parties and without careful discussion.

In my opinion, the Court of Appeals correctly held that this case fell into the category in which independent evidence of antiunion motive is required to sustain a violation. . . . Nor is the employer's conduct here, like the super-seniority plan in *Erie Resistor, supra*, such that an unlawful motive can be found by "an application of the common-law rule that a man is held to intend the foreseeable consequences of his conduct." *Radio Officers* v. *Labor Board*, 347 U.S. 17, 45. The differences between the facts of this case and those of *Erie Resistor* are, as the parties recognize, so significant as to preclude analogy. Unlike the granting of super-seniority, the vacation pay policy here had no potential long-term impact on the bargaining situation. The vacation policy was not employed as a weapon against the strike as was the super-seniority plan. Notice of the date of required presence for vacation pay eligibility was not given until after the date had passed. The record shows clearly that Great Dane had no need to employ any such policy to combat the strike, since it had successfully replaced almost all of the striking employees. The Trial Examiner rejected all union claims that particular actions by Great Dane demonstrated antiunion animus. In these circumstances, the Court of Appeals found no substantial evidence of a violation of § 8(a)(3).

Plainly the Court is concerned lest the strikers in this case be denied their "rights" under the collective bargaining agreement that expired at the commencement of the strike. Equally plainly, a suit under § 301 is the proper manner by which to secure these "rights," if they indeed exist. I think it inappropriate to becloud sound prior interpretations of § 8(a)(3) simply to reach what seems a sympathetic result.

Questions

1. Do you read the opinion of the Court to place the burden of proof, or at least the burden of going forward, upon the employer in every Section 8(a)(3) case? If not, what was the Court saying? If so, was not the opinion a radical departure from other cases dealing with Section 8(a)(3)?

2. In an omitted part of the dissenting opinion, it was stated that the employer had a good faith contract argument. The dissent argued that if the employees had a contract right, they had to seek redress through the usual contract remedies. If there was no contract right, the dissent then argued what you have read. Are you persuaded? Especially, is the dissent's distinction of *Erie Resistor* useful? After all, didn't the employer in *Erie Resistor* have a very strong motive in adopting its plan—the motive of keeping its business in operation?

3. What efforts can the employer make to induce the strikers to return to work other than threaten them with loss of their jobs through permanent replacements? Can it offer the strikers something not offered during negotiations? In *NLRB* v. *Crompton-Highland Mills, Inc.*, 337 U.S. 217, 24 LRRM 2088 (1949), the Supreme Court upheld the Board's determination that increases in wages not offered first to the union violated the Act. See *NLRB* v. *Katz*, page 395, *infra*.

4. Using the majority's reasoning, can you imagine anything more "inherently destructive" of the right to strike than termination of employment for exercising that right? If that is so, how can an employer meet the burden of justifying the use of permanent—rather than temporary—replacements? Has *Mackay* been overturned, as the dissent feared?

5. In *NLRB* v. *Fleetwood Trailer Co., Inc.*, 389 U.S. 375, 66 LRRM 2737 (1967), the Supreme Court was faced with the issue of whether unreplaced economic strikers retained some reinstatement rights although

there were no jobs available for them at the end of the strike. In the case, the employer's business had been sufficiently affected by the strike that it had need for far fewer employees at the end of the strike than it had employed prior to the strike. Over the few months following the end of the strike, the business was rebuilt, but the employer did not give the former strikers any preference in filling positions as they became available. The Board held that the refusal to reemploy the strikers violated the Act. The Supreme Court affirmed. In its reasoning, the Court said, "In some situations, 'legitimate and substantial business justifications' for refusing to reinstate employees who engaged in an economic strike have been recognized. One is when the jobs claimed by the strikers are occupied by workers hired as permanent replacements during the strike in order to continue operations. *NLRB* v. *Mackay Radio & Telegraph Co.*" Are you surprised that *Mackay* survived the apparent doctrinal shift found in *Great Dane?*

6. Can there be any question, regardless of your doubts about *Mackay* and its progeny, that, short of a reversal of that case's dictum, Enderby Company (in the problem) could properly replace the strikers permanently?

7. Since *Fleetwood,* the NLRB has held that even where an economic (non-unfair labor practice) striker has been permanently replaced, the striker can retain a priority for recall if she requests reemployment at the end of her strike activities. The employer could refuse subsequent employment only if the employee had found permanent employment elsewhere or the employer had a good business (non-labor-related) reason for refusing to employ her subsequently. *Laidlaw Corp.,* 171 NLRB 1366, 68 LRRM 1252 (1968), 414 F.2d 99, 71 LRRM 3054 (9th Cir. 1969). Moreover, when reemployed, the employee is entitled to full seniority. *Globe Molded Plastic Co.,* 204 NLRB 1041, 83 LRRM 1460 (1973).

Do these subsequent developments, especially *Globe Molded Plastic,* reflect an insensitivity to the interests of strikebreakers? What recourse, if any, do "permanent" replacements have if—at the end of a strike—the union and employer agree to put strikers back to work at the expense of the strikebreakers?

b. May Enderby Subcontract in Lieu of Hiring Replacements?

Accepting the *Mackay* doctrine as the basis for analysis of the remainder of the Enderby problem, page 364, is the subcontracting of the delivery work to another employer a lawful extension of the *Mackay* privilege?

1. Is it significant that the subcontracting involves another employer? Why might that be so? Because the scope of the labor dispute might become broader than is consistent with sound labor policy?

2. Would it matter whether all of the drivers and helpers of Enderby had gone on strike? What justification could there be for "permanently replacing" nonstriking drivers and helpers? Should the employer have *more* freedom to subcontract rather than to replace permanently? On the other hand, to what protection from the Act are the nonstrikers entitled? See Section 7.

3. Should it matter whether the subcontracting is permanent or temporary? First, is this a question more properly asked of the *Mackay* doctrine itself? Whatever can be said for permitting the parties to engage in economic warfare, is there something paradoxical about lawful severance of the employer-employee relationship due to the collective bargaining which has as its purpose stabilizing that employer-employee relationship? Second, the subcontracting may be distinguishable from the *Mackay* practice in the following respect: an employer may not be able to hire individual replacements without promising permanency. Is it so likely that a subcontractor cannot be found without a similar promise?

4. Certainly the possibility of using subcontracting as an alternative to replacing strikers permanently adds considerable strength to the employer's bargaining position, at least in those cases where it would want to take advantage of that option. Just how much added strength depends on many factors, does it not? What would the factors be? How does one measure them? Who is to measure them? Can the Board, or the courts? Would it be sound as a matter of administrative efficiency to resolve these matters in the unfair labor practice hearing? Would it be possible to resolve them rationally?

5. What relevance, if any, does Section 9(c)(3) have to the suggested extension of *Mackay*?

6. If the subcontracting is a lawful extension of *Mackay,* does that conclusion cut in favor of *Mackay's* retention or of its abolition?

c. Was Enderby Obligated to Bargain With the Union About the Subcontracting?

Although your study of the meaning of the duty to bargain in good faith must be postponed, one cannot leave the Enderby case without recognizing some questions posed by the duty to bargain required by Sections 8(a)(5) and 8(d) of the Act. The following questions anticipate the problem, "About What Do We Have to Bargain?", page 418, *infra*. For a moment, let us accept that an employer does not have to reach a collective agreement with the union. Section 8(d). Let us assume further, as the facts of the problem suggest, that there has been nothing improper about Enderby's contribution to the nonproductive negotiations. That is, the employer and the union simply have not been able to reach an agreement. In what conceivable sense has the employer failed to bargain?

1. Has the employer failed to negotiate about the subcontracting? To answer that question, must you not first ask: Does subcontracting fall within the scope of matters about which the employer must bargain? If you answer that affirmatively, must you not ask the next question: Does the employer fail to bargain when the union has not asked that the matter be taken up? And, finally, you must ask: Must the employer bargain about *this* economic weapon used in *this* case, before it can be put into effect?

2. To answer the first question, a preliminary question should be posed: Must an employer bargain about anything and everything the union seeks to discuss? And, conversely, must the union bargain about all matters that the employer raises? If you answered those questions in the affirmative,

then obviously the employer must bargain about subcontracting. But if you answered in the negative, why did you do so? Are those reasons relevant to determining whether subcontracting must be negotiated before being implemented?

Section 8(d) provides that the parties in collective bargaining must negotiate about "wages, hours, and other terms and conditions of employment." Is subcontracting within that particular scope? If not, must the employer bargain about subcontracting anyway?

3. If you have reached the conclusion that subcontracting is something about which the employer must bargain, must it do so when the union has not requested bargaining? Is it conceivable that there are some matters over which the employer is free to act unilaterally until the union objects or demands bargaining? And that there are other propositions about which the employer must consult with the union before it implements them? If such a distinction exists, what factors are relevant to devising a standard for the distinction?

4. There are difficulties with requiring the employer to bargain about such matters. When does the duty arise? For how long must it negotiate before it is free to go ahead? Or is it never free to implement the plan? How much of this is affected by the fact that there is a strike? By the fact that the products of an employer are perishable?

5. Does it make a difference that the employer's action in this case is most clearly a response to a strike? Why should the parties not be forced by the Act to bargain about the economic weapons they choose to use? Do you think notice in advance of the use of economic weapons would be helpful to collective bargaining?

d. Does the Union Have any Economic Recourse to Combat Enderby's Subcontracting?

In Chapter 7, you shall study the legal limitations upon union economic pressure against persons other than the employer with whom the union has its dispute. Nevertheless, the Enderby problem raises some questions in anticipation of that study.

Can the union picket Fukumoto, who was the hauler who obtained the contract? Can the union picket Fukumoto wherever it does business, whether or not it is Enderby business? What possible reason is there for prohibiting such picketing? To limit the effects of the labor dispute so that not too much of the economy is involved? Is it an adequate response to say that Enderby has already expanded the dispute by subcontracting? Does this justify further expansion to involve fourth parties dealing with the third party (the subcontractor)? See Chapter 7, *infra*.

Is picketing in violation of Section 8(b)(4)(B) unprotected by Section 7? If the union pickets the subcontractors, may the employer discharge those employees if their picketing is in violation of Section 8(b)(4)(B)? If the union has asked this question, how would you have answered? Do you think the employees made the decision about where to picket? Do you think they were aware of the unlawfulness of their conduct? Does the employer have remedies other than discharging the employees? See Sections 10(1) and 303. Do you think there is something improper about the employees' seeking the protection of the very Act which they are violating? Review the cases following *Local 1229*, page 344, *supra*. Further guidance is provided in Chapter 7.

3. BARGAINING, SLOWDOWNS, AND EMPLOYER RESPONSES

Sam Houston Company Problem
The Case of the Unwilling or Tired Workers

Recently, the Sam Houston Gun Manufacturing Co. consulted you regarding the following matter. The company wants to know what sanctions, either through governmental agencies or through self-help, are available to stop, or interfere with, the effectiveness of the employees' conduct described below.

The Sam Houston Gun Manufacturing Co. has been a leading manufacturer of many sorts of weapons that eject relatively small missiles at great speeds. These products include various rifles, shotguns, and sidearms. For the past six years, the employees who work in the plant and who operate the machinery that manufactures the products have been represented by Local 40 of the Amalgamated Gun Makers of America. During those six years, the company and AGMA have signed two three-year contracts dealing with the employees' hours, pay, and other terms and conditions of employment. Each has had a broad no-strike clause. The more recent contract expired several weeks ago.

For more than two months prior to the recent contract's expiration, the union and the company have attempted to negotiate a new contract. They have been unable to do so. One of the matters in dispute is whether increased productivity during the past two years justified a substantial increase in salaries. Two years ago, the company installed new machinery that was far more efficient than the predecessor machinery. As a result the company is producing far more guns per employee than in the past. The employees and the union insist that hourly wages should reflect this increase. The company has been of the view that the company's own capital has been the sole cause of the increase in productivity, and the employees should not insist on doubling the cost to the company for having purchased the machinery.

Since the day after the recent contract expired, the company has been virtually certain that the employees in the plant have been engaging in a slowdown. That is, although the workers report for work and stay on the premises and in their work positions as usual, production has fallen off sharply. In fact, production has almost fallen to the level that existed at the time just prior to the purchase of the new machinery. A careful check of the employees by watchful supervisors and foremen and an assessment of the productivity of certain machines lead the company to the conclusion that 10 identifiable employees are primarily responsible for the slowdown. Two of the 10 are shop stewards, and two others are on the local union's negotiations team.

Alice Trembles, president of Sam Houston, is outraged and wants to discharge these workers. However, she recognizes the possible consequences of such action. The employees may strike. This is the last thing Trembles wants. She has received a large contract with the government and wants to fill it as soon as possible. If she does not succeed in filling it within the next 45 days, she will lose it. On the other hand, the slowdown will preclude completion of the contract for a considerable time beyond the 45 days.

In light of the need to keep the operations going, Trembles wants to know if there is any way she can use government institutions to enjoin the workers and union, or at least have their conduct declared unlawful. If the government offers her no solace, what can she lawfully do? If she has to lose the government contract because of the slowdown, she would like to rid herself of the offending employees. Short of that, she at least would like to reciprocate in kind the economic pressure which is resulting from the slowdown and placing considerable pressure on the company to capitulate to the union's demands at the bargaining table.

a. NLRB Remedies

As you already know, conduct of employees as such is not designated as unlawful under the Act. Thus, unless the action of the employees can be attributed to the union, there is no need to consider further the possible application of the Act. In order to prove union responsibility, what factors do you think would be relevant and persuasive if, as is likely, you will be unable to obtain an open admission from the union that the slowdown is occurring let alone that it is occurring under union auspices?

Assuming you can prove that the union should be held responsible for the slowdown, what provisions of the Act do you think are violated by the conduct of the union?

NLRB v. Insurance Agents International Union AFL-CIO

Supreme Court of the United States, 1960
361 U.S. 478, 45 LRRM 2704

MR. JUSTICE BRENNAN delivered the opinion of the Court.

This case presents an important issue of the scope of the National Labor Relations Board's authority under § 8(b)(3) of the National Labor Relations Act, which provides that "It shall be an unfair labor practice for a labor organization or its agents . . . to refuse to bargain collectively with an employer, provided it is the representative of his employees. . . ." The precise question is whether the Board may find that a union, which confers with an employer with the desire of reaching agreement on contract terms, has nevertheless refused to bargain collectively, thus violating that provision, solely and simply because during the negotiations it seeks to put economic pressure on the employer to yield to its bargaining demands by sponsoring on-the-job conduct designed to interfere with the carrying on of the employer's business.

Since 1949 the respondent Insurance Agents' International Union and the Prudential Insurance Company of America have negotiated collective bargaining agreements covering district agents employed by Prudential in 35 States and the District of Columbia. The principal duties of a Prudential district agent are to collect premiums and to solicit new business in an assigned locality known in the trade as his "debit." He has no fixed or regular working hours except that he must report at his district office two mornings a week and remain for two or three hours to deposit his collections, prepare and submit reports, and attend meetings to receive sales and other instructions. He is paid commissions on collections made and on new policies written; his only fixed compensation is a weekly payment of $4.50 intended primarily to cover his expenses.

In January 1956 Prudential and the union began the negotiation of a new contract to replace an agreement expiring in the following March. Bargaining was carried on continuously for six months before the terms of the new contract were agreed upon on July 17, 1956. It is not questioned that, if it stood alone, the record of negotiations would establish that the union conferred in good faith for the purpose and with the desire of reaching agreement with Prudential on a contract.

However, in April 1956, Prudential filed a § 8(b)(3) charge of refusal to bargain collectively against the union. The charge was based upon actions of the union and its members outside the conference room, occurring after the old contract expired in March. The union had announced in February that if agreement on the terms of the new contract was not reached when the old contract expired, the union members would then participate in a "Work Without A Contract" program—which meant that they would engage in certain planned, concerted on-the-job activities designed to harass the company.

A complaint of violation of § 8(b)(3) issued on the charge and hearings began before the bargaining was concluded. It was developed in the evidence that the union's harassing tactics involved activities by the member agents such as these: refusal for a time to solicit new business, and refusal (after the writing of new business was resumed) to comply with the company's reporting procedures; refusal to participate in the company's "May Policyholder's Month Campaign"; reporting late at district offices the days the agents were scheduled to attend them, and refusing to perform customary duties at the offices, instead engaging there in "sit-in-mornings," "doing what comes naturally" and leaving at noon as a group; absenting themselves from special business conferences arranged by the company; picketing and distributing leaflets outside the various offices of the company on specified days and hours as directed by the union; distributing leaflets each day to policyholders and others and soliciting policyholders' signatures on petitions directed to the company; and presenting the signed policyholders' petitions to the company at its home office while simultaneously engaging in mass demonstrations there.

. . .

First, The bill which became the Wagner Act included no provision specifically imposing a duty on either party to bargain collectively. Senator Wagner thought that the bill required bargaining in good faith without such a provision. However, the Senate Committee in charge of the bill concluded that it was desirable to include a provision making it an unfair labor practice for an *employer* to refuse to bargain collectively in order to assure that the Act would achieve its primary objective of requiring an employer to recognize a union selected by his employees as their representative. It was believed that other rights guaranteed by the Act would not be meaningful if the employer was not under obligation to confer with the union in an effort to arrive at the terms of an agreement.

. . .

However, the nature of the duty to bargain in good faith thus imposed upon employers by § 8(5) of the original Act was not sweepingly conceived. The Chairman of the Senate Committee declared: "When the employees have chosen their organization, when they have selected their representatives, all the bill proposes to do is to escort them to the door of their employer and say, 'Here they are, the legal representatives of your employees.' What happens behind those doors is not inquired into, and the bill does not seek to inquire into it."

The limitation implied by the last sentence has not been in practice maintained—practically, it could hardly have been—but the underlying purpose of the remark has remained the most basic purpose of the statutory provision. That purpose is the making effective of the duty of management to extend recognition to the union; the duty of management to bargain in good faith is essentially a corollary of its duty to recognize the union. Decisions under this provision reflect this. . . .

But at the same time, Congress was generally not concerned with the substantive terms on which the parties contracted. Obviously there is tension between the principle that the parties need not contract on any specific terms and a practical enforcement of the principle that they are bound to deal with each other in a serious attempt to resolve differences and reach a common ground. And in fact criticism of the Board's application of the "good-faith" test arose from the belief that it was forcing employers to yield to union demands if they were to avoid a successful charge of unfair labor practice. Thus, in 1947 in Congress the fear was expressed that the Board had "gone very far, in the guise of determining whether or not employers had bargained in good faith, in setting itself up as the judge of what concessions an employer must make and of the proposals and counterproposals that he may or may not make." Since the Board was not viewed by Congress as an agency which should exercise its powers to arbitrate the parties' substantive solutions of the issues in their bargaining, a check on this apprehended trend was provided by writing the good-faith test of bargaining into § 8(d) of the Act. . . .

Second. At the same time as it was statutorily defining the duty to bargain collectively, Congress, by adding § 8(b)(3) of the Act through the

Taft-Hartley amendments, imposed that duty on labor organizations. Unions obviously are formed for the very purpose of bargaining collectively; but the legislative history makes it plain that Congress was wary of the position of some unions, and wanted to ensure that they would approach the bargaining table with the same attitude of willingness to reach an agreement as had been enjoined on management earlier. It intended to prevent employee representatives from putting forth the same "take it or leave it" attitude that had been condemned in management.

Third. It is apparent from the legislative history of the whole Act that the policy of Congress is to impose a mutual duty upon the parties to confer in good faith with a desire to reach agreement, in the belief that such an approach from both sides of the table promotes the overall design of achieving industrial peace. Discussion conducted under that standard of good faith may narrow the issues, making the real demands of the parties clearer to each other, and perhaps to themselves, and may encourage an attitude of settlement through give and take. The mainstream of cases before the Board and in the courts reviewing its orders, under the provisions fixing the duty to bargain collectively, is concerned with insuring that the parties approach the bargaining table with this attitude. But apart from this essential standard of conduct, Congress intended that the parties should have wide latitude in their negotiations, unrestricted by any governmental power to regulate the substantive solution of their differences.

. . . The presence of economic weapons in reserve, and their actual exercise on occasion by the parties, is part and parcel of the system that the Wagner and Taft-Hartley Acts have recognized. Abstract logical analysis might find inconsistency between the command of the statute to negotiate toward an agreement in good faith and the legitimacy of the use of economic weapons, frequently having the most serious effect upon individual workers and productive enterprises, to induce one party to come to the terms desired by the other. But the truth of the matter is that at the present statutory stage of our national labor relations policy, the two factors—necessity for good-faith bargaining between parties, and the availability of economic pressure devices to each to make the other party incline to agree on one's terms—exist side by side. . . .

For similar reasons, we think the Board's approach involves an intrusion into the substantive aspects of the bargaining process—again, unless there is some specific warrant for its condemnation of the precise tactics involved here. The scope of § 8(b)(3) and the limitations on Board power which were the design of § 8(d) are exceeded, we hold, by inferring a lack of good faith not from any deficiencies of the union's performance at the bargaining table by reason of its attempted use of economic pressure, but solely and simply because tactics designed to exert economic pressure were employed during the course of the good-faith negotiations. Thus the Board in the guise of determining good or bad faith in negotiations could regulate what economic weapons a party might summon to its aid. And if the Board could regulate the choice of economic weapons that may be used as part of collective bargaining, it would be in a position to exercise considerable influence upon the substantive terms on which the parties contract. . . .

Fourth. The use of economic pressure, as we have indicated, is of itself not at all inconsistent with the duty of bargaining in good faith. But in three cases in recent years, the Board has assumed the power to label particular union economic weapons inconsistent with that duty. The Board freely (and we think correctly) conceded here that a "total" strike called by the union would not have subjected it to sanctions under § 8(b)(3), at least if it were called after the old contract, with its no-strike clause, had expired. . . .

(a) The Board contends that the distinction between a total strike and the conduct at bar is that a total strike is a concerted activity protected against employer interference by §§ 7 and 8(a)(1) of the Act, while the activity at bar is not a protected concerted activity. We may agree *arguendo* with the Board that this Court's decision in the *Briggs-Stratton* case, *Automobile Workers* v. *Wisconsin Board,* 336 U.S. 235, establishes that the employee conduct here was not a protected concerted activity. On this assumption the employer could have discharged or taken other appropriate disciplinary action against the employees participating in these "slow-down," "sit-in," and arguably unprotected disloyal tactics. But surely that a union activity is not protected against disciplinary action does not mean that it constitutes a refusal to bargain in good faith. The reason why the ordinary economic strike is not evidence of a failure to bargain in good faith is not that it constitutes a protected activity but that, as we have developed, there is simply no inconsistency between the application of economic pressure and good-faith collective bargaining. . . .

(b) The Board contends that because an orthodox "total" strike is "traditional" its use must be taken as being consistent with § 8(b)(3); but since the tactics here are not "traditional" or "normal," they need not be so viewed. Further, the Board cites what it conceives to be the public's moral condemnation of the sort of employee tactics involved here. But again we cannot see how these distinctions can be made under a statute which simply enjoins a duty to bargain in good faith. Again, these are relevant arguments when the question is the scope of the concerted activities given affirmative protection by the Act. But as we have developed, the use of economic pressure by the parties to a labor dispute is not a grudging exception to some policy of completely academic discussion enjoined by the Act; it is part and parcel of the process of collective bargaining. On this basis, we fail to see the relevance of whether the practice in question is time-honored or whether its exercise is generally supported by public opinion. It may be that the tactics used here deserve condemnation, but this would not justify attempting to pour that condemnation into a vessel not designed to hold it. . . .

Fifth. These distinctions essayed by the Board here, and the lack of relationship to the statutory standard inherent in them, confirm us in our conclusion that the judgment of the Court of Appeals, setting aside the order of the Board, must be affirmed. For they make clear to us that when the Board moves in this area, with only § 8(b)(3) for support, it is functioning as an arbiter of the sort of economic weapons the parties can use in seeking to gain acceptance of their bargaining demands. It has sought to introduce some standard of properly "balanced" bargaining power, or some new distinction of justifiable and unjustifiable, proper and "abusive" economic weapons into the collective bargaining duty imposed by the Act. The Board's assertion of power under § 8(b)(3) allows it to sit in judgment upon every economic weapon the parties to a labor contract negotiation employ, judging it on the very general standard of that section, not drafted with reference to specific forms of economic pressure. We have expressed our belief that this amounts to the Board's entrance into the substantive aspects of the bargaining process to an extent Congress has not countenanced.

It is one thing to say that the Board has been afforded flexibility to determine, for example, whether an employer's disciplinary action taken against specific workers is permissible or not, or whether a party's conduct at the bargaining table evidences a real desire to come into agreement. The statute in such areas clearly poses the problem to the Board for its solution. And specifically we do not mean to question in any way the Board's powers to determine the latter question, drawing inferences from the conduct of the parties as a whole. It is quite another matter, however, to say that the Board has been afforded flexibility in picking and choosing which economic devices of labor and management shall be branded as unlawful. Congress has been rather specific when it has come to outlaw particular economic weapons on the part of unions.

But the activities here involved have never been specifically outlawed by Congress. To be sure, the express prohibitions of the Act are not exclusive—if there were any questions of a stratagem or device to evade the policies of the Act, the Board hardly would be powerless. But it is clear to us that the Board needs a more specific charter than § 8(b)(3) before it can add to the Act's prohibitions here.

. . .

Affirmed.

Questions

1. Although we are postponing a study of the obligation to bargain in good faith, one question should be asked: Can a slowdown be any evidence of a union's stalling in negotiations until the effects of the slowdown have taken hold?

2. Can you think of any economic pressure—standing alone—which would convince you that the party using the weapon was bargaining in bad faith? How about appeals by the employer to the employees that the union is not serving their interests? Or employer promises to negotiate directly with the employees resulting in greater benefits than through collective bargaining? How about an increase in wages without the employer's first notifying or consulting with the union? How about the reduction of wages during negotiations? Or a lockout? In what way, if any, are these weapons distinguishable from the slowdown?

3. The Court rejects the Board's effort to balance economic weapons in *Insurance Agents*. Is this consistent with the language and decisions in *Erie Resistor, Great Dane, Fleetwood*, and even *Mackay*? Can one reconcile the apparent disparity?

4. In any event, in light of *Insurance Agents*, you can have no doubt regarding the Houston Company Problem on page 378, can you, that AGMA's slowdown, at least standing alone, was not a violation of the union's duty to bargain in good faith? In light of the reasoning of the Court, and considering the language of the statute, do you think the slowdown constitutes a violation of any other section of the Act?

b. State Remedies for the Employer

Do you think there ought to be some remedy for the employer in the courts for some sort of tort or breach of implied contract based on the employees' interference with the efficient conduct of the company? What theory or theories can you conceive? In addition to those possible common-law remedies, many states have special laws and agencies to deal with labor relations. Solace for Alice Trembles may be found there.

Might there be some preemption problems if the state provides remedies for the sort of conduct involved in the Houston Company hypothetical case? Might your answer to this question be affected by what you understood the NLRA's treatment of this conduct was? For example, if the Act does outlaw the conduct, are the considerations the same as if the Act protected it? What if the Act does neither? In *Auto Workers v. Wisconsin Employment Relations Board*, 336 U.S. 245, 23 LRRM 2361 (1949), referred to in *Insurance Agents*, the Supreme Court held that a state labor agency could legally enjoin intermittent work stoppages by a union in support of negotiation demands.

Machinists, Lodge 76 v. Wisconsin Employment Relations Commission

Supreme Court of the United States, 1976
427 U.S. 132, 92 LRRM 2881

MR. JUSTICE BRENNAN delivered the opinion of the Court.

The question to be decided in this case is whether federal labor policy pre-empts the authority of a state labor relations board to grant an employer covered by the National Labor Relations Act an order enjoining a union and its members from continuing to refuse to work overtime pursuant to a union policy to put economic pressure on the employer in negotiations for renewal of an expired collective-bargaining agreement.

. . .[During negotiations for a new collective bargaining contract and after the old contract had been terminated by the employer pursuant to that contract, the employer unilaterally eliminated some union privileges, and later threatened to institute unilaterally proposals it had made at the bargaining table. The union responded with a concerted employee refusal to work all the hours the employer wanted. The employer disciplined no one.]

Instead, while negotiations continued, the employer filed a charge with the National Labor Relations Board that the Union's resolution violated § 8(b)(3) of the National Labor Relations Act. The Regional Director dismissed the charge. . . . However, the employer also filed a complaint before the Wisconsin Employment Relations Commission. . . . The Commission . . . entered an order that the Union . . . "[i]mmediately cease and desist from authorizing, encouraging or condoning any concerted refusal to accept overtime assignments. . . ." The Wisconsin Circuit Court affirmed and entered judgment enforcing the Commission's order. The Wisconsin Supreme Court affirmed the Circuit Court. We reverse.

. . .

[A] line of pre-emption analysis has been developed in cases focusing upon the crucial inquiry whether Congress intended that the conduct involved be unregulated because left "to be controlled by the free play of economic forces," *NLRB* v. *Nash-Finch Co.*, 404 U.S. 138, 144, 78 LRRM 2967, 2969 (1971). Concededly this inquiry was not made in 1949 in the so-called *Briggs-Stratton* case, *Automobile Workers* v. *Wisconsin Board*, 336 U.S. 245, 23 LRRM 2361 (1949), the decision of this Court heavily relied upon the court below in reaching its decision that state regulation of the conduct at issue is not pre-empted by national labor law. . . .

However, the *Briggs-Stratton* holding that state power is not pre-empted as to peaceful conduct neither protected by § 7 nor prohibited by § 8 of the federal Act, a holding premised on the statement that "[t]his conduct is either governable by the State or it is entirely ungoverned," was undercut by subsequent decisions of this Court. For the Court soon recognized that a particular activity might be "protected" by federal law not only where it fell within § 7, but also when it was an activity that Congress intended to be "unrestricted by *any* governmental power to regulate" because it was among the permissible "economic weapons in reserve . . . actual exercise [of which] on occasion by the parties is part and parcel of the system that the Wagner and Taft-Hartley Acts have recognized." *NLRB* v. *Insurance Agents*, 361 U.S., at 488, 489, 45 LRRM at 2708, 2709 (emphasis added). "[T]he legislative purpose may . . . dictate that certain activity 'neither protected nor prohibited' be privileged against state regulation." *Hanna Mining Co.* v. *Marine Engineers*, 382 U.S., at 187, 60 LRRM at 2475.

. . .

[In *Local 20, Teamsters, Chauffeurs & Helpers Union* v. *Morton*, 377 U.S. 252 (1964), we] held pre-empted the application of state law to award damages for peaceful union secondary picketing. Although *Morton* involved conduct neither "protected nor prohibited" by § 7 or § 8 of the NLRA, we recognized the necessity of an inquiry whether "Congress occupied the field and closed it to state regulation.". . .

. . . Whether self-help economic activities are employed by employer or union, the crucial inquiry regarding pre-emption is the same: whether "the exercise of plenary state authority to curtail or entirely prohibit self-help would frustrate effective implementation of the Act's processes."

III

There is simply no question that the Act's processes would be frustrated in the instant case were the State's ruling permitted to stand. The employer in this case invoked the Wisconsin law because unable to overcome the union tactic with its own economic self-help means. Although it did employ economic weapons putting pressure on the union when it terminated the previous agreement, *supra*, at 2, it apparently lacked sufficient economic strength to secure its bargaining demands under "the balance of power between labor and management expressed in our national labor policy," *Teamsters Union v. Morton*, 377 U.S., at 260. But the economic weakness of the affected party cannot justify state aid contrary to federal law for, "as we have developed, the use of economic pressure by the parties to a labor dispute is not a grudging exception [under] . . . the [federal] Act; it is part and parcel of the process of collective bargaining." *Insurance Agents*, 361 U.S., at 495. . . .

Our decisions hold that Congress meant that these activities, whether of employer or employees, were not to be regulable by States any more than by the NLRB, for neither States nor the Board are "afforded flexibility in picking and choosing which economic devices of labor and management would be branded as "unlawful." *Ibid.* Rather, both are without authority to attempt to "introduce some standard of properly 'balanced' bargaining power," *id.*, at 497, or to define "what economic sanctions might be permitted negotiating parties in an 'ideal' or 'balanced' state of collective bargaining." *Id.*, at 500. . . .

. . .We hold today that the ruling of *Briggs-Stratton*, permitting state regulation of partial strike activities such as are involved in this case is likewise "no longer of general application."

. . .

Since *Briggs-Stratton* is today overruled, and as we hold further that the Union's refusal to work overtime is peaceful conduct constituting activity which must be free of regulation by the States if the congressional intent in enacting the comprehensive federal law of labor relations is not to be frustrated, the judgment of the Wisconsin Supreme Court is

Reversed.

c. Employer's Self-Help Remedies

i. Discharge

If we make the assumption that neither the Act's unfair labor practice provisions nor state law, if applicable, outlaws the union's conduct in the Houston Company problem, what sanctions are available to the employer to respond to the union's efforts to coerce it into agreeing to the wage demands? For example, can the employer discharge the 10 employees most involved in the slowdown? In the early years of the Act, the Board seemed to answer this question, "No." However, in *Auto Workers v. Wisconsin Employment Relations Board*, 336 U.S. 245, 23 LRRM 2361 (1949), the

Supreme Court (by a 5-to-4 majority) indicated that discharge was available to the employer subjected to a slowdown. In that case, after bargaining became deadlocked, the employees engaged in 27 work stoppages over a five-month period in order to bring pressure on the employer. Throughout all of this, the union did not make clear what concessions the employer had to make to avoid this pressure. The Court held that it was within the proper jurisdiction of the state to forbid such employee-union conduct. In reaching this conclusion, the Court had to find that the activity of the employees was not protected by Section 7 of the Act and, therefore, the state regulation was not preempted.

The Court said:

> "If we are to read § 13 as we are urged to do, to make the strike an absolute right and the definition to extend the right to all other variations of the strike, the effect would be to legalize beyond the power of any state or federal authorities to control not only the intermittent stoppages such as we have here but also the slowdown and perhaps the sit-down strike as well. [Citation omitted.] And this is not all; the management also would be disabled from any kind of self-help to cope with these coercive tactics of the union except to submit to its undeclared demands. . . .[I]f the rights here asserted are rights conferred by the . . . Act, it is hard to see how the management can take any steps to resist or combat them without incurring the sanctions of the Act." 336 U.S. at 264, 23 LRRM at 2361.

The Court then concluded that the Act neither forbade nor protected the stoppages, and therefore the states could outlaw them.

Questions

1. Is it necessary to conclude that if the conduct is protected by Sections 7 and 13 of the Act, the employer is precluded from any and all responses to the union conduct? Consider, for example, the following: Does the Court's reasoning mean an employer cannot respond in any effective way to a strike by employees? Or may it continue to operate its business? May the employer stockpile in advance of a strike? May it hire replacements to keep the business in operation? May these replacements be permanent? May the employer lock out employees before they strike? May it put into effect the proposals made during collective bargaining, at least after that process has had a fair opportunity to produce agreement? If your answer to any of these questions is "Yes," isn't the *Auto Workers* Court incorrect in its conclusion that the employer is necessarily forced to submit meekly without retaliation to all protected activities?

2. Perhaps we should look for some other basis for the Court's conclusion. Can it be that the union and employees are being exposed to sanctions because what they are doing is thought to be new and different? Because what they are doing is not "nice"? Why should that make any difference?

3. Or was the Court merely saying that this particular weapon in the hands of the employees was too powerful? Before you decide whether you agree with that assessment of the slowdown or intermittent work stoppage techniques, don't you first have to ask yourself what weapons are available to the employer? And don't you also have to ask: Who is to determine what is "too powerful"? And how is that proved?

4. In *Elk Lumber Co.*, 91 NLRB 333, 26 LRRM 1493 (1950), the Board held that a slowdown by unorganized employees to protest a decrease in wages was not protected by the Act. The Board said:

> "The test . . . is whether the particular activity is so indefensible as to warrant the employer in discharging the participating employees. Either an unlawful objective or the adoption of improper means of achieving it may deprive employees engaged in concerted activities of the protection of the Act. . . . In effect, [the slowdown] constituted a refusal on their part to accept the terms of employment set by their employer without engaging in a stoppage, but to continue rather to work on their own terms."

We see once again a return to the "improper means" test of the common law. Whether or not you agree that it may be necessary to assess the propriety of concerted activities to determine their protection under Section 7, do you agree with the premises of the Board in decrying the slowdown? Are these premises even consistent with the purposes of the Act?

5. Are the *Auto Workers* and *Elk Lumber* cases still "good law"? Reconsider *Local 1229, IBEW*, page 344, *supra, Washington Aluminum*, page 349, *supra, Insurance Agents*, page 379, *supra*, and *Lodge 76*, page 385, *supra*. Consider, also, the following material.

ii. Lockout

American Ship Building Co. v. NLRB*

Supreme Court of the United States, 1964
380 U.S. 300, 58 LRRM 2672

Mr. Justice Stewart delivered the opinion of the Court.

The American Ship Building Company seeks review of a decision of the United States Court of Appeals for the District of Columbia Circuit enforcing an order of the National Labor Relations Board which found that the company had committed an unfair labor practice under §§ 8(a)(1) and (3) of the National Labor Relations Act. The question presented is . . . whether an employer commits an unfair labor practice . . . when he temporarily lays off or "locks out" his employees during a labor dispute to bring economic pressure in support of his bargaining position.

*See Meltzer, *The Lockout Cases*, 1965 Supreme Court Rev. 87.

Since 1952 the employer has engaged in collective bargaining with a group of eight unions. Prior to the negotiations here in question, the employer had contracted with the unions on five occasions, each agreement having been preceded by a strike. The particular chapter of the collective bargaining history with which we are concerned opened shortly before May 1, 1961, when the unions notified the company of their intention to seek modification of the current contract. . . .

[A]fter extended negotiations, the parties separated without having resolved substantial differences on the central issues dividing them and without having specific plans for further attempts to resolve them—a situation which the trial examiner found was an impasse. Throughout the negotiations, the employer displayed anxiety as to the unions' strike plans, fearing that the unions would call a strike as soon as a ship entered the Chicago yard or delay negotiations into the winter to increase strike leverage. The union negotiator consistently insisted that it was his intention to reach an agreement without calling a strike; however, he did concede incomplete control over the workers—a fact borne out by the occurrence of a wildcat strike in February 1961. Because of the danger of an unauthorized strike and the consistent and deliberate use of strikes in prior negotiations, the employer remained apprehensive of the possibility of a work stoppage.

In light of the failure to reach an agreement and the lack of available work, the employer decided to lay off certain of its workers. On August 11 the employees received a notice which read: "Because of the labor dispute which has been unresolved since August 1, 1961, you are laid off until further notice." . . . Negotiations were resumed shortly after these layoffs and continued for the following two months until a two-year contract was agreed upon. . . . The employees were recalled the following day.
. . .

In analyzing the status of the bargaining lockout under §§ 8(a)(1) and (3) of the National Labor Relations Act, it is important that the practice with which we are here concerned be distinguished from other forms of temporary separation from employment. No one would deny that an employer is free to shut down his enterprise temporarily for reasons of renovation or lack of profitable work unrelated to his collective bargaining situation. Similarly, we put to one side cases where the Board has concluded on the basis of substantial evidence that the employer has used a lockout as a means to injure a labor organization or to evade his duty to bargain collectively. What we are here concerned with is the use of a temporary layoff of employees solely as a means to bring economic pressure to bear in support of the employer's bargaining position, after an impasse has been reached. This is the only issue before us, and all that we decide.[8]

To establish that this practice is a violation of § 8(a)(1), it must be shown that the employer has interfered with, restrained, or coerced employees

[8]Contrary to the views expressed in a concurring opinion filed in this case, we intimate no view whatever as to the consequences which would follow had the employer replaced its employees with permanent replacements or even temporary help. Cf. *Labor Board* v. *Mackay Radio & Telegraph Co.*, 304 U.S. 333.

in the exercise of some right protected by § 7 of the Act. The Board's position is premised on the view that the lockout interferes with two of the rights guaranteed by § 7: the right to bargain collectively and the right to strike. In the Board's view, the use of the lockout "punishes" employees for the presentation of and adherence to demands made by their bargaining representatives and so coerces them in the exercise of their right to bargain collectively. It is important to note that there is here no allegation that the employer used the lockout in the service of designs inimical to the process of collective bargaining. There was no evidence and no finding that the employer was hostile to its employees' banding together for collective bargaining or that the lockout was designed to discipline them for doing so. It is therefore inaccurate to say that the employer's intention was to destroy or frustrate the process of collective bargaining. What can be said is that it intended to resist the demands made of it in the negotiations and to secure modification of these demands. We cannot see that this intention is in any way inconsistent with the employees' rights to bargain collectively.

Moreover, there is no indication, either as a general matter or in this specific case, that the lockout will necessarily destroy the unions' capacity for effective and responsible representation. The unions here involved have vigorously represented the employees since 1952, and there is nothing to show that their ability to do so has been impaired by the lockout. Nor is the lockout one of those acts which are demonstrably so destructive of collective bargaining that the Board need not inquire into employer motivation, as might be the case, for example, if an employer permanently discharged his unionized staff and replaced them with employees known to be possessed of a violent antiunion animus. . . .

The Board has taken the complementary view that the lockout interferes with the right to strike protected under §§ 7 and 13 of the Act in that it allows the employer to pre-empt the possibility of a strike and thus leave the union with "nothing to strike against." Insofar as this means that once employees are locked out, they are deprived of their right to call a strike against the employer because he is already shut down, the argument is wholly specious, for the work stoppage which would have been the object of the strike has in fact occurred. It is true that recognition of the lockout deprives the union of exclusive control of the timing and duration of work stoppages calculated to influence the result of collective bargaining negotiations, but there is nothing in the statute which would imply that the right to strike "carries with it" the right exclusively to determine the timing and duration of all work stoppages. The right to strike as commonly understood is the right to cease work—nothing more. No doubt a union's bargaining power would be enhanced if it possessed not only the simple right to strike but also the power exclusively to determine when work stoppages should occur, but the Act's provisions are not indefinitely elastic, content-free forms to be shaped in whatever manner the Board might think best conforms to the proper balance of bargaining power.

. . .

Section 8(a)(3) prohibits discrimination in regard to tenure or other conditions of employment to discourage union membership. Under the words of the statute there must be both discrimination and a resulting discouragement of union membership. It has long been established that a finding of violation under this section will normally turn on the employer's motivation. . . . [W]e have consistently construed the section to leave unscathed a wide range of employer actions taken to serve legitimate business interests in some significant fashion, even though the act committed may tend to discouraage union membership. . . .

[T]his lockout does not fall into that category of cases arising under § 8(a)(3) in which the Board may truncate its inquiry into employer motivation. As this case well shows, use of the lockout does not carry with it any necessary implication that the employer acted to discourage union membership or otherwise discriminate against union members as such. The purpose and effect of the lockout were only to bring pressure upon the union to modify its demands. Similarly, it does not appear that the natural tendency of the lockout is severely to discourage union membership while serving no significant employer interest. In fact, it is difficult to understand what tendency to discourage union membership or otherwise discriminate against union members was perceived by the Board. There is no claim that the employer locked out only union members, or locked out any employee simply because he was a union member; nor is it alleged that the employer conditioned rehiring upon resignation from the union. It is true that the employees suffered economic disadvantage because of their union's insistence on demands unacceptable to the employer, but this is also true of many steps which an employer may take during a bargaining conflict, and the existence of an arguable possibility that someone may feel himself discouraged in his union membership or discriminated against by reason of that membership cannot suffice to label them violations of § 8(a)(3) absent some unlawful intention. The employer's permanent replacement of strikers *(Labor Board v. Mackay Radio & Telegraph Co., supra),* his unilateral imposition of terms *(Labor Board v. Tex-Tan, Inc.,* 318 F.2d 472, 479–482), or his simple refusal to make a concession which would terminate a strike—all impose economic disadvantage during a bargaining conflict, but none is necessarily a violation of § 8(a)(3).

To find a violation of § 8(a)(3), then, the Board must find that the employer acted for a proscribed purpose. Indeed, the Board itself has always recognized that certain "operative" or "economic" purposes would justify a lockout. But the Board has erred in ruling that only these purposes will remove a lockout from the ambit of § 8(a)(3), for that section requires an intention to discourage union membership or otherwise discriminate against the union. There was not the slightest evidence and there was no finding that the employer was actuated by a desire to discourage membership in the union as distinguished from a desire to affect the outcome of the particular negotiations in which it was involved. . . .

The Board has justified its ruling in this case and its general approach to the legality of lockouts on the basis of its special competence to weigh the competing interests of employers and employees and to accommodate these interests according to its expert judgment. "The Board has reasonably concluded that the availability of such a weapon would so substantially tip the scales in the employer's favor as to defeat the Congressional purpose of placing employees on a par with their adversary at the bargaining table." To buttress its decision as to the balance struck in this particular case, the Board points out that the employer has been given other weapons to counterbalance the employees' power of strike. The employer may permanently replace workers who have gone out on strike, or, by stockpiling and subcontracting, maintain his commercial operations while the strikers bear the economic brunt of the work stoppage. Similarly, the employer can institute unilaterally the working conditions which he desires once his contract with the union has expired. Given these economic weapons, it is argued, the employer has been adequately equipped with tools of economic self-help.

There is of course no question that the Board is entitled to the greatest deference in recognition of its special competence in dealing with labor problems. In many areas its evaluation of the competing interests of employer and employee should unquestionably be given conclusive effect in determining the application of §§ 8(a)(1), (3), and (5). However, we think that the Board construes its functions too expansively when it claims general authority to define national labor policy by balancing the competing interests of labor and management.

While a primary purpose of the National Labor Relations Act was to redress the perceived imbalance of economic power between labor and management, it sought to accomplish that result by conferring certain affirmative rights on employees and by placing certain enumerated restrictions on the activities of employers. The Act prohibited acts which interfered with, restrained, or coerced employees in the exercise of their rights to organize a union, to bargain collectively, and to strike; it proscribed discrimination in regard to tenure and other conditions of employment to discourage membership in any labor organization. The central purpose of these provisions was to protect employee self-organization and the process of collective bargaining from disruptive interferences by employers. Having protected employee organization in countervailance to the employers' bargaining power, and having established a system of collective bargaining whereby the newly coequal adversaries might resolve their disputes, the Act also contemplated resort to economic weapons should more peaceful measures not avail. Sections 8(a)(1) and (3) do not give the Board a general authority to assess the relative economic power of the adversaries in the bargaining process and to deny weapons to one party or the other because of its assessment of that party's bargaining power. In this case the Board has, in essence, denied the use of the bargaining lockout to the employer because of its conviction that use of this device would give the employer "too much power." In so doing, the Board has stretched §§ 8(a)(1) and (3) far beyond their functions of protecting the rights of employee organization and collective bargaining. . . .

Reversed

Questions

1. Is an employer free to lock out its employees during collective bargaining when there is no impasse? Remember the Court's apparent disapproval of "take-it-or-leave-it" bargaining in *Insurance Agents*? But also remember that the union in *Insurance Agents* engaged in its economic pressure before there was an impasse. By the way, what is an impasse?

2. The Court comes close to equating the employer's lockout with the union's strike. Must the statute be read in this way? How would you respond to the argument that the "right" to strike was Congress's way of giving the employees an adequate economic response to the employer's inherent power derived from its corporate status, capital, and resources? Is the Court's answer to this argument satisfactory?

3. The Court repeats the "anti-balancing" rhetoric of *Insurance Agents* and scolds the NLRB for balancing economic weapons. What is the Board supposed to do? Is this rhetoric consistent with other opinions you have read? Didn't the Court itself "balance" in *American Ship Building*? And in other cases? Is it possible that Congress wanted the Court, not the Board, to balance?

4. Does *Mackay* permit an employer to replace permanently the employees it has locked out pursuant to *American Ship Building*? See *NLRB* v. *Brown*, 380 U.S. 278, 58 LRRM 2663 (1965), where the Court, in overruling the Board, held it lawful for employers in an association to respond to a whipsaw strike of one employer by locking out and employing temporary replacements.

5. In light of *Insurance Agents* and *Washington Aluminum*, on the one hand, and *American Ship Building* on the other, can you have any rational doubt that the *Auto Workers* and *Elk Lumber* cases have no vitality? After all, the final possible argument to be made for those cases has been destroyed if it is true that the employer can respond to the slowdown with its own economic weapons, short of discharge. Moreover, if you take seriously the Court's declaration of war against the balancing of economic weapons, it should not matter that the employer may be helpless in the face of the slowdown by the workers. And, yet, given the reasoning in *Elk Lumber*, page 389, *supra*, one can still suspect Board disapproval of a slowdown.

iii. Permanent Replacement

Assume that the Sam Houston Gun Manufacturing Company would run too great a legal risk to justify discharging the employees identified as participants in the slowdown. Can the employer use the *Mackay* doctrine to replace the troublemakers? In a somewhat analogous situation, the Board and the courts have allowed the employer a somewhat watered-down *Mackay* privilege. When truck drivers refuse to cross picket lines at other employers' premises, they are refusing to do part of their work. In such cases, the Board has held that the refusals to cross the lines are protected because they constitute a classic concerted activity about which the Act surely gives protection. Some Courts of Appeals have upheld the

Board. Other courts, however, relying either on the notion that the drivers' employer is uninvolved in the labor dispute and has no control over its resolution or on the rationale that the drivers' refusals to cross picket lines is a partial strike, have held that such activities are unprotected. For the Board and the courts which hold the refusals to cross a protected activity, the question of replacements remains. The Board has reasoned that the burden is on the employer to demonstrate that a "business need to replace the employees is such as clearly to outweigh the employees' right to engage in protected activity that an invasion of the statutory right is justified." *Overnite Transportation Co.,* 154 NLRB 1271, 60 LRRM 1134 (1965), *modified,* 364 F.2d 682, 62 LRRM 2502 (D.C. Cir. 1966). Does this formulation make sense in the picket-line cases? If so, are there differences in the slowdown situation at Sam Houston Gun Co.?

iv. Reduction in Pay or Other Benefits

NLRB v. Katz*

Supreme Court of the United States, 1962
369 U.S. 736, 50 LRRM 2177

Mr. Justice Brennan delivered the opinion of the Court.
Is it a violation of the duty "to bargain collectively" imposed by § 8(a)(5) of the National Labor Relations Act for an employer, without first consulting a union with which it is carrying on bona fide contract negotiations, to institute changes regarding matters which are subjects of mandatory bargaining under § 8(d) and which are in fact under discussion? The National Labor Relations Board answered the question affirmatively in this case, in a decision which expressly disclaimed any finding that the totality of the respondents' conduct manifested bad faith in the pending negotiations.
A divided panel of the Court of Appeals for the Second Circuit denied enforcement of the Board's cease-and-desist order, finding in our decision in *Labor Board* v. *Insurance Agents' Union,* 361 U.S. 477, a broad rule that the statutory duty to bargain cannot be held to be violated, when bargaining is in fact being carried on, without a finding of the respondent's subjective bad faith in negotiating. . . .
[During negotiations, the parties discussed, among other things, merit increases and sick leave. Prior to an impasse, the employer instituted changes that promoted this litigation.]
The duty "to bargain collectively" enjoined by § 8(a)(5) is defined by § 8(d) as the duty to "meet . . . and confer in good faith with respect to wages, hours, and other terms and conditions of employment." Clearly, the duty thus defined may be violated without a general failure of subjective good faith; for there is no occasion to consider the issue of good faith

---

*See Schatzki, *The Employer's Unilateral Act—A Per Se Violation—Sometimes,* 44 Tex. L. Rev. 470 (1966).

if a party has refused even to negotiate *in fact*—"to meet . . . and confer"— about any of the mandatory subjects. A refusal to negotiate *in fact* as to any subject which is within § 8(d), and about which the union seeks to negotiate, violates § 8(a)(5) though the employer has every desire to reach agreement with the union upon an over-all collective agreement and earnestly and in all good faith bargains to that end. We hold that an employer's unilateral change in conditions of employment under negotiation is similarly a violation of § 8(a)(5), for it is a circumvention of the duty to negotiate which frustrates the objectives of § 8(a)(5) much as does a flat refusal.

The unilateral actions of the respondent illustrate the policy and practical considerations which support our conclusion.

We consider first the matter of sick leave. A sick-leave plan had been in effect since May 1956, under which employees were allowed ten paid sick-leave days annually and could accumulate half the unused days, or up to five days each year. Changes in the plan were sought and proposals and counterproposals had come up at three bargaining conferences. In March 1957, the company, without first notifying or consulting the union, announced changes in the plan, which reduced from ten to five the number of paid sick-leave days per year, but allowed accumulation of twice the unused days, thus increasing to ten the number of days which might be carried over. This action plainly frustrated the statutory objective of establishing working conditions through bargaining. Some employees might view the change to be a diminution of benefits. Others, more interested in accumulating sick-leave days, might regard the change as an improvement. If one view or the other clearly prevailed among the employees, the unilateral action might well mean that the employer had either uselessly dissipated trading material or aggravated the sick-leave issue. On the other hand, if the employees were more evenly divided on the merits of the company's changes, the union negotiators, beset by conflicting factions, might be led to adopt a protective vagueness on the issue of sick leave, which also would inhibit the useful discussion contemplated by Congress in imposing the specific obligation to bargain collectively.

Other considerations appear from consideration of the respondents' unilateral action in increasing wages. At the April 4, 1957, meeting the employers offered, and the union rejected, a three-year contract with an immediate across-the-board increase of $7.50 per week, to be followed at the end of the first year and again at the end of the second by further increases of $5 for employees earning less than $90 at those times. Shortly thereafter, without having advised or consulted with the union, the company announced a new system of automatic wage increases whereby there would be an increase of $5 every three months up to $74.99 per week; an increase of $5 every six months between $75 and $90 per week; and a merit review every six months for employees earning over $90 per week. It is clear at a glance that the automatic wage increase system which was instituted unilaterally was considerably more generous than that which had shortly theretofore been offered to and rejected by the union. Such action conclusively manifested bad faith in the negotiations, and so would have violated § 8(a)(5) even on the Court of Appeals' interpretation, though no additional evidence of bad faith appeared. An employer is not required to lead with his best offer; he is free to bargain. But even after an impasse is reached he has no license to grant wage increases greater than any he has ever offered the union at the bargaining table, for such action is necessarily inconsistent with a sincere desire to conclude an agreement with the union.[12]

The respondents' third unilateral action related to merit increases, which are also a subject of mandatory bargaining. . . . The matter of merit increases had been raised at three of the conferences during 1956 but no final understanding had been reached. In January 1957, the company, without notice to the union, granted merit increases to 20 employees out of the approximately 50 in the unit, the increases ranging between $2 and $10. This action too must be viewed as tantamount to an outright refusal to negotiate on that subject, and therefore as a violation of § 8(a)(5), unless the fact that the January raises were in line with the company's long-standing practice of granting quarterly or semiannual merit reviews—in effect, were a mere continuation of the status quo—differentiates them from the wage increases and the changes in the sick-leave plan. We do not think it does. Whatever might be the case as to so-called "merit raises" which are in fact simply automatic increases to which the employer has already committed himself, the raises here in question were in no sense automatic, but were informed by a large measure of discretion. There simply is no way in such case for a union to know whether or not there has been a substantial departure from past practice, and therefore the union may properly insist that the company negotiate as to the procedures and criteria for determining such increases.

It is apparent from what we have said why we see nothing in *Insurance Agents* contrary to the Board's decision. The union in that case had not in any way whatever foreclosed discussion of any issue, by unilateral actions or otherwise. The conduct complained of consisted of partial-strike tactics designed to put pressure on the employer to come to terms with the union negotiators. We held that Congress had not, in § 8(b)(3), the counterpart of § 8(a)(5), empowered the Board to pass judgment on the legitimacy of any particular economic weapon used in support of genuine negotiations. But the Board *is* authorized to order the cessation of behavior which is in effect a refusal to negotiate, or which directly obstructs or inhibits the actual process of discussion, or which reflects a cast of mind against reaching agreement. Unilateral action by an employer without prior discussion with the union does amount to a refusal to negotiate about the affected conditions of employment under negotiation, and must of necessity obstruct bargaining, contrary to the congressional policy. It will often disclose an unwillingness to agree with the union. It will rarely be justified by any reason of substance. It follows that the Board may hold such unilateral action to be an unfair labor practice in violation

[12]Of course, there is no resemblance between this situation and one wherein an employer, after notice and consultation, "unilaterally" institutes a wage increase identical with one which the union has rejected as too low. See *Labor Board* v. *Bradley Washfountain Co.*, 192 F.2d 144, 150–152; *Labor Board* v. *Landis Tool Co.*, 193 F.2d 279.

of § 8(a)(5), without also finding the employer guilty of overall subjective bad faith. While we do not foreclose the possibility that there might be circumstances which the Board could or should accept as excusing or justifying unilateral action, no such case is presented here.

The judgment of the Court of Appeals is reversed and the case is remanded with direction to the court to enforce the Board's order.

It is so ordered.

Questions

1. Should it make a difference whether the employer proposed the change during collective bargaining? Whether the bargaining process has had a fair opportunity to produce agreement before it unilaterally put the changes into effect?

2. Is *Katz* consistent with *American Ship Building*? With *Insurance Agents*? If the key to understanding *Katz* is to determine whether the unilateral acts "foreclosed discussion," are you persuaded by the conclusion that the *Katz* opinion reaches?

3. If you reached the conclusion that the Sam Houston Gun Manufacturing Co. could lock out, why should it not be able to reduce wages in a manner commensurate with the reduction in production? Or reduce wages even more? Or lock out partially? Compare *Hilton-Davis Chemical Co.*, 185 NLRB 241, 75 LRRM 1036 (1970) (refusal to go to arbitration over grievances which had arisen during the hiatus between collective agreements, both of which had arbitration clauses; held: no unfair labor practice), *Local 155 Molders Union v. NLRB*, 442 F.2d 742, 76 LRRM 2133 (D.C. Cir. 1971) (tactical unilateral decreases in economic benefits; held: NLRB correctly found an unfair labor practice), and *NLRB v. Great Falls Employers' Council*, 277 F.2d 772, 46 LRRM 2060 (9th Cir. 1960) (employer association locked out its employees in response to a whipsaw strike. When the locked-out employees attempted to collect unemployment benefits, the association recalled the workers for 16 hours each week, thus disqualifying the employees for the unemployment benefits; held: the NLRB incorrectly found an unfair labor practice).

Note

In light of these Supreme Court cases, are you confident the employer, Sam Houston Gun Manufacturing Co., can or cannot discharge the employees engaged in the slowdown? That it can or cannot lock out? That it can or cannot unilaterally reduce benefits? That it can or cannot hire permanent replacements for employees it has locked out?

To a considerable extent, the Board and the appellate courts have given their answers to these questions. For example, it seems safe to conclude at this time that in the eyes of the Board and appellate courts, "partial strikes" (*i.e.,* slowdowns, intermittent stoppages, refusals to do overtime, and the like) are unprotected activities, and participants may be lawfully discharged. However, the employer is probably precluded from unilaterally decreasing benefits ("partial lockouts"). In *Darling & Co.,* 171 NLRB 801, 68 LRRM 1133 (1968), *aff'd sub nom. Lane v. NLRB,* 418 F.2d 1208, 72 LRRM 2439 (D.C. Cir. 1969), the Board and court held that, at least in some circumstances, a lockout prior to impasse was lawful, although the employer admittedly acted to force the union to make concessions at the bargaining table.

Note the strange result of these developments. The parties are reduced to all-or-nothing weapons, which are most disruptive of "industrial peace" and of commerce and are most injurious to the parties. Are you satisfied with this consequence? If not, who is to blame? And what better solution is there?

The Sam Houston Gun Manufacturing Co. is in a difficult spot. If it resorts to institutional remedies, the time will pass when the company can meet its government contract deadline. If the company resorts to retaliation, it may be faced with a full strike which will cost it the loss of the contract. In other words, does the company have any realistic solution to its problem other than capitulating to the union's demands if the company is determined to keep the government contract? If so, is this a bad state of affairs?

C. THE DUTY TO BARGAIN IN GOOD FAITH*

White v. NLRB

United States Court of Appeals, Fifth Circuit, 1958
255 F.2d 564, 42 LRRM 2001

TUTTLE, Circuit Judge.

This is a petition by the individual petitioners, doing business as White's Uvalde Mines, to review and set aside an order of the National Labor Relations Board, and a cross-request by the Board that the order be enforced.

. . .

. . . [The issue is] whether, in an otherwise unassailable attitude of collective bargaining, the employer may nevertheless be found guilty of a failure to bargain in good faith solely upon a consideration of the content of the proposals and counter proposals of the parties. In other words may the charge of refusal to bargain in good faith be sustained solely by reference to the terms of the employment contract which management finally says it is willing to sign if such proposed contract could fairly be found to be one which would leave the employees in no better state than they were without it. For the purpose of considering this question we may

---

*Cox, *The Duty to Bargain in Good Faith,* 71 HARV. L. REV. 1401 (1958); Fleming, *The Obligation to Bargain in Good Faith,* 47 VA. L. REV. 988 (1961); Feinsinger, *The National Labor Relations Act and Collective Bargaining,* 57 MICH. L. REV. 807 (1959); Gross, Cullen, and Hanslowe, *Good Faith in Labor Negotiations: Tests and Remedies,* 53 CORNELL L. REV. 1009 (1968).

assume that the Board could find that the terms of the contract insisted on by the company requiring the surrender by the employees of their right to strike and their agreeing to leave to management the right to hire and fire and fix wages in return for agreements by the company respecting grievances and security that gave the union little, if any, real voice in these important aspects of employment relations would in fact have left the union in no better position than if it had no contract. It is perfectly apparent that the company representatives approached the bargaining table with a full understanding of their obligations to meet with, and discuss with, representatives of the employees any terms and conditions of employment that either party put forward; that they must at least expose themselves to such argument and persuasion as could be put forward, and that they must try to seek an area of agreement at least as to some of the terms of employment; that if they were able to arrive at such agreement they must be willing to reduce it to writing and sign it. It is of some significance that at the fourth of the six bargaining sessions, when challenged by the employees' bargaining agent the company's managing partner signed the company's proposed complete contract and tendered it to the union, which declined to accept it. The question is: Can the company's insistence on terms overall favorable to it in net result be taken as proof that it did not approach the bargaining table in good faith, but that it approached the bargaining table only to give the outward sign of compliance when it had already excluded the possibilty of agreement?
. . .

We start with the statute which states specifically that the "obligation [to bargain collectively] does not compel either party to agree to a proposal or require the making of a concession." . . .[3]

[3]It would extend this opinion too greatly to outline in detail the proposals and counter proposals and the responses of the parties to them at the seven different bargaining sessions. However, it would seem that the statement of the criticized actions of the company, as enumerated by counsel for the Board in its brief, is as strong a presentation of the Board's views as is available. With some comments added by the Court, the brief says:

"A fair summary of the Company's bargaining in this case reveals the following:

"1. The Company, while insisting on a 'no strike' clause with provisions for union liability in the case of breach, at first resisted a corresponding 'no lockout' clause, and after agreeing to such a clause refused at all times to agree to a provision calling for corresponding liability in the event of its breach.

"2. As the courts have recognized, a union's contractual waiver of its statutory right to strike is normally accompanied by a provision that disputes between the parties will be settled by grievance procedures and arbitration rather than by such 'self-help' measures as strikes. But the Company in this case coupled its insistence on a no-strike clause with an insistence that matters going to arbitration must be decided in the Company's favor if there was any evidence that the Company's position was not arbitrary or capricious. Such limited arbitration would leave the Union 'hamstrung' in a dispute with the Company, unable to strike or to secure a review on the merits by the arbitrators.

"3. The Company at no time acceded to any proposal for the selection of a neutral arbitrator, in the event the arbitrators chosen by the Union and the Company could not agree. [The company proposal was that the two arbitrators select the third.]

"4. In the absence of any contract, the Company could not lawfully change its wage rates or grant merit increases or alter shop rules relating to working conditions without first bargaining with the Union over those changes. But the Company insisted, as a condition of the contract, that the Union surrender its right to bargain about those matters, and leave the Company free to act in a manner which, but for the contract, would be violative of the law.

"5. Although the Company professed to find the matters of house rentals and physical examinations 'of no importance,' it insisted that the contract contain no provision as to the

Thus the Board is saying that although the statute says no concession need be made and no item need be agreed upon, if a company fails to concede *anything* substantial, then this is too much, and such failure amounts to bad faith.

The language of the Courts is not, as it cannot be, in construing this difficult statute, entirely clear, but we find no case which precisely supports the proposition here asserted by the Board. The principal basis of the Board's attack here is the broad management function clause and the failure to agree to a real arbitration clause in which the arbitrators have final powers. The remaining provisions criticized by the Board could not conceivably be considered as proof of bad faith by the petitioners. . . .

. . .

If [a broad management prerogatives] clause is not per se proof of failure to bargain in good faith then *a fortiori* insistence on physical examination by the company's own doctor, refusal to include terms of a Christmas bonus, a refusal to grant specified wage increases, refusal to "freeze" rent and utility charges on company-owned houses and like issues could not either separately or collectively constitute such proof.

. . .

We do not hold that under no possible circumstances can the mere content of the various proposals and counterproposals of management and union be sufficient evidence of a want of good faith to justify a holding to that effect. We can conceive of one party to such bargaining procedure suggesting proposals of such a nature or type or couched in such objectionable language that they would be calculated to disrupt any serious negotiations. . . .

Union's right to bargain over the rental rates of Company houses, and further insisted that the contract require the employees to submit to a physical examination by the Company doctor, whose word as to employment would be final. The Company's intransigent attitude over matters which it regarded as unimportant is itself suggestive of a want of good faith. [The company insisted that these matters were important to it, but not to the employees, because in neither respect had there been any complaint as to the company's attitude.]

"6. The Company rejected the Union's request that the contract provide for bargaining over the annual bonus, although in the absence of a contract such bonuses are matters over which bargaining is required. *NLRB* v. *Niles-Bement-Pond Co.*, 199 F.2d 713, 31 LRRM 2057 (C.A. 2).

"7. Admitting that its minimum wage rate was substantially lower than comparable rates in the area, the Company at first 'stood pat' on wages, and eventually offered an increase to less than that embodied in the amendment to the federal wage and hour law, then being debated in Congress. [The statement that the Company admitted its minimum rate was substantially lower than comparable rates is strongly contested by the Company. The proposed increase was a minimum of 90 cents per hour, which was the minimum actually enacted months later.]

"8. Notwithstanding substantial concessions by the Union in the course of the negotiations, the Company characterized the Union's second proposal as 'about the same' as its first one, and the Union's third proposal as 'not substantially different.' Such a denial of the realities of the Union's efforts to compromise differences hardly comports with a good faith desire to bargain.

"9. Granting little beyond such bare requirements as a provision against discrimination, the Company took the attitude, expressed by its chief negotiator, that 'we are giving the contract, and that is something.' This attitude, we submit falls far short of what this Court has described as 'a duty . . . to enter into discussion with an open and fair mind, and a sincere purpose to find a basis of agreement touching wages and hours and conditions of employment, and if found to embody it in a contract as specific as possible . . .' *Globe Cotton Mills* v. *NLRB*, 103 F.2d 91, 94, 4 LRRM 621."

Rives, Circuit Judge.
I respectfully dissent.

. . .

Collective bargaining is at the very heart and core of the Labor Management Relations Act. If, in any particular case, effective collective bargaining is not had and cannot be required, then in that case the Act is nothing. If follows that there must be some protection against "merely going through the motions of negotiating," "a predetermined resolve not to budge from an initial position," "surface bargaining" accompanied by "a purpose to defeat it and wilful obstruction of it," "shadow boxing to a draw," "giving the Union a runaround while purporting to be meeting with the Union for the purpose of collective bargaining."

Nowhere has the rule been better stated than by Judge Russell for this Circuit in *Majure* v. *National Labor Relations Board*, 5th Cir., 1952, 198 F.2d 735, 739, 30 LRRM 2441:

> " . . . It is true, of course, that the employer was not required to accept the union's proposal, nor to make any concession, or counter-proposal. However, the employer was required to bargain in good faith. This Court held in *American National Insurance Co.* v. *NLRB*, 187 F.2d 307, 27 LRRM 2405, affirmed by the Supreme Court in *NLRB* v. *American National Insurance Co.*, 343 U.S. 395, 30 LRRM 2147, that the obligation of the employer to bargain in good faith does not require the yielding of positions fairly maintained, nor permit the Board, under the guise of a finding of bad faith, to require the employer to contract in a way which the Board might deem proper. Nevertheless, the requirement of good faith in such bargaining is imposed by the statute. The dividing line between the right to the exercise of good faith and independent judgment and to maintain the resultant position with firmness, with no obligation of retreat, and nevertheless obey the statutory command to bargain in good faith must, in the nature of such right, and yet obligation, be frequently difficult of ascertainment and establishment. It has not been easy in the present case. In such cases there is danger that the negotiating parties may have their freedom of contract as to substance restricted or destroyed by a construction of their conduct as an evidence of bad faith. However, judicial ingenuity has devised but one standard, or test, which, recognizing the problem, yet seeks to insure reconciliation of privilege and obligation. This rule requires fair appraisal of the circumstances and the particular facts of the particular case. *NLRB* v. *American National Insurance Company*, *supra*.
>
> "Applying the rule here, we think the circumstances of this case support the Board's finding that the employer, while freely conferring, did not approach the bargaining table with an open mind and purpose to reach an agreement consistent with the respective rights of the parties."

Chief Judge Magruder, speaking for the First Circuit in *NLRB* v. *Reed & Prince Mfg. Co.*, 1953, 205 F.2d 131, 134, 135, 32 LRRM 2225, made an admirable expression of the same principle:

"It is true, as stated in *NLRB* v. *American National Ins. Co.*, 1952, 343 U.S. 395, 404, 30 LRRM 2147, that the Board may not 'sit in judgment upon the substantive terms of collective bargaining agreements.' But at the same time it seems clear that if the Board is not to be blinded by empty talk and by the mere surface motions of collective bargaining, it must take some cognizance of the reasonableness of the positions taken by an employer in the course of bargaining negotiations. Thus if an employer can find nothing whatever to agree to in an ordinary current-day contract submitted to him, or in some of the union's related minor requests, and if the employer makes not a single serious proposal meeting the union at least part way, then certainly the Board must be able to conclude that this is at least some evidence of bad faith, that is, of a desire not to reach an agreement with the union. In other words, while the Board cannot force an employer to make a 'concession' on any specific issue or to adopt any particular position, the employer is obliged to make *some* reasonable effort in *some* direction to compose his differences with the union, if § 8(a)(5) is to be read as imposing any substantial obligation at all."

Chief Judge Chase, speaking for the Second Circuit in *NLRB* v. *Century Mfg., Co.*, 1953, 208 F.2d 84, 88, 33 LRRM 2061, said:

" . . . The respondent made no proposals of its own as a basis for negotiation on such subjects. They were all, however, proper subjects for collective bargaining and while the respondent was, indeed, free to reject the union's demands in the exercise of its business judgment the failure to do little more than reject them was indicative of a failure to comply with its statutory requirement to bargain in good faith."

Under all of the authorities, in determining whether *either* an employer or a labor organization has failed to bargain in good faith, the Board must necessarily consider its conduct at the bargaining table, and whether it has acted reasonably or arbitrarily.

In the present case, the Company insisted on a no-strike clause with provisions for Union liability in the case of breach. It further insisted that matters going to arbitration must be decided in the Company's favor if there is any evidence that the Company's position was not arbitrary or capricious. It declined to accede to any proposal for the selection of a neutral arbitrator in the event the arbitrators chosen by the Union and the Company could not agree. While thus insisting that the Union waive its statutory right to strike, the Company declined to give any substitute, such as effective arbitration. In the recent case of *Textile Workers* v. *Lincoln Mills*, 1957, 353 U.S. 448, 455, 40 LRRM 2113, the Supreme Court said: "Plainly the agreement to arbitrate grievance disputes is the *quid pro quo* for an agreement not to strike."

Even without a contract, the Company could not lawfully change its wage rates, grant merit increases, or alter shop rules relating to working conditions without first bargaining with the Union. Nevertheless, the Company insisted that the Union surrender its right to bargain about those matters and leave the Company free to act as it saw fit. There are many other instances of arbitrary and unreasonable action set forth in the fair and careful intermediate report of the Trial Examiner and the decision of the Board, which leave me convinced that the Board had a rational basis for its conclusion that the Company failed to bargain in good faith. The other violations on the part of the Company make that conclusion all the more reasonable. In my opinion, that is a conclusion peculiarly within the province of the Board and which the Board is more competent to arrive at than is this Court. I therefore, respectfully dissent.

Questions

1. Assume an employer insists upon the following contract, already signed by the employer: "*Section 1.* The employer recognizes the union as the exclusive bargaining representative of the employer's employees for wages, hours, and other terms and conditions of employment. *Section 2.* The union delegates to the employer unilateral control of wages, hours, and other terms and conditions of employment."

Does *White* authorize such negotiations? If not, what standard distinguishes the hypothetical from *White*? If so, what does the statute require, other than each party being willing to sign an agreement?

2. Assume White's Uvalde Mines had met regularly with the union, been polite, agreed to nothing more than recognition of the union, and made no counterproposals. Is that more or less clearly a violation than the hypothetical posed in question "1"?

What if the employer made different proposals at successive meetings, so that the apparent agreements of earlier meetings were constantly set aside.

3. Do you see a difference between the *White* case and the hypotheticals in questions "1" and "2" on the one hand, and an employer who makes it "unjustifiably" difficult for the union and employer to meet regularly? Or, consider the employer who says to the union, "I'll listen to all you have to say, but I'll not explain anything. Maybe I'll agree, and maybe I won't." The employer agrees to some union demands but not to all. No agreement is reached.

4. In light of what you have read in Part B of this chapter, in what way do the answers to questions "1," "2," and "3" matter to the parties?

NLRB v. General Electric Co.

United States Court of Appeals, Second Circuit, 1969
418 F.2d 736, 72 LRRM 2530

IRVING R. KAUFMAN, Circuit Judge.

Almost ten years after the events that gave rise to this controversy, we are called upon to determine whether an employer may be guilty of bad faith bargaining, though he reaches an agreement with the union, albeit on the company's terms. We must also decide if the company committed three specific violations of the duty to bargain by failing to furnish information requested by the union, by attempting to deal separately with IUE locals, and by presenting a personal accident insurance program on a take-it-or-leave-it basis.

. . .

THE BARGAINING BACKGROUND

General Electric . . . employed about 250,000 men and women; of these only 120,000 were unionized. The IUE . . . represented some 70,000 of the 120,000 unionized GE employees, formally grouped in more than 105 bargaining units, and was far and away the largest single union with whom GE dealt. . . .

. . . In 1946, negotiations reached an impasse and resulted in a serious and crippling strike. GE eventually capitulated, and agreed to a settlement that it later characterized as a "debacle," and beyond the company's ability to meet.

. . .

[Thereafter, the company's bargaining] plan was threefold. GE began by soliciting comments from its local management personnel on the desires of the work force, and the type and level of benefits that they expected. These were then translated into specific proposals, and their cost and effectiveness researched, in order to formulate a "product" that would be attractive to the employees, and within the Company's means. The last step was the most important, most innovative, and most often criticized. GE took its "product"—now a series of fully-formed bargaining proposals—and "sold" it to its employees and the general public. Through a veritable avalanche of publicity, reaching awesome proportions prior to and during negotiations, GE sought to tell its side of the issues to its employees. It described its proposals as a "fair, firm offer," characteristic of its desire to "do right voluntarily," without the need for any union pressure or strike. In negotiations, GE announced that it would have nothing to do with the "blood-and-threat-and-thunder" approach, in which each side presented patently unreasonable demands, and finally chose a middle ground that both knew would be the probable outcome even before the beginning of the bargaining. . . .

Henceforth, GE would hold nothing back when it made its offer to the Union; it would take all the facts into consideration, and make that offer it thought right under all the circumstances. Though willing to accept Union suggestions based on facts the Company might have overlooked, once the basic outlines of the proposal had been set, the mere fact that the Union disagreed would be no ground for change. . . .

To bring its position home to its employees, GE utilized a vast network of plant newspapers, bulletins, letters, television and radio announcements, and personal contacts through management personnel.

Side by side with its policies of "doing right voluntarily" through a "firm, fair offer," GE also pursued a policy of guaranteeing uniformity among unions, and between union and non-union employees. Thus all unions received substantially the same offer, and unrepresented employees were assured that they would gain nothing through representation that they would not have had in any case. Prior to 1960, GE held up its proposed benefits for unrepresented employees until the unions agreed, or until the old contract with the Union expired.

. . . In practice, the IUE has dealt with the company through its General Electric Conference Board, composed of delegates from IUE locals. Under the Union constitution, the Conference Board may call strikes, make contract proposals, and conclude agreements, regardless of an individual local's consent. GE has dealt with, and recognized the status of, the Conference Board since 1950, although the national agreements frequently provided that some matters, usually minor, would be left to local agreement. . . .

III

THE 1960 NEGOTIATIONS

Since the linchpin of the "Boulware approach" was to bring GE's side of the story home to its employees and to the general public, it began in the latter part of 1959 to advise its Employment Relations Managers of the subjects that they should be prepared to discuss with employees. This was effected through various media, including plant publications and personal contact. General arguments in favor of keeping GE competitive through low costs, and the advantage of receiving GE benefits without having to wait for Union officials to approve them, were among the suggestions presented.

Informal meetings were first held in January, 1960, and Union and Company subsequently joined in preparing a body of information. Neither side felt any inclination to complain of want of cooperation at this stage. GE, in fact, took pains to suggest alternate information when the precise form the Union desired was unavailable.

Before another planned informal meeting in June, 1960, GE notified the IUE by letter that as of July it would institute a contributory group accident and life insurance plan for all employees, but if the Union objected, only unrepresented employees would receive the benefits. The Union protested that the Company had to bargain before making such a unilateral change, but GE insisted that the 1955 IUE-GE Pension and Insurance agreement waived all such requirements. The Union still objected, and the program was put into effect only for unrepresented employees.

At the June meeting, the Union stated its proposals, as they then stood. Without much discussion, other than some minor clarifications, Philip D. Moore, GE's Union Relations Service Manager and chief negotiator, called the proposals "astronomical" in cost, "ridiculous," and not designed for early settlement.

Following the presentation of these proposals, the early publicity phase of the Boulware approach swung into high gear. Employing virtually all media, from television and radio, to newspaper, plant publications and personal contact, the Company urged employees and the public to regard the Union demands as "astronomical" (then and later a favored Company term), and likely to cost many GE employees their jobs through increased foreign competition. GE, on the other hand, announced it would in time make a fair and "firm" offer that would give employees no reason to allow union leadership to impose a strike. The basic theme was that the Company, and not the Union, was the best guardian and protector of the employees' interests.

The IUE also tried its hand at publicity, including an "IUE Caravan" that travelled from city to city, and occasional articles in the International Union's newspaper. In scope and effectiveness, however, they were far outshadowed by the Company's massive campaign.

From July 19 to August 11, the Union presented its specific proposals on employment security, to which the Company replied with general expressions of disapproval, or simply rejected. GE spent the next five meetings delivering prepared presentations on the general causes of economic instability, which the Union branded as a waste of time.

In subsequent meetings, the Company's posture remained unchanged. It would comment generally on some Union demands, and consider them in formulating its offer, but would not commit itself in any way. While it complained that the IUE proposals were excessive, it replied to Union requests for cost estimates with "we talk about the level of benefits," or that the proposals cost "a lot." GE would not indicate the total cost of a settlement it considered reasonable ("we talk level of benefits"); the Union in turn refused to rank its demands by priority, describing them all as "musts." Indeed the entire early period—and the later negotiations as well—were characterized by an air of rancor on both sides, which provided each with welcome opportunities to downgrade the other in communications to Union members.

GE finally revealed its own proposal informally on August 29. While expressing distress at some features of the offer, Union negotiators urged the Company to delay publicizing its "firm, fair" offer, so that its position would not be frozen before the IUE had an opportunity to examine it and offer changes. GE refused, agreeing only to hold up most of the prepared and packaged publicity until after formal presentation of the offer on the next day.

Union officials frequently renewed their requests for cost information during the ensuing month of negotiations. GE consistently refused to estimate the cost of its proposal or of any of its elements, so that the Union might reallocate its demands. When pressed for some of the highly-touted GE cost studies, Moore frequently slipped into the "level of benefits" format, and generally showed no interest in presenting alternate information that was available and would have served the Union's needs.

There are few modifications made in the original GE offer. The Company did propose an extra week's vacation after 25 years in exchange for a smaller wage increase; but Union officials had indicated at the outset that they were uninterested in paring down what they considered an already inadequate wage offer. Despite this, and in the face of the departure by

Union officials for their national conference, GE publicized the "new" offer heavily in employee communications.

After declaring late in September that the "whole offer" was "on the table," GE contrary to prior practice, brought its position home by making its three per cent wage increase offer effective for unrepresented employees before the end of the contract or IUE acceptance. Two days later GE also put its pension and insurance proposals into effect, despite IUE President James Carey's complaint that this would "inhibit" any subsequent modifications.

On September 21, Federal Mediation Service officials began to sit in on the negotiations at the request of the Union. Their presence does not appear to have measurably aided the negotiations. The Union, in response to Company complaints that the IUE proposals were too costly, submitted a written request for information on the cost per employee of the GE pension and insurance plans, as well as the number of employees who could be expected to benefit from GE's vacation and income extension proposals. The request was refused in part, and the remainder was not complied with until after the strike, when the information would be of no substantial value to the Union.

Similar difficulties confronted the Union in its efforts to change the effective date of the pension and insurance plans. The Company proposed a January 1 date for the first increase in pension and insurance benefits; the Union in turn suggested that the increase in benefits should coincide with the beginning of the contract. GE shifted its ground back and forth: first it claimed that the earlier date would be too costly; then it said that it was talking "level of benefits" and not cost; then it argued that prior contracts had always provided for pension increases on the first of the year. When this last ground proved to be incorrect, one GE negotiator promised to "consider" the October date, although he insisted the January date was "appropriate." During that afternoon, however, even this concession was withdrawn, and later explanations included describing January again as "appropriate," and "the time that you make all the resolutions for the New Year."

Union officials complained that "it is just because we request something that you would refuse to give it," and subsequent Company explanations served to support, rather than to undercut, this feeling. On September 28, with three scheduled meetings left before the end of the contract, a Union negotiator, seeking to salvage something of the earlier IUE Supplemental Unemployment Benefits proposal, suggested a local option plan under which some of the funds the Company had allocated to wage increases and its income extension offer could be diverted to supplement unemployment compensation. He was clear that nothing was to be added to the Company's costs. Moore responded, "After all our month of bargaining and after telling the employees before they went to vote that this is it, we would look ridiculous to change it at this late date; and secondly the answer is no." A few moments later Moore reiterated his belief that "we would look ridiculous if we changed it." Hilbert, for GE, later gave three reasons why the Company would not consider the proposal—and two of them were that it would make GE "look foolish in the eyes of employees and others. . . ."

GE on September 29 rejected a Union offer to maintain the status quo under the old contract until a new one was signed, specifically refusing the cost-of-living escalator clause, and stating that it would "consider" later Union-related terms such as dues checkoff. A strike (which took place on October 2, except for the Schenectady Local, which joined October 6) was clearly imminent. Although claiming to be uncertain about truce terms with national IUE negotiators, GE headquarters on September 29 authorized its Schenectady Employee Relations Manager, Stevens, to offer all the pre-existing terms of the contract (except for the cost-of-living term) to the local. Stevens did so in statements to Union members and to the local Business Agent, Jandreau. A similar offer was made to the Pittsfield local, and broadly publicized there.

By October 10, the Company (after the Union had filed an unfair labor practice charge) made the same offer to the Union's national negotiators, for any locals that returned to work. Despite rejection by the Union at the national level, the Company proceeded to deal directly with local officials, and to urge acceptance of the offer. When local officials demurred, as, for example, at Lynn, Massachusetts, publicity was aimed at the employees themselves, criticizing the local officials' stand on the "truce." Similar events occurred at Waterford, Louisville, Bridgeville, and Syracuse.

Throughout the course of the strike, GE communications to the employees emphasized the personal character of the Union leaders' conduct, and threatened loss of jobs to plants that returned to work late. Negotiations were held during the strike until October 19, when the Company declared that an impasse had been reached. During that period, GE refused to give the IUE definitive contract language until the Union had chosen which of the options it preferred, and until it gave its unqualified approval of the Company proposal.

On October 21, it became clear that Union capitulation was near. The Company, which had previously refused to delete the retraining provision from its offer, felt free to relax its position, and granted the Union's request to permit a local option on retraining. While refusing a joint strike settlement agreement, which both parties would sign, GE did propose a unilateral "letter of intent," indicating that it was in agreement with most of the Union settlement proposals. On October 22, the Union capitulated completely, signing a short form memorandum agreement (they had not yet seen the complete contract language to which they were agreeing), and the Company alone issued its letter of intent. The strike ended on October 24.

Two matters were left open for settlement: seniority for transferred employees, and dues checkoffs. Neither, when finally settled, represented more than an adjustment to take account of NLRB decisions that rendered the original form of the agreement of dubious legality. Some minor changes also followed, none of any considerable significance.

The only other events of importance occurred at the Augusta, Georgia plant. On October 5, the plant manager sent a letter to the four employees on strike (at that time the only ones), warning them that their employment would be terminated and replacements hired if they did not return to work. On October 13, however, he sent them telegrams, retracting the earlier letter as to job termination, but indicating the replacements would be hired. More employees (twenty in all) joined the strike after October 5, and on October 24 the Company refused their unconditional offer to return to work. It did, however, give physical examinations to three of the employees, and rehired the two who passed.

IV.

THE SPECIFIC UNFAIR LABOR PRACTICES

A. UNILATERAL INSURANCE PROPOSAL

On June 1, 1960, before the reopening of negotiations, but after GE had agreed to meet with the Union on June 13 to hear its proposals, the Company notified the Union by letter that it would unilaterally institute a personal accident insurance proposal. Under the Company plan, the insurance would go into effect on July 1, would be paid wholly by the employees, and would be in addition to existing insurance coverage provided by GE. If the IUE objected, GE would not offer the insurance to its members; it would, however, make it available to other employees regardless of the stand taken by the IUE.

Prior to the June 13 meeting, GE publicized the new insurance proposal, along with the information that enrollment would take place later in the month. At the meeting, the Union objected strenuously to GE's failure to bargain over the insurance, claiming that it was clearly a bargainable issue, which GE had a duty to discuss with Union representatives.

Under the 1955–1960 Pension and Insurance Agreement, each party waived the right to require the other to bargain as to pensions or insurance matters except during the stated renegotiation period—which, barring waiver, was months off.

Read expansively, and without any attention to the purpose of the section, the combination of 8(d) and the Pension Agreement might appear to protect any action that GE might take with respect to insurance during the term of the agreement. In *Equitable Life Insurance Co.*, 133 NLRB 1675 (1961), however, the Board took the view that 8(d) was designed to protect the status quo; it was to be used as a shield, not as a sword.

. . . [T]here are serious objections to permitting one party to an agreement unilaterally to hold out this type of inducement to the other. It creates divisive tensions within the Union; employees with hazardous occupations will favor the proposal, while those with routine tasks will object. Whichever way the Union moves, it loses ground with some part of its constituency. Union democracy is not furthered by permitting the Company to pick the Union apart piece by piece. The same point may be made where there are both union and non-union employees. If the Union refuses the benefit, then it may appear, at least in the short run, to have disadvantaged its members vis-à-vis non-members. Thus it may be forced to sacrifice long-term goals to avoid short-term dissatisfaction.

In the context of this case, where the Company's tactics seemed so clearly designed to show the employees that the Union could win them nothing more than the Company was prepared to offer, it is even more apparent that a unilateral offer—over which the Union may not bargain—diminishes the rewards and the importance of the bargaining at the end of the contract period. Thus the Union's ability to function as a bargaining representative is seriously impaired. Indeed, such conduct amounts to a declaration on the part of the Company that not only the Union, but the process of collective bargaining itself may be dispensed with. Cf. *Equitable Life Ins. Co.*, 133 NLRB 1675, 1693 (1961).

. . . The dilemma created by an employer exists whether he uses it crudely or subtly; it is inherent in a take-it-or-leave-it bargaining approach. True, GE did not capitalize on the Union's refusal; but through its enrollment program late in June, and by the unavoidable controversy that the issue itself raised in Union ranks, the Company was able to profit from the situation without exploiting it outright. The rationale of the Board's *Equitable* rule reaches at least that far. Once it is clear that the party who disrupts the status quo cannot rely on section 8(d) to protect his conduct, then unilateral action over a mandatory matter, joined to a refusal to bargain, represents a straightforward rejection of the collective bargaining principle in fact. See *NLRB* v. *Katz*, 369 U.S. 736 (1962).

B. REFUSAL TO FURNISH INFORMATION

. . . [During negotiations, there was a pattern] in which the Union would propose a particular benefit, Company negotiators would label it as "astronomical," or "costly," and when pressed by the Union for figures to back up their cost criticisms, would respond with "we talk level of benefits, not costs."

. . .

The cases that have dealt with the difficult problem of giving meaning to "bargaining in good faith" are instructive. In *NLRB* v. *Truitt Manufacturing Co.*, 351 U.S. 149, 38 LRRM 2042 (1956), the company claimed that a wage increase of over 2½ cents per hour would put it out of business, but refused to furnish the Union with any indication of its financial status. The Supreme Court, in finding that the Company had committed an unfair labor practice, commented.

> "Good-faith bargaining necessarily requires that claims made by either bargainer should be honest claims. This is true about an asserted inability to pay an increase in wages. If such an argument is important enough to present in the give and take of bargaining, it is important enough to require some sort of proof of its accuracy."

Moreover, it is not always necessary that the Company put the cost of its proposals in issue, or even refuse Union demands on the ground that they are too costly. In *Sylvania Electric Products, Inc.* v. *NLRB*, 358 F.2d 591 (1st Cir.), *cert. denied*, 385 U.S. 852, 63 LRRM 2236 (1966), the court decided (without raising the issue of cost justifications by the company) that pension and insurance costs (which it labeled "collateral" issues) should be made available to the Union where it wished to weigh the value of such plans against an increase in take-home pay. This is particularly true, of course, where the Company contributes to the plan, thus in effect substituting it for wages. . . .

. . . There can be no question that the information available would have assisted the Union here; GE committed an unfair labor practice in withholding it.

C. BARGAINING DIRECTLY WITH LOCALS

As we have pointed out above, GE and the IUE had a consistent pattern of national negotiations for over ten years before the 1960 strike. There can be little doubt that the Board's finding that GE recognized and dealt with the IUE–GE Conference Board as representative of all IUE locals was both supported by substantial evidence and correct.

Once the strike was imminent, however, GE abandoned this pattern, and dealt separately with several of the IUE locals.

. . .

The Trial Examiner and the Board agreed that in each instance GE committed an unfair labor practice when it went behind the backs of the national negotiators and offered separate peace settlements to locals. *Medo Photo Supply Corp.* v. *NLRB*, 321 U.S. 678, 14 LRRM 581 (1944) sustains this conclusion. In *Medo*, several employees who appeared to represent a majority met with their employer to express their dissatisfaction with the union representing them. They offered to abandon it if their wages were increased. When the Employer treated with the dissenting employees, the Court held, he violated section 9(a) of the Act (bargaining representatives of the union are "exclusive"). Therefore, he committed unfair labor practices under sections 8(a)(1) and 8(a)(5). *Medo* instructs that it does not matter who initiates the bypassing of the bargaining representatives. Subsequent cases appear to have applied the doctrine even where the offer to the local or to the employees was no better than that made to the bargaining representative. We have, under similar circumstances, condemned efforts by an employer to take a matter up with his employees, where their bargaining representative had already taken a stand on the matter.

[The court concluded that in all but one of the incidents involving GE communications to locals, the Board correctly found the conduct to violate the Act. In one instance, the court found the letter sent to the local to be wholly informational and not an attempt to reach a separate agreement with the local. Therefore, in the interest of free speech, that single communication was not violative of the Act.]

V.

OVERALL FAILURE TO BARGAIN IN GOOD FAITH

We now approach the most troublesome and most vigorously contested of the charges. In addition to the three specific unfair labor practices, GE is also charged with an overall failure to bargain in good faith, compounded like a mosaic of many pieces, but depending not on any one alone. They are together to be understood to comprise the "totality of the circumstances." . . .

The Board . . . [found] an overall failure of good faith bargaining in GE's conduct. Specifically, the Board found that GE's bargaining stance and conduct, considered as a whole, were designed to derogate the Union in the eyes of its members and the public at large. This plan had two major facets: first, a take-it-or-leave-it approach ("firm, fair offer") to negotiations in general which emphasized both the powerlessness and uselessness of the Union to its members, and second, a communications program that pictured the Company as the true defender of the employees' interests, further denigrating the Union, and sharply curbing the Company's ability to change its own position.

The Board relies both on the unfair labor practices already discussed and on several other specific instances to show that GE had developed a pattern of conduct inconsistent with good faith bargaining. . . .

GE argues forcefully that it made so many concessions in the course of negotiations—concessions which, under section 8(d), it was not obliged to make—that its good faith and the absence of a take-it-or-leave-it attitude were conclusively proven, despite any contrary indicia on which the Trial Examiner and the Board rely. The dissent proceeds under the misapprehension that we consider lack of major concessions as evidence of bad faith. Rather, we discuss them only because while the absence of concessions would not prove bad faith, their presence would, as GE claims, raise a strong inference of good faith. On close examination, however, few of the alleged concessions turn out to have a great deal of substance.

The Company's stand, however, would be utterly inexplicable without the background of its publicity program. Only when viewed in that context does it become meaningful. . . . GE, the Trial Examiner found, chose to rely "entirely" on its communications program to the virtual exclusion of genuine negotiations, which it sought to evade by any means possible. Bypassing the national negotiators in favor of direct settlement dealings with employees and local officials forms another consistent thread in this pattern. The aim, in a word, was to deal with the Union through the employees, rather than with the employees through the Union.

. . .

The most telling effect of GE's marketing campaign was not on the Union, but on GE itself. Having told its employees that it had made a "firm, fair offer," that there was "nothing more to come," and that it would not change its position in the face of "threats" or a strike, GE had in effect rested all on the expectation that it could institute its offer without significant modification. Properly viewed, then, its communications approach determined its take-it-or-leave-it bargaining strategy. Each was the natural complement of the other; if either were substantially changed, the other would in all probability have to be modified as well.

. . .

The petition for review is denied, and the petition for enforcement of the Board's order is granted.

WATERMAN, Circuit Judge, concurred.

FRIENDLY, Circuit Judge (concurring and dissenting).

I agree with my brothers that by refusing to furnish cost information and by bargaining with locals during the strike, GE violated § 8(a)(5) of the National Labor Relations Act. I do not believe it also violated the Act by submitting a contributory personal accident insurance plan to the Union and declining to bargain about it until the time for reopening of negotiations. . . .

. . . [As to the overall bad faith issue] the majority of the Board was at pains to emphasize that its finding . . . was not based upon identifiable acts or failures to act that GE could avoid in the future but rather upon our review of (1) the Respondent's entire course of conduct, (2) its failure to furnish relevant information, (3) its attempts to deal separately with locals and to bypass the national bargaining representative, (4) the manner of its presentation of the accident insurance proposal, (5) the disparagement of the Union as bargaining representative by the communication program, (6) its conduct of the negotiations themselves, and (7) its attitude or approach as revealed by all these factors.

Such attempts to restrict communications (item 5) and lay down standards with respect to bargaining techniques, attitudes and approaches (items (6) and (7)), bring the Board into collision with § 8(c) and (d) and the important policies they embody. It is easy to understand that anyone reviewing this enormous record would emerge with a good deal of sympathy for the situation of the Union and distaste for the tactics of the employer; no one likes to see a person who regards himself as in a strong position pushing it unduly, even though the fairness of GE's offer is not challenged. But the Act does not empower the Board to translate such feelings into a finding of an unfair labor practice, and judicial sanction of such efforts to intrude into areas which Congress left to the parties may in the long run be quite as detrimental to unions as to employers. See *NLRB* v. *Insurance Agents' Int'l Union*, 361 U.S. 477, 45 LRRM 2705 (1960).

. . .

I would grant enforcement with respect to the failure to furnish information and the bargaining with locals, and would otherwise deny.

Notes

1. Was the company's communications and publicity campaign with its employees an unlawful circumvention of the company's duty to bargain with the union?

Reread *J.I. Case Co. v. NLRB,* page 105, *supra.*

a. Does the *Case* decision give any lessons about the freedom of the employer to negotiate with the employee rather than with the union? If it does, do you read the opinion to preclude the employer from talking to its employees about their desires and needs?

b. In the *Medo* decision cited by the court, page 412, *supra,* the Supreme Court affirmed the Board's finding of an unlawful refusal to bargain in a situation where an employer refused to bargain with a certified union at all after the following occurrences: An apparent majority of the employees solicited a wage increase, which was granted, and the employees then told the employer they no longer wanted the union.

Does the *Medo* case make it clear that General Electric violated the statute by its publicity campaign? Was it unlawful, at least, for the company supervisors to obtain information from employees as to their needs and desires? Or is it significant that General Electric, unlike the employer in *Medo,* was not attempting to destroy the union's majority status, and it was willing to negotiate with the union after it had discussed matters first with the employees? Put differently, do you think *Medo*'s bottom is to be found in the destruction of the union's majority status, the dealings with the individual employees, or both? If the violation in *Medo* is based on the employer's dealing with the individual employees, how is it distinguishable from the General Electric practice?

c. Review the materials in Chapter 3 dealing with Section 8(c) of the Act. What relevance do they have to this problem? Are you persuaded that the employer has the same freedom to communicate with its employees after a union is recognized and during negotiations with the employees' representative as it has in a campaign to persuade its employees to vote against union representation? Should it have the same freedom?

2. Why were the company's dealings with the local unions an unlawful attempt to circumvent the company's duty to negotiate with the international?

Is there any difference between the employer's circumvention of the recognized union by negotiating with subparts of the union and its dealing with the individual employees? In the *General Electric* situation, some (although not all) of the locals with which the company dealt were certified by the Board to represent the employees of the particular local plants. If all the locals involved in the direct dealing with General Electric had been so certified, would that make any difference? Should one consider the collective bargaining history of General Electric, the international union, and the locals? Is it controlling that the parties accepted the international as the bargaining representative of the local employees?

3. Why was the company's refusal to produce cost information about the pension and insurance proposals a violation of Section 8(a)(5)?

a. In the *Truitt* case, page 411, *supra,* cited by the *General Electric* court, the Supreme Court affirmed the Board's decision that an employer who claimed it could not afford a request made by a union during collective bargaining was required to provide information to support that claim of inability to pay, at least when the union requested that information. While the Court stated that it was not creating a *per se* rule, the only evidence of "bad faith" on the part of the *Truitt* employer, in fact, was the refusal to produce the relevant records. In the process of reaching this result, the Court said that claims in collective bargaining must be "honest claims." Do you agree? Does your answer turn on your understanding of "honest claims"?

Shortly after *Truitt*, the Supreme Court, in reversing a lower court decision, held in a *per curiam* opinion that an employer had an obligation to supply a recognized union with wage information in order that the union could play an informed role in the administration of an already existing collective agreement. *NLRB* v. *F.W. Woolworth*, 352 U.S. 938, 39 LRRM 2151 (1956). After the *General Electric* facts were developed and heard, the Supreme Court reaffirmed the *Woolworth* holding and stated than an employer violates the Act when it refuses to furnish relevant information to a union which is processing a grievance under an existing collective agreement, even if it is possible for the union to get the same information through the arbitration process. *NLRB* v. *Acme Industrial Co.*, 385 U.S. 432, 64 LRRM 2069 (1967).

Nevertheless, the Court held that the employer in *Detroit Edison Co.* v. *NLRB*, 440 U.S. 301, 100 LRRM 2728 (1979), lawfully refused to disclose to a union an aptitude test and aptitude test scores of individual employees, even though such information arguably was relevant to the union's processing of promotion grievances. Although the employer offered to furnish the test and the answer sheets to an industrial psychologist, selected by the union to evaluate them independently, and offered to turn over to the union the test scores of individual employees for any employees who would sign waivers releasing the company psychologist from his pledge to keep such information confidential, the union refused to accept these offers. Noting that the company had a reasonable concern for the secrecy of the aptitude test, the Court held that the Board abused its discretion when it ordered the company to turn over the test and the answer sheets directly to the union. The Court further agreed with the company that its willingness to disclose individual test scores to the union, only if the examinees consented, satisfied the company's obligation under Section 8(a)(5). Relevant to this ruling is the observation of the Court that "[t]he sensitivity of any human being to disclosure of information that may be taken to bear on his or her basic competence is sufficiently well known to be an appropriate subject of judicial notice."

b. If one defines *per se* violative conduct in the duty-to-bargain context as conduct which constitutes a violation, regardless of the accused's state of mind, is General Electric's refusal to produce records such a violation? When an employer unilaterally changes working conditions, does that constitute a *per se* violation in the same sense? See *NLRB* v. *Katz*, page 395, *supra*. What about the "take-it-or-leave-it" bargaining?

It is clear, is it not, that certain conduct is *per se* unlawful? *E.g.*, the employer who refuses to meet the union, or the employer who refuses to sign a contract once it is agreed upon, or the employer who negotiates with its employees rather than with the union. See Section 8(d); *H. J. Heinz* v. *NLRB*, 311 U.S. 514, 7 LRRM 291 (1941); *Medo*, page 412, *supra*.

c. Is the *Truitt* rule conducive to sound collective bargaining? Or does it encourage the parties to attempt to "trap" each other into a technical mistake of some sort which will serve the "trapper" in some future proceeding? If the latter is likely, is that a happy impact on collective bargaining?

d. You have no doubt, have you, that—given *Truitt*—General Electric's refusal to produce the requested information was violative of the Act?

4. Did the overall conduct of the company justify the court's finding that the company had failed to bargain in "good faith"?

a. What standard do you understand the *General Electric* court is applying to find a violation of the duty to bargain in "good faith"? Does the Supreme Court use the same standard in cases like *Insurance Agents*, page 379, *supra*, or *Katz*, page 395, *supra*? What standard ought to be used? Consider the following standards and whether any make sense: (i) The party must enter negotiations with a desire to reach an agreement; (ii) the party must enter negotiations with no desire not to reach an agreement; (iii) the party must enter negotiations with an open mind, that is, with a willingness to listen to and consider what the other party has to say; (iv) the party must not enter negotiations in a self-created position which precludes it from making concessions to the other party.

b. What factors are relevant in assessing whether a party has met the standard? The Board and the courts have, from time to time, looked to the following to get some insight into the party's subjective state of mind. Which of them do you think is relevant? Useful? Authorized by the statute as an area of inquiry?

   (i) Independent violations of the Act;
  (ii) *Per se* violations of Section 8(a)(5) or 8(b)(3);
 (iii) Evidence of stalling on the part of one party to the negotiations;
 (iv) Refusal to make any concessions on any matter whatsoever;
  (v) The reasonableness of the party's proposals;
 (vi) The reasonableness of the party's bargaining "manners" (*e.g.*, did the party explain its position, did it listen to the other's position).

c. Was General Electric's conduct violative of the "good faith" requirements of the Act? If so, on what basis?

(i) If the basis for a "bad faith" finding is that the employer was unwilling to make concessions, what meaning do you give Section 8(d), which states that the duty to bargain ". . . does not compel either party to agree to a proposal or require the making of a concession"? If the failure to make any significant concession is the basis for your conclusion, does this place the government in the role of arbitrator? Is this desirable? What standards would be applicable? In light of the Act as it is presently written, should the Board, or the courts, assume the role of arbitrator?

Finally, if the basis of your conclusion that the company violated the Act is the failure to make concessions, does this mean a party must be dishonest at the bargaining table in order to comply with the statute? Is that desirable? What about *Truitt*'s mandate that "[g]ood-faith bargaining necessarily requires that claims made by either bargainer should be honest claims?"

(ii) In light of the company's public posture, can it be said that the company had placed itself in the position of not being able to make any significant concession? Or that this position was the equivalent of bargaining with a closed mind? If so, can this properly be the basis for the finding of a violation?

(iii) Is the court holding that an employer must make concessions? Is the court holding that an employer cannot communicate its views of ongoing negotiations to its employees? Is the court holding that a combination of these two elements is not lawful?

(iv) Whatever is the meaning of *General Electric* and of "good faith," could the company have accomplished its objectives as well without running afoul of the law? If so, was General Electric guilty of more than what one might call a breach of etiquette? Should that be deemed a violation of law?

5. Although we shall postpone full discussion of the duty to bargain during the term of a collective agreement, we should consider briefly that issue as it was raised in the *GE* case. Once the employer proposed the pension change, what options were open to the union? The dissent reasons that the union could accept or reject, but not insist on discussions about the proposal. Could the union have insisted the matter go to arbitration? Assuming (as did all members of the court) that GE could not put the new pension plan into effect without notifying the union, what is the purpose of notification? Even if the dissent reads Section 8(d) and the collective agreement correctly insofar as it does not require the employer to negotiate about pensions, may the situation be different if the *employer* raises the new issue?

D. SUBJECT MATTER OF COLLECTIVE BARGAINING*

Problem: About What Do We Have to Bargain?

Emily Ployer is the owner and president of the Ployer Plow Company. Her employees are represented by the International Association of Plow Makers. Ployer is of the view that during the past three years the union has greatly abused the grievance and arbitration procedures existing under the soon-to-expire contract. As a result, Ployer believes that she has been forced to spend a lot of unnecessary time and money in defending company decisions in arbitration; and, in the apparent belief that the union will always intervene, the employees have become almost arrogant in their behavior. Moreover, Ployer feels she has compromised on some unjustifiable grievances solely to avoid any further expense.

Ployer has told you, her attorney, that she will not agree to sign a new contract unless something is done about this grievance-arbitration "mess." It was suggested to her by a friend at the Chamber of Commerce that she insist on a contract clause which would stipulate that no grievance

*See Cox and Dunlop, *Regulation of Collective Bargaining by the National Labor Relations Board*, 63 HARV. L. REV. 389 (1950).

could be processed under the contractual procedures until the individual involved in the grievance has signed a grievance form. Ployer believes that a large number of the employees have always hidden behind the union's presence, and, therefore, such a proposal would significantly reduce the number of grievances filed.

Although you were not sure about the proposal, you advised Ployer to go ahead and suggest it to the union.

At the first meeting with the union, Ployer was given a copy of the union's demands. Most of the union's requests were wholly predictable, but, much to Ployer's surprise, the union included a demand to create a joint company-union panel which would deal with broad decisions for the company regarding its policies and practices in marketing and advertising. At that meeting, Ployer had time to glance at the demands, and upon seeing this one, she demanded to know what it was all about and where did the union "get off sticking its nose into my business" in such a fashion. Ployer now tells you that the union responded that the major reason, in its judgment, for a declining trend in Ployer's gross income is selling in the wrong markets. Apparently she was so enraged by the proposal that she did not listen too carefully, but she says she believes the union argued that the place to make much more money was through direct sales to the large farms and construction firms (which use Ployer's bulldozers), rather than through sales to wholesalers and retailers. The meeting ended with an understanding to meet again in three days. Ployer sought you out immediately.

Ployer tells you that under no circumstances will she agree even to talk about the subject matter the union is attempting to bring into the negotiations. Moreover, she is incredulous that the federal law would force her to talk about it.

What advice can you give Ployer regarding the following questions: (1) Does she have to respond at all to the merits of the union's unique proposal? (2) Can she insist that the union stop talking about it? (3) Can she charge the union with violating the law for bringing the matter up? (4) If no agreement on these matters is reached and an impasse occurs, what follows a strike? Can Ployer fire or permanently replace the strikers if she refuses to discuss the matter despite several union requests to do so?

In light of these questions, do you have any second thoughts about the advice you gave Ployer regarding the proposal to require employees' signatures on grievance forms? Why? Or is the situation different?*

Are you satisfied that the legal issue raised by the union's (International Association of Plow Makers) demands in the problem is the same as the one raised by the employer's (Emily Ployer)? First, you do not doubt, do you, that both proposals, if agreed upon, are lawful? But does Ployer's proposal, at least if insisted upon over the union's objection, run counter to the policy, if not the letter, of Section 9 of the Act? The union's proposal does not raise the same considerations. On the other hand, although the union's proposal does have some relationship to the employ-

*Some of the facts of the problem are suggested by *Bethlehem Steel Co.* v. *NLRB*, 320 F.2d 615, 53 LRRM 2878 (3d Cir. 1963).

ees' interest, it is further removed than the employer's proposal, is it not, from the matters traditionally considered in collective bargaining—that is, more removed from the employer-employee (or union) relationship? If the force of law can compel the employer to bargain about marketing and advertising policy, is there anything about which the union cannot insist on bargaining? Is that desirable?

NLRB v. Wooster Division of Borg-Warner Corp.

Supreme Court of the United States, 1958
356 U.S. 342, 42 LRRM 2034

Mr. Justice Burton delivered the opinion of the Court.

. . . [Following a Board election and during negotiations for a first contract, the] employer insisted that its collective-bargaining contract with certain of its employees include: (1) a "ballot" clause calling for a pre-strike secret vote of those employees (union and nonunion) as to the employer's last offer, and (2) a "recognition" clause which excluded, as a party to the contract, the International Union which had been certified by the National Labor Relations Board as the employees' exclusive bargaining agent, and substituted for it the agent's uncertified local affiliate. The Board held that the employer's insistence upon either of such clauses amounted to a refusal to bargain, in violation of § 8(a)(5) of the National Labor Relations Act, as amended. The issue turns on whether either of these clauses comes within the scope of mandatory collective bargaining as defined in § 8(d) of the Act. For the reasons hereafter stated, we agree with the Board that neither clause comes within that definition. Therefore, we sustain the Board's order directing the employer to cease insisting upon either clause as a condition precedent to accepting any collective-bargaining contract.

. . .

From the time that the company first proposed these clauses, the employees' representatives . . . made it clear that each was wholly unacceptable. The company's representatives made it equally clear that no agreement would be entered into by it unless the agreement contained both clauses. In view of this impasse, there was little further discussion of the clauses, although the parties continued to bargain as to other matters. . . . Finally, on May 5, the Local, upon the recommendation of International, gave in and entered into an agreement containing both controversial clauses.

. . .

Read together, [Sections 8(a)(5) and 8(d)] establish the obligation of the employer and the representative of its employees to bargain with each other in good faith with respect to "wages, hours, and other terms and conditions of employment. . . ." The duty is limited to those subjects, and within that area neither party is legally obligated to yield. *Labor Board* v. *American Insurance Co.*, 343 U.S. 395. As to other matters, however, each party is free to bargain or not to bargain, and to agree or not to agree.

The company's good faith has met the requirements of the statute as to the subjects of mandatory bargaining. But that good faith does not license the employer to refuse to enter into agreements on the ground that they do not include some proposal which is not a mandatory subject of bargaining. We agree with the Board that such conduct is, in substance, a refusal to bargain about the subjects that are within the scope of mandatory bargaining. This does not mean that bargaining is to be confined to the statutory subjects. Each of the two controversial clauses is lawful in itself. Each would be enforceable if agreed to by the unions. But it does not follow that, because the company may propose these clauses, it can lawfully insist upon them as a condition of any agreement.

Since it is lawful to insist upon matters within the scope of mandatory bargaining and unlawful to insist upon matters without, the issue here is whether either the "ballot" or the "recognition" clause is a subject within the phrase "wages, hours, and other terms and conditions of employment" which defines mandatory bargaining. The "ballot" clause is not within that definition. It relates only to the procedure to be followed by the employees among themselves before their representative may call a strike or refuse a final offer. It settles no term or condition of employment—it merely calls for an advisory vote of the employees. It is not a partial "no-strike" clause. A "no-strike" clause prohibits the employees from striking during the life of the contract. It regulates the relations between the employer and the employees. See *Labor Board* v. *American Insurance Co.* The "ballot" clause, on the other hand, deals only with relations between the employees and their unions. It substantially modifies the collective-bargaining system provided for in the statute by weakening their independence of the "representative" chosen by the employees. It enables the employer, in effect, to deal with its employees rather than with their statutory representative. Cf. *Medo Photo Corp.* v. *Labor Board*, 321 U.S. 678.

The "recognition" clause likewise does not come within the definition of mandatory bargaining. The statute requires the company to bargain with the certified representative of its employees. It is an evasion of that duty to insist that the certified agent not be a party to the collective-bargaining contract. The Act does not prohibit the voluntary addition of a party, but that does not authorize the employer to exclude the certified representative from the contract.

. . .

MR. JUSTICE FRANKFURTER joins this opinion insofar as it holds that insistence by the company on the "recognition" clause, in conflict with the provisions of the Act requiring an employer to bargain with the representative of his employees, constituted an unfair labor practice. He agrees with the views of MR. JUSTICE HARLAN regarding the "ballot" clause. The subject matter of that clause is not so clearly outside the reasonable range of industrial bargaining as to establish a refusal to bargain in good faith, and is not prohibited simply because not deemed to be within the rather vague scope of the obligatory provisions of § 8(d).

MR. JUSTICE HARLAN, whom MR. JUSTICE CLARK and MR. JUSTICE WHITTAKER join, concurring in part and dissenting in part.

I agree that the company's insistence on the "recognition" clause constituted an unfair labor practice, but reach that conclusion by a different route from that taken by the Court. However, in light of the finding below that the company bargained in "good faith," I dissent from the view that its insistence on the "ballot" clause can support the charge of an unfair labor practice.

. . .

Preliminarily, I must state that I am unable to grasp a concept of "bargaining" which enables one to "propose" a particular point, but not to "insist" on it as a condition to agreement. The right to bargain becomes illusory if one is not free to press a proposal in good faith to the point of insistence. Surely adoption of so inherently vague and fluid a standard is apt to inhibit the entire bargaining process because of a party's fear that strenuous argument might shade into forbidden insistence and thereby produce a charge of an unfair labor practice. This watered-down notion of "bargaining" which the Court imports into the Act with references to matters not within the scope of § 8(d) appears as foreign to the labor field as it would to the commercial world. To me all of this adds up to saying that the Act limits *effective* "bargaining" to subjects within the three fields referred to in § 8(d), that is "wages, hours, and other terms and conditions of employment," even though the Court expressly disclaims so holding.

I shall discuss my difficulties with the Court's opinion in terms of the "ballot" clause. The "recognition" clause is subject in my view to different considerations.

I.

At the start, I question the Court's conclusion that the "ballot" clause does not come within the "other terms and conditions of employment" provision of § 8(d). The phrase is inherently vague and prior to this decision has been accorded by the Board and courts an expansive rather than a grudging interpretation. Many matters which might have been thought to be the sole concern of management are now dealt with as compulsory bargaining topics. And since a "no-strike" clause is something about which an employer can concededly bargain to the point of insistence, I find it difficult to understand even under the Court's analysis of this problem why the "ballot" clause should not be considered within the area of bargaining described in § 8(d). . . .

. . .

Of course, an employer or union cannot insist upon a clause which would be illegal under the Act's provisions, *Labor Board* v. *National Maritime Union*, 175 F.2d 686, or conduct itself so as to contravene specific requirements of the Act. *Medo Photo Supply Corp.* v. *Labor Board*, 321 U.S. 678. But here the Court recognizes, as it must, that the clause is lawful under the Act, and I think it clear that the company's insistence upon it violated no statutory duty to which it was subject. The fact that the employer here *did* bargain with the union over the inclusion of the "ballot" clause in the proposed agreement distinguishes this case from the situation involved in the *Medo Photo Supply Corp.* case, where an employer, without the sanction of a labor agreement contemplating such action, negotiated *directly* with its employees in reference to wages.

Fibreboard Paper Products Corp. v. NLRB*

Supreme Court of the United States, 1964
379 U.S. 203, 57 LRRM 2609

MR. CHIEF JUSTICE WARREN delivered the opinion of the Court.

This case involves . . . whether the "contracting out" of work being performed by employees in the bargaining unit is a statutory subject of collective bargaining. . . .

. . . [T]he Union gave timely notice of its desire to modify . . . [an existing] contract and sought to arrange a bargaining session with Company representatives. . . . Efforts by the Union to schedule a bargaining session met with no success until . . . four days before the expiration of the contract, when the Company notified the Union of its desire to meet.

The Company, concerned with the high cost of its maintenance operation, had undertaken a study of the possibility of effecting cost savings by engaging an independent contractor to do the maintenance work. At the . . . meeting, the Company informed the Union that it had determined that substantial savings could be effected by contracting out the work upon expiration of its collective bargaining agreements with the various labor organizations representing its maintenance employees. The Company delivered to the Union representatives a letter which stated in pertinent part:

> "For some time we have been seriously considering the question of letting out our Emeryville maintenance work to an independent contractor, and have now reached a definite decision to do so effective August 1, 1959.
>
> "In these circumstances, we are sure you will realize that negotiation of a new contract would be pointless. However, if you have any questions, we will be glad to discuss them with you."

. . .

By July 30, the Company had selected Fluor Maintenance, Inc., to do the maintenance work. . . .

The Company . . . distributed a letter stating that "since we will have no employees in the bargaining unit covered by our present Agreement, negotiation of a new or renewed Agreement would appear to us to be pointless." On July 31, the employment of the maintenance employees

---

*See Rabin, *Fibreboard and the Termination of Bargaining Unit Work: The Search for Standards in Defining the Scope of the Duty to Bargain*, 71 COLUM. L. REV. 803 (1971); Rabin, *The Decline and Fall of Fibreboard*, 24 N.Y.U. CONF. ON LABOR 237 (1972).

represented by the Union was terminated and Fluor employees took over. That evening the Union established a picket line at the Company's plant.
. . .

[The NLRB held that the company had violated Section 8(a)(5) by its unilaterial act of subcontracting.]

The inclusion of "contracting out" within the statutory scope of collective bargaining also seems well designed to effectuate the purposes of the National Labor Relations Act. One of the primary purposes of the Act is to promote the peaceful settlement of industrial disputes by subjecting labor-management controversies to the mediatory influence of negotiation. The Act was framed with an awareness that refusals to confer and negotiate had been one of the most prolific causes of industrial strife. To hold, as the Board has done, that contracting out is a mandatory subject of collective bargaining would promote the fundamental purpose of the Act by bringing a problem of vital concern to labor and management within the framework established by Congress as most conducive to industrial peace.

The conclusion that "contracting out" is a statutory subject of collective bargaining is further reinforced by industrial practices in this country. While not determinative, it is appropriate to look to industrial bargaining practices in appraising the propriety of including a particular subject within the scope of mandatory bargaining. Industrial experience is not only reflective of the interests of labor and management in the subject matter but is also indicative of the amenability of such subjects to the collective bargaining process. Experience illustrates that contracting out in one form or another has been brought, widely and successfully, within the collective bargaining framework. Provisions relating to contracting out exist in numerous collective bargaining agreements, and "[c]ontracting out work is the basis of many grievances; and that type of claim is grist in the mills of the arbitrators." *United Steelworkers* v. *Warrior & Gulf Nav. Co.*, 363 U.S. 574, 584.
. . .

The facts of the present case illustrate the propriety of submitting the dispute to collective negotiation. The Company's decision to contract out the maintenance work did not alter the Company's basic operation. The maintenance work still had to be performed in the plant. No capital investment was contemplated; the Company merely replaced existing employees with those of an independent contractor to do the same work under similar conditions of employment. Therefore, to require the employer to bargain about the matter would not significantly abridge his freedom to manage the business. . . .

We are thus not expanding the scope of mandatory bargaining to hold, as we do now, that the type of "contracting out" involved in this case—the replacement of employees in the existing bargaining unit with those of an independent contractor to do the same work under similar conditions of employment—is a statutory subject of collective bargaining under § 8(d). Our decision need not and does not encompass other forms of "contracting out" or "subcontracting" which arise daily in our complex economy.

II.

The only question remaining is whether, upon a finding that the Company had refused to bargain about a matter which is a statutory subject of collective bargaining, the Board was empowered to order the resumption of maintenance operations and reinstatement with back pay. We believe that it was so empowered.

. . .

There has been no showing that the Board's order restoring the *status quo ante* to insure meaningful bargaining is not well designed to promote the policies of the Act. Nor is there evidence which would justify disturbing the Board's conclusion that the order would not impose an undue or unfair burden on the Company.

. . .

The judgment of the Court of Appeals is

Affirmed.

MR. JUSTICE STEWART, with whom MR. JUSTICE DOUGLAS and MR. JUSTICE HARLAN join, concurring.

. . . An enterprise may decide to invest in labor-saving machinery. Another may resolve to liquidate its assets and go out of business. Nothing the Court holds today should be understood as imposing a duty to bargain collectively regarding such managerial decisions, which lie at the core of entrepreneurial control. Decisions concerning the commitment of investment capital and the basic scope of the enterprise are not in themselves primarily about conditions of employment, though the effect of the decision may be necessarily to terminate employment. If, as I think clear, the purpose of § 8(d) is to describe a limited area subject to the duty of collective bargaining, those management decisions which are fundamental to the basic direction of a corporate enterprise or which impinge only indirectly upon employment security should be excluded from that area.

Applying these concepts to the case at hand, I do not believe that an employer's subcontracting practices are, as a general matter, in themselves conditions of employment. Upon any definition of the statutory terms short of the most expansive, such practices are not conditions—tangible or intangible—of any person's employment. The question remains whether this particular kind of subcontracting decision comes within the employer's duty to bargain. On the facts of this case, I join the Court's judgment, because all that is involved is the substitution of one group of workers for another to perform the same task in the same plant under the ultimate control of the same employer. . . .

. . .

. . . It is possible that in meeting these problems [caused by automation] Congress may eventually decide to give organized labor or government a far heavier hand in controlling what until now have been considered the prerogatives of private business management. That path would mark a sharp departure from the traditional principles of a free enterprise economy. Whether we should follow it is, within constitutional limitations, for Congress to choose. But it is a path which Congress certainly did not choose when it enacted the Taft-Hartley Act.

Questions

1. Surely there is a difference between the *Borg-Warner* situation, where the employer did bargain with the union about all subjects, and the *Fibreboard* situation, where the employer evaded bargaining altogether. Insofar as the doctrine of *Borg-Warner* applies to employers who do engage in bargaining on all issues, is the doctrine enforceable?

a. To respond to that question, one must first understand the doctrine. Does the statute compel bargaining about "wages, hours, and other terms and conditions of employment" *only,* or is the scope of Section 8(d) "wages, hours, and other terms and conditions of employment" *among other things*?

b. What are "wages, hours, and other terms and conditions of employment"? Are you satisfied with the standards set out in either *Borg-Warner* or *Fibreboard*? Not only are the standards very vague, but the factors which will be relevant in order to apply the standards may be very difficult, if not impossible, to assess. How is one to know when the employer's refusal to negotiate about a particular subject will be a "prolific cause of industrial strife," or when its bargaining will be "most conducive to industrial peace"? While one can make some assessment about how frequently certain kinds of clauses appear in collective agreements, are we to read this factor as an alternative ground, or a required concurrent ground, under the *Fibreboard* formula? How frequently must the relevant clause appear in contracts throughout the nation? Or throughout the relevant industry?

c. Given the vagueness of the *Fibreboard* gloss on *Borg-Warner,* there are very real dangers to the parties. If Ployer (in the problem on page 418), decides to fight for her proposal to an impasse, or refuses entirely to discuss the union's proposal, and a strike ensues, she may want to know whether she can permanently replace the strikers. Can she? As you know, that turns on whether she has committed an unfair labor practice which caused the strike. Has she? Is there any sure way she can know in advance? Yet the cost to her may be astronomical if she guesses incorrectly. Conversely, what assurances can the union give the striking employees that Ployer cannot permanently replace them?

d. What does the doctrine of *Borg-Warner* mean with respect to what actually transpires at the collective bargaining table? If a matter is not "mandatory," may the proposing party raise the issue more than once? If so, how often? So long as the issue is abandoned before impasse? So long as other matters also have not been resolved? Can the party hint at its proposal but never suggest with clear language that it is the *sine qua non* to agreement? For example, what is the difference between the following four postures? (i) "This permissive proposal is the *sine qua non* to agreement"; (ii) "This permissive proposal is the most important issue in these negotiations"; (iii) "This permissive proposal is very important, but we will not insist"; and (iv) "All proposals are part of a total package—everything affects everything else." Are all four outlawed? If only some, but not all, are prohibited, then negotiations become a game. And, if all four are outlawed, how can a party lawfully raise a permissive subject of bargaining in an effective fashion?

e. In representing Ployer, do you think you could devise a method which would allow Ployer to raise her proposal, never mention it again until the union itself might raise the issue, and yet never reach agreement without the union's agreeing to the proposal? If you can, what do you think of the lines being drawn? Think of the care with which one must speak during negotiations to avoid pitfalls. And think of the care with which the other party will attempt to "trap" the first. Is this conducive to sound collective bargaining? To development of trust between the parties? What do you think Ployer and the union must think of such lawmaking? Do you find yourself in an uncomfortable ethical situation? What advice can you give Ployer in light of such administrative and judicial reasoning?

f. Why are these issues not left to the bargaining power of the parties? If the proposing party is economically strong enough and urgently desires its proposals, it will succeed in getting its proposals into the contract, will it not? Short of a proposal that transcends the limits of legality or contravenes clear policies of the Act (might not *Borg-Warner* have been analyzed by the Court on that basis?), would it not be simpler to leave these matters to the parties and keep the government out of negotiations where the parties are ready to discuss all issues?

2. What are mandatory subjects of bargaining? Certainly, the Board and the courts are agreed that anything which can be characterized as "wages" clearly falls within the mandate of Section 8(d), *e.g.*, pay scales, incentive pay, prices (when they reflect virtually only the employees' pay), severance pay, holidays and vacations, insurance, and pension plans. More debate centers upon whether bonuses, meals, and housing fall within the rubric of "mandatory subjects" of bargaining. In those situations, the surrounding circumstances may determine whether the particular subject is mandatory. Other terms and conditions of employment which are deemed mandatory are the following: grounds for discharge or discipline, seniority, layoffs and recall, hiring halls, plant rules, work loads, no-strike clauses, arbitration and grievance procedures, in-plant cafeteria and machine vending food prices and services, and management prerogative clauses (but, if such a clause is "too" broad, the clause may become "permissive"; does this make any sense?), subcontracting (depending on the circumstances), relocations and "partial closings" (perhaps), and the effects of closings, of sales of businesses, of subcontracting and the like, on employees.

"Permissive subjects for bargaining" include the following: whether to terminate or sell a business (how is that consistent with the idea that subcontracting and plant relocations may be mandatory?), performance bonds, bargaining units broader than the one for which the union has been authorized to bargain in those particular negotiations, interests of retired employees, employer contributions to an industry promotion fund, internal union affairs, and a proposal to arbitrate a new contract if the parties are unable to negotiate one ("interest arbitration"). Of course it is also improper for a party to insist on negotiating about illegal proposals.

Can anyone make rational sense of the distinctions apparently being made?

What of Ployer's proposal that all employees sign the grievances—is that an internal union matter or is it part of the grievance procedure? What of the union's proposal regarding advertising and marketing: Is it analogous to contributions to industry promotion funds? However one characterizes the proposals in the Ployer case, is it not clear that the employer has a real interest in the way the grievances are handled? Is it not also distinctly possible that the union and employees may have an equally real interest in the marketing and advertising practices of the company? If that is true, does it make sense to give either party lawful standing to refuse to bargain about such matters?

3. For how long must an employer negotiate about a mandatory matter before it can act? Does the concept of impasse adapt to the immediate needs of the employer?

First National Maintenance Corp. v. NLRB

Supreme Court of the United States, 1981
452 U.S. 666, 107 LRRM 2705

JUSTICE BLACKMUN delivered the opinion of the Court.

Must an employer, under its duty to bargain in good faith "with respect to wages, hours, and other terms and conditions of employment," §§ 8(d) and 8(a)(5) of the National Labor Relations Act, negotiate with the certified representative of its employees over its decision to close a part of its business? In this case, the National Labor Relations Board (the Board) imposed such a duty on petitioner with respect to its decision to terminate a contract with a customer, and the United States Court of Appeals, although differing over the appropriate rationale, enforced its order.

I

Petitioner, First National Maintenance Corporation (FNM), is a New York corporation engaged in the business of providing housekeeping, cleaning, maintenance, and related services for commercial customers in the New York City area. It supplies each of its customers, at the customer's premises, contracted-for labor force and supervision in return for reimbursement of its labor costs (gross salaries, FICA and FUTA taxes, and insurance) and payment of a set fee. It contracts for and hires personnel separately for each customer, and it does not transfer employees between locations.

During the Spring of 1977, petitioner was performing maintenance work for the Greenpark Care Center, a nursing home in Brooklyn. Its written agreement dated April 28, 1976, with Greenpark specified that Greenpark "shall furnish all tools, equipment [*sic*], materials, and supplies," and would pay petitioner weekly "the sum of five hundred dollars plus the gross weekly payroll and fringe benefits." Its weekly fee, however, had been reduced to $250 effective November 1, 1976. The contract prohibited Greenpark from hiring any of petitioner's employees during the term of the contract and for 90 days thereafter. Petitioner employed approximately 35 workers in its Greenpark operation.

Petitioner's business relationship with Greenpark, seemingly, was not very remunerative or smooth. In March 1977, Greenpark gave petitioner the 30 days' written notice of cancellation specified by the contract, because of "lack of efficiency." This cancellation did not become effective, for FNM's work continued after the expiration of that 30-day period. Petitioner, however, became aware that it was losing money at Greenpark. On June 30, by telephone, it asked that its weekly fee be restored at the $500 figure and, on July 6, it informed Greenpark in writing that it would discontinue its operations there on August 1 unless the increase were granted. By telegram on July 25, petitioner gave final notice of termination.

While FNM was experiencing these difficulties, District 1199, National Union of Hospital and Health Care Employees, Retail, Wholesale and Department Store Union, AFL-CIO (the union), was conducting an organization campaign among petitioner's Greenpark employees. On March 31, 1977, at a Board-conducted election, a majority of the employees selected the union as their bargaining agent. On July 12, the union's vice president, Edward Wecker, wrote petitioner, notifying it of the certification and of the union's right to bargain, and stating: "We look forward to meeting with you or your representative for that purpose. Please advise when it will be convenient." Petitioner neither responded nor sought to consult with the union.

On July 28, petitioner notified its Greenpark employees that they would be discharged 3 days later. Wecker immediately telephoned petitioner's secretary-treasurer, Leonard Marsh, to request a delay for the purpose of bargaining. Marsh refused the offer to bargain and told Wecker that the termination of the Greenpark operation was purely a matter of money, and final, and that the 30-days' notice provision of the Greenpark contract made staying on beyond August 1 prohibitively expensive. Wecker discussed the matter with Greenpark's management that same day, but was unable to obtain a waiver of the notice provision. Greenpark also was unwilling itself to hire the FNM employees because of the contract's 90-day limitation on hiring. With nothing but perfunctory further discussion, petitioner on July 31 discontinued its Greenpark operation and discharged the employees.

The union filed an unfair labor practice charge against petitioner, alleging violations of the Act's §§ 8(a)(1) and (5). After a hearing held upon the Regional Director's complaint, the administrative law judge made findings in the union's favor. . . .

. . .

The National Labor Relations Board adopted the administrative law judge's findings. . . .

The United States Court of Appeals for the Second Circuit, with one judge dissenting in part, enforced the Board's order. . . .

Some management decisions, such as choice of advertising and promotion, product type and design, and financing arrangements, have only an indirect and attenuated impact on the employment relationship. See *Fibreboard*, 379 U.S., at 223 (STEWART, J., concurring). Other management decisions, such as the order of succession of layoffs and recalls, production quotas, and work rules, are almost exclusively "an aspect of the relationship" between employer and employee. *Chemical Workers*, 404 U.S., at 178. The present case concerns a third type of management decision, one that had a direct impact on employment, since jobs were inexorably eliminated by the termination, but had as its focus only the economic profitability of the contract with Greenpark, a concern under these facts wholly apart from the employment relationship. This decision, involving a change in the scope and direction of the enterprise, is akin to the decision whether to be in business at all, "not in [itself] primarily about conditions of employment, though the effect of the decision may be necessarily to terminate employment." *Fibreboard*, 379 U.S., at 223 (STEWART, J., concurring). Cf. *Textile Workers* v. *Darlington Co.*, 380 U.S. 263, 268 (1965) ("an employer has the absolute right to terminate his entire business for any reason he pleases"). At the same time, this decision touches on a matter of central and pressing concern to the union and its member employees: the possibility of continued employment and the retention of the employees' very jobs.

Petitioner contends it had no duty to bargain about its decision to terminate its operations at Greenpark. This contention requires that we determine whether the decision itself should be considered part of petitioner's retained freedom to manage its affairs unrelated to employment. The aim of labeling a matter a mandatory subject of bargaining, rather than simply permitting, but not requiring, bargaining, is to "promote the fundamental purpose of the Act by bringing a problem of vital concern to labor and management within the framework established by Congress as most conducive to industrial peace," *Fibreboard*, 379 U.S., at 211. The concept of mandatory bargaining is premised on the belief that collective discussions backed by the parties' economic weapons will result in decisions that are better for both management and labor and for society as a whole. This will be true, however, only if the subject proposed for discussion is amenable to resolution through the bargaining process. Management must be free from the constraints of the bargaining process to the extent essential for the running of a profitable business. It also must have some degree of certainty beforehand as to when it may proceed to reach decisions without fear of later evaluations labeling its conduct an unfair labor practice. Congress did not explicitly state what issues of mutual concern to union and management it intended to exclude from mandatory bargaining. Nonetheless, in view of an employer's need for unencumbered decisionmaking, bargaining over management decisions that have a substantial impact on the continued availability of employment should be required only if the benefit, for labor-management relations and the collective bargaining process, outweighs the burden placed on the conduct of the business. . . .

III

A

Both union and management regard control of the decision to shut down an operation with the utmost seriousness. As has been noted, however, the Act is not intended to serve either party's individual interest, but to foster in a neutral manner a system in which the conflict between these interests may be resolved. It seems particularly important, therefore, to consider whether requiring bargaining over this sort of decision will advance the neutral purposes of the Act.

A union's interest in participating in the decision to close a particular facility or part of an employer's operations springs from its legitimate concern over job security. The Court has observed: "The words of [§ 8(d)] . . . plainly cover termination of employment which . . . necessarily results" from closing an operation. *Fibreboard*, 379 U.S., at 210. The union's practical purpose in participating, however, will be largely uniform: it will seek to delay or halt the closing. No doubt it will be impelled, in seeking these ends, to offer concessions, information, and alternatives that might be helpful to management or forestall or prevent the termination of jobs. It is unlikely, however, that requiring bargaining over the decision itself, as well as its effects, will augment this flow of information and suggestions. There is no dispute that the union must be given a significant opportunity to bargain about these matters of job security as part of the "effects" bargaining mandated by § 8(a)(5). And, under § 8(a)(5), bargaining over the effects of a decision must be conducted in a meaningful manner and at a meaningful time, and the Board may impose sanctions to insure its adequacy. A union, by pursuing such bargaining rights, may achieve valuable concessions from an employer engaged in partial closing. It also may secure in contract negotiations provisions implementing rights to notice, information, and fair bargaining.

Moreover, the union's legitimate interest in fair dealing is protected by § 8(a)(3), which prohibits partial closings motivated by anti-union animus, when done to gain an unfair advantage. *Textile Workers* v. *Darlington Co.*, 380 U.S. 263 (1965). Under § 8(a)(3) the Board may inquire into the motivations behind a partial closing. An employer may not simply shut down part of its business and mask its desire to weaken and circumvent the union by labeling its decision "purely economic."

Thus, although the union has a natural concern that a partial closing decision not be hastily or unnecessarily entered into, it has some control over the effects of the decision and indirectly may ensure that the decision itself is deliberately considered. It also has direct protection against a partial closing decision that is motivated by an intent to harm a union.

Management's interest in whether it should discuss a decision of this kind is much more complex and varies with the particular circumstances.

If labor costs are an important factor in a failing operation and the decision to close, management will have an incentive to confer voluntarily with the union to seek concessions that may make continuing the business profitable. At other times, management may have great need for speed, flexibility, and secrecy in meeting business opportunities and exigencies. It may face significant tax or securities consequences that hinge on confidentiality, the timing of a plant closing, or a reorganization of the corporate structure. The publicity incident to the normal process of bargaining may injure the possibility of a successful transition or increase the economic damage to the business. The employer also may have no feasible alternative to the closing, and even good-faith bargaining over it may be both futile and cause the employer additional loss.

There is an important difference, also, between permitted bargaining and mandated bargaining. Labeling this type of decision mandatory could afford a union a powerful tool for achieving delay, a power that might be used to thwart management's intentions in a manner unrelated to any feasible solution the union might propose. . . .

While evidence of current labor practice is only an indication of what is feasible through collective bargaining, and not a binding guide, that evidence supports the apparent imbalance weighing against mandatory bargaining. We note that provisions giving unions a right to participate in the decisionmaking process concerning alteration of the scope of an enterprise appear to be relatively rare. Provisions concerning notice and "effects" bargaining are more prevalent. . . .

Further, the presumption analysis adopted by the Court of Appeals seems ill suited to advance harmonious relations between employer and employee. An employer would have difficulty determining beforehand whether it was faced with a situation requiring bargaining or one that involved economic necessity sufficiently compelling to obviate the duty to bargain. If it should decide to risk not bargaining, it might be faced ultimately with harsh remedies forcing it to pay large amounts of backpay to employees who likely would have been discharged regardless of bargaining, or even to consider reopening a failing operation. Also, labor costs may not be a crucial circumstance in a particular economically-based partial termination. And, in those cases, the Board's traditional remedies may well be futile. If the employer intended to try to fulfill a court's direction to bargain, it would have difficulty determining exactly at what stage of its deliberations the duty to bargain would arise and what amount of bargaining would suffice before it could implement its decision. If an employer engaged in some discussion, but did not yield to the union's demands, the Board might conclude that the employer had engaged in "surface bargaining," a violation of its good faith. A union, too, would have difficulty determining the limits of its prerogatives, whether and when it could use its economic powers to try to alter an employer's decision, or whether, in doing so, it would trigger sanctions from the Board. . . .

We conclude that the harm likely to be done to an employer's need to operate freely in deciding whether to shut down part of its business purely for economic reasons outweighs the incremental benefit that might be gained through the union's participation in making the decision,[22] and we hold that the decision itself is *not* part of § 8(d)'s "terms and conditions" over which Congress has mandated bargaining.[23]

B

In order to illustrate the limits of our holding, we turn again to the specific facts of this case. First, we note that when petitioner decided to terminate its Greenpark contract, it had no intention to replace the discharged employees or to move that operation elsewhere. Petitioner's sole purpose was to reduce its economic loss, and the union made no claim of anti-union animus. In addition, petitioner's dispute with Greenpark was solely over the size of the management fee Greenpark was willing to pay. The union had no control or authority over that fee. The most that the union could have offered would have been advice and concessions that Greenpark, the third party upon whom rested the success or failure of the contract, had no duty even to consider. These facts in particular distinguish this case from the subcontracting issue presented in *Fibreboard*. Further, the union was not selected as the bargaining representative or certified until well after petitioner's economic difficulties at Greenpark had begun. We thus are not faced with an employer's abrogation of ongoing negotiations or an existing bargaining agreement. Finally, while petitioner's business enterprise did not involve the investment of large amounts of capital in single locations, we do not believe that the absence of "significant investment or withdrawal of capital," *General Motors Corp., GMC Truck & Coach Div.*, 191 NLRB, at 952, is crucial. The decision to halt work at this specific location represented a significant change in petitioner's operations, a change not unlike opening a new line of business or going out of business entirely.

The judgment of the Court of Appeals, accordingly, is reversed and the case is remanded to that court for further proceedings consistent with this opinion.

It is so ordered.

JUSTICE BRENNAN, with whom JUSTICE MARSHALL joins, dissenting:
. . .

As this Court has noted, the words "terms and conditions of employment" plainly cover termination of employment resulting from a management decision to close an operation. *Fibreboard Paper Products Corp.* v. *NLRB*, 379 U.S. 203, 210 (1964). As the Court today admits, the decision to close an operation "touches on a matter of central and pressing concern to the union and its member employees." Moreover, as the Court today

---

[22]In this opinion we of course intimate no views as to other types of management decisions, such as plant relocations, sales, other kinds of subcontracting, automation, etc., which are to be considered on their particular facts. . . .

[23]Despite the contentions of *amicus* AFL-CIO our decision in *Order of Railroad Telegraphers* v. *Chicago & N.W.R. Co.*, 362 U.S. 330 (1960), does not require that we find bargaining over this partial closing decision mandatory. . . . The mandatory scope of bargaining under the Railway Labor Act and the extent of the prohibition against injunctive relief contained in Norris-La Guardia are not coextensive with the National Labor Relations Act and the Board's jurisdiction over unfair labor practices. . . .

further concedes, Congress deliberately left the words "terms and conditions of employment" indefinite, so that the NLRB would be able to give content to those terms in light of changing industrial conditions. In the exercise of its congressionally delegated authority and accumulated expertise, the Board has determined that an employer's decision to close part of its operations affects the "terms and conditions of employment" within the meaning of the Act, and is thus a mandatory subject for collective bargaining. Nonetheless, the Court today declines to defer to the Board's decision on this sensitive question of industrial relations, and on the basis of pure speculation reverses the judgment of the Board and of the Court of Appeals. I respectfully dissent.

The Court bases its decision on a balancing test. It states that "bargaining over management decisions that have a substantial impact on the continued availability of employment should be required only if the benefit, for labor-management relations and the collective-bargaining process, outweighs the burden placed on the conduct of the business." I cannot agree with this test, because it takes into account only the interests of *management*; it fails to consider the legitimate employment interests of the workers and their union. This one-sided approach hardly serves "to foster in a neutral manner" a system for resolution of these serious, two-sided controversies.

Even if the Court's statement of the test were accurate, I could not join in its application, which is based solely on speculation. Apparently, the Court concludes that the benefit to labor-management relations and the collective-bargaining process from negotiation over partial closings is minimal, but it provides no evidence to that effect. The Court acknowledges that the union might be able to offer concessions, information, and alternatives that might obviate or forestall the closing, but it then asserts that "[i]t is unlikely, however, that requiring bargaining over the decision . . . will augment this flow of information and suggestions." Recent experience, however, suggests the contrary. Most conspicuous, perhaps, were the negotiations between Chrysler Corporation and the United Auto Workers, which led to significant adjustments in compensation and benefits, contributing to Chrysler's ability to remain afloat. Even where labor costs are not the direct cause of a company's financial difficulties, employee concessions can often enable the company to continue in operation—if the employees have the opportunity to offer such concessions.*

The Court further presumes that management's need for "speed, flexibility, and secrecy" in making partial closing decisions would be frustrated by a requirement to bargain. In some cases the Court might be correct. In others, however, the decision will be made openly and deliberately, and considerations of "speed, flexibility, and secrecy" will be inapposite. Indeed, in view of management's admitted duty to bargain over

---

*Indeed, in this case, the Court of Appeals found: "On the record, . . . there is sufficient reason to believe that, given the opportunity, the union might have made concessions, by accepting reduction in wages or benefits (take-backs) or a reduction in the work force, which would in part or in whole have enabled Greenpark to give FNM an increased management fee. At least, if FNM had bargained over its decision to close, that possibility would have been tested, and management would still have been free to close the Greenpark operation if bargaining did not produce a solution."

the effects of a closing, it is difficult to understand why additional bargaining over the closing itself would necessarily unduly delay or publicize the decision.

I am not in a position to judge whether mandatory bargaining over partial closings *in all cases* is consistent with our national labor policy, and neither is the Court. The primary responsibility to determine the scope of the statutory duty to bargain has been entrusted to the NLRB, which should not be reversed by the courts merely because they might prefer another view of the statute. I therefore agree with the Court of Appeals that employers presumptively have a duty to bargain over a decision to close an operation, and that this presumption can be rebutted by a showing that bargaining would be futile, that the closing was due to emergency financial circumstances, or that, for some other reason, bargaining would not further the purposes of the National Labor Relations Act. I believe that this approach is amply supported by recent decisions of the Board. . . .

Questions

1. In advising employers or unions, what advice would you give about the requirement, if any, to bargain regarding an employer's desire to subcontract some of its business? Is there a possible reconciliation between *Fibreboard*'s facts (which were tantamount to an employer's undermining the union employees) and *First National Maintenance*'s (which removed the employer—and any possibility of profit—from the business which created the work formerly done by the discharged employees)? Or, has *Fibreboard* been, for all practical purposes, overruled?

2. Was not *First National Maintenance*'s dissent correct in its observation that the majority's balancing of interests was one-sided? Notice the majority balanced the "benefit, for labor-management relations and collective-bargaining process" against "the burden placed on the conduct of business." Why do the interests of the employees, who are losing their jobs, not get on the scales of law and justice? Compare the tone of the majority with the majority opinion in *Bell Aerospace*, page 88, *supra*. Can it be that, despite Congressional enactments, a majority of the Court cannot conceive of unions being good and useful institutions? Does this remind you of the old common law cases? Why don't judges like unions?

3. Was not the dissent also correct in suggesting that the majority's litany of all the terrible consequences (for the employer) that will follow collective bargaining just "ain't necessarily so"?

4. In a more detailed and articulate way, the majority adopted the standard previously used by several Courts of Appeals, to wit, the issue proposed for negotiations was "at the heart of entrepreneurial decision-making." Isn't the following the real issue: Is this a matter of direct, immediate, substantial concern to the employees? If so, why shouldn't the courts agree with the Board's approach? Is there a real danger to the freedom of employers to run their own businesses? That has been the employers' complaint since the inception of the Act about every provision

that limited employer freedom. How much interference is there when the Act is interpreted not to require agreement, but only negotiations? To put the matter differently, and in a manner almost entirely opposite to what the Court did, should not the standard for these cases be the following: The more important the issue to the employees (and, often, the bigger the decision of the employer), the more clearly the employer is obligated to give notice and the opportunity to negotiate? Other considerations, such as the nature of the impact of the required bargaining on the employer, are relevant to the quality and quantity of negotiations expected of the employer, but ought not to be relevant to the initial question whether the employer should offer at all to bargain.

5. Are there positive values to the "mandatory-permissive" dichotomy?

First, it cannot be doubted, can it, that certain unilateral changes by one party to the collective bargaining relationship ought to be deemed an evasion of the duty to bargain and hence a violation of the Act? Review *Katz*, page 395, *supra*, as well as *Fibreboard*. However, one can conceive of many items over which only one party ordinarily would have control. For example, at least until one party objects, should not each party have unilateral control over who will be the next president of its own organization? Does the mandatory-permissive distinction serve some function in determining when one party must give notice and an opportunity to bargain before initiating a change?

6. In Chapter 1, B, the present-day problems of the application of antitrust laws to labor unions and labor relations are explored. One of the issues that has plagued the courts over the years has been the difficulty in defining what joint conduct of employers and unions falls within the labor exemption of the antitrust laws. One can imagine a contract between a union and management which has as an aim the limitation of competition between that employer and other employers. Sometimes, the union has a distinct interest in protecting the employees it represents when it enters into such a contract. Should courts "weigh" the interest of the union, if it has one, against the anticompetitive consequences of the arrangement between the union and the employer? Moreover, how does one define the union interest?

7. In recent years, the Supreme Court appears to have settled on the idea that, if a matter is "wages, hours, or other terms or conditions of employment," it is a proper subject for bargaining and the resulting contract cannot normally be held a violation of the antitrust laws. In *Local Union 189, Amalgamated Meat Cutters* v. *Jewel Tea Co.*, page 60, *supra*, the Supreme Court was faced with a claim that a collective contract which limited the marketing hours of meat departments in food stores violated the Sherman Act. Three members of the Court stated that "the issue . . . is whether the marketing-hours restriction, like wages, and unlike prices, is so intimately related to wages, hours, and working conditions that the unions' successful attempt to obtain that provision through bona fide, arm's-length bargaining in pursuit of their own labor union policies, and not at the behest of or in combination with nonlabor groups, falls within the protection of the national labor policy and is therefore exempt from the Sherman Act." 381 U.S. at 689–90, 59 LRRM 2380–81. The same

members of the Court concluded that the contractual provision was "well within the realm of 'wages, hours, and other terms and conditions of employment.' " Note that the quoted language puts restrictions on the freedom of unions even to negotiate on wages, hours, and terms and conditions of employment.

[Three other members of the Court concurred to form a majority, holding the union had not violated the Sherman Act.]

In a companion case, the same three members of the Court held that if a union agreed with an employer association to obtain the same wage settlement from the association's competitors for the purpose of driving the competition out of business, this action fell within the prohibitions of the Sherman Act. It is not clear from the opinion whether the three were holding that the provision dealing with other employers fell outside the scope of mandatory bargaining, or that the contract was violative of the antitrust laws if the intent was to drive the other employers out of business. A fair reading of the opinion is that the three justices said both. *United Mine Workers* v. *Pennington*, page 56, *supra.*

The three who concurred in *Jewel Tea* dissented in *Pennington* on the ground that anything that can be characterized as "wages, hours, and other terms and conditions of employment" cannot fall within the antitrust prohibitions. This is so, regardless of the union's motives, since it "is precisely in this area . . . that Congress has recognized that unions have a substantial, direct, and basic interest of their own to advance." 381 U.S. at 720, 59 LRRM at 2394. These three justices could not conceive of the disputed matter not being a mandatory subject of bargaining if rational and open discussion is to be the product of the national labor laws.

More recently, the Supreme Court expanded its view of "wages, hours, and other terms and conditions of employment" to include, at least in the context of the case, price fixing for the charges to be paid orchestras. The Court decided that unlike "most industries, except for [a small charge to cover social security, unemployment insurance, and other expenses] there are no . . . costs contributing to the price" of orchestras other than the wages of the orchestra members. *American Federation of Musicians* v. *Carroll*, page 73, *supra*. Therefore, the price fixing is tantamount to setting wages, and is lawful. Has the Court opened the door?

Consider the *Truitt* doctrine, page 415, *supra*. Can you reconcile it with the Court's decision in *Pennington*? How does an employer tell a union it can afford the union's demands only if its competitors also raise their employees' salaries? How can a union respond to such a position? In light of *Pennington*, is rational and honest collective bargaining a possibility in industries where wages constitute a major portion of the employers' expenses?

8. Given the *Truitt* doctrine (which requires, sometimes, the disclosure of information), the mandatory-permissive dichotomy may serve as a standard for relevancy of requested information.

9. The language, the approach, and the tone of *First National Maintenance* make clear that Ployer can refuse entirely to discuss the union's marketing and advertising scheme. *Borg-Warner* suggests the union can similarly refuse to negotiate about Ployer's grievance proposal. Unless the

parties use their respective economic strength in an oblique and dishonest way to force some horsetrading of positions on mandatory subjects in return for the strongly desired permissive proposals, the issues about which the parties care the most will be kept completely off the bargaining table.

Observation

You have now read the significant law which has been poured into the vessel of the duty to bargain in good faith. What, if anything, do you think has been accomplished? Do you believe employers and unions enter into contracts that are much different from contracts that would have been reached if there were no statutory duty to bargain in good faith? If not, why the mandated "dance"? If so, Congress, the Board, and the Supreme Court have affected the freedom of parties to make their own economic deals. If government is planning the economy, would it be better for the task to be done more consciously?

The dilemma posed by these last questions may explain the equally perplexing problem posed by the search for a meaningful remedy to failures to bargain in good faith.

E. THE NEED FOR A MEANINGFUL REMEDY*

In 1970, the National Labor Relations Board held that it did not have the authority under the Act to order an employer to reimburse its employees for the benefits they would have received if the employer had not refused to bargain with the employees' collective bargaining agent.

1. As you read the following opinion, consider whether you agree with the majority's opinion. What is your assessment after reading some of the excerpts from other cases which are set out after the *Ex-Cell-O* opinion?

2. Does the Board have the authority to use such a remedy, at least in some cases? In which cases?

3. Is it a wise remedy? Assuming the Board has the authority to use the remedy, should it do so? When?

Ex-Cell-O Corp.

National Labor Relations Board, 1970

185 NLRB 107, 74 LRRM 1740

DECISION AND ORDER

[The union won an election to which the employer filed objections. After the Board overruled the objections, the employer refused to bar-

*See Gross, Cullen and Hanslowe, *Good Faith in Labor Negotiations: Tests and Remedies*, 53 CORNELL L. REV. 1009 (1968); St. Antoine, *A Touchstone for Labor Board Remedies*, 14 WAYNE L. REV. 1039 (1968).

gain. The trial examiner held that the employer had violated Section 8(a)(5). In addition the trial examiner ordered the company to compensate its employees for monetary losses incurred as a result of its unlawful conduct.]

We have given most serious consideration to the Trial Examiner's recommended financial reparations Order, and are in complete agreement with his finding that current remedies of the Board designed to cure violations of Section 8(a)(5) are inadequate. A mere affirmative order that an employer bargain upon request does not eradicate the effects of an unlawful delay of 2 or more years in the fulfillment of a statutory bargaining obligation. It does not put the employees in the position of bargaining strength they would have enjoyed if their employer had immediately recognized and bargained with their chosen representative. It does not dissolve the inevitable employee frustration or protect the Union from a loss of employee support attributable to such delay. The inadequacy of the remedy is all the more egregious where . . . the employer . . . [has] raised "frivolous" issues in order to postpone or avoid its lawful obligation to bargain. We have weighed these considerations most carefully. For the reasons stated below, however, we have reluctantly concluded that we cannot approve the Trial Examiner's Recommended Order that Respondent compensate its employees for monetary losses incurred as a consequence of Respondent's determination to refuse to bargain until it had tested in court the validity of the Board's certification.

Section 10(c) of the Act . . . is not so broad, . . . as to permit the punishment of a particular respondent or a class of respondents. Nor is the statutory direction to the Board so compelling that the Board is without discretion in exercising the full sweep of its power, for it would defeat the purposes of the Act if the Board imposed an otherwise proper remedy that resulted in irreparable harm to a particular respondent and hampered rather than promoted meaningful collective bargaining. Moreover, . . . the Board's grant of power does not extend to compelling agreement. It is with respect to these three limitations upon the Board's power to remedy a violation of Section 8(a)(5) that we examine the UAW's requested remedy in this case.

The Trial Examiner concluded that the proposed remedy was not punitive, that it merely made the employees partially whole for losses occasioned by the Respondent's refusal to bargain. . . . [T]here is no contention that this Respondent acted in a manner flagrantly in defiance of the statutory policy. On the contrary, the record indicates that this Respondent responsibly fulfills its legally established collective-bargaining obligations. It is clear that Respondent merely sought judicial affirmance of the Board's decision that the election of October 22, 1964, should not be set aside on the Respondent's objections. In the past whenever an employer has sought court intervention in a representation proceeding the Board has argued forcefully that court intervention would be premature, that the employer had an unquestioned right under the statute to seek court review of any Board order before its bargaining obligation became final. Should this procedural right in 8(a)(5) cases be tempered by a large monetary liability in the event the employer's posi-

tion in the representation case is ultimately found to be without merit? Of course, an employer or a union, which engages in conduct later found in violation of the Act, does so at the peril of ultimate conviction and responsibility for a make-whole remedy. But the validity of a particular Board election tried in an unfair labor practice case is not, in our opinion, an issue on the same plane as the discharge of employees for union activity or other conduct in flagrant disregard of employee rights. There are wrongdoers and wrongdoers. Where the wrong in refusing to bargain is, at most, a debatable question, though ultimately found a wrong, the imposition of a large financial obligation on such a respondent may come close to a form of punishment for having elected to pursue a representation question beyond the Board and to the courts.
. . .

In our opinion, however, the crucial question to be determined in this case relates to the policies which the requested order would effectuate. . . .

It is argued that . . . the requested remedy merely would require an employer to compensate employees for losses they incurred as a consequence of their employer's *failure to agree* to a contract he *would* have agreed to *if* he had bargained in good faith. In our view, the distinction is more illusory than real. . . . The fact that the contract, so to speak, is "written in the air" does not diminish its financial impact upon the recalcitrant employer who, willy-nilly, is forced to accede to terms never mutually established by the parties. . . .

Much as we appreciate the need for more adequate remedies in 8(a)(5) cases, we believe that, as the law now stands, the proposed remedy is a matter for Congress, not the Board. . . .

MEMBERS McCULLOCH and BROWN, dissenting in part:

Although concurring in all other respects in the Decision and Order of the Board, we part company with our colleagues on the majority in that we would grant the compensatory remedy recommended by the Trial Examiner. Unlike our colleagues, we believe that the Board has the statutory authority to direct such relief and that it would effectuate the policies of the Act to do so in this case. . . .

The Supreme Court, in its consideration of the Board's remedial powers, has consistently interpreted Section 10(c) as allowing the Board wide discretion in fashioning remedies. . . .

The declared policy of the Act is to promote the peaceful settlement of disputes by encouraging collective bargaining and by protecting employee rights. To accomplish this purpose, Board remedies for violations of the Act should, on one hand, have the effect of preventing the party in violation from so acting in the future, and from enjoying any advantage he may have gained by his unlawful practices. But they must also presently dissipate the effects of violations on employee rights in order that the employees so injured receive what they should not have been denied. . . .

The Board has already recognized in certain refusal-to-bargain situations that the usual bargaining order is not sufficient to expunge the effects of an employer's unlawful and protracted denial of its employees' right to bargain. Though the bargaining order serves to remedy the loss of the legal right and protect its exercise in the future, it does not remedy the financial injury which may also have been suffered. In a number of situations the Board has ordered the employer who unlawfully refused to bargain to compensate its employees for their resultant financial losses. Thus, some employers unlawfully refuse to sign after an agreement. . . .

Similarly, in *American Fire Apparatus Co.*,[36] the employer violated Section 8(a)(5) by unilaterally discontinuing payment of Christmas bonuses, and the Board concluded that only by requiring the bonuses to be paid could the violation be fully remedied. . . .

And in *Fibreboard Paper Products Corp.*, the employer unilaterally contracted out its maintenance operations in violation of Section 8(a)(5). The Board concluded that an order to bargain about this decision could not, by itself, adequately remedy the effects of the violation. It further ordered the employer to reinstate the employees and to make them whole for any loss of earnings suffered on account of the unlawful conduct. The Supreme Court upheld the compensatory remedy. . . .

The question now before us is whether a reimbursement order is an appropriate remedy for other types of unlawful refusals to bargain. On the basis of the foregoing analysis regarding Section 10(c), we believe that the Board has the power to order this type of relief. Further, . . . we are of the view that the compensatory remedy is appropriate and necessary in this case. . . .

. . .

A study by Professor Philip Ross shows that a contract is signed in most situations where the employer honors its duty to bargain without delay, but that the chance of a contract being signed is cut in half if the case must go to court enforcement of a bargaining order. In the interim, of course, the employees are deprived of their rightful union representation and the opportunity to bargain over their terms and conditions of employment, while at the same time their employers may gain a monetary advantage over their competitors who have complied with their legal duty.

. . .

In these refusal-to-bargain cases there is at least a legal injury. Potential employee losses incurred by an employer's refusal to bargain in violation of the Act are not limited to financial matters such as wages. Thus, it is often the case that the most important employee gains arrived at through collective bargaining involve such benefits as seniority, improved physical facilities, a better grievance procedure, or a right to arbitration. Therefore, even the remedy we would direct herein is not complete. . . .

This type of compensatory remedy is in no way forbidden by Section 8(d). It would be designed to compensate employees for injuries incurred by them by virtue of the unfair labor practices and would not require the employer to accept the measure of compensation as a term of any contract which might result from subsequent collective bargaining. The remedy contemplated in no way "writes a contract" between the

---

[36] 160 NLRB 1318, *enf'd*, 380 F.2d 1005 (C.A. 8).

employer and the union, for it would not specify new or continuing terms of employment and would not prohibit changes in existing terms and conditions. All of these would be left to the outcome of bargaining, the commencement of which would terminate Respondent's liability.

Furthermore, this compensatory remedy is not a punitive measure. It would be designed to do no more than reimburse the employees for the loss occasioned by the deprivation of their right to be represented by their collective-bargaining agent during the period of the violation. . . .

. . . [U]ncertainty as to the amount of loss does not preclude a make-whole order proposed here, and some reasonable method or basis of computation can be worked out as part of the compliance procedure. These cannot be defined in advance, but there are many methods for determining the measurable financial gain which the employees might reasonably have expected to achieve, had the Respondent fulfilled its statutory obligation to bargain collectively. The criteria which prove valid in each case must be determined by what is pertinent to the facts. Nevertheless, . . . [there are many] methods for measuring such loss. . . .

H.K. Porter Co. v. NLRB

Supreme Court of the United States, 1970

397 U.S. 99, 73 LRRM 2561

[The Board had held that the employer had failed to bargain in good faith when it refused to agree to a check-off arrangement because the payment of union dues was the "union's business." After a remand from the court of appeals in which the court suggested it, the Board ordered, as a remedy for the company's failure to bargain, the employer to agree to the check-off arrangement. The court of appeals affirmed.]

Mr. Justice Black delivered the opinion of the Court.

. . .

In 1947 Congress reviewed the experience under the Act and concluded that certain amendments were in order. . . . Accordingly, Congress amended the provisions defining unfair labor practices and said in § 8(d) that: [The Court quoted Section 8(d).]

In discussing the effect of that amendment, this Court said it is "clear that the Board may not, either directly or indirectly, compel concessions or otherwise sit in judgment upon the substantive terms of collective bargaining agreements." *NLRB* v. *American Ins. Co.*, 343 U.S. 395, 404 (1952). Later this Court affirmed that view stating that "it remains clear that § 8(d) was an attempt by Congress to prevent the Board from controlling the settling of the terms of collective bargaining agreements." *NLRB* v. *Insurance Agents*, 361 U.S. 477, 487 (1960). The parties to the instant case are agreed that this is the first time in the 35-year history of the Act that the Board has ordered either an employer or a union to agree to a substantive term of a collective-bargaining agreement.

We may agree with the Court of Appeals that as a matter of strict, literal interpretation that section refers only to deciding when a violation has occurred, but we do not agree that that observation justifies the conclusion that the remedial powers of the Board are not also limited by the same considerations that led Congress to enact § 8(d). It is implicit in the entire structure of the Act that the Board acts to oversee and referee the process of collective bargaining, leaving the results of the contest to the bargaining strengths of the parties. It would be anomalous indeed to hold that while § 8(d) prohibits the Board from relying on a refusal to agree as the sole evidence of bad-faith bargaining, the Act permits the Board to compel agreement in that same dispute. The Board's remedial powers under § 10 of the Act are broad, but they are limited to carrying out the policies of the Act itself. One of these fundamental policies is freedom of contract. While the parties' freedom of contract is not absolute under the Act, allowing the Board to compel agreement when the parties themselves are unable to agree would violate the fundamental premise on which the Act is based—private bargaining under governmental supervision of the procedure alone, without any official compulsion over the actual terms of the contract.

In reaching its decision the Court of Appeals relied extensively on the equally important policy of the Act that workers' rights to collective bargaining are to be secured. In this case the court apparently felt that the employer was trying effectively to destroy the union by refusing to agree to what the union may have considered its most important demand. Perhaps the court, fearing that the parties might resort to economic combat, was also trying to maintain the industrial peace that the Act is designed to further. But the Act as presently drawn does not contemplate that unions will always be secure and able to achieve agreement even when their economic position is weak, or that strikes and lockouts will never result from a bargaining impasse. It cannot be said that the Act forbids an employer or a union to rely ultimately on its economic strength to try to secure what it cannot obtain through bargaining. It may well be true, as the Court of Appeals felt, that the present remedial powers of the Board are insufficiently broad to cope with important labor problems. But it is the job of Congress, not the Board or the courts, to decide when and if it is necessary to allow governmental review of proposals for collective-bargaining agreements and compulsory submission to one side's demands. The present Act does not envision such a process.

The judgment is reversed and the case is remanded to the Court of Appeals for further action consistent with this opinion.

Reversed and remanded.

Mr. Justice Douglas, with whom Mr. Justice Stewart concurs, dissenting.

The Court correctly describes the general design and main thrust of the Act. It does not encompass compulsory arbitration; the Board does not sit to impose what it deems to be the best conditions for the collective-bargaining agreement; the obligation to bargain collectively "does not compel either party to agree to a proposal or require the making of a concession." § 8(d) of the Act.

Yet the Board has the power, where one party does not bargain in good faith, "to take such affirmative action . . . as will effectuate the policies" of the Act. § 10(c) of the Act.

Here the employer did not refuse the checkoff for any business reason, whether cost, inconvenience, or what not. Nor did the employer refuse the checkoff as a factor in its bargaining strategy, hoping that delay and denial might bring it in exchange favorable terms and conditions. Its reason was a resolve to avoid reaching any agreement with the union.

In those narrow and specialized circumstances, I see no answer to the power of the Board in its discretion to impose the checkoff as "affirmative action" necessary to remedy the flagrant refusal of the employer to bargain in good faith.

The case is rare, if not unique, and will seldom arise. I realize that any principle once announced may in time gain a momentum not warranted by the exigencies of its creation. But once there is any business consideration that leads to a denial of a demand or any consideration of bargaining strategy that explains the refusal, the Board has no power to act. Its power is narrowly restricted to the clear case where the refusal is aimed solely at avoidance of any agreement. Such is the present case. Hence, with all respect for the strength of the opposed view, I dissent.

Questions

1. Can you conceive of a violation of the Act based solely on the employer's refusal to agree to a single proposal? If not, is *H.K. Porter* an example of an already bad case making even more bad law?

2. What remedy *is* the Court approving? Will the company be in contempt of court if it does not agree to the check-off proposal? If so, is that a different remedy from the one the Board ordered? If not, is there any remedy at all for the "violation"?

3. Does the Board have the authority it disclaims in *Ex-Cell-O*?

a. Are you persuaded that Section 8(d) precludes the remedy rather than merely a finding that the company had violated Section 8(a)(5)? In *NLRB* v. *Thayer Co.*, 213 F.2d 748, 34 LRRM 2250 (1st Cir. 1954), the court of appeals held that even if activity of employees was unprotected, indeed, unlawful, the Board could properly order their reinstatement under Section 10(c) of the Act in order to remedy unfair labor practices of the employer. In *Blades Mfg. Corp.*, 144 NLRB 561, 566–67, 54 LRRM 1087, 1089–90 (1963), the Board accepted the *Thayer* doctrine and, in order to remedy a violation of Section 8(a)(5), ordered reinstatement of employees who had engaged in concerted activity, whether or not that activity was protected by Section 7. In these cases, especially *Thayer* where the employees arguably engaged in unlawful activity, does Section 10(c)'s prohibition on Board-ordered reinstatement of employees discharged for "cause" create more serious problems than Section 8(d)'s prohibition, which is not aimed at Board remedies at all?

b. In *NLRB* v. *Rutter-Rex Mfg. Co.*, 396 U.S. 258, 72 LRRM 2881 (1969), the Supreme Court stated that, where there was unusual delay in the Board processes following the determination that the employer had unlawfully discharged employees, the burden fell on the wrongdoing employer to compensate the wronged employees for wages lost during that delay, rather than on the innocent employees to suffer the loss of wages. What relevance does this have to the Board's determination in *Ex-Cell-O*?

c. In *NLRB* v. *Strong*, 393 U.S. 357, 70 LRRM 2100 (1969), the Supreme Court held that an employer had to pay its employees monies that it would have been contractually obligated to pay if it had not unlawfully refused to sign the proposed collective contract. What relevance does this have to the Board's determination in *Ex-Cell-O*?

d. In *International Union of Electricians* v. *NLRB* (Tiidee Products, Inc.), 426 F.2d 1243, 73 LRRM 2870 (D.C. Cir. 1970), the employer refused to bargain with the certified union because it had objections to the election which the court characterized as "patently frivolous." A majority of the court refused to accept the Board's refusal to issue the type of order sought in *Ex-Cell-O*, and remanded the case for further consideration. In addition to the reasons given by the *Ex-Cell-O* dissent for urging the remedy, the court majority pointed out that the present system of permitting Board and judicial review of election certification resulted in unnecessary and unjustified use of valuable institutional resources which could be better spent adjudicating justly difficult cases. Is this a proper consideration for a court to take into account in urging a particular remedy in this case?

e. Is the proposed remedy a "penalty," and thereby precluded by the Act?

f. Does the proposed remedy violate the employer's "right" to seek judicial review of the Board's determination in representation proceedings? If so, does that mean the remedy is properly available in cases where employers fail to bargain in other ways?

g. Is assessment of the remedy too speculative?

4. Assuming the Board does have the authority to grant the remedy, is it wise for the Board to do so?

a. What reasons are there for imposing the remedy? Should the remedy be used in every refusal-to-bargain case? If not, what factors should be taken into account to determine in which cases the remedy should be invoked? The nature and egregiousness of the unfair labor practices? Their effects? Should exercising the "right" to judicial review of Board representation proceedings ever be such a case? Can one distinguish between "frivolous" challenges to elections and more substantial objections?

b. What objections are there to the use of the remedy, even assuming the Board's authority to invoke it?

(1) There is not sufficient need for the remedy.

(2) The remedy is too immense.

(3) The remedy effectively places the Board in the role of an arbitrator.

(4) The remedy may freeze future positions taken by the employer in future negotiations, and in any event, the remedy will greatly affect the substance of the future negotiations.

(5) Assessing the amount due under the remedy would be an undue burden on the Board and the parties.

(6) The remedy will be a further inducement to each party to engage in bargaining which will have as its purpose causing the other party to commit an unfair labor practice.

(7) Can the following be argued successfully? Since the essential force for granting higher wages to employees through their union is the threat of a strike, and since the employees can strike to protest the employer's refusal to bargain and obtain whatever wages the Board might eventually assess pursuant to the proposed remedy, the employees have lost nothing they could not have had by either threatening to strike or actually striking.

5. Should Congress amend the Act to permit, or to require, the Board to use the *Ex-Cell-O* remedy?

6. At the present time, for most failures to bargain in good faith, are there any significant remedies other than deprivation of the *Mackay* privilege for offending employers and an "unprotected" designation for concerted acts in support of an offending union?

5. The Collective Bargaining Agreement: Its Nature and Administration

Problem

Assume that the Enderby Company is subject to the jurisdiction of the NLRB and that the NLRB will exercise its jurisdiction under its "jurisdictional yardsticks." Assume also that the union and company have executed a collective bargaining agreement for a term of three years.

The company sends the following memorandum concerning "operation of the laboratory" to the union's business agent.

"As you may know, the operation of the laboratory has been a recurrent problem for management. Since our expertise lies in the production aspect of the business, and not in materials testing, we have been unable to run the laboratory on an efficient, economical, and controlled basis. Accordingly, we have discontinued operations of the testing laboratory, effective immediately. All laboratory testing will now be performed by Dunbar Testing, Inc., an independent concern. We have leased the laboratory space to Dunbar on a two-year basis and have sold the necessary equipment to it. We expect that Dunbar will perform its operations on our premises, but it will not be required to do so.

"We are pleased to advise you that Dunbar has agreed to hire 15 of the 20 technicians who presently work in the laboratory and that it will do so on the basis of seniority. Under the provisions of the collective bargaining agreement now in force, particularly the management rights clause thereof, the company is entitled to take the action in question without prior permission of, or consultation with, the union. Since the action in question is not mentioned in our contract, we are not restricted from taking such managerial action. I am sure that you recognize that all rights not restricted by the agreement are reserved to management.

"Nevertheless, as a courtesy to you, and in the interest of good labor relations, we have chosen to advise you of our decision. While this action does not constitute a layoff under the seniority provisions of the contract, we will follow the contractual provisions with regard to the placement of the five laboratory technicians who will not be hired by Dunbar. It is our earnest hope that the employees displaced by this change in operations may be absorbed into the regular work force.

447

"P.S. Please note that the *management rights* section of our agreement states that 'Except as expressly limited by specific provisions of this agreement the company retains the sole exclusive right to manage the business and to exercise every right or power necessary or incidental thereto. The exercise of such rights shall not be subject to arbitration.' "

Questions

1. If you are representing the company, would you have advised that this letter be sent to the union? Is the company's underlying philosophy as to the nature of the agreement sound?

2. If you were representing the union, how would you characterize the nature of the collective bargaining agreement?

3. Is the company's position consistent with the Supreme Court's decision in *Fibreboard*?

There are several possible courses of action which are available to the union in this problem. For example, the union could file a grievance and process it to arbitration, or strike, or seek to bargain with the company over the conduct in question, or file an unfair labor practice charge with the NLRB. The student should evaluate the advantages and disadvantages of each possible course of action in light of the materials presented in this chapter.

A. INTRODUCTION—NATURE OF THE AGREEMENT

Although collective bargaining agreements are often referred to as "contracts," it is clear that traditional contract doctrines may not provide sound answers to many questions that may arise under collective bargaining agreements. The legal nature of a collective agreement must be considered. Questions of interpretation and enforcement of collective agreements are inextricably intertwined with the nature of the agreement. For example, it is commonly said that an arbitrator must interpret the agreement, *i.e.*, an arbitrator should interpret provisions according to the agreement of the parties. Yet, as in the case of statutes, the parties do not foresee all possible questions that may arise. Can the arbitrator properly decide a grievance on the basis of past practice or on the basis of a sound labor relations policy if the agreement is silent on the particular matter? Another question is whether an employee, who is covered by an agreement but who is not a party to the agreement, may enforce the agreement in court or by arbitration if the union is unwilling to assist the employee? The common law of contracts may not provide a safe guide for answering these questions.

When the collective bargaining agreement does not expressly refer to a matter in dispute between the parties, company and union representatives frequently express conflicting views as to the nature of the collective bargaining agreement. Company representatives often rely, particularly in arbitration, on a "reserved rights" theory, *i.e.*, that all rights not specifically restricted by the collective bargaining agreement are retained by management. On the other hand, union representatives often contend in such cases that past practice is an implied part of the agreement. Note the conflict of these views as expressed in the following excerpts from talks given at the Ninth Annual Meeting of the National Academy of Arbitrators.

COMPANY REPRESENTATIVE: ". . . To read into the mere act of signing a contract implications that may never have been considered by either party is repugnant to the basic concept of the collective bargaining agreement that it is a voluntary act of the parties. That can be avoided only by interpreting the contract as the parties write it—an instrument containing specific and limited restrictions on the functions that management would otherwise be free to exercise. To the extent that the parties have not seen fit to limit management's sphere of action, management's rights are unimpaired by the contract."

UNION REPRESENTATIVE: "I cannot agree . . . that management's reserved rights were all-embracing to the exclusion of any labor right. The bit of historical fiction that some of my management colleagues attempt to write is neither accurate nor well-founded. As I understand it, it goes something like this: First, there was management. Its power was supreme. Then came unions [which] challenged this absolute power. Management's rights are diminished only to the extent that labor's challenge is measured, the story goes, only by specific contract clauses wherein a right is specifically established for labor. No other right for labor exists.

"I cannot agree to this appraisal of the reserved rights of management. The law of the land has established labor's right to bargain collectively over wages, hours, and working conditions. Bargaining implies that each party can agree or not agree and that a bargain is necessary if business is to be done. Management controls the property and the tools; unions represent the labor necessary to utilize the property and the tools. If the property and tools are not available, labor cannot produce. If labor is not available, the property and tools cannot be used for production. Because both are needed, a bargain is needed.

"Usually the bargain is reduced to writing. The written document does not represent labor's imposition on mangement's reserved rights; rather it represents the basis on which both parties agree to go forward. In examining the meaning of an agreement, it is proper to inquire about the conditions under which the bargain took place with a presumption that the normal practices which did exist are expected to continue except as the agreement would require or justify alteration and except as conditions make such past circumstances no longer feasible or appropriate. Both parties have rights to stability and protection from unbargained changes in wages, hours, and working conditions."

Consider the validity of these positions in light of the materials in this chapter.

Willard Wirtz has stated that "our first and probably most basic difficulty has been in appreciating the differences between collective bargaining agreements and ordinary commercial contracts. The fact that they are called 'contracts' has led us to try to fit them into the familiar mode of Willistonian concepts." Wirtz, *Collective Bargaining: Lawyers' Role in Negotiations and Arbitrations,* 34 A.B.A.J. 547, 548 (1948). Also see Feller, *A General Theory of the Collective Agreement,* 61 Calif. L. Rev. 663 (1973); Summers, *Collective Agreements and the Law of Contracts,* 78 Yale L.J. 525 (1969); and Shulman, *Reason, Contract, and Law in Labor Relations,* 68 Harv. L. Rev. 999 (1955).

As you read the following materials, try to identify aspects of a collective bargaining agreement that distinguish it from a commercial contract. Also review the Court's comments in *J.I. Case Co.* v. *NLRB,* page 105, *supra,* on the nature of a collective bargaining agreement.

Cox, The Legal Nature of Collective Bargaining Agreements*

. . . There are no settled rules governing rights and remedies under collective bargaining agreements. Whether judges apply existing contract doctrines blindly or accommodate the law to the needs of the industrial world will depend upon the imagination and attitude of labor lawyers.

The starting point is sure to be the familiar rules of contract law. . . .

Voluntarism and bargain are . . . significant ingredients of a collective bargaining agreement. The law leaves the employer and the collectivity of employees free to agree or refrain from agreement subject only to the obligation that they bargain in good faith. The terms of the bargain are not determined by the government; in this respect both management and labor enjoy much greater freedom than a utility or insurance company dealing with the public.

In fact neither the employer nor the employees collectively have the freedom to disagree which characterizes typical contracts between business firms and individuals. Sooner or later the employer and employees must strike some kind of a bargain. For both the costs of delay can be very heavy. The compulsion has two relevant consequences. First, it partially explains the gaps and deliberate ambiguities in collective bargaining agreements which create distinctive problems of interpretation. The pressure to reach an agreement is so great that the parties are willing to contract although each knows that the other places a different meaning on the words and they share only the common intent to postpone the issue and take a gamble upon an arbitrator's ruling if decision is required. Second, the importance of having some agreement means that the arbitrator can hardly say that there was no meeting of the minds upon the question before him, and therefore there was no contract, and that the parties should go back and negotiate a solution.

These consequences of the practical compulsion to sign and preserve collective agreements mean that interpretation must assume a more creative role than in most commercial or property litigation. . . .

*Reprinted by permission from Cox, *The Legal Nature of Collective Bargaining Agreements,* 57 MICH. L. REV. 1 (1958). Copyright © 1958 by the Michigan Law Review Association.

A unique characteristic of a collective bargaining agreement is the number of people affected. The habit of speaking of a triangular relationship involving employer, labor union, and individual employees obscures the number of employees and the complexity of their interests. Under some contracts the number of individual employees reaches tens of thousands; it is usually more than fifty. The identity of the employees may change from day to day; Joe Smith quits but Annie Jones is hired. Often several employees have conflicting interests, as where the claim is that some are being permitted to deprive others of work by doing jobs outside of their own classification. The second party—the labor union or collective bargaining representative—is in a very real sense only the third party—the individual employees—acting as an organized group through its agents and constitutional processes. Thus, if we think of the union as an agent and the employees as principals, we have the paradox that the agent is only the principals acting as an organization. The group interests, however, may conflict with the claims of individuals because several classes of individuals have divergent interests, because the demands of group organization and coherence clash with individual self-interest, or even because the union officialdom is not immediately responsive to the wishes of a numerical majority of the members. Since experience offers no factual parallel to these arrangements, no other legal conception is quite analogous.

A group cannot function effectively without rules for its government. When the group is a wholly voluntary association it may adopt its own rules, but under collective bargaining the group is only partly voluntary and the Railway Labor and Naional Labor Relations Acts provide rules for its government. NLRA Section 9(a) provides that the representatives designated by a majority of the employees in a bargaining unit shall be the exclusive representatives of all the employees in the unit. The National Labor Relations Board defines the bargaining unit and determines when and how the representative shall be chosen.

These outside rules seriously disturb any effort to analyze collective bargaining agreements according to the elementary principles of contract and agency. Under the principle of majority rule dissident members of the appropriate unit lose the power to act for themselves, unlike any ordinary principal to an agency relation. The practicalities of group organization deprive even a majority of the power to discharge their representative at will; although the ordinary agency is always revocable, a bargaining representative can be ousted only upon certain occasions. The agreements executed by the employer with the bargaining representative not only fix a man's wages but they may compel him to contribute a portion of his earnings to a trust fund, compel his retirement or change his seniority without his consent. In my opinion the union may even compromise accrued claims under an existing contract, but the point may be doubtful.

Efforts have been made to assimilate all these cases to familiar contract law by saying that when an employee works in a bargaining unit covered by a collective agreement he enters into a voluntary contract of hire which incorporates its provisions. The words can be made to fit, but the formula has the taste of fiction. The individual employee may not even know whether the workers are represented by a labor union. Probably he does not know many of the major terms of the collective bargaining agreement. It may be said that this is also true of the farmer who insures his barn or the professor who ships his books by railway express, but I submit that Justice Stone provided us with a truer insight when he said, "Congress has seen fit to clothe the bargaining representative with powers comparable to those possessed by a legislative body both to create and restrict the rights of those whom it represents."

. . .

In the community of the shop the collective bargaining agreement serves a function fairly comparable to the role of the Federal Trade Commission Act or National Labor Relations Act in the whole community. It is an instrument of government as well as an instrument of exchange. The point is highly important both in evolving substantive law and . . . in matters of interpretation.

The governmental nature of a collective bargaining agreement results partly from the number of people affected and the diversity of their interests. Harry Shulman aptly suggested other determining conditions:

"[The collective bargaining agreement] is not the typical offer and acceptance which normally is the basis for classroom or text discussions of contract law. It is not an undertaking to produce a specific result; indeed, it rarely speaks of the ultimate product. It is not made by parties who seek each other out to make a bargain from scratch and then go his own way. The parties to a collective agreement . . . meet in their contract negotiations to fix the terms and conditions of their collaboration for the future."

Perhaps "collaboration" is too optimistic a word. Perhaps there is a "typical" contract only in the sense that economists have a model. The point which Shulman caught and I am seeking to emphasize is that the collective agreement governs complex, many-sided relations between large numbers of people in a going concern for very substantial periods of time. "The trade agreement thus becomes, as it were, the industrial constitution of the enterprise setting forth the broad general principles upon which the relationship of employer and employee is to be conducted."

. . .

One consequence is that many provisions of the labor agreement must be expressed in general and flexible terms. The concept of "just cause" is an obvious illustration. Sometimes it is not possible to do more than establish an appropriate set of procedures for resolving certain issues; witness the provisions for fixing work loads and piece rates in many of the textile contracts. A collective agreement rarely expresses all the rights and duties falling within its scope. One simply cannot spell out every detail of life in an industrial establishment, or even of that portion which both management and labor agree is a matter of mutual concern.

It is largely for these reasons that collective bargaining agreements provide their own administrative or judicial machinery. Of course arbitration long antedates collective bargaining and there are thousands of commercial contracts and construction contracts under which arbitration is a daily occurrence. Sometimes, as in a large scale government construction contract, the functions of the "arbitrator" may resemble his functions under a labor agreement. By and large, however, there is this distinct difference: the commercial arbitrator finds facts—did the cloth meet the sample—while the labor arbitrator necessarily pours meaning into the general phrases and interstices of a document written somewhat in the generalities of basic regulatory legislation. Furthermore, because management and employees are involved in continuing relationships, it is at least possible for the arbitrator's ruling to become a body of subordinate rules for the future conduct of the enterprise. I say "subordinate rules" because the contract may change them. They are rather like the judge-made law—the rubrics which the judges put upon statutes, the precepts which govern where the statute is silent, the context into which new bits of statutory law will be intruded.

Of course this body of shop law is not made up exclusively or even largely of arbitration decisions. "The parties to a collective agreement start in a going enterprise with a store of amorphous methods, attitudes, fears and problems." The agreement "is based upon a mass of unstated assumptions and practices as to which the understanding of the parties may actually differ." The assumptions and practices which have prevailed in the past and as they develop in the future are not only the background of the agreement but the flesh and blood which gives it meaning.

Individual workers would receive the most protection against arbitrary treatment under the theory that the provisions of a collective bargaining agreement relating to wages and hours become effective by incorporation into bilateral contracts of hire between the employer and each employee. On the other hand it seems to me that giving the union control over all claims arising under the collective agreement comports so much better with the functional nature of a collective bargaining agreement. . . . Allowing an individual to carry a claim to arbitration whenever he is dissatisfied with the adjustment worked out by the company and the union treats issues which arise in the administration of a contract as if there were always a "right" interpretation to be divined from the instrument. It discourages the kind of day-to-day cooperation between company and union which is normally the mark of sound industrial relations—a relationship in which grievances are treated as problems to be solved and contract clauses are only guideposts in a dynamic human relationship. When the interests of several groups conflict, or future needs run contrary to present desires, or when the individual's claim endangers group interests, the union's function is to resolve the competition by reaching an accommodation or striking a balance. The process is political. It involves a melange of power, numerical strength, mutual aid, reason, prejudice, and emotion. Limits must be placed on the authority of the group, but within the zone of fairness and rationality this method of self-government probably works better than the edicts of any outside arbiter. . . .

The governmental nature of a collective bargaining agreement should have predominant influence in its interpretation. The generalities, the deliberate ambiguities, the gaps, the unforeseen contingencies, the need for a rule although the agreement is silent—all require a creativeness quite unlike the attitude of one construing a deed or a promissory note or a three-hundred page corporate trust indenture. Perhaps the requisite attitude can be suggested by likening the interpretation of a collective agreement to the construction of a basic statute creating an administrative agency, although the analogy may assume too readily that the "look-in-dictionary" school of statutory interpretation has given way to willingness to read basic statutes "not as theorems of Euclid but with some imagination of the purposes which lie behind them."

The interpretation of a statute is the proliferation of a purpose. In a sense it is misleading to speak of the legislative intent. No one supposes that the tens of senators and hundreds of representatives who vote for a bill have one common state of mind. I trust, also, that arbitrators who speak of "the intent of the parties" do not mean to imply that they are concerned with the secret, unexpressed intent of either party. Those who listen seriously to the testimony of negotiators concerning what they understood or supposed or intended run the risk of imposing upon one side the unilateral suppositions of the other. The true standard of interpretation must be objective. To speak of intent as if the congressmen or negotiators had reached a conclusion upon the specific issue is also misleading. The troublesome issues during the administration of a statute or contract are usually those which the authors either refused to face or failed to anticipate. Yet to speak of intent, when the word is properly understood, serves two useful functions. It reminds the interpreter that the statute or contract is a purposive instrument. The metaphor also cautions the interpreter that it is his duty to effectuate the will of the Congress—or of the parties to the contract—even though he himself might reach an infinitely wiser decision. What the interpreter must strive to do, therefore, is to give the instrument the application which the author would have provided if he had consciously determined the issue.

In the case of a statute the best guide to this meaning is its policy or purpose. . . .

Many questions of interpretation can be handled in this fashion under collective bargaining agreements. . . .

Unfortunately, many of the most important questions of interpretation are not soluble by reference to the fundamental purposes of the collective agreement—at least not in the sense in which that term is usually understood. . . .

Suppose that an employee is discharged for what the union thinks is insufficient cause during the term of a collective bargaining agreement which contains most of the customary provisions, including recognition, seniority, grievance, and arbitration clauses but which imposes no express limitation upon the management's power to discharge. Of course the exact words of the contract make a difference but one reading the opinions gets the feeling that it is not the language which leads courts to deny relief while arbitrators examine the merits of the discharge. In *Coca-Cola Bottling Co. of Boston* Saul Wallen reasoned that ". . . the meaning of the contract, when viewed as a whole, is that a limitation on the employer's right to discharge was created with the birth of the instrument. Both the necessity for maintaining the integrity of the contract's component parts and the very nature of collective bargaining agreements are the basis for this conclusion."

There is little force to the argument that the implication of a clause limiting discharges to cases of just cause is necessary to preserve the integrity of a seniority clause or grievance procedure. The integrity of the seniority and grievance clauses would not be affected by the arbitrary and capricious discharge of a junior employee who had no grievance.

Mr. Wallen's reliance upon "the very nature of collective bargaining agreements" cuts much deeper. He thereby asserts that a company which signs a collective bargaining agreement automatically assumes some obligations and submits certain management actions to the jurisdiction of the arbitrator even though the agreement says nothing about them. The dissenting member of the arbitration board spoke the truth when he protested that the majority "have taken a contract which contained no language which could possibly be construed as a limitation on the Company's right of discharge and have implied a very stringent limitation on that right," but this assertion did not meet the basic contention that employees had rights cognizable by the arbitrator in addition to those which the contract expressly gave them.

Some of the subcontracting cases which have been so much debated in recent years raise the same kind of issues although others may turn upon narrower reasoning. Suppose that a manufacturer of heavy steam valves is a party to a contract which makes no mention of subcontracting but contains, in addition to the arbitration clause, such customary provisions as a recognition clause, a seniority clause, a discharge clause and a schedule of wage rates. The manufacturer sublets the machining of certain parts to an independent concern instead of following his previously unbroken practice of doing all his own production. There are layoffs and a reduction of overtime. The union protests that the contract has been violated and takes the case to arbitration. There is precedent for the view that subcontracting is a reserved right of management. There are also decisions upholding the union's contention on grounds reminiscent of Mr. Wallen's reasoning in the *Coca-Cola* case:

> ". . . the Recognition clause, where considered together with the Wage clause, the Seniority clauses, and other clauses establishing standards for covered jobs and employees limits the Company's right to subcontract during the term of the Contract. . . . To allow the Company, . . . to lay off the employees and transfer the work to employees not covered by the agreed standards would subvert the contract and destroy the meaning of the collective bargaining relation."

I suggested earlier that the collective bargaining agreement, unlike most other contracts, is an instrument of government because it regulates diverse affairs of many people with conflicting interests over a substantial period of time. One can phrase the basic problem of interpretation in the discharge and subcontracting cases by saying that the parties differ with respect to the kind of government which they propose to establish. Is it a monarchy except insofar as the employer has assumed the obligations explicitly stated or fairly implied from the contract? Or has the whole realm of matters of mutual concern to employer and employees been brought within the joint authority of the company and union under a regime in which the legislative process is performed in annual contract negotiations and the executive and judicial process is carried out under a grievance procedure ending in arbitration? Usually the realm of matters of mutual concern is divided, part to be regulated by the employer and part to be governed by joint authority under the regime established by the contract. The issue then becomes, which matters are regulated by one form of government and which by the other. Did the Coca-Cola contract move discharges into the area of collective bargaining, i.e., of joint responsibility, or were they left to the sole responsibility of management? What about subcontracting? It is to the basic conflict over the size of the area subject to joint responsibility that I refer when I speak of the lack of a common purpose on the part of both management and labor to which questions of interpretation can be referred. Going a step further, I suggest that this is the very essence of large parts of a collective bargaining agreement—it has the nature of an armed truce in a continuing struggle, yet the armistice line has not been put on a map.

Before discussing the significance of this highly tentative conclusion I should like to insist upon two distinctions. First, I submit that problems of the kinds illustrated by the discharge and subcontracting cases will sometimes yield to analysis in terms of familiar contract principles. The notion that ordinary commercial contracts spell out all their obligations is a silly canard. Every contract, whether a typical commercial contract or a labor agreement contains "an implied covenant of good faith and fair dealing." One who sells a retail milk business impliedly promises that he will not solicit former customers. A lease of coal lands in exchange for a schedule of royalties implies an obligation to mine the coal diligently. Under the Coca-Cola-type contract there should be no hesitation in setting aside a discharge aimed at circumventing seniority or defeating a grievance even though the contract says nothing about discharges because such a discharge destroys the right of the employees to have the fruits of their bargain. Upon this familiar principle of contracts one might fairly conclude in the absence of other evidence that the provisions of a collective bargaining agreement establishing wages and labor standards imply an obligation not to seek a substitute labor supply at lower wages or inferior standards. The implied promise would prohibit subcontracting for this purpose. But there are limitations to the covenant of honesty and fair dealing. A manufacturer who sells goods when the price is high is not precluded from doubling his output because this would impair the value of the buyer's purchase. A collective bargaining agreement does not imply a promise that the employer will not deprive the union and the employees of its benefits by closing an obsolete plant or dropping an unprofitable line of business. Similarly, the implied covenant of good faith and fair dealing can hardly be supposed to reach subcontracting which is based upon business considerations other than the cost of acquiring labor under the collective agreement. In such a case either management is free to act or some limitation must be found in the very nature of a collective bargaining agreement.

The second distinction which I wish to press is a differentiation between (1) implying obligations within the general area of terms and conditions of employment brought under the regime of the collective bargaining agreement and (2) implying restrictions upon management by drawing the boundary line more favorably to the union. One could put the discharge and subcontracting cases in more familiar terms than I have used by saying that the critical issue is whether a collective bargaining agreement is simply a document by which the union and the employees have imposed upon management limited restrictions of its otherwise absolute right to manage the enterprise, so that an employee's claim must always fail unless he can point to a specific contract provision on which the claim is founded. But this reserved-rights phraseology obscures the very distinction which I wish to press. Management and labor are certainly free to bring some areas of mutual concern under the regime of collective bargaining and to assign others exclusively to management. This is true as a matter of legal theory, and the freedom is exercised as a matter of practical living. Within the area put under the regime of collective bargaining, however, it is hardly practicable to make the contract the exclusive source of rights, remedies and duties. There are too many people, too many problems, too many unforeseeable contingencies, too many variations—one cannot reduce all the rules governing the community of an industrial plant to fifteen or even fifty pages. The logic of the governmental nature of the process of collective bargaining therefore creates a strong presumption that within the sphere of collective bargaining the parties, if they had thought about it, would have acknowledged the need and therefore the existence of a common law of the shop which furnishes the context of, and also implements, the agreement. Interpretation should give effect to this presumption arising from the very nature of a collective agreement unless the agreement states a contrary rule in pretty plain language.

A good many people experienced in management may spontaneously challenge the statement that the contract cannot be the exclusive guide to all questions arising thereunder but I suspect that when pressed, most of them will concede the accuracy of my presumption in the only sense in which I intend it. Many contracts limit the employer's right to discharge employees to cases where there is "just cause" but say nothing about the power to impose lesser discipline. Does anyone deny an arbitrator appointed under such a contract the power to decide whether there was just cause for a disciplinary layoff even though his jurisdiction is limited to the "interpretation and application of any provision of this agreement"? Again, suppose that a contract fixes a seven-day time limit upon the appeal of grievances from the foreman's ruling and that the employee and shop steward wait ten days to appeal upon the strength of the personnel director's specific assurance that the company will not enforce the time limit. Surely there are only a few stern literalists who would deny the grievance without examining the merits if the company invoked the time limit as a bar to arbitration. The customary disposition would be to ignore the time limit upon grounds of waiver or estoppel. These doctrines obviously grant remedies, if not rights, based upon notions of justice which are not spelled out in the agreement. And does not an arbitrator resort to such a body of law when he grants reinstatement with back pay as a remedy for an unjustified discharge?

Occasionally arbitrators and courts have come into conflict because of the court's failure to perceive this need for an industrial jurisprudence within the area of labor-management relations brought under the joint authority of management and labor. . . .

The imperative which requires a body of "common law" in the area marked off by the contract for government under the regime established by the contract has no place in deciding what area has been marked off. There is nothing in the function of a collective bargaining agreement which makes the reserved management rights view, when confined to this issue, either more or less serviceable than the opposing view sometimes espoused by labor unions. Nor can guidance be found in an underlying purpose or intent unless those words include a purpose to strike a compromise, for on this issue management and union usually stand in opposition. Where then is the judge or arbitrator to turn in deciding the discharge or subcontracting question, or any other issue concerning the scope of area marked off for government under the contract but on which the contract is silent?

I have no answer to these questions—only a conviction that the search is one which ought to be pursued more consciously in general terms, even though the answer is the pot of gold at the end of the rainbow. Ideally the parties should write the answer into the contract, for the choice is theirs, but often the difference of opinion is too deep and too enduring for either party to express in writing even its temporary acceptance of the position of the other. . . .

. . . In the discharge case it would not be implausible to conclude, if the words of the contract are otherwise blind, that review of discharges to determine whether there is just cause is more consistent with a contract granting other forms of job security and industrial justice than is the reservation of untrammelled power to discharge for any reason which the employer deems sufficient. The plausibility is less, if indeed there is any, in the case of subcontracting or shift schedules. . . .

B. ADMINISTRATION: GRIEVANCE PROCEDURE AND ARBITRATION

1. DESCRIPTION OF THE PROCESS

After the collective bargaining agreement has been negotiated, differences inevitably arise during the term of the agreement as to how it should be interpreted and applied. Most of these differences will not have been anticipated by the parties. These disputes which arise during the term of a contract are settled through the operation of a grievance procedure which is set out in the contract itself. A study by the U.S. Bureau of Labor Statistics has revealed that 99 percent of 1,717 major contracts provided for a grievance procedure.

A typical grievance procedure will have the following characteristics. It will define the "grievances" which are subject to the procedure. Thus, a grievance may be broadly defined as "any complaint" by an employee "in connection with his work" or it may be more narrowly confined to "disputes arising over the interpretation or application of the terms of this agreement." The procedure may require that a grievance be filed by an employee or group of employees, or it may enable the union, or perhaps even the employer, to invoke the procedure.

The grievance procedure will then usually specify the various steps to be followed in processing the grievance. For example, the grievance may be taken up initially by the shop steward representing the aggrieved employee and the employee's foreman. If the grievance is not satisfactorily adjusted by them, then it will move to progressively higher echelons of responsibility on both sides. Many contracts contain time limitations within which a grievance must be taken to the next higher level. Some contracts require that the grievance be filed in writing initially, others that it be reduced to writing at a certain step. In either event, printed forms are normally used.

Under many contracts involving large numbers of employees, the practice is to set aside a certain time each week, *e.g.,* Friday afternoon, for a fairly high level union and company discussion of an accumulation of grievances which have not been settled in earlier steps of the procedure. Many contracts also provide that the time spent by union officer/employees in the processing of grievances is compensable working time.

Literally hundreds of thousands of disputes over the terms and conditions of employment in America are resolved annually through the system of negotiation and settlement made available by the grievance procedure. For those disputes which cannot be resolved by the parties themselves through the grievance procedure, the collective bargaining agreement will normally provide for resolution through impartial arbitration. The BLS study referred to above revealed that about 95 percent of the contracts in the survey contained provisions for arbitration as the terminal step in the grievance procedure. The arbitration process began to be used to a considerable extent during World War II by the War Labor Board, and since that time has come to be accepted and recognized as a standard technique for the final settlement of contract disputes and grievances.

The reasons for the development and increased use of arbitration are clear. Neither the judicial process nor resort to economic warfare is a practical method of resolving disputes over contract interpretation and application. Litigation is too slow, expensive, and technical; furthermore, most judges have little understanding of industrial relations. Strikes or other forms of economic pressure involve too much economic waste and personal hardship to be used with any frequency. The large number of contract interpretation disputes and the continuing relationship between the parties require a better method of solution. Arbitration offers greater speed, less expense, more flexibility, and a more rational and knowledge-able result than any alternative, and does not interfere with the continuity of the enterprise. Exact figures are not available, but a good estimate is that by the mid-1970s 12 to 15 thousand arbitration awards were handed down annually by arbitrators and arbitration boards.

The parties themselves determine in their negotiations the scope and coverage of the arbitration provisions of the agreement. The arbitration clause may or may not be coextensive with the grievance procedure. The "standard" arbitration clause applies to "disputes concerning the application and interpretation of the provisions of this agreement." On the other hand, the parties may specifically exclude certain matters from arbitration in their contract, or they may limit the remedial power of the arbitrator with respect to other matters. Typically the contract will provide that the arbitrator "shall have no power to add to, subtract from, or otherwise modify the terms of this agreement." The parties also usually specifically agree in the contract that they will accept the award of the arbitrator as "final and binding."

Some contracts provide for hearing and decision by a tripartite board composed of one member from each side and a third neutral member. For obvious reasons, such boards usually render split decisions, but it is sometimes helpful in a complex or technical case for the neutral member to have the assistance of the two partisan members after the hearing is over. Far more frequently the case will be heard and decided by a single arbitrator. In the great majority of cases, the single arbitrator will be chosen ad hoc for the particular grievance. If a large number of employees are covered by the contract and arbitration occurs with frequency, the parties may choose a permanent umpire to hear all their cases. Obviously, a permanent umpire can acquire a familiarity with the parties and their employment problems that an ad hoc arbitrator could not possess. Consider the advantages and disadvantages of use of a single arbitrator versus a tripartite board, and the advantages and disadvantages of use of an ad hoc arbitrator versus a permanent umpire. What advice on these matters would you give to a client who is engaged in negotiations for a new contract?

The arbitrator may be chosen by the parties on the basis of their personal knowledge of available arbitrators. Or the parties may request a panel of three, five, or seven qualified arbitrators in their area from either of two sources: the Federal Mediation and Conciliation Service, an agency of the U.S. Government, or the American Arbitration Association, a private nonprofit organization. Both sources maintain lists of several hundred qualified arbitrators throughout the nation. Although there is a growing number of full-time professionals, most arbitrators are lawyers or professors of law, labor economics, or some related subject, who arbitrate on a part-time basis.

Once the arbitrator is selected, arrangements will be made by mutual consent for the time and place of the hearing. The hearing will usually be held in a company conference room or a nearby hotel or motel room. Most arbitration hearings are completed in one or at most two days; longer hearings are exceptional. Normally, the arbitrator knows virtually nothing about the case before the hearing; most arbitrators consider themselves lucky if they have been given a copy of the contract in advance.

The issue may be submitted to the arbitrator at the beginning of the hearing in a "submission agreement" or it may be delineated in the grievance procedure papers. Occasionally the actual issue for the arbitrator will not emerge until well after the hearing has begun. The parties may or may not be represented by attorneys. Frequently the union's case will be presented by the business agent or an international representative; the company may be represented by the personnel or industrial relations manager. The hearing itself follows the general format of a court trial, but is much more informal. Both parties usually will make an opening statement setting forth their positions. Except in disciplinary cases, when the burden is on the company to justify its action, the union representing the grievant(s) will proceed first with its witnesses and documentary evidence. Witnesses usually are present in the hearing room without restriction.

When the union has completed its case, the company will then put on its own witnesses and evidence. All witnesses on both sides are fully subject to cross-examination. The parties may then proceed in turn as long as either side has anything it wishes to present. Since the arbitrator is an experienced and informed specialist, the rules of evidence which govern jury trials are not applicable. Objections may be made to proffered evidence, but the arbitrator usually confines the objection to the probative value of the evidence rather than to its admissibility. It is not infrequent, at the end of a witness' testimony, or at the end of the hearing, for the arbitrator to propound a series of questions to bring out information not previously adduced which he thinks he may need in deciding the case. In many cases the parties arrange for a court reporter, in which case the arbitrator will be provided with a copy of the transcript to use in deciding the case. If there is no reporter, the parties must rely on the arbitrator to take notes which, unless the arbitrator knows shorthand (a rarity), are necessarily incomplete. Nevertheless, a reporter is not used for most cases. Consider the advantages and disadvantages involved in the use of a reporter. What advice on this matter would you give to a client?

There are four practices concerning the filing of briefs. In many cases no briefs are filed. In a few cases prehearing briefs are filed with the arbitrator by the parties. In some cases briefs are exchanged at the hearing. In some cases posthearing briefs are filed. What are the advantages and disadvantages involved in each of these four practices? Under AAA rules the arbitrator has 30 days from the close of the case to render his decision. Frequently, however, busy arbitrators are required to obtain extensions of time. In rendering his decision, the arbitrator will give an award (analogous to the judgment of a court) which will be accompanied by an opinion setting forth the facts and the arguments together with an explanation of his decision. Since arbitration is a private matter between the parties, an arbitrator cannot reveal his award and opinion without their consent. With their consent he may submit his decisions to various publishing companies which publish bound volumes of arbitrator's decisions, appropriately categorized and indexed.

For their services arbitrators typically charge $350–$500 per day for travel, hearing, and decisional time, plus actual expenses. Most contracts provide that the cost of the arbitrator's services will be borne equally by the parties. The total cost to the parties, of course, includes not only the time spent by numerous people in the preparation and presentation of the case but also the attorney's and court reporter's fees, where applicable. Both of these, more often than not, are more expensive than the arbitrator.

Today arbitration is a highly professionalized service. In 1946 the National Academy of Arbitrators was founded. Since that time the Academy has delineated and promoted the performance and ethical standards to which its members are expected to subscribe. Membership is carefully screened, and today totals several hundred. Professionalization has been enhanced by a large amount of study, analysis, and critical commentary on every aspect of the arbitration process. The literature available is enormous and shows no signs of slackening in output. Some of the more useful works for beginners, as well as the experienced, are Elkouri and Elkouri, How Arbitration Works (1973); Fleming, The Labor Arbitration Process (1965); the Annual Proceedings of the National Academy of Arbitrators, published by BNA; and the Arbitration Journal, a quarterly published by the American Arbitration Association.

It must be emphasized that the arbitration process just summarized deals with grievance disputes which arise during the term of the contract and which usually center on differences in the meaning and application of the terms of the contract. An entirely different use of arbitration is in the resolution of bargaining disputes. If the parties are unable to agree during negotiations on the substantive terms to be included in their contract, they may decide to submit their differences to arbitration rather than resorting to economic contest. As would be expected, however, this kind of arbitration finds far less favor with the parties and is used far more rarely than grievance arbitration. A BLS survey of 1,717 contracts revealed that less than 2 percent of the contracts provided for arbitration of bargaining disputes.

The most common types of grievances appealed to arbitration involve discharge or suspension of an employee, seniority questions, and rates of pay. Other types of grievances involve work assignments, safety, subcontracting, vacation pay, holiday pay, etc. Many discharge cases generate much emotion. The parties may have stronger feelings about the discharge or reinstatement of a single employee than they do about a wage case involving many employees and a large sum of money. Thus, it is interesting to note the results of a study of 207 individual grievants in 145 establishments who had been discharged by their employers but who were reinstated by arbitrators. The results of the study are reflected in the following excerpts from Ross, *The Arbitration of Discharge Cases: What Happens After Reinstatement,* published in Critical Issues in Arbitration 21, 42–44 (1957):

"The most significant variable revealed in the questionnaires is seniority status. A majority of the grievants had five years or less seniority at the time of discharge. A majority of the short-service men did not take advantage of reinstatement, or were terminated after reinstatement. Those reinstated employees deemed unsatisfactory were practically all relatively junior, and a majority had less than two years at the time of discharge. Almost all the employees who encountered disciplinary troubles after reinstatement were in the junior group.

"About sixty percent of the grievants were discharged over dramatic and conspicuous episodes such as illegal strikes, assaults and acts of insubordination. The theory of corrective discipline has never been satisfactorily expounded in relation to this kind of offense, although it is clear enough with respect to continuing problems of a gradual character.

"The decision to reinstate was not typically based on a finding of innocence, or a refusal to find guilt. The most common grounds for reinstatement were that mitigating circumstances should be recognized, that discharge was an excessive penalty, and that the employer had failed to pursue a consistent disciplinary policy. Moreover, about seventy percent of the grievants were reinstated with no back pay or only partial retroactivity. Thus it is apparent that the discharge case most frequently becomes a review of the reasonableness of management's action rather than a trial of guilt or innocence.

"Ten percent of the employees did not return. Another twenty percent lasted less than a year. Fifty percent are no longer employed. But the normal rate of labor turnover in industry must be taken into account. Probably the reinstated employee is not more likely than other employees to resign, but is more likely to be discharged again.

"From an operational standpoint, about two-thirds of the cases have worked out well. Employers say that two-thirds of the reinstated employees have proved satisfactory. About sixty percent have reportedly made normal occupational progress, although there is reason to believe that the reinstated employee is less likely to be promoted. Seventy percent have presented no further disciplinary problems. The attitude of supervisors has been favorable or neutral in about seventy percent of the cases. The reinstated employee's attitude is described as good in about sixty percent of the cases. Since reinstatement creates a delicate human situation in the shop at best, these responses indicate a generally mature and far-sighted adjustment to the difficulties.

"A rather small proportion of the union questionnaires was returned.

"Nonetheless, it is surely of some significance that the unions did not complain of unfair treatment in a single case. In virtually every case the union reported that supervisors as well as grievants have displayed sound and favorable attitudes.

"Employers now believe that the decision to reinstate was correct in thirty-nine percent of the cases. By way of explanation, they stress principally the favorable outcome of the reinstatements. Employers disagree with sixty-one percent of the decisions, chiefly on the merits as they stood at the time of discharge. Thus the employer is more likely to approve of a reinstatement that works out well, and almost certain to disapprove of one that works out poorly.

"The unions agreed with the decision, and considered it worthwhile to have arbitrated the grievance, in almost every case. Unions believe they have a primary duty to support a discharged employee unless the merits of the discharge are clear."

2. COMPARATIVE NOTE

In many other industrial relations systems, adjudication of grievances has not been left in the hands of private arbitral tribunals.

In Canada, where institutional arrangements most closely resemble those of the United States, labor relations statutes typically provide that: (a) the parties must write no-strike and arbitration clauses into collective agreements, (b) in the event of their failure to do so, standard form clauses are deemed to be included, and (c) arbitrators enjoy certain procedural powers, including the right to administer oaths, subpoena witnesses, and enforce awards by registering them in court. See, *e.g.,* Ontario Labor Relations Act, Rev. Stat. Ont. 1960, c. 202, as amended, Sections 33, 34. However, the operation of the system otherwise closely conforms to the United States model.

In a number of European countries, labor courts perform some functions analogous to our arbitration boards (as well as many other functions). For example, in France the labor courts (*conseils de prud' hommes*) have jurisdiction only over disputes relating to individual employment contracts, in Germany over both individual and collective agreement disputes, and in Sweden over collective agreement disputes only.

The composition of these labor courts varies considerably. The French *conseils de prud' hommes* are decentralized geographically and by occupation, and bipartite, with provision for participation by a local judge to break a deadlock. In Germany and Sweden, labor courts are tripartite and presided over by law-trained neutrals with judicial rank.

Procedures likewise differ, with each country, formally or informally, placing some emphasis on compromise and conciliation prior to adjudication, to a greater extent than is common in the United States. Procedures at the adjudicative stage tend to be less formal, speedier, and cheaper than in the United States.

For a survey of the characteristics of these tribunals, and an analysis of their potential relevance to American labor law, see Aaron, *Labor Courts: Western European Models and Their Significance for the United States,* 16 UCLA L. Rev. 847 (1969) and Fleming, *The Labor Court Idea,* 65 Mich. L. Rev. 1551 (1967). For a fuller treatment see Aaron (ed.), Dispute Settlement Procedures in Five Western European Countries (1970).

C. JUDICIAL INTERVENTION

Section 301 of the Taft-Hartley Act was adopted partly in response to the fact that in some states a union could not be sued as a legal entity. A reading of Section 301, however, shows that its terms are not limited to suits by employers against unions. Although this section is applicable to a suit by an employer against a union for violation of a contract, unions have also used this section in suits against employers—as demonstrated by some of the following cases.

Section 301 also may be applicable to a suit by a union against a union. In *Plumbers* v. *Plumbers Local 334*, 452 U.S. 615, 107 LRRM 2715 (1981), the Supreme Court of the United States held that the constitution of an international union is a contract between labor organizations within the meaning of Section 301(a), and that a federal district court had jurisdiction over an action by a local union which alleged that the international union violated its constitution by ordering consolidation of some local unions. Writing for the majority of the Court, Justice Brennan noted that it was difficult, prior to 1947, to sue unions in state courts because of their status as unincorporated associations, that Congress wanted to make unions legally accountable for their contracts, and that Congress therefore conferred jurisdiction on federal courts, through Section 301(a), to enforce contracts made by labor organizations. Chief Justice Burger, and Justices Stevens and Rehnquist, dissented. Chief Justice Burger agreed that a union constitution is a contract. But he contended that it is a contract between a union and its members, and that union constitutions are not "contracts . . . between . . . labor organizations" under Section 301(a).

1. Agreements to Arbitrate and Arbitration Awards

By a common-law rule of ancient vintage agreements to arbitrate were freely revocable by either party; they were not specifically enforceable and their breach did not give rise to substantial damages. This common-law approach, developed in the context of commercial arbitration to protect the jurisdiction of the courts, was applied uncritically in more modern times to agreements to arbitrate in collective bargaining contracts. Some states have changed the rule by statute, and the United States Arbitration Act, enacted in 1925, 9 U.S.C. Sections 1–208 (1970), makes an agreement to arbitrate enforceable. But there is dispute over whether such statutes are applicable to agreements to arbitrate in collective bargaining contracts as distinguished from agreements to arbitrate in commercial or other types of contracts. On the other hand, an arbitration award was enforceable under the common law.

Textile Workers Union of America v. Lincoln Mills of Alabama

Supreme Court of the United States, 1957
353 U.S. 448, 40 LRRM 2113

Mr. Justice Douglas delivered the opinion of the Court.
Petitioner-union entered into a collective bargaining agreement in 1953 with respondent-employer, the agreement to run one year and from

year to year thereafter, unless terminated on specified notices. The agreement provided that there would be no strikes or work stoppages and that grievances would be handled pursuant to a specified procedure. The last step in the grievance procedure—a step that could be taken by either party—was arbitration.

This controversy involves several grievances that concern work loads and work assignments. The grievances were processed through the various steps in the grievance procedure and were finally denied by the employer. The union requested arbitration, and the employer refused. Thereupon the union brought this suit in the District Court to compel arbitration.

The District Court concluded that it had jurisdiction and ordered the employer to comply with the grievance arbitration provisions of the collective bargaining agreement. The Court of Appeals reversed by a divided vote. 230 F.2d 81. It held that, although the District Court had jurisdiction to entertain the suit, the court had no authority founded either in federal or state law to grant the relief. The case is here on a petition for a writ of certiorari which we granted because of the importance of the problem and the contrariety of views in the courts.

The starting point of our inquiry is § 301 of the Labor Management Relations Act of 1947, 61 Stat. 156, 29 U.S.C. § 185. . . .

There has been considerable litigation involving § 301 and courts have construed it differently. There is one view that § 301(a) merely gives federal district courts jurisdiction in controversies that involve labor organizaions in industries affecting commerce, without regard to diversity of citizenship or the amount in controversy. Under that view § 301(a) would not be the source of substantive law; it would neither supply federal law to resolve these controversies nor turn the federal judges to state law for answers to the questions. Other courts—the overwhelming number of them—hold that § 301(a) is more than jurisdictional—that it authorizes federal courts to fashion a body of federal law for the enforcement of these collective bargaining agreements and includes within that federal law specific performance of promises to arbitrate grievances under collective bargaining agreements. Perhaps the leading decision representing that point of view is the one rendered by Judge Wyzanski in *Textile Workers Union* v. *American Thread Co.*, 113 F. Supp. 137. That is our construction of § 301(a), which means that the agreement to arbitrate grievance disputes, contained in this collective bargaining agreement, should be specifically enforced.

From the face of the Act it is apparent that § 301(a) and § 301(b) supplement one another. Section 301(b) makes it possible for a labor organization, representing employees in an industry affecting commerce, to sue and be sued as an entity in the federal courts. Section 301(b) in other words provides the procedural remedy lacking at common law. Section 301(a) certainly does something more than that. Plainly, it supplies the basis upon which the federal district courts may take jurisdiction and apply the procedural rule of § 301(b). The question is whether § 301(a) is more than jurisdictional.

The legislative history of § 301 is somewhat cloudy and confusing. But there are a few shafts of light that illuminate our problem.

The bills, as they passed the House and the Senate, contained provisions which would have made the failure to abide by an agreement to arbitrate an unfair labor practice. S. Rep. No. 105, 80th Cong., 1st Sess., pp. 20–21, 23; H.R. Rep. No. 245, 80th Cong., 1st Sess., p. 21. This feature of the law was dropped in Conference. As the Conference Report stated, "Once parties have made a collective bargaining contract the enforcement of that contract should be left to the usual processes of the law and not to the National Labor Relations Board." H.R. Conf. Rep. No. 510, 80th Cong., 1st Sess., p. 42.

Both the Senate and the House took pains to provide for "the usual processes of the law" by provisions which were the substantial equivalent of § 301(a) in its present form. Both the Senate Report and the House Report indicate a primary concern that unions as well as employees should be bound to collective bargaining contracts. But there was also a broader concern—a concern with a procedure for making such agreements enforceable in the courts by either party. At one point the Senate Report, *supra*, p. 15, states, "We feel that the aggrieved party should also have a right of action in the Federal courts. Such a policy is completely in accord with the purpose of the Wagner Act which the Supreme Court declared was 'to compel employers to bargain collectively with their employees to the end that an employment contract, binding on both parties, should be made. . . .' "

Congress was also interested in promoting collective bargaining that ended with agreements not to strike. The Senate Report, *supra*, p. 16 states:

"If unions can break agreements with relative impunity, then such agreements do not tend to stabilize industrial relations. The execution of an agreement does not by itself promote industrial peace. The chief advantage which an employer can reasonably expect from a collective labor agreement is assurance of uninterrupted operation during the term of the agreement. Without some effective method of assuring freedom from economic warfare for the term of the agreement, there is little reason why an employer would desire to sign such a contract.

"Consequently, to encourage the making of agreements and to promote industrial peace through faithful performance by the parties, collective agreements affecting interstate commerce should be enforceable in the Federal courts. Our amendment would provide for suits by unions as legal entities and against unions as legal entities in the Federal courts in disputes affecting commerce."

Thus collective bargaining contracts were made "equally binding and enforceable on both parties." *Id.*, at p. 15. As stated in the House Report, *supra*, p. 6, the new provision "makes labor organizations equally responsible with employers for contract violations and provides for suit by either against the other in the United States district courts." To repeat, the Senate Report, *supra*, p. 17, summed up the philosophy of § 301 as follows: "Statutory recognition of the collective agreement as a valid, binding, and enforceable contract is a logical and necessary step. It will promote a higher degree of responsibility upon the parties to such agreements, and will thereby promote industrial peace."

Plainly the agreement to arbitrate grievance disputes is the quid pro quo for an agreement not to strike. Viewed in this light, the legislation does more than confer jurisdiction in the federal courts over labor organizations. It expresses a federal policy that federal courts should enforce these agreements on behalf of or against labor organizations and that industrial peace can be best obtained only in that way.

To be sure, there is a great medley of ideas reflected in the hearings, reports, and debates on this Act. Yet, to repeat, the entire tenor of the history indicates that the agreement to arbitrate grievance disputes was considered as quid pro quo of a no-strike agreement. And when in the House the debate narrowed to the question whether § 301 was more than jurisdictional, it became abundantly clear that the purpose of the section was to provide the necessary legal remedies. Section 302 of the House Bill, the substantial equivalent of the present § 301, was being described by Mr. Hartley, the sponsor of the bill in the House:

> "MR. BARDEN. Mr. Chairman, I take this time for the purpose of asking the Chairman a question, and in asking the question I want it understood that it is intended to make a part of the record that may hereafter be referred to as history of the legislation.
>
> "It is my understanding that section 302, the section dealing with equal responsibility under collective bargaining contracts in strike actions and proceedings in district courts contemplates not only the ordinary lawsuits for damages but also such other remedial proceedings, both legal and equitable, as might be appropriate in the circumstances; in other words, proceedings could, for example, be brought by the employers, the labor organizations, or interested individual employees under the Declaratory Judgments Act in order to secure declarations from the Court of legal rights under the contract.
>
> "MR. HARTLEY. The interpretation the gentleman has given of that section is absolutely correct." 93 Cong. Rec. 3656–3657.

It seems, therefore, clear to us that Congress adopted a policy which placed sanctions behind agreements to arbitrate grievance disputes, by implication rejecting the common-law rule, discussed in *Red Cross Line* v. *Atlantic Fruit Co.,* 264 U.S. 109, against enforcement of executory agreements to arbitrate. We would undercut the Act and defeat its policy if we read § 301 narrowly as only conferring jurisdiction over labor organizations.

The question then is, what is the substantive law to be applied in suits under § 301(a)? We conclude that the substantive law to apply in suits under § 301(a) is federal law, which the courts must fashion from the policy of our national labor laws. See Mendelsohn, *Enforceability of Arbitration Agreements Under Taft-Hartley Section 301,* 66 Yale L.J. 167. The Labor Management Relations Act expressly furnishes some substantive law. It points out what the parties may or may not do in certain situations. Other problems will lie in the penumbra of express statutory mandates. Some will lack express statutory sanction but will be solved by looking at the policy of the legislation and fashioning a remedy that will effectuate that policy. The range of judicial inventiveness will be determined by the nature of the problem. See *Board of Commissioners v. United States*, 308 U.S. 343, 351. Federal interpretation of the federal law will govern, not state law. Cf. *Jerome v. United States*, 318 U.S. 101, 104. But state law, if compatible with the purpose of § 301, may be resorted to in order to find the rule that will best effectuate the federal policy. See *Board of Commissioners v. United States, supra*, at 351–352. Any state law applied, however, will be absorbed as federal law and will not be an independent source of private rights.

It is not uncommon for federal courts to fashion federal law where federal rights are concerned. See *Clearfield Trust Co. v. United States*, 318 U.S. 363, 366–367; *National Metropolitan Bank v. United States*, 323 U.S. 454. Congress has indicated by § 301(a) the purpose to follow that course here. There is no constitutional difficulty. Article III, § 2, extends the judicial power to cases "arising under . . . the Laws of the United States. . . ." The power of Congress to regulate these labor-management controversies under the Commerce Clause is plain. *Houston & Texas R. Co. v. United States*, 234 U.S. 342; *Labor Board v. Jones & Laughlin Corp.*, 301 U.S. 1. A case or controversy arising under § 301(a) is, therefore, one within the purview of judicial power as defined in Article III.

The question remains whether jurisdiction to compel arbitration of grievance disputes is withdrawn by the Norris-LaGuardia Act, 47 Stat. 70, 29 U.S.C. § 101. Section 7 of that Act prescribes stiff procedural requirements for issuing an injunction in a labor dispute. The kinds of acts which had given rise to abuse of the power to enjoin are listed in § 4. The failure to arbitrate was not a part and parcel of the abuses against which the Act was aimed. Section 8 of the Norris-LaGuardia Act does, indeed, indicate a congressional policy toward settlement of labor disputes by arbitration, for it denies injunctive relief to any person who has failed to make "every reasonable effort" to settle the dispute by negotiation, mediation, or "voluntary arbitration." Though a literal reading might bring the dispute within the terms of the Act (see Cox, *Grievance Arbitration in the Federal Courts*, 67 Harv. L. Rev. 591, 602–604), we see no justification in policy for restricting § 301(a) to damage suits, leaving specific performance of a contract to arbitrate grievance disputes to the inapposite procedural requirements of that Act. Moreover, we held in *Virginian R. Co. v. System Federation*, 300 U.S. 515, and in *Graham v. Brotherhood of Firemen*, 338 U.S. 232, 237, that the Norris-LaGuardia Act does not deprive federal courts of jurisdiction to compel compliance with the mandates of the Railway Labor Act. The mandates there involved concerned racial discrimination. Yet those decisions were not based on any peculiarities of the Railway Labor Act. We followed the same course in *Syres v. Oil Workers International Union*, 350 U.S. 892, which was governed by the National Labor Relations Act. There an injunction was sought against racial discrimination in application of a collective bargaining agreement; and we allowed the injunction to issue. The congressional policy in favor of the enforcement of agreements to arbitrate grievance disputes being clear, there is no reason to submit them to the requirements of § 7 of the Norris-LaGuardia Act.

A question of mootness was raised on oral argument. It appears that since the date of decision in the Court of Appeals respondent has terminated its operations and has contracted to sell its mill properties. All work in the mill ceased in March, 1957. Some of the grievances, however, ask for back pay for increased workloads; and the collective bargaining agreement provides that "the Board of Arbitration shall have the right to adjust compensation retroactive to the date of the change." Insofar as the grievances sought restoration of workloads and job assignments, the case is, of course, moot. But to the extent that they sought a monetary award, the case is a continuing controversy.

The judgment of the Court of Appeals is reversed and the cause is remanded to that court for proceedings in conformity with this opinion.

MR. JUSTICE BLACK took no part in the consideration or decision of this case.

MR. JUSTICE BURTON and MR. JUSTICE HARLAN concur in the result.

Notes

1. In his dissent in *Lincoln Mills* Justice Frankfurter wrote a 25-page opinion, with a 61-page appendix of legislative history, in support of his conclusions that Section 301 was purely jurisdictional, that jurisdiction could not properly be based on the existence of a federal question, and that Section 301 was beyond the scope of Article III of the Constitution since diversity of citizenship was not required.

2. Despite *Lincoln Mills*, in *UAW-CIO* v. *Hoosier Cardinal Corp.*, 383 U.S. 696, 61 LRRM 2545 (1966), the Court declined to use "judicial inventiveness" to provide a national statute of limitations for actions under Section 301. The Court upheld application of an Indiana six-year statute of limitations to an employees' suit for vacation pay. But see note 5 on page 674.

Problem

The union files a grievance alleging that subcontracting of laboratory work by Enderby Company violates the agreement. In the course of grievance discussion the company cites the management rights clause which reads as follows: "Except as expressly limited by specific provisions of this agreement the company retains the sole exclusive right to manage the business and to exercise every right or power necessary or incidental thereto. The exercise of such rights shall not be subject to arbitration." Management argues that this clause permits the action in question, and that no specific provision of the agreement prevents it. The union argues that subcontracting of bargaining unit work violates the following provision of the contract: "*Recognition.* The company recognizes the union as the exclusive bargaining agent for all its employees as specified in the certification of representation in NLRB case 26–RC–1729."

When grievance discussions fail to resolve the problem, the union files a demand for arbitration with the local office of the American Arbitration Association, which, under the agreement, is designated to supply a list of arbitrators and handle the administrative details of setting up the arbitration. The company refuses to submit the question to arbitration, asserting that under the last sentence of the management rights clause the matter is not arbitrable.

The union brings an action against the company in federal district court under Section 301 of the LMRA to compel arbitration.

Questions

1. If you were the law clerk to the district judge, would you advise the judge to order the parties to proceed to arbitration? On what authority?

2. If you were representing the company, how would you have drafted a clause to keep matters of this sort from going to arbitration? Is it tactically advantageous to raise questions of arbitrability before the court rather than before an arbitrator?

The Trilogy

The next three principal cases were decided by the Court at the same time in 1960. They are known as "The Trilogy."

In *American Manufacturing* the Court repudiates the *Cutler-Hammer* doctrine which had developed in New York where, by statute, agreements to arbitrate were enforceable. Under the *Cutler-Hammer* doctrine a court, in passing on the question of arbitrability before requiring arbitration, could refuse to order arbitration of disputes which it thought were clearly without merit. Subsequent to the decision in *American Manufacturing* the *Cutler-Hammer* doctrine was rejected in New York by amendment of the state law.

United Steelworkers of America v. American Manufacturing Co.

Supreme Court of the United States, 1960
363 U.S. 564, 46 LRRM 2414

MR. JUSTICE DOUGLAS delivered the opinion of the Court.

This suit was brought by petitioner union in the District Court to compel arbitration of a "grievance" that petitioner, acting for one Sparks, a union member, had filed with the respondent, Sparks' employer. The employer defended on the ground (1) that Sparks is estopped from making his claim because he had a few days previously settled a workmen's compensation claim against the company on the basis that he was permanently partially disabled, (2) that Sparks is not physically able to do the work, and (3) that this type of dispute is not arbitrable under the collective bargaining agreement in question.

The agreement provided that during its term there would be "no strike," unless the employer refused to abide by a decision of the arbitrator. The agreement sets out a detailed grievance procedure with a provision for arbitration (regarded as a standard form) of all disputes between the parties "as to the meaning, interpretation and application of the provisions of this agreement."[1]

The agreement reserves to the management power to suspend or discharge any employee "for cause."[2] It also contains a provision that the employer will employ and promote employees on the principle of seniority "where ability and efficiency are equal." Sparks left his work due to an injury and while off work brought an action for compensation benefits. The case was settled, Sparks' physician expressing the opinion that the injury had made him 25 percent "permanently partially disabled." That was on September 9. Two weeks later the union filed a grievance which charged that Sparks was entitled to return to his job by virtue of the seniority provision of the collective bargaining agreement. Respondent refused to arbitrate and this action was brought. The District Court held that Sparks, having accepted the settlement on the basis of permanent partial disability, was estopped to claim any seniority or employment rights and granted the motion for summary judgment. The Court of Appeals affirmed, 264 F.2d 624, for different reasons. After reviewing the evidence it held that the grievance is "a frivolous, patently baseless one, not subject to arbitration under the collective bargaining agreement." *Id.*, at 628. The case is here on a writ of certiorari, 361 U.S. 881.

Section 203(d) of the Labor Management Relations Act, 1947, 61 Stat. 154, 29 U.S.C. § 173(d), states, "Final adjustment by a method agreed upon by the parties is hereby declared to be the desirable method for settlement of grievance disputes arising over the application or interpretation of an existing collective-bargaining agreement. . . ." That policy can be effectuated only if the means chosen by the parties for settlement of their differences under a collective bargaining agreement is given full play.

[1]The relevant arbitration provisions read as follows:

"Any disputes, misunderstandings, differences or grievances arising between the parties as to the meaning, interpretation and application of the provisions of this agreement, which are not adjusted as herein provided, may be submitted to the Board of Arbitration for decision. . . .

"The arbitrator may interpret this agreement and apply it to the particular case under consideration but shall, however, have no authority to add to, subtract from, or modify the terms of the agreement. Disputes relating to discharges or such matters as might involve a loss of pay for employees may carry an award of back pay in whole or in part as may be determined by the Board of Arbitration.

"The decision of the Board of Arbitration shall be final and conclusively binding upon both parties, and the parties agree to observe and abide by same. . . ."

[2]"The Management of the works, the direction of the working force, plant layout and routine of work, including the right to hire, suspend, transfer, discharge or otherwise discipline any employee for cause, such cause being: infraction of company rules, inefficiency, insubordination, contagious disease harmful to others, and any other ground or reason that would tend to reduce or impair the efficiency of plant operation; and to lay off employees because of lack of work, is reserved to the Company, provided it does not conflict with this agreement. . . ."

A state decision that held to the contrary announced a principle that could only have a crippling effect on grievance arbitration. The case was *International Assn. of Machinists* v. *Culter-Hammer, Inc.*, 271 App. Div. 917, 67 N.Y.S.2d 317, *aff'd*, 297 N.Y. 519, 74 N.E.2d 464. It held that "If the meaning of the provision of the contract sought to be arbitrated is beyond dispute, there cannot be anything to arbitrate and the contract cannot be said to provide for arbitration." 271 App. Div., at 918, 67 N.Y.S.2d, at 318. The lower courts in the instant case had a like preoccupation with ordinary contract law. The collective agreement requires arbitration of claims that courts might be unwilling to entertain. In the context of the plant or industry the grievance may assume proportions of which judges are ignorant. Yet, the agreement is to submit all grievances to arbitration, not merely those that a court may deem to be meritorious. There is no exception in the "no strike" clause and none therefore should be read into the grievance clause, since one is the quid pro quo for the other. The question is not whether in the mind of the court there is equity in the claim. Arbitration is a stabilizing influence only as it serves as a vehicle for handling any and all disputes that arise under the agreement.

The collective agreement calls for the submission of grievances in the categories which it describes, irrespective of whether a court may deem them to be meritorious. In our role of developing a meaningful body of law to govern the interpretation and enforcement of collective bargaining agreements, we think special heed should be given to the context in which collective bargaining agreements are negotiated and the purpose which they are intended to serve. See *Lewis* v. *Benedict Coal Corp.*, 361 U.S. 459, 468. The function of the court is very limited when the parties have agreed to submit all questions of contract interpretation to the arbitrator. It is confined to ascertaining whether the party seeking arbitration is making a claim which on its face is governed by the contract. Whether the moving party is right or wrong is a question of contract intepretation for the arbitrator. In these circumstances the moving party should not be deprived of the arbitrator's judgment, when it was his judgment and all that it connotes that was bargained for.

The courts, therefore, have no business weighing the merits of the grievance, considering whether there is equity in a particular claim, or determining whether there is particular language in the written instrument which will support the claim. The agreement is to submit all grievances to arbitration, not merely those which the court will deem meritorious. The processing of even frivolous claims may have therapeutic values of which those who are not a part of the plant environment may be quite unaware.

The union claimed in this case that the company had violated a specific provision of the contract. The company took the position that it had not violated that clause. There was, therefore, a dispute between the parties as to "the meaning, interpretation and application" of the collective bargaining agreement. Arbitration should have been ordered. When the judiciary undertakes to determine the merits of a grievance under the guise of interpreting the grievance procedure of collective bargaining agreements, it usurps a function which under that regime is entrusted to the arbitration tribunal.

Reversed.

MR. JUSTICE FRANKFURTER and MR. JUSTICE WHITTAKER concur in the result.

MR. JUSTICE BLACK took no part in the consideration or decision of this case.

United Steelworkers of America v. Warrior & Gulf Navigation Co.

Supreme Court of the United States, 1960
363 U.S. 574, 46 LRRM 2416

MR. JUSTICE DOUGLAS delivered the opinion of the Court.

Respondent transports steel and steel products by barge and maintains a terminal at Chickasaw, Alabama, where it performs maintenance and repair work on its barges. The employees at that terminal constitute a bargaining unit covered by a collective bargaining agreement negotiated by petitioner union. Respondent between 1956 and 1958 laid off some employees, reducing the bargaining unit from 42 to 23 men. This reduction was due in part to respondent contracting maintenance work, previously done by its employees, to other companies. The latter used respondent's supervisors to lay out the work and hired some of the laid-off employees of respondent (at reduced wages). Some were in fact assigned to work on respondent's barges. A number of employees signed a grievance which petitioner presented to respondent, the grievance reading:

"We are hereby protesting the Company's actions, of arbitrarily and unreasonably contracting out work to other concerns, that could and previously has been performed by Company employees.

"This practice becomes unreasonable, unjust and discriminatory in lieu [*sic*] of the fact that at present there are a number of employees that have been laid off for about 1 and ½ years or more for allegedly lack of work.

"Confronted with these facts we charge that the Company is in violation of the contract by inducing a partial lock-out, of a number of the employees who would otherwise be working were it not for this unfair practice."

The collective agreement had both a "no strike" and a "no-lockout" provision. It also had a grievance procedure which provided in relevant part as follows:

"Issues which conflict with any Federal statute in its application as established by Court procedure or matters which are strictly a function of management shall not be subject to arbitration under this section.

"Should differences arise between the Company and the Union or its members employed by the Company as to the meaning and application of the provisions of this Agreement, or should any local trouble of any kind arise, there shall be no suspension of work on account of such differences but an earnest effort shall be made to settle such differences immediately in the following manner:

"A. For Maintenance Employees:
"First, between the aggrieved employees, and the Foreman involved;
"Second, between a member or members of the Grievance Committee designated by the Union, and the Foreman and Master Mechanic.
. . .

"Fifth, if agreement has not been reached the matter shall be referred to an impartial umpire for decision. The parties shall meet to decide on an umpire acceptable to both. If no agreement on selection of an umpire is reached, the parties shall jointly petition the United States Conciliation Service for suggestion of a list of umpires from which selection will be made. The decision of the umpire shall be final."

Settlement of this grievance was not had and respondent refused arbitration. This suit was then commenced by the union to compel it.

The District Court granted respondent's motion to dismiss the complaint. 168 F. Supp. 702. It held after hearing evidence, much of which went to the merits of the grievance, that the agreement did not "confide in an arbitrator the right to review the defendant's business judgment in contracting out work." *Id.*, at 705. It further held that "the contracting out of repair and maintenance work, as well as construction work, is strictly a function of management not limited in any respect by the labor agreement involved here." *Ibid.* The Court of Appeals affirmed by a divided vote, 269 F.2d 633, the majority holding that the collective agreement had withdrawn from the grievance procedure "matters which are strictly a function of management" and that contracting out fell in that exception. The case is here on a writ of certiorari. 361 U.S. 912.

We held in *Textile Workers* v. *Lincoln Mills*, 353 U.S. 448, that a grievance arbitration provision in a collective agreement could be enforced by reason of § 301(a) of the Labor Management Relations Act and that the policy to be applied in enforcing this type of arbitration was that reflected in our national labor laws. *Id.*, at 456, 457. The present federal policy is to promote industrial stabilization through the collective bargaining agreement. *Id.*, at 453–454. A major factor in achieving industrial peace is the inclusion of a provision for arbitration of grievances in the collective bargaining agreement.

Thus the run of arbitration cases, illustrated by *Wilko* v. *Swan*, 346 U.S. 427, becomes irrelevant to our problem. There the choice is between the adjudication of cases or controversies in courts with established procedures or even special statutory safeguards on the one hand and the settlement of them in the more informal arbitration tribunal on the other. In the commercial case, arbitration is the substitute for litigation. Here arbitration is the substitute for industrial strife. Since arbitration of labor disputes has quite different functions from arbitration under an ordinary commercial agreement, the hostility evinced by courts toward arbitration of commercial agreements has no place here. For arbitration of labor disputes under collective bargaining agreements is part and parcel of the collective bargaining process itself.

The collective bargaining agreement states the rights and duties of the parties. It is more than a contract; it is a generalized code to govern a myriad of cases which the draftsmen cannot wholly anticipate. See Shulman, *Reason, Contract, and Law in Labor Relations,* 68 Harv. L. Rev. 999, 1004–1005. The collective agreement covers the whole employment relationship. It calls into being a new common law—the common law of a particular industry or of a particular plant. As one observer has put it:

> ". . . [I]t is not unqualifiedly true that a collective bargaining agreement is simply a document by which the union and employees have imposed upon management limited, express restrictions of its otherwise absolute right to manage the enterprise, so that an employee's claim must fail unless he can point to a specific contract provision upon which the claim is founded. There are too many people, too many problems, too many unforeseeable contingencies to make the words of the contract the exclusive source of rights and duties. One cannot reduce all the rules governing a community like an industrial plant to fifteen or even fifty pages. Within the sphere of collective bargaining, the institutional characteristics and the governmental nature of the collective-bargaining process demand a common law of the shop which implements and furnishes the context of the agreement. We must assume that intelligent negotiators acknowledged so plain a need unless they stated a contrary rule in plain words."

A collective bargaining agreement is an effort to erect a system of industrial self-government. When most parties enter into contractual relationship, they do so voluntarily, in the sense that there is no real compulsion to deal with one another, as opposed to dealing with other parties. This is not true of the labor agreement. The choice is generally not between entering or refusing to enter into a relationship, for that in all probability preexists the negotiations. Rather it is between having that relationship governed by an agreed-upon rule of law or leaving each and every matter subject to a temporary resolution dependent solely upon the relative strength, at any given moment, of the contending forces. The mature labor agreement may attempt to regulate all aspects of the complicated relationship, from the most crucial to the most minute over an extended period of time. Because of the compulsion to reach agreement and the breadth of the matters covered, as well as the need for a fairly concise and readable instrument, the product of negotiations (the written document) is, in the words of the late Dean Shulman, "a compilation of diverse provisions: some provide objective criteria almost automatically applicable; some provide more or less specific standards which require reason and judgment in their application; and some do little more than leave problems to future consideration with an expression of hope and good faith." Shulman, *supra,* at 1005. Gaps may be left to be filled in by reference to the practices of the particular industry and of the various shops covered by the agreement. Many of the specific practices which underlie the agreement may be unknown, except in hazy form, even to the negotiators. Courts and arbitration in the context of most commercial contracts are resorted to because there has been a breakdown in the working relationship of the parties; such resort is the unwanted exception. But the grievance machinery under a collective bargaining agreement is at the very heart of the system of industrial self-government. Arbitration is the means of solving the unforeseeable by molding a system of private law for all the problems which may arise and to provide for their solution in a way which will generally accord with the variant needs and desires of the parties. The processing of disputes through the grievance machinery is actually a vehicle by which meaning and content are given to the collective bargaining agreement.

Apart from matters that the parties specifically exclude, all of the questions on which the parties disagree must therefore come within the scope of the grievance and arbitration provisions of the collective agreement. The grievance procedure is, in other words, a part of the continuous collective bargaining process. It, rather than a strike, is the terminal point of a disagreement.

The labor arbitrator performs functions which are not normal to the courts; the considerations which help him fashion judgments may indeed be foreign to the competence of courts.

"A proper conception of the arbitrator's function is basic. He is not a public tribunal imposed upon the parties by superior authority which the parties are obliged to accept. He has no general charter to administer justice for a community which transcends the parties. He is rather part of a system of self-government created by and confined to the parties. . . ." Shulman, *supra,* at 1016.

The labor arbitrator's source of law is not confined to the express provisions of the contract, as the industrial common law—the practices of the industry and the shop are equally a part of the collective bargaining agreement although not expressed in it. The labor arbitrator is usually chosen because of the parties' confidence in his knowledge of the common law of the shop and their trust in his personal judgment to bring to bear considerations which are not expressed in the contract as criteria for judgment. The parties expect that his judgment of a particular grievance will reflect not only what the contract says but, insofar as the collective bargaining agreement permits, such factors as the effect upon productivity of a particular result, its consequence to the morale of the shop, his judgment whether tensions will be heightened or diminished. For the parties' objective in using the arbitration process is primarily to further their common goal of uninterrupted production under the agreement, to make the agreement serve their specialized needs. The ablest judge cannot be expected to bring the same experience and competence to bear upon the determination of a grievance, because he cannot be similarly informed.

The Congress, however, has by § 301 of the Labor Management Relations Act, assigned the courts the duty of determining whether the reluctant party has breached his promise to arbitrate. For arbitration is a matter of contract and a party cannot be required to submit to arbitration any dispute which he has not agreed so to submit. Yet, to be consistent with congressional policy in favor of settlement of disputes by the parties through the machinery of arbitration, the judicial inquiry under § 301 must be strictly confined to the question whether the reluctant party did agree to arbitrate the grievance or did agree to give the arbitrator power to make the award he made. An order to arbitrate the particular grievance should not be denied unless it may be said with positive assurance that the arbitration clause is not susceptible of an interpretation that covers the asserted dispute. Doubts should be resolved in favor of coverage.[7]

We do not agree with the lower courts that contracting-out grievances were necessarily excepted from the grievance procedure of this agreement. To be sure, the agreement provides that "matters which are strictly a function of management shall not be subject to arbitration." But it goes on to say that if "differences" arise or if "any local trouble of any kind" arises, the grievance procedure shall be applicable.

Collective bargaining agreements regulate or restrict the exercise of management functions; they do not oust management from the performance of them. Management hires and fires, pays and promotes, supervises and plans. All these are part of its function, and absent a collective bargaining agreement, it may be exercised freely except as limited by public law and by the willingness of employees to work under the particular, unilaterally imposed conditions. A collective bargaining agreement may treat only with certain specific practices, leaving the rest to management but subject to the possibility of work stoppages. When, however, an absolute no-strike clause is included in the agreement, then in a very real sense everything that management does is subject to the agreement, for either management is prohibited or limited in the action it takes, or if not, it is protected from interference by strikes. This comprehensive reach of the collective bargaining agreement does not mean, however, that the language, "strictly a function of management," has no meaning.

"Strictly a function of management" might be thought to refer to any practice of management in which, under particular circumstances prescribed by the agreement, it is permitted to indulge. But if courts, in order to determine arbitrability, were allowed to determine what is permitted and what is not, the arbitration clause would be swallowed up by the exception. Every grievance in a sense involves a claim that management has violated some provision of the agreement.

Accordingly, "strictly a function of management" must be interpreted as referring only to that over which the contract gives management

---

[7]It is clear that both under the agreement in this case and that involved in *American Manufacturing Co.* . . . , the question of arbitrability is for the courts to decide. . . . Where the assertion by the claimant is that the parties excluded from court determination not merely the decision of the merits of the grievance but also the question of its arbitrability, vesting power to make both decisions in the arbitrator, the claimant must bear the burden of a clear demonstration of that purpose.

complete control and unfettered discretion. Respondent claims that the contracting out of work falls within this category. Contracting out work is the basis of many grievances; and that type of claim is grist in the mills of the arbitrators. A specific collective bargaining agreement may exclude contracting out from the grievance procedure. Or a written collateral agreement may make clear that contracting out was not a matter for arbitration. In such a case a grievance based solely on contracting out would not be arbitrable. Here, however, there is no such provision. Nor is there any showing that the parties designed the phrase "strictly a function of management" to encompass any and all forms of contracting out. In the absence of any express provision excluding a particular grievance from arbitration, we think only the most forceful evidence of a purpose to exclude the claim from arbitration can prevail, particularly where, as here, the exclusion clause is vague and the arbitration clause quite broad. Since any attempt by a court to infer such a purpose necessarily comprehends the merits, the court should view with suspicion an attempt to persuade it to become entangled in the construction of the substantive provisions of a labor agreement, even through the back door of interpreting the arbitration clause, when the alternative is to utilize the services of an arbitrator.

The grievance alleged that the contracting out was a violation of the collective bargaining agreement. There was, therefore, a dispute "as to the meaning and application of the provisions of this Agreement" which the parties had agreed would be determined by arbitration.

The judiciary sits in these cases to bring into operation an arbitral process which substitutes a regime of peaceful settlement for the older regime of industrial conflict. Whether contracting out in the present case violated the agreement is the question. It is a question for the arbiter, not for the courts.

Reversed.

MR. JUSTICE FRANKFURTER concurs in the result. MR. JUSTICE BLACK took no part in the consideration of the case. MR. JUSTICE WHITTAKER dissents.

Note

In *Nolde Bros.* v. *Bakery Workers*, 430 U.S. 243, 94 LRRM 2753 (1977), the Court held that an employer may have a duty to arbitrate a dispute based on events occurring after expiration of the collective bargaining agreement. In that case the contract (which provided for submission of all grievances to arbitration) terminated on August 27. The employer then closed his plant on August 31. Shortly thereafter the displaced employees sought severance pay under the terms of the expired agreement. The Court required the employer to arbitrate the claim for severance pay, holding that the presumptions favoring arbitrability must be negated expressly or by clear implication where the dispute is over an obligation arguably created by the provisions of an expired contract. The Court viewed the resolution of the claim for severance pay as hinging on the interpretation of the contract clause providing for severance pay. The Court added that it would not speculate as to the arbitrability of post-termination contractual claims which are not asserted within a reasonable time after the contract's expiration.

If the provision for arbitration extends beyond expiration of the collective bargaining agreement, should a no-strike clause in that agreement be deemed to extend beyond expiration of the contract? In *Goya Foods, Inc.*, 238 NLRB 1465, 1466–67, 99 LRRM 1282, 1283–84 (1978), the NLRB noted that "In *Nolde* the Supreme Court adopted the rule that the contractual duty to arbitrate disputes arising out of or during the term of a collective bargaining agreement extends beyond the date of expiration of that agreement . . . ," and that it would "be anomalous if an employer, who would be contractually bound to arbitrate a certain dispute after contract expiration, could still be subjected to economic pressure that would be protected." Finding that "the no-strike clause . . . has coterminous application with [the] duty to arbitrate," the Board concluded that employees who were discharged because they went on strike the day after expiration of the collective bargaining agreement (to protest the discharge of co-workers shortly before expiration of the contract) were not entitled to reinstatement because such strike was unprotected. The Board reasoned that: "The agreement 'lives' on in the duty to arbitrate; so should the duty not to strike live on to the extent of the duty to arbitrate over issues created by or arising out of the expired agreement."

Problem

Assume that, in order to avoid litigation or as a result of rulings by a federal district court or by the NLRB, the Enderby Company agrees to arbitrate the question of the right of the company to subcontract its laboratory work to Dunbar Testing, Inc., an independent concern.

Questions

1. How should the arbitrator decide the case? Assume that the contract between the union and the Enderby Company contains a typical management rights provision and a typical recognition of the union provision. What other criteria would be helpful to the arbitrator?

2. Should the arbitrator hold that the union acquiesced in management's right to take the action in question if the union sought but failed to obtain language limiting the right to control bargaining unit work? How could the union have prevented such a demand from backfiring against it now?

3. If the union attempts to introduce testimony at the arbitration hearing to explain how it interpreted the dropping of such a demand, should the arbitrator permit such testimony over the objection of the company?

4. If a federal district court rules in a Section 301 proceeding to compel arbitration that the grievance is arbitrable, may the arbitrator rule that it is not arbitrable?

5. If the arbitrator sustains the grievance and orders Enderby Company to discontinue the subcontracting, what standards should be employed by a federal district court which is asked by Enderby Company to vacate the award?

6. May an arbitrator properly rely on external law (such as the NLRA or the Civil Rights Act) as *a* basis, or *the* basis, for an arbitration award? Or should the arbitrator base the award solely on the terms of the collective bargaining agreement? These questions should be considered in greater depth in connection with subsequent sections of this chapter which deal with Board Deferral to Arbitration Awards and Relationship of Arbitration and Title VII.

United Steelworkers of America v. Enterprise Wheel and Car Corp.

Supreme Court of the United States, 1960
363 U.S. 593, 46 LRRM 2423

Mr. Justice Douglas delivered the opinion of the court.

Petitioner union and respondent during the period relevant here had a collective bargaining agreement which provided that any differences "as to the meaning and application" of the agreement should be submitted to arbitration and that the arbitrator's decision "shall be final and binding on the parties." Special provisions were included concerning the suspension and discharge of employees. The agreement stated:

"Should it be determined by the Company or by an arbitrator in accordance with the grievance procedure that the employee has been suspended unjustly or discharged in violation of the provisions of this Agreement, the Company shall reinstate the employee and pay full compensation at the employee's regular rate of pay for the time lost."

The agreement also provided:

". . . It is understood and agreed that neither party will institute *civil suits or legal proceedings* against the other for alleged violation of any of the provisions of this labor contract; instead all disputes will be settled in the manner outlined in this Article III—Adjustments of Grievances."

A group of employees left their jobs in protest against the discharge of one employee. A union official advised them at once to return to work. An official of respondent at their request gave them permission and then rescinded it. The next day they were told they did not have a job any more "until this thing was settled one way or the other."

A grievance was filed; and when respondent finally refused to arbitrate, this suit was brought for specific enforcement of the arbitration provisions of the agreement. The District Court ordered arbitration. The arbitrator found that the discharge of the men was not justified, though their conduct, he said, was improper. In his view the facts warranted at most a suspension of the men for 10 days each. After their discharge and before the arbitration award the collective bargaining agreement had expired. The union, however, continued to represent the workers at the plant. The arbitrator rejected the contention that expiration of the agreement barred reinstatement of the employees. He held that the provision of the agreement above quoted imposed an unconditional obligation on the employer. He awarded reinstatement with back pay, minus pay for a 10-day suspension and such sums as these employees received from other employment.

Respondent refused to comply with the award. Petitioner moved the District Court for enforcement. The District Court directed respondent to comply. 168 F. Supp. 308. The Court of Appeals, while agreeing that the District Court had jurisdiction to enforce an arbitration award under a collective bargaining agreement, held that the failure of the award to specify the amounts to be deducted from the back pay rendered the award unenforceable. That defect, it agreed, could be remedied by requiring the parties to complete the arbitration. It went on to hold, however, that an award for back pay subsequent to the date of termination of the collective bargaining agreement could not be enforced. It also held that the requirement for reinstatement of the discharged employees was likewise unenforceable because the collective bargaining agreement had expired. 269 F.2d 327. We granted certiorari. 351 U.S. 929.

The refusal of courts to review the merits of an arbitration award is the proper approach to arbitration under collective bargaining agreements. The federal policy of settling labor disputes by arbitration would be undermined if courts had the final say on the merits of the awards. As we stated in *United Steelworkers of America* v. *Warrior & Gulf Navigation Co.*, decided this day, the arbitrators under these collective agreements are indispensable agencies in a continuous collective bargaining process. They sit to settle disputes at the plant level—disputes that require for their solution knowledge of the custom and practices of a particular factory or of a particular industry as reflected in particular agreements.

When an arbitrator is commissioned to interpret and apply the collective bargaining agreement, he is to bring his informed judgment to bear in order to reach a fair solution of a problem. This is especially true when it comes to formulating remedies. There the need is for flexibility in meeting a wide variety of situations. The draftsmen may never have thought of what specific remedy should be awarded to meet a particular contingency. Nevertheless, an arbitrator is confined to interpretation and application of the collective bargaining agreement; he does not sit to dispense his own brand of industrial justice. He may of course look for guidance from many sources, yet his award is legitimate only so long as it draws its essence from the collective bargaining agreement. When the arbitrator's words manifest an infidelity to this obligation, courts have no choice but to refuse enforcement of the award.

The opinion of the arbitrator in this case, as it bears upon the award of back pay beyond the date of the agreement's expiration and reinstatement, is ambiguous. It may be read as based solely upon the arbitrator's view of the requirements of enacted legislation, which would mean that he exceeded the scope of the submission. Or it may be read as embodying a construction of the agreement itself, perhaps with the arbitrator looking to "the law" for help in determining the sense of the agreement. A mere ambiguity in the opinion accompanying an award, which permits the inference that the arbitrator may have exceeded his authority, is not a reason for refusing to enforce the award. Arbitrators have no obligation to the court to give their reasons for an award. To require opinions free of ambiguity may lead arbitrators to play it safe by writing no supporting opinions. This would be undesirable for a well-reasoned opinion tends to engender confidence in the integrity of the process and aids in clarifying the underlying agreement. Moreover, we see no reason to assume that this arbitrator has abused the trust the parties confided in him and has not stayed within the areas marked out for his consideration. It is not apparent that he went beyond the submission. The Court of Appeals' opinion refusing to enforce the reinstatement and partial back pay portions of the award was not based upon any finding that the arbitrator did not premise his award on his construction of the contract. It merely disagreed with the arbitrator's construction of it.

The collective bargaining agreement could have provided that if any of the employees were wrongfully discharged, the remedy would be reinstatement and back pay up to the date they were returned to work. Respondent's major argument seems to be that by applying correct principles of law to the interpretation of the collective bargaining agreement it can be determined that the agreement did not so provide, and that therefore the arbitrators's decision was not based upon the contract. The acceptance of this view would require courts, even under the standard arbitration clause, to review the merits of every construction of the contract. This plenary review by a court of the merits would make meaningless the provisions that the arbitrator's decision is final, for in reality it would almost never be final. This underlines the fundamental error which we have alluded to in *United Steelworkers of America* v. *American Manufacturing Co.,* decided this day. As we there emphasized, the question of interpretation of the collective bargaining agreement is a question for the arbitrator. It is the arbitrator's construction which was bargained for; and so far as the arbitrator's decision concerns construction of the contract, the courts have no business overruling him because their interpretation of the contract is different from his.

We agree with the Court of Appeals that the judgment of the District Court should be modified so that the amounts due the employees may be definitely determined by arbitration. In all other respects we think the judgment of the District Court should be affirmed. Accordingly, we reverse the judgment of the Court of Appeals, except for that modification, and remand the case to the District Court for proceedings in conformity with this opinion.

It is so ordered.

MR. JUSTICE FRANKFURTER concurs in the result. MR. JUSTICE BLACK took no part in the consideration of the case. MR. JUSTICE WHITTAKER dissents.

Notes on Professional Responsibility

1. In *Enterprise Wheel,* Mr. Justice Douglas suggested that the arbitrator "is to bring informed judgment to bear in order to reach a fair solution of a problem." Since arbitrators are normally selected by the parties—on either an ad hoc basis, or for the duration of an agreement—there is at least a risk that they may try to maintain their acceptability by not giving offense to either party. This might include such innocuous matters as the diplomatic framing of the language of an award, or much more serious matters such as giving a borderline decision to one side because it has already experienced a string of losses at the hands of the same arbitrator.

By and large, arbitrators try to avoid this type of distortion of the adjudicative process. However, because feelings in labor relations controversies tend to run deep, the parties are sometimes quick to draw conclusions of bias. This, in turn, creates a special burden on the arbitrator to hold himself beyond reproach.

In doing so, paradoxically, he may become somewhat less useful as a contributor to industrial peace and justice. For example, suppose the parties to an arbitration are mismatched, one being represented by a skilled professional, the other by an incompetent layman. The arbitrator may well be tempted to conduct the hearing so as to minimize the advantage of the one side or prejudice to the other—but can he do so without risking his reputation for even-handedness? Or, to take another example, the arbitrator may hear part of a case and develop a strong sense that fairness requires a particular result, although the language of the agreement does not. Would he not impair his own status as an impartial adjudicator if during a recess in the hearing, he tried to informally persuade the parties to settle the case?

2. The Code of Professional Responsibility for Arbitrators of Labor-Management Disputes provides that "[t]he arbitrator's responsibility does not extend to the enforcement of an award," and that ". . . an arbitrator should not voluntarily participate in legal enforcement proceedings." A survey of arbitrators who heard 100,000 cases over a period of 20 years shows that only 234 (.002 percent) of the awards were challenged in court, that in 14 cases the arbitrator was subpoenaed to testify or to produce records, and that in seven cases the arbitrator was sued for damages. The Chronicle of the National Academy of Arbitrators, Vol. III, Number 1, p. 1 (1977). In most cases an attempt to vacate an arbitrator's award is unsuccessful. An arbitrator's motion to quash a subpoena relating to his award is likely to be successful. And it appears that no arbitrator has been held personally liable in damages because of his award.

Debate About the Trilogy

Justice Douglas' opinions, particularly in *Warrior and Gulf*, have been criticized from many points of view. Almost all critics have agreed that some of his assumptions are of questionable validity although there is considerable debate concerning how far off the mark he was. In order to appreciate the dimensions of the debate and to be able to respond to the points made, list all of the factual premises implicit or explicit in the opinions.

What support, if any, does Justice Douglas have for these assumptions?

Dunau, Review of Hays's Book*

Judge Hays's central and surprising thesis is that labor arbitration is not fit to survive. Basic to the indictment is his conviction that a "system of adjudication in which the judge depends for his livelihood, or for a substantial part of his livelihood or even for substantial supplements to his regular income, on whether he pleases those who hire him to judge is *per se* a thoroughly undesirable system." Judge Hays would substitute a simplified system of judicial administration said to preserve the procedural flexibility of arbitration without sacrificing the independence of judgment supposed to inhere in the judge's tenure. For those who still prefer arbitration as a means of resolving their contract controversies, he would insist that adherence to the institution depend entirely on the voluntary action of the parties, with courts withholding enforcement of both the executory promise to arbitrate and the rendered award. One measure of Judge Hays's deeply held yet retrogressive view is that even at common law, while the promise to arbitrate was generally not judicially enforceable, courts would compel compliance with an award issued in a completed proceeding in which the parties had voluntarily participated.

But for Judge Hays's thorough knowledgeability, born of years of experience as a teacher, arbitrator and judge, it would be simple to dismiss his views as cranky. His high credentials, however, require examination of the merits of his position. And the analysis might as well begin by acknowledging that his indictment is not without at least a modicum of factual support. It is probable that some arbitrators at some times have consciously based decision upon what they deemed would better promote their economic self-interest in maintaining their acceptability to those who select arbitrators. The importance of this excrescence can, however, be easily overstated. Some lawyers at some times have recommended courses of action better designed to fatten their fees than to serve their clients'

*Reprinted by permission from Dunau, *Review of Hays's Book*, 35 THE AM. SCHOLAR 774–78 (1966). Copyright © 1966 by THE AMERICAN SCHOLAR. This review is by Bernard Dunau, a nonarbitrator labor lawyer.

Benjamin Aaron also criticizes Hays's book in 42 WASH. L. REV. 969 (1967), and Saul Wallen criticizes this book in 81 HARV. L. REV. 507 (1967). The book in question is LABOR ARBITRATION: A DISSENTING VIEW by Paul R. Hays (1966).

interests; some doctors at some times have recommended courses of treatment better designed to enhance their profits than their patients' health; some judges at some times have taken bribes. Yet no one for that reason suggests that the services of lawyers, doctors or judges should be abolished. It is hard to see why arbitrators as a class should be condemned for a default not unique to them but unhappily indigenous to human behavior however disinterested the calling is supposed to be.

Labor arbitrators are not our only adjudicators who are not immunized from the reality of economic self-interest and the temptation to yield to it. While federal judges have life tenure during good behavior, many state judges are elected to office; and federal and state agency heads, exercising highly important adjudicatory functions in such tribunals as the National Labor Relations Board, the Federal Trade Commission, the Civil Aeronautics Board and the Federal Communications Commission, are appointed for terms ranging from five to seven years. Inherent in the desire for reelection or reappointment are distractions from disinterested judgment at least as potent as any that face an arbitrator. Many an appointee has paid the price of his independence by incurring the disfavor of a power bloc sufficiently influential to prevent his reappointment, and it is highly likely that many an appointee has been tempted to temper his judgment, and some have doubtless yielded, to avoid fatal disfavor. In some respects the situation of the arbitrator is indeed happier than that of the judge or agency head facing periodic reelection or reappointment. An established arbitrator who becomes *persona non grata* with one or another union or employer will ordinarily have other unions and employers who are still content with his services. He can count on continuing appointment, however shifting the identity of the particular parties who choose him. An arbitrator can thus survive disfavor and therefore need not fear that extinction is its consequence.

But the weakness of Judge Hays's thesis is more fundamental than any of these considerations. It lies instead in the quality of a good judge, whether his forum is judicial, administrative or arbitral. He requires, as Judge Hays says, "knowledge, training, skill, intelligence and character." And of these character is preeminent—the patience to hear the tedious controversy through without flagging attention and without irritability; the manners to probe positions incisively and to suffer stupidity without manifesting disrespect or impoliteness; the humility to withhold reaching a final determination until the parties have completed their presentation even though the point seems evident almost immediately; the drive to understand even apparent wrongheadedness to be sure that the controversy is truly comprehended; and the passion for a just result within the legal or contractual limitations that circumscribe the judge's authority to decide. A judge with these qualities will be alert to guard against the intrusion of economic self-interest and by his wariness can avoid yielding to it. A judge without these qualities has much more wrong with him than exposure to the temptation. For a judge with deficient qualifications, economic self-interest is not even the most important of the impediments to judicious performance. He may fall in with his prejudice for or against a class, movement or interest, surrender to the pressure of community feeling, or curry social or political esteem. He may be arrogant, stupid, insolent or self-righteous. And so, in relationship to the totality of attributes that makes a good judge, the impediment inherent in economic self-interest is not overly significant. It is unfortunately true that the level of judging, whether judicial, administrative or arbitral, is in the overall quite mediocre, but for those who have worked in all three forums the arbitrator does not suffer by comparison. Among union and employer representatives who select arbitrators, the encomium bestowed on the good arbitrator is that "he calls them as he sees them," and any system of adjudication would be hard pressed to profess or practice a higher ideal.

As a preface to his condemnation of labor arbitration, Judge Hays severely criticizes the Supreme Court's panegyrical description of the arbitrator's talents and role (*Steelworkers* v. *American Mfg. Co.*, 363 U.S. 564 [1960]; *Steelworkers* v. *Warrior & Gulf Nav. Co.*, 363 U.S. 754 [1960]; *Steelworkers* v. *Enterprise Wheel and Car Corp.*, 363 U.S. 593 [1960]). The censure is merited but misses the transcendent problem that the Supreme Court faced. The need overriding all others that confronted the Court was to formulate a standard to coordinate the work of judge and arbitrator granting the fitness of labor arbitration as an adjudicatory method. This the Court accomplished by cleanly and unequivocally divorcing inquiry into the merits of the dispute (the arbitrator's function) from the question of whether the parties had promised to submit the dispute to arbitration (the court's function). And the arbitrator's determination of the merits is not to be displaced by the court upon a proceeding to confirm or set aside the award. This sound and workable accommodation preserved the arbitral process from the damage that heavy judicial review threatened. The Supreme Court's "extravagant praise for arbitration" is at worst a rhetorical flourish emphasizing for the judiciary that its displeasure with the merits of a claim or an arbitrator's decision of it is no reason for a court to stand in the way of arbitration or its result.

The point is illustrated by Judge Hays's bland statement that a "lower Connecticut court vacated on public policy grounds an award reinstating an employee who had been discharged for gambling on the premises of the employer." Judge Hays cites this case among others in approving judicial review of arbitration awards on the basis of public policy. But there is a story behind this Connecticut case that Judge Hays does not tell. The arbitrator in that case had found that the evidence was insufficient to establish that the employee had gambled on company premises. The arbitrator had also found that the employee had certain gambling articles in his possession within the plant but concluded that possession itself should not be "considered gambling 'on the premises' . . . ." And the arbitrator determined that, while possession of gambling articles was a criminal offense under Connecticut law, the collective bargaining agreement should not be construed to incorporate the statutory prohibition as just cause for discharge. It was an award based on this reasoning that the lower Connecticut court voided as "contrary to public policy." The arbitrator was Paul R. Hays.

Torrington Co. v. Metal Products Workers Union Local 1645

United States Court of Appeals, Second Circuit, 1966
362 F.2d 677, 62 LRRM 2495

LUMBARD, Chief Judge:

This appeal presents the question whether an arbitrator exceeded his authority under the collective bargaining agreement between The Torrington Company (Torrington) and Metal Products Workers Union Local 1645, UAW, AFL-CIO (the Union), in ruling that the agreement contained an implied provision, based upon prior practice between the parties, that Torrington would allow its employees up to one hour off with pay to vote each election day. The District Court for the District of Connecticut held that "the arbitrator exceeded and abused his authority when he attempted to read into the agreement this implied contractual relationship," and it vacated and set aside the arbitrator's award. We affirm.

In its company newsletter of December 1962, Torrington announced that it was discontinuing its twenty-year policy of permitting employees time off with pay to vote on election days. This policy had been unilaterally instituted by the company and was not a part of the then-existing collective bargaining agreement, which contained an extremely narrow arbitration provision. The Union did not attempt to arbitrate this issue. Rather, on April 9, 1963, it filed a many-faceted complaint with the National Labor Relations Board which included a charge that the unilateral change of election day policy constituted an unfair labor practice.

The Union later dropped this charge, and the Board dismissed the entire complaint on July 29, 1963. In August, the parties began negotiations for a new collective bargaining agreement, as the old contract was due to expire September 27, 1963. At the first meeting, Torrington informed the Union that it did not intend to reestablish its paid time off for voting policy. The Union responded by including a contrary provision in its written demands presented at a meeting in August or early September.

At this point, the record is somewhat unclear as to the circumstances surrounding the negotiations. We know that in the written proposals made by Torrington (September 26) and by the Union (October 25), *each* suggested that the old contract be continued with specific amendments, none of which involved the election day policy. We know that a long and costly strike began when the old contract expired on September 27, that some employees worked during the strike, and that those employees were not given paid time off for the November 1963 elections. And it is conceded by all that the current contract, signed on January 18, 1964, contained, like the old, no mention of paid time off for voting.

When the 1964 elections became imminent, Torrington's understanding of its rights under the new contract was revealed by a union flier to the employees dated November 2, 1964. The Union reported that, "The Torrington Company has again stated that you will *not* be allowed the one hour time off for voting this year." This time, however, the Union was armed with a new weapon, for the new contract contained a much less restrictive arbitration clause.[2] Thus, on December 17, 1964, the Union filed the grievance which underlies this case. . . .

In his written decision, the arbitrator first held that the dispute was arbitrable under the new contract's arbitration clause even though the contract contained no express provision for paid time off for voting, a decision which is not challenged. . . . He then ruled that the benefit of paid time off to vote was a firmly established practice at Torrington, that the company therefore had the burden of changing this policy by negotiating with the Union, and that in the negotiations which culminated in the current bargaining agreement the parties did not agree to terminate this practice. Finding further that this employee benefit was not within management's prerogative under the "management functions" clause of the contract, the arbitrator held that employees who took time off to vote on November 3, 1964, or who worked on that day and had received an election benefit in 1962 must be paid a comparable benefit for Election Day 1964.

The company petitioned to vacate the award. Judge Clarie agreed with the arbitrator that the practice at issue had been long established at Torrington prior to 1963. But he also found that, "Throughout the negotiations [of 1963–1964], the plaintiff employer persistently reiterated its position not to grant this benefit [in the new contract]." Commenting that, "Labor contracts generally affirmatively state the terms which the contracting parties agree to; not what practices they agree to discontinue," Judge Clarie held that the arbitrator had gone outside the terms of the contract and thus had exceeded his authority by reading the election day benefit into the new contract after the parties had negotiated the issue but had made no such provision in that contract.

The essence of the Union's argument on appeal is that, in deciding that the arbitrator exceeded his authority in making this award, the District Court exceeded the scope of its authority and improperly examined the merits of the arbitrator's award. The Union relies on the language in *United Steelworkers of America* v. *Enterprise Wheel & Car Corp.*, 363 U.S. 593, 596, 46 LRRM 2423, 2425 (1960), the third of the famous *Steelworkers* trilogy in which the Supreme Court outlined the proper role of the judiciary in labor arbitration cases, to the effect that the courts are not "to review the merits of an arbitration award."

[2]Relevant portions of Article V of the agreement are as follows:
"*Section 1.*—If a grievance is not settled after it has been processed through the three (3) steps described in Article IV above, and if it is a grievance with respect to the interpretation or application of any provisions in this contrcat and is not controlled by Section 1 of Article XIV, (Management) it may be submitted to arbitration in the manner herein provided. . . .
"*Section 3.*—The arbitrator shall be bound by and must comply with all of the terms of the agreement and he shall have no power to add to, delete from, or modify, in any way, any of the provisions of this agreement. The arbitrator shall not have the authority to determine the right of employees to merit increases. The arbitrator shall have no authority to set or determine wages except as provided by Section 21 of Article VI, Wages.
"*Section 4.*—The decision of the arbitrator shall be binding on both parties during the life of this agreement unless the same is contrary, in any way, to law."

I.

It is now well settled that a grievance is arbitrable "unless it may be said with positive assurance that the arbitration clause is not susceptible of an interpretation that covers the asserted dispute." *United Steelworkers of America* v. *Warrior & Gulf Nav. Co.*, 363 U.S. at 582–83, 46 LRRM at 2419–2420. A less settled question is the appropriate scope of judicial review of a specific arbitration award. Although the arbitrator's decision on the merits is final as to questions of law and fact, his authority is contractual in nature and is limited to the powers conferred in the collective bargaining agreement.[5] For this reason, a number of courts have interpreted *Enterprise Wheel* as authorizing review of whether an arbitrator's award exceeded the limits of his contractual authority. . . .

Torrington contends that the arbitrator exceeded his authority in this case by "adding" the election day bonus to the terms of the January 1964 agreement. However, the arbitrator held that such a provision was implied by the prior practice of the parties. In some cases, it may be appropriate exercise of an arbitrator's authority to resolve ambiguities in the scope of a collective bargaining agreement on the basis of prior practice, since no agreement can reduce all aspects of the labor-management relationship to writing. However, while courts should be wary of rejecting the arbitrator's interpretation of the implications of the parties' prior practice, the mandate that the arbitrator stay within the confines of the collective bargaining agreement, footnote 5 *supra*, requires a reviewing court to pass upon whether the agreement authorizes the arbitrator to expand its express terms on the basis of the parties' prior practice. Therefore, we hold that the question of an arbitrator's authority is subject to judicial review, and that the arbitrator's decision that he has authority should not be accepted where the reviewing court can clearly perceive that he has derived that authority from sources outside the collective bargaining agreement at issue. See *Textile Workers Union of America* v. *American Thread Co.*, 291 F.2d 894 (4 Cir. 1961).[6]

II.

Unfortunately, as the dissenting opinion illustrates, agreeing upon these general principles does not make this case any easier. Certain it is

---

[5]"[The arbitrator] does not sit to dispense his own brand of industrial justice. He may of course look for guidance from many sources, yet his award is legitimate only so long as it draws its essence from the collective bargaining agreement. When the arbitrator's words manifest an infidelity to this obligation, courts have no choice but to refuse enforcement of the award." *United Steelworkers of America* v. *Enterprise Wheel & Car Corp.*, 363 U.S. at 597, 46 LRRM at 2425.

[6]Of course, it can be argued that our decision authorizes an impermissible review of the "merits" in a case where the principal issue was whether the arbitrator should find an implied substantive obligation in the contract, see Meltzer, *The Supreme Court, Arbitrability, and Collective Bargaining,* 28 U. CHI. L. REV. 464, 484–85 (1961), but we think this position is contrary to *Enterprise Wheel.* See note 5 *supra.* The question of the arbitrator's authority is really one of his contractual jurisdiction, and the courts cannot be expected to place their stamp of approval upon his action without making some examination of his jurisdiction to act. As stated above, we think more exhaustive judicial review of this question is appropriate

that Torrington's policy of paid time off to vote was well established by 1962. On this basis, the arbitrator ruled that the policy must continue during the 1964 agreement because Torrington did not negotiate a contrary policy into that agreement. To bolster his decision, the arbitrator noted that Torrington's written demands of September 26, 1963, constituted the first occasion on which either party did not expressly insist that its election day position be adopted. Therefore, he concluded, it was the company which removed this question "from the table" and the company cannot complain if its policy under the old contract is now continued.

We cannot accept this interpretation of the negotiations. In the first place, as Judge Clarie stated, labor contracts generally state affirmatively what conditions the parties agree to, more specifically, what restraints the parties will place on management's freedom of action. While it may be appropriate to resolve a question never raised during negotiations on the basis of prior practice in the plant or industry, it is quite another thing to assume that the contract confers a specific benefit when that benefit was discussed during negotiations but omitted from the contract. . . .

The arbitrator's primary justification for reading the election day benefit into the 1964 agreement was that such a benefit corresponded to the parties' prior practice. But in this the arbitrator completely ignored the fact that the company had revoked that policy almost ten months earlier, by newsletter to the employees in December 1962 and by formal notice to the Union in April 1963. It was within the employer's discretion to make such a change since the narrow arbitration clause in the previous collective bargaining agreement precluded resort to arbitration by the Union. And there was no showing that Torrington's announcement was merely a statement of bargaining position and was not a seriously intended change in policy.

In light of this uncontroverted fact, and bearing in mind that the arbitrator has no jurisdiction to "add to" the 1964 agreement, we do not think it was proper to place the "burden" of securing an express contract provision in the 1964 contract on the company. At the start of negotiations, Torrington announced its intent to *continue* its previous change of election day policy. This was an express invitation to the Union to bargain with respect to this matter. After the Union failed to press for and receive a change in the 1964 agreement, the company was surely justified in applying in November 1964 a policy it had rightfully established in 1962, and had applied in November 1963 (during the strike).

In our opinion, the Union by pressing this grievance has attempted to have "added" to the 1964 agreement a benefit which it did not think sufficiently vital to insist upon during negotiations for the contract which ended a long and costly strike. We find this sufficiently clear from the facts as found by the arbitrator to agree with the district court that the arbitra-

---

after the award has been made than before the award in a suit to compel arbitration; in this way, the court receives the benefit of the arbitrator's interpretive skills as to the matter of his contractual authority. See *Livingston v. John Wiley & Sons, Inc.*, 313 F.2d 52, 59 n. 5 (2 Cir. 1963), *aff'd*, 376 U.S. 543, 55 LRRM 2769 (1964).

tor exceeded his authority by ruling that such a benefit was implied in the terms of that agreement. . . .

FEINBERG, Circuit Judge (dissenting). . . .

The arbitrator assumed that a collective bargaining agreement can include terms or conditions not made explicit in the written contract. This proposition is correct. In a prior appeal involving these same parties and this same contract, this court said that the arbitration clause of the agreement could be applicable to a recall grievance if there were "some special agreement making it applicable or . . . some custom or common understanding which has that effect." This is a clear statement of the view that it is proper to look beyond the terms of a labor contract in interpreting it. In *United Steelworkers of America* v. *Warrior & Gulf Nav. Co.*, 363 U.S. 574, 580, 46 LRRM 2416, 2419 (1960), the Supreme Court said: "Gaps [in the 'written document'] may be left to be filled in by reference to the practices of the particular industry and of the various shops covered by the agreement." Moreover, the difference between the earlier (1961–1963) and the new contract in this case is most significant. The arbitration article in the earlier contract contained the following limitations on the arbitrator's power:

> "The Company's decisions will stand and will not be over-ruled by any arbitrator unless the arbitrator can find that the Company misinterpreted or violated the express terms of the agreement.
> . . .
> "No point not covered by this contract shall be subject to arbitration. . . ."

After a 16-week strike in which the scope of the arbitration clause was an important issue (which, in itself, is unusual), these limitations on the arbitrator's power were excluded in the new contract. This was a clear recognition by the parties that there can be "implied" as well as "express" terms in the agreement. In this case, the arbitrator held that pay for time off for voting was a benefit which was such "an implied part of the contract." If so, then, of course, the arbitrator did not "add to, delete from, or modify, in any way, any of the provisions of this agreement" in violation of the arbitration clause.

Thus, the arbitrator looked to prior practice, the conduct of the negotiation for the new contract and the agreement reached at the bargaining table to reach his conclusion that paid time off for voting was "an implied part of the contract." From all of this, I conclude that the arbitrator's award "draws its essence from the collective bargaining agreement" and his words do not "manifest an infidelity to this obligation." Once that test is met, the inquiry ends. Whether the arbitrator's conclusion was correct is irrelevant because the parties agreed to abide by it, right or wrong. Nevertheless, the majority has carried the inquiry further and concerned itself with a minute examination of the merits of the award, which we are enjoined not to do. . . .

Note

Although the percentage of arbitration awards challenged in court is very low and although most challenges to arbitration awards in court are unsuccessful, the courts have vacated arbitration awards in a number of cases (many of which have been criticized on the ground that the courts violated the guidelines of *Enterprise Wheel*). One 20-year survey of federal court decisions where arbitration awards involving discharge (the subject most commonly arbitrated) were challenged on the ground that the arbitrators exceeded their contractual authority showed that only 18 such awards were vacated in the period 1960-1980. Eleven of these awards that were vacated were at the circuit court level, and six of these awards were decided by the Sixth Circuit. Fogel, *Court Review of Discharge Arbitration Awards*, 37 Arb. J. 22, 33 (1982).

Questions

1. If you were the arbitrator, how would you have decided *Torrington*? Did the majority of the court in *Torrington* properly apply the basic principles of the Trilogy?
2. If you wished to become an arbitrator, how should you seek to become acceptable as an arbitrator to labor and employer representatives? There is no single or easy answer to this question. Nevertheless, a survey of members of the National Academy of Arbitrators (published in Appendix C in the Proceedings of the 24th Annual Meeting of the National Academy of Arbitrators, 1971) and a survey of individuals admitted to the Academy between 1970 and 1975 (published as Appendix D in the Proceedings of the 29th Annual Meeting of the National Academy of Arbitrators, 1976) provide some general suggestions for those who seek to become arbitrators.
3. Critics assert that under modern trends the arbitration process involves increasing delay, increasing cost, and creeping legalism. Although there is no legal requirement that unions or employers be represented by lawyers in labor arbitration proceedings, the parties are frequently represented by lawyers in such proceedings. How does the use of lawyers as representatives of the parties in arbitration tend to increase delay, cost, and creeping legalism?

2. NO-STRIKE PROMISES

Problem

The union files a grievance to protest the Enderby Company's subcontracting of laboratory work. The union also calls a strike, which cripples the entire operation, to protest the subcontracting. The company immediately brings an action against the union seeking an injunction for breach of the no-strike clause in the agreement, which provides: *"Strikes and Lockouts.* The parties agree that during the term of this agreement there shall be no strikes or other interference with work and no lockouts."

The state court issues an injunction *ex parte.* When served with the court's order, the union's attorney removes the case to federal district court and moves to dissolve the injunction pursuant to Section 4 of the Norris-LaGuardia Act. The judge for the federal district court sets the matter down for immediate hearing in his chambers.

Questions

1. What should the judge do?
2. What contentions will each side raise in support of its position?

Local 174, Teamsters v. Lucas Flour Co.

Supreme Court of the United States, 1962
369 U.S. 95, 49 LRRM 2717

[In May, 1958, an employee named Welsch was discharged for "unsatisfactory work" after he ran a new fork lift truck off a loading platform onto some railroad tracks, damaging it. The union struck to force the employer to reinstate him. After a strike of eight days, Welsch's discharge was submitted to arbitration under the collective bargaining contract in effect at the time, which provided that:

["Article II. The Employer reserves the right to discharge any man in his employ if his work is not satisfactory.

["Article XIV. Should any difference as to the true interpretation of this agreement arise, same shall be submitted to a Board of Arbitration. . . .[T]he decision of the said Board of Arbitration shall be binding. It is further agreed by both parties hereto that during such arbitration, there shall be no suspension of work.

["Should any difference arise between the employer and the employee, same shall be submitted to arbitration by both parties. Failing to agree, they shall mutually appoint a third person whose decision shall be final and binding."

[The Arbitration Board sustained the discharge of Welsch. Meanwhile, the employer sued the union in the Superior Court of Washington for business losses sustained during the strike. A judgment in favor of the employer for $6501.20 was affirmed by Department One of the Supreme Court of Washington, which held (1) that Section 301 neither pre-empted state jurisdiction nor foreclosed application of state substantive law, and (2) that applying the principles of state law, the strike violated the contract because it attempted to coerce the employer to forego his contractual right to discharge for unsatisfactory work.

[JUSTICE STEWART, delivering the opinion of the Court, found that the state court had jurisdiction over the litigation even though it was within the purview of Section 301(a), but that federal law should have been applied rather than state law. Nevertheless, he went on to find that application of principles of federal labor law resulted in affirmance of the judgment below.]

Whether, as a matter of federal law, the strike which the union called was a violation of the collective bargaining contract is thus the ultimate issue which this case presents. It is argued that there could be no violation in the absence of a no-strike clause in the contract explicitly covering the subject of the dispute over which the strike was called. We disagree.

The collective bargaining contract expressly imposed upon both parties the duty of submitting the dispute in question to final and binding arbitration. In a consistent course of decisions the Courts of Appeals of at least five Federal Circuits have held that a strike to settle a dispute which a collective bargaining agreement provides shall be settled exclusively and finally by compulsory arbitration constitutes a violation of the agreement. The National Labor Relations Board has reached the same conclusion. *W. L. Mead, Inc.*, 113 NLRB 1040. We approve that doctrine. To hold otherwise would obviously do violence to accepted principles of traditional contract law. Even more in point, a contrary view should be completely at odds with the basic policy of national labor legislation to promote the arbitral process as a substitute for economic warfare. See *United Steelworkers* v. *Warrior & Gulf Nav. Co.*, 363 U.S. 574.

What has been said is not to suggest that a no-strike agreement is to be implied beyond the area which it has been agreed will be exclusively covered by compulsory terminal arbitration. Nor is it to suggest that there may not arise problems in specific cases as to whether compulsory and binding arbitration has been agreed upon, and, if so, as to what disputes have been made arbitrable. But no such problems are present in this case. The grievance over which the union struck was, as it concedes, one which it had expressly agreed to settle by submission to final and binding arbitration proceedings. The strike which it called was a violation of that contractual obligation.

Affirmed.

MR. JUSTICE BLACK, dissenting. . . .

The Court now finds—out of clear air, so far as I can see—that the union, without saying so in the agreement, not only agreed to arbitrate such differences, but also promised that there would be no strike while arbitration of a dispute was pending under this provision. And on the basis of its "discovery" of this additional unwritten promise by the union, the Court upholds a judgment awarding the company substantial damages for a strike in breach of contract.

. . . In view of the fact that [one] provision contains an explicit promise by the union "that during such arbitration, there shall be no suspension of work," it seems to me plain that the parties in this contract, knowing how to write a provision binding a union not to strike, deliberately included a no-strike clause with regard to disputes over broad questions of contractual interpretation and deliberately excluded such a clause with regard to the essentially factual disputes arising out of the application of the contract in particular instances. And there is not a word anywhere else in this agreement which indicates that this perfectly sensible contractual framework for handling these two different kinds of disputes was not intended to operate in the precise manner dictated by the express language of the two arbitration provisions. . . .

. . . The implication found by the Court thus flows neither from the contract itself, nor so far as this record shows, from the intention of the parties. In my judgment, an "implication" of that nature would better be described as a rigid rule of law that an agreement to arbitrate has precisely the same effect as an agreement not to strike—a rule of law which introduces revolutionary doctrine into the field of collective bargaining.

Notes

1. Query: How can the union protect itself against the result of this decision? Does *Lucas Flour* affect the bargaining process, as does the Trilogy, but in the opposite direction?

2. The holding in *Lucas Flour* is premised upon "accepted principles of traditional contract law" and the federal policy of promoting arbitration as an alternative to economic action. To what extent does traditional contract law explain the result? What set of rules does the Court have in mind?

In relation to the needs of federal law, what is the source of the federal policy on which the Court relies? Most important, to what extent is a strike or any act of self help inconsistent with a promise to arbitrate?

3. In *Packinghouse Workers* v. *Needham Packing Co.,* 376 U.S. 247, 55 LRRM 2580 (1964), the union called a strike to protest the discharge of an employee. Approximately 200 of 600 employees walked out. When they refused to return to work, the employer discharged the strikers and hired replacements. The union filed grievances over the initial discharge and the subsequent discharges. The employer refused to arbitrate these grievances, claiming that the union's alleged breach of the no-strike clause in the agreement released the employer from any duty to arbitrate. When the union sued to compel arbitration, the employer counterclaimed for damages. The Court held that the alleged breach of the no-strike clause did not release the employer from its duty to arbitrate the union's claim that the employees had been wrongfully discharged. Although the Court noted that the employer could continue with its claim for damages against the union, the Court left open two questions: (a) the legal effect that the arbitrator's decision would have on the court action for damages, and (b) "whether a fundamental and long-lasting change in the relationship of the parties prior to the demand for arbitration would be a circumstance which, alone or among others, would release an employer from his promise to arbitrate."

4. Most collective bargaining agreements contain a no-strike clause. One question that may arise concerns the matter of who may render the union liable as an entity for breach of a no-strike clause. It has been held that the responsibility of the union for acts of its officers and members is measured by the ordinary doctrines of agency law. *United Mine Workers* v. *Gibbs*, 383 U.S. 715, 61 LRRM 2561 (1966).

Carbon Fuel Co. v. Mine Workers

Supreme Court of the United States, 1979
444 U.S. 212, 102 LRRM 3017

MR. JUSTICE BRENNAN delivered the opinion of the Court.

The question for decision in this case is whether an International Union, which neither instigates, supports, ratifies, or encourages "wildcat" strikes engaged in by Local Unions in violation of a collective-bargaining agreement, may be held liable in damages to an affected employer if the Union did not use all reasonable means available to it to prevent the strikes or bring about their termination.

Petitioner, Carbon Fuel Company, and respondent, United Mine Workers of America (UMWA), were parties to the National Coal Wage Agreements of 1968 and 1971, collective-bargaining agreements covering, *inter alia,* workers at petitioner's several coal mines in southern West Virginia. Forty-eight unauthorized or "wildcat" strikes were engaged in by three Local Unions at petitioner's mines from 1969 to 1973. Efforts of District 17, a regional subdivision of UMWA, to persuade the miners not to strike and to return to work were uniformly unsuccessful.[1]

Petitioner brought this suit pursuant to § 301 of the Labor-Management Relations Act of 1947 (the Taft-Hartley Act), as amended, 29 U.S.C. § 185, in the District Court for the Southern District of West Virginia. UMWA, District 17, and the three Local Unions were named defendants. The complaint sought injunctive relief[2] and damages, alleging that the strikes were in violation of the two collective-bargaining agreements. The case was tried before a jury. The trial judge found as a matter of law that the strikes violated the agreements. The trial judge also instructed the jury, over objection of UMWA and District 17, that those defendants might be found liable in damages to petitioner "[i]f you find from a preponderance of the evidence that the International and District Unions did not use all reasonable means available to them to prevent work

---

[1]The facts relevant to the participation of the District and International in the wildcat strikes can be briefly stated. As recently as 1966 the International expressed its intention to discipline "wildcatters." The District and International were promptly notified of each strike. In each instance a District representative arranged for a meeting of the striking Local and directed the members to return to work. Often the representative advised the members that the International and District could take disciplinary action against participants in illegal, unauthorized strikes. If the strike did not end after the first meeting a second meeting was called. Most strikes ended in the first one or two days. No strike lasted longer than six days. From concern that such action might only aggravate a bad situation, no disciplinary action was taken against the strikers. There is however no suggestion that the District's efforts to end the strikes were not in good faith.

[2]The contracts have expired, and the question of injunctive relief is out of the case.

stoppages or strikes from occurring in violation of the contract or to terminate any such work stoppages or strikes after they began. . . ." (App. 197.) Verdicts in different amounts were returned against UMWA, District 17, and the three Local Unions.

On appeal, the Court of Appeals for the Fourth Circuit vacated in part the judgments against the three Local Unions but otherwise affirmed those judgments.[3] However, the Court of Appeals vacated the judgments against UMWA and District 17, and remanded to the District Court with directions to dismiss the case against those defendants. . . .

. . .

Petitioner argues that the obligation of UMWA and District 17 to use all reasonable means to prevent and end unauthorized strikes in violation of the collective-bargaining agreement is either (a) implied in law because the agreement contains an arbitration provision or (b) in any event is to be implied from the provision of the agreement that the parties "agree and affirm that they will maintain the integrity of this contract. . . ." We find no merit in either argument.

A

Insofar as petitioner's argument relies on the history of § 301 and the congressional plan to prevent and remedy strikes in breach of contract by encouraging arbitration, the legislative history is clear that Congress limited the responsibility of unions for strikes in breach of contract to cases when the union may be found responsible according to the common-law rule of agency.[5]

Section 301(a) makes collective-bargaining agreements judicially enforceable. *Textile Workers* v. *Lincoln Mills*, 353 U.S. 448, 40 LRRM 2113 (1957). At the same time, Congress gave careful attention to the problem of strikes during the term of a collective-bargaining agreement, but stopped short of imposing liability upon a union for strikes not authorized, participated in, or ratified by it. Rather, to effectuate § 301(a), the Taft-Hartley Act provided in § 301(b) that a union "shall be bound by the acts of its agents," and in § 301(e) provided that the common law of agency shall govern "in determining whether one person is acting as an 'agent' for another person." In explaining § 301(e) Senator Taft stated, 93 CONG. REC. 4022 (1947):

> "If the wife of a man who is working at a plant receives a lot of telephone messages, very likely it cannot be proved that they came from the union. *There is no case then. There must be legal proof of agency in the case of Unions as in the case of corporations. . . .*" (Emphasis supplied.)

[3]Review of the judgments against the Locals was not sought here.

[5]An international union, of course, is responsible under § 301 for any authorized strike if such strike violates any term of the contract, whether express or implied. See, *e.g., Gateway Coal Co.* v. *UMWA*, 414 U.S. 368, 85 LRRM 2049 (1974); *Boys Markets, Inc.* v. *Retail Clerks Union*, 398 U.S. 235, 74 LRRM 2257 (1970). Our holding in Part A of this opinion does not affect the content, as implied by law, of arbitration clauses. Rather, we are addressing the wholly different issue of whether an international or district union may be held legally responsible for locals' unilateral actions which are concededly in violation of the locals' responsibilities under the contract.

Congress' reason for adopting the common-law agency test, and applying to unions the common-law doctrine of *respondeat superior,* follows the lead of Chief Justice Taft in *Coronado Coal Co.* v. *UMWA,* 268 U.S. 295, 304 (1925), that to find the union liable "it must be clearly shown . . . that what was done was done by their agents in accordance with their fundamental agreement of association." The common-law agency test replaced the very loose test of responsibility incorporated in § 2(2) of the original 1935 National Labor Relations Act under which the term "employer" included "any person acting in the interest of an employer. . . ." 49 Stat. 436.[6]

Petitioner makes the distinct argument that we should hold the International liable for its *own* failure to respond to the Local's strike. In the face of Congress' clear statement of the limits of an international union's legal responsibility for the acts of one of its local unions, it would be anomalous to hold that an international is nonetheless liable for its failure to take certain steps in response to actions of the local. Such a rule would pierce the shield that Congress took such care to construct. Accordingly, we reject petitioner's suggestion that Congress' policy in favor of arbitration extends to imposing an obligation on the respondents, which agreed to arbitrate grievances, to use reasonable means to try to control the locals' actions in contravention of that agreement.

The Court of Appeals stated: "There was no evidence presented in the district court that either the District or International Union instigated, supported, ratified, or encouraged any of the work stoppages. . . ." 582 F.2d at 1351. Under Art. XVI, § 1, of the UMWA constitution, the Local Unions lacked authority to strike without authorization from UMWA. (App. 195.) Moreover, UMWA had repeatedly expressed its opposition to wildcat strikes. Petitioner thus failed to prove agency as required by §§ 301(b) and (e), and we therefore agree with the Court of Appeals that ". . . under these circumstances it was error for the [District Court] to deny the motions of these defendants for directed verdicts." 582 F.2d at 1351.

B

We turn next to petitioner's argument that even if the no-strike obligation to be implied from the promise to resolve disputes by arbitration did not carry with it the further step of implying an obligation on UMWA and District 17 to use all reasonable efforts to end an unauthorized strike, that obligation should nevertheless be implied from the contract provision obligating UMWA and District 17 to "maintain the integrity of this contract. . . ."

In the 1947 Taft-Hartley Act Congress sought to promote numerous policies. One policy of particular importance—if not the overriding one— was the policy of free collective bargaining. . . .

---

[6]At the same time, Congress applied to unions the common-law doctrine of *respondeat superior* rather than the more restrictive test of union responsibility under § 6 of the Norris-LaGuardia Act, which requires "clear proof of *actual* participation in, or *actual* authorization of such acts, or of ratification of such acts after *actual* knowledge thereof." 29 U.S.C. § 106 (emphasis supplied).

The contractual provision to which petitioner looks to create the alleged union duty to use "all reasonable means" to end wildcat strikes is the promise to "maintain the integrity of this contract." Petitioner argues that the promise, intended to get disputes into arbitration, is meaningless if the UMWA and District 17 have no obligation to exert their best efforts to force the miners to live up to the contracts.

The bargaining history of the contracts completely answers petitioner's argument. The parties directly addressed the issue early in their bargaining history and, after first including such an obligation, specifically deleted it from their agreement. The first agreement between the parties, in 1941, contained an explicit no-strike clause. In order to avoid liability under § 301 for contract breaches, UMWA negotiated the deletion of the no-strike provision from the 1947 contract. Instead, the coverage of the contract was limited to employees "able and willing to work," and the parties agreed that all disagreements would be settled through arbitration or collective bargaining. In 1950 the contract was again rewritten. The "able and willing" provision was dropped and replaced by a promise "to maintain the integrity of this contract and *to exercise their best efforts through available disciplinary measures* to prevent stoppages of work by strike or lockout." (Emphasis supplied.)

Because the Union did not want to surrender its freedom to decide what measures to take or not to take in dealing with unauthorized strikes, it negotiated the deletion of the "best efforts through available disciplinary measures" clause. . . . The new provision in the 1952 contract, which was carried forward into the 1968 and 1971 contracts essentially unchanged as to this issue, read as follows:

> "The United Mine Workers of America and the Operators agree and affirm that they will maintain the integrity of this contract and that all disputes and claims which are not settled by agreement shall be settled by the machinery provided in the 'Settlement of Local and District Disputes' section of the Agreement unless national in character in which event the parties shall settle such disputes by free collective bargaining as heretofore practiced in the industry, it being the purpose of this provision to provide for the settlement of all such disputes and claims through the machinery in this contract provided and by collective bargaining without recourse to the courts."

It makes no sense to assume that the parties thought the new language subsumed the deleted provision. Had that been their intention, there would have been no reason to alter the contract.

The inescapable conclusion to be drawn from their bargaining history is that, whatever the integrity clause may mean, the parties purposely decided not to impose on the Union an obligation to take disciplinary or other actions to get unauthorized strikers back to work. It would do violence to the bargaining process and the national policy furthering free collective bargaining to impose by judicial implication a duty upon UMWA and District 17 that the parties in arms-length bargaining first included and then purposely deleted.

Moreover, since the deletion but before 1968 or 1971 when these agreements were reached, two Courts of Appeals construed this contract as not imposing liability on the Union for wildcat strikes and as not requiring UMWA to take any action with regard to such strikes. . . . If these interpretations did not accord with the parties' understanding of their contract, they had ample opportunity to make their own understanding explicit. Failure to do so strongly suggests the parties incorporated the courts' interpretation of the agreements.

Affirmed.

Atkinson v. Sinclair Refining Co.

Supreme Court of the United States, 1962
370 U.S. 238, 50 LRRM 2433

[The respondent, Sinclair Refining Company, employed 1700 men at its East Chicago Refinery, who were represented by the Oil, Chemical and Atomic Workers and its local. In February 1959, the company docked three employees a total of $2.19. As a result, alleged the company, a thousand employees struck for two days. The company instituted a three-count action for injunction and damages in the Federal District Court. Count I sought $12,500 damages for breach of a no-strike clause against the international and the local under Section 301. Count II, invoking diversity jurisdiction, sought damages against 24 union committeemen, who "contrary to their duty to plaintiff to abide by such contract, and maliciously confederating and conspiring together to cause the plaintiff expense and damage, and to induce breaches of said contract, and to interfere with performance thereof by the said labor organizations, and the affected employees, and to cause breaches thereof, individually and as officers, committeemen and as agents of said labor organizations, fomented, assisted and participated in a strike or work stoppage. . . ." Count III sought injunctive relief, and was decided in a separate opinion.

[The defendants moved to dismiss and stay the proceedings on the grounds that the issues raised were referable to arbitration under the collective agreement, and that some issues were involved in grievances which had been filed and were in arbitration. The District Court refused to dismiss or stay Count I and Count II, but was reversed by the Court of Appeals. The Supreme Court granted certiorari.]

MR. JUSTICE WHITE delivered the opinion of the Court. . . .

I

We have concluded that Count I should not be dismissed or stayed. Count I properly states a cause of action under § 301 and is to be governed by federal law. *Local 174* v. *Lucas Flour Co.,* 369 U.S. 95, 102–104; *Textile Workers Union* v. *Lincoln Mills,* 353 U.S. 448. Under our decisions, whether or not the company was bound to arbitrate, as well as what issues it must arbitrate, is a matter to be determined by the Court on the basis of the contract entered into by the parties. . . . We think it unquestionably clear that the contract here involved is not susceptible to a construction that the company was bound to arbitrate its claim for damages against the union for breach of the undertaking not to strike.

While it is quite obvious from other provisions of the contract that the parties did not intend to commit all of their possible disputes and the whole scope of their relationship to the grievance and arbitration procedures established in Article XXVI, that article itself is determinative of the issue in this case since its precludes arbitration boards from considering any matters other than employee grievances. After defining a grievance as "any difference regarding wages, hours or working conditions between the parties hereto or between the Employer and an employee covered by this working agreement," Article XXVI provides that the parties desire to settle employee grievances fairly and quickly and that therefore a stated procedure "must be followed." The individual employee is required to present his grievance to his foreman, and if not satisfied there, he may take his grievance to the plant superintendent who is to render a written decision. There is also provision for so-called Workmen's Committees to present grievances to the local management. If the local superintendent's decision is not acceptable, the matter is to be referred for discussion between the President of the International and the Director of Industrial Relations for the company (or their representatives), and for decision by the Director alone. If the Director's decision is disputed, then "upon request of the President or any District Director" of the international, a local arbitration board may be convened and the matter finally decided by this board.

Article XXVI then imposes the critical limitation. It is provided that local arbitration boards "shall consider only individual or local employee or local committee grievances arising under the application of the currently existing agreement." There is not a word in the grievance and arbitration article providing for the submission of grievances by the company. Instead, there is the express, flat limitation that arbitration boards should consider only employee grievances. Furthermore, the article expressly provides that arbitration may be invoked only at the option of the union. At no place in the contract does the union agree to arbitrate at the behest of the company. The company is to take its claims elsewhere, which it has now done.

The union makes a further argument for a stay. Following the strike, and both before and after the company filed its suit, 14 of the 24 individual defendants filed grievances claiming reimbursement for pay withheld by the employer. The union argues that even though the company need not arbitrate its claim for damages, it is bound to arbitrate these grievances; and the arbitrator, in the process of determining the grievants' right to reimbursement, will consider and determine issues which also underlie the company's claim for damages. Therefore, it is said that a stay of the court action is appropriate.

We are not satisfied from the record now before us, however, that any significant issue in the damage suit will be presented to and decided by an arbitrator. The grievances filed simply claimed reimbursement for pay

due employees for time spent at regular work or processing grievances. . . .

The District Court must decide whether the company is entitled to
damages from the union for breach of contract. The arbitrator, if arbitration occurs, must award or deny reimbursement in whole or in part to all
or some of the 14 employees. His award, standing alone, obviously would
determine no issue in the damage suit. If he awarded reimbursement to
the employees and if it could be ascertained with any assurance that one of
his subsidiary findings was that the 14 men had not participated in a
forbidden work stoppage—the critical issue according to the union's
brief—the company would nevertheless not be foreclosed in court since,
even if it were bound by such a subsidiary finding made by the arbitrator,
it would be free to prove its case in court through the conduct of other
agents of the union. In this state of the record, the union has not made out
its case for a stay.

For the foregoing reasons, the lower courts properly denied the union's
motion to dismiss Count I or stay it pending arbitration of the employer's
damage claim.

II

We turn now to Count II of the complaint, which charged 24 individual
officers and agents of the union with breach of the collective bargaining
contract and tortious interference with contractual relations. The District
Court held that under § 301 union officers or members cannot be held
personally liable for union actions, and that therefore "suits of the nature
alleged in Count II are no longer cognizable in state or federal courts."
The Court of Appeals reversed, however, ruling that "Count II stated a
cause of action cognizable in the courts of Indiana and, by diversity,
maintainable in the District Court."

We are unable to agree with the Court of Appeals, for we are convinced
that Count II is controlled by federal law and that it must be dismissed on
the merits for failure to state a claim upon which relief can be granted.

Under § 301 a suit for violation of the collective bargaining contract in
either a federal or state court is governed by federal law . . . and Count II
on its face charges the individual defendants with a violation of the no-
strike clause. . . .

It is universally accepted that the no-strike clause in a collective agreement at the very least establishes a rule of conduct or condition of
employment the violation of which by employees justifies discipline or
discharge. . . . The conduct charged in Count II is therefore within the
scope of a "violation" of the collective agreement.

As well as charging a violation of the no-strike clause by the individual
defendants, Count II necessarily charges a violation of the clause by the
union itself. The work stoppage alleged is the identical work stoppage for
which the union is sued under Count I and the same damage is alleged as
is alleged in Count I. Count II states that the individual defendants acted
"as officers, committeemen and agents of the said labor organizations" in
breaching and inducing others to breach the collective bargaining con-

tract. Count I charges the principal, and Count II charges the agents for acting on behalf of the principal. . . . Count II, like Count I, is thus a suit based on the union's breach of its collective bargaining contract with the employer, and therefore comes within § 301(a). When a union breach of a contract is alleged, that the plaintiff seeks to hold the agents liable instead of the principal does not bring the action outside the scope of § 301.

Under any theory, therefore, the company's action is governed by the national labor relations law which Congress commanded this Court to fashion under § 301(a). We hold that this law requires the dismissal of Count II for failure to state a claim for which relief can be granted— whether the contract violation charged is that of the union or that of the union plus the union officers and agents.

When Congress passed § 301, it declared its view that only the union was to be made to respond for union wrongs, and that the union members were not subject to levy. Section 301(b) has three clauses. One makes unions suable in the Courts of the United States. Another makes unions bound by the acts of their agents according to conventional principles of agency law (cf. § 301(e)). At the same time, however, the remaining clause exempts agents and members from personal liability for judgments against the union (apparently even when the union is without assets to pay the judgment). The legislative history of § 301(b) makes it clear that this third clause was a deeply felt congressional reaction against the *Danbury Hatters* case (*Loewe* v. *Lawlor, 208 U.S. 274; Lawlor* v. *Loewe,* 235 U.S. 522), and an expression of legislative determination that the aftermath (*Loewe* v. *Savings Bank of Danbury,* 236 F. 444 (C.A. 2d Cir.)) of that decision was not to be permitted to recur. In that case, an antitrust treble damage action was brought against a large number of union members, including union officers and agents, to recover from them the employer's losses in a nationwide, union-directed boycott of his hats. The union was not named as a party, nor was judgment entered against it. A large money judgment was entered, instead, against the individual defendants for participating in the plan "emanating from headquarters" (235 U.S., at 534), by knowingly authorizing and delegating authority to the union officers to do the acts involved. In the debates, Senator Ball, one of the Act's sponsors, declared that § 301, "by providing that the union may sue and be sued as a legal entity, for a violation of contract, and that liability for damages will lie against union assets only, will prevent a repetition of the *Danbury Hatters* case, in which many members lost their homes" (93 Cong. Rec. 5014). See also 93 Cong. Rec. 3839, 6283; S. Rep. No. 105, 80th Cong., 1st Sess. 16.

Consequently, in discharging the duty Congress imposed on us to formulate the federal law to govern § 301(a) suits, we are strongly guided by and do not give a niggardly reading to § 301(b). "We would undercut the Act and defeat its policy if we read § 301 narrowly" (*Lincoln Mills,* 353 U.S., at 456). We have already said in another context that § 301(b) at least evidences "a congressional intention that the union as an entity, like a corporation, should in the absence of agreement be the sole source of recovery for injury inflicted by it" (*Lewis* v. *Benedict Coal Corp.,* 361 U.S.

459, 470). This policy cannot be evaded or truncated by the simple device of suing union agents or members, whether in contract or tort, or both, in a separate count or in a separate action for damages for violation of a collective bargaining contract for which damages the union itself is liable. The national labor policy requires and we hold that when a union is liable for damages for violation of the no-strike clause, its officers and members are not liable for these damages. Here, Count II, as we have said, necessarily alleges union liability but prays for damages from the union agents. Where the union has inflicted the injury it alone must pay. Count II must be dismissed.

The case is remanded to the District Court for further proceedings not inconsistent with this opinion.

Notes

1. Does it make any difference if the arbitration clause in the agreement is worded differently from the arbitration clause in *Atkinson*? If the arbitration clause is worded differently, may the employer be required to arbitrate a claim for damages for breach of a no-strike clause?

In *Drake Bakeries, Inc.* v. *Local 50, American Bakery Workers*, 370 U.S. 254, 50 LRRM 2440 (1962), the company sued for damages and the union moved for and received a stay pending arbitration. The Supreme Court affirmed. The contract provided that "[t]he parties agree that they will promptly attempt to adjust all complaints, disputes or grievances arising between them involving questions of interpretation or application of any cause or matter covered by this contract or any act or conduct or relation between the parties hereto, directly or indirectly." The language of the grievance procedure made it clear that either party could invoke it and that either party could seek arbitration.

The Court said: "If the union did strike in violation of the contract, the employer is entitled to its damages; by staying this action, pending arbitration, we have no intention of depriving it of those damages. We simply remit the company to the forum it agreed to use for processing its strike damage claims. That forum, it is true, may be very different from a courtroom, but we are not persuaded that the remedy there will be inadequate." The Court rejected the argument that the union's breach of the no-strike clause relieved the company of its obligation to arbitrate. Justice Harlan, dissenting, argued that since arbitrators have less expertise in the assessment of damages than courts and since their awards are not self-enforcing, the arbitration clause should not be construed to include damage claims.

2. In *Complete Auto Transit, Inc.*, v. *Reis*, 451 U.S. 401, 107 LRRM 2145 (1981), the Supreme Court agreed (seven to two) with the Court of Appeals that Congress did not intend through Section 301 to create a cause of action for damages against individual union members for breach of a no-strike agreement. The Court said:

"In *Atkinson* v. *Sinclair Refining Co.* . . . the Court held that § 301(a) . . . does not authorize a damages action against individual union officers and members when their union is liable for violating a no-strike clause in a collective-bargaining agreement. We expressly reserved the question whether an employer might maintain a suit for damages against 'individual defendants acting not in behalf of the union but in their personal and nonunion capacity' where their 'unauthorized, individual action' violated the no-strike provision of the collective-bargaining agreement. . . .

". . . [T]he legislative history of § 301 . . . reveals Congress' intent to shield individual employees from liability for damages arising from their breach of the no-strike clause of a collective-bargaining agreement, whether or not the union participated in or authorized the illegality. Indeed, Congress intended this result, even though it might leave the employer unable to recover for his losses. . . ."

Noting that Section 301(b) forbids a money judgment against a union from being enforced against individual union members, the Court says that Section 301(b) reflects a congressional reaction to the *Danbury Hatters* case. (The litigation in *Danbury Hatters* is summarized under Count II in *Atkinson.*)

The Court recognizes that "§ 301(b) explicitly addresses only union-authorized violations of a collective bargaining agreement," but it concludes that the legislative history of Section 301(b) shows that "Congress meant to exclude individual strikers from damages liability, whether or not they were authorized by their union to strike," and that "Congress deliberately chose to allow a damages remedy for breach of the no-strike provision of a collective-bargaining agreement only against *unions,* not *individuals,* and, as to unions, only when they participated in or authorized the strike."

In footnote 18 the Court indicates that employers must look to "the significant array of other remedies available to employers to achieve adherence to collective-bargaining agreements": an action for damages against the union "where responsibility may be traced to the union for the contract breach"; discharge of employees who unlawfully walk off the job; asking the union to discipline its members; or injunctive relief when the underlying dispute giving rise to the breach of the no-strike provision is subject to binding arbitration.

Do you agree with Justice Powell's statements in a concurring opinion that "in reality, more often than not, each of these remedies is illusory" and that "the result of the absence of remedies is a lawless vacuum"?

3. Should an employer be allowed to punish union officials more severely than rank-and-file union members for participating in a strike which violates a collective bargaining agreement? In *Metropolitan Edison Co.* v. *NLRB*, 460 U.S. ___, 112 LRRM 3265 (1983), the Supreme Court held that, in the absence of a "clear and unmistakable" waiver of the statutory protection of the union officials from discrimination, an employer may not lawfully impose greater discipline on union officers

than on rank-and-file union members who participate in a strike which violates a no-strike clause in a collective bargaining agreement.

In this case the contract between the employer (Metropolitan Edison Co., which was constructing a nuclear power generating station at Three Mile Island) and the union (the IBEW) provided that the union and its members "agree that during the term of this agreement there shall be no strikes or walkouts by the Brotherhood or its members." When IBEW members refused to cross a picket line established by another union at the construction site, the employer ordered the IBEW president to cross the picket line to demonstrate the IBEW obligation to comply with the no-strike clause. He refused to do so. After four hours, he and the union vice president achieved a settlement of the problem. The employer disciplined all its employees who refused to cross the picket line by imposing 5- to 10-day suspensions on them except for the union president and vice president who received 25-day suspensions (and a warning that any future participation in unlawful work stoppages would result in their immediate discharge) because they failed to attempt to end the strike by crossing the picket line. The employer stressed the fact that two arbitration awards had upheld its imposition of greater discipline on union officers who had participated in prior illegal strikes, on the ground that union officers have an affirmative duty to enforce the no-strike clause.

Noting that this case did not present the question of whether an employer may impose stricter penalties on union officials who are leaders of an unlawful strike and that the NLRB did not question the employer's right to impose the same discipline on the union officers as was imposed on the others who failed to honor the no-strike clause, the Court holds that an employer may not unilaterally define the actions a union official is required to take to enforce a no-strike clause and penalize him for his failure to comply. Reasoning that discrimination against union officials adversely affects protected employee interests in violation of Section 8(a)(3) because it may deter qualified employees from seeking union office, the Court observes that failure to comply with the employer's directions to cross the picket line would put the officer's job in jeopardy while compliance with the order might diminish the respect and authority necessary to perform his job as a union official. The Court agrees that a union lawfully may bargain away the statutory right protecting union officers from discrimination (by agreeing to require union officials to take affirmative steps to end unlawful work stoppages), but the Court held that the two prior arbitration awards in this case did not constitute a clear and unmistakable waiver of such statutory rights.

Since the Court indicates that violation of a contract provision which requires union officials to take affirmative steps to end an unlawful work stoppage may justify more severe punishment of a union officer for such a violation, is such a policy likely to deter a union from agreeing to such a contract clause? If a union states that it will agree to such a contract clause only if an exculpatory clause (providing that no union officer may be disciplined for any alleged violation of the contract clause) is added, can it validly be argued that the union is bargaining in bad faith?

Boys Markets, Inc. v. Retail Clerks Union, Local 770

Supreme Court of the United States, 1970
398 U.S. 235, 74 LRRM 2257

MR. JUSTICE BRENNAN delivered the opinion of the Court.
In this case we re-examine the holding of *Sinclair Refining Co.* v. *Atkinson,* 370 U.S. 195, 50 LRRM 2420 (1962), that the anti-injunction provisions of the Norris-LaGuardia Act preclude a federal district court from enjoining a strike in breach of a no-strike obligation under a collective bargaining agreement even though that agreement contains provisions enforceable under Section 301(a) of the Labor Management Relations Act for binding arbitration of the grievance dispute concerning which the strike was called. The Court of Appeals for the Ninth Circuit, considering itself bound by *Sinclair,* reversed the grant by the District Court for the Central District of California of petitioner's prayer for injunctive relief. . . . Having concluded that *Sinclair* was erroneously decided and that subsequent events have undermined its continuing validity, we overrule that decision and reverse the judgment of the Court of Appeals.

I

In February 1969, at the time of the incidents that produced this litigation, petitioner and respondents were parties to a collective bargaining agreement which provided *inter alia,* that all controversies concerning its interpretation or application should be resolved by adjustment and arbitration procedures set forth therein and that, during the life of the contract, there should be "no cessation or stoppage of work, lock-out, picketing or boycotts. . . ." The dispute arose when petitioner's frozen foods supervisor and certain members of his crew who were not members of the bargaining unit began to rearrange merchandise in the frozen food cases of one of petitioner's supermarkets. A union representative insisted that the food cases be stripped of all merchandise and be restocked by union personnel. When petitioner did not accede to the union's demand, a strike was called and the union began to picket petitioner's establishment. Thereupon petitioner demanded that the union cease the work stoppage and picketing and sought to invoke the grievance and arbitration procedures specified in the contract.
The following day, since the strike had not been terminated, petitioner filed a complaint in California Superior Court seeking a temporary restraining order, a preliminary and permanent injunction, and specific performance of the contractual arbitration provision. . . . Shortly thereafter, the union removed the case to the federal district court and there made a motion to quash the state court's temporary restraining order. . . . Concluding that the dispute was subject to arbitration under the collective bargaining agreement and that the strike was in violation of the contract, the District Court ordered the parties to arbitrate the underlying dispute and simultaneously enjoined the strike, all picketing in the vicinity of

petitioner's supermarket, and any attempts by the union to induce the employees to strike or to refuse to perform their services.

II

At the outset, we are met with respondent's contention that *Sinclair* ought not to be disturbed because the decision turned on a question of statutory construction which Congress can alter at any time. Since Congress has not modified our conclusions in *Sinclair*, even though it has been urged to do so, respondent argues that principles of *stare decisis* should govern the present case.

We do not agree that the doctrine of *stare decisis* bars a re-examination of *Sinclair* in the circumstances of this case. We fully recognize that important policy considerations militate in favor of continuity and predictability in the law. Nevertheless, as Mr. Justice Frankfurter wrote for the Court "[S]*tare decisis* is a principle of policy and not a mechanical formula of adherence to the latest decision, however recent and questionable, when such adherence involves collision with a prior doctrine more embracing in its scope, intrinsically sounder, and verified by experience." *Helvering* v. *Hallock*, 309 U.S. 106, 119 (1940). See *Swift & Co.* v. *Wickham*, 382 U.S. 111, 116 (1965). It is precisely because *Sinclair* stands as a significant departure from our otherwise consistent emphasis upon the congressional policy to promote the peaceful settlement of labor disputes through arbitration and our efforts to accommodate and harmonize this policy with those underlying the anti-injunction provisions of the Norris-LaGuardia Act that we believe *Sinclair* should be reconsidered. Furthermore, in light of developments subsequent to *Sinclair*, in particular our decision in *Avco Corp.* v. *Aero Lodge 735*, 390 U.S. 557 (1968), it has become clear that the *Sinclair* decision does not further but rather frustrates realization of an important goal of our national labor policy.

Nor can we agree that conclusive weight should be accorded to the failure of Congress to respond to *Sinclair* on the theory that congressional silence should be interpreted as acceptance of the decision. The Court has cautioned that "[i]t is at best treacherous to find in congressional silence alone the adoption of a controlling rule of law." *Girouard* v. *United States*, 328 U.S. 61, 69 (1946). Therefore, in the absence of any persuasive circumstances evidencing a clear design that congressional inaction be taken as acceptance of *Sinclair*, the mere silence of Congress is not a sufficient reason for refusing to reconsider the decision. *Helvering* v. *Hallock, supra*, at 119–120.

III

From the time *Textile Workers Union* v. *Lincoln Mills*, 353 U.S. 448 (1957), was decided, we have frequently found it necessary to consider various substantive and procedural aspects of federal labor contract law and questions concerning its application in both state and federal courts. *Lincoln Mills* held generally that "the substantive law to apply in suits under § 301(a) is federal law, which the courts must fashion from the policy of our national labor laws," 353 U.S., at 456, and more specifically that a union can obtain specific performance of an employer's promise to arbitrate grievances. We rejected the contention that the anti-injunction proscriptions of the Norris-LaGuardia Act prohibited this type of relief, noting that a refusal to arbitrate was not "part and parcel of the abuses against which the Act was aimed," *id.*, at 458, and that the Act itself manifests a policy determination that arbitration should be encouraged. See 29 U.S.C. § 108. Subsequently in the *Steelworkers Trilogy* we emphasized the importance of arbitration as an instrument of federal policy for resolving disputes between labor and management and cautioned the lower courts against usurping the functions of the arbitrator.

Serious questions remained, however, concerning the role which state courts are to play in suits involving collective bargaining agreements. Confronted with some of these problems in *Charles Dowd Box Co.* v. *Courtney,* 368 U.S. 502 (1962), we held that Congress clearly intended *not* to disturb the pre-existing jurisdiction of the state courts over suits for violations of collective bargaining agreements. We noted that the "clear implication of the entire record of the congressional debates in both 1946 and 1947 is that the purpose of conferring jurisdiction upon the federal district courts was not to displace, but to supplement, the thoroughly considered jurisdiction of the courts of the various States over contracts made by labor organizations." *Id.,* at 511.

Shortly after the decision in *Dowd Box,* we sustained, in *Teamsters Local 174* v. *Lucas Flour Co.,* 369 U.S. 95 (1962), an award of damages by a state court to an employer for a breach by the union of a no-strike provision in their contract. While emphasizing that "in enacting § 301 Congress intended doctrines of federal labor law uniformly to prevail over inconsistent local rules," *id.,* at 104, we did not consider the applicability of the Norris-LaGuardia Act to state court proceedings because the employer's prayer for relief sought only damages and not specific performance of a no-strike obligation.

Subsequent to the decision in *Sinclair,* we held in *Avco Corp.* v. *Aero Lodge No. 735, supra,* that § 301(a) suits initially brought in state courts may be removed to the designated federal forum under the federal question removal jurisdiction delineated in 28 U.S.C. § 1441. In so holding, however, the Court expressly left open the questions whether state courts are bound by the anti-injunction proscriptions of the Norris-LaGuardia Act and whether federal courts, after removal of a § 301(a) action, are required to dissolve any injunctive relief previously granted by the state courts. See generally *General Electric Co.* v. *Local Union 191,* 413 F.2d 964 (C.A. 5th Cir. 1969) (dissolution of state injunction required). Three Justices who concurred expressed the view that *Sinclair* should be reconsidered "upon an appropriate future occasion." 390 U.S., at 562 (STEWART, J., concurring).

The decision in *Avco,* viewed in the context of *Lincoln Mills* and its progeny, has produced an anomalous situation which, in our view, makes urgent the reconsideration of *Sinclair.* The principal practical effect of *Avco* and *Sinclair* taken together is nothing less than to oust state courts of jurisdiction in § 301(a) suits where injunctive relief is sought for breach of a no-strike obligation. Union defendants can, as a matter of course, obtain removal to a federal court, and there is obviously a compelling incentive for them to do so in order to gain the advantage of the strictures upon injunctive relief which *Sinclair* imposes on federal courts. The sanctioning of this practice, however, is wholly inconsistent with our conclusion in *Dowd Box* that the congressional purpose embodied in § 301(a) was to *supplement,* and not to encroach upon, the preexisting jurisdiction of the state courts. It is ironic indeed that the very provision which Congress clearly intended to provide additional remedies for breach of collective bargaining agreements has been employed to displace previously existing state remedies. We are not at liberty thus to depart from the clearly expressed congressional policy to the contrary.

On the other hand, to the extent that widely disparate remedies theoretically remain available in state, as opposed to federal, courts, the federal policy of labor law uniformity elaborated in *Lucas Flour Co.,* is seriously offended. This policy, of course, could hardly require, as a practical matter, that labor law be administered identically in all courts, for undoubtedly a certain diversity exists among the state and federal systems in matters of procedural and remedial detail, a fact which Congress evidently took into account in deciding not to disturb the traditional jurisdiction of the States. The injunction, however, is so important a remedial device, particularly in the arbitration context, that its availability or nonavailability in various courts will not only produce rampant forum-shopping and maneuvering from one court to another but will also greatly frustrate any relative uniformity in the enforcement of arbitration agreements.

Furthermore, the existing scheme, with the injunction remedy technically available in the state courts but rendered inefficacious by the removal device, assigns to removal proceedings a totally unintended function. While the underlying purposes of Congress in providing for federal question removal jurisdiction remain somewhat obscure, there has never been a serious contention that Congress intended that the removal mechanism be utilized to foreclose completely remedies otherwise available in the state courts. Although federal question removal jurisdiction may well have been intended to provide a forum for the protection of federal rights where such protection was deemed necessary or to encourage the development of expertise by the federal courts in the interpretation of federal law, there is no indication that Congress intended by the removal mechanism to effect a wholesale dislocation in the allocation of judicial business between the state and federal courts. Cf. *City of Greenwood* v. *Peacock,* 384 U.S. 808 (1966).

It is undoubtedly true that each of the foregoing objections to *Sinclair-Avco* could be remedied either by overruling *Sinclair* or by extending that decision to the States. While some commentators have suggested that the solution to the present unsatisfactory situation does lie in the extension of the *Sinclair* prohibition to state court proceedings, we agree with Chief Justice Traynor of the California Supreme Court that "whether or not Congress could deprive state courts of the power to give such [injunctive] remedies when enforcing collective bargaining agreements, it has not attempted to do so either in the Norris-LaGuardia Act or Section 301." *McCarroll* v. *Los Angeles County Dist. Council of Carpenters,* 49 Cal. 2d 45, 61, 315 P.2d 322, 332 (1957), *cert. denied,* 355 U.S. 932 (1958). See, *e.g, American Dredging Co.* v. *Marine Local 25,* 338 F.2d 837 (C.A. 3d Cir. 1964), *cert. denied,* 380 U.S. 935 (1965); *Shaw Electric Co.* v. *I.B.E.W.,* 418 Pa. 1, 208 A.2d 769 (1965).

An additional reason for not resolving the existing dilemma by extending *Sinclair* to the States is the devastating implications for the enforceability of arbitration agreements and their accompanying no-strike obligations if equitable remedies were not available. As we have previously indicated, a no-strike obligation, express or implied, is the *quid pro quo* for any undertaking by the employer to submit grievance disputes to the process of arbitration. See *Textile Workers Union of America* v. *Lincoln Mills, supra,* 353 U.S., at 455.

An incentive for employers to enter into such an arrangement is necessarily dissipated if the principal and most expeditious method by which the no-strike obligation can be enforced is eliminated. While it is of course true, as respondent contends, that other avenues of redress, such as an action for damages, would remain open to an aggrieved employer, an award of damages after a dispute has been settled is no substitute for an immediate halt to an illegal strike. Furthermore, an action for damages prosecuted during or after a labor dispute would only tend to aggravate industrial strife and delay an early resolution of the difficulties between employer and union.

Even if management is not encouraged by the unavailability of the injunction remedy to resist arbitration agreements, the fact remains that the effectiveness of such agreements would be greatly reduced if injunctive relief were withheld. Indeed, the very purpose of arbitration procedures is to provide a mechanism for the expeditious settlement of industrial disputes without resort to strikes, lock-outs, or other self-help measures. This basic purpose is obviously largely undercut if there is no immediate, effective remedy for those very tactics which arbitration is designed to obviate. Thus, because *Sinclair,* in the aftermath of *Avco,* casts serious doubt upon the effective enforcement of a vital element of stable labor-management relations—arbitration agreements with their attendant no-strike obligations—we conclude that *Sinclair* does not make a viable contribution to federal labor policy.

IV

We have also determined that the dissenting opinion in *Sinclair* states the correct principles concerning the accommodation necessary between the seemingly absolute terms of the Norris-LaGuardia Act and the policy considerations underlying § 301(a), 370 U.S., at 215. Although we need not repeat all that was there said, a few points should be emphasized at this time.

The literal terms of § 4 of the Norris-LaGuardia Act must be accommodated to the subsequently enacted provisions of § 301(a) of the Labor-

Management Relations Act and the purposes of arbitration. Statutory interpretation requires more than concentration upon isolated words; rather, consideration must be given to the total corpus of pertinent law and the policies which inspired ostensibly inconsistent provisions. See *Richards* v. *United States*, 369 U.S. 1, 11 (1962); *Mastro Plastics Corp.* v. *NLRB*, 350 U.S. 270, 285, 37 LRRM 2587 (1956); *United States* v. *Hutcheson*, 312 U.S. 219, 235, 7 LRRM 267 (1941).

The Norris-LaGuardia Act was responsive to a situation totally different from that which exists today. In the early part of this century, the federal courts generally were regarded as allies of management in its attempt to prevent the organization and strengthening of labor unions; and in this industrial struggle the injunction became a potent weapon which was wielded against the activities of labor groups. The result was a large number of sweeping decrees, often issued *ex parte*, drawn on an *ad hoc* basis without regard to any systematic elaboration of national labor policy. See *Drivers' Union* v. *Lake Valley Co.*, 311 U.S. 91, 102 (1940).

In 1932 Congress attempted to bring some order out of the industrial chaos that had developed and to correct the abuses which had resulted from the interjection of the federal judiciary into union-management disputes on the behalf of management. See Declaration of Public Policy, Norris-LaGuardia Act, § 2, 47 Stat. 70 (1932). Congress, therefore, determined initially to limit severely the power of the federal courts to issue injunctions "in any case involving or growing out of any labor dispute. . . ." 47 Stat. 70. Even as initially enacted, however, the prohibition against federal injunctions was by no means absolute. See Norris-LaGuardia Act, §§ 7, 8, 9, 47 Stat. 70 (1932). Shortly thereafter Congress passed the Wagner Act, designed to curb various management activities which tended to discourage employee participation in collective action.

As labor organizations grew in strength and developed toward maturity, congressional emphasis shifted from protection of the nascent labor movement to the encouragement of collective bargaining and to administrative techniques for the peaceful resolution of industrial disputes. This shift in emphasis was accomplished, however, without extensive revision of many of the older enactments, including the anti-injunction section of the Norris-LaGuardia Act. Thus it became the task of the courts to accommodate, to reconcile the older statutes with the more recent ones.

A leading example of this accommodation process is *Brotherhood of R. R. Trainmen* v. *Chicago River & Ind. R. R.*, 353 U.S. 30 (1957). There we were confronted with a peaceful strike which violated the statutory duty to arbitrate imposed by the Railway Labor Act. The Court concluded that a strike in violation of a statutory arbitration duty was not the type of situation to which the Norris-LaGuardia Act was responsive, that an important federal policy was involved in the peaceful settlement of disputes through the statutorily-mandated arbitration procedure, that this important policy was imperiled if equitable remedies were not available to implement it, and hence that Norris-LaGuardia's policy of nonintervention by the federal courts should yield to the overriding interest in the successful implementation of the arbitration process.

The principles elaborated in *Chicago River* are equally applicable to the present case. To be sure, *Chicago River* involved arbitration procedures established by statute. However, we have frequently noted, in such cases as *Lincoln Mills*, the *Steelworkers Trilogy*, and *Lucas Flour*, the importance which Congress has attached generally to the voluntary settlement of labor disputes without resort to self-help and more particularly to arbitration as a means to this end. Indeed, it has been stated that *Lincoln Mills*, in its exposition of § 301(a), "went a long way towards making arbitration the central institution in the administration of collective bargaining contracts."

The *Sinclair* decision, however, seriously undermined the effectiveness of the arbitration technique as a method peacefully to resolve industrial disputes without resort to strikes, lockouts, and similar devices. Clearly employers will be wary of assuming obligations to arbitrate specifically enforceable against them when no similarly efficacious remedy is available to enforce the concomitant undertaking of the union to refrain from striking. On the other hand, the central purpose of the Norris-LaGuardia Act to foster the growth and viability of labor organizations is hardly retarded—if anything, this goal is advanced—by a remedial device which merely enforces the obligation that the union freely undertook under a specifically enforceable agreement to submit disputes to arbitration. We conclude, therefore, that the unavailability of equitable relief in the arbitration context presents a serious impediment to the congressional policy favoring the voluntary establishment of a mechanism for the peaceful resolution of labor disputes, that the core purpose of the Norris-LaGuardia Act is not sacrificed by the limited use of equitable remedies to further this important policy, and consequently that the Norris-LaGuardia Act does not bar the granting of injunctive relief in the circumstances of the instant case.

V

Our holding in the present case is a narrow one. We do not undermine the vitality of the Norris-LaGuardia Act. We deal only with the situation in which a collective bargaining contract contains a mandatory grievance adjustment or arbitration procedure. Nor does it follow from what we have said that injunctive relief is appropriate as a matter of course in every case of a strike over an arbitrable grievance. The dissenting opinion in *Sinclair* suggested the following principles for the guidance of the district courts in determining whether to grant injunctive relief—principles which we now adopt: "A District Court entertaining an action under § 301 may not grant injunctive relief against concerted activity unless and until it decides that the case is one in which an injunction would be appropriate despite the Norris-LaGuardia Act. When a strike is sought to be enjoined because it is over a grievance which both parties are contractually bound to arbitrate, the District Court may issue no injunctive order until it first holds that the contract *does* have the effect; and the employer should be ordered to arbitrate, as a condition of his obtaining an injunction against the strike. Beyond this, the District Court must, of course, consider whether issuance of an injunction would be warranted under ordinary principles of equity—whether breaches are occurring and will continue, or have been threatened and will be committed; whether they have caused or will cause irreparable injury to the employer; and whether the employer will suffer more from the denial of an injunction than will the union from its issuance." 370 U.S., at 228. (Emphasis in original.)

In the present case there is no dispute that the grievance in question was subject to adjustment and arbitration under the collective bargaining agreement and that the petitioner was ready to proceed with arbitration at the time an injunction against the strike was sought and obtained. The District Court also concluded that, by reason of respondent's violations of its no-strike obligation, petitioner "has suffered irreparable injury and will continue to suffer irreparable injury." Since we now overrule *Sinclair*, the holding of the Court of Appeals in reliance on *Sinclair* must be reversed. Accordingly, we reverse the judgment of the Court of Appeals and remand the case with directions to enter a judgment affirming the order of the District Court.

It is so ordered.

[MR. JUSTICE STEWART concurred. Although he supported the majority in *Sinclair* in 1962, he changed his mind during the interim period and concurred with the majority in *Boys Markets*. He noted the aphorism that "Wisdom too often never comes, and so one ought not to reject it because it comes late."]

MR. JUSTICE BLACK, dissenting.

Congress in 1932 enacted the Norris-LaGuardia Act, § 4 of which with exceptions not here relevant, specifically prohibited federal courts in the broadest and most comprehensive language from issuing any injunctions, temporary or permanent, against participation in a labor dispute. Subsequently, in 1947, Congress gave jurisdiction to the federal courts in "[s]uits for violation of contracts between an employer and a labor organization." Although this subsection, § 301(a) of the Taft-Hartley Act explicitly waives the diversity and amount-in-controversy requirements for federal jurisdiction, it says nothing at all about granting injunctions. Eight years ago this Court considered the relation of these two statutes: after full briefing and argument, relying on the language and history of the Acts, the Court decided that Congress did not wish this later statute to impair in any way Norris-LaGuardia's explicit prohibition against injunctions in labor disputes. *Sinclair Refining Co.* v. *Atkinson*, 370 U.S. 195 (1962).

Although Congress has been urged to overrule our holding in *Sinclair*, it has steadfastly refused to do so. Nothing in the language or history of the two Acts has changed. Nothing at all has changed, in fact, except the membership of the Court and the personal views of one Justice. I remain of the opinion that *Sinclair* was correctly decided, and, moreover, that the prohibition of the Norris-LaGuardia Act is close to the heart of the entire federal system of labor regulation. In my view *Sinclair* should control the disposition of this case.

Even if the majority were correct, however, in saying that *Sinclair* misinterpreted the Taft-Hartley and Norris-LaGuardia Acts, I should be compelled to dissent. I believe that both the making and the changing of laws which affect the substantial rights of the people are primarily for Congress, not this Court. Most especially is this so when the laws involved are the focus of strongly held views of powerful but antagonistic political and economic interests. The Court's function in the application and interpretation of such laws must be carefully limited to avoid encroaching on the power of Congress to determine policies and make laws to carry them out.

. . . Of course, when this Court first interprets a statute, then the statute becomes what this Court has said it is. Such an initial interpretation is proper, and unavoidable, in any system in which courts have the task of applying general statutes in a multitude of situations. B. Cardozo, The Nature of the Judicial Process 112–115 (1921). The Court undertakes the task of interpretation, however, not because the Court has any special ability to fathom the intent of Congress, but rather because interpretation is unavoidable in the decision of the case before it. When the law has been settled by an earlier case then any subsequent "reinterpretation" of the statute is gratuitous and neither more nor less than an amendment: it is no different in effect from a judicial alteration of language that Congress itself placed in the statute. . . .

The legislative effect of the Court's reversal is especially clear here. In *Sinclair* the Court invited Congress to act if it should be displeased with the judicial interpretation of the statute. . . .

Congress, however, did not act, thus indicating at least a willingness to leave the law as *Sinclair* had construed it. It seems to me highly inappropriate for this Court now, eight years later, in effect to enact the amendment that Congress has refused to adopt.

I do not believe that the principle of *stare decisis* forecloses all reconsiderations of earlier decisions. In the area of constitutional law, for example, where the only alternative to action by this Court is the laborious process of constitutional amendment and where the ultimate responsibility rests with this Court, I believe reconsideration is always proper. . . .

Even on statutory questions the appearance of new facts or changes in circumstances might warrant re-examination of past decisions in exceptional cases under exceptional circumstances. In the present situation there are no such circumstances. . . .

The only "subsequent event" to which the Court can point is our decision in *Avco Corp.* v. *Aero Lodge 735*, 390 U.S. 557 (1968). The Court must recognize that the holding of *Avco* is in no way inconsistent with *Sinclair*. As we said in *Avco, supra*, at 561: "The nature of the relief available after jurisdiction attaches is, of course, different from the question whether there is jurisdiction to adjudicate the controversy." The Court contends, however, that the result of the two cases taken together is the "anomalous situation" that no-strike clauses become unenforceable in state courts, and this is inconsistent with "an important goal of our national labor policy."

Avco does make any effort to enforce a no-strike clause in a state court removable to a federal court, but it does not follow that the no-strike clause is unenforceable. Damages may be awarded; the union may be forced to arbitrate. And the employer may engage in self-help. The Court would have it that these techniques are less effective than an injunction. That is doubtless true. But the harshness and effectiveness of injunctive relief—and opposition to "government by injunction"—were the precise reasons for the congressional prohibition in the Norris-LaGuardia Act. The effect of the *Avco* decision is, indeed, to highlight the limited remedial powers of federal courts. But if the Congress is unhappy with these powers as this Court defined them, then the Congress may act; this Court should not. The members of the majority have simply decided that they are more sensitive to the "realization of an important goal of our national labor policy" than the Congress or their predecessors on this Court.

The correct interpretation of the Taft-Hartley Act, and even the goals of "our national labor policy," are less important than the proper division of functions between the branches of our Federal Government. The Court would do well to remember the words of John Adams, written in the Declaration of Rights in the Constitution of the Commonwealth of Massachusetts:

> "The judicial [department] shall never exercise the legislative and executive powers, or either of them: to the end it may be a government of laws and not of men."

I dissent.

Notes

1. In *Gateway Coal Co.* v. *United Mine Workers*, 414 U.S. 368, 85 **LRRM** 2049 (1974), the contract arbitration clause applied not only to disputes over interpretation of the contract but also to "any local trouble of any kind aris[ing] at the mine." There was no express no-strike clause. The union, refusing arbitration, struck over the alleged safety hazard created by the company's retention of two foremen who had falsely recorded mine air flow figures. The district court enjoined the strike and ordered arbitration, in the meantime suspending the two foremen. The court of appeals reversed, holding that there was a public policy against compulsory arbitration of safety disputes.

The Supreme Court held that the dispute was arbitrable under the contract and *Warrior & Gulf*, that under *Lucas Flour* there was an implied agreement not to strike over the dispute, and that a *Boys Markets* injunction against the strike was therefore proper. The Court recognized that Section 502 of the LMRA was a "limited exception to an express or an implied no-strike obligation," but held that "an honest belief" in the existence of "abnormally dangerous conditions for work" was not sufficient. A union relying on Section 502 must present "ascertainable, objective evidence" of the dangerous work condition.

Query: What would be the precise issue before the arbitrator?

2. *Boys Markets* seems to lay at rest the question whether the Norris-LaGuardia Act prevents federal judicial enforcement of an arbitrator's cease and desist order, *i.e.*, such enforcement is permissible.

3. A question not laid to rest is whether the new federal law which it enunciates is applicable in all respects to the state courts. Specifically, before issuing an injunction, must a state court make the same kind of findings that were made by the district court in the *Boys Markets* case and noted by Justice Brennan in the last part of his opinion? The question is important because even in some states with anti-injunction laws, such as New York and Pennsylvania, a strike in breach of a no-strike clause is held not to be a "labor dispute" and thus enjoinable. See Aaron, *Labor Injunctions in the State Courts—Part I: A Survey*, 50 Va. L. Rev. 951, 981 (1964).

Comment on the Developing Federal Common Law

In *Boys Markets*, the Supreme Court stressed that *Sinclair* v. *Atkinson* (interpreting Norris-LaGuardia to prohibit the enjoining of strikes in breach of contract) stands as a significant departure from the otherwise consistent efforts to promote the peaceful settlement of labor disputes through arbitration.

The statement indicates the Court's interest in industrial peace, an interest that has caused it sometimes to override freedom of contract—*Lucas Flour, John Wiley* (which is considered in the next section of this chapter), *Gateway Coal*, and the Trilogy itself. These decisions make two critical assumptions:

(a) Industrial peace can be achieved through the imposition of federal law—often allegedly interpreting the agreement—when the result is or may be at variance with the intentions of the parties.

The "quid pro quo" language, first enunciated in *Lincoln Mills*, may have been a device to find Section 301 constitutional. There was considerable evidence in legislative history that no-strike clauses should be enforceable. If so, and if no-strike clauses are the quid pro quo for arbitration clauses, it follows that arbitration clauses should be enforced. The first rule to be developed under the "law" of Section 301 was that such clauses should be specifically enforced.

The quid pro quo "device" in *Lincoln Mills*, if that is what it was, has subsequently developed a life of its own, most clearly reflected in *Lucas Flour* (where the Court implied a no-strike clause coextensive with an express arbitration clause). It seems that that which is most consistent with the Court's view of responsible collective bargaining will be found to exist even if the Court must imply the existence of an important clause hardly omitted by inadvertence.

Will arbitration continue to be a preferred avenue for the settlement of disputes (i) when most disputes reach arbitration under a federal presumption of arbitrability; (ii) when awards can only be reversed if the arbitrator's *words* manifest an infidelity to the agreement; (iii) when an arbitration clause survives a change of employer through merger, etc.;

(iv) when agreement on an arbitration clause creates an implied no-strike clause equally as broad which may lead to a damage award or injunction for "breach" of this implied clause? (Compare the Court's cavalier attitude to freedom of contract in this area to its abhorrence of contract making by the NLRB in cases involving an employer's violation of Section 8(a)(5) and in cases involving the obligations of a successor employer.)

(b) The Court can accurately gauge whether or not its rulings will effectuate the federal policy encouraging the avoidance of labor strife. As implied above, peace is problematical when purchased in the face of the intentions of the parties. The interest in arbitration could decrease given the federal baggage, presumptions, and implied clauses, which now come freighted on the arbitration vehicle. Moreover, the policy referred to by the Court is *judicial*, not legislative, policy.

Professor Wellington has indicated that strikes over grievable issues are rare but occur when feelings run extremely high. If this is so, query whether the legal rules serve a deterrence function. Even if they do, he argues that the dispute will merely be postponed for resolution subsequent to the expiration of the agreement. (Yet, this "cooling off" period could be helpful, lending "a measure of rationality to the resolution of disputes." See Gould, *On Labor Injunctions, Unions, and the Judges: The Boys Markets Case*, 1970 Sup. Ct. Rev. 215, 225–27.)

It is also possible that to the extent the Court has encouraged arbitration in order to avoid labor strife, it has too optimistically viewed the impact of law. Have the decisions encouraged the adoption of arbitration clauses? It would be interesting to check the spread of arbitration clauses in light of Supreme Court decisions. Considerable arbitration existed before the Trilogy in the early 1960s, and the interest in the private settlement of disputes may have little to do with Court decisions. Evidence suggests that arbitration clauses gained wide acceptance even during the period when *Sinclair* prevented the enjoining of strikes in breach of no-strike clauses! Thus, the Bureau of Labor Statistics noted in 1964 that approximately 94 percent of agreements negotiated contained arbitration clauses. BLS Bull. No. 1425–1, Grievance Procedures, p. 1 (1964).

More relevant, perhaps, is the need to provide quick and relatively inexpensive resolution of contract disputes. Indeed, there is considerable grumbling in union ranks over the delay and cost of arbitration today. Arbitration serves other functions, of course, but it is not clear that interest in this mode of dispute resolution has any relation to the legal rules developed under Section 301.

Another question goes to the heart of the Court's position: How dysfunctional are strikes over grievable matters? In the situation of contract making, the emphasis is on freedom of contract and not industrial peace. Yet, most strikes occur here, and the NLRA expressly protects strikes as a vehicle for the fair resolution of disputes. The Court has protected strikes in response to an employer's unfair labor practices even though the procedures of the Act exist to remedy these violations and, indeed, were designed to avoid strife over such violations. Nevertheless, "unfair labor practice" strikers receive more protection than economic strikers. Moreover, such strikes may be protected even if a no-strike promise has been made.

The NLRA recognized that strikes could be functional, ironically, in the cause of industrial peace. Can the law effectively shut off strikes over white-hot issues? Even if this is possible, is something lost? If strikes are enjoinable, or subject to damage awards, might not other, more subtle, devices be used to put pressure on the employer? There is evidence that this occurs. But the main concern in these comments is with the Court's assumption that strife is dysfunctional.

Boys Markets is a decision the parties can live with. The point made here, however, is that *Sinclair* was at variance with federal policy enunciated since *Lincoln Mills only if* every decision must be resolved in favor of industrial peace (the Court's notions of industrial peace and short-run peace to boot).

Thus, whether or not industrial peace is purchased by the Supreme Court decisions discussed here, the issue is whether the cost is too high. The strike, after all, is a device to resolve disputes and, although we might prefer other kinds of dispute resolving procedures, it is generally protected by the NLRA.

Buffalo Forge *and Sympathy Strikes*

The issue in *Buffalo Forge Co.* v. *Steelworkers*, 428 U.S. 397, 92 LRRM 3032 (1976), was whether a federal court may enjoin a sympathy strike pending an arbitrator's decision as to whether the strike was forbidden by the express no-strike clause contained in the collective bargaining agreement to which the striking union was a party.

In this case the company operated three separate plant and office facilities in the Buffalo, N.Y. area. For some years the production and maintenance (P & M) employees at these three locations were represented by the Steelworkers. The contracts applicable to the P & M employees contained no-strike clauses as well as grievance and arbitration provisions for settling disputes over the interpretation and application of the contracts. Shortly before the dispute in question arose, the union was also certified to represent the company's "office clerical-technical" (O & T) employees at these three locations. After several months of negotiations for a first collective bargaining agreement failed to produce an agreement, the O & T employees struck and established picket lines at all three locations. The P & M employees honored the O & T picket lines and stopped work at the three plants. The employer took the position that a strike by the P & M employees violated the no-strike clause in the contract applicable to the P & M employees. The employer "offered to arbitrate any dispute which led to the planned strike."

The employer sought a temporary restraining order and other relief in federal district court. The employer claimed that the question of whether the P & M employees' work stoppage violated the no-strike clause was itself arbitrable. The federal district court refused to issue a temporary restraining order. The district court found that the P & M employees were engaged in a sympathy action in support of the O & T employees, and that Section 4 of the Norris-LaGuardia Act precluded an injunction because the P & M employees' strike was not over an "arbitrable grievance" and hence was not within the "narrow" exception to the Norris-LaGuardia Act established in *Boys Markets*. On appeal the parties stipulated that the union had authorized and directed the P & M work stoppage, and that the O & T employees' strike and picket line were bona fide, primary, and legal. The court of appeals agreed with the district court that no injunction should be issued.

In a 5-to-4 decision the majority of the Supreme Court affirmed the judgment of the court of appeals. The majority opinion, written by Mr. Justice White, agreed with the employer that the issue of whether the sympathy strike by the P & M employees violated the no-strike clause was arbitrable, that the employer was entitled to a court order requiring the union to arbitrate if the union refused to do so, and that the employer could obtain an injunction to enforce the arbitration award if the award found that the sympathy strike violated the no-strike clause. But the majority of the Court agreed with the district court and the court of appeals that the employer was not entitled to an injunction against the sympathy strike (while the issue of whether this strike violated the no-strike clause was pending in arbitration) because the strike had not been precipitated by a dispute which was subject to binding arbitration, *i.e.*, the strike was not over a grievance which was arbitrable.

The majority of the Court reasoned as follows:

". . . The driving force behind *Boys Markets* was to implement the strong congressional preference for the private dispute settlement mechanisms agreed upon by the parties. Only to that extent was it held necessary to accommodate § 4 of the Norris-LaGuardia Act to § 301 of the Labor Management Relations Act and to lift the former's ban against the issuance of injunctions in labor disputes. Striking over an arbitrable dispute would interfere with and frustrate the arbitral processes by which the parties had chosen to settle a dispute. The *quid pro quo* for the employer's promise to arbitrate was the union's obligation not to strike over issues that were subject to the arbitration machinery. Even in the absence of an express no-strike clause, an undertaking not to strike would be implied where the strike was over an otherwise arbitrable dispute. *Gateway Coal Co.* v. *United Mine Workers, supra*; *Teamsters Local* v. *Lucas Flour Co.*, 369 U.S. 95, 49 LRRM 2717 (1962). Otherwise, the employer would be deprived of his bargain and the policy of the labor statutes to implement private resolution of disputes in a manner agreed upon would seriously suffer.

"*Boys Markets* plainly does not control this case. The District Court found, and it is not now disputed, that the strike was not *over* any dispute between the Union and the employer that was even remotely subject to the arbitration provisions of the contract. The strike at issue was a sympathy strike in support of sister unions negotiating with the employer; neither its causes nor the issue underlying it were subject to the settlement procedures provided by the contract between the employer and respondents. The strike had neither the purpose nor the effect of denying or evading an obligation to arbitrate or of depriving the employer of his bargain. Thus, had the contract not contained a no-strike clause or had the clause expressly excluded sympathy strikes, there would have been no possible basis for implying from the existence of an arbitration clause a promise not to strike that could have been violated by the sympathy strike in this case. *Gateway Coal Co.* v. *Mine Workers, supra*, at 383.[10]

"Nor was the injunction authorized solely because it was alleged that the sympathy strike called by the Union violated the express no-strike provision of the contract. Section 301 of the Act assigns a major role to the courts in enforcing collective bargaining agreements, but aside from the enforcement of the arbitration provisions of such contracts, within the limits permitted by *Boys Markets*, the Court has never indicated that the courts may enjoin actual or threatened contract violations despite the Norris-LaGuardia Act. In the course of enacting the Taft-Hartley Act, Congress rejected the proposal that the Norris-LaGuardia Act's prohibition against labor-dispute injunctions be lifted to the extent necessary to make injunctive remedies available in federal courts for the purpose of enforcing collective bargaining agreements. The allegation of the complaint that the Union was breaching its obligation not to strike did not in itself warrant an injunction. . . ."

MR. JUSTICE STEVENS, with whom MR. JUSTICE BRENNAN, MR. JUSTICE MARSHALL, and MR. JUSTICE POWELL joined, dissented as follows:

"A contractual undertaking not to strike is the union's normal *quid pro quo* for the employer's undertaking to submit grievances to binding arbitration. The question in this case is whether that *quid pro quo* is severable into two parts—one which a federal court may enforce by injunction and another which it may not.

"Less than three years ago all eight of my Brethren joined in an opinion which answered that question quite directly by stating that whether a district court has authority to enjoin a work stoppage 'depends on whether the union was under a contractual duty not to

"[10]To the extent that the Court of Appeals and other courts have assumed that a mandatory arbitration clause implies a commitment not to engage in sympathy strikes, they are wrong.

"*Gateway Coal Co.* v. *United Mine Workers, supra*, itself furnishes no additional support for the employer here. In that case, after finally concluding that the dispute over which the strike occurred was arbitrable within the meaning of the arbitration clause contained in a contract which did not also contain a no-strike clause, the Court implied an undertaking not to strike based on *Teamsters Local* v. *Lucas Flour Co., supra*, and permitted an injunction against the strike based on the principles of *Boys Markets*. The critical determination in *Gateway* was that the dispute was arbitrable. This was the fulcrum for implying a duty not to strike over that dispute and for enjoining the strike the union had called. Of course, the authority to enjoin the work stoppage depended on 'whether the union was under a contractual duty not to strike.' 414 U.S., at 380. But that statement was made only preparatory to finding an implied duty not to strike. The strike was then enjoined only because it was over an arbitrable dispute. The same precondition to a strike injunction also existed in *Boys Markets*. Absent that factor, neither case furnishes the authority to enjoin a strike solely because it is claimed to be in breach of contract and because this claim is itself arbitrable."

strike.' " *Gateway Coal Co.* v. *United Mine Workers*, 414 U.S. 368, 380, 85 LRRM 2049.[1]

"The Court today holds that only a part of the union's *quid pro quo* is enforceable by injunction.[2] The principal bases for the holding are (1) the Court's literal interpretation of the Norris-LaGuardia Act; and (2) its fear that the federal judiciary would otherwise make a 'massive' entry into the business of contract interpretation heretofore reserved for arbitrators. The first argument has been rejected repeatedly in cases in which the central concerns of the Norris-LaGuardia Act were not implicated. The second is wholly unrealistic[3] and was implicitly rejected in *Gateway Coal* when the Court held that 'a substantial question of contractual interpretation' was a sufficient basis for federal equity jurisdiction. 414 U.S., at 384. That case held that an employer might enforce a somewhat ambiguous *quid pro quo*; today the Court holds that a portion of the *quid pro quo* is unenforceable no matter how ambiguous it may be. With all respect, I am persuaded that a correct application of the reasoning underlying the landmark decision in *Boys Markets, Inc.* v. *Clerks Union* requires a different result. . . ."

Notes

1. What are the most persuasive policy arguments in support of the holding of the majority in *Buffalo Forge*? In support of the dissent? Does *Buffalo Forge* preclude an action by an employer against a union for damages for an alleged breach of a no-strike clause as a result of a sympathy strike? May the employer discipline employees who engage in a sympathy strike in violation of a no-strike clause? Cf. *U.S. Steel Corp.*, 264 NLRB No. 10, 111 LRRM 1200 (1982), where the Board says that a no-strike clause normally will be read to prohibit only those strikes which are over disputes covered by the arbitration provisions of the contract, and that, under a principle of coterminous application, sympathy strikes are not normally encompassed by broad no-strike clauses because the dispute

[1]"The Court read *Boys Markets* to conclude that '§ 301(a) empowers a federal court to enjoin violations of a contractual duty not to strike.' 414 U.S., at 381. There was no dissent from that proposition."

[2]"The enforceable part of the no-strike agreement is the part relating to a strike 'over an arbitrable dispute.' In *Gateway Coal*, however, my Brethren held that the district court had properly entered an injunction that not only terminated a strike pending an arbitrator's decision of an underlying safety dispute, but also 'prospectively required both parties to abide by his resolution of the controversy.' *Id.*, at 373. A strike in defiance of an arbitrator's award would not be 'over an arbitrable dispute'; nevertheless, the Court today recognizes the propriety of an injunction against such a strike. . . ."

[3]"The Court's expressed concern that enforcing an unambiguous no-strike clause by enjoining a sympathy strike might 'embroil the district courts in massive preliminary injunction litigation.'. . . is supposedly supported by the fact that 21 million American workers were covered by over 150,000 collective-bargaining agreements in 1972. These figures give some idea of the potential number of grievances that may arise, each of which could lead to a strike which is plainly enjoinable under *Boys Markets*. These figures do not shed any light on the number of sympathy strikes which may violate an express no-strike commitment. In the past several years over a dozen such cases have arisen. . . . Future litigation of this character would, of course, be minimized by clarifying amendments to existing no-strike clauses."

which causes the sympathy strike is not arbitrable under the contract with the broad no-strike clause. Thus, the Board holds that an employer who has a broad no-strike clause in his contract with the Union may be precluded from imposing discipline on employees engaged in a sympathy strike because the strike may be deemed to be outside the coverage of the no-strike clause. Should *Buffalo Forge* be viewed as applicable to the question of imposition of discipline on employees?

2. Suppose that an employer seeks an injunction in a state court against a strike, and that, for some reason, the case is not removed to federal court. Assume further that the strike is not over an arbitrable grievance, and, thus, that a federal court could not enjoin the activity under *Buffalo Forge*. May the state court enjoin the strike on the reasoning that Norris-LaGuardia is not applicable to a state court because this statute is based on congressional power under the Constitution to regulate the jurisdiction of inferior federal courts? Such a holding would encourage forum shopping since employers would seek injunctions in state courts rather than federal courts. If the state court can enjoin, then the very same problems which seemingly bothered Justice Brennan in *Boys Markets* are all present. If the state court cannot enjoin the strike, then it must be because the Norris-LaGuardia Act has become part of Section 301 law and, as such, is binding on state courts. But if this is so, why was this proposition not adopted in *Boys Markets* itself? As the critics of *Buffalo Forge* have noted, Norris-LaGuardia does not distinguish between strikes based on a response to arbitrable or nonarbitrable grievances.

3. Suppose that an employer commits an unfair labor practice (in violation of Section 8(a)(5) of the NLRA) by unilaterally deciding to use part-time employees on a separate seniority schedule. The agreement contains a broad no-strike clause and a broad arbitration clause. Although the union could file a grievance and process it to arbitration, the union decides instead to strike to protest the unfair labor practice. Should a federal district court grant an injunction to the employer?

3. RIGHTS AND OBLIGATIONS OF SUCCESSORS

Assume that a company and a union representing the company's employees execute a five-year collective bargaining agreement. What rights and obligations arise if the union is displaced by another union before the agreement expires? What rights and obligations arise if the company is displaced by another employer (by merger, sale, or some other means) before the agreement expires? Consider these questions in light of the following materials.

a. Successor Union

The leading case on the question of the effect of a change in union representation upon an existing collective bargaining agreement is *American Seating Co.*, 106 NLRB 250, 32 LRRM 1439 (1953). In that case the UAW was certified in September 1949, and on July 1, 1950, it executed a three-year contract with the company. Two years later the Pattern Makers petitioned for an election in a small craft unit which was included in the UAW certification and contract. At that time two years was the maximum period under contract bar rules. An election was ordered which the Pattern Makers won. After certification they requested bargaining, but the company replied that the existing contract with the UAW was still in full force and effect and remained binding on all employees, including patternmakers, until its expiration on July 1, 1953. In the subsequent 8(a)(5) proceeding, the company contended that the certification of the Pattern Makers merely resulted in the substitution of a new bargaining representative for patternmakers, with the substantive terms of the contract remaining unchanged. The company argued that the UAW was the agent of the patternmakers when the 1950 contract was executed and that the patternmakers, as principals, were bound notwithstanding that they had changed their agent.

The Board concluded that the company had violated Section 8(a)(5) under the following reasoning. The assumption that "common-law principles of agency control the relationship of exclusive bargaining representative to employees in an appropriate unit" was "unwarranted" and overlooked "the unique character of that relationship" under the NLRA.

"If the Respondent's contention is sound, a certified bargaining representative might be deprived of effective statutory power as to the most important subjects of collective bargaining for an unlimited number of years as the result of an agreement negotiated by an unwanted and repudiated bargaining representative. There is no provision in the statute for this kind of emasculated certified bargaining representative. Moreover, the rule urged by the Respondent seems hardly calculated to reduce 'industrial strife' by encouraging the 'practice and procedure of collective bargaining,' the declared purpose of the National Labor Relations Act. . . . We hold that, for the reasons which led the Board to adopt the rule that a contract of unreasonable duration is not a bar to a new determination of representatives, such a contract may not bar full statutory collective bargaining."

What conflicting statutory policies are applicable to this type of situation?

Consistent with the above result, it has been held that the superseded contracting union retains no rights under the former contract as to the employees covered by the new contract. See *Modine Manufacturing Co.* v. *Association of Machinists*, 216 F.2d 326, 35 LRRM 2003 (6th Cir. 1954).

b. Successor Employer

In *NLRB* v. *Burns International Security Services*, 406 U.S. 272, 80 LRRM 2255 (1972), the Court held that an employer, who replaced another employer, was not bound to honor the terms of the collective bargaining agreement between the predecessor employer and the union representing the latter's employees, but that the new employer, who had hired its predecessor's employees, had a duty to bargain with the union over the terms and conditions of the employees. In that case the new employer did not purchase anything from the predecessor employer. They were competitors, each bidding for a service contract to provide plant protection services to a third party. The Court said that:

". . . in a variety of circumstances involving a merger, stock acquisition, reorganization, or assets purchase, the Board might properly find as a matter of fact that the successor had assumed the obligations under the old contract. Such a duty does not, however, ensue as a matter of law from the mere fact that an employer is doing the same work in the same place with the same employees as his predecessor. . . ."

In *Burns* the Court identified the following policy considerations which are applicable to its refusal to require a union or a successor employer to honor the provisions of a collective bargaining agreement executed with a predecessor employer:

"We also agree with the Court of Appeals that holding either the union or the new employer bound to the substantive terms of an old collective-bargaining contract may result in serious inequities. A potential employer may be willing to take over a moribund business only if he can make changes in corporate structure, composition of the labor force, work location, task assignment, and nature of supervision. Saddling such an employer with the terms and conditions of employment contained in the old collective-bargaining contract may make these changes impossible and may discourage and inhibit the transfer of capital. On the other hand, a union may have made concessions to a small or failing employer that it would be unwilling to make to a large or economically successful firm. The congressional policy manifest in the Act is to enable the parties to negotiate for any protection either deems appropriate, but to allow the balance of bargaining advantage to be set by economic power realities. Strife is bound to occur if the concessions that must be honored do not correspond to the relative economic strength of the parties."

In connection with a related problem the Court has held that the bona fide purchaser of a business, who purchased the business with knowledge that his predecessor has committed an unfair labor practice in discharging an employee, may be required by the Board to reinstate the employee with back pay. Both employers are jointly and severally liable for the back pay. *Golden State Bottling Co., Inc.* v. *NLRB*, 414 U.S. 164, 84 LRRM 2839 (1973). The Court recognized that the potential liability of a successor employer for remedying an unfair labor practice "is a matter which can be reflected in the price that he pays for the business or he may secure an indemnity clause in the sales contract. . . ."

Problem

The following memo is sent from the union's assistant general counsel to the union's general counsel:

"I'm concerned that our arbitration action against the Enderby Company is not going to prevent the subcontracting of lab work to Dunbar from the Enderby Company. I suggest we bring an arbitration action also against Dunbar as a successor. We then would argue, under the *Wiley* v. *Livingston* doctrine, that even if Enderby has the contractual right to turn the work over to Dunbar, Dunbar as successor is bound to honor the terms and conditions of the original agreement with us. What do you think of this approach?"

Questions

1. What do you think of the proposal?
2. Does Dunbar buy its way into a successorship problem if it hires 15 of Enderby's 20 lab technicians? Would Dunbar violate 8(a)(3) by not hiring them?

The reasoning in *Burns* (which dealt with the rights and obligations of a successor-employer in the context of an alleged unfair labor practice) was inconsistent to some extent with the reasoning of the Court in the earlier case of *Wiley* v. *Livingston*, 376 U.S. 543, 55 LRRM 2769 (1964) (which dealt with the duty of a successor employer to arbitrate with a union under a predecessor employer's contract with the union). This conflict gave rise to the following case.

Howard Johnson Co. v. Detroit Joint Board

Supreme Court of the United States, 1974
417 U.S. 249, 86 LRRM 2449

MR. JUSTICE MARSHALL delivered the opinion of the Court.

Once again we are faced with the problem of defining the labor law obligations of a "successor" employer to the employees of his predecessor. In this case, petitioner Howard Johnson Company is the bona fide purchaser of the assets of a restaurant and motor lodge. Respondent Union was the bargaining representative of the employees of the previous operator, and had successfully concluded a collective-bargaining agreement with him. In commencing its operation of the restaurant, Howard Johnson hired only a small fraction of the predecessor's employees. The question presented in this case is whether the Union may compel Howard Johnson to arbitrate, under the arbitration provision of the collective-bargaining agreement signed by its predecessor, the extent of its obligations under that agreement to the predecessor's employees.

Prior to the sale at issue here, the Grissom family . . . had operated a Howard Johnson's Motor Lodge and an adjacent Howard Johnson's Restaurant in Belleville, Michigan, under franchise agreements with the petitioner. Employees at both the restaurant and motor lodge were represented by the respondent Hotel & Restaurant Employees & Bartenders International Union. The Grissoms had entered into separate collective-bargaining agreements with the Union covering employees at the two establishments. Both agreements contained dispute settlement procedures leading ultimately to arbitration. Both agreements also provided that they would be binding upon the employer's "successors, assigns, purchasers, lessees or transferees."

On June 16, 1972, the Grissoms entered into an agreement with Howard Johnson to sell it all of the personal property used in connection with operation of the restaurant and motor lodge. The Grissoms retained ownership of the real property, leasing both premises to Howard Johnson. Howard Johnson did not agree to assume any of the Grissom's obligations, except for four specific contracts relating to operation of the restaurant and motor lodge. On June 28, Howard Johnson mailed the Grissoms a letter, which they later acknowledged and confirmed, clarifying that "[i]t was understood and agreed that the Purchaser . . . would not recognize and assume any labor agreements between the Sellers . . . and any labor organizations," and that it was further agreed that "the Purchaser does not assume any obligations or liabilities of the Sellers resulting from any labor agreements. . . ."

Transfer of operation of the restaurant and motor lodge was set for midnight, July 23, 1972. On July 9, the Grissoms notified all of their employees that their employment would terminate as of that time. The Union was also notified of the termination of the Grissom's business. On July 11, Howard Johnson advised the Union that it would not recognize the Union or assume any obligations under the existing collective-bargaining agreements.

After reaching agreement with the Grissoms, Howard Johnson began hiring its own work force. It placed advertisements in local newspapers, and posted notices in various places, including at the restaurant and motor lodge. It began interviewing prospective employees on July 10, hired its first employees on July 18, and began training them at a Howard Johnson's facility in Ann Arbor on July 20. Prior to the sale, the Grissoms had 53 employees. Howard Johnson commenced operations with 45 employees, 33 engaged in the restaurant and 12 in the motor lodge. Of these, only nine of the restaurant employees and none of the motor lodge employees had previously been employed by the Grissoms. None of the supervisory personnel employed by the Grissoms were hired by Howard Johnson.

. . .

. . . At a hearing before the District Court on August 7, the Grissoms admitted that they were required to arbitrate in accordance with the terms of the collective-bargaining agreements they had signed and that an order compelling arbitration should issue. On August 22, the District Court . . . held that Howard Johnson was also required to arbitrate the extent of its obligations to the former Grissom employees. The court denied, however, the Union's motion for a preliminary injunction requiring the Company to hire all the former Grissom employees, and granted a stay of its arbitration order pending appeal. Howard Johnson appealed

the order compelling arbitration, but the Court of Appeals affirmed. . . .
We reverse.

Both courts below relied heavily on this Court's decision in *John Wiley &*
Sons v. *Livingston,* 376 U.S. 543, 55 LRRM 2769 (1964). In *Wiley,* the
Union representing the employees of a corporation which had disappeared through a merger sought to compel the surviving corporation,
which had hired all of the merged corporation's employees and continued to operate the enterprise in a substantially identical form after the
merger, to arbitrate under the merged corporation's collective-bargaining agreement. As *Wiley* was this Court's first experience with the difficult
"successorship" question, its holding was properly cautious and narrow:

> "We hold that the disappearance by merger of a corporate employer
> which has entered into a collective bargaining agreement with a union
> does not automatically terminate all rights of the employees covered by
> the agreement, and that, in appropriate circumstances, present here,
> the successor employer may be required to arbitrate with the union
> under the agreement." *Id.,* at 548, 55 LRRM, at 2772.

Mr. Justice Harlan, writing for the Court, emphasized "the central role of
arbitration in effectuating national labor policy" and preventing industrial strife, and the need to afford some protection to the interests of the
employees during a change of corporate ownership. *Id.,* at 549, 55
LRRM, at 2772.

The courts below recognized that the reasoning of *Wiley* was to some
extent inconsistent with our more recent decision in *NLRB* v. *Burns*
International Security Services, 406 U.S. 272, 80 LRRM 2255 (1972). Burns
was the successful bidder on a contract to provide security services at a
Lockheed Aircraft plant, and took a majority of its employees from the
ranks of the guards employed at the plant by the previous contractor,
Wackenhut. In refusing to enforce the Board's order finding that Burns'
failure to honor the substantive provisions of the collective-bargaining
agreement negotiated with Wackenhut was an unfair labor practice, we
emphasized that freedom of collective bargaining—"private bargaining
under governmental supervision of the procedure alone, without any
official compulsion over the actual terms of the contract"—was a "fundamental premise" of the federal labor laws [citation omitted], and that it
was therefore improper to hold Burns to the substantive terms of a
collective-bargaining agreement which it had neither expressly nor
impliedly assumed. *Burns* also stressed that holding a new employer
bound by the substantive terms of the pre-existing collective-bargaining
agreement might inhibit the free transfer of capital, and that new employers must be free to make substantial changes in the operation of the
enterprise. [citation omitted]

The courts below held that *Wiley* rather than *Burns* was controlling here
on the ground that *Burns* involved an NLRB order holding the employer
bound by the substantive terms of the collective-bargaining agreement,
whereas this case, like *Wiley,* involved a § 301 suit to compel arbitration.
Although this distinction was in fact suggested by the Court's opinion in
Burns [citation omitted], we do not believe that the fundamental policies

outlined in *Burns* can be so lightly disregarded. In *Textile Workers Union* v. *Lincoln Mills*, 353 U.S. 448, 40 LRRM 2113 (1957), this Court held that § 301 of the Labor Management Relations Act authorized the federal courts to develop a federal common law regarding enforcement of collective-bargaining agreements. But *Lincoln Mills* did not envision any freewheeling inquiry into what the federal courts might find to be the most desirable rule, irrespective of congressional pronouncements. Rather, *Lincoln Mills* makes clear that this federal common law must be "fashion[ed] from the policy of our national labor laws.". . .

It would be plainly inconsistent with this view to say that the basic policies found controlling in an unfair labor practice context may be disregarded by the courts in a suit under § 301, and thus to permit the rights enjoyed by the new employer in a successorship context to depend upon the forum in which the Union presses its claims. Clearly the reasoning of *Burns* must be taken into account here.

We find it unnecessary, however, to decide in the circumstances of this case whether there is any irreconcilable conflict between *Wiley* and *Burns*. We believe that even on its own terms, *Wiley* does not support the decision of the courts below. The Court in *Burns* recognized that its decision "turn [ed] to a great extent on the precise facts involved here." 406 U.S., at 274, 80 LRRM, at 2226. The same observation could have been made in *Wiley*, as indeed it could be made in this case. In our development of the federal common law under § 301, we must necessarily proceed cautiously, in the traditional case-by-case approach of the common law. Particularly in light of the difficulty of the successorship question, the myriad factual circumstances and legal contexts in which it can arise, and the absence of congressional guidance as to its resolution, emphasis on the facts of each case as it arises is especially appropriate. The Court was obviously well aware of this in *Wiley*, as its guarded, almost tentative statement of its holding amply demonstrates.

When the focus is placed on the facts of these cases, it becomes apparent that the decision below is an unwarranted extension of *Wiley* beyond any factual context it may have contemplated. Although it is true that both *Wiley* and this case involve § 301 suits to compel arbitration, the similarity ends there. *Wiley* involved a merger, as a result of which the initial employing entity completely disappeared. In contrast, this case involves only a sale of some assets, and the initial employer remains in existence as a viable corporate entity, with substantial revenues from its lease of the motor lodge and restaurant to Howard Johnson. Although we have recognized that ordinarily there is no basis for distinguishing among mergers, consolidations, or purchases of assets in the analysis of successorship problems, see *Golden State Bottling Co.* v. *NLRB*, 414 U.S. 168, 182–183 n. 5, 84 LRRM 2839, 2844–2845 n. 5 (1973), we think these distinctions are relevant here, for two reasons. First, the merger in *Wiley* was conducted "against a background of state law which embodied the general rule that in merger situations the surviving corporation is liable for the obligations of the disappearing corporation," *Burns, supra*, 406 U.S., at 286, 80 LRRM at 2230, which suggests that holding *Wiley* bound to arbitrate under its predecessor's collective-bargaining agreement may have been fairly within the reasonable expectations of the parties. Second, the disappearance of the original employing entity in the *Wiley* merger meant that unless the union were afforded some remedy against *Wiley*, it would have no means to enforce the obligations voluntarily undertaken by the merged corporation, to the extent that those obligations vested prior to the merger or to the extent that its promises were intended to survive a change of ownership. Here, in contrast, because the Grissom corporations continue as viable entities with substantial retained assets, the union does have a realistic remedy to enforce their contractual obligations. Indeed, the Grissoms have agreed to arbitrate the extent of their liability to the union and their former employees; presumably this arbitration will explore the question whether the Grissoms breached the successorship provisions of their collective-bargaining agreements, and what the remedy for this breach might be.[3]

Even more important, in *Wiley* the surviving corporation hired *all* of the employees of the disappearing corporation. Although, under *Burns*, the surviving corporation may have been entitled to make substantial changes in its operation of the enterprise, the plain fact is that it did not. As the arbitrator in *Wiley* subsequently stated:

> "Although the Wiley merger was effective on October 2, 1961, the former Interscience employees continued to perform the same work on the same products under the same management at the same work place as before the change in the corporate employer." *Interscience Encyclopedia, Inc.*, 55 Lab.Arb. 210, 218 (1970).

The claims which the union sought to compel Wiley to arbitrate were thus the claims of Wiley's employees as to the benefits they were entitled to receive in connection with their employment. It was on this basis that the Court in *Wiley* found that there was the "substantial continuity of identity in the business enterprise," 376 U.S., at 551, 55 LRRM at 2773, which it held necessary before the successor employer could be compelled to arbitrate.

Here, however, Howard Johnson decided to select and hire its own independent work force to commence its operations of the restaurant and motor lodge.[5] It therefore hired only nine of the 53 former Grissom employees and none of the Grissom supervisors. The primary purpose of the Union in seeking arbitration here with Howard Johnson is not to protect the rights of Howard Johnson's employees; rather, the Union

---

[3] The Union apparently did not explore another remedy which might have been available to it prior to the sale, *i.e.*, moving to enjoin the sale to Howard Johnson on the ground that this was a breach by the Grissoms of the successorship clauses in the collective-bargaining agreements. See *National Maritime Union v. Commerce Tankers Corp.*, 325 F.Supp. 360 (S.D.N.Y. 1971), *vacated*, 457 F.2d 1127 (CA2 1972). The mere existence of the successorship clauses in the bargaining agreements between the Union and the Grissoms, however, cannot bind Howard Johnson either to the substantive terms of the agreements or to the arbitration clauses thereof, absent the continuity required by *Wiley*, when it is perfectly clear the Company refused to assume any obligations under the agreements.

[5] It is important to emphasize that this is not a case where the successor corporation is the "alter ego" of the predecessor, where it is "merely a disguised continuance of the old employer." [citation omitted] Such cases involve a mere technical change in the structure or identity of the employing entity, frequently to avoid the effect of the labor laws, without any substantial change in its ownership or management. In these circumstances, the courts have

primarily seeks arbitration on behalf of the former Grissom employees who were *not* hired by Howard Johnson. It is the Union's position that Howard Johnson was bound by the pre-existing collective-bargaining agreement to employ all of these former Grissom employees, except those who could be dismissed in accordance with the "just cause" provision or laid-off in accordance with the seniority provision. It is manifest from the Union's efforts to obtain injunctive relief requiring the Company to hire all of these employees that this is the heart of the controversy here. Indeed, at oral argument, the Union conceded that it would be making the same argument here if Howard Johnson had not hired any of the former Grissom employees, and that what was most important to the Union was the prospect that the arbitrator might order the Company to hire all of these employees.

What the Union seeks here is completely at odds with the basic principles this Court elaborated in *Burns*. We found there that nothing in the federal labor laws "requires that an employer . . . who purchases the assets of a business be obligated to hire all of the employees of the predecessor though it is possible that such an obligation might be assumed by the employer." [citations omitted] *Burns* emphasized that "[a] potential employer may be willing to take over a moribund business only if he can make changes in corporate structure, composition of the labor force, . . . and nature of supervision." 406 U.S., at 287–288, 80 LRRM, at 2231. We rejected the Board's position in part because "[i]t would seemingly follow that employees of the predecessor would be deemed employees of the successor, dischargeable only in accordance with provisions of the contract and subject to the grievance and arbitration provisions therof. Burns would not have been free to replace Wackenhut's guards with its own except as the contract permitted." *Id.*, at 388, 80 LRRM, at 2231. Clearly, *Burns* establishes that Howard Johnson had the right not to hire any of the former Grissom employees, if it so desired.[8] The Union's effort to circumvent this holding by asserting its claims in a § 301 suit to compel arbitration rather than in an unfair labor practice context cannot be permitted.

We do not believe that *Wiley* requires a successor employer to arbitrate in the circumstances of this case.[9] The Court there held that arbitration

---

had little difficulty holding that the successor is in reality the same employer and is subject to all the legal and contractual obligations of the predecessor. [citations omitted]

There is not the slightest suggestion in this case that the sale of the restaurant and motor lodge by the Grissoms to Howard Johnson was in any sense a paper transaction without meaningful impact on the ownership or operation of the enterprise. . . .

8. . . . Of course, it is an unfair labor practice for an employer to discriminate in hiring or retention of employees on the basis of union membership or activity under § 8(a)(3) of the NLRA. Thus, a new owner could not refuse to hire the employees of his predecessor solely because they were union members or to avoid having to recognize the union. See *Burns, supra,* 406 U.S., at 280–281 n. 5. [citations omitted]

9. . . . The question whether Howard Johnson is a "successor" is simply not meaningful in the abstract. Howard Johnson is of course a successor employer in the sense that it succeeded to operation of a restaurant and motor lodge formerly operated by the Grissoms. But the real question in each of these "successorship" cases is, on the particular facts, what are the legal obligations of the new employer to the employees of the former owner or their representative. The answer to this inquiry requires analysis of the interests of the new

could not be compelled unless there was "substantial continuity of identity in the business enterprise" before and after a change of ownership, for otherwise the duty to arbitrate would be "something imposed from without, not reasonably to be found in the particular bargaining agreement and the acts of the parties involved." 376 U.S., at 551, 55 LRRM, at 2773. This continuity of identity in the business enterprise necessarily includes, we think, a substantial continuity in the identity of the work force across the change in ownership. The *Wiley* Court seemingly recognized this, as it found the requisite continuity present there in reliance on the "wholesale transfer" of Interscience employees to Wiley. *Ibid.* This view is reflected in the emphasis most of the lower courts have placed on whether the successor employer hires a majority of the predecessor's employees in determining the legal obligations of the successor in § 301 suits under *Wiley*. This interpretation of *Wiley* is consistent also with the Court's concern with affording protection to those employees who are in fact retained in "the transition from one corporate organization to another" from sudden changes in the terms and conditions of their employment, and with its belief that industrial strife would be avoided if these employees' claims were resolved by arbitration rather than by "the relative strength . . . of the contending forces." [citation omitted] At the same time, it recognizes that the employees of the terminating employer have no legal right to continued employment with the new employer, and avoids the difficulties inherent in the union's position in this case. This holding is compelled, in our view, if the protection afforded employee interests in a change of ownership by *Wiley* is to be reconciled with the new employer's right to operate the enterprise with his own independent labor force.

Since there was plainly no substantial continuity of identity in the work force hired by Howard Johnson with that of the Grissoms, and no express or implied assumption of the agreement to arbitrate, the courts below erred in compelling the Company to arbitrate the extent of its obligations to the former Grissom employees. Accordingly, the judgment of the Court of Appeals must be reversed.

MR. JUSTICE DOUGLAS dissented.

Notes

1. If a court decides that a successor employer is required to arbitrate with a union under a contract which the union has executed with the predecessor employer, may the arbitrator properly decide that the successor employer is not bound by the terms of such contract? Do you agree with the holding of Arbitrator B. Roberts (in the arbitration proceeding which

---

employer and the employees and of the policies of the labor laws in light of the facts of each case and the particular legal obligation which is at issue, whether it be the duty to recognize and bargain with the union, the duty to remedy unfair labor practices, the duty to arbitrate, etc. There is, and can be, no single definition of "successor" which is applicable in every legal context. A new employer, in other words, may be a successor for some purposes and not for others. [citations omitted]

followed the Court's decision in *Wiley*) that the collective bargaining agreement between the union and the predecessor company ceased to be enforceable after the employees of the predecessor moved to the successor's quarters and commingled with the employees of the successor? *Interscience Encyclopedia, Inc.*, 55 LA 210 (1970). Should the employees be deemed to have any contractual rights against the successor (on such matters as seniority, severance pay, and vacation pay) after a merger of employers or after an assignment of assets by one company to another in payment of a debt? See *Weber Truck & Warehouse*, 66 LA 1029 (1976), and *High Point Sprinkler*, 67 LA 239 (1976).

2. In *McGuire* v. *Humble Oil & Refining Co.*, 355 F.2d 352, 61 LRRM 2410 (2d Cir. 1966), a retail fuel company in Brooklyn sold its fuel oil accounts, trucks, and some equipment to Humble. The fuel company employed 24 drivers and mechanics represented by the Teamsters. Most of these 24 employees were hired by Humble, which had a contract with an independent union covering over 500 Humble employees in the New York area (including about 350 drivers and mechanics). Shortly after the sale, the Teamsters filed grievances against Humble under the contract between the Teamsters and the fuel company, which contained an arbitration clause. The Teamsters protested Humble's refusal to recognize the Teamsters as the representative of the employees formerly employed by the fuel company, and Humble's refusal to abide by the wage and other provisions of the Teamsters contract with the fuel company. Humble refused the Teamsters' demand to arbitrate. While a Section 301 action to enforce arbitration was pending, the NLRB held that the fuel company's employees who had been hired by Humble had become a part of the larger bargaining unit represented by the independent union. Do you agree with the federal district court (which ordered arbitration)? Or the court of appeals (which refused to order arbitration)?

3. In *John Wiley & Sons* v. *Livingston*, 376 U.S. 543, 549, 55 LRRM 2769 (1964), the Court said that:

> "The objectives of national labor policy, reflected in established principles of federal law, require that the rightful prerogative of owners independently to arrange their businesses and even eliminate themselves as employers be balanced by some protection to the employees from a sudden change in the employment relationship."

A transfer of ownership may affect employee interests in the job security functions of a grievance clause in a collective bargaining agreement, in other contractual benefits and in the seniority system by which they were earned. But the Court's concern for such employee interests, which was expressed in *Wiley*, is certainly less evident in *Burns* and in *Howard Johnson*. The shift in policy is reflected in *Howard Johnson* where the Court attempts to distinguish *Wiley*.

If *Burns* and *Wiley* continue to coexist (as suggested in *Howard Johnson*), a collective bargaining agreement may not survive a transfer of ownership for purposes of Section 8(a)(5) of the NLRA, but it may survive for Section 301 purposes. Does it make any sense for the contract to be binding under one statutory provision but not under the other?

D. ROLE OF THE NLRB

1. The Contract and the NLRB

What bearing, if any, does the existence of a collective bargaining agreement have on the role of the NLRB? When the Taft-Hartley amendments to the NLRA were considered by Congress in 1947, Congress rejected a bill which would have given the NLRB unfair labor practice jurisdiction over all breaches of collective bargaining agreements. Does this legislative history indicate that the existence of a collective bargaining agreement forecloses the Board from exercising power over a matter to which the agreement is applicable? Or should the Board exercise its statutory power and ignore the collective bargaining agreement? If the Board should proceed with its statutory functions and should not ignore the existence of a contract, to what extent may the Board properly consider the terms of the contract as distinguished from the terms of the NLRA? If a collective bargaining agreement provides for an arbitrator to resolve unsettled grievances involving interpretation and/or application of the agreement, may the Board interpret and/or apply the agreement? These questions may arise in various contexts. Consider these questions in light of the following materials.

Carey v. Westinghouse Electric Corp.

Supreme Court of the United States, 1964
375 U.S. 261, 55 LRRM 2042

[The IUE, representing the production and maintenance employees at the plant where the dispute arose, filed a grievance in which it asserted that technical employees who were represented by another union were performing production and maintenance work. The IUE's agreement with the company contained a grievance procedure leading to arbitration. Westinghouse refused to arbitrate the grievance on the ground that the controversy presented a representation matter for the NLRB. The IUE's petition to the state courts of New York for an order compelling arbitration was denied. The Court of Appeals held that the matter was within the exclusive jurisdiction of the NLRB since it involved a definition of bargaining units.]

MR. JUSTICE DOUGLAS delivered the opinion of the Court. . . .

We have here a so-called "jurisdictional" dispute involving two unions and the employer. But the term "jurisdictional" is not a word of a single meaning. In the setting of the present case this "jurisdictional" dispute could be one of two different, though related, species: either—(1) a controversy as to whether certain work should be performed by workers in one bargaining unit or those in another; or (2) a controversy as to which union should represent the employees doing a particular work. If this controversy is considered to be the former, the National Labor Relations Act does not purport to cover all phases and stages of it. While

§ 8(b)(4)(D) makes it an unfair labor practice for a union to strike to get an employer to assign work to a particular group of employees rather than to another, the Act does not deal with the controversy anterior to a strike nor provide any machinery for resolving such a dispute absent a strike. The Act and its remedies for "jurisdictional" controversies of that nature come into play only by a strike or a threat of a strike. Such conduct gives the Board authority under § 10(k) to resolve the dispute.

Are we to assume that the regulatory scheme contains an hiatus, allowing no recourse to arbitration over work assignments between two unions but forcing the controversy into the strike stage before a remedy before the Board is available? The Board, as admonished by § 10(k), has often given effect to private agreements to settle disputes of this character; and that is in accord with the purpose as stated even by the minority spokesman in Congress—"that full opportunity is given the parties to reach a voluntary accommodation without governmental intervention if they so desire." 93 Cong. Rec. 4035; 2 Leg. Hist. LMRA (1947) 1046.

As Judge Fuld, dissenting below said: "The underlying objective of the national labor laws is to promote collective bargaining agreements and to help give substance to such agreements through the arbitration process."

Grievance arbitration is one method of settling disputes over work assignments; and it is commonly used, we are told. To be sure, only one of the two unions involved in the controversy has moved the state courts to compel arbitration. So unless the other union intervenes, an adjudication of the arbiter might not put an end to the dispute. Yet the arbitration may as a practical matter end the controversy or put into movement forces that will resolve it. The case in its present posture is analogous to *Whitehouse* v. *Illinois Central R. Co.*, 349 U.S. 366, where a railroad and two unions were disputing a jurisdictional matter, when the National Railroad Adjustment Board served notice on the railroad and one union of its assumption of jurisdiction. The railroad, not being able to have notice served on the other union, sued in the courts for relief. We adopted a hands-off policy, saying, "Railroad's resort to the courts had preceded any award, and one may be rendered which could occasion no possible injury to it." *Id.*, at 373.

Since § 10(k) not only tolerates but actively encourages voluntary settlements of work assignment controversies between unions, we conclude that grievance procedures pursued to arbitration further the policies of the Act.

What we have said so far treats the case as if the grievance involves only a work assignment dispute. If, however, the controversy be a representational one, involving the duty of an employer to bargain collectively with the representative of the employees as provided in § 8(a)(5), further considerations are necessary. Such a charge, made by a union against the employer, would, if proved, be an unfair labor practice, as § 8(a)(5) expressly states. Or the unions instead of filing such a charge might petition the Board under § 9(c)(1) to obtain a clarification of the certificates they already have from the Board; and the employer might do the same. . . .

If this is truly a representation case, either IUE or Westinghouse can move to have the certificate clarified. But the existence of a remedy before the Board for an unfair labor practice does not bar individual employees from seeking damages for breach of a collective bargaining agreement in a state court, as we held in *Smith* v. *Evening News Assn.*, 371 U.S. 195. We think the same policy considerations are applicable here; and that a suit either in the federal courts, as provided by § 301(a) of the Labor Management Relations Act of 1947 (*Textile Workers* v. *Lincoln Mills*, 353 U.S. 448), or before such state tribunals as are authorized to act (*Charles Dowd Box Co.* v. *Courtney*, 368 U.S. 502; *Teamsters Local* v. *Lucas Flour Co.*, 369 U.S. 95) is proper, even though an alternative remedy before the Board is available, which, if invoked by the employer, will protect him.

The policy considerations behind *Smith* v. *Evening News Assn.* . . . are highlighted here by reason of the blurred line that often exists between work assignment disputes and controversies over which of two or more unions is the appropriate bargaining unit. It may be claimed that A and B, to whom work is assigned as "technical" employees, are in fact "production and maintenance" employees; and if that charge is made and sustained the Board, under the decisions already noted, clarifies the certificate. But IUE may claim that when the work was assigned to A and B, the collective agreement was violated because "production and maintenance" employees, not "technical" employees, were entitled to it. As noted, the Board clarifies certificates where a certified union seeks to represent additional employees; but it will not entertain a motion to clarify a certificate where the union merely seeks additional work for employees already within its unit. . . .

As the Board's decisions indicate, disputes are often difficult to classify. In the present case the Solicitor General, who appears amicus, believes the controversy is essentially a representational one. So does Westinghouse. IUE on the other hand claims it is a work assignment dispute. Even if it is in form a representation problem, in substance it may involve problems of seniority when layoffs occur (see Sovern, *Section 301 and the Primary Jurisdiction of the NLRB*, 76 Harv. L. Rev. 529, 574–575 (1963)) or other aspects of work assignment disputes. If that is true, there is work for the arbiter whatever the Board may decide.

If by the time the dispute reaches the Board, arbitration has already taken place, the Board shows deference to the arbitral award, provided the procedure was a fair one and the results not repugnant to the Act. . . .

Should the Board disagree with the arbiter, by ruling, for example, that the employees involved in the controversy are members of one bargaining unit or another, the Board's ruling would, of course, take precedence; and if the employer's action had been in accord with that ruling, it would not be liable for damages under § 301. But that is not peculiar to the present type of controversy. Arbitral awards construing a seniority provision, or awards concerning unfair labor practices, may later end up in conflict with Board rulings. Yet, as we held in *Smith* v. *Evening News Assn.* . . . the possibility of conflict is no barrier to resort to a tribunal other than the Board.

However the dispute be considered—whether one involving work assignments or one concerning representation—we see no barrier to use of the arbitration procedure. If it is a work assignment dispute, arbitration conveniently fills a gap and avoids the necessity of a strike to bring the matter to the Board. If it is a representation matter, resort to arbitration may have a pervasive, curative effect even though one union is not a party.

By allowing the dispute to go to arbitration its fragmentation is avoided to a substantial extent; and those conciliatory measures which Congress deemed vital to "industrial peace" (*Textile Workers* v. *Lincoln Mills, supra,* at 455) and which may be dispositive of the entire dispute, are encouraged. The superior authority of the Board may be invoked at anytime. Meanwhile the therapy of arbitration is brought to bear in a complicated and troubled area.

Reversed.

MR. JUSTICE GOLDBERG took no part in the consideration or decision of this case.

MR. JUSTICE HARLAN, concurring.

I join the Court's opinion with a brief comment. As is recognized by all, neither position in this case is without its difficulties. Lacking a clear-cut command in the statute itself, the choice in substance lies between a course which would altogether preclude any attempt at resolving disputes of this kind by arbitration, and one which at worst will expose those concerned to the hazard of duplicative proceedings. The undesirable consequences of the first alternative are inevitable, those of the second conjectural. As between the two, I think the Court at this early stage of experience in this area rightly chooses the latter.

MR. JUSTICE BLACK, with whom MR. JUSTICE CLARK joins, dissenting. . . .

I agree with the New York court and would affirm its judgment. Stripped of obscurantist arguments, this controversy is a plain, garden-variety jurisdictional dispute between two unions. The Court today holds, however, that the National Labor Relations Act not only permits but compels Westinghouse to arbitrate the dispute with only one of the two warring unions. Such an arbitration could not, of course, bring about the "final and binding arbitration of grievances and disputes" that the Court says contributes to the congressional objectives in passing the Labor Act. Unless all the salutary safeguards of due process of law are to be dissipated and obliterated to further the cause of arbitration, the rights of employees belonging to the Federation should not, for "policy considerations," be sacrificed by an arbitration award in proceedings between IUE and Westinghouse alone. Although I do not find the Court's opinion so clear on the point as I would like, I infer that it is not holding that this misnamed "award" would be completely final and binding on the Federation and its members. What the Court does plainly hold, however—that "the weight of the arbitration award is likely to be considerable, if the Board is later required to rule on phases of the same dispute"—seems only a trifle less offensive to established due process concepts. And this means, I suppose, that this same award, ex parte as to Federation, must be given that same or greater weight in any judicial review of the Board's final order involving the same "phases of the same dispute."

Moreover, the Court holds that suits for damages can be filed against the employer in state courts or federal courts under § 301 of the Taft-Hartley Act for the "unfair labor practice" of failing to bargain with the right union when two unions are engaged in a jurisdictional dispute. The employer, caught in that jurisdictional dispute, is ordinarily in a helpless position. He is trapped in a cross-fire between two unions. All he can do is guess as to which union's members he will be required by an arbitrator, the Labor Board, or a court to assign to the disputed jobs. If he happens to guess wrong, he is liable to be mulcted in damages. I assume it would be equally difficult for him to prophesy what award an arbitrator, the Labor Board, or a judge will make as to guess how big a verdict a court or a jury would give against him. It must be remembered that the employer cannot make a choice which will be binding on either an arbitrator, the Board, or a court. The Court's holding, thus subjecting an employer to damages when he has done nothing wrong, seems to me contrary to the National Labor Relations Act as well as to the basic principles of common everyday justice.

The result of all this is that the National Labor Relations Board, the agency created by Congress finally to settle disputes in the interest of industrial peace, is to be supplanted in part by so-called arbitration which in its very nature cannot achieve a final adjustment of those disputes. One of the main evils it had been hoped the Labor Act would abate was jurisdictional disputes between unions over which union members would do certain work. The Board can make final settlements of such disputes. Arbitration between some but not all the parties cannot. I fear that the Court's recently announced leanings to treat arbitration as an almost sure and certain solvent of all labor troubles has been carried so far in this case as unnecessarily to bring about great confusion and to delay final and binding settlements of jurisdictional disputes by the Labor Board, the agency which I think Congress intended to do that very job.

I would affirm.

Notes

1. Under *Carey* should the Board give significant weight to the arbitrator's decision? In the arbitration proceeding that followed *Carey* the arbitrator decided that the case involved a representation issue. He divided the jobs in dispute between the two unions on the basis of the wage rates. But Westinghouse filed a petition with the NLRB to clarify the two bargaining units. In rendering its decision the Board did not follow the arbitrator's award. *Westinghouse Electric Corp.*, 162 NLRB 768, 64 LRRM 1082 (1967).

2. One of the factors considered by the NLRB in making jurisdictional awards is the agreements of the parties. As stated by the NLRB in *J.A. Jones Construction Co.*, 135 NLRB 1402, 49 LRRM 1684 (1962):

"The Board will consider all relevant factors in determining who is entitled to the work in dispute, e.g., the skills and work involved, certifications by the Board, company and industry practice, agreements between unions and between employers and unions, awards of arbitrators, joint boards and the AFL-CIO in the same or related cases, the assignment made by the employer, and the efficient operation of employer's business. This list of factors is not meant to be exclusive, but is by way of illustration. The Board cannot at this time establish the weight to be given the various factors. Every decision will have to be an act of judgment based on common sense and experience rather than on precedent. It may be that later, with more experience in concrete cases, a measure of weight can be accorded to earlier decisions."

In *Precrete, Inc.*, 136 NLRB 1072, 49 LRRM 1932 (1962), relative labor costs were considered as one factor. In disputes concerning work done by the operation of new machinery, the Board has considered the fact that the work was previously performed by one group of employees through different techniques; this has been called the "substitution of function" or "loss of job" test. *E.g.*, *Philadelphia Inquirer*, 142 NLRB 36, 52 LRRM 1504 (1963). Although the preference of the employer is only one of the factors, analysis of the Board's decisions reveals that in the overwhelming majority of the cases, the award made by the Board has supported the employer's assignment of the work.

3. Assume that IUE in *Carey* has won its arbitration case and that the Federation has thereafter obtained a different result in an arbitration under its contract with Westinghouse. Can this type of conflict be avoided by bringing both unions before an arbitrator in the same proceeding?

In *Glass Cutters League* v. *American St. Gobain*, 428 F.2d 353, 74 LRRM 2749 (3d Cir. 1970), the League (a union) instituted a Section 301 action to require the company to arbitrate a grievance which alleged that "[t]he company is in violation of the contract by assigning to employees outside the League's contractual bargaining unit the work of setting and adjusting cutting heads on cutting machines." The disputed work was assigned to employees represented by the Ceramics Union which had a separate collective bargaining agreement with the company. Prior to answering the complaint, the company filed a motion under Federal Rules of Civil Procedure 19 and 21 to require the joinder of the Ceramics Union as an additional party defendant. The court of appeals approved the federal district court's order which called for the joinder of the Ceramics Union in the action pending before the federal district court and the federal district court's dismissal of the League's complaint because of the League's failure to join the Ceramics Union. Although the court of appeals recognized that no ruling requiring trilateral arbitration had been made by the court below, the court of appeals stated that the federal district court "clearly would have authority to provide for joint arbitration of a labor dispute." The court cited *CBS* v. *Broadcasting Ass'n*, 414 F.2d 1236, 72 LRRM 2140 (2d Cir. 1969), which approved a federal district court order compelling joint arbitration of a work assignment dispute between an employer and two unions. However, in the latter case one of the unions had agreed to arbitrate its dispute before the arbitrator who had been chosen by the employer and the other union to arbitrate their dispute.

What are the arguments for and against a court order requiring tri-lateral arbitration of a work assignment dispute between an employer and two unions? See Jones, *An Arbitral Answer to a Judicial Dilemma: The Carey Decision and Trilateral Arbitration of Jurisdictional Disputes*, 11 UCLA L. Rev. 327 (1964); Bernstein, *Nudging and Shoving All Parties to a Jurisdictional Dispute Into Arbitration: The Dubious Procedure of National Steel*, 78 Harv. L. Rev. 784 (1965); Jones, *On Nudging and Shoving the National Steel Arbitration Into a Dubious Procedure*, 79 Harv. L. Rev. 327 (1965).

4. Cf. *Transportation-Communication Employees Union* v. *Union Pacific R.R.*, 385 U.S. 157, 63 LRRM 2481 (1966), *rehearing denied*, 380 U.S. 1032 (1967), where the Supreme Court agreed with the lower courts that a work assignment award of the National Railroad Adjustment Board should not be enforced. In this case the Telegraphers claimed before the NRAB that a railroad had incorrectly awarded certain work to Railway Clerks. The Clerks, given notice of the proceedings, refused to partici-pate. The NRAB held that the Telegraphers were entitled to the work. But the Supreme Court reasoned that the NRAB could not determine the whole dispute without considering the Clerks' contract. The case was remanded to the NRAB to offer the Clerks another opportunity to participate and to determine the whole dispute by consideration of both contracts.

Jacobs Manufacturing Co.

National Labor Relations Board, 1951
94 NLRB 1214, enforced, 196 F.2d 680, 30 LRRM 2098 (2d Cir. 1952)

[In July 1948, the company and the UAW (CIO) executed a two-year contract which by its terms could be reopened one year after its execution date for a discussion of "wage rates." In July 1949, the union invoked this reopening clause and gave written notice of wage demands. These included a request for a wage increase, a request that the company take over the full cost of an existing group health insurance program, and a request for the establishment of a pension plan. At the time of negotia-tions in 1948 the company and the union had discussed changes in the insurance program and had agreed to increase certain of the benefits as well as the costs. However, neither the changes nor the insurance pro-gram were mentioned in the agreement. No pension plan was in effect in the plant, and the subject was not discussed during the 1948 negotiations, nor was it mentioned in the contract.

[At reopening in 1949, the employer refused to discuss either the insurance program or a pension plan, arguing that Section 8(d) of the Act states that the duty to bargain does not require either party "to discuss or agree to any modification of the terms and conditions contained in a contract for a fixed period, if such modification is to become effective before such terms and conditions can be reopened under the provisions of the contract." The existence of the health and welfare program in its present form and the nonexistence of a pension plan were terms and conditions "contained" in the contract; to change the former and institute the latter would constitute a "modification" not covered by the reopening clause, which was limited to "wage rates."

[The union countered by demanding that the employer discuss its demands as to health and welfare and pensions under the contract grievance procedure. The employer refused to do so on the ground that proposals to alter the substantive terms and conditions of employment were not grievances within the meaning of the agreement.

[The Board unanimously supported the company's position that neither the reopening clause nor the grievance procedure of the agreement required it to discuss or bargain over the proposed change in the health and welfare plan or the institution of the pension plan. Indeed, Member Murdock stopped there on the basis of a finding of fact that the only issue which had been raised between the parties was whether the contract required the employer to bargain on the union's demands.

[However, the other four Board members found from the evidence that the company's position was that since the contract did not obligate it to bargain, it was excused by Section 8(d) from the duties of Section 8(a)(5) and had no present obligation to discuss the matters at all. Thus, they came squarely to grips with the question of the scope of the statutory duty.

[Members Houston and Styles held that while either party may refuse to bargain as to the written terms of the contract, a term or condition of employment is not "contained" in a contract unless it has been integrated and embodied in a writing. Accordingly, as to such "unwritten" terms, the obligation remains on both parties, unless they have agreed not to bargain about such subjects during the term of the agreement. Thus the company was obligated to discuss not only the matter of pensions but also the union's group insurance demand.

[Member Reynolds disagreed with Members Houston and Styles as to the employer's duty to bargain with respect to both subjects. He argued that legislative history supported an interpretation of Section 8(d) as excusing either party from bargaining on any matter during the life of the contract except as its express terms require, and that the "unwritten" terms and conditions of employment existing at the time a contract is executed are part of the status quo, which the parties by implication adopt as an essential element of the collective bargaining agreement; any change amounts to a modification of that agreement.

[The opinion of Chairman Herzog, who agreed with Members Houston and Styles as to the pension plan, explaining his disagreement with them as to the matter of group insurance, follows.]

I believe that this Respondent was *not* under a duty to discuss the Union's *group insurance* demand. The individual views which lead me, by a different road, to the result reached on this issue by Members Reynolds and Murdock, are as follows:

Unlike the issue of pensions, concerning which the contract is silent and the parties did not negotiate at all in 1948, the subject of group insurance was fully discussed while the Respondent and the Union were negotiating the agreement. True, that agreement is silent on the subject, so it cannot literally be said that there is a term "contained in" the 1948 contract relating to the group insurance program. The fact remains that during the negotiations which preceded its execution, the issue was consciously explored. The record reveals that the Union expressly requested that the preexisting program be changed so that the Respondent would assume its entire cost, the very proposal that was again made as part of the 1949 mid-term demand which gave rise to this case. The Respondent rejected the basic proposal on this first occasion, but agreement was then reached—although outside the written contract—to increase certain benefits under the group insurance program.

In my opinion, it is only reasonable to assume that rejection of the Union's basic proposal, coupled in this particular instance with enhancement of the substantive benefits, constituted a part of the contemporaneous "bargain" which the parties made when they negotiated the entire 1948 contract. In the face of this record as to what the parties discussed and did, I believe that it would be an abuse of this Board's mandate to throw the weight of Government sanction behind the Union's attempt to disturb, in mid-term, a bargain sealed when the original agreement was reached.

[The pertinent part of the Board's order, supported by Chairman Herzog and Members Houston and Styles, was a direction to the employer to bargain collectively with respect to rates of pay, wages, and hours of employment, including the subject of a pension plan or program. The Court of Appeals granted enforcement, specifically rejecting the interpretation given to Section 8(d) by Member Reynolds. *NLRB* v. *Jacobs Manufacturing Co.*, 196 F.2d 680 (2d Cir. 1952).]

Note

In a later case, involving workload, the Board said that "although . . . statutory rights may be 'waived' by collective bargaining, . . . such a waiver 'will not readily be inferred.' . . . [T]here must be a 'clear and unmistakable showing' that the waiver occurred." *Beacon Piece Dyeing & Finishing Co.*, 121 NLRB 953, 956, 42 LRRM 1489, 1490 (1958). Although the Board has taken the position that a waiver may be shown by evidence other than a specific contract provision, it is not clear as to exactly what evidence the Board will accept (other than a specific contract provision) to show a waiver.

NLRB v. C & C Plywood Corp.

Supreme Court of the United States, 1967
385 U.S. 421, 64 LRRM 2065

MR. JUSTICE STEWART delivered the opinion of the Court.
The respondent employer was brought before the National Labor Relations Board to answer a complaint that its inauguration of a premium

pay plan during the term of a collective agreement, without prior consultation with the union representing its employees, violated the duties imposed by §§ 8(a)(5) and (1) of the National Labor Relations Act. The Board issued a cease-and-desist order, rejecting the claim that the respondent's action was authorized by the collective agreement.[2] The Court of Appeals for the Ninth Circuit refused, however, to enforce the Board's order. It reasoned that a provision in the agreement between the union and the employer, which "arguably" allowed the employer to institute the premium pay plan, divested the Board of jurisdiction to entertain the union's unfair labor practice charge. We granted certiorari to consider a substantial question of federal labor law.

In August 1962, the Plywood, Lumber, and Saw Mill Workers Local No. 2405 was certified as the bargaining representative of the respondent's production and maintenance employees. The agreement which resulted from collective bargaining contained the following provision:

"Article XVII

"WAGES

"A. A classified wage scale has been agreed upon by the Employer and Union, and has been signed by the parties and thereby made a part of the written agreement. The Employer reserves the right to pay a premium rate over and above the contractual classified wage rate to reward any particular employee for some special fitness, skill, aptitude or the like. The payment of such a premium rate shall not be considered a permanent increase in the rate of that position and may, at sole option of the Employer, be reduced to the contractual rate. . . ."

The agreement also stipulated that wages should be "closed" during the period it was effective and that neither party should be obligated to bargain collectively with respect to any matter not specifically referred to in the contract.[4] Grievance machinery was established, but no ultimate arbitration of grievances or other disputes was provided.

Less than three weeks after this agreement was signed, the respondent posted a notice that all members of the "glue spreader" crews would be paid $2.50 per hour if their crews met specified biweekly (and later weekly) production standards, although under the "classified wage scale" referred to in the above quoted Art. XVII of the agreement, the members

---

[2]The NLRB's order directed respondent to bargain with the union upon the latter's request and similarly to rescind any payment plan which it had unilaterally instituted.

[4]"Article XIX

"WAIVER OF DUTY TO BARGAIN:

"The parties acknowledge that during negotiations which resulted in this Agreement, each had the unlimited right and opportunity to make demands and proposals with respect to any subject matter of collective bargaining, and that the understanding and agreements arrived at by the parties after the exercise of that right and opportunity are set forth in this Agreement. Therefore, the Employer and Union, for the life of this Agreement, each voluntarily and unqualifiedly waives the right and each agree that the other shall not be obligated to bargain collectively with respect to any subject matter not specifically referred to or covered in this Agreement, even though such subjects or matters may not have been within the knowledge or contemplation of either or both of the parties at the time they negotiated or signed this Agreement."

of these crews were to be paid hourly wages ranging from $2.15 to $2.29, depending upon their function within the crew. When the union learned of this premium pay plan through one of its members, it immediately asked for a conference with the respondent. During the meetings between the parties which followed this request, the employer indicated a willingness to discuss the terms of the plan, but refused to rescind it pending those discussions.

It was this refusal which prompted the union to charge the respondent with an unfair labor practice in violation of §§ 8(a)(5) and (1). The trial examiner found that the respondent had instituted the premium pay program in good-faith reliance upon the right reserved to it in the collective agreement. He, therefore, dismissed the complaint. The Board reversed. Giving consideration to the history of negotiations between the parties,[6] as well as the express provisions of the collective agreement, the Board ruled the union had not ceded power to the employer unilaterally to change the wage system as it had. For while the agreement specified different hourly pay for different members of the glue spreader crews and allowed for merit increases for "particular employee[s]," the employer had placed all the members of these crews on the same wage scale and had made it a function of the production output of the crew as a whole.

In refusing to enforce the Board's order, the Court of Appeals did not decide that the premium pay provision of the labor agreement had been misinterpreted by the Board. Instead, it held the Board did not have jurisdiction to find the respondent had violated § 8(a) of the Labor Act, because the "existence . . . of an unfair labor practice [did] not turn entirely upon the provisions of the Act, but arguably upon a good-faith dispute as to the correct meaning of the provisions of the collective bargaining agreement. . . ."

The respondent does not question the proposition that an employer may not unilaterally institute merit increases during the term of a collective agreement unless some provision of the contract authorizes him to do so. See *Labor Board* v. *J.H. Allison & Co.*, 165 F.2d 766 (C.A. 6th Cir.), *cert. denied*, 335 U.S. 814. Cf. *Beacon Piece Dyeing Co.*, 121 NLRB 953 (1958). The argument is, rather, that since the contract contained a provision which *might* have allowed the respondent to institute the wage plan in question, the Board was powerless to determine whether that provision *did* authorize the respondent's action, because the question was one for a state or federal court under § 301 of the Act.

In evaluating this contention, it is important first to point out that the collective bargaining agreement contained no arbitration clause. The contract did provide grievance procedures, but the end result of those procedures, if differences between the parties remained unresolved, was

---

[6]The trial examiner found that "quite some time prior" to the execution of the contract, the respondent's general manager had proposed an "incentive bonus system" within the department where the glue spreader crews worked. The union's representative, however, declared that the union would not agree to such a plan. Sometime later in the negotiations, the respondent again made reference to the fact that it was "giving thought" to incentive pay, but the trial examiner was unable to conclude that this reference was related to the premium pay provision that eventually appeared in the contract.

economic warfare, not "the therapy of arbitration." *Carey* v. *Westinghouse Corp.*, 375 U.S. 261, 272. Thus, the Board's action in this case was in no way inconsistent with its previous recognition of arbitration as "an instrument of national labor policy for composing contractual differences." *International Harvester Co.*, 138 NLRB 923, 926 (1962), *aff'd sub nom. Ramsey* v. *Labor Board*, 327 F.2d 784 (C.A. 7th Cir.), *cert. denied*, 377 U.S. 1003.

The respondent's argument rests primarily upon the legislative history of the 1947 amendments to the National Labor Relations Act. It is said that the rejection by Congress of a bill which would have given the Board unfair labor practice jurisdiction over all breaches of collective bargaining agreements shows that the Board is without power to decide any case involving the interpretation of a labor contract. We do not draw that inference from this legislative history.

When Congress determined that the Board should not have general jurisdiction over all alleged violations of collective bargaining agreements and that such matters should be placed within the jurisdiction of the courts, it was acting upon a principle which this Court had already recognized.

"The Railway Labor Act, like the National Labor Relations Act, does not undertake governmental regulation of wages, hours, or working conditions. Instead it seeks to provide a means by which agreement may be reached with respect to them." *Terminal Railroad Ass'n* v. *Brotherhood of Railroad Trainmen*, 318 U.S. 1, 6.

To have conferred upon the National Labor Relations Board generalized power to determine the rights of parties under all collective agreements would have been a step toward governmental regulation of the terms of those agreements. We view Congress' decision not to give the Board that broad power as a refusal to take this step.

But in this case the Board has not construed a labor agreement to determine the extent of the contractual rights which were given the union by the employer. It has not imposed its own view of what the terms and conditions of the labor agreement should be. It has done no more than merely enforce a statutory right which Congress considered necessary to allow labor and management to get on with the process of reaching fair terms and conditions of employment—"to provide a means by which agreement may be reached." The Board's interpretation went only so far as was necessary to determine that the union did not agree to give up these statutory safeguards. Thus, the Board, in necessarily construing a labor agreement to decide this unfair labor practice case, has not exceeded the jurisdiction laid out for it by Congress. . . .

If the Board in a case like this had no jurisdiction to consider a collective agreement prior to an authoritative construction by the courts, labor organizations would face inordinate delays in obtaining vindication of their statutory rights. Where, as here, the parties have not provided for arbitration, the union would have to institute a court action to determine the applicability of the premium pay provision of the collective bargaining agreement.[15] If it succeeded in court, the union would then have to go back to the Labor Board to begin an unfair labor practice proceeding. It is not unlikely that this would add years to the already lengthy period required to gain relief from the Board. Congress cannot have intended to place such obstacles in the way of the Board's effective enforcement of statutory duties. For in the labor field, as in few others, time is crucially important in obtaining relief. *Amalgamated Clothing Workers* v. *Richman Bros. Co.*, 348 U.S. 511, 526 (dissenting opinion).

The legislative history of the Labor Act, the precedents interpreting it, and the interest of its efficient administration thus all lead to the conclusion that the Board had jurisdiction to deal with the unfair labor practice charge in this case. We hold that the Court of Appeals was in error in deciding to the contrary.

The remaining question, not reached by the Court of Appeals, is whether the Board was wrong in concluding that the contested provision in the collective agreement gave the respondent no unilateral right to institute its premium pay plan. In reaching this conclusion, the Board relied upon its experience with labor relations and the Act's clear emphasis upon the protection of free collective bargaining. We cannot disapprove of the Board's approach. For the law of labor agreements cannot be based upon abstract definitions unrelated to the context in which the parties bargained and the basic regulatory scheme underlying that context. See Cox, *The Legal Nature of Collective Bargaining Agreements*, 57 Mich. L. Rev. 1 (1958). Nor can we say that the Board was wrong in holding that the union had not forgone its statutory right to bargain about the pay plan inaugurated by the respondent. For the disputed contract provision referred to increases for "particular employee[s]," not groups of workers. And there was nothing in it to suggest that the carefully worked out wage differentials for various members of the glue spreader crew could be invalidated by the respondent's decision to pay all members of the crew the same wage. . . .

Reversed and remanded.

Note

If a grievance is filed during the term of a collective bargaining agreement to protest management's action on a matter to which the grievance

---

[15]The precise nature of the union's case in court is not readily apparent. If damages for breach of contract were sought, the union would have difficulty in establishing the amount of injury caused by respondent's action. For the real injury in this case is to the union's status as bargaining representative, and it would be difficult to translate such damage into dollars and cents. If an injunction were sought to vindicate the union's contractual rights, the problem of the applicability of the Norris-LaGuardia Act would have to be faced. A federal injunction issuing from a court with § 301 jurisdiction might be barred by § 7 of that Act. See *International Union of Electrical Workers* v. *General Electric Co.*, 341 F.2d 571 (C.A. 2d Cir.); *Local No. 861* v. *Stone & Webster Corp.*, 163 F. Supp. 894 (D.C. W.D. La.). Cf. *Sinclair Refining Co.* v. *Atkinson*, 370 U.S. 195; *Publishers Ass'n* v. *New York Mailers' Union*, 317 F.2d 624 (C.A. 2d Cir.), *cert. granted*, 375 U.S. 901, *judgment vacated in part for dismissal as moot*, 376 U.S. 775. Whether a state injunction might be similarly barred in suits governed by federal law, *Teamsters Local* v. *Lucas Flour Co.*, 869 U.S. 95, is an open question. See *Charles Dowd Box Co.* v. *Courtney*, 368 U.S. 502, 514, n. 8. Thus, it may be that the only remedy in court which would be available to the union would be a suit for a declaratory judgment, assuming such a suit in these circumstances would be maintainable under state or federal law.

procedure is applicable, may the company properly insist that the union follow the agreed-upon grievance procedure? Or may the union insist, under Section 8(a)(5), that the company "bargain" over the matter outside the scope of the grievance procedure? In *Timken Roller Bearing Co.* v. *NLRB*, 161 F.2d 949, 20 LRRM 2204 (6th Cir. 1947), the court stated that "[a]djustment of grievances by conferences between grievance representatives of management and grievance committees of the union and leading, in the event of failure, to arbitration, is itself a bargaining process. . . ."

Allied Chemical and Alkali Workers v. Pittsburgh Plate Glass Co.

Supreme Court of the United States, 1971
404 U.S. 157, 78 LRRM 2974

[An employee health insurance plan, in which retired employees participated, was negotiated by the union and the company. Upon enactment of Medicare by Congress, the union sought midterm bargaining to renegotiate the insurance benefits for retired employees. The company, contending that Medicare made the insurance program useless and that benefits for retirees were not a mandatory subject for collective bargaining, offered to pay the supplemental Medicare program premium for each retiree who would withdraw from the negotiated insurance plan. Fifteen of 190 retirees accepted the offer. The union, asserting that the company could not unilaterally substitute Medicare coverage for the negotiated plan, filed unfair labor practice charges. The NLRB found a violation of 8(a)(5), but the Sixth Circuit refused to enforce the cease-and-desist order. The Supreme Court found that "benefits of already retired employees" (as distinguished from "benefits of active employees") are not a mandatory subject of collective bargaining, and affirmed the order of the court of appeals.]

MR. JUSTICE BRENNAN delivered the opinion of the Court.

The question remains whether the Company committed an unfair labor practice by offering retirees an exchange for their withdrawal from the already negotiated health insurance plan. After defining "to bargain collectively" as meeting and conferring "with respect to wages, hours, and other terms and conditions of employment," § 8(d) of the Act goes on to provide in relevant part that "where there is in effect a collective-bargaining contract covering employees in an industry affecting commerce, the duty to bargain collectively shall also mean that no party to such contract shall terminate or modify such contract" except upon (1) timely notice to the other party, (2) an offer to meet and confer "for the purpose of negotiating a new contract or a contract containing the proposed modifications," (3) timely notice to the Federal Mediation and Conciliation Service and comparable state or territorial agencies of the existence of a "dispute," and (4) continuation "in full force and effect [of] . . . all the terms and conditions of the existing contract . . . until [its] expiration date. . . ." The Board's trial examiner ruled that the Company's action in offering retirees a change in their health plan did not amount to a "modification" of the collective-bargaining agreement in violation of § 8(d), since the pensioners had merely been given an additional option which they were free to accept or decline as they saw fit. The Board rejected that conclusion on the ground that there were several possible ways of adjusting the negotiated plan to the Medicare provisions and the Company "modified" the contract by unilaterally choosing one of them. The Company now urges, in effect, that we adopt the views of the trial examiner. We need not resolve, however, whether there was a "modification" within the meaning of § 8(d), because we hold that even if there was, a "modification" is a prohibited unfair labor practice only when it changes a term that is a mandatory rather than a permissive subject of bargaining.

Paragraph (4) of § 8(d), of course, requires that a party proposing a modification continue "in full force and effect . . . all the terms and conditions of the existing contract" until its expiration. Viewed in isolation from the rest of the provision, that language would preclude any distinction between contract obligations that are "terms and conditions of employment" and those that are not. But in construing § 8(d), "we must not be guided by a single sentence or member of a sentence, but look to the provisions of the whole law, and to its object and policy." Seen in that light, § 8(d) embraces only mandatory topics of bargaining. The provision begins by defining "to bargain collectively" as meeting and conferring "with respect to wages, hours, and other terms and conditions of employment." It then goes on to state that "the duty to bargain collectively shall also mean" that mid-term unilateral modifications and terminations are prohibited. Although this part of the section is introduced by a "proviso" clause, it quite plainly is to be construed *in pari materia* with the preceding definition. Accordingly, just as § 8(d) defines the obligation to bargain to be with respect to mandatory terms alone, so it prescribes the duty to maintain only mandatory terms without unilateral modification for the duration of the collective-bargaining agreement.

The relevant purpose of § 8(d) which emerges from the legislative history of the Act together with the text of the provision confirms this understanding. . . . The provisions to make contract violations an unfair labor practice . . . were rejected with the explanation that "[o]nce parties have made a collective bargaining contract the enforcement of that contract should be left to the usual processes of the law and not to the National Labor Relations Board." The purpose of the proscription of unilateral midterm modifications and terminations in § 8(d) cannot be, therefore, simply to assure adherence to contract terms. As far as unfair-labor-practice remedies are concerned, that goal was to be achieved through other unfair-labor-practice provisions which were rejected in favor of customary judicial procedures.

The structure and language of § 8(d) point to a more specialized purpose than merely promoting general contract compliance. The conditions for a modification or termination set out in paragraphs (1) through (4) plainly are designed to regulate modifications and terminations so as to facilitate agreement in place of economic warfare. Thus, the party desiring to make a modification or termination is required to serve a written notice on the other party, offer to meet and confer, notify mediation and conciliation agencies if necessary, and meanwhile maintain contract relations. Accordingly, we think we accurately described the relevant aim of § 8(d) when we said in *Mastro Plastics Corp.* v. *National Labor Relations Board*, 350 U.S., at 284, that the provision "seeks to bring about the termination and modification of collective-bargaining agreements without interrupting the flow of commerce or the production of goods. . . ."

If that is correct, the distinction that we draw between mandatory and permissive terms of bargaining fits the statutory purpose. By once bargaining and agreeing on a permissive subject, the parties, naturally, do not make the subject a mandatory topic of future bargaining. When a proposed modification is to a permissive term, therefore, the purpose of facilitating accord on the proposal is not at all in point, since the parties are not required under the statute to bargain with respect to it. The irrelevance of the purpose is demonstrated by the irrelevance of the procedures themselves of § 8(d). Paragraph (2), for example, requires an offer "to meet and confer with the other party for the purpose of negotiating the proposed modifications." But such an offer is meaningless if a party is statutorily free to refuse to negotiate on the proposed change to the permissive term. The notification to mediation and conciliation services referred to in paragraph (3) would be equally meaningless, if required at all. We think it would be no less beside the point to read paragraph (4) of § 8(d) as requiring continued adherence to permissive as well as mandatory terms. The remedy for a unilateral mid-term modification to a permissive term lies in an action for breach of contract, not in an unfair-labor-practice proceeding.[24]

As a unilateral mid-term modification of a permissive term such as retirees' benefits does not, therefore, violate § 8(d), the judgment of the Court of Appeals is

Affirmed.

Mr. Justice Douglas dissents.

Note

In addition to *Pittsburgh Plate Glass*, two other Supreme Court decisions interpret the provisions of Section 8(d) dealing with modification, notice, and termination. In *NLRB* v. *Lion Oil Co.*, 352 U.S. 282, 39 LRRM 2296 (1957), it was held that the notice and waiting requirements of Section 8(d) are not violated "where a contract provides for negotiation and adoption of modifications at an intermediate date during its term, and a strike in support of modification demands occurs after the date on which such modifications may become effective—and after the 60-day notice

---

[24]It does not appear whether the collective-bargaining agreement involved in this case provided for arbitration that would have been applicable to this dispute. We express no opinion, therefore, on the relevance of such a provision to the question before us.

period has elapsed—but prior to the terminal date of the contract." The Court reasoned that Congress meant "expiration date" in Section 8(d) to encompass both the final termination date of the contract and any intermediate reopening date. In *Mastro Plastics Corp.* v. *NLRB*, 350 U.S. 270, 37 LRRM 2587 (1956), the Court held that since an unfair labor practice strike is not to terminate or modify the contract, Section 8(d) does not deprive individuals of their status as employees if, within the waiting period prescribed by Section 8(d)(4), they strike solely against unfair labor practices of their employer. The Court also held that a typical no-strike clause waives only the right to strike for economic benefits, and not the right to strike solely against unfair labor practices by the employer.

Los Angeles Marine Hardware Co. v. NLRB

United States Court of Appeals, Ninth Circuit, 1979
602 F.2d 1302, 102 LRRM 2498

WRIGHT, Circuit Judge.
Los Angeles Marine Hardware Co. (LA Marine) and California Marine Hardware Co. (Cal Marine), both divisions of Mission Marine Associates (Mission) petition for review of a National Labor Relations Board (Board) order adopting the decision of the Administrative Law Judge (ALJ).

The order states, in part, that: (a) Mission, LA Marine and Cal Marine are employers and, collectively, constitute a single employing enterprise within the meaning of § 2(2) of the National Labor Relations Act; (b) they violated §§ 8(a)(1) and (5) and § 8(d) of the Act by repudiating the terms and conditions of a collective bargaining agreement (CBA or agreement) with the union; and (c) they violated §§ 8(a)(1) and (3) by the resultant discharge and refusal to reinstate 23 employees.

We grant the Board's cross-appeal for enforcement.

Mission, a holding company, owned LA Marine, a separate corporation. In November 1976, Mission reorganized the corporations it held and made them operating divisions. One of those divisions, the Hardware Distribution Group, includes LA Marine and Cal Marine. It is headed by General Manager Richard Zajic, a vice-president of Mission.

Cal Marine was an inactive shell prior to March 1977. LA Marine's activities centered in two market areas, recreational sales and commercial fishing. Recreational sales represented more than 80 percent of LA Marine's total sales by early 1977.

The bargaining relationship between LA Marine and the union dated back at least to 1956. LA Marine was the only Mission subsidiary to sign the collective bargaining agreement at issue.

Despite efficiency measures, LA Marine faced a sizable potential operating loss. In part, this was due to the high union wages it was paying. During the 1975 collective bargaining negotiations, Zajic, Mission's Hardware Group General Manager, attempted unsuccessfully to obtain economic relief from the union in the recreational sales area.

Zajic and Jack D. Cox, the union's Secretary-Treasurer, met several times during January and February 1977. They discussed LA Marine's intention to relocate its San Pedro recreational sales operations. Zajic proposed a new contract for the relocation, but the union declined to discuss the matter further in light of the existing agreement.

Zajic announced Mission's decision to move LA Marine's recreational sales operation to San Dimas and San Fernando on March 1, 1977. Although union workers were terminated, Mission announced its intention to contribute to the union trust fund and take applications for employment at its new locations. The union replied that the relocation, motivated by an attempt to avoid the CBA, would constitute an unfair labor practice.

On the same day, Mission activated Cal Marine, the inactive corporate shell, to conduct the relocated recreational sales operations of LA Marine. Cal Marine employees have the same job classifications and performed the same type of work as did the LA Marine employees in recreational sales prior to the relocation. The wages and benefits at the new warehouses, however, are approximately $3 per hour less than those agreed upon in the CBA between LA Marine and the union.

LA Marine ceased its operations in San Pedro and transferred its equipment and supplies to Cal Marine's San Dimas and San Fernando locations in April 1977. The new locations are 50 to 60 miles from San Pedro.

DISCUSSION

. . .

SINGLE EMPLOYER:

The Board's findings of unfair labor practices turn initially upon their determination that LA Marine and Cal Marine constitute a single employing enterprise under § 2(2) of the Act. . . .

The four criteria for determining the existence of an integrated enterprise are: (1) interrelation of operations, (2) common management, (3) centralized control of labor relations, and (4) common ownership or financial control. *Radio Union* v. *Broadcast Service*, 380 U.S. 255, 256, 58 LRRM 2545 (1965). The first three factors carry the most weight and particularly significant is the common control of labor.

Here, each of the *Radio Union* criteria is satisfied. . . .
. . .

There is substantial evidence on the record as a whole to support the conclusion that Cal Marine is merely continuing LA Marine's recreational sales operation under a different name. As a result, LA Marine and Cal Marine are a single employing enterprise under § 2(2) of the Act.[3]

---

[3]The employer argues that the Board erred in not applying the accretion principle. This argument is without merit because an accretion requires the addition of new employees to an

UNFAIR LABOR PRACTICES:

Mission relocated LA Marine's recreational sales operation because of its dissatisfaction with labor costs imposed by the CBA. Its motivation was strictly economic and was not based upon unlawful considerations. The inquiry, however, does not stop here.

The employers were bound to a collective bargaining agreement which was not scheduled to expire until 1979. The agreement covered the union's recreational sales employees. This is different from most relocation cases in that the relocation here took place during the effective period of the agreement. The Board's findings are predicated upon this mid-term repudiation.

After negotiations failed, the employers moved the San Pedro bargaining unit work to San Dimas and San Fernando without the union's consent. In conjunction with the relocation, it instituted less favorable wages at the new locations and abandoned the then existing CBA as to the recreational sales operation. This was done despite the fact that Mission, LA Marine and Cal Marine are a single employing enterprise.

The Board found, in part, that LA Marine and Cal Marine violated §§ 8(d), 8(a)(3) and (5) of the Act by: (1) discharging and refusing to reinstate LA Marine employees; (2) closing the San Pedro facility and relocating the recreational sales operation in an attempt to withdraw work from the bargaining unit; (3) refusing to apply the terms and conditions of the CBA to the new Cal Marine employees; (4) withdrawing recognition of the union as the collective bargaining representative of those employees, and (5) modifying unlawfully the CBA, in midterm, without the consent of the union. Its findings were correct.

The employers argue that they neither repudiated nor modified the CBA in midterm because the agreement applies to the San Pedro area only. This is their primary defense to the unfair labor violations. They rely upon language in the CBA preamble which states:

> THIS MASTER AGREEMENT is made and entered into by and between CHAUFFEURS, SALES DRIVERS, WAREHOUSEMEN AND HELPERS UNION LOCAL 572, IBT, hereinafter referred to as the "Union," and C.J. HENDRY COMPANY, MARINE HARDWARE COMPANY AND SEASIDE SUPPLY STORES, INC., *on behalf of their operations located at San Pedro, California and vicinity,* . . . (emphasis added).

The employers contend that this is a clear waiver by the union and limits the geographical application of the agreement. They argue that if their construction of the preamble is correct, they did not commit any unfair labor practices.

The language cited is not a geographical limitation, but merely the parties' descriptive recitation of the physical location of the facilities at the

---

already existing unit. Here, there was a transfer of the recreational sales operation. *NLRB* v. *Sunset House,* 415 F.2d 545, 547, 72 LRRM 2283 (9th Cir. 1969). In addition, the Board's discretion in applying this principle is broad. *NLRB* v. *Hospital and Institutional Workers, etc.,* 577 F.2d 649, 653, 99 LRRM 2431 (9th Cir. 1978).

time of the negotiations. The language appears only in the preamble of the agreement, and not in the recognition clause. The agreement's effectiveness is not limited expressly to the San Pedro area, nor is there evidence that the parties intended such a limitation.

An employer cannot alter mandatory contractual terms during the effective period of the agreement without the consent of the union. *Chemical Workers* v. *Pittsburgh Glass*, 404 U.S. 157, 159, 183–88, 78 LRRM 2974 (1971). As a result, the employers' actions here amounted to a midterm repudiation of the CBA, in violation of §§ 8(d) and 8(a)(1) and (5) of the Act.

Such a repudiation is not excused because the employer acted in good faith or was motivated solely by economic necessity. Nor is an employer relieved of its duty to recognize the union by relocating its business, when the relocation is an unfair labor practice. To permit such a result would allow an employer to do indirectly what cannot be done directly under the Act.

The Board properly found that the employer violated Sections 8(d), 8(a)(1) and (5) of the Act.

The Board found also a violation of §§ 8(a)(1) and (3) of the Act because the employers terminated 23 LA Marine recreational sales employees as a direct result of their attempt to abandon the CBA.

. . . When the employer's conduct is "inherently destructive," anti-union motivation is presumed to exist. *Great Dane*, 388 U.S. at 33–34, 65 LRRM at 2466. . . .

. . .

The employers did not carry the burden of justifying their actions. On balance, the employers' desire to escape the financial burden they contracted for voluntarily is not an adequate business justification that would excuse the unlawful terminations.

Finally, the employers argue that even if they violated § 8(a)(3) of the Act, eight of the terminated employees were not discriminatees. The employers contend that Gondolfi, Castignolia, Newel, Donatoni, Davi and Williamson could have used their seniority to obtain positions at the reorganized LA Marine, and Isaacs and Amos would have been terminated in any event.

These arguments are without merit with respect to seven of the eight employees. There is substantial evidence on the record as a whole to support the Board's findings that the employer repudiated the CBA. There is no evidence that these employees would have retired or been fired had the employers not violated the Act. Consequently, these persons are discriminatees and are entitled to reinstatement.

We do not take a position as to Newell because the matter was not reached below. . . .

DEFERRAL TO ARBITRATION:

The employers requested that the Board defer to arbitration the question whether the language in the agreement's preamble was a descriptive recitation or a geographic limitation. The Board correctly denied this request.

We note the long recognized national labor policy favoring arbitration. The policy has much less force, however, in this procedural context.

The employer has not sued to compel the union to submit to arbitration. Such actions are cognizable under § 301 of the Labor Management Relations Act of 1947. . . .

Here, the Board brought an enforcement proceeding against the employer under § 10 of the Act. Section 10(a) of the Act gives the Board power to prevent unfair labor practices, unaffected by any other means agreed to by the parties. The Board can exercise its jurisdiction without regard to potential or pending arbitration proceedings.

Although the Board *may* defer the exercise of its authority to contractually establish arbitral processes, it is not compelled to do so. Here, the Board decided that deferral would not further the policies of the Act in light of the allegations that the employer repudiated the collective bargaining relationship.

The Board did not abuse its discretion. . . .

We grant enforcement of the Board's order.

Excerpt from Daily Labor Report on *Milwaukee Spring*

1984 DLR 16:AA-1

The mere existence of a wage scale set by a union contract does not prevent an employer from transferring work outside the bargaining unit during the life of the agreement, a divided NLRB holds (268 NLRB No. 87 (1984)). Reversing a 1982 holding, the Board dismisses a complaint based on charges filed by the United Auto Workers against the Milwaukee Spring Division of Illinois Coil Spring Company. During the term of the union contract, the company sought to relocate work from a union plant to a nonunion facility to escape the contract's labor costs. "[W]e have searched the contract in vain for a provision requiring bargaining unit work to remain in Milwaukee," the Board says. Chairman Dotson and Members Hunter and Dennis sign the ruling.

Member Zimmerman, the Board's lone Carter Administration appointee, files a dissent. He concludes that the employer's decision to relocate assembly work from one plant to another was a mandatory subject of bargaining: "[A]s the [employer's] decision was motivated solely by its desire to avoid the wage provisions of the contract, I would find that [Milwaukee Spring] is prohibited from implementing its decision without the union's consent during the term of the collective bargaining agreement."

The Board majority declares that it is not empowered to rewrite collective bargaining agreements: "Language recognizing the union as the bargaining agent 'for all production and maintenance employees in the company's plant at Milwaukee, Wisconsin,' does not state that the functions that the unit performs must remain in Milwaukee. No doubt parties could draft such a clause; indeed, work-preservation clauses are commonplace. It is not for the Board, however, to create an implied work-preservation clause in every American labor agreement based on wage and benefits or recognition provisions, and we expressly decline to do so."

[Since the Board majority found that no contract provision was violated, they found that Section 8(d) of the Act was not violated.]

The Board decision [involves reconsideration of its earlier decision in] the *Milwaukee Spring* case. The case arose in January 1982 when management asked Auto Workers Local 547 to forgo a scheduled wage increase and to grant other concessions. Two months later, the company announced its intention to relocate the assembly operations. The move would have resulted in the layoff of 32 employees. The parties stipulated that the proposed transfer was based on economic considerations, rather than antiunion animus. The Board describes the original *Milwaukee Spring* decision [finding a violation of the NLRA] as a "radical departure" from the traditional course of collective bargaining. The majority warns that the Zimmerman dissent "adds to the collective-bargaining agreement terms not agreed to by the parties and forecloses the exercise of rational economic discussion and decision-making which ultimately accrue to the benefit of all parties."

The majority overrules earlier Board decisions in *Los Angeles Marine Hardware*, *Boeing*, and *University of Chicago*. In a footnote, the Board adds that it does not find it necessary to decide whether the work relocation was a subject of bargaining.

The Board says the original decision in *Milwaukee Spring* effectively discouraged truthful midterm bargaining over decisions to transfer unit work. It explains that an employer contemplating a plant relocation would supply the union only with reasons unrelated to labor costs to avoid giving the union a veto power over the decision. Unaware that labor costs were a factor in management's decision, the union would be unlikely to volunteer wage concessions. "Even if the union offered to consider wage concessions, the employer might hesitate to discuss such suggestions for fear that bargaining with the union over the union's proposals would be used as evidence that labor costs had motivated the relocation decision," the Board says. The majority outlines the practical impact of its holding:

> "We believe our holding today avoids this dilemma and will encourage the realistic and meaningful collective bargaining that the Act contemplates. Under our decision, an employer does not risk giving a union veto power over its decision regarding relocation and should therefore be willing to disclose all factors affecting its decision. Consequently, the union will be in a better position to evaluate whether to make concessions. Because both parties will no longer have an incentive to refrain from frank bargaining, the likelihood that they will be able to resolve their differences is greatly enhanced."

Dissenting Member Zimmerman reasons that the relocation was simply an indirect attempt to modify contractually promised wage rates—a modification forbidden by Section 8(d) of the Act. He submits that management "voluntarily obligated itself to pay a certain amount of wages to employees performing assembly work during the term of the contract, and it cannot avoid this obligation merely by unilaterally relocating the work to another of its facilities, just as it could not by unilaterally reducing the wage rate."

2. NLRB Deference to Contractual Procedures

In the Trilogy the Supreme Court adopted a number of principles which have required the lower courts to defer to the role of the arbitrator on many issues. *United Steelworkers v. American Mfg. Co.*, 363 U.S. 564, 46 LRRM 2414 (1960); *United Steelworkers v. Warrior & Gulf Navigation Co.*, 363 U.S. 574, 46 LRRM 2416 (1960): *United Steelworkers v. Enterprise Wheel & Car Corp.*, 363 U.S. 593, 46 LRRM 2423 (1960). Nevertheless, despite the laudatory words used by the Supreme Court about arbitration in the Trilogy, the Court noted, in *NLRB v. Acme Industrial Co.*, 285 U.S. 432, 436, 64 LRRM 2069 (1967), that those cases "dealt with the relationship of courts to arbitrators," but that "the relationship of the Board to the arbitration process is of quite a different order."

In *Acme* the union sought information from the employer concerning the movement of machinery from the plant, in order to determine whether there had been a violation of the collective bargaining agreement. The employer refused to comply with the request, claiming that the information was not relevant under the contract, which was subject to arbitration. The Board found that the employer's refusal was a violation of Section 8(a)(5), and the Supreme Court agreed, holding that the Trilogy did not "automatically" require the Board to defer to the arbitrator. The Court saw no threat to the power which the parties had given the arbitrator to make binding interpretations of the collective bargaining agreement. It viewed the Board's order to supply the requested information as a desirable aid to the arbitration process. The Court said that the Board had not made "a binding construction of the labor contract. It was only acting upon the probability that the desired information was relevant. . . . This discovery-type standard decided nothing about the merits of the union's contractual claims. . . . Far from intruding upon the preserve of the arbitrator, the Board's action was in aid of the arbitral process." The Court also noted Section 10(a) of the NLRA, which provides that the Board's power to deal with unfair labor practices shall not be affected by any other means of adjustment that has been established by agreement.

During the term of a collective bargaining agreement a dispute may arise over a matter which could be the subject of an unfair labor practice charge and also the subject of a grievance which could be processed under the contract through the grievance procedure to arbitration. Such a dispute could involve, for example, an alleged discriminatory discharge or a unilateral action by the employer which allegedly violates the contract and changes a term or condition of employment. Should the union be free to choose which remedy to pursue? Should it be entitled to "two bites at the apple" (an opportunity to prevail before the Board and/or an arbitrator)? Does the Board have the power to interpret provisions of the agreement applicable to these matters? Does an arbitrator have the power to interpret and apply the NLRA? Should the Board defer to the arbitrator? Should the arbitrator defer to the Board? Consider these questions in light of the following materials.

a. Board Deferral to Arbitration Awards

The Board has honored many arbitration awards which meet the *Spielberg* standards. In *Spielberg Mfg. Co.*, 112 NLRB 1080, 1082, 36 LRRM 1152 (1955), the Board dismissed a complaint (involving strikers whose discharge had been upheld in arbitration because of their misconduct) on the reasoning that "the [arbitration] proceedings appear to have been fair and regular, all parties had agreed to be bound, and the decision of the arbitration panel is not clearly repugnant to the purposes and policies of the Act. In these circumstances we believe that the desirable objective of encouraging the voluntary settlement of labor disputes will best be served by our recognition of the arbitrators' award." Application of this doctrine to discharge cases is criticized in Atleson, *Disciplinary Discharges, Arbitration and NLRB Deference*, 20 Buffalo L. Rev. 355 (1971).

Further elaboration on the *Spielberg* reasoning was provided in *International Harvester Co.*, 138 NLRB 923, 927, 51 LRRM 1155 (1962), where the Board said that:

> "If complete effectuation of the Federal policy is to be achieved, . . . the Board . . . should give hospitable acceptance to the arbitral process as 'part and parcel of the collective bargaining process itself,' and voluntarily withhold its undoubted authority to adjudicate unfair labor practice charges involving the same subject matter, unless it clearly appears that the arbitration proceedings were tainted by fraud, collusion, unfairness, or serious procedural irregularities or that the award was clearly repugnant to the purposes and policies of the Act."

This decision was affirmed, *sub nom. Ramsey* v. *NLRB*, 327 F.2d 784, 55 LRRM 2441 (7th Cir. 1964), *cert. denied*, 377 U.S. 1003, 56 LRRM 2544 (1964), where the court recognized that the Board has discretion to defer to the decision of an arbitrator. With respect to a claim of procedural irregularity, the court said at 787:

> "Petitioner contends, inter alia, that his rights were denied since he was not given notice of the arbitration hearing and did not appear there. We disagree. There is no statutory or constitutional right of an employee to be present at an arbitration hearing. It appears that the company fully and adequately defended petitioner's position at the hearing."

Nevertheless, consider in the light of the remaining materials in this chapter the question of whether the *Spielberg* policy of deference to arbitration awards can be justified. Is there a hierarchy of statutory rights, some of which can be lost through arbitration?

Should the union be allowed "to reserve" some arguments and evidence (which could properly have been presented to the arbitrator) so that the union may later claim before the Board (if the union loses the arbitration case) that the arbitrator did not "clearly decide the issue"? In order to discourage dual litigation before the NLRB and arbitrators, a majority of the Board held, in *Electronic Reproduction Service Corp.*, 213 NLRB 758, 87 LRRM 1211 (1974), that an arbitration award involving the discipline or discharge of an employee should be honored where a union could have, but did not, introduce evidence of unlawful discrimination at the arbitration hearing (unless the failure to present such evidence was due to a bona fide reason other than a desire to try the same case before two forums). But *Electronic Reproduction Service Corp.* was overruled by the Board in *Suburban Motor Freight*, 247 NLRB 146, 103 LRRM 413 (1980), which holds that the Board will not defer to an arbitration award in employee discipline cases unless the party urging deferral shows that the unfair labor practice issue before the Board was presented to, and considered by, the arbitrator. Although the Board notes that *Electronic Reproduction* promoted the statutory purpose of encouraging collective bargaining relationships, the Board says that the rule of this case did not give proper weight to the equally important purpose of protecting employees in the exercise of their statutory rights.

Inland Steel Co.

National Labor Relations Board, 1982
263 NLRB No. 147, 111 LRRM 1193

. . . we agree with the Administrative Law Judge's conclusion that it is appropriate here to dismiss the 8(a)(3) and (1) complaint by deferring to an arbitration award which held that Respondent acted for proper cause when it terminated Jessie Kauffman for falsifying her employment application. The General Counsel has alleged a violation of the Act because Respondent's discovery of Kauffman's falsification resulted from a personnel investigation begun when her union and other protected activities brought her name to Respondent's attention. The arbitrator found, however, that Respondent had no discriminatory intent in pursuing its investigation of Kauffman and that its discharge action was consistent with a long-established company rule.

The parties clearly litigated the statutory issue of discrimination before the arbitrator and he clearly considered that issue in deciding Kauffman's grievance. In addition, we agree with the Administrative Law Judge that the arbitration award satisfies the requirements of *Spielberg Manufacturing Company*, 112 NLRB 1080, 36 LRRM 1152 (1955). In particular, we emphasize our agreement that the arbitration award is not, as our dissenting colleague contends, "clearly repugnant" to the purposes and policies of the Act.

The test of repugnancy under *Spielberg* is not whether the Board would have reached the same result as an arbitrator, but whether the arbitrator's award is palpably wrong as a matter of law. Based on the record before the arbitrator here, a trier of fact could have inferred that Respondent initiated the investigation of Kauffman's personnel file for the purpose of discovering a reason to discharge her. Contrary to arguments made by the General Counsel and our dissenting colleague, however, Board law does not compel the drawing of such an inference. There is no per se illegality in commencing an investigation of an employee who has come to an employer's attention by engaging in union and other protected concerted activities, and disciplinary action based on such an investigation does not fall within the narrow class of "inherently destructive" acts which violate Section 8(a)(3) and (1) of the Act even without proof of specific discriminatory intent.

Based on the foregoing, we conclude that the General Counsel has failed to demonstrate that the arbitration award upholding Kauffman's discharge is contrary to a clear and consistent line of Board and judicial precedent, and consequently is not clearly repugnant to the Act. Accordingly, we shall dismiss the complaint.

JENKINS, Member, dissenting:
. . .

Jessie Kauffman filed a written application for employment with Respondent on February 8, 1978. The application stated . . . that false statements of fact were grounds for discharge. To avoid rejection as over-qualified for the craft position she sought, Kauffman omitted from her application the four years she spent at Cornell University and stated instead that she was employed in a retail store during that time. On February 23, Respondent hired her and in May closed its investigation of her application.

Kauffman joined the Union and became an organizer and leading proponent of its women's committee. She wrote articles in the Union's newspaper and engaged in various projects concerned with sex discrimination, and in this context brought upon herself the specific attention of Respondent's upper management personnel. On June 5, 1979, Kauffman addressed the East Chicago Human Rights Commission (ECHRC) as a member of the Union's women's committee and as an employee of Respondent. She told the Commission that Respondent engaged in discriminatory practice and asked how to prove such discrimination against women and minorities. Respondent's coordinator of manpower planning and utilization, Vincent Soto, attended this meeting, as was his custom, and arrived too late to hear Kauffman's name, but did hear her remarks about Respondent. Soto attempted to learn Kauffman's name after the meeting but failed to do so. Soto reported Kauffman's remarks, and those of another employee, to the staff of his section and its supervisor, Mezey, as "disparaging." On June 15, Mezey and Soto attended an ECHRC conference on affirmative action, where Soto and Mezey both saw Kauffman, and Soto objected publicly to Kauffman's inquiries about Respondent's affirmative action plan.

The next Monday, June 18, the first working day following the ECHRC conference, Mezey and Soto reviewed Kauffman's personnel file. This is the critical event in this case, for Mezey testified before the arbitrator that he reviewed Kauffman's personnel file because he was curious and ". . . made natural inquiries . . . about her, her career and her [Union] involvement . . . that if she was . . . going to be active in the Union [he] ought to be aware of Jessie Kauffman." Before the Administrative Law Judge, Mezey gave an entirely new reason, i.e., that he was concerned whether ". . . she was having problems in her department because of her vociferous display against Inland Steel or against its employment process." Significantly, Mezey was undaunted by the fact that Kauffman's file showed her to be a good employee without any problems or complaints, and nevertheless instigated a full investigation of her references. Consequently, on August 14, 1979, Respondent discharged Kauffman for the false statements in her employment application revealed by this investigation, in accordance with its established practice.

. . .

Respondent investigated Kauffman's employment application because it learned of her protected activity, and the discharge which followed therefore violated Section 8(a)(3) of the Act. The Board has consistently so held, and so the arbitrator's decision herein is contrary to Board precedent and repugnant to the purpose and policies of the Act, and therefore is unworthy of deference. For all these reasons, I would find that Respondent violated Section 8(a)(3) of the Act by discharging Kauffman.

U.S. Steel Corp.

National Labor Relations Board, 1982
264 NLRB No. 10, 111 LRRM 1200

. . . Charging Party Eugene Goldenfeld was employed as a journeyman motor inspector by Respondent at its Gary Works facility. Goldenfeld was a member of a bargaining unit represented by Steelworkers Local 1014 and covered by a collective-bargaining agreement between the Steelworkers and Respondent. The agreement contains no-strike and grievance and arbitration provisions, the pertinent language of which reads as follows:

"SECTION 4—RESPONSIBILITIES OF THE PARTIES

. . .

"3. There shall be no strikes, work stoppages, or interruptions or impeding of work. No officer or representative of the Union shall authorize, instigate, aid, or condone any such activities. No employee shall participate in any such activities.

"4. The applicable procedures of the Agreement will be followed for the settlement of all complaints or grievances.

. . .

"SECTION 6—ADJUSTMENT OF COMPLAINTS AND GRIEVANCE

"B. DEFINITIONS

"1. 'Complaints' as used in this Agreement shall be interpreted to mean a request or complaint.

"2. 'Grievance' as used in this Agreement is limited to a complaint of an employee which involves the interpretation or application of, or compliance with, the provisions of this Agreement."

The contract then outlines a four-step complaint and grievance procedure, with appeal from the fourth step to arbitration. "Complaints" are processed through the first two steps of the procedure, but only "grievances" may proceed beyond the second step.

The Elgin, Joliet and Eastern Railroad, herein called EJE, maintains tracks, offices, and switching facilities at Respondent's Gary Works facility. On September 26, 1978, members of BRAC [Brotherhood of Railway & Airline Clerks] employed by EJE set up picket lines at several of the entrances to the Gary Works. The picket lines were established to protest EJE's contributions to a strike insurance fund which was being used to support the Norfolk and Western Railroad in resisting a strike by BRAC. There is no contention here that the BRAC picket lines at the Gary Works were unlawful.

Goldenfeld was scheduled to work the 7 a.m. to 3 p.m. shift on September 26. When he arrived at work that morning, Goldenfeld noticed the picketing and, after ascertaining its source, decided not to cross the lines and report for duty. After Goldenfeld telephoned his supervisor to inform him that he would not work behind the BRAC picket lines, Goldenfeld called Jack Parton, president of Steelworkers Local 1014. Goldenfeld, who is an active participant in union affairs, tried unsuccessfully to persuade Parton that the Steelworkers should honor the BRAC picket lines and encourage its members to do the same. Goldenfeld did not ask Parton for his interpretation of the no-strike clause in the collective-bargaining agreement.

Later on the morning of September 26, Goldenfeld prepared a leaflet concerning the picketing for distribution to Respondent's employees. The leaflet reads:

"Picket Lines mean: Don't Cross!
"VICTORY TO THE RAIL STRIKE!
"Union members at Gary Works were confronted Tuesday by picketing E J & E workers, members of the Brotherhood of Railway and Airline Clerks (BRAC). BRAC has been on strike against the Norfolk and Western (N & W) railroad for 78 days and Tuesday's nationwide picketing of over 70 rail lines was designed to force the N & W to the bargaining table. At U.S. Steel Gary Works and South Works (Chicago), United Transportation Union (UTU) members on the 'J' have been honoring the pickets, while scabbing foremen are trying to keep a few trains running.

"I will not cross these lines. Honoring a picket line is the most elementary duty of union members. The hard fight to organize unions in this country was victorious because workers refused to cross each others' strike lines. They learned that a picket line is a battle line in the class struggle and crossing that line sabotages the fight for the unrestricted right to strike.

"It is outrageous that while rail employees are refusing to cross, our Steelworkers Union Leadership has refused to instruct members to stay out and respect the lines. This scab policy divides the labor movement and strengthens the companies. As a Steelworker honoring the BRAC lines, I call on our union to defend all workers who may be victimized by the Company for their act of solidarity with the strike.

"1978 is the year of the coal miners' strike. They learned from bitter experience the importance of honoring picket lines. Their strike showed that militant labor solidarity—mass picketing, honoring picket lines, refusing to handle struck goods and equipment—can successfully defy no-strike restrictions and government strikebreaking.

"Right now, the rail companies are getting anti-strike injunctions from the federal courts. Rail workers must not allow this government's strike-breaking attempt to intimidate them. Carry the strike through to victory! The USWA and the rest of the labor movement must come to the aid of the BRAC strike with whatever acts of militant labor solidarity that are necessary to win the strike.

"VICTORY TO THE RAIL CLERKS!

"DOWN WITH GOVERNMENT STRIKEBREAKING INJUNCTIONS

"PICKET LINES MEAN: DON'T CROSS!

"Gene Goldenfeld, Coke Plant

"September 26, 1978

"labor donated"

Goldenfeld distributed this leaflet to Respondent's employees at the Gary Works on both September 26 and 27. During the morning of September 27, Goldenfeld again called a supervisor and reported off from work upon encountering BRAC pickets at some entrances of the Gary Works plant. The supervisor informed Goldenfeld that he was suspended for three days—September 27, 28, and 29. The suspension notice stated that the discipline was assessed for violating plant rule 7, which provides:

"The following offenses may be cause for suspension preliminary to discharge. . . .

. . .

"7. Absence from duty without notice to, and permission from, Superintendent or Foreman, except in case of sickness or cause beyond the employee's control of a nature that prevents his giving notice."

The BRAC picketing at the Gary Works ended on the evening of September 29. Goldenfeld returned to work on September 30, his suspension period having been completed. On that day, however, Respondent issued a second suspension to Goldenfeld, for a period of 35 days. This additional suspension resulted from Goldenfeld's distribution of the "Victory" leaflet described above, and the suspension notice identified Goldenfeld's "offense" as engaging in "activities designed to encourage other employees to violate" the no-strike provisions of the contract.

With the support of Local 1014, Goldenfeld filed and pursued grievances regarding his suspensions. Ultimately, the grievances were presented to an arbitrator. At the arbitration hearing, the Union contended that Goldenfeld was engaged in protected concerted activity when he honored the BRAC picket lines and distributed his leaflet, and, therefore, Respondent's disciplining of him violated the National Labor Relations

Act. Respondent took the position that the broad no-strike clause of the collective-bargaining agreement constituted a waiver by the Union of Goldenfeld's right to engage in sympathy strikes or to honor a picket line. The arbitrator denied the grievances, finding that Goldenfeld's activity was not protected by the Act inasmuch as the collective-bargaining contract prohibited unit employees from engaging in sympathy strikes and from encouraging other employees to do so. The arbitrator reasoned that since the parties agreed that the question of whether the no-strike clause covered sympathy strikes was an arbitrable issue, it necessarily followed that sympathy strikes were encompassed within the contractual arbitration provision, and as such were covered by the no-strike obligation.
. . .

Discussion and Conclusions: There are, as the parties stipulated, no significant factual issues to be resolved. The threshold legal issue to be decided is whether the arbitration award satisfies the *Spielberg* standards for deferral. We conclude that it does not because we find that the award is clearly repugnant to the purposes and policies of the Act. It is well established that the Board does not defer to an arbitration award where it contravenes unfair labor practice principles of the Act. . . .

For the reasons set forth below, we find that the arbitrator's award in the instant case conflicts with Board law regarding contractual waivers of the right to strike. Accordingly, we refuse to defer to that award.

The Board and the courts repeatedly have held that a waiver of the right to engage in sympathy strikes will not be inferred simply from a broad, general no-strike clause in a contract, but that such a waiver must be clear and unmistakable. Where, as here, the contractual no-strike language does not expressly prohibit sympathy strikes, a waiver of the right to engage in such strikes may be established by bargaining history or other extrinsic evidence showing the parties' clear intent. The arbitrator in this case found such extrinsic evidence merely from the willingness of the parties to litigate the strike waiver issue under the arbitration provisions of the collective-bargaining agreement. There is no legal basis for this mode of analysis.

A no-strike clause normally will be read to prohibit only those strikes which are over disputes covered by the contractual arbitration procedure. Under this principle, known as the doctrine of coterminous application, the Board and the courts consistently have refused to find sympathy strikes to be encompassed in broad no-strike pledges on the ground that the dispute which sparks the sympathy strike is not arbitrable under the sympathy strikers' contract with their employer[6]. . . . It is nothing more than an exercise in circular reasoning to determine, as the arbitrator did here, that the parties' willingness to arbitrate the issue of whether sympa-

---

[6]It is obvious from the dissenting opinion that Chairman Van de Water and Member Hunter disagree with this well-established Board and judicial principle. Accordingly, they erroneously begin their analysis of the arbitrator's award with the assumption that, based solely on the broad no-strike language of the contract, the arbitrator had "at least a reasonable basis for finding that the right to refuse to cross a picket line had been waived." On the contrary, Board and judicial precedent hold that, without more, the arbitrator had no reasonable basis for finding a waiver.

thy strikes are covered by the no-strike clause ineluctably leads to the conclusion that the no-strike language was applicable to the sympathy strike in question because the issue was subject to the arbitration clause.

Thus, rather than undertaking the correct approach of attempting to discern whether there was any evidence indicating a waiver of the right to engage in sympathy strikes, the arbitrator focused on the arbitrability of the scope of the no-strike provision. In this and in most cases involving asserted sympathy strike waivers, the dispute as to the meaning of the no-strike clause presents an arbitrable issue. That fact, however, does not automatically bring sympathy strikes [within] the ambit of such clauses. The arbitrator framed the question presented to him in such a manner as to make only one answer possible, and therefore did not, in fact, resolve the issue before him.

It is thus apparent that the arbitrator did not apply the "clear and unmistakable waiver" test, and, contrary to the Board's clear holding that no-strike language is not sufficient, per se, to establish a waiver, he relied solely on such language as the basis for finding a waiver.[7] Since we find the arbitrator's mode of analysis unacceptable, we reject the result he reached by way of that invalid reasoning. Accordingly, as the arbitrator's award is based on a standard which conflicts with Board law, the award is clearly repugnant to the policies and purposes of the Act and is not a proper basis for deferral under *Spielberg*.

. . .

. . . The Supreme Court has held that employees' statutory rights are not to be so subordinated to contractual arbitration procedures. *Barrentine* v. *Arkansas-Best Freight System, Inc.*, 450 U.S. 728, 24 WH Cases 1284 (1981); *Alexander* v. *Gardner-Denver Co.*, 415 U.S. 36, 7 FEP Cases 81 (1974). Although *Barrentine* and *Alexander* involve statutory rights arising under the Fair Labor Standards Act and Title VII of the Civil Rights Act of 1964, at the very least they stand for the proposition that the mere fact that a contractual issue has been resolved in arbitration does not end the inquiry into related statutory issues by the authority charged with enforcement of that statute.

Turning to the merits, we perceive no express contractual language or evidence of bargaining history to support a waiver of Goldenfeld's right to engage in sympathy strikes. The contract does not refer to sympathy strikes, nor does it contain a picket line clause. There is no evidence that the parties ever discussed sympathy strikes during bargaining, and the parties' history of implementation of the grievance-arbitration provisions does not show a waiver of the employees' right to strike in sympathy. Similarly, we discern no waiver of Goldenfeld's right to distribute leaflets regarding the BRAC picketing. The relevant contractual language prohibits only officers and representatives of the Union—not employees—from authorizing, instigating, aiding, or condoning strikes and work stoppages. Goldenfeld was neither an officer nor a representative of the

---

[7]Thus, in his decision, the arbitrator stated that the no-strike clause was "plainly worded and sweeping in scope," and that the collective-bargaining agreement appeared "on the surface and in straight-forward langauge" to prohibit Goldenfeld from refusing to work because of the presence of a picket line.

Union at the time he distributed his leaflets. In any event, since the sympathy strike is not encompassed by the contractual prohibitions, the leafletting concerning that strike also is not covered. It is well settled that leaflets urging employees to engage in protected activities are themselves protected.

We also find no merit in Respondent's argument that Goldenfeld was not engaged in concerted activity. Goldenfeld was acting in concert with the employees he was seeking to have join him in honoring the picket lines when he refused to cross those lines and when he distributed his leaflet in support of the striking workers.

In sum, we conclude that Goldenfeld was engaged in protected concerted activity when he honored the BRAC picket lines and distributed his leaflet, and that the no-strike provisions of the collective-bargaining agreement did not waive his right to engage in those activities.[11] Accordingly, we find that Respondent's suspension of Goldenfeld violated Section 8(a)(1) of the Act.

VAN DE WATER, Chairman, and HUNTER, Member, dissenting:
. . .

The collective-bargaining agreement between Respondent and the United Steelworkers of America contains the following no-strike provision cited by the arbitrator:

"There shall be no strikes, work stoppages, or interruption or impeding of work. No officer or representative of the Union shall authorize, instigate, aid, or condone any such activities. No employee shall participate in any such activities."

The arbitrator found that "the contract appears to prohibit the conduct in which the Grievant was engaged when he refused to work because of the presence of the picket line" and concluded that "since the Grievant's otherwise protected right to observe the picket lines established on behalf of the Norfolk Western strikers was waived by his bargaining agent when it executed this Agreement, with its broad no strike and arbitration clauses, his conduct was a work stoppage which breached Section 4 of the Agreement." Based in part on the language of the leaflet handed out by Goldenfeld, including, "Picket Lines Mean: Don't Cross!" the arbitrator found that Goldenfeld intended to induce fellow employees to honor the picket lines. Accordingly, the arbitrator found that the leaflet was tantamount to an "impeding of work" in violation of the no-strike provision and concluded, "The protection which might otherwise be applicable to such activity under the National Labor Relations Act was waived when the

---

[11] We likewise reject Respondent's related contention that Goldenfeld was not engaged in protected activity inasmuch as the collective-bargaining agreement waived his right to go to the Board. The contractual language relied on by Respondent in support of this assertion reads as follows: "The provisions of this Agreement constitute the sole procedure for the processing and settlement of any claim by an employee or the Union of a violation by the Company of this Agreement." It is well established that the Board will not apply the *Spielberg* deferral doctrine to issues involving employees' access to the Board's processes as protected by Sec. 8(a)(4) of the Act. *Filmation Associates, Inc.*, 227 NLRB 1721, 94 LRRM 1470 (1977). Moreover, the waiver language in question clearly does not purport to cover statutory claims, only contractual ones.

Union agreed to the no strike provisions of the Agreement, and the Company was justified in disciplining him for his actions."

The majority declined to defer because in their view the award "contravenes unfair labor practice principles of the Act," because "the arbitrator's mode of analysis [is] unacceptable" and because the award "does not comport with our unfair labor practice decisions." The majority decision, in our opinion, applies an improper deferral standard rather than the "clearly repugnant standard" of *Spielberg Manufacturing Company*, 112 NLRB 1080, 36 LRRM 1152 (1955), which we would apply.

Although, as stated by the majority, the Board does not infer that a general no-strike provision waives the right of employees to honor third-party picket lines, the question of waiver ultimately turns on the interpretation of the contract. From the broad language of the no-strike provision herein, the arbitrator had at least a reasonable basis for finding that the right to refuse to cross a picket line had been waived. That the majority would interpret the contract differently than the arbitrator is not grounds under *Spielberg* for refusing to defer. Indeed, it is the arbitrator's interpretation that Respondent and the Union have bargained for and that Goldenfeld, by filing a grievance, has requested.

For the foregoing reasons, we would find that the arbitrator had an arguable basis for finding waiver and, accordingly, that Goldenfeld's honoring the picket line was arguably unprotected. Similarly, Goldenfeld's leafletting to induce other employees to honor the picket line was arguably unprotected. As the arbitrator's award is susceptible to a permissible interpretation, it cannot, in our opinion, be characterized as clearly repugnant to the purposes and policies of the Act. Accordingly, we would defer to the grievance arbitration award and dismiss the complaint in its entirety.

b. *Pre-Arbitral Deferral by Board*

Problem

The union files a charge with the regional director of the NLRB, alleging that the Enderby Company's action in subcontracting its laboratory operation violates NLRA Section 8(a)(5) in that (1) the company failed to bargain as to the decision itself and (2) it failed to bargain properly about the impact of its decision since it did not give the union adequate advance notice of the decision to permit meaningful negotiations as to impact. The union appends affidavits to its charge setting forth the facts. The NLRB assigns a field examiner to investigate the charge. He obtains all the factual data through interviews with the parties.

Upon conclusion of the investigation the company attorney writes a "letter brief" to the NLRB, urging that a complaint not be issued. After setting out the facts the letter concludes:

"Our statutory obligation was limited to bargaining over the effects of our decision to terminate laboratory operations. Whatever the extent of our statutory obligation to bargain, the union has plainly acquiesced in our right to take the action in question during the effective period of the collective bargaining agreement. This is apparent from the management rights provision in the agreement, which provides that 'Except as expressly limited by specific provisions of this agreement the company retains the sole exclusive right to manage the business and to exercise every right or power necessary or incidental thereto.'

"In addition, the union acquiesced in our right when it sought but failed to obtain the following provision in negotiations for the present agreement: 'No job category or work shift shall be abolished or curtailed by a factor of more than 10 percent without prior consultation with the union as to the necessity of such action and the disposition of the employees so affected. Further, in the event that following such consultation the company determines to implement such course of action it allow a grace period of 30 days before terminating any employee affected unless such employee shall in the interim have secured other employment.'

"The union should not be permitted to obtain through Board processes what it was unable to obtain in negotiations. Furthermore, under the *Collyer* decision the union is limited to the agreement in asserting any rights it may have and must pursue this matter through the grievance and arbitration process. The relevant provision of the agreement is: '*Arbitration.* Any dispute between the company and the union concerning the interpretation or application of a specific provision of this agreement shall be subject to the grievance procedure contained herein, and if, unresolved, shall be subject to binding arbitration.' We are willing to arbitrate the dispute. Accordingly, the Board is without jurisdiction to consider this charge."

Questions

1. Assume that you are an attorney in the regional office of the NLRB. The charge has been placed on the regional director's "agenda" for determination as to whether to issue a complaint. What do you advise?
2. If a complaint issues, what relief should be sought?

Collyer Insulated Wire

National Labor Relations Board, 1971
192 NLRB 837, 77 LRRM 1931

[The contract between the company and union in this case contains a grievance-arbitration procedure (providing for binding arbitration) and a no-strike provision. Production employees have historically been compensated on an incentive basis. The contract provides for a job evaluation plan and for the adjustment of rates, subject to the grievance procedure, during the term of the contract. For skilled maintenance tradesmen, the contract establishes nonincentive rates. It also provides for changes in those rates pursuant to the job evaluation plan where there are changes in or additions to the duties. During the term of the contract, the company unilaterally increased the wage rates for skilled maintenance tradesmen, reassigned certain job duties, and increased the wage rates for extruder operators.

[No grievances were filed by the union or its members to protest the unilateral changes in wages and working conditions made by the company. But the union filed an unfair labor practice charge, claiming that the unilateral changes violated Section 8(a)(5). The company contended that it was authorized, under the collective bargaining agreement and the course of dealing under that contract, to make the changes.]

Opinion of CHAIRMAN MILLER AND MEMBER KENNEDY:

. . . We agree with Respondent's contention that this dispute is essentially a dispute over the terms and meaning of the contract between the Union and Respondent. For that reason . . . the dispute should have been resolved pursuant to the contract and we shall dismiss the complaint. . . . We conclude that the Board is vested with authority to withhold its processes in this case, and that the contract here made available a quick and fair means for the resolution of this dispute including, if appropriate, a fully effective remedy for any breach of contract which occurred. We conclude, in sum, that our obligation to advance the purposes of the Act is best discharged by the dismissal of this complaint.

In our view, disputes such as these can better be resolved by arbitrators with special skill and experience in deciding matters arising under established bargaining relationships than by the application by this Board of a particular provision of our statute. The necessity for such special skill and expertise is apparent upon examination of the issues arising from Respondent's actions with respect to the operator's rates, the skill factor increase, and the reassignment of duties relating to the worm gear removal. Those issues include, specifically: (a) the extent to which these actions were intended to be reserved to the management, subject to later adjustment by grievance and arbitration; (b) the extent to which the skill factor increase should properly be construed, under article IX of the agreement, as a "change in the general scale of pay" or, conversely, as "adjustments in individual rates . . . to remove inequalities or for other proper reason"; (c) the extent, if any, to which the procedures of article XIII governing new or changed jobs and job rates should have been made applicable to the skill factor increase here; and (d) the extent to which any of these issues may be affected by the long course of dealing between the parties. The determination of these issues, we think, is best left to discussions in the grievance procedure by the parties who negotiated the applicable provisions or, if such discussions do not resolve them, then to an arbitrator chosen under the agreement and authorized by it to resolve such issues.

The Board's authority, in its discretion, to defer to the arbitration process has never been questioned by the courts of appeals, or by the Supreme Court. Although Section 10(a) of the Act clearly vests the Board with jurisdiction over conduct which constitutes a violation of the provisions of Section 8, notwithstanding the existence of methods of "adjustment or prevention that might be established by agreement," nothing in the Act intimates that the Board must exercise jurisdiction where such methods exist. . . .

The policy favoring voluntary settlement of labor disputes through arbitral processes finds specific expression in Section 203(d) of the LMRA, in which Congress declared:

> "Final adjustment by a method agreed upon by the parties is hereby declared to be the desirable method for settlement of grievance disputes arising over the application or interpretation of an existing collective-bargaining agreement."

And of course disputes under Section 301 of the LMRA called forth from the Supreme Court the celebrated affirmation of that national policy in the *Steelworkers trilogy*.

Admittedly neither Section 203 nor Section 301 applies specifically to the Board. However labor law as administered by the Board does not operate in a vacuum isolated from other parts of the Act, or, indeed, from other acts of Congress. In fact the legislative history suggests that at the time the Taft-Hartley amendments were being considered, Congress anticipated that the Board would "develop by rules and regulations, a policy of entertaining under these provisions only such cases . . . as cannot be settled by resort to the machinery established by the contract itself, voluntary arbitration. . . ."

The question whether the Board should withhold its process arises, of course, only when a set of facts may present not only an alleged violation of the Act but also an alleged breach of the collective-bargaining agreement subject to arbitration. Thus, this case like each such case compels an accommodation between, on the one hand, the statutory policy favoring the fullest use of collective bargaining and the arbitral process and, on the other, the statutory policy reflected by Congress' grant to the Board of exclusive jurisdiction to prevent unfair labor practices.

We address the accommodations required here with the benefit of the Board's full history of such accommodations in similar cases. From the start the Board has, case by case, both asserted jurisdiction and declined, as the balance was struck on particular facts and at various stages in the long ascent of collective bargaining to its present state of wide acceptance. Those cases reveal that the Board has honored the distinction between two broad but distinct classes of cases, those in which there has been an arbitral award, and those in which there has not.

In the former class of cases the Board has long given hospitable acceptance to the arbitral process. . . .

In those cases in which no award had issued, the Board's guidelines have been less clear. At times the Board has dealt with the unfair labor practice, and at other times it has left the parties to their contract remedies. . . .

Jos. Schlitz Brewing Company is the most significant recent case in which the Board has exercised its discretion to defer. . . .

The circumstances of this case, no less than those in *Schlitz*, weigh heavily in favor of deferral. Here, as in *Schlitz*, this dispute arises within the confines of a long and productive collective-bargaining relationship. The parties before us have, for 35 years, mutually and voluntarily resolved the conflicts which inhere in collective bargaining. Here, as there, no claim is made of enmity by Respondent to employees' exercise of protected rights. Respondent here has credibly asserted its willingness to resort to arbitration under a clause providing for arbitration in a very broad range of disputes and unquestionably broad enough to embrace this dispute.

Finally, here, as in *Schlitz*, dispute is one eminently well suited to resolution by arbitration. The contract and its meaning in present circumstances lie at the center of this dispute. In contrast, the Act and its policies become involved only if it is determined that the agreement between the parties, examined in the light of its negotiating history and the practices of the parties thereunder, did not sanction Respondent's right to make the disputed changes, subject to review if sought by the Union, under the contractually prescribed procedure. That threshold determination is clearly within the expertise of a mutually agreed-upon arbitrator. In this regard we note especially that here, as in *Schlitz*, the dispute between these parties is the very stuff of labor contract arbitration. The competence of a mutually selected arbitrator to decide the issue and fashion an appropriate remedy, if needed, can no longer be gainsaid.

We find no basis for the assertion of our dissenting colleagues that our decision here modifies the standards established in *Spielberg* for judging the acceptability of an arbitrator's award. . . .

Member Fanning's dissenting opinion incorrectly characterizes this decision as instituting "compulsory arbitration" and as creating an opportunity for employers and unions to "strip parties of statutory rights."

We are not compelling any party to agree to arbitrate disputes arising during a contract term, but are merely giving full effect to their own voluntary agreements to submit all such disputes to arbitration, rather than permitting such agreements to be sidestepped and permitting the substitution of our processes, a forum not contemplated by their own agreement.

Nor are we "stripping" any party of "statutory rights." The courts have long recognized that an industrial relations dispute may involve conduct which, at least arguably, may contravene both the collective agreement and our statute. When the parties have contractually committed themselves to mutually agreeable procedures for resolving their disputes during the period of the contract, we are of the view that those procedures should be afforded full opportunity to function. The long and successful functioning of grievance and arbitration procedures suggests to us that in the overwhelming majority of cases, the utilization of such means will resolve the underlying dispute and make it unnecessary for either party to follow the more formal, and sometimes lengthy, combination of administrative and judicial litigation provided for under our statute. At the same time, by our reservation of jurisdiction, *infra*, we guarantee that there will be no sacrifice of statutory rights if the parties' own processes fail to function in a manner consistent with the dictates of our law. This approach, we believe, effectuates the salutary policy announced in

Spielberg, which the dissenting opinion correctly summarizes as one of not requiring the "serious machinery of the Board where the record indicates that the parties are in the process of resolving their dispute in a manner sufficient to effectuate the policies of the Act."

We are especially mindful, finally, that the policy of this Nation to avoid industrial strife through voluntary resolution of industrial disputes is not static, but is dynamic. The years since enactment of Section 203(d) have been vital ones, and the policy then expressed has helped to shape an industrial system in which the institution of contract arbitration has grown not only pervasive but, literally, indispensable. The Board has both witnessed and participated in the growth, a complex interaction where the growth and arbitration in response to Congress' will has called forth and nurtured gradually broader conceptions of the basic policy. The Supreme Court which in *Lincoln Mills*, first upheld the enforceability of agreements to arbitrate disputes has recently, in *Boys Markets, Inc.* v. *Retail Clerks*, suggested that arbitration has become "the central institution in the administration of collective bargaining contracts." After *Boys Market* it may truly be said that where a contract provides for arbitration, either party has at hand legal and effective means to ensure that the arbitration will occur. We believe it to be consistent with the fundamental objectives of Federal law to require the parties here to honor their contractual obligations rather than, by casting this dispute in statutory terms, to ignore their agreed-upon procedures.

Without prejudice to any party and without deciding the merits of the controversy, we shall order that the complaint herein be dismissed, but we shall retain jurisdiction for a limited purpose. Our decision represents a developmental step in the Board's treatment of these problems and the controversy here arose at a time when the Board decisions may have led the parties to conclude that the Board approved dual litigation of this controversy before the Board and before an arbitrator. We are also aware that the parties herein have not resolved their dispute by the contractual grievance and arbitration procedure and that, therefore, we cannot now inquire whether resolution of the dispute will comport with the standards set forth in *Spielberg, supra*. In order to eliminate the risk of prejudice to any party we shall retain jurisdiction over this dispute solely for the purpose of entertaining an appropriate and timely motion for further consideration upon a proper showing that either (a) the dispute has not, with reasonable promptness after the issuance of this decision, either been resolved by amicable settlement in the grievance procedure or submitted promptly to arbitration, or (b) the grievance or arbitration procedures have not been fair and regular or have reached a result which is repugnant to the Act.

Views of Other Board Members

Member Brown concurred in *Collyer*, but he expressed serious doubts about deferring to arbitration in representation cases. Member Fanning and Member Jenkins dissented in separate opinions.

Do the following policy arguments, suggested by the dissenting opinions, outweigh the arguments in support of the above opinion?

a. The majority's position verges on compulsory arbitration. The contract in *Collyer* gives the parties the *right* to file grievances and to present their disputes to an arbitrator. The contract does not make it clear that the grievance-arbitration machinery is to be the exclusive forum for resolving contract disputes. There is no indication that the union or its members voluntarily desire to use this machinery. Voluntarism has been the essence of labor arbitration, not compulsion.

b. The majority's decision may discourage the use of the arbitral process, since many may decide that they cannot afford the luxury of such "voluntary" arbitration. The parties may eliminate arbitration and no-strike provisions from their agreements.

c. The majority decision announces a new standard for the non-assertion of jurisdiction, embracing a whole class of employers who have entered contracts with unions containing a grievance-arbitration clause. To the extent that the Board retains jurisdiction in the instant case, it adopts a new policy of dual litigation—before an arbitrator and before the Board. The majority's position is contrary to Section 10(a) and Section 14(c)(1).

d. Arbitrators are employed to adjudicate private rights by interpreting and applying collective bargaining agreements. They are reluctant to intrude into the area of public rights and national labor policy. Those questions are the prime concern of the Board, which can provide such remedies as a cease-and-desist order and an order to post notices. Since the arbitrator decides contractual questions and the Board decides statutory questions, an arbitrator may render a decision under the contract which is inconsistent with statutory rights. For example, where a contract is silent, or speaks only obliquely, on a given subject, an arbitrator might hold that unilateral action on this matter is permissible under the contract. But the Board would hold that further negotiation is required in the absence of a clear and unmistakable waiver by the union.

e. Legitimate interests of individual workers or managers may not be protected because of a lack of funds to process cases. Small unions or financially weak companies may be "arbitrated to death." Time and expense may be increased by the necessity of filing a charge with the Board within six months of the alleged violation to prevent Section 10(b) from barring Board review of the award under *Spielberg*. To this must be added the time and expense of the Board proceeding if the award is challenged.

f. Arbitration can be invoked only by the union, and not by the individual. Since arbitration is not available to aggrieved individuals, their rights may be sacrificed. The majority decision may encourage parties to provide in their agreements that alleged violations of the NLRA will be arbitrated. But the public interest will not receive proper protection.

g. Cases such as *Collyer* are an insignificant part of the Board's workload, averaging only about two per year during 1960–70. The Board's new policy will reduce the workload of the Board by only a minuscule amount.

Note

What additional arguments may be made for or against the *Collyer* deferral doctrine? See Getman, Collyer Insulated Wire: *A Case of Misplaced Modesty,* 49 Ind. L.J. 57 (1973); Schatzki, *NLRB Resolution of Contract Dispute Under Section 8(a)(5),* 50 Tex. L. Rev. 225 (1972); Sherman, *Comments on NLRB and Arbitration,* published in Proceedings of the Twenty-Seventh Annual Meeting of the National Academy of Arbitrators 138 (1975); Zimmer, *Wired for* Collyer: *Rationalizing NLRB and Arbitration Jurisdiction,* 48 Ind. L.J. 141 (1972).

Continuing Controversy Over **Collyer**

The sharp controversy over the question of the validity and desirability of the *Collyer* doctrine continued among the members of the Board. Two cases decided at the same time, *Roy Robinson Chevrolet,* 228 NLRB 828, 94 LRRM 1474 (1977), and *General American Trans. Corp.,* 228 NLRB 808, 94 LRRM 1483 (1977), reflect a three-way split among members of the Board.

In *Roy Robinson* the complaint alleged that the company violated Section 8(a)(5) by closing its body shop and discharging body shop employees without prior notice to and bargaining with the IAM, the bargaining representative of the employees. The company asserted that the issue should be referred to arbitration under *Collyer.* The majority of the Board found that the Administrative Law Judge erred when he refused to refer the dispute to the grievance-arbitration provisions of the agreement. Members Penello and Walther relied on the deferral procedure under *Collyer.* Murphy, who was then Chairman of the Board, concurred. She noted that the complaint alleged a violation of only Section 8(a)(5) and that no independent violation of Sections 8(a)(1) or 8(a)(3) was alleged. Members Fanning and Jenkins dissented.

Murphy's opinion in *Roy Robinson* calls for deferral of complaints alleging violations of Sections 8(a)(5) and 8(b)(3), but no deferral for complaints alleging violations of Sections 8(a)(3), 8(a)(1), 8(b)(1)(A), and 8(b)(2). In response to her distinction between "individual" and "collective" rights, the dissenting opinion in *Roy Robinson* says:

"Nor are we persuaded by the Chairman's distinction between 'individual' rights under Section 8(a)(1) and (3) and 'collective' or 'group' or 'union' rights under Section 8(a)(5), leading her not to defer in the former cases, and to defer in the latter. It is possible that an 8(a)(5) violation involving 'course of conduct,' 'surface bargaining,' or refusal to recognize or meet the union may be considered a 'collective' or 'union' right more than an 'individual' one, but this type of case is never a candidate for deferral, since a contract (almost by definition) does not exist for an arbitrator to interpret. The 8(a)(5) cases which are considered for deferral are those in which the employer unilaterally takes some action contrary to, or not authorized by, the collective-bargaining agreement which affects some of his employees adversely in their terms and conditions of employment. The right of the employees to protection against such action is individual as well as collective, and it is not necessary that a violation extend to more than one employee for it to be cognizable under the statute. . . .

"The 'individual vs. collective' distinction is not strengthened by arguing that 8(a)(5) violations which are deferred arise out of the contract made by the 'group' (union) with the employer. Discharges under Section 8(a)(3) have at least equal 'collective' character, for violations occur only when the purpose is to encourage or discourage 'union' (*i.e.*, 'group') support or activity. Indeed, the fact that the entire statute is directed toward protecting the right to engage in, or refrain from, 'concerted' activities eliminates any substance in the attempted distinction. . . ."

General American Trans. Corp.

National Labor Relations Board, 1977
228 NLRB 808, 94 LRRM 1483

[The complaint alleged that Soape, the union's area steward, was discharged in violation of Sections 8(a)(3) and 8(a)(1). The Administrative Law Judge denied deferral. He relied on several factors (including the unwillingness of Soape, the charging party, to go to arbitration and the General Counsel's opposition to deferral). Although the majority of the Board agreed that this case should not be deferred to the grievance-arbitration procedure of the collective bargaining contract, no member of the Board based the refusal to defer on the reasons given by the Administrative Law Judge.

[The employer contended that Soape was laid off solely because of lack of work. The contract between the employer and the Boilermakers' Union provided a grievance-arbitration procedure for dealing with "any questions involving the intent, application or interpretation of this agreement. . . ." Another provision stated that "[i]n the exercise of the functions of management, the contractor shall have the right to . . . layoff employees because of lack of work or for other legitimate reasons . . . provided, however, that the contractor will not use these rights for the purposes of discrimination against any employee."

[The General Counsel contended that Soape was discharged because of his union or protected concerted activities, since Soape had taken time off from work to attend area contract negotiations and had filed a complaint with OSHA. The findings of the Administrative Law Judge are as follows: Soape had notified his foreman when he was hired that his union duties would include time off from work; he told his foreman in advance that he was going to attend area contract negotiations; he had previously been absent for union business with the foreman's knowledge and permission; the foreman told a job applicant that he would be hired in Soape's place because Soape was taking too much time on union business; the foreman knew that Soape had called OSHA; testimony of the employer's regional manager showed that he was convinced that Soape was discharged because he took a trip to attend contract negotiations; there was no probative evidence that Soape was terminated for lack of work.]

Opinion of MEMBERS FANNING and JENKINS:

. . . Although we agree with the Administrative Law Judge that this case should not be deferred to arbitration, our rejection of deferral is predicated on our longstanding opposition to the policy established by *Collyer* and its progeny, and is not based merely on the particular circumstances of the instant case. As we pointed out initially in our dissenting opinions in *Collyer*, and thereafter reiterated in dissenting from the extension of the *Collyer* policy to cases involving alleged violations of sections of the Act other than Section 8(a)(5), we believe that the Board has a statutory duty to hear and to dispose of unfair labor practices and that the Board cannot abdicate or avoid its duty by seeking to cede its jurisdiction to private tribunals. As we have repeatedly pointed out, Section 10(a) of the Act is explicit that the Board's power to prevent unfair labor practices "shall not be affected by any other means of adjustment or prevention that has been or may be established by agreement, law, or otherwise. . . ." Such a lack of power in the Board to make the public interest in the vindication of statutory rights "a plaything of private treaty and interpretation" is further underlined by the decision of Congress, reflected in Section 14(c)(1), limiting the extent to which the Board may exercise its discretion to refuse jurisdiction over any "class or category of employers." Moreover, as we observed in our dissenting opinion in *McLean Trucking Company*, 202 NLRB 710, 715–716, 82 LRRM 1652 (1973):

> "When Congress thought it desirable that the Board defer its statutory duties to arbitration, it knew how to say so clearly, and did so in Section 10(k) of the Act, dealing with jurisdictional disputes. But even in the instance of an explicit description of arbitration, the Board's attempt to remit jurisdictional disputes to private tribunals by refusing to decide, as it is now doing in *Collyer*, was cut short by the Supreme Court. *NLRB* v. *Radio Engineers Union (CBS)*, 364 U.S. 573, 47 LRRM 2332. Thus it seems obvious that Congress wanted no deferral of matters arising under other sections of the Act, and that such deferral has been foreclosed."

Aside from the Board's lack of power to subcontract to private tribunals the adjudication of rights that arise solely by virtue of our Act, we believe the facts of the instant case convincingly demonstrate why, on practical as well as policy grounds. the *Collyer* doctrine of deferral has failed.

In the first place, as we noted in dissenting from the result reached in *National Radio Company, Inc.*, 198 NLRB 527, 80 LRRM 1718 (1972), the lead case in which the *Collyer* majority ordered deferral in the context of an alleged discriminatory discharge in violation of Section 8(a)(3), our Act explicitly protects employees from on-the-job discrimination because they have engaged in, or have refrained from engaging in, union activities. The protection thus afforded employees by the Act is clearly an individual, as contrasted with a union or group, right. In the instant case, instead of pursuing arbitration, a route which for a myriad of reasons he concluded would prove futile, Charging Party Soape chose to seek vindication of his statutory rights before the Board. Were we to order deferral in these circumstances, there would be nothing voluntary about the arbitration to which Charging Party Soape would be forced. Hence the voluntary nature of arbitration, long trumpeted by the *Collyer* enthusiasts as the main reason for deferral, is revealed as a sham in cases, like the instant case, where the charging party is an individual discriminatee seeking to enforce his individual rights.

This case is also instructive insofar as it illustrates the uncertainty, indeed the outright confusion that has attended the efforts of the *Collyer* advocates to stretch their original justification for deferral to cover nearly every conceivable situation. Thus, as we have had frequent occasion to point out, even had we accepted the rationale for deferral as initially propounded in the *Collyer* decision, in subsequent cases the *Collyer* adherents repeatedly ignored record facts that clearly militated against deferral. In so doing, they so blurred the announced guidelines and criteria under which the *Collyer* policy was to be applied as to make almost any case in which they found a contract and an arbitration clause a likely candidate for deferral.

As we noted in dissenting from the result reached in *Joseph T. Ryerson & Sons, Inc.*, 199 NLRB 461, 81 LRRM 1261, (1972), and similar cases, the *Collyer* adherents, by indicating that they would defer in any case where the contract incorporates sections of the Act and contains an arbitration clause, in effect invited parties to seek to contract themselves out of the Act, thus stripping employees of the protection afforded by the Act. Indeed, the dissenters here point to a vague "no purposes of discrimination" statement in the contract in the instant case as a justification for insulating this Employer's unlawful conduct from the Board's processes. They also assert that because of the existence of this statement in the contract an arbitrator "would necessarily have to decide the very issue before the Board." What our colleagues really mean, however, is that if this case were deferred they would *presume* that the arbitrator decided the statutory issue, and decided it correctly, merely because this type of clause is in the contract. That this is the substance underlying their rhetoric is demonstrated by their assertion that because arbitrators often decide whether "just cause" for a discharge exists, the arbitrator thereby also decides whether the cause was in fact union activity. Logically and in fact, the two issues are not connected at all, and in the classic discriminatory discharge case are quite separate; "just cause" for discharge may exist (and often exists with respect to perhaps most employees), and may be the pretextual justification for the discharge. But the issue is whether this was the true reason for the discharge, or whether the true reason was union support, and the "just cause" conclusion of an arbitrator does not begin to resolve this. . . .

The *Collyer* adherents cite figures showing that from May 1973 through December 1975 a total of 1,632 cases had been deferred under *Collyer*. Of those, an arbitration award issued in 473, and 437 were settled short of arbitration. Of those 473 where an award was made, our Regional Offices on request examined 159 (about a third) for compliance with *Spielberg* standards, revoking deferral in 33 (over 20 percent) and securing violation-settlement agreements in 24 of those. The dissenters cite these figures to establish that their doctrine is a successful and effective means of reducing the Board's workload while preserving statutory rights and voluntary resolution of disputes. The message these figures convey to us is a quite different one: half these deferred cases disappeared from view, with no assurance of any kind that any statutory rights involved had received any consideration or protection; nearly half the remainder, *i.e.*, about one quarter, were settled short of arbitration, and these probably would have been settled short of appeal to the Board even had they not been deferred; and of the one quarter which went to arbitration, it was necessary that the Board examine over a third, and over one out of five of the awards examined proved to have flouted the Act. During this same period of time, 80,152 "C" or violation cases were filed with the Board, so the total *Collyer* deferrals amounted to about 2 per cent of our workload. These figures make it plain to us that *Collyer* is not assuring protection of statutory rights and that it is costing us some effort in reviewing awards and in determining which cases to defer. The reduction in our workload is insignificant and the sacrifice of statutory protection is substantial. We do not regard this trade-off as compatible with our responsibility to administer and apply the Act.

For all of the foregoing reasons, we affirm the Administrative Law Judge's conclusion that deferral is not appropriate.

MURPHY, Chairman, concurring:

I agree with the Administrative Law Judge and with my colleagues, that the substantive issues joined by the pleadings herein—*i.e.*, whether Respondent discharged employee Soape because of his union or other protected concerted activities in violation of Section 8(a)(3) and (1) of the Act—are not suitable for deferral to the parties' contractual grievance-arbitration machinery under the principles enunciated in *Collyer* and *National Radio*. I disagree, however, with that portion of their rationale which argues that the Board lacks statutory authority to defer any unfair labor practice allegation to the parties' agreed-upon means of resolution.

In my concurring opinion in *Roy Robinson Chevrolet*, issued this day, I expressed my agreement with the threshold holding in *Collyer, supra*, that the Board has the necessary discretionary authority under the Act to defer to the parties' contractual grievance-arbitration machinery certain unfair labor practice allegations growing out of differences between them as to the interpretation and/or application of their collective-bargaining agreement. I reached this conclusion substantially for the reasons articulated in *Collyer*. I also stated, however, that I would not exercise this discretionary authority in every instance where the alleged unfair labor practice might also be a contract violation and where the parties have an agreement calling for binding arbitration of all contract disputes. Rather, I indicated that the Board should stay its processes in favor of the parties' grievance arbitration machinery only in those situations where the dispute is essentially between the contracting parties and where there is no alleged interference with individual employees' basic rights under Section 7 of the Act. Complaints alleging violations of Section 8(a)(5) and 8(b)(3) fall squarely into this category, while complaints alleging violations of Section 8(a)(3), 8(a)(1), 8(b)(1)(A), and 8(b)(2) clearly do not. As discussed more fully below, in the former category the dispute is principally between the contracting parties—the employer and the union—while in the latter the dispute is between the employee on the one hand and the employer and/or the union on the other. In cases alleging violations of Section 8(a)(5) and 8(b)(3), based upon conduct assertedly in derogation of the contract, the principal issue is whether the complained-of conduct is permitted by the parties' contract. Such issues are eminently suited to the arbitral process, and resolution of the contract issue by an arbitrator will, as a rule, dispose of the unfair labor practice issue. On the other hand, in cases alleging violations of Section 8(a)(1), 8(a)(3), 8(b)(1)(A), and 8(b)(2), although arguably also involving a contract violation, the determinative issue is not whether the conduct is permitted by the contract, but whether the conduct was unlawfully motivated or whether it otherwise interfered with, restrained, or coerced employees in the exercise of the rights guaranteed them by Section 7 of the Act. In these situations, an arbitrator's resolution of the contract issue will not dispose of the unfair labor practice allegation.[11] Nor is the arbitration process suited for resolving employee complaints of discrimination under Section 7. Accordingly, for the reasons discussed below, I find that our decision in *National Radio, supra,* was an unwise extension of the *Collyer* deferral policy into an area in which the Board should retain its preeminence. That decision and its progeny must, therefore, be reversed.

The distinction which I draw between purely contractual issues which I would defer to arbitration under the *Collyer* rationale and those which I would not so defer are based upon statutory, as well as policy and practical, considerations.

The National Labor Relations Act, as amended, is predicated upon two national policy objectives which the Board is charged with effectuating. These dual statutory purposes are stated in the last paragraph of Section 1 of the Act as follows:

[11]Contrary to my dissenting colleagues' assertion, I do not question the competence of arbitrators to decide issues involving the interpretation and/or application of collective-bargaining agreements. Rather I question whether arbitration is the most desirable forum in which to decide whether an employee's Sec. 7 rights have been violated. My colleagues state that "the issue most often resolved by arbitrators is that of just cause for the imposition of discipline, *which frequently also requires the arbitrator to decide whether the cause was in fact union or concerted activities."* (Emphasis supplied.) In cases involving alleged interference with Sec. 7 rights, however, the issue which the Board must *always* decide is whether the imposition of discipline was motivated by the employee's union or protected concerted activity. And in deciding that issue the Board relies upon its wealth of expertise in interpreting Sec. 7 of the Act. . . .

Furthermore, arbitrators in fact are not qualified to decide unfair labor practice issues. For such issues must be decided by persons who have been qualified by the Civil Service Commission as hearing examiners under Sec. 11 of the Administrative Procedures Act, 5 U.S.C. Sec. 557. See also NLRB Rules and Regulations and Statements of Procedure, Series 8, as amended, Secs. 101.10, 101.11, 102.35 (i).

"It is hereby declared to be the policy of the United States to eliminate the causes of certain substantial obstructions to the free flow of commerce and to mitigate and eliminate these obstructions when they have occurred by encouraging the practice and procedure of collective bargaining and by protecting the exercise by workers of full freedom of association, self-organization, and designation of representatives of their own choosing, for the purpose of negotiating the terms and conditions of their employment or other mutual aid or protection."

In formulating its deferral policy, the majority in *Collyer* relied upon the first of the above policy objectives; namely, that obstructions to the free flow of commerce can be eliminated or mitigated "by encouraging the practice and procedure of collective bargaining." The majority concluded, on the facts of that case, that the national policy favoring the practice and procedure of collective-bargaining agreement to resolve their differences with respect to the interpretation of such contract by utilizing the procedures established by them for that purpose. I fully agree with that theory where, as in *Collyer* and in *Roy Robinson Chevrolet, supra,* the underlying issue raised by the parties, in a context free from mutual enmity, is whether the employer's unilateral changes in working conditions were permissible under the contract. Resolution of that issue depends upon an interpretation of the bargaining agreement. And, while I believe that the Board, too, is competent to interpret and apply such agreement, I find no compelling reason for doing so where the parties themselves have contractually opted for a method of resolving such disputes. In neither of the above-cited cases was it alleged that the employer's unilateral changes in working conditions were made with an intent to encourage or discourage union activities or otherwise interfered with the employees' individual rights under Section 7 of the Act. Indeed, had such additional allegations been raised in good faith, I would not have deemed the cases appropriate for deferral to the parties' grievance-arbitration procedures.

For, in addition to the statutory policy relied on by the *Collyer* majority, Section 1 of the Act states that it is the policy of Congress to eliminate or mitigate obstructions to the free flow of commerce "by protecting the exercise by workers of full freedom of association, self-organization, and designation of representatives of their own choosing, for the purpose of negotiating the terms and conditions of their employment or other mutual aid or protection." In *Mastro Plastics Corp.,* the Supreme Court explained that "[t]he two policies [listed in Section 1 of the Act] are complementary. They depend for their foundation upon assurance of 'full freedom of association.' *Only after that is assured* can the parties turn to effective negotiation as a means of maintaining 'the normal flow of commerce and . . . the full production of articles and commodities. . . .'" (Emphasis in the original.) Since genuine collective bargaining cannot take place until the employees' full freedom of association is assured, we would do violence to both congressional policies by deferring to the parties' grievance-arbitration machinery a dispute alleging that one of the contracting parties has interfered with the employees' "full freedom of association."

The right of employees to full freedom of association is, after all, the cornerstone of all Section 7 rights and the protection of those rights is the very reason for the Board's existence. Therefore, I believe it would not further the fundamental aims of the National Labor Relations Act to defer to arbitration disputes alleging interference with the employees' Section 7 rights, even though such dispute may also involve an underlying disagreement between the parties as to the meaning and/or application of their contract. Although the rights enumerated in, and guaranteed by, Section 7 of the Act are phrased in terms of individual rights of employees, they have long been recognized as public rights enforceable by governmental rather than private action. Interference with these rights, or employment discrimination intended to encourage or discourage the free exercise of these rights, is an unfair labor practice under Section 8(a)(1) and (3) if committed by an employer, and under Section 8(b)(1)(A) and (2) if committed by a labor organization. Statutory rights, unlike rights created by contract, cannot lawfully be reduced or eliminated either by the employer, the union, or by both. By the same token, an allegation that an employee's statutory rights have been invaded by the employer, the union, or by both ought not to be adjudicated by the very party or parties charged with the wrongdoing. To the contrary, Congress having declared that certain labor practices are unfair, entrusted the Board with preeminent authority to prevent such practices. Section 10(a) states:

"The Board is empowered, as hereinafter provided, to prevent any person from engaging in any unfair labor practice (listed in Section 8) affecting commerce. This power shall not be affected by any other means of adjustment or prevention that has been or may be established by agreement, law or otherwise."

Even where a collective-bargaining agreement exists in which the employer and the union have established grievance machinery providing for final resolution of all disputes arising under the contract, such contract cannot lawfully strip the employees of their statutory rights, nor the Board of its obligation to protect these rights. . . .

The dissenters erroneously imply that I disagree with the policy of *Spielberg Manufacturing Company*, 112 NLRB 1080, 36 LRRM 1152 (1955). On the contrary, I believe that deferral to an arbitrator's award is appropriate under the *Spielberg* guidelines where all of the parties, including the affected employee, have voluntarily submitted their dispute to the arbitrators.[20] I will not, however, compel an unwilling party to go to arbitration if that party charges that employee *Section 7 rights have been violated.*

There are also compelling policy and practical considerations for declining to defer to the parties' contractual grievance-arbitration

---

[20]Indeed, I would honor an arbitrator's award under the *Spielberg* guidelines even if the award resulted from deferral by our Regional Offices under the prevailing *Collyer* policy.

machinery any dispute which alleges interference with, or discrimination grounded on, an employee's exercise of Section 7 rights. These rights, as stated, are public rights which, in my judgment, must be protected by the Board in its public capacity of giving effect to the declared public policy of the Act. Rights under a collective-bargaining agreement, on the other hand, are private rights created by the contract and enforceable under procedures established by the contract for that purpose and by suits under Section 301 of the Labor-Management Relations Act. A dispute as to the meaning and/or applicability of the contract is essentially one between the contracting parties—the employer and the union—in which the employee has virtually no role to play. Thus, an employee who feels aggrieved by some action of the employer can file a grievance under the contract but has no standing to compel the union to process the grievance through arbitration if the grievance is resolved against the employee. Arbitration is a costly process and unions for the most part lack the resources necessary to fully investigate and prosecute to arbitration every grievance filed. Indeed, short of a failure to fairly represent, unions have wide discretion in determining which grievances to pursue to arbitration and which to abandon or to trade off in favor or some other advantage. Even where the union proceeds to arbitration on an employee's grievance, the aggrieved employee is but an outsider—a third party—to such proceeding, having no standing to participate as a party, to have counsel different from union counsel, to examine witnesses, or to submit evidence. Finally, the arbitrator is generally authorized only to determine the contract issue presented by the grievance, i.e., whether the employee engaged in the conduct for which he or she was assertedly disciplined and whether the contract permitted such discipline for that conduct. If the employee claimed that the discipline was in reprisal for having engaged in protected concerted activities under Section 7, the arbitrator either would not or could not reach that issue without exceeding the power given him by the contract.

In sum, I shall continue to defer to arbitration those cases involving only contract interpretation issues, as in *Roy Robinson Chevrolet*. But I shall not defer to arbitration in those cases which involve unfair labor practices allegations affecting individual rights under Section 7 of the Act.[22] Since the instant case is of the latter type, being concerned with whether Respondent's motive in discharging employee Soape was his union or other protected concerted activities, I find that the matter should not be deferred to arbitration and I agree with my colleagues' finding that the Respondent violated Section 8(a)(3) and (1) by the said discharge.

PENELLO and WALTHER, Members, dissenting:

Inasmuch as we believe that this case should be deferred to arbitration under the *Collyer* doctrine, we find it unnecessary to determine whether

---

[22] I note that my colleagues reach different interpretations of the same statistical information concerning cases deferred under the *Collyer* policy. Inasmuch as these statistics do not differentiate between cases involving alleged violations of Sec. 8(a)(5), in which I would defer, and those involving alleged 8(a)(3) violations, in which I shall not defer, they are not significant and are inconclusive at best. In any event, as is often said, statistics tend to support the position of the party offering them.

the Administrative Law Judge correctly decided that the Charging Party, Perry Soape, Jr., was discriminatorily discharged. . . .

Members Fanning and Jenkins would not defer for the reasons stated in their dissenting opinions in *Collyer* and repeatedly reiterated since; namely, "that the Board has a statutory duty to hear and to dispose of unfair labor practices and that the Board cannot abdicate or avoid its duty by seeking to cede its jurisdiction to private tribunals." Chairman Murphy does not agree with this lack-of-power theory. On the contrary, she agrees with us, essentially for the reasons set forth in the majority opinion of *Collyer*, that the Board has discretionary authority under the Act to defer disputes arising under the parties' collective-bargaining agreement to the grievance-arbitration machinery established by such agreement. However, she would exercise that discretionary authority only in cases involving alleged violations of Section 8(a)(5) and 8(b)(3). She would not defer cases alleging violations of Section 8(a)(1), 8(a)(3), 8(b)(1)(A), and 8(b)(2). Inasmuch as the present case involves an alleged violation of Section 8(a)(3), she would therefore not defer this case to arbitration.

The arguments of Members Fanning and Jenkins against all deferral have been considered and rejected repeatedly by both the Board and the courts. We need not take them up again. However, the Chairman's position needs answering.

Collyer involved only an 8(a)(5) situation. Nevertheless, in his concurring opinion, which reflected his many years of experience in administering the Act as Regional Director and Board Member, Member Brown indicated that the deferral process should be given a broad sweep. He said in words that are extremely relevant (192 NLRB at 845):

"The deferral policy should be applied to disputes covered by the collective-bargaining agreement and subject to arbitration whether the disputes involve alleged violations of Section 8(a)(5), (3), or (1) or whether brought by the employer, the union, or an employee. It is inconsistent with the statutory policy favoring arbitration for the Board to resolve disputes which, while cast as unfair labor practices, essentially involve disputes with respect to the interpretation or application of the contract and which the arbitrator can put to rest. That the employer and union are bound by their agreement is fundamental to collective bargaining. I also believe that an employee is bound by the acts of his bargaining agent. If an employee could initiate and repudiate the acts of his duly designated representative at his whim, the statutory objective of fostering voluntary settlements by parties to collective-bargaining agreements cannot be attained. This was not intended by Congress and is contrary to the fundamental purposes of the Act." [Citations omitted.]

In *National Radio Company, Inc.*, 198 NLRB 527, 80 LRRM 1718 (Members Fanning and Jenkins dissenting), the Board extended the *Collyer* doctrine to a case involving an alleged discriminatory discharge of a union official. The Board explained the reason for this extension as follows (198 NLRB at 531–532):

"The question whether, in fact, the policies and purposes of the Act will be furthered by abstention here and in similar cases is more complex. The crucial determinant is, we believe, the reasonableness of the assumption that the arbitration procedure will resolve this dispute in a manner consistent with the standards of *Spielberg*. As we noted in *Collyer*, contract grievances and arbitration procedures have become an integral part of virtually all collective-bargaining contracts in this country. Though arbitration like all systems for the resolution of disputes has its imperfections, the demand for and resort to services of skilled arbitrators has increased at a steady and heartening rate. The issue most often resolved by arbitrators is that of just cause for the imposition of discipline. Indeed, it is largely the insistence of unions upon procedures to protect employees against arbitrary treatment that has led to the modern ubiquity of contractual grievance and arbitration procedures. Wholly aside from considerations arising from the increasing caseload before this five-man Board, we believe the purposes of the Act are well served by encouraging the parties to those contracts to resolve their disputes without government intervention. The reference in *Carey* to the 'therapy of arbitration' is not simply rhetorical. The relationship of contracting parties is strengthened by the experience of mutual reliance on contract procedures. The intervention of this Board, by contrast, can sometimes be an unsettling force." [Citations omitted.]

The Board noted two factors which justified its belief that abstention was proper: (1) the parties had had a long-established, stable, and productive bargaining relationship; and (2) although the 8(a)(3) allegation subsumed union animus, there was no pattern of action subversive of Section 7 rights. The facts in this case are identical. . . .

The Chairman has now substantially emasculated the court-approved *Collyer* doctrine for reasons which we do not regard as valid. The Chairman says that in cases involving 8(a)(1), 8(a)(3), 8(b)(1)(A), and 8(b)(2) violations an arbitrator's resolution of the contract issue will not dispose of the unfair labor practice allegations and that the arbitration process is not suited for resolving employee complaints of discrimination under Section 7. This is a strange doctrine in view of the Board's experience under *Spielberg* and volumes of arbitrator's decisions. In *Spielberg*, the Board said that it would accept an arbitrator's award made pursuant to a contract arbitration procedure as dispositive of related unfair labor practices if the awards met certain standards. Pursuant thereto, the Board has in fact dismissed 8(a)(1) and (3) allegations because of *Spielberg* arbitral awards. As to the allegation that the arbitration process is not suited for resolving complaints of discrimination under Section 7, this presumably means that arbitrators are not competent to decide such issues. With all due respect to the Chairman, we cannot subscribe to this notion. As the Board majority said in *National Radio Company*, 198 NLRB at 531–532, 80 LRRM 1718, the issue most often resolved by arbitrators is that of just cause for the imposition of discipline, which frequently also requires the arbitrator to decide whether the cause was in fact union or concerted activities. . . .

The Chairman finds justification for thus bifurcating the *Collyer* doctrine by the language of Section 1 of the Act which says that the policy of the Act is: (1) to encourage the "practice and procedure of collective bargaining," and (2) to protect the "exercise by workers of full freedom of association, self-organization, and designation of representatives of their own choosing, for the purpose of negotiating the terms and conditions of their employment or other mutual aid or protection." Arbitration, the Chairman says, is appropriate to the first objective but not to the second. In support the Chairman cites the *Mastro Plastics* case. In *Mastro Plastics*, employees struck in protest against employer unfair labor practices which involved violations of Section 8(a)(1), (2), and (3). The employer contended, inter alia, that the strike was unprotected because in violation of a no-strike clause in an existing collective-bargaining contract. The Supreme Court rejected this claim holding that the no-strike clause did not waive the employees' right to strike against the "flagrant" interference with the employees' protected right to select their own bargaining representative. It was in the light of the "flagrant" unfair labor practices of the employer which were destructive of any collective-bargaining relationship that the court said (350 U.S. at 280):

> "The two policies [set forth in section 1] are complementary. They depend for their foundation upon assurance of 'full freedom of association.' *Only after that is assured* can the parties turn to effective negotiation as a means of maintaining 'the normal flow of commerce and . . . the full production of articles and commodities. . . .' "

The present case does not involve any such situation as existed in *Mastro Plastics*. In no sense can it be said that the aim or result of the discharge of Soape was to destroy the collective-bargaining relationship with the incumbent union. Rather, if there did exist an unlawful motive in Soape's layoff it was the result not of company policy but of an aberration by a minor supervisor. Certainly the Union did not consider that the discharge undermined its position or prestige for it expressed disapproval of Soape's approach to the Board for redress and instead declared that he should file a grievance under the contract.[38] The Union was thus upholding the collective-bargaining process by insisting that Soape take up its grievance pursuant to the provisions of the collective-bargaining agreement. In so doing, the Union was affirming the underlying objective of the labor laws which, as the Supreme Court has stated, is to promote collective-bargaining agreements and to give substance to those agreements through the arbitration process.

[38]On December 27, 1974 a union official wrote Soape:

"I regret that it is necessary for me to advise you that the avenue you have taken concerning NLRB is entirely out of order since you did not in any way utilize any of the mechanics available to you under our working agreement.

"And I request that you cease and desist from this course and file your grievance under Article 22 of the NTM agreement. This, of course is your prerogative, but if you insist in maintaining your present position, it will be necessary that I maintain a complete hands-off policy concerning this matter."

The Chairman also argues that Section 7 rights are public rather than private rights, that Section 10(a) entrusts the Board with exclusive authority to protect those rights, and that a collective-bargaining agreement cannot lawfully strip the employees of their statutory rights nor the Board of its obligation to protect those rights. This argument is pretty much the argument which has been repeatedly advanced by Members Fanning and Jenkins, and the conclusion drawn therefrom repeatedly rejected by the Board majority and the courts. To take up the argument piecemeal: no one disputes that Section 7 rights are public rather than private rights and that the Board is charged with protecting those rights in the public interest. But the Section 7 public rights of individuals includes the right "to bargain collectively through representatives of their own choosing," and this right is vindicated by Section 8(a)(5) and 8(b)(3), yet the Chairman is prepared to defer to arbitration cases involving alleged violations of those sections. The reference to Section 10(a) seems to be advanced to justify a conclusion that the Board lacks discretion to defer to arbitration at least some alleged unfair labor practice violations. This seems to be contradictory to the opening paragraphs of the Chairman's concurring opinion in this case and in her concurring opinion in *Roy Robinson Chevrolet.*

Nor is the Board stripping the employees of their statutory rights or repudiating its obligation to protect those rights by deferring suitable cases to arbitration. In *National Radio* the Board, in rejecting this argument of abdication, said (198 NLRB 531):

"We may not abdicate our statutory duty to prevent and remedy unfair labor practices. Yet, once an exclusive agent has been chosen by employees to represent them, we are charged with a duty fully to protect the structure of collective representation and the freedom of the parties to establish and maintain an effective and productive relationship.

"In this context, abstention simply cannot be equated with abdication. We are, instead, adjuring the parties to seek resolution of their dispute under the provisions of their own contract and thus fostering both the collective relationship and the Federal policy favoring voluntary arbitration and dispute settlement. And by reserving jurisdiction we preserve the right of the Charging Party to seek from us vindication of statutory rights should the arbitration reach a result not tolerable under the statute."

The Board has not deferred cases to arbitration in an indiscriminate manner, nor has it been insensitive to the statutory rights of employees in deciding whether to defer and whether to give effect to an arbitration award. The standard it has used is reasonable belief that arbitration procedures would resolve the dispute in a manner consistent with the criteria of *Spielberg*. Thus, it has refused to defer where the interests of the union which might be expected to represent the employee filing the unfair labor practice charge are adverse to those of the employee, or where the respondent's conduct constitutes a rejection of the principles of collective bargaining. And where, after deferral, the respondent has refused to proceed to arbitration, the Board has rescinded the deferral and decided the case on the merits. Finally, if for any reason the arbitrator's award fails to meet the *Spielberg* standards, as for example, that it is repugnant to the policies of the Act, the Board will not give it effect.

The Chairman refers to alleged "practical considerations" to justify a refusal to defer to arbitration. Thus, she says that "Arbitration is a costly process and unions for the most part lack the resources necessary to fully investigate and prosecute to arbitration every grievance filed." There are several answers to this argument. In the first place, if a union has agreed that disputes are to be handled by a specific grievance-arbitration procedure, it is not in a position to complain about costs when it is called upon to live up to its agreement. In the second place, not all unions are poor and unable to defray the costs of arbitration. In the third place, the union involved in this case is not pleading poverty and is not opposed to having Soape's dispute submitted to the contract grievance-arbitration procedure. On the contrary, it has told Soape in no uncertain terms that it should be so submitted. In the fourth place, if a grievance is submitted it may be resolved without ever reaching the arbitration stage.

The Chairman also complains about the right of a union to represent employees in grievance and arbitration procedures to the exclusion of the employees involved. This complaint is really directed at the nature of the collective-bargaining process itself. The Board, which has the responsibility of fostering collective bargaining, ought not itself undermine that process by permitting the employee to ignore the bargaining representative short of finding that the union is not fairly representing the employee.[47] In this case, there is no evidence that the Union is prepared to sacrifice Soape's rights to the benefit of other employees or that it will not fairly represent him.

Finally, the Chairman says that an arbitrator is generally authorized to determine only the contract issue presented by the grievance, i.e., whether the employee engaged in the conduct for which he was disciplined and whether the contract permitted such discipline, but could not decide whether the discipline, if so claimed, was in reprisal for having engaged in protected concerted activities. Whatever the validity of this argument as a general proposition, it has no application to the present case, for the collective-bargaining contract in this case in listing the causes for "proper discharge" contains the following proviso:

". . . The Contractor will not use these rights for the purposes of discrimination against any employee."

---

[47] In *Acuff* v. *United Papermakers and Paperworkers Union, AFL-CIO*, 404 F.2d 169, 69 LRRM 2828 (C.A. 5, 1969), cited by the Chairman, the court denied a motion by employees who had been discharged to intervene in a suit brought by the bargaining representative to compel arbitration of the discharges. The court said:
"The issue in this case is fundamental, yet simple. In order to effectuate the purposes of the labor statutes employees are empowered to organize. This, of course, has resulted in enormous benefits but entails certain burdens as well. One of these is that to some extent the interests of particular individuals are subordinated to the interests of the group both at the contract negotiation stage and thereafter. . . . This is necessary if a union is to function efficiently. As a result, a union may properly determine not to pursue a member's grievance to the arbitration stage at all." [404 F.2d at 171.]

Under the proviso the arbitrator in deciding the contract issue would necessarily have to decide the very issue before the Board, i.e., whether Soape was discriminated against for impermissible reasons.

In an unpublished Board study of the effect of *Collyer* over a 2½ year period, from May 1973 through December 31, 1975, a total of 1,632 cases had been deferred by the Board's Regional Offices under *Collyer*. Arbitrators' decisions issued in 473 of these cases. Of these 473 decisions, the Regions scrutinized 159 at the request of the charging parties in light of the *Spielberg* standards. On 33 occasions, the Regions revoked the *Collyer* deferrals either because the respondents refused to proceed to arbitration or the arbitration awards were deficient under the *Spielberg* standards. In 24 of these 33 instances, issuance of a complaint was made unnecessary by the respondent's signing of a settlement agreement. Further, of the 1,632 deferred cases, 437 were settled through the contract grievance procedure without the need of proceeding to arbitration. The study concludes:

> "As between processing a dispute as a grievance vis-à-vis an unfair labor practice, the evidence that 437 cases were subsequently adjusted by the parties, themselves, following deferral by the Regional Office suggests that *Collyer* has forced the parties to rely less on the NLRB and more on collective bargaining via the contractual grievance machinery to settle certain disputes. Moreover, this same evidence indicates that there is a 50/50 chance of resolving the dispute short of arbitration. When it is necessary to arbitrate, however, the data indicates that arbitration, much like Board litigation, is a victim of delay."

Relevant to the problem of deferral are the Board's own statistics as to elapsed time from the time of deferral to the time of the issuance of the arbitrator's decision. According to the study previously mentioned, the median time for the issuance of an arbitration decision following deferral by the Regional Office is 140 days. In comparison, the elapsed time from the issuance of a complaint by the Regional Office to the issuance of a decision by the Board is approximately twice as long.

The statistics by this Agency indicate that *Collyer* works, that it has encouraged the use of contract grievance-arbitration procedures and thus encouraged collective bargaining itself, that it has speeded up the disposition of some disputes, that it has resulted in the settlement of many grievance procedures making arbitration unnecessary, and that it has lightened the workload of the board.[48]

---

[48]In citing the deferral statistics to show, in their view, that *Collyer* has failed because it has not significantly reduced the Board's caseload, Members Fanning and Jenkins confuse an incidental benefit of deferral (caseload reduction) with the purpose of deferral (collective-bargaining encouragement). Deferral requires parties (including individuals who are bound by the acts of their bargaining agent) to abide by their agreement to settle their disputes themselves through the collective-bargaining process. The statistics show that of 1,632 cases deferral has been revoked in only 33 cases, or 2 percent of the time. Thus, deferral has had a 98-percent success rate in achieving its purpose. And these figures do not reflect those disputes which the parties, looking to *Collyer*, have settled themselves without resort to the Board. We think that deferral has had a significant and beneficial impact in furthering the major purpose of the Act, to encourage the practice and procedure of collective bargaining.

The reasons advanced by the Chairman for cutting back the *Collyer* doctrine are no more persuasive than those advanced by Members Fanning and Jenkins, as we have shown. Accordingly, we dissent.

Excerpt from Daily Labor Report on *United Technologies Corp.* and *Olin Corp.*

1984 DLR 16:A-1

By a vote of 3-1, NLRB adopts a broad policy of deferring to grievance-arbitration machinery, including cases involving alleged interference with employee rights under [Sections 7, 8(a)(1), 8(a)(3), and 8(a)(5) of the NLRA]. In a prearbitral case involving United Technologies Corporation of Hartford, Conn., (268 NLRB No. 83 (1984)), the Board dismisses an unfair labor practice complaint, finding instead that the purposes of the Act can best be effectuated by having the dispute resolved by an arbitrator selected under the parties' collective bargaining agreement.

In a separate ruling, the Board sets new standards in which it will honor arbitration decisions already rendered rather than decide unfair labor practice questions that grow out of the same set of facts presented to the arbitrator. The Board dismisses a complaint based on charges involving a Niagara, N.Y., plant owned by Olin Corporation (268 NLRB No. 86 (1974)). Chairman Dotson and Members Hunter and Dennis join to form the majority in both cases. Member Zimmerman protests his colleagues' reversal of several major rulings. He warns that the Board is "needlessly sacrific[ing] basic safeguards for individual employee rights under the Act."

In *United Technologies*, the new Board majority—Dotson, Hunter, and Dennis—votes to overrule *General American* and return to what it regards as the correct policy first announced in the landmark 1971 ruling of *Collyer Insulated Wire*, and the 1972 *National Radio* decision. The Board describes *General American* as an abrupt change which

"essentially emasculated the Board's deferral policy. . . . Simply stated, *Collyer* worked well because it was premised on sound legal and pragmatic considerations. Accordingly, we believe it deserves to be resurrected and infused with renewed life. It is fundamental to the concept of collective bargaining that the parties to a collective-bargaining agreement are bound by the terms of their contract. Where an employer and a union have voluntarily elected to create a dispute resolution machinery culminating in final and binding arbitration, it is contrary to the basic principles of the Act for the Board to jump into the fray prior to an honest attempt by the parties to resolve their disputes through that machinery. For dispute resolution under the grievance-arbitration process is as much a part of collective bargaining as the act of negotiating the contract. In our view, the statutory purpose of encouraging the practice and procedure of collective bargaining is ill-served by permitting the parties to ignore their agreement and to petition this Board in the first instance for remedial relief."

The *United Technologies* case involves allegations that management harassed and threatened a grievant in an attempt to intimidate her into withdrawing a grievance. The employee had filed a grievance claiming that her foreman had engaged in an "act of aggression"—that he threw a bag of parts at her. The grievance statement sought a "cease and desist" remedy and asked that the foreman "be properly instructed as to his attitude in employee-management relations." The foreman's supervisor told the employee that the company had been nice to her in the past and failed to discipline her even though she was responsible for a lot of rejects.

The Board concludes that the underlying facts make the case "eminently well suited for deferral." It stresses that the dispute involves a statement by a single foreman made to a single employee and a shop steward during the course of a routine first-step grievance meeting. The union contract clearly establishes that such disputes are subject to the grievance-arbitration provisions, the Board says. It adds that the employer has expressed its willingness to arbitrate the dispute.

In the companion case involving Olin Corporation, the Board restates its adherence to the 1955 *Spielberg* decision, favoring deferral to arbitrator's rulings, but the Board adopts standards announced in a dissent by Member Hunter in the 1982 ruling in *Procopo, Inc.* The following standards will be applied for deferral to arbitration awards: (1) the contractual issue is factually parallel to the unfair labor practice issue, and (2) the arbitrator was presented generally with the facts relevant to resolving the unfair labor practice.

The Board adds that in determining whether an award is "clearly repugnant" to the Act under the *Spielberg* test, the Board will not require that the arbitrator's award be "totally consistent with Board precedent. Unless the award is 'palpably wrong,' i.e., unless the arbitrator's decision is not susceptible to an interpretation consistent to the Act, we will defer." The Board also places a heavy burden on the NLRB general counsel to establish that the arbitral process was defective and that the award is unworthy of deferral. "[T]he burden of persuasion rests," the Board says, "with the General Counsel to demonstrate that there are deficiencies in the arbitral process requiring the Board to ignore the determination of the arbitrator and subject the case to de novo review."

Zimmerman contends that under the standard of the *Procopo* dissent, the Board will defer to the arbitrator's award even if the arbiter failed to consider and pass on the unfair labor practice issue. In unusually strong terms, Member Zimmerman denounces as a "canard" the majority's assertion that it has not totally overruled *Suburban Motor Freight, Procopo*, and similar holdings. He contends that the majority's presumption that the arbiter has resolved the unfair labor practice issue extends beyond permissible statutory bounds and constitutes an abdication of the Board's "responsibility to protect employees' rights and the public interest by preventing and remedying unfair labor practices."

All the members agree, however, that the arbitrator's award in the *Olin* case is worthy of deferral. The case involves a sickout by some 43 members of the Oil, Chemical and Atomic Workers. The company fired the union president for participating in the work stoppage in violation of the no-strike clause of the union contract. The arbitrator upheld the discharge since the union contract specifically barred union officers from causing or permitting work stoppages.

E. RELATIONSHIP OF ARBITRATION AND TITLE VII

Alexander v. Gardner-Denver Co.

Supreme Court of the United States, 1974
415 U.S. 36, 7 FEP Cases 81

[In this case an employee, discharged on the ground of poor work, claimed that he was really discharged because of his race. The collective bargaining agreement prohibited racial discrimination and required "proper cause" for a discharge. The employee's grievance was processed to arbitration. Although the claim of race discrimination was submitted to the arbitrator, he did not mention it in his award which found "just cause" for the discharge based on poor work of the employee. The employee also was unsuccessful in protesting his discharge before a state civil rights commission and the EEOC.]

Mr. Justice Powell delivered the opinion of the Court.

This case concerns the proper relationship between federal courts and the grievance-arbitration machinery of collective-bargaining agreements in the resolution and enforcement of an individual's rights to equal employment opportunities under Title VII of the Civil Rights Act of 1964. Specifically, we must decide under what circumstances, if any, an employee's statutory right to a trial *de novo* under Title VII may be foreclosed by prior submission of his claim to final arbitration under the nondiscrimination clause of a collective-bargaining agreement. . . .

Congress enacted Title VII of the Civil Rights Act of 1964 to assure equality of employment opportunities by eliminating those practices and devices that discriminate on the basis of race, color, religion, sex, or national origin. Cooperation and voluntary compliance were selected as the preferred means for achieving this goal. To this end, Congress created the Equal Employment Opportunity Commission and established a procedure whereby existing State and local equal employment opportunity agencies, as well as the Commission, would have an opportunity to settle disputes through conference, conciliation, and persuasion before the aggrieved party was permitted to file a lawsuit. In the Equal Employment Opportunity Act of 1972 Congress amended Title VII to provide the Commission with further authority to investigate individual charges of discrimination, to promote voluntary compliance with the requirements of Title VII, and to institute civil actions against employers or unions named in a discrimination charge.

Even in its amended form, however, Title VII does not provide the Commission with direct powers of enforcement. The Commission cannot adjudicate claims or impose administrative sanctions. Rather, final responsibility for enforcement of Title VII is vested with federal courts. The Act authorizes courts to issue injunctive relief and to order such affirmative action as may be appropriate to remedy the effects of unlawful employment practices. Courts retain these broad remedial powers despite a Commission finding of no reasonable cause to believe that the Act has been violated. Taken together, these provisions make plain that federal courts have been assigned plenary powers to secure compliance with Title VII.

In addition to reposing ultimate authority in federal courts, Congress gave private individuals a significant role in the enforcement process of Title VII. Individual grievants usually initiate the Commission's investigatory and conciliatory procedures. And although the 1972 amendment to Title VII empowers the Commission to bring its own actions, the private right of action remains an essential means of obtaining judicial enforcement of Title VII. In such cases, the private litigant not only redresses his own injury but also vindicates the important congressional policy against discriminatory employment practices. . . .

Pursuant to this statutory scheme, petitioner initiated the present action for judicial consideration of his rights under Title VII. The District Court and the Court of Appeals held, however, that petitioner was bound by the prior arbitral decision and had no right to sue under Title VII. Both courts evidently thought that this result was dictated by notions of election of remedies and waiver and by the federal policy favoring arbitration of labor disputes, as enunciated by this Court in *Textile Workers Union* v. *Lincoln Mills,* 353 U.S. 448, 40 LRRM 2113 (1957), and the *Steelworkers* Trilogy. . . . We disagree.

Title VII does not speak expressly to the relationship between federal courts and the grievance-arbitration machinery of collective-bargaining agreements. It does, however, vest federal courts with plenary powers to enforce the statutory requirements; and it specifies with precision the jurisdictional prerequisites that an individual must satisfy before he is entitled to institute a lawsuit. In the present case, these prerequisites were met when petitioner (1) filed timely a charge of employment discrimination with the Commission, and (2) received and acted upon the Commission's statutory notice of the right to sue. There is no suggestion in the statutory scheme that a prior arbitral decision either forecloses an individual's right to sue or divests federal courts of jurisdiction.

In addition, legislative enactments in this area have long evinced a general intent to accord parallel or overlapping remedies against discrimination. In the Civil Rights Act of 1964, 42 U.S.C. § 2000e *et seq.,* Congress indicated that it considered the policy against discrimination to be of the "highest priority." Consistent with this view, Title VII provides for consideration of employment-discrimination claims in several forums. See 42 U.S.C. § 2000e-5(b) (EEOC); 42 U.S.C. § 2000e-5(c) (State and local agencies); 42 U.S.C. § 2000e-5(f) (federal courts). And, in general, submission of a claim to one forum does not preclude a later submission to another. Moreover, the legislative history of Title VII manifests a congressional intent to allow an individual to pursue independently his rights under both Title VII and other applicable state and federal statutes.[9] The clear inference is that Title VII was designed to supplement, rather than supplant, existing laws and institutions relating to employment discrimination. In sum, Title VII's purpose and procedures strongly suggest that an individual does not forfeit his private cause of action if he first pursues his grievance to final arbitration under the nondiscrimination clause of a collective-bargaining agreement.

In reaching the opposite conclusion, the District Court relied in part on the doctrine of election of remedies.[10] That doctrine, which refers to situations where an individual pursues remedies that are legally or factually inconsistent, has no application in the present context. In submitting his grievance to arbitration, an employee seeks to vindicate his contractual right under a collective-bargaining agreement. By contrast, in filing a lawsuit under Title VII, an employee asserts independent statutory rights accorded by Congress. The distinctly separate nature of these contractual and statutory rights is not vitiated merely because both were violated as a result of the same factual occurrence. And certainly no inconsistency results from permitting both rights to be enforced in their respectively appropriate forums. The resulting scheme is somewhat analogous to the procedure under the National Labor Relations Act, as amended, where disputed transactions may implicate both contractual and statutory rights. Where the statutory right underlying a particular claim may not be abridged by contractual agreement, the Court has recognized that consideration of the claim by the arbitrator as a contractual dispute under the collective-bargaining agreement does not preclude subsequent consideration of the claim by the National Labor Relations Board as an unfair labor practice charge or as a petition for clarification of the union's representation certificate under the Act. *Carey* v. *Westinghouse Corp.*, 375 U.S. 261, 55 LRRM 2042 (1964). Cf. *Smith* v. *Evening News Assn.*, 371 U.S. 195, 51 LRRM 2646 (1962). There, as here, the relationship between the forums is complementary since consideration of the claim by both forums may promote the policies underlying each. Thus,

---

[9]For example, Senator Joseph Clark, one of the sponsors of the bill, introduced an interpretive memorandum which stated: "Nothing in Title VII or anywhere else in this bill affects the rights and obligations under the NLRA or the Railway Labor Act. . . . Title VII is not intended to and does not deny to any individual, rights and remedies which he may pursue under other federal and state statutes. If a given action should violate both Title VII and the National Labor Relations Act, the National Labor Relations Board would not be deprived of jurisdiction." 110 Cong. Rec. 7207 (1964). Moreover, the Senate defeated an amendment which would have made Title VII the exclusive federal remedy for most unlawful employment practices. 110 Cong. Rec. 13650–13652 (1964). And a similar amendment was rejected in connection with the Equal Employment Opportunity Act of 1972. See H.R. 9247, 92d Cong., 1st Sess. (1971). See also 2 U.S. Code Cong. & Admin. News. 92d Cong., 2d Sess. (1972), pp. 2137, 2179, 2181–2182. The report of the Senate Committee responsible for the 1972 Act explained that neither the "provisions regarding the individual's right to sue under Title VII, nor any of the provisions of this bill, are meant to affect existing rights granted under other laws." S. Rep. No. 415, at 24, 92d Cong., 1st Sess. (1971). For a detailed discussion of the legislative history of the 1972 Act, see Sape and Hart, *Title VII Reconsidered: The Equal Opportunity Act of 1972*, 40 GEO. WASH. L. REV. 824 (1972).

[10] . . . The policy reasons for rejecting the doctrines of election of remedies and waiver in the context of Title VII are equally applicable to the doctrines of *res judicata* and collateral estoppel.

the rationale behind the election of remedies doctrine cannot support the decision below.[14]

We are also unable to accept the proposition that petitioner waived his cause of action under Title VII. To begin, we think it clear that there can be no prospective waiver of an employee's rights under Title VII. It is true, of course, that a union may waive certain statutory rights related to collective activity, such as the right to strike. . . . These rights are conferred on employees collectively to foster the processes of bargaining and properly may be exercised or relinquished by the union as collective-bargaining agent to obtain economic benefits for unit members. Title VII, on the other hand, stands on plainly different ground; it concerns not majoritarian process, but an individual's right to equal employment opportunities. Title VII's strictures are absolute and represent a congressional command that each employee be free from discriminatory practices. Of necessity, the rights conferred can form no part of the collective-bargaining process since waiver of these rights would defeat the paramount congressional purpose behind Title VII. In these circumstances an employee's rights under Title VII are not susceptible to prospective waiver.

The actual submission of petitioner's grievance to arbitration in the present case does not alter the situation. Although presumably an employee may waive his cause of action under Title VII as part of a voluntary settlement, mere resort to the arbitral forum to enforce contractual rights constitutes no such waiver. Since an employee's rights under Title VII may not be waived prospectively, existing contractual rights and remedies against discrimination must result from other concessions already made by the union as part of the economic bargain struck with the employer. It is settled law that no additional concession may be exacted from any employee as the price for enforcing those rights.

Moreover, a contractual right to submit a claim to arbitration is not displaced simply because Congress also has provided a statutory right against discrimination. Both rights have legally independent origins and are equally available to the aggrieved employee. This point becomes apparent through consideration of the role of the arbitrator in the system of industrial self-government.[16]

---

[14]Nor can it be maintained that election of remedies is required by the possibility of unjust enrichment through duplicative recoveries. Where, as here, the employer has prevailed at arbitration, there of course can be no duplicative recovery. But even in cases where the employee has first prevailed, judicial relief can be structured to avoid such windfall gains. Furthermore, if the relief obtained by the employee at arbitration were fully equivalent to that obtainable under Title VII, there would be no further relief for the court to grant and hence no need for the employee to institute suit.

[16]See Meltzer, *Labor Arbitration and Overlapping and Conflicting Remedies for Employment Discrimination*, 39 U. CHI. L. REV. 30, 32–35 (1971); Meltzer, *Ruminations About Ideology, Law, and Arbitration*, 34 U. CHI. L. REV. 545 (1967). As the late Dean Shulman stated:

"A proper conception of the arbitrator's function is basic. He is not a public tribunal imposed upon the parties by superior authority which the parties are obliged to accept. He has no general charter to administer justice for a community which transcends the parties. He is rather part of a system of industrial self-government created by and confined to the parties. He serves their pleasure only, to administer the rule of law established by their collective agreement." Shulman, *Reason, Contracts and Law in Labor Relations*, 68 HARV. L. REV. 999, 1000 (1955).

As the proctor of the bargain, the arbitrator's task is to effectuate the intent of the parties. His source of authority is the collective-bargaining agreement, and he must interpret and apply that agreement in accordance with the "industrial common law of the shop" and the various needs and desires of the parties. The arbitrator, however, has no general authority to invoke public laws that conflict with the bargain between the parties:

"[A]n arbitrator is confined to interpretation and application of the collective bargaining agreement; he does not sit to dispense his own brand of industrial justice. He may of course look for guidance from many sources, yet his award is legitimate only so long as it draws its essence from the collective bargaining agreement. When the arbitrator's words manifest an infidelity to his obligation, courts have no choice but to refuse enforcement of the award." *United Steelworkers of America* v. *Enterprise Wheel & Car Corp.*, 363 U.S., at 597, 46 LRRM, at 2425.

If an arbitral decision is based "solely on the arbitrator's view of the requirements of enacted legislation," rather than on an interpretation of the collective-bargaining agreement, the arbitrator has "exceeded the scope of his submission," and the award will not be enforced. *Ibid.* Thus the arbitrator has authority to resolve questions of contractual rights, and this authority remains regardless whether certain contractual rights are similar to, or duplicative of, the substantive rights secured by Title VII.

The District Court and the Court of Appeals reasoned that to permit an employee to have his claim considered in both the arbitral and judicial forums would be unfair since this would mean that the employer, but not the employee, was bound by the arbitral award. In the District Court's words, it could not "accept a philosophy which gives the employee two strings to his bow when the employer has only one." This argument mistakes the effect of Title VII. Under the *Steelworker's Trilogy*, an arbitral decision is final and binding on the employer and employee, and judicial review is limited as to both. But in instituting an action under Title VII, the employee is not seeking review of the arbitrator's decision. Rather, he is asserting a statutory right independent of the arbitration process. An employer does not have "two strings to his bow" with respect to an arbitral decision for the simple reason that Title VII does not provide employers with a cause of action against employees. An employer cannot be the victim of discriminatory employment practices.

The District Court and the Court of Appeals also thought that to permit a later resort to the judicial forum would undermine substantially the employer's incentive to arbitrate and would "sound the death knell for arbitration clauses in labor contracts." Again, we disagree. The primary incentive for an employer to enter into an arbitration agreement is the union's reciprocal promise not to strike. As the Court stated in *Boys Markets, Inc.* v. *Retail Clerks Union*, 398 U.S. 235, 248, 74 LRRM 2257, 2261 (1970), "a no strike obligation, express or implied, is the *quid pro quo* for an undertaking by an employer to submit grievance disputes to the process of arbitration." It is not unreasonable to assume that most employers will regard the benefits derived from a no-strike pledge as outweighing whatever costs may result from according employees an arbitral remedy against discrimination in addition to their judicial remedy under Title VII. Indeed, the severe consequences of a strike may make an arbitration clause almost essential from both the employees and the employer's perspective. Moreover, the grievance-arbitration machinery of the collective-bargaining agreement remains a relatively inexpensive and expeditious means for resolving a wide range of disputes, including claims of discriminatory employment practices. Where the collective-bargaining agreement contains a nondiscrimination clause similar to Title VII, and where arbitral procedures are fair and regular, arbitration may well produce a settlement satisfactory to both employer and employee. An employer thus has an incentive to make available the conciliatory and therapeutic process of arbitration which may satisfy an employee's perceived need to resort to the judicial forum, thus saving the employer the expense and aggravation associated with a lawsuit. For similar reasons, the employee also, has a strong incentive to arbitrate grievances, and arbitration may often eliminate those misunderstandings or discriminatory practices that might otherwise precipitate resort to the judicial forum.

Respondent contends that even if a preclusion rule is not adopted, federal courts should defer to arbitral decisions on discrimination claims where: (i) the claim was before the arbitrator; (ii) the collective-bargaining agreement prohibited the form of discrimination charged in the suit under Title VII; and (iii) the arbitrator has authority to rule on the claim and to fashion a remedy.[17] Under respondent's proposed rule, a court would grant summary judgment and dismiss the employee's action if the above conditions were met. The rule's obvious consequence in the present case would be to deprive the petitioner of his statutory right to attempt to establish his claim in a federal court.

At the outset, it is apparent that a deferral rule would be subject to many of the objections applicable to a preclusion rule. The purpose and procedures of Title VII indicate that Congress intended federal courts to exercise final responsibility for enforcement of Title VII; deferral to arbitral decisions would be inconsistent with that goal. Futhermore, we have long recognized that "the choice of forums inevitably affects the scope of the substantive right to be vindicated." Respondent's deferral rule is necessarily premised on the assumption that arbitral processes are commensurate with judicial processes and that Congress impliedly intended federal courts to defer to arbitral decisions on Title VII issues. We deem this supposition unlikely.

Arbitral procedures, while well suited to the resolution of contractual disputes, make arbitration a comparatively inappropriate forum for the final resolution of rights created by Title VII. This conclusion rests first on the special role of the arbitrator, whose task is to effectuate the intent of the parties rather than the requirements of enacted legislation. Where the collective-bargaining agreement conflicts with Title VII, the arbitra-

[17]Brief of Respondent, at 37. Respondent's proposed rule is analogous to the NLRB's policy of deferring to arbitral decisions on statutory issues in certain cases. See *Spielberg Manufacturing Co.*, 112 NLRB 1080, 1082, 36 LRRM 1152 (1955).

tion must follow the agreement. To be sure, the tension between contractual and statutory objectives may be mitigated where a collective-bargaining agreement contains provisions facially similar to those of Title VII. But other facts may still render arbitral processes comparatively inferior to judicial processes in the protection of Title VII rights. Among these is the fact that the specialized competence of arbitrators pertains primarily to the law of the shop, not the law of the land.[18] Parties usually choose an arbitrator because they trust his knowledge and judgment concerning the demands and norms of industrial relations. On the other hand, the resolution of statutory or constitutional issues is a primary responsibility of courts, and judicial construction has proven especially necessary with respect to Title VII, whose broad language frequently can be given meaning only by reference to public law concepts.

Moreover, the fact-finding process in arbitration usually is not equivalent to judicial fact-finding. The record of the arbitration proceedings is not as complete; the usual rules of evidence do not apply; and rights and procedures common to civil trials, such as discovery, compulsory process, cross-examination, and testimony under oath, are often severely limited or unavailable. . . .And as this Court has recognized, "[a]rbitrators have no obligation to the court to give their reasons for an award." Indeed, it is the informality of arbitral procedure that enables it to function as an efficient, inexpensive, and expeditious means for dispute resolution. This same characteristic, however, makes arbitration a less appropriate forum for final resolution of Title VII issues than the federal courts.[19]

It is evident that respondent's proposed rule would not allay these concerns. Nor are we convinced that the solution lies in applying a more demanding deferral standard. . . . As respondent points out, a standard that adequately insured effectuation of Title VII rights in the arbitral forum would tend to make arbitration a procedurally complex, expensive, and time-consuming process. And judicial enforcement of such a standard would almost require courts to make *de novo* determinations of the employees' claims. It is uncertain whether any minimal savings in judicial time and expense would justify the risk to vindication of Title VII rights.

A deferral rule also might adversely affect the arbitration system as well as the enforcement scheme of Title VII. Fearing that the arbitral forum cannot adequately protect their rights under Title VII, some employees may elect to bypass arbitration and institute a lawsuit. The possibility of

[18]. . . Significantly, a substantial proportion of labor arbitrators are not lawyers. This is not to suggest, of course, that arbitrators do not possess a high degree of competence with respect to the vital role in implementing the federal policy favoring arbitration of labor disputes.

[19]A further concern is the union's exclusive control over the manner and extent to which an individual grievance is presented. In arbitration, as in the collective-bargaining process, the interests of the individual employee may be subordinated to the collective interests of all employees in the bargaining unit. Moreover, harmony in interest between the union and the individual employee cannot always be presumed, especially where a claim of racial discrimination is made. And a breach of the union's duty of fair representation may prove difficult to establish. In this respect, it is noteworthy that Congress thought it necessary to afford the protections of Title VII against unions as well as employers.

voluntary compliance or settlement of Title VII claims would thus be reduced, and the result could well be more litigation, not less.

We think, therefore, that the federal policy favoring arbitration of labor disputes and the federal policy against discriminatory employment practices can best be accommodated by permitting an employee to pursue fully both his remedy under the grievance-arbitration clause of a collective-bargaining agreement and his cause of action under Title VII. The federal court should consider the employee's claim *de novo*. The arbitral decision may be admitted as evidence and accorded such weight as the court deems appropriate.[21]

The judgment of the Court of Appeals is Reversed.

Notes

1. *Alexander* does not, on its facts, involve the relationship of the NLRB to arbitration. *Alexander* involves the relationship between federal courts and grievance-arbitration machinery with respect to an individual's rights under Title VII of the Civil Rights Act of 1964. Nevertheless, what arguments can be made on the basis of the reasoning in *Alexander* and in *Barrentine* (set forth in the following Note) that the *Collyer* doctrine, with or without the modifications made by Murphy's opinion in *Robinson* and *General American*, is invalid?

2. In *Barrentine* v. *Arkansas-Best Freight Systems*, 450 U.S. 728, 24 WH Cases 1284 (1981), the Supreme Court held that submission of a wage claim to binding arbitration under a collective bargaining agreement (which resulted in an award for the employer) did not bar a subsequent suit, based on the same facts, under the Fair Labor Standards Act. The Court found that the rights asserted by the employees under the statute were independent of the collective bargaining process, and that these rights devolved on the employees as individual workers, not as members of a collective organization. In this case truck drivers claimed that their employer violated the Fair Labor Standards Act by failing to compensate them for time spent on pretrip safety inspections. Noting that the statutory enforcement scheme granted employees broad access to the courts, the Supreme Court held that an employee's right to a minimum wage and to overtime under the Act cannot be abridged or waived by a collective bargaining agreement.

---

[21]We adopt no standards as to the weight to be accorded an arbitral decision, since this must be determined in the court's discretion with regard to the facts and circumstances of each case. Relevant factors include the existence of provisions in the collective-bargaining agreement that conform substantially with Title VII, the degree of procedural fairness in the arbitral forum, adequacy of the record with respect to the issue of discrimination, and the special competence of particular arbitrators. Where an arbitral determination gives full consideration to an employee's Title VII rights, a court may properly accord it great weight. This is especially true where the issue is solely one of fact, specifically addressed by the parties and decided by the arbitrator on the basis of an adequate record. But courts should ever be mindful that Congress, in enacting Title VII, thought it necessary to provide a judicial forum for the ultimate resolution of discriminatory employment claims. It is the duty of courts to assure the full availability of this forum.

Quoting from *Gardner-Denver*, the Court extended its holding in *Gardner-Denver* to employees who seek recovery under the Fair Labor Standards Act following an adverse arbitration award arising out of the same facts. The Court pointed out that an employee's rights under the Act might be lost if arbitration of his wage claim precluded a later suit in federal court, because the arbitrator must effectuate the intent of the parties rather than enforce the statute and because the arbitrator is often powerless to grant an aggrieved employee as broad a range of relief. Under the Fair Labor Standards Act a court can award actual and liquidated damages, reasonable attorney's fees and costs, but the arbitrator can only award the compensation authorized by the wage provisions of the collective bargaining agreement. On the other hand, the Court said, in footnote 22, that: "We do not hold that an arbitral decision has no evidentiary bearing on a subsequent FLSA action in court. As we decided in *Gardner-Denver*, such a decision may be admitted into evidence. . . ." The Court then quoted the famous footnote 21 in *Gardner-Denver*.

A dissenting opinion by Chief Justice Burger states that "the Court ought not to be oblivious to desperately needed changes to keep the federal courts from being inundated with disputes of a kind that can be handled more swiftly and more cheaply by other methods." The opinion asserts that allowing an employee who has a relatively simple wage claim to resort to the federal courts, when an established, simple, and less costly grievance and arbitration procedure can resolve the claim, will increase costs and consume judicial time unnecessarily. The opinion also distinguishes a dispute over wages under the FLSA, where the union and the employee are traditional allies, from a race discrimination case like *Gardner-Denver*.

Comment on Conflicting Forums*

Conduct which is covered by a grievance that is arbitrable under a collective bargaining agreement may also be subject to litigation in some other forum. Thus, there is the possibility of a conflict in the decisions of the two forums. . . .

Those who engage in arbitration . . . ought to be aware of the fact that various broad theories have been advanced on the subject of the relationship of law to the role of the arbitrator. Under one view a collective bargaining agreement should be deemed to incorporate all existing law, and therefore the arbitrator should consult the law in order to interpret the agreement. Under a second view the arbitrator is a creature of the parties, and the arbitrator should simply interpret the agreement in accordance with their intent without regard to statutory law. Under a third view the arbitrator should not normally be concerned about statutory law, but he should not direct a party to violate an express prohibition of law. Nevertheless, despite the popularity of this topic as a subject for

*Sherman, *Conflicting Forums*, 95 LRRM 194 (1977). This paper was delivered as a talk at an Arbitration Conference on June 13, 1977, which was sponsored by Temple University and the American Arbitration Association.

discussion and debate at labor-management conferences, it is my view that these broad theories are not very helpful in resolving the vast majority of cases.

In my experience arbitration cases arising in private industry tend to fall into the following six categories:

1. The first category embraces the typical case, which simply involves a claim of violation of the collective bargaining agreement and does not involve any realistic possibility of litigation in any other forum. Most arbitration cases do not involve conduct which would constitute a valid basis for a claim for relief under statutory law, and there is no problem of a possible conflicting decision by another forum.

2. A second category differs from the first only in the sense that the parties may note, as part of the *background* for the arbitration case, that the company has taken certain action because of some statute. For example, the company may have installed equipment because of rulings of the Environmental Protection Agency. But the issue before the arbitrator, which could involve some question concerning job classification, does not require the arbitrator to consider or construe statutory law, and there is no problem of conflicting forums in this category of cases.

3. In a third category of cases the parties may agree that the arbitrator should construe a statute to resolve the case before him. For example, there may be a broad relevant contract clause which the parties mention briefly, but both parties may then proceed to rely specifically on statutory law, such as a law requiring the wearing of safety glasses. In such cases, there is no problem as to whether the arbitrator should rely on statutory law.

4. A fourth category of cases is similar to the third. The parties may copy statutory language, such as Section 8(a)(3) of the NLRA, and insert it in the collective bargaining agreement. When a case is arbitrated under this language, both parties are likely to rely on statutory precedents, and the arbitrator may properly do so. In fact, not to do so would invite the NLRB to ignore the award under the *Spielberg* standards. The parties also may rely on statutory precedents when arbitrating cases under contract language which has been taken from Title VII of the Civil Rights Act or from the FLSA or from OSHA.

5. A fifth category of cases involves arbitration of a case under *ambiguous* contract language where the position of one party on contract interpretation is consistent with a relevant statute and where the position of the other party on contract interpretation is inconsistent with the relevant statute. Most arbitrators would probably adopt the position which is consistent with the statute. . . .

6. The sixth category consists of cases which involve a direct and specific conflict between the contract and a statute. For the following reasons I submit that such cases are very rare unless the parties and the arbitrator go out of their way to find such a conflict:

(a) Collective bargaining agreements usually provide benefits over and above those required by statute, and not in conflict with the law.

(b) Almost all cases fall in one of the five categories that I have previously listed and are distinguishable from the sixth category.

(c) Parties frequently state the issue in arbitration carefully so as to avoid a ruling in conflict with statutory law.

(d) In 25 years of arbitrating over 1,000 cases I have never had a case which could not be handled properly by treating it as not falling in this sixth category. . . .

Note on Professional Responsibility

The materials in this chapter show examples of situations where an arbitrator's award may be vacated or ignored (*e.g.*, *Torrington*, failure to meet *Spielberg* standards, and *Alexander*). An award also may be vacated because of failure of the arbitrator to make a required disclosure to the parties.

The ethical responsibilities of arbitrators received judicial scrutiny in a case in which the neutral member of a tripartite arbitration tribunal, which determined a commercial dispute over an alleged breach of contract, sporadically rendered engineering consulting services to one of the parties. Although he had rendered no such services for about a year prior to the arbitration, over the preceding four or five years the neutral's consulting fees from this disputant had amounted to some $12,000. The facts of this relationship were unknown to the other disputant, were not revealed during the arbitration proceeding, and did not become known until after the award had been made. A petition filed in federal court asserted that under Section 10 of the United States Arbitration Act the award should be set aside because it was "procured by corruption, fraud, or undue means" or because there was "evident partiality . . . in the arbitrators." The trial court found that this neutral arbitrator's conduct was impartial and fair. At the trial, petitioner's counsel admitted that even had he known of the arbitrator's prior relationship, he probably would not have objected. A federal district court refused to vacate the award. Its decision was affirmed by the Court of Appeals for the First Circuit. The Supreme Court reversed, six to three, holding that an arbitrator "must not only be unbiased but must avoid even the appearance of bias." *Commonwealth Coatings Corp.* v. *Continental Casualty Co.*, 393 U.S. 145 (1968).

Cf. the Code of Professional Responsibility for Arbitrators of Labor-Management Disputes, which provides that "[b]efore accepting an appointment, an arbitrator must disclose directly or through the administrative agency involved, any current or past managerial, representational, or consultative relationship with any company or union involved in a proceeding in which he or she is being considered for appointment or has been tentatively designated to serve. . . . Prior to acceptance of an appointment, an arbitrator must disclose . . . any personal relationship or other circumstance . . . which might reasonably raise a question as to the arbitrator's impartiality. . . . If the circumstances requiring disclosure are not known to the arbitrator prior to acceptance of appointment, disclosure must be made when such circumstances become known to the arbitrator." See Sherman, *Arbitrator's Duty of Disclosure*, 31 U. Pitt. L. Rev.

377 (1970), and Sherman, *Labor Arbitrator's Duty of Disclosure—A Sequel,* 32 U. Pitt. L. Rev. 167 (1970).

Problem

Enderby Company and the union mutually agree upon C.D. Connor, a former practicing attorney and now a full-time labor arbitrator, to arbitrate the question of the right of the company to subcontract laboratory work. While he is reviewing the briefs of the parties after the conclusion of the hearing, Arbitrator Connor realizes that about 15 years ago, when he was in practice with a large law firm, Black Plastics (the predecessor of Enderby) was a client of the firm. Connor was never assigned to work for Black Plastics and never had any dealings with Black Plastics through his old firm. Connor decides that in view of the long passage of time, the fact that his relationship with Black Plastics was so indirect, and that Enderby and not Black Plastics is a party to this arbitration, no disclosure to the parties is called for. His judgment is reinforced by the fact that it would be wasteful to reopen the case if he were disqualified by the parties and that he had already made up his mind when he realized his past association. He decides in favor of Enderby.

Questions

1. Should Connor have made a disclosure to the parties?
2. If the union now learns of Connor's past association, is this a valid basis to vacate the award? What if this association could have been discovered by the union through a reasonably easy search of Connor's background?
3. At the conclusion of the arbitration hearing, and with the union's consent, the Enderby Company's attorney drove Arbitrator Connor to the airport. On the way the attorney said to Connor: "Please don't take this the wrong way, but I'm going to look like a damn fool if we lose this one, because I told our client in negotiations that the management rights clause which we agreed to would protect us in cases like this." What was Connor's professional obligation at this point?

F. INDIVIDUAL'S RIGHTS IN ADMINISTRATION OF CONTRACT

Should an individual employee be deemed to have a vested right to use the grievance and arbitration provisions of an applicable collective agreement?

Suppose that the employer does not wish to negotiate the grievance with the employee in the absence of the union. May the employee compel him to do so? The Conference Committee Report, H.R. Rep. 510, 80th

Cong., 1st Sess. 46 (1947) stated that "[b]oth the House bill and the Senate amendment amended Section 9(a) of the existing law to specifically authorize employers to settle grievances presented by individual employees or groups of employees, so long as the settlement is not inconsistent with any collective bargaining contract in effect." The Second Circuit, holding that a declaratory judgment action is proper under Section 301 of LMRA, nevertheless held that Section 9(a) "does not confer upon an individual grievant the power, enforceable in a court of law, to compel the employer to arbitrate his [discharge] grievance. . . . Despite Congress' use of the word 'rights' . . . we are convinced that the proviso was designed merely to confer upon the employee the privilege to approach his employer. . . . The proviso was apparently designed to safeguard . . . the employer who voluntarily processed employee grievances. . . . 'The office of a proviso is seldom to create substantive rights and obligations; it carves exceptions out of what goes before.' Cox, *Rights Under a Labor Agreement*, 69 Harv. L. Rev. 601, 624 (1956)." *Black-Clawson Co.* v. *Int'l Ass'n of Machinists*, 313 F.2d 179, 184–85, 52 LRRM 2038 (1962).

In 1975 the Supreme Court finally spoke of the proviso, in a footnote to *Emporium Capwell Co.* v. *Western Addition Community Organization*, 420 U.S. 50, 88 LRRM 2660. "The intendment of the proviso is to permit employees to present grievances and to authorize the employer to entertain them without opening itself to liability for dealing directly with employees in derogation of the duty to bargain only with the exclusive bargaining representative, a violation of Section 8(a)(5). . . . The Act nowhere protects this 'right' by making it an unfair labor practice for an employer to refuse to entertain such a presentation, nor can it be read to authorize resort to economic coercion. This matter is fully explicated in *Black-Clawson Co.* v. *Machinists*. . . ." And in *Vaca* v. *Sipes*, 368 U.S. 171, 65 LRRM 2369 (1967), the Court noted that "[s]ome have suggested that every individual employee should have the right to have his grievance taken to arbitration," but the Court stated that ". . . we do not agree that the individual employee has an absolute right to have his grievance taken to arbitration regardless of the provisions of the applicable agreement." Moreover, it has been held, despite the proviso to Section 9(a), that an individual employee does not have the right to counsel of his own choosing to represent him at an arbitration hearing, since the parties to the proceeding are the union and the employer. *Blake* v. *USM Corp.*, 94 LRRM 2509 (D. N.H. 1977).

Although the individual employee cannot compel the employer to negotiate a grievance directly with the employee, to what extent has the Court in *Emporium* answered the question as to whether the employer is authorized to deal directly with the employee (in the absence of the bargaining representative) if the employer chooses to do so?

The proviso to Section 9(a) of the original Wagner Act simply stated that "any individual or a group of employees shall have the right at any time to present grievances to their employer." In *Hughes Tool Co.*, 56 NLRB 981, 982, 14 LRRM 165 (1944), *enf'd*, 147 F.2d 69, 15 LRRM 852 (5th Cir. 1945), the Board held that an individual employee could appear on behalf of himself at every stage of the grievance procedure, that the exclusive bargaining representative was entitled to be present and negotiate at each stage, that "any dissatisfied party may carry the grievance through subsequent machinery until the established grievance procedure is exhausted," and that the individual "cannot present grievances under any procedure except that provided in the contract." On the other hand, in *NLRB* v. *North American Aviation, Inc.*, 136 F.2d 898, 12 LRRM 806 (9th Cir. 1943), the court construed the proviso to allow the employer to process all grievances without the presence of the union at the request of individual employees. The court approved dual methods of handling grievances—one provided by the collective agreement, the other provided by the employer's notice that he would process grievances independently of the agreement.

In 1947 Congress amended the proviso to Section 9(a) by adding its present language. For an analysis of the impact of the 1947 amendments on the pre-1947 cases, see Sherman, *The Individual and His Grievance—Whose Grievance Is It?* 11 U. Pitt. L. Rev. 35 (1949). Has the Supreme Court in *Emporium* clearly delineated the precise nature of the roles and rights of the employer and the union under the proviso to Section 9(a) when the employer desires to use his authority under the proviso "to entertain" grievances from individual employees?

Still another question is whether a union may make a binding settlement of the employee's grievance with the employer. In *Elgin, Joliet & Eastern Ry.* v. *Burley*, 325 U.S. 711, 16 LRRM 749 (1945), the company defended a suit by 10 employees under the Railway Labor Act for back wages on the ground that the employees' grievances had been compromised and settled with the union. The Court held the defense insufficient, stating (p. 738): "For an award to affect the employee's rights, therefore, more must be shown than that the collective agent appeared and purported to act for him. It must be that in some legally sufficient way he authorized it to act in his behalf." The Court also noted the distinction under Railway Labor Act provisions between the handling of disputes concerning the making of collective agreements and disputes over grievances. The 1947 debates over Taft-Hartley amendments suggest that Congress intended to write into the new law the same rights of an individual over his grievance as the Court recognized in *Burley*. However, it should be noted that grievance forms signed by employees frequently authorize the union to act on behalf of grievants. Moreover, more recent cases have tended to treat this type of problem under the heading of the union's duty of fair representation (to be considered in the next chapter).

6. The Union's Duty to Protect Employee Status

A. THE DUTY OF FAIR REPRESENTATION

A legally recognized or certified union under Section 9(a) becomes the exclusive bargaining representative for all employees within the bargaining unit. This status provides the union with critical legislative and administrative power affecting each employee's working life. The selection of a union as bargaining representative diminishes the ability of individual employees to deal directly with the employer. The employer is barred from bargaining with groups other than the union, and economic pressure not sanctioned by the union is often held to be unprotected activity.

The power to bargain includes the ability to negotiate an agreement setting out terms and conditions of employment binding on each employee. Since federal policy grants unions this exclusive legislative role, it is sensible to argue that this power should not be exercised in an arbitrary or a discriminatory manner. The Supreme Court early found that implicit in the policy of Section 9(a) was a union duty to represent all employees fairly.

The duty is generally easier to state than to apply. Unions are usually not homogeneous groups of employees without conflicting group and individual interests. Bargaining, for instance, initially involves the preparation of bargaining demands, an intra-organizational negotiation process which, like collective bargaining itself, involves trading some issues for others. Not all employees will view alternative proposals as equally valuable. A wage increase, for instance, may be desired by younger employees more than additions to pension or health plans. One's view of equity will, moreover, often be affected by the perceived personal value of one bargaining goal over another, and any particular union choice may be opposed as unfair by some group of employees. The union's determination of its primary bargaining goals and the actual contractual resolution will to some extent, therefore, be political.

Governmental intervention, although required to some extent, must also be tempered by the need to preserve the union's status as an institution free from unwarranted governmental restraints. The right to organize was designed to encourage collective bargaining, and one primary objective of the NLRA was the protection and economic advancement of workers without direct governmental regulation of working conditions.

This section will deal with the uneasy tension between the federal obligation to protect employees from the arbitrary exercise of union power and the concurrent need to preserve the integrity of unions and their independence from governmental interference.

Most of the litigation involving the union's duty to fairly represent employees has involved the union's day-to-day responsibility to administer the collective agreement. The union's power to interpret the agreement and its discretion to grieve the company's action, perhaps bringing the matter to arbitration, also involves the conflict between institutional or majority interests and the expectations of employees. The situation is made considerably more complex, however, because an employee's claim to equity in this situation usually rests upon an alleged breach of the agreement, a legally recognized interest arguably independent of the union's legislative power.

Employee complaints about the operation of the grievance procedure usually involve either the union's failure to process the grievance, perhaps the refusal to submit it for arbitral resolution, or the union's resolution of the dispute which the employee finds unsatisfactory. The union's failure to act could have been based upon improper considerations, such as the employee's lack of union membership, intra-union political activity, race or sex, or clearly legitimate factors such as perceived lack of merit. An unsatisfactory settlement could also result from hostile discrimination, a belief in the grievance's lack of merit, or from the trading of grievances or other issues.

Two arguably separate legal issues are involved. First, to what extent is a union obliged to grieve or arbitrate an employee's claim of contract infringement? Second, irrespective of the union's good faith, to what extent may an employee apply to some forum for review of the breach of contract issue? As we shall see, these issues are intertwined. Both issues involve the extent to which the law should intervene in the private administration of the grievance process, a process given enormous stature by the Supreme Court decisions discussed in the preceding chapter. The recognition of individual rights may be thought to interfere at some point with the strong federal policies supporting the private resolution of contractual disputes.

The Taft-Hartley Act specifically provided another avenue for regulating union power over employee work opportunities. Employees are given the right to refrain from union activities, and the statute attempts to insulate job interests from an employee's relationship with a union. Later sections of this chapter will deal with these matters as well as their relationship to the duty of fair representation.

A third area of regulation, employment discrimination, is dealt with by Title VII of the Civil Rights Act of 1964. This area is given detailed treatment in Unit 3 of this series on Labor Relations and Social Problems. Finally, the Labor-Management Reporting and Disclosure Act of 1959 (Landrum-Griffin) protects union members' democratic rights to speak, vote, and participate in union affairs as well as providing means to hold officers accountable to the membership.

Summers, Union Powers and Workers' Rights*†

I

THE UNION'S POWER OVER THE INDIVIDUAL

. . .

Unions are first and foremost collective bargaining agencies. Their principal function is to speak for workers in negotiating terms of employment, to exercise the collective strength of workers in obtaining concessions, and to bind the workers by making collective contracts. The union's power over the individual, therefore, is measured largely by the impact which its bargaining has on the economic life of the employee. The force of this impact depends upon two separate factors: the breadth of bargaining—that is, the number of terms of employment which a union defines by its agreement; and the power of binding representation—that is, the degree to which an individual is bound by his union's decisions and is compelled to speak only through his union.

A. THE BREADTH OF BARGAINING

The area of bargaining varies so greatly from industry to industry, from union to union, and from employer to employer that accurate generalizations are impossible. However, a quick look at some of the more customary contract provisions will suffice to illustrate the extensive powers which unions exercise over the economic welfare of individual workers.

First, unions bargain to determine who shall work. Most commonly known are the closed shop, union preference, or hiring hall agreements. Far more significant, however, is the common seniority clause. Although it does not control who shall be hired in the first instance, it rigidly controls the order in which individuals shall be laid off. Furthermore, by requiring recall of employees on layoff before new hirings, seniority may severely limit the job opportunities of new workers seeking to enter the trade. In short, the seniority clause which the union obtains determines who shall work and who shall not.

Second, unions bargain to determine the amount of wages each employee will receive. The collective contract governs not only the level of wages, but customarily provides for a complex wage structure with wide differentials between job classifications, automatic increases and premium pay. . . .

Third, the union helps govern the individual every hour of his working day. The contract sets shift hours which call him to work, describes job classifications which define his work, and provides the offenses for which he may be disciplined. Through the union's grievance procedure he can

*Reprinted by permission from Summers, *Union Powers and Workers' Rights*, 49 MICH. L. REV. 805, 806–16 (1951). Copyright © 1951 by Michigan Law Review Association.
†Footnotes omitted.

protest against dangerous machines, poor ventilation, or overbearing foremen. If he is discharged the union can seek his reinstatement. . . .

The union's power to bargain does not give it unrestrained power to govern the terms and conditions of employment, for management must agree to those terms. However, the union does make significant policy decisons which vitally affect every employee. . . . The total concessions which can be obtained at the bargaining table are limited, but the union has a substantial power of choice between possible alternatives. The union's choice determines the worker's welfare. If the concessions are inadequate the union has a more drastic decision to make—whether to surrender or to strike. The union decides whether the individual shall forego his claim for future pensions or sacrifice his present savings. As the strike progresses, it is the union which decides whether the claims shall be compromised or further sacrifices required.

The extensive power of unions to regulate the lives of individuals does not arise solely from the union's own strength. The Railway Labor Act, the National Labor Relations Act, and similar state statutes provide affirmative legal protection for organizational activity and collective action. . . .

Unions are not only shielded by the armor of the law, but are armed with the authority of government. Under the Wagner Act and other labor relations acts, they are designated by government as instruments for effectuating broad social policies and economic regulation. The National Labor Relations Board, by defining the appropriate bargaining unit, allocates the industrial territory for the exercise of union power. By officially certifying a union, the board constitutes it the statutory representative of all employees in the unit and vests it with the power to bargain for those employees. The board then compels the employer, under threat of severe penalties, to meet with the union and bargain in good faith. The employer is barred from establishing terms of employment unilaterally, but must first negotiate with the union. Within a wide but yet undefined area, he is compelled to share with the union the power of making any decisions affecting employees. . . . Furthermore, the union can demand that the employer divulge information as to employment practices, merit increases, and wage payments. Unions, in bargaining, are not private organizations but are governmental agencies garbed with the cloak of legal authority to represent all employees in the unit and armed with the legal right to participate in all decisions affecting terms and conditions of employment.

B. BINDING REPRESENTATION

The impact of the union upon an individual lies not only in the wide range of its bargaining, but in the tightness with which its decisions bind the individual. The union's grant of power lies in Section 9(a) of the National Labor Relations Act, which provides: "Representatives designated . . . by the majority of employees in a unit . . . shall be the exclusive representative of all employees in such unit for purposes of collective bargaining. . . ."

The completeness of the union's power to bind individuals is indicated by three Supreme Court decisions. In *J. I. Case Co.* v. *NLRB*, 321 U.S. 332, 14 LRRM 501 (1944), the Court held that the union's power to bargain could not be limited by prior contracts made in good faith between the employer and the individual. The union's power was supreme, and though the individual may still contract for matters beyond the union's scope, the breadth of union power leaves small room for individual bargaining. In *Order of Railroad Telegraphers* v. *Railway Express Agency, Inc.*, 321 U.S. 342, 14 LRRM 506 (1944), the union had made a contract providing that each telegrapher be paid for each car of fruit switched at his station. Because of re-routing, this resulted in exorbitant payments to some telegraphers. To correct this, the employer made agreements with individual employees to establish new rates which would yield the amount contemplated by the contract. The court held these agreements invalid. The union's power to bargain extended not only to general standards, but to each employee's peculiar situation. Only through the union could any changes in terms of employment be made. In *Medo Photo Supply Corp.* v. *NLRB*, 321 U.S. 678, 14 LRRM 581 (1944), a majority of the employees attempted to ignore the union and meet with the employer as a group to negotiate an agreement. The court held that so long as a union is designated the bargaining agent, no agreement can be made except through that union. It is not the majority but the designated union which holds the bargaining power.

In short, these cases hold that a union which has been designated as bargaining agent can destroy individual contracts made previously, even though made in good faith; it can void individual contracts made subsequently, even though made to adjust contract terms to fit special needs; and it can prevent the employer from negotiating any agreement with a group of his employees, even though they constitute a majority.

This power of the union continues so long as it is the designated agent. If it is not certified, the employees may be able to escape by revoking their authorization before a contract is made. If it is certified, under Section 9(c)(3) it has an irrevocable power for one year and can be unseated only by new representation proceedings. Whether certified or not, if the union obtains a contract, its irrevocable power may be extended for as long as three years. Whether the union is still approved by the majority is irrelevant. Its power continues. The significance of the one-year rule and the contract bar doctrine is that, like the *Medo* case, they point an unerring finger at the locus of power. The power to bargain is not vested in the majority, but in the union as an entity wholly apart from the governed employees.

It is, of course, true that the union must have been authorized by a majority of the employees in the unit. With rare exceptions it continues to represent the majority. However, this does not lessen its impact on the lives of individuals, for its decisions bind both majority and minority alike. . . . Although these rights are the very foundation of a man's right to his job and have been acquired by many years of work, they are subservient to union power.

Thus far we have dealt only with the union's power to bind the individual by negotiation of an agreement. However, the union's control does not end here. The contract requires constant interpretation and day-to-day application; it has gaps which require further negotiation; and it is not self-enforcing but calls for constant vigilance to insure that every employee enjoys full rights. The primary instrument for additions, interpretations, and enforcement is the grievance machinery, and that machinery is completely controlled by the union. The individual files his complaint with the union steward, it is appealed through a union shop committee, is pleaded by union officers, and is arbitrated before a union-approved arbitrator. The individual's claim may be surrendered or compromised by the union at any step. His relief is largely dependent on the union's enthusiasm for his cause. [Editor's Note: See discussion of Section 9(a) in Chapter 5.]

C. THE NATURE OF UNION POWER

Enough has been said to indicate the breadth and depth of union power. As collective bargaining agents, unions help determine when a man shall work, what he shall do, how much he shall make, when he shall have holidays and the terms on which he shall retire. As exclusive representative, the union alone speaks for him in obtaining these terms, and he can speak only through the union. Even his personal grievances are not free of the union's controlling hand.

It is now necessary to state more explicitly the nature of union power. A union, in bargaining, acts as the representative of all workers within an industrial area. It weighs alternatives and determines policies which vitally affect all those whom it represents. It negotiates a contract which becomes the basic law of that industrial community. In making those laws, the union acts as the worker's economic legislature. After the laws have been made, the union is charged with their enforcement, and through its grievance procedure helps judge their interpretation and application. It is the worker's policeman and judge. The union is, in short, the employee's economic government. The union's power is the power to govern. Only if we fully appreciate this cardinal fact and keep it clearly in mind can we critically evaluate the rights which an individual should have within the union.

All of the foregoing has emphasized the submergence of the individual under a tide of organizational control. This does not, however, constitute a criticism of collective bargaining nor a denial of the propriety of union power. The submergence of the individual came not with the Wagner Act in 1935, but with the industrial revolution in 1800; for it was not unions but the factory system which destroyed the individuality of the worker. In an industrial economy with large scale production and a chronic scarcity of jobs, the individual's power to bargain for himself became an empty fiction. Concentrations of capital, made possible by the corporate structure, placed in the hands of employers the power to determine who should work and at what wage. The employer's word was law. The worker retained full freedom—to submit or starve. The advent of unions has not

changed the inescapable character of modern industry that an individual's economic life is governed by forces beyond himself. Collective
bargaining does not alter the amount of power which is exercised over the
individual. It only shifts its source.

. . .

1. NEGOTIATION AND FAIR REPRESENTATION

Steele v. Louisville & Nashville Railroad Co.

Supreme Court of the United States, 1944

323 U.S. 192, 15 LRRM 708

MR. CHIEF JUSTICE STONE delivered the opinion of the Court.

The question is whether the Railway Labor Act, 48 Stat. 1185, 45 U.S.C.
§§ 151 *et seq.*, imposes on a labor organization, acting by authority of the
statute as the exclusive bargaining representative of a craft or class of
railway employees, the duty to represent all the employees in the craft
without discrimination because of their race, and, if so, whether the
courts have jurisdiction to protect the minority of the craft or class from
the violation of such obligation.

. . .

The allegations of the bill of complaint, so far as now material, are as
follows: Petitioner, a Negro, is a locomotive fireman in the employ of
respondent Railroad, suing on his own behalf and that of his fellow
employees who, like petitioner, are Negro firemen employed by the Railroad. Respondent Brotherhood, a labor organization, is, as provided
under § 2, Fourth of the Railway Labor Act, the exclusive bargaining
representative of the craft of firemen employed by the Railroad and is
recognized as such by it and the members of the craft. The majority of the
firemen employed by the Railroad are white and are members of the
Brotherhood, but a substantial minority are Negroes who, by the constitution and ritual of the Brotherhood, are excluded from its membership. As
the membership of the Brotherhood constitutes a majority of all firemen
employed on respondent Railroad, and as under § 2, Fourth the members because they are the majority have the right to choose and have
chosen the Brotherhood to represent the craft, petitioner and other
Negro firemen on the road have been required to accept the Brotherhood
as their representative for the purposes of the Act.

On March 28, 1940, the Brotherhood, purporting to act as representative of the entire craft of firemen, without informing the Negro firemen
or giving them opportunity to be heard, served a notice on respondent
Railroad and on twenty other railroads operating principally in the south-
eastern part of the United States. The notice announced the Brotherhood's desire to amend the existing collective bargaining agreement in
such manner as ultimately to exclude all Negro firemen from the service.
By established practice on the several railroads so notified only white
firemen can be promoted to serve as engineers, and the notice proposed
that only "promotable," *i.e.*, white, men should be employed as firemen or

assigned to new runs or jobs or permanent vacancies in established runs or jobs.

On February 18, 1941, the railroads and the Brotherhood, as representative of the craft, entered into a new agreement which provided that not more than 50 percent of the firemen in each class of service in each seniority district of a carrier should be Negroes; that until such percentage should be reached all new runs and all vacancies should be filled by white men; and that the agreement did not sanction the employment of Negroes in any seniority district in which they were not working. The agreement reserved the right of the Brotherhood to negotiate for further restrictions on the employment of Negro firemen on the individual railroads. On May 12, 1941, the Brotherhood entered into a supplemental agreement with respondent Railroad further controlling the seniority rights of Negro firemen and restricting their employment. The Negro firemen were not given notice or opportunity to be heard with respect to either of these agreements which were put into effect before their existence was disclosed to the Negro firemen.

Until April 8, 1941, petitioner was in a "passenger pool," to which one white and five Negro firemen were assigned. These jobs were highly desirable in point of wages, hours and other considerations. Petitioner had performed and was performing his work satisfactorily. Following a reduction in the mileage covered by the pool, all jobs in the pool were, about April 1, 1941, declared vacant. The Brotherhood and the Railroad, acting under the agreement, disqualified all the Negro firemen and replaced them with four white men, members of the Brotherhood, all junior in seniority to petitioner and no more competent or worthy. As a consequence petitioner was deprived of employment for sixteen days and then was assigned to more arduous, longer, and less remunerative work in local freight service. In conformity to the agreement, he was later replaced by a Brotherhood member junior to him, and assigned work on a switch engine, which was still harder and less remunerative, until January 3, 1942. On that date, after the bill of complaint in the present suit had been filed, he was reassigned to passenger service.

. . .

The Supreme Court of Alabama took jurisdiction of the cause but held on the merits that petitioner's complaints stated no cause of action. . . . It thought that the Brotherhood was empowered by the statute to enter into the agreement of February 18, 1941, and that by virtue of the statute the Brotherhood has power by agreement with the Railroad both to create the seniority rights of petitioners and his fellow Negro employees and to destroy them. It construed the statute, not as creating the relationship of principal and agent between the members of the craft and the Brotherhood, but as conferring on the Brotherhood plenary authority to treat with the Railroad and enter into contracts fixing rates of pay and working conditions for the craft as a whole without any legal obligation or duty to protect the rights of minorities from discrimination or unfair treatment, however gross. Consequently it held that neither the Brotherhood nor the Railroad violated any rights of petitioner or his fellow Negro employees by negotiating the contracts discriminating against them.

If, as the state court has held, the Act confers this power on the bargaining representative of a craft or class of employees without any commensurate statutory duty toward its members, constitutional questions arise. For the representative is clothed with power not unlike that of a legislature which is subject to constitutional limitations on its power to deny, restrict, destroy or discriminate against the rights of those for whom it legislates and which is also under an affirmative constitutional duty equally to protect those rights. If the Railway Labor Act purports to impose on petitioner and the other Negro members of the craft the legal duty to comply with the terms of a contract whereby the representative has discriminatorily restricted their employment for the benefit and advantage of the Brotherhood's own members, we must decide the constitutional questions which petitioner raises in his pleading.

But we think that Congress, in enacting the Railway Labor Act and authorizing a labor union, chosen by a majority of a craft, to represent the craft, did not intend to confer plenary power upon the union to sacrifice, for the benefit of its members, rights of the minority of the craft, without imposing on it any duty to protect the minority. Since petitioner and the other Negro members of the craft are not members of the Brotherhood or eligible for membership, the authority to act for them is derived not from their action or consent but wholly from the command of the Act. . . .

By the terms of the Act, § 2, Fourth, the employees are permitted to act "through" their representative, and it represents them "for the purposes of" the Act. Sections 2, Third, Fourth, Ninth. The purposes of the Act declared by § 2 are the avoidance of "any interruption to commerce or to the operation of any carrier engaged therein," and this aim is sought to be achieved by encouraging "the prompt and orderly settlement of all disputes concerning rates of pay, rules, or working conditions." Compare *Texas & New Orleans R. Co.* v. *Brotherhood of Clerks*, 281 U.S. 548, 569. These purposes would hardly be attained if a substantial minority of the craft were denied the right to have their interests considered at the conference table and if the final result of the bargaining process were to be the sacrifice of the interests of the minority by the action of a representative chosen by the majority. The only recourse of the minority would be to strike, with the attendant interruption of commerce, which the Act seeks to avoid.

Section 2, Second, requiring carriers to bargain with the representative so chosen, operates to exclude any other from representing a craft. *Virginian R. Co.* v. *System Federation, supra* [300 U.S. 545]. The minority members of a craft are thus deprived by the statute of the right, which they would otherwise possess, to choose a representative of their own, and its members cannot bargain individually on behalf of themselves as to matters which are properly the subject of collective bargaining. *Order of Railroad Telegraphers* v. *Railway Express Agency*, 321 U.S. 342, and see under the like provisions of the National Labor Relations Act *J. I. Case Co.* v. *Labor Board*, 321 U.S. 332, and *Medo Photo Supply Corp.* v. *Labor Board*, 321 U.S. 678.

. . .

Unless the labor union representing a craft owes some duty to represent nonunion members of the craft, at least to the extent of not discriminating against them as such in the contracts which it makes as their representative, the minority would be left with no means of protecting their interests or, indeed, their right to earn a livelihood by pursuing the occupation in which they are employed. While the majority of the craft chooses the bargaining representative, when chosen it represents, as the Act by its terms makes plain, the craft or class, and not the majority. The fair interpretation of the statutory language is that the organization chosen to represent a craft is to represent all its members, the majority as well as the minority, and it is to act for and not against those whom it represents. It is a principle of general application that the exercise of a granted power to act in behalf of others involves the assumption toward them of a duty to exercise the power in their interest and behalf, and that such a grant of power will not be deemed to dispense with all duty toward those for whom it is exercised unless so expressed.

We think that the Railway Labor Act imposes upon the statutory representative of a craft at least as exacting a duty to protect equally the interests of the members of the craft as the Constitution imposes upon a legislature to give equal protection to the interests of those for whom it legislates. Congress has seen fit to clothe the bargaining representative with powers comparable to those possessed by a legislative body both to create and restrict the rights of those whom it represents, cf. *J. I. Case Co.* v. *Labor Board, supra,* 335, but it has also imposed on the representative a corresponding duty. We hold that the language of the Act to which we have referred, read in the light of the purposes of the Act, expresses the aim of Congress to impose on the bargaining representative of a craft or class of employees the duty to exercise fairly the power conferred upon it in behalf of all those for whom it acts, without hostile discrimination against them.

This does not mean that the statutory representative of a craft is barred from making contracts which may have unfavorable effects on some of the members of the craft represented. Variations in the terms of the contract based on differences relevant to the authorized purposes of the contract in conditions to which they are to be applied, such as differences in seniority, the type of work performed, the competence and skill with which it is performed, are within the scope of the bargaining representation of a craft, all of whose members are not identical in their interest or merit. . . . Without attempting to mark the allowable limits of differences in the terms of contracts based on differences of conditions to which they apply, it is enough for present purposes to say that the statutory power to represent a craft and to make contracts as to wages, hours and working conditions does not include the authority to make among members of the craft discriminations not based on such relevant differences. Here the discriminations based on race alone are obviously irrelevant and invidious. Congress plainly did not undertake to authorize the bargaining representative to make such discriminations. . . .

The representative which thus discriminates may be enjoined from so doing, and its members may be enjoined from taking the benefit of such discriminatory action. No more is the Railroad bound by or entitled to take the benefit of a contract which the bargaining representative is prohibited by the statute from making. In both cases the right asserted, which is derived from the duty imposed by the statute on the bargaining representative, is a federal right implied from the statute and the policy which it has adopted. It is the federal statute which condemns as unlawful the Brotherhood's conduct. . . .

So long as a labor union assumes to act as the statutory representative of a craft, it cannot rightly refuse to perform the duty, which is inseparable from the power of representation conferred upon it, to represent the entire membership of the craft. While the statute does not deny to such a bargaining labor organization the right to determine eligibility to its membership, it does require the union, in collective bargaining and in making contracts with the carrier, to represent nonunion or minority union members of the craft without hostile discrimination, fairly, impartially, and in good faith. Wherever necessary to that end, the union is required to consider requests of nonunion members of the craft and expressions of their views with respect to collective bargaining with the employer and to give to them notice of and opportunity for hearing upon its proposed action. . . .

. . . There is no administrative means by which the Negro firemen can secure separate representation for the purposes of collective bargaining.

In the absence of any available administrative remedy, the right here asserted, to a remedy for breach of the statutory duty of the bargaining representative to represent and act for the members of a craft, is of judicial cognizance. That right would be sacrificed or obliterated if it were without the remedy which courts can give for breach of such a duty or obligation and which it is their duty to give in cases in which they have jurisdiction. . . .

We conclude that the duty which the statute imposes on a union representative of a craft to represent the interests of all its members stands on no different footing and that the statute contemplates resort to the usual judicial remedies of injunction and award of damages when appropriate for breach of that duty.

The judgment is accordingly reversed and remanded for further proceedings not inconsistent with this opinion.

Reversed.

MR. JUSTICE BLACK concurs in the result.

MR. JUSTICE MURPHY, concurring.

The economic discrimination against Negroes practiced by the Brotherhood and the railroad under color of Congressional authority raises a grave constitutional issue that should be squarely faced.

The utter disregard for the dignity and the well-being of colored citizens shown by this record is so pronounced as to demand the invocation of constitutional condemnation. To decide the case and to analyze the statute solely upon the basis of legal niceties, while remaining mute and placid as to the obvious and oppressive deprivation of constitutional guarantees, is to make the judicial function something less than it should be.

The constitutional problem inherent in this instance is clear. Congress, through the Railway Labor Act, has conferred upon the union selected by a majority of a craft or class of railway workers the power to represent the entire craft or class in all collective bargaining matters. While such a union is essentially a private organization, its power to represent and bind all members of a class or craft is derived solely from Congress. The Act contains no language which directs the manner in which the bargaining representative shall perform its duties. But it cannot be assumed that Congress meant to authorize the representative to act so as to ignore rights guaranteed by the Constitution. Otherwise the Act would bear the stigma of unconstitutionality under the Fifth Amendment in this respect. For that reason I am willing to read the statute as not permitting or allowing any action by the bargaining representative in the exercise of its delegated powers which would in effect violate the constitutional rights of individuals.

If the Court's construction of the statute rests upon this basis, I agree. But I am not sure that such is the basis. Suffice it to say, however, that this constitutional issue cannot be lightly dismissed. The cloak of racism surrounding the actions of the Brotherhood in refusing membership to Negroes and in entering into and enforcing agreements discriminating against them, all under the guise of Congressional authority, still remains. No statutory interpretations can erase this ugly example of economic cruelty against colored citizens of the United States. Nothing can destroy the fact that the accident of birth has been used as the basis to abuse individual rights by an organization purporting to act in conformity with its Congressional mandate. Any attempt to interpret the Act must take that fact into account and must realize that the constitutionality of the statute in this respect depends upon the answer given.

The Constitution voices its disapproval whenever economic discrimination is applied under authority of law against any race, creed or color. A sound democracy cannot allow such discrimination to go unchallenged. Racism is far too virulent today to permit the slightest refusal, in the light of a Constitution that abhors it, to expose and condemn it wherever it appears in the course of a statutory interpretation.

Notes

1. As Justice Murphy implies, the duty of fair representation, found to be implied in the Railway Labor Act, may have been created to avoid reaching a constitutional issue. How would you phrase that issue? See Wellington, *Union Democracy and Fair Representation: Federal Responsibility in a Federal System*, 67 Yale L.J. 1327 (1958).

2. Does the Court provide a workable standard for the duty created in *Steele*? Beyond the cases of obviously arbitrary and unconscionable action as in *Steele*, how meaningful is a standard calling for union action which is "without hostile discrimination . . . and in good faith"?

The Court's statement that a union has powers, and therefore obligations, similar to legislative bodies, arguably implies an equal-protection standard. Would this standard adequately respond to the interests involved?

3. Is it actually the statute that grants the union in *Steele* its power to affect nonmembers?

The union and railroad employers may have bargained and reached collective agreements covering firemen long before the passage of the Railway Labor Act. The statute, therefore, cannot be said to be the *source* of the union's power to adversely affect black firemen. What function is served by basing the duty upon implied obligations stemming from federal law?

The Court states that a minority of employees in a bargaining unit are deprived by the statute of their right of separate representation. What is the minority's right actually worth in this situation?

Without a union, the employer would possess unchecked power over workers' job rights. Can it be said, then, that the basis of the duty is the protection against job loss? It is interesting to note that common-law courts often intervened in union discipline or expulsion situations (but not in admission-to-the-union cases) when the union controlled job opportunities. Compare *Heasley* v. *Operative Plasterers*, 324 Pa. 257, 188 A. 206 (1936); *James* v. *Marinship Corp.*, 25 Cal.2d 721, 155 P.2d 329 (1944); *Phalen* v. *Theatrical Protective Union*, 22 N.Y.2d 34, 290 N.Y.S.2d 881, 238 N.E.2d 295 (1968); see generally, Summers, *The Right to Join a Union*, 47 Colum. L. Rev. 33 (1947). Yet, employers at the same time were under no restrictions in regard to hiring and tenure of employment except in rare situations where a written employment contract existed.

4. The black firemen in *Steele* were not permitted to become members of the union because of the discriminatory admission policy which would now violate Title VII of the Civil Rights Act of 1964. Other than Title VII, however, no other federal law provides that employees have a right to join the union which represents them, and *Steele* did not interpret the duty of fair representation to include the right to be a member. See NLRA Section 8(b)(1)(A). Can employees' valid job interests adequately be protected without membership? How valuable is the right of nonmembers to receive "notice of and opportunity for hearing" on proposed collective bargaining?

The Court's "conception of fair representation without participation rests on a particular model of the collective bargaining process: a non-participatory conception, in which the bargaining agent stands at a distance from the rank and file." An alternative conception was presented by the NAACP's amicus brief: "It is a basic conception of labor relations and of the trade union movement that collective bargaining is a system whereby all employees . . . participate by a democratic representative system of self-government in the determination of their conditions of employment." See K. Klare, *The Quest for Industrial Democracy and the Struggle Against Racism: Perspectives from Labor Law and Civil Rights Law*, 61 Or. L. Rev. 157, 190 (1982).

5. As the following excerpted case demonstrates, the duty of fair representation was extended to the National Labor Relations Act.

A federal statute enacted during World War II provided that employees should receive seniority credit for their military service when returning to their preservice positions. The contract between Ford Motor Company and UAW extended this concept by giving seniority credit for military service prior to employment. The effect was to give higher seniority to employees who were employed after Huffman, thus reducing his relative seniority and leading to layoffs which would not otherwise have occurred. The Supreme Court considered whether the union had violated its duty of fair representation in *Ford* v. *Huffman*, 345 U.S. 330, 31 LRRM 2548 (1953):

". . . Any authority to negotiate derives its principal strength from a delegation to the negotiators of a discretion to make such concessions and accept such advantages as, in the light of all relevant considerations, they believe will best serve the interests of the parties represented. A major responsibility of negotiators is to weigh the relative advantages and disadvantages of differing proposals. . . . The bargaining representative, whoever it may be, is responsible to, and owes complete loyalty to, the interests of all whom it represents. In the instant controversy, International represented, with certain exceptions not material here, all employees at the Louisville works, including both the veterans with, and those without, prior employment by Ford, as well as the employees having no military service. Inevitably differences arise in the manner and degree to which the terms of any negotiated agreement affect individual employees and classes of employees. The mere existence of such differences does not make them invalid. The complete satisfaction of all who are represented is hardly to be expected. A wide range of reasonableness must be allowed a statutory bargaining representative in serving the unit it represents, subject always to complete good faith and honesty of purpose in the exercise of its discretion.

"Compromises on a temporary basis, with a view to long-range advantages, are natural incidents of negotiation. Differences in wages, hours and conditions of employment reflect countless variables. Seniority rules governing promotions, transfers, layoffs, and similar matters may, in the first instance, revolve around length of competent service. Variations acceptable in the discretion of bargaining representatives, however, may well include differences based upon such matters as the unit within which seniority is to be computed, the privileges to which it shall relate, the nature of the work, the time at which it is done, the fitness, ability or age of the employees, their family responsibilities, injuries received in course of service, and time or labor devoted to related public service, whether civil or military, voluntary or involuntary. . . .

". . . It is not necessary to define here the limits to which a collective-bargaining representative may go in accepting proposals to promote the long-range social or economic welfare of those it represents. Nothing in the National Labor Relations Act, as amended, so limits the vision and action of a bargaining representative that it must disregard public policy and national security. Nor does anything in that Act compel a bargaining representative to limit seniority clauses solely to the relative lengths of employment of the respective employees. . . ."

6. Is it sufficient that the union reasonably believes its actions are in the best interests of the membership irrespective of the impact of the union's actions on employee expectations? Suppose the union had bargained for a substantially different seniority arrangement in exchange for a wage increase? If bargaining is viewed as a practical settlement of conflicting employee interests, can the union's actions ever violate a rationality standard?

7. Company A purchases a local rival, Company B (which continues to run itself for six months), and then shuts it down. Assume that the union represents the employees at both firms. The union considers whether to create a combined seniority list which will accord Company B employees seniority only from the date of acquisition, thereby threatening their continued employment, or to base seniority on the relevant date of hire at their respective firm (dovetailing). Would the union violate its duty if either option were chosen? One court stated that the test in a similar case was whether the union's decision was in good faith *and* reached a fair and reasonable solution of the merger problem. *O'Donnell* v. *Pabst Brewing,* 12 Wis.2d 491, 107 N.W.2d 484 (1961). Would either of the solutions noted above be "fair and reasonable"? Are courts suited for such determinations?

Indeed, there are more than two options since dovetailing and endtailing can be structured or even combined in a variety of ways.

Could a union referendum fairly resolve the issue, even though the result would predictably favor the larger group of employees? Should the union, in part a political institution, be held to a standard more rigorous than a good faith attempt to satisfy a majority of its members? If more than political muscle or majority desires are required, how would you phrase the appropriate standard? Is some objective justification, beyond placating desires of the majority, required when minority interests are adversely affected? For an argument that no principled theory of fair representation has been developed, see Freed, Polsby, Spitzer, *Unions, Fairness, and the Conundrums of Collective Choice,* 56 S. Cal. L. Rev. 461 (1983).

8. The difficulty of upsetting a negotiated agreement or settlement has led to increased scrutiny of the union's bargaining procedure leading to an agreement. To what extent must the union convey the employer's positions to the membership during negotiations or accurately inform members of the contents of the agreement prior to a ratification vote?

In *Teamsters, Local 860* v. *NLRB,* 652 F.2d 1022, 107 LRRM 2174 (D.C. Cir. 1981), the union represented warehousemen and a unit of 13 clerical employees. Twelve of the 13 were women. Prior to the commencement of negotiations, the clericals notified the union that they desired the same wage increase demanded by the warehousemen. During negotiations, the employer repeatedly asserted that such an increase for the clerical employees would result in the elimination of the entire unit. Nevertheless, the union persisted in demanding the increase without consulting the clericals. The employer ultimately acceded to the wage increase, and the employees voted to accept the new contract. Subsequently, the employer terminated the clerical unit, permanently laying off the employees in that unit. The NLRB rejected the charge that the union, motivated by sex discrimination, made an express agreement with the employer to eliminate the unit. It did hold, however, that the union violated Section 8(b)(1)(A) "by persisting in demanding a wage increase it knew would result in their termination." The appellate court affirmed, holding that "the Union had a duty to inform its membership of management's position so that they, in turn, could make an informed reassessment of their wage demand. The Union's failure to apprise the clericals of the ultimate danger and risk of job loss created by their wage demand was clearly an arbitrary action and constituted a breach of duty."

In *Farmer* v. *ARA Services, Inc.*, 660 F.2d 1096, 108 LRRM 2145 (6th Cir. 1981), the union was held to violate its duty by negotiating an agreement which substantially disadvantaged female employees and whose terms were "not adequately explained to the membership prior to ratification or which varied from the terms as explained." But uncertainty continues with respect to the union's duty to inform members of the content and effect of agreements prior to ratification. In *Deboles* v. *TWA*, 552 F.2d 1005, 94 LRRM 3237 (3d Cir. 1977), the union's intentionally false statements concerning its efforts to obtain retroactive systemwide seniority rights were held not to breach its duty because there was no evidence that the false statements materially affected the result of the vote.

2. Fair Representation and Contract Administration

Whatever the appropriate standard in negotiation, it is arguable that a more rigorous standard is required when an employee's asserted claim is based on a written agreement. The decision on bargaining goals is in part a political decision, and no set of goals or priorities will satisfy all employees. An employee's contractual claim, however, will involve strong employee expectations and the traditional legal claim that agreements should be enforced. Moreover, Section 9(a) suggests that the administration of agreements is legally different from negotiation as it protects an employee's access to the employer. (The value of this "right" will be dealt with later in this section.) It is possible, however, to view contract administration merely as part of the bargaining process, granting unions the power to bargain away or settle employee claims so long as such action is taken in good faith.

An employee's standing to sue for breaches of the collective bargaining agreement under Section 301 of the NLRA was recognized by the Supreme Court in *Smith* v. *Evening News Ass'n*, 371 U.S. 195, 51 LRRM 2646 (1962). As will become clear later in this section, however, this right is substantially limited by a contractual grievance system and the union's administrative power over such a system.

All these questions involve the basic problem of reconciling the need to protect individual interests with the often conflicting institutional concerns of the contracting parties.

The subsequent problem and the *Hildreth* case suggest that the line between negotiation and administration is not a glaringly bright one. Although negotiation generally looks to the future, it can also involve the resolution of existing problems. Similarly, grievance processing settles existing workplace disputes, but the results may also establish a pattern for future settlements.

Problem: Shaker Redi-Mix Cement Co.

Due to a change of operations at Crumbly Cement Company, the Shaker Redi-Mix Company will assume much of the work previously done by Crumbly. Teamsters Local 632 represents the employees of Shaker and Crumbly.

The officers of Local 632 determined that an "absorption" of Crumbly will occur under the collective bargaining agreement between the Teamsters and the two cement companies. The seniority clause of the collective bargaining agreement provides that "in the event that the employer absorbs the business of another . . . , the seniority of the employees absorbed or affected thereby shall be determined by mutual agreement between the employer and the unions involved." Controversies arising from such matters are to be resolved by arbitration. Using the "absorption" clause of the contract, the union decided to dovetail seniority lists; that is, a new seniority list would be created combining employees of Crumbly and Shaker based upon their initial date of employment at their respective companies.

Since the 20 Shaker employees generally have less seniority and are younger than the 49 Crumbly employees, the union's decision effectively protects Crumbly employees and adversely affects Shaker employees.

Shaker Company would prefer to keep its regular employees and, along with the Shaker employees, feels that there has been no "absorption" within the meaning of the contract. Therefore, they argue, the union has no authority to affect the seniority of the Shaker employees.

Because of Shaker Company's opposition to dovetailing, the local submits a grievance under the contractual grievance procedure. Since the Shaker employees' job opportunities will be severely affected if the union's position is upheld in arbitration, the employees seek to intervene and seek your assistance. It is apparent that the Shaker employees are unwilling to rely solely on the sympathetic presentation of their interests by the Shaker Company.

One problem is that immediate action is required because the union's grievance will be arbitrated within the next two months. A further problem, irrespective of whether you can intervene or not, arises if the arbitrator should decide an "absorption" has indeed occurred. Can the Shaker employees challenge this determination? How? What is the union's obligation to its membership when any decision will adversely affect part of its membership?

Union News Co. v. Hildreth

United States Court of Appeals, Sixth Circuit, 1961
295 F.2d 658, 48 LRRM 3084

O'SULLIVAN, Circuit Judge.

This is an appeal by defendant-appellant, Union News Company, from a judgment for $5,000.00 entered upon a jury verdict in favor of plaintiff-appellee, Gladys Hildreth. Her complaint charged that she had been discharged from defendant's employ without just cause, in breach of a collective bargaining agreement between defendant and the Hotel and Restaurant Employees and Bartenders International Union, AFL, Detroit Local Joint Executive Board, hereinafter referred to as the Union. Damages awarded included wages lost by plaintiff between her discharge and the time of trial and damages she claims she will suffer through loss of seniority as defendant's employee.

Defendant operated a soda fountain and lunch counter at the Michigan Central Railroad terminal at Detroit. Plaintiff was one of a crew of eleven or twelve persons employed at said counter. She had been employed at the Detroit terminal for about ten years, and was a member of the Union. During the period of plaintiff's employment, the Union was the designated exclusive bargaining representative of defendant's employees. The current agreement between the Union and defendant, dated October 15, 1957, was to run for one year with the usual provision for automatic yearly renewals unless terminated by either party.

Material and relevant to the issues on this appeal are the following paragraphs of the Collective Bargaining Agreement:

"14. No regular employee covered by this Agreement shall be discharged except for just cause. In the event of a claim by the Union that an employee has been discharged without just cause, such claim must be filed with the manager of the unit within five (5) days and disposed of by him within five (5) days thereafter. If the matter cannot be satisfactorily adjusted between the Union and the employer's manager, the same shall be promptly referred to the employer's home office at 131 Varick Street, New York City.

"15. Any and all questions and discussions which at any time may arise affecting the employees of the employer shall be taken up with the manager of the unit involved at such time and place as will be mutually agreed upon between the Union and the manager.

. . .

"17. During the term of this agreement, any question arising hereunder which cannot be directly and satisfactorily adjusted between the Union and the employer shall be referred to a Committee which shall consist of one member representing the Union, one representing the employer, and a third member to be mutually agreed upon by the employer and the Union, and the decision of any two (2) members of such Committee shall be final and binding upon the parties hereto."

On March 14, 1958, plaintiff was laid off by defendant. Her layoff matured into a discharge as discussed hereinafter. For a period of 9 to 12 months prior to plaintiff's discharge, the manager of defendant's enterprise was concerned about its cost experience at the counter where plaintiff worked. There was evidence that in the type of business there being carried on, efficient and honest work by counter employees should result in food costs being something less than 40 percent of the amount of gross sales; that a percentage of 35 to 37 percent in that regard is considered good; and that where the cost of merchandise reaches a figure above 40 percent of the amount of gross sales, it is indicative of a "poor operation" resulting from mishandling of merchandise and money by employees. Such mishandling could include dishonesty. From January, 1957, through February, 1958, this percentage was running rather uniformly above the 40 percent figure and was the cause of continuing discussions between defendant's manager and the Union. Defendant was unable to ascertain which of, and how many of, its counter employees were guilty of misconduct causing its bad experience. Its manager suggested to the Union that the only solution was the replacement of all, or some of, the crew. The Union refused at first, suggesting less drastic measures such as talking to the girls and telling defendant's manager to "do the best you can and we will look into it further." Conditions did not improve, and in early 1958 defendant's manager opened its books to the business agents of the Union who made their own examination and analysis of defendant's continuing problem. In February, 1958, the food cost percentage was the highest, but one, of any of the preceding 12 months. Union representatives made their own analysis of the records of defendant and concluded that some action had to be taken to remedy the situation. Defendant's manager suggested that the entire crew on the soda and lunch counter be replaced. The Union representative felt that such action was too drastic and between the Union agent and defendant's manager, it was agreed that five of the counter employees be given a three day layoff and be replaced by new employees. There was then to be a trial period of ten days to two weeks to see whether such change of crew would bring about an improvement. It was agreed that if improvement came it would demonstrate that the laid off employees were, at least partially, the cause of the trouble. In such case, the laid off employees would not be rehired. It was further agreed that if conditions did not improve following the layoff, such experience would exculpate the laid off employees of fault and they would be rehired and paid the wages lost during the period of the layoff. The laid off employees were replaced by other members of the Union. Following the replacement of the five employees, one of whom was the plaintiff, defendant's operation did improve and for the month of March the percentage of food costs to sales dropped from 43.46 percent for February to 39.90 percent for March and to 35.90 percent for April. This percentage remained below 40 percent for the entire balance of

1958, except for the month of August. In the week following the layoff, the cash receipts of the counter in question were $250.00 more than the final week with the old crew. After about ten days of the new operation, the Union agreed with defendant that it had proved its point and the replacement of the five employees became permanent. On the trial, plaintiff, to some extent, challenged the validity of the conclusions of the Union and defendant as to the significance of the food cost figures. However, there was no evidence of bad faith in the reliance of the Union and defendant upon such analysis.

After learning that she had been replaced, plaintiff took the matter up with her Union. On March 24th, a meeting was had at which the Union and defendant's representatives were present, as well as plaintiff and the other replaced employees. At this meeting, defendant's representative told plaintiff that she was laid off under Code No. 12, which meant "change of crew without prejudice." Such a termination of employment, the company representative said, would not disqualify plaintiff for unemployment compensation. When first laid off, she was told that it was for the good of the Union News Company, with mention being made of the bad condition at the fountain. She was told that the matter had already been cleared with the Union. Except for this meeting of March 24, plaintiff made no further contact with defendant until her attorney wrote a letter to it some months later. Plaintiff continued for a time to press for action by her Union. She was told that the Union was convinced that her discharge was for just cause. With the other discharged girls, she met with Union officers at the various levels of authority, and with the Union's grievance committee. This committee referred the matter to the Executive Board of the Union, and final consideration of it was had at a meeting of the Executive Board in June following the discharge. Plaintiff was present at this meeting. No action was taken by the Board and no grievance was ever presented by the Union on Plaintiff's behalf.

. . .

Plaintiff's complaint averred, inter alia, that the Union Local 705 was her "statutory collective bargaining representative and agent"; that her cause of action was bottomed upon the Union's contract with defendant; that she was discharged on March 14, 1958, "without just cause in violation of the terms and conditions of said contract of employment"; that "plaintiff has made numerous and several attempts to invoke the remedies provided by the grievance procedure, including arbitration, but defendant Union News Company has wholly refused, failed and neglected to discuss said grievance with plaintiff's collective bargaining representative or to permit plaintiff to present her grievance to it as provided by 29 U.S.C.A. § 159, commonly known as the Taft-Hartley Act."

The defendant's answer, with amendment thereto, denied that plaintiff was discharged without cause; denied that it refused to discuss plaintiff's grievance or to permit her to present her grievance; and affirmatively averred that plaintiff was guilty of carelessness "amounting to dishonesty or malfeasance in the handling of funds and merchandise of the defendant, which resulted in financial loss to defendant" and that the discharge of plaintiff "was agreed and consented to by . . . Local 705. . . ."

. . .

Before discussion of the legal questions involved, we should add that there was no proof directly connecting plaintiff, individually, with dishonesty, wrong-doing, or malfeasance. We further, preliminarily, observe that in our opinion there was no evidence from which a jury could find that in agreeing to lay off and then discharge plaintiff and her co-workers in an effort to solve defendant's problems, there was any fraud, bad faith or collusion on the part of, or between, the Union's and defendant's agents. We do not think that the inability of defendant to place individual responsibility for its difficulties on plaintiff impairs the validity of our conclusion in this regard, nor prevents the discharge of plaintiff and her fellow workers being "for just cause." An employer should not be foreclosed from applying a remedy to stop a continuing loss merely because it cannot identify and isolate the particular source, or sources, of such loss. We state also that what was done by the Union and defendant after plaintiff's discharge could not, in our opinion, be relied upon as evidence of fraud, bad faith or collusion in the prior mutual agreement to terminate plaintiff's employment.

Defendant's motion for a directed verdict at the close of plaintiff's evidence, renewed after proofs were closed, was denied. This ruling, with others, makes up the questions involved on this appeal. Because we are of the opinion that defendant was entitled to a directed verdict of no cause of action, we do not reach other errors charged as ground for reversal.

It is our conclusion that, considering the statutory authority of the Union as the bargaining agent, the language of the collective bargaining agreement, and the undisputed facts as to the good faith bargaining between Union and defendant, it was within the authority of the Union as bargaining agent to agree with defendant that there was just cause for plaintiff's discharge. Her discharge following, and pursuant to, such agreement was not a breach of contract by defendant.

. . . Plaintiff's right of action, if any, must arise from the terms of the contract between the Union and the employer. Not only the sentence of that contract which provides against discharge without cause, but all other relevant provisions of the contract and existing law, must be respected in determining whether, in this case, plaintiff has established a cause of action for breach of such contract. . . . Whatever protection against discharge inured to plaintiff was the consequence of the *collective* action of plaintiff's Union. The Union, chosen as the statutory bargaining agent of plaintiff and defendant's other employees, is declared by statute to "be the exclusive representative(s) of all of the employees (in such unit) for the purposes of collective bargaining in respect to rates of pay, wages, hours of employment, or other conditions of employment: . . ." (Title 29 U.S.C.A. § 159 [a]).

The question, then, for decision here is whether such statutory power, in combination with the terms of the bargaining contract, authorized the Union and defendant to mutually conclude, as a part of the bargaining process, that the circumstances shown by the evidence provided just cause for the layoff and discharge of plaintiff and other of defendant's employees. We conclude that it did. Unless such bilateral decisions, made in good faith, and after unhurried consideration between a Union and an employer, be sustained in court, the bargaining process is a mirage, without the efficacy contemplated by the philosophy of the law which makes its use compulsory.

. . .

The National Labor Relations Board emphasizes the continuing duty of the employer to bargain concerning the administration of a contract, "It is now well settled that the statutory duty to bargain collectively does not close with the execution of the collective agreement. The employer is under the further duty to negotiate with the accredited bargaining agency concerning the modification, *interpretation* and *administration* of the *existing* agreement." *Carroll's Transfer Co.,* 56 NLRB 935, 937. ". . . [T]he execution of a collective contract does not end the process of collective bargaining. . . . the *interpretation* and *administration* of a contract already made and the settlement of disputes arising under any such contract are properly regarded as within the sphere of collective bargaining." *Consolidated Aircraft Corp.,* 47 NLRB 694, 706. Professor Archibald Cox in his learned and comprehensive treatise "Rights Under a Labor Agreement" (69 Harvard Law Review 601, 622) says, "It is also settled law that the Union's right to bargain and the employer's correlative duties are not limited to the negotiation of an agreement. Both the NLRB and the courts have consistently held that to refuse to discuss grievances and questions of contractual interpretation violates Section 8(a)(5)."

The *interpretation* of a contract by the parties thereto is not done as a matter of academic interest or in a vacuum. Interpretation is employed where there are facts to which such an interpretation is to be applied. Here the contract forbade discharge except for just cause. A condition arose which called for an interpretation of such clause. The employer disclosed to the Union the facts which the company felt would constitute just cause for the discharge of some of its employees. After an investigation and appraisal of such facts, the bargaining agent agreed that such facts constituted just cause. For our conclusion we do not rely upon the fact that, after plaintiff's discharge, the Union failed to present or process a grievance on her behalf, nor upon the then expressed opinion of its representatives that her discharge was for just cause. We are aware of the authorities which have held that the collective bargaining agent's authority does not extend to a retroactive determination that a discharge was for just cause or to the waiver or settlement of an existing grievance. *Elgin, Joliet & Eastern Railway Co.* v. *Burley,* 325 U.S. 711, 761, 16 LRRM 749 (1945); . . . Neither do we rely upon authorities which have held that under such a contract as the one here involved only the Union can process a grievance and if a Union refuses or neglects to do so, an aggrieved employee is without remedy against his employer.

We turn, then to the specific terms of the contract in this case to see whether what was done here was within the power of the contracting parties. The first sentence of paragraph 14 contains the prohibition against discharge "except for just cause." The next sentence of the paragraph provides that "[i]n the event of a claim *by the Union* that an employee has been discharged without just cause" certain procedures are to follow. Nothing is said about a claim by the *employee* to the same effect. Paragraph 15 provides that "any and all questions and discussions which at any time may arise *affecting the employees* of the employer *shall* be taken up with the manager of the unit involved at such time and place as will be mutually agreed upon between *the Union* and the manager." The discussion between the representatives of the Union and defendant concerning the prospective layoff and discharge of some of defendant's employees was a matter "affecting the employees" and obeyed the command of such paragraph.

Paragraph 17 provides that "[d]uring the term of this agreement *any question* arising hereunder which cannot be directly and satisfactorily adjusted between *the Union and the employer* shall be referred to a committee. . . ." Such committee is given authority to make a binding determination. It should be noted that the responsibility of implementing the contract's terms is, in each case, placed with the Union. Procedure to call into question a discharge is provided only in the event "of a claim *by the Union* that an employee has been discharged without just cause." We are impressed that a fair reading of these provisions discloses the contract's intent that the parties thereto had authority to do what was done here. The employer, in keeping with its duty to bargain on all matters, presented its problems to the Union. It did not act hastily or unilaterally. The Union, on behalf of its members, refused initially to permit the discharge of defendant's employees. It urged further and less drastic methods. Discussion of defendant's problems continued for many months with submission by defendant to the Union of data which defendant asserted demonstrated that some discharges had to be made. The Union made its own study of this material and concluded that action had to be taken. It refused, however, to allow the defendant to discharge all of the employees in the unit and suggested a layoff of half of them with their ultimate discharge if their replacement with new employees proved the company's point. The defendant acquiesced in the Union's suggestion and the layoffs and discharges were carried out in strict compliance with the programme agreed upon. We consider that the Union was acting in the *collective* interest of those who by law and contract the Union was charged with protecting.

. . .

The fact that in the case at bar the agreement by the Union to permit defendant to discharge plaintiff and others was not reduced to a written agreement or memorandum does not detract from its legality.

Professor Cox reviews what has been decided by the courts to date on this subject (69 Harvard Law Review 601) and what that distinguished scholar considers desirable in labor contracts and in courts' construction of rights growing out of them. He says:

> "All this suggests that the bargaining rights of the majority representatives are as broad *in the administration of a collective agreement as in its negotiation*." (p. 622)

"In my judgment the interests of the individual will be better protected on the whole by first according legal recognition to the group interest in contract administration and then strengthening the representative's awareness of its moral and legal obligations to represent all employees fairly than by excluding the union in favor of an individual cause of action. Consequently, I would lean toward finding such an intention in an ambiguous agreement." (p. 657)

We find no precise precedent for our decision, but believe it comports with legal principle and is consonant with the beneficial objectives of collective bargaining, now so important a tool in the continuing efforts to strengthen the position of the individual through collective action. Unless those upon whom is placed the responsibility for protecting collective interests are given the authority needed to discharge such responsibility, the entire process is of doubtful worth. Under the philosophy of collective responsibility an employer who bargains in good faith should be entitled to rely upon the promises and agreements of the Union representatives with whom he must deal under the compulsion of law and contract. The collective bargaining process should be carried on between parties who can mutually respect and rely upon the authority of each other.

. . . The judgment of the district court is reversed and a new trial ordered.

———————

A petition for certiorari was denied in a case based upon the same event but brought by a different plaintiff. *Simmons* v. *Union News Co.,* 341 F.2d 531, 58 LRRM 2521 (6th Cir.), *cert. denied,* 382 U.S. 884, 60 LRRM 2255 (1965). A portion of Mr. Justice Black's dissent follows:

"Although this Court has gone very far in some of its cases with reference to the power of a collective bargaining union to process the personal grievances of its members, it has not yet gone so far as to say that where there is a personal grievance for breach of a collective bargaining agreement, the employee can be deprived of an independent judicial determination of the claim by an agreement between the union and the employer that no breach exists. But this is exactly what was done to petitioner and Miss Hildreth. Though I dissented in *Republic Steel Corp.* v. *Maddox,* 379 U.S. 650 [58 LRRM 2193], I was, and still am of the belief that the majority opinion purported to preserve the right of an employee to sue his employer if his union refused to press his grievances. However, I fear that the decisions below in the Hildreth case and in this one go a long way toward effectively destroying whatever redress this Court left the individual employee in *Maddox.* The courts below refused to make their own determination of whether Miss Hildreth's and petitioner's discharges were made for 'just cause.' Instead, they allowed the employer's defense that 'just cause' was simply what the employer and the union jointly wanted it to be. While we often say that nothing is decided by a denial of certiorari, all of us know that a denial of certiorari in this case, following the denial of certiorari in the *Hildreth* case, will undoubtedly lead people to believe, and I fear with cause, that this Court is now approving such a forfeiture of contractual claims of individual employees.

"This case points up with great emphasis the kind of injustice that can occur to an individual employee when the employer and the union have such power over the employee's claim for breach of contract. Here no one has claimed from the beginning to the end of the *Hildreth* lawsuit or this lawsuit that either of these individuals was guilty of any kind of misconduct justifying her discharge. Each was one of twelve employees engaged in the operation of a lunch counter. In the *Hildreth* case respondent's supervisor testified that he had no knowledge that any of the employees discharged were in any way responsible for the lunch counter's unsuccessful operation. The manager of the lunch counter stated that he did not know of 'one single thing' that Miss Hildreth had done to reduce the counter's profits. We must assume that had petitioner here been given an opportunity to try her case, the same facts would have appeared. Moreover, petitioner alleges that she was prepared to show that subsequent to her discharge, the office girl who counted the money received at the lunch counter was found to be embezzling those funds and was discharged for it. Miss Hildreth had worked for respondent for nine and one-half years, and petitioner for fifteen years, prior to their discharges. There is no evidence that respondent had ever been dissatisfied with their work before the company became disappointed with its lunch counter about a year prior to the discharges. Yet both were discharged for 'just cause,' as determined not by a court but by an agreement of the company and the union.

"I would not construe the National Labor Relations Act as giving a union and an employer any such power over workers. In this case there has been no bargain made on behalf of all the workers represented by the union. Rather there has been a sacrifice of the rights of a group of employees based on the belief that some of them might possibly have been guilty of some kind of misconduct that would reduce the employer's profits. Fully recognizing the right of the collective bargaining representative to make a contract on the part of the workers for the future, I cannot believe that those who passed the Act intended to give the union the right to negotiate away alleged breaches of a contract claimed by individual employees.

"The plain fact is that petitioner has lost her job, not because of any guilt on her part, but because there is a suspicion that some one of the group which was discharged was guilty of misconduct. The sum total of what has been done here is to abandon the fine, old American ideal that guilt is personal. Our system of jurisprudence should not tolerate imposing on the innocent punishment that should be laid on the guilty. If the construction of the labor law given by the courts below is to stand, it should be clearly and unequivocally announced by this Court so that Congress can, if it sees fit, consider this question and protect the just claims of employees from the joint power of employers and unions." 382 U.S. at 886–888.

Questions

1. The case of Gladys Hildreth seems appalling even to those sympathetic to the institutional needs of unions. The result is also disturbing because the common "just cause" standard for employer discipline is almost universally deemed to require some personal fault on the part of the employee. The "just cause" limitation on managerial discretion is one of the most significant results of collective bargaining and one of the primary reasons for union organization. The standard surely imposes some limit on managerial power to discipline. Does the action become fairer or less subject to review because *both* contracting parties agreed upon the action taken?

Would the union have been liable for a breach of the duty of fair representation had it been sued rather than the employer? Would the union's action be remediable on an arbitrariness standard if the union held a good faith belief that the discharge of five employees would maintain employment for other employees? The case poignantly suggests the limitations of a doctrine based solely on good faith and the absence of hostile discrimination, standards that do not consider the impact of the union's action upon employees.

2. Does the court hold that the contracting parties *amended* the agreement and, therefore, the action was within their power? Or does it hold that the action taken was based upon an *interpretation* of the agreement? If the latter, does the court feel it cannot review the merits if the result was reached in good faith, or does the court actually review and find that "just cause" for discharge exists? What should be the court's role?

What if the agreement contained a clause permitting the discharge of some or all employees in a particular unit when there is reason to believe theft has occurred even though individual guilt cannot be established? Since the right alleged to have been infringed is contractual, could Ms. Hildreth object if the agreement permitted her discharge? How is this situation different from the *Hildreth* case?

3. If there is some review of the parties' interpretation of their agreement, how can this be justified? Are courts well equipped for this purpose?

In the article extracted below, Professor Cox argues that if the parties can make binding settlements, free of judicial scrutiny, there is a greater chance of uniform application of the agreement. Does this argument apply to *Hildreth*?

Cox, Rights Under a Labor Agreement*

In my opinion the needs of the industrial community would be served best by leaving management and union free to determine by the terms of their collective bargaining agreement what shall be the respective rights

*Reprinted by permission from Cox, *Rights Under a Labor Agreement*, 69 HARV. L. REV. 601, 618–19, 625–27 (1956). Copyright © 1956 by the Harvard Law Review Association.

of the union and the individual in its administration. The law could fill any gap resulting from the parties' failure to manifest a reasonably clear intention by formulating presumptions based upon considerations of fairness and convenience mixed with an informed hunch as to the "intent" of the transaction. If this approach is sound, it should embrace three propositions.

(1) The employer and bargaining representative are free to determine by contract in the collective agreement who shall have the right to enforce and settle claims arising out of the employer's failure to observe the agreed conditions of employment. In other words, the power to compromise claims, the right to sue for breach of contract, and the necessity of exhausting a grievance procedure shall be determined by asking what character of rights the parties intended to create when they negotiated the agreement.

(2) Unless a contrary intention is manifest, the employer's obligations under a collective bargaining agreement which contains a grievance procedure controlled by the union shall be deemed to run solely to the union as the bargaining representative, to be administered by the union in accordance with its fiduciary duties to employees in the bargaining unit. The representative can enforce the claim. It can make reasonable binding compromises. It is liable for breaches of trust in a suit by the employee beneficiaries.

(3) Unless a contrary intention is manifest, a collective agreement which contains no grievance procedure shall be deemed a bilateral contract between the employer and union which contemplates the execution of further bilateral contracts of employment between the employer and individual workers incorporating the wage scale and other conditions of employment set forth in the collective agreement. The union may sue on the collective agreement to enforce the closed shop, check-off, and similar provisions inuring to its benefit as an organization, but only individuals may prosecute or settle claims based upon failure to observe the stipulated conditions of employment. . . .

Collective Bargaining Policies.—Apart from statute there are strong reasons for concluding that the bargaining representative ought to have power under a broad industrial agreement to control the prosecution of claims for breach of contract, whether by pressing grievances, invoking arbitration, or instituting legal proceedings.

(1) The union is sometimes the only party qualified to prosecute the claim, either because its participation is necessary to implement the promise as in the case of the proposed job evaluation study, or because the violation has not injured an identifiable individual, as in some cases of subcontracting. The group interest is often involved to an equal degree when there is past damage to an identifiable individual.

(2) Many grievances result from failure to foresee a problem at the time of contract negotiations. When the contingency arises and conflicting views are asserted, the issue is nominally framed by the past but the truly important question may be, "What rule shall hereafter govern our conduct in these circumstances?" The group may be affected by the future implications of the ruling to an extent that far outweighs the

individual claims to damages. . . . The union is the natural spokesman for future implications. Nor can adjudication of past rights be separated from rule making for the future. Both pertain to the interstices of the contract. The parties—and when they fail, an arbitrator—can successfully project general standards upon specific occasions because they are required to make their determinations within a given framework. The process works precisely because the same decision must be both an adjudication of the past and a rule for the future. To separate the two would either take the rule-making function out of the framework of the contract or else produce the unacceptable incongruity of two interpretations upon the same set of facts.

(3) Many claims of contract violation affect employees other than those who were directly damaged by nonperformance. . . .

(4) Vesting the union with control of all grievances increases the likelihood of uniformity and therefore reduces "a potential source of competitions and discriminations that could be destructive of the entire structure of labor relations in the plant.". . .

(5) Competition between rival groups of employees can be troublesome to an employer not only because of the resulting unrest in the plant but also because it deters the bargaining representative from taking what the employer may consider a "responsible position." Public officials and arbitrators no less than employers constantly remind union officials that they have a duty to discountenance disruptive and frivolous claims.

(6) When the interests of several groups conflict, or future needs run contrary to present desires, or when the individual's claim endangers group interests, the union's function is to resolve the competition by reaching an accommodation or striking a balance. The process is political. It involves a melange of power, numerical strength, mutual aid, reason, prejudice, and emotion. Limits must be placed on the authority of the group, but within the zone of fairness and rationality this method of self-government probably works better than the edicts of any outside arbiter. A large part of the daily grist of union business is resolving differences among employees poorly camouflaged as disputes with the employer.

Note

The employee's contract action under Section 301 of the Labor-Management Relations Act (LMRA) is often limited by a contractual grievance system made the "exclusive" method of resolving such disputes. An employee's action will be subject to "exhaustion" of the contractual grievance system. In *Republic Steel Corp.* v. *Maddox,* 379 U.S. 650, 58 LRRM 2193 (1965), the Court held that an employee must, as a general rule, attempt to use the grievance procedure in the collective agreement before bringing suit for severance pay in a state court under a contract subject to Section 301(a). The Court recognized that "[i]f the union refuses to press or only perfunctorily presses the individual's claim, differences may arise as to the forms of redress then available." *Id.* at 652, 58 LRRM 2194. But the Court concluded that the union must at least be afforded an opportunity to act on the employee's behalf.

Should the matter be taken to arbitration, and resolved adversely to the employee, the significance of the contractual claim is not clear. Arbitral awards under Section 301 will receive only minimal review, although it is possible to read *Humphrey* v. *Moore*, which follows, as a modification of those restrictions. A fair representation action may, of course, lie against the union. The value of that action, however, may be limited by the measure of damages and the fact that the employee's basic concern will often be job reinstatement and not monetary compensation.

Humphrey, thus, involves the viability of a contract action when the grievance system has been exhausted as well as the scope of the duty of fair representation.

Humphrey v. Moore

Supreme Court of the United States, 1964
375 U.S. 335, 55 LRRM 2031

[When Dealers Transport Company absorbed the southern operations of the E. & L. Transport Company, a Joint Conference Committee, consisting of employer and union representatives, decided that the seniority of the affected employees should be dovetailed. The employees of both companies were represented by the same local union, the president of which was Paul Priddy. Moore, one of Dealers' employees, sought an injunction in a Kentucky state court against implementation of the committee's decision. He claimed that the committee exceeded its power under the existing collective bargaining agreement in making the decision to dovetail the seniority lists, and that the decision of the committee resulted from dishonest union conduct in breach of its duty of fair representation. The Kentucky Court of Appeals enjoined the implementation of the committee's decision. The majority of the Supreme Court agreed with the Kentucky court's observation that Moore's action was in the nature of an action to enforce a collective bargaining agreement.]

Mr. Justice White delivered the opinion of the Court.

. . . [T]his action is one arising under § 301 of the Labor Management Relations Act and is a case controlled by federal law . . . even though brought in the state court. *Local 174, Teamsters* v. *Lucas Flour Co.*, 369 U.S. 95; *Smith* v. *Evening News Ass'n*, 371 U.S. 195. Although there are differing views on whether a violation of the duty of fair representation is an unfair labor practice under the Labor Management Relations Act, it is not necessary for us to resolve that difference here. Even if it is, or arguably may be, an unfair labor practice, the complaint here alleged that Moore's discharge would violate the contract and was therefore within the cognizance of federal and state courts. *Smith* v. *Evening News Ass'n, supra,* subject, of course, to the applicable federal law.

We now come to the merits of this case.

II

If we assume with Moore and the courts below that the Joint Conference Committee's power was circumscribed by § 5 and that its interpretation of the section is open to court review, Moore's cause is not measurably advanced. For in our opinion the section reasonably meant what the Joint Commission said or assumed it meant. There was an absorption here within the meaning of the section and that section did deal with jobs as well as with seniority. . . .

The power of the Joint Conference Committee over seniority gave it power over jobs. It was entitled under § 5 to integrate the seniority lists upon some rational basis, and its decision to integrate lists upon the basis of length of service at either company was neither unique nor arbitrary. On the contrary, it is a familiar and frequently equitable solution to the inevitably conflicting interests which arise in the wake of a merger or an absorption such as occurred here. The Joint Conference Committee's decision to dovetail seniority lists was a decision which § 5 empowered the committee to make.

Neither do we find adequate support in this record for the complaint's attack upon the integrity of the union and of the procedures which led to the decision. Although the union at first advised the Dealers drivers that they had nothing to worry about but later supported the E & L employees before the Joint Conference Committee, there is no substantial evidence of fraud, deceitful action or dishonest conduct. Priddy's early assurances to Dealers employees were not well founded, it is true; but Priddy was acting upon information then available to him, information received from the company which led him to think there was no trade or exchange involved, no "absorption" which might bring § 5 into play. Other sections of the contract, he thought, would protect the jobs of Moore and his fellow drivers. Consistent with this view, he also advised E & L employees that the situation appeared unfavorable for them. However, when he learned of the pending acquisition by Dealers of E & L operating authority in Louisville and of the involvement of other locations in the transaction, he considered the matter to be one for the Joint Committee. Ultimately he took the view that an absorption was involved, that § 5 did apply and that dovetailing seniority lists was the most equitable solution for all concerned. We find in this evidence insufficient proof of dishonesty or intentional misleading on the part of the union. And we do not understand the court below to have found otherwise.

The Kentucky court, however, made much of the antagonistic interests of the E & L and Dealers drivers, both groups being represented by the same union, whose president supported one group and opposed the other at the hearing before the Joint Conference Committee. But we are not ready to find a breach of the collective bargaining agent's duty of fair representation in taking a good faith position contrary to that of some individuals whom it represents nor in supporting the position of one group of employees against that of another. . . . Just as a union must be free to sift out wholly frivolous grievances which would only clog the grievance process, so it must be free to take a position on the not so frivolous disputes. Nor should it be neutralized when the issue is chiefly between two sets of employees. Conflict between employees represented by the same union is a recurring fact. To remove or gag the union in these cases would surely weaken the collective bargaining and grievance processes.

As far as this record shows, the union took its position honestly, in good faith and without hostility or arbitrary discrimination. After Dealers absorbed the Louisville business of E & L, there were fewer jobs at Dealers than there were Dealers and E & L drivers. One group or the other was going to suffer. If any E & L drivers were to be hired at Dealers either they or the Dealers drivers would not have the seniority which they had previously enjoyed. Inevitably the absorption would hurt someone. By choosing to integrate seniority lists based upon length of service at either company, the union acted upon wholly relevant considerations, not upon capricious or arbitrary factors. The evidence shows no breach by the union of its duty of fair representation.

There is a remaining contention. Even though the union acted in good faith and was entitled to take the position it did, were the Dealers employees, if the union was going to oppose them, deprived of a fair hearing by having inadequate representation at the hearing? Dealers employees had notice of the hearing; they were obviously aware that they were locked in a struggle for jobs and seniority with the E & L drivers, and three stewards representing them went to the hearing at union expense and were given every opportunity to state their position. Thus the issue is in reality a narrow one. There was no substantial dispute about the facts concerning the nature of the transaction between the two companies. It was for the Joint Conference Committee initially to decide whether there was an "absorption" within the meaning of § 5 and, if so, whether seniority lists were to be integrated and the older employees of E & L given jobs at Dealers. The Dealers employees made no request to continue the hearing until they could secure further representation and have not yet suggested what they could have added to the hearing by way of facts or theory if they had been differently represented. The trial court found it "idle speculation to assume that the result would have been different had the matter been differently presented." We agree.

Moore has not, therefore, proved his case. Neither the parties nor the Joint Committee exceeded their power under the contract and there was no fraud or breach of duty by the exclusive bargaining agent. The decision of the committee, reached after proceedings adequate under the agreement, is final and binding upon the parties, just as the contract says it is. *Drivers Union* v. *Riss & Co.*, 372 U.S. 517.

The decision below is reversed and the cases are remanded for further proceedings not inconsistent with this opinion.

It is so ordered.

Mr. Justice Douglas.

I agree for the reasons stated by my Brother Goldberg, that this litigation was properly brought in the state court but on the merits I believe that no cause of action has been made out for the reasons stated by the Court.

MR. JUSTICE GOLDBERG, with whom MR. JUSTICE BRENNAN joins, concurring in the result.

I concur in the judgment and in the holding of the Court that since "Moore has not . . . proved his case . . . ," the decision below must be reversed. *Supra.* I do not, however, agree that Moore stated a cause of action arising under § 301(a) of the Labor Management Relations Act, 61 Stat. 156, 29 U.S.C. § 185(a). It is my view rather that Moore's claim must be treated as an individual employee's action for a union's breach of its duty of fair representation—a duty derived not from the collective bargaining contract but from the National Labor Relations Act as amended. . . .

. . . A mutually acceptable grievance settlement between an employer and a union, which is what the decision of the Joint Committee was, cannot be challenged by an individual dissenting employee under § 301(a) on the ground that the parties exceeded their contractual powers in making the settlement. It is true that this Court, in a series of decisions dealing with labor arbitrations, has recognized that the powers of an arbitrator arise from and are defined by the collective bargaining agreement. . . . Thus the existing labor contract is the touchstone of an arbitrator's powers. But the power of the union and the employer jointly to settle a grievance dispute is not so limited. The parties are free by joint action to modify, amend, and supplement their original collective bargaining agreement. They are equally free, since "[t]he grievance procedure is . . . a part of the continuous collective bargaining process," to settle grievances not falling within the scope of the contract. *Id.,* at 581. In this case, for example, had the dispute gone to arbitration, the arbitrator would have been bound to apply the existing agreement and to determine whether the merger-absorption clause applied. However, even in the absence of such a clause, the contracting parties—the multiemployer unit and the union—were free to resolve the dispute by amending the contract to dovetail seniority lists or to achieve the same result by entering into a grievance settlement. The presence of the merger-absorption clause did not restrict the right of the parties to resolve their dispute by joint agreement applying, interpreting, or amending the contract. There are too many unforeseeable contingencies in a collective bargaining relationship to justify making the words of the contract the exclusive source of rights and duties. . . .

It is wholly inconsistent with this Court's recognition that "[t]he grievance procedure is . . . a part of the continuous collective bargaining process," *United Steelworkers of America* v. *Warrior & Gulf Navigation Co.,* 363 U.S., at 581, to limit the parties' powers to settle grievances to the confines of the existing labor agreement, or to assert, as the Court now does, that an individual employee can claim that the collective bargaining contract is violated because the parties have made a grievance settlement going beyond the strict terms of the existing contract. . . .

MR. JUSTICE HARLAN, concurring in part and dissenting in part.

I agree with the Court's opinion and judgment insofar as it relates to the claim that the Joint Conference Committee exceeded its authority under the collective bargaining agreement. Although it is undoubtedly true as a general proposition that bargaining representatives have power to alter the terms of a contract with an employer, the challenge here is not to a purported exercise of such power but to the validity of a grievance settlement reached under proceedings allegedly not authorized by the terms of the collective agreement. Moreover, a committee with authority to settle grievances whose composition is different from that in the multiunion-multiemployer bargaining unit cannot be deemed to possess power to effect changes in the bargaining agreement. When it is alleged that the union itself has engaged or acquiesced in such a departure from the collective bargaining agreement, I can see no reason why an individually affected employee may not step into the shoes of the union and maintain a § 301 suit himself. . . .

[Mr. Justice Harlan noted that insofar as plaintiff's claim was based upon unfair representation, a duty implicit in the NLRA, the Court had to decide whether that cause of action fell within the preemption doctrine.]

Questions

1. Would this decision have helped Gladys Hildreth? That is, would *Humphrey* provide judicial review of the merits of Ms. Hildreth's contractual claim? If so, how can this case be reconciled with cases like *Enterprise Wheel* which strictly limit the judicial power to review arbitration awards? The *Hildreth* court suggested that breach of the duty of fair representation was the only ground upon which a mutually agreed upon settlement could be challenged. To what extent does *Humphrey* v. *Moore* alter this view?

Should it matter for purposes of review whether the contracting parties purport to amend the agreement or purport to interpret the agreement pursuant to the contractual grievance system? Mr. Justice Goldberg argues that a "mutually acceptable grievance settlement" cannot be challenged by an employee under Section 301. What then becomes of the individual employee's legally recognized right to litigate contract violations under Section 301? Would this right exist if no settlement was reached by the contracting parties? What if the contract provided an arbitration procedure, but the union failed or refused to bring the issue to arbitration?

2. The import of *Humphrey* is unclear since Mr. Justice White's opinion only assumes, without deciding, that the parties' interpretation of Section 5 is open to judicial scrutiny. What is the result of accepting Mr. Justice Goldberg's view? What values are promoted—what assumptions are made about the needs of collective bargaining?

3. The problem of protecting individual employees is compounded by the arbitration system generally used in trucking. Instead of a neutral arbitrator, employees appeal to joint employer-union committees composed of equal numbers of employer and union representatives. Joint

committee decisions are often given the same deference by courts as awards by neutral arbitrators. The members of the panels often have relationships with the employers and union officials appearing before them. Resolution depends upon agreement by both union and employer representatives, and it is thought that lobbying as well as trading of grievances frequently occurs. In addition, hearings and deliberations, even in complicated cases, are short and the record is extremely sparse. See P. Tobias, *Individual Employee Suits for Breach of the Labor Agreement and the Union's Duty of Fair Representation,* 5 Toledo L. Rev. 514, 540–43 (1974).

Comment on Individual Rights

The leading exponent of recognizing a grievance as an affirmative right is Professor Summers. His views are reflected in the following excerpts.

Summers, Individual Rights in Collective Agreements and Arbitration*

Both the National Labor Relations Act and the Railway Labor Act express the basic national policy of reliance on collective bargaining as a system of industrial government. Section 301 is but a segment of the statutory framework supporting and shaping that system, and the courts in constructing rules to govern the rights of individual employees should seek to further, not frustrate, the purposes of collective bargaining. But the purposes to be furthered are not simply those of the collective entities—union and management. The controlling purposes are those of the statute, for collective bargaining, a private institution, is charged with a public function.[125]

Collective bargaining as conceived by the statute vests in the union collective power to enable it to bargain effectively with the employer, but the purpose of giving the union that power is to benefit the employees. The function of the collective agreement is not only to stabilize the relationship of the collective parties, but also to establish terms and conditions of employment for the employees. Nor are the interests of the employees conceived in narrow economic terms, for one of the dominant purposes of collective bargaining is to protect employees from arbitrary or unequal treatment—to bring a sense of justice to the workplace. The role of the collective agreement is to substitute general rules for unchanneled discretion; wages are not based on whimsy but on established rates,

---

*Reprinted by permission from Clyde W. Summers, *Individual Rights in Collective Agreements and Arbitration,* 37 N.Y.U. L. Rev. 362, 389–97 (1962). Copyright © 1962 by New York University.

[125]Congress, in amending § 9(a), made clear that it did not believe that exclusive control by the union over grievances was essential for collective bargaining to fulfill the statutory purpose. At the very least, § 9(a) upholds contracts which deny unions such exclusive control. Indeed, the legislative history makes it unmistakably clear that Congress considered such contracts preferable. •

layoffs are not governed by favoritism but by seniority provisions, discharges are not based upon vindictive bias but upon just cause after objective inquiry. As the Labor Study Group of the Committee for Economic Development has so well stated:

> "A major achievement of collective bargaining, perhaps its most important contribution to the American workplace, is the creation of a system of industrial jurisprudence, a system under which employer and employee rights are set forth in contractual form and disputes over the meaning of the contract are settled through a rational grievance process usually ending, in the case of unresolved disputes, with arbitration. The gains from this system are especially noteworthy because of their effect on the recognition and dignity of the individual worker."[126]

The needs of collective bargaining, thus conceived, inevitably look two ways—toward the interests of the collective parties and their relationship, and toward the interests of the employees and their individual rights. The need for an effective union to obtain benefits and establish rules carries with it a need for individuals to receive those benefits according to the rules. The need for the collective parties to resolve disputes and meet changed conditions during the contract has a concurrent need for the individual to be fairly treated according to general rules. In framing the legal rules, the multiple needs of collective bargaining cannot be fully served by looking only to the collective relationship; for one of the major functions of collective bargaining may be frustrated if the employees' interest in fair and equal treatment under established rules is not given significant weight.

If the law looks only to the needs and desires of union and management, it may give little protection to the individual. Both of the collective parties are primarily concerned with managing their relationship, and that is simplified by giving the union exclusive control over the prosecution of grievances. Three uses of the grievance procedure in managing the collective relationship are particularly relevant in defining individual rights. First, the grievance procedure is used to complete the collective agreement. Contract provisions may be intentionally silent or vague, or they may unwittingly leave gaps, include inconsistent terms, or fail to foresee future problems. Whatever its source, ambiguity reveals that the agreement is incomplete and requires continued bargaining. The forum for bargaining is the grievance procedure, and the unsettled rule is illustrated by a particular grievance. The process of completion is akin to the original negotiation of the agreement, and the collective parties have primary interests in evolving the general rule to fill out the agreement. But this bargaining process is more confined than the original negotiation, for the parties normally expect that the grievance will be settled

---

[126]Comm. for Economic Development, The Public Interest in National Labor Policy 32 (1961). The importance of the collective agreement and its observance for the individual is underlined by § 104 of the LMRDA, which requires that the union provide employees with copies of the collective agreement. One of the purposes of this provision was to enable employees to insist that the collective agreement be followed and their rights not bartered away by the union officers.

within the range of reasonable interpretations which can be drawn from guides in the agreement, and if they are unable to settle the dispute, it will be resolved by arbitration.[127]

Second, the grievance procedure may be used to change the collective agreement and serve the needs of flexibility.[128] During cutbacks in employment the employer may lay off all women employees and retain men with lesser seniority or impose layoffs instead of spreading the work as required by the seniority clause. The union, by refusing to appeal the grievances, accepts an informal modification of the agreement. The purposes of both collective parties are served by the freedom to improvise exceptions to the general rules of the agreement. Of course, the line between changing the contract and completing the contract is indistinct, but the line is crossed when the settlement is beyond the range of reasonable interpretation of the agreement or contravenes a previously established rule. The indistinctness of the dividing line does not obliterate the essential difference in the two uses of the grievance procedure.

Third, the grievance procedure may be used as a clearing house for balancing off unrelated claims. Grievances may be bargained against each other, the employer granting one in return for the union's surrendering another. This may serve a useful and legitimate function, but also can raise serious problems. . . . When the grievance procedure becomes clogged, large numbers of grievances may be settled in a wholesale exchange. Thus in *Elgin, Joliet,* the union's surrender of back pay claims was part of a package settlement of sixty-one different grievances.

From the union's institutional viewpoint, exclusive control over grievances enhances the union's prestige and authority. Through the prosecution of grievances it can daily demonstrate its effectiveness as guardian of the employee's interests; successful settlement builds bonds of loyalty from those benefited; and refusal to process underscores the union's authority. Conversely, grievances settled with individual or other unions makes the majority union appear unnecessary, if not ineffective, and creates conflicting loyalties. More importantly, the union as representative of all the employees has a collective interest in the individual's claim. If the claim is granted, it may be at the expense of other employees—seniority, promotion, and job assignment cases are only the most obvious examples. If the claim is denied, it may provide a precedent which casts a cloud over other employees' rights. The union has not only an interest but a responsibility to protect the other employees' rights. In addition, it has a

---

[127]For an analysis of the dual role of the grievance procedure in "legislating" new employment standards and "administering" established standards, particularly with reference to individual rights, see Dunau, *Employee Participation in the Grievance Aspect of Collective Bargaining,* 50 COLUM. L. REV. 731, 747–51 (1950).

[128]One of the arguments most commonly used against recognition of individual rights under the collective agreement is that "a prime function of the grievance procedure is to secure uniformity in interpreting the agreement and building up a 'law of the plant' with respect to matters not spelled out in the agreement." *Ostrofsky v. United Steelworkers,* 171 F. Supp. 782, 790 (D. Md. 1959). See discussion in Cox, *Individual Enforcement of Collective Bargaining Agreements,* 8 LAB. L.J. 850, 855 (1957). This argument puts the shoe on the wrong foot, for it is the individual who insists on uniformity—that he be treated according to the "law of the plant" which governs all others under the agreement. It is the collective parties who insist on exceptions, variations and departure from uniformity.

separable institutional interest that the bargain it has made not be remade or frittered away by individual action.

From management's viewpoint, vesting exclusive control over grievances in the union simplifies contract administration. Friction and distrust on the part of the union are reduced, and all grievances are funneled though a single established procedure which orders appeals up the chain of management control. Most important, it simplifies management's obtaining definite answers to questions arising under the collective agreement. Grievances settled with the union cannot return to haunt management in the form of individual claims; dispensations granted by union officers cannot be challenged by individual employees. The employer can proceed with full security, for the union's control over the grievance procedure shields him from possible liability to his employees.

These needs and desires of the collective parties, and their use of the grievance procedure to manage their collective relationship are all served by giving the union exclusive control over the grievance procedure. Obviously, not all of these needs are equally compelling nor the desires worthy of fulfillment in the same measure. More important, however, many of these needs do not require such totality of union control, or may be adequately met through other methods. The purpose here is only to identify the principal collective needs, not to prescribe the measure or method of meeting them. That must be done through specifying the design of the substantive law.

The needs of collective bargaining look also to the interests of the employees and their individual rights. In simple economic terms, the individual's interest is often of first magnitude, for more than three-fourths of the cases coming to the courts involve seniority rights or disciplinary discharges. The individual's very livelihood is at stake. In personal terms, loss of seniority undermines his sense of security, and discharge darkens his good name. Making the union the exclusive representative for processing grievances subordinates those interests of individual employees and endangers interests which collective bargaining purposes to protect.

The grievance procedure is particularly susceptible to abuse, for through it individuals or groups may be singled out for arbitrary treatment. . . . Most grievances involve some factual issue, and the union, by rejecting the employees' version, can act "responsible" and wear the face of fairness.

The individual's interest may more often be vitiated without vindictiveness or deliberate discrimination. Incomplete investigation of the facts, reliance on untested evidence, or colored evaluation of witnesses may lead the union to reject grievances which more objective inquiry would prove meritorious. Union officials burdened with institutional concerns may be willing to barter unrelated grievances or accept wholesale settlements if the total package is advantageous, even though some good grievances are lost. Concern for collective interests and the needs of the enterprise may dull the sense of personal injustice. Thus in *Union News Co.* v. *Hildreth,* the management of a restaurant found that the food costs were out of line with past experience, a fact indicating wastage, serving too large portions, or theft. Unable to discover who or what was at fault, management picked five of the twelve employees at random and replaced them. When food costs appeared to go down, this was taken as proof that the culprits had been caught and the five employees were discharged. The union agreed that "just cause" had been shown and refused to process a grievance on behalf of the discharged employees.

Although the frequence of unfairness in grievance handling is impossible to measure, there is no doubt that the danger to the individual can be substantial. Within union groups cliques are not uncommon, political rivalries are often sharp and factional fights are bitter. Refusal to process grievances or "botching" them is a subtle but effective weapon. Seniority grievances are vulnerable to group pressures, and "horse-trading" of grievances can become commonplace. That these are real dangers is evidenced by the few studies made[139] and confirmed by leading commentators.[140]

Beyond these dangers of malice, majority intolerance, or official insensitivity, there are less tangible, but more pervasive values. One of the functions of collective bargaining is to replace vagrant discretion with governing rules. The individual, by his ability to insist that those general rules be observed, gains an assurance of fair and equal treatment and a sense of dignity and individual worth. If the union, by *ad hoc* settlement, can set aside the rule and bar the aggrieved individual from access to any neutral tribunal, these values are denied. What is involved, and what collective bargaining seeks to bring to industrial life, are elemental notions of due process—the right of a person to be governed by the law of the land and the right to be heard in his own cause.

Although union and management may fear that transplanting such notions of due process into our system of industrial government will complicate their collective relationship, experience under the Railway Labor Act suggests that those fears may prove unfounded. The collective parties greeted the *Elgin, Joliet*[141] decision with alarums that it would "shackle" the unions, "cause a breakdown of grievance handling" and jeopardize the whole process of orderly adjustment of disputes. However, no such consequences followed. The right of the individual to carry his case to the Adjustment Board is now accepted and the rules of notice, hearing and fair tribunal have proved livable.

The interests of the collective parties and the interests of the individual employees do not stand in simple opposition to each other; they cannot be

---

[139]See *ABA Report on Individual Grievances*, 33, 41–44, 50 Nw. U.L. Rev. at 153–56. In this study questionnaires were sent to over 1,000 labor lawyers. Out of 175 replies, two-thirds stated that in their experience they found that meritorious grievances were at times ignored or surrendered because of political pressures within the union. See also Fleming, *Some Problems of Due Process and Fair Procedure in Labor Arbitration*, 13 Stan. L. Rev. 235 (1961); Schubert, *Individual Rights in the Grievance Procedure of the Railway Labor Act* (1961) (unpublished study in Yale Law Library); Comment, *Railroad Labor Disputes and the National Railroad Adjustment Board*, 18 U. Chi. L. Rev. 303 (1951).

[140]Cox, *Individual Enforcement of Collective Bargaining Agreements*, 8 Lab. L.J. 850, 854 (1957); Dunau, *Employee Participation in the Grievance Aspect of Collective Bargaining*, 50 Colum. L. Rev. 731, 759 (1950); Sherman, *The Individual and His Grievance—Whose Grievance Is It?*, 11 U. Pitt. L. Rev. 35, 49 (1949).

[141]*Elgin, J. & E. Ry. v. Burley*, 325 U.S. 711 (1945), *aff'd on rehearing*, 327 U.S. 661 (1946).

lumped for weighing on the scale of judgment to determine whether individuals should or should not have rights under collective agreements. The interests do not clash directly, and the choice is not whether the union should have complete control or the individual full independence. We are not required to choose between polar alternatives; we are rather required to work out an accommodation of the multiple needs of collective bargaining as conceived by our national labor laws. The significant inquiry is what structure of legal rules can be designed which will best serve all of the multiple needs of collective bargaining, and to what extent can the varied interests be mediated by details in the design. This is the task of the next section.

IV

THE STRUCTURE OF SUBSTANTIVE LAW

From these varied sources which project the national labor policy, the courts must build a body of federal substantive law defining the relative rights of individual employees and unions under the collective agreement. The state courts are as much bound by this responsibility as the federal courts, and their task is made more difficult by the clutter of precedents which have largely ignored controlling federal concerns. The incomplete words of Section 9(a), the suggestive experiences under the Railway Labor Act, and the diverse needs of collective bargaining provide no ready-made blueprint. From these, however, emerge three guiding rules which provide a basic framework for the law.

First, the individual employee is bound by the substantive terms of the collective agreement. He cannot bargain individually to vary the contract or set it aside; he can only demand compliance with its terms. He cannot deny the union's power to make a binding agreement; he can only insist that when the agreement is made, he shall not be denied its benefits. The very essence of the individual's claim is that the terms and conditions of his employment are governed by the collective agreement and that neither he, nor the union, nor the employer can refuse to live by it.

The collective agreement by which the individual and the collective parties are governed is not limited to the four corners of the written instrument. It is the whole agreement, including industrial customs, established practices, understandings and precedents which infuse the contractual words with life and meaning. The collective agreement inevitably includes incomplete terms and unresolved ambiguities; and the individual's rights, like those of the collective parties, are subject to these gaps and uncertainties. The individual whose claim is disputed cannot insist on his interpretation; he can only insist on access to an appropriate procedure through which that dispute can be resolved. In this sense, the individual's right under a collective agreement is essentially procedural— the right of access to a tribunal, court or arbitrator, to have his substantive claims determined and enforced.

Second, the union has a substantial interest in the settlement of all individual claims arising under the collective agreement. The employee and the employer cannot make a binding settlement without the consent of the union, nor can they submit their dispute to a tribunal without making the union a party. The union has a right to be heard on behalf of other employees and its institutional interests.

But this right of the union has more than procedural significance, particularly when the individual's claim arises out of a gap or ambiguity in the collective agreement. If the union supports management's interpretation, this will be highly persuasive to the court or arbitrator so long as the interpretation is within the range of reasonableness as determined by the words, practices and precedents of the parties. Thus the collective parties will remain a dominant voice in completing the terms of the agreement, thereby satisfying in substantial measure this need of collective bargaining.

Third, the collective parties can change the general rules governing the terms and conditions of employment, either by negotiating a new agreement or by formally amending the old. The individual has no right to have the contract remain unchanged; his right is only to have it followed until it is changed by proper procedures. Although contract making (or amending) and contract administration are not neatly severable, they are procedurally distinct processes. Most union constitutions prescribe the method of contract ratification, and it is distinct from grievance settlement; the power to make and amend contracts is not placed in the same hands as the power to adjust grievances. Indeed, many union constitutions expressly bar any officer from ratifying any action which constitutes a breach of any contract. Through the ability to change the agreement, the collective parties retain a measure of flexibility. They are not free, however, to set aside general rules for particular cases, nor are they free by informal processes to replace one general rule with a contrary one.

Problem

The Enderby Company employs a small number of truck drivers to ship certain products to various points in Pennsylvania, Ohio, and New York. Truck drivers making long hauls are customarily reimbursed for their motel expenses.

Recently, two employees of Enderby received a notice of discharge which alleged that they had falsified motel receipts on various days in the preceding month. Their union, Teamsters Local 1108, secured their reinstatement pending resolution of the matter in "Detroit." Detroit is the headquarters of the district arbitration panel, the Central Conference Automobile Transporters Joint Arbitration Committee, which is composed of equal numbers of employer representatives and teamsters officials.

In the arbitration proceeding, the sole piece of evidence of wrongdoing was a short letter by the owner of a motel in Batavia, New York, which reads as follows:

"Statement: On the evening of 4/14/78 V. Mum and G. Arid paid $5.20 each for lodging. V. Mum and G. Arid were given a receipt—each in the amount of $7.28."

Despite representations of honesty by the employees, the joint arbitration panel upheld the discharges under the collective agreement. The agreement generally provides for discharge for cause only after a written warning notice, but discharge for dishonesty, drunkeness, or recklessness dispenses with the prior warning requirement.

The employees urged the Teamster International Representative for their area to schedule a new hearing. The attempts proved successful, and a "new hearing" was listed on the agenda for the June 15 meeting of the Joint Committee.

In the meantime the employees sought private counsel, since the Local had provided no assistance. Their attorney secured a sworn statement from the motel owner indicating that his short letter to Enderby was based solely on a file card prepared by his night clerk. He had no personal knowledge of wrongdoing. Indeed, since his night clerk had quit, he did not know if any dishonesty actually occurred.

On June 15, the Chairman of the Joint Committee held that the sworn statement presented no new evidence and that the case was closed. The attorney protested that a hearing on new evidence was not the same as a new hearing, but the protestation fell on deaf ears.

Has the union breached its statutory duty? May the discharged employees bring a Section 301 action against the employer? To what extent may a court review the joint union-employer determination?

Vaca v. Sipes

Supreme Court of the United States, 1967
386 U.S. 171, 64 LRRM 2369

[Upon return from sick leave Owens was discharged for poor health. To secure his reinstatement, a grievance was filed and processed through the first four steps of the grievance procedure. The medical evidence of his fitness to work was conflicting. The union sent Owens to a doctor at union expense to support its position in a possible arbitration proceeding, but this examination did not support Owens' claim. When the union refused to take the grievance to arbitration because of insufficient medical evidence to support grievant's position, Owens instituted suit against the union in a state court of Missouri. Owens alleged that the union had "arbitrarily, capriciously and without just or reasonable reason or cause" refused to take his grievance to arbitration under the bargaining agreement's grievance procedures. Owens also filed a second suit against Swift, the Company, for breach of contract. This suit remained pending at the pretrial stage.

[A jury awarded Owens $7,000 compensatory damages and $3,300 punitive damages in his action against the union. After the trial judge had set the verdict aside on the ground that the NLRB had exclusive jurisdiction of the controversy, the Supreme Court of Missouri reversed and reinstated the verdict. During the appeal Owens died; respondent, administrator of his estate, was substituted.

[The majority opinion of the United States Supreme Court holds that the NLRB did not have exclusive jurisdiction over this controversy, and that the preemption doctrine does not apply to the alleged breach of union's duty of fair representation in this case. Thus the state court had jurisdiction. On the other hand, since the majority opinion finds that federal law governs this type of case and since governing federal standards were not applied, the judgment of the Supreme Court of Missouri was reversed.]

II

. . . Petitioners challenge the jurisdiction of the Missouri courts on the ground that the alleged conduct of the Union was arguably an unfair labor practice and within the exclusive jurisdiction of the NLRB. Petitioners rely on *Miranda Fuel Co.*, 140 NLRB 181 (1962), *enforcement denied*, 326 F.2d 172 (C.A. 2d Cir. 1963), where a sharply divided Board held for the first time that a union's breach of its statutory duty of fair representation violates NLRA § 8(b), as amended. With the NLRB's adoption of *Miranda Fuel*, petitioner's argue, the broad preemption doctrine defined in *San Diego Building Trades Council* v. *Garmon*, 359 U.S. 236, becomes applicable. For the reasons which follow, we reject this argument.

It is now well established that, as the exclusive bargaining representative of the employees in Owens' bargaining unit, the Union had a statutory duty fairly to represent all of those employees, both in its collective bargaining with Swift . . . and in its enforcement of the resulting collective bargaining agreement. . . . It is obvious that Owens' complaint alleged a breach by the Union of a duty grounded in federal statutes, and that federal law therefore governs his cause of action. . . .

Although NLRA § 8(b) was enacted in 1947, the NLRB did not until *Miranda Fuel* interpret a breach of a union's duty of fair representation as an unfair labor practice. In *Miranda Fuel*, the Board's majority held that NLRA § 7 gives employees "the right to be free from unfair or irrelevant or invidious treatment by their exclusive bargaining agent in matters affecting their employment," and "that Section 8(b)(1)(A) of the Act accordingly prohibits labor organizations, when acting in a statutory representative capacity, from taking action against any employee upon considerations or classifications which are irrelevant, invidious, or unfair," 140 NLRB, at 185. The Board also held that an employer who "participates" in such arbitrary union conduct violates § 8(a)(1), and that the employer and the union may violate §§ 8(a)(3) and 8(b)(2), respectively, "when, for arbitrary or irrelevant reasons or upon the basis of an unfair classification, the union attempts to cause or does cause an employer to derogate the employment status of an employee." *Id.*, at 186. . . .

A. In *Garmon*, this Court recognized that the broad powers conferred by Congress upon the National Labor Relations Board to interpret and to enforce the complex Labor Management Relations Act necessarily imply that potentially conflicting "rules of law, of remedy, and of administration" cannot be permitted to operate. 359 U.S., at 242. . . . [Here Mr. Justice White notes Congressional and judicial exceptions to the doctrines of primary jurisdiction and preemption.] Consequently, as a general rule, neither state nor federal courts have jurisdiction over suits directly involving "activity [which] is arguably subject to § 7 or § 8 of the Act." *San Diego Building Trades Council* v. *Garmon*, 359 U.S., at 235.

This pre-emption doctrine, however, has never been rigidly applied to cases where it could not fairly be inferred that Congress intended exclusive jurisdiction to lie with the NLRB. . . .

. . . While these exceptions in no way undermine the vitality of the pre-emption rule where applicable, they demonstrate that the decision to pre-empt federal and state court jurisdiction over a given class of cases must depend upon the nature of the particular interests being asserted and the effect upon the administration of national labor policies of concurrent judicial and administrative remedies.

A primary justification for the pre-emption doctrine—the need to avoid conflicting rules of substantive law in the labor relations area and the desirability of leaving the development of such rules to the administrative agency created by Congress for that purpose—is not applicable to cases involving alleged breaches of the union duty of fair representation. The doctrine was judicially developed in *Steele* and its progeny, and suits alleging breach of the duty remained judicially cognizable long after the NLRB was given unfair labor practice jurisdiction over union activities by the L.M.R.A. Moreover, when the Board declared in *Miranda Fuel* that a union's breach of its duty of fair representation would henceforth be treated as an unfair labor practice, the Board adopted and applied the doctrine as it had been developed by the federal courts. . . . Finally, as the dissenting Board members in *Miranda Fuel* have pointed out, fair representation duty suits often require review of the substantive positions taken and policies pursued by a union in its negotiation of a collective bargaining agreement and in its handling of the grievance machinery; as these matters are not normally within the Board's unfair labor practice jurisdiction, it can be doubted whether the Board brings substantially greater expertise to bear on these problems than do the courts, which have been engaged in this type of review since the *Steele* decision.

In addition to the above considerations, the unique interests served by the duty of fair representation doctrine have a profound effect, in our opinion, on the applicability of the pre-emption rule to this class of cases. The federal labor laws seek to promote industrial peace and the improvement of wages and working conditions by fostering a system of employee organization and collective bargaining. . . . The collective bargaining system as encouraged by Congress and administered by the NLRB of necessity subordinates the interests of an individual employee to the collective interests of all employees in a bargaining unit. . . . This Court recognized in *Steele* that the congressional grant of power to a union to act as exclusive collective bargaining representative, with its corresponding reduction in the individual rights of the employees so represented, would raise grave constitutional problems if unions were free to exercise this power to further racial discrimination. 323 U.S., at 198–199. Since that landmark decision, the duty of fair representation has stood as a bulwark to prevent arbitrary union conduct against individuals stripped of traditional forms of redress by the provisions of federal labor law. Were we to hold, as petitioners and the government urge, that the courts are preempted by the NLRB's *Miranda Fuel* decision of this traditional supervisory jurisdiction, the individual employee injured by arbitrary or discriminatory union conduct could no longer be assured of impartial review of his complaint, since the Board's General Counsel has unreviewable discretion to refuse to institute an unfair labor practice complaint. See *United Electrical Contractors Ass'n* v. *Ordman*, No. 29879, C.A. 2d Cir., Sept. 23, 1966, *cert. denied*, 35 U.S. L. Week 3243 (Jan. 17, 1967).[8] The existence of even a small group of cases in which the Board would be unwilling or unable to remedy a union's breach of duty would frustrate the basic purposes underlying the duty of fair representation doctrine. For these reasons, we cannot assume from the NLRB's tardy assumption of jurisdiction in these cases that Congress, when it enacted N.L.R.A. § 8(b) in 1947, intended to oust the courts of their traditional jurisdiction to curb arbitrary conduct by the individual employee's statutory representative.

B. There are also some intensely practical considerations which foreclose preemption of judicial cognizance of fair representation duty suits, considerations which emerge from the intricate relationship between the duty of fair representation and the enforcement of collective bargaining contracts. For the fact is that the question of whether a union has breached its duty of fair representation will in many cases be a critical issue in a suit under L.M.R.A. § 301 charging an employer with a breach of contract. To illustrate, let us assume a collective bargaining agreement that limits discharges to those for good cause and that contains no grievance, arbitration or other provisions purporting to restrict access to the courts. If an employee is discharged without cause, either the union or the employee may sue the employer under L.M.R.A. § 301. Under this section, courts have jurisdiction over suits to enforce collective bargaining agreements even though the conduct of the employer which is challenged as a breach of contract is also arguably an unfair labor practice within the jurisdiction of the NLRB. *Garmon* and like cases have no application to § 301 suits. . . .

The rule is the same with regard to preemption where the bargaining agreement contains grievance and arbitration provisions which are intended to provide the exclusive remedy for breach of contract claims. If an employee is discharged without cause in violation of such an agreement, that the employer's conduct may be an unfair labor practice does not preclude a suit by the union against the employer to compel arbitra-

---

[8] The public interest in effectuating the policies of the federal labor laws, not the wrong done the individual employee, is always the Board's principal concern in fashioning unfair labor practice remedies. See N.L.R.A. § 10(c) as amended, 29 U.S.C., § 160(c); *Phelps Dodge Corp.* v. *NLRB*, 313 U.S. 177. Thus, the General Counsel will refuse to bring complaints on behalf of injured employees where the injury complained of is "insubstantial."

tion of the employee's grievance; the adjudication of the claim by the arbitrator; or a suit to enforce the resulting arbitration award. . . .

However, if the wrongfully discharged employee himself resorts to the courts before the grievance procedures have been fully exhausted, the employer may well defend on the ground that the exclusive remedies provided by such a contract have not been exhausted. Since the employee's claim is based upon breach of the collective bargaining agreement, he is bound by terms of that agreement which govern the manner in which contractual rights may be enforced. For this reason, it is settled that the employee must at least attempt to exhaust exclusive grievance and arbitration procedures established by the bargaining agreement. *Republic Steel Corp.* v. *Maddox,* 379 U.S. 650. However, because these contractual remedies have been devised and are often controlled by the union and the employer, they may well prove unsatisfactory or unworkable for the individual grievant. The problem then is to determine under what circumstances the individual employee may obtain judicial review of his breach-of-contract claim despite his failure to secure relief through the contractual remedial procedures.

An obvious situation in which the employee should not be limited to the exclusive remedial procedures established by the contract occurs when the conduct of the employer amounts to a repudiation of those contractual procedures. . . . In such a situation (and there may of course be others), the employer is estopped by his own conduct to rely on the unexhausted grievance and arbitration procedures as a defense to the employee's cause of action.

We think that another situation when the employee may seek judicial enforcement of his contractual rights arises if, as is true here, the union has sole power under the contract to invoke the higher stages of the grievance procedure, *and* if, as is alleged here, the employer-plaintiff has been prevented from exhausting his contractual remedies by the union's *wrongful* refusal to process the grievance. It is true that the employer in such a situation may have done nothing to prevent exhaustion of the exclusive contractual remedies to which he agreed in the collective bargaining agreement. But the employer has committed a wrongful discharge in breach of that agreement, a breach which could be remedied through the grievance process to the employee-plaintiff's benefit were it not for the union's breach of its statutory duty of fair representation to the employee. To leave the employee remediless in such circumstances would, in our opinion, be a great injustice. We cannot believe that Congress, in conferring upon employers and unions the power to establish exclusive grievance procedures, intended to confer upon unions such unlimited discretion to deprive injured employees of all remedies, for breach of contract. Nor do we think that Congress intended to shield employers from the natural consequences of their breaches of bargaining agreements by wrongful union conduct in the enforcement of such agreements. . . .

For these reasons, we think the wrongfully discharged employee may bring an action against his employer in the face of a defense based upon the failure to exhaust contractual remedies, provided the employee can prove that the union as bargaining agent breached its duty of fair representation in its handling of the employee's grievance. We may assume for present purposes that such a breach of duty by the union is an unfair labor practice, as the NLRB and the Fifth Circuit have held. The employee's suit against the employer, however, remains a § 301 suit, and the jurisdiction of the courts is no more destroyed by the fact that the employee, as part and parcel of his § 301 action, finds it necessary to prove an unfair labor practice by the union, than it is by the fact that the suit may involve an unfair labor practice by the employer himself. The court is free to determine whether the employee is barred by the actions of his union representative, and, if not, to proceed with the case. And if, to facilitate his case, the employee joins the union as a defendant, the situation is not substantially changed. . . . And, insofar as adjudication of the union's breach of duty is concerned, the result should be no different if the employee, as Owens did here, sues the employer and the union in separate actions. There would be very little to commend a rule which would permit the Missouri courts to adjudicate the Union's conduct in an action against Swift but not in an action against the Union itself.

For the above reasons, it is obvious that the courts will be compelled to pass upon whether there has been a breach of the duty of fair representation in the context of many § 301 breach-of-contract actions. If a breach of duty by the union and a breach of contract by the employer are proven, the court must fashion an appropriate remedy. Presumably, in at least some cases, the union's breach of duty will have enhanced or contributed to the employee's injury. What possible sense could there be in a rule which would permit a court that has litigated the fault of employer and union to fashion a remedy only with respect to the employer? Under such a rule, either the employer would be compelled by the court to pay for the union's wrong—slight deterrence, indeed, to future union misconduct— or the injured employee would be forced to go to two tribunals to repair a single injury. Moreover, the Board would be compelled in many cases either to remedy injuries arising out of a breach of contract, a task which Congress has not assigned to it, or to leave the individual employee without remedy for the union's wrong.[12] Given the strong reasons for not pre-empting duty of fair representation suits in general, and the fact that the courts in many § 301 suits must adjudicate whether the union has breached its duty, we conclude that the courts may also fashion remedies for such a breach of duty. . . .

III

Petitioners contend, as they did in their motion for judgment notwithstanding the jury's verdict, that Owens failed to prove that the Union

---

[12]Assuming for the moment that Swift breached the collective bargaining agreement in discharging Owens and that the Union breached its duty in handling Owens' grievance, this case illustrates the difficulties that would result from a rule pre-empting the courts from remedying the Union's breach of duty. If Swift did not "participate" in the Union's unfair labor practice, the Board would have no jurisdiction to remedy Swift's breach of contract. Yet a Court might be equally unable to give Owens full relief in a § 301 suit against Swift. Should the court award damages against Swift for Owens' full loss, even if it concludes that part of that loss was caused by the Union's breach of duty? Or should it award Owens only

breached its duty of fair representation in its handling of Owens' grievance. Petitioners also argue that the Supreme Court of Missouri, in rejecting this contention, applied a standard that is inconsistent with governing principles of federal law with respect to the Union's duty to an individual employee in its processing of grievances under the collective bargaining agreement with Swift. We agree with both contentions.

. . . [T]he question which the Missouri Supreme Court thought dispositive of the issue of liability was whether the evidence supported Owens' assertion that he had been wrongfully discharged by Swift, regardless of the Union's good faith in reaching a contrary conclusion. This was also the major concern of the plaintiff at trial; the bulk of Owens' evidence was directed at whether he was medically fit at the time of discharge and whether he had performed heavy work after that discharge.

A breach of the statutory duty of fair representation occurs only when a union's conduct toward a member of the collective bargaining unit is arbitrary, discriminatory, or in bad faith. . . . There has been considerable debate over the extent of this duty in the context of a union's enforcement of the grievance and arbitration procedures in a collective bargaining agreement. . . . Some have suggested that every individual employee should have the right to have his grievance taken to arbitration. Others have urged that the Union be given substantial discretion (if the collective bargaining agreement so provides) to decide whether a grievance should be taken to arbitration, subject only to the duty to refrain from patently wrongful conduct such as racial discrimination or personal hostility.

Though we accept the proposition that a union may not arbitrarily ignore a meritorious grievance or process it in perfunctory fashion, we do not agree that the individual employee has an absolute right to have his grievance taken to arbitration regardless of the provisions of the applicable collective bargaining agreement. . . . In providing for a grievance and arbitration procedure which gives the union discretion to supervise the grievance machinery and to invoke arbitration, the employer and the union contemplate that each will endeavor in good faith to settle grievances short of arbitration. Through this settlement process, frivolous grievances are ended prior to the most costly and time-consuming step in the grievance procedures. Moreover, both sides are assured that similar complaints will be treated consistently, and major problem areas in the interpretation of the collective bargaining contract can be isolated and perhaps resolved. And finally, the settlement process furthers the interest of the union as statutory agent and as coauthor of the bargaining agreement in representing the employees in the enforcement of that agreement. . . .

If the individual employee could compel arbitration of his grievance regardless of its merit, the settlement machinery provided by the contract would be substantially undermined, thus destroying the employer's confi-

---

partial recovery hoping that the Board will make him whole? These remedy problems are difficult enough when one tribunal has all parties before it; they are impossible if two independent tribunals, with different procedures, time limitations, and remedial powers must participate.

dence in the union's authority and returning the individual grievant to the vagaries of independent and unsystematic negotiation. Moreover, under such a rule, a significantly greater number of grievances would proceed to arbitration.[15] This would greatly increase the cost of the grievance machinery and could so over-burden the arbitration process as to prevent it from functioning successfully. . . . It can well be doubted whether the parties to collective bargaining agreements would long continue to provide for detailed grievance and arbitration procedure of the kind encouraged by L.M.R.A. § 203(d), *supra*, if their power to settle the majority of grievances short of the costlier and more time-consuming steps was limited by a rule permitting the grievant unilaterally to invoke arbitration. Nor do we see substantial danger to the interests of the individual employee if his statutory agent is given the contractual power honestly and in good faith to settle grievances short of arbitration. For these reasons, we conclude that a union does not breach its duty of fair representation, and thereby open up a suit by the employee for breach of contract, merely because it settled the grievance short of arbitration.

For these same reasons, the standard applied here by the Missouri Supreme Court cannot be sustained. For if a union's decision that a particular grievance lacks sufficient merit to justify arbitration would constitute a breach of the duty of fair representation because a judge or jury later found the grievance meritorious, the union's incentive to settle such grievances short of arbitration would be seriously reduced. The dampening effect on the entire grievance procedure of this reduction of the union's freedom to settle claims in good faith would surely be substantial. Since the union's statutory duty of fair representation protects the individual employee from arbitrary abuses of the settlement device by providing him with recourse against both employer (in a § 301 suit) and union, this severe limitation on the power to settle grievances is neither necessary nor desirable. Therefore, we conclude that the Supreme Court of Missouri erred in upholding the verdict in this case solely on the ground that the evidence supported Owens' claim that he had been wrongfully discharged.

B. Applying the proper standard of union liability to the facts of this case, we cannot uphold the jury's award, for we conclude that as a matter of federal law the evidence does not support a verdict that the Union breached its duty of fair representation. . . .

. . . Having concluded that the individual employee has no absolute right to have his grievance arbitrated under the collective bargaining agreement at issue, and that a breach of the duty of fair representation is not established merely by proof that the underlying grievance was meritorious, we must conclude that that duty was not breached here.

---

[15]Under current grievance practices, an attempt is usually made to keep the number of arbitrated grievances to a minimum. An officer of the National Union testified in this case that only one of 967 grievances filed at all of Swift's plants between September and October 1963 was taken to arbitration. And the AFL-CIO *amicus* brief reveals similar performances at General Motors Company and United States Steel Corporation, two of the Nation's largest unionized employers; less than .05% of all written grievances filed during a recent period at General Motors required arbitration, while only 5.6% of the grievances processed beyond the first step at United States Steel were decided by an arbitrator.

IV

In our opinion, there is another important reason why the judgment of the Missouri Supreme Court cannot stand. Owens' suit against the Union was grounded on his claim that Swift had discharged him in violation of the applicable collective bargaining agreement. In his complaint, Owens alleged "that, as a direct result of said wrongful breach of said contract, by employer. . . . Plaintiff was damaged in the sum of Six Thousand, Five Hundred ($6,500.00) Dollars per year, continuing until the date of trial." For the Union's role in "preventing Plaintiff from completely exhausting administrative remedies," Owens requested, and the jury awarded, compensatory damages for the above-described breach of contract plus punitive damages of $3,000. R., at 6. We hold that such damages are not recoverable from the Union in the circumstances of this case.

The appropriate remedy for a breach of a union's duty of fair representation must vary with the circumstances of the particular breach. In this case, the employee's complaint was that the Union wrongfully failed to afford him the arbitration remedy against his employer established by the collective bargaining agreement. But the damages sought by Owens were primarily those suffered because of the employer's alleged breach of contract. Assuming for the moment that Owens had been wrongfully discharged, Swift's only defense to a direct action for breach of contract would have been the Union's failure to resort to arbitration, . . . and if that failure was itself a violation of the Union's statutory duty to the employee, there is no reason to exempt the employer from contractual damages which he would otherwise have had to pay. The difficulty lies in fashioning an appropriate scheme of remedies.

Petitioners urge that an employee be restricted in such circumstances to a decree compelling the employer and the union to arbitrate the underlying grievance. It is true that the employee's action is based on the employer's alleged breach of contract plus the union's alleged wrongful failure to afford him his contractual remedy of arbitration. For this reason, an order compelling arbitration should be viewed as one of the available remedies when a breach of the union's duty is proved. But we see no reason inflexibly to require arbitration in all cases. In some cases, for example, at least part of the employee's damages may be attributable to the union's breach of duty, and an arbitrator may have no power under the bargaining agreement to award such damages against the union. In other cases, the arbitrable issues may be substantially resolved in the course of trying the fair representation controversy. In such situations, the court should be free to decide the contractual claim and to award the employee appropriate damages or equitable relief.

A more difficult question is, what portion of the employee's damages may be charged to the union; in particular, may an award against a union include, as it did here, damages attributable solely to the employer's breach of contract? We think not. Though the union has violated a statutory duty in failing to press the grievance, it is the employer's unrelated breach of contract which triggered the controversy and which caused this portion of the employee's damages. The employee should have no difficulty recovering these damages from the employer, who cannot, as we have explained, hide behind the union's wrongful failure to act; in fact, the employer may be (and probably should be) joined as a defendant in the fair representation suit, as in *Humphrey* v. *Moore, supra.* It could be a real hardship on the union to pay these damages, even if the union were given a right of indemnification against the employer. With the employee assured of direct recovery from the employer, we see no merit in requiring the union to pay the employer's share of the damages.[18]

The governing principle, then, is to apportion liability between the employer and the union according to the damage caused by the fault of each. Thus, damages attributable solely to the employer's breach of contract should not be charged to the union, but increases if any in those damages caused by the union's refusal to process the grievance should not be charged to the employer. In this case, even if the Union had breached its duty, all or almost all of Owens' damages would still be attributable to his allegedly wrongful discharge by Swift. For these reasons, even if the Union here had properly been found liable for a breach of duty, it is clear that the damage award was improper.

Reversed.

MR. JUSTICE FORTAS, with whom THE CHIEF JUSTICE and MR. JUSTICE HARLAN join, concurring in the result.

1. In my view, a complaint by an employee that the union has breached its duty of fair representation is subject to the exclusive jurisdiction of the NLRB. It is a charge of unfair labor practice. [citations omitted] There is no basis for failure to apply the pre-emption principles in the present case, and, as I shall discuss, strong reason for its application. The relationship between the union and the individual employee with respect to the processing of claims to employment rights under the collective bargaining agreement is fundamental to the design and operation of federal labor law. It is not "merely peripheral," as the Court's opinion states. It "presents difficult problems of definition of status, problems which we have held are precisely 'of a kind most wisely entrusted initially to the agency charged with day-to-day administration of the Act as a whole.' " *Iron Workers* v. *Perko, supra,* 373 U.S., at 706. Accordingly, the judgment of the Supreme Court of Missouri should be reversed and the complaint dismissed for this reason and on this basis. I agree, however, that if it were assumed that jurisdiction of the subject matter exists, the judgment would still have to be reversed because of the use by the Missouri court of an

---

[18]We are not dealing here with situations where a union has affirmatively caused the employer to commit the alleged breach of contract. In cases of that sort where the union's conduct is found to be an unfair labor practice, the NLRB has found an unfair labor practice by the employer, too, and has held the union and the employer jointly and severally liable for any back pay found owing to the particular employee who was the subject of their joint discrimination. *E.g., Imparato Stevedoring Corp.,* 113 NLRB 883, 36 LRRM 1401 (1955); *Squirt Distrib. Co.,* 92 NLRB 1667, 27 LRRM 1303 (1951); *H. M. Newman,* 85 NLRB 725, 24 LRRM 1463 (1949). Even if this approach would be appropriate for analogous § 301 and breach-of-duty suits, it is not applicable here. Since the Union played no part in Swift's alleged breach of contract and since Swift took no part in the Union's alleged breach of duty, joint liability for each wrong would be unwarranted.

improper standard for measuring the union's duty, and the absence of evidence to establish that the union refused further to process Owens' grievance because of bad faith or arbitrarily.

. . .

3. If we look beyond logic and precedent to the policy of the labor relations design which Congress has provided, court jurisdiction of this type of action seems anomalous and ill-advised. We are not dealing here with the interpretation of a contract or with an alleged breach of an employment agreement. As the Court in effect acknowledges, we are concerned with the subtleties of a union's statutory duty faithfully to represent employees in the unit, including those who may not be members of the union. The Court—regrettably, in my opinion—ventures to state judgments as to the metes and bounds of the reciprocal duties involved in the relationship between the union and the employee. In my opinion, this is precisely and especially the kind of judgment that Congress intended to entrust to the Board and which is well within the preemption doctrine that this Court has prudently stated. . . . The nuances of union-employee and union-employer relationship are infinite and consequential, particularly when the issue is as amorphous as whether the union acted "in bad faith or arbitrarily" which the Court states as the standard applicable here. In all reason and in all good judgment, this jurisdiction should be left with the Board and not be placed in the courts, especially with the complex and necessarily confusing guidebook that the Court now publishes.

Accordingly, I join the judgment of reversal, but on the basis stated.

Mr. Justice Black, dissenting.

The Court today opens slightly the courthouse door to an employee's incidental claim against his union for breach of its duty of fair representation, only to shut it in his face when he seeks direct judicial relief for his underlying and more valuable breach-of-contract claim against his employer. This result follows from the Court's announcement in this case, involving an employee's suit against his union, of a new rule to govern an employee's suit against his employer. The rule is that before an employee can sue his employer under § 301 of the L.M.R.A. for a simple breach of his employment contract, the employee must prove not only that he attempted to exhaust his contractual remedies, but that his attempt to exhaust them was frustrated by "arbitrary, discriminatory or . . . bad faith" conduct on the part of his union. With this new rule and its result, I cannot agree.

. . .

. . . Today the Court holds that an employee with a meritorious claim has no absolute right to have it either litigated or arbitrated. Fearing that arbitrators would be overworked, the Court allows unions unilaterally to determine not to take a grievance to arbitration—the first step in the contract grievance procedure at which the claim would be presented to an impartial third party—as long as the union decisions are neither "arbitrary" nor "in bad faith." The Court derives this standard of conduct from a long line of cases holding that "a breach of the statutory duty of fair representation occurs only when the union's conduct toward a member of the collective bargaining unit is arbitrary, discriminatory, or in bad faith." What the Court overlooks is that those cases laid down this standard in the context of situations where the employee's sole or fundamental complaint was against the union. There was not the slightest hint in those cases that the same standard would apply where the employee's primary complaint was against his employer for breach of contract and where he only incidentally contended that the union's conduct prevented the adjudication, by either court or arbitrator, of the underlying grievance. . . . Either the employee should be able to sue his employer for breach of contract after having attempted to exhaust his contractual remedies, or the union should have an absolute duty to exhaust contractual remedies on his behalf. The merits of an employee's grievance would thus be determined by either a jury or an arbitrator. Under today's decision it will never be determined by either.

. . . I simply fail to see how the union's legitimate role as statutory agent is undermined by requiring it to prosecute all serious grievances to a conclusion or by allowing the injured employee to sue his employer after he has given his union a chance to act on his behalf.

Henceforth, in almost every § 301 breach-of-contract suit by an employee against an employer, the employee will have the additional burden of proving that the union acted "arbitrarily or in bad faith." The Court never explains what is meant by this vague phrase or how trial judges are intelligently to translate it to a jury. Must the employee prove that the union in fact acted arbitrarily, or will it be sufficient to show that the employee's grievance was so meritorious that a reasonable union would not have refused to carry it to arbitration? Must the employee join the union in his § 301 suit against the employer, or must he join the employer in his unfair representation suit against the union? However these questions are answered, today's decision, requiring the individual employee to take on both the employer and the union in every suit against the employer and to prove not only that the employer breached its contract, but that the union acted arbitrarily, converts what would otherwise be a simple breach-of-contract action into a three-ring donnybrook. It puts an intolerable burden on employees with meritorious grievances and means they will frequently be left with no remedy. Today's decision, while giving the worker an ephemeral right to sue his union for breach of its duty of fair representation, creates insurmountable obstacles to block his far more valuable right to sue his employer for breach of the collective bargaining agreement.

Notes

1. The union's good faith determination to forego arbitration does not necessarily indicate that the employees' otherwise legally cognizable Section 301 claim is without merit. Why, then, should the contractual claim be lost because of the union's decision not to arbitrate?

If the employer is entitled to rely on the union's good faith administration of the grievance process, why can the employer be sued when the union *does* breach the federal standard? Does any legitimate employer interest, or interest in effective grievance administration, turn on whether the union's decision not to arbitrate is made fairly?

Whose interests are served by this doctrine? What is the effect upon the union? Is the result likely to strengthen the union's discretion with regard to decisions on arbitration or, rather, to induce the union to arbitrate claims it would rather forego? The Court certainly did not intend the latter result. Indeed, the Court uses the fear of clogged grievance channels to deny employees the right to independently grieve or to sue the employer in the absence of a union breach of its duty.

Consider whether any alternative actually affects the incidence of grievance processing. The number of grievances employees file may turn on a variety of factors having nothing to do with law, such as the production process, changes in methods of production or supervision, or political infighting within the union. See A. Gouldner, Patterns of Industrial Bureaucracy (1954); Atleson, *Work Group Behavior and Wildcat Strikes: The Causes and Functions of Industrial Civil Disobedience*, 34 Ohio St. L.J. 751, 776–809 (1973). Union processing will be affected by a number of variables, including, but certainly not limited to, estimated cost and presumed merit. Unions are often accused of processing nonmeritorious grievances to avoid the charge of being "too soft" or having "sold out." See D. Jones, Arbitration and Industrial Discipline 127–142 (1961). On the other hand, of course, officers' images are not enhanced by a losing record. Will the result in *Vaca* affect any of these pressures? Would they be avoided by giving individual employees the right to arbitrate their own grievances where the union refuses to do so?

2. The most important legacy of *Vaca* is the Court's dictum stressing the crucial connection between an alleged breach of the duty of fair representation (DFR) when no arbitration has occurred and a Section 301 action. The result of *Vaca* is that the union's refusal to arbitrate must be arbitrary or in bad faith no matter who the employee sues, for the Court makes the union's DFR violation a condition precedent to the employee's contract action. The preemption issue was relevant since the NLRB had begun to enforce the duty of fair representation under Section 8(b)(1)(A). The Court, however, supplemented its holding that NLRB preemption did not exist by positing a situation where an employee sued the employer on contract grounds. It seems ironic that the Court's preemption discussion expresses concern that the employee have some forum to present a fair representation action, unrestricted by the discretionary power of the NLRB's General Counsel, yet makes the contract action depend upon the union's behavior which may be beyond the employee's control. Does this suggest that federal policy is more concerned with DFR actions than breach of contract claims? Are DFR claims, based upon the NLRA, more important than all other violations of the NLRA whch *are* subject to the General Counsel's discretion?

3. Few agreements provide that employees may invoke the grievance process or seek arbitration without union approval. The Court holds that Section 9(a) does not provide a right to use the grievance procedure irrespective of a contractual provision. What significance remains, then,

to the Section 9(a) proviso that employees may present grievances to their employer? See *Emporium Capwell Co.,* p. 353.

4. An important problem after *Vaca* is the extent to which the DFR will mandate standards of union performance. Consider the following situations:

(a) What burden is placed upon the union to investigate the facts of the dispute before deciding that no merit exists? Note the union's efforts in *Vaca.* Does the failure to investigate involve the "perfunctory" handling of grievances? Reconsider the Enderby problem, page 644, *supra.*

(b) The union agrees to arbitrate, but fails to process the claim within the contractual time period, and the employer insists on timely grievance processing. Assume that no personal hostility or bad faith can be proved. See *Schum* v. *South Buffalo Ry. Co.,* 496 F.2d 328, 86 LRRM 2459 (2d Cir. 1974).

Although grievance processing cannot be expected to be error free, some degree of integrity can be required. A clear division exists, however, as to the degree to which unions are to be excused for negligent behavior or inadequate representation when the union seemingly acts in good faith. Some courts require subjective bad faith, and reject any test based upon errors in judgment or the manner with which grievances are presented.

Recently, however, courts have been increasingly more willing to hold that arbitrary or substandard representation violates the standard despite the union's good faith and the absence of hostility. These decisions have found violations where grievances were negligently filed beyond contractual time limits, the arbitration presentation was inadequately prepared or presented, or where the union failed to investigate claims before declining to process them. See, *e.g., Figueroa de Arroyo* v. *Sindicato de Trabajadores Packinghouse,* 425 F.2d 281, 74 LRRM 2028 (1st Cir. 1970); *Griffin* v. *UAW,* 469 F.2d 181, 81 LRRM 2485 (4th Cir. 1972). But see, *Ruzicka* v. *General Motors Corp.,* 649 F.2d 1207, 107 LRRM 2726 (6th Cir. 1981). Do these holdings apply a tort standard of due care, or are these holdings merely cases of "perfunctory handling" of grievances cited in *Vaca* as violative of the duty? On the other hand, would such a holding "create an unacceptable high risk of collusion between union and employee, both of whom may share the ultimate goal of reinstatement of the employee"? *Hoffman* v. *Lanza,* 658 F.2d 519, 108 LRRM 2311 (7th Cir. 1981).

(c) An employee writes an article in a political newspaper criticizing both the union and the company. He is subsequently discharged for violating a company rule prohibiting false or malicious statements. The union agrees to grieve and, subsequently, to arbitrate the matter. The union's lawyer read the article for the first time shortly before the arbitration hearing was to begin. During the hearing, the attorney conceded the validity of the employer's rule and its validity under the First Amendment, although the company's production was overwhelmingly defense related and the federal government owned nearly all the land, building, machinery, and equipment. The union attorney also failed to object to the arbitrator's hostile and often offensive questioning, which frequently focused on the grievant's political beliefs.

The arbitrator denied the grievance, and plaintiff sued both his union and employer for breach of contract and violation of the duty of fair representation. Is the union liable? Will the award be overturned? See *Holodnak v. Avco Corp., Avco-Lycoming Div.*, 381 F. Supp. 191, 87 LRRM 2237 (D. Conn. 1974), *modified*, 514 F.2d 285, 88 LRRM 2950 (2d Cir. 1975).

(d) In many situations collective agreements specify which employees are to receive certain benefits, e.g., promotions, shift, or vacation preference, usually based on seniority. What is the union's duty in a situation in which its successful sponsorship of A's grievance will result in the loss of a promotion or other job advantage for B? Does B have a right to participate in the arbitration proceeding on A's grievance?

5. To what extent may the merits of plaintiff's grievance be considered in deciding the reasonableness of a union's decision not to arbitrate? Is it reasonable to interpret *Vaca* to mean that the merits of the individual's claim are always irrelevant? See Levy, *The Collective Bargaining Agreement as a Limitation on Union Control of Employee Grievances*, 118 U. Pa. L. Rev. 1036 (1970). The Fourth Circuit has stated that "proof of a grievance's merit is circumstantial evidence that the failure to process the claim constituted bad faith." *Harrison* v. *UTU*, 530 F.2d 558, 561, 90 LRRM 3265, 3268 (1975). See also, *Price* v. *Teamsters*, 457 F.2d 605, 80 LRRM 2636 (3d Cir. 1972). Is this a sound approach? Is this approach consistent with the holding in *Vaca* that the jury could not base Owens' recovery on a finding that he had been wrongfully discharged?

6. Do the policies inherent in *Vaca* permit a union to refuse to arbitrate a grievance which is admittedly valid? Clearly, there are situations in which a union might reasonably feel that the individual's interest is outweighed by group or institutional interests. The Court's stress on the need for economy and efficiency of the grievance process could suggest that even meritorious grievances can be validly rejected in certain circumstances.

(a) L. Sayles and G. Strauss, in The Local Union (rev. ed. 1967), describe some situations in which grievances were not processed despite their acknowledged merit. In one situation the union declined to grieve because a wage increase, although contractually required, would "take the pressure off" the company in forthcoming negotiations to grant a general wage increase for the entire department. *Id.*, 41. In a second situation, the gain to one group of employees, the grievants, would have been at the direct expense of another group of employees, *Id.*, 28. The grinding and cutting departments could perform roughly the same work. During a decline in business, grinders' work was transferred to cutters, resulting in layoffs and a grievance by grinders.

(b) The union acknowledges the probable validity of grievant's claim that she is due $17.50 on a management mistake on overtime, although management rejects the notion. The problem is not likely to recur, however, and arbitration, the next step, would cost the union approximately $500. See *Curth* v. *Faraday, Inc.*, 401 F. Supp. 678, 90 LRRM 2735 (E.D. Mich. 1975).

7. Professor Summers' argument rests upon the belief that employees have a contractual right under Section 301 to sue for violations of the collective agreement. Professor Feller has argued that this position, partially accepted in *Vaca*, rests upon an erroneous view of the agreement. Between employer and employee, he argues, no contractual obligations exist. Rather, he argues, the agreement sets out the rules of the workplace, rules which are only enforceable through the grievance procedure. The employees' only claim is to the use of that procedure, which is enforceable through a fair representation action against the union to compel it to employ the grievance process. See Feller, *A General Theory of the Collective Bargaining Agreement*, 61 Calif. L. Rev. 663, 774–817 (1973).

8. If the union decides to process the grievance, should it as a policy matter have the power to settle or compromise individual claims if based upon a good faith effort to protect or promote group interests, even to the prejudice of individual grievants? This approach would view the union as fiduciary for group interests but not necessarily for an individual employee. It is probable that most unions assume they possess this power and that most contracting parties intend to grant the union this power under the grievance process. If so, how much weight should be given to these expectations?

Is an approach more favorable to individual interests likely to change union behavior or employee and union assumptions? How threatened would the grievance process be by such an approach? The DFR, it should be remembered, stems from Section 9(a) of the Act, and was created to protect minority interests. Consider these situations:

(a) When the agreement expired, a backlog of 60 grievances existed. Most concerned the proper allocation of overtime, and a few involved disciplinary discharges. Negotiations on a successor agreement stalled, and a strike ensued. Eventually, a new agreement was reached on condition that the unresolved grievances would be "washed out." The union and a majority of its members agreed on this bargain.

(b) What if grievances are traded for satisfactory resolution of other grievances? The union agrees to drop A's grievance in exchange for a satisfactory resolution of B's. See *Harrison* v. *UTU*, 530 F.2d 558, 90 LRRM 3265 (4th Cir. 1975); *Local 13, ILWU* v. *PMA*, 441 F.2d 1061, 77 LRRM 2160 (9th Cir. 1971) ("The deliberate sacrifice of a particular employee as a consideration for other objectives must be a concession that the union cannot make.")

9. The Court suggests that the union's failure to arbitrate will not foreclose the employee's contract action in some situations. A common exception to the exhaustion of remedies doctrine is futility. Could such an excuse even be relevant in an employee's contract action? See, *e.g.*, *Glover* v. *St. Louis-San Francisco Ry. Co.*, 393 U.S. 324, 70 LRRM 2097 (1969).

Under the Railway Labor Act, employees have the statutory right to appeal adverse employer actions to the Railway Adjustment Board. See 45 U.S.C. Section 153; *Andrews* v. *Louisville & Nashville Ry. Co.*, 406 U.S. 320, 80 LRRM 2240 (1972). Unlike the *Vaca* situation, then, an employee's failure to exhaust remedies under the RLA is personal. What if the employee is unaware that a statutory right of appeal exists? If the union assures the employee that it will appeal, but negligently fails to process the appeal within the statutory time period, should the employee's reliance on union action excuse the failure to exhaust? Does this case involve considerations not present in *Vaca*? See *Schum* v. *South Buffalo Ry. Co.*, 496 F.2d 328, 86 LRRM 2459 (2d Cir. 1974); *Ruzicka* v. *General Motors Corp.*, 523 F.2d 306, 90 LRRM 2497 (6th Cir. 1975).

10. Should an employee, as a condition to a DFR action, be required to exhaust internal union appeal procedures? Many courts have required exhaustion, which must rest on notions about inherent judicial power and a policy favoring private resolution of disputes. If the union has refused to process plaintiff's grievance, and a DFR action is a condition precedent to a Section 301 action against the employer, what is served by another layer of exhaustion? Consider the following decision.

Clayton v. Automobile Workers

Supreme Court of the United States, 1981
451 U.S. 679, 107 LRRM 2385

[The plaintiff brought an action alleging that the union violated its duty of fair representation by failing to arbitrate the plaintiff's grievance and that the employer breached the agreement by discharging him without just cause. Plaintiff sought reinstatement from the employer and monetary relief from both defendants. Plaintiff did not file a timely internal union appeal from his local's determination not to seek arbitration of his grievance. The court of appeals held that the failure to pursue internal union appeals procedures was fatal to the plaintiff's claim against the union but did not bar his action against the employer because the internal appeals procedure could not result in either reinstatement or reactivation of his grievance. The Supreme Court held that "where an internal union appeals procedure cannot result in reactivation of the employee's grievance or an award of the complete relief sought in his § 301 suit, exhaustion will not be required with respect to either the suit against the employer or the suit against the union."]

BRENNAN, J.:

. . .

. . . Clayton's employer and union contend that exhaustion of the UAW procedures, like exhaustion of contractual grievance and arbitration procedures, will further national labor policy and should be required as a matter of federal common law. Their argument, in brief, is that an exhaustion requirement will enable unions to regulate their internal affairs without undue judicial interference and that it will also promote the broader goal of encouraging private resolution of disputes arising out of a collective-bargaining agreement.

We do not agree that the policy of forestalling judicial interference with internal union affairs is applicable to this case.[13] This policy has been strictly limited to disputes arising over *internal* union matters such as those involving the interpretation and application of a union constitution. . . . Here Clayton's dispute against his union is based upon an alleged breach of the union's duty of fair representation. This allegation raises issues rooted in statutory policies extending far beyond internal union interests. . . .

Our analysis, then, focuses on that aspect of national labor policy that encourages private rather than judicial resolution of disputes arising over collective-bargaining agreements. Concededly, a requirement that aggrieved employees exhaust internal remedies might lead to nonjudicial resolution of some contractual grievances. For example, an employee who exhausts internal union procedures might decide not to pursue his § 301 action in court, either because the union offered him a favorable settlement, or because it demonstrated that his underlying contractual claim was without merit. However, we decline to impose a universal exhaustion requirement lest employees with meritorious § 301 claims be forced to exhaust themselves and their resources by submitting their claims to potentially lengthy internal union procedures that may not be adequate to redress their underlying grievances.

. . . [C]ourts have discretion to decide whether to require exhaustion of internal union procedures. In exercising this discretion, at least three factors should be relevant: first, whether union officials are so hostile to the employee that he could not hope to obtain a fair hearing on his claim; second, whether the internal union appeals procedures would be inadequate either to reactivate the employee's grievance or to award him the full relief he seeks under § 301; and third, whether exhaustion of internal procedures would unreasonably delay the employee's opportunity to obtain a judicial hearing on the merits of his claim. If any of these factors are found to exist, the court may properly excuse the employee's failure to exhaust.

Clayton has not challenged the finding of the lower courts that the UAW internal appeals procedures are fair and reasonable. He concedes that he could have received an impartial hearing on his claim had he exhausted the internal union procedures. . . . Accordingly, our inquiry turns to the second factor, whether the relief available through the union's internal appeals procedures is adequate.

In his suit under § 301, Clayton seeks reinstatement from his employer and monetary relief from both his employer and his union. Although the UAW Constitution does not indicate on its face what relief is available through the internal union appeals procedures, the parties have stipulated that the Public Review Board can award backpay in an appropriate

---

[13]This policy has its statutory roots in § 101(a)(4) of the Landrum-Griffin Act, 29 U.S.C. § 411(a)(4), which is part of the subchapter of the Act entitled "Bill of Rights of Members of Labor Organizations." Section 101(a)(4) provides:

"No labor organization shall limit the right of any member thereof to institute an action in any court, . . . *Provided,* That any such member may be required to exhaust reasonable hearing procedures (but not to exceed a four-month lapse of time) within such organization, before instituting legal . . . proceedings against such organizations or any officer thereof.

case. . . . It is clear, then, that at least some monetary relief may be obtained through the internal appeals procedure.[17]

It is equally clear that the union can neither reinstate Clayton in his job, nor reactivate his grievance. Article IX of the collective-bargaining agreement between Local 509 and ITT Gilfillan provides that the union may obtain arbitration of a grievance only if it gives "notice . . . to the Company in writing within fifteen (15) working days after the date of the Company's decision at Step 3 of the Grievance Procedure." By the time Clayton learned of his union's decision not to pursue the grievance to arbitration, this 15-day time limit had expired. Accordingly, the union could not have demanded arbitration even if the internal appeal had shown Clayton's claim to be meritorious. The union was bound by its earlier decision not to pursue Clayton's grievance past the third stage of the grievance and arbitration procedure.[18] For the reasons that follow, we conclude that these restrictions on the relief available through the internal UAW procedures render those procedures inadequate.[19]

Where internal union appeals procedures can result in either complete relief to an aggrieved employee or reactivation of his grievance, exhaustion would advance the national labor policy of encouraging private resolution of contractual labor disputes. In such cases, the internal union procedures are capable of fully resolving meritorious claims short of the judicial forum. Thus, if the employee received the full relief he requested through internal procedures, his § 301 action would become moot, and he would not be entitled to a judicial hearing. Similarly, if the employee obtained reactivation of his grievance through internal union procedures, the policies underlying *Republic Steel* would come into play, and the employee would be required to submit his claim to the collectively-bargained dispute-resolution procedures.[21] In either case, exhaustion of internal remedies could result in final resolution of the employee's contractual grievance through private rather than judicial avenues.

By contrast, where an aggrieved employee cannot obtain either the substantive relief he seeks or reactivation of his grievance, national labor policy would not be served by requiring exhaustion of internal remedies. In such cases, exhaustion would be a useless gesture: it would delay

---

[17]The record does not indicate whether this monetary relief includes backpay only, or whether it also may include prospective monetary relief and incidental or punitive damages, relief that Clayton is apparently seeking in his § 301 action.

[18] . . .

Although most collective-bargaining agreements contain similarly strict time limits for seeking arbitration of grievances, there are some exceptions. The UAW informs us that "[s]ome employers and unions have, through collective bargaining, agreed to allow the reinstatement of withdrawn grievances where a union tribunal reverses the union's initial decision. This is true, for example, in the current UAW contracts with the major automobile and agricultural implement manufacturers." UAW Brief 18, n. 40. In such cases, the relief available through the union's internal appeal procedures would presumably be adequate.

[19]Accordingly, we need not discuss the third factor, whether exhaustion of the union's otherwise adequate internal appeals procedures would unreasonably delay the employee's opportunity to obtain a judicial hearing on the merits of his claim.

[21]In addition, by reactivating the grievance, the union might be able to rectify the very wrong of which the employee complains—a breach of the duty of fair representation caused by the union's refusal to seek arbitration—and the employee would then be unable to satisfy the precondition to a § 301 suit against the employer.

judicial consideration of the employee's § 301 action, but would not eliminate it. The employee would still be required to pursue judicial means to obtain the relief he seeks under § 301. Moreover, exhaustion would not lead to significant savings in judicial resources, because regardless of the outcome of the internal appeal, the employee would be required to prove *de novo* in his § 301 suit that the union breached its duty of fair representation and that the employer breached the collective-bargaining agreement. . . .

In reliance upon the Court of Appeals' opinion in this case, the UAW contends that even if exhaustion is not required with respect to the employer, it should be required with respect to the union, because the relief Clayton seeks *against the union* in his § 301 suit is available through internal union procedures. We disagree. While this argument might have force where the employee has chosen to bring his § 301 suit only against the union, the defense should not be available where, as here, the employee has filed suit against both the union and the employer. A trial court requiring exhaustion with respect to the suit against the union, but not with respect to the suit against the employer, would be faced with two undesirable alternatives. If it stayed the action against the employer pending resolution of the internal appeals procedures, it would effectively be requiring exhaustion with respect to the suit against the employer, a result we have held would violate national labor policy. Yet if it permitted the action against the employer to proceed, and tolled the running of the statute of limitations in the suit against the union until the internal procedures had been exhausted, it could very well find itself with two separate § 301 suits, based on the same facts, proceeding at different paces in its courtroom. As we suggested in *Vaca* v. *Sipes*, this is a result that should be avoided if possible. The preferable approach is for the court to permit the employee's § 301 action to proceed against both defendants, despite the employee's failure to exhaust, unless the internal union procedures can reactivate the grievance or grant the relief that would be available in the employee's § 301 suit against both defendants.

III

. . .

In this case, the internal union appeals panels cannot reactivate Clayton's grievance and cannot grant Clayton the reinstatement relief he seeks under § 301. We therefore hold that Clayton should not have been required to exhaust internal union appeals procedures prior to bringing suit against his union and employer under § 301.

Affirmed in part, reversed in part.

JUSTICE POWELL, with whom THE CHIEF JUSTICE joins, dissenting:
. . .
. . . I would hold that in the circumstances of this case no issue concerning the breach of the union's statutory duty of fair representation properly can be said to arise *at all*. The union has not made a final determination whether to pursue arbitration on Clayton's behalf. Clayton should

not be able to claim a breach of duty by the union until the union has had a full opportunity to make this determination. No such opportunity exists until Clayton exhausts the procedures available for resolving that question. Thus, as Clayton cannot claim a breach of duty by the union, he cannot bring a breach of contract suit under § 301 against his employer.

In my view, the asserted distinction in a tripartite case such as this one between contractual and internal union remedies, is immaterial. The situation presented in this case is well within the doctrine, underlying *Republic Steel Corp.* v. *Maddox*, 379 U.S. 650 (1965), that employees must pursue all procedures established for determining whether a union will go forward with a grievance. . . .

JUSTICE REHNQUIST, with whom THE CHIEF JUSTICE, JUSTICE STEWART and JUSTICE POWELL join, dissenting:

. . .

. . .[N]o prior case of this Court has held that exhaustion should not be required unless the internal union remedies can provide all the substantive relief requested or reactivation of the grievance. The principal difficulty with the Court's opinion lies in its framing of this second criterion which reflects much too narrow a view of the purposes of the exhaustion defense and the benefits which will likely result from requiring exhaustion in a case where a union has established a means for reviewing the manner in which it has represented an employee during a grievance.

The exhaustion of intraunion remedies, even where those remedies cannot provide reinstatement or reactivation of a grievance, does promote private resolution of labor disputes. Resort to the intraunion appeals procedures provides the union with its first opportunity to focus on the issue of fair representation—as opposed to the alleged breach of the collective-bargaining agreement. Resort to the union appeals procedures gives the union an opportunity to satisfy the employee that its decision not to pursue a grievance was correct. If successful on this score, litigation is averted. Where a union determines through its appeals procedure that it mishandled an employee's grievance, litigation may also be averted because at that point both the union and the employer have a strong incentive to pursue private resolution of the grievance. Even where a collective-bargaining agreement does not provide for reactivation of a grievance, it is reasonable to assume that many employers, when confronted with both a determination by a union that it had breached its duty of fair representation and the immediate prospect of an employee commencing litigation, would seriously consider voluntarily reactivating the grievance procedure to avoid the additional burden and costs of litigation. Should litigation nonetheless occur, exhaustion may well have narrowed the factual and legal issues to be decided and thus result in a savings of judicial resources. A fact that should also not be discounted is that the conscientious handling by a union of an employee's intraunion appeal cannot help but enhance the union's prestige with its employees. Cf. *Republic Steel Corp.* v. *Maddox*, 379 U.S. 650, 653 (1965). Exhaustion promotes union democracy and self-government as well as the broader policy of non-interference with internal union affairs. A union's incentive to maintain internal procedures which provide substantial procedural protection and which can afford significant substantive relief will be greatly undermined if an employee can simply bypass the procedures at will.

The error in the Court's analysis results in part from its apparent belief that intraunion remedies must provide a complete substitute for either the courts or the contract grievance procedure in order to be deemed "adequate." The purpose of intraunion remedies, however, is quite different. These remedies are provided to facilitate or encourage the private resolution of disputes, not to be a complete substitute for the courts. Intraunion remedies can serve this purpose so long as they have the capacity to address whether the union wrongfully handled the grievance. Obviously, if a union appeals procedure cannot address this question, exhaustion should not be required.

An additional question which is also of great importance is whether a union should ever be found to have breached its duty of fair representation where a union member shuns an appeals procedure which is both mandated by the union constitution and established for the purpose of allowing the union to satisfy its duty of fair representation. It seems to me not at all unreasonable to say that a union should have the right to require its members to give it the first opportunity to correct its own mistakes. . . .

Section 101(a)(4) reflects what I believe to be the reasonable compromise Congress reached when trying to balance two somewhat competing interests—furtherance of the national labor policy in favor of private resolution of disputes on the one hand and the desire not to unduly burden or "exhaust" an individual employee with time-consuming procedures on the other. It is fair to say that § 101(a)(4) represents Congress' judgment that limiting access to the courts for at least 4 months is not an unreasonable price to pay in exchange for the previously mentioned benefits exhaustion may provide.

The language of § 101(a)(4) also goes a long way to satisfy the third prong of the test set forth by the Court today. Exhaustion of internal union procedures should not be required where such would unreasonably delay an employee's opportunity to obtain a judicial hearing on the merits of his claim. Intraunion procedures which take years to complete serve no worthwhile purpose in the overall scheme of promoting the prompt and private resolution of claims. But a requirement that an employee not be permitted to go to court without first having pursued an intraunion appeal for at least 4 months does substantially further this national labor policy without placing any unfair burden on an employee. As such, I think all interested parties would be well served by a requirement that employees exhaust their intraunion procedures for this limited period of time prescribed by Congress.

Damages in DFR Cases

In *Czosek* v. *O'Mara*, 397 U.S. 25, 73 LRRM 2481 (1970), furloughed employees brought an action against a railroad and their union, alleging a wrongful discharge by the company under the Railway Labor Act, and a breach of duty of fair representation by the union. The Supreme Court affirmed a dismissal of the complaint against the railroad for failure to exhaust administrative remedies under the Act, subject to an amendment of the complaint on remand to allege that the company was somehow implicated in the union's alleged discrimination. In response to union fears that it would be held liable for all damages suffered by the employees, the Supreme Court said that

". . .judgment against petitioners can in any event be had only for those damages which flowed from their own conduct. Assuming a wrongful discharge by the employer independent of any discriminatory refusal by the union to process grievances based on the discharge, damages against the union for loss of employment are unrecoverable except to the extent that its refusal to handle the grievances added to the difficulty and expense of collecting from the employer."

Despite the language in *Czosek* v. *O'Mara*, the Court in a recent 5-4 decision held that the employer is only liable for back pay that accrues *prior* to a hypothetical date upon which an arbitrator would have issued an award had the union taken the dispute to arbitration. *Bowen* v. *United States Postal Service*, 51 USLW 4051, 459 U.S. 212, 112 LRRM 2281 (1983). A union which fails to take a grievance to arbitration and thereby breaches its duty is primarily liable for all damages after this time. The employer remains liable, but only secondarily. Many prior appellate courts had read the language and meaning of both *Vaca* and *Czosek* to mean that unions which breached their obligations by refusing to proceed to arbitration are only liable to the extent that misconduct "add[s] to the difficulty and expense of collecting from the employer."

The heart of the Court's rationale is as follows:

"Although each party participates in the grievance procedure, the union plays a pivotal role in the process since it assumes the responsibility of determining whether to press an employee's claims. The employer, for its part, must rely on the union's decision not to pursue an employee's grievance. For the union acts as the employee's exclusive representative in the grievance procedure, as it does in virtually all matters involving the terms and conditions of employment. Just as a nonorganized employer may accept an employee's waiver of any challenge to his discharge as a final resolution of the matter, so should an organized employer be able to rely on a comparable waiver by the employee's exclusive representative.

"There is no unfairness to the union in this approach. By seeking and acquiring the exclusive right and power to speak for a group of employees, the union assumes a corresponding duty to discharge that responsibility faithfully—a duty which it owes to the employees whom it represents and on which the employer with whom it bargains may rely. When the union, as the exclusive agent of the employee, waives arbitration or fails to seek review of an adverse decision, the employer should be in substantially the same position as if the employee had had the right to act on his own behalf and had done so. Indeed, if the employer could not rely on the union's decision, the grievance procedure would not provide the 'uniform and exclusive method for [the] orderly settlement of employee grievances,' which the Court has recognized is essential to the national labor policy.[15]

"The principle announced in *Vaca* reflects this allocation of responsibilities in the grievance procedure—a procedure that contemplates that both employer and union will perform their respective obligations. In the absence of damages apportionment where the default of both parties contributes to the employee's injury, incentives to comply with the grievance procedure will be diminished. Indeed, imposing total liability solely on the employer could well affect the willingness of employer to agree to arbitration clauses as they are customarily written.

"Nor will requiring the union to pay damages impose a burden on the union inconsistent with national labor policy. It will provide an additional incentive for the union to process its members' claims where warranted. This is wholly consistent with a union's interest. It is a duty owed to its members as well as consistent with the union's commitment to the employer under the arbitration clause."

The effect of *Bowen* is that the union's misconduct not only removes the Court-imposed bar to a Section 301 action against the employer, but also effectively "insulates the employer from further backpay liability" even if the union's misconduct is totally unrelated to the decision to discharge the employee. In what way does the employer rely on a union's decision *not* to process a grievance? Does an employer open itself up to open-ended liability whenever it discharges an employee? Why are employees not retained on the job until an arbitration proceeding is held?

What effect will this holding have on a union's decision whether to proceed to arbitration? If the dissenters are correct in believing that unions will be motivated to "take many unmeritorious grievances to arbitration simply to avoid exposure to the new breach-of-duty liability," does the result not conflict with the policy basis of *Vaca*? What is the reason for treating the union's breach of its duty as terminating, at least as far as

---

[15]Under the dissent's analysis, the employer may not rely on the union's decision not to pursue a grievance. Rather it can prevent continued liability only by reinstating the discharged employee. . . . This leaves the employer with a dubious option: it must either reinstate the employee promptly or leave itself exposed to open-ended liability. If this were the rule, the very purpose of the grievance procedure would be defeated. It is precisely to provide the exclusive means of resolving this kind of dispute that the parties agree to such a procedure and national labor policy strongly encourages its use. . . .

"When the union has breached its duty of fair representation, the dissent justifies its rule by arguing that "only the employer ha[s] the continuing ability to right the wrong by reinstating" the employee, an ability that the union lacks. . . . But an employer has no way of knowing that a failure to carry a grievance to arbitration constitutes a breach of duty. Rather than rehiring, as the dissent suggests, the employer reasonably could assume that the union had concluded the discharge was justified. The union would have the option, if it realized it had committed an arguable breach of duty, to bring its default to the employer's attention. Our holding today would not prevent a jury from taking such action into account. . . .

"Moreover, the rule urged by the dissenting opinion would allow the union and the employee, once the case goes to trial, to agree to a settlement pursuant to which the union would acknowledge a breach of its duty of fair representation in exchange for the employee's undertaking to look to his employer for his entire recovery. Although we may assume that this would not occur frequently, the incentive the dissent's rule would provide to agree to such a settlement demonstrates its unsoundness."

primary liability is concerned, the employer's liability for a wrongful discharge? The heart of the employee's action, after all, is the attempt to retain a job, and the action against the union is undertaken only because *Vaca* requires it.

What types of damages can be secured? Attorneys' fees? Mental distress? See *Harrison* v. *UTU*, 530 F.2d 558, 90 LRRM 3265 (4th Cir. 1975) (attorneys' fees); *Richardson* v. *CWA*, 443 F.2d 974, 77 LRRM 2566 (8th Cir. 1971) (mental stress).

In *IBEW* v. *Foust*, 442 U.S. 42, 101 LRRM 2365 (1979), the Supreme Court held that punitive damages may not be awarded against a union which breaches its duty of fair representation. The union had failed to file a timely grievance after plaintiff's discharge for failing to properly request an extension of a medical leave of absence. A jury awarded plaintiff $40,000 in damages and $75,000 in punitive damages. The court, in an opinion by Justice Marshall, held that "punitive damages could impair the financial stability of unions and unsettle the careful balance of individual and collective interests which this Court has previously articulated in the unfair representation area." In addition, the Court noted that the possibility of punitive damages might deter unions from screening out frivolous claims or making fair settlements. Four members of the Court objected to the creation of a *per se* rule in the context of a case in which the union's conduct was only negligent, preferring to permit such damages to be awarded for egregious conduct. Has *Foust* now been undercut by *Bowen?*

The difficulty of securing DFR damages against a union makes it more incumbent upon an employee's attorney to bring an action against the employer. It is foreseeable, then, that pressure will be created to expand the "excuses" allowed under *Vaca* in order to expand the permissible range of Section 301 actions against employers.

The result of *Vaca* is that employees must bring actions against their union and employer when no arbitration has occurred, often before a jury, and perhaps in state court. Does this solution adequately meet the federal interests in fair representation? In efficient grievance processing? Would interests be better served by reading Section 9(a) to give individuals the right to grieve irrespective of union desires?

Hines v. Anchor Motor Freight, Inc.

Supreme Court of the United States, 1976
424 U.S. 554, 91 LRRM 2481

[The facts in the previous Enderby problem are loosely based on an actual case. After nine years, the Supreme Court resolved one of the issues in this dispute in *Hines* v. *Anchor Motor Freight Inc., i.e.,* whether a Section 301 action can be maintained against the employer when the discharges were upheld in arbitration but plaintiffs challenge the fairness of their union's representation in the arbitration proceeding.

[The relevant portions of the decision follow.]

MR. JUSTICE WHITE delivered the opinion of the Court.

The issue here is whether a suit against an employer by employees asserting breach of a collective-bargaining contract was properly dismissed where the accompanying complaint against the union for breach of duty of fair representation has withstood the union's motion for summary judgment and remains to be tried.

. . .

Section 301 of the Labor Management Relations Act, 29 U.S.C. § 185, provides for suits in the district courts for violation of collective-bargaining contracts between labor organizations and employers without regard to the amount in controversy. This provision reflects the interest of Congress in promoting "a higher degree of responsibility upon the parties to such agreements. . . ." S. Rep. No. 105, 80th Cong., 1st Sess., 17 (1947). The strong policy favoring judicial enforcement of collective-bargaining contracts was sufficiently powerful to sustain the jurisdiction of the district courts over enforcement suits even though the conduct involved was arguably or would amount to an unfair labor practice within the jurisdiction of the National Labor Relations Board. . . . Section 301 contemplates suits by and against individual employees as well as between unions and employers; and contrary to earlier indications § 301 suits encompass those seeking to vindicate "uniquely personal" rights of employees such as wages, hours, overtime pay, and wrongful discharge. *Smith* v. *Evening News Ass'n* [371 U.S. 195] at 198–200 (1962). Petitioners' present suit against the employer was for wrongful discharge and is the kind of case Congress provided for in § 301.

Collective-bargaining contracts, however, generally contain procedures for the settlement of disputes, through mutual discussion and arbitration. These provisions are among those which are to be enforced under § 301. Furthermore, Congress has specified in § 203(d), 61 Stat. 154, 29 U.S.C. § 173(d), that "[f]inal adjustment by a method agreed upon by the parties is declared to be the desirable method for settlement of grievance disputes. . . ." This congressional policy "can be effectuated only if the means chosen by the parties for settlement of their differences under a collective-bargaining agreement is given full play." [*United*] *Steelworkers* v. *American Mfg. Co.*, 363 U.S. 564, 566 (1960). Courts are not to usurp those functions which collective-bargaining contracts have properly "entrusted to the arbitration tribunal." *Id.*, at 569. They should not undertake to review the merits of arbitration awards but should defer to the tribunal chosen by the parties finally to settle their disputes. Otherwise "plenary review by a court of the merits would make meaningless the provisions that the arbitrator's decision is final, for in reality it would almost never be final." *United Steelworkers* v. *Enterprise Corp.*, 363 U.S. 593, 599 (1960).

Pursuant to this policy, we later held that an employee could not sidestep the grievance machinery provided in the contract and that unless he attempted to utilize the contractual procedures for settling his dispute with his employer, his independent suit against the employer in the District Court would be dismissed. *Republic Steel Corp.* v. *Maddox*, 379 U.S. 650 (1965). *Maddox* nevertheless distinguished the situation where "the

union refuses to press or only perfunctorily presses the individual's claim.
. . . See *Humphrey* v. *Moore*, 375 U.S. 335; *Labor Board* v. *Miranda Fuel Co.*,
326 F.2d 132." [*Maddox*, 379 U.S. at 652] (footnote omitted).

The reservation in *Maddox* was well advised. The federal labor laws, in
seeking to strengthen the bargaining position of the average worker in an
industrial economy, provided for the selection of collective-bargaining
agents with wide authority to negotiate and conclude collective-bargaining agreements on behalf of all employees in appropriate units, as well as
to be the employee's agent in the enforcement and administration of the
contract. Wages, hours, working conditions, seniority and job security
therefore become the business of certified or recognized bargaining
agents, as did the contractual procedures for the processing and settling
of grievances, including those with respect to discharge.

Even though under *Vaca* the employer may not insist on exhaustion of
grievance procedures when the union has breached its representation
duty, it is urged that when the procedures have been followed and a
decision favorable to the employer announced, the employer must be
protected from relitigation by the express contractual provision declaring
a decision to be final and binding. We disagree. The union's breach of
duty relieves the employee of an express or implied requirement that
disputes be settled through contractual grievance procedures; if it
seriously undermines the integrity of the arbitral process the union's
breach also removes the bar of the finality provisions of the contract.

It is true that *Vaca* dealt with a refusal by the union to process a
grievance. It is also true that where the union actually utilizes the grievance and arbitration procedures on behalf of the employee, the focus is
no longer on the reasons for the union's failure to act but on whether,
contrary to the arbitrator's decision, the employer breached the contract
and whether there is substantial reason to believe that a union breach of
duty contributed to the erroneous outcome of the contractual proceedings. But the judicial remedy in *Humphrey* v. *Moore* was sought after the
adverse decision of the joint arbitration committee. Our conclusion in
that case was not that the committee's decision was unreviewable. On the
contrary, we proceeded on the basis that it was reviewable and vulnerable
if tainted by breach of duty on the part of the union, even though the
employer had not conspired with the union. The joint committee's decision was held binding on the complaining employees only after we determined that the union had not been guilty of malfeasance and that its
conduct was within the range of acceptable performance by a collective-
bargaining agent, a wholly unnecessary determination if the union's
conduct was irrelevant to the finality of the arbitral process.[9]

---

[9]*Czosek* v. *O'Mara*, 397 U.S. 25 (1970), which arose under the Railway Labor Act, 44 Stat.
577, as amended, 45 U.S.C. § 151 *et seq.*, involved a claim that a railroad had wrongfully
deprived plaintiff of his seniority and that the union had failed in its duty to protest. The suit
against the union was sustained by the Court of Appeals, but dismissal of the claim against
the railroad was affirmed absent allegation that the company had participated in the union's
breach. In affirming the judgment we upheld the Court of Appeals' ruling against the
union, but did not reach the question whether the railroad was properly dismissed over the
employee's objections, since the latter did not challenge the judgment in this respect.

In *Vaca* "we accept[ed] the proposition that a union may not arbitrarily ignore a meritorious grievance or process it in a perfunctory fashion," 386 U.S., at 191, and our ruling that the union had not breached its duty of fair representation in not pressing the employee's case to the last step of the grievance process stemmed from our evaluation of the manner in which the union had handled the grievance in its earlier stages. Although "the union might well have breached its duty had it ignored [the employee's] complaint or had it processed the grievance in a perfunctory manner," "the Union conclude[d] that arbitration would be fruitless and that the grievance should be dismissed" only after it had "processed the grievance into the fourth step, attempted to gather sufficient evidence to prove [the employee's] case, attempted to secure for [him] less vigorous work at the plant, and joined in the employer's efforts to have [him] rehabilitated." *Id.*, at 914.

Anchor would have it that petitioners are foreclosed from judicial relief unless some blameworthy conduct on its part disentitles it to rely on the finality rule. But it was Anchor that originated the discharges for dishonesty. If those charges were in error, Anchor has surely played its part in precipitating this dispute. Of course, both courts below held there were no facts suggesting that Anchor either knowingly or negligently relied on false evidence. As far as the record reveals it also prevailed before the joint committee after presenting its case in accordance with what were ostensibly wholly fair procedures. Nevertheless there remains the question whether the contractual protection against relitigating an arbitral decision binds employees who assert that the process has fundamentally malfunctioned by reason of the bad-faith performance of the union, their statutorily imposed collective-bargaining agent.

Under the rule announced by the Court of Appeals, unless the employer is implicated in the Union's malfeasance or has otherwise caused the arbitral process to err, petitioners would have no remedy against Anchor even though they are successful in proving the Union's bad faith, the falsity of the charges against them and the breach of contract by Anchor by discharging without cause. This rule would apparently govern even in circumstances where it is shown that a union has manufactured the evidence and knows from the start that it is false; or even if, unbeknownst to the employer, the union has corrupted the arbitrator to the detriment of disfavored union members. As is the case where there has been a failure to exhaust, however, we cannot believe that Congress intended to foreclose the employee from his § 301 remedy otherwise available against the employer if the contractual processes have been seriously flawed by the union's breach of its duty to represent employees honestly and in good faith and without invidious discrimination or arbitrary conduct.

It is urged that the reversal of the Court of Appeals will undermine not only the finality rule but the entire collective-bargaining process. Employers, it is said, will be far less willing to give up their untrammeled right to discharge without cause and to agree to private settlement procedures. But the burden on employees will remain a substantial one, far too heavy in the opinion of some. To prevail against either the company or the

Union, petitioners must show not only that their discharge was contrary to the contract but must also carry the burden of demonstrating breach of duty by the Union. As the District Court indicated, this involves more than demonstrating mere errors in judgment.

Petitioners are not entitled to relitigate their discharge merely because they offer newly discovered evidence that the charges against them were false and that in fact they were fired without cause. The grievance processes cannot be expected to be error-free. The finality provision has sufficient force to surmount occasional instances of mistake. But it is quite another matter to suggest that erroneous arbitration decisions must stand even though the employee's representation by the union has been dishonest, in bad faith or discriminatory; for in that event error and injustice of the grossest sort would multiply. The contractual system would then cease to qualify as an adequate mechanism to secure individual redress for damaging failure of the employer to abide by the contract. Congress has put its blessing on private dispute settlement arrangements provided in collective agreements, but it was anticipated, we are sure, that the contractual machinery would operate within some minimum levels of integrity. In our view, enforcement of the finality provision where the arbitrator has erred is conditioned upon the Union's having satisfied its statutory duty fairly to represent the employee in connection with the arbitration proceedings. Wrongfully discharged employees would be left without jobs and without a fair opportunity to secure an adequate remedy.

Except for this case the Courts of Appeals have arrived at similar conclusions. As the Court of Appeals for the Ninth Court put it in *Margetta* v. *Pam Pam Corp.*, 501 F.2d 179, 180 (1974): "To us, it makes little difference whether the union subverts the arbitration process by refusing to proceed as in *Vaca* or follows the arbitration trail to the end, but in doing so subverts the arbitration process by failing to fairly represent the employee. In neither case does the employee receive fair representation."

Petitioners, if they prove an erroneous discharge and the Union's breach of duty tainting the decision of the joint committee, are entitled to an appropriate remedy against the employer as well as the Union. It was error to affirm the District Court's final dismissal of petitioners' action against Anchor. To this extent the judgment of the Court of Appeals is reversed.

So ordered.

MR. JUSTICE STEVENS took no part in the consideration or decision of this case.

MR. JUSTICE STEWART, concurring.

I agree with the Court that proof of breach of the Union's duty of fair representation will remove the bar of finality from the arbitral decision that Anchor did not wrongfully discharge the petitioners. See *Vaca* v. *Sipes*, 386 U.S. 171, 194; *Humphrey* v. *Moore*, 375 U.S. 335, 348–351. But this is not to say that proof of breach of the Union's representation duty would render Anchor potentially liable for backpay accruing between the time of the "tainted" decision by the grievance committee and a subsequent "untainted" determination that the discharges were, after all, wrongful.

If an employer relies in good faith on a favorable arbitral decision, then his failure to reinstate discharged employees cannot be anything but rightful, until there is a contrary determination. Liability for the intervening wage loss must fall not on the employer but on the Union. Such an apportionment of damages is mandated by *Vaca's* holding that "damages attributable solely to the employer's breach of contract should not be charged to the union, but increases if any in those damages caused by the union's refusal to process the grievance should not be charged to the employer." 386 U.S., at 197–198. To hold an employer liable for back wages for the period during which he rightfully refuses to rehire discharged employees would be to charge him with a contractual violation on the basis of conduct precisely in accord with the dictates of the collective agreement.

[The dissenting opinion of Mr. JUSTICE REHNQUIST is omitted.]

Questions

1. Does *Hines* unduly undercut the "finality" principle of arbitration decisions? What interests, if any, are harmed by permitting a suit against the employer in this case? Why did the union, although a defendant, argue for the result reached?

2. If the union is found to have acted unfairly, and the company is found to have breached the agreement, what damages will be assessed and against whom?

3. Does the Court in *Hines* clarify the meaning of *Humphrey* v. *Moore?* Did the Court in *Humphrey* review the merits of the "absorption" determination because it was "tainted" by the union's breach of its duty?

4. Does the decision suggest what standard of performance unions must maintain in arbitration proceedings? Review the Enderby Problem on page 644 Does *Hines* affect the role of the arbitrator?

5. There is no federal statute of limitations expressly applicable to DFR cases or to Section 301 breach of contract actions. The Supreme Court has generally assumed that Congress intended the courts to apply the most closely analogous state statute. *Auto Workers* v. *Hoosier Corp.,* 383 U.S. 696 (1966). The result meant that essentially federal actions were governed by state statutes of limitations, and doubt often existed concerning which of a state's statutes was most applicable.

In 1981 the Court was confronted with a hybrid DFR-Section 310 situation similar to *Hines,* and it held that New York's 90-day period for actions to vacate arbitration awards applies rather than the state's six-year statute governing breach of contract actions. *United Parcel Service, Inc.* v. *Mitchell,* 451 U.S. 56, 107 LRRM 2001 (1981). The analogy to an action to vacate an arbitration award was imperfect, and the short limitation period effectively restricted the right of aggrieved employees to vindicate federal rights. Recognizing these problems, the Court overturned *Mitchell* in 1983, holding that the six-month period in Section 10(b) of the NLRA would be adopted for all *Vaca-Hines* type cases. *DelCostello* v. *Teamsters*, 462 U.S. ___, 113 LRRM 2737 (1983).

When an adverse arbitration award is rendered, is the union now obliged to notify the grieving employee of the applicable statute of limitations? How else might an employee be informed that only a short time exists in which to challenge the award, the employer's action or even the manner in which the union presented or researched the case? The same questions could be raised concerning the union's obligation when it decides not to proceed to arbitration.

B. EMPLOYEE STATUS AND UNION MEMBERSHIP UNDER THE NLRA

Section 8(a)(3) is designed to protect employees from discriminatory employer action based on membership or nonmembership in a labor organization. In 1947 Congress added Section 8(b)(2), which prohibits a union from causing an employer to discriminate against employees in violation of 8(a)(3). Both sections *permit* discrimination based upon nonmembership only where there is a union security clause, pursuant to the proviso of Section 8(a)(3), and membership is denied or terminated for "failure to tender the periodic dues and the initiation fees uniformly required as a condition of acquiring or retaining membership."

This section will deal with particular aspects of the union's duties to employees under Section 8(b)(2), and the next section will contrast these duties with the union's duty of fair representation under the NLRA. The Supreme Court first considered the scope of these restrictions in *Radio Officers* v. *NLRB*, 347 U.S. 17, 33 LRRM 2417 (1954). Although the Court adopted a broad reading of "discrimination," "encourage," and "membership," later decisions have followed more tortuous paths, as the decisions in Chapter 4 indicate. Most relevant to our purposes here is the holding that union "membership" encompasses any "participation in union activities" within the protection of Section 7: "The policy of the Act is to insulate employees' jobs from their organizational rights. Thus §§ 8(a)(3) and 8(b)(2) were designed to allow employees to freely exercise their right to join unions, be good, bad, or indifferent members, or abstain from joining any union without imperiling their livelihood. The only limitation Congress has chosen to impose on this right is specified in the proviso to § 8(a)(3). . . . " *Id.* at 40.

1. UNION SECURITY

Under a closed shop agreement, the employer is barred from hiring anyone except members of the appropriate union and must discharge any employee who does not remain a member in good standing throughout the contractual term. Such agreements were generally frowned upon by the courts, as *Plant* v. *Woods* indicates. The Wagner Act, however, provided that enforcement of union security agreements was not to be considered as prohibited discrimination. Congress did not declare such agreements lawful; legality was considered a matter of state law.

The law of union security was substantially revised in 1947 as the following extract describes.

Morris, Union Security*

The Taft-Hartley changes in the NLRA significantly weakened the status of union security agreements. The 1947 Act amended Section 7 to guarantee employees' rights to *refrain* from union membership and activity; the proviso to Section 8(a)(3), the amended version of former Section 8(3), was modified to outlaw the closed shop (i.e., where initial employment is conditioned upon union membership), while permitting the union shop (which requires only that employees become union members after hire).

Moreover, the 1947 statute created the present Section 8(b), which provides that certain union activities are unfair labor practices. Among those bearing on union security, Section 8(b)(1)(A) makes it an unfair labor practice for a union to "restrain or coerce . . . employees in the exercise of the rights guaranteed in Section 7" (e.g., the right to refrain from joining a union), and Section 8(b)(2) makes it unlawful for a union

> to cause or attempt to cause an employer to discriminate against an employee in violation of [Section] 8(a)(3) or to discriminate against an employee with respect to whom membership in [the union] has been denied or terminated on some ground other than his failure to tender the periodic dues and the initiation fees uniformly required as a condition of acquiring or retaining membership.

In addition, Section 8(b)(5) prohibits unions from requiring employees covered by union security clauses to pay "excessive or discriminatory" initiation fees.

The most controversial of the Taft-Hartley amendments was Section 14(b), which permits states to prohibit "agreements requiring membership in a labor organization as a condition of employment." Thus, as explained more fully below, Section 14(b) withholds federal preemption from state "right-to-work" laws, i.e., measures which regulate or outlaw union security agreements that are otherwise privileged under Section 8(a)(3) of the Act.

Section 302 of the Taft-Hartley Act is also relevant to union security agreements in one respect. While it generally prohibits employers from paying money to unions, Subsection (c)(4) exempts voluntary dues checkoff systems from this prohibition. Thus, under Section 302(c)(4), an employer may lawfully agree with a collective bargaining representative to deduct union dues from employees' pay and remit them directly to the union so long as certain conditions are met: The employee must have

---

*Reprinted by permission from Charles J. Morris (ed.), THE DEVELOPING LABOR LAW. 1362–63 (2d ed. 1983). Copyright © 1983 by the American Bar Association. Footnotes omitted.

authorized the dues deduction in writing, and the authorization cannot be irrevocable for a period longer than one year or beyond the termination date of the applicable collective bargaining agreement, whichever occurs earlier.

Examples of Union Security Provisions

The most important means by which unions attempt to establish their own strength with respect to employers, other unions, and workers are the so-called "union security provisions" frequently included in collective bargaining agreements. These provisions generally fall into the following categories:

The union shop. Under union-shop agreements, employers are permitted to hire workers on the open market, but all new employees must join the union within a specified period and must continue their membership in good standing throughout the life of the agreement. Failure to do so results automatically in discharge by the employer.

Example: "It shall be a condition of employment that all employees of the Employer covered by this agreement who are members of the Union in good standing on the effective date of this agreement shall remain members in good standing; that those who are not members on the effective date of this agreement shall, on or before the thirtieth day following the effective date of this agreement, become and remain members of the Union; and that all employees hired on or after the effective date shall, on or before the thirtieth day following the beginning of such employment, become and remain members in good standing in the Union."

The preferential shop. Some agreements provide that preference in employment shall be given to union members. Under such agreements the employer is free to hire workers on the open market only if no suitable union members are supplied within a specified period of time. A preferential-hiring provision may be incorporated as a supplement to a union-shop agreement. In that event, the union security provision as a whole has practically the same effect as a closed shop.

Example: "It is agreed that in hiring new employees the employer shall give preference to union members but in the event union members are not available, new members may be hired from any source."

Maintenance of membership. In order to avoid the compulsory aspects of the closed and the union shop, some employers and unions have agreed upon maintenance of membership as a compromise. The National War Labor Board employed this means of adjustment during World War II. Under this arrangement, membership in the union is not required of new employees; they may join or not, as they prefer. Once they do join, however, they are obligated to maintain their union membership in good standing for the life of the collective agreement as a condition of employment. Some maintenance-of-membership provisions specify an "escape period," usually at the end of the contract term, during which time members may withdraw from the union with impunity.

The agency shop. In recent years there has come into use a clause relating exclusively to the payment to the union by nonunion employees of a sum of money equal to that paid by union members, as initiation fees and dues. Membership in the union is expressly made noncompulsory, but the payment of these sums is made a condition of continued employment by management.

Example: "All employees shall, as a condition of continued employment, pay to the Union, the employee's exclusive bargaining representative, an amount of money equal to that paid by other employees in the bargaining unit who are members of the Union, which shall be limited to an amount of money equal to the Union's regular and usual initiation fees, and its regular and usual dues and its general and uniform assessments."

The checkoff. The checkoff is also a form of union security. It is a device whereby employers aid unions by insuring the collection of dues and initiation fees (and sometimes fines and assessments) with a minimum of trouble to the union. The employer makes a deduction from the paychecks of those employees who have dues obligations and transmits the amounts so deducted to the union. The deduction can be automatic and compulsory, or it can be made only upon the consent of the individual employee. Such consent can be written or oral, revocable or irrevocable. Section 302(c)(4) of the LMRA restricts the permissible form of the checkoff.

Section 19 of the NLRA provides that persons who hold religious objections to joining or financially supporting a union need not do so as a condition of employment. Although Section 19, as adopted in 1974, was limited to employees of health care institutions, in late 1980 Congress extended the rights in Section 19 to all employees covered by the Act. Thus, the words ". . . of a health care institution" in the first line of Section 19 have been deleted. Pub. L. No. 96–593 (1980). See 106 LRRM 58 (1981).

Notes

1. The 1958 agreement between the United Auto Workers and General Motors provided for a maintenance of membership and the union shop. These provisions were not operative, however, in Indiana, where state law prohibited making union membership a condition of employment. The union in 1959 proposed an agency shop for Indiana plants after an Indiana court held that an agency shop clause, requiring the payment of union dues and initiation fees but not requiring actual membership, was permissible under the state's "right to work" law. Under the proposal, all employees who wished to join would be admitted. Those who chose not to join would make the required payments, share in union strike benefits and other benefits, but could not attend union meetings, participate in union affairs, or vote upon the ratification of negotiated agreements. General Motors refused to discuss the proposal on the ground that Section 8(a)(3) permitted only an agreement requiring "membership" as a

condition of employment, whereas the union's proposal required the payment of dues but not membership. The NLRB charged General Motors with a refusal to bargain. The court of appeals, surprisingly, upheld the employer's contention. The Supreme Court reversed in *NLRB* v. *General Motors*, 373 U.S. 734, 54 LRRM 2313 (1963). The Court found no evidence that Congress intended in 1947 to abolish, not only the closed shop, but all other union security arrangements otherwise lawful. The Court discussed the extent to which "membership" was actually required under 8(a)(3):

". . . [T]he 1947 amendments not only abolished the closed shop but also made significant alterations in the meaning of 'membership' for the purposes of union-security contracts. Under the second proviso to § 8(a)(3), the burdens of membership upon which employment may be conditioned are expressly limited to the payment of initiation fees and monthly dues. It is permissible to condition employment upon membership, but membership, insofar as it has significance to employment rights, may in turn be conditioned only upon payment of fees and dues. 'Membership' as a condition of employment is whittled down to its financial core. This Court has said as much before in *Radio Officers' Union* v. *Labor Board*, 347 U.S. 17, 41:

" 'This legislative history clearly indicates that Congress intended to prevent utilization of union security agreements for any purpose other than to compel payment of union dues and fees. Thus Congress recognized the validity of unions' concern about "free riders," i.e., employees who receive the benefits of union representation but are unwilling to contribute their fair share of financial support to such union, and gave unions the power to contract to meet that problem while withholding from unions the power to cause the discharge of employees for any other reason. . . .'

"We are therefore confident that the proposal made by the union here conditioned employment upon the practical equivalent of union 'membership,' as Congress used that term in the proviso to § 8(a)(3). The proposal for requiring the payment of dues and fees imposes no burdens not imposed by a permissible union shop contract and compels the performance of only those duties of membership which are enforceable by discharge under a union shop arrangement. If an employee in a union shop unit refuses to respect any union-imposed obligations other than the duty to pay dues and fees, and membership in the union is therefore denied or terminated, the condition of 'membership' for § 8(a)(3) purposes is nevertheless satisfied and the employee may not be discharged for nonmembership even though he is not a formal member. Of course, if the union chooses to extend membership even though the employee will meet only the minimum financial burden, and refuses to support or 'join' the union in any other affirmative way, the employee may have to become a 'member' under a union shop contract, in the sense that the union may be able to place him on its rolls. The agency shop arrangement proposed here removes that choice from the union and places the option of membership in the employee while still requiring the same monetary support as does the union shop. Such a difference between the union and agency shop may be of great importance in some contexts, but for present purposes it is more formal than real. To the extent that it has any significance at all it serves, rather than violates, the desire of Congress to reduce the evils of compulsory unionism while allowing financial support for the bargaining agent. . . ."

2. Does the "agency shop" differ in any significant way from the "union shop"? Suppose under a union shop clause an employee tenders dues and initiation fees, yet refuses to attend meetings or take the membership oath, or even tenders a formal resignation from the union? *Hershey Foods Corp.*, 207 NLRB 897, 85 LRRM 1004 (1973), enf'd, 513 F.2d 1083, 89 LRRM 2126 (9th Cir. 1975); *Marlin Rockwell Corp.*, 114 NLRB 553, 36 LRRM 1592 (1955); *Union Starch & Refining Co.*, 87 NLRB 779, 25 LRRM 1176, 1366 (dissenting opinion) (1949), enf'd, 186 F.2d 1008, 27 LRRM 2342 (7th Cir. 1951), cert. denied, 342 U.S. 815, 28 LRRM 2625 (1951).

Is an employee who has been lawfully suspended or expelled from the union required to tender monthly dues to maintain her job under a union shop provision? What if the dues are accepted? See *Steelworkers, Local 4186 (McGraw-Edison)*, 181 NLRB 992, 73 LRRM 1570 (1970).

If employees are denied membership and subsequently refuse to pay the equivalent of union dues pursuant to an agency shop clause, may the union seek their discharge under 8(b)(2) or 8(b)(1)(A)? Would it matter if the agreement contained a union, rather than an agency, shop clause? See *Local 1104, Communications Workers* v. *NLRB*, 520 F.2d 411, 89 LRRM 3028 (2d Cir. 1975).

3. Consider Grodin and Beeson, *State Right-to-Work Laws and Federal Labor Policy*, 52 Calif. L. Rev. 95, 96 n. 6 (1964):

"The term 'right-to-work' is normally used to describe statutes or constitutional provisions that prohibit the requirement of union membership as a condition of employment. [Nineteen states now] have such laws. . . . The constitutionality of such laws was upheld in *Plumbers Union* v. *Graham*, 345 U.S. 192 (1953). [See also *Lincoln Federal Labor Union* v. *Northwestern Iron and Metal Co.*, 335 U.S. 525 (1949).] Right-to-work laws differ widely, however, with respect to scope and remedies. Some consist simply of a constitutional amendment to the effect that the right of persons to work shall not be denied or abridged on account of membership or nonmembership in any labor organization. . . . Most laws declare agreements in conflict with that policy unlawful. . . . In addition, some laws prohibit: (1) 'combinations' or 'conspiracies' to deprive persons of employment because of nonmembership . . . (2) strikes or picketing for the purpose of inducing an illegal agreement . . . (3) denial of employment to any persons because of membership or nonmembership . . . (4) conspiracy to cause the discharge or denial of employment to an individual by inducing other persons to refuse to work with him because he is a non-member. . . . With respect to remedies, most laws provide for damages to persons injured by a violation . . . many provide for injunctions . . . and some make violation a misdemeanor subject to criminal penalties. . . . Many right-to-work laws appear to go beyond a prohibition against making union membership or non-membership a condition of employment. . . . [S]ome laws proscribe requirements of membership in or 'affiliation with' a labor organization as a condition of employment. . . . Many expressly prohibit a requirement that an individual pay 'dues, fees, or other charges of any kind to a union as a condition of employment.' . . . Several contain a prohibition against compelling a person to join a union or strike against his will by threatened or actual interference with his person, family, or property. . . . Even further afield, some laws appear to sanction individual bargaining in the face of collective bargaining. . . . In addition to the right-to-work states, some states have laws regulating union security agreements more restrictively than does federal law, without prohibiting them. . . ."

4. If state law forbids the agency shop, can a union successfully argue that a contractual provision of that type is still permissible since Section 14(b) of the National Labor Relations Act only gives states the power to ban "agreements requiring membership in a labor organization"? In *Retail Clerks* v. *Schermerhorn*, 373 U.S. 746, 751, 53 LRRM 2318 (1963), the Supreme Court concluded:

"The connection between the Section 8(a)(3) proviso and Section 14(b) is clear. Whether they are perfectly coincident, we need not now decide, but unquestionably they overlap to some extent. At the very least, the agreements requiring 'membership' in a labor union which are expressly permitted by the proviso are the same 'membership' agreements expressly placed within the reach of state law by Section 14(b). It follows that the *General Motors* case rules this one. . . ."

5. Left unresolved in the first *Schermerhorn* opinion was the question whether state courts have jurisdiction to provide remedies for the violation of state laws prohibiting union security arrangements. The preemption doctrine, as stated in *San Diego Council* v. *Garmon*, 359 U.S. 236, 43 LRRM 2838 (1959), holds that where action is "arguably subject to Section 7 or Section 8 of the Act, the States as well as the federal courts must defer to the exclusive competence of the NLRB."

In a second opinion, *Retail Clerks* v. *Schermerhorn*, 375 U.S. 96, 54 LRRM 2612 (1963), the Court rejected the argument from *Garmon* that the federal remedy is exclusive:

"It is argued that that course is necessary, if uniformity is to be achieved. But Section 14(b) gives the States power to outlaw even a union-security agreement that passes muster by federal standards. Where Congress gives state policy that degree of overriding authority, we are reluctant to conclude that it is nonetheless enforceable by the federal agency in Washington."

However, a balance was struck to achieve an accommodation of state and federal jurisdiction:

". . .[P]icketing in order to get an employer to execute an agreement to hire all-union labor in violation of a state union-security statute lies exclusively in the federal domain . . . because state power, recognized by Section 14(b), begins only with actual negotiation and execution of the type of agreement described by Section 14(b). Absent such an agreement, conduct arguably an unfair labor practice would be a matter for the National Labor Relations Board under *Garmon*."

What basis is there in the underlying purposes of the preemption doctrine for drawing the line the Court has drawn?

6. Consider Grodin and Beeson, *State Right-to-Work Laws and Federal Labor Policy*, 52 Calif. L. Rev. 95, 107 (1964):

"State right-to-work laws have frequently been invoked in such cases [as] the discriminatory operation of a hiring hall, the discharge of an employee because of his union membership or nonmembership when no agreement is involved, picketing to force the discharge of non-union employees and the hiring of union members, and other actions which the Board would find to violate the [National] Act. Discrimination of this kind, indeed, is more prevalent than the enforcement of a closed shop contract, for few employers and unions enter into such obviously illegal agreements."

Does *Schermerhorn II* apply in these cases, giving the state courts jurisdiction concurrent with that of the NLRB?

2. Hiring Halls

In industries where work tends to be of short duration and with a variety of employers, notably construction, longshore, and maritime, unions have developed job referral systems called hiring halls. The union-operated hall may be the exclusive method through which employers obtain employees, although some arrangements permit employers to hire through other channels. The hiring halls provide a rough approximation of industrial seniority and provide an alternative to arbitrary employer hiring methods.

Hiring halls, however, can be abused by favoring union members, those who are active union participants or simply friends or relatives. Discrimination on the basis of membership would violate Sections 8(b)(2) and 8(a)(3), but, even without explicit membership discrimination, the very existence of a hiring hall will encourage employees to join the union for fear that nonmembership will adversely affect job opportunities.

Hiring halls in some industries are known to operate in effect like closed shops. W. Haber & H. Levinson, Labor Relations & Productivity in the Building Trades (1956); Rains, *Construction Trades Hiring Halls*, 10 Lab. L.J. 363 (1959). The fate of the NLRB's attempt to regulate hiring hall practices in the late 1950s is dealt with in the following case.

Local 357, International Brotherhood of Teamsters v. NLRB

Supreme Court of the United States, 1961
365 U.S. 667, 47 LRRM 2906

Mr. Justice Douglas delivered the opinion of the Court.

Petitioner union (along with the International Brotherhood of Teamsters and a number of other affiliated local unions) executed a three-year collective bargaining agreement with California Trucking Associations, which represented a group of motor truck operators in California. The provisions of the contract relating to hiring of casual or temporary employees were as follows:

"Casual employees shall, wherever the Union maintains a dispatching service, be employed only on a seniority basis in the Industry whenever such senior employees are available. An available list with seniority status will be kept by the Unions, and employees requested will be dispatched upon call to any employer who is a party to this Agreement. Seniority rating of such employees shall begin with a minimum of three months service in the Industry, *irrespective of whether such employee is or is not a member of the Union.*

"Discharge of any employee by any employer shall be grounds for removal of any employee from seniority status. No casual employee shall be employed by any employer who is a party to this Agreement in violation of seniority status if such employees are available and if the dispatching service for such employees is available. The employer shall first call the Union or the dispatching hall designated by the Union for such help. In the event the employer is notified that such help is not available, or in the event the employees called for do not appear for work at the time designated by the employer, the employer may hire from any other available source." (Emphasis added.)

Accordingly the union maintained a hiring hall for casual employees. One Slater was a member of the union and had customarily used the hiring hall. But in August 1955 be obtained casual employment with an employer who was party to the hiring-hall agreement without being dispatched by the union. He worked until sometime in November of that year, when he was discharged by the employer on complaint of the union that he had not been referred through the hiring-hall arrangement.

Slater made charges against the union and the employer. Though, as plain from the terms of the contract, there was an express provision that employees would not be discriminated against because they were or were not union members, the Board found that the hiring-hall provision was unlawful per se and that the discharge of Slater on the union's request constituted a violation by the employer of § 8(a)(1) and § 8(a)(3) and a violation by the union of § 8(b)(2) and § 8(b)(1)(A) of the National Labor Relations Act, as amended by the Taft-Hartley Act. . . . The . . . Board's ruling in Mountain Pacific Chapter, 119 NLRB 883 . . . rendered in 1958, departed from earlier rulings and held, Abe Murdock dissenting, that the hiring-hall agreement, despite the inclusion of a nondiscrimination clause, was illegal per se.

[The following excerpts from the Mountain Pacific opinion state the Board's reasoning:

"The Respondent's do not, nor could they, argue that this contract does not make employment conditional upon union approval, for a more complete and outright surrender of the normal management hiring prerogative to a union could hardly be phrased in contract language. . . .

"From the standpoint of the working force generally—those who, for all practical purposes, can obtain jobs only through the grace of the Union or its officials—it is difficult to conceive of anything that would encourage their subservience to union activity, whatever its form, more than this kind of hiring-hall arrangement. Faced with this hiring-hall contract, applicants for employment may not ask themselves what skills, experiences, or virtues are likely to win them jobs at the hands of AGC contracting companies. Instead their concern is, and must be: What, about themselves, will probably please the Unions or their agents? How can they conduct themselves best to conform with such rules and policies as Unions are likely to enforce? In short, how to ingratiate themselves with the Union, regardless of what the Employer's desires or needs might be. . . .

"Here the very grant of work at all depends solely upon union sponsorship, and it is reasonable to infer that the arrangement displays and enhances the Union's power and control over the employment status. Here all that appears is unilateral union determination and subservient employer action with no above-board explanation as to the reason for it, and it is reasonable to infer that the Union will be guided in its concession by an eye towards winning compliance with a membership obligation or union fealty in some other respect. The Employers here have surrendered all hiring authority to the Union and have given advance notice via the established hiring hall to the world at large that the Union is arbitrary master and is contractually guaranteed to remain so. From the final authority over hiring vested in the Respondent Union by the three AGC chapters, the inference of encouragement of union membership is inescapable." 119 NLRB at 894–896.]

The Board went on to say that a hiring-hall arrangement to be lawful must contain protective provisions. Its views were stated as follows:

"We believe, however, that the inherent and unlawful encouragement of union membership that stems from unfettered union control over the hiring process would be negated, and we would find an agreement to be nondiscriminatory on its face, only if the agreement explicitly provided that:

"(1) Selection of applicants for referral to jobs shall be on a nondiscriminatory basis and shall not be based on, or in any way affected by, union membership, bylaws, rules, regulations, constitutional provisions, or any other aspect or obligation of union membership policies, or requirements.

"(2) The employer retains the right to reject any job applicant referred by the union.

"(3) The parties to the agreement post in places where notices to employees and applicants for employment are customarily posted, all provisions relating to the functioning of the hiring arrangement, including the safeguards that we deem essential to the legality of an exclusive hiring agreement." Id., 897.

The Board recognizes that the hiring hall came into being "to eliminate wasteful, time-consuming, and repetitive scouting for jobs by individual workmen and haphazard uneconomical searches by employers." Id., 896, N. 8. The hiring hall at times has been a useful adjunct to the closed shop. But Congress may have thought that it need not serve that cause, that in fact it has served well both labor and management—particularly in the maritime field and in the building and construction industry. In the latter the contractor who frequently is a stranger to the area where the work is done requires a "central source" for his employment needs; and a man looking for a job finds in the hiring hall "at least a minimum guarantee of continued employment."

Congress has not outlawed the hiring hall, though it has outlawed the closed shop except within the limits prescribed in the provisos to § 8(a)(3). Senator Taft made clear his views that hiring halls are useful, that they are not illegal per se, that unions should be able to operate them so long as they are not used to create a closed shop:

"In order to make clear the real intention of Congress, it should be clearly stated that the hiring hall is not necessarily illegal. The employer should be able to make a contract with the union as an employment agency. The union frequently is the best employment agency. The employer should be able to give notice of vacancies and in the normal course of events to accept men sent to him by the hiring hall. He should not be able to bind himself, however, to reject nonunion men if they apply to him; nor should he be able to contract to accept men on a rotary-hiring basis. . . .

". . . The National Labor Relations Board and the courts [in early decisions] did not find hiring halls as such illegal, but merely certain practices under them. The Board and the court found that the manner in which the hiring halls operated created in effect a closed shop in violation of the law. Neither the law nor these decisions forbid hiring halls, even hiring halls operated by the unions as long as they are not so operated as to create a closed shop with all of the abuses possible under such an arrangement, including discrimination against employees, prospective employees, members of union minority groups, and operation of closed union." S. Rep. No. 1827, 81st Cong., 2d Sess., pp. 13, 14.

There being no express ban of hiring halls in any provisions of the Act, those who add one, whether it be the Board or the courts, engage in a legislative act. The Act deals with discrimination either by the employers or unions that encourages or discourages union membership. . . .

But surely discrimination cannot be inferred from the face of the instrument when the instrument specifically provides that there will be no discrimination against "casual employees" because of the presence or absence of union membership. The only complaint in the case was by Slater, a union member, who sought to circumvent the hiring-hall agreement. When an employer and the union enforce the agreement against union members, we cannot say without more that either indulges in the kind of discrimination to which the Act is addressed.

It may be that the very existence of the hiring hall encourages union membership. We may assume that it does. The very existence of the union has the same influence. When a union engages in collective bargaining and obtains increased wages and improved working conditions, its prestige doubtless rises and, one may assume, more workers are drawn to it. When a union negotiates collective bargaining agreements that include arbitration clauses and supervises the functioning of those provisions so as to get equitable adjustments of grievances, union membership may also be encouraged. The truth is that the union is a service agency that probably encourages membership whenever it does its job well. But . . . the only encouragement or discouragement of union membership banned by the Act is that which is "accomplished by discrimination."

Nothing is inferrable from the present hiring-hall provision except that employer and union alike sought to route "casual employees" through the union hiring hall and required a union member who circumvented it to adhere to it.

It may be that hiring halls need more regulation than the Act presently affords. As we have seen, the Act aims at every practice, act, source or institution which in fact is used to encourage and discourage union membership by discrimination in regard to hire or tenure, term or condition of employment. Perhaps the conditions which the Board attaches to hiring-hall arrangements will in time appeal to the Congress. Yet, where Congress has adopted a selective system for dealing with evils, the Board is confined to that system. . . . Where, as here, Congress has aimed its sanctions only at specific discriminatory practices, the Board cannot go further and establish a broader, more pervasive regulatory scheme. . . .

The present agreement for a union hiring hall has a protective clause in it, as we have said; and there is no evidence that it was in fact used unlawfully. We cannot assume that a union conducts its operations in violation of law or that the parties to this contract did not intend to adhere to its express language. Yet we would have to make those assumptions to agree with the Board that it is reasonable to infer the union will act discriminatorily. . . .

Reversed.

MR. JUSTICE FRANKFURTER took no part in the consideration or decision of this case.

[The concurring opinion of HARLAN, J., with whom STEWART, J., joined is omitted.]

MR. JUSTICE CLARK, dissenting.

I cannot agree with the casual treatment the Court gives to the "casual employee" who is either unable to get employment or is fired therefrom because he has not been cleared by a union hiring hall. Inasmuch as the record, and the image of a hiring hall which it presents, are neglected by the Court, a short resumé of the facts is appropriate.

Lester Slater, the complainant, became a "casual employee" in the truck freight business in 1953 or early 1954. He approached an employer but was referred to the union hiring hall. There the dispatcher told him to see Barney Volkoff, an official of the union, whose office in the union headquarters building was some three miles away. Describing his visit to Volkoff, Slater stated that "(I) just give him (Volkoff) the money to send back East to pay up my dues back there for the withdrawal card, . . . and I went right to the (hiring) hall and went to work." However, this was but the beginning of Slater's trouble with the hall. After some difficulty with one of his temporary employers (Pacific Intermountain Express), the hall refused to refer Slater to other employers. In order to keep employed despite the union hall's failure to dispatch him, Slater relied on a letter from John Annand, an International Representative of the union, stating that "you may seek work wherever you can find it in the freight industry without working through the hiring hall." It was this letter that obtained Slater his employment with Los Angeles-Seattle Motor Express, where he was characterized by its dock foreman as being "a good worker." After a few months employment, the Business Agent of the union (Victor Karaty) called on the Los Angeles-Seattle Motor Express, advising that it could not hire Slater "any longer here without a referral card"; that the company would "have to get rid of Slater, and if (it) . . . didn't, that he was going to tie the place up in a knot, (that he) would pull the men off." Los Angeles-Seattle Motor Express fired Slater, telling him that "(We) . . . can't use you now until you get this straightened out with the union. Then come back; we will put you to work." He then went to the union, and was again referred to Volkoff who advised, "I can't do anything for this job." Upon being shown the Annand letter, Volkoff declared "I am the union." On later occasions when Slater attempted to get clearance from Volkoff he was asked "How come you weren't out on that—didn't go out on the picket line?" (Apparently the Union had been on a strike.) Slater testified, "I told him that nobody asked me to. I was out a week. I thought the strike was on. The hall was closed. The guys told me there weren't no work." The landlady of Slater also approached Volkoff in an effort to get him cleared and she testified that "I asked Mr. Barney Volkoff what he had against Lester Slater and why he was doing this to him." And she quoted him as saying: "For a few reasons, óne is about the P.I.E. (Pacific Intermountain Express) . . . (a)nother thing, he is an illiterate." She further testified that "he (Volkoff) didn't like the way he dressed. And he (Volkoff) fussed around and fussed around." He therefore refused to "route," as the Court calls it, Slater through the union hiring hall.

. . . The word "discrimination" in the section, as the Board points out and I agree, includes not only distinctions contingent upon "the presence or absence of union membership," but all differences in treatment regardless of their basis. This is the "cause" portion of the section. But § 8(a)(3) also includes an "effect" clause which provides that the intended or inherent effect of the discrimination must be "to encourage or discourage [union] membership." The section has, therefore, a divided structure. Not all discriminations violate the section, but only those the effect of which is encouragement or discouragement of union membership. . . . Each being a requirement of the section, both must be present before an unfair labor practice exists. On the other hand, the union here contends, and the Court agrees, that there can be no "discrimination" within the section *unless it is based on* union membership, *i.e.,* members treated one way, nonmembers another, with further distinctions, among members, based on good standing. Through this too superficial interpretation, the Court abuses the language of the Congress and unduly restricts the scope of the proscription so that it forbids only the most obvious "hard-sell" techniques of influencing employee exercise of § 7 rights.

Even if we could draw no support from prior cases, the plain and accepted meaning of the word means to distinguish or differentiate. Without good reason, we should not limit the word to mean to distinguish in a particular manner (*i.e.,* on the basis of union membership or activity) so that a finding that the hall dispatched employees without regard to union membership or activity bars a finding of violation. The mere fact that the section *might* be read in the manner suggested by the union does not license such a distortion of the clear intent of the Congress, *i.e.,* to prohibit all auxiliaries to the closed shop, and all pressures on employee free choice, however subtly they are established or applied. . . .

Given that interpretation of the word "discrimination," it becomes necessary to determine the class of employee involved, and then whether *any* differences in treatment within that class are present. The Board found the class affected by the union hiring hall to be that group which was qualified, in the sense of ability, to do the work required by the employer and who had applied for work through the hiring hall. Obviously, not all of those who apply receive like treatment. Not all applicants receive referral cards. Clearly, then, the class applying to the hiring hall is itself divided into two groups treated differently—those cleared by the union and those who were not. The next question is whether the contract requiring and endorsing that discrimination or differentiation is designed to, or inherently tends to, encourage union membership. If it does, then § 8(a)(3) has been violated. . . .

I would hold that there is not only a reasonable likelihood, but that it must inescapably be concluded under this record, that, without the safeguards at issue, a contract conditioning employment *solely upon union referral* encourages membership in the union by that very distinction itself. . . .

Mr. Justice Whittaker joins in . . . this dissent.

Notes

1. Are there any circumstances under which the Board can now find an exclusive hiring hall provision to violate Section 8(b)(2)?

Obviously, unions cannot give preferential treatment to union members. The parties, however, can base referrals upon length of work experience or residence in particular locations. May preference be given to workers unemployed due to a strike called by their union or workers who have successfully passed a union administered skills test? See generally Gorman, Basic Text on Labor Law 666–70 (1976).

2. May the union lawfully charge nonmembers a service fee for the use of a hiring hall? If so, can the fee equal union dues or must it bear a closer relationship to the specific costs of operating the hall?

3. Consider Summers, *A Summary Evaluation of the Taft-Hartley Act*, 11 Indus. & Lab. Rel. Rev. 405, 409–10 (1958):

"The real failure of the law is that it has not been obeyed. The closed shop and hiring hall are still standard practice in the construction industry and are only thinly disguised in printing, longshore, and maritime. In the building trades the established practice of the unions and employers is to ignore the law, pay any claims filed, and keep away from the courts. The very industries in which the abuses were most severe have not changed their ways.

"The moral here again is that it is difficult to legislate against union-management cooperation, but the problem runs much deeper. The closed shop, closed union, and hiring hall—an inseparable trilogy—persist because of practical needs of both unions and employers. In inudstries where employment is short-term, seniority structures are impossible. Those workers who are established in the industry seek priority of job rights by requiring that new entrants wait until established workers are employed. The auto worker, the steel worker, and even the office worker has his seniority clause which gives him job priority. In these industries there is no 'free labor market'; a man cannot get a job where he wants it. For the hodcarrier, the bricklayer, or the carpenter, the closed shop trilogy provides his substitute for seniority. The statute attempted to wipe out all this and substituted nothing in its place. This desperate need for job priority cannot thus be wished away with a wand of words. The employer's need is nearly as compelling. In these industries the employer needs a pool of labor on which to draw on short notice; he cannot advertise or even maintain an adequate personnel department. The hiring hall is a practical and proven solution.

"The Taft-Hartley Act gave no recognition to these stubborn economic facts. Where there were genuine economic needs of the parties, it attempted to create a vacuum. It blandly assumed that, if the union were prohibited from having a closed shop, the employers would protect the individuals. The signal lesson of the Taft-Hartley Act is that when the union's needs are acute, and when the employer's needs or desires for cooperation are strong, legal measures must be carefully constructed to permit the creating of new institutions to meet the genuine needs."

4. Longshoreman's work is allocated through a union-run hiring hall so as to give first preference to registered longshoremen, designated as Class A longshoremen, and second preference to Class B, or limited registered workers. Class A registrants are usually union members; class B registrants usually are not. Unregistered workers—"casuals"—are dispatched if Class A or Class B workers are not available.

To qualify for registration as a "B" longshoreman, a worker needs the sponsorship of a class "A" worker. Is this policy a violation of Section 8(b)(1)(A) or 8(b)(2)? Could it more properly be treated as a fair representation matter? See *ILWU, Local 13* v. *NLRB, 183* NLRB 221, 74 LRRM 1532 (1970).

C. THE NLRB AND THE DUTY OF FAIR REPRESENTATION

In 1962 the NLRB asserted that it had jurisdiction over a charge that a union violated its duty of fair representation. *Miranda Fuel Co., Inc.,* 140 NLRB 181, 51 LRRM 1584 (1962) involved a union's attempt to force one of its members to forfeit his contract seniority on the basis of a provision in the collective bargaining agreement. After being placed at the bottom of the seniority list because of union pressure on the company, the member filed a complaint alleging that the union had caused the employer to discriminate against him without proper cause. The Board agreed, by reading the duty of fair representation into the employees' Section 7 rights of mutual self-organization and individual protection and then concluding that discrimination, even though unrelated to union activity, had the foreseeable effect of encouraging union membership, thereby establishing union violations of Sections 8(b)(1)(A) and 8(b)(2) and derivative employer violations of Sections 8(a)(1) and 8(a)(3).

The Court of Appeals for the Second Circuit refused to enforce the Board's order, however, holding that the alleged discrimination would neither encourage nor discourage union membership, *NLRB* v. *Miranda Fuel Co.,* 326 F.2d 172, 54 LRRM 2715 (CA 2 1963). Only one judge expressly rejected the Board's conclusion that discrimination for reasons unrelated to union activity would support violations of Sections 8(b)(1)(A), 8(b)(2), 8(a)(1), and 8(a)(3). The judge who concurred in the result did not find it necessary to reach this question and the third member of the panel limited his dissent to an argument that the Board should be sustained because the union's conduct violated Sections 8(a)(3) and 8(b)(2).

In contrast, a panel of the Court of Appeals for the Fifth Circuit unanimously upheld a Board finding that refusal to process black workers' complaints and grievances concerning wages and segregated plant facilities constituted a violation of Section 8(b)(1)(A) in that the union restrained employees in the exercise of their Section 7 right to bargain collectively and be represented by their chosen representatives without invidious discrimination. Unlike the *Steele* case, the black employees were members of the union and the collective bargaining agreement was neutral on its face. Thus, the union's practices under the agreement were alleged to be discriminatory.

"... The mere fact that Local 12's conduct may not have directly resulted in encouraging or discouraging union membership does not persuade us to alter our determination, for the language of section 8(b)(1)(A), unlike certain other provisions of Section 8, is not restricted to discrimination which encourages or discourages union membership.

"It is upon this point that we must respectfully decline to concur in the reasoning of Judge Medina in *NLRB* v. *Miranda Fuel Co., supra,* that since 8(b)(3) was intended as merely a counterpart of the employer's duty to bargain collectively under Section 8(a)(5), and since Section 8(b)(2) requires a showing of discrimination by the employer under Section 8(a)(3) which serves to encourage or discourage union membership, Congress must have intended that the application of Section 8(b)(1)(A) should also be limited to conduct affecting union membership. This argument that Section 8(b)(1)(A) should thus be restricted because Section 7 rights are limited by these other enforcement provisions of Section 8 is, as has been pointed out by one commentator in this area, to allow 'the remedial tail to wag the substantive dog.' Blumrosen, *supra* note 11 [omitted], at 1510. As exclusive bargaining representative, Local 12 had the duty to represent fairly *all* employees, union members and non-members alike. To adopt a narrow interpretation of Section 8(b)(1)(A) which would only protect the comprehensive Section 7 right of employees to bargain collectively in those cases involving union conduct which encourages or discourages union membership would to a large degree render such right meaningless in the area of union administration of the bargaining agreement. Indeed, it is only through the day-to-day administration of individual grievances that employee rights achieved in the negotiated bargaining contract are placed in a definitive context, and through which specific individual claims find a vital means of protection." *Local Union No. 12, United Rubber, Cork, Linoleum & Plastic Wkrs. of America* v. *NLRB,* 368 F.2d 20–21 (CA 6 1966).

The court did not need to determine whether such conduct violated Sections 8(b)(2) and (3). Judicial consideration of 8(b)(3) as the basis for proscribing union conduct arose from the Board's decision in *Independent Metal Workers Union (Hughes Tool Co.),* 147 NLRB 1573, 56 LRRM 1289 (1964), in which the union's failure to process an employee's grievance because of his race was deemed an unfair labor practice. The Board indicated, moreover, that court enforcement of the duty in *Steele* resulted from the lack of administrative enforcement machinery under the RLA.

The Board's decision in *Miranda* is analyzed approvingly in Blumrosen, *The Worker and Three Phases of Unionism: Administrative Control of the Worker Union Relationship,* 61 Mich. L. Rev. 1435, 1516 (1963) and Sovern, *Race Discrimination and the National Labor Relations Act: The Brave New World of Miranda,* NYU Sixteenth Annual Conference on Labor 3 (1963). For a critical comment, see Murphy, *The Duty of Fair Representation Under Taft-Hartley*, 30 Mo. L. Rev. 373 (1965); see also Professor Sovern's article, written prior to *Miranda*, which concludes that "unhappily, Section 7 says nothing about the right to be represented fairly." *The National Labor Relations Act and Racial Discrimination*, 62 Colum. L. Rev. 563 (1962). For a discussion of *Miranda* and *Rubber Workers* in a constitutional framework, see Note, *Racially Discriminatory Union Conduct: Constitutional Commands for the NLRB*, 56 Iowa L. Rev. 1044, 1054–57 (1971).

Hughes Tool Co.

National Labor Relations Board, 1964
147 NLRB 1573, 56 LRRM 1289

[In October 1961, Locals 1 and 2 of the Independent Metal Workers Union were certified as joint bargaining representative. At this time the unions and the company were operating under a two-year contract negotiated in 1959. This contract provided for Group I jobs open only to white employees, and Group II jobs open only to black employees, with separate lines of progression and demotion that prevented transfer from one group to the other. After the 1961 certification, the two locals met and agreed on most of the matters to be presented to the company in negotiating a new contract. Local 2 wanted a proposal that would eliminate racial discrimination in job opportunities, but no agreement was reached. In December, 1961, the company and Local 1 executed a document "amending and extending" the 1959 contract. Local 2 objected, but the agreement was put into effect over its protest. Also in December the company and Local 1 agreed to create new apprenticeships in the plant, and in February 1962, they were posted for bids. Davis, a black employed since 1942 and treasurer of Local 2, bid for an apprenticeship. The company refused to include his name on the list of applicants, notwithstanding protest by Local 2's grievance committee. Davis' request to Local 1 to intercede for him was ignored. A charge was filed upon which complaint issued charging violation of Section 8(b)(1)(A). Local 2 also filed a motion to rescind the 1961 certification. The two cases were consolidated.]

Report of the Trial Examiner. . . .

General Counsel's basic contention is that Local 1's failure to process Davis' grievance constituted restraint and coercion in the exercise of Section 7 rights. Reliance is placed on such cases as *Peerless Tool and Engineering Co.*, 111 NLRB 853, 858, *enforced*, 231 F.2d 298 (C.A. 7), *cert. den.*, 352 U.S. 833, and *M. Eskin & Son*, 135 NLRB 666, enforced as to the union respondent [312 F.2d 108] (C.A. 2, January 7, 1963).

In those cases the unions involved conditioned the processing of grievances on the employees' engaging in a certain activity which the unions demanded of them. Although the cases stand for the well-settled proposition that the bargaining representative has the duty of accepting and processing grievances on which its aid is requested by an employee it represents (see also *Conley v. Gibson*, 355 U.S. 41, 45–46), their applicability here is considerably diminished by the fact that in those cases the Section 7 right involved was the right to refrain from union activity.

No such right is involved here. What is involved here, instead, is Davis' right under Section 7 to have the bargaining agent represent him. If a labor organization which is the exclusive bargaining representative declines to process the grievance of a member of the unit, it has to that extent refused to represent him, and hence it has restrained or coerced him in his exercise of his right to be represented. In essence this is the analysis of the Board majority in *Miranda Fuel Company*, 140 NLRB No. 7. . . .

In my opinion, Local 1's refusal to process Davis' grievance also violated Section 8(b)(3) of the Act. That section requires the statutory-bargaining representative to bargain collectively with an employer. The processing of grievances is, of course, a part of the bargaining function. *Conley* v. *Gibson, supra*. A refusal to process a grievance is, therefore, a refusal to bargain. This does not mean, of course, that the bargaining representative must fight every grievance to the bitter end. As noted above, Local 1 might reasonably have found, after brief investigation, that the grievance was unmeritorious because other applicants were better qualified. But the record is clear that Local 1 did not make even this much inquiry into the matter, and refused to handle Davis' grievance for reasons unrelated to his qualifications for the job.

It may be argued that the duty to bargain prescribed by Section 8(b)(3) is a duty the union owes to employers, not to employees in the unit. But nothing in the statutory language requires such a limitation on the union's duty; certainly the employer's corresponding duty runs both to the union and to the employee in the unit. See *Louisville Refining Co.*, 4 NLRB 844–860–1, *enforced*, 102 F.2d 678 (C.A. 6). If, for example, a union which represents a majority, should seek to make a "members only" contract, it would appear to be violating its duty to bargain on behalf of all. In that example, it would be dealing with an employer, and hence plainly violating Section 8(b)(3). In the instant case it is, in effect, acting on behalf of "members only" when it refuses to deal with the employer concerning Davis' grievance, and its inaction is as much, if not more, of a refusal to bargain than would be its action on behalf of a minority. Cf. Cox, *The Duty of Fair Representation*, 2 Villanova L. Rev. 151, 172–174. Since, as is well settled, the majority union has a statutory obligation to represent all employees in the unit fairly in collective bargaining, I find that a breach of that duty is a breach of the duty to bargain. . . .

Finally, the majority of the Board held in *Miranda Fuel Co.*, 140 NLRB No. 7, that a labor organization violates Section 8(b)(2) when "for arbitrary or irrelevant reasons or upon the basis of an unfair classification the union attempts to cause or does cause an employer to derogate the employment status of an employee," and that "union membership is encouraged or discouraged whenever a union causes an employer to affect an individual's employment status." What is said in *Miranda* with respect to union *action* would appear equally applicable to *inaction* which was founded upon "arbitrary or irrelevant reasons or upon the basis of an unfair classification."

Decision of the Board. . . .

With respect to the unfair labor practice case, we agree with the Trial Examiner for the reasons stated by him that Local No. 1, by its failure to entertain in any fashion or to consider the grievance filed by an employee in the bargaining unit, Ivory Davis, and by its outright rejection of Davis' grievance for reasons of race, violated Section 8(b)(1)(A), 8(b)(2), and 8(b)(3) of the Act.

We further agree with the Trial Examiner, contrary to the Charging Party's contention, that the validity of the racially discriminatory contracts between Local No. 1 and the Company was not placed in issue by the complaint in the unfair labor practice case. Similarly, racial segregation in union membership was not placed in issue in *that* case. This conclusion is not to be construed, however, as a disagreement on our part with the contentions of the Charging Party that the negotiation of racially discriminatory terms or conditions of employment by a statutory bargaining representative violates Section 8(b) of the Act and that racial segregation in membership, when engaged in by such a representative, cannot be countenanced by a Federal Agency and may violate Section 8(b).

We would be content to terminate our discussion of the unfair labor practice case at this point and to rely, as we do, upon the Trial Examiner's treatment of the issues, but the separate opinion of Chairman McCulloch and Member Fanning, in which they disagree with us at length, necessitates additional comments in this majority opinion.

With respect to the Section 8(b)(1)(A) violation, the separate opinion relies upon cases which were advanced by the General Counsel for consideration by the Trial Examiner. The latter's discussion of the subject in his Intermediate Report casts much doubt upon the applicability of the cases. Moreover, as we understand the separate opinion, our colleagues would find an 8(b)(1)(A) violation only because the Negro employee, Ivory Davis, who is a member of the Negro local of Independent Metal Workers Union, is not a member of Local No. 1, the Respondent.

In other words, our colleagues appear to say that, in another factual context, when a statutory bargaining representative does not practice segregation or other racial restrictions in membership, such representative may refuse, on racial grounds as distinguished from nonmembership grounds, to consider a meritorious grievance of a Negro in the bargaining unit, seeking by such refusal to keep Negro employees in inferior jobs, and that such refusal does not violate Section 8(b)(1)(A). We cannot concur in our colleagues' view of the law. We rely instead upon the Trial Examiner's reasoning in finding a violation of Section 8(b)(1)(A).

The separate opinion utilizes this case as an opportunity to reiterate and enlarge the dissenters' views in *Miranda Fuel Co., Inc.*, 140 NLRB 181. We need not detail the bases of our disagreement. We note only a few facts. When the Supreme Court enunciated the duty of fair representation in *Steele* [323 U.S. 192] and *Tunstall* [323 U.S. 210], which were Railway Labor Act cases, the Court emphasized in each case the lack of an administrative remedy as a reason for holding that Federal courts constitute a forum for relief from breaches of the duty.

In this connection, it should be noted that provisions of the Railway Labor Act which are substantially identical to certain unfair labor practice provisions of the National Labor Relations Act are enforceable by the Federal courts, not by an administrative agency. When the Labor Board, in recognition of the *Steele* and *Tunstall* doctrines, held that under the Wagner Act statutory bargaining representatives owe to their constituents a duty to represent fairly, the Board's holding necessarily was confined to representation proceedings because the Board had no power to issue an order against a labor organization. After enactment of the Taft-Hartley Act, however, an administrative remedy became available in our view and in the view of various legal scholars . . . as well as in briefs amici in this case and before the Court of Appeals in *NLRB* v. *Miranda Fuel Co., Inc.*, 326 F.2d 172 (C.A. 2). Moreover, a majority of the panel of the Court which decided that case expressly refrained from determining whether a breach of the duty of fair representation violates Section 8(b)(1)(A), and the Supreme Court said recently that the question is open, *Humphrey* v. *Moore*, 375 U.S. 335, 344, as indeed our dissenting colleagues concede. . . .

Turning to the representation case, we join the separate opinion of our colleagues in holding that the Pioneer Bus doctrine requires that the certification issued jointly to Locals Nos. 1 and 2 on October 18, 1961, be rescinded because the certified organizations executed contracts based on race and administered the contracts so as to perpetuate racial discrimination in employment. The separate opinion fails, however, to treat two issues which are of crucial importance today. First, the separate opinion disregards certain constitutional limitations upon the Board's powers. Second, the separate opinion fails to join in overturning an outmoded and fallacious doctrine which the Board established long ago.

Specifically, we hold that the Board cannot validly render aid under Section 9 of the Act to a labor organization which discriminates racially when acting as a statutory bargaining representative. Cf. *Shelley* v. *Kraemer*, 334 U.S. 1; *Hurd* v. *Hodge*, 334 U.S. 24; *Bolling* v. *Sharpe*, 347 U.S. 497.

We hold too, in agreement with the Trial Examiner, that the certification should be rescinded because Locals Nos. 1 and 2 discriminated on the basis of race in determining eligibility for full and equal membership and segregated their members on the basis of race. In the light of the Supreme Court decisions cited herein and others to which the Board adverted in *Pioneer Bus*, we hereby expressly overrule such cases as *Atlanta Oak Flooring Co.*, 62 NLRB 973; *Larus & Brother Co.*, 62 NLRB 1075; and other cases epitomized by the language of the Board's Tenth Annual Report, . . . insofar as such cases hold that unions which exclude employees from membership on racial grounds, or which classify or segregate members on racial grounds, may obtain or retain certified status under the Act.

We are not confronted at this time, as we were in *Pioneer Bus*, with a new petition for certification, and thus we have no present occasion for prescribing a notice such as that recommended by the Trial Examiner as a condition for certification.[30] We intimate no disapproval of that recommendation, however, and we shall entertain it if occasion to do so should arise. We also commend it to the consideration of the Regional Director in the event that he should be called upon to issue a certification of representatives at this plant.

CHAIRMAN MCCULLOCH and MEMBER FANNING concurring in part and dissenting in part.

We join with the majority members in adopting the Trial Examiner's recommendation for the rescission of the certification. However, we do so because of the discriminatory contract negotiated by the certified unions and the employer. We find it unnecessary at this time to pass on the other grounds relied upon by the Trial Examiner in making his recommendation.

We also join with the majority in holding that Respondent violated Section 8(b)(1)(A), but we rest this conclusion on a ground different from that of the majority. We do not agree with the majority that Respondent violated Section 8(b)(2) and (3). . . .

One of the allegations of the complaint is that Respondent refused to process Ivory Davis' grievance because he was not a member of Respondent Local 1. In its answer, Respondent admits that it refused to process the grievance and a reason for its refusal was Davis' nonmembership in Local 1. This refusal to represent him in a grievance matter because of his nonmembership was to this extent predicated upon a consideration specifically condemned by the Act, and therefore prima facie restrained or coerced him in violation of Section 8(b)(1)(A).

Respondent urges three grounds to justify its refusal to press Davis' grievance. They are: (1) the grievance had no merit because of contractual provisions; (2) a clause in the constitution of the Independent, which was not waived by Local 2, precluded it from handling the grievance; and (3) in the past the Company had refused to process grievances presented by a joint grievance committee unless the grievance pertained to members of both Locals. We find all these defenses to be without merit. . . .

Accordingly, we find that Respondent Local 1 restrained and coerced Ivory Davis in violation of Section 8(b)(1)(A) of the Act.

In making this finding we do not rely, as does the majority, on a violation of the duty of fair representation. Our reasons are as follows: . . . Neither Section 7 nor Section 8(b)(1)(A) mentions a duty of fair representation. The majority in the *Miranda* case, reaffirmed here, found a right to fair representation implied in Section 7 on the basis of the

---

[30]The Trial Examiner's recommended notice read: "Notice to all Employees: This labor organization has been certified by the National Labor Relations Board as the bargaining representative of the employees in the unit described below. The certification is conditioned upon our not discriminating against any employee because of his race or color, both with respect to membership in this labor organization on terms fully equal to those afforded any member and with respect to terms and conditions of employment and opportunities for advancement under any contract we may negotiate with management. Any person who believes that this labor organization is not observing a policy of nondiscrimination should bring the matter to the attention of the National Labor Relations Board, Washington 25, D.C., or the Board's Regional Office in Houston."—ED.

bargaining representative's implied duty of fair representation derived from its status as bargaining representative under Section 9.

There are a number of reasons why this conclusion based on verbal logic does not, in our opinion, represent the intent of Congress, which is after all the goal of statutory construction. Section 7 was part of the Wagner Act which in its unfair labor practice section was aimed only at employer conduct. The Wagner Act also contained the present Section 9(a). It hardly seems reasonable to infer, in these circumstances, that Section 7 contained a protected implied right to fair representation against the bargaining representative, when the entire Wagner Act did not make any conduct by a labor organization unlawful. Section 7 was continued substantially unchanged in the Taft-Hartley Act except for the addition of the "right to refrain" clause, which is not material to our problem. Although the Taft-Hartley Act added union unfair labor practices to the list of prohibited conduct, neither the Act nor the legislative history contains any mention of the duty of fair representation, despite the fact that the *Steele* and *Wallace* decisions were well known, having issued 3 years previously. Again, although in the interval between the dates of the Taft-Hartley and Landrum-Griffin Acts, there were additional court decisions and articles by learned commentators in the law journals dealing with the legal problems of fair representation, Congress made no change in the wording of Section 7, and ignored the problem completely in adding a "Bill of Rights" section to the existing statute. If Congress had really intended that violation of the duty of fair representation should be an unfair labor practice, it would seem that the 1959 revision afforded it an opportunity to clear up the uncertainty. Instead it remained silent. We do not believe that realistically this silence can be interpreted as in any way favorable to the contention that the right to fair representation is a protected Section 7 right. There are practical reasons for believing that, if there had been any contemporary understanding that the Act had made it an unfair labor practice for a union to fail in its duty of fair representation, the opposition would have been both strong and loud.

There is another and more important reason why the Board should not undertake to police a union's administration of its duties without a clear mandate from Congress. The purpose of the Act is primarily to protect the organizational rights of employees. But apart from the obligation to bargain in good faith, "Congress intended that the parties would have wide latitude in their negotiations, unrestricted by any governmental power to regulate the substantive solution of their differences." Before *Miranda,* it was assumed that contract or grievance decisions by employers and unions were immune from examination by the Board unless they were influenced by union considerations. But, under the underlying reasoning of the *Miranda* majority and that of the present decision, the Board is now constituted a tribunal to which every employee who feels aggrieved by a bargaining representative's action, whether in contract negotiations or in grievance handling, may appeal, regardless of whether the decision has been influenced in whole or in part by consideration of union membership, loyalty, or activity.

The Board must determine on such appeal, without statutory standards, whether the representative's decision was motivated by "unfair or irrelevant or invidious" considerations and therefore to be set aside, or was within the "wide range of reasonableness . . . allowed a statutory representative in serving the unit it represents. . . ," and to be sustained. Inevitably, the Board will have to sit in judgment on the substantive matters of collective bargaining, the very thing the Supreme Court has said the Board must not do, and in which it has no special experience or competence. This is not exaggeration. The duty of fair representation covers more than racial discrimination. *Miranda* itself did not involve a race issue and since *Miranda*, the Board has had to decide a number of other cases where allegations of violation of the duty of fair representation rested on other than racial grounds, with many more such cases disposed of at the regional level. . . .

What we are confronted with is an important question of policy which should be resolved not by logomachy, but by a careful weighing of alternatives in the light of the ends to be achieved. Where specific statutory rights or prohibitions are not involved, should enforcement of the duty of fair representation be left to the courts, to the Board, or both? In such circumstances, should cases of breach of this duty insofar as they involve race discrimination be treated differently from breaches involving non-racial factors? If a separate agency is created to handle the task of eliminating employment discrimination by unions and employers based on race, should the Board have a duty in this field? If so, what should it be? To ask these questions is to appreciate that the problem with which we are presented is legislative to be resolved by the Congress and not by an administrative body whose duty it is only to administer the law which Congress has written.

Accordingly, we would rest our finding of a violation of 8(b)(1)(A) not on non-performance of the duty of fair representation, but on those other considerations present in this case which Congress brought within the unfair labor practice ambit of the statute. . . .

In our dissent in *Miranda,* we expressed the view that 8(b)(2) outlaws only discrimination related to "union membership, loyalty, the acknowledgment of union authority or the performance of union obligations." This position was endorsed by a majority holding of the Court of Appeals in reversing the Board decision in *Miranda.* We adhere to that view. . . .

The majority has adopted the Trial Examiner's finding that Respondent Union's refusal to process Ivory Davis' grievance also violated Section 8(b)(3). It seems to us that Section 8(b)(3) prescribes a duty owed by a union to employers and not to employees. . . .

The legislative history of Section 8(b)(3) shows conclusively that this Section was intended to be a counterpart of Section 8(a)(5), and under the latter the bargaining duty is owed entirely to the union. Thus the House Report on the proposal which became 8(b)(3) said: "The standards and definitions which have been discussed in relation to Section 2(11) apply in the case of unions, as well as in the case of employers. The duty to bargain now becomes mutual. This, the committee believes, will promote equality and responsibility in bargaining." Similarly, the House Conference

Report commenting on 8(b)(3) said: "This provision . . . imposed upon labor organizations the same duty which under Section 8(a)(5) . . . was imposed on employers." The same understanding is reflected by the Supreme Court. . . .

Questions

1. As a matter of legislative interpretation, what significance should be given to congressional silence in 1947 concerning the duty of fair representation? Does this silence, despite the *Steele* decision only three years before, indicate that the duty is not within Section 8(b)(1)(A)? What significance should be given to the passage of the LMRDA (Landrum-Griffin) in 1959 which provided individual union members with rights in relation to their union?

2. How convincing is the dissenters' argument that the Board is "embarking on a wholly new field of activity for which it has had no preparation. . . ."? Are the dissenters asserting that courts have more competence with respect to these matters?

3. Although the Supreme Court has not directly passed upon the propriety of the NLRB's jurisdiction in this area, the Court assumed that the Board had jurisdiction in discussing the preemption issue in *Vaca* v. *Sipes*. At the present time, then, the DFR can presumably by enforced either through court action or through an NLRB complaint. What is gained by concurrent jurisdiction over the DFR? Is there any other section of Section 8(b) which provides a sounder basis for the duty?

4. When a union unlawfully refuses to process a grievance, the union usually cannot then arbitrate the grievance because of contractual time bars. The usual NLRB remedy is to require the union to compensate the grievant for any loss of wages from the date of the unlawful refusal to process the grievance until the grievant obtains substantially equivalent employment. Is this a satisfactory remedy? Although the grievant can sue the employer for breach of contract under Section 301, are there other NLRB remedies available to resolve the situation? Should the NLRB order the employer to arbitrate? Can this be done in the absence of an employer unfair labor practice? Do you see any problem in union representation of the grievant in arbitration? How could these problems be avoided?

5. May a union which operates an exclusive hiring hall properly refer minority workers, departing from the normal contractual procedure, because the employers have received warnings from state agencies that current minority employment does not meet an existing affirmative action plan? Assume that some of the minority applicants referred pursuant to these requests are given preference over nonminority applicants with superior referral rights under the contract, but that the employers face the loss of existing government contracts if they do not hire more minority workers. Is it relevant that the affected nonminority applicants may have other remedies under the contract or under civil rights legislation?

Comment on Employment Discrimination and the NLRB

Whatever section is appropriately used, it has been clear since *Steele* that distinctions based upon race or ethnicity are inconsistent with the union's statutory duties. This standard has been applied to situations other than union unfair labor practice situations. In *NLRB* v. *Mansion House Center Management Corp.*, 473 F.2d 471, 82 LRRM 2608 (8th Cir. 1973), the court held that a union's racially discriminatory membership practices were a legitimate defense to the employer's refusal to bargain. The court believed that the union's duty was of constitutional dimension and, thus, federal law could not be used to enforce such a union's bargaining status.

The Board has enforced the duty in representation situations, and *Mansion House* might be seen as the logical result of decisions which deny or revoke certification in similar cases. The Board, for instance, will waive the normal contract bar rule for representation elections when the agreement contains facially discriminatory provisions or when locals are organized on racial lines. *Pioneer Bus Co.*, 140 NLRB 54, 51 LRRM 1546 (1962). Similarly, the Board will revoke the certification of a union which discriminates on the basis of race in contract negotiation, grievance processing, or membership. *Hughes Tool Co.*, 147 NLRB 1573, 56 LRRM 1289 (1964).

In 1974, a majority of the Board held that the Constitution barred the issuance of a certification to a union found guilty of invidious discrimination. *Bekins Moving & Storage Co.*, 211 NLRB 138, 86 LRRM 1323 (1974). The Board held that a precertification inquiry should be made into the union's "willingness and capacity" to fairly represent all employees if the employer makes a timely motion after the union wins the election. *Bekins*, however, has now been overruled. *Handy Andy, Inc.*, 228 NLRB 447, 94 LRRM 1354 (1977); *Bell & Howell Co.*, 230 NLRB 420, 95 LRRM 1333 (1977) (sex discrimination). The Board now believes that certification does not involve federal approval of a union's discriminatory behavior. Alleged invidious discrimination can be more properly determined in unfair labor practice proceedings. Although *Mansion House* arose in an unfair labor practice proceeding, its status is doubtful—the Board in overruling *Bekins* noted that the Board's recognition of bargaining status, through an election *or* bargaining order, merely indicates that a majority in an appropriate unit has chosen that representative and the employer is obliged to bargain with it.

A union which denies job opportunities or benefits on the basis of sex violates Sections 8(b)(1)(A) or 8(b)(2). The most liberal holding to date is *Local 106, Glass Bottle Blowers Ass'n*, 210 NLRB 943, 86 LRRM 1257 (1974), enf'd, 520 F.2d 693, 89 LRRM 3020 (6th Cir. 1975), where a violation of 8(b)(1)(A) was found where dual locals were maintained for each sex and male and female grievances were separately processed. The agreement did not discriminate against women, and grievances of women were apparently processed. The NLRB, however, held that the maintenance of separate locals and the creation of separate grievance processes inherently generated a feeling of inferiority and adversely affected employee working conditions. The Board noted that separate grievance processing also could adversely affect working conditions because the nongrieving local would be denied participation in the grieving local's action, an action whose resolution will affect all employees. See also *Pacific Maritime Ass'n,* 209 NLRB 519, 85 LRRM 1389 (1974) (violation to operate hiring hall which refuses to refer women as casual laborers); *Petersen* v. *Rath Packing Co.,* 461 F.2d 312, 80 LRRM 2833 (8th Cir. 1972) (creation of "male only" jobs into which laid-off women cannot "bump").

What is the soundest doctrinal base for the unfair labor practice in *Glass Bottle Blowers:*

(1) The union's maintenance of separate locals and grievance channels are per se violations of 8(b)(1)(A)?

(2) The violation exists only because a nexus exists between the discrimination and the restraint or coercion of Section 7 rights?

(3) Separate representation is inherently unequal and, thus, the violation should be based on the union's duty of fair representation?

Would the choice of any of these approaches affect a situation where an employer, allegedly engaging in racial or sex discrimination, is charged with violating 8(a)(3)?

The NLRB has held that sex and race discrimination by an *employer* does not necessarily violate Sections 8(a)(1) or 8(a)(3). In *Jubilee Mfg. Co.,* 202 NLRB 272, 272, 82 LRRM 1482, 1484 (1973), the Board stated that there must be "a nexus between the alleged discriminatory conduct and the interference with, or restraint of, employees in the exercise of those rights protected by the Act." The Board held that discrimination did not necessarily interfere with the exercise of Section 7 rights. The decision was the NLRB's answer to the D.C. Circuit which had previously held that an employer who discriminates on the basis of race deters the exercise of Section 7 rights by, first, creating "an unjustified clash of interests between groups of workers which tends to reduce the likelihood and the effectiveness of their working in concert to achieve their legitimate goals under the Act," and, second, by generating an "apathy or docility" in the victims which deters the assertion of employee rights. *United Packinghouse Workers* v. *NLRB,* 416 F.2d 1126, 1135, 70 LRRM 2489, 2495 (D.C. Cir), *cert. denied sub nom. Farmers' Cooperative Compress* v. *United Packinghouse Workers,* 396 U.S. 903, 72 LRRM 2658 (1969). Does the approach of the NLRB or the court comport more with statutory policy and reality?

Can *Jubilee* and *Glass Bottle Blowers* be distinguished? Consider the fact that employers who participate in union-instigated discrimination, for instance, by cooperating with an illegal hiring hall arrangement, violate Sections 8(a)(1) and 8(a)(3). *Houston Maritime Ass'n,* 168 NLRB 615, 66 LRRM 1337 (1967); *Pacific Maritime Ass'n,* 209 NLRB 519, 85 LRRM 1389 (1974). Should the employer be in a better position under the NLRA because it discriminates alone instead of jointly with the union? Is it sufficient to say that unions, since they represent employees, have statutory obligations not possessed by employers? *Glass Bottle Blowers Ass'n, supra.* Note that other remedies exist for union or employer unlawful discrimination. See Unit 3 of this series of books.

Legislative history provides little assistance. Congress specifically refused to make racial discrimination an unfair labor practice, and it probably did not have such discrimination in mind when 8(a)(1) was enacted. The same, however, could be said about union obligations under 8(b)(1)(A). Although it is not at all clear that the duty of fair representation, created by judicial action, is properly an unfair labor practice when the duty is breached, it seems too late in the day to seriously question the issue. Given this duty, there is no doubt that the union's statutory authority includes a duty to avoid arbitrary conduct. Does the union's special statutory role provide a basis for distinguishing employer discrimination?

Truck Drivers and Helpers, Local Union 568 v. NLRB

United States Court of Appeals, District of Columbia Circuit, 1967
379 F.2d 137, 65 LRRM 2309

McGOWAN, Circuit Judge:

. . .

The issues here were generated by the Company's acquisition of another trucking company in Shreveport, Louisiana, and its subsequent action in unifying the terminals from which each had formerly operated in that city. The acquired business had used for some years a facility known as the Abbey Street terminal; and the Teamsters were the recognized bargaining representative of its approximately 30 employees working as drivers and dockworkers at that terminal. The Company's terminal was in another part of the city. Known as the Airport Drive terminal, its 50 workers were represented by UTE.

Some two years after the original acquisition, the Company notified the two unions of its intention to close the older and more inefficient Abbey Street terminal, and to consolidate all Shreveport operations at the Airport Drive terminal. The Company met with the unions, and, on September 1, 1964, agreement was reached that the Company would initiate representation proceedings to determine which of the two unions the majority of the combined employees wished to represent them all. It was also agreed that the existing contract of the winning union would apply to all of the employees. The agreement further comprehended an undertaking by the Company to negotiate with the successful union on all issues "arising from the integration of employees and/or the closing of the Abbey Street terminal."

UTE promptly convened meetings of its members at which it addressed itself immediately and decisively to the critical question of what seniority principles should be applied in consolidating the two working forces. UTE officers represented that it would never agree to the dovetailing of the seniority lists, as would be the case if the Teamsters won. They prepared and exhibited comparative lists, one placing all UTE employees above the Teamsters, and the other integrating the two groups on the basis of individual seniority. Although there appeared to be no factual basis for doing so, they represented that about 15 jobs would be abolished by reason of the merger; and they noted that some 15 or 16 Teamsters had higher seniority than UTE members. The latter were assured that UTE would protect them at all events against these contingencies by an adamant position on seniority integration. UTE put this in writing by a letter distributed on September 9, the day before the consent election.[1] This letter was by way of comment upon a letter previously distributed by the Teamsters which stated that "whichever union wins the election will be under a duty of representing fairly all the employees in the bargaining unit"; and which went on to suggest that that duty could be discharged by the dovetailing of the rosters. UTE won the election on September 10 by a narrow margin, but the Teamsters filed objections. The Regional Director, after the hearing, sustained the one of these objections founded upon the seniority representations. He set aside the election, and ordered a new one to be held. . . .

The Board's finding of a Section 8(b)(1)(A) violation against UTE rests upon essentially undisputed facts. But to proceed from these facts to this finding requires preliminary consideration of at least two substantial legal questions. The first is whether a union's refusal fairly to represent all of the employees in its bargaining unit can constitute an unfair labor practice cognizable under the Act. The second is whether a union's adamant stand against the dovetailing of seniority lists can be a violation of that duty of fair representation. . . .

As for the second question, the standards to be applied in determining what union acts of commission or omission are in violation of its duty of fair representation under the Act remain largely to be drawn. Only recently has the Board begun to articulate the characteristics of unfair representation as it has begun more actively to entertain complaints of this nature. On the narrow question before us, we need not concern ourselves with what may eventually prove to be the precise contours of a union's duty fairly to represent all of the employees for whom it speaks, for there are cases which indicate that union action taken solely for considerations of political expediency, and unsupported by any rational argument whatsoever, is in violation of representational responsibilities. In *Ferro* v. *Railway Express Agency, Inc.*, 296 F.2d 847 (2d Cir. 1961), the trial court had dismissed a complaint brought against their union by workers who, after losing their jobs in a merger, had sought positions elsewhere in the system under a contract permitting them to follow their work. The union negotiated a settlement excluding them, allegedly because it desired to discriminate in favor of a politically stronger local. The Court of Appeals, stating that "it is not proper for a bargaining agent in representing all of the employees to draw distinctions among them

---

[1]The letter concluded:

"Even if seniority is dovetailed, you know a majority of UTE employees will go to the bottom of the board should the Teamsters win.

"When the Union of Transportation Employees wins the election, the Teamsters Union will have no bargaining rights and no say-so at all. You can rest assured that the Union of Transportation Employees will *never* agree that its members will go to the bottom of any seniority list and that your seniority will be respected and protected against all others. Do not be fooled by long, legal, complicated letters. This is a plain statement of the position of the Union of Transportation Employees." [Emphasis in original.]

which are based upon their political power within the union," directed that the plaintiffs' complaint under the Railway Labor Act be reinstated. *Id.* at 851. Similarly, in *Gainey v. Brotherhood of Railway and Steamship Clerks*, 313 F.2d 318, 324 (1963), the Third Circuit characterized the "arbitrary sacrifice of a group of employees' rights in favor of another stronger or more politically favored group" as one of the major categories of cases comprised within the *Steele* doctrine.

The merger situation poses notoriously difficult problems in accommodating the interests of theretofore independent groups of employees. It frequently, although by no means invariably in an expanding economy, raises the dread spectre of job-loss for workers with relatively long records of stable employment. Many different formulae for reconciliation have been attempted, and more have been suggested, as methods for alleviating the discord over seniority when two groups of employees are joined. It is not our function to prefer one as against any other. But it seems clear to us, as it did to the Board on the undisputed evidence before it, that UTE has renounced any good faith effort to reconcile the interests of the employees formerly at the Abbey Street depot with those of the Airport Drive terminal. It raised no questions with respect to the merits of dovetailing, such as that some jobs are more difficult of execution or require more training than others.[10] There has been no indication that the Abbey Street operation was unsuccessful and that its employees, had they not followed the work to Airport Drive, would have lost their job altogether. UTE has, in sum, failed to come forward with any reason at all for preferring the Airport Drive employees other than the purely political motive of winning an election by a promise of preferential representation to the numerically larger number of voters.

That UTE's fulfillment, if it won the election, of its campaign promise to discriminate against the Teamster employees would constitute an unfair labor practice does not finally resolve the precise issue before us. Here there is only threatened action, promised by a union which is not yet an exclusive bargaining agent. Neither *United Rubber Workers* nor the Board's decision in *Miranda* resolves this issue. In each of those cases the union had been for some time the exclusive bargaining agent, and any

[10]The Board may legitimately measure other proposals for handling the problems occasioned by merging the seniority rosters by a dovetailing standard, as experience has demonstrated it generally to be an equitable and feasible solution in other situations. See *e.g.*, Humphrey v. Moore, 375 U.S. 335, 347, 55 LRRM 2031, 2037 (1964) and authorities cited in footnote 10; O'Donnell v. Pabst Brewing Co., 12 Wis.2d 491, 107 N.W.2d 484 (1961), *cf.* Kent v. CAB, 204 F.2d 263 (2d Cir.), *cert. denied*, 346 U.S. 826, 32 LRRM 2750 (1953); Kahn, *supra*, at 373–78. The condemnations of refusal to dovetail are legion. *E.g.*, Commercial Telegraphers' Union v. Western Union Telegraph Co., 53 F.Supp. 90, 96 (1943); In re City of Green Bay, Wisconsin, 44 LAB. ARB. 311, 315 (1965); Blumrosen, *Union-Management Agreements Which Harm Others*, 10 JOURNAL OF PUBLIC LAW 345, 371 (1961). Apparently most employees have come to accept dovetailing as the preferred procedure when mergers occur. In discussing the fair representation duty in a hypothetical merger situation, Professor Wellington has concluded that "where company A acquired company B, and the B employees were treated as new employees for the purpose of seniority, the union would be in a breach of duty. Although position on the seniority ladder is subject to revision, bargaining for its total elimination seems clearly outside the expectation of the employee community. Some sort of dovetailing would accordingly be required to approximate community expectation." Wellington, *Union Democracy and Fair Representation: Federal Responsibility in a Federal System*, 67 YALE L.J. 1327, 1360–61 (1958).

duty to represent all employees in its unit had, by definition, already attached. Here neither UTE nor the Teamsters had as yet become the exclusive bargaining agent for all employees at the consolidated Airport Drive operation.

Thus the question is whether *threatened* action which *would* violate a union's fair representation duty constitutes an unfair labor practice. To this specific point no court has addressed itself, and we find in this regard scant assistance from decisions of the Board. Cf. *Local 55, St. Louis Offset Printing Union, AFL-CIO (Mendle Press)*, 130 NLRB 324 (1961), where a union threat to induce an employer to take retaliatory action was found violative of Section 8(b)(1)(A). Because UTE is not yet the exclusive bargaining agent for all of the employees in the unit, it is necessary to find other circumstances indicating coercion or restraint of Section 7 rights in order to affirm the existence of an unfair labor practice under Section 8(b)(1)(A).

Those circumstances, we think, consist in this: UTE has not only pledged itself to violate its fair representation duty in the future, but that very commitment presently restrains the employees of the bargaining unit in the exercise of their Section 7 right to freedom of choice in the selection or rejection of a bargaining representative. The combination of (1) the promise of illegal action and (2) the contribution of that illegal promise to impairment of freedom of choice leads us here to affirm the Board's finding that UTE has committed an unfair labor practice. . . .

We think the Board could conclude that this campaign activity by UTE inevitably introduced improper influences into the election process tantamount to the restraint or coercion contemplated by Section 7. By holding out the inducement of seniority preferences to the UTE employees, UTE conceivably restrained some Teamster members from expressing a choice for UTE which they might otherwise have had or, as is more probably the case, it may have made the alternative of no union at all appear to be the lesser evil. It may well have had a similarly restraining effect upon some UTE members who may have been attracted to the Teamsters by the generally more advantageous terms of the Teamster contract with the Company. Because interjection of what would be an illegal union policy into the campaign may have coerced members of both unions into thinking they had best sit tight with their current representation, it seems probable that employees were restrained from the full exercise of "the complete and unhampered freedom of choice which the Act contemplates." *International Ass'n of Machinists, Tool & Die Workers Lodge No. 35* v. *NLRB*, 311 U.S. 72, 80, 7 LRRM 282, 286 (1940). . . .

Questions

1. Assume that the UTE wins the election and an agreement is reached which bases seniority upon the date of hire at the Airport Drive Terminal. The employees, formerly represented by the Teamsters, now find themselves at the bottom of a combined seniority list and facing possible layoff. Has the UTE violated its duty to fairly represent these employees? Does

the agreement violate 8(b)(2) by discriminating against employees based upon union affiliation?

2. How would you distinguish the union's duty under Section 8(b)(1)(A) and under 8(b)(2)? Do these sections provide analytically distinguishable obligations? Hiring hall and union security cases are normally dealt with under Section 8(b)(2) as the earlier materials indicate, and the focus is usually on the existence of improper encouragement of union membership. The DFR, on the other hand, was originally created as a protection for nonmembers but has been applied to members as well. Moreover, as *Radio Officers* indicates, the scope of 8(b)(2) is broader than mere membership or nonmembership, but also applies to union attempts to force members to comply with intra-union procedures. The following questions attempt to raise this issue in a variety of contexts.

(a) Collective bargaining agreements commonly grant union stewards superseniority in matters of layoff and recall. Unions are concerned about the continuity of union leadership, the efficient operation of the grievance procedure and the protection of union representatives from discriminatory treatment. See Wortman, *Superseniority—Myth or Reality*, 18 Lab. L.J. 195, 199 (1967). Although seniority is based only on contract, is it nevertheless consistent with 8(b)(1)(A) and 8(b)(2) to make continued employment in particular situations turn not on strict seniority but on one's status as union steward? The Supreme Court has stated that "[a] provision for the retention of union chairmen beyond the routine requirements of seniority is not at all uncommon and surely ought not to be deemed arbitrary or discriminatory." *Aeronautical Indus. Dist. Lodge 727 v. Campbell*, 337 U.S. 521, 528, 24 LRRM 2173, 2176 (1949). Since the justification for such clauses is based on union interests as well as the continued effectiveness of the grievance procedure, is the issue different from those faced in fair representation cases?

The Board has held that clauses which grant superseniority to union officers, but which extend to employee benefits beyond layoff and recall, *e.g.*, promotions, shift selection, overtime assignments, choice of vacation periods, are presumptively invalid under Section 8(a)(3) because they encourage union activity. *Dairylea Cooperative, Inc.*, 219 NLRB 656, 89 LRRM 1737 (1975), enf'd sub nom. *NLRB v. Teamsters Local 338*, 531 F.2d 1162, 91 LRRM 2929 (2d Cir. 1976). The Board justified a superseniority clause limited to layoff and recall because it "furthers the effective administration of bargaining agreements on the plant level by encouraging the continued presence of the steward on the job." Any discrimination caused was merely "an incidental side effect" of the general benefit to all employees. A broader clause, however, would require special justification. Moreover, clauses will be held invalid if they apply to officers who do not have responsibilities which require their on-the-job presence to further the administration of the agreement. *NLRB v. Gutton Electro-Voice*, 112 LRRM 1361 (1983).

Why should a broad superseniority clause fall outside the "wide range of reasonableness" allowed unions in seniority matters? Is recognition of union service less worthy than recognition of premilitary service in *Ford v. Huffman*? Does such a clause encourage membership more than a hiring hall arrangement? Might a union justifiably determine that enticements are necessary to encourage employees to become stewards? See L. Sayles and G. Strauss, The Local Union 24–33 (rev. ed. 1967), on the burdens of a union steward. Does a broad clause cover matters which are irrelevant to the steward's role in contract administration or, rather, are these benefits necessary to protect stewards against possible employer recrimination? Is the Board or a court in a better position than the union, in the absence of any finding of bad faith, to determine the needs of the union or the grievance process? How do these cases differ from fair representation cases?

(b) A bylaw of the American Federation of Musicians prohibits union members from working with nonmembers. If the existence of such a clause induces an employer to hire union members exclusively, has Section 8(a)(3) been violated? Section 8(b)(2) requires some union action to "cause" the employer to violate 8(a)(3). The Second Circuit has held that "some direct approach to the employer, or some conduct aimed at him," is required to fall within the ambit of 8(b)(2). Glasser v. NLRB, 395 F.2d 401, 406, 68 LRRM 2239, 2243 (2d Cir. 1968). Thus, the maintenance and internal enforcement of the bylaw alone did not violate the Act. Would situations be likely to exist where the very existence of such a bylaw, known to an employer, would encourage discrimination based upon membership? Is it relevant to ask whether membership is open to all who apply? Aside from 8(b)(2) problems, would the employer's actions violate 8(a)(3)? See Musicians Local 802, 176 NLRB 198, 71 LRRM 1228 (1969).

Is such a bylaw a violation of the union's duty to fairly represent all musicians, including nonmembers? See Comment, Closed Shop Union Bylaws Under the NLRA, 37 U. Chi. L. Rev. 778 (1970).

Does the bylaw violate 8(b)(1)(A) by forcing employees to forego the Section 7 right to "refrain" from union activities under Section 7? Scofield v. NLRB, 394 U.S. 423, 70 LRRM 3105 (1969); see generally, Atleson, Union Fines and Picket Lines: The NLRA and Union Disciplinary Power, 17 UCLA L. Rev. 681 (1970); Gould, Some Limitations Upon Union Disciplinary Power Under the NLRA: The Radiations of Allis-Chalmers, 1970 Duke L.J. 1067.

(c) The employer hires replacements during a strike, informing them that they are "permanent replacements." The dispute ends with a new agreement and an understanding that all strikers will be rehired. The strikebearers are laid off, and they file a complaint alleging violations of Sections 8(a)(1), 8(a)(3), 8(b)(1)(A), and 8(b)(2).

The problem is complicated by NLRB v. Mackay Radio and Telegraph Co., supra, page 365, which permits permanent replacements in the first instance, an action which logically conflicts with the policies inherent in Sections 8(a)(1) and 8(a)(3). If the employer may replace strikers to maintain production, may the union correspondingly seek the reinstatement of strikers to protect its members and its institutional interests? Does such action force an employer to discriminate on the grounds of union activity or membership in violation of 8(a)(3)? The union's duty of fair representation extends to all employees within the unit and thus, somewhat uncomfortably, includes strikebearers. Has the union acted unfairly?

Do these problems suggest that 8(b)(2) problems can be treated as part of the union's broad fiduciary obligations under the duty of fair representation? Or is there independent significance to 8(b)(2)?

D. PREEMPTION AND INDIVIDUAL EMPLOYEE RIGHTS

Amalgamated Ass'n of Street, Electric Railway & Motor Coach Employees v. Lockridge

Supreme Court of the United States, 1971
403 U.S. 274, 77 LRRM 2501

MR. JUSTICE HARLAN delivered the opinion of the Court.
. . .

I

Respondent, Wilson P. Lockridge, has obtained in the Idaho courts a judgment for $32,678.56 against petitioners, Northwest Division 1055 of the Amalgamated Association of Street, Electric Railway and Motor Coach Employees of America and its parent international association,[1] on the grounds that, in procuring Lockridge's discharge from employment, pursuant to a valid union security clause in the applicable collective bargaining agreement, the Union breached a contractual obligation embodied in the Union's constitution and bylaws.

From May 1943 until November 2, 1959, Lockridge was a member of petitioner Union and employed within the State of Idaho as a bus driver for Western Greyhound Lines, or its predecessor. At the time of Lockridge's dismissal from the Union, § 3(a) of the collective bargaining agreement in effect between the Union and Greyhound provided:

"All present employees covered by this contract shall become members of the ASSOCIATION [Union] not later than thirty (30) days following its effective date and shall remain members as a condition precedent to continued employment. This section shall apply to newly hired employees thirty (30) days from the date of their employment with the COMPANY." App. 88.

In addition, § 91 of the Union's Constitution and General Laws provided, in pertinent part, that:

---

[1]The local and its parent are, of course, separate legal entities for many purposes and were joined as codefendants below so that each appears as a petitioner in this Court. However, both will be jointly described throughout this opinion as "the petitioner" or "the Union" since the parent was held liable on the theory that it was responsible for the acts of the local here involved, not on the basis of any separate acts committed only by the parent.

"All dues . . . of the members of this Association are due and payable on the first day of each month for that month. . . . They must be paid by the fifteenth of the month in order to continue the member in good standing. . . . A member in arrears for his dues . . . after the fifteenth day of the month is not in good standing . . . and where a member allows his arrearage . . . to run into the second month before paying the same, he shall be debarred from benefits for one month after payment. Where a member allows his arrearage . . . to run over the last day of the second month without payment, he does thereby suspend himself from membership in this Association. . . . Where agreements with employing companies provide that members must be in continuous good financial standing, the member in arrears one month may be suspended from membership and removed from employment, in compliance with the terms of the agreement." App., 91–92.

Prior to September 1959, Lockridge's dues had been deducted from his paycheck by Greyhound, pursuant to a checkoff arrangement. During that year, however, Lockridge and a few other employees were released at their request from the checkoff, and thereby became obligated to pay their dues directly to the Union's office in Portland, Oregon. On November 2, 1959, C.A. Bankhead, the treasurer and financial secretary of the union local, suspended Lockridge from membership on the sole ground that since respondent had not yet paid his October dues he was therefore in arrears contrary to § 91. Bankhead simultaneously notified Greyhound of this determination and requested that Lockridge be removed from employment. Greyhound promptly complied. Lockridge's wife received notice of the suspension from membership in early November, while her husband was on vacation, and on November 10, 1959, tendered Bankhead a check to cover respondent's dues for October and November, which Bankhead refused to accept.

This chain of events, combined with the disparity between the above-quoted terms of the collective bargaining agreement and the union constitution and general laws, generated this lawsuit. Lockridge has contended, and the Idaho courts have so held, that because he was less than two months behind in his payment of dues, respondent had not yet "suspended himself from membership" within the meaning of the Union's rules, but instead had merely ceased to be a "member in good standing." And, because the collective-bargaining agreement required only that employees "remain members," those courts held that neither that agreement nor the final sentence of § 91 justified the Union's action in procuring Lockridge's discharge. Therefore, the Idaho courts have held, Lockridge's dismissal violated a promise, implied in law, that the union would not seek termination of his employment unless he was sufficiently derelict in his dues payments to subject him to loss of his job under the terms of the applicable collective bargaining agreement.

Although the trial court made no formal findings of fact on this score, it appears likely that the Union procured Lockridge's dismissal in the mistaken belief that the applicable union security agreement with Greyhound did in fact, require employees to remain members in good standing and that the Union insisted on what it thought was a technically valid position because it was piqued by Lockridge's obtaining his release from the checkoff. The trial court did find specifically that "almost without exception" it had been the past practice of this local division of the Union merely to suspend delinquent members from service, rather than stripping them of membership, and to put them back to work without loss of seniority when their dues were paid.

Lockridge initially made some efforts, with Bankhead's assistance, to obtain reinstatement in the Union but these proved unsuccessful. No charges were filed before the National Labor Relations Board. Instead, Lockridge filed suit in September 1960 in the Idaho State District Court against the Union and Greyhound, which was later dropped as a party. That court, on the Union's motion, dismissed the complaint in April 1961 on the grounds that it charged the Union with the commission of an unfair labor practice and consequently fell within the exclusive jurisdiction of the NLRB. A year later, the Idaho Supreme Court reversed, holding that the state courts had jurisdiction under this Court's decision in *Association of Machinists* v. *Gonzales*, 356 U.S. 617 (1958), and remanded for trial on the merits. *Lockridge* v. *Amalgamated Assn. of St. El. Ry. & M.C. Emp.*, 84 Idaho 201, 369 P.2d 1006 (1962).

In 1965 Lockridge filed a second amended complaint which has since served as the basis for this lawsuit. Its first count alleged that[:]

> "[I]n suspending plaintiff from membership in the [Union] which resulted in plaintiff's loss of employment, the [Union] . . . acted wantonly, wilfully and wrongfully and without just cause, and . . . deprived plaintiff of his . . . employment with Greyhound Corporation that accrued to him and would accrue to him by reason of his employment, seniority and experience, and plaintiff has been harassed and subject to mental anguish. . . ." App., 46–47.

Count Two, sounding squarely in contract, alleged that[:]

> "[I]n wrongfully suspending plaintiff from membership in the [Union], which resulted in plaintiff's discharge from employment with the Greyhound Corporation, the [Union] . . . acted wrongfully, wantonly, wilfully and maliciously and without just cause and violated the constitution and general laws of the [Union] which constituted a contract between the plaintiff as a member thereof and the [Union], and as a result of said breach of contract plaintiff has been deprived of his . . . employment with . . . Greyhound Corporation . . . and plaintiff has been embarrassed and subjected to mental anguish. . . ." App. 48.

The complaint sought damages in the amount of $212,000 "and such other and further relief as to the court may appear meet and equitable in the premises." *Ibid.*

After trial, the Idaho District Court found the facts as stated above and held that they did, indeed, amount to a breach of contract. The court felt itself bound by the prior determination of the Idaho Supreme Court to consider that it might properly exercise jurisdiction over the controversy and to "decide [the] case on the theories of" *Machinists* v. *Gonzales, supra.*

Consequently, the trial judge concluded that Lockridge was entitled to a decree restoring him to membership in the Union, "although plaintiff has never sought such a remedy." Lockridge was also awarded $32,678.56 as compensation for wages actually lost due to his dismissal from Greyhound's employ, but his requests for future damages arising from continued loss of employment, compensation for loss of seniority or fringe benefits, and punitive damages were all denied. On appeal the Idaho Supreme Court affirmed, over one dissenting vote, except that it also ordered restoration of respondent's seniority rights. 93 Idaho 294, 460 P.2d 719 (1969). Having granted certiorari for the reasons stated at the outset of this opinion, we now reverse.

II

A

. . .

. . . On their face, the above-quoted provisions of the Act [Sections 8(b)(2), 8(b)(1)(A), 8(a)(3)] at least arguably either permit or forbid the union conduct dealt with by the judgment below. For the evident thrust of this aspect of the federal statutory scheme is to permit the enforcement of union security clauses, by dismissal from employment, only for failure to pay dues. Whatever other sanctions may be employed to exact compliance with those internal union rules unrelated to dues payment, the Act seems generally to exclude dismissal from employment. See *Radio Officers' Union* v. *National Labor Relations Bd.*, 347 U.S. 17 (1954). Indeed, in the course of rejecting petitioner's preemption argument, the Idaho Supreme Court stated that, in its opinion, the Union "did most certainly violate 8(b)(1)(A), did most certainly violate 8(b)(2) . . . and probably caused the employer to violate 8(a)(3)." 93 Idaho, at —, 460 P.2d at 724. Thus, given the broad preemption principle enunciated in *Garmon*, the want of state court power to resolve Lockridge's complaint might well seem to follow as a matter of course.

The Idaho Supreme Court, however, concluded that it nevertheless possessed jurisdiction in these circumstances. That determination, as we understand it, rested upon three separate propositions, all of which are urged here by respondent. The first is that the Union's conduct was not only an unfair labor practice, but a breach of its contract with Lockridge as well. . . . In other words *Garmon*, the state court and respondent assert, states a principle applicable only where the state law invoked is designed specifically to regulate labor relations; it has no force where the State applies its general common law of contracts to resolve disputes between a union and its members. Secondly, it is urged that the facts that might be shown to vindicate Lockridge's claim in the Idaho state courts differ from those relevant to proceedings governed by the National Labor Relations Act. It is said that the conduct regulated by the Act is union and employer discrimination; general contract law takes into account only the correctness of competing interpretations of the language embodied in agreements. . . . Finally, there recurs throughout the state court opinion, and the arguments of respondent here, the theme that the facts of the instant case render it virtually indistinguishable from *Association of Machinists* v. *Gonzales*, 356 U.S. 617 (1958), where this Court upheld the exercise of state court jurisdiction in an opinion written only one Term prior to *Garmon*, by the author of *Garmon* and which was approvingly cited in the *Garmon* opinion itself.

We do not believe that any of these arguments suffice to overcome the plain purport of *Garmon* as applied to the facts of this case. However, we have determined to treat these considerations at some length because of the understandable confusion, perhaps in a measure attributable to the previous opinions of this Court, they reflect over the jurisdictional bases upon which the *Garmon* doctrine rests.

. . . The rationale for preemption . . . rests in large measure upon our determination that when it set down a federal labor policy Congress plainly meant to do more than simply to alter the then-prevailing substantive law. It sought as well to restructure fundamentally the processes for effectuating that policy, deliberately placing the responsibility for applying and developing this comprehensive legal system in the hands of an expert administrative body rather than the federalized judicial system. . . .

A second factor that has played an important role in our shaping of the preemption doctrine has been the necessity to act without specific congressional direction. The precise extent to which state law must be displaced to achieve those unifying ends sought by the national legislature has never been determined by the Congress. This, has, quite frankly, left the Court with few available options. We cannot declare preempted all local regulation that touches or concerns in any way the complex interrelationships between employees, employers, and unions; obviously, much of this is left to the States. Nor can we proceed on a case-by-case basis to determine whether each particular final judicial pronouncement does, or might reasonably be thought to, conflict in some relevant manner with federal labor policy. This Court is ill-equipped to play such a role and the federal system dictates that this problem be solved with a rule capable of relatively easy application, so that lower courts may largely police themselves in this regard. Equally important, such a principle would fail to take account of the fact . . . that simple congruity of legal rules does not, in this area, prove the absence of untenable conflict. Further, it is surely not possible for this Court to treat the National Labor Relations Act section by section, committing enforcement of some of its provisions wholly to the NLRB and others to the concurrent domain of local law. Nothing in the language or underlying purposes of the Act suggests any basis for such distinctions. Finally, treating differently judicial power to deal with conduct protected by the Act from that prohibited by it would likewise be unsatisfactory. Both areas equally involve conduct whose legality is governed by federal law, the application of which Congress committed to the Board, not courts.

. . .

The failure of alternative analyses and the interplay of the foregoing policy considerations, then, led this Court to hold in *Garmon*, 359 U.S., at 244:

"When it is clear or may fairly be assumed that the activities which a State purports to regulate are protected by § 7 of the National Labor Relations Act, or constitute an unfair labor practice under § 8, due regard for the federal enactment requires that state jurisdiction must yield. To leave the States free to regulate conduct so plainly within the central aim of federal regulation involves too great a danger of conflict between power asserted by Congress and requirements imposed by state law."

Upon these premises, we think that *Garmon* rather clearly dictates reversal of the judgment below. None of the propositions asserted to support that judgment can withstand an application, in light of those factors that compelled its promulgation, of the *Garmon* rule.

Assuredly the proposition that Lockridge's complaint was not subject to the exclusive jurisdiction of the NLRB because it charged a breach of contract rather than an unfair labor practice is not tenable. Preemption, as shown above, is designed to shield the system from conflicting regulation of conduct. It is the conduct being regulated, not the formal description of governing legal standards, that is the proper focus of concern. Indeed, the notion that a relevant distinction exists for such purposes between particularized and generalized labor law was explicitly rejected in *Garmon* itself. 359 U.S., at 244.

The second argument, closely related to the first, is that the state courts, in resolving this controversy, did deal with different conduct, *i.e.*, interpretation of contractual terms, than would the NLRB which would be required to decide whether the Union discriminated against Lockridge. At bottom, of course, the Union's action in procuring Lockridge's dismissal from employment is the conduct which Idaho courts have sought to regulate. Thus, this second point demonstrates at best that Idaho defines differently what sorts of such union conduct may permissibly be proscribed. This is to say either that the regulatory schemes, state and federal, conflict (in which case preemption is clearly called for) or that Idaho is dealing with conduct to which the federal Act does not speak. If the latter assertion was intended, it is not accurate. As pointed out in Part II A, *supra*, the relevant portions of the Act operate to prohibit a union from causing or attempting to cause an employer to discriminate against an employee because his membership in the union has been terminated "on some ground other than" his failure to pay those dues requisite to membership. This has led the Board routinely and frequently to inquire into the proper construction of union regulations in order to ascertain whether the union properly found an employee to have been derelict in his dues-paying responsibilities, where his discharge was procured on the asserted grounds of nonmembership in the union. . . . That a union may in good faith have misconstrued its own rules has not been treated by the Board as a defense to a claimed violation of § 8(b)(2). In the Board's view, it is the fact of misapplication by a union of its rules, not the motivation for that discrimination, that constitutes an unfair labor practice. . . .

From the foregoing, then, it would seem that this case indeed represents one of the clearest instances where the *Garmon* principle, properly understood, should operate to oust state court jurisdiction. There being no doubt that the conduct here involved was arguably protected by § 7 or prohibited by § 8 of the Act, the full range of very substantial interests the preemption doctrine seeks to protect are directly implicated here.

However, a final strand of analysis underlies the opinion of the Idaho Supreme Court, and the position of respondent, in this case. Our decision in *Association of Machinists* v. *Gonzales*, 356 U.S. 617 (1958), it is argued, fully survived the subsequent reorientation of preemption doctrine effected by the *Garmon* decision, providing, in effect, an express exception for the exercise of judicial jurisdiction in cases such as this.

The fact situation in *Gonzales* does resemble in some relevant regards that of the instant case. . . . Gonzales prevailed on his breach of contract theory and was awarded damages for wages lost due to the revocation of membership as well as a decree providing for his reinstatement in the union. This Court confirmed the California courts' power to award the monetary damages, the only aspect of the action below challenged in this Court. The primary rationale for the result reached was that California should be competent to "fill out," 356 U.S., at 620, the reinstatement remedy by utilizing "the comprehensive relief of equity," *id.*, at 621, which the Board did not fully possess. Secondarily, it was said that the lawsuit "did not purport to remedy or regulate union conduct on the ground that it was designed to bring about employer discrimination against an employee, the evil the Board is concerned to strike at as an unfair labor practice under § 8(b)(2)." *Id.*, at 622.

Although it was decided only one Term subsequent to *Gonzales*, *Garmon* clearly did not fully embrace the technique of the prior case. It was precisely the realization that disparities in remedies and administration could produce substantial conflict, in the practical sense of the term, between the relevant state and federal regulatory schemes and that this Court could not effectively and responsibly superintend on a case-by-case basis the exertion of state power over matters arguably governed by the National Labor Relations Act that impelled the somewhat broader formulation of the preemption doctrine in *Garmon*. It seems evident that the full-blown rationale of *Gonzales* could not survive the rule of *Garmon*. Nevertheless, *Garmon* did not cast doubt upon the result reached in *Gonzales*, but cited it approvingly as an example of the fact that state court jurisdiction is not preempted "where the activity regulated was a merely peripheral concern of the . . . Act." 359 U.S., at 243.

Against this background, we attempted to define more precisely the reach of *Gonzales* within the more comprehensive framework *Garmon* provided in the companion cases of *Plumbers Union* v. *Borden*, 373 U.S. 690 (1963), and *Iron Workers* v. *Perko*, 373 U.S. 701 (1963).

Borden had sued his union in state courts, alleging that the union had arbitrarily refused to refer him to a particular job which he had lined up. He recovered damages, based on lost wages, on the grounds that this conduct constituted both tortious interference with his right to contract for employment and a breach of promise, implicit in his membership arrangement with the union, not to discriminate unfairly against any member or deny him the right to work. Perko had obtained a large money judgment in the Ohio courts on proof that the union had conspired, without cause, to deprive him of employment as a foreman by demanding his discharge from one such position he had held and representing to others that his foreman's rights had been suspended. We held both Perko's and Borden's judgments inconsistent with the *Garmon* rule essentially for the same reasons we have concluded that Lockridge could not, consistently with the *Garmon* decision, maintain his lawsuit in the state courts. We further held there was no necessity to "consider the present vitality of [the *Gonzales*] rationale in the light of more recent decisions," because in those cases, unlike *Gonzales*, "the crux of the action[s] . . . concerned alleged interference with the plaintiff's existing or prospective employment relations and was not directed to internal union matters." Because no specific claim for restoration of membership rights had been advanced, "there was no permissible state remedy to which the award of consequential damages for loss of earnings might be subordinated." *Perko*, 373 U.S., at 705. See also *Borden*, 373 U.S., at 697.

In sum, what distinguished *Gonzales* from *Borden* and *Perko* was that the former lawsuit "was focused on purely internal union matters," *Borden, supra*, at 697, a subject the National Labor Relations Act leaves principally to other processes of law. The possibility that, in defining the scope of the union's duty to Gonzales, the state courts would directly and consciously implicate principles of federal law was at best tangential and remote. In the instant case, however, this possibility was real and immediate. To assess the legality of his union's conduct toward Gonzales the California courts needed only to focus upon the union's constitution and by-laws. Here, however, Lockridge's entire case turned upon the construction of the applicable union security clause, a matter as to which, as shown above, federal concern is pervasive and its regulation complex. The reasons for Gonzales' deprivation of union membership had nothing to do with matters of employment, while Lockridge's cause of action and claim for damages was based solely upon the procurement of his discharge from employment. It cannot plausibly be argued, in any meaningful sense, that Lockridge's lawsuit "was focused upon purely internal matters." Although nothing said in *Garmon* necessarily suggests that States cannot regulate the general conditions which unions may impose on their membership, it surely makes crystal clear that *Gonzales* does not stand for the proposition that resolution of any union-member conflict is within state competence so long as one of the remedies provided is restoration of union membership. This much was settled by *Borden* and *Perko*, and it is only upon such an unwarrantably broad interpretation of *Gonzales* that the judgment below could be sustained.

III

. . .

In his brief before this Court, respondent has argued for the first time since this lawsuit was started that two of these exceptions to the *Garmon* principle independently justify the Idaho courts' exercise of jurisdiction over this controversy. First, Lockridge contends that his action, properly viewed, is one to enforce a collective-bargaining agreement. Alternatively, he asserts the suit, in essence, was one to redress petitioner's breach of its duty of fair representation. As will be seen, these contentions are somewhat intertwined.

. . . Indeed, in *Vaca v. Sipes*, 386 U.S. 171 (1967), we held that an action seeking damages for injury inflicted by a breach of a union's duty of fair representation was judicially cognizable in any event, that is, even if the conduct complained of was arguably protected or prohibited by the National Labor Relations Act and whether or not the lawsuit was bottomed on a collective agreement. Perhaps Count One of Lockridge's second amended complaint could be construed to assert either or both of these theories of recovery. However, it is unnecessary to pass upon the extent to which *Garmon* would be inapplicable if it were shown that in these circumstances petitioner not only breached its contractual obligations to respondent, but did so in a manner that constituted a breach of the duty of fair representation. For such a claim to be made out, Lockridge must have proved "arbitrary or bad faith conduct on the part of the union." *Vaca v. Sipes, supra,* at 193. There must be "substantial evidence of fraud, deceitful action or dishonest conduct.". . . Whether these requisite elements have been proved is a matter of federal law. Quite obviously, they were not even asserted to be relevant in the proceedings below. As the Idaho Supreme Court stated in affirming the verdict for Lockridge, "[t]his was a misinterpretation of a contract. Whatever the underlying motive for expulsion might have been, this case had been submitted and tried on the interpretation of the contract, not on a theory of discrimination." Thus, the trial judge's conclusion of law in sustaining Lockridge's claim specifically incorporates the assumption that the Union's "acts . . . were predicated solely upon the ground that [Lockridge] had failed to tender periodic dues in conformance with the requirements of the union Constitution and employment contract as they interpreted [it]. . . ." App., 66. Further, the trial court excluded as irrelevant petitioner's proffer of evidence designed to show that the union's interpretation of the contract was reasonably based upon its understanding of prior collective bargaining agreements negotiated with Greyhound. . . .

Nor can it be fairly argued that our resolution of respondent's final contentions entails simply attaching variegated labels to matters of equal substance. We have exempted § 301 suits from the *Garmon* principle because of the evident congressional determination that courts should be free to interpret and enforce collective bargaining agreements even where that process may involve condemning or permitting conduct arguably subject to the protection or prohibition of the National Labor Relations Act. The legislative determination that courts are fully competent to resolve labor relations disputes through focusing on the terms of a collective bargaining agreement cannot be said to sweep within it the same conclusion with regard to the terms of union-employee contracts that are said to be implied in law. That is why the principle of *Smith v. Evening News* is applicable only to those disputes that are governed by the terms of the collective bargaining agreement itself.

Similarly, this Court's refusal to limit judicial competence to rectify a breach of the duty of fair representation rests upon our judgment that such actions cannot, in the vast majority of situations where they occur, give rise to actual conflict with the operative realities of federal labor policy. The duty of fair representation was judicially evolved, without the participation of the NLRB, to enforce fully the important principle that no individual union member may suffer invidious, hostile treatment at the hands of the majority of his coworkers. Where such union conduct is proved it is clear, beyond doubt, that the conduct could not be otherwise regulated by the substantive federal law. And the fact that the doctrine was originally developed and applied by courts, after passage of the Act, and carries with it the need to adduce substantial evidence of discrimination that is intentional, severe and unrelated to legitimate union objectives ensures that the risk of conflict with the general congressional policy favoring expert, centralized administration, and remedial action is tolerably slight. *Vaca* v. *Sipes, supra*, at 180–181. So viewed, the duty of fair representation, properly defined, operates to limit the scope of *Garmon* where the sheer logic of the preemption principle might otherwise cause it to be extended to a point where its operation might be unjust. *Vaca* v. *Sipes, supra*, at 182–183. If, however, the congressional policies *Garmon* seeks to promote are not to be swallowed up, the very distinction, embedded within the instant lawsuit itself, between honest, mistaken conduct, on the one hand, and deliberate and severely hostile and irrational treatment, on the other, needs strictly to be maintained.

IV

Finally, we deem it appropriate to discuss briefly two other considerations underlying the conclusion we have reached in this case. First, our decision must not be taken as expressing any views on the substantive claims of the two parties to this controversy. Indeed, our judgment is, quite simply, that it is not the task of federal or state courts to make such determinations. Secondly, in our explication of the reasons for the *Garmon* rule, and the various exceptions to it, we noted that, although largely of judicial making, the labor relations preemption doctrine finds its basic justification in the presumed intent of Congress. While we do not assert that the *Garmon* doctrine is without imperfection, we do think that it is founded on reasoned principle and that until it is altered by congressional action or by judicial insights that are born of further experience with it, a heavy burden rests upon those who would, at this late date, ask this Court to abandon *Garmon* and set out again in quest of a system more nearly perfect. A fair regard for considerations of *stare decisis* and the coordinate role of the Congress in defining the extent to which federal legislation preempts state law strongly support our conclusion that the basic tenets of *Garmon* should not be disturbed.

For the reasons stated above, the judgment below is:

Reversed.

Mr. Justice Douglas, dissenting.

I would affirm this judgment on the basis of *Machinists* v. *Gonzales*, 356 U.S. 617, rather than overrule it. I would not extend *San Diego Building Trades Council* v. *Garmon*, 359 U.S. 236, so as to make Lockridge, the employee, seek his relief in faraway Washington, D.C., from the National Labor Relations Board.

When we hold that a grievance is "arguably" within the jurisdiction of the National Labor Relations Board and remit the individual employee to the Board for remedial relief, we impose a great hardship on him, especially where he is a lone individual not financed out of a lush treasury. I would allow respondent recourse to litigation in his home town tribunal and not require him to resort to an elusive remedy in distant and remote Washington, D.C., which takes money to reach.

He has six months within which to file an unfair labor practice charge with the Regional Director and serve it upon the other party. If he does not file within six months, the claim is barred. 29 U.S.C. § 160(b). . . . [See 29 CFR § 101 et seq. for the new regulations, procedures, and limitations.]

From the viewpoint of an aggrieved employee, there is not a trace of equity in this long-drawn, expensive remedy. If he musters the resources to exhaust the administrative remedy, the chances are that he too will be exhausted. If the General Counsel issues a complaint, then he stands in line for some time waiting for the Board's decision. If the General Counsel refuses to act, then the employee is absolutely without remedy. . . .

When we tell a sole individual that his case is "arguably" within the jurisdiction of the Board, we in practical effect deny him any remedy. I repeat what I said before. "When the basic dispute is between a union and an employer, any hiatus that might exist in the jurisdictional balance that has been struck can be filled by resort to economic power. But when the union member has a dispute with his union, he has no power on which to rely." *Association of Journeymen* v. *Borden*, 373 U.S. 690, 699–700 (dissenting).

Garmon involved a union-employer dispute. It should not be extended to the individual employee who seeks a remedy for his grievance against his union.

. . .

MR. JUSTICE WHITE, with whom THE CHIEF JUSTICE joins, dissenting.

. . .

. . . [I]t is time to recognize that Congress has not federalized the entire law of labor relations, even labor-management relations, and that within the area occupied by federal law neither Congress, this Court nor the National Labor Relations Board itself has, in the name of uniformity, insisted that the agency always be the exclusive expositor of federal policy in the first instance. . . .

I

[Justice White discusses the following exceptions to the Board's primary jurisdiction and the application of federal law: Board acceptance of arbitrator's awards based on behavior which is also an alleged unfair labor practice; enforcement of collective bargaining agreements and of the duty of fair representation by the judiciary notwithstanding concurrent Board jurisdiction of the alleged unfair labor practice; federal or state jurisdiction of damage claims under Section 303 of the LMRA; and state court jurisdiction following Board declination to act on "non-policy" grounds under Section 14(c)(2).]

. . .

Even though federal law is pervasive in labor-management relations, state law is preserved in some respects. At first blush, it might seem that these matters present no problems of uniformity, for there is no national law being applied. But the simple fact that Congress and this Court have deferred to the States in these areas indicates a subordination of the interest in uniformity to the interests of the States. By making the matter one of state law, Congress has not only authorized multiformity on the subject, but practically guaranteed it. The results, as far as uniformity is concerned, are no different than if the States applied federal law with abandon. For example, the controversial § 14(b) of the Taft-Hartley Act . . . has authorized States to choose for themselves whether to require or permit union shops. This allows the States to regulate union or agency shop clauses . . . so that union insistence on a security agreement as part of a collective bargaining agreement may be prohibited in one State and protected or even encouraged in another. The policy choice made by Congress on this matter necessarily subordinated uniformity in national law to what were perceived to be overriding concerns of the States.

. . . Again, it is entirely possible that some States will require a greater showing of violence than others before awarding damages, so that behavior which violently seeks to coerce union membership will be prohibited in one State and allowed in another. But the interest in uniformity is subordinated to the larger interests that persons injured by such violence have preserved to them whatever remedies state law may authorize.

. . .

Until today, *Int'l Ass. of Machinists* v. *Gonzales, supra,* had been thought to stand for the proposition that *Garmon* did not reach cases "when the possibility of conflict with federal policy is . . . remote," 350 U.S. 617, 621. But with today's emasculation of *Gonzales,* there is probably little that remains of it. *Linn* v. *Plant Guard Workers,* 383 U.S. 53 (1966), was ostensibly based in part on this rationale, 383 U.S., at 59–61, but it was equally bottomed on *Laburnum Construction* and other cases upholding state power to regulate matters of "overriding state interest" such as violence or, as in *Linn,* defamation. I see no reason why this exception has not, for all practical purposes, thus expired. In my view, however, and for the reasons set forth in Part II, *Gonzales* controls this case.[3]

. . .

---

[3]With all respect, the majority's attempt to distinguish the instant case from *Gonzales* is unpersuasive. According to the majority, "The reasons for Gonzales' deprivation of union membership had nothing to do with matters of employment, while Lockridge's cause of action and claim for damages was based solely upon the procurement of his discharge from employment." Slip op., at 21. In the first place, Lockridge squarely alleged that his damages

. . . The unmistakable focus of both the NLRA and the LMRA is on labor management relations, rather than union-member relations, as such.

During the 1950's there came to light various patterns of union abuse of power, and in the Labor Management Reporting and Disclosure Act of 1959 (LMRDA) . . . Congress acted to correct these evils by directly addressing itself to some aspects of union-member affairs. The LMRDA provides a "bill of rights," which gives union members the right to participate in union affairs, to speak freely, and to be protected from arbitrary discipline. It also imposes certain requirements on unions to disclose their financial affairs, regulates union elections, and safeguards labor organizations against unscrupulous agents or officers. Throughout the Act are provisions for civil or criminal enforcement of the Act in federal courts. See 73 Stat. 523, 525, 529–530, 531, 534, 536, 537, 539. But in a crucial departure from what the Court has held the legislative intention was in regulating *labor-management* relations, the Congress declared:

> "Except as specifically provided to the contrary, nothing in this Act shall reduce or limit the responsibilities of any labor organization or any officer . . . or other representative of a labor organization . . . under any other Federal law or under the laws of any State and, *except as explicitly provided to the contrary, nothing in this Act shall take away any right or bar any remedy to which members of a labor organization are entitled under such other Federal law or law of any State.*" § 603(a), 73 Stat. 540, 29 U.S.C. § 523 (emphasis added).

. . .

The LMRDA was a major effort by Congress to regulate the rights and responsibilities of the union-member relationship as such, but, as shown by § 603(a), it was clearly not an attempt to make federal law the exclusive arbiter of this relationship. In *Gonzales* the Court noted that "the protection of union members in their rights as members from arbitrary conduct by unions and union officers has not been undertaken by federal law. . . ." 356 U.S., at 620. Though in the following year the LMRDA certainly "undertook" to protect members in important respects, it specifically disavowed any notion of preempting state law and thus left unimpaired the *Gonzales'* conclusion that state law has a proper role in union-member disputes.[5]

. . .

---

had been caused by suspension from union membership contrary to the constitution and laws of the union; his cause of action was bottomed upon this breach of duty by the union. More importantly, it is inaccurate to imply, as the foregoing quoted statement does, that *Lockridge* is somehow different from *Gonzales* in that Gonzales' "deprivation of union membership" did not result in his loss of employment. The *Gonzales* Court said, "[t]he evidence adduced at the trial showed that plaintiff, *because* of his loss of membership, was unable to obtain employment and was *thereby* damaged. . . . [T]his damage was not charged nor treated as the result of an unfair labor practice but *as a result* of the breach of contract." 356 U.S., at 622, n.*. (Quoting the California court's opinion.) (Emphasis added.)

[5]The majority's opinion simply refuses to face this issue. There is no "absence of a contrary expression of intention from Congress," as the majority contends. See p. 13, at

Like many States, Idaho construes the union-member relation to be a contractual one, defined by the constitution and bylaws of the union. As such, the contracts are enforceable through the State's traditional common-law jurisdiction. Here, Lockridge was discharged for alleged non-payment of dues in accordance with the union constitution and brought suit alleging that he had in fact not been unduly tardy and that the union's action was a breach of the contract. The face of the complaint did not implicate federal law. If the Idaho court were allowed to proceed it would not have purported to adjudicate an unfair labor practice by reference to federal law but, if it found the conduct unprotected by federal law, see Part III *infra*, would have enforced rights and obligations created by the union constitution. The Court nevertheless holds that because the union conduct alleged in the complaint also constitutes, or arguably so, an unfair labor practice, the controversy must be adjudicated by the National Labor Relations Board. I find little in the Court's opinion to convince me that Congress intended this result. With all respect, I agree with *Gonzales* that this result is at best "abstractly justifiable, as a matter of wooden logic." 356 U.S., at 619.

Furthermore, this Court's decision in *Smith* v. *Evening News, supra,* seems contrary to the result reached today. *Smith* held that suits to enforce the collective bargaining agreement could be brought in state or federal courts under § 301 notwithstanding the fact that the conduct alleged would also constitute an unfair labor practice. Thus, courts enforcing *Smith*-type actions are dealing in contract rights, not unfair labor practices. There seems little reason why suits for breach of the union-member contract cannot similarly be brought in state courts (or in federal courts in diversity actions), notwithstanding the alternate nature of the behavior as an unfair labor practice.

III

I have attempted to show in Part II that invocation of *Garmon*-type preemption is inappropriate where a union member brings suit against a union for breach of the union's constitution or bylaws. Wholly apart from such considerations, however, I cannot agree with the opinion of the Court because it reaffirms the *Garmon* doctrine as applied to conduct arguably protected under § 7, as well as to that arguably prohibited under § 8. The essential difference, for present purposes, between activity which is arguably prohibited and that which is arguably protected is that a hearing on the latter activity is virtually impossible unless one deliberately commits an unfair labor practice. In a typical unfair practice case, by alleging conduct arguably prohibited by § 8 the charging party can at least present the General Counsel with the facts, and if the General Counsel issues a complaint, the charging party can present the Board with the facts and arguments to support the claim. But for activity which is

n. 5. When Congress addressed itself to union-member relations as such it specifically preserved existing state remedies even though there may be federal remedies to redress the same conduct.

arguably protected, there is no provision for an authoritative decision by the Board in the first instance; yet the *Garmon* rule blindly preempts other tribunals. . . .

MR. JUSTICE BLACKMUN also dissents for the basic reasons set forth by MR. JUSTICE DOUGLAS and MR. JUSTICE WHITE in their respective dissenting opinions.

Questions

1. Assuming that in *Lockridge* the actions of the employer and union are "arguably prohibited" by the NLRA, what dangers to federal interests exist in the allowance of Lockridge's state court action? Is the basic concern that the "arguably prohibited conduct" may actually not be federally proscribed at all, and, therefore, the conduct may be intended to be free of all legal restraint?

2. Does *Wisconsin Employment Relations Commission, supra,* page 385, suggest revisions of approach or result in *Lockridge?* The Court noted one "line of pre-emption analysis," focusing on whether Congress intended the conduct to be free of all regulation. The conduct in *Lockridge* would not seem to fall within this category. The Court also posed a second dimension, one "based predominantly upon the primary jurisdiction of the Board." Was this the basis for *Lockridge?* What if Lockridge, like another Greyhound employee, had filed a charge but it had been dismissed by the NLRB? Were the underlying issues in the state action the kind that require NLRB expertise? One issue involved an interpretation of the union shop clause; another involved the union's constitutional provisions dealing with the effect of a default of regular dues. If NLRB expertise is not required, is there any other ground upon which Washington law could be preempted?

3. Has the Court adequately distinguished *Gonzales?* Didn't *Lockridge,* like *Gonzales,* involve a construction of union constitutional provisions rather than the union security clause? Lockridge challenged, not the clause, but its application to him. Both cases involved a loss of employment, but arguably the loss of employment in Lockridge was used only as a measure of damages rather than being the "crux" of the case. If the state action was, as the Court suggests, based upon the union security clause, why was Section 301 not an adequate basis of state jurisdiction?

4. Compare *Vaca* v. *Sipes, supra,* page 645, where the Court rejected NLRB exclusivity in a case which, like *Lockridge,* involved a union-member dispute. Justice Harlan distinguished *Vaca,* since fair representation involves "deliberate and severely hostile and irrational treatment" whereas *Lockridge,* at worst, involved "honest, mistaken conduct." Does this distinction relate to the policies involved in preemption?

5. Since DFR actions are not subject to preemption, what if Lockridge had simply framed his complaint in DFR terms? If most union discrimination cases, involving membership or other union considerations, can be framed as DFR cases, the preemption hurdle can seemingly be easily

avoided. To overcome this problem, would it make sense to preempt only "traditional" 8(b) claims, such as union discrimination for nonmembership or for intraunion activities? See Bryson, *A Matter of Wooden Logic: Labor Law Preemption and Individual Rights*, 51 Tex. L. Rev. 1037, 1109 (1973). Is this a workable or a wise solution?

6. Lockridge was suspended for being one day late, and the union had ignored his subsequent check for the dues arrears. Why should the union have acted this way, even if its action is contractually permissible? Is it relevant that Lockridge had previously revoked his checkoff authorization? Would this be relevant to a fair representation action in federal or state court? Would this type of action interfere less with NLRA administration than the action Lockridge actually brought?

7. Is it relevant that actions brought by individual employees against their employer or union are often brought by attorneys who usually do not represent unions or employers and, thus, may have little experience with the field?

8. What if Lockridge had filed an unfair labor practice charge? Under Sections 8(a)(3) and 8(b)(2), discharge could only result from the termination of union membership if he was terminated because of his "failure . . . to tender the periodic dues . . . uniformly required as a condition of . . . retaining membership. . . ." Lockridge had lost his good standing, but he had not yet lost his status as a member under the union constitution and the collective agreement. See generally, Lesnick, *Preemption Reconsidered: The Apparent Reaffirmation of Garmon*, 72 Colum. L. Rev. 469 (1972); Cox, *Labor Law Preemption Revisited*, 85 Harv. L. Rev. 1337 (1972).

9. Hill is a carpenter and a member of a union which operates an exclusive hiring hall. He alleges that due to differences over internal union policies he was discriminated against in referrals to employers. In addition, he was subject to a campaign of personal vilification and harassment. What avenues of relief exist?

(a) Can Hill file valid charges with the NLRB under Sections 8(b)(1)(A) or 8(b)(2)?

(b) Can Hill bring a valid fair representation action in state or federal court? What about a breach of contract action under Section 301?

(c) Would an action for the intentional infliction of mental distress lie in state court if it did not involve lost wages due to discrimination in hiring hall referrals? See *Farmer* v. *Carpenters, Local 25*, 45 USLW 4263, 94 LRRM 2759, 2765 (1977), where the Supreme Court held that the state tort action is not preempted so long as the action is "either unrelated to employment discrimination or a function of the particularly abusive manner in which the discrimination is accomplished or threatened rather than a function of the actual or threatened discrimination itself."

7. Statutory Regulation of Union Economic Pressure

A. ORGANIZATIONAL PICKETING

Problem

You are an associate in the office of the General Counsel of the United Factory Workers Union. Assume that an initial organizing drive is taking place at the Enderby Company. You have been asked to respond to the following memo from the General Counsel.

"Ruth Blair, one of our organizers, called me this morning to advise that the Enderby organizing campaign is not going very well. After an early flurry of card signing, we've come almost to a standstill. Ruth thinks that this is the result of a strong anti-union campaign by Enderby, including conduct which in her opinion crosses the line and constitutes unfair labor practices. The discharge of two of our key union adherents, on stated grounds of excessive absenteeism and poor production, has further chilled the union drive. Ruth thinks that she can establish that some of this activity violates the Act. There is a good chance for a bargaining order under *Gissel* if we go that route.

"However, Ruth does not want to incur the long delays involved in using the election-*Gissel* procedure. She has spoken to the local Teamsters union. She is convinced that if a picket line were put up in front of Enderby, key deliveries would not be made. This might put pressure on Enderby, if not to recognize the union, at least to stop its unfair campaign and give the election machinery a chance. It might also persuade some of the employees that a continuing organizational struggle will hurt Enderby, and that it might be better to sign authorization cards and support the union in order to resolve this matter.

"Would you please advise me whether we can engage in picketing for this purpose under Section 8(b)(7) of the Act? Specifically, will such conduct be enjoined, or will it force us into an election? And if it does, must we proceed to election in face of these employer violations of the Act, or may we block the election by filing charges against the employer? Ruth also wants to know how the picket signs should be phrased. Do you see any ethical problems in assisting in wording the signs to achieve a favorable result?"

Eagerly, you consult the murky text of 8(b)(7), mastering, within an hour, its structure and content. Then you delve into the statutory history and some of the key cases. Miraculously, you come across the following document.

Section 8(b)(7) Dialogue
. . . at a cast party

MAIN CLAUSE: Congress was wise to include 8(b)(7) in its 1959 amendments. Before we came along it was possible for a union which did not yet represent a majority of the employees to put economic pressure on the company through picketing. The company, afraid this would mess up deliveries, or at least be bad public relations, would agree to recognize the union, perhaps making sure first that the initial collective bargaining agreement was an easy one to live with. That kind of pressure is bad because it pressures employees to join a union without a chance to exercise their free choice in an election. Until 8(b)(7) came along, this kind of activity was resolved by tort doctrines, in cases like *Plant* v. *Woods.** Of course, there were First Amendment questions, but the Supreme Court made clear in *Teamsters* v. *Vogt*** that overriding state concerns justified limitations on such picketing. Now, of course, 8(b)(7) occupies the field, and any state efforts at regulation would run up against the preemption doctrine.

PROVIDED FURTHER: It's a good thing that I'm in the statute. I preserve the constitutional rights you would have taken away. All a union has to do is design its picket signs to make clear that the purpose of the picketing is to advise the public that the company is nonunion.

MAIN CLAUSE: That isn't so, Provided Further. As I read our statute you have a very limited role in labor relations. You apply, the words say, when "*the* purpose" of the picketing is to advise the public. Now most organizational picketing, as I see it, has a dual purpose: maybe to advise the public, but more critically, to force the employer to bargain with the union. So I think your section saves only the activity that has purely a publicity purpose.

PROVIDED FURTHER: You've had too many bloody literalisms at this party. If you think I apply only when the picketing is solely informational, then I'm superfluous.

MAIN CLAUSE: You said it, not I.

PROVIDED FURTHER: No, I'm serious. Picketing that is for the sole purpose of advising the public literally cannot at the same time have a recognitional object. Purely informational picketing, if there is such a thing, does not fit within the main clause of 8(b)(7). 8(b)(7) would not apply at all, and the picketing would not need my protection to be immune from regulation. That is why I say that, unless Congress simply meant to add a few more meaningless words to an already convoluted

---

Plant v. *Woods* appears in Chapter 1, A, *supra.*
** 354 U.S. 284, 40 LRRM 2208 (1957). *Vogt* is discussed in Chapter 3, A, *supra.*

statute, it must have meant for the "provided further" clause to operate in those situations in which the union seeks recognition, but also desires to advise the public that the company is nonunion. At the very least the consumer ought to have the information that the company has no union, so that he or she can refuse to deal with the company if he or she chooses.

MAIN CLAUSE: You are saying, then, that a union that pickets for recognition, as defined in the main clause of 8(b)(7), may exempt its activity from regulation merely by giving it an informational aspect. Now that seems dishonest. Isn't it too easy for the union to manufacture a motive to save its picketing?

PROVIDED FURTHER: I assume the union can't make it all up, but must have a bona fide interest in advising the public.

MAIN CLAUSE: With all respect, you dissemble. I don't think unions are at all concerned with the publicity aspect of their picketing. They want to stop deliveries. Now what happens when a union asks its lawyer how to draft its signs to comply with 8(b)(7)? Do you think the lawyer is going to say, "Now don't you engage in publicity appeals unless you really mean it"? Even if law students are taught that it is unethical to draw up a sign reflecting a phony motive, won't a lawyer feel silly telling this to his client? Won't he be afraid of losing the client?

PROVIDED FURTHER: You are a hard, cynical concatenation of words, but I suppose the triggering paragraph of a section like ours has to be tough, or else violators of the Act would escape our net. Now on the ethical question, let me tell you what the ABA Code of Professional Responsibility says:

"Canon 7
"A lawyer should represent a client zealously within the bounds of the law.
"Disciplinary Rule DR 7–102: (A) In his representation of a client a lawyer shall not:

. . .

"(6) Participate in the creation or preservation of evidence when he knows or it is obvious that the evidence is false."

I have enjoyed meeting you on the grounds of logic and policy in figuring out how our section treats informational picketing, but the evening wears on, so I give you authority. Have a look at *Smitley, d/b/a/ Crown Cafeteria* v. *NLRB*, 327 F.2d 351, 55 LRRM 2302 (9th Cir. 1964). There you will find the court affirms a Board decision which gives me my due as a proviso. I'd rather recite Yeats at this party, but let me quote you a little DUNIWAY, J., from the *Smitley* case:

"Petitioners urge that if the picketing has as 'an object' recognition or organization, then it is still illegal, even though it has 'the purpose' of truthfully advising the public, etc., within the meaning of the second proviso to subparagraph (C). It seems to us, as it did to the Board, that to so construe the statute would make the proviso meaningless. The hard realities of union-employer relations are such that it is difficult, indeed almost impossible, for us to conceive of picketing falling within the terms of the proviso that did not also have as 'an object' obtaining a contract with the employer. This is normally the ultimate objective of any union in relation to an employer who has employees whose jobs fall within the categories of employment that are within the jurisdiction of the union, which is admittedly the situation here."

MAIN CLAUSE: Courts don't help us very much when they cut the heart out of a statute by giving effect to little provisos like you.

UNLESS . . .: Watch your tongue, Main Clause. Thanks to "little provisos" like me, even though I don't go under that name, your job is much easier. We "unless" clauses like to hide in the thicket near the end of a statutory clause and turn the whole meaning around. Now look at me. I can undo in a sentence or so all the damage caused by Provided Further. You see, if "such picketing," that is, Provided Further's kind of tactics, has an effect of interfering with the employer's operations, say, by inducing employees not to work or suppliers not to deliver, then 8(b)(7) is violated in spite of Provided Further.

PROVIDED FURTHER: Yes, you are a pernicious sort. No thanks to you, the statute is a tease. It promises protection of First Amendment rights through my proviso, but renders it an illusion when your clause comes into play.

UNLESS . . .: Every student of labor law and constitutional law knows that there is speech and then there is something more than speech. The appeals that you would protect, especially when carried out with pickets, are not just an exchange in the marketplace of ideas. They are signals for action, unthinking action of the sort not encompassed by the rationale of the First Amendment. When I step in, it is only because speech has gone beyond its legitimate boundaries as pure speech.

PROVIDED FURTHER: Would you stop all activity protected under my clause simply because some truck driver working for a solitary supplier happens to respect the appeal?

UNLESS . . .: You must think I'm unreasonable. Isolated instances won't trigger application of my clause. See *Barker Bros.* v. *NLRB*, 328 F.2d 431, 55 LRRM 2544 (9th Cir. 1964).

MAIN CLAUSE: Then, ladies and gentlemen, can we all agree that Provided Further and Unless give us a tidy accommodation between the kind of speech which appeals to the public and that which goes beyond pure speech and undercuts the lofty purposes of 8(b)(7)?

ALL: Perhaps.

ATEBESEVENA (8(b)(7)(A)): Thank goodness my sister Atebesevenbe (8(b)(7)(B)) and I are pure and simple. We have no provisos, no unlesses, and care not for motives and ethics. We simply say that if a union has been recognized in such a manner that an election would be barred, or if a valid election has been held within the past 12 months, then all picketing is barred under 8(b)(7). No further questions are asked. In this respect we are closely akin to our cousin Atebeforce (8(b)(4)(C)), who deals with certified unions and sets up pretty much the same rule.

MAIN CLAUSE: You are too simple and not pure enough. Before we can deal with you we must face a threshold question. For whether we deal with the picketing under parts A, B, or C, it must first be established that the picketing is recognitional picketing and not something else.

ATEBESEVENBE: But everybody knows. . . .

MAIN CLAUSE: No, everybody doesn't know that there is picketing that looks like recognitional picketing but really isn't. Now once upon a time, before we words went into the big statute book, the courts saw a distinction between organizational and recognitional picketing. The former was tolerated by most courts on the ground that it was sort of a prelude to a real push for recognition and didn't entail the dangers of recognitional picketing. Now that is a hard line to draw, and wisely our statute eliminates the distinction. Picketing which has recognition as its goal, whether immediately or ultimately, comes within the proscriptions of our section. Even so, unions have managed to escape our net by disclaiming any interest whatever in recognition, and by contending that they are interested rather in improving area standards or some noble sounding thing like that. It seems to me a big loophole was opened up in the *Houston Building Case (Claude Everett)*, 136 NLRB 321, 49 LRRM 1757 (1962), where a union was able to get away with using the following picket sign:

> "Houston Building and Construction Trades Council, AFL-CIO, protests substandard wages and conditions being paid on this job by Claude Everett Company. Houston Building and Construction Trades Council does not intend by this picket line to induce or encourage the employees of any other employer to engage in a strike or concerted refusal to work."

PROVIDED FURTHER: But don't you think that Congress was not concerned with such activity when it enacted 8(b)(7)?

MAIN CLAUSE: Maybe not. But once again I think it is too easy for unions and their lawyers to fabricate a purpose which masks their true intent. Or perhaps the union will try to take advantage of the ill-chosen term "to picket" at the beginning of 8(b)(7) and will use other devices not literally proscribed, like handbilling, to achieve its goal. Fortunately, the Board and courts have treated such activity, where it has a coercive or "signal" effect rather than a persuasive one, as within the proscription of 8(b)(7).

ATEBESEVENCE (8(b)(7)(C)): What a dull party. Don't you realize that all the action is under 8(b)(7)(C)? Most 8(b)(7) cases don't involve prior recognition, certification, or elections. Rather, they deal with a union which pickets for recognition but fails to petition for an election. I'm not an unreasonable clause, and I effect a nice compromise. I give the unions a little leeway to do their thing, but I draw the line at too much picketing. At that point I insist they go to an election if they want to keep picketing.

PROVIDED: What a mischievous piece of legislation you are! You pronounce to the world that a union may picket for 30 days without filing a petition, but not if 30 days is unreasonably long. Is it 30 days or isn't it? Who is to say what is a reasonable time? How can a lawyer intelligently advise a client how the Board will handle picketing which runs 28 days?

ATEBESEVENCE: Well, we generally give the union 30 days unless the employer is hurting. . . .

UNLESS . . .: Ah.

PROVIDED FURTHER: More hypocrisy. We respect free speech until it becomes effective.

ATEBESEVENCE: I was about to say that we curtail the free period where improper means, such as intimidation, are used, or violence results.

PROVIDED: Well, you still give me trouble. I am supposed to set up an expedited election once "such a petition" has been filed. I really don't know what that means. Is "such a petition" one filed within the 30-day reasonable time period, or is it one filed outside it?

ATEBESEVENCE: We'd better go slowly. First of all, nothing happens under 8(b)(7)(C) unless the employer files a charge. The Board does not police recognitional picketing on its own. This is not such a trivial point, for as a practical matter the employer may be reluctant to file such a charge, as we shall see in a moment.

PROVIDED: All right, but now let's suppose that on the 28th day of picketing the employer files a charge and that under the circumstances picketing for 28 days without filing a petition was not an unreasonable period of time.

ATEBESEVENCE: Now your expedited election machinery goes into effect.

PROVIDED: I have trouble seeing this. The union's conduct is still conduct which does not violate 8(b)(7) for it has not exceeded the 30-day reasonable time marker.

ATEBESEVENCE: True, the union's conduct doesn't violate 8(b)(7)(C). But the very next sentence says that when such a petition is filed, that is, one which is filed within the 30-day reasonable time frame, an expedited election shall be held. You see, we don't bar recognitional picketing of reasonable duration. But the price the union must pay for this concession is to move into an expedited election procedure if the employer files a charge.

PROVIDED: I guess I see all that. But where is the petition that triggers the expedited election? Don't you need one to invoke this machinery?

ATEBESEVENCE: Absolutely. But it can be an RM petition filed by the employer. Or the union, upon receipt of the 8(b)(7) charge, may decide to file a petition within the 30-day reasonable time period.

PROVIDED: Why on earth would it do that?

ATEBESEVENCE: Because if it doesn't, the picketing will go beyond the 30-day reasonable time frame without a petition having been filed, the opportunity for an expedited election will have been lost, and the union will be enjoined from further picketing. In short, if the picketing goes beyond 30 days without a petition being filed, the effect of an 8(b)(7) charge is to cause the picketing to be enjoined. If, on the other hand, the petition is filed within 30 days, the only effect of the 8(b)(7) charge is to move the election into the expedited system.

UNLESS . . .: This means that a union can get perhaps 28 days of unlimited economic pressure on the employer, petition on the 29th day, and still be free of 8(b)(7)'s restraints. This enables it to continue to picket until the election is held. At that point, if the union wins we don't worry about 8(b)(7). And if the union loses, then the unqualified bar on picketing takes effect under 8(b)(7)(B). But meanwhile, it seems to me, the union gets an awfully long period in which to picket as though 8(b)(7) did not exist.

PROVIDED: That troubles me. It also troubles me that any union that is impatient with the timetable of union elections has only to picket for 30 days and file a petition, which would seem to mandate an expedited election. That seems a devious way to force a quick election.

ATEBESEVENCE: Maybe that suggests that the real problem is with our cumbersome election machinery. Perhaps if new labor legislation is enacted, the speed of the election process will do away with much of the need of expedited elections under 8(b)(7). Anyway, a union can't get an expedited election merely by manipulating the statute that way. The expedited election machinery is triggered by the employer's filing of an 8(b)(7)(C) charge, together with its RM petition or an RC petition filed by the union. This really leaves the use of the expedited election route up to the employer. If the employer needs the time that it takes to hold an ordinary election to mount an effective campaign against the union, then it will have to think twice about going to an expedited election as the price of containing the union's pressure.

MAIN CLAUSE: What you seem to be saying is that quicker routine election procedures would eliminate the need for the 8(b)(7) expedited route. What do we lose by the expedited procedure? Does the Board ignore important unit determination questions?

PROVIDED: Of course not. We still must follow the mandate of Section 9(a). But we save time by eliminating some of the procedural hassles, like showing of interest.

TENNEL (10(l)): Can I get an injunction against a union that pickets for, say, 25 days, if that is an unreasonable period of time?

MAIN CLAUSE: Who invited you?

TENNEL: No 8(b)(7) party is complete without me. I provide the enforcement machinery. I can restrain 8(b)(7) picketing. Indeed, I get priority over all other cases.

PROVIDED FURTHER: This is astonishing. You mean to tell me that if a union guesses wrong and pickets for 25 days without filing a petition, and 25 days turns out under the circumstances to be an unreasonable period of time, you can enjoin the picketing?

TENNEL: Certainly.

PROVIDED: But what happens to my expedited election?

TENNEL: Nothing. Because no petition has been filed. And if one finally is filed, it will be too late. Not within a reasonable period of time. So you don't have "such a petition" on which to act.

ATEBESEVENCE: The beauty of our section is that it leaves so much to chance. The union which pickets without a petition being filed cannot be sure that the employer will propel it into an expedited election. The employer who files an 8(b)(7) charge will not know whether the union will simply cease picketing, or will accept the challenge and move to a quick election. And neither party can predict accurately whether a shorter period than 30 days will be applicable. But basically the section works well. See if you now understand the classic explanation, in *Blinne Construction*,

135 NLRB 1153, 49 LRRM 1638 (1962). It's in all the casebooks, and it says:

> "The expedited election procedure is applicable, of course, only in a § 8(b)(7)(C) proceeding, *i.e.*, where an 8(b)(7)(C) unfair labor practice charge has been filed. Congress rejected efforts to amend the provisions of § 9(c) of the Act so as to dispense generally with preelection hearings. Thus, in the absence of an 8(b)(7)(C) unfair labor practice charge, a union will not be enabled to obtain an expedited election by the mere device of engaging in recognition or organization picketing and filing a representation petition. And on the other hand, a picketing union which files a representation petition pursuant to the mandate of § 8(b)(7)(C) and to avoid its sanctions will not be propelled into an expedited election, which it may not desire, merely because it has filed such a petition. In both the above situations, the normal representation procedures are applicable; the showing of a substantial interest will be required, and the preelection hearing directed in § 9(c)(1) will be held.
>
> "This, in our considered judgment, puts the expedited election procedure prescribed in the first proviso to subparagraph C in its proper and intended focus. That procedure was devised to shield aggrieved employers and employees from the adverse effects of prolonged recognition or organizational picketing. Absent such a grievance, it was not designed either to benefit or to handicap picketing activity. . . ."

Let's try it another way. Here's an excerpt from Morris, The Developing Labor Law, 1098-99 (2d ed. 1983):

> "Section 8(b)(7)(C) establishes two routes for dealing with proscribed picketing, depending on whether a petition is filed. If a petition is filed, there will be no violation of subparagraph (C) and the picketing may continue during the processing of the petition. If a Section 8(b)(7)(C) charge is also filed by the employer, the petition may be processed by the expedited election procedure. However, the expedited election procedure may be invoked only by an *employer's* Section 8(b)(7)(C) charge; otherwise, unions could obtain expedited elections simply by picketing or perhaps by having sympathetic employees file Section 8(b)(7)(C) charges. If an election is directed, the Section 8(b)(7)(C) charge will be dismissed because the election resolves the representation question. If the union is not certified and it continues to picket for a proscribed object, Section 8(b)(7)(B) will be activated. If the union is certified, Section 8(b)(7) ceases to apply.
>
> "For various reasons both the union and the employer may decide not to file a petition. The employer, for example, may not wish to risk calling an election which it might lose; or it may decide that activating the expedited election procedure by an "RM" petition and a Section 8(b)(7)(C) charge will not shorten the time during which proscribed picketing is permitted. Upon the expiration of 30 days of proscribed picketing without the filing of a petition, a Section 8(b)(7)(C) charge will proceed solely along the unfair labor practice route; a petition filed thereafter, or lingering Section 8(a)(1) or (3) violations, will not affect the

issue. If the regional director 'has reasonable cause to believe the charge is true and that a complaint should issue,' he is required to petition a federal district court for an injunction."

PROVIDED FURTHER: One last point. Suppose a union gets propelled into an expedited election, but finds that the employer has committed certain unfair labor practices which might cause the union to lose the election. In a normal election the union can "block" the election; that is, hold it up until the charges are resolved. What happens in an expedited situation?

PROVIDED: If the union files its petition within 30 days or within a reasonable period of time, it can utilize the "blocking" technique as in any ordinary election. In that way the picketing continues, but the election may be delayed. But if the union goes beyond the 30-day mark without filing a petition, the pendency of those charges is not going to affect the Board's determination to seek a 10(1) injunction.

MAIN CLAUSE: But suppose the union now argues that it was not picketing to gain recognition at all, but was picketing to protest the employer's unfair labor practices? Can't the union get the best of all possible worlds that way? Engage in picketing, avoid an expedited election, and put the employer to the task of defending unfair labor practice charges?

PROVIDED FURTHER: I think I'm going to have a hangover tomorrow. I'm going home.

Note on Section 8(f)

Section 8(f) of the Act permits an employer and a union engaged in the building trades to enter into a "prehire" agreement. Such an agreement, which may be made even before the union has established its majority status, may require as a condition of employment membership in the union after the seventh day of employment.

In *NLRB* v. *Iron Workers (Higdon Contracting Co.)*, 434 U.S. 335, 97 LRRM 2333 (1978), the Court in a divided opinion held that picketing by a union to enforce a prehire agreement valid under Section 8(f) is nevertheless a violation of Section 8(b)(7)(C) where the union fails to petition for an election within 30 days. The Court upheld the Board's view that until the union actually attains majority support in the relevant unit, "the pre-hire agreement is voidable and does not have the same stature as a collective-bargaining agreement. . . ." Accordingly, the picketing is not exempt under Section 8(b)(7)(C) as picketing to enforce a contract, but is "the legal equivalent of picketing to require recognition as the exclusive agent. . . ."

Justices Stewart, Blackmun, and Stevens dissented. In their words, "when an employer in the construction industry does choose to enter a § 8(f) prehire agreement, there is nothing in the provisions or policies of national labor law that allows the employer, or the Board, to dismiss the agreement as a nullity. Yet in this case the Court holds that both the Board and the employer may do precisely that."

Some of the concerns expressed by the dissenters in *Higdon* were addressed by a unanimous Court in *Iim McNeff, Inc.* v. *Todd*, ____ U.S. ____, 113 LRRM 2113 (1983). In *McNeff*, the employer, a construction subcontractor, entered into a prehire agreement with the union in which the employer agreed to make contributions on behalf of covered employees to a fringe benefit trust fund. When the employer attempted to renege, the Court held the agreement was enforceable under Section 301 of the Act. The Court explained that *Higdon* barred picketing to enforce a prehire agreement because the picketing might interfere with employee free choice in the selection of a bargaining representative. However, "union enforcement, by way of a § 301 suit, of money obligations incurred by an employer under a prehire contract prior to its repudiation does not impair the right of employees to select their own bargaining agent." On the other hand, "however limited the binding effect of a prehire agreement may be, it strains both logic and equity to argue that a party to such an agreement can reap its benefits and then avoid paying the bargained for consideration." U.S. at ____, 113 LRRM at 2117.

B. SECONDARY PRESSURES

1. INTRODUCTION

Suppose that negotiations between Enderby Industries and the United Factory Workers Union fail to produce agreement on a new contract, and the union strikes. The strike is not very effective because some of the Enderby employees ignore the strike call and report to work, and the company is able to secure replacements for those who honor the strike. The union decides that it must escalate the economic pressure, and sets up a picket line outside the plant. As trucks approach Enderby for the purpose of delivering supplies or picking up completed products, the truck drivers, all organized employees of other concerns, refuse to cross the picket lines. Since Enderby cannot obtain supplies or make deliveries, it is now under strong pressure to settle its dispute with the union.

You might conclude that there is nothing wrong with this sort of economic pressure. You have already been through the debate in Chapter 4 over the extent to which the Government should regulate the use of economic weapons by the parties; the present example involves an extension of those considerations. Perhaps you will conclude that if Enderby finds the economic pressure too compelling, it has only to accede to the union's demands.

But what about the trucking companies attempting to carry on their regular business with Enderby? They are not at all concerned with Enderby's labor problems; yet as a practical matter they find themselves enmeshed in Enderby's labor dispute, for they are unable to carry on their own business. Does the law afford them any protection in such a situation?

There is consensus that, as a theoretical matter, the employer who occupies a position of neutrality with respect to another's labor dispute should be immune from the pressures generated by that dispute. But consider the situation we have been describing. If the picketing is proscribed because it enmeshes a neutral employer, does this not unfairly insulate Enderby from the economic pressures normally incident to a labor dispute? Obviously the problem involves a balancing of competing sets of interests.

Consider how you would balance these interests as the pressure is applied at points further away from the physical site of the Enderby plant.

(i) Enderby delivers its completed products to a retailer for sale. Pickets follow the truck to the retail store and remain there while the truck is unloaded. Employees of the neutral retailer, seeing the pickets, refuse to report to work.

(ii) The picketing described in (i) is ineffective, and the goods are unloaded. They are sold to the public by the neutral retailer. The union pickets the store, asking consumers not to buy any goods sold by the store because the store deals with products manufactured by Enderby, with whom the union has a labor dispute.

(iii) The Enderby products are component parts for manufacture of completed television sets by a neutral employer. The union asks the employees of the neutral manufacturer not to work on products which contain components manufactured by Enderby.

What kind of accommodation is reasonable in each of these situations? The Act speaks to these problems in Section 8(b)(4), an impenetrable jungle of commas, subsections, and provisos. A preliminary reading should be ventured at this point, particularly of 8(b)(4)(A) and (B) (which entails reading all the words separated by commas before those subsections and all the provisos after them). With some perseverance you will soon see that motive plays some role in the structure of 8(b)(4), and that a union is not supposed to put pressure on one employer for the purpose of inducing it not to do business with another. As you read the materials in this section, you will have to decide what role motive should play in resolving these problems.

Although this is normally referred to as the "secondary boycott" provision of the Act, the term "secondary" does not appear in the statute. Indeed, the only hint of a primary-secondary dichotomy is in the use of the term "primary" in the proviso to 8(b)(4)(B). It may be helpful to use the term "offending employer" to describe the employer with whom the union has its dispute (i.e., the primary employer) and "neutral employer" to describe the other employer (i.e., the secondary employer) who is brought into the dispute.

A useful point of departure for your analysis is to treat economic activity that occurs on the premises of the offending employer as presumptively valid, even though it has an adverse impact on neutral employers. The force of this rule is explored more closely in subpart (4) of this section, particularly in *Electrical Workers (General Electric)* at page 747. As the economic activity moves away from the situs of the offending employer to that of a neutral employer, the accommodation of interests becomes more difficult. This is admittedly a simplistic analysis, but it is a useful way to get a "beginning handle" on a complex problem that is difficult to follow. For a detailed and critical analysis of the distinctions the Board and courts are seeking to draw between lawful primary and unlawful secondary activity, see Lesnick, *The Gravamen of the Secondary Boycott*, 62 Colum. L. Rev. 1363 (1962).

The fact that the union's complaint is a political one, not directed at any employer's labor policies, does not immunize the union's conduct from the reach of the Act. In *Longshoremen* v. *Allied International, Inc.*, 456 U.S. 212, 110 LRRM 2001 (1982), the union refused to handle Soviet cargo as a protest against the Russian invasion of Afghanistan. While the union's objective was "understandable and even commendable," it placed a burden on the neutral employer—in this case an importer of Russian wood products, who, as a result of the boycott, suffered damages when it was forced to renegotiate its contracts. The Court characterized this as "just such a burden, as well as a widening of industrial strife, as the secondary boycott provisions were designed to prevent." 456 U.S. at 223, 110 LRRM at 2005.

What, then, makes this conduct subject to the Act? Would the result be different if a citizens group urged employees not to handle such cargo? Does this mean that union members' political rights are impaired by the fact that the activity occurs in the context of collective bargaining?

The initial question for consideration is whether the asserted "neutral" really is neutral, hence entitled to the protections of the Act.

2. ALLY DOCTRINE

Problem

Enderby Company has a close working relationship with Umaya Electronics, a manufacturer of television sets and other communication devices. In fact, the principal stockholder of Enderby has a substantial, though not controlling, stock interest in Umaya. Under its arrangement with Umaya, Enderby manufactures molded plastic consoles to Umaya's specifications, and Umaya completes the television sets by installing the necessary electronic parts. Enderby also provides certain smaller rubber and plastic components for the television sets. The consoles and parts are normally shipped to Wagner Warehouse, an independently owned facility some five miles from the Enderby Plant. These parts are routinely stored there and sent on to Umaya as needed.

Enderby is now engaged in difficult negotiations with the United Factory Workers Union for a successor to an expired agreement. In anticipation of a possible strike, Enderby discusses the following courses of conduct with counsel.

(i) Increase the production of the items in question and accelerate shipments to Wagner Warehouse. Then, if there is a strike and picketing at Enderby, the goods can be shipped to Umaya from Wagner Warehouse.

(ii) Locate other manufacturers who can perform the component rubber and plastic work. Advise Umaya of these alternative sources of production and promise to reimburse Umaya for any production costs in excess of those that would be incurred if Enderby did the work. Provide technical assistance and specifications to these other manufacturers, if needed.

Please advise Enderby whether these plans will work. Specifically, will the union be able to set up a lawful picket line at either Wagner, Umaya, or the other manufacturers if these plans are carried out?

Sears, Roebuck & Co.

National Labor Relations Board, 1971
190 NLRB 143, 77 LRRM 1060

SUPPLEMENTAL DECISION

Briefly, this case arose as follows. Sears sells carpet and various other forms of floor coverings from several Denver area locations. It offers these products either installed or uninstalled. When, as is usually the case, a customer purchases installed floor covering or carpeting, the customer pays Sears for both the material and a charge for the installation. Sears in turn assigns the task of installation to one of a number of installer enterprises with which it is in contractual relationship and pays that installer an agreed-upon rate for his service.

In July 1968 the Respondent attempted to organize one of the installer enterprises, Joe and Eddie's Carpet Service, and in connection therewith, picketed briefly at the home of a customer where carpeting was being installed by that enterprise. In August 1968 Respondent renewed picketing, but at Sears' locations, and effectively stopped or delayed various deliveries.

In the previous Decision in this case we found, in agreement with the Trial Examiner, that the Respondent violated Section 8(b)(4)(i) and (ii)(B) of the Act by picketing Sears, with an unlawful object of forcing Sears to cease doing business with certain floor covering installers with whom the Respondent had a dispute. That finding was predicated upon our conclusions, also in agreement with the Trial Examiner, that the floor covering installers were independent contractors and not employees of Sears, and that there was no basis for finding Sears to be an "ally" of the installers in their dispute with the Respondent.

While accepting the Board's conclusion that the installers were independent contractors, the court was of the opinion that the Board nevertheless had not sufficiently considered the question whether Sears was in fact a neutral in the dispute. The court thus deemed it necessary to determine (1) whether Sears was truly a neutral in an economic sense and (2) whether Sears' possible interest in whether the installers were unionized was sufficient to preclude finding any such neutrality.

The details of the relationship between Sears and the installers have been set forth at considerable length in the Trial Examiner's Decision, in the Board's previous Decision, and in the court's Decision as well. In summary, the installers perform no work at Sears' locations beyond picking up carpet and installation orders; operate out of their own homes; utilize their own trucks, tools, and equipment; hire their own employees, where necessary, at rates of pay which are not determined by Sears; are responsible for repair or damage which may be caused during installation; establish their own hours and schedules; schedule and reschedule jobs directly with the customers without notice to Sears; subcontract jobs without prior approval or knowledge of Sears; in practice do extra work for customers without Sears' approval; generally perform work without instructions or guidelines; and, if a job is more difficult or time consuming than estimated by Sears, change the prices quoted by Sears to the customer. In addition we note the following circumstances established by the evidence before us. The installers here work for firms other than Sears who sell installed carpet and at least to that extent are in competition with Sears; the installers can and do turn down work for Sears; and there are no employees of Sears performing functions which are the same as or similar to those of the installers.

While we accept the view of the court, we are convinced that this case falls within the ambit of *Denver Building and Construction Trades Council.** It is unquestionably true, as the court suggests, that Sears has a competitive interest in the amounts charged by the installers for their services, and that Sears is thus concerned with whether those installers join a labor organization, insofar as such circumstance might affect the fees charged by the installers. However, the same interest or lack of neutrality would be presumable on the part of Sears concerning the labor costs of a steel manufacturer which supplied a hardware producer which in turn produces and supplies Sears with items for sale on a competitive market. In sum, we do not believe that such an economic interest requires a conclusion that a firm is not neutral for the purposes of Section 8(b)(4)(i) and (ii)(B) where, as here, the record so clearly shows the independent contractor status of the installers, and the manner in which they secure and perform their work for Sears; the absence of Sears' employees doing the same work; the fact that the installers can and do turn down work offered by Sears; and the fact that they work for other companies.

Accordingly, upon reconsideration, we affirm our Decision and Order as published in 176 NLRB No. 120.

MEMBER FANNING, dissenting:

The court has remanded this case to give the Board an opportunity to consider whether the conditions under which carpet installers (found by the Board and the court to be independent contractors) perform installation of carpets sold by Sears gives the Respondent Union a legitimate interest in bringing direct pressure against Sears in its efforts to combat the substandard wages under which the carpets are installed.

---

*341 U.S. 675, 28 LRRM 2108 (1951). This case is discussed in subpart (5), starting on p. 755 in this chapter.

The court suggests that the economic relationship between Sears and its installers is such that Sears is not a neutral in an economic sense in the dispute between the Union and the installers over their performance of installation work at substandard wages. This seems clearly to be so. Sears sells both carpeting and the installation service, the latter under a contract with the customer that obligates Sears, as a continuing relationship with more than 60 installers in the Denver area who are obligated to accept all work that Sears furnishes with certain exceptions not relevant here. Sears determines the time within which the installation is to be made, sets the price of the installation, bills and collects from the customer, and retains the right to inspect and approve the installation and to require installers to correct defective work at the installer's expense. Sears and the installer together set the cost to Sears of the installer's services. Quite obviously, the sale of installation services grants Sears to increase its volume of carpet and floor covering sales. As that volume increases, the amount of work available to installers increases. In essence, Sears and its installers are engaged in a common venture involving the sale and installation of carpets. The success of that venture for each depends to a considerable extent on the performance of the other and can only be carried out through an integration of the operations of both.

My colleagues conclude that the relationship involved herein falls within the ambit of *NLRB* v. *Denver Building and Construction Trades Council* because Sears' interest in whether or not its installers are organized is no greater than its interest in whether employees of the manufacturers of the carpets are organized. I cannot agree. Sears' relationship with its installers is significantly different from its relationship with manufacturers of the carpets. In the case of the manufacturer, it may well be true that Sears' willingness to purchase its products will depend to a significant extent on the labor costs incorporated in the price charged Sears and that union wages may increase those costs. Nevertheless, Sears has no say in the setting of those wages. With respect to the carpet installers, however, Sears has not only a direct interest in the carpet installers' labor charges, it has a substantial, if not the dominant, role in the setting of those charges. More than that, it also has the primary role in setting the price to be charged to the retail customer who purchases— from Sears itself—the installation services. Significantly, as the court pointed out, it appears that Sears makes a profit on the installation charges. Moreover, the carpet installers agree to accept all jobs within a defined geographical area tendered them by Sears, and agree that they will not do work for Sears' customers which is not specifically authorized by Sears.

The continuing nature of the relationship, the substantial role played by Sears in the establishment of the installers' wages, and its power through assignment to compel installers to work only for Sears, leads me to agree with the court that the *Denver Building and Construction Trades Council* decision is not controlling on the question of whether the Union's pressures on Sears in its efforts to raise the substandard wages of the installers is unlawful secondary or lawful primary activity. There seems to me to be a crucial distinction between the relationship involved here and the normal relationship between contractors and their subcontractors in the building and construction industry. In such a relationship, the general contractor undertakes to perform a construction contract and generally subcontracts various parts of that work to subcontractors, usually on a bid basis. At the conclusion of the project they go their separate ways for the subcontractor does not bind himself to a general contractor on a continuing basis. Here, in contrast, the installers do bind themselves to Sears under 3-year contracts to take all the work that Sears assigns to them. There is no guarantee of the amount of work for that depends on Sears' volume of carpet sales, which in turn depends in substantial part on Sears' willingness and ability to provide installation service to the buyer. Whether or not Sears and the installer may properly be called allies as that concept has found expression in previous decisions is of less importance than is the fact that Sears is directly involved in the setting of the labor costs of the installation services.

In the final analysis, Respondent Union seeks to avoid the wage cutting or depressing effect on Sears' use of nonunion installers in two ways. First, through direct organization of the installers, and second, through direct pressure on Sears by picket line advertisement of the fact that Sears' carpets are installed by workmen receiving substandard wages. Whether Sears grants an increase in the installers' charges to the level of union wages in unilateral response to the Union's picket line pressures or as a result of negotiations with unionized installers, it is apparent that it necessarily must be involved as a direct participant in the settlement of this labor dispute. In these circumstances, it is unrealistic to classify Sears as a neutral third person to the dispute, and I would find that the Union's pressures against Sears do not constitute unlawful secondary activity.

Comment on the Ally Doctrine

The *Sears* case illustrates only one of several bases upon which a showing of ally status may be predicated. Essentially, the argument is that the so-called ally performs an integrated production function which is important to the other employer (in this case the "neutral" Sears). Thus, the neutral has a real concern with (and probably exerts an influence on) the wage structure of the asserted ally. This is probably the least promising branch on which to hang ally status, as illustrated by *J.G. Roy & Sons* v. *NLRB*, 251 F.2d 771, 41 LRRM 2445 (1st Cir. 1958). In that case the union called a strike against Roy Construction on the grounds that Roy Construction was purchasing lumber from a nonunion lumber company (Roy Lumber), owned by the same interests. The union's defense to what would otherwise surely be prohibited activity under 8(b)(4) was that the two Roy companies were allied both in terms of integration of operations and common ownership. The Board's finding of ally status on the basis of integration of operations was reversed by the court with the following observation:

"The Board's 'straight line operation' doctrine derived from its own decision in *National Union of Marine Cooks and Stewards (Irwin-Lyons Lumber Co.)*, 87 NLRB 54 (1949). In that case the primary employer was engaged in logging operations while the secondary employer transported all of the logs from the primary employer's logging site to its sawmill. Both employers were commonly owned, and unlike the instant case, the president and active operating head of both companies was the same man. The secondary employer's operations were an absolutely essential and integral part of the primary employer's enterprise. In contrast to this, Roy Construction's purchases of millwork from Roy Lumber constitute a very small part of the total sales and purchases of both companies and were not part of a 'unified production effort.' To characterize the Roy Construction and Roy Lumber Companies as a 'straight line operation' because of this purchase of millwork would be a strained interpretation of the facts in order that they might fit within the doctrine adopted by the Board in the Irwin-Lyons case. See *Alpert* v. *United Brotherhood of Carpenters, etc.*, D.C. Mass. 1956, 143 F.Supp. 371 (wherein a temporary injunction was granted against the Union upon request of the regional director of the Board under authority of Sec. 10(1) of the Act in earlier proceedings in this case)."

As you think about this analysis, and the limitations it places on the union's ability to apply economic pressure, reconsider the unit determination questions in Chapter 2 and the extent to which they turn on product integration. Do the findings of separate unit status for separate plants on the basis of lack of product integration unduly insulate the employer from economic pressure? Are the unit determinations consistent with the approach to ally status under 8(b)(4)?

A more common basis for finding ally status is an arrangement under which the "neutral" employer takes over work which the primary employer is unable to perform because of the strike. The classic illustration is the *Royal Typewriter* case (*NLRB* v. *Business Machines and Office Union*, 228 F.2d 553, 37 LRRM 2219 (2d Cir. 1955)). The primary employer, Royal, was unable to fulfill its warranty obligations to its customers because its employees were on strike. When a customer under warranty required repair work, Royal advised the customer to select an independent repair company listed in the directory, and to obtain a receipt for services rendered. Royal would either pay the other repair company directly or reimburse the customer for his expenses. The union then picketed four independent repair concerns who were performing repairs for Royal customers under the reimbursement arrangement described above. The court reversed the Board's conclusion that such picketing violated Section 8(b)(4):

"We approve the 'ally' doctrine which had its origin in a well reasoned opinion by Judge Rifkind in the Ebasco case, *Douds* v. *Metropolitan Federation of Architects, Engineers, Chemists & Technicians, Local 231*, D.C.S.D.N.Y. 1948, 75 F.Supp. 672, 676. Ebasco, a corporation engaged in the business of providing engineering services, had a close business relationship with Project, a firm providing similar services. Ebasco subcontracted some of its work to Project and when it did so Ebasco supervised the work of Project's employees and paid Project for the time spent by Project's employees on Ebasco's work plus a factor for overhead and profit. When Ebasco's employees went on strike, Ebasco transferred a greater percentage of its work to Project, including some jobs that had already been started by Ebasco's employees. When Project refused to heed the Union's requests to stop doing Ebasco's work, the Union picketed Project and induced some of Project's employees to cease work. On these facts Judge Rifkind found that Project was not 'doing business' with Ebasco within the meaning of § 8(b)(4)(A) and that the Union had therefore not committed an unfair labor practice under that section. He reached this result by looking to the legislative history of the Taft-Hartley Act and to the history of the secondary boycotts which it sought to outlaw. He determined that Project was not a person 'wholly unconcerned in the disagreement between an employer and his employees' such as § 8(b)(4)(A) was designed to protect. This result has been described as a proper interpretation of the Act by its principal sponsor, Senator Taft, 95 Cong. Rec. (1949) 8709, and President Eisenhower in his January 1954 recommendations to Congress for revision of the Act included a suggestion which would make this rule explicit.

"Here there was evidence of only one instance where Royal contacted an independent (Manhattan Typewriter Service, not named in the complaint) to see whether it could handle some of Royal's calls. Apart from that incident there is no evidence that Royal made any arrangement with an independent directly. It is obvious, however, that what the independents did would inevitably tend to break the strike. As Judge Rifkind pointed out in the Ebasco case: 'The economic effect upon Ebasco's employees was precisely that which would flow from Ebasco's hiring strikebreakers to work on its own premises.' And at 95 Cong. Rec. (1949) page 8709 Senator Taft said:

" 'The spirit of the Act is not intended to protect a man who in the last case I mentioned is cooperating with a primary employer and taking his work and doing the work which he is unable to do because of the strike.' "

Finally, ally status may be found in common ownership, but, as with the "straight line" theory of integrated operations, this approach does not usually succeed in legitimizing the economic pressure. It is well illustrated by *Miami Newspaper Printing Pressmen* v. *NLRB*, 322 F.2d 405, 53 LRRM 2629 (D.C. Cir. 1963). In that case the union, which was engaged in contract negotiations with the Miami Herald, sought to put economic pressure on the paper by picketing, but the paper was able to continue publishing. The union then picketed the Detroit Free Press, a newspaper owned by the same Knight Newspaper chain. This strike was successful, but it was enjoined as a violation of Section 8(b)(4). The court said:

"It is asserted that Knight Newspapers, Inc., is not a truly neutral or unallied employer within the meaning of the statute. The Union points first to the circumstance of common ownership. This, of course, appears clearly from the record. But both the Board and the courts have consistently and repeatedly held that common ownership alone does not suffice for this purpose. There must be something more in the form of common control, as it is usually phrased, denoting an actual, as distinct from merely a potential, integration of operations and management policies. Two business enterprises, although commonly owned, do not for that reason alone become so allied with each other as to lift the congressional ban upon the extension of labor strife from the one to the other.

"Although the Union argues that common ownership alone is sufficient to justify its bringing the Free Press within the orbit of its legitimate strike pressure, it does not—as it cannot—rest, in the last analysis, on this claim. It asserts that the facts as found by the Board disclose what it calls 'common management,' so sweeping in scope as to warrant the direction of the Union's force against the Free Press for the purpose of forcing the Herald to accede to its demands. . . .

"These two metropolitan daily newspapers appear to have had separate and largely unrelated lives of their own, despite their common ownership. Published hundreds of miles apart in two distinctive urban communities of the United States, each paper went its way under independent direction supplied locally, as they must have done in order to be successfully responsive to the varying needs of their two unrelated readerships. A newspaper reflects in significant measure the peculiar personality of its locale. To the extent that it does so in fact, its commercial success is to that degree correspondingly assured. Wise publishers know this to be true and shape their arrangements and policies accordingly. This appears to be the case here."

The *Miami Newspaper* decision cited *J.G. Roy,* discussed *supra,* in which the court held that the common ownership involved in *Roy* did not by itself make the separate Roy enterprises allies.

Suppose, however, as is the case in some cities, the two major newspapers are owned by the same chain. If the union has a dispute with the morning paper, may it picket the afternoon paper? In short, does the wide geographical separation between Miami and Detroit make a difference? Suppose the advertising and circulation revenues of the struck morning paper were simply picked up by a fatter afternoon paper with wider circulation. Does this make the two papers allies, assuming common ownership, even if the parent corporation makes no effort to divert revenues from one paper to the other? Do you think common ownership is essential to finding ally status when one paper so clearly reaps the monetary benefits of a strike against the other? Why?

Are you convinced that the Board and courts have taken the proper factors into consideration in determining ally status in the three types of situations described in this comment? What tests would you suggest?

3. Common Situs Picketing

Problem

Assume that in the Enderby Problem, page 735, Umaya and Wagner are not deemed allies of Enderby. Assume further that some of the "stockpiled" goods at Wagner Warehouse are shipped on to Umaya. Does Enderby have a sufficient presence at Wagner and Umaya, in the form of its goods, that the union may lawfully follow its dispute with Enderby to Umaya and Wagner? If so, how must the union word its picket signs?

The Moore Dry Dock *Rules*

The definitive case dealing with the union's right to follow a dispute with an offending employer to the situs of a neutral employer is popularly known as *Moore Dry Dock (Sailors Union of the Pacific)*, 92 NLRB 547, 27 LRRM 1108 (1950). The offending employer, Samsoc, a shipping company, owned a vessel called the *Phopho.* The Union's dispute with Samsoc concerned its hiring of nonunion seamen under a foreign-flag-of-convenience arrangement. Samsoc delivered the *Phopho* to a neutral employer, Moore Dry Dock, for conversion into a bulk gypsum carrier. The contract between Moore and Samsoc provided that during the last two weeks of the conversion, Samsoc "shall have the right to put a crew on board the vessel for training purposes, provided, however, that such crew shall not interfere in any way with the work of conversion." After the conversion work had been 90 percent completed, Samsoc placed a crew aboard the *Phopho* for the purpose of readying it for sea. At this point the union placed pickets outside the entrance to the Moore shipyard. The Board held by a 3-to-2 majority that by carefully confining its picketing to the dispute with Samsoc, the union was not engaged in secondary activity in violation of 8(b)(4). The following excerpts from the opinion indicate the theoretical justification for allowing the picketing, and mark out the practical guidelines a union must follow in such a situation in order to avoid a charge of unlawful secondary activity.

"Section 8(b)(4)(A) is aimed at secondary boycotts and secondary strike activities. It was not intended to proscribe primary action by a union having a legitimate labor dispute with an employer. Picketing at the premises of a primary employer is traditionally recognized as primary action even though it is 'necessarily designed to induce and encourage third persons to cease doing business with the picketed employer.' . . .

" . . . Hence, if Samsoc, the owner of the S.S. *Phopho,* had had a dock of its own in California to which the *Phopho* had been tied up while undergoing conversion by Moore Dry Dock employees, picketing by the Respondent at the dock site would unquestionably have constituted *primary* action, even though the Respondent might have expected that the picketing would be more effective in persuading Moore employees not to work on the ship than to persuade the seamen aboard the *Phopho* to quit that vessel. The difficulty in the present case arises therefore, not because of any differences in picketing objectives,[5] but from the fact that the *Phopho* was not tied up at its own dock, but at that of Moore, while the picketing was going on in front of the Moore premises.

"In the usual case, the *situs* of a labor dispute is the premises of the primary employer. Picketing of the premises is also picketing of the *situs;* the test of legality of picketing is that enunciated by the Board in the *Pure Oil* and *Ryan Construction* cases. But in some cases the *situs* of the dispute may not be limited to a fixed location; it may be ambulatory. Thus in the *Schultz* case, a majority of the Board held that the truck upon which a truck driver worked was the *situs* of a labor dispute between him and the owner of the truck. Similarly, we hold in the present case that, as the *Phopho* was the place of employment of the seamen, it was the *situs* of the dispute between Samsoc and the Respondent over working conditions aboard that vessel.

"When the *situs* is ambulatory, it may come to rest temporarily at the premises of another employer. The perplexing question is: Does the right to picket follow the *situs* while it is stationed at the premises of a secondary employer, when the only way to picket that *situs* is in front of the secondary employer's premises? Admittedly, no easy answer is possible. Essentially the problem is one of balancing the right of a union to picket at the site of its dispute as against the right of a secondary employer to be free from picketing in a controversy in which it is not directly involved.

"When a secondary employer is harboring the *situs* of a dispute between a union and a primary employer, the right of neither the union to picket nor of the secondary employer to be free from picketing can be absolute. The enmeshing of premises and *situs* qualifies both rights. In the kind of situation that exists in this case, we believe that picketing of the premises of a secondary employer is primary if it meets the following conditions: (a) The picketing is strictly limited to times when the *situs* of dispute is located on the secondary employer's premises; (b) at the time of the picketing the primary employer is engaged in its normal business at the *situs;* (c) the picketing is limited to places reasonably close to the location of the *situs;* and (d) the picketing discloses clearly that the dispute is with the primary employer. All these conditions were met in the present case. . . . " 92 NLRB at 547–49.

A close reading of the balance of the majority opinion in *Moore Dry Dock* suggests that a crucial factor in permitting the union to follow the *Phopho* to the shipyard was that the crew was aboard preparatory to the voyage at the time the picketing occurred. Had the crew not been aboard, the majority would have proscribed the picketing. Do you agree with the following criticism of this distinction, as set forth in the dissent?

[5] 'Plainly, the object of all picketing at all times is to influence third persons to withhold their business or services from the struck employer. In this respect there is no distinction between lawful primary picketing and unlawful secondary picketing proscribed by Section 8(b)(4)(A).' International Brotherhood of Teamsters, etc. (Schultz Refrigerated Service, Inc.).

"The majority hold, however, that Moore in granting Samsoc permission to train a crew aboard the *Phopho* in the last stages of that ship's conversion thereby forfeited all right to protection under Section 8(b)(4)(A). We think such an interpretation of that section of the amended Act puts a severe and unreasonable restraint upon the operations of a secondary employer whenever that employer, as a gesture of cooperation, extends the slightest contract privilege to a primary employer with which it does business at a time when neither is engaged in a labor dispute. By extending the above small courtesy to Samsoc, Moore made unnecessary an additional loss of time in readying the ship for its voyage that would be entailed if the work were postponed until after the *Phopho* left Moore's drydock. An earlier voyage for the *Phopho*, made possible by Moore's action, actually facilitated the free flow of commerce which this Act is designed to protect and encourage; but the effect of the decision of the majority will be to hamper the achievement of such objectives." 92 NLRB at 556.

For a period in the development of the *Moore Dry Dock* standard, the Board viewed the existence of a home base at which the union could picket the primary employer as evidence that the union's motive in following the work to a neutral situs was to place pressure on the neutral employer. This factor, once elevated to a "fifth rule" in *Brewery & Beverage Drivers, Local 67 (Washington Coca-Cola Bottling Works)*, 107 NLRB 299 (1953), enf'd, 220 F.2d 380, 35 LRRM 772 (D.C. Cir. 1955), is now merely one of the many considerations that bear upon the legality of picketing at a common situs. *IBEW, Local 861 (Plauche Electric, Inc.)*, 135 NLRB 250, 49 LRRM 1446 (1962).

Independent evidence of motive may play a role in determining that picketing is unlawful even where it complies with *Moore Dry Dock* standards. For example, in *IBEW, Local 441 (Rollins Communications)*, 222 NLRB 99, 91 LRRM 1348 (1976), conversations between the union and the neutral employer, in which the union stated that it would withdraw its pickets if the neutral would give a written commitment to stop using the primary contractor at the jobsite, led the Board to conclude that the union's activity was secondary. But how should the union respond if the neutral employer asks it what it must do to get rid of the pickets? This point troubled the court of appeals when it remanded the case to the Board, *IBEW, Local 441 v. NLRB*, 510 F.2d 1274, 1277, 88 LRRM 3438 (1975). Some light may be shed on this question when you read the *Servette* case at page 759.

Sometimes a common situs problem may be analyzed alternatively under the ally doctrine. For example, suppose Enderby routinely ships and stores completed products in a wholly independent warehouse, Wagner Warehouse. In a labor dispute with Enderby, the union might picket Wagner on a theory that the presence of Enderby products at Wagner Warehouse makes the latter a common situs. Alternatively, it could urge that storage is an integral part of Enderby's operations, hence Wagner is an ally. Each approach, if it works, entails a different consequence. An ally is treated, for picketing purposes, as the equivalent of the primary employer. Thus, the union has the freedom it would have if engaged in primary picketing. But if the union's picketing can only be justified on common situs grounds, then its activity is subject to the restrictions of *Moore Dry Dock*.

A good illustration of the overlap in theories may be seen in the *Auburndale Freezer* litigation, in which the primary employer, much the same as in the Enderby problem, stored its completed products at a wholly independent warehouse. The Board upheld the union's right to picket at the warehouse under *Moore Dry Dock* standards on the theory that the primary employer had a presence there in the form of its stored products, which were an integral part of its operations. The Fifth Circuit reversed, holding that the Board's theory as to the "presence" of the primary employer's goods was an unwarranted extension of the common situs doctrine. Could the Board have better justified its result under the ally doctrine on the theory of straight-line integration of operations? See *Steelworkers Local 6991 (Auburndale Freezer Corp.)*, 177 NLRB 791, 71 LRRM 1503 (1969), *rev'd sub nom. Auburndale Freezer Corp. v. NLRB*, 434 F.2d 1219, 75 LRRM 2752 (5th Cir. 1970), *cert. denied*, 402 U.S. 1013, 77 LRRM 2386 (1971).

4. RESERVED GATE PICKETING

Problem

When bargaining commenced between Enderby Company and the United Factory Workers, Enderby's attorney, McCormick, asked his associate to respond to the following memo.

"In the event that the union calls a strike against us, we will be vulnerable to pressure upon some of our suppliers, contractors and the like. I understand, of course, that this kind of secondary pressure has been held in general to be an unavoidable consequence of the union's right to engage in primary activity here. But I wonder what steps we can take to minimize this pressure by insulating these neutrals from primary activity at Enderby. For example, will it do us any good to set up 'reserved gates' through which the employees of these neutral employers must enter? The specific suppliers and others that we are concerned about are:

"(a) Rufus Roofers. Rufus has signed a contract with Enderby to repair the roofs of both plants, which are in bad condition as the result of a tough winter.

"(b) Anglin Trucking. They deliver to Enderby by truck most of the raw rubber and plastic used in the manufacturing process.

"(c) Zampino Construction. They are engaged by the industrial park, in which Enderby is located, to perform a wide variety of construction work which benefits all the tenants, such as sewage, road and parking lot maintenance, installation of power lines, etc. Enderby's rental fees cover this basic work. If special work is required, all tenants are assessed on a pro rata basis, depending upon the extent to which they are benefited by the improvement or repair.

"(d) Red Hook Railroad. Their trains carry supplies into the industrial park (as shown on the map in Chapter 3); cars are delivered directly to Enderby or to other tenants of the park."

What steps could the union take to maximize its legitimate pressure on these neutrals?

Local 761, Electrical Workers v. NLRB

Supreme Court of the United States, 1961
366 U.S. 667, 48 LRRM 2210

MR. JUSTICE FRANKFURTER delivered the opinion of the Court.

Local 761 of the International Union of Electrical, Radio and Machine Workers, AFL-CIO, was charged with a violation of § 8(b)(4)(A) of the National Labor Relations Act, as amended by the Taft-Hartley Act, 61 Stat. 136, 141, 29 U.S.C.A. § 158(b)(4)(A), upon the following facts.

General Electric Corporation operates a plant outside of Louisville, Kentucky, where it manufactures washers, dryers, and other electrical household appliances. The square-shaped, thousand-acre, unfenced plant is known as Appliance Park. A large drainage ditch makes ingress and egress impossible except over five roadways across culverts, designated as gates.

Since 1954, General Electric sought to confine the employees of independent contractors, described hereafter, who work on the premises of the Park, to the use of Gate 3-A and confine its use to them. The undisputed reason for doing so was to insulate General Electric employees from the frequent labor disputes in which the contractors were involved. Gate 3-A is 550 feet away from the nearest entrance available for General Electric employees, suppliers, and deliverymen. Although anyone can pass the gate without challenge, the roadway leads to a guardhouse where identification must be presented. Vehicle stickers of various shapes and colors enable a guard to check on sight whether a vehicle is authorized to use Gate 3-A. Since January 1958, a prominent sign has been posted at the gate which states: "Gate 3-A For Employees Of Contractors Only—G.E. Employees Use Other Gates." On rare occasions, it appears, a General Electric employee was allowed to pass the guardhouse, but such occurrence was in violation of company instructions. There was no proof of any unauthorized attempts to pass the gate during the strike in question.

The independent contractors are utilized for a great variety of tasks on the Appliance Park premises. Some do construction work on new buildings; some install and repair ventilating and heating equipment; some engage in retooling and rearranging operations necessary to the manufacture of new models; others do "general maintenance work." These services are contracted to outside employers either because the company's employees lack the necessary skill or manpower, or because the work can be done more economically by independent contractors. The latter reason determined the contracting of maintenance work for which the Central Maintenance department of the company bid competitively with the contractors. While some of the work done by these contractors had on occasion been previously performed by Central Maintenance, the findings do not disclose the number of employees of independent contractors who were performing these routine maintenance services, as compared with those who were doing specialized work of a capital-improvement nature.

The Union, petitioner here, is the certified bargaining representative for the production and maintenance workers who constitute approximately 7,600 of the 10,500 employees of General Electric at Appliance Park. On July 27, 1958, the Union called a strike because of 24 unsettled grievances with the company. Picketing occurred at all the gates, including Gate 3-A, and continued until August 9 when an injunction was issued by a Federal District Court. The signs carried by the pickets at all gates read: "Local 761 On Strike G. E. Unfair." Because of the picketing, almost all of the employees of independent contractors refused to enter the company premises.

Neither the legality of the strike or of the picketing at any of the gates except 3-A nor the peaceful nature of the picketing is in dispute. The sole claim is that the picketing before the gate exclusively used by employees of independent contractors was conduct proscribed by § 8(b)(4)(A).

The Trial Examiner recommended that the Board dismiss the complaint. He concluded that the limitations on picketing which the Board had prescribed in so-called "common situs" cases were not applicable to the situation before him, in that the picketing at Gate 3-A represented traditional primary action which necessarily had a secondary effect of inconveniencing those who did business with the struck employer. He reasoned that if a primary employer could limit the area of picketing around his own premises by constructing a separate gate for employees of independent contractors, such a device could also be used to isolate employees of his suppliers and customers, and that such action could not relevantly be distinguished from oral appeals made to secondary employees not to cross a picket line where only a single gate existed.

The Board rejected the Trial Examiner's conclusion, 123 NLRB 1547. It held that, since only the employees of the independent contractors were allowed to use Gate 3-A, the Union's object in picketing there was "to enmesh these employees of the neutral employers in its dispute with the Company," thereby constituting a violation of § 8(b)(4)(A) because the independent employees were encouraged to engage in a concerted refusal to work "with an object of forcing the independent contractors to cease doing business with the Company."

. . .

I.

Section 8(b)(4)(A) of the National Labor Relations Act provides that it shall be an unfair labor practice for a labor organization

". . . to engage in, or to induce or encourage the employees of any employer to engage in, a strike or a concerted refusal in the course of their employment to use, manufacture, process, transport, or otherwise handle or work on any goods, articles, materials, or commodities or to perform any services, where an object thereof is: (A) forcing or requiring . . . any employer or other person . . . to cease doing business with any other person. . . ."

This provision could not be literally construed; otherwise it would ban most strikes historically considered to be lawful, so-called primary activity. "While § 8(b)(4) does not expressly mention 'primary' or 'secondary' disputes, strikes or boycotts, that section often is referred to in the Act's legislative history as one of the Act's 'secondary boycott sections.' " *National Labor Relations Board* v. *Denver Building & Const. Trades Council,* 341 U.S. 675, 686, 28 LRRM 2108, 2113 (1951). "Congress did not seek, by § 8(b)(4), to interfere with the ordinary strike. . . ." *National Labor Relations Board* v. *International Rice Milling Co.,* 341 U.S. 665, 672, 28 LRRM 2105, 2108 (1951). The impact of the section was directed toward what is known as the secondary boycott whose "sanctions bear, not upon the employer who alone is a party to the dispute, but upon some third party who has no concern in it." *International Brotherhood of Electrical Workers, Local 501* v. *National Labor Relations Board,* 2 Cir., 181 F.2d 34, 37. Thus the section "left a striking labor organization free to use persuasion, including picketing, not only on the primary employer and his employees but on numerous others. Among these were secondary employers who were customers or suppliers of the primary employer and persons dealing with them . . . and even employees of secondary employers so long as the labor organization did not . . . 'induce or encourage the employees of any employer to engage in a strike or a concerted refusal in the course of their employment', . . . *National Labor Relations Board* v. *Local 294, International Brotherhood of Teamsters,* 2 Cir., 284 F.2d 887, 889.

But not all so-called secondary boycotts were outlawed in § 8(b)(4)(A). "The section does not speak generally of secondary boycotts. It describes and condemns specific union conduct directed to specific objectives. Employees must be induced; they must be induced to engage in a strike or concerted refusal; an object must be to force or require their employer or another person to cease doing business with a third person. Thus, much that might argumentatively be found to fall within the broad and somewhat vague concept of secondary boycott is not in terms prohibited."

Important as is the distinction between legitimate "primary activity" and banned "secondary activity," it does not present a glaringly bright line. The objectives of any picketing include a desire to influence others from withholding from the employer their services or trade. See *Sailors' Union of the Pacific (Moore Dry Dock),* 92 NLRB 547. "[I]ntended or not, aimed for or not, employees of neutral employers do take action sympathetic with strikers and do put pressure on their own employers." *Seafarers International Union, etc.* v. *National Labor Relations Board,* 105 U.S. App. D.C. 211, 265 F.2d 585, 590. "It is clear that, when a union pickets an employer with whom it has a dispute, it hopes, even if it does not intend, that all persons will honor the picket line, and that hope encompasses the employees of neutral employers who may in the course of their employment (deliverymen and the like) have to enter the premises." *Id.*, at page 591. "Almost all picketing, even at the situs of the primary employer and surely at that of the secondary, hopes to achieve the forbidden objective, whatever other motives there may be and however small the chances of success." *Local 294, supra*, 284 F.2d at page 890. But picketing which induces secondary employees to respect a picket line is not the equivalent of picketing which has an object of inducing those employees to engage in concerted conduct against their employer in order to force him to refuse to deal with the struck employer. *Labor Board* v. *International Rice Milling, supra.*

However difficult the drawing of lines more nice than obvious, the statute compels the task. Accordingly, the Board and the courts have attempted to devise reasonable criteria drawing heavily upon the means to which a union resorts in promoting its cause. Although "[n]o rigid rule which would make . . . [a] few factors conclusive is contained in or deducible from the statute," *Sales Drivers* v. *Labor Board*, 229 F.2d 514, 517,[3] "[i]n the absence of admissions by the union of an illegal intent, the nature of acts performed shows the intent." *Seafarers International Union, supra*, at 591.

The nature of the problem, as revealed by unfolding variant situations, inevitably involves an evolutionary process for its rational response, not a quick, definitive formula as a comprehensive answer. And so, it is not surprising that the Board has more or less felt its way during the 14 years in which it has had to apply § 8(b)(4)(A), and has modified and reformed its standards on the basis of accumulating experience. "One of the purposes which lead to the creation of such boards is to have decisions based upon evidential facts under the particular statute made by experienced officials with an adequate appreciation of the complexities of the subject which is entrusted to their administration." *Republic Aviation Corp.* v. *Labor Board*, 324 U.S. 793, 800. . . .

II.

The early decisions of the Board following the Taft-Hartley amendments involved activity which took place around the secondary employer's premises. For example, in *Wadsworth Building Co., supra*, the union set up a picket line around the situs of a builder who had contracted to purchase prefabricated houses from the primary employer. The Board found this to be illegal secondary activity. In contrast, when picketing took place around the premises of the primary employer, the Board regarded this as valid primary activity. In *Oil Workers International Union (Pure Oil Co.)*, 84 NLRB 315, Pure had used Standard's dock and employees for loading its oil onto ships. The companies had contracted that, in case of a strike against Standard, Pure employees would take over the loading of Pure oil. The union struck against Standard and picketed the

---

[3]See also Labor Board v. General Drivers, Local 968, 225 F.2d 205.

dock, and Pure employees refused to cross the picket line. The Board held this to be a primary activity, although the union's action induced the Pure employees to engage in a concerted refusal to handle Pure products at the dock. The fact that the picketing was confined to the vicinity of the Standard premises influenced the Board not to find that an object of the activity was to force Pure to cease doing business with Standard, even if such was a secondary effect. . . .

In *United Electrical Workers (Ryan Construction Corp.)*, 85 NLRB 417, Ryan had contracted to perform construction work on a building adjacent to the Bucyrus plant and inside its fence. A separate gate was cut through the fence for Ryan's employees which no employee of Bucyrus ever used. The Board concluded that the union—on strike against Bucyrus—could picket the Ryan gate, even though an object of the picketing was to enlist the aid of Ryan employees, since Congress did not intend to outlaw primary picketing.

"When picketing is wholly at the premises of the employer with whom the union is engaged in a labor dispute, it cannot be called 'secondary' even though as is virtually always the case, an object of the picketing is to dissuade all persons from entering such premises for business reasons. It makes no difference whether 1 or 100 other employees wish to enter the premises. It follows in this case that the picketing of Bucyrus premises, which was primary because in support of a labor dispute *with Bucyrus*, did not lose its character and become 'secondary' at the so-called Ryan gate because Ryan employees were the only persons regularly entering Bucyrus premises at that gate." 85 NLRB, at 418. See also *General Teamsters (Crump, Inc.)*, 112 NLRB 311.

Thus, the Board eliminated picketing which took place around the situs of the primary employer—regardless of the special circumstances involved—from being held invalid secondary activity under § 8(b)(4)(A).

However, the impact of the new situations made the Board conscious of the complexity of the problem by reason of the protean forms in which it appeared. This became clear in the "common situs" cases—situations where two employers were performing separate tasks on common premises. The *Moore Dry Dock* case, *supra*, laid out the Board's new standards in this area. There, the union picketed outside an entrance to a dock where a ship, owned by the struck employer, was being trained and outfitted. Although the premises picketed were those of the secondary employer, they constituted the only place where picketing could take place; furthermore, the objectives of the picketing were no more aimed at the employees of the secondary employer—the dock owner—than they had been in the *Pure Oil* and *Ryan* cases. The Board concluded, however, that when the situs of the primary employer was "ambulatory" there must be a balance between the union's right to picket and the interest of the secondary employer in being free from picketing. It set out four standards for picketing in such situations which would be presumptive of valid primary activity: (1) that the picketing be limited to times when the situs of dispute was located on the secondary premises, (2) that the primary employer be engaged in his normal business at the situs, (3) that the picketing take place reasonably close to the situs, and (4) that the picketing clearly disclose that the dispute was only with the primary employer. These tests were widely accepted by reviewing federal courts. . . .

As is too often the way of law or, at least, of adjudications, soon the *Dry Dock* tests were mechanically applied so that a violation of one of the standards was taken to be presumptive of illegal activity. For example, failure of picket signs clearly to designate the employer against whom the strike was directed was held to be violative of § 8(b)(4)(A). . . .

In *Local 55 (PBM)*, 108 NLRB 363, the Board for the first time applied the *Dry Dock* test, although the picketing occurred at premises owned by the primary employer. There, an insurance company owned a tract of land that it was developing, and also served as the general contractor. A neutral subcontractor was also doing work at the site. The union, engaged in a strike against the insurance company, picketed the entire premises, characterizing the entire job as unfair, and the employees of the subcontractor walked off. The Court of Appeals for the Tenth Circuit enforced the Board's order which found the picketing to be illegal on the grounds that the picket signs did not measure up to the *Dry Dock* standard that they clearly disclose that the picketing was directed against the struck employer only. 218 F.2d 226.

The Board's application of the *Dry Dock* standards to picketing at the premises of the struck employer was made more explicit in *Retail Fruit & Vegetable Clerks (Crystal Palace Market)*, 116 NLRB 856. The owner of a large common market operated some of the shops within, and leased out others to independent sellers. The union, although given permission to picket the owner's individual stands, chose to picket outside the entire market. The Board held that this action was violative of § 8(b)(4)(A) in that the union did not attempt to minimize the effect of its picketing, as required in a common-situs case, on the operations of the neutral employers utilizing the market. "We believe . . . that the foregoing principles should apply to all common situs picketing, including cases where, as here, the picketed premises are owned by the primary employer." 116 NLRB, at 859. The *Ryan* case, *supra*, was overruled to the extent it implied the contrary. The Court of Appeals for the Ninth Circuit, in enforcing the Board's order, specifically approved its disavowance of an ownership test. 249 F.2d 591. The Board made clear that its decision did not affect situations where picketing which had effects on neutral third parties who dealt with the employer occurred at premises occupied solely by him. "In such cases, we adhere to the rule established by the Board . . . that more latitude be given to picketing at such separate primary premises than at premises occupied in part (or entirely) by secondary employers." 116 NLRB, at 860, n. 10.

In rejecting the ownership test in situations where two employers were performing work upon a common site, the Board was naturally guided by this Court's opinion in *Rice Milling*, in which we indicated that the location of the picketing at the primary employer's premises was "not necessarily conclusive" of its legality. 341 U.S. at 671. Where the work done by the secondary employees is unrelated to the normal operations of the primary employer, it is difficult to perceive how the pressure of picketing the entire situs is any less on the neutral employer merely because the picketing takes place at property owned by the struck employer. The application of the *Dry Dock* tests to limit the picketing effects to the employees of the employer against whom the dispute is directed carries out the "dual congressional objectives of preserving the right of labor organizations to bring pressure to bear on offending employers in primary labor disputes and of shielding unoffending employers and others from pressures in controversies not their own." *Labor Board* v. *Denver Building Council, supra,* at 692.

III.

From this necessary survey of the course of the Board's treatment of our problem, the precise nature of the issue before us emerges. With due regard to the relation between the Board's function and the scope of judicial review of its rulings, the question is whether the Board may apply the *Dry Dock* criteria so as to make unlawful picketing at a gate utilized exclusively by employees of independent contractors who work on the struck employer's premises. The effect of such a holding would not bar the union from picketing at all gates used by the employees, suppliers, and customers of the struck employer. Of course an employer may not, by removing all his employees from the situs of the strike, bar the union from publicizing its cause, see *Local 618, Automotive, Petroleum, etc.* v. *National Labor Relations Board,* 8 Cir., 249 F.2d 332. The basis of the Board's decision in this case would not remotely have that effect, nor any such tendency for the future.

The Union claims that, if the Board's ruling is upheld, employers will be free to erect separate gates for deliveries, customers, and replacement workers which will be immunized from picketing. This fear is baseless. The key to the problem is found in the type of work that is being performed by those who use the separate gate. It is significant that the Board has since applied its rationale, first stated in the present case, only to situations where the independent workers were performing tasks unconnected to the normal operations of the struck employer—usually construction work on his buildings. In such situations, the indicated limitations on picketing activity respect the balance of competing interests that Congress has required the Board to enforce. On the other hand, if a separate gate were devised for regular plant deliveries, the barring of picketing at that location would make a clear invasion on traditional primary activity of appealing to neutral employees whose tasks aid the employer's everyday operations. The 1959 Amendments to the National Labor Relations Act, which removed the word "concerted" from the boycott provisions, included a proviso that "nothing contained in this clause (B) shall be construed to make unlawful, where not otherwise unlawful, any primary strike or primary picketing." 29 U.S.C. (Supp. I, 1959) § 158(b)(4)(B), 29 U.S.C.A. § 158(b)(4)(B). The proviso was directed against the fear that the removal of "concerted" from the statute might be interpreted so that "picketing at the factory violates Section 8(b)(4)(A) because the pickets induce the truck drivers employed by the trucker not to perform their usual services where an object is to compel the trucking firm not to do business with the . . . manufacturer during the strike." Analysis of the bill prepared by Senator Kennedy and Representative Thompson, 105 Con.Rec. 16589.

In a case similar to the one now before us, the Court of Appeals for the Second Circuit sustained the Board in its application of § 8(b)(4)(A) to a separate-gate situation. "There must be a separate gate marked and set apart from other gates; the work done by the men who use the gate must be unrelated to the normal operations of the employer and the work must be of a kind that would not, if done when the plant were engaged in its regular operations, necessitate curtailing those operations." *United Steelworkers of America, AFL-CIO* v. *National Labor Relations Board*, 2 Cir., 289 F.2d 591, 595. These seem to us controlling considerations.

IV.

The foregoing course of reasoning would require that the judgment below sustaining the Board's order be affirmed but for one consideration, even though this consideration may turn out not to affect the result. The legal path by which the Board and the Court of Appeals reached their decisions did not take into account that if Gate 3-A was in fact used by employees of independent contractors who performed conventional maintenance work necessary to the normal operations of General Electric, the use of the gate would have been a mingled one outside the bar of § 8(b)(4)(A). In short, such mixed use of this portion of the struck employer's premises would not bar picketing rights of the striking employees. While the record shows some such mingled use, it sheds no light on its extent. It may well turn out to be that the instances of these maintenance tasks were so insubstantial as to be treated by the Board as *de minimis*. We cannot here guess at the quantitative aspect of this problem. It calls for Board determination. For determination of the questions thus raised, the case must be remanded by the Court of Appeals to the Board.
Reversed.

Question

In the previous Problem, Enderby was the offending (primary) employer, seeking to minimize the effect of union pressure upon its suppliers and contractors. But what if the roles are reversed and the union has a dispute with one of those suppliers or contractors? For example, if the union has a dispute with Rufus Roofers, it may want to set up pickets outside Enderby's premises in the hope that the pressure on Enderby will cause it to terminate its arrangement with Rufus. How may the union legitimately achieve this objective? What can Enderby do to insulate itself from such pressure? Reconsider *General Electric* and *Moore Dry Dock*.

5. Construction Industry Problems

The lines drawn in *General Electric* tend to blur in the construction industry. In the first place, the construction industry generally involves a "common" situs, where both neutral and primary employers carry out their work. Contrast this with *General Electric*, where the neutral employer comes to the situs of the primary employer. Second, there is usually a contractor-subcontractor relationship on the construction job, which the picketing unions contend really constitutes a single employer situation for purposes of applying pressure. Finally, there are intensely practical problems arising from the customs of the industry and the political positions of the unions involved. These cannot be explored here. But the peculiarities of the construction industry setting will be examined in the context of two important cases.

In *NLRB* v. *Denver Building Council*, 341 U.S. 675, 28 LRRM 2108 (1951), the general contractor was organized while a particular subcontractor was not. The union sought to change the subcontractor's status, and to this end picketed the entire job. Its sign read: "This Job Unfair to Denver Building and Construction Trades Council." The result of the picketing was that all the union employees walked off the job, while the employees of the subcontractor continued to work. Eventually, the general contractor terminated the subcontractor in order to get on with the job.

If the general contractor and the subcontractor are viewed as the same employer, or at the very least as occupying some sort of ally status, then the union's pressure creates no problems from a legal standpoint. The union, in demanding that the general contractor not hire nonunion labor through the device of a nonunion subcontractor, can be viewed as merely putting pressure on the offending (primary) employer, the general contractor. However, the Court held that "the business relationship" between independent contractors is too well established in the law to be overridden without clear language doing so, and refused to treat the two as a single employer. On this aspect of the case Justices Douglas and Reed dissented, arguing that the union's right to put pressure on the general contractor was thwarted by the fortuity of a particular business arrangement.

But if the general contractor and subcontractor are viewed as separate employers, the union can lawfully put pressure on the general contractor only if its dispute is with the general contractor. However, the Court concluded that the union's real complaint was with the subcontractor's employment of nonunion workers. As such, the union was actually seeking to compel the neutral general contractor to terminate its relationship with the subcontractor, hence its activity violated the Act.

But if the union's dispute was essentially with the subcontractor, the union could have, under *Moore Dry Dock*, confined its activity to the localized situs of the subcontractor's activity. The general contractor would, of course, utilize reserve gates to contain the situs of the subcontractor. However, the issue of limited location was never reached in this case as the picketing was blanket.

The reverse situation was faced in *Building & Construction Trades Council of New Orleans (Markwell & Hartz, Inc.)*, 155 NLRB 319, 60 LRRM 1296 (1965). This time the general contractor was not organized while the subcontractors were. The union picketed the job with a sign reading:

> Markwell and Hartz
> General Contractor
>
> Does Not Have a Signed Agreement with
> the Building and Construction Trades
> Council of New Orleans
> AFL-CIO

Under a traditional primary-secondary approach, as explained in the *General Electric* case, this pressure on the primary general contractor would be lawful even if it had an effect on the neutral subcontractors. Further, under *General Electric*, efforts to "gate out" the subcontractors would be unavailing, as that case holds that the primary employer must suffer pressures on his neutral suppliers and others who normally do business with him.

But in *Markwell & Hartz*, in a 3-to-2 decision, the Board refused to extend that aspect of *General Electric* to a common situs construction setting. Thus, when the general contractor set up a reserve gate for the subcontractors, the union's picketing at the reserve gate, which resulted in the subcontractor's unionized employees walking off the job, was held to be unlawful secondary pressure on the neutral subcontractor. The critical portion of the Board's opinion states:

"Unlike *General Electric* and *Carrier Corp.*, both of which involved picketing *at the premises of a struck manufacturer*, the picketing in the instant case occurred at a construction project on which M & H, the primary employer, was but one of several employers operating on premises owned and operated by a third party, the Jefferson Parish Water Works. Picketing of neutral and primary contractors under such conditions, has been traditionally viewed as presenting a 'common situs' problem.

"Over the years, the distinction between common situs picketing and that which occurs at premises occupied solely by the struck employer has been a guiding consideration in Board efforts to strike a balance between the competing interests underlying the boycott provisions of the Act. Mindful of the fact that 'Congress did not seek, by Section 8(b)(4), to interfere with the ordinary strike,' the Board has given wide latitude to picketing and related conduct confined to the sole premises of the primary employer. On the other hand, in the interest of shielding 'unoffending employers' from disputes not their own, the Board has taken a more restrictive view of common situs picketing, requiring that it be conducted so as 'to minimize its impact on neutral employees insofar as this can be done without substantial impairment of the effectiveness of the picketing in reaching the primary employees.'

"In accordance with the foregoing, the Board, in determining whether a labor organization, when picketing a common situs, has taken all reasonable precaution to prevent enmeshment of neutrals, traditionally applies the limitations set forth in the *Moore Dry Dock* case. In our opinion application of these standards to all common situs situations, including those, which like the instant case, involve picketing of gates reserved exclusively for neutral contractors on a construction project, serves the 'dual congressional objectives' underlying the boycott provisions of the Act.

"The instant facts, when considered in the light of the legislative history and decisional precedent, do not warrant a departure from our long-established policy with respect to common situs picketing. Quite to the contrary, our continued adherence to the *Moore Dry Dock* standards in such cases comports with the clear expression of Congress, in enacting the 'primary strike and picketing' proviso, that said proviso '. . . does not eliminate, restrict, or modify the limitations on picketing at the site of a primary dispute that are in existing law.'[14] Nor do the Supreme Court's decisions in *General Electric* and *Carrier* detract from our conclusions in this regard; for, the mere fact that picketing of a neutral gate *at premises of a struck employer*, may in proper circumstances be lawful primary action, does not require a like finding when a labor organization applies *direct* pressure upon secondary employers engaged on a common situs. That the Supreme Court had no intention of overriding this historic distinction is evidenced by its express approval of the *Moore Dry Dock* standards, and its observation that the *General Electric* case did not present a common situs situation to which the *Moore Dry Dock* standards should apply. It is plain, therefore, that the Court did not seek to interfere with the Board's traditional approach to common situs problems; rather, the Court's decisions in *General Electric* and *Carrier Corp.* merely represent an implementation of the concomitant policy that lenient treatment be given to strike action taking place at the separate premises of a struck employer.'"

---

[14]As indicated by the following statement on the part of the House conferees, the enactment of specific language protecting primary activity was accompanied by express preservation of the *Denver Building Trades* and *Moore Dry Dock* cases:
'. . . the amendment adopted by the committee of conference contains a provision "that nothing contained in clause (B) of this paragraph (4) shall be construed to make unlawful, where not otherwise unlawful, any primary strike or primary picketing." The purpose of this provision is to make it clear that the changes in Section 8(b)(4) do not overrule or qualify the present rules of law permitting picketing at the site of a primary labor dispute. This provision does not eliminate, restrict, or modify the limitations on picketing at the site of a primary labor dispute that are in existing law. See, for example, NLRB v. Denver Building and Construction Trades Council, et al. (341 U.S. 675 (1951)); . . . Moore Drydock Co. (81 NLRB 1108) [sic]; . . . 1 Leg. Hist. 942 (1959).' "

The differentiated treatment of secondary activity in the construction industry would have ended under the ill-fated common situs bill that was passed by Congress in 1976 but suffered from a change of heart in the White House. The bill, which would have added several tortuous byways (nine "provided furthers" in a single section!) to a statute already described as labyrinthian, in effect treated contractors and subcontractors as a single employer with respect to picketing at a construction site.

For a recent Board decision applying the *Moore Dry Dock* and *General Electric* standards, see *Teamsters, Local 83 (Allied Concrete, Inc.)*, 231 NLRB 1097, 96 LRRM 1165 (1977). In that case a supplier of concrete drove its truck onto the job site through a gate reserved for suppliers. The pickets (in dispute with the supplier) followed the truck through the gate, at which point employees of the general contractor walked off the job. A majority upheld the picketing under *Moore Dry Dock* standards. The two dissenting Board members would have limited the picketing to the gate itself, which would sanitize its impact on the general contractor's employees.

The case quite plainly reveals how closely the lines may be drawn in these cases. Surely, under *Markwell & Hartz*, the union would not be allowed to picket at the gate reserved for employees of the general contractor. But if the union is denied the right to follow the truck onto the premises, its right to engage in primary activity (against the trucking company) is rendered ineffectual. Should activity directed at a supplier of a general contractor, as distinguished from a subcontractor on the job, be treated under the *General Electric* rule or under the rules developed for common situs situations?

6. Consumer Picketing and Distribution of Handbills

Problems

(a) Suppose that Enderby's products are shipped to Umaya, but Umaya is held not to be an ally of Enderby, nor is there a sufficient Enderby "presence" at Umaya to justify picketing there on *Moore Dry Dock* grounds. Is there nevertheless an overriding First Amendment interest which entitles the union at Enderby to take its dispute to the public? For example, suppose Umaya has an outlet store at which it sells its products. May the union post pickets at the store carrying signs which urge the public not to buy Umaya television sets because they contain component parts produced by Enderby, which is "unfair" to its employees?

(b) Suppose that as a result of a strike at Enderby, supported by the company's cafeteria workers, Enderby is no longer able to provide cafeteria service to its employees. In order to feed its managerial employees, who are staffing the plant in the absence of the strikers and performing some production work, Enderby hires the Jolly Frog to bring in lunches for its executives. May the union lawfully post pickets in front of the Jolly Frog urging customers not to patronize the establishment because it is assisting Enderby in a strike-breaking effort?

NLRB v. Servette, Inc.

Supreme Court of the United States, 1964
377 U.S. 46, 55 LRRM 2957

MR. JUSTICE BRENNAN delivered the opinion of the Court.

Respondent Servette, Inc., is a wholesale distributor of specialty merchandise stocked by retail food chains in Los Angeles, California. In 1960, during a strike which Local 848 of the Wholesale Delivery Drivers and Salesmen's Union was conducting against Servette, the Local's representatives sought to support the strike by asking managers of supermarkets of the food chains to discontinue handling merchandise supplied by Servette. In most instances the representatives warned that handbills asking the public not to buy named items distributed by Servette would be passed out in front of stores which refused to cooperate, and in a few cases handbills were in fact passed out. A complaint was issued on charges by Servette that this conduct violated subsections (i) and (ii) of § 8(b)(4) of the National Labor Relations Act, as amended. . . .

The Court of Appeals correctly read the term "individual" in subsection (i) as including the supermarket managers,[4] but it erred in holding that the Local's attempts to enlist the aid of managers constituted inducement of the managers in violation of the subsection. . . . In the instant case . . . the Local, in asking the managers not to handle Servette items, was not attempting to induce or encourage them to cease performing their managerial duties in order to force their employers to cease doing business with Servette. Rather, the managers were asked to make a managerial decision which the Board found was within their authority to make. Such an appeal would not have been a violation of § 8(b)(4)(A) before 1959, and we think that the legislative history of the 1959 amendments makes it clear that the amendments were not meant to render such an appeal an unfair labor practice.

The 1959 amendments were designed to close certain loopholes in the application of § 8(b)(4)(A) which had been exposed in Board and court decisions. Thus, it had been held that the term "the employees of any employer" limited the application of the statute to those within the statutory definitions of "employees" and "employer." Section 2(2) of the National Labor Relations Act defines "employer" to exclude the federal and state governments and their agencies or subdivisions, nonprofit hospitals, and employers subject to the Railway Labor Act. 29 U.S.C. § 152(2). The definition of "employee" in § 2(3) excludes agricultural laborers, supervisors, and employees of an employer subject to the Railway Labor Act. 29 U.S.C. § 152(3). Furthermore, since the section proscribed only inducement to engage in a strike or "concerted" refusal to

---

[4]The Board reached a contrary conclusion on the authority of its decision in *Carolina Lumber Co.*, 130 NLRB 1438, 1443, which viewed the statute as distinguishing "low level" supervisors from "high level" supervisors, holding that inducement of "low level" supervisors is impermissible but inducement of "high level" supervisors is permitted. We hold today that this is not the distinction drawn by the statute, rather, the question of the applicability of subsection (i) turns upon whether the union's appeal is to cease performing employment services, or is an appeal for the exercise of managerial discretion.

perform services, it had been held that it was violated only if the inducement was directed at two or more employees. To close these loopholes, subsection (i) substituted the phrase "any individual employed by any person" for "the employees of any employer," and deleted the word "concerted." The first change was designed to make the provision applicable to refusals by employees who were not technically "employees" within the statutory definitions, and the second change was intended to make clear that inducement directed to only one individual was proscribed. But these changes did not expand the type of conduct which § 8(b)(4)(A) condemned, that is, union pressures calculated to induce the employees of a secondary employer to withhold their services in order to force their employer to cease dealing with the primary employer.

Moreover, the division of § 8(b)(4) into subsections (i) and (ii) by the 1959 amendments has direct relevance to the issue presented by this case. It had been held that § 8(b)(4)(A) did not reach threats of labor trouble made to the secondary employer himself. Congress decided that such conduct should be made unlawful, but only when it amounted to conduct which "threaten[s], coerce[s] or restrain[s] any person"; hence the addition of subsection (ii). The careful creation of separate standards differentiating the treatment of appeals to the employees of the secondary employer not to perform their employment services, from appeals for other ends which are attended by threats, coercion or restraint, argues conclusively against the interpretation of subsection (i) as reaching the Local's appeals to the supermarket managers in this case. If subsection (i), in addition to prohibiting inducement of employees to withhold employment services, also reaches an appeal that the managers exercise their delegated authority by making a business judgment to cease dealing with the primary employer, subsection (ii) would be almost superfluous. Harmony between (i) and (ii) is best achieved by construing subsection (i) to prohibit inducement of the managers to withhold their services from their employer, and subsection (ii) to condemn an attempt to induce the exercise of discretion only if the inducement would "threaten, coerce, or restrain" that exercise.

We turn finally to the question whether the proviso to amended § 8(b)(4) protected the Local's handbilling. The Court of Appeals, following its decision in *Great Western Broadcasting Corp.* v. *Labor Board*, 310 F.2d 591 (CA 9th Cir.), held that the proviso did not protect the Local's conduct, because, as a distributor, Servette was not directly involved in the physical process of creating the products, and thus "does not produce any products." The Board on the other hand followed its ruling in *Lohman Sales Co.*, 132 NLRB 901, that products "produced by an employer" included products distributed, as here, by a wholesaler with whom the primary dispute exists. We agree with the Board. The proviso was the outgrowth of a profound Senate concern that the unions' freedom to appeal to the public for support of their case be adequately safeguarded. We elaborated the history of the proviso in *Labor Board* v. *Fruit & Vegetable Packers, Local 760*, decided today. It would fall far short of achieving this basic purpose if the proviso applied only in situations where the union's labor dispute is with the manufacturer or processor. Moreover, a primary target of the 1959 amendments was the secondary boycotts conducted by the Teamsters Union, which ordinarily represents employees not of manufacturers, but of motor carriers. There is nothing in the legislative history which suggests that the protection of the proviso was intended to be any narrower in coverage than the prohibition to which it is an exception, and we see no basis for attributing such an incongruous purpose to Congress.

The term "produced" in other labor laws was not unfamiliar to Congress. Under the Fair Labor Standards Act, the term is defined as "produced, manufactured, mined, handled, or in any other manner worked on . . ." 29 U.S.C. § 203(j), and has always been held to apply to the wholesale distribution of goods. The term "production" in the War Labor Disputes Act has been similarly applied to a general retail department and mail-order business. The Court of Appeals' restrictive reading of "producer" was prompted in part by the language of § 8(b)(4)(B), which names as a proscribed object of the conduct defined in subsections (i) and (ii) "forcing or requiring any person to cease . . . dealing in the products of any other *producer, processor,* or *manufacturer.*" (Italics supplied.) In its decision in *Great Western Broadcasting Corp.* v. *Labor Board, supra,* the Court of Appeals reasoned that since a "processor" and a "manufacturer" are engaged in the physical creation of goods, the word "producer" must be read as limited to one who performs similar functions. On the contrary, we think that "producer" must be given a broader reach, else it is rendered virtually superfluous.

Finally, the warnings that handbills would be distributed in front of noncooperating stores are not prohibited as "threats" within subsection (ii). The statutory protection for the distribution of handbills would be undermined if a threat to engage in protected conduct were not itself protected.

Note

Servette was held to be a "producer" within the meaning of the proviso even though it did not manufacture the items that it distributed to the supermarkets. The Board has also treated as producers primary employers who supply services such as maintenance and advertising. The Supreme Court recently noted that the coverage of the proviso is "broad enough to include almost any primary dispute that might result in prohibited secondary activity," *DeBartolo Corp.* v. *NLRB,* 463 U.S. ___, 113 LRRM 2953 (1983). Nevertheless, the Court held, unless the primary employer's product is also "distributed by" the affected secondary employer, the proviso does not protect the handbilling.

In *DeBartolo* the union had a dispute with a building contractor who had been retained by a department store in the shopping center owned by DeBartolo. The union distributed handbills asserting that the contractor was paying substandard wages and urging customers not to patronize any of the stores in the mall "until DeBartolo publicly promised that all construction at the mall would be done by contractors who pay their employees fair wages and fringe benefits." DeBartolo told the union it would not oppose this handbilling if it were limited to the contractor and the department store. But when the union persisted in its broader appeal, DeBartolo filed charges with the NLRB. In dismissing the complaint, the Board concluded that the union's handbilling was protected by the publicity proviso to Section 8(b)(4).

In reaching its decision, the Board relied heavily upon the Court's broad definition of "producer" in the earlier *Servette* decision. However, the *DeBartolo* court noted that its focus in *Servette* had only been on the term "producer," and not on the additional requirement for application of the proviso that the product be "distributed by another employer." The Court assumed for purposes of its opinion that the offending contractor was indeed a "producer" within the meaning of the proviso. However, there was no evidence that the contractor's product "was being distributed by DeBartolo" or any of the other shopping center co-tenants. While the Board had relied upon the theory that the other tenants would derive substantial benefit from the contractor's work, describing it as a "symbiotic" relationship, the Court concluded, "that form of analysis would almost strip the distribution requirement of its limiting effect."

The case was remanded to the Board to determine whether the union's conduct fell within the terms of Section 8(b)(4)(ii)(B), since the Board's decision had rested solely on the scope of the proviso. Consider the materials which follow. Further, in light of these materials, was the scope of the proviso necessarily relevant to a decision in *Servette*?

NLRB v. Fruit & Vegetable Packers & Warehousemen, Local 760

Supreme Court of the United States, 1964
377 U.S. 58, 55 LRRM 2961

MR. JUSTICE BRENNAN delivered the opinion of the Court.

Under § 8(b)(4)(ii)(B) of the National Labor Relations Act, as amended, it is an unfair labor practice for a union "to threaten, coerce, or restrain any person," with the object of "forcing or requiring any person to cease using, selling, handling, transporting, or otherwise dealing in the products of any other producer . . . or to cease doing business with any other person. . . ." A proviso excepts, however, "publicity, *other than picketing*, for the purpose of truthfully advising the public . . . that a product or products are produced by an employer with whom the labor organization has a primary dispute and are distributed by another employer, as long as such publicity does not have an effect of inducing any individual employed by any person other than the primary employer in the course of his employment to refuse to pick up, deliver, or transport any goods, or not to perform any services, at the establishment of the employer engaged in such distribution." (Italics supplied.) The question in this case is whether the respondent unions violated this section when they limited their secondary picketing of retail stores to an appeal to the customers of the stores not to buy the products of certain firms against which one of the respondents was on strike.

Respondent Local 760 called a strike against fruit packers and warehousemen doing business in Yakima, Washington. The struck firms sold Washington State apples to the Safeway chain of retail stores in and about Seattle, Washington. Local 760, aided by respondent Joint Council, instituted a consumer boycott against the apples in support of the strike. They placed pickets who walked back and forth before the customers' entrances of 46 Safeway stores in Seattle. The pickets—two at each of 45 stores and three at the 46th store—wore placards and distributed handbills which appealed to Safeway customers, and to the public generally, to refrain from buying Washington State apples, which were only one of numerous food products sold in the stores.[3]

Before the pickets appeared at any store, a letter was delivered to the store manager informing him that the picketing was only an appeal to his customers not to buy Washington State apples, and that the pickets were being expressly instructed "to patrol peacefully in front of the consumer entrances of the store, to stay away from the delivery entrances and not to interfere with the work of your employees, or with deliveries to or pickups from your store." A copy of written instructions to the pickets—which included the explicit statement that "you are also forbidden to request that the customers not patronize the store"—was enclosed with the letter. Since it was desired to assure Safeway employees that they were not to cease work, and to avoid any interference with pickups or deliveries, the pickets appeared after the stores opened for business and departed before the

---

[3]The placard worn by each picket stated: "To the Consumer: Non-Union Washington State apples are being sold at this store. Please do not purchase such apples. Thank you. Teamsters Local 760, Yakima, Washington."

A typical handbill read:

"DON'T BUY
WASHINGTON STATE
APPLES

The 1960 Crop of Washington State
Apples is Being Packed by Non-Union Firms

Included in this non-union operation are twenty-six firms in the Yakima Valley with which there is a labor dispute. These firms are charged with being

UNFAIR

by their employees who, with their union, are on strike and have been replaced by non-union strikebreaking workers employed under substandard wage scales and working conditions.

In justice to these striking union workers who are attempting to protect their living standards and their right to engage in good-faith collective bargaining, we request that you

DON'T BUY
WASHINGTON STATE
APPLES

Teamsters Union Local 760
Yakima, Washington

This is not a strike against any store or market.

(P.S.—PACIFIC FRUIT & PRODUCT CO. is the only firm packing Washington State Apples under a union contract.)"

stores closed. At all times during the picketing, the store employees continued to work, and no deliveries or pickups were obstructed. Washington State apples were handled in normal course by both Safeway employees and the employees of other employers involved. Ingress and egress by customers and others was not interfered with in any manner.

A complaint issued on charges that this conduct violated § 8(b)(4) as amended. The case was submitted directly to the National Labor Relations Board on a stipulation of facts and the waiver of a hearing and proceedings before a Trial Examiner. The Board held, following its construction of the statute in *Upholsterers Frame & Bedding Workers Twin City Local No. 61*, 132 NLRB 40, that "by literal wording of the proviso [to Section 8(b)(4)] as well as through the interpretive gloss placed thereon by its drafters, consumer picketing in front of a secondary establishment is prohibited." 132 NLRB 1172, 1177. Upon respondents' petition for review and the Board's cross-petition for enforcement, the Court of Appeals for the District of Columbia Circuit set aside the Board's order and remanded. The court rejected the Board's construction and held that the statutory requirement of a showing that respondents' conduct would "threaten, coerce, or restrain" Safeway could only be satisfied by affirmative proof that a substantial economic impact on Safeway had occurred, or was likely to occur as a result of the conduct. Under the remand the Board was left "free to reopen the record to receive evidence upon the issue whether Safeway was in fact threatened, coerced, or restrained."

The Board's reading of the statute—that the legislative history and the phrase "other than picketing" in the proviso reveal a congressional purpose to outlaw all picketing directed at customers at a secondary site— necessarily rested on the finding that Congress determined that such picketing always threatens, coerces or restrains the secondary employer. We therefore have a special responsibility to examine the legislative history for confirmation that Congress made that determination. Throughout the history of federal regulation of labor relations, Congress has consistently refused to prohibit peaceful picketing except where it is used as a means to achieve specific ends which experience has shown are undesirable. "In the sensitive area of peaceful picketing Congress has dealt explicitly with isolated evils which experience has established flow from such picketing." *National Labor Relations Board* v. *Drivers etc. Local Union [639]*, 362 U.S. 274, 284, 45 LRRM 2975, 2979 (1960). We have recognized this congressional practice and have not ascribed to Congress a purpose to outlaw peaceful picketing unless "there is the clearest indication in the legislative history," *ibid.*, that Congress intended to do so as regards the particular ends of the picketing under review. Both the congressional policy and our adherence to this principle of interpretation reflect concern that a broad ban against peaceful picketing might collide with the guarantees of the First Amendment.

We have examined the legislative history of the amendments to § 8(b)(4), and conclude that it does not reflect with the requisite clarity a congressional plan to proscribe all peaceful consumer picketing at secondary sites, and particularly, any concern with peaceful picketing when it is limited, as here, to persuading Safeway customers not to buy Washington State apples when they traded in the Safeway stores. All that the legislative history shows in the way of an "isolated evil" believed to require proscription of peaceful consumer picketing at secondary sites was its use to persuade the customers of the secondary employer to cease trading with him in order to force him to cease dealing with, or to put pressure upon, the primary employer. This narrow focus reflects the difference between such conduct and peaceful picketing at the secondary site directed only at the struck product. In the latter case, the union's appeal to the public is confined to its dispute with the primary employer, since the public is not asked to withhold its patronage from the secondary employer, but only to boycott the primary employer's goods. On the other hand, a union appeal to the public at the secondary site not to trade at all with the secondary employer goes beyond the goods of the primary employer, and seeks the public's assistance in forcing the secondary employer to cooperate with the union in its primary dispute. This is not to say that this distinction was expressly alluded to in the debates. It is to say, however, that the consumer picketing carried on in this case is not attended by the abuses at which the statute was directed. [The Court then considered the legislative history of the 1959 amendments to the LMRA and concluded that Congress, in enacting these amendments, was not concerned with curtailing certain kinds of consumer boycotts. This portion of the opinion, heavily edited, follows.]

When major labor relations legislation was being considered in 1958 the closing of these loopholes [certain provisions of the act not relevant to our discussion] was important to the House and to some members of the Senate. . . . The Administration introduced such a bill, and it was supported by Senators Dirksen and Goldwater. Senator Goldwater, an inconsistent proponent of stiff boycott curbs, also proposed his own amendments. We think it is especially significant that neither Senator, nor the Secretary of Labor in testifying in support of the Administration's bill, referred to consumer picketing as making the amendments necessary. Senator McClellan, who also offered a bill to curb boycotts, mentioned consumer picketing but only such as was "pressure in the form of dissuading customers *from dealing with* secondary employers." (Emphasis supplied.) It was the opponents of the amendments who, in expressing fear of their sweep, suggested that they might proscribe consumer picketing. Senator Humphrey first sounded the warning early in April. Many months later, when the Conference bill was before the Senate, Senator Morse, a conferee, would not support the Conference bill on the express ground that it prohibited consumer picketing. But we have often cautioned against the danger, when interpreting a statute, of reliance upon the views of its legislative opponents. In their zeal to defeat a bill, they understandably tend to overstate its reach. "The fears and doubts of the opposition are no authoritative guide to the construction of legislation. It is the sponsors that we look to when the meaning of the statutory words is in doubt." *Schwegmann Bros.* v. *Calvert Distillers Corp.*, 341 U.S. 384, 394–395. The silence of the sponsors of amendments is pregnant with significance since they must have been aware that consumer picketing as such had been held to be outside the reach of § 8(b)(4). We are faithful to our practice of respecting the congressional policy of legislating only against clearly identified abuses of peaceful picketing when we conclude that the Senate neither specified the kind of picketing here involved as an abuse, nor indicated any intention of banning all consumer picketing.

The House history is similarly beclouded, but what appears confirms our conclusion. . . .

Senator Kennedy presided over the Conference Committee. He and Congressman Thompson prepared a joint analysis of the Senate and House bills. This analysis pointed up the First Amendment implications of the broad language in the House revisions of § 8(b)(4) stating,

> "The prohibition [of the House bill] reaches not only picketing but leaflets, radio broadcasts and newspaper advertisements, thereby interfering with freedom of speech.
>
> . . .
>
> ". . . one of the apparent purposes of the amendment is to prevent unions from appealing to the general public as consumers for assistance in a labor dispute. This is a basic infringement upon freedom of expression."

This analysis was the first step in the development of the publicity proviso, but nothing in the legislative history of the proviso alters our conclusion that Congress did not clearly express an intention that amended § 8(b)(4) should prohibit all consumer picketing. Because of the sweeping language of the House bill, and its implications for freedom of speech, the Senate conferees refused to accede to the House proposal without safeguards for the right of unions to appeal to the public, even by some conduct which might be "coercive." The result was the addition of the proviso. But it does not follow from the fact that some coercive conduct was protected by the proviso, that the exception "other than picketing" indicates that Congress had determined that all consumer picketing was coercive.

No Conference Report was before the Senate when it passed the compromise bill, and it had the benefit only of Senator Kennedy's statement of the purpose of the proviso. He said that the proviso preserved "the right to appeal to consumers by methods other than picketing asking them to refrain from buying goods made by nonunion labor *and* to refrain from trading with a retailer who sells such goods. . . . We were not able to persuade the House conferees to permit picketing in front of that secondary shop, but were able to persuade them to agree that the unions shall be free to conduct informational activity short of picketing. In other words, the union can hand out handbills at the shop . . . and can carry on all publicity short of having ambulatory picketing. . . ." (Italics supplied.) This explanation does not compel the conclusion that the Conference Agreement contemplated prohibiting any consumer picketing at a secondary site beyond that which urges the public, in Senator Kennedy's words, to "refrain from trading with a retailer who sells such goods." To read into the Conference Agreement, on the basis of a single statement, an intention to prohibit all consumer picketing at a secondary site would depart from our practice of respecting the congressional policy not to prohibit peaceful picketing except to curb "isolated evils" spelled out by the Congress itself.

Peaceful consumer picketing to shut off all trade with the secondary employer unless he aids the union in its dispute with the primary employer, is poles apart from such picketing which only persuades his customers not to buy the struck product. The proviso indicates no more than that the Senate conferees' constitutional doubts led Congress to authorize publicity other than picketing which persuades the customers of a secondary employer to stop all trading with him, but not such publicity which has the effect of cutting off his deliveries or inducing his employees to cease work. On the other hand, picketing which persuades the customers of a secondary employer to stop all trading with him was also to be barred.

In sum, the legislative history does not support the Board's finding that Congress meant to prohibit all consumer picketing at a secondary site, having determined that such picketing necessarily threatened, coerced or restrained the secondary employer. Rather, the history shows that Congress was following its usual practice of legislating against peaceful picketing only to curb "isolated evils."

This distinction is opposed as "unrealistic" because, it is urged, all picketing automatically provokes the public to stay away from the picketed establishment. The public will, it is said, neither read the signs and handbills, nor note the explicit injunction that "This is not a strike against any store or market." Be that as it may, our holding today simply takes note of the fact that Congress has never adopted a broad condemnation of peaceful picketing, such as that urged upon us by petitioners, and an intention to do so is not revealed with that "clearest indication in the legislative history," which we require. *National Labor Relations Board* v. *Drivers, etc. Local Union, supra.*

We come then to the question whether the picketing in this case, confined as it was to persuading customers to cease buying the product of the primary employer, falls within the area of secondary consumer picketing which Congress did clearly indicate its intention to prohibit under § 8(b)(4)(ii). We hold that it did not fall within that area, and therefore did not "threaten, coerce, or restrain" Safeway. While any diminution in Safeway's purchases of apples due to a drop in consumer demand might be said to be a result which causes respondents' picketing to fall literally within the statutory prohibition, "it is a familiar rule that a thing may be within the letter of the statute and yet not within the statute, because not within its spirit nor within the intention of its makers." *Holy Trinity Church* v. *United States,* 143 U.S. 457, 459. When consumer picketing is employed only to persuade customers not to buy the struck product, the union's appeal is closely confined to the primary dispute. The site of the appeal is expanded to include the premises of the secondary employer, but if the appeal succeeds, the secondary employer's purchases from the struck firms are decreased only because the public has diminished its purchases of the struck product. On the other hand, when consumer picketing is employed to persuade customers not to trade at all with the secondary employer, the latter stops buying the struck product, not because of a falling demand, but in response to pressure designed to inflict injury on his business generally. In such case, the union does more than merely follow the struck product; it creates a separate dispute with the secondary employer.

We disagree therefore with the Court of Appeals that the test of "to threaten, coerce, or restrain" for the purposes of this case is whether Safeway suffered or was likely to suffer economic loss. A violation of § 8(b)(4)(ii)(B) would not be established, merely because respondents' picketing was effective to reduce Safeway's sales of Washington State apples, even if this led or might lead Safeway to drop the item as a poor seller.

The judgment of the Court of Appeals is vacated and the case is remanded with direction to enter judgment setting aside the Board's order. It is so ordered.

Judgment of Court of Appeals vacated and case remanded with directions.

MR. JUSTICE BLACK, concurring.

Because of the language of § 8(b)(4)(ii)(B) of the National Labor Relations Act and the legislative history set out in the opinions of the Court and of my Brother Harlan, I feel impelled to hold that Congress, in passing this section of the Act, intended to forbid the striking employees of one business to picket the premises of a neutral business where the purpose of the picketing is to persuade customers of the neutral business not to buy goods supplied by the struck employer. Construed in this way, as I agree with Brother Harlan that it must be, I believe, contrary to his view, that the section abridges freedom of speech and press in violation of the First Amendment.

"Picketing," in common parlance and in § 8(b)(4)(ii)(B), includes at least two concepts: (1) patrolling, that is, standing or marching back and forth or round and round on the streets, sidewalks, private property, or elsewhere, generally adjacent to someone else's premises; (2) speech, that is, arguments, usually on a placard, made to persuade other people to take the picketers' side of a controversy. See Mr. Justice Douglas concurring in *Bakery & Pastry Drivers* v. *Wohl*, 315 U.S. 769, 775. See also *Hughes* v. *Superior Court*, 339 U.S. 460, 464–465, and concurring opinions at 469. While "the dissemination of information concerning the facts of a labor dispute must be regarded as within that area of free discussion that is guaranteed by the Constitution," *Thornhill* v. *Alabama*, 310 U.S. 88, 102, patrolling is, of course, conduct, not speech, and therefore is not directly protected by the First Amendment. It is because picketing includes patrolling that neither *Thornhill* nor cases that followed it lend "support to the contention that peaceful picketing is beyond legislative control." *Giboney* v. *Empire Storage & Ice Co.*, 336 U.S. 490, 499–500. Cf. *Schneider* v. *State*, 308 U.S. 147, 160–161. However, when conduct not constitutionally protected, like patrolling, is intertwined, as in picketing, with constitutionally protected free speech and press, regulation of the non-protected conduct may at the same time encroach on freedom of speech and press. In such cases it is established that it is the duty of courts, before upholding regulations of patrolling, "to weigh the circumstances and to appraise the substantiality of the reasons advanced in support of the regulation of the free enjoyment of the rights" of speech and press. . . .

In short, we have neither a case in which picketing is banned because the picketers are asking others to do something unlawful nor a case in which *all* picketing is, for reasons of public order, banned. Instead, we have a case in which picketing, otherwise lawful, is banned only when the picketers express particular views. The result is an abridgement of the freedom of these picketers to tell a part of the public their side of a labor controversy, a subject the free discussion of which is protected by the First Amendment.

I cannot accept my Brother Harlan's view that the abridgement of speech and press here does not violate the First Amendment because other methods of communication are left open. This reason for abridgement strikes me as being on a par with holding that governmental suppression of a newspaper in a city would not violate the First Amendment because there continue to be radio and television stations. First Amendment freedoms can no more validly be taken away by degrees than by one fell swoop. . . .

MR. JUSTICE HARLAN, whom MR. JUSTICE STEWART joins, dissenting. . . .

Nothing in the statute lends support to the fine distinction which the Court draws between general and limited product picketing. The enactment speaks pervasively of threatening, coercing, or restraining any person; the proviso differentiates only between modes of expression, not between types of secondary consumer picketing. For me, the Court's argument to the contrary is very unconvincing. . . .

[A detailed discussion of the legislative history is omitted.]

Under my view of the statute the constitutional issue is therefore reached. Since the Court does not discuss it, I am content simply to state in summary form my reasons for believing that the prohibitions of § 8(b)(4)(ii)(B), as applied here, do not run afoul of constitutional limitations. This Court has long recognized that picketing is "inseparably something more [than] and different" from simple communication. *Hughes* v. *Superior Court*, 339 U.S. 460, 464. Congress has given careful and continued consideration to the problems of labor-management relations, and its attempts to effect an accommodation between the right of unions to publicize their position and the social desirability of limiting a form of communication likely to have effects caused by something apart from the message communicated, are entitled to great deference. The decision of Congress to prohibit secondary consumer picketing during labor disputes is, I believe, not inconsistent with the protections of the First Amendment, particularly when, as here, other methods of communication are left open.

Contrary to my Brother Black, I think the fact that Congress in prohibiting secondary consumer picketing has acted with a discriminating eye is the very thing that renders this provision invulnerable to constitutional attack. That Congress has permitted other picketing which is likely to have effects beyond those resulting from the "communicative" aspect of picketing does not, of course, in any way lend itself to the conclusion that Congress here has aimed to "prevent dissemination of information about the facts of a labor dispute." Even on the highly dubious assumption that the "non-speech" aspect of picketing is always the same whatever the particular context, the social consequences of the "non-communicative" aspect of picketing may certainly be thought desirable in the case of "primary" picketing and undesirable in the case of "secondary" picketing, a judgment Congress has indeed made in prohibiting secondary but not primary picketing.

I would enforce the Board's order.

"Give me some of whatever the bleeding hearts are boycotting."

Drawing by D. Reilly; © 1972
The New Yorker Magazine, Inc.

Questions

1. Is Justice Brennan's analysis in *Tree Fruits* (shortened name for the *Fruit & Vegetable Packers & Warehousemen* case above) of the legislative history merely wishful thinking?
2. Is the distinction at the end of the opinion, between persuasion not to buy the product and persuasion not to deal at all with the secondary employer, also wishful?
3. How should the case have been decided?

NLRB v. Retail Clerks, Local 1001

Supreme Court of the United States, 1980
447 U.S. 607, 104 LRRM 2567

MR. JUSTICE POWELL delivered the opinion of the Court.

The question is whether § 8(b)(4)(ii)(B) of the National Labor Relations Act forbids secondary picketing against a struck product when such picketing predictably encourages consumers to boycott a neutral party's business.

I

Safeco Title Insurance Co. underwrites real estate title insurance in the State of Washington. It maintains close business relationships with five local title companies. The companies search land titles, perform escrow services, and sell title insurance. Over 90 percent of their gross incomes derives from the sale of Safeco insurance. Safeco has substantial stockholdings in each title company, and at least one Safeco officer serves on each company's board of directors. Safeco, however, has no control over the companies' daily operations. It does not direct their personnel policies, and it never exchanges employees with them.

Local 1001 of the Retail Store Employees Union became the certified bargaining representative for certain Safeco employees in 1974. When contract negotiations between Safeco and the Union reached an impasse, the employees went on strike. The Union did not confine picketing to Safeco's office in Seattle. The Union also picketed each of the five local title companies. The pickets carried signs declaring that Safeco had no contract with the Union,[2] and they distributed handbills asking consumers to support the strike by cancelling their Safeco policies.

. . . [Safeco] charged that the Union had engaged in an unfair labor practice by picketing in order to promote a secondary boycott against the title companies. The Board agreed. It found the title companies to be neutral in the dispute between Safeco and the Union. The Board then concluded that the Union's picketing violated § 8(b)(4)(ii)(B) of the

---

[2]The picket signs read:

"SAFECO NONUNION
DOES NOT EMPLOY MEMBERS OF
OR HAVE CONTRACT WITH
RETAIL STORE EMPLOYEES LOCAL 1001."

National Labor Relations Act. The Union had directed its appeal against Safeco insurance policies. But since the sale of those policies accounted for substantially all of the title companies' business, the Board found that the Union's action was "reasonably calculated to induce customers not to patronize the neutral parties at all." The Board therefore rejected the Union's reliance upon *NLRB* v. *Fruit Packers (Tree Fruits)*, which held that § 8(b)(4)(ii)(B) allows secondary picketing against a struck product. It ordered the Union to cease picketing and to take limited corrective action.

The United States Court of Appeals for the District of Columbia Circuit set aside the Board's order. . . .

We granted a writ of certiorari to consider whether the Court of Appeals correctly understood § 8(b)(4)(ii)(B) as interpreted in *Tree Fruits*. Having concluded that the Court of Appeals misapplied the statute, we now reverse and remand for enforcement of the Board's order.

II

. . .

In *Tree Fruits,* the Court held that § 8(b)(4)(ii)(B) does not prohibit all peaceful picketing at secondary sites. There, a union striking certain Washington fruit packers picketed large supermarkets in order to persuade consumers not to buy Washington apples. Concerned that a broad ban against such picketing might run afoul of the First Amendment, the Court found the statute directed to an " 'isolated evil.' " The evil was use of secondary picketing "to persuade the customers of the secondary employer to cease trading with him in order to force him to cease dealing with, or to put pressure upon, the primary employer." Congress intended to protect secondary parties from pressures that might embroil them in the labor disputes of others, but not to shield them from business losses caused by a campaign that successfully persuades consumers "to boycott the primary employer's goods." Thus, the Court drew a distinction between picketing "to shut off all trade with the secondary employer unless he aids the union in its dispute with the primary employer" and picketing that "only persuades his customers not to buy the struck product." The picketing in that case, which "merely follow[ed] the struck product," did not " 'threaten, coerce, or restrain' " the secondary party within the meaning of § 8(b)(4)(ii)(B).

Although *Tree Fruits* suggested that secondary picketing against a struck product and secondary picketing against a neutral party were "poles apart," the courts soon discovered that product picketing could have the same effect as an illegal secondary boycott. In *Hoffmann ex rel. NLRB* v. *Cement Masons Local 337*, 468 F.2d 1187 (CA 9 1972), *cert. denied*, 411 U.S. 986 (1973), for example, a union embroiled with a general contractor picketed the housing subdivision that he had constructed for a real estate developer. Pickets sought to persuade prospective purchasers not to buy the contractor's houses. The picketing was held illegal because purchasers "could reasonably expect that they were being asked not to transact any business whatsoever" with the neutral developer. "[W]hen a union's interest in picketing a primary employer at a 'one product' site, [directly conflicts] with the need to protect . . . neutral employers from the labor disputes of others," Congress has determined that the neutrals' interests should prevail. *Id.*, at 1191.[7]

Cement Masons highlights the critical difference between the picketing in this case and the picketing at issue in *Tree Fruits*. The product picketed in *Tree Fruits* was but one item among the many that made up the retailer's trade. If the appeal against such a product succeeds, the Court observed, it simply induces the neutral retailer to reduce his orders for the product or "to drop the item as a poor seller." The decline in sales attributable to consumer rejection of the struck product puts pressure upon the primary employer, and the marginal injury to the neutral retailer is purely incidental to the product boycott. The neutral therefore has little reason to become involved in the labor dispute. In this case, on the other hand, the title companies sell only the primary employer's product and perform the services associated with it. Secondary picketing against consumption of the primary product leaves responsive consumers no realistic option other than to boycott the title companies altogether. If the appeal succeeds, each company "stops buying the struck product, not because of a falling demand, but in response to pressure designed to inflict injury on [its] business generally." Thus, "the union does more than merely follow the struck product; it creates a separate dispute with the secondary employer." Such an expansion of labor discord was one of the evils that Congress intended § 8(b)(4)(ii)(B) to prevent.

As long as secondary picketing only discourages consumption of a struck product, incidental injury to the neutral is a natural consequence of an effective primary boycott. But the Union's secondary appeal against the central product sold by the title companies in this case is "reasonably calculated to induce customers not to patronize the neutrals at all." 226 NLRB, at 757.[8] The resulting injury to their businesses is distinctly different from the injury that the Court considered in *Tree Fruits*. Product picketing that reasonably can be expected to threaten neutral parties with ruin or substantial loss simply does not square with the language or the purpose of § 8(b)(4)(ii)(B). Since successful secondary picketing would put the title companies to a choice between their survival and the severance of their ties with Safeco, the picketing plainly violates the statutory ban on the coercion of neutrals with the object of "forcing or requiring

[7] The so-called merged product cases also involve situations where an attempt to follow the struck product inevitably encourages an illegal boycott of the neutral party. . . .

[8] . . .

We do not disagree with Mr. Justice Brennan's dissenting view that successful secondary product picketing may have no greater effect upon a neutral than a legal primary boycott. But when the neutral's business depends upon the products of a particular primary employer, secondary product picketing can produce injury almost identical to the harm resulting from an illegal secondary boycott. See generally Duerr, Developing a Standard for Secondary Consumer Picketing, 26 Lab.L.J. 585 (1975). Congress intended § 8(b)(4)(ii)(B) to protect neutrals from that type of coercion. Mr. Justice Brennan's view that the legality of secondary picketing should depend upon whether the pickets "urge only a boycott of the primary employer's product," would provide little or no protection. No well-advised union would allow secondary pickets to carry placards urging anything other than a product boycott. Section 8(b)(4)(ii)(B) cannot bear a construction so inconsistent with the congressional intention to prevent neutrals from becoming innocent victims in contests between others.

[them] to cease . . . dealing in the [primary] produc[t] . . . or to cease doing business with" the primary employer.[11]

III

The Court of Appeals suggested that application of § 8(b)(4)(ii)(B) to the picketing in this case might violate the First Amendment. We think not. Although the Court recognized in *Tree Fruits* that the Constitution might not permit "a broad ban against peaceful picketing," the Court left no doubt that Congress may prohibit secondary picketing calculated "to persuade the customers of the secondary employer to cease trading with him in order to force him to cease dealing with, or to put pressure upon, the primary employer." Such picketing spreads labor discord by coercing a neutral party to join the fray. In *Electrical Workers v. NLRB*, 341 U.S. 694, 705 (1951), this Court expressly held that a prohibition on "picketing in furtherance of [such] unlawful objectives" did not offend the First Amendment. We perceive no reason to depart from that well-established understanding. As applied to picketing that predictably encourages consumers to boycott a secondary business, § 8(b)(4)(ii)(B) imposes no impermissible restrictions upon constitutionally protected speech.

Accordingly, the judgment of the Court of Appeals is reversed and the case is remanded with directions to enforce the National Labor Relations Board's order.

So ordered.

[Justices Blackmun and Stevens each concurred in separate opinions in which each expressed concern about the constitutional ramifications of the majority's decision. Both Justices concluded, however, that the regulation in the present case would not violate the First Amendment.

[Justice Brennan dissented in an opinion joined by Justices White and Marshall. To the dissenters, the majority decision "stunts *Tree Fruits* by declaring that secondary site picketing is illegal when the primary employer's product at which it is aimed happens to be the only product which the secondary retailer distributes." A portion of the dissenting opinion follows:]

Tree Fruits addressed this problem by focusing upon whether picketing at the secondary site is directed at the primary employer's product, or whether it more broadly exhorts customers to withhold patronage from the full range of goods carried by the secondary retailer, *including those goods originating from nonprimary sources.* The *Tree Fruits* test reflects the distinction between economic damage sustained by the secondary firm

---

[11]The picketing in *Tree Fruits* and the picketing in this case are relatively extreme examples of the spectrum of conduct that the Board and the courts will encounter in complaints charging violations of § 8(b)(4)(ii)(B). If secondary picketing were directed against a product representing a major portion of a neutral's business, but significantly less than that represented by a single dominant product, neither *Tree Fruits* nor today's decision necessarily would control. The critical question would be whether, by encouraging customers to reject the struck product, the secondary appeal is reasonably likely to threaten the neutral party with ruin or substantial loss. Resolution of the question in each case will be entrusted to the Board's expertise.

solely by virtue of its dependence upon the primary employer's goods, and injuries inflicted upon interests of the secondary firm that are unrelated to the primary dispute—injuries that are calculated to influence the secondary retailer's conduct with respect to the primary dispute.

The former sort of harm is simply the result of union success in its conflict with the primary employer. The secondary firm is hurt only insofar as it entwines its economic fate with that of the primary employer by carrying the latter's goods. To be sure, the secondary site may be a battleground; but the secondary retailer, in its own right, is not enlisted as a combatant.

The latter kind of economic harm to the secondary firm, however, does not involve merely the necessary commercial fallout from the primary dispute. Appeals to boycott nonprimary goods sold by a secondary retailer place more at stake for the retailer than the risk it has assumed by handling the primary employer's product. Four considerations indicate that this broader pressure is highly undesirable from the standpoint of labor policy. First, nonprimary product boycotts distort the strength of consumer response to the primary dispute; the secondary retailer's decision to continue purchasing the primary employer's line becomes a function of consumer reaction to the primary conflict *amplified* by the impact of the boycott upon nonprimary goods. *Tree Fruits, supra,* at 72, and n. 20. Second, although it seems proper to compel the producer or retailer of an individual primary product to internalize the costs of labor conflict engendered in the course of the item's production, a nonprimary product boycott may unfairly impose multiple costs upon the secondary retailer who does not wish to terminate his relationship with the primary employer. Third, nonprimary product boycotts attack interests of the secondary firm that are not derivative of the interests of the primary enterprise; because the retailer thereby becomes an independent disputant, the primary labor controversy may be aggravated and complicated. Finally, by affecting the sales of nonprimary goods handled by the secondary firm, the disruptive effect of the primary dispute is felt even by those businesses that manufacture and sell nonprimary products to the secondary retailer.

These sound reasons support *Tree Fruits'* conclusion that the legality of secondary site picketing should turn upon whether the union pickets urge only a boycott of the primary employer's product.[2] Concomitantly, *Tree Fruits* expressly rejected the notion that the coerciveness of picketing should depend upon the extent of loss suffered by the secondary firm through diminished purchases of the primary product. Nevertheless, the Court has now apparently abandoned the *Tree Fruits* approach, choosing instead to identify coerciveness with the percentage of the secondary firm's business made up by the primary product. . . .

[2]Because a "merged product" consists in part of nonprimary products, the prohibition of "merged product" boycotts follows as a matter of logic and of policy from *Tree Fruits'* primary product boycott test. Thus, "merged product" cases do not support the Courts view that certain purely primary product boycotts are proscribed by the National Labor Relations Act. In fact, "merged product" boycotts are wholly different than primary product boycotts against single product retailers. "Merged product" boycotts need not entail a total withholding of patronage from the secondary retailer, which may carry other, nonmerged products.

Note on Conglomerates

Suppose that Enderby is but one component of a conglomerate enterprise, and that the conglomerate headquarters sets labor relations policies for all its component divisions. If the United Factory Workers Union has a labor dispute with Enderby, may it lawfully involve other companies within the conglomerate? For example, should the union be allowed to picket another component on the theory that if Enderby is shut down the conglomerate will simply invest its assets in another portion of the enterprise? Does this give the other component companies ally status under the doctrine discussed in part 2 *supra,* and should they as a result be unable to shield themselves from labor pressure under Section 8(b)(4)?

The Board is just beginning to wrestle with the set of problems arising from conglomerate organization in American industry. For example, in *Steelworkers (Pet, Inc.),* the Steelworkers union had a dispute with Hussmann, a refrigeration manufacturer which was a subsidiary of the giant Pet Food conglomerate. The union called for a nationwide boycott of all Pet products and services, many of which were known by popular brand names. Pet filed charges under Section 8(b)(4), claiming that the union's pressure against Pet and its subsidiaries was unlawfully directed at persons "neutral" in the union's dispute with Hussmann.

The Board did not address the "neutrality" issue. Rather, it concluded that the union's picketing was protected under the publicity proviso of Section 8(b)(4) as truthfully advising the public that the products were produced by an employer (Hussmann) with whom the union had a primary dispute. The critical finding to bring the proviso into play was that Hussmann was a "producer" of the products and services of Pet and its subdivisions. Based on the Court's *Servette* decision and the decisions cited in that case (see pages 759–761), the Board broadly defined "product."

Steelworkers (Pet, Inc.)

National Labor Relations Board, 1979
244 NLRB 96, 102 LRRM 1046

. . .

The General Counsel and the Charging Party contend that Respondent violated Section 8(b)(4)(ii)(B) of the Act by calling for a total consumer boycott of Pet and its subsidiaries and divisions. They argue that the handbilling and other publicity used in an attempt to achieve that end constitutes restraint and/or coercion within the meaning of subparagraph (ii) of Section 8(b)(4) of the Act, since it was directed against Pet and certain specified subsidiaries and divisions which they allege to be "neutral" persons. The General Counsel further argues that the object of Respondent's conduct was to induce or influence consumers to cease doing business with Pet and its subsidiaries and divisions, with the intended consequence of causing a diminution of business between Pet's divisions and their suppliers and distributors and a cessation of business between the various divisions of Pet, and that said objective is therefore proscribed by paragraph (B) of Section 8(b)(4) of the Act. Both the General Counsel and the Charging Party contend that because a requisite "producer-distributor" relationship between Pet and its subsidiaries and divisions and Hussmann does not exist, the publicity proviso offers no immunity to Respondent's conduct. Finally, they contend that a finding that Respondent's conduct is unprotected by the publicity proviso would not be an unconstitutional abridgment of free speech.

Respondent argues that the Board in the *Hearst Corporation, supra,* and similar cases, applied an improper test to determine the neutrality of an employer under Section 8(b)(4) of the Act. Respondent urges that the proper test is whether the supposed neutral has a direct economic interest in the outcome of the primary's dispute with the union and contends that Pet and its subsidiaries and divisions, having such an economic interest, are not neutrals. Respondent further argues that the handbilling and other activities constitute neither unlawful restraint nor coercion and that Section 8(b)(4)(B) was not intended to reach the type of conduct involved herein. Affirmatively, Respondent asserts that the alleged unlawful conduct is protected by the publicity proviso of Section 8(b)(4), citing *NLRB* v. *Servette, Inc.,* and *International Brotherhood of Teamsters, Chauffeurs, Warehousemen and Helpers of America, Milk Drivers and Dairy Employees Local 537 (Jack M. Lohman, d/b/a Lohman Sales Company),* in that Hussmann substantially contributes to Pet and its subsidiaries and divisions and vice versa. Respondent also asserts that the first amendment to the Constitution further protects the conduct at issue. For these reasons, Respondent contends that the complaint should be dismissed in its entirety.

DISCUSSIONS OF LAW AND CONCLUSIONS

The proscription of Section 8(b)(4)(ii)(B), making it unlawful to "threaten, coerce, or restrain any person" where an object thereof is to force such person to cease doing business with any other person, is limited in its reach by the publicity proviso of Section 8(b)(4). That proviso immunizes from statutory proscription:

"... publicity, other than picketing, for the purpose of truthfully advising the public, including consumers and members of a labor organization, that a product or products are produced by an employer with whom the labor organization has a primary dispute and are distributed by another employer, as long as such publicity does not have an effect of inducing any individual employed by any person other than the primary employer in the course of his employment to refuse to pick up, deliver, or transport any goods, or not to perform any services, at the establishment of the employer engaged in such distribution."

For the reasons set forth below, we find that Respondent's handbilling and other conduct comes under the umbrella of the publicity proviso.[23]

[23]Thus, assuming without deciding, that Respondent's conduct falls within the proscription of Section 8(b)(4)(ii)(B) of the Act, it is nevertheless not unlawful because it comes within the purview of the publicity proviso and is therefore immunized from statutory proscription. Accordingly, we find the complaint should be dismissed whether or not Respondent's conduct constitutes restraint and/or coercion and even if it was directed against "neutral"

A consumer boycott falls outside the protection of the proviso if (1) it results in refusals by employees, other than those of the primary employer, to pick up, deliver, or transport goods or to perform services or (2) the publicity is untruthful. If either situation obtains the publicity proviso is inapplicable.

As to (1), the parties stipulated, and we find, that at no time did Respondent's alleged unlawful conduct have the effect of inducing any individual employed by any persons, other than Hussmann, to refuse, in the course of his employment, to pick up, deliver, or transport any goods, or not to perform any services.

As to (2), the General Counsel and Respondent entered into a stipulation that Respondent's advertisements and handbills are neither misleading nor untruthful. The Charging Party, on the other hand, refused to join in this stipulation and in its brief to the Board contends that Respondent's advertisements and handbills are in fact misleading and untruthful in that (a) none of the products listed is produced by Hussmann, the primary employer to the dispute with Respondent, and (b) Respondent does not have a primary dispute with the producer of any of the products listed. These contentions, however, are really addressed to the claim that the products listed by Respondent are not "produced" by Hussmann within the meaning of the publicity proviso, rather than to the truthfulness of the advertisements and handbills. The Charging Party has not established that these materials were on their face untruthful, *i.e.*, that they substantially departed from fact or intended to deceive. Thus, the materials accurately state that members of Respondent were "on strike at Hussmann Refrigerator" and that Hussmann is owned by, or is a part of, Pet. In view of the above, we find no merit to the Charging Party's contentions regarding the truthfulness of the materials at issue.

The central question for resolution, therefore, is whether Respondent's conduct falls within the bounds of the proviso or, more specifically, whether Hussmann constitutes a "producer" within the meaning of the proviso vis-à-vis the products of Pet and its other subsidiaries and divisions as a result of the diversified corporate relationship existent between Hussmann, Pet, and its other subsidiaries and divisions. The Board and the courts have heretofore liberally interpreted the terms "products," "produced," and "distributed" as used in the proviso. In *Lohman Sales Company, supra* at 906–908, the Board analyzed the words "product" and "produced" as they are naturally interpreted and found, inter alia, that a product need not be tangible, and that, since labor is the prime requisite of one who produces, an employer who applies his labor in the form of "capital, enterprise, and service" to the product, in the initial or intermediate stages of the marketing of the product, is a producer of the product. Whatever notion thereafter existed that the proviso applies only to situations where a union's labor dispute is with a manufacturer or processor engaged in the physical creation of goods was laid to

persons. We shall not, therefore, further discuss or pass upon the contentions of the parties concerning the legality of Respondent's conduct within the context of subparagraph (ii) or paragraph (B) of Section 8(b)(4) of the Act.

rest by the Supreme Court in *NLRB* v. *Servette Inc.*, *supra*. Noting that the proviso was an outgrowth of a profound Senate desire to adequately safeguard a union's freedom to appeal to the public for support of its case, the Court approved the Board's earlier finding in *Lohman Sales Company*, *supra*, that products "produced by an employer" include products distributed by a wholesaler with whom the primary dispute exists. The Court went on to say (377 U.S. at 55):

> "There is nothing in the legislative history which suggests that the protection of the proviso was intended to be any narrower in coverage than the prohibition to which it is an exception, and we see no basis for attributing such an incongruous purpose to Congress."

Thereafter, the Board, considering *Great Western Broadcasting Corp.*, on remand from the Ninth Circuit, found that *Servette* sustained the Board's holding enunciated in *Lohman* "that 'producer,' as used in the proviso, encompasses anyone who enhances the economic value of the product ultimately sold or consumed; *i.e.*, for the purpose of the proviso, no distinction is drawn between processors, distributors, and those supplying services" (150 NLRB at 472, 58 LRRM at 1019). Further, the Board found that (150 NLRB at 472, 58 LRRM at 1019):

> "Since the Court has stated that the protection of the proviso is not 'any narrower in coverage than the prohibition to which it is an exception,' and since the prohibition of Section 8(b)(4)(B) covers the performances of services as well as processing or distribution of physical products, it follows that the proviso likewise applies to the performance of services."

Additionally, the Board reaffirmed the principle, originally enunciated in *Middle South Broadcasting Co.*, *supra* at 1705, 1715–17, that the proviso was intended to permit a consumer boycott of the secondary's entire business and not merely a boycott of the product involved in the primary dispute.

From the foregoing, it is apparent that a union can lawfully urge, via handbilling or other nonpicketing publicity, a total consumer boycott of a neutral employer, so long as the primary employer has at some stage produced, in the sense of applying capital, enterprise, or service, a product of the neutral employer. Applying these principles to the facts herein, we find that as a result of its relationship with the diversified Pet enterprise, Hussmann applies capital, enterprise, and service to Pet and its other subsidiaries and divisions. We therefore conclude that Hussmann is a "producer" of the products of Pet and its other subsidiaries and divisions as that term is used in the publicity proviso and that Respondent's total consumer boycott of said products is thus exempt from the proscriptions of Section 8(b)(4) of the Act.

Diversified corporations, by their very nature, are composed of operations which provide support for and contribute to one another. The contributions of each to the others may vary considerably. However, all add to the diversification which enables the enterprise as a whole to weather economic assault on any one of its operations. All contribute profits, either actual or potential, which enhance the value of the enterprise and foster its economic viability. All contribute a measure of goodwill.

Pet perceives itself as just such a diversified corporation, with its divisions and subsidiaries supporting each other. Thus, Boyd F. Schenk, chairman of the board and president of Pet, stated in the document entitled "Pet, Incorporated," discussed *supra*:

"Pet is a diversified company with varied operations and businesses serving many aspects of American life. . . . This diversity allows Pet great flexibility in keeping pace with constantly changing economic and social trends and makes us a stronger, more vital organization."

Hussmann is clearly a major part of this Pet enterprise and as such a producer of Pet products within the terms of the proviso. Hussmann provides part of the diversification which contributes to the success of Pet and its other operations. Hussmann's acclaimed high sales and earnings generate income which inures to the benefit of Pet and to Pet's effort to maintain its other subsidiaries.[32] The goodwill earned by Hussmann likewise enhances the reputation of all Pet operations. Consequently, Hussmann variously contributes to the operation of Pet as a whole and to each of its subsidiaries and divisions and thus is a producer of all Pet enterprises products in the sense that "producer," is used in the proviso as interpreted by the Supreme Court in *Servette* and subsequent Board decisions.

Having found Hussmann to be a producer of all the products of Pet and its subsidiaries and divisions, we find that Respondent's handbilling and other nonpicketing publicity urging a total consumer boycott of said products and services is protected by the second proviso of Section 8(b)(4).

Accordingly, we shall dismiss the complaint in its entirety.

The Court of Appeals reversed the Board's decision in *Pet, Inc.* v. *NLRB*. It distinguished the Pet situation from those in which courts had previously found producer status:

Pet, Inc. v. NLRB

United States Court of Appeals, Eighth Circuit, 1981
641 F.2d 545, 106 LRRM 2477

. . .

We first consider whether the Union's conduct fell within the proviso, or, more specifically, whether Hussmann is a "producer" of the products of Pet. Both the Board and federal courts have given the term "producer" a broader meaning than manufacturer or processor.

----

[32]For example, by participating in the national accounts maintained by Pet, Hussmann obviously contributes to the likelihood of their perpetuation and thus to the benefit of other subsidiaries. Similarly, Hussmann's capital contributions to Pet enable Pet to adhere to its apparent policy of financing all substantial debts of its subsidiaries.

In *Lohman Sales Co.*, 132 NLRB 901, 48 LRRM 1429 (1961), a union struck a company which was engaged in the wholesale distribution of cigarettes, other tobacco products, and candies. The striking employees distributed handbills in front of stores which stocked products that Lohman distributed, advising the public of the strike and requesting the public not to purchase tobacco products or candy at the stores. Before the NLRB Lohman contended that it did not produce the products, but only handled products manufactured by others, and thus the proviso should not apply to the union's handbilling. The NLRB rejected this contention and dismissed the complaint, stating:

"[L]abor is the prime requisite of one who produces. A wholesaler, such as Lohman, need not be the actual manufacturer to add his labor in the form of capital, enterprise, and service to the product he furnishes the retailers. In this sense, therefore, Lohman, as the other employers who 'handled' the raw materials of the product before him, is one of the producers of the cigarettes distributed by his customers. A contrary view would attach a special importance to one form of labor over another and attempt to isolate fabricators of products from those who otherwise add to its value." 132 NLRB at 907, 48 LRRM at 1432 (emphasis omitted).

Lohman Sales Co. was approved by the Supreme Court in *NLRB v. Servette, Inc.*, 377 U.S. 46, 55, 55 LRRM 2957 (1964). *Servette* also was a case in which the primary labor dispute was with a wholesaler, and the union asked the public not to purchase the merchandise the wholesaler distributed. The Court stated:

"The proviso was the outgrowth of a profound Senate concern that the unions' freedom to appeal to the public for support of their case be adequately safeguarded. . . . It would fall far short of achieving this basic purpose if the proviso applied only in situations where the union's labor dispute is with the manufacturer or processor. . . . There is nothing in the legislative history which suggests that the protection of the proviso was intended to be any narrower in coverage than the prohibition to which it is an exception, and we see no basis for attributing such an incongruous purpose to Congress.
"The term 'produced' in other labor laws was not unfamiliar to Congress. Under the Fair Labor Standards Act, the term is defined as 'produced, manufactured, mined, handled, or in any other manner worked on . . . ,' 29 U.S.C. § 203(j), and has always been held to apply to the wholesale distribution of goods." 377 U.S. at 55–56.

In *Great Western Broadcasting Corp.* v. *NLRB*, 356 F.2d 434, 61 LRRM 2364 (9th Cir. 1966), *enforcing* 150 NLRB 467, 58 LRRM 1019 (1964), *cert. denied*, 384 U.S. 1002, 62 LRRM 2392 (1966), there was a strike at a television station. The union requested sponsors not to advertise on the station during the strike. The union later passed out leaflets, naming those sponsors who continued to advertise on the station. The Ninth Circuit held that the union's handbilling activity was protected by the proviso, and that the station was a "producer" of the products and services it advertised. The court noted the incongruity of regarding the television as a producer of services such as banking, inasmuch as the proviso refers to products which are "distributed" by another employer. The court stated that "the Supreme Court has spoken in such broad terms in *Servette* that we think the incongruity . . . may not control the ultimate decision." 356 F.2d at 436.

Although all of the three cases discussed above support a broad reading of the proviso, we do not regard them as dispositive of the present case. *Lohman Sales Co., Servette* and *Great Western Broadcasting* all found that the primary was a "producer" when the primary was directly involved in the promotion and/or distribution of products of the secondary.[3] In all three cases, the primary worked on specific products. In the present case Hussmann does not work on any specific products of Pet.

In spite of the absence of any direct relationship of Hussmann's operations to any specific product of Pet, the Board found Hussmann was still a "producer" of Pet's products, reasoning as follows:

> "[A]s a result of its relationship with the diversified enterprise, Hussmann applies capital, enterprise, and service to Pet and its other subsidiaries and divisions. . . .
>
> "Diversified corporations, by their very nature, are composed of operations which provide support for and contribute to one another. The contributions of each to the others may vary considerably. However, all add to the diversification which enables the enterprise as a whole to weather economic assault on any one of its operations. All contribute profits, either actual or potential, which enhance the value of the enterprise and foster its economic viability. All contribute a measure of goodwill.
>
> . . .
>
> ". . . Hussmann provides part of the diversification which contributes to the success of Pet and its other operations. Hussmann's acclaimed high sales and earnings generate income which inures to the benefit of Pet and to Pet's effort to maintain its other subsidiaries. The goodwill earned by Hussmann likewise enhances the reputation of all Pet operations. Consequently, Hussmann variously contributes to the operation of Pet as a whole and to each of its subsidiaries and divisions and thus is a producer of all Pet enterprises products in the sense that 'producer' is used in the proviso as interpreted by the Supreme Court in *Servette* and subsequent Board decisions."

We are mindful of the Supreme Court's admonition that if the Board's "construction of a statute is reasonably defensible, it should not be rejected merely because the court might prefer another view of the statute." *Ford Motor Co. v. NLRB*, 441 U.S. 488, 497, 101 LRRM 2222 (1979). We think that the present case is one of those rare instances in which the Board's interpretation is unreasonable and must be rejected. First, we think it totally at odds with any normal interpretation of the

---

[3]Another case to the same effect is *Middle South Broadcasting*, 133 NLRB 1698, 49 LRRM 1042 (1961).

word "produce" to say that because Hussmann's profits inure to the benefit of Pet, Hussmann produces Pet's products. We find the connection between Pet's products and Hussmann to be highly attenuated. Should Pet sell Hussmann tomorrow, Pet would manufacture, distribute, and promote its products the same way it is doing now.

Secondly, we do not think that the Board's decision flows from *Servette, supra,* because the Supreme Court was not there considering a case in which the primary-subsidiary's products and services were unrelated to the secondary-parent's products. We note in particular the Court's comment, quoted earlier, that "[t]he term 'produced' in other labor laws was not unfamiliar to Congress. Under the Fair Labor Standards Act, the term is defined as 'produced, manufactured, mined, handled, or in any other manner worked on. . . ,' 29 U.S.C. § 203(j) . . . ." 377 U.S. at 55–56. Hussmann does not work on any of the products of Pet.

Accordingly, we reverse the decision of the Board that the Union's publicity activities fell within the proviso. Pet has asked us to consider three other issues not ruled upon by the Board. The first two, whether Pet and its subsidiaries are separate "persons" from Hussmann for purposes of Section 8(b)(4), and whether the Union's publicity fell within the prohibition of Section 8(b)(4)(ii), are questions initially committed to the discretion of the Board under Section 10(a), which empowers the Board "to prevent any person from engaging in any unfair labor practice . . ." listed in Section 8. 29 U.S.C. § 160(a) (1976). These questions are not trivial and are not free from difficulty. They could be decided by the Board in such a way that it will become unnecessary for us to reach the third issue which is whether, if the Union's conduct is prohibited by Section 8(b)(4)(ii), the Union's first amendment rights are violated. In the circumstances, we decline to pass upon any of the three issues not ruled upon by the Board.

Reversed and remanded for further proceedings.

The court remanded the case to the Board for determination of those issues not faced by the Board when it decided the case under the publicity proviso. Thus it is an open question whether Pet and its subsidiaries should be considered neutrals in the union's dispute with Hussmann. Should a conglomerate and its subsidiaries automatically forfeit neutrality status under the Act with respect to labor relations activities of its subsidiaries and affiliates?

Additional light may be cast upon the scope of Section 8(b)(4)(B) when the Board reconsiders the *DeBartolo* case. In *DeBartolo,* the union, which had a primary dispute with a building contractor constructing a store within a shopping mall, handbilled consumers urging them not to patronize other tenants in the mall until the owner, DeBartolo, took steps to replace the offending contractor. The Board found a "symbiotic" relationship between the contractor and the mall tenants, and held the handbilling protected under the publicity proviso of Section 8(b)(4), 252 NLRB 99, 108 LRRM 2729 (1981). The Supreme Court reversed the

Board in *DeBartolo Corp.* v. *NLRB,* 463 U.S. ___, 113 LRRM 2953 (1983). It concluded that while the contractor might be considered a "producer" for purposes of the proviso, it could not be said that its product was "distributed by" DeBartolo or the other tenants, hence the proviso did not shelter the union's activity. The Court remanded the case to the Board, which had decided it solely on the basis of the publicity proviso, to determine whether Section 8(b)(4)(B) prohibited the activity in question.

Consider the following excerpts from a daily labor reporting service regarding union efforts to organize Litton Industries:

"UNIONS SEEK HELP FROM NLRB, CONGRESS
IN CAMPAIGN AGAINST LITTON INDUSTRIES

"A coalition of unions next week will step up its campaign against Litton Industries, Inc., a conglomerate it accuses of repeated labor law violations.

"Representatives of eight unions will meet on April 20 with NLRB General Counsel William A. Lubbers to discuss a request that the Board consider Litton as a single employer when cases are brought against the many subsidiaries of the firm.

"On the same day, the House Education and Labor Subcommittee on Labor-Management Relations will begin hearings on H.R. 1743 which would debar willful labor law violators from federal contracts. Later that day unions and other groups will sponsor a rally against Litton at the George Washington University School of Government and Business. A faculty member at that school is on Litton's board of directors.

"According to union organizers, Litton and its subsidiaries have demonstrated a pattern of labor law violations dating back 20 years. Data compiled by the unions show 18 instances in which NLRB or the courts have found Litton guilty of violating the National Labor Relations Act and 19 more cases settled by the company after the Board issued complaints. Another three cases were overturned by appeals courts, and seven cases still are pending.

"Two major frustrations encountered by unions in their dealings with Litton are the highly diversified nature of the company, which sometimes makes it difficult even to discover if a subsidiary actually is owned by Litton, and the tendency of Litton to enter informal settlements shortly before a case is to go to trial before the Board. While such settlements may provide the relief sought by unions, they usually do not take effect until months or even years after the violations occurred and there are no mechanisms to enforce the settlements, the unions say. . . ." No. 73 *Daily Labor Report* (BNA) A-1 (1983).

Assuming these facts are true, do they suffice to deprive Litton and its subsidiaries of the neutrality protections of the Act? What factors should the Board consider in determining if there is "a common control of labor relations policy at the corporate level"? How do these factors differ from those discussed in Chapter 2 in connection with the Board's determination whether a single store in a retail chain is an appropriate bargaining unit?

How should the labor laws be changed, if at all, to deal with conglomerates? By allowing unions to bring wider economic pressure under Section 8(b)(4)? By providing for broader remedial orders which cut across the entire conglomerate, to remedy systemic unfair labor practices? By changes in unit determination rules? For a perceptive study of the conglomerate phenomenon, see Craypo, *Collective Bargaining in the Conglomerate Firm: Litton's Shutdown of Royal Typewriter*, 29 Ind. Lab. Rel. Rev. 3 (1975).

7. "Hot Cargo" Agreements

Problem

The Factory Workers Union is concerned about an increasing tendency of U.S. manufacturers to import rubber components from abroad, where they are not produced by union employees. In its collective bargaining agreement with Enderby the union now has a clause prohibiting the employer from subcontracting work "of the type now normally performed by bargaining unit members." May the union lawfully expand this clause to bar the employer from using component parts not manufactured in unionized plants? How should this clause be worded? If it is violated, what may the union do? Arbitrate? Strike?

National Woodwork Manufacturer's Ass'n v. NLRB

Supreme Court of the United States, 1967
386 U.S. 612, 64 LRRM 2801

Mr. Justice Brennan delivered the opinion of the Court.

Frouge Corporation, a Bridgeport, Connecticut concern, was the general contractor on a housing project in Philadelphia. Frouge had a collective bargaining agreement with the Carpenter's International Union under which Frouge agreed to be bound by the rules and regulations agreed upon by local unions with contractors in areas in which Frouge had jobs. Frouge was therefore subject to the provision of a collective bargaining agreement between the Union and an organization of Philadelphia contractors, the General Building Contractors Association, Inc. A sentence in a provision of that agreement entitled Rule 17 provides that ". . . no member of the District Council will handle . . . any doors . . . which have been fitted prior to being furnished on the job. . . ." Frouge's Philadelphia project called for 3,600 doors. Customarily, before the doors could be hung on such projects, "blank" or "blind" doors would be mortised for the knob, routed for the hinges, and beveled to make them fit between jambs. These are tasks traditionally performed in the Philadelphia area by the carpenters employed on the jobsite. However, precut and prefitted doors ready to hang may be purchased from door manufacturers. Although Frouge's contract and job specifications did not call for premachined doors, and "blank" or "blind" doors could have been ordered, Frouge contracted for the purchase of premachined doors from a Pennsylvania door manufacturer which is a member of the National Woodwork Manufacturers Association, petitioner in No. 110 and respondent in No. 111. The Union ordered its carpenter members not to hang the doors when they arrived at the jobsite. Frouge thereupon withdrew the prefabricated doors and substituted "blank" doors which were fitted and cut by his carpenters on the jobsite.

The National Woodwork Manufacturers Association and another filed charges with the National Labor Relations Board against the Union alleging that by including the "will not handle" sentence of Rule 17 in the collective bargaining agreement the Union committed the unfair labor practice under § 8(e) of entering into an "agreement . . . whereby . . . [the] . . . employer . . . agrees to cease or refrain from handling . . . any of the products of any other employer. . . ." and alleging further that in enforcing the sentence against Frouge, the Union committed the unfair labor practice under § 8(b)(4)(B) of "forcing or requiring any person to cease using . . . the products of any other . . . manufacturer. . . ."

I. Even on the doubtful premise that the words of § 8(e) unambiguously embrace the sentence of Rule 17, this does not end inquiry into Congress' purpose in enacting the section. It is a "familiar rule, that a thing may be within the letter of the statute and yet not within the statute, because not within its spirit, nor within the intention of its makers." *Holy Trinity Church* v. *United States*, 143 U.S. 457, 459. That principle has particular application in the construction of labor legislation which is "to a marked degree, the result of conflict and compromise between strong contending forces and deeply held views on the role of organized labor in the free economic life of the Nation and the appropriate balance to be struck between the uncontrolled power of management and labor to further their respective interests." *Local 1976, United Brotherhood of Carpenters* v. *Labor Board*, 357 U.S. 93, 99–100, 42 LRRM 2243.

Strongly held opposing views have invariably marked controversy over labor's use of the boycott to further its aims by involving an employer in disputes not his own. But congressional action to deal with such conduct has stopped short of proscribing identical activity having the object of pressuring the employer for agreements regulating relations between him and his own employees. That Congress meant §§ 8(e) and 8(b)(4)(B) to prohibit only "secondary" objectives clearly appears from an examination of the history of congressional action on the subject. . . .

Judicial decisions interpreting the broad language of § 8(b)(4)(A) of the Taft-Hartley Act uniformly limited its application to such "secondary" situations. This limitation was in "conformity with the dual Congressional objectives of preserving the right of labor organizations to bring pressure to bear on offending employers in primary labor disputes and of shielding unoffending employers and others from pressures in controversies not their own." *Labor Board* v. *Denver Bldg. Trades Council*, 341 U.S. 675, 692, 28 LRRM 2108. This Court accordingly refused to read § 8(b)(4)(A) to ban traditional primary strikes and picketing having an impact on neutral employers even though the activity fell within its sweeping terms. *Labor Board* v. *International Rice Milling Co.*, 341 U.S. 665, 28 LRRM 2105; see *Local 761, Electrical Workers Union* v. *Labor Board*, 366 U.S. 667, 48

LRRM 2210. Thus, however severe the impact of primary activity on neutral employers, it was not thereby transformed into activity with a secondary objective. . . .

Despite this virtually overwhelming support for the limited reading of § 8(b)(4)(A), the Woodwork Manufacturers Association relied on *Allen Bradley Co.* v. *Local 3, Electrical Workers*, 325 U.S. 797, 16 LRRM 798 as requiring that the successor section, § 8(b)(4)(B), be read as proscribing the District Council's conduct in enforcing the "will not handle" sentence of Rule 17 against Frouge. The Association points to the references to *Allen Bradley* in the legislative debates leading to the enactment of the predecessor § 8(b)(4)(A). We think that this is an erroneous reading of the legislative history. *Allen Bradley* held violative of the antitrust laws a combination between Local 3 of the International Brotherhood of Electrical Workers and both electrical contractors and manufacturers of electrical fixtures in New York City to restrain the bringing in of such equipment from outside the city. The contractors obligated themselves to confine their purchases to local manufacturers, who in turn obligated themselves to confine their New York City sales to contractors employing members of the local, this scheme supported by threat of boycott by the contractors' employees. While recognizing that the union might have had an immunity for its contribution to the trade boycott had it acted alone, citing *Hutcheson, supra,* the Court held immunity was not intended by the Clayton or Norris-LaGuardia Acts in cases in which the union's activity was part of a larger conspiracy to abet contractors and manufacturers to create a monopoly. . . .

. . . Third, even on the premise that Congress meant to prohibit boycotts such as that in *Allen Bradley* without regard to whether they were carried on to affect labor conditions elsewhere, the fact is that the boycott in *Allen Bradley* was carried on, not as a shield to preserve the jobs of Local 3 members, traditionally a primary labor activity, but as a sword, to reach out and monopolize all the manufacturing job tasks for Local 3 members. It is arguable that Congress may have viewed the use of the boycott as a sword as different from labor's traditional concerns with wages, hours, and working conditions. But the boycott in the present cases was not used as a sword; it was a shield carried solely to preserve the members' jobs. We therefore have no occasion today to decide the questions which might arise where the workers carry on a boycott to reach out to monopolize jobs or acquire new job tasks when their own jobs are not threatened by the boycotted product.[19]

II. The Landrum-Griffin Act amendments in 1959 were adopted only to close various loopholes in the application of § 8(b)(4)(A) which had been exposed in Board and court decisions. We discussed some of these loopholes, and the particular amendments adopted to close them, in *Labor Board* v. *Servette, Inc.,* 377 U.S. 46, 51–54, 55 LRRM 2957. We need not repeat that discussion here, except to emphasize, as we there said, that "these changes did not expand the type of conduct which § 8(b)(4)(A)

---

[19]We likewise do not have before us in these cases, and express no view upon, the antitrust limitations, if any, upon union-employer work-preservation or work-extension agreements. See *United Mine Workers* v. *Pennington,* 381 U.S. 657, 662–665.

condemned, that is, union pressures calculated to induce the employees of a secondary employer to withhold their services in order to force their employer to cease dealing with the primary employer." Id., at 52–53.

Section 8(e) simply closed still another loophole. In *Local 1976, United Brotherhood of Carpenters* v. *Labor Board (Sand Door)*, 357 U.S. 93, 42 LRRM 2243, the Court held that it was no defense to an unfair labor practice charge under § 8(b)(4)(A) that the struck employer had agreed, in a contract with the union, not to handle nonunion material. However, the Court emphasized that the mere execution of such a contract provision (known as a "hot cargo" clause because of its prevalence in Teamsters Union contracts), or its voluntary observance by the employer, was not unlawful under § 8(b)(4)(A). Section 8(e) was designed to plug this gap in the legislation by making the "hot cargo" clause itself unlawful. The *Sand Door* decision was believed by Congress not only to create the possibility of damage actions against employers for breaches of "hot cargo" clauses, but also to create a situation in which such clauses might be employed to exert subtle pressures upon employers to engage in "voluntary" boycotts. Hearings in late 1958 before the Senate Select Committee explored seven cases of "hot cargo" clauses in Teamsters union contracts, the use of which the Committee found conscripted neutral employers in Teamster organizational campaigns.

This loophole closing measure likewise did not expand the type of conduct which § 8(b)(4)(A) condemned. Although the language of § 8(e) is sweeping, it closely tracks that of § 8(b)(4)(A), and just as the latter and its successsor § 8(b)(4)(B) did not reach employees' activity to pressure their employer to preserve for themselves work traditionally done by them, § 8(e) does not prohibit agreements made and maintained for that purpose.

However, provisos were added to § 8(e) to preserve the *status quo* in the construction industry, and exempt the garment industry from the prohibitions of §§ 8(e) and 8(b)(4)(B). This action of the Congress is strong confirmation that Congress meant that both §§ 8(e) and 8(b)(4)(B) reach only secondary pressures. If the body of § 8(e) applies only to secondary activity, the garment industry proviso is a justifiable exception which allows what the legislative history shows it was designed to allow, secondary pressures to counteract the effects of sweat-shop conditions in an industry with a highly integrated process of production between jobbers, manufacturers, contractors and subcontractors. First, this motivation for the proviso sheds light on the central theme of the body of § 8(e), from which the proviso is an exception. Second, if the body of that provision and § 8(b)(4)(B) were construed to prohibit primary agreements and their maintenance, such as those concerning work preservation, the proviso would have the highly unlikely effect, unjustified in any of the statute's history, of permitting garment workers, but garment workers only, to preserve their jobs against subcontracting or prefabrication by such agreements and by strikes and boycotts to enforce them. Similarly, the construction industry proviso, which permits "hot cargo" agreements only for job-site work, would have the curious and unsupported result of allowing the construction worker to make agreements preserving his traditional tasks against job-site prefabrication and subcontracting, but not against nonjob-site prefabrication and subcontracting. On the other hand, if the heart of § 8(e) is construed to be directed only to secondary activities, the construction proviso becomes, as it was intended to be, a measure designed to allow agreements pertaining to certain secondary activities on the construction site because of the close community of interests there, but to ban secondary-objective agreements concerning nonjob-site work, in which respect the construction industry is no different from any other. The provisos are therefore substantial probative support that primary work preservation agreements were not to be within the ban of § 8(e). . . .

In addition to all else, "the silence of the sponsors of [the] Amendments is pregnant with significance. . . ." *Labor Board* v. *Fruit & Vegetable Packers, supra,* . . . . Before we may say that Congress meant to strike from workers' hands the economic weapons traditionally used against their employers' efforts to abolish their jobs, that meaning should plainly appear. "[I]n this era of automation and onrushing technological change, no problems in the domestic economy are of greater concern than those involving job security and employment stability. Because of the potentially cruel impact upon the lives and fortunes of the working men and women of the Nation, these problems have understandably engaged the solicitous attention of government, of responsible private business, and particularly of organized labor." *Fibreboard Paper Prods. Corp.* v. *Labor Board*, 379 U.S. 203, 225, 57 LRRM 2609 (concurring opinion of Stewart, J.). We would expect that legislation curtailing the ability of management and labor voluntarily to negotiate for solutions to these significant and difficult problems would be preceded by extensive congressional study and debate, and consideration of voluminous economic, scientific, and statistical data. The silence regarding such matters in the Eighty-sixth Congress is itself evidence that Congress, in enacting §8(e), had no thought of prohibiting agreements directed to work preservation. In fact, since the enactment of § 8(e), both the Subcommittee on Employment and Manpower of the Senate Committee on Labor and Public Welfare, and the Subcommittee on Unemployment and the Impact of Automation and the Select Subcommittee on Labor of the House Committee on Education and Labor have been extensively studying the threats to workers posed by increased technology and automation, and some legislation directed to the problem has been passed. We cannot lightly impute to Congress an intent of § 8(e) to preclude labor-management agreements to ease these effects through collective bargaining on this most vital problem created by advanced technology.

Moreover, our decision in *Fibreboard Paper Prods. Corp., supra,* implicitly recognizes the legitimacy of work preservation clauses like that involved here. Indeed, in the circumstances presented in *Fibreboard,* we held that bargaining on the subject was made mandatory by § 8(a)(5) of the Act, concerning as it does "terms and conditions of employment." *Fibreboard* involved an alleged refusal to bargain with respect to the contracting-out of plant maintenance work previously performed by employees in the bargaining unit. The Court recognized that the "termination of employment which . . . necessarily results from the contracting-out of work performed by members of the established bargaining unit," *supra*, at 210, is "a problem of vital concern to labor and management . . . ," *supra*, at 211. We further noted, *supra*, at 211–212:

> "Industrial experience is not only reflective of the interests of labor and management in the subject matter but is also indicative of the amenability of such subjects to the collective bargaining process. Experience illustrates that contracting out in one form or another has been brought, widely and successfully, within the collective bargaining framework. Provisions relating to contracting out exist in numerous collective bargaining agreements, and '[c]ontracting out work is the basis of many grievances; and that type of claim is grist in the mills of the arbitrators.' *United Steelworkers* v. *Warrior & Gulf Nav. Co.*, 363 U.S. 574, 584, 46 LRRM 2416."

See *Local 24, Teamsters Union* v. *Oliver*, 358 U.S. 283, 294, 43 LRRM 2374. It would therefore be incongruous to interpret § 8(e) to invalidate clauses over which the parties may be mandated to bargain and which have been successfully incorporated through collective bargaining in many of this Nation's major labor agreements.

Finally, important parts of the historic accommodation by Congress of the powers of labor and management are §§ 7 and 13 of the National Labor Relations Act, passed as part of the Wagner Act in 1935 and amended in 1947. The former section assures to labor "the right . . . to bargain collectively through representatives of their own choosing, and to engage in other concerted activities for the purpose of collective bargaining or other mutual aid or protection. . . . " Section 13 preserves the right to strike, of which the boycott is a form, except as specifically provided in the Act. In the absence of clear indicia of congressional intent to the contrary, these provisions caution against reading statutory prohibitions as embracing employee activities to pressure their own employers into improving the employees' wages, hours, and working conditions. See *Labor Board* v. *Drivers Union*, 362 U.S. 274, 45 LRRM 2975; *Labor Board* v. *International Rice Milling Co.*, *supra*, at 672–673; *Labor Board* v. *Denver Bldg. Trades Council*, *supra*, at 687; *Mastro Plastics* v. *Labor Board*, *supra*, at 284, 287.

The Woodwork Manufacturers Association and *amici* who support its position advance several reasons, grounded in economic and technological factors, why "will not handle" clauses should be invalid in all circumstances. Those arguments are addressed to the wrong branch of government. It may be "that the time has come for re-evaluation of the basic content of collective bargaining as contemplated by the federal legislation. But that is for Congress. Congress has demonstrated its capacity to adjust the Nation's labor legislation to what, in its legislative judgment, constitutes the statutory pattern appropriate to the developing state of labor relations in the country. Major revisions of the basic statute were enacted in 1947 and 1959. To be sure, then, Congress might be of the opinion that greater stress should be put on . . . eliminating more and more economic weapons from the . . . [Union's] grasp. . . . But Congress' policy has not yet moved to this point. . . . " *Insurance Agents' International Union* v. *Labor Board,* 361 U.S. 477, 500, 45 LRRM 2705.

III. The determination whether the "will not handle" sentence of Rule 17 and its enforcement violated § 8(e) and § 8(b)(4)(B) cannot be made without an inquiry into whether, under all the surrounding circumstances, the Union's objective was preservation of work for Frouge's employees, or whether the agreements and boycott were tactically calculated to satisfy union objectives elsewhere. Were the latter the case, Frouge, the boycotting employer, would be a neutral bystander, and the agreement or boycott would, within the intent of Congress, become secondary. There need not be an actual dispute with the boycotted employer, here the door manufacturer, for the activity to fall within this category, so long as the tactical object of the agreement and its maintenance is that employer, or benefits to other than the boycotting employees or other employees of the primary employer thus making the agreement or boycott secondary in its aim. The touchstone is whether the agreement or its maintenance is addressed to the labor relations of the contracting employer *vis-a-vis* his own employees. This will not always be a simple test to apply. But "[h]owever difficult the task of drawing lines more nice than obvious, the statute compels the task." *Local 761, Electrical Workers* v. *Labor Board,* 366 U.S. 667, 674, 48 LRRM 2210.

That the "will not handle" provision was not an unfair labor practice in this case is clear. The finding of the Trial Examiner, adopted by the Board, was that the objective of the sentence was preservation of work traditionally performed by the jobsite carpenters. This finding is supported by substantial evidence, and therefore the Union's making of the "will not handle" agreement was not a violation of § 8(e).

Similarly, the Union's maintenance of the provision was not a violation of § 8(b)(4)(B). The Union refused to hang prefabricated doors whether or not they bore a union label, and even refused to install prefabricated doors manufactured off the jobsite by members of the Union. This and other substantial evidence supported the finding that the conduct of the Union on the Frouge jobsite related solely to preservation of the traditional tasks of the jobsite carpenters.

The judgment is affirmed in No. 110, and reversed in No. 111.

It is so ordered.

Note on Work Preservation and Technological Change

In *NLRB* v. *Plumbers Local 638 (Austin Co.),* 429 U.S. 507, 94 LRRM 2628 (1977), a split decision, the union represented steamfitters employed by the subcontractor on a construction project. When certain air control units came through with fitting work already done in the factory, the union refused to install them, contending that under a clause of the collective bargaining agreement with the subcontractor, this fitting was to be done on the jobsite by steamfitters. The Court held this conduct unlawful, distinguishing *National Woodwork* on the basis that the installation involved was mandated in the general contractor's job specifications.

Since the subcontractor had no control over these specifications, the union's conduct was deemed to be directed not at the subcontractor, but at the general contractor. The subcontractor, powerless to effect the desired changes, was thus considered neutral.

National Woodwork involved an agreement to preserve work readily found to belong traditionally to carpenters at the jobsite. But how should Section 8(b)(4) and Section 8(e) be applied when the technological change is so substantial that it is difficult to determine whether the work in question is within the domain of the complaining employees?

The Supreme Court faced this issue in *NLRB* v. *Longshoremen's Ass'n.* The dispute involved a collective bargaining response to the introduction of containerization, a development which the Court agreed was "the single most important innovation in ocean transport since the steamship displaced the schooner" (447 U.S. at 495). The use of containers allowed the shipper to avoid costly and time-consuming loading and unloading formerly done at the piers by longshoremen. It also "drastically reduced" the volume of work of longshoremen.

In a series of collective bargaining agreements over the course of a decade, the Longshoremen's Union (ILA) and various shipping associations responded to the introduction of this new technology by providing, essentially, that only longshoremen could load and unload containers within a 50-mile radius of the port. If a container was handled by other than longshoremen, the offender was required to pay $1,000 per container as liquidated damages. In addition, shipping companies had to pay a royalty on containers covered by the rules which passed over piers intact.

The rules exempted certain kinds of containers, such as those loaded by the owner of the goods (as opposed to a freight consignor, for example), loaded outside the 50-mile radius, or warehoused locally for over 30 days.

In *Longshoremen's Ass'n.* two freight consolidators loaded containers within the 50-mile radius. When shipping association members who handled these goods were subjected to liquidated damages under the collective bargaining agreement, they ceased doing business with the consolidators. The consolidators in turn challenged the rules as hot cargo agreements prohibited by Section 8(e) and the parties' actions to enforce these agreements as secondary boycotts under Section 8(b)(4)(B).

The Board held that this activity violated the Act. It concluded that the rules were "not valid work-preservation clauses in that traditionally the off-pier stuffing and stripping of containers was performed by consolidating companies and not longshoremen. Since the work was not traditional longshore work and had never been performed by longshoremen, the Rules which required the shipping companies to stop doing business with consolidators did not have a lawful work-preservation object." 236 NLRB 525 at 526 (1978).

The Board concluded that since the work was not historically that of longshoremen, the purpose of the collective bargaining rule was to acquire work traditionally performed by others. Thus it was forbidden secondary activity.

The Court disagreed with the Board's conclusion as well as its approach. Portions of its opinion follow:

NLRB v. Longshoremen's Ass'n

Supreme Court of the United States, 1980
447 U.S. 490, 104 LRRM 2552

. . . Whether an agreement is a lawful work preservation agreement depends on "whether, under all the surrounding circumstances, the Union's objective was preservation of work for [bargaining unit] employees, or whether the [agreement was] tactically calculated to satisfy union objectives elsewhere. . . . The touchstone is whether the agreement or its maintenance is addressed to the labor relations of the contracting employer *vis-à-vis* his own employees." *National Woodwork* [386 U.S. 612], at 644–645 (footnotes omitted). Under this approach, a lawful work preservation agreement must pass two tests: First, it must have as its objective the preservation of work traditionally performed by employees represented by the union. Second, the contracting employer must have the power to give the employees the work in question—the so-called "right of control" test of *Pipefitters* [429 U.S. 507]. The rationale of the second test is that if the contracting employer has no power to assign the work, it is reasonable to infer that the agreement has a secondary objective, that is, to influence whoever does have such power over the work. "Were the latter the case, [the contracting employer] would be a neutral bystander, and the agreement or boycott would, within the intent of Congress, become secondary." *National Woodwork, supra,* at 644–645.

But in many cases it is not so easy to find the starting point of the analysis. Work preservation agreements typically come into being when employees' traditional work is displaced, or threatened with displacement, by technological innovation. The national labor policy expresses a preference for addressing "the threats to workers posed by increased technology and automation" by means of "labor-management agreements to ease these effects through collective bargaining on this most vital problem created by advanced technology." *National Woodwork, supra,* 386 U.S., at 641, 642. In many instances, technological innovation may change the method of doing the work, instead of merely shifting the same work to a different location. One way to preserve the work of the employees represented by the union in the face of such a change is simply to insist that the innovation not be adopted and that the work continue to be done in the traditional way. The union in *National Woodwork* followed this tactic and negotiated an agreement in which the employer agreed not to use prefabricated materials. We held that agreement was lawful under §§ 8(e) and 8(b)(4)(B). But the protection Congress afforded to work preservation agreements cannot be limited solely to employees who respond to change with intrasigence. Congress, in enacting § 8(e), did not intend to protect only certain kinds of work preservation agreements; rather, it "had no thought of prohibiting agreements directed to work preservation," *National Woodwork, supra,* at 640. The work preservation doctrine, then, must also apply to situations where unions attempt to accommodate change while preserving as much of their traditional work patterns as possible. When this is the case the inquiry must be more refined and the analysis more discriminating. . . .

The Board's approach reflects a fundamental misconception of the work preservation doctrine as it has been applied in our previous cases. Identification of the work at issue in a complex case of technological displacement requires a careful analysis of the traditional work patterns that the parties are allegedly seeking to preserve, and of how the agreement seeks to accomplish that result under the changed circumstances created by the technological advance. The analysis must take into account "all the surrounding circumstances," *National Woodwork,* 386 U.S., at 644, including the nature of the work both before and after the innovation. In a relatively simple case, such as *National Woodwork* or *Pipefitters,* the inquiry may be of rather limited scope. Other, more complex cases will require a broader view, taking into account the transformation of several interrelated industries or types of work; this is such a case. Whatever its scope, however, the inquiry must be carefully focused: to determine whether an agreement seeks no more than to preserve the work of bargaining unit members, the Board must focus on the work of the bargaining unit employees, not on the work of other employees who may be doing the same or similar work, and examine the relationship between the work as it existed before the innovation and as the agreement proposes to preserve it.

The Board, by contrast, focused on the work done by the employees of the charging parties, the truckers and consolidators, after the introduction of containerized shipping. It found that work was similar to work those employees had done before the innovation, and concluded that ILA was trying to acquire the traditional work of those employees. That conclusion ignores the fact that the impact of containerization occurred at the interface between ocean and motor transport; not surprisingly, the work of stuffing and stripping containers is similar to work previously done by both longshoremen and truckers. The Board's approach would have been entirely appropriate in considering an agreement to preserve the work of truckers' employees, but it misses the point when applied to judge this contract between the ILA and the shipowner employers.

By focusing on the work as performed, after the innovation took place, by the employees who allegedly have displaced the longshoremen's work, the Board foreclosed—by definition—any possibility that the longshoremen could negotiate an agreement to permit them to continue to play any part in the loading or unloading of containerized cargo. For the very reason the Rules were negotiated was that longshoremen do not perform that work away from the pier, and never have. Thus it is apparent that under the Board's approach, in the words of the Court of Appeals, the "work preservation doctrine is sapped of all life." 198 U.S. App. D.C., at 176, 613 F.2d, at 909.

. . .

Thus the Board's determination that the work of longshoremen has historically been the loading and unloading of ships should be only the beginning of the analysis. The next step is to look at how the contracting parties sought to preserve that work, to the extent possible, in the face of a massive technological change that largely eliminated the need for cargo handling at intermediate stages of the intermodal transportation of goods, and to evaluate the relationship between traditional longshore work and the work which the Rules attempt to assign to ILA members. This case presents a much more difficult problem than either *National Woodwork* or *Pipefitters* because the union did not simply insist on doing the work as it had always been done and try to prevent the employers from using container ships at all—though such an approach would have been consistent with *National Woodwork* and *Pipefitters*. Instead, ILA permitted the great majority of containers to pass over the piers intact, reserving the right to stuff and strip only those containers that would otherwise have been stuffed or stripped locally by anyone except the beneficial owner's employees. The legality of the agreement turns, as an initial matter, on whether the historical and functional relationship between this retained work and traditional longshore work can support the conclusion that the objective of the agreement was work preservation rather than the satisfaction of union goals elsewhere.

Respondents assert that the stuffing and stripping reserved for the ILA by the Rules is functionally equivalent to their former work of handling break-bulk cargo at the pier. Petitioners-intervenors, on the other hand, argue that containerization has worked such fundamental changes in the industry that the work formerly done at the pier by both longshoremen and employees of motor carriers has been completely eliminated.

These questions are not appropriate for initial consideration by reviewing courts. They are properly raised before the Board, whose determinations are, of course, entitled to deference. Since the Board has not had an opportunity to consider these questions in relation to a proper understanding of the work at issue, we will not address them here. We emphasize that neither our decision nor that of the Court of Appeals implies that the result of the Board's reconsideration of this case is foreordained. Viewing the work allegedly to be preserved by the Rules from the proper perspective, the Board will be free to determine whether the Rules represent a lawful attempt to preserve traditional longshore work, or whether, instead, they are "tactically calculated to satisfy union objectives elsewhere," *National Woodwork*, 386 U.S., at 644. This determination will, of course, be informed by an awareness of the congressional preference for collective bargaining as the method for resolving disputes over dislocations caused by the introduction of technological innovations in the workplace, see *id.*, at 641–642. Thus, in judging the legality of a thoroughly bargained and apparently reasonable accommodation to technological change, the question is not whether the Rules represent the most rational or efficient response to innovation, but whether they are a legally permissible effort to preserve jobs.

[The Board gained strange bedfellows for its position in the persons of Chief Justice Burger and Justice Rehnquist, who suddenly found themselves deferring to the Board's expertise. Brief excerpts from the Chief Justice's opinion, in which Justices Stewart, Rehnquist, and Stevens joined, follow:]

This case turns on the definition of the work in controversy. If viewed exclusively from the perspective of the ILA, without regard to other aspects of the transportation industry or to the evolutionary changes in methods of doing business, the work can be characterized broadly as the loading and unloading of vessels; that gives the contract Rules on Containers a plausible work preservation objective sufficient to escape what would otherwise be a violation of § 8(e) of the National Labor Relations Act. If viewed from the perspective of the consolidators and motor carriers—many of whose employees are also union members—the objective is not preservation of traditional longshoremen's work but a claim to work historically and traditionally performed by teamsters, truckers, and similar inland laborers. Which of these perspectives is chosen, in turn, depends on the view taken of the nature and function of a "container."

This is where the Court's analysis runs astray. To the Court, the work-in-controversy problem in the instant case is simply analogous to that involved in *National Woodwork Manufacturers Assn.* v. *NLRB,* 386 U.S. 612 (1967), or *NLRB* v. *Pipefitters,* 429 U.S. 507 (1977), although the Court disclaims this. Compare *ante,* at 2315–2316 with *ante,* at 2316. But viewing the work in controversy, as we should, "under all the surrounding circumstances," *National Woodwork, supra,* 386 U.S., at 644, the Court's analysis simply will not "wash." A door may be a door in the carpenter's world, and a pipe may be a pipe to the plumber, but a "container" can be seen as sometimes like the hold of a ship, sometimes like the trailer of a truck—and sometimes an independent component.

Because of the many functions of a container, it affects both sea and land transportation systems. The Court apparently recognizes the complexities involved, see *ante,* at 2316, n. 23, but does not seem to respond to the logical inferences as did the Board, which has a vast reservoir of experience with day-to-day industrial operations. We cannot blink the reality of this technological innovation, nor can we, as the Court does, focus merely on one aspect of the work it has affected. The Board understood the complexities involved here; consequently, it invalidated only that part of the Rules on Containers whose primary effect was to influence the loading and unloading of containers functioning away from the pier as truck trailers. See 231 NLRB 351 (1977) and 236 NLRB 525 (1978). The Court's failure to appreciate this distinction and unwillingness to concede its significance underscores the reason why reviewing courts must give weight to the Board's long and intimate experience with the workings of the industries implicated. See, *e.g., Pipefitters, supra,* 429 U.S., at 531–532. Calling the issue one of law does not make it so.

On remand, the Board concluded that most of the rules in question had a lawful work preservation objective, although some, relating to "short-stopping and traditional warehousing practices have an illegal work acquisition objective." *Longshoremen,* 266 NLRB No. 54, 112 LRRM 1305 (1983).

8. Relationship to Antitrust Problems

It would be worthwhile at this time to review the materials in Chapter 1, B, on antitrust laws, particularly the *Connell Construction* case at page 67. That case involved a union demand that a general contractor agree that subcontracts would be let only to subcontractors who were parties to the union's current collective bargaining agreement. The Court held that the resulting agreement could be the basis of a federal antitrust suit. It specifically rejected the union's claim that the agreement was protected under Section 8(e) of the Act, and that it constituted a defense to the antitrust claim. That aspect of the case appears below.

Connell Construction Co., Inc. v. Plumbers and Steamfitters, Local 100

Supreme Court of the United States, 1974
421. U.S. 616, 89 LRRM 2401

Mr. Justice Powell delivered the opinion of the Court. . . .

III

Local 100 nonetheless contends that the kind of agreement it obtained from Connell is explicitly allowed by the construction-industry proviso to § 8(e) and that antitrust policy therefore must defer to the NLRA. The majority in the Court of Appeals declined to decide this issue, holding that it was subject to the "exclusive jurisdiction" of the NLRB. 483 F.2d, at 1174. This Court has held, however, that the federal courts may decide labor law questions that emerge as collateral issues in suits brought under independent federal remedies, including the antitrust laws. We conclude that § 8(e) does not allow this type of agreement.

Local 100's argument is straightforward: the first proviso to § 8(e) allows "an agreement between a labor organization and an employer in the construction industry relating to the contracting or subcontracting of work to be done at the site of the construction, alteration, painting, or repair of a building, structure, or other work." Local 100 is a labor organization, Connell is an employer in the construction industry, and the agreement covers only work "to be done at the site of construction, alteration, painting or repair of any building, structure, or other works." Therefore, Local 100 says, the agreement comes within the proviso. Connell responds by arguing that despite the unqualified language of the proviso, Congress intended only to allow subcontracting agreements within the context of a collective-bargaining relationship; that is, Congress did not intend to permit a union to approach a "stranger" contractor and obtain a binding agreement not to deal with nonunion subcontractors. On its face, the proviso suggests no such limitation. This Court has held, however, that § 8(e) must be interpreted in light of the statutory setting and the circumstances surrounding its enactment:

> "It is a 'familiar rule, that a thing may be within the letter of the statute and yet not within the statute, because not within its spirit, nor within the intention of its makers.' *Holy Trinity Church* v. *United States*, 143 U.S. 457, 459." *National Woodwork Mfrs. Ass'n* v. *NLRB*, 386 U.S. 612, 619 (1967).

Section 8(e) was part of a legislative program designed to plug technical loopholes in § 8(b)(4)'s general prohibition of secondary activities. In § 8(e) Congress broadly proscribed using contractual agreements to achieve the economic coercion prohibited by § 8(b)(4). See *National Woodwork Mfrs. Ass'n, supra,* at 634. The provisos exempting the construction and garment industries were added by the Conference Committee in an apparent compromise between the House bill, which prohibited all "hot cargo" agreements, and the Senate bill, which prohibited them only in the trucking industry. Although the garment-industry proviso was supported by detailed explanations in both Houses, the construction-industry proviso was explained only by bare references to "the pattern of collective bargaining" in the industry. It seems, however, to have been adopted as a partial substitute for an attempt to overrule this Court's decision in *NLRB* v. *Denver Building & Construction Trades Council,* 341 U.S. 675 (1951). Discussion of "special problems" in the construction industry, applicable to both the § 8(e) proviso and the attempt to overrule *Denver Building Trades,* focused on the problems of picketing a single nonunion subcontractor on a multiemployer building project, and the close relationship between contractors and subcontractors at the jobsite. Congress limited the construction-industry proviso to that single situation, allowing subcontracting agreements only in relation to work done on a jobsite. In contrast to the latitude it provided in the garment-industry proviso, Congress did not afford construction unions an exemption from § 8(b)(4)(B) or otherwise indicate that they were free to use subcontracting agreements as a broad organizational weapon. In keeping with these limitations, the Court has interpreted the construction-industry proviso as

> "a measure designed to allow agreements pertaining to certain secondary activities on the construction site because of the close community of interests there, but to ban secondary-objective agreements concerning nonjobsite work, in which respect the construction industry is no different from any other." *National Woodwork Mfrs. Ass'n,* 386 U.S., at 638–639 (footnote omitted).

Other courts have suggested that it serves an even narrower function:

> "[T]he purpose of the Section 8(e) proviso was to alleviate the frictions that may arise when union men work continuously alongside nonunion men on the same construction site." *Drivers Local 695* v. *NLRB,* 124 U.S. App. D.C. 93, 99, 361 F.2d 547, 553 (1966).

See also *Denver Building Trades*, 341 U.S., at 692–693 (Douglas, J., dissenting); *Essex County and Vicinity District Council of Carpenters* v. *NLRB*, 332 F.2d 636, 640 (CA 3 1964).

Local 100 does not suggest that its subcontracting agreement is related to any of these policies. It does not claim to be protecting Connell's employees from having to work alongside nonunion men. The agreement apparently was not designed to protect Local 100's members in that regard, since it was not limited to jobsites on which they were working. Moreover, the subcontracting restriction applied only to the work Local 100's members would perform themselves and allowed free subcontracting of all other work, thus leaving open a possibility that they would be employed alongside nonunion subcontractors. Nor was Local 100 trying to organize a nonunion subcontractor on the building project it picketed. The union admits that it sought the agreement solely as a way of pressuring mechanical subcontractors in the Dallas area to recognize it as the representative of their employees.

If we agreed with Local 100 that the construction-industry proviso authorizes subcontracting agreements with "stranger" contractors, not limited to any particular jobsite, our ruling would give construction unions an almost unlimited organizational weapon. The unions would be free to enlist any general contractor to bring economic pressure on nonunion subcontractors, as long as the agreement recited that it only covered work to be performed on some jobsite somewhere. The proviso's jobsite restriction then would serve only to prohibit agreements relating to subcontractors that deliver their work complete to the jobsite.

It is highly improbable that Congress intended such a result. One of the major aims of the 1959 Act was to limit "top-down" organizing campaigns, in which unions used economic weapons to force recognition from an employer regardless of the wishes of his employees. Congress accomplished this goal by enacting § 8(b)(7), which restricts primary recognitional picketing, and by further tightening § 8(b)(4)(B), which prohibits the use of most secondary tactics in organizational campaigns. Construction unions are fully covered by these sections. The only special consideration given them in organizational campaigns is § 8(f), which allows "prehire" agreements in the construction industry, but only under careful safeguards preserving workers' rights to decline union representation. The legislative history accompanying § 8(f) also suggests that Congress may not have intended that strikes or picketing could be used to extract prehire agreements from unwilling employers.

These careful limits on the economic pressure unions may use in aid of their organizational campaigns would be undermined seriously if the proviso to § 8(e) were construed to allow unions to seek subcontracting agreements, at large, from any general contractor vulnerable to picketing. Absent a clear indication that Congress intended to leave such a glaring loophole in its restrictions on "top-down" organizing, we are unwilling to read the construction-industry proviso as broadly as Local 100 suggests. Instead, we think its authorization extends only to agreements in the context of collective-bargaining relationships and, in light of congressional references to the *Denver Building Trades* problem, possibly to common-situs relationships on particular jobsites as well.

Finally, Local 100 contends that even if the subcontracting agreement is not sanctioned by the construction-industry proviso and therefore is illegal under § 8(e), it cannot be the basis for antitrust liability because the remedies in the NLRA are exclusive. This argument is grounded in the legislative history of the 1947 Taft-Hartley amendments. Congress rejected attempts to regulate secondary activities by repealing the anti-trust exemptions in the Clayton and Norris-LaGuardia Acts, and created special remedies under the labor law instead. It made secondary activities unfair labor practices under § 8(b)(4), and drafted special provisions for preliminary injunctions at the suit of the NLRB and for recovery of actual damages in the district courts. § 10(*l*) of the NLRA, 49 Stat. 453, as added, 61 Stat. 149, as amended, 29 U.S.C. § 160(*l*), and § 303 of the Labor Management Relations Act, 61 Stat. 158, as amended, 29 U.S.C. § 187. But whatever significance this legislative choice has for antitrust suits based on those secondary activities prohibited by § 8(b)(4), it has no relevance to the question whether Congress meant to preclude antitrust suits based on the "hot cargo" agreements that it outlawed in 1959. There is no legislative history in the 1959 Congress suggesting that labor-law remedies for § 8(e) violations were intended to be exclusive, or that Congress thought allowing antitrust remedies in cases like the present one would be inconsistent with the remedial scheme of the NLRA.

We therefore hold that this agreement, which is outside the context of a collective-bargaining relationship and not restricted to a particular jobsite but which nonetheless obligates Connell to subcontract work only to firms that have a contract with Local 100, may be the basis of a federal antitrust suit because it has a potential for restraining competition in the business market in ways that would not follow naturally from elimination of competition over wages and working conditions.

Note on Application of Section 8(e) to Union Signatory Subcontracting Clauses not Limited to Particular Jobsites

As the *Connell* court observes, Section 8(e) shelters agreements pertaining to a construction job site because of "the close relationship between contractors and subcontractors at the jobsite," 421 U.S. at 629–630, 89 LRRM at 2406. The *Connell* decision notes that some courts have construed Section 8(e) even more narrowly, as intended only to alleviate frictions that may arise when union and nonunion employees work together at the same job site. But the Court rejected this narrower basis for application of Section 8(e) in *Woelke & Romero Framing, Inc.* v. *NLRB*, 456 U.S. 645, 110 LRRM 2377 (1982). *Woelke* involved two separate labor disputes, consolidated for decision. In one, the union demanded a clause which would prohibit the employer, a framing subcontractor, from in turn subcontracting work to any firm not a signatory to a collective bargaining agreement with the union. When the employer refused to agree, the union picketed the work site. The other case involved a similar restriction, agreed to by an association of general contractors; this was challenged by another contractors' association as violating Section 8(e).

While Section 8(e) literally applies to and shelters agreements of the sort described, the employers in *Woelke* argued that the provision must be construed, as the Court stated in *Connell*, "in light of the statutory setting and the circumstances surrounding its enactment." In *Connell*, it will be recalled, the Court went beyond a literal reading of the Section 8(e) exemption and limited its application to agreements sought or obtained in the context of a collective bargaining relationship. The employers in *Woelke* argued that

"Congress designed the proviso to solve the problems that arise when union and nonunion workers are employed at the same jobsite. Thus, it should be interpreted to protect only those agreements that are limited in application to construction projects where both union and nonunion workers are employed." 456 U.S. 654, 110 LRRM 2380.

After an extensive review of the legislative history, the Court concluded that Congress did not intend to apply Section 8(e) so narrowly. Rather, Section 8(e) was intended to validate contemporaneous subcontracting arrangements, and "there is ample evidence that Congress believed that union signatory contract clauses of the type at issue here were part of the pattern of collective bargaining in the construction industry."

The Court also rejected the employers' argument that validation of union signatory clauses would encourage "top down" organizing, one of the concerns of Congress when it enacted Section 8(e) and of the *Connell* court when it held the union's efforts unlawful in that case. The *Woelke* court acknowledged that the subcontracting clauses in question might lead employers to force their employees to join the union, so that the subcontractor could get work under the union signatory provision. But while the Court agreed that Congress intended to limit "top down" organizing, it concluded that

"we believe that Congress endorsed subcontracting agreements obtained in the context of a collective bargaining relationship—and decided to accept whatever top-down pressure such clauses might entail. Congress concluded that the community of interests on the construction job-site justified the top-down organizational consequences that might attend the protection of legitimate collective-bargaining objectives." 456 U.S. at 663, 110 LRRM at 2384.

The student should realize that even though such a clause may be sheltered under Section 8(e), a union may not be able to use picketing to enforce it. Such activity may violate Section 8(b)(4)(B) under the principles of *Denver Building Trades,* set out at page 755, *supra.* Thus, a union must rely upon voluntary compliance or contractual enforcement to achieve the objectives of a union signatory subcontracting clause.

9. REMEDIES

Sections 8(b)(4) and 8(e) are enforced through unfair labor practice proceedings and also through the "mandatory" injunction provisions of Section 10(l). In addition, Section 303 authorizes damage suits for violations of Section 8(b)(4). Either the primary or any secondary employer may sue under Section 303. *United Brick & Clay Workers* v. *Deena Artware,* 198 F.2d 637, 30 LRRM 2485 (6th Cir. 1952). The Section 303 remedy is independent of the unfair labor practice proceeding. *International Longshoreman's and Warehousemen's Union* v. *Juneau Spruce Corp.,* 342 U.S. 237, 29 LRRM 2249 (1952). Thus, a Board finding of a Section 8(b)(4) violation is not a prerequisite to Section 303 relief; indeed, damages may be awarded even though the Board finds no violation of Section 8(b)(4). *United Brick & Clay Workers* v. *Deena Artware, supra.*

Attorney's fees incurred in bringing proceedings before the Board under Section 8(b)(4) are not recoverable under Section 303. The Court held in *Summit Valley Industries* v. *Carpenters,* 456 U.S. 903, 110 LRRM 2441 (1982) that Section 303 did not satisfy the "American Rule" for attorney's fees by a "specific and explicit" provision, nor did Congress intend to expand the term "damages" in Section 303(b) to encompass attorney's fees.

When the Board finds that an agreement violates Section 8(e), it normally orders the parties to cease and desist from its enforcement. But damages, such as the reimbursement of money paid pursuant to an unlawful agreement, are not part of the Board's normal arsenal of remedies, except in cases where the payment is coerced, for example, by a strike, or in other "especially egregious" situations. The Board points out that damages may be recovered in a judicial proceeding under Section 303 of the Act.

The Court upheld this position in *Larry Shepard* v. *NLRB,* 459 U.S. ____, 112 LRRM 2369 (1983). In order to get work as a trucker, Shepard was required to join the union and pay an initiation fee and dues. He did so under protest, and later succeeded in overturning the requirement as a violation of Section 8(e). But he was unsuccessful before the Board in obtaining a refund of the fees and dues he paid under the illegal agreement.

A key to the Court's reasoning may be found in Justice Rehnquist's majority opinion:

> "The Board is not a court; it is not even a labor court; it is an administrative agency charged by Congress with the enforcement and administration of the federal labor laws. While a prayer for 'complete relief' might find a receptive ear in a court of general jurisdiction, it is well settled that there are wide differences between administrative agencies and courts.
>
> . . .
>
> "We find nothing in the language or structure of the Act that requires the Board to reflexively order that which a complaining party may

regard as 'complete relief' for every unfair labor practice." 459 U.S. at ____, 112 LRRM at 2372.

Justice O'Connor dissented.

The responsibility of the union for acts of its officers and members is measured by the ordinary doctrines of agency, as noted in Chapter 5. *United Mine Workers* v. *Gibbs*, 383 U.S. 715, 61 LRRM 2561 (1966). Punitive damages cannot be awarded under Section 303, and state law has been preempted by Section 303 in damage suit actions based on peaceful union secondary activity. *Teamsters Local 20* v. *Morton,* 377 U.S. 252, 56 LRRM 2225 (1964). But since state authority is not preempted as to acts of violence, punitive damages may be awarded under state law for violent secondary activity. However, if the suit is in federal court, the agency requirement will apply. *United Mine Workers* v. *Gibbs, supra.*

C. FEATHERBEDDING

Baker, Some Heroic Toilers of Yore*

Labor has had many heroes and innovators besides George Meany and President Nixon, and while no one would wish to deprive those two of their due in glory this Labor Day weekend, it is only fair that we recall a few of the others.

One of the most revered is Kpoppos, an ancient Cretan Minotaur-herder who invented featherbedding after helping herd the Minotaur into the labyrinth at Knossos.

Kpoppos and his colleague, Kmommos, were sitting on a rocky hillside outside Knossos one afternoon watching the Minotaur chew on an offering of Athenian youth when Kmommos asked the now historic question: "What are you going to do for a living when they finish the labyrinth?"

"With that question," Kpoppos wrote in his autobiography, "the scales fell from my eyes." Once the Minotaur was safely sealed into the labyrinth, Minotaur-herders would no longer be needed to protect it from wolves on the mountainside or restrain it from descending into Knossos and chewing on the local Cretan youth.

Kpoppos, who had never mastered any trade except Minotaur-herding, left Kmommos in charge of the monster and went down to the labyrinth. Meeting with Kbobbos, one of the skilled labyrinth dovetailers, he pointed out that they would both be permanently out of work once the labyrinth was finished.

Kbobbos immediately saw the point, for he had no job training for anything except dovetailing labyrinth corners. Neither had any of the other labyrinth dovetailers.

---

*An article by Russell Baker appearing in *The New York Times*, September 3, 1972, p. E 13. © by The New York Times Company. Reprinted by permission.

Next day at a meeting with King Minos, Kpoppos threatened a strike by Minotaur-herders and labyrinth-builders unless jobs were provided for them in perpetuity. King Minos said he did not know where Perpetuity was and, in any case, did not intend to build any labyrinths there for any more Minotaurs. He was "fed up" with the present Minotaur, he said, and if Queen Pasiphae presented him with a new one she was going to hear from his lawyers.

The King quickly changed his tune when Kpoppos signaled Kmommos to walk off the job and let the Minotaur come to town for dinner. In the resulting contract, the King agreed to keep everybody on the payroll, with cost-of-living escalators, until the fall of Rome.

Note

In *American Newspaper Publishers Ass'n* v. *NLRB*, 345 U.S. 100, 31 LRRM 2422 (1953), the question was "whether a labor organization engages in an unfair labor practice, within the meaning of § 8(b)(6) . . . , when it insists that newspaper publishers pay printers for reproducing advertising matter for which the publishers ordinarily have no use." Conceding that the practice of "setting bogus" was a wasteful procedure, the Court nevertheless held that there was no unfair labor practice because the practice calls for payment only for services for work actually performed as distinguished from payment "for services which are not performed or not to be performed." The Court relied on legislative history, noting that the Taft-Hartley bill as it passed the House condemned practices which required an employer to employ persons in excess of the number reasonably required by him but that such provision was not finally adopted by Congress. Accord: *NLRB* v. *Gamble Enterprises*, 345 U.S. 117, 31 LRRM 2428 (1953), where the union demanded, as a condition of allowing traveling orchestras to appear on a local theater's programs, that a local orchestra also be hired to play.

D. JURISDICTIONAL OR WORK ASSIGNMENT DISPUTES

The term jurisdictional dispute describes two types of problems: first, there is the issue of representation—which union, if any, will represent a group of employees—and, second, there is the issue of work assignments—which group of employees will be assigned to perform certain job tasks. In this section we are looking at the way in which the NLRA regulates clashes about work assignments.

The relevant statutory provisions are Sections 8(b)(4)(D) and 10(k). Section 8(b)(4)(D) makes it an unfair labor practice for a labor organization to use economic pressure to force the assignment of particular work to one group of employees, unless the employer is refusing to honor a representation order of the Board. This form of regulation is a familiar one. But in addition to making use of economic pressure subject to unfair labor practice proceedings, Congress created an unusual means for expeditious resolution of work assignment disputes under Section 10(k). After a Section 8(b)(4)(D) charge has been filed, the work assignment dispute is to be resolved through a Board hearing or adjustment by the parties themselves. Under Section 10(k) the Board is required to hold a hearing to decide which group of employees is entitled to the work. If the parties comply with the Board's decision, the Section 8(b)(4)(D) charge is dismissed. Alternatively, the parties may avoid a Board determination and resolve the dispute themselves by notifying the Board within 10 days after the Section 8(b)(4)(D) charge is filed that they have adjusted the dispute or have agreed on a method to adjust the dispute. Voluntary settlement will result in dismissal of the Section 8(b)(4)(D) charge. The policies underlying this unusual procedure are discussed in the excerpts from the following law review articles.

Player, Work Assignment Disputes Under Section 10(k): Putting the Substantive Cart Before the Procedural Horse*

At first glance a jurisdictional dispute manifests only a bitter struggle for power between two or more greedy unions. Further analysis, however, reveals other important interests at stake. Both the employer and the NLRB, for example, have a substantial interest in the outcome of jurisdictional disputes and the methods that bring about their resolution. Furthermore, there are interests of both employees and their local unions that do not always coincide with those of the national and international unions.

The employer has an obvious interest in maintaining the efficiency of his operations. When he creates a new job he understandably prefers to assign it to the employee who is most likely to render the best performance at the least expense. To implement this interest, the employer must consider many economic variables. First, of course, he must balance the skills of his employees against the labor costs that accompany expertise. A highly skilled employee, for example, may yield prolific output of a high quality, but his skills will no doubt cost more in wages than would those of a less able craftsman. An employer, however, must also look beyond the individual's isolated performance to the efficiency of the operation as a whole. Assigning a new job to a particular group of employees may fragment or confuse overall plant operations. Additionally, an employer must attempt to eliminate idle time, unnecessary overtime, undue movement of employees, dual supervision, and other wasteful practices that detract from the overall efficiency of his production.

In addition to his interest in operational efficiency, however, the employer may also find motivation to deal with the collective representative of his employees that will cause him the least trouble. To the extent that strong and assertive unions are likely to demand higher wages for performing a newly created job, this interest is a component of his profit-

*Reprinted by permission from Player, *Work Assignment Disputes Under Section 10(k): Putting the Substantive Cart Before the Procedural Horse*, 52 Tex. L. Rev. 417, 420–22 (1974). Copyright © 1974 by Texas Law Review Publications, Inc.

maximization interest. But the master may have other reasons for favoring cooperative unions. He may wish to eliminate a highly organized craft union that has troubled other areas of his operations; he may award jobs to a union that is near death, hoping to inherit unrepresented employees; or he may just perversely dislike one of the unions vying for the job. These hidden employer interests, which certainly violate the spirit of the section 8(a)(3) ban on employer discrimination, are important to any method of resolving jurisdictional disputes that takes employer interest into account.

Individual employee and local union interests also play a part in jurisdictional disputes. An individual employee is obviously anxious to remain employed. As his employer implements technological changes, however, he may prefer one of the newer jobs, or the elimination of his old job may force him to seek a new area of expertise. Similarly, his union shares this interest in expanding into new job fields. A union's strength is directly proportional to the number of workers it represents. The union may thus fear obsolescence as much as the employees themselves, and it can enhance its prestige among other workers by placing its members in new jobs. The local union's interest, however, may not precisely correspond to the national or international union's objectives. For example, since the national will not feel the pinch of a single plant's job changes as acutely as the local, the national may be more inclined to avoid fratricidal warfare. Awards that are satisfactory to the international thus may be totally unacceptable to the individual employee and his local.

The NLRB has two important interests in jurisdictional battles. Congress has addressed the work assignment dispute, indicating a desire to end those fights with minimum harm to individual employers and national productivity. Congress believed that disputes could be more effectively resolved with permanence and a minimum of economic bloodshed if the parties themselves, rather than the Government, imposed the solution. Congress also presumably intended that jurisdictional problems consume the least possible administrative time and energy. The NLRB thus has an interest in expediency as well as a duty to implement the statutory scheme. These two goals can, of course, conflict. Overly hasty action on the part of the Board can result in inadvertent violations of the policy underlying section 8(b)(4)(D). Undue deliberation and delay on the other hand can nullify the purpose of section 10(k).

All parties have an interest in rapid resolution of jurisdictional disputes. Long jurisdictional strikes can delay an employer's fulfillment of contract obligations or even cause him to cease operations altogether. These economic losses seem particularly harsh when an employer faces the certainty of a strike regardless of the union he picks to fill a new job. If an employer can procure an injunction against a strike, he may complete his work and eliminate the new job before the protracted NLRB procedure determines which union has a right to fill the position. Since undue delay can only result in the kind of industrial strife that the National Labor Relations Act meant to avoid, Congress provided a procedure for resolving work assignment disputes that encourages the conflicting parties to waive the burdensome administrative machinery and seek their own solutions to their own problems. In a time of overburdened courts and agencies, the Board and courts should do everything possible to implement this congressional policy of discouraging litigation.

Leslie, The Role of the NLRB and the Courts in Resolving Union Jurisdictional Disputes*

SUBSTANTIVE PROBLEMS

During the 12 years following the passage of Section 8(b)(4)(D), the Board, contending that deciding substantive terms of employment were not its business, refused to decide the merits of jurisdictional disputes. The Board affirmed the employer's preference unless he was acting contrary to a Board's certification or a collective bargaining agreement. In the 1961 *CBS* decision [364 U.S. 573, 47 LRRM 1226 (1961)], the Supreme Court ordered the Board to decide jurisdictional disputes on the merits in Section 10(k) hearings.

The evidence is persuasive that the Board has never complied with the Supreme Court's direction. Soon after *CBS* the Board identified several factors that it would consider in deciding a jurisdictional dispute in a Section 10(k) hearing. Included among the factors were area practice, national practice, the union's traditional and historical claims to the work, cost, efficiency, employer preference and collective bargaining agreements. Yet throughout the 15 years since *CBS*, commentators have routinely observed that the employer's preference is affirmed in the overwhelming majority of Section 10(k) decisions, thus in effect continuing the Board's pre-*CBS* practice. The Ninth Circuit has recently given judicial recognition to the propensity of the Board to routinely affirm the employer's assignment, although surprisingly the court did not disapprove but rather remanded for a more explicit recognition of the practice.

In those few cases where the employer's preference is not affirmed by the Board, one can usually find a special reason. For example, in the above-mentioned Ninth Circuit case the employer shifted his assignment after strike pressure from a competing union, and the Board, repeating its litany of factors, affirmed the employer's initial assignment. The Board's apparent guess that the employer's real preference was for the union members granted the work in the absence of strike pressure proved incorrect and the employer took the case to the court of appeals.

While many employers making work assignments surely consider questions of safety, skill and efficiency, area practice and the strike, as the Board professes to do, a 95 percent coincidence between Board awards and employer preferences is too high to be explained on the grounds that the Board and the employers are considering the same factors. The Board is apparently trying to free the employer and the industry of the

*Reprinted by permission from Leslie, *The Role of the NLRB and the Courts in Resolving Union Jurisdictional Disputes*, 75 COLUM. L. REV. 1470, 1490–1493, 1505–1508 (1975). Copyright © 1975 by the Directors of the Columbia Law Review Association, Inc.

strike pressure that would be felt if the union without the employer's assignment were given the Section 10(k) award but the employer refused to assign them the work. The war on jurisdictional disputes has been referred to as a "holy war," and the Board has taken up weapons against the heathen.

There are several problems with this Board practice. First, because it in fact avoids a decision on the merits, it is contrary to the Supreme Court's mandate in *CBS*. Second, it undermines the integrity of the Board and lends support to those who feel that the Board is more of a political entity than an independent quasi-judicial tribunal. Third, it leaves unfulfilled the congressional policy of giving parties to a jurisdictional dispute a tribunal for an independent settlement, and so frustrates unions and their members. This, in turn, may tempt them to resort to covert and unlawful forms of retaliation against employers.

Even if there were something to be said for routinely affirming the employer's assignment of the work, it is not always clear who the employer is, especially in the construction industry. Consider, for example, a strike by carpenters over a general contractor's subcontracting of work—including work traditionally claimed by the carpenters—to a sheet metal worker subcontractor. The carpenters refuse to enter the job site, and they picket. Assuming this is a jurisdictional dispute rather than a work preservation case, the carpenters have violated Section 8(b)(4)(D) no matter which employer they are striking unless they win the Section 10(k) award. Either the general contractor, the carpentry subcontractor, or the sheet metal subcontractor must be considered the assigner of work in the Section 10(k) hearing. Since the general contractor made the initial decision to subcontract the work to a sheet metal subcontractor rather than a carpentry subcontractor, in actual practice he is the one assigning the work. But once the subcontract is let, the Board will consider the sheet metal subcontractor as the assigning employer. At the Section 10(k) hearing, the sheet metal subcontractor will be able to show that he has a collective bargaining agreement only with the Sheet Metal Workers Union and will also show that if he must hire carpenters to do only one portion of the work for which he has subcontracted, then he may have to pay them for standing around while the sheet metal workers do other tasks. Thus, the decision to identify the sheet metal subcontractor as the assigning employer is outcome determinative in this typical sort of Section 10(k) hearing.

If the general contractor were considered the assigning employer, union recognition, certifications or collective bargaining agreements probably would not favor either the sheet metal workers or the carpenters. Furthermore, it may well be that the particular piece of work being assigned could be done either by the sheet metal workers or the carpenters as a part of their routine tasks. If so, safety, skills, efficiency and costs would be of considerable importance in making the Section 10(k) determination if the general contractor were considered the assigning employer. Were these factors to cancel out, the Board would be left with the employer's preference and the historical or area practice of assigning the work. It is difficult in such a situation to see why the general contractor's preference should be given substantial weight, since he is really only deciding which subcontractor should take the profit for this particular work. Treating the subcontractor as the assigning employer ignores construction industry reality that many of these disputes are not merely between unions but between specialty subcontractors. Perhaps industrial peace would be furthered most by an examination of area practice and an award to the appropriate union, at least when the other factors seem balanced.

. . .

THE BOARD AND VOLUNTARY SETTLEMENTS

NLRB v. Plasterers' Local 79. In *Plasterers' Local 79* [404 U.S. 116, 78 LRRM 2897 (1971)], the Supreme Court held that the Board should hold a Section 10(k) hearing and issue a Section 8(b)(4)(D) finding where the two unions involved in a jurisdictional dispute are bound to a voluntary method of settling the dispute but the employer is not. In reaching its decision, the Court had to come to grips with the fuzzy relationship between Section 8(b)(4)(D) and Section 10(k) of the Act. Section 8(b)(4)(D) prohibits the union from striking to gain work "unless [the] employer is failing to conform to an order . . . of the Board determining the bargaining representative for employees performing such work. . . ." Section 10(k) provides that whenever a union is charged with violating Section 8(b)(4)(D) the Board must hold a Section 10(k) hearing and determine the dispute. The last sentence of Section 10(k) reads: "Upon compliance by the parties to the dispute with the decision of the Board or upon such voluntary adjustment of the dispute, such charge shall be dismissed." The Court of Appeals in *Plasterers' Local 79* reasoned that since the employer was not bound to award the work in accordance with the Board's Section 10(k) decision, the reference to "parties" in the last sentence of Section 10(k) could not include the employer. There is some merit in this argument, for, if the striking union prevailed in the Section 10(k) hearing, the Board would not find a Section 8(b)(4)(D) violation even though the employer involved was unwilling to assign the work to the prevailing union.

The Supreme Court reversed, however, holding that the employer involved in a jurisdictional dispute was to be considered a "party" and that a voluntary adjustment mechanism which had failed to include the employer would not require the Board to forego a Section 10(k) hearing. The court noted that while many employers caught in jurisdictional disputes between unions are neutral as to which union finally secures the work, many other employers are not. A work assignment may have a substantial economic effect because of differences in efficiency or wage rate. The Court might even have gone further and noted, as have some commentators, that many jurisdictional disputes in the construction industry are as much disputes between two specialty subcontractors as they are disputes between two unions.

The Court held that "parties to the dispute" must be given a "common sense" meaning and so rejected the Court of Appeals' rationale. It reasoned that a Section 10(k) award standing alone binds neither the employer nor the union because no cease and desist order is issued, although the Court admitted that practically speaking the Section 10(k) award decides whether or not the union will prevail in the subsequent Section 8(b)(4)(D) hearing. As a matter of statutory construction, the critical point of the opinion is its holding that the dismissal of the Board proceedings that occurs when a Section 10(k) award goes to a striking union is not done pursuant to the last part of Section 10(k), but pursuant to the language of Section 8(b)(4)(D) which speaks in terms of the employer "failing to conform to an order . . . of the Board."

Plasterers' Local 79 was decided by a unanimous court and is unlikely to be overruled. But in my view, it was wrongly decided. The Court's construction that the subsequent dismissal is pursuant to Section 8(b)(4)(D) when the striking union wins the Section 10(k) award would render the last sentence of Section 10(k) surplusage. By itself, this would not be objectionable since the statutory provisions are so poorly drafted that attempts to achieve semantic consistency may result in frustrating the Act's policies. What is debatable is the Court's resolution of the underlying policies.

The Court reasoned that the employer should be considered a "party" to the dispute because of his interest in which group performs the work. This analysis gives controlling weight to an employer interest which the Court, in light of the purpose of the Act, should not have protected. The employer in most jurisdictional disputes has two interests. First, he has an interest in removing himself from the dilemma of being caught between two warring factions, each of whom will strike if he gives the work to the other. Second, the employer has an interest in seeing that the work assignment finally goes according to his preference. Both the legislative history and the nature of Sections 8(b)(4)(D) and 10(k) indicate that Congress intended to protect the first interest. But nothing suggests that Congress was mandating the Board to protect the employer's economic interest in securing his own work assignment. Indeed, it would have been extraordinary had Congress evinced such an intent. The NLRA is a framework within which unions and employers are to hammer out their own terms and conditions of employment, going to the warfare mat if necessary, but reaching voluntary agreements whenever possible. Extracting the employer from competing work stoppages is one thing; to suggest that the Board is also in the business of protecting the employer's substantive interest in securing this particular condition of employment injects a measure of bias making Sections 8(b)(4)(D) and 10(k) the most remarkable ones of the Act.

When two unions by their own voluntary settlement mechanism remove the employer's danger of being caught between them and, as a result, the voluntary mechanism sends forth one union to do battle with the employer over the work assignment, the policies of Sections 8(b)(4)(D) and 10(k) are fully satisfied. The only interest remaining to the employer is that of protecting his own work assignment and this should be worked out in the market place.

E. NATIONAL EMERGENCY DISPUTES

1. TAFT-HARTLEY PROCEDURE

One of the most controversial features of the Taft-Hartley Act is the procedure for settlement of national emergency disputes. Sections 208 through 210 of the Labor Management Relations Act of 1947 provide for injunctions against strikes or lockouts affecting an industry engaged in interstate commerce which are so serious as to imperil the national health or safety. Section 212 makes this procedure inapplicable to any matter which is subject to the provisions of the Railway Labor Act.

Section 206 provides that if the President of the United States finds that a national emergency strike or lockout has occurred or is threatened, he may appoint a board of inquiry to investigate the issues and report their findings. The board submits a report to the President, but it is specifically prohibited from making any recommendations. After receiving the report, the President files it with the Federal Mediation and Conciliation Service (FMCS), and he may then direct the Attorney General to seek an injunction against the strike or lockout. If the appropriate district court finds that a national emergency dispute exists (affects an entire industry or a substantial part thereof engaged in interstate commerce and imperils the national health or safety), the court may issue an injunction restraining the strike or lockout.

Upon issuance of the injunction, the parties must attempt to settle their dispute with the help of the FMCS. If at the end of 60 days the parties have not reached a settlement, the board of inquiry reports to the President on the progress of the negotiations, including a statement of each party's position and the employer's last offer. This report is made available to the public. During the next 15 days the NLRB conducts a secret ballot vote of the employees to determine whether they wish to accept the employer's last offer of settlement. Within 5 days after the "final offer" vote (80 days after the issuance of the injunction), the NLRB certifies the results to the Attorney General, who must then have the injunction discharged. The final step is a report to Congress by the President on the status of the dispute. He may recommend congressional action.

The Taft-Hartley national emergency dispute provisions do not prohibit strikes. An 80-day "cooling off" period is imposed during which time it is contemplated that the parties will settle the dispute through negotiation. If, after the 80-day injunction is vacated, the dispute has not been settled, the parties are free to strike or lockout as the case may be, unless further limitations are imposed upon them by Congress.

In several of the cases in which an injunction has been sought under the Taft-Hartley national emergency dispute provisions, the constitutionality of the procedure has been assailed. In *Steelworkers* v. *United States*, 361 U.S. 39, 45 LRRM 2209 (1959), the Court rejected a contention that these provisions violate the constitutional limitation which prohibits courts from exercising powers of a legislative or executive nature. Although a great deal of the evidence in this case involved the meaning of "national health," the Court never reached this issue since the evidence was sufficient to establish that the strike endangered the national safety. Thus it is not clear whether national health means only physical health of the citizenry or whether it also comprehends the economic health of the country. In this case the union also argued that a selective reopening of some of the steel mills would suffice to fulfill specific defense needs. But the Court held that the statute cannot be construed to require the Government to formulate a reorganization of the industry to satisfy its defense needs without the complete reopening of the closed facilities.

Mr. Justice Douglas dissented on the ground that the record did not support the issuance of a broad injunctive order totally prohibiting the strike and that the case should be remanded to the district court for particularized findings as to exactly how the strike imperiled the national health and what plants needed to be reopened to produce the quantity of steel needed for national safety. "If the federal court is to be merely an automaton stamping the papers an Attorney General presents, the judicial function rises to no higher level than an IBM machine." 361 U.S. 39, 71.

In 1971, for the first time, a federal district court refused to issue an injunction requested by the Government. The strike was against grain elevators in Chicago. The court held that the strike did not affect an entire industry or substantial part thereof, and that the national health or safety would not be imperiled by continuation of the strike. *United States* v. *International Longshoremen's Local 418*, 335 F.Supp. 501 (N.D. Ill. 1971), *stay denied*, 78 LRRM 2801 (7th Cir. 1971).

2. CRITICISMS OF THE PRESENT PROCEDURES

The national emergency provisions of the Taft-Hartley Act were not used from 1972 through 1977. Between 1947 and 1972 these provisions were invoked 34 times. Over two million workers were affected by application of these provisions. In only 29 cases, however, was an injunction sought and obtained. In many cases settlement of the dispute was reached during the 80-day period. Well over one half of all emergency disputes occurred in three industries—stevedoring (10), aircraft-aerospace (5), and atomic energy (4). See U.S. Department of Labor Summary Report on National Emergency Disputes Under the Labor-Management Relations Act, 1947–72. In 1978 the national emergency provisions of the Taft-Hartley Act were invoked in connection with the longest coal industry strike in the history of the United States (111 days). However, a temporary restraining order against the strike was not enforced, and the parties reached a negotiated settlement of the dispute shortly after the board of inquiry issued a report.

Votes on the employer's last offer have been conducted and completed in 14 cases. In every case the employer's last offer was rejected by the voters.

In general, the criticisms of current provisions of the law for handling national emergency disputes are:

(a) The fact-finding process usually operates *pro forma* simply for the purpose of obtaining the injunction, which is the opposite of the deliberation needed. The way the statute is designed, the injunction cannot be obtained until the appointed board has made some findings of fact.

(b) The board of inquiry is not authorized to make recommendations. Since it is accepted by many that recommendations by a fact-finding board are the ultimate goal of the process, this lack of power in a Taft-Hartley board constitutes a limitation upon the usefulness of the process itself.

(c) The concept of "national emergency" is too loosely defined.

(d) The last offer vote has been tried and found wanting. It simply serves as a means of solidifying the disputing employees against the employer's position.

(e) Experience has indicated that the process of collective bargaining is usually not carried on effectively during the 80-day period of the injunction. Where settlements have taken place during this period, often they have come from outside pressures, as in the 1959 steel dispute, rather than from collective bargaining. Further, in case the dispute is not settled during the 80-day period, the parties are right back where they started, and there is no further process immediately available to the Government to avert an emergency work stoppage.

(f) The terms of the statute are too definite. The parties know exactly what can happen to them. Thus, there is no threat hanging over their heads of some alternative processes which may be applied to them if they do not settle their dispute without a work stoppage. This criticism is made by those who favor the "choice of procedures" approach to emergency disputes.

(g) The apparent purpose of the Taft-Hartley provisions is to allow time for the public to react to the demands of the parties and thus to bring about a settlement through the medium of public pressure. There is substantial doubt that public opinion actually makes much difference in the settlement of such disputes, especially when no recommendations for settlement may be made.

(h) Allowing a strike to be carried on for a time and then stopping it by the 80-day injunction applies economic pressure unevenly to the parties, usually unfavorably to the union. Thus, in the steel dispute of 1959, there was a work stoppage for 116 days. The strikers, without pay checks, were under serious economic pressure during all this period. Yet the companies, because of anticipatory stockpiling, were not under serious pressure until just before the Taft-Hartley provisions were invoked. It was not until the dwindling stockpile created a "national emergency" that the companies also began to feel heavy economic pressure.

For critical evaluation of the current law see Jones, *Toward a Definition of "National Emergency Dispute,"* 1971 Wis. L. Rev. 700; Jones, *The National Emergency Disputes Provisions of the Taft-Hartley Act: A View From a Legislative Draftsman's Desk,* 17 W. Res. L. Rev. 133 (1965); Williams, *Settlement of Labor Disputes in Industries Affected With a National Interest,* 49 A.B.A.J. 862 (1963).

3. STATE REGULATION OF EMERGENCY DISPUTES

State statutes dealing with emergency disputes may be preempted by federal law. In *Amalgamated Ass'n of Street, Electric Railway & Motor Coach Employees* v. *Wisconsin Board*, 340 U.S. 383, 27 LRRM 2395 (1951), the Court held that the Wisconsin Public Utility Anti-Strike Law, which made it a misdemeanor for public utility employees to engage in a strike which would cause an interruption of an essential public utility service, conflicted with the NLRA and was therefore invalid under the Supremacy Clause of the Constitution.

The Taft-Hartley emergency dispute provisions do not, of course, preempt regulation of strikes against the state as an employer. But in *Amalgamated Ass'n of Street, Electric Railway & Motor Coach Employees* v. *Missouri*, 374 U.S. 74, 53 LRRM 2394 (1963), it was held that a state could not convert a private strike into a strike against the state by a *pro forma* government seizure of a privately owned public utility. The Court reasoned as follows:

"First, whatever the status or the title to the properties of Kansas City Transit, Inc., acquired by the State as a result of the Governor's executive order, the record shows that the State's involvement fell far short of creating a state-owned and operated utility whose labor relations are by definition excluded from the coverage of the National Labor Relations Act. The employees of the company did not become employees of Missouri. Missouri did not pay their wages, and did not direct or supervise their duties. No property of the company was actually conveyed, transferred, or otherwise turned over to the State. Missouri did not participate in any way in the actual management of the company, and there was no change of any kind in the conduct of the company's business. As summed up by the Chairman of the State Mediation Board: 'So far as I know the company is operating now just as it was two weeks ago before the strike.'

"Secondly, the *Wisconsin Board* case decisively rejected the proposition that a state enactment affecting a public utility operating in interstate commerce could be saved from a challenge based upon a demonstrated conflict with the standards embodied in a federal law simply by designating it as 'emergency legislation.' There the Court said that where 'the state seeks to deny entirely a federally guaranteed right which Congress itself restricted only to a limited extent in case of national emergencies, however serious, it is manifest that the state legislation is in conflict with federal law.' 340 U.S., at 394.

"The short of the matter is that Missouri, through the fiction of 'seizure' by the State, has made a peaceful strike against a public utility unlawful, in direct conflict with federal legislation which guarantees the right to strike against a public utility, as against any employer engaged in interstate commerce. In forbidding a strike against an employer covered by the National Labor Relations Act, Missouri has forbidden the exercise of rights explicitly protected by § 7 of that Act. Collective bargaining, with the right to strike at its core, is the essence of the federal scheme. As in *Wisconsin Board*, a state law which denies that right cannot stand under the Supremacy Clause of the Constitution.

"It is hardly necessary to add that nothing we have said even remotely affects the right of a State to own or operate a public utility or any other business, nor the right or duty of the chief executive or legislature of a State to deal with emergency conditions of public danger, violence, or disaster under appropriate provisions of the State's organic or statutory laws." 374 U.S. at 81–83.

4. Alternatives

a. Fact-Finding and Recommendation of Terms of Settlement

As noted earlier, the present Taft-Hartley "national emergency" provisions are criticized by many persons because the fact-finding board is forbidden to make recommendations for settlement of the labor dispute it is considering. A number of impartial observers believe that if these critical disputes were submitted to a fact-finding process which included recommendations for settlement announced by the board, the process would be much more effective than it now is. The belief is that reasonable terms of settlement, widely publicized, would tend to force the disputants to settle along the lines of the recommendation. President Truman, who made no secret of his dislike of the national emergency provisions of Taft-Hartley (although he invoked them several times), used the device of fact-finding with recommendations in the 1949 steel dispute. Under the Railway Labor Act, emergency boards not only find facts, but they also make recommendations for settlement.

b. Compulsory Arbitration

Some form of compulsory settlement by Government of critical labor disputes has become the norm in most of the free countries of the world. This process may or may not take the form of arbitration, but the significant fact is that the Government does have the final authority to promulgate a settlement which must be accepted by the disputants. In Australia and New Zealand this use of governmental power has a long tradition, and the free European countries have come to it as well, though in less specific and detailed form.

There have been some earlier experiments in the United States with the compulsory arbitration of emergency labor disputes. The theory behind them is that there are certain industries where strikes cannot be tolerated. The purpose, then, is to force the parties to submit their dispute to an impartial board of arbitration whose award will be binding upon them. This was the established means of dealing with labor disputes during World War II under the War Labor Disputes Act, 57 Stat. 163 (1943), 50 U.S.C. App. Section 1501 (1946).

Compulsory arbitration is criticized because, some authorities argue, it tends to defeat collective bargaining. If a third party (such as an arbitrator) makes the final decision, each side is likely to take an extreme position, expecting the arbitrator to "split the difference."

c. Government Seizure

During World War II, government seizure was used to end strikes in critical industries. In most cases the Army or Navy took possession, operating the plant through the regular management but with the terms of employment fixed by the Government. This device was almost exclusively a wartime expedient for enforcing decisions of the National War Labor Board.

In 1952 President Truman seized the steel mills when the companies refused to accept the recommendations of the Wage Stabilization Board, but in *Youngstown Sheet & Tube Co.* v. *Sawyer*, 343 U.S. 579, 587, 30 LRRM 2172 (1952), the Supreme Court held the seizure to be unconstitutional. Justice Black, delivering the opinion of the Court, held that in the absence of any statute granting him the power, the President had no constitutional power to order the seizure of the industry. He did not have the power as Commander in Chief "to take possession of private property in order to keep labor disputes from stopping production. This is a job for the Nation's lawmakers, not for its military authorities." Nor was this power inherent in his position as chief executive.

The kind of seizure involved in enforcement of the orders of the War Labor Disputes Act during World War II and the steel dispute which culminated in the *Youngstown* case must be distinguished from seizure of a business to prevent an "emergency" strike when the seizure is viewed as an end in itself. In the former situations, seizure is simply an enforcing device designed to pressure the parties into acceptance of a settlement which comes from some other source. Under the War Labor Disputes Act it was the War Labor Board. In the steel controversy, it was the Wage Stabilization Board. Seizure for its own sake without any provision of law designed to establish a recommended or compelled settlement is sometimes advocated as a device to be used in emergency situations. It should be noted, however, that the result of seizure in such circumstances is that the workers are simply ordered by the seizure not to strike, but then are left to continue the process of collective bargaining. This means that the workers are forced to bargain with their bargaining strength emasculated.

d. The Choice-of-Procedures Approach

One criticism of the present national emergency provisions of the Taft-Hartley Act is that they are so definite that the parties know exactly what will happen to them. Critics argue that the most effective device is to have a number of possible choices of action available in order to keep the parties in doubt as to what may happen if they do not resolve the dispute on their own. See Wirtz, *The "Choice of Procedures" Approach to National Emergency Disputes*, in Emergency Disputes and National Policy, 149 (Bernstein, Enarson, and Fleming, eds. 1955); Shultz, *The Massachusetts Choice-of-Procedures Approach to Emergency Disputes*, 10 Indus. & Lab. Rel. Rev. 358 (1957).

Thus, some suggest that the President should have the option to establish a cooling-off period and, if desirable, to extend this period while mediation takes place, or to order fact-finding with recommendations, or to order compulsory arbitration, or to order government seizure, or to order partial operation of an industry. What other options might be added to this list? Another proposal involves "either-or" arbitration (sometimes referred to as "final offer selection"). Under this proposal a board of arbitration would have the duty of choosing in full one of the final offers of the parties. The board would decide which party's final offer is more reasonable. That offer would then become the final and binding settlement. What are the advantages and disadvantages of this proposal?

5. VOLUNTARY ARBITRATION OF INTEREST DISPUTES

Voluntary arbitration of new contract terms is used more widely in the public sector than in the private sector. But arbitration of new contract terms has been used in some local transit disputes and in the newspaper industry. Moreover, use of this device in recent years in the basic steel industry prevented a situation from arising which could have resulted in a national emergency strike.

Adoption of the ENA (Experimental Negotiating Agreement) in the basic steel industry was a significant development in labor-management relations. Under this agreement (first adopted by the Steelworkers and the 10 major steel producers for use in 1974, and readopted for use in connection with negotiations in 1977 and in 1980) the parties agreed that they would submit most disputed issues to an arbitration panel if normal collective bargaining failed, rather than resorting to a test of economic strength by strike or lockout. The arbitration panel, composed of three veteran labor arbitrators plus one union representative and one employer representative, would then impose a binding settlement on the parties for a three-year term. But ENA provided that the following issues would be excluded from arbitration: local working conditions (involving such matters as established crew sizes, locker room facilities and parking lots), union membership and checkoff provisions, cost-of-living provisions, the uniformity or lack of uniformity of wages among plants, minimum agreed-upon wage increases and a bonus of $150 for the employees, no-strike and no-lockout provisions, and the management rights provision. Special procedures were adopted to deal with local issues involving a given plant. Under specified conditions a strike or lockout could take place over local issues at a plant. Management estimated that the minimum guarantees set forth in ENA for 1977 involved an increase of over 26 percent in hourly employment costs for the next three years, before the parties even started their negotiations for a new contract in 1977.

A new national contract was negotiated by the parties in 1974 and in 1977, thus making it unnecessary to submit any issues to arbitration. However, the existence of ENA undoubtedly created pressures on the parties to settle through collective bargaining rather than resorting to the uncertainties of arbitration.

In 1977 ENA was the subject of widespread publicity. In the campaign for the presidency of the Steelworkers in early 1977, the losing candidate claimed that ENA was a sellout to management, that the union had lost its negotiating power, and that ENA was too high a price to pay for labor peace. Supporters of ENA, however, pointed to the disadvantages of the system used prior to 1974. The parties engaged in contract negotiations every three years. Because of the threat or fear of a strike, customers of the steel producers engaged in stockpiling. This process resulted in a temporary expanded use of labor and the purchase of foreign imports prior to the expiration of the old contract. If the union went on strike, steelworkers obviously were not working. But even if the union did not strike, many steelworkers were not working after the conclusion of negotiations. Many steelworkers were laid off while the customers used up the stockpiled inventory. And many customers continued to use foreign imports, resulting in fewer jobs for steelworkers. ENA was designed to provide stability of production and employment, to avoid industry-wide strikes and government intervention, to avoid a strike-hedge steel-inventory buildup, and to arrest foreign steel imports. ENA was not renewed for use in connection with expiration of the next two basic steel collective bargaining agreements—in 1983 and in 1986. But important customers, particularly in the automobile industry, exerted pressure on major steel producers and the Steelworkers to reach agreement in 1983 without a strike by statements that they would consider buying foreign steel if the U.S. supply was not guaranteed, and an agreement was reached without a strike long before expiration of the prior agreement.

Table of Cases

Cases presented in text or partial text are in italic type. Other cases—those discussed or merely cited—are in roman type. References are to pages.

819

Topical Index

825

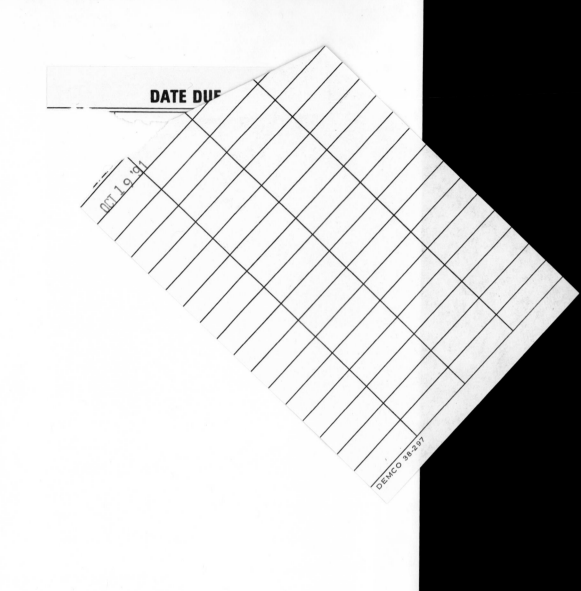